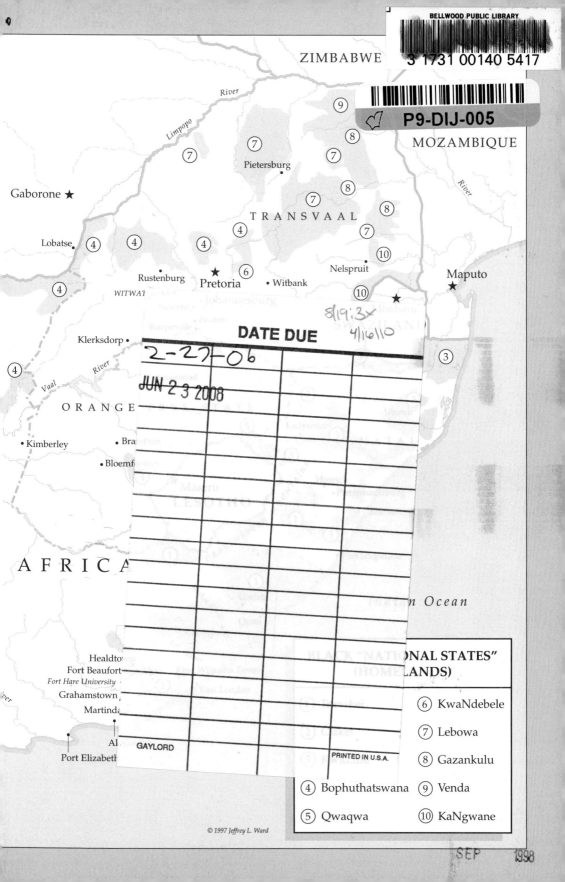

ZIMBABWE

MOZAMBIQUE

River

Limpopo

⑨

⑦ ⑧

⑦ Pietersburg

⑧

Gaborone ★

⑦ ⑧

T R A N S V A A L ⑧

⑦

④

Lobatse ④ ④ ④

⑩

④ Rustenburg ★ ⑥ Nelspruit

Pretoria • Witbank Maputo ★

WITWAT

④ Klerksdorp •

⑩ ★ ③

Vaal *River*

8/19:3x

DATE DUE 4/16/10

O R A N G E

• Kimberley • Bra

• Bloemf

A F R I C A

n Ocean

Healdto

Fort Beaufort

Fort Hare University

Grahamstown

Martinda

A

Port Elizabeth

BLACK "NATIONAL STATES"
(HOMELANDS)

⑥ KwaNdebele

⑦ Lebowa

⑧ Gazankulu

④ Bophuthatswana ⑨ Venda

⑤ Qwaqwa ⑩ KaNgwane

© 1997 Jeffrey L. Ward

DOUBLEDAY
CELEBRATES
100 YEARS OF
EXCELLENCE

Robert Kinloch Massie

Loosing
the Bonds

The United States
and South Africa
in the
Apartheid Years

NAN A. TALESE

DOUBLEDAY

New York   London   Toronto   Sydney   Auckland

PUBLISHED BY NAN A. TALESE
an imprint of Doubleday
a division of Bantam Doubleday Dell Publishing Group, Inc.
1540 Broadway, New York, New York 10036

DOUBLEDAY is a trademark of Doubleday, a division of
Bantam Doubleday Dell Publishing Group, Inc.

Book design by Paul Randall Mize
Endpaper map by Jeffrey L. Ward

Library of Congress Cataloging-in-Publication Data

Massie, Robert Kinloch, August 17, 1956
Loosing the bonds : the United States and South Africa in the
apartheid years / Robert Kinloch Massie. — 1st ed.
        p.   cm.
Includes bibliographical references (p.   ) and index.
1. United States—Relations—South Africa. 2. South Africa—
Relations—United States. 3. Disinvestment—South Africa.
4. Investments, American—South Africa. 5. Corporate divestiture—
South Africa. 6. Apartheid—South Africa. I. Title.
        E183.8.S6M28   1997
        327.73068—dc20   96-27126
                        CIP

1   3   5   7   9   10   8   6   4   2

For my sons,
Samuel and John

Is this not the fast that I choose?
To loose the bonds of injustice
To undo the thongs of the yoke
To let the oppressed go free?
—Isaiah 58:6

Contents

x   *Contents*

INTRODUCTION

The Mottled Mirror

ON JUNE 6, 1966, the Democratic senator from the state of New York, Robert F. Kennedy, stood in front of several hundred white students at the University of Cape Town, South Africa. "I come here today because of my deep interest in and affection for a land settled by the Dutch in the seventeenth century," he began, "a land taken over by the British, and at last independent; a land in which the native inhabitants were at first subdued and relations with whom are a problem to this day; a land which defined itself on a hostile frontier; a land which was once an importer of slaves and now must struggle to wipe out the last traces of that form of bondage." Kennedy paused briefly for effect. "I refer, of course," he said, "to the United States of America."

Kennedy's words captured the odd intersection between the histories of South Africa and the United States, two countries born of European curiosity and greed, imbued with high principle yet scarred by racial cruelty, and destined to influence each other's wobbly modern path toward justice. Though each country has its own distinctive history and though the differences in size and population are vast, their national characters and racial predicaments have continually invited comparison. Political leaders, social commentators, and average citizens have all, from time to time, glanced over at the other country in search of some revealing image. They have searched for different things: for excuses and examples, warnings and prophecies, heroes and villains, reassurance and reproach. Each country has served as a refuge for the imagination of the other, a mottled mirror in which anxious souls have found the portraits they have most admired and feared.

The roots of this mutual interest can be traced to the early similarities and contacts between the two colonies. Both nations arose from the Western search for wealth. Long before the first outposts took root on American and African soil, young European explorers boarded cramped wooden vessels and launched themselves, like fifteenth-century astronauts, onto the roiling dangers of the deep. In mission after mission Portuguese explorers pushed down the African coastline until they finally rounded the southern tip and found the sea route to India. Annoyed by the achievements of his neighbors, the Spanish king then sent Christopher Columbus hurtling toward the setting sun until he collided with an unexpected continent. Though these early explorers touched foreign soil, drank from foreign springs, traded and stole from the foreign beings they encountered, they always reboarded their ships, hauled up their sails, and left.

Five generations after these first journeys, when the coastlines had been traced and the sea routes mapped, the idea of permanently depositing European settlers took hold. In 1609 Henry Hudson sailed up the stately river that would later bear his name under orders from the world's largest multinational corporation at the time, the Dutch East India Company. By 1626 Dutch settlers had begun to build New Amsterdam, complete with gabled houses and a star-shaped fort, on the southern tip of Manhattan island. Twenty-five years later, the directors of the same Dutch East India Company decided to set up a provisioning station north of the Cape of Good Hope. They commissioned Jan van Riebeeck, a merchant and physician, and on April 6, 1652, van Riebeeck led his fleet into the protected waters below the colossus known as Table Mountain, lowered his boats, and went ashore. Soon he and his crew had tilled gardens and laid foundations for a granary, a hospital, and a star-shaped fort almost identical to the one on Manhattan island. Van Riebeeck was keenly aware of his counterparts in North America, writing just a month after his arrival that the African soil was far superior to that of New Amsterdam, "where the forest is first to be destroyed before anything can be planted."

Like their American equivalents, the settlers of Cape Town—or Kaapstad, as it was known in Dutch—relied heavily on commerce with the indigenous peoples. Most of the trading was with the Khoikhoi, a cattle-herding people whom the Europeans called Hottentots. For a time harmony reigned between the settlers and the inhabitants, as the Europeans bartered for their own needs and those of the sailors who stopped en route to India. Within less than a decade, however, the settlers began to press the Khoikhoi to work on their burgeoning farms. When the Khoikhoi refused, the settlers, desperate for laborers, received permission from the home office to import slaves from other parts of Africa.

Over the next half century the number of slaves and settlers rapidly increased. With each new influx the colonists pushed farther out from Kaapstad and seized larger swatches of territory. The Khoikhoi, watching their herding land disappear, decided that their early hospitality had been a mistake and attacked the settlers. The Europeans, armed with superior weapons, repeatedly crushed the poorly organized uprisings. By the beginning of the eighteenth century, the Khoikhoi, subdued by force and decimated by smallpox, were working for the settlers as farm laborers, domestic servants, and artisans. There followed enough intermarriage, intermingling, and rape to guarantee that within a few decades most families had ancestors on both sides of the racial divide.

The colony's economy, like that of America, centered on farming, though the region lacked the accessible interior waterways that helped make American agriculture a booming business. Nonetheless the Dutch farmers, or *boers* as they called themselves, continued to expand their holdings while the directors of the Dutch East India Company gradually ceded authority. Every month ships disgorged new settlers, many of them Protestants fleeing religious persecution in Europe. The burghers of Kaapstad moved quickly to assimilate them by requiring them to speak Dutch and shepherding them into the care of the Dutch Reformed churches whose clergy were on salary to the Dutch East India company. Moving outward from the edges of the settlement, itinerant stock farmers known as *trekboers* pushed steadily into the territories around the Cape, north through the Hex River Pass into the massive plateau known as the Great Karoo, southeast toward Mossel Bay, eastward to the Great Brak River. With each advance they came in contact with more indigenous peoples who, like the Khoikhoi, battled them until forced to acquiesce.

By the end of the eighteenth century Kaapstad had become not only an attractive way station but a place with enough population to warrant its own trade—even with distant places like New England. Yankee merchants, finding themselves blocked by tariffs from many European markets, fanned out across the seas in search of trading partners. When they discovered that the people of Kaapstad had a taste for American products, the merchants transformed their African-bound ships into floating New England general stores, selling everything from hams to violins. Trading vessels were not the only American ships floating off for Kaapstad. Every year a fleet of whalers left the harbors of New Bedford and Nantucket and set course southeast across eleven thousand miles of open ocean. When the Americans arrived off the coast of southern Africa they found whales everywhere—from the coast of Mozambique to an inlet on the Atlantic side where so many sperm whales came to feed that the Dutch had named it Walvis Bay—Whale Bay. Each year the Americans killed sperm whales by the hundreds. By the end of the eighteenth century American traders and whalers were so common that one of the piers in Kaapstad was known as the "American wharf."

More than one visiting Yankee thought that his compatriots should repeat the Dutch experiment and establish an American settlement up the coast from Kaapstad. In June 1796 Captain Benjamin Stout, a relative of U.S. President John Adams, was shipwrecked when a huge storm hurled his India-bound ship, the *Hercules,* onto the rocks at the mouth of the Mzimvubu River. Stout's dramatic narrative of his calamity and rescue exhibited the conflicting humanitarian and mercantile impulses that would run through American attitudes toward South Africa for the next two centuries. Stout vigorously denounced the abuses of the settlers against the indigenous Africans he had met, whom he described as "a race of unoffending mortals, long persecuted by those enlightened savages who, under the names of Christians and Dutchmen, settled themselves by violence on the southern promontory." Stout particularly objected to the settlers' habit of "hunting these unfortunate Natives as they do the lion and the panther." At the same time, Stout recognized the region's economic value and implored the president of the United States to establish an American colony on South African soil.

Though President Adams and his successors were too busy building a new republic on one continent to think of setting up outposts on another, the king of England had no such reserve. In 1795 officers of the British navy took advantage of Napoleon's occupation of the Netherlands to swoop down on Kaapstad. Avoiding the cannon perched on the Fort of Good Hope, the British deposited several companies of soldiers on the wide sandy beaches on the northern side of Table Bay. The soldiers marched south across the flats, defeated the local militia, and secured the town. The occupation lasted eight years, after which a treaty briefly returned the town to the Dutch. The British, however, had set their sights on controlling the southern tip of Africa and returned with a permanent military force in 1806.

With British rule came British law. In 1807 Parliament banned the slave trade, depriving the Dutch farmers of their most valued source of labor. In Cape Town, as it was now known, magistrates replaced the existing hodgepodge of Dutch Roman law and frontier codes with British jurisprudence. The Dutch burghers, long accustomed to meting out unsupervised punishment to their servants, bridled when they suddenly had to appear before British judges to answer formal charges of abuse. In one famous case, a roughneck settler named Frederick Bezuidenhout fled back to his farm rather than show up in court. When the British sent Khoikhoi soldiers to arrest him, he fired on them and they shot him dead. His brother then stirred up a rebellion on the frontier until the British finally tracked the leaders down and handed them to the local prosecutor, Jacob Glen Cuyler, a Dutch-speaking Tory who had grown up in America and whose father had been mayor of Albany, New York. The leaders of the insurrection were eventually condemned to death, taken to the gallows, and hanged in a row. The combined weight of their bodies snapped the gallows beam and sent the men tumbling to the ground, half-strangled, where they twitched and writhed until the executioners dragged them back up and hanged them a second time. The incident horrified the spectators and became an enduring symbol of the Boers' resistance to what they perceived as the monstrous alliance between Briton and black.

The Dutch community, who increasingly referred to themselves as *Afrikaners,* reserved special fury for the British missionaries who were busily befriending the mixed-race or "Coloured" families in town and the African communities in the bush. The conflict arose in part from differences in theology. The Boers hewed to the stern dictates of Calvinist predestination, which viewed mission, conversion, and salvation as God's chores. British clerics, in contrast, split into those who embraced the stodgy platitudes of state religion and those who had been touched by the swirling fervors of evangelicalism. The latter group forged out to remote farms and frontiers with the message of salvation through Christ and culture. Such commitment to personal conversion threatened the social, political, and economic order of the Cape colony, for even the most conservative colonist had to acknowledge that a fellow Christian, white or black, deserved better treatment than a heathen.

In 1828 a Scottish clergyman named John Philip published a scathing attack on the Boers' treatment of their workers in his book *Researches in South Africa.* Philip's views—and his appeal for more missionaries— eventually reached the United States. In response to a letter from a student at Princeton Theological Seminary, Philip strongly encouraged Americans to come and serve as missionaries to the Zulu and other indigenous peoples of South Africa. After publishing his plea and receiving an abundant response, the American Board of Commissioners for Foreign Missions, the missionary arm of the Congregational Church, finally selected six married men—Daniel Lindley, Alexander Wilson, Aldin Grout, Henry Venable, George Champion, and Newton Adams— to travel with their wives to southern Africa. The twelve young people departed from Boston on December 3, 1834, on board the bark *Burlington.* The days preceding the departure were marked by heroic preaching and tearful goodbyes, since few of their friends expected the missionaries to return from a continent filled with savages, wild animals, and disease. Brimming with hope and piety, the Americans sailed blithely into one of the most explosive political environments in the world.

The distant Zulus to whom the Americans dedicated themselves had just come through two decades of wrenching civil war. Climate changes had forced local tribes to fight for land and water, and the conflicts had gradually melded the disparate bands into a highly militarized nation under the leadership of Shaka, a man of legendary physical prowess and military genius. Equipping his men with short-stabbing spears, drilling them in battle tactics, shaping them into disciplined regiments, or *impis,* Shaka formed a standing army of more than forty thousand warriors whom he used to take control of an area the size of Portugal. Shaka's warriors ruthlessly seized cattle, leveled villages, disrupted agriculture, and forced thousands of terrified refugees up into the desert or down toward the white settlements. Shaka's reign began as it ended, in blood, when his half brother Dingane assassinated him in September 1828.

Dingane tried to hold Shaka's empire together, but he could not prevent some pieces of it from breaking off, including a large block under Mzilikazi, who led his people beyond the Vaal River. When the Americans arrived in Cape Town and learned of this split, they divided themselves in half. Lindley, Wilson, and Venable set their course for the "interior Zoolahs" under Mzilikazi, while Grout, Champion, and Adams headed for the "maritime Zoolahs" under Dingane. It took the Americans more than a year to make their way from Cape Town up the coast and across the land where they finally encountered the people whose salvation they so earnestly sought.

Even as the Americans made their way across the broken terrain, another social upheaval was erupting among the Dutch settlers in the Cape colony. By the mid-1830s, thousands of Dutch burghers—perhaps a quarter of all those living in the colony—had decided that after three decades they had had enough of British meddling and moralizing. The influx of new immigrants from England had sharply reduced the lands available for the sons of Dutch farmers. Many of the Dutch also rejected the growing British tolerance of the Coloured and African residents. "It is not so much their freedom that drove us to such lengths," wrote Anna Steenkamp, the niece of one of the movement's leaders, "as their being placed on an equal footing with Christians, contrary to the laws of God and the natural distinction of race and religion." Defying the leaders of their church, who refused to allow any clergy to accompany them, the disgruntled Dutch citizens loaded covered oxcarts with their portable possessions and set out in a search for new land that became known as the Great Trek. Over many months these *voortrekkers* trundled slowly to the northeast, farther and farther across the mammoth arid plateau of southern Africa.

The missionaries found themselves in the same position that many Americans would later occupy—caught between principle and prudence, black and white. Their first efforts at conversion met with no success. At the little mission station in Mzilikazi's territory, Alexander Wilson struggled throughout the winter to care for the many ill and feverish members of his party. In September 1836 his wife died, becoming the first white woman to be buried in the region. A few months later the missionaries' efforts collapsed completely when two hundred Voortrekker horsemen, in retaliation for a cattle raid, swept down and attacked the village in which they were living. With every shot, the missionaries wrote later, "the thought would rush on our minds, there falls one, and another, and another of the poor heathen of whose salvation we once had some hope. . . . In a few minutes we were in the midst of a slaughter." After the Voortrekkers had finished, they seized nearly six thousand cattle and urged the missionaries to withdraw with them to avoid Mzilikazi's retribution. The Americans—shocked, demoralized, and frightened—made the fateful decision to abandon their station and depart with the attackers. For many years Mzilikazi would recall this act as proof that the loyalties of the white missionaries did not truly lie with his people.

To the south an equally violent conflict was brewing as another contingent of Voortrekkers, under the leadership of Piet Retief, moved into the territory controlled by Dingane. At the town of Umlazi, Retief encountered the missionary Daniel Lindley, who by this time had learned enough Zulu to help Retief compose a letter to Dingane. In his letter Retief demanded that Dingane cede a large portion of his territory to the Boer settlers and warned the Zulu king that if he did not agree he would suffer the fate of Mzilikazi's people. When Retief received no reply from Dingane, he took a band of armed men on horseback to the Zulu capital in February 1838 to force the king's acceptance. Dingane admired the Boers' horses and guns—neither of which he had ever seen before—and gave his visitors the impression that he would grant their territorial demands. Two days later Dingane invited his guests to a farewell party at which his warriors seized the Boers, dragged them to a hill outside the town, and crushed their skulls with rocks, all within the full and horrified view of an English missionary who had been allowed to camp nearby. Leaving their bodies on a hilltop to be eaten by vultures, Dingane's army ran all night and day and fell upon the main party of Voortrekkers, killing forty more white men, fifty-six white women, one hundred eighty-five white children, and more than two hundred Coloured servants at what is still known as the Place of Weeping. Over the next six months Dingane attacked every Boer settlement he could find and nearly drove the Voortrekkers from the region.

Not until November could the Boers send in a military assembly of five hundred men under the command of Andries Pretorius. The commandos encountered nearly ten thousand Zulu warriors at a river embankment. Facing such a force, the Boers knew they could not avoid battle and prayed for divine assistance. On December 16, 1838, the outnumbered soldiers barricaded themselves behind a tight circle of wagons, or *laager,* next to the Ncome River. As the Zulus charged across the river and attacked in massive ranks from the grassy plain, the Voortrekkers leveled their cannons and mowed them down with grapeshot. Those warriors who made it past the cannons encountered a hail of disciplined musket fire. When three successive assaults failed, the Zulus retreated in disarray, leaving thousands of their compatriots dead on the battlefield. Observing the oozing scarlet streaks in the waters of the Ncome, the uninjured Boers renamed it Blood River.

The outbreak of fighting forced the American missionaries to reconsider their choices. George Champion agonized for days whether he should leave his mission station and take his nearly hysterical wife back to the coastal towns. Dingane sent a special envoy to invite them to stay, but Champion finally packed his bags and left. He feared that the mercurial king might change his mind and then "we might in some way be counted of abettors of the king's enemies and like others treacherously slain." "To retire for the present at least," he wrote shortly afterward, "was, we thought, the better part of Christian prudence and the voice of God." His departure turned out to be permanent; he returned to the United States, became a pastor in Dover, Massachusetts, and died shortly afterward of tuberculosis at the age of thirty-one. Aldin Grout, whose wife had died in Africa, went back to the United States, remarried, and returned with his new wife to South Africa several years later to serve among the Zulus in Natal. Grout eventually developed the first consistent written form of Zulu and became a champion of Zulu rights, collecting evidence to disprove the white settlers' insistence that the Zulus had arrived in the region only after it had been claimed by the Europeans.

Newton Adams and Daniel Lindley decided to stay in South Africa, though Lindley radically changed focus. Having encountered several bands of Voortrekkers, Lindley worried about the absence of clergy to provide the settlers with moral guidance. "Unless they come under religious instruction," he wrote to the American Board of Commissioners for Foreign Missions, "they will overturn everything in this country." When the Voortrekkers asked him to serve as their pastor, Lindley accepted, offering his supervisors the explanation that this career would also eventually benefit the Zulus to whom he had originally been sent. "The cheapest, speediest, easiest way to convert the heathen," Lindley wrote with a characteristically American mix of idealism and efficiency, "is to convert the white ones first." For the next six years Lindley served as pastor to the Voortrekkers and proclaimed the virtues of the gospel in broken Dutch to the most famous figures in the pantheon of Afrikaner nationalism. In gratitude for his efforts, the Afrikaner settlers eventually named two towns after Lindley, the American preacher from Pennsylvania who had become their spiritual leader.

While the missionaries struggled to find a place on the turbulent frontier, each shift of the wind and tide brought more settlers to southern Africa's shores. Though the British government controlled trade with its navy and its tariffs, the Cape colony continued to expand its business with the American states. The temperate climate of the Western Cape prompted many farmers to plant vineyards and make wine, a pursuit that created a demand for American-made barrel hoops and staves. Oars milled in Massachusetts lined most of Cape Town's rowboats. The rapid expansion of shoemaking in New England turned the United States into the leading importer of Cape hides and skins. By 1850 G. S. Holmes and Company, the first American firm in South Africa, was shipping two hundred thousand skins a year to Boston alone. Farmers on South Africa's eastern frontier prized the Eagle plow and other Yankee tools for their simplicity and adaptability. At mid-century, trade had become so brisk that several ships did nothing but commute between the two countries. One took advantage of the opposing seasons and sped from snowbound Boston to sunbaked Cape Town so that the residents of southern Africa could cool their seasonal drinks with ice cubes cut from New England lakes. Americans, in turn, bought most of the Cape's leather and wool. As a result, during the Civil War many Union soldiers wore boots made from South African cows and slept under blankets woven from South African sheep.

Though they traded with Union ships before and during the Civil War, residents of Cape Town generally favored the underdog Confederacy and once got to witness a Civil War sea battle right in Table Bay. The confederate ship *Alabama,* a rigged steamer under the command of Captain Ralph Semmes, spent several months cruising the waters off the Azores, seizing and burning fifty-three Union merchant ships. The harm to Union commerce was severe; in addition to the loss of the cargo, insurance rates skyrocketed, and many shipowners were forced to transfer their vessels to British registry. In the summer of 1862, Semmes sailed to Cape Town in search of more Union ships, and en route he captured six more, including a clipper ship that he pressed into Confederate military service. In August 1862, a large Union bark, the *Sea Bride,* sailed into Table Bay and encountered the *Alabama,* which was lying in wait under false British colors. In full view of the town's excited populace, the Confederate ship fired a few shots, captured the *Sea Bride,* and then docked in Cape Town, where Semmes and his crew were greeted as heroes. Though the British government had decided to remain officially neutral, the governor allowed the *Alabama* to take on fuel and provisions and thereby to elude the U.S.S. *Vanderbilt,* the Union warship that had been sent to put a stop to the Confederate raids. The residents of Cape Town immortalized the incident in a folk song, "Daar Kom die Alabama" (Here Comes the Alabama) that remains popular to this day.

In the second half of the nineteenth century, prospectors and explorers began discovering that beneath the rolling fields of grazing sheep lay unexpected riches. The discoveries heightened tension between the British in the Cape colony and the Dutch in their rugged little republics. Since the Great Trek, the Afrikaners had continued to push inward to the central high veld, founding the Orange Free State and moving in fits and starts across the Vaal River to the area they called the Transvaal. The colonial authorities in Cape Town could not decide whether to pursue these stubborn settlers or to leave them to the exacting task of building and defending farms on the frontier. Their interest rose when they learned that water-borne diamonds had been found on the banks of the Vaal River in 1867. Soon afterward news came that the remnants of several primordial volcanoes had been discovered and that within the bluish ground of their worn-down stacks could be found diamonds by the thousands. The news promised spectacular wealth to those who could gain control of the land. Cecil Rhodes and other flamboyant capitalists rushed to buy as much land as they could and goaded the British government to seize the regions in which ownership with the Boers was disputed. The British government finally agreed, annexed the Transvaal in 1877, and instantly stumbled into war with the small but still hardy Zulu nation. The Boers in the Transvaal watched with mixed emotions as imperial troops sustained painful early defeats. The most spectacular rout occurred in January 1879 at the Battle of Isandlwana when twenty thousand Zulu warriors raced over the rolling hills and annihilated a British force of twelve hundred. In later encounters, however, British cavalry, artillery, machine guns, and experience took their toll on the Zulu regiments. The British eventually captured the Zulu king, Cetshwayo, and sent him to London, where he was wined and dined in exile until he returned years later to serve as a puppet monarch.

The Boers, satisfied that the British had defeated a durable enemy for them, then attacked the British themselves. The first Anglo-Boer war lasted only a few months. In every military encounter the Boer commandos, all skilled horsemen and crack shots, decimated the columns of British conscripts as they trudged along looking for an army to engage. The British, deciding that these ornery farmers were just not worth the trouble, again relinquished their control of the Transvaal. The Boers, however, had another invasion with which to contend, one that proved

much harder to defeat. After an English immigrant named Edward Button had discovered alluvial gold in the eastern Transvaal in 1871, hundreds of prospectors had flooded into the area and found lumps ranging
from small grains to the colossal twelve-pound Peacock Nugget. The
boom was brief; within a few years the supply had dried up and the
prospectors had dispersed.

In 1886, however, another Englishman, George Harrison, found a
large outcropping of gold ore on a farm in the Witwatersrand in the
heart of the Transvaal. His discovery triggered a gold rush every bit as
tumultuous as the one that had transformed California thirty-seven
years earlier. Thousands of would-be millionaires rushed in from around
the world and fell frantically on the region to stake tents and claims. The
city of Johannesburg appeared almost overnight as the same kind of
rough, bustling, high-stakes outpost commonly found on the American
frontier. Indeed, many of the new arrivals came from the United States.
One was William P. McKinley, son of the man who would soon become
president of the United States. Another was Samuel Height, a native of
Mississippi who became U.S. consul in Johannesburg and opened the
city's first hotel. Freeman Cobb of Massachusetts made a good living
importing stagecoaches that had been retired from the gold fields of
California. A couple of Americans went to work for the Transvaal government to help write regulations, while a small army of pimps and
prostitutes arrived from Manhattan, fleeing an anti-Tammany crackdown on vice.

At the top of the social pyramid—above the prospectors, fortune
seekers, merchants, and swindlers—was the mining engineer. Because
the United States had built mines in its western territories for more than
a generation, American equipment was the most advanced and American engineers the most sought after in the world. Huge fortunes could
be made if the engineers picked the right spot to dig. "The importance
of the services rendered by American engineers in the development of
the Rand [Witwatersrand] can hardly be overestimated," wrote one observer. "Upon their signature to reports capital was raised or shares rose
to several times their nominal value." Such skill brought great financial
rewards. "South Africa seems to be the heaven of the American scientific mining engineer," wrote Mark Twain, who visited Johannesburg
during the boom. "He gets the choicest places, and keeps them. His
salary is not based upon what he would get in America but apparently
upon what a whole family of him would get there."

For more than fifty years after the Civil War, American engineers
came regularly to South Africa. Some rose to prominence within South
African firms, including Gardner F. Williams of Saginaw, Michigan, who
eventually became the general manager of the giant De Beers diamond

company. The most famous American mining engineer in South African history was John Hays Hammond. The son of an army officer who had been sent to California at the time of the gold rush, Hammond had studied at Yale and the University of Freiburg before returning to the American West to build his reputation as a mine examiner. Even before he arrived in South Africa he had had a colorful career that had gone from encounters with Wyatt Earp in Tombstone, Arizona, to a honeymoon dinner hosted by President Rutherford B. Hayes at the White House. By the time Hammond reached South Africa in 1893 at the age of thirty-eight, he was considered one of the top engineers in the world, with experience in mines from Mexico to Idaho. Hammond first took a job with one diamond baron, Barney Barnato, and then with his archrival Cecil Rhodes. Hammond persuaded Rhodes that instead of digging gold from the surface one could follow the reef underground, a feat thought technically impossible until that point. Rhodes sold his open-mine holdings, bought the tracts nearby that permitted him to pursue deep mining, and increased his wealth to a fabulous degree.

Hammond eventually got tangled up in a political fiasco in which a friend of Cecil Rhodes, Dr. Leander Starr Jameson, tried to fabricate an internal rebellion against the Transvaal republic in which the mines were located and then lead an expeditionary force to "rescue" British citizens and seize control of the territory. The episode—known as the Jameson Raid—ended in disaster. Jameson's forces were rapidly defeated by the unexpectedly hardy Boers, and John Hays Hammond found himself in prison along with seven other Americans on charges of high treason. Transvaal President Paul Kruger, a bearded biblical fundamentalist who literally believed that the world was flat, took a stern view and sentenced Hammond and the other ringleaders to hang. Only after appeals came in from around the world did Kruger relent and commute their sentences to life imprisonment.

One day while Hammond was languishing in prison and his supporters were haggling on a price that might buy his freedom, Mark Twain dropped by. Twain chatted with the prisoners, inspected the jail, and spoke to reporters after his visit. When the reporters asked about the conditions, Twain joked that compared to the Nevada mining camps, Hammond's prison was luxurious. The facilities were so attractive, Twain continued, that he was considering taking advantage of them to rest his tired nerves and seek relief from his creditors. The South African reporters, not familiar with Twain's brand of humor, dutifully printed his remarks, which produced an outcry in the Afrikaner press and a sudden increase in the severity with which the prisoners were treated.

Kruger eventually brought the price of release down to $125,000 per prisoner, and Cecil Rhodes paid Hammond's fine. A few weeks later Hammond and his wife returned to the United States, where Hammond continued his lucrative career as an engineer and became actively involved in Republican politics as a confidant of President William Howard Taft. The bitterness stirred up by Cecil Rhodes's connection to the Jameson Raid—and Kruger's suspicion that it all had somehow been a plot of the British government—brewed for three years and then exploded into the Boer War, in which the rugged and skillful Afrikaner guerrillas confronted the massive power of the British army.

Many on the European continent and in the United States viewed Great Britain as an imperialist bully out to crush a plucky underdog. Many Americans saw the Afrikaners' battle against Great Britain as a replay of their own war of independence. Nearly three thousand schoolboys in Philadelphia signed a message of support for the Boer cause and sent a sixteen-year-old messenger boy to deliver it to President Kruger. A specially formed Irish-American brigade traveled from Chicago to enlist in the Transvaal army. In 1900 John F. Fitzgerald, a congressman from Massachusetts and the grandfather of future president John F. Kennedy, introduced a resolution in Congress proclaiming that the Boers "would make a valuable addition to the citizenship of the United States, being a sturdy, self-reliant, intelligent people." In the event of their defeat, Fitzgerald said, the United States government should send steamships to southern Africa "to transport to the United States the burghers of the Transvaal Republics, or so many of them as may desire to emigrate, in order that they may take up land in the public domain of the United States." At the same time, Paul Kruger told a visiting American journalist, Richard Harding Davis, that the United States government should intervene on behalf of the Boers.

Relying on their topographical knowledge, excellent horsemanship, and good aim, the Boer commandos struck repeatedly at the slow-moving columns of British troops. When the British realized that the Afrikaners were inflicting unexpectedly deep wounds, they shifted to more brutal tactics. The British government imported hundreds of thousands of fresh soldiers. They invaded and burned more than thirty thousand Boer farms to deny the guerrillas sustenance and rest. They carted off Boer women and children and interned them in what they called concentration camps, under such horrendous conditions that starvation reduced children to skeletons and dysentery killed one-third of all the women and children in a single year. In all, more than twenty-six thousand internees died, including more than twenty thousand children and young teenagers, an outrage that for decades left many Afrikaners filled with bitterness. After three years, the British won the Boer War, but at a steep cost. They had committed nearly half a million men and had sustained, by one estimate, seventy thousand fatalities, all to defeat a tiny corps of men on horseback. In May 1902 the adversaries signed the Treaty of Vereeniging, in which the leaders of the Boer republics grudgingly accepted British rule in return for the protection of their language and the promise that Britain would not grant the vote to Africans.

While the warring white factions settled their differences, the seeds that had been planted by British and American missionaries were beginning to bear fruit in the form of a newly educated African elite. After Daniel Lindley had finished serving as the pastor to the Voortrekkers, he returned to his original task of ministering to the Zulus. Through raw persistence and the willingness of the British government to grant the mission stations large blocks of land with funds to administer them, the American efforts to convert the local population finally began to succeed. The early adherents to Christianity were often social outcasts; many of them had been dispossessed of their land through tribal power struggles. When Shaka's regiments killed Dube, the chief of the Qadi, his wife and young son eventually found refuge with Lindley. The son, James Dube, grew up on the mission station and became an ordained minister and a prosperous farmer and trader who amassed enough wealth to send his own son, John, to receive an education in the United States. John Dube finally arrived in the United States in 1887, made his way to Ohio, and enrolled at Oberlin College.

Dube was the first of a stream of young Africans who, believing that education was the key to advancement, made a pilgrimage to American schools. They were encouraged in this effort by prominent Americans who came to South Africa at the end of the nineteenth century. The Orpheus McAdoo Singers, an African American singing group, visited South Africa three times in the 1890s and electrified more than a thousand audiences. Africans throughout the country marveled not only at the African Americans' music but at their self-confident urbanity. How were these sons and daughters of American slaves able to move so easily as honorary whites among South African society? It was because, many Africans concluded, American Negroes were more educated and advanced than their African counterparts.

The singers had a huge impact not only on African culture but also in opening up educational and religious connections between American and South African blacks, as seen in the remarkable story of Charlotte Manye, a young African woman born in 1871 and raised in the vicinity of Kimberley. By the time she was a teenager, Manye was an accomplished soprano who was so impressed by the McAdoo Singers that she joined a similar South African choir and traveled to both England and the United States. Midway through her second tour of America the choir ran out of money, leaving the singers stranded in Cleveland. The African Methodist Episcopal (AME) Church intervened and half a dozen of the students, including Manye, ended up enrolling at Wilberforce College in Xenia, Ohio. At the time, Wilberforce was the center of the most educated and affluent black community in America. There Manye became a student of W. E. B. Du Bois, who had just returned from completing his training in Germany, and was treated by the leading couple on campus—Bishop Benjamin Arnett and his wife—like their own daughter. She completed her bachelor of science in 1901, becoming the first black South African woman in history to receive a bachelor's degree. Soon afterward she and her new husband, another South African student, Marshall Maxeke, returned to South Africa where they began setting up schools through Natal and the Transvaal. The Maxekes became the leaders of the black South African Christian elite; Charlotte founded the South African Women's Missionary Society and led a women's protest against the early pass laws.

It was through Manye that another important connection between America and South Africa grew. When Manye wrote a letter to her sister in Johannesburg about the wonders of Wilberforce, her sister showed it to Mangena Mokona, a leader of the newly independent or "Ethiopian" church. Mokona wrote to Bishop Henry MacNeal Turner of the American AME Church in 1895 asking if he could invite additional students to the United States "who will become teachers after completing their studies there." Soon afterward the South Africans sent a representative, James Dwane, to explore the possibility of direct affiliation between the American and South African churches. Bishop Turner reciprocated in 1898. As he swept through the country during his five-week tour, he ordained more than sixty-five new clergy and offered to help African students come to the United States. Thus through these and other connections, dozens of Africans made their way across the Atlantic Ocean—some under the auspices of the church, some having scraped together the money themselves—to obtain an American education.

The education they received included all of the tangled contradictions and crosscurrents about race that were operating in America at the time. On the one hand, the black American elite believed that the key to black advancement was education. They largely accepted the premise, articulated by many whites, that the main barrier to full participation by blacks in American society was a lack of preparedness, and they were determined to demonstrate through their learning and achievement that they were qualified. At the same time, others harbored doubts about the uncritical acceptance of the goals and values of white society and about the manner in which black education was increasingly being designed to prepare blacks for vocational and industrial careers. The most difficult question for this cadre of educated blacks in both the United States and South Africa lay in their own status in relation to their race: were they the voice and vehicle for black emancipation or a buffering elite whose nominal advancement could be used to shield whites from the demands of huge uneducated black majorities?

The Africans who studied in the United States brought these questions back to South Africa when they returned. John Dube, who was impressed by the philosophy of vocational advancement advocated by Booker T. Washington, returned from Oberlin to Natal, where he set up the Ohlange Institute, a technical school modeled on Washington's Tuskegee Institute. In the aftermath of the Boer War, as it became clear that the British-Dutch reconciliation would leave no room for black political rights, the black elite began to press for changes using the methods they had learned: articles, resolutions, and deputations. In 1910, under the strong direction of the British government, the white leaders of the Cape colony, the territory of Natal, and the Afrikaner republics finally agreed to create a single country—the Union of South Africa—whose constitution explicitly barred voting by Africans. The black elite, realizing that the democratic principles which they had absorbed in England and the United States had been betrayed, searched frantically for other methods to bring their influence to bear.

The key seemed to be to form a new organization, and so in 1912 several hundred members of the educated elite came together and formed the South African Native National Congress, a group designed to transcend all tribal differences in South Africa and bring the interests of Africans as a whole to bear on the political process. One of the founders of the group was Pixley Ka Seme, an African who had studied in the United States and received a law degree from Columbia University. For their first president the delegates chose John Dube, thus creating one of the more peculiar ironies of South African history. For John Dube, the first president of the organization that would later be renamed the African National Congress, was the spiritual and intellectual progeny of American missionaries, and not just any missionaries, but Daniel Lindley, who had also been pastor to the Voortrekkers. And so, in a strange way, the founders of both Afrikaner nationalism and the African National Congress, the two movements that would battle over the future of South Africa for most of the twentieth century, can be said to have been blessed by the same pair of American hands.

The story that follows—of America's relationship with South Africa in the second half of the twentieth century—is the tale of two countries with comparable histories struggling to overcome legacies of racial injustice and using each other for symbolic counterpoint in the attempt. In each nation the struggle forced citizens to ponder their personal values and national identity. During the course of several decades concern over South Africa's system of racial discrimination spread across the United States, from churches to universities, from state capitols to corporate boardrooms, from protests in the streets to deliberations in the White House. Transnational organizations such as corporations and churches, whose members exhibit loyalties that transcend civic borders, became the conduits for a debate that moved back and forth between the countries. Religious institutions used their far-flung networks to amplify the muted voices of protest and carry them straight into the heart of American elites. American firms, by building and trading in South Africa, found themselves increasingly enmeshed in that country's political realities and pressed to defend their actions abroad in light of the beliefs they professed at home. In an era of increased global interdependence, the South African case offers a critical example of how information can increase accountability and change the behavior of firms and nations.

In the United States the campaigns to end American involvement in South Africa took many forms, though the most common was to urge institutions to sell their stock (or divest) in companies operating in South Africa in order to persuade those companies to withdraw (or disinvest) from South Africa. As a piece of American social and political history, the anti-apartheid movement in the United States can be understood in many ways. It can be seen, for example, as the natural extension of America's turbulent concern about civil rights and racial justice into the international sphere, brought about in part by the increasing power and prominence of African American elected officials and the discovery by liberal religious groups of new methods to influence corporate policy. It can be understood as a grassroots seizure of the initiative in foreign policy comparable to the movement against the Vietnam War. It can also, less charitably, be viewed as a massive distraction, in which members of the white elite, from students to politicians to executives, chose to demonstrate their abhorrence of discrimination on the other side of the world rather than confront the enduring effects of racism in the United States.

This is also a chronicle of the advance of democracy, not only in South Africa but also in America. With regard to the federal government, it is a cautionary lesson about the limits of leadership—of American presidents too preoccupied with the cold war to back their words with deeds, of legislators whose intentions were often eviscerated by their unspoken prejudice, and of bureaucrats so eager to appear "realistic" that they found ways to excuse the inexcusable. Yet failure at the federal level triggered a vigorous response elsewhere, as citizens and officials in smaller venues took up the debate. In doing so they pushed innumerable colleges, churches, foundations, and other mediating institutions in new directions. As the leaders of such organizations were goaded by their constituents to articulate policy toward South Africa, they discovered that they could not remain silent without appearing culpable. Reasons had to be offered, and before they could be offered, they had to be found. Thus for thousands of American institutions the debate inspired lengthy internal deliberations in which policy and morality were weighed, balanced, and fused. Indeed, these same organizations found themselves reconsidering the matter year after year. Each time, they steadily augmented their knowledge and moved toward greater engagement. The analysis of how public questioning can stir institutional response, how moral deliberation is combined with policy formulation in defining institutional identity and purpose, and how organizations can be coaxed through incremental stages of commitment can help us understand new dimensions of democratic discourse in a contemporary economy.

Additional lessons can be drawn from South Africa's eventual response to external pressure, including that of economic sanctions. Though for years the South African government insisted, and many Westerners agreed, that South Africa was so wealthy and powerful that it would never be influenced by economic pressure, the historical evidence is now overwhelmingly to the contrary. Every economist, government official, and business leader in contemporary South Africa agrees that the government's policies were so cumbersome and senseless that they imposed a stiff tax on the country's economy. Former officials from the white regime now readily acknowledge that South Africa could not have sustained its racial policies without the financial, technological, and psychological support of foreign companies and countries. The gradual tightening of the economic noose, far from bringing the intensification of Afrikaner resolve predicted by so many foreign policy professionals, in fact limited the choices available to the government, cleaved its constituents into bickering factions, destroyed business confidence, and led directly to the peaceful resolution of what many had predicted would eventually erupt into racial war.

In tracing the role of various social and economic forces in changing South Africa, one must not overlook the tenacity and courage of particular individuals. Some of them—like Nelson Mandela, Helen Suzman, and Desmond Tutu—became known to the world. Others—like Timothy Smith, Jennifer Davis, and Randall Robinson—are not nearly as familiar. These persons, like the tens of thousands of others who participated on both sides of the Atlantic, are not stick heroes, but flesh and blood human beings whose lives were filled with their own confusions, uncertainties, and imperfections. As participants tried to position themselves along the spectrum from withdrawal to collaboration, many morally ambiguous viewpoints surfaced. Complex figures, torn between confrontation and cooperation, emerged within the government and the liberation movements; within the American activist groups and their corporate counterparts; within the U.S. government at all levels; within the South African homelands, army, universities, press, and even prisons.

Each of the interwoven biographical portraits presented in this book is designed to sketch out how complex forces—background, training, race, intellect, and social position—can coalesce within an individual. Each example suggests how purposive decisions and happenstance interact in the formation of a committed life. In addition to serving as a literary mechanism for illustrating moral complexity, some of the portraits are of people who exerted two particular forms of influence: first, by becoming political symbols to others and, second, by exercising exceptional control over the actual course of events. Though personality is not the only potent force shaping the great tides of history, at key points it can be decisive. Anyone who doubts this should ponder the lives of men like Hendrik Verwoerd and Nelson Mandela, two mortal human beings who, through the depth of their convictions, altered the history of their country and of the world. It is to their story—and to that of the hundreds of thousands of human beings who believed in them—that we now turn.

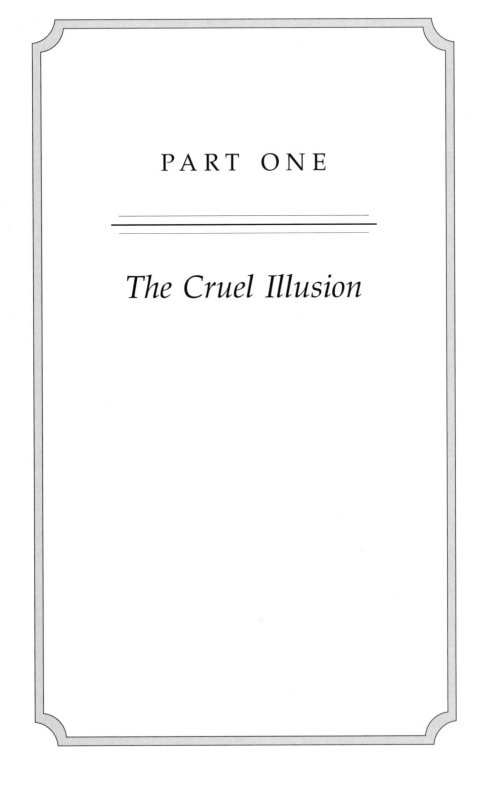

PART ONE

The Cruel Illusion

O N E

Rival Dreams of Nationhood

The problem of the twentieth century is the problem of the color-line—the relation of the darker to the lighter races of men in Asia and Africa, in America and the islands of the sea.
   —W. E. B. Du Bois

THIRTY MILES east of Cape Town, nestled among lush vineyards and overshadowed by dark blue mountains, lies the graceful university town of Stellenbosch. Along its broad streets stand row after row of Cape Dutch houses with thick wooden doors, gabled roofs, and whitewashed walls dappled by the interplay of oak leaves and African sunlight. At the center of town stands the *moederkerk*, the mother church, beneath whose needle-point spire generations of Afrikaner leaders married and prayed and assured each other of the righteousness of their convictions. In a strange historical twist, the town that had been named after Simon van der Stel, a man of mixed race who was one of the colony's first governors, became the intellectual and spiritual center of white supremacy in South Africa. From among the students at the University of Stellenbosch came some of its most ardent disciples and from the faculty came its most zealous prophet, Hendrik Frensch Verwoerd.

For nearly thirty years Verwoerd's single-minded brilliance and overpowering personality helped to transform South Africa, a mishmash of colonies and polities with a legacy of racial injustice, into a modern and mechanized racist state. Astonishingly, Verwoerd was not an Afrikaner by birth. He was born on September 8, 1901, along the canals of Amsterdam. His father, Wilhelm, was a simple Dutch grocer who longed to become an overseas missionary. When Wilhelm read about the suffering of the Afrikaners during the Boer War, he raised money for their relief. At the end of the conflict, Wilhelm packed up his wife and two sons, took the steamship to South Africa, and placed himself at the service of the Dutch Reformed Church. In Wynberg, near the southern slopes of Table Mountain, he found employment as a building contractor and did missionary work among the local "Coloured" population, the mixed-race descendants of colonists, slaves, and indigenous peoples of the Cape. In 1910 he qualified as a missionary and was sent by the church fathers to Bulawayo, a small town in southern Rhodesia. In Rhodesia young Hendrik attended an English-speaking school where, despite his strong Dutch accent, he excelled. As a youth Hendrik loathed the British anthem and other trappings of colonial rule, believing that one day South Africa should free itself from the empire and establish its own republic. As Verwoerd recalled years later, "ever since I was in short pants, I was a nationalist and a republican."

In 1917 Wilhelm Verwoerd transported his family hundreds of miles south to the tiny Orange Free State town of Brandfort, where he took a job as a religious book salesman. Their new hometown was already feeling the effects of recent laws passed by the white legislators who governed the Union of South Africa. The Natives Land Act of 1913 had introduced mandatory territorial segregation, decreeing that thousands of independent black farmers and sharecroppers had no right to own land in areas now formally declared "white" and restricting them to increasingly overpopulated and impoverished "reserves." Empowered by the law, many white farmers in the Orange Free State were evicting black sharecroppers for squatting on their newly claimed land.

Living for the first time in a predominantly Afrikaner environment, young Hendrik found himself in the midst of a broad social movement to increase the self-identity and pride of his adopted people. Only a few years before, in 1914, former Boer War general H. M. "Barry" Hertzog had established the Nationalist Party. The next year, Afrikaans communities had been troubled when former Boer War heroes who opposed South Africa's support for England in the First World War were arrested, and several young rebels were executed by the government for treason. About the same time a rash of new magazines promoting respect for Afrikaner history and culture appeared, and by 1917, the year Verwoerd arrived, many of these publications were switching from Dutch to the simpler dialect of Afrikaans as the language of the Afrikaner *volk*.

The following year Hendrik Verwoerd completed high school and took his national university exams, scoring first in the province and fifth in all of South Africa. In 1919 Hendrik traveled southwest to the Cape Province and enrolled at the University of Stellenbosch, recently declared a *volksuniversiteit* (people's university) by Afrikaner nationalists. He told his parents at the time that he intended to study in the school of theology and become a *dominee,* an ordained minister in the Dutch Reformed Church. At the university Verwoerd further proved himself a brilliant student. Surrounded at the university by peers whose families had participated in the great events of Afrikaner history, Verwoerd intensified his commitment to the cause of Afrikaner identity; indeed, it may have been the very lack of a nationalist patrimony that fueled his future passion.

During his studies Verwoerd showed an early interest in both politics and linguistic nationalism. When Jan Christian Smuts, former Boer War hero who had been elected prime minister, used the South African army to suppress a revolt by white mine workers known as the Rand Rebellion, Verwoerd joined in student debates about the event. He soon became head of the student union, where he requested a visiting orchestra to remove the British anthem from its repertoire. Verwoerd also changed his course of study from theology to psychology and entered the doctoral program, where he wrote his dissertation in Afrikaans.

After completing his Ph.D. at the age of twenty-three, Verwoerd turned down a substantial scholarship to Oxford and accepted a much smaller grant in 1925 to study in Hamburg, Leipzig, and Berlin, the leading academic centers of German psychology. After marrying his college girlfriend, Betsie Schoombie, when she came to meet him in Europe, he traveled with his new wife to England and eventually to the United States, where they spent several months. Verwoerd was fascinated with the American idea that scientific insights into psychology could be used to improve social problems, particularly through the newly emerging profession of social work. He visited factories, schools, and psychological laboratories, including one at Harvard. Betsie worked as his secretary, making appointments on the telephone and struggling through nausea that was later revealed to be caused by her first pregnancy. Verwoerd also tried to learn about American attitudes toward race; during their visit to New York City he and Betsie even made a special pilgrimage to Harlem, where they attended a performance of *Porgy and Bess.* While still in the United States, Verwoerd received a telegram informing him that he had been appointed a professor of applied psychology at the University of Stellenbosch; he and Betsie made arrangements to return to South Africa as quickly as possible.

While Verwoerd had been soaking up the culture of the Weimar Republic and learning about America, politics in South Africa had entered a newly turbulent period. In part because of his involvement in the Rand Rebellion, Jan Christian Smuts lost the election of 1924, ceding the prime ministership to Barry Hertzog. Juggling the interests of white mine owners, farmers, and industrialists, the new government enacted legislation favoring whites. Hertzog pushed through the Colour Bar Act to reserve skilled jobs for white mine workers; wooed struggling white farmers with a host of subsidies; and protected local industries with high tariff barriers. Hertzog filled his cabinet with Boer War veterans and tried through a variety of means to wrest dominion of the economy away from British interests. By 1926 Hertzog had increased his standing among Afrikaans voters by securing a declaration by the British Crown in which South Africa was declared to have absolute autonomy and equal status with England.

During this period the government also increased its control over Africans. In 1927 Hertzog approved the Native Administration Act, which extended discriminatory legislation first fashioned by the British in Natal over every province except the Cape. In doing so, the white government gave itself the power to define territorial boundaries, appoint chiefs, change the composition of tribes, and relocate villages at will. Through such measures Hertzog's government gradually accumulated the legislative authority to control black labor according to the needs of white farmers and mine owners. Though Hertzog desperately wanted to eliminate what he viewed as a blot on South Africa's purity— the continuing legal ability of a few Africans to vote in the overwhelmingly white elections in Cape Town—for the moment he had to bide his time.

In 1927 Hendrik Verwoerd, then only twenty-five years old, returned from overseas to Stellenbosch, where he taught courses on everything from psychological theory to problems of business management and advertising. He continued to exhibit a keen interest in American methods and scholarship and published one of his earliest articles in the *American Journal of Psychology.* Verwoerd's knowledge was enhanced by the steady stream of American social scientists who visited and taught in South Africa under a program administered by the Carnegie Foundation. According to his lecture notes Verwoerd veered away from the abstractions of German psychological theory and toward what he considered the more pragmatic American approach.

Intent on solidifying his academic position, Verwoerd did not yet exhibit the focused interest in nationalist politics that would later mark his career. Nor, when measured by the standard of his community, was he a racial extremist. He rejected the idea, popular in America and Germany at the time, that variations in test scores proved that some races were biologically inferior to others. Verwoerd preferred to talk about the distinctive cultural traits of "nationalities," rather than the innate biological differences among "races." "The Arab is fatalist; the southern Italian is emotionally unstable; the Japanese and French are philosophical; and the Scandinavian is boring," he announced in his introductory lecture on sociology. Though these views were, in some sense, moderate for the period, Verwoerd, like most white South Africans, strongly supported social segregation of blacks and whites. Among his students Verwoerd quickly developed a reputation for his broad knowledge and intimidating style. He would enter a classroom exactly thirty seconds after the bell had rung, speak with only a few notes for the full class period while the students scribbled furiously, and then walk out the instant the bell signaled the end of class. On the rare occasions when students dared to interrupt him with a question, he answered in a hurried and disdainful voice.

In October 1929 the American stock market crash sent financial shock waves around the globe. Within a year South Africa's industrial and commercial sectors had crumpled and mineral exports collapsed, sending the country into depression. As the crisis deepened, so did the poverty of rural Afrikaners. The double burden of severe drought and falling export prices drove thousands of white farmers and sharecroppers off the land. In 1932 the Carnegie Commission sponsored a study of poverty in South Africa that focused exclusively on the white population and completely ignored the destitution facing other races. Of the 1,800,000 white citizens of South Africa 300,000, or almost twenty percent, were considered extremely poor; the percentage of the Afrikaner population in poverty was between a quarter and a third. The economic strain created the same tumultuous politics in South Africa as in other countries at the time. Angry workers grumbled that the capitalists had deliberately engineered the depression to force down their wages and bring in lower-paid blacks. Segregationists shuddered at the sight of white farm girls moving to the city to take jobs as maids for wealthy Indian families. Under such pressures opinions similar to those growing in Germany took shape in South Africa: politicians, joined by intellectuals, began articulating an ideology that harped on historical grievances, promoted cultural integrity and racial purity, and blamed the nation's problems on particular ethnic groups.

At the University of Stellenbosch Verwoerd's interest in the problem of "poor whiteism" accelerated his shift from psychology to sociological theory. In 1932 he established the first department of sociology and social work in South Africa. In 1934 he became a member of the fifteen-year-old secret Afrikaner society the Broederbond (Brotherhood), though to admit him the leaders had to waive the requirement that members' parents and grandparents had to have been born in South Africa. That same year Verwoerd helped to organize the three-day gathering of Afrikaners that launched his political career. The gathering, known as the Volkscongres (People's Congress), had been called to discuss the "poor white question" highlighted by the Carnegie Commission Report. The conference was opened by the minister of labour and brought together a range of organizations concerned about white poverty. Verwoerd, who chaired its socioeconomic committee, achieved prominence by delivering the first speech. In his address he criticized Afrikaners for failing to do more to help their compatriots. Though most poor whites were Afrikaners, most welfare and philanthropic organizations—with the exception of several women's groups—were run by English speakers. In addition, Verwoerd continued, Afrikaners were not focusing on the real source of white unemployment, which was the excessive numbers of Coloured and African workers competing for white jobs. To lower white unemployment, he said, the state should meet the economic needs of the white community first. "Where a particular privilege for the poor white causes a difficulty, however increasing, for the non-white, there must be no hesitation in choosing it," Verwoerd proclaimed. "If someone should be unemployed, it should be the native."

Officials at the Volkscongres were captivated by this young scholar who seemed so insightful about Afrikaner problems. At the end of the conference they appointed him to a small committee created to implement the Volkscongres's resolutions; within a short time he rose to chairman. Under Verwoerd's direction the committee spawned a host of new organizations to promote Afrikaner self-reliance. In 1935 the committee decided to start a new newspaper in the Transvaal that would become "the feather in the hat of Afrikanerdom." To serve as the editor, the Reverend Daniel F. Malan and other nationalist leaders turned to their academic star, Verwoerd. It was a fateful choice that moved Verwoerd decisively from the role of analyst to that of advocate. Verwoerd resigned from his university post, packed up his family, and moved north to Johannesburg to oversee the preparations for the new newspaper, which he had decided to call *Die Transvaler*. Throughout 1937 he set his mind to learning the politics of the region and the trade of editor. Verwoerd ordered a new printing press from the United States and was deeply disappointed when the ship carrying it sank in the Atlantic. Overcoming the delay, he proudly displayed the first issue on October 1, 1937.

For the next eleven years the newspaper became the instrument through which Verwoerd trumpeted his views on Afrikaner nationalism, racial segregation, and a South African republic independent from Britain. Verwoerd also used the newspaper as a vehicle for anti-Semitism. In 1936, he organized and spoke at a rally to protest the arrival by ship of five hundred German Jewish refugees who were fleeing Hitler's persecution. In the maiden issue of *Die Transvaler* he wrote a six-thousand-word article on "the Jewish question," in which he displayed his genius for promoting prejudice as altruism. Since Jews refused to assimilate into their host cultures, he argued, they should not, for their own benefit, be permitted to come to South Africa because this would inevitably lead to a rise in anti-Semitism. Moreover, Verwoerd continued, their presence would harm Afrikaner economic advancement, since Jews compete with Afrikaners and poison the commercial atmosphere with their anti-Christian ethics. To his amazement Verwoerd found that Jewish owners of small businesses, when they became aware of his views, declined to advertise in his paper. In response Verwoerd publicly threatened businessmen who refused to purchase advertisements with a boycott of their shops by Afrikaners, followed by a campaign of "open warfare." From then on, Verwoerd vented his spleen on "the Jewish problem" in almost every edition.

Throughout 1937 and 1938 Verwoerd's attention was drawn to another project of the Volkscongres: a centennial commemoration of the Battle of Blood River. The Afrikaner nationalists wanted to use the occasion to focus attention on Afrikaner culture and to mobilize their followers to combat white poverty. The organizers planned many public events—including a partial reenactment of the Great Trek itself—all of which would culminate in the dedication of the site of a colossal new monument to the Voortrekkers on a hill in Pretoria. As the commemorative oxcarts rolled and bumped from town to town, they ignited a blaze of nationalist passion. Hundreds of men and women took time off from work, gathered their families into restored oxcarts, and joined the swelling ranks of pilgrims heading for Pretoria. Throughout the nation old Boer attire became the rage, especially among the young. The women donned ankle-length chintz dresses and old-fashioned bonnets while the men dug out their grandfathers' corduroy suits, colorful jerkins, and brocaded waistcoats. Verwoerd himself grew a full mustacheless beard like that of Paul Kruger.

Displays of popular nationalist fervor were quickly followed up with a summit to plan the Afrikaners' progress toward economic power. Appeals to save the living descendants of the Voortrekkers sparked the idea of an economic *volkscongres* in 1939, at which Verwoerd was a prominent participant. Discussions ranged from how to mobilize Afrikaner capital and people's banks to the organization of pro-nationalist, anti-Communist trade unions. This second gathering led to the promotion of Afrikaner business and the formation of large investment corporations that would concentrate economic power in the hands of the Afrikaner middle class.

For Verwoerd and his allies, the success of the centennial celebration and the congresses implied that an Afrikaner republic was no longer a pipe dream; the question boiled down to engineering a break with Great

Britain. By this time the two former political opponents Jan Smuts and Barry Hertzog had joined forces in an uneasy coalition known as the Fusion government, but as Europe moved steadily toward war the tensions between them increased. Smuts saw Hitler as a despot feeding off popular rage; Hertzog viewed him as the legitimate voice of an oppressed people. Smuts shared England's view that Hitler's aggression needed to be contained; Hertzog, under pressure from Malan and his former political colleagues, wanted South Africa to remain neutral. The fragile pact between Smuts and Hertzog held until September 1939 when war finally exploded between Germany and England. When the British governor asked Hertzog to join the Allies, the prime minister refused and the parliament instantly voted him out of office. At the urgent request of the governor, Jan Smuts stepped forward and after a fifteen-year hiatus again became prime minister of South Africa.

Under Smuts the South African government moved firmly to the side of the Allies. In the early stages of the conflict everyone believed that South Africa would have little to do except protect the Cape sea route. The collapse of France and the penetration of Italian battalions into northern Africa forced Smuts to send troops. The government trained 135,000 white soldiers—almost a quarter of all eligible white males in South Africa. The 70,000 African and Coloured soldiers found themselves in support roles, since the government did not want to trust them with rifles. South African troops helped to recapture Ethiopia, seize Madagascar, and fight Rommel's Afrika Korps in Libya and Egypt. The 6th South African Armoured Division joined the American Fifth Army in the invasion of Italy. In all, more than 200,000 uniformed South Africans served in World War II and more than 5,000 died, half of them black.

Verwoerd and Malan, though unhappy about South Africa's entry into the war, were delighted with Hertzog's abrupt exit from the government, for they knew that it would heal the split between Hertzog and Malan. In December 1939, Hertzog's and Malan's followers joined in an emotional rally at the Voortrekker monument to mark the beginning of a newly unified Nationalist Party. From then on, Verwoerd fired up his printing presses and set his newspaper steaming on a fiercely pro-republican, anti-British course. He denounced the conflict as "England's war" and repeatedly called for a withdrawal from the "hopeless struggle" and for a separate peace with Germany. In 1940, when German bombers pounded English cities in preparation for invasion, Verwoerd chortled in print that "Britain has lost the war. This is not only my opinion; it is my wish."

When some of his fellow Afrikaners expressed concerns over a possible invasion of Holland, Verwoerd dismissed their fears as British propaganda; when the Nazis swept through the Netherlands, Verwoerd refused to condemn them except to worry that their actions might cause an increase in Jewish immigration to South Africa. Throughout 1941, in the expectation of a German victory, Verwoerd and other members of the Broederbond wrote a draft constitution for a "Christian national republic" that could be adopted by a newly independent South African republic. "In obedience to God Almighty and His Holy Word," began the text, which Verwoerd printed in *Die Transvaler* in 1942, "the Afrikaans people acknowledge their national destiny, as embodied in the Voortrekker past, for the Christian development of South Africa." They would establish a government founded on "the principles of justice of the Holy Scriptures" rather than the "British-Jewish liberalism" that underlay parliamentary democracy. In later years, when challenged about his involvement in the draft constitution, Verwoerd daintily sidestepped the question, dismissing it as the product of a "group of young intellectuals" that never became the official platform of the Nationalist Party.

Despite Verwoerd's criticism of the Allies, he never openly favored Hitler, for two reasons. The first was prudence: the Nazis, after all, were the official enemies of a South African government at war; to speak in their favor was to court a charge of treason. The second was politics: the Nationalist Party's focus was on obtaining power in South Africa, a process jeopardized by the emergence of an Afrikaner organization that was fully and openly pro-Nazi. The group, known as the Ossewa Brandwag (OB, Oxcart Sentinels), had been formed in October 1938, just before the centennial, with the originally benign purpose of promoting Afrikaner culture. Within a few months the leaders of the OB had transformed their growing cadres into an enthusiastically fascist movement. In early 1941 Dr. J. F. J. van Rensburg, a friend of Joseph Goebbels and an open admirer of Adolf Hitler, became commandant general of the OB. He modeled the organization closely on Hitler's storm troopers, breaking the group into highly disciplined paramilitary units, drilling the members in uniform, and using them to attack political opponents on all sides. Van Rensburg and the other leaders of the Ossewa Brandwag berated the Smuts government for its craven service to the British war against the Germans and criticized Nationalist Party officials for offering only meek resistance.

Verwoerd, though eager to avoid another rift among Afrikaner nationalists so soon after the Malan-Hertzog division had been mended, realized that the OB's violent tactics were harming the cause of Afrikaner political advancement. At the moment Verwoerd's party was trying to enlist support from diverse groups, the Ossewa Brandwag's pro-Nazi activism and clear contempt for democracy were threatening to alienate important Afrikaner communities and trigger repression by the government. Smuts had already been sufficiently concerned about the OB's activities that he had called in the members' rifles and banned them from government jobs. While Verwoerd worked privately with the Broederbond and with the leaders of the Nationalist Party to patch together several temporary agreements that would keep the OB in the Nationalist Party's fold, he also publicly condemned the group's commitment to national socialism as "un-Afrikaans" and the organization as "anti-volk." OB members responded by threatening Nationalist members and even launched an attack on Verwoerd's office at *Die Transvaler.*

The final break came in 1942, when a founding member of the OB, the Reverend C. R. Kotze, challenged van Rensburg to repudiate his increasingly violent anti-Semitism. Nationalist Party leaders, eager for a reason to squelch van Rensburg, instantly declared that membership in the OB was no longer compatible with membership in the Nationalist Party. The OB responded with threats against the Nationalists and increasing sabotage against the South African government. At this point Smuts finally decided to act: in September South African police swept through the country and arrested hundreds of OB leaders. The prisoners were interned in large rural prison camps for more than a year. With the leaders of the OB under lock and key, Smuts called for a new election in 1943; his United Party won by a large majority. The Nationalists also enjoyed electoral success: they eliminated all the small splinter parties that had been vying for Afrikaner support, captured sixty-eight percent of the Afrikaner vote nationwide, and increased their parliamentary presence from twenty-eight to forty-three seats to become the official opposition.

As in the United States, the manufacturing demands of war snapped South Africa out of economic depression and into rapid economic growth. When white workers left factory jobs and boarded ships for the front, plant managers urgently recruited and trained thousands of Asian, Indian, Coloured, and African workers to fill their spots. Families of all races streamed in from the country to the industrial heartland south of Johannesburg, cramming into the dense ramshackle townships ringing the cities. With the assistance of the members of the small but active Communist Party, the workers coalesced into unions and political groups and pressed for recognition. As the war progressed, Hertzog's carefully constructed system of national segregation began to decay. Factory foremen broke the color bar while government inspectors looked the other way; urban Africans entered the cities more freely as police eased enforcement of the identity card requirements and movement restrictions known as the pass laws; and families desperate for a place to live built unauthorized squatter camps next to the townships without opposition from the state. To the young men who arrived in Cape Town and Johannesburg from their rural birthplaces, it seemed that the war against fascism abroad had also corroded the iron edifice of oppression at home.

One of those who came to Johannesburg during the war was a tall, trim young man whose name and fate would one day be inseparably linked with the struggle for racial justice. Nelson Rolihlahla Mandela was born on July 18, 1918, at Mvezo, a tiny village on the banks of the Mbashe River in the Transkei. His father, Gadla Henry Mphakanyiswa, was chief of Mvezo, adviser to the Thembu kings, and husband to four wives, of whom Nelson's mother, Nosekeni Fanny, was the third. When the boy was born, his father presciently named him Rolihlahla—"troublemaker." Soon afterward a white magistrate deposed his father as chief, forcing his mother to move to Qunu, a small enclave of huts in a grassy valley crisscrossed by little streams. It was, Mandela would recall, "a village of women and children; most of the men spent the greater part of the year working on remote farms or in the mines along the Reef." By the age of five Mandela was working as a herd-boy, looking after sheep and goats, and when he was seven his mother decided to send him to the little schoolhouse on a hillside near Qunu. Until then Mandela had worn only a blanket, but on the day before his first day of school his father gave him a pair of his own trousers cut off at the knees and tightened at the waist with a piece of string. "I must have been a comical sight," Mandela remembered, "but I have never owned a suit I was prouder to wear than my father's cut-off pants." The next day his teacher announced that they would be learning English and that she was going to give each of them an English name to which they would answer in school. Mandela's name, she announced to him without explanation, would be Nelson.

In 1927, when Mandela was nine, his father suddenly fell ill and died. Shortly afterward his mother took Nelson to live with Chief Jongintaba Dalindyebo, the acting regent of the Thembu people. Mandela's father had supported the chief when the time had come to choose a regent, and the chief decided to repay the favor by becoming Nelson's guardian. Mandela was delighted with his life at the "Great Place" of Mqhekezwini. He wore new clothes purchased for him by the chief, rode horses, plowed the fields, and played with his new friends and adoptive family. The twin poles that quickly came to govern his life were the church and the chieftaincy. He attended the Methodist mission school and marveled at the energy and influence of the local pastor, Reverend Matyolo. To the young Mandela "virtually all of the achievements of Africans seemed to have come about through the missionary work of the church." At the same time, he could not help noticing the tensions between the institutions. In school Mandela followed a British curriculum that taught about the heroic white victories of the settlers over the indigenous peoples in the nineteenth century "kaffir wars," whereas at night he heard a different version. Under the arching, star-encrusted African sky Nelson would listen as the old men sat around the fire and told stories about African leaders—Hintsa and Makana among the AmaXhosa, Dingane and Bambatha among the Zulu—who had fought valiantly until crushed by an alien military force. Mandela's notion of leadership was also profoundly influenced by observing the regent's behavior when he called a meeting to discuss matters of importance to the tribe. Any Thembu male could participate in the discussion, and many did, coming from afar on foot and on horseback. The regent, surrounded by his most senior advisers, would thank everyone for coming, outline the topic of discussion, and then remain silent, often for hours, until the topic had been fully discussed. At that point the regent would sum up what he had heard or, if consensus had not been achieved, propose another meeting. From watching his mentor, Mandela learned that "a leader is like a shepherd. He stays behind the flock, letting the most nimble go out ahead, whereupon all the others follow, not realizing that all along they are being directed from behind."

At sixteen, Mandela and his close friend, the regent's son Justice, both underwent the traditional Xhosa circumcision ceremony that marked their official passage into manhood. Shortly afterward the regent sent him to Clarkebury Boarding Institute, another mission school, to prepare him to follow in his father's footsteps and serve as an adviser to the Thembu kings. There Mandela learned that his connections to the tribal elite would not prevent him from being judged on his own academic abilities. In 1937—the same year that Verwoerd published the first issue of *Die Transvaler*—the nineteen-year-old Mandela joined the regent's son Justice at Healdtown, a Methodist college in Fort Beaufort. After a year of preparatory studies, the two young men then moved to the University College at Fort Hare, at the time the only residential center of higher education for blacks in South Africa.

Based in the town of Alice in the Eastern Cape, Fort Hare had been founded by Scottish missionaries twenty years before. Though it had only a hundred and fifty students, Mandela remembered, "for young black South Africans like myself, it was Oxford and Cambridge, Harvard and Yale, all rolled into one." They came to study with men like D. D. T. Jabavu, who had earned his degree at the University of London and was the first member of the staff when the school opened, and Z. K. Matthews, the son of a miner who had been influenced by Booker T. Washington's philosophy of persistence and who taught anthropology and law. Both men had a long record of public opposition to discrimination in South Africa; they both embodied the conviction that advances in education would lead to increased political power.

For Mandela, Fort Hare represented an entirely new level of contact with Western ideas and practices. Though already in his twenties he had never before encountered flush toilets, hot showers, toothbrushes, or pajamas. He quickly made contact with several older students who helped him adjust and whose friendship would influence him for the rest of his life. One was a cousin, Kaiser Matanzima, a third-year student who helped Mandela find his way around and even split his allowance with him so that Mandela would have some spending money. Another was a young science student from Pondoland, Oliver Tambo. A year older than Mandela, Tambo had gone to St. Peter's secondary school in Johannesburg on a scholarship, passed his national exams in the first rank, and journeyed to Alice to get his undergraduate degree on the road, he hoped, to ordination to the Anglican priesthood. The two young men met during their weekly excursions as members of the Student Christian Association to teach Bible classes in neighboring villages.

At Fort Hare, Mandela's political consciousness rose rapidly. In the evening Mandela and new friends gathered around the radio to hear news of the Second World War and to listen to Winston Churchill's stirring speeches. When Jan Smuts came to speak at Fort Hare, Mandela was thrilled. "I cared more that he had helped found the League of Nations, promoting freedom around the world," Mandela recalled, "than the fact that he had repressed freedom at home."

Mandela's forceful personality and impatience sometimes led him into trouble. When the college administration tried to reduce the powers of the Student Representative Council, to which Mandela recently had been elected, Mandela organized a protest. In response the university's principal called Mandela into his office and told him that unless he abandoned his effort, he would be expelled. Mandela agonized about whether he was sacrificing his entire career for an abstract moral principle, and then decided, with his cousin Kaiser's support, that he should not back down. The next day the principal sent him back to his guardian, Chief Dalindyebo, who was furious. His mentor told Mandela that he would have to abandon the protest, return to the college, and settle down. To stabilize him, the chief also decided that his son Justice and his ward Nelson should both be married. "He loved me very much and looked after me as diligently as my father had," Mandela remembered. "But he was no democrat and did not think it worth while to consult me about a wife. He had selected a girl, fat and dignified, paid the bride-price and arranged for the wedding." Not only was Mandela not in love with her, but she was actually in love with Justice. After unsuccessfully trying to dissuade the chief, the two young men decided to flee to Johannesburg.

Traveling by bus and train, Nelson and Justice made their way north through the undulating green hills of Natal and on to the high plateau of the Transvaal. When they arrived in Johannesburg, they traded on the chief's reputation to get them started. Mandela eventually found a small room in Alexandra, the bustling African township on the northeastern side of Johannesburg, and took a job as night watchman for Crown Mines. Every evening, armed with a heavy wooden club known as a *knobkerrie,* Mandela guarded the gate of the huge hostels where thousands of miners who labored a mile below ground lived and slept. In the township Mandela swiftly made friends, the most important of whom was a gifted and tenacious man named Walter Sisulu, who was also from the Transkei. Sisulu, the son of an African mother and a white father, was several years older than Mandela. He had received a strict religious upbringing and had traveled to Johannesburg some years earlier looking for work. By the time Mandela met him, Sisulu had already dug gold out of the bowels of the earth with a pick and shovel, worked as a "kitchen-boy" for a white family, been fired from several factories for protesting unjust practices, and started a small real estate agency that dealt in the few properties that Africans were still permitted to own. Sisulu liked Mandela and worked to set him up. He gave Mandela a job in the agency, loaned him money to finish his undergraduate degree by correspondence, bought him a new suit for the graduation ceremony, helped him enroll in part-time legal studies at the University of the Witwatersrand in Johannesburg, and got him a job with the white law firm of Witkin, Sidelsky, and Eidelman. Sisulu also introduced Mandela to his soft-spoken young cousin Evelyn Ntoko Mase, a nurse at City Deep Mine Hospital, whom Mandela married shortly afterward.

Mandela enjoyed working in the law office. Lazar Sidelsky, the Polish Jew who had brought him into the firm, treated Mandela well and even him gave him one of his suits, which Mandela wore every day for five years. Sidelsky often took Mandela aside and lectured him on the importance of getting an education and of staying out of politics. At the same time, Mandela made friends with the only other African who worked in the office, Gaur Radebe, who surreptitiously urged him to become a Communist. Mandela declined. "I was not inclined to join any political organization," Mandela recalled, "and the advice of Mr. Sidelsky was still ringing in my ears. I was also quite religious, and the party's antipathy to religion put me off." Even in the liberal haven of the law firm, Mandela still had to endure incidents of prejudice. He had made friends with a young white woman who worked as a typist and she sometimes asked him if he had any dictation for her. On one occasion when Mandela was dictating a letter, a white man entered the firm's offices. The secretary, not wanting the client to think that Mandela was her superior, pulled out some coins from her purse and handed them to him. "Nelson," she said primly, "please go out and get me some hair shampoo from the chemist." Mandela, to avoid humiliating her, did the errand.

Mandela was delighted when his old college friend Oliver Tambo returned to Johannesburg to teach science at St. Peter's, Tambo's alma mater; the two of them had already spent hours with Walter Sisulu discussing South Africa's future. Sisulu had long been a member of the African National Congress (ANC) and he urged his younger friends to join because, he insisted, it was the organization that one day would free their people. This was far from obvious. The ANC was still mostly an elite group of intellectuals who did not command universal support among Africans. Populist critics like I. B. Tabata had fiercely attacked the ANC for its willingness to participate in the Natives' Representative Council set up by Hertzog as an alternative to allowing Africans to vote. To restore the ANC's claim to preeminence among South African resistance groups, delegates to a conference at the beginning of World War II elected a new president, a physician named Alfred Bitini Xuma.

Xuma, like John Dube, had trained in the United States, graduating from Tuskegee Institute and a medical school in Minnesota before serving his residency in Scotland. While in the United States he had met and married his first wife, whom he brought back to South Africa in the late 1920s. When she died a few years later, Xuma launched a search for a new American bride and, after years of courtship by mail, persuaded Madie Hall, the daughter of a distinguished North Carolina family and an officer of the YWCA, to become his wife. By the time he took control of the ANC, Xuma was a prominent member of the South African educated elite; Mandela had paid him a visit shortly after arriving in Johannesburg to ask for help in finding a job. As soon as Xuma was elected president, he immediately took steps to revitalize the group. He strengthened the national organization's power by requiring unity among the provincial branches. He launched a million-member drive, which, though it did not reach its goal, nevertheless built morale. He pushed through a new constitution in 1943 that formally opened the ANC to persons of all races. He established coalitions and closer working relationships with Indian and Coloured activists. He reorganized and improved the group's finances, although despite its prominence the ANC never had more than a few thousand dollars.

Like millions around the world, Xuma believed that the defeat of Hitler would bring a new international order that would change the political balance in South Africa. To be ready, Xuma wanted the ANC to have a list of proposals. He formed a committee of African intellectuals, with Z. K. Matthews as chairman, and asked them to draft a Bill of Rights. When it was completed in 1943, the document called for "the freedom of the African people from all discriminatory laws whatsoever" and was couched in liberal, Western terms. They sent it to Prime Minister Smuts, who looked it over but dismissed it as "unrealistic." To Smuts, Xuma's efforts to promote African rights seemed comparable to Verwoerd's endless carpings in the pages of *Die Transvaler;* both men were partisan extremists who did not have the best interests of the entire country at heart. The salvation of the country lay in rational paternalism, in which the benevolent judgment of a senior statesman—namely Smuts—would control the crude bigotry of the Nationalists and compensate the disfranchised races by seeing to their interests better than they could do themselves.

Though Xuma nurtured the hope that after the war Smuts would be persuaded to enter a new dispensation, a group of young and impatient African activists began to meet to discuss how both men could be prodded to move more quickly. The group included the three friends Mandela, Sisulu, and Tambo and a host of others whose names would become synonymous with resistance: Anton Lembede, Govan Mbeki, Robert Sobukwe, Nthato Motlana, and Peter Mda. Though from different African ethnic groups, the young men shared many experiences. Most had been trained in mission schools and believed in intellectual rigor, personal commitment, and democratic rights. Many had been teachers and had then gone on into professions: Lembede, like Mandela and Tambo, was a lawyer; Motlana a physician. For months the men met and debated, honing their vision of the future of their country. Reflecting on that period of his life, Oliver Tambo said, "We were never really young. There were no dances, hardly a cinema, only meetings and discussions, every night and every weekend."

Although they supported the ANC, the young men believed that the movement needed an internal spark plug to keep the engine firing at a high rate. Many pointed to the vital role the Broederbond had played in bringing energy, unity, and discipline to the Afrikaner drive for power. In 1943 they decided to form a similar organization—though it was not secret—which they named the African National Congress Youth League. The purpose, they agreed, would be to galvanize the African National Congress into becoming "the symbol and embodiment of the African's will to present a united front against all forms of oppression." In March 1944 they published a manifesto, written by Mda and Mandela, called the "Programme of Action," in which they called for majority rule but specifically rejected the notion popular among some Africans that the goal should be to drive the whites into the sea. The next month they elected leaders: Lembede became president and Tambo secretary. When they went to Xuma and proposed affiliation with the national ANC, Xuma warily agreed.

When peace came in the summer of 1945, the members of the African National Congress pressed Smuts for change. Smuts, who was busy helping to create the United Nations, deflected their overtures. The prime minister signaled his postwar intentions most strongly in March 1946, when he introduced into parliament the Asiatic Land Tenure Act and Indian Representation Bill, which gave the government the power to dictate where Indians could work, trade, and live. To protest the "ghetto bills," the Indian community organized a series of passive resistance councils to hold demonstrations and by June more than two thousand Indians had been arrested.

The unhappiness of millions of African workers who had been frustrated throughout the war by low pay, expensive supplies, and arduous working and living conditions could not be contained for long. In August 1946 more than seventy thousand miners went on strike, threatening South Africa's lucrative mineral exports. The government broke the strike with troops, who beat and fired on the workers, killing twelve and wounding twelve hundred. Soon afterward the ANC-dominated Natives' Representative Council (NRC) formally demanded that the government abolish the pass laws, recognize African trade unions, and repeal the most repressive sections of the Native Administration Act of 1927. Smuts could not respond to the striking miners or the NRC representatives personally because, ironically, he was in Paris helping to draft the new International Declaration of Human Rights.

Verwoerd, Malan, and the other members of the Nationalist Party also welcomed the end of the war because they knew it would free Afrikaner patriots from detention and remove the taint of treason that had surrounded their advocacy of neutrality. They churned out articles, speeches, and pamphlets that played on the resentments of white veterans who had returned from far-flung posts to find their jobs and their cities occupied by persons of different races. Smuts, much like his British counterpart, Winston Churchill, expected that the glow bestowed by the Allied victory would more than compensate for voters' residual dissatisfaction with the privations of war. As a Boer War veteran, he believed he retained the support of most Afrikaners; as a supporter of Great Britain in both world wars, he had attracted most of those of English descent into the ranks of the United Party. To strengthen his popularity, Smuts invited the British royal family to make a formal state visit to South Africa. In February 1947, King George VI and his family, including the future Queen Elizabeth II, arrived in South Africa and were greeted with enthusiastic pomp. Hendrik Verwoerd, still ardently in favor of an Afrikaner republic independent from England, was so infuriated by the visit that he refused to mention the royal family in the pages of *Die Transvaler*. On the day of the king's arrival in Johannesburg, Verwoerd deigned only to warn his readers that the presence of certain visitors from overseas might cause a traffic jam in the city.

As 1947 drew to a close, Smuts, confident of his personal popularity, decided the time had come to renew his mandate by calling an election for May. The Nationalists leapt to the challenge. Throughout the campaign, Nationalist Party candidates ferociously attacked Smuts and his party as too weak to stand up to Communism or to the *swart gevaar,* the black threat. After years of emphasizing the differences between the English and the Afrikaner, they tried a new tactic, that of stressing "European" unity. In every tract and at every rally, the candidates proclaimed that only the Nationalists had the will, the vision, and the strength to preserve three centuries of white culture and dominance. They vowed to eliminate the social laxity that had poisoned the country during the war; to circumscribe the rights of those who were not the proper heirs of European culture and privilege; to redraw fading lines, rebuild barriers, and reproduce the purity of yesteryear that Verwoerd and the other revisionists had largely fabricated. They would do all of this, they shouted, because they believed in the fundamental principle of separateness of the races, the principle known in Afrikaans as *apartheid.*

On May 26, 1948, the white voters of South Africa went to the polls. The Nationalists believed that they would end up with more members in parliament and worried when they learned that the United Party was leading. The next day, they and all the citizens of South Africa were shocked to learn the truth: though the United Party had received more votes overall, the massive support of rural Afrikaner voters, voting district by district, had given the Nationalist Party a five-seat majority in parliament. Even the old lion himself, Jan Smuts, had been defeated in his own district. Two days later Smuts, the man who had dominated South African politics for fifty years, resigned as prime minister. The governor general turned to the leader of the Nationalist Party, the Rev. Daniel F. Malan, and asked him to form the government that would lead South Africa into the future.

For D. F. Malan, Hendrik Verwoerd, and the other members of the Nationalist Party, the electoral success of 1948 vindicated a century of toil. The *volk* had triumphed, retrieving the power that had been wrongfully snatched away by the British Empire. The Nationalists knew that they would need to move quickly to solidify their control of the country and give bone and sinew to the vaporous campaign slogan of "apartheid." The forces of assimilation had gained ground alarmingly during the war. Boys of Boer and British ancestry had fought together against the Nazis and were coming home with new respect for one another. Tens of thousands of men and women of all races and ethnic backgrounds had crowded into the cities, found work in factories, and settled side by side. Smuts's United Party, though no longer in power, remained a forceful opponent.

The Nationalists swiftly consolidated their parliamentary margin by giving the 24,000 white inhabitants of South West Africa, who had previously been unrepresented in parliament, six newly created seats in the House of Assembly (the lower house of parliament), all of which were then won by Nationalist Party candidates. They also created the legal tools with which to disentangle South Africa's interracial clumps and construct the idyllic segregated community of which they dreamed. They began with the Prohibition of Mixed Marriages Act of 1949, a measure designed to halt the miscegenation that had been part of South African culture from its inception. They passed the Group Areas Act in June of 1950 to confine the residences of persons of different races to officially designated areas. This prompted a debate about who should qualify as the member of one race or another, a debate that led to the Population Registration Act, which required every person within South Africa's borders to obtain an official designation of race. To implement this law, the Nationalist parliament created a ponderous bureaucracy to sort the residents of South Africa into official categories. The agency bureaucrats then had to develop regulations and genealogical standards for the thousands of persons whose race could not be determined by the cursory glance of an Afrikaner functionary. One of the most ridiculous procedures was the "pencil in the hair" test. White officials stuck pencils in the hair of applicants and then asked them to bend over. If the curls were tight enough to hold the pencil, the person was deemed African; if the pencil fell to the floor, the verdict was Coloured.

In 1950, to constrain the noisiest opponents of apartheid, Nationalist Party members approved the Suppression of Communism Act. The primary target of the legislation, the South African Communist Party, had been a small but active source of political dissent for more than twenty years. After a brief period in the 1920s during which Communists unsuccessfully tried to attract the support of white workers with the slogan "Workers of the World Unite for a White South Africa," party leaders had decided that the greatest hope for socialist revolution lay with the African majority. Throughout the 1930s and 1940s white Communists had followed a strict policy of nonracialism, criticized the United Party's support of the war, and worked to organize African and Coloured workers into unions.

Ideologically the Communists and the Nationalists formed a strangely complementary pair. Both insisted that there was a necessary connection between a nonracial society and a socialist society; for Communists this was a virtue, for Nationalists a threat. The breadth and depth of Nationalist anxieties about dissent was evident in the Suppression of Communism Act, a law that brushed aside most judicial safeguards and dramatically expanded the power of the state. Under the act, the state president could declare any organization unlawful if he was satisfied that it was engaged in activities calculated to further any of the aims of Communism. Under this formulation, even a pro-capitalist group became vulnerable to government prosecution if it worked for the elimination of racial discrimination, because this goal was shared by Communists. Leaders of organizations could be banned from attending gatherings or forbidden to write or be quoted, even after death. The leaders of the United Party, stung by their loss at the polls in 1948 and the death of Jan Smuts in 1950, not only consented to the new legislation but went one better, arguing that anyone supporting Communism should be considered guilty of high treason. Shortly before the law went into effect, the South African Communist Party officially disbanded, though its members continued to meet secretly and to exert an influence on the resistance movement for some years afterward. These developments did not bode well for other anti-apartheid groups. "Today it is the Communist Party," Oliver Tambo wrote prophetically. "Tomorrow it will be our trade unions, our Indian Congress, and our African National Congress."

Hendrik Verwoerd, unlike many of the Nationalist Party candidates, had lost his 1948 bid for election to parliament from the district of Alberton by 171 votes. For a moment Verwoerd seemed destined to observe the triumph of his adopted people from outside the government. Daniel Malan rescued him soon afterward by appointing him to a seat in the South African Senate. In August 1948 Verwoerd resigned his position as editor of *Die Transvaler* and busied himself with the affairs of parliament's upper house. His friends maintained pressure on the prime minister to bring Verwoerd into the cabinet and in October 1950 Malan agreed. By this time Malan had realized that the success of the Nationalist Party depended on the success of apartheid and that apartheid would require the passage and implementation of an enormous web of laws. Having listened to Verwoerd's abundant opinions on the subject for years, Malan decided to give the professor his chance. On the 19th of October 1950 the prime minister appointed Hendrik Verwoerd minister of native affairs.

On hearing the news, an overjoyed Verwoerd ran home to his wife and told her, "My dear wife, I am now actually the Great Induna!"—the chief of all chiefs. Verwoerd was not exaggerating. As a result of the powers conferred on him by the white legislature, Verwoerd knew he would exercise autocratic control over four-fifths of the residents of South Africa, "a vast black empire independent of Parliament," as one writer put it. His word would be law for eight million Africans, whether they tilled on farms or toiled in cities. Verwoerd could outlaw any African organization; govern the movement, employment, and residence of Africans in any part of the country by decree; and relocate tribes at will. He would have absolute power over village chiefs, local superintendents, and regional commissioners. It was a social scientist's dream: this former professor now had eight million subjects on whom he could experiment without obtaining their consent.

From the first day of his appointment, Verwoerd seized his new responsibilities "like a giant unchained," in the words of one observer. He labored from dawn until long after dusk, leading discussions, quizzing assistants, poring through dusty files. On evenings and weekends Verwoerd stuffed his car with reports that he carefully annotated at home in his study. With each passing day, a more complete plan for South Africa's future took shape in his mind. It would extend the principles of apartheid into every sphere: primary education, housing, family life, vocational training, employment, medical care, ethnic culture, industrial development, and even defense. Weaving strands from his prior academic and political experiences, Verwoerd steadily fashioned a canopy under which all of South Africa's problems, he believed, could be included and resolved. According to his friends, critics, and biographers, Verwoerd never suffered from any reservations about the rectitude of his actions. Asked by a reporter some years later whether his many responsibilities did not strain him or give him ulcers, Verwoerd replied that they did not. Why not? asked the reporter. Because, replied Verwoerd, "I do not have the nagging doubt of ever wondering whether I am perhaps wrong."

Verwoerd, of course, did not act alone. The views he promoted had support throughout Afrikanerdom—from the churches to the universities, from the factories to the farms. In the early 1950s he was still just one member of a cabinet, one voice in a chorus. Yet as both contemporary witnesses and subsequent history testify, he exerted an influence over South African politics for the next sixteen years out of all proportion with what one might expect of a single man. His power flowed directly from the depth of his confidence and the breadth of his vision, both of which inspired and rallied his colleagues at moments when their commitment to white supremacy might otherwise have flagged. Verwoerd succeeded partly through raw force of personality, but even more through his exceptional ability to buttress every proposal, no matter how outlandish, with layers of moral and quasi-scientific argument. Every inequitable edict he presented as necessary to prevent the unjust domination of the white minority by the black majority. Every restriction on the civil liberties or rights of Africans he defended as necessary for the protection of Western, democratic, and white civilization. Every incident of brutality by the police and army he explained away as necessary measures to guard all South Africans—black and white—from revolutionaries who refused to accept the natural racial harmony of the nation.

Though Verwoerd held fast to a personal belief in the racial superiority of whites to all other races, he was wary of relying on simple racial prejudice or retooled social Darwinism to advance his cause. To avoid the pitfalls of arguments based on race, Verwoerd brilliantly relocated the justification for white domination into a new sphere, that of culture. His logic often paralleled the work of German anthropologists and mission theorists, who believed that missionaries should not attempt to alter the culture of the people with whom they worked. They opposed British and American efforts to teach English; to build schools and hospitals; and to encourage the adoption of Western etiquette and practices. Though apparently benevolent, such cultural sensitivity also had adverse effects, since it required missionaries to withhold medical, educational, economic, and technological resources deemed to be culturally "inappropriate." Perversely, the theory of distinctive cultures often ended up more imperialist than its English counterpart, since it maintained a stark boundary of dominion permeable to the members of the "more advanced" culture but impenetrable to those it claimed to protect.

Verwoerd deftly argued that the principle of cultural purity that undergirded apartheid would be beneficial for everyone. The government's measures would not only preserve white culture but would also guard the cultures of the Indian, Asian, Coloured, and African peoples from inappropriate European contamination. Verwoerd's theories, born in academia and raised in the intoxicating fervor of editorial advocacy, grew to maturity in the Department of Native Affairs. For decades Verwoerd had been a strong proponent of Afrikaner culture, but now, after his party's political triumph, he could look beyond his parochial borders and claim the role of protector of both Afrikaner culture and the English way of life in South Africa. Verwoerd transformed himself from the defender of the Dutch against the hostile English to the defender of the European against the hostile African; from the advocate of the Afrikaner to the champion of the white race. Though Verwoerd detested the squeamishness of his predecessors, he freely borrowed their ideas and prescriptions. From the British Lagden Commission at the turn of the century, Verwoerd accepted the idea of breaking South Africa into white and black regions. From Hertzog and the experiences of the economic depression of the 1930s, he drew the belief that the protection of white labor from black competition was necessary and desirable. From Smuts he plucked the rhetoric of enlightened paternalism, under which Verwoerd tried to hide every new restrictive policy. Out of these intellectual traditions and past examples, Verwoerd gradually constructed a plan for the permanent white domination of his country, a plan which would eventually be given its own title—"grand apartheid."

Despite the Nationalist Party's success, Verwoerd knew that his ideas about South Africa's future would be controversial, so he laid them before the legislature in pieces. In doing so, he adopted an unusual strategy, casting each component of his plan on the legislative shore in such a tidal wave of detail that his opponents were completely engulfed. Members of the opposition groaned when they saw Verwoerd's broad figure take the podium in parliament. Like his days at the University of Stellenbosch, Verwoerd treated his listeners with disdain. One observer described his delivery as that of a "patient schoolmaster who had to explain a difficult lesson to the class"; another said he resembled "a professor reaching down to a group of disappointing students." Unfettered in parliament by the limitations of fixed class periods, Verwoerd held forth at mind-numbing length. In one of his earliest speeches, he droned in a reedy, inflectionless voice for four hours. At first the end of his speeches brought an explosion of rebuttals from the opposition, but Verwoerd wore them all down with a blend of courteous irony, patient reiteration, and absolute indefatigability. On one occasion a hapless member asked Verwoerd one question to which Verwoerd replied for half a day.

His condescending demeanor and obfuscatory tactics entertained his supporters, infuriated his opponents, and amused the press. Over time Verwoerd's fantastic prolixity intimidated the legislators, who knew that to ask him a question was to destroy any prospect of conducting business for hours. Even when politicians and journalists openly complained and snickered, Verwoerd remained impervious. So complete was his self-confidence, in fact, that he felt no shame in lecturing other members of the government to keep their remarks brief. "Long political speeches are wearisome," he told one group. "Short and pithy sermons are therefore worth more than long, drawn out ones."

However high-handed Verwoerd's treatment of the elected members of his own legislature might have been, he had, in his own mind, demonstrated respect by his willingness to answer their questions at all. To the millions of Africans under his command he believed he owed no such duty. Rural Africans, in his view, were childlike creatures who had difficulty perceiving and pursuing their best interests. To Verwoerd these interests were obvious: Africans should work for the white man when the white man needed it, but otherwise they should maintain their own picturesque culture, free from the unhealthy effects of white civilization. To counteract the influence of industrial society, which had thrown Africans from all over the country together, eroding ethnic boundaries, Verwoerd set out to revive an effort first pioneered by the British to re-tribalize Africans and to use tribal leaders as an extension of the government's authority. After announcing that chiefs would be the source of authority for Africans, Verwoerd put them on the government payroll and sent them to special schools to learn how to govern according to the requirements of the Department of Native Affairs.

Verwoerd also labored to revitalize tribal customs. Whenever he visited an African community, he notified the village leaders that he wished to be honored in the "traditional way." When he entered a village, a prearranged chorus would shout "Sebeloke!" (the patron) and Verwoerd would process inside in a blaze of pageantry. Moving to the center of the village, Verwoerd would receive a wooden carving or other gift from the chief. Sometimes a specially composed hymn of praise would be recited to him while the entire village listened respectfully. Verwoerd's aides would then ostentatiously distribute sugar, salt, and tobacco to the chief and his officers, fabric to the wives, and boxes of candy to the children. After the exchange of gifts, Verwoerd would join his hosts in a meal around a central fire. As they squatted in a circle, crunching chicken bones, sipping homemade beer, and scooping porridge from a common pot, Verwoerd would garrulously instruct his audience, carefully selecting simple metaphors and allegories that he thought would reach their minds. Before departing, Verwoerd would stroll among the children and pose for the government photographers. These pictures served double duty: they demonstrated to detractors that Africans responded well to benevolent control and reminded supporters that such savage peoples could never be integrated into the civilized white world.

To Verwoerd such visits typified the proper relationship between whites and the other races of South Africa. Like a slaveholder in the American South, Verwoerd felt magnanimous toward those who meekly accepted their inferior status and gratefully received the tokens of white paternalism. Conversely, he detested Africans who believed in equality. In his view the efforts by English, American, and other missionaries to build schools for Africans had been a disastrous mistake. The Africans emerging from these schools and coming to the cities were freaks of nature, persons deluded with fantasies of equality that their own biology and sociology rendered impossible. At best, they were cultural traitors who undermined the otherwise happy tribal societies; at worst, revolutionaries whose goal was a murderous seizure of power.

Like all Nationalists, Verwoerd believed that Africans and other races should not be given the slightest toehold in the white parliamentary system. He moved quickly to neutralize the advisory Natives' Representative Council on which sat so many members of the African National Congress. In December 1950, less than two months after he became minister of native affairs, Verwoerd traveled to the Orlando location in the South West township that would later become known by its acronym, Soweto. In his usual doctrinaire manner Verwoerd lectured Professor Z. K. Matthews and the other members of the council about his vision for South Africa and urged the group to agree that apartheid was a desirable political goal. "Must the future development of the Bantu and white societies take place together, or separated as far as possible?" Verwoerd asked. "If the answer is together, then it should be clearly realized that rivalry and clashes will take place everywhere. As long as the points of contact are small, as at present, friction and clashes will be less evident."

The more intermixture there was, Verwoerd warned, the stronger the clashes between races would become. "In such clashes the whites will come off best, at least for a long time, and the non-white will come off second best in every sphere," Verwoerd predicted. "This will inevitably cause in him growing resistance and resentment." Blacks would not be satisfied with a limited share in the political life of the country but would want equal voting rights, he said. They would want the same condition in the social, economic, and other fields, which in time would bring mixed residence, mixed working, mixed living, and ultimately mixture of the races, in spite of the known pride of the European and the Bantu in the purity of their ancestry.* Verwoerd insisted that the only alternative to such a horrendous outcome would be to find a plan that would allow both populations to develop to their full potential yet avoid conflict. To Verwoerd, the answer was obvious: "The only possible way out . . . is that both should accept development apart from each other."

When Verwoerd finished speaking, Z. K. Matthews rose to his feet. With dignity and reserve, the professor told the minister that Africans had not been allowed to express their views on the plan and would never accept the unilateral imposition of it by whites. Another council mem-

---

* "Bantu" is a technical name for the language group that encompasses the languages and dialects of the majority of Africans in South Africa, much like "Romance" includes French, Spanish, and Italian. By extension, the term was used by whites, often disparagingly, to describe individuals or groups who spoke a Bantu language. In its full political usage under Verwoerd, the term implied a culture separated from white civilization by unbridgeable gaps of language, history, and development.

ber, Selope Thema, attacked Verwoerd for wanting to create a network of territorial "zoos" for African people. The council decisively rejected his ideas and Verwoerd left. A few months later he issued a statement that the council was "not an effective body to represent the real interests of the Bantu people" and abolished it outright.

Though Verwoerd found no support for his views among the African, Indian, and Coloured organizations, he attracted increasing interest among whites in his reformulation of apartheid into a doctrine of "separate development." To any group of listeners—in the press, at dinner parties, before the legislature, or over a village fire—Verwoerd tirelessly propounded this new vision of the future. The Afrikaners had a distinctive culture formed over three hundred years in South Africa. Other groups—from wandering African tribes to marauding English imperialists—had tried unsuccessfully to destroy it. Since that culture was continuously threatened by political, economic, and demographic forces, it needed to be preserved through political power. This drive for cultural purity was a positive development for all groups within South Africa, since a segregated society would protect them from mutual corruption. "The Nationalist Afrikaner is not an oppressor because he knows what it means to be suppressed," he told parliament. "We know what it means to fight for freedom. We realize that the Natives must also be given the opportunity to develop along their own lines under the guidance of the European, instead of becoming imitators of the white man."

In pressing his case, Verwoerd skillfully adjusted his argument for different audiences. When speaking to whites, he stressed that the Afrikaner and British, though born of different ethnic roots, had to protect their common "European culture" from alien customs. To Africans, he denied the notion of racial unity or common culture and insisted that they be separated into tribal categories such as Xhosa, Sotho, Zulu, and Tswana. Thus the same idea—cultural integrity—enabled Verwoerd to argue simultaneously in favor of ethnic unity for whites and ethnic diversity for blacks. The logical results were bizarre: those of English and Afrikaner descent, whose mother tongues are only somewhat related, could live in the same neighborhoods because they were all Europeans; Xhosa and Zulu peoples, whose languages are close cognates, had to be forcibly separated because they were culturally distinct.

Guided by Verwoerd's plan and goaded by his energy, the Nationalist Party parliament in Cape Town forged link after link in a chain of racist restrictions. In 1951 the government approved the Bantu Authorities Act, which established a new hierarchical system of government for the African reserves that could be controlled directly by Verwoerd in Pretoria. In 1952 the legislature passed the Native Act, which technically required all persons to possess and carry reference books containing identity, tax receipts, and other important information but was applied solely, and with severe penalties for noncompliance, to Africans. In 1953 it approved the Bantu Labor Act, which prohibited strikes of any sort by Africans. For Verwoerd it was a period of great creativity and optimism. He could see what many of his colleagues could not: that each piece of legislation brought the country closer to the realization of his design and the resolution of South Africa's most insoluble problems.

For Africans, the 1948 triumph of the Nationalist Party had brought disillusionment and reevaluation. A. B. Xuma had already decided that the African National Congress needed to broaden its opposition to the white government. In 1947 he had entered into a formal agreement with two other physicians, Dr. Yusuf Dadoo of the Transvaal Indian Congress and Dr. G. M. Naicker of the Natal Indian Congress. Many attacked the "doctors' pact"—the government from the right and more radical groups from the left—and a race riot in Durban in January 1949 nearly destroyed it. A few weeks later the executive committees of the Indian and African congresses urgently met to patch up the coalition as best they could.

In July 1947 Mandela and Anton Lembede were discussing Youth League business when Lembede suddenly complained of a severe pain in his stomach. Mandela drove him to the hospital, but the care was so abysmal that Lembede, who was only thirty-three years old, died that same night. Deeply shaken, the remaining members of the Youth League regrouped and elected a new slate of officers. Peter Mda became the new president, Oliver Tambo vice president, and Nelson Mandela secretary. Under their guidance the membership and financial resources of the Youth League swelled rapidly. After the 1948 election, the officers of the Youth League concluded that Xuma was being altogether too cautious. The spontaneity of the miners' strike and the vigor of the Indian passive resistance movement had persuaded the members of the Youth League that Africans across the country could be inspired to join mass protests against the new policy of apartheid. When Xuma failed to capitalize on this sentiment in the first year of Malan's rule, the Youth League plotted to unseat him. Shortly before the annual African National Congress convention in December 1949, the officers of the Youth League went to Xuma with an ultimatum: either he immediately would have to adopt the Youth League's assertive Programme of Action as the blueprint for resistance to apartheid or they would sponsor a drive to remove him from office at the convention.

When Xuma spurned their offer, Mda and Tambo located an outside candidate, Dr. James Moroka, who was so unfamiliar with the ANC that he kept calling it the African National "Council." When the ANC Youth

League brought their nominee to the floor of the national conference, the vote split along generational lines: the older delegates supported Xuma, the younger ones Moroka. Moroka won by a slim margin and became the new president general of the ANC. Even more important, the delegates elevated Walter Sisulu to the post of secretary general—by a majority of one. The Youth League, founded only a few years before as a small pressure group, had achieved a decisive position within the ANC, whose national executive committee now included not only their own members but also an eclectic mix of Communists, traditionalists, and liberals. The young men were delighted with their new prominence. Writing in the Youth League's journal, *Lodestar,* Nelson Mandela commented that in the past the ANC leaders had acted "in the apparent hope that by pleading their cause they would persuade the authorities to change their hearts and extend to them all the rights they were demanding"; now, he said, the ANC would exert pressure to "compel the authorities to grant their demands. . . . We have a powerful ideology capable of capturing the imaginations of the masses. . . . Our duty is now to carry that ideology fully to them."

Despite the Nationalist government's later portrayal of ANC members as political extremists, the leaders saw themselves as moderate democrats who always had to combat a host of more strident organizations such as the All African Convention (AAC) and the Non-European Unity Movement (NEUM). The divisions between the groups cut along many lines: race, class, geography, ideology, power base, religion, and strategy. The African National Congress of the late 1940s was an elite movement of African professionals; the Unity Movement, though composed almost exclusively of intellectuals, held to a Trotskyite doctrine of the power of the "masses." The African National Congress had its strongest following in Johannesburg and the Eastern Cape; the Unity Movement drew its largest following from the Western Cape. The officers of the Youth League had an "Africanist" streak and believed that their primary responsibility was to Africans; the Unity Movement was dominated by Coloureds who thought that the movement offered the only legitimate mechanism to coalesce the aversion to apartheid felt by all racial groups. Many of the ANC leaders had been educated in mission schools and retained a strong commitment to Christianity; the majority of Unity Movement members were atheists and viewed Christianity as a tool of oppression. The leaders of the ANC were pragmatic about the means to achieve the clear goal of a universal democratic franchise; the leaders of the Unity Movement demanded strict "noncollaboration" as a precondition to the apocalyptic advent of a new socialist society.

Until 1950, neither the members of the Unity Movement nor those of the African National Congress were eager to work with the South African Communist Party. Though both groups suspected that the Communists had a hidden agenda, the ANC and the Unity Movement criticized the Communists from opposite directions. The leaders of the ANC resisted the Communists' insistence that South Africa's racial discrimination was solely the result of class struggle, and they feared that the Communists intended to use the drive for national liberation as a stepping-stone to socialist revolution. The Unity Movement, on the other hand, believed that the Communists were committed not to "true socialism" but to whatever dogma was currently propounded by the Soviet government. Despite repeated efforts throughout the 1940s to reconcile and unite these disparate groups, a last marathon negotiation in April 1949 ended in failure.

With Moroka and the Youth League guiding the African National Congress, relations with the Communists grew more turbulent. In keeping with their promise to take more direct action, the Youth League leaders planned a national work stoppage for May 1, 1950. A few days later they were enraged to learn that an ad hoc group formed of members of the Indian Congress, the Transvaal ANC, and the Communist Party had called for a similar action on the same day in Johannesburg to protest the arrest of some of their leaders. Eager to thwart this challenge to the ANC's dominance, Mandela and others feverishly rushed around and disrupted meetings, clashed with Communist organizers, and denounced the plan in print, demanding that Africans ignore the call to protest. At the same time the Malan government rapidly issued new restrictions on demonstrations and deployed two thousand police in Johannesburg on the first of May.

Despite these limitations, more than half of the African workers in the Johannesburg region stayed home on May 1. The protest remained peaceful until the end of the day, when police attacks and shootings set off sporadic rioting. Afterward Mandela and his associates marveled at what they had seen. "That day," he later recalled, "was a turning point in my life, both in understanding through first-hand experience the ruthlessness of the police and in being deeply impressed by the support the African workers had given to the May Day call." The Youth Leaguers felt new respect for the actions of uneducated workers and the determination of the Communists. Given the success of the Johannesburg strike, the ANC national executive committee decided to try the technique across the entire country. They called for a work stoppage on June 26, 1950, to mark a National Day of Mourning and Protest. This time the officials of the ANC, the Indian Congress, and the Communist Party created a coordinating committee to plan the event. Tensions among the groups eased even more when Nelson Mandela met Cape

Town's Moses Kotane, a member of the ANC executive committee and secretary of the Communist Party, who had recently been issued a government banning order that tightly restricted his words and movements. Mandela decided that Kotane was "really a Nationalist" and the two became personal friends. The new political partnership proved fruitful: on June 26 there were partial work stoppages in Johannesburg and Cape Town and strong stay-aways in Port Elizabeth, Durban, and Alexandra township. Though employers in Durban fired a thousand workers in retaliation, it seemed to leaders in all racial groups that the activists had found a potent new weapon.

The Nationalist Party government lost no time responding to the disturbances. They strengthened labor regulations and broadened police powers. They also moved forward aggressively with segregationist legislation aimed at the Coloured population, sparking another wave of protests. Eager to weaken the United Party and to remove the last remnant of interracial political participation, the Malan government submitted the Separate Representation of Voters Act to parliament in 1951. The measure was designed to strip thousands of Coloured citizens in the region around Cape Town of their vote. The proposal triggered a storm of protest, not only among Coloured leaders but also among whites. A former South African war hero and Battle of Britain flying ace, A. G. "Sailor" Malan (no relation to the prime minister), gathered hundreds of followers into a brigade of "torch commandos" who marched at night through Cape Town and illumined the city with portable flames. Liberal women, many of them of English descent, banded together into an organization known as the Black Sash, a name derived from their practice of wearing diagonal black strips of cloth as they stood silently on street corners and held signs denouncing the Nationalists' attack on the constitution.

In late 1950, just a few weeks after Hendrik Verwoerd took control of the Department of Native Affairs, Nelson Mandela became the national president of the African National Congress Youth League. The thirty-two-year-old lawyer knew that after persuading the African National Congress to follow their Programme of Action, the Youth Leaguers had to prove that the plan would work. During the early months of 1951 Mandela, Sisulu, and the others argued about tactics, particularly that of nonviolent resistance. Could nonviolent civil disobedience spark the imagination and participation of millions of Africans throughout the country? What other alternatives could succeed against an overwhelmingly armed police force? How would they find, train, organize, and support volunteers to commit acts of civil disobedience?

The government inadvertently settled the dispute among the ANC leaders when Malan announced that it was planning a massive celebration of the three hundredth anniversary of Jan van Riebeeck's arrival in Cape Town for April 6, 1952. In response, the ANC leaders decided to organize a nonviolent Defiance Campaign to challenge the growing web of apartheid laws and regulations. The delegates to the ANC's annual convention in December 1951 approved the plan but set the beginning of the campaign for June 26, 1952, the second anniversary of the 1950 work stoppage, to give themselves almost three more months to organize. Nelson Mandela was selected national volunteer in chief to coordinate all the activities of the campaign; Maulvi Cachalia, whose father had been deeply involved in the South African protests organized by Gandhi in 1907, became his deputy.

To inform the prime minister of their intentions and to urge him to reconsider his policies, Moroka and Sisulu wrote Malan a letter on January 21, 1952. They reminded him of the decades of conscientious effort by the members of the ANC to achieve their aims through legitimate constitutional means. They explained that instead of responding favorably, the government had systematically tightened controls to the point where the matter had become one of "life and death to the people." The African National Congress could not remain silent any longer, for such silence would betray the trust of their followers. Accordingly, if the government did not repeal the segregationist laws, the ANC would go forward with a national campaign of protest. The prime minister did not reply; instead the ANC leaders received an angry letter from his private secretary, who scolded them for not addressing their concerns through the proper channels, that is, to Hendrik Verwoerd.

By this time Mandela had already spent months traveling around South Africa to cities and townships, villages and industrial sites, to explain nonviolence and to solicit volunteers for the campaign. Having just obtained his driver's license—a rarity for Africans at the time— Mandela sometimes traveled in his Oldsmobile. Other times he took the train, though he sometimes found himself stranded late in the evening in small rural towns where no restaurant, taxi, or hotel would serve an African. In such cases he would have to walk miles in the hope of finding an African family who would take him in for the night. Day after day he explained to gatherings of potential recruits that the authorities would be provocative and harsh. The volunteers would have to be dignified and disciplined at all times, he told them. At the end of each talk he held a political altar call, asking the listeners to come forward and sign up; through dozens of such meetings he built a roster of volunteers.

Mandela did not restrict his appeals to Africans. He also traveled with Cachalia to Durban to secure the support of the Indian community. He was moved when large groups of Indians listened attentively and responded to his call. His emerging faith in Indian, Coloured, and white activists began to outweigh his distrust of working with other racial groups. Reflecting at the time on the preparations for the campaign, he commented that "we can now say unity between the non-European people in this country has become a living reality." Mandela also knew from the Indian resistance of 1946 that the Africans had much to learn from Indian activists. Indeed, the tactics of the Defiance Campaign had been drawn beyond South Africa from the Gandhian techniques that had won India its independence from the British Empire only three years before. Though Mandela preached on behalf of nonviolence, his endorsement was more pragmatic than moral. "The state was far more powerful than we," he wrote later, "and any attempts at violence by us would be devastatingly crushed. . . . I saw nonviolence not as an inviolable principle but as a tactic to be used as the situation demanded."

On June 26, 1952, thousands of South Africans of all races systematically defied apartheid. In cities from the Eastern Cape to the Transvaal they publicly burned their passes and gathered in integrated groups; entered whites-only waiting rooms and bathrooms in train stations; and marched into restricted restaurants, hotels, buses, and neighborhoods. Though all the early demonstrations were completely peaceful, the police responded violently. Nelson Mandela watched a policeman break a friend's ankle by throwing him down a flight of stairs. When Mandela protested, the policeman kicked him. Mandela spent the next two days in jail, his first real experience of imprisonment. The jail was "squalid, dark, and dingy," he recalled, "but we were all together and so impassioned and spirited that I barely noticed my surroundings."

As the campaign continued, the authorities cracked down harder. In late July, armed police raided ANC homes and offices throughout the country, arrested Moroka, Mandela, Sisulu, Dadoo, Cachalia, and others, and charged them under the Suppression of Communism Act with furthering the aims of Communism. When the trial date arrived in November, the government prosecutors argued that the leaders of the Defiance Campaign had planned a violent overthrow of the government. The ANC defendants were shocked to find that their president, James Moroka, had dissociated himself from the other defendants and hired his own defense attorney. When Moroka took the witness stand he publicly renounced the principles of the ANC. "Asked whether he thought there should be equality between black and white in South Africa," Mandela wrote later, "Dr. Moroka replied that there would never be such a thing. We felt like slumping in our seats." Moroka's lawyer pleaded for leniency for his client by pointing to Moroka's financial assistance in the education of rural white farm boys. Despite this setback the trial turned out relatively well for the defendants. The judge rejected the prosecutor's key arguments and found the leaders guilty only of "statutory Communism," which had "nothing to do with Communism as it is commonly known." To accommodate the government, he sentenced them to nine months in prison and then suspended the sentences on the condition that they cease their political activities.

By December, after six months of repeated challenges to the apartheid laws, the leaders of the National Party* government showed no signs of conceding. The Defiance Campaign had not received wide coverage in the international press and few foreign governments had expressed support for its goals. Employers had responded to protest strikes by firing thousands of workers. Police had jailed more than eight thousand protesters; many remained in prison at the end of the year. Officials of the Malan government, unhappy at the outcome of the ANC trial, slapped banning orders—strict prohibitions from speaking in public or attending meetings—on more than one hundred leaders of the Defiance Campaign. Finally, the government approved more severe punishments: any person caught in any act "by way of protest or in support of any campaign against any law" could be sentenced to three years in prison. To cool the ardor of the campaign's youthful volunteers, the government also reintroduced flogging as a penalty for public dissent.

Though the South African judiciary occasionally tried to rebuke the National Party for its disregard of basic civil liberties, Malan and his cabinet smashed every one of the courts' efforts to rein them in. Unlike the situation in the United States, where civil disobedience and economic boycotts could complement a legal drive to secure constitutionally guaranteed rights, South African activists had no deep-rooted egalitarian principles or constitutional documents on which to draw—indeed, the founding document of the Union of South Africa explicitly restricted African rights. Despite these limitations, anti-apartheid lawyers persuaded the courts in 1951 and 1952 that the Nationalist laws requiring separate electoral rolls for the races were invalid. Malan responded by pushing a bill through parliament that declared the legislative branch a higher authority than the judiciary on such matters. When lawyers for the Defiance Campaign defendants garnered a court ruling that public facilities of differing quality for different races violated standards of equity, Malan's party swiftly passed the Separate Amenities Act, which specified that facilities such as bathrooms, buses, waiting rooms, restaurants, and so on *should* vary in quality for the different races.

Despite the government's unrelenting severity, the Defiance Campaign proved a boon to the African National Congress. Tens of thou-

---

* The name of the party was changed from Nationalist to National after mergers with several smaller factions in 1951.

sands across the country now recognized the ANC as the leading opponent of apartheid. The number of official members of the ANC shot up
in a year from a few thousand to more than one hundred thousand
people. Perhaps most important, the exuberance, commitment, and success created by the protests finally freed the leaders of the African National Congress from the remnants of their historical fidelity to public
decorum and parliamentary procedure. "The ANC emerged as a truly
mass-based organization with an impressive corps of experienced activists who had braved the police, the courts, and the jails," Mandela later
wrote. "The stigma usually associated with imprisonment had been removed." After their release from prison, the Youth League members
decided that Moroka's obsequiousness had undermined his ability to
lead the movement. They turned instead to Albert Luthuli, the chief of a
small Zulu community near the Groutville mission station, just north of
Durban on the Indian Ocean.

Not long before, when Luthuli had been elected president of the
Natal branch of the ANC, W. W. M. Eiselen, Verwoerd's deputy, summoned Luthuli for an audience. Luthuli's involvement with the ANC,
Eiselen said bluntly, was inconsistent with his responsibilities as a tribal
chief. He would have to choose between the positions. Several weeks
later Luthuli told the government that he refused to resign from either
post, so Verwoerd immediately deposed him as chief of the mission
reserve. When the members of the Amakholwa tribe heard, they asked
the local native commissioner what would happen when the new chief
was appointed, since they were all members of the ANC. Luthuli's refusal to bow enhanced his reputation not only in his community but
among ANC activists across the country. Though the government eventually found a compliant figurehead to replace him, Luthuli continued
to use the title of chief as a form of protest against Verwoerd's action.

Unlike Xuma, who had nurtured a patrician distaste for public demonstrations, or Moroka, who had feared that such actions would spiral
out of control, Luthuli strongly endorsed the new ANC attempts to
work with other groups and attract mass popular support, even though
he knew that this would attract increased government oppression.
Luthuli was a devout Christian who believed that unjust suffering and
sacrifice on the part of those struggling for political rights would prove a
powerful moral force, strong enough to move the hearts of the white
community.

The evidence for the moral sensitivity of the white community in the
face of National Party policies was, at best, mixed. When the National
Party called for elections in 1953, the members of the United Party
chose to attack the government's candidates from the right, arguing that
Verwoerd's proposals for separate development would mean carving up

South Africa and delivering large slices of "white territory" to the Africans. National Party candidates in turn played on fears stimulated by the Defiance Campaign and won a large victory throughout the country. To Malan and to Verwoerd the election results signaled strong support for apartheid, and they planned to accelerate its implementation. In disgust at the United Party's stance and the National Party's victory, a small number of white politicians broke off to form the anti-apartheid Liberal Party. Among their number was Alan Paton, whose novel *Cry, the Beloved Country,* about the life of a humble Zulu Anglican priest under apartheid, had become an international best-seller in 1950.

The outpouring of mass support for the Defiance Campaign in 1952 and the victory of the apartheid government in 1953 presented the leaders of the African National Congress with two tenacious problems, the first organizational and the second ideological. In the years since its inception its small roster, professional membership, modest budget, and regional concentration had meant that the ANC could be managed with short chains of command and direct communication. The leaders came from a small pool of activists who knew each other well and could rely on interpersonal loyalties to sustain them under political duress. The explosive numerical and geographical growth in membership that accompanied the Defiance Campaign produced the same administrative problems for the ANC as it would for any political or commercial organization. Luthuli, Sisulu, and Mandela had to consider how to set up standard procedures, disseminate information and instructions, channel criticism, outwit informants, and reach consensus with supporters scattered in pockets around a vast country. No longer could they rely on fervent leaflets, mass meetings, and word-of-mouth messages between leaders to combat Verwoerd's accelerating machine.

Mandela pondered the problem for some time and then proposed a new system, a hybrid network of democratic councils and revolutionary cells. Members would be organized into local street committees, who would elect representatives to a wider group, then to a citywide body, and finally to a regional council. The ANC leaders liked the proposal, known as the M (for Mandela) plan, and agreed to implement it. When they tried, they immediately ran into serious practical problems. Members of the ANC, like all Africans, had to struggle daily with the exhausting task of surviving in a highly discriminatory and economically oppressive society. Africans had to travel long distances from the country to the urban communities to find work; when they arrived, they had to locate housing and employment. Most who found jobs had to rise early in the morning and catch crowded, uncomfortable government buses to carry them from the township on the distant edges of the cities to the white factories, shops, or households where they worked. The white employers saw no difficulty in keeping their African employees for long hours in return for low pay, and at the end of the day the workers would return on another tightly packed, creaking bus to their homes. Then came all the normal responsibilities of life—finding and preparing food, washing clothes, cleaning and repairing the home, caring for children, and meeting responsibilities to the wider family. As apartheid stiffened, the time, resources, and energy that Africans could offer to the political struggle dropped. In South Africa, as in many countries around the world, the regime ruled not only through force but through fatigue.

The practical obstacles encountered by the leaders of the African National Congress increased dramatically under the constant barrage of harassment, surveillance, and arrests to which they were subjected by the police. The minister of native affairs churned out reams of new regulations to circumscribe the rights and actions of all Africans. The minister of justice imposed banning orders on those who showed signs of leadership, and as the years wore on the restrictions listed in those banning orders grew more and more detailed and stifling. Luthuli was banned immediately after his election as ANC president and Mandela was restricted by law to Johannesburg and ordered not to speak in public for more than a year. As soon as the old banning orders expired, the government immediately imposed new ones.

Despite these burdens Nelson Mandela managed to complete both his legal education (by correspondence) and his required apprenticeship. During the year of the Defiance Campaign, the thirty-four-year-old opened a practice with Oliver Tambo in a small office on the second floor of a building near the magistrates' court in Johannesburg. The new laws and regulations passed by the government and the vigor with which they were enforced by the police propelled hundreds of Africans through the small door marked MANDELA AND TAMBO. "To reach our desks each morning Nelson and I ran the gauntlet of patient queues of people overflowing from the waiting-room into the corridors," Tambo later recalled. Most normal actions and aspirations had been criminalized by the government. Everything from owning a piece of land to brewing beer was tightly regulated, and any infringement could lead to prison.

Tambo and Mandela struggled to handle as many cases as they could. Mandela's persistence won him grudging respect from some white court officers and attorneys. When the Transvaal Law Society petitioned the Supreme Court to have Mandela disbarred for his involvement in the Defiance Campaign because it was activity "which did not conform to the standards of conduct expected from members of an honorable profession," a prominent white lawyer defended him and persuaded the Supreme Court to reject the petition. Despite such occasional displays of support or their periodic courtroom victories, neither Mandela nor Tambo ever forgot that the judicial system was fundamentally tilted against them. "In the courts we were treated courteously by many officials but we were very often discriminated against by some and treated with resentment and hostility by others," Mandela recalled. "We were constantly aware that no matter how well, how correctly, how adequately we pursued our career of law, we could not become a prosecutor, or a magistrate, or a judge. . . . As attorneys we often dealt with officials whose competence and attainments were no higher than ours, but whose superior position was maintained and protected by a white skin."

In the aftermath of the Defiance Campaign the burden of Mandela's case load and his new responsibilities as the leader of the Transvaal ANC began to affect his family and his marriage. Not long after their marriage in 1944, Nelson and Evelyn had moved to 8115 Orlando West, a small brick structure that Mandela would view as home for the next forty-five years. In their nine years of marriage they had had four children, one of whom died at ten months. By 1953 the two had started to drift apart. Mandela had been molded as a patriarch and thought that the care of children was his wife's responsibility. He often left his home before dawn and returned hours after the children had gone to sleep, prompting his five-year-old son Thembi to ask Evelyn one day, "Where does Daddy live?" During the Defiance Campaign Mandela traveled for weeks at a time, spent long days at his law office in town, and attended interminable evening meetings. Evelyn, in the meantime, had become a midwife and a passionate Jehovah's Witness. She distributed *The Watchtower* to her neighbors and urged Mandela to abandon his work with the ANC in order to prepare for Armageddon. "I tried to persuade her of the necessity of the struggle, while she attempted to persuade me of the value of religious faith," Mandela wrote years later. "We also waged a battle for the minds and hearts of the children. She wanted them to be religious, and I thought they should be political." In 1955 Evelyn demanded that her husband choose between her and the ANC. When Mandela was released from one of his stints in jail, he returned to find his house stripped bare: Evelyn had packed everything, taken the children, and left. The marriage was over, but it planted a permanent seed of self-doubt in Mandela about whether his political convictions were worth the price that his loved ones were forced to pay. Eventually Evelyn returned to the Transkei where Mandela's cousin Kaiser Matanzima helped her to get back on her feet.

The ANC's organizational difficulties, though troublesome, were not as serious as its ideological problems. Even after the Defiance Campaign, the African National Congress did not have a clearly articulated set of beliefs. They had slipped free from the tenets of parliamentary liberalism and moved into street activism, but unlike the Communists and members of other more radical groups, they did not have an overarching doctrine to link goals, strategy, and tactics. For many years this ideological flexibility had been an advantage, for it had permitted the African National Congress to welcome many points of view under its nationalist umbrella. Nonetheless, the leaders of the ANC knew that if they were to sustain the excitement that their bold challenge to the government had whipped up, they would need a new vision.

The idea that captured the minds of the leaders took form in August 1953 in the home of the venerable ANC leader Professor Z. K. Matthews. Matthews had just returned from a year as a visiting professor at Union Theological Seminary in New York City, where he had followed closely the growing postwar interest in race in the United States and had begun to consider how to apply what he had learned. When he returned to South Africa, he quickly identified the ideological gap that threatened to undermine the gains of the Defiance Campaign. Matthews proposed that the ANC sponsor a series of large public meetings across the country to discuss and articulate the future of South Africa. He suggested that the meetings be open to all races and all political parties, even the Nationalists. When Matthews formally advanced the idea at the ANC's annual conference in December 1953, the delegates strongly approved.

To coordinate the eighteen-month planning of the national event, the ANC leaders endorsed the formation of a National Action Council made up of eight representatives, two from each racial group. This arrangement infuriated many. Africanists in the ANC complained that the structure of the council allowed three minority racial groups—who even in combination did not equal the number of Africans—to control three-quarters of the votes and thus effectively to dictate the direction of the campaign to the majority population. White liberals worried about the extensive participation of the Congress of Democrats, an organization filled with white Communists who were determined to bend the thinking, language, and strategies of the group toward Marxism.

Despite the contentious atmosphere, the sponsoring organizations moved forward with their plans to involve as many people as possible in the convention. To solicit the participation and ideas from members of all races, the National Action Council issued a "Call to a Congress of the People" and invited everyone to help plan South Africa's future. Tens of thousands of pamphlets circulated through the country asking "If you could make the laws, what would you do? How would you set about making South Africa a happy place for all the people who live in it?" The members of the council tried, with mixed success, to set up a national network of local and regional committees to solicit, collect, and digest the suggestions. In some parts of the country the invitation produced thousands of ideas; some people scribbled on small pieces of paper, school exercise books, or the back of the leaflet itself. In other areas the committees had to think up ideas on their own. Gradually the suggestions filtered up to the national organization, which passed them to a drafting committee to weave into a single document. Working under fierce pressure, the members of the drafting committee struggled to reconcile the collection of haphazard, conflicting ideas. Only days before the national convention was to take place, they produced a draft of a document they called the "Freedom Charter."

On June 26, 1955, more than three thousand delegates assembled in an open, grassy meadow in Kliptown, a small Coloured community on the rim of the African township of Soweto, about fifteen miles southwest of Johannesburg. As Albert Luthuli noted with satisfaction, for the first time in South African history a widely diverse group from many races and political persuasions had come together to confer about the country's future. One hundred and twelve whites, 230 Coloureds, 320 Indians, and nearly 2,500 Africans mingled and talked—a living, swirling rejection of apartheid. Despite the diversity, everywhere one saw the triumphant colors of the African National Congress: green for the verdant land, gold for the mineral wealth, and black for the majority of the population. As a British journalist described the day, one could find "large African grandmothers, wearing Congress skirts, Congress blouses, or Congress *doeks* (berets) on their heads; young Indian wives, with glistening saris and shawls embroidered with Congress colors; grey old African men, with walking sticks and Congress arm-bands; young city workers from Johannesburg, with broad hats, bright American ties and narrow trousers; smooth Indian lawyers and businessmen, moving confidently among the crowd in well-cut suits; and a backcloth of anonymous African faces, listening impassively to the hours of speeches that are the staple of every Congress meeting." Dozens of plainclothes security police mingled with the representatives, taking notes and surreptitiously photographing the participants. Hovering inconspicuously at the edge of the crowd were Nelson Mandela and Walter Sisulu, who despite their banning orders had come to see the fruition of more than a decade of hard organizing.

The primary order of business for the assembly was the reading, discussion, and approval of the Freedom Charter. The charter began with a simple statement: "We, the people of South Africa, declare for all our country and the world to know that South Africa belongs to all who live in it, black and white, and that no government can justly claim authority unless it is based on the will of the people." However straightforward such a statement might seem in retrospect, it was highly controversial at the time. To the members of the ANC who longed for an African nation, this was a dangerous concession to other racial groups; to Nationalists, it was a revolutionary assault on apartheid. The charter then proceeded to make ten vigorous declarations, each followed by four or five sentences offering specific goals or rights within the category. Under the heading "The People Shall Govern!" the charter stated that "every man and woman shall have the right to vote for and stand as a candidate for all bodies which make laws." Under the section "All Shall Be Equal before the Law!" the charter stipulated that "no one shall be imprisoned, deported, or restricted without a fair trial" and "all laws which discriminate on grounds of race, color, or belief shall be repealed."

For the members of the Nationalist government, such political and legal rights were anathema, but the most enduring internal controversies about the provisions of the Freedom Charter have centered on its economic provisions. In some cases the charter lapsed into the vague, optimistic promises of any party platform—"There shall be Houses, Security, and Comfort!"; "The Doors of Learning and of Culture Shall Be Opened!"—which spoke more to the anger and deprivation of those who had experienced the brunt of National Party discrimination than to a specific program. In its most hotly debated section, which begins "The People Shall Share in the Country's Wealth!," the charter zeroed in on chronic economic disparities and proposed a massive redistribution of property, resources, and privileges. "The national wealth of our country, the heritage of all South Africans, shall be restored to the people," the charter declared. "The mineral wealth beneath the soil, the banks, and the monopoly industry shall be transferred to the ownership of the people as a whole; all other industries and trade shall be controlled to assist the well-being of the people; and all people shall have equal rights to trade where they choose, to manufacture and to enter all trades, crafts, and professions."

To liberals, this was more evidence of the influence of Communists, an opinion reinforced when they heard prominent delegates praise the Soviet Union or read congratulatory messages from Chinese leader Zhou En-lai. In later years this economics clause of the Freedom Charter would be interpreted by hardliners in both the ANC and the National Party as evidence of the commitment of the African organization to a centralized socialist economy. But Nelson Mandela, writing a year after the Kliptown conference, insisted that the need to exert economic control was a temporary measure designed to correct past exploitation and ensure the success of the political effort. "It is true that in demanding the nationalization of the banks, the gold mines, and the land the Charter strikes a fatal blow at the financial and gold-mining monopolies

and farming interest," he wrote. "But such a step is absolutely imperative and necessary because the realization of the charter is inconceivable
. . . until the monopolies are first smashed up and the national wealth
of the country turned over to the people." Mandela insisted that the
result would be a new, more vibrant market economy based on private
ownership. "The breaking up . . . of these monopolies will open up
fresh fields for the development of a non-European bourgeois class," he
concluded. "For the first time in the history of the country the non-
European bourgeoisie will have the opportunity to own in their own
name and right mills and factories; [thus] trade and private enterprise
will bloom and flourish as never before."

For nearly two days the organizers methodically read each clause of
the Freedom Charter aloud, pausing after each provision to permit discussion by various speakers and extemporaneous comments from the
delegates. After a period of debate the crowd then adopted the clauses
with a show of hands and a shout of "Afrika!" By three-thirty in the
afternoon of the second day, the delegates had worked their way
through eight sections and were about to begin the section on housing
when one organizer rushed to the microphone and announced to the
crowd, "Armed police are approaching. We do not know what they
want." To keep the crowd calm, he asked them all to rise and sing the
anthem of the African National Congress, "Nkosi Sikelel' iAfrika."

> Lord, bless Africa
> Let her horn be raised
> Listen to our prayers
> Lord bless, we, her children
>
> Come spirit, come Holy Spirit
> Lord bless,
> We, her children

Suddenly fifteen white members of the government's Special Branch,
surrounded by a large group of policemen armed with Sten guns,
mounted the platform. One took the microphone and announced that
all persons were to remain until the officials could identify everyone. To
prevent anyone from departing, a double cordon of heavily armed constables immediately encircled the crowd. Mounted police galloped off to
patrol the perimeter for stragglers.

The participants finished their hymn:

> God bless our nation
> Do away with wars and trouble
> Bless it, bless it,

Bless it, Lord
Our nation, our nation

The police carefully searched those who had been sitting on the platform and seized every piece of paper and roll of film they found. They swept through the crowd, stuffing boxes with literature and money from the tables set up by different organizations. They pulled down banners and posters and filed them away as evidence, including two notices from the food stall identifying "Soup with Meat" and "Soup without Meat." As darkness fell, the police erected tables, some for Europeans and others for non-Europeans, lit portable lamps, and began laboriously taking the name of every participant. Before being permitted to leave, every person was searched; any papers the police discovered were sealed in an envelope with the person's name on it. In addition to being searched and interrogated, every European was photographed. By eight o'clock the police had finished and sent everyone home.

Despite its abrupt and somber end, the Congress of the People at Kliptown accomplished much of what it had been designed to do. The event had brought together a politically, racially, and economically diverse group of South Africans and united them in their opposition to the National government's program of apartheid. It had refined the disparate aspirations of thousands of individuals throughout the country and forged them into a creed for the next generation of anti-apartheid activists. It also marked an important transition for the African National Congress, which in the years to come would claim to be the guardian of the Freedom Charter and thus the representative of all South Africans in the struggle for a new political order.

For most of its participants, the Congress of the People and the Freedom Charter projected a brief, bright ray of hope into a darkening political landscape. The leaders of the National Party government, emboldened by their decisive victory in the parliamentary elections of 1953, displayed diminishing tolerance for such seditious interracial gatherings. In 1954 the aging Daniel Malan finally retired as prime minister and was replaced by the extreme Nationalist Johannes Gerhardus Strijdom. As soon as Strijdom came to office, the new prime minister, with Verwoerd's support, moved speedily to implement one of the most controversial and brutal pieces of apartheid: the forcible removal of thousands of African and Coloured families from the homes and interspersed urban communities in which they had lived for generations. Verwoerd particularly loathed Sophiatown, a section of Johannesburg where Africans of all ethnic backgrounds had bought land and built houses since the late nineteenth century. From the beginning it had been a thriving center of urban African culture, a culture that was increasingly influenced by American music, literature, and language. The Nationalists hated everything about Sophiatown—its ethnic mix, its cultural exuberance, its threatening urban permanence. It could not be disentangled or tamed, Verwoerd decided, so it had to wiped from the face of the earth. On February 10, 1955, four months before Kliptown, Verwoerd sent two thousand police armed with machine guns into the town. The police entered the homes of a hundred families, ordered the residents to bring all their possessions outside, and threw their furniture, clothes, dishes, and possessions into the backs of trucks. They then drove the families to the other side of the city and dumped them with all their worldly goods in front of rows of little brick huts. Over the following year the police ejected thousands of Africans from property they had owned for half a century; Verwoerd told parliament the action was a routine slum-clearing mission. Trevor Huddleston, a white Anglican priest who worked in a parish in Sophiatown and later wrote an internationally famous book about his experience, said that in the destruction of Sophiatown, South Africa lost "not only a place but an ideal." Verwoerd felt differently; as government bulldozers plowed the Africans' homes into the dirt, the minister of native affairs told parliament that the residents had "gone singing" to Meadowlands and then announced that the area would be rebuilt as a white suburb known as Triomf, or Triumph.

Throughout the 1950s, increasing support from his party and from the white electorate encouraged Verwoerd to reveal his diagnosis of South Africa's ills and his proposed remedies more plainly. The essential problem, he insisted, was that too many Africans, under the pressures of taxation and severe poverty, were flowing from the rural reserves to the urban areas looking for work. While in the urban areas, they intermingled dangerously with other African ethnic groups and other races. Such mixing and urbanization would inevitably result, Verwoerd explained, in the destruction not only of European culture but of all the other cultures from which the different races came. To make matters worse from Verwoerd's perspective, certain irresponsible schools, churches, and parties blindly promoted this trend as desirable.

The ideal solution, in Verwoerd's mind, was radical physical separation of the races. To achieve complete apartheid, however, he faced serious structural barriers from within the European community. After three hundred years the white residents of South Africa had become dependent on the enormous pool of cheap black workers conveniently squatting on the outskirts of the all-white cities. Businesspeople did not want to give up their inexpensive African employees. Local governments would not forgo the large labor-intensive projects that they could tackle because they had so many workers who could be paid so little. Middle-class white families could not imagine what they would do without the cooks, gardeners, and maids who lived in backyard shacks or appeared after dawn to work a ten-hour day. However much Verwoerd might have liked the voters to emulate his own family and eschew black servants, however much he would have liked to create a state within whose physical boundaries only whites resided—a transplanted Holland grafted onto the tip of the African continent—he knew that this could never be done. Thus, because apartheid could never be reduced solely to a question of physical boundaries, he had to inject racial segregation into every sphere of life. For Verwoerd the solution to South Africa's problem lay in a massive imposition of state control, backed by an aggressive police force, on every social sector; only this, he believed, would succeed in arresting and reverting the degenerative course along which South Africa was sliding.

Verwoerd focused heavily on education as a mechanism of social control. In 1951 a National Party commission headed by W. W. M. Eiselen had issued a report, "Education for Natives as a Separate Race." The report had recommended that the principles of "Bantu education" be centralized administration of the schools, creation of an obligatory curriculum for the different races, increased use of African languages to preserve African ethnic differences, and restriction of secondary and tertiary education to the African reserves. This last measure would force parents to send children who had finished primary school back to the reserves in order to ease the growth of the African urban population. Most important, said the committee, was that the educational system should be designed to be more "culturally appropriate" for Africans and to teach every African child that "there is no place for him in the European community above certain forms of labor."

Verwoerd had pronounced himself delighted with the report and then launched an attack on the nation's mission schools, which constituted ninety-five percent of the forty-five hundred schools open to Africans. The mission schools, he sneered, were committed to the production of "black Englishmen." In 1953 the members of parliament, at Verwoerd's behest, took control of African education away from the churches, the local governments, and the minister of education and gave it solely to Verwoerd. During the debate in parliament in September 1953, Verwoerd vowed that he would use his autocratic powers to ensure that "Natives will be taught from childhood to realize that equality with Europeans is not for them. . . . racial relations cannot improve if the wrong type of education is given to Natives. They cannot improve if the result of Native education is the creation of a frustrated people who . . . have expectations in life which circumstances in South Africa do not allow to be fulfilled."

As soon as he had control of the educational system Verwoerd swiftly expelled blacks from previously integrated universities, downgraded or closed facilities for black teachers, and imposed a national curriculum to indoctrinate Africans to accept their permanently subservient position. To persuade local communities that "Bantu education" was a positive development, he created local parent advisory committees; at the same time, he reduced government financial support and required African parents to pay steep new fees on the grounds that such fees would give the parents greater influence over their children's education.

Verwoerd's innovations provoked sharp but sporadic reactions from African parents and teachers around the country. In some areas they tried, with the help of the churches, to form new alternative schools. Parent and teacher groups also goaded the national ANC into approving a school boycott. On Tuesday, April 12, 1954, in a campaign organized by the ANC Youth League, thousands of children withdrew from their schools in the Johannesburg area. By Wednesday, April 13, the boycott had widened to include several more thousand children from neighboring townships. On Thursday, Verwoerd struck back, announcing that all children who were not back in school by Monday, April 25, would be barred from any further education for the rest of their lives. By Friday the boycott reached its peak, with more than ten thousand children absent. Over the weekend, however, the grim implications of Verwoerd's threat sank in and on Monday some parents sent their children back. By the time Verwoerd's deadline arrived, nearly seven thousand children were still out of school and he formally expelled them all.

Verwoerd's attack on education was a necessary but not a sufficient component in his drive to implement apartheid. Equally important was his proposal that each African resident of South Africa, as part of his or her racial classification, be designated a citizen of one of the tribal reserves or "homelands" scattered across the country. It did not matter to Verwoerd that millions of Africans had been born in the urban townships and had never set foot in the impoverished rural territories to which they would be assigned. With characteristic deftness, Verwoerd presented his plan in contradictory ways to different audiences. To Africans he preached the sanctity of culture, which, he tirelessly insisted, could be preserved only by offering the Africans territories in which they could rule according to their own customs. Separate development, he said, was a generous, visionary solution that responded to the aspirations of African nationalists. If Africans would cooperate, he told them, the future would brighten as the citizens of the homelands gradually demonstrated their capacity for "responsible" government and received political independence from South Africa. Though it was true that Africans would continue to be barred from owning property or operating

businesses within the white country of South Africa, in their own homelands no such barriers would exist. An adept application of pressures on
the accelerator of homeland opportunity and the brake of urban restrictions would, in Verwoerd's opinion, drive the nation toward the segregated ideal.

To calculate when South Africa would reach its goal, Verwoerd had
developed his own model of demographic growth, manufacturing needs,
and labor migration and had projected it well into the twenty-first century. In the first stage, as South Africa's manufacturing industries grew,
African workers would continue to flow out of the rural areas and into
the industrial Vaal Triangle around Johannesburg and into the urban
centers on the coast. Gradually, as the labor needs in white factories
declined and the economic opportunities in the homelands increased,
the flow would slowly and eventually revert, so that Africans would
move back to the homelands in search of work. Verwoerd predicted in
the 1950s that the magic year in which the movement would reverse
would be 1978—a generation away.

Despite his vision of African "independence" through a confederation of tiny African states floating inside a white country, Verwoerd
remained adamant that the arrangement would never threaten white
dominance. Whereas to Africans he emphasized the attractive outcome
of eventual independence, to whites he stressed the lengthy process. "It
is essential, as far as the African is concerned, to start off from a tribal
system, which is what he knows and then gradually work towards Western conceptions of democratic government," Verwoerd told parliament
at one point. "The peoples of Africa cannot be transplanted suddenly
into a Western form of society. The process has to be gradual." To his
detractors from the right, who argued that he was giving away too much,
he responded that many of the territories, such as Bophuthatswana in
the north and KwaZulu in the east, were hopelessly fragmented into
dozens of pieces surrounded by white strongholds. Only in a few politically irrelevant places, such as in the Transkei in the Eastern Cape,
would white property owners actually have to cede property to African
authorities.

Subsequent defenders of Verwoerd's vision have insisted that his
plans were benign and fair, a genuine attempt to create a separate but
equal collection of communities in which distinct cultures could flourish.
Yet Verwoerd undercut such an interpretation with his own words and
deeds. Years later, when his political power was so great that he no
longer needed to obscure any aspect of his policy, Verwoerd described
his true intentions with breathtaking bluntness. "Reduced to its simplest
form the problem is nothing less than this: we want to keep South Africa
white," he told the House of Assembly. " 'Keeping it white' can only

mean one thing, namely white domination. This means not 'leadership,' not 'guidance,' but 'control,' and 'supremacy.' If we agreed that it is the desire of the people that the white man should be able to continue to protect himself by retaining white domination . . . we say that it can be achieved by separate development."

Even in the 1950s, while Verwoerd was still publicly propounding the material benefits that Africans would derive from separate development, he was also taking careful bureaucratic steps to castrate the economic potential of the homelands. In 1952 he appointed the Tomlinson Commission to examine the requirements for the independent economic development of the homelands. The committee members labored for two years and produced an enormously detailed study. Verwoerd was so displeased with the findings that he squelched their release until 1956. When the report was finally published, the summary alone reached almost four thousand pages and the conclusion, even after Verwoerd's intervention, was still stark. The homelands were so impoverished, the members of the commission concluded, that only a colossal influx of capital could create a modestly functioning manufacturing or extractive economy.

Verwoerd considered this ridiculous. The whites had pulled themselves up by their bootstraps on the same inhospitable terrain, he thought; let the Africans show what they could do without the guidance and support of Europeans. His ahistorical view overlooked the prodigious sums of money from Europe and America that had been pumped into South Africa for more than two centuries to build its cities, mines, and factories. Verwoerd deliberately blocked European businesses from setting up factories within the homelands in order to prevent Africans from benefiting from "white" capital and taxes. Instead he proposed in 1955 that white managers set up factories just outside the homelands so that African workers could cross over in the day, staff the factories, and return to their destitute preserves at night. Verwoerd also disregarded the artificial boost given to his people by the discovery of fabulous mineral wealth in the dirt—none of which, by design, would be available to any African resident of a homeland. Finally, he overlooked the benefits whites had derived from the Africans themselves, who for centuries had been bullied into shouldering the most backbreaking and dangerous of jobs at the lowest of wages. So implacably was Verwoerd committed to white supremacy that he ignored the lessons of his own history. Of the commission's suggested minimum financing to bring economic vitality to the homelands, Verwoerd set aside less than two percent.

Verwoerd understood that his actions in education and in the homelands would not have their intended effects on the African population for some years. Pending those results, he pumped up the machinery of state repression and control. Africans were still moving around inside the country and within the urban areas to what he considered an alarming degree. Verwoerd and Strijdom tightened the net of restrictions known as "influx control," which required Africans to obtain multiple government permits for residence, work, and travel. Verwoerd extended the pass laws to African women, provoking a huge confrontation with crowds of women who almost forced him to back down.

Though Verwoerd did not take the lead on every piece of apartheid legislation that came before the assembly, he strongly supported them all. He encouraged passage of the 1956 Industrial Conciliation Act, which prohibited Africans from being members of registered trade unions and allowed the minister of labour to regulate the racial composition of employment in most areas and occupations. He approved when parliament tightened the policy of job reservation, which allotted the most highly skilled and best-paying jobs to whites. He endorsed the final expurgation of the few remaining Coloured voters from the electoral rolls in the Cape Province. And in 1957 he applauded when parliament passed the Immorality Act, which made sexual intercourse between persons of different races a criminal act.

Verwoerd ran into some of the stiffest resistance when he added what became known as the "church clause" to the Native Laws Amendment Bill. This provision prohibited racially integrated church services and required all clergy to obtain special government permits for mixed congregations. Though the Dutch Reformed Church remained silent, the leaders of the Anglican, Presbyterian, and Roman Catholic Churches announced that they would disobey the law if it were passed. On receipt of the church leaders' letter, Verwoerd instructed his secretary to respond and exhort them to desist from "any further participation in this most unnecessary agitation." When the bill was presented to parliament, Verwoerd explained that the segregation of religious services was necessary to prevent the worship, order, and rest of Europeans from being disturbed by Africans. He also insisted that only a penalty of imprisonment would be sufficient to deter agitators. Though Verwoerd was forced to accept some mild amendments, the members of parliament approved the bill. Armed with this new weapon against the churches, Verwoerd warned a few months later that "we will use an iron hand with regard to mixed gatherings aimed at undermining the government's apartheid policy."

That hand struck the leaders of anti-apartheid organizations across the country within a few months of the end of the Congress of the People. Because of the government's apparent dissatisfaction with the evidence collected at Kliptown, in September 1955 police launched the biggest raid in South African history, bursting into homes and offices of

activists throughout the country, seizing every scrap of paper that could remotely be incriminating. Then, a little over a year later, the government struck again. On December 5, 1956, police throughout the country burst into homes at dawn, arrested 156 people, and took them to the Fort, Johannesburg's old prison, where they immediately were segregated by race. Thus, in a strange twist, ANC leaders such as Mandela, Luthuli, Sisulu, and Tambo, who had been separated for months under banning orders, found themselves herded into common cells in which they had long hours to catch up and confer. After two weeks of imprisonment they were taken down to the courthouse with the other defendants and charged with high treason. The prosecutors announced that they would demonstrate that the defendants had intended to overthrow the government by revolution and institute a Communist state. The main evidence would be the writings of the defendants, the evidence gathered at Kliptown and in the police raids, and, most important, the Freedom Charter. The penalty, if they were convicted, would be life imprisonment or execution.

After substantial wrangling, the defense team won bail for the defendants. Those who lived in Johannesburg could return to their homes. From then on for several years, Mandela and the others had to rise every morning and drive from the township up to Pretoria, nearly forty miles away, to sit in court all day while the government and the defense lawyers engaged in their exhausting maneuvers. Though supporters established a defense fund and helped in whatever ways they could, the leaders found themselves financially encumbered and physically pinned by the proceedings.

During the pretrial hearings, which alone lasted for twenty months, the leaders of the African National Congress continued to organize and encourage resistance to the apartheid laws and other oppressive measures as best they could. Having been denied most forms of political expression, opponents of apartheid experimented with economic tactics. In 1957 when the government bus company raised the fare for township workers to travel to their jobs in the cities, the workers instituted a boycott reminiscent of the one which had successfully desegregated the bus system the year before in Montgomery, Alabama, under the leadership of Martin Luther King Jr. For months the bus riders in Alexandra township walked to work or hitched rides until the government finally retracted the increase. A stay-away organized for June 26, 1957, disrupted white businesses in several urban areas. Later the ANC organized a highly successful potato boycott to protest the horrendous abuse of African prisoners whom the state penitentiary distributed to local farmers as free labor. As the months wore on, the Treason Trials took a growing personal toll on the defendants. Oliver Tambo, who for decades

had nurtured the hope of being ordained an Anglican priest and had only recently been approved for ordination by Bishop Ambrose Reeves, had to abandon the dream. Virtually all of the defendants lost their jobs and had to exhaust their savings to stay afloat. Some, like Nelson Mandela, watched their families and marriages split apart permanently under the strain.

Several months into the Treason Trials, Mandela was driving out of Soweto past Baragwanath Hospital when he noticed a young woman standing on the sidewalk waiting for the bus. "I was struck by her beauty," Mandela recalled, "and I turned my head to get a better look at her, but my car had gone by too fast." A few weeks later Mandela was startled when the same woman stopped at his law office to consult with Oliver Tambo about a legal matter. The next day he took her to a local Indian restaurant, where she drank innumerable glasses of water to compensate for her first encounter with curry. Her name, he learned, was Nomzamo Winnifred Madikizela. Her African name, Nomzamo, meant "one who undergoes trials." Her European name, Winnifred, had been selected by her father, a history teacher from Pondoland, who had long admired the German people. One of eleven children, she had lost her mother at an early age, studied at a mission school, moved to Johannesburg, completed her studies at the Jan Hofmeyr School of Social Work, and become the first black female social worker at Baragwanath Hospital. During the entire lunch people came up to Mandela to ask him questions, consult with him, shake his hand. When they left the restaurant it took them half an hour to walk to the car because so many people stopped him. Returning to the office, he found another mob of supplicants, so he drove Winnie out into the veld so they could be alone.
    Winnie had initially been attracted to the ideological fervor of the Non-European Unity Movement, but her affiliation with Nelson plunged her into the swirling center of the African National Congress. For the next months, the two seized whatever time they could, chatting on the way to political meetings or while Nelson exercised at the local gym. In June 1958 Mandela applied for a relaxation of his banning orders and was granted permission to leave Johannesburg for a few days. He, Winnie, and a group of friends drove to Pondoland and the two were married in a church in Bizana. After the ceremony was over, according to Xhosa custom, they should then have driven to Nelson's home in the Transkei to complete the wedding and finish eating their cake. Because Mandela's leave was about to expire, the newlyweds instead had to rush back to Johannesburg. Winnie carefully wrapped up the piece of cake and set it aside until the day she and Nelson could finish the ceremony.

□   □   □   □

From the start their marriage was overshadowed by ominous changes in the political climate. Shortly before the wedding the National Party had called for an election; candidates throughout the country had touted the success of apartheid and had vowed to strengthen *blanke baasskap*—"white boss-ship." Verwoerd, in his many campaign speeches, continued to propound his vision of a white South African republic, freed from England and from the Commonwealth. He brushed aside objections that segregation might mean slower economic growth, arguing that he would rather see South Africa "poor and white than rich and mixed." The success of the republic, he insisted, depended on the success of apartheid. "A republic in South Africa would be of no value to us," he proclaimed on the stump, "if we allowed it to slip into the hands of the Natives."

When the votes from the 1958 election were counted, the Nationalists had won a crushing victory, increasing their parliamentary majority by ten more delegates. The election helped undercut the dwindling United Party and all but wiped out the band of English-speaking liberals who had formed the Progressive Federal Party. After ten years in power, the Nationalist leaders had much to celebrate. The Afrikaner people had emerged as the dominant political force in South Africa. The vague slogan of apartheid had been translated through hundreds of laws and regulations into a system of strict racial segregation in all walks of life— from the home to the factory, from the restaurant to the ballot box— and was backed by an invigorated police and military. Parliamentary opposition had been reduced as increasing numbers of white voters, including those of English descent, shifted their support to Nationalist policies and candidates. Anti-apartheid activists from other racial groups had been immobilized by the Treason Trials, which concluded twenty months of pretrial hearings and began in earnest in August 1958. Though charges against sixty-one of the original defendants, including Luthuli and Tambo, were dropped, ninety-one of those remaining were officially charged with high treason. The prosecutor was Oswald Pirow, a close friend of J. F. J. van Rensburg, the pro-Nazi leader of the Ossewa Brandwag. Despite the presence at the trial of a delegation of observers from the International Commission of Jurists, the leaders of most foreign governments limited their objections to rhetoric. At their tenth anniversary in power, the leaders of the Nationalist government predicted confidently that they would establish permanent white supremacy in their country.

That confidence was shaken briefly on August 24, 1958, when, only four months after the election and a few weeks after the opening of the Treason Trials, the prime minister, Johannes Strijdom, suddenly died.

For more than two weeks members of the press, the government, and the business community speculated uneasily about who the new leader of the National Party and government would be. On September 2, 1958, the top officials of the party, all members of the Broederbond, caucused behind closed doors. The decision took slightly more than two hours; at twelve-forty in the afternoon, the doors of the caucus room opened. The members of the government assembled solemnly on the Senate steps and announced to the world that the next prime minister of South Africa would be Hendrik Verwoerd.

TWO

Crisis and Recovery
(1958–1962)

Politics, as a practice, whatever its professions, has always been the systematic organization of hatreds.
—HENRY ADAMS

HENDRIK VERWOERD saw his elevation to prime minister as the convergence of personal, national, and divine destiny. Standing in the spring sunshine on the Senate steps in view of towering Table Mountain, Verwoerd told reporters he believed that "the will of God was revealed in the ballot." To calm the fears of those who remembered Verwoerd's wartime opposition to the parliamentary system, the new prime minister went on the radio that evening and publicly committed himself to democracy. "No one need doubt for a moment that it will always be my aim to uphold the democratic institutions of our country," he told his millions of listeners. "It is one of the most treasured possessions of Western civilization." With chilling obliviousness to his own behavior toward those who disagreed with him, Verwoerd promised that public dissent would be tolerated. "The will of the people may not be impaired," he said, "and the right of people who have other convictions to express their views will be maintained."

In the same speech, Verwoerd identified his two main objectives: the creation of an independent republic and the implementation of separate development. Despite a decade of National Party rule, each of these proposals remained controversial. The idea of inaugurating a South African republic—that is, removing the queen of England as the titular head of state, eliminating the role of the British governor general, and creating a fully sovereign nation with features reminiscent of the early

Boer republics—was anathema to most South Africans of English descent. For them, the ties to England held tremendous emotional and commercial value; to break these off and stride back into the narrow-minded recesses of historical Afrikanerdom seemed ruinous. Moreover, most English speakers worried that a separation from Great Britain would lead to eviction from the British Commonwealth, though Verwoerd vigorously argued that India's transition to a republic had not.

The white community also continued to disagree sharply about separate development. For white liberals, the primary objection remained moral, though electoral slippage in the 1958 elections had reduced their potency. For white conservatives, Verwoerd had already treaded dangerously with his vague promises of development and independence for the African reserves. Verwoerd triggered an outcry within the first year of his prime ministry when he submitted the Promotion of Bantu Self-Government Act to parliament. Up to then Verwoerd had talked of separate development primarily in economic terms; now he was suddenly taking steps to transfer limited political decision making to the reserves. Ultraconservatives screeched that Verwoerd intended to partition South Africa and steal land from whites, and in an act of political expediency the United Party joined the hue and cry.

From his first speech as prime minister, Verwoerd insisted that the policy of separate development was being misunderstood. Only through this policy could the weak be protected from the strong and the minority protected from the majority, he said. Such a formulation again revealed Verwoerd's rhetorical prowess: by asserting an intuitively fair principle (the weak should be protected) and by failing to specify the parties, he allowed whites to embrace logically and emotionally contradictory views. For those whites who felt threatened, the "weak" could be understood as the white minority who needed protection from the majority of Africans. For those whites who felt powerful, the "weak" could be the uncultured natives who needed protection from the overpowering European or from each other.

He made other changes in his rhetoric. In the past Verwoerd had drawn from the standard Afrikaner grab bag of stereotypes to attack his enemies. In his writings he had caricatured opponents as arrogant British imperialists, grasping foreign capitalists, meddling missionaries, avaricious Jewish immigrants, narrow-minded Indians, lazy and cunning Coloureds, and spineless liberals. Now, as prime minister, Verwoerd adopted a simpler formula: white unity must stand against black nationalism, capitalism against Communism. And, as always, he presented his proposals as benevolent. "Separation, whether it be residential, territorial, or social, does not envisage oppression," he told his listeners in that first speech. "It envisages full opportunities for all, which opportunities can be enjoyed only to the extent to which the person or group in various stages are capable of doing so. . . . The policy of separate development is designed for happiness, security, and the stability provided by having one's own home, language, and administration—for the Bantu as well as the whites."

Verwoerd saw a vital link between the goal of republic and that of separate development, a link which would lead to a new and more potent formula for regional white supremacy. Under separate development the line between white and black would no longer be grounded in differences of religion, race, or culture. Verwoerd believed that each of these three distinctions could be captured and transformed by a fourth: that of citizenship. Under his plan whites would become the only citizens of the Republic of South Africa; Africans, assigned arbitrarily to the fragmented landlocked reserves, sometimes referred to as "bantustans," would become citizens of tiny independent homelands. Once the bond of common nationality was destroyed, Verwoerd knew, the discussion of white-black relations could be shifted into the morally remote language of foreign policy. By transforming South African blacks from fellow citizens into foreigners, separate development offered the chance of securing white privilege forever in an internationally acceptable manner. In the weeks after his maiden speech as prime minister, the Afrikaner press praised Verwoerd as a "man of steel," a "passionate patriot," and a man of "brilliant talents." Most of the English and foreign press, however, denounced the choice and accused Verwoerd of racial and political extremism. Verwoerd dismissed the criticisms, noting a few weeks later that "the important thing is that I was elected."

Verwoerd immediately set about consolidating his power. He stuffed the cabinet with loyal members of the Broederbond. He courted sympathetic members of the press by inviting them to Groote Schuur, the "Big Barn," an elegant white Dutch mansion in Cape Town that had been built by Cecil Rhodes and now served as the prime minister's official residence. While Betsie served tea and home-baked sweet cakes on the shaded veranda below Table Mountain, Verwoerd dazzled his listeners with his plans for the future. Verwoerd was determined to secure his identity as the *volksleier,* the "people's leader," a title which the Nationalists had first conferred on Daniel Malan in 1941 and had modeled on that of the Führer. The *volksleier* was, in the words of one of Verwoerd's biographers, "a superman, infallible, austere, God-chosen, and beyond criticism. . . . He is the guardian of the white race, of the honor and glory of Afrikanerdom, the personification of the national hero repulsing the enemies of the people."

Only two days before becoming prime minister, Verwoerd had auditioned for the role of *volksleier* in an effusive eulogy to Strijdom in the

Afrikaner newspaper *Dagbreek en Sondagnuus*. The true *volksleier,* he wrote, "is never a tyrant, never dishonest, self-centered, power-greedy. He is filled with patriotism, noble ideals, and uses only those means to achieve his ends which he can reconcile with his Christian conscience. It is not hate which determines his conduct towards his fellow man but love, hope, the search for a better and freer future, free as a state, free from secret ties, free from racial strife, so that everyone can be happy and free from hate because everyone is united in one—yes, one—patriotism." Two days later his colleagues gave him the role. Verwoerd was elated. Armed with the convictions he had held for much of his adult life; propelled by the certainty that his pleas had been consecrated by history, by the electorate, and by God; and empowered by his elevation to a position of unchallenged political power, Hendrik Verwoerd seized the chance to save his people by creating the most perfectly segregated society the world had ever seen.

Verwoerd's ascendance triggered a crisis within the African National Congress. To the more radical activists, his rise to power proved that a half century of nonviolent protests had accomplished nothing. Even the recent predictions by leaders of the African National Congress had been disproved by events. Walter Sisulu, for example, had written just eighteen months earlier that the National Party had "reached its high-water mark. There is no possibility of the Nationalists growing stronger than they are at present." Now the most fanatical proponent of apartheid had taken control of the party, the police, and the government.

The question was what to do. In the 1940s the answer had seemed easy to the young leaders of the ANC Youth League: the ANC should commit to a forceful campaign of nonviolent resistance that would steadily increase the pressure on the government and ignite the consciences of thoughtful whites throughout the land. But by 1958 the men who had clamored for change were now running the African National Congress themselves. Behind them lay a solid decade of energetic struggle, including the Programme of Action, the Day of Mourning, the work stoppages and strikes, the Defiance Campaign, the Freedom Charter, and hundreds of other, smaller acts and expressions of resistance. Despite the vigor of their efforts, the leaders of the African National Congress could only watch in anguish as a new tide of apartheid swept over them and smothered their gains. The officials of the National Party had responded to their every move with more restrictive legislation, bannings, harassment, arrests, and brutality. The response of the white voters in three national elections—1948, 1953, and 1958—had not been one of shock but of increasing approval of Nationalist positions and candidates.

There were still some, like Albert Luthuli, who believed that fundamental change in South Africa could come through persuasion, not violence. He and others pointed to the small number of whites who had embraced the cause of African liberation—students, clergy, liberals, and Communists—as evidence of the underlying generosity of the white race. Such leaders harbored the hope that African protests would embolden the few liberals in parliament to go beyond their proposal for a franchise limited to qualified Africans. They continued to believe that someday a decisive portion of the white population would become so horrified by the implications of apartheid that they would reject privilege, embrace justice, and undermine the government. After Verwoerd's first speech as prime minister, the hopes for such a white conversion waned quickly. The discontent that throughout the 1950s had simmered just below the surface of the African National Congress bubbled up as critics demanded that the ANC either change tactics or get results.

One of the most ardent critics was thirty-four-year-old Robert Sobukwe, an instructor in African languages at the University of the Witwatersrand in Johannesburg. Sobukwe had been born in 1924 in the predominantly Afrikaner town of Graaf Reinet in the Cape. His father had received some elementary education and worked as a day laborer and wood merchant, serving on the weekends as a lay preacher for the Methodist Church. Sobukwe's mother had received no formal schooling but raised her six children in a highly religious and disciplined household; her influence was such that in later years Robert became a Methodist lay preacher and his brother became an Anglican bishop. Robert was an excellent student, earning scholarships to high school and to the University of Fort Hare, where he joined the ANC Youth League. When he graduated, he moved to the Transvaal and got a job as a high school teacher, from which he was soon fired for giving speeches in favor of the Defiance Campaign. In 1954 Sobukwe moved to Johannesburg and began teaching at the University of the Witwatersrand. In the small, swirling political circles in the city he came into contact with the leadership of the African National Congress, particularly with its Africanist faction, led by P. K. Leballo. Sobukwe was immediately recognized as a man of considerable intellectual talents—his friends called the pipe-smoking academic "the Prof"—and he soon became the editor of the faction's newspaper, the *Africanist.*

Ever since the Defiance Campaign Robert Sobukwe had observed the decisions of Mandela, Sisulu, Luthuli, and the others with increasing dismay. Sobukwe worried that as the men had risen into positions of regional and national leadership they, like their predecessors, had become cautious. He also feared that they had cozied up too closely with other racial groups, especially whites. The key to African liberation,

Sobukwe felt, was to develop the unity, identity, and commitment of Africans. Luthuli dismissed such Africanist views as a step backward and referred to Sobukwe and his circle as the "right wing" of the ANC movement. Sobukwe, for his part, felt that ANC leaders were being duped and drained by allies who did not really care about the needs of Africans. However much whites might want to help, the Africanists grumbled, they always did so by trying to take control. Moreover, many of the whites, like Joseph Slovo and his wife, Ruth First, were also Communists. The willingness of the ANC leaders to work with such people and to include calls for nationalization in the Freedom Charter were signs of the dilution of the movement and the repudiation of the Youth League's original anti-Communist position. Finally, Sobukwe and his circle believed that Sisulu, Tambo, Mandela, and the others had abandoned the Youth League's Programme of Action, which he and the others in his group believed had been shaped by the Africanist convictions of Anton Lembede.

For Sobukwe these errors were more than unfortunate; they were potentially disastrous. They stank of timidity at a time that called for temerity. The whole world could see that Africa was in the midst of a massive revolution, throwing off the chains of European colonialism and establishing new, independent African states. Sobukwe and his followers admired young, dynamic leaders like Tom Mboya of Kenya and Kwame Nkrumah, who had become the first president of independent Ghana in 1957. African office clerks kept pictures of Nkrumah in their cubbyholes; during the South African bus boycott, which took place at the time of Ghana's independence, the strikers had shouted "Ghana!" as a rallying cry. This was not the time to be dallying with other races and alien ideologies, the Africanists believed; it was the moment for a bold move that would ignite the African gunpowder strewn through the cities and the reserves.

The ANC leaders steadily rebuffed the claims by Sobukwe, Leballo, and the other Africanists. They argued that the Africanists' ideas misrepresented the facts, could not be implemented, and smacked of a "fanatical African racialism and denunciation of everything that is not African," in Walter Sisulu's words. Despite the running debate over the organization and provisions of the Freedom Charter, Sobukwe and the other Africanist remained loyal throughout the decade to the African National Congress. When the Treason Trials ended, the Africanists became increasingly dissatisfied. Through 1957 and 1958 Sobukwe watched as the courts sapped the ANC defendants' time and energy just as Verwoerd was pressing his programs with increasing speed. To make matters worse, in Sobukwe's view, the ANC leaders were not responding forcefully but were wasting efforts on pitiful projects such as attempting to assist the United Party in the election of 1958. When the United Party failed to capture parliament and Verwoerd rose to become prime minister, Sobukwe could stand it no longer. In November 1958, at the annual conference of the African National Congress, just two months after Verwoerd's elevation, the Africanists tried to elect their own candidates to ANC leadership positions. When this failed, Sobukwe announced that he and his followers would break away and form a new and truly African liberation movement, the Pan-Africanist Congress (PAC).

The seceding group held their first conference in April 1959 in an Orlando communal hall festooned with signs and banners demanding "Africa for Africans" and "Imperialists Quit Africa." The delegates promptly elected Sobukwe president; in his inaugural address, Sobukwe laid out the vision of the PAC. "We aim politically at government of the Africans, by Africans, for Africans, with everybody who owes his only loyalty to Africa and who is prepared to accept the democratic rule of an African majority." Sobukwe told the group, "We guarantee no minority rights because we think in terms of individuals not groups." Sobukwe rejected the ANC's claim that colonialism in South Africa was different from that in the rest of Africa and he publicly expressed his support for Kwame Nkrumah's dream of a "United States of Africa."

Sobukwe, flush with enthusiasm, greatly overestimated the receptiveness of the African population to his ideas and organization. He boldly predicted that his organization would collect 100,000 members by the beginning of 1960 and that South Africa would be free from white domination by 1963. The reality was more stark; by December 1959, the first anniversary of Sobukwe's break with the ANC, the faction was struggling along with little funds and less than a quarter of the expected membership. When the leaders of the African National Congress announced a new nationwide demonstration against the pass laws for March 31, 1960, Sobukwe tried to wrench the initiative back by declaring a mass PAC protest for March 21.

Because the PAC leaders anticipated that they would trigger a mass uprising, in only a few townships did local PAC activists work hard to elicit support. Sobukwe himself spent his time traveling to South Africa's industrial centers to publicize the campaign. In speech after speech he urged his listeners to leave their pass books at home, boycott their work, and present themselves in large groups at police stations for arrest. The protests must be nonviolent, Sobukwe insisted; if the police asked them to disperse, they should do so. The point, he told the crowds, was to pack the jails and to break the pass laws; if the police refused to arrest them, then they would have scored a victory.

Sobukwe was not alone in believing that the tide of freedom sweeping the African continent could not be held back by Verwoerd. Delegates at the United Nations headquarters in New York City had proclaimed 1960 the "year of Africa." "Revolution . . . is obviously coming to this country—and will obviously be successful—within the next five years," wrote Kirkpatrick Sale, a correspondent for the *Chicago Tribune,* in 1961, reflecting the views of many American journalists. The Western powers were increasingly directing their gaze away from postwar reconstruction to the needs and demands of the emerging states. The British, in particular, had made the transformation of their ties with former colonies a centerpiece of their foreign policy. To demonstrate this commitment the British prime minister, Harold Macmillan, undertook a month-long trip through Africa. In the first week of February 1960, while Robert Sobukwe was crisscrossing the country and Winnie and Nelson Mandela were celebrating the birth of their first daughter, Zenani, Macmillan arrived in South Africa to participate in the celebration of the golden anniversary of the Union of South Africa.

On February 3, 1960, Macmillan stood in the large paneled dining room in the parliament building in Cape Town and addressed the members of both South African houses. He began with a sweeping assessment of the role of nationalism in world history and described how he had been deeply impressed by the power of that same nationalist sentiment in every African country. "The wind of change," Macmillan announced dramatically, "is blowing through this continent." Britain viewed these changes as positive, he said, because such a historical force could not be stopped. Accordingly, since the war, Great Britain had agreed to grant independence to India, Pakistan, Ceylon, Ghana, and Nigeria, and it intended to do so for other countries in Africa.

For the British government, said Macmillan, the goal was to assist in the creation of societies which allowed citizens an increasing share in political power and responsibilities and in which individual merit was the only criterion for political and economic achievement. "As a fellow member of the Commonwealth we always try, and I think have succeeded, in giving to South Africa our full support and encouragement," Macmillan told the members of parliament, "but I hope you won't mind my saying frankly that there are some aspects of your policies which make it impossible for us to do this without being false to our own deep convictions about the political destinies of free men to which in our own territories we are trying to give effect."

Verwoerd was sitting to Macmillan's left, below an immense portrait of the members of the 1910 national convention who had brought political unity to the warring white factions of South Africa. As he listened to Macmillan's lengthy speech, Verwoerd's face blanched. The instant Macmillan had finished, Verwoerd leapt to the podium, scolded the prime minister for not telling him what he had intended to say, and delivered a thirty-minute rebuttal. "If our policies were rightly understood," Verwoerd told his guest, "it would be seen that what we are attempting to do is not at variance with the new direction in Africa, but is in the fullest accord with it." Verwoerd then repeated the Nationalists' cherished myth: since the whites had arrived in South Africa first, they should be allowed to rule it without interference from late-arriving Africans. "We see ourselves as part of the Western world, a true white state in Africa," Verwoerd concluded to applause. "We look upon ourselves as indispensable to the white world." Verwoerd returned to Groote Schuur to find a deluge of congratulatory telegrams. In his memoir, Macmillan noted grimly that throughout the trip, in public and in private, Verwoerd had been absolutely implacable. "It was only during these days that I began to realize to the full extent the degree of obstinacy, amounting really to fanaticism, which Dr. Verwoerd brought to the consideration of his policies," wrote Macmillan later. "I had the unusual experience of soon noticing that nothing one could say or put forward would have the smallest effect upon the views of this determined man."

On Monday, March 21, the turnout for the PAC protest was poor. In Port Elizabeth and Durban in the Eastern Cape, where loyalty to the African National Congress remained strong, there were no demonstrations at all. In Johannesburg, Sobukwe and 150 others presented themselves without their passes at the police station, where they were instantly thrown in jail. In the United States, Martin Luther King Jr. and others had used such arrests and imprisonments to draw attention to their cause; because of the American legal limits on detentions, they were often released on bail within days or at most weeks. The tactic had also been used in South Africa and until that point the remaining legal and civil protections had prevented the police from holding the protesters indefinitely. What Sobukwe could not have known when he presented himself for his sacrificial arrest was that events elsewhere in the nation would prompt the government to eliminate those vestigial liberties and keep him imprisoned for the next seventeen years.

In other urban areas around the country, the response to Sobukwe's call was spotty. Indeed, the campaign would almost certainly have gone unnoticed by anyone outside of South Africa if it had not been for a small township on the border of the Transvaal and Orange Free State. The township, known as Sharpeville, was part of a cluster of African communities whose residents worked in the steel mills and industrial factories around Vereeniging, the town where the treaty ending the Boer War had been signed. PAC organizers had concentrated on the area, regularly driving the fifty miles down from Johannesburg to drum up support. On the day of the protest they had persuaded the African drivers to enforce the stay-away by refusing to drive residents to work. In the townships of Evaton and Vanderbiljpark, the demonstrations at the police stations had taken place without incident; hundreds of Africans had gone to the police station and the police had refused to arrest them.

In Sharpeville, however, the police's tactic of using low-flying military aircraft to intimidate the crowd seemed to attract more people, and several thousand gathered in the huge compound outside the wire fence of the police station. The crowd was unarmed but restless and showed no signs of dispersing. The nervous police called in reinforcements, who arrived inside a convoy of British-made Saracen armored troop carriers. By midday there were more than three hundred heavily armed white police inside the enclosure facing an encircling crowd of Africans fifteen times larger. At one-fifteen a scuffle broke out near the front gate; a police officer was shoved to the ground. Without warning the other policemen raised their submachine guns and fired directly into the crowd at short range.

Though the government later claimed that the police fired for no more than a few seconds, eyewitnesses reported that the police seemed determined to take as long as necessary to mow down the crowd. Humphrey Tyler, a white South African reporter from the liberal magazine *Drum,* watched as a policeman standing on top of an armored troop carrier fired his Sten gun "in a wide arc from his hip as though he were panning a movie camera." Two other officers next to him helped him with their pistols. The police and the government later claimed that many in the crowd had been armed, but Tyler reported that at the time he had looked carefully and afterward he had studied photographs and he had not found a single weapon.

The crowd retreated in a panic. Wounded men and women screamed in pain and tried in desperation to drag themselves out of range. One terrified young boy covered his head with his coat in the apparent belief that it could protect him from the bullets. "When the shooting started it did not stop until there was no living thing on the huge compound in front of the police station," Tyler reported. By the time the chattering gunfire ceased, sixty-nine people had been shot dead. One hundred eighty-six others, including forty women and eight children, had been seriously wounded. Almost all of the bullet holes were found in the victims' backs. When asked about the carnage, a senior police official told a *New York Times* reporter, "I don't know how many we've shot, but if they do these things, they must learn the hard way."

The next day, news of the "Sharpeville massacre" exploded onto the front pages of newspapers around the world. The editors of *Newsweek* magazine put the story on the cover and coupled it with a long feature on the political and social status of the American Negro. Republicans in the Eisenhower administration, facing increasing criticism about their treatment of racial issues at home and abroad and gazing at a presidential election in seven months, moved speedily to condemn the South African government. Assistant Secretary of State for African Affairs Joseph Satterthwaite wrote an unusually strong statement that was rapidly communicated to the South African government.

Within hours of the massacre Prime Minister Verwoerd went to the House of Assembly to report to the members of parliament. He said that ANC and PAC propaganda had provoked Africans to try the impossible and challenge the authority of the state. The police had exercised remarkable restraint, Verwoerd continued, and should be congratulated for being so firm and using force only where they had no choice. The members of parliament should not be excessively alarmed by the events, he continued, since similar disturbances had erupted in other parts of Africa. The fault, he insisted, lay with the violent tactics of the ANC and the PAC, who had dragged people out of their homes and forced them to come to the demonstrations. Verwoerd later told the delegates that international accusations that the government had acted like a police state were false; instead, he said, "the riots in which law-abiding Bantu are dragged in . . . convince everybody that protection by a greatly increased police force within the Bantu residential area is essential."

On March 30 and 31 the delegates to the United Nations Security Council met in special session to debate the Sharpeville massacre and the policy of apartheid. The South African ambassador, Bernardus Fourie, at first left the room to protest the body's interference in his country's internal affairs, but he later returned to tell the delegates that "the police were attacked with a variety of weapons: *pangas* [machetes], axes, iron-bars, knives, sticks, and firearms. Indeed, shots were fired at the police before the police returned fire in order to defend their own lives and also to forestall what might have been greater and more tragic bloodshed. . . . I need hardly say how deeply the Union government regrets that there was this tragic loss of life." When several delegates proposed that the Security Council approve economic and political sanctions against the Verwoerd government, the British ambassador announced that he would veto the move. The Security Council eventually passed a measure which "deplored" the violence, asked South Africa to end apartheid, and instructed Secretary General Dag Hammarskjöld to "consult" with the South African government. U.S. ambassador Henry Cabot Lodge, acting on orders from Secretary of State Christian Herter, voted in favor of the watered-down resolution; both Britain and France abstained. In South Africa Verwoerd dismissed the efforts by the United Nations as interference in domestic matters, telling the members of

parliament that he failed "to see how local police action for the maintenance of law and order could possibly be construed as endangering
international peace and security." In any case, such actions by the
United Nations were counterproductive, he said, because they would
only encourage the agitators and lead to more violence.

When the Anglican bishop of Johannesburg asked Verwoerd to appoint a commission of inquiry, the prime minister flatly refused. Only
when Verwoerd received the communication from the United States did
he relent and appoint a judge, who later declined to apportion responsibility for the event. Throughout the turbulent days that followed, Verwoerd seemed unconcerned by the deaths of the Africans; they seemed,
if anything, to foster new resolve. Within days he had slapped a ban on
public meetings, ordered the nighttime arrests of more than eighteen
thousand people of all races, and called up reserve troops. As he grimly
told parliament, "We will see to it that we remain in power in this white
South Africa."

During the week after Sharpeville, the mood of crisis increased daily.
In Johannesburg, Treason Trial defendants Mandela, Sisulu, Slovo, and
Duma Nokwe, the secretary general of the ANC, met frantically in a
series of all-night meetings. In Cape Town, a confrontation of momentous proportions was taking shape. For years state officials had subjected the city's relatively small African population to more restrictions
than they imposed elsewhere in the country. Under ever-tightening influx control regulations, township residents were frequently harassed
and deported back to the impoverished reserves. More than twenty-two
thousand people were squeezed into Langa, a township only ten miles
from the city center, where the PAC had established several branches.
On March 21, several thousand men stayed away from work to attend
large meetings. By the afternoon, the police, after goading the crowds to
anger with baton charges, opened fire, killing two and wounding forty-
nine. Over the next few days rioting broke out in Langa and support for
the stay-away increased. While workers in other regions returned to
work, ninety-five percent of Cape Town's workforce participated in the
second week of the strike.

The ANC leaders, on hearing the news from Cape Town, decided it
was time for their banned president, Chief Albert Luthuli, to do something dramatic. Nokwe went to see Luthuli, who was in Johannesburg to
testify in the Treason Trials, and suggested that he defy Verwoerd.
Luthuli agreed and on March 27 he publicly set his passbook aflame and
urged all Africans to join him. When tens of thousands did so, the
minister of justice announced that the police would temporarily suspend
arrests for pass violations. The ANC leaders, believing that they had
won an important concession and sensing their momentum, called for a

national day of mourning to commemorate the victims of Sharpeville and Langa, followed by nationwide strikes. Africans throughout the country responded, shutting down the cities of Johannesburg, Port Elizabeth, and Durban. The next day, fifty thousand people attended a funeral for the victims of police action in Langa. Two days later, the township was plunged into crisis by a brutal police raid, and township residents decided to march to parliament in protest.

Since most of the PAC leaders in Cape Town had been arrested, the task of leading the demonstration into the city fell to an unlikely candidate named Philip Kgosana. Kgosana was twenty-three years old, small in stature, and only six years out of primary school. Originally from Pretoria, he had been sent a thousand miles south to attend the University of Cape Town on a scholarship. Before leaving for college he had heard Robert Sobukwe speak in Johannesburg, and when Sobukwe came through Cape Town trying to organize the March protest, Kgosana had offered his services. After the events of March 21, Kgosana had spent three days in jail; when he was released, he immediately led a march down to the Caledon Square police station to urge the release of the others. At the police station he negotiated with Colonel I. P. S. Terblanche, who agreed not to have the marchers arrested for pass law violations if they would return peacefully to their homes.

On the morning of Wednesday, March 30, more than twenty thousand rough-hewn African workers walked around the base of Table Mountain into the heart of the city of Cape Town. They intended to march directly to parliament, which was in session, to demand the release of their leaders. Kgosana had to hitch a ride and arrived late at the head of this human lava flow. Despite his youth and his undignified short pants (the uniform of a high school student that penury forced him to wear), the crowd responded to him instantly. This was even more remarkable when one considers the ethnic difference between Kgosana and his followers. Kgosana was from the Sotho tribe in the northern territories; the workers were overwhelmingly southern Xhosa. Kgosana spoke Xhosa imperfectly, as a fifth language. Yet, as he later told a commission of inquiry, "When I told them to sit down, they sat down. When I told them to stand up, they stood up." With such immense influence over a huge body of committed followers moving into the center of the white government, Kgosana for a few hours that morning held the future of South Africa in his hands. A reporter for the *New York Times,* Joseph Lelyveld, later suggested that under different circumstances the moment might have become the South African equivalent of the storming of the Bastille. It did not because the crowds were so committed to nonviolence, Kgosana so trusting, and the government so treacherous.

As the crowd approached the center of the city, eyewitnesses recalled its somber, dignified mood. There were no raised fists, no thrown stones, no shouting. When the marchers arrived, they discovered a line of steel-helmeted troops gripping automatic rifles with fixed bayonets. Behind the soldiers sat a row of dun-colored Saracen armored vehicles drawn up bumper to bumper in front of parliament. Kgosana, following the relentlessly repeated instructions of Sobukwe to avoid provocations and violence, viewed the scene and decided to switch the destination of the march back to the central police station at Caledon Square, where many of the PAC leaders were being held.

At the front door of the station Kgosana again encountered the craggy-faced Afrikaner police commander, Colonel Terblanche. Kgosana asked to see the justice minister to communicate their grievances. The police commander told him that the minister was "at lunch." Kgosana asked when he could see him. Terblanche replied that if Kgosana asked the crowd to disperse he would arrange an appointment that afternoon. When Kgosana continued to press his advantage, Terblanche insisted that this "gentleman's agreement" was the only proper way to see the minister of justice. Kgosana finally agreed, turned around, and called for silence in the crowd. The murmurs of the thousands in front of him ceased. Kgosana explained the agreement, reminded the crowd of Sobukwe's call to nonviolence, and asked them to disperse and return to the townships. The workers quietly turned and headed home.

At four-forty-five that afternoon Kgosana returned with a delegation of four PAC activists to present their point of view to the minister of justice. When they arrived, they were instantly arrested and thrown into prison. Because of the South African government's strict control of the press, the newspapers made no more mention of the march, its leaders, or their fate. The minister of justice even refused to answer official questions from members of parliament about whether Kgosana had been arrested or not. From the standpoint of the thousands of Africans who had obeyed Kgosana, he, like his mentor Robert Sobukwe, had simply disappeared.

Verwoerd, having thwarted a direct challenge to his rule, moved with characteristic decisiveness to reestablish control over the country. On the day of Kgosana's march, Verwoerd declared a state of emergency. Heavily armed white troops rushed in and set up positions on the sandy flats around the Langa and Nyanga townships. The soldiers cut off all electricity and water to the African communities and then went in and brutally attacked anyone suspected of supporting the strike. After four days the resistance of the unarmed inhabitants was crushed.

Verwoerd was especially determined to break the back of his political opponents. On April 7 he reinstated the pass laws and ordered the police to begin arresting those who did not have proper identification. On April 8, with the support of the timorous United Party leaders, he rammed through parliament the Unlawful Organizations Act, which allowed him to declare any existing organization illegal and to prosecute any members for having participated in the organization even before the law was passed. With this new authority, Verwoerd instantly banned the African National Congress and the Pan-Africanist Congress. He had the Treason Trial defendants who had been free on bail seized, stuffed them into filthy, overcrowded cells, and gave them putrid food. Mandela passed the long hours between court appearances trying to teach himself Afrikaans, while Sisulu learned shorthand. After conferring with his colleagues, Tambo escaped Verwoerd's net and slipped across the border to begin a new life as the head of the African National Congress in exile.

On Saturday, April 9, after more than two weeks of national tumult, Verwoerd returned to his normal schedule and resumed his speaking tour in favor of a South African republic. He appeared at the Rand Easter Show, an annual agricultural fair, and told a crowd of thirty thousand that they should be as bold in building the future as the Voortrekkers had been in the past. After the prime minister had inspected some cattle, he returned to his seat to officiate at an award ceremony. Within minutes, a fifty-year-old white farmer named David Beresford Pratt approached the dais. "Dr. Verwoerd!" called Pratt. As Verwoerd turned to speak to him, Pratt pulled a revolver from his jacket and fired two bullets at point-blank range into Verwoerd's face. The first entered the prime minister's right cheek and fractured his upper and lower jawbone. The second struck him in the neck below the right ear. The force of the bullets hurled Verwoerd back against the row of chairs behind him.

In the bedlam that followed, the police seized Pratt, gathered up Verwoerd's limp body, and rushed the prime minister to the hospital. In the emergency room the doctors examined the prime minister with deep pessimism. As they stanched the bleeding and inspected his wounds more closely, they were stunned to discover that the first bullet had not entered the brain at all. Even more astonishing, the second bullet, which they had expected to be lethal, had traversed Verwoerd's skull but had somehow missed the facial nerve, the joint between the upper and lower jawbone, and the carotid artery. The physicians told the waiting government officials and reporters that Verwoerd had escaped death only by a miracle.

Though the press, following the government's urgings, painted Pratt as a madman, the truth was more complex. Pratt was a world-famous cattle breeder who lived in a large mansion in Magaliesberg and had been married twice, the second time to a Dutch woman. After his second wife left him and returned to Holland, he went to Europe to try to persuade her to return. When he was unsuccessful he returned dejectedly to South Africa. He told the court that upon his arrival home he was horrified by the new security measures that had been imposed by the National Party. After he saw a police van loaded with African women prisoners arrested under the emergency regulations, he told the judge, he felt "a violent urge to shoot at apartheid—the striking monster that was gripping the throat of South Africa and preventing South Africa from achieving its rightful place among the nations." In his last public statement he appealed to the court and to all South Africans to move quickly to abandon apartheid. The court found him mentally disordered and unfit to stand trial. Pratt was placed in a mental hospital in Bloemfontein and a year later was found choked to death with a sheet around his neck on the floor of his hospital room. The government issued a terse statement that he had committed suicide.

Verwoerd's reputation as a man of prodigious tenacity rose sharply after the assassination attempt. In less than two months, he made a complete recovery from the bullet wounds and returned to a full schedule. His brush with death also strengthened his conviction "that the protection of Divine Providence was accorded me with a purpose, a purpose which concerns South Africa too," as he told parliament a few weeks after the attempt. "May it be given to me to fulfill that task faithfully." In the ensuing years Verwoerd's fixity of purpose led his supporters to nickname him "the man of granite" and his detractors, including members of the opposition party, to speculate on whether he had gone mad. Some voiced their concerns publicly: a prominent Afrikaner member of the United Party, Major Piet Van Der Byl, denounced Verwoerd in parliament as a "paranoiac." When the presiding officer ordered him to retract his remarks as a breach of legislative etiquette, Van der Byl refused. "I cannot withdraw it; it is true. It is my duty to the country to say this," he retorted and stalked angrily off the floor of the chamber.

Despite Verwoerd's ability to control much of South African society, one sphere eluded both his understanding and his will: that of the economy. The country, despite its fabulous deposits of minerals, gems, and gold, was still struggling to evolve from its agrarian and mining origins into a full-fledged industrial power. To succeed, South Africa needed foreign trade, foreign investment, and foreign technology, all of which were jeopardized by the explosive events of the early 1960s.

South Africa's economic dependence on foreign capital stretched back to the arrival of the first Europeans, who had been sent out not by a government but by one of the earliest multinational firms, the Dutch

East India Company. For more than a century the company had privately controlled and administered the Cape Province as an investment. For many reasons—including the distance from Europe, the indigenous resistance, and the inhospitable terrain—the region seemed unpromising, of value to the firm for its location but not for its wealth. When diamonds were discovered in the 1860s and thousands of prospectors flooded into Kimberley, in the northern Cape, they drew with them the attention of European investors. The early prospectors staked their claims on seven-foot-square open-air parcels, which they excavated by hand like an archaeological dig. The excess dirt was removed through a fantastic web of wires and pulleys, with each plot assigned a bucket that could be hauled directly to the rim. Slower prospectors found themselves working on top of small square towers of dirt as their neighbors carved away the surrounding plots. The workers went "up and down at every step, jumping here on to a narrow wall and skipping there across a deep dividing channel," wrote British novelist Anthony Trollope, who visited the site in 1877, "as though some diabolically ingenious architect had contrived a house with five hundred rooms, not one of which should be on the same floor."

The need for foreign capital was small at first, because the technology was relatively simple and could be paid for out of reinvested profits. Within a few years the prospectors and their African laborers had sliced through the strata and created an immense, gaping cavity a mile wide and fifteen hundred feet deep. As they cut into bedrock, they struck water, which at first they pumped out. In time the water defeated them, forced them to abandon their plots, and slowly filled what became known as Kimberley's Deep Hole. At this point the more enterprising prospectors turned to foreign money to pay for the conversion to subterranean mining and to reduce competition by buying up other small diamond companies. Mine owners by the dozens scrambled to persuade investors, primarily in London, to back their schemes. The master of this process turned out to be Cecil Rhodes, the founder of De Beers Mining Company, who in the end successfully seized control of his most aggressive competitor, Kimberley Mines, with the help of a million-pound loan from the British Rothschilds.

The discovery of gold shortly afterward increased dramatically the need for capital and gave an advantage to those who had already developed the financial contacts and the organizational structure to conduct subterranean mining. Though the mining experts decided that the Witwatersrand reef was extensive, there were many barriers to its successful exploitation. To begin, the gold was not lying just below the surface, as the earliest diamonds had been, but was buried deep beneath the soil. As a report by the Chamber of Mines later described it, "imagine a solid mass of rock tilted . . . like a fat, twelve hundred page dictionary lying at an angle. The gold-bearing reef would be thinner than a single page, and the amounts of gold contained therein would hardly cover a couple of commas in the entire book." To get at those gold deposits, which might be as small as a few grains of rice in a rock as large as an automobile, the miners had to drill and blast a gargantuan human anthill out of solid rock. As they burrowed with picks, hammers, and ear-shattering drills through the crust of the planet, the temperature in the cramped, dark tunnels rose sharply. New laborers sometimes panicked with claustrophobia when brought below the surface and introduced to the sweltering, tenebrous world in which they would be compelled to spend their waking hours.

The mining companies who scrambled to exploit the gold deposits had to solve one complex technical problem after another: how to locate the best places to dig to find the reef; how to dig vertical shafts and construct elevators to transport thousands of miners thousands of feet below the surface rapidly; how to get enough air down into the shafts so that the miners would not asphyxiate; how to bring to the surface the rubble which the miners had chopped and dynamited from the face of the vein; how to crush the rubble and extract the gold; and how to dispose of the mountainous tailings brought forth from the depths. Before the mine owners could do any of these things, they had to find the money to pay for these operations, which might have to function for months or even years before enough gold had been removed to earn a profit. Here the early mining capitalists faced a particularly bedeviling problem that limited the return they and any potential investors could make on the venture: the fixed international price of gold.

In this regard gold differed dramatically from diamonds. The market for diamonds had been subject to wild fluctuations in price according to the erratic patterns of supply and demand. When the price of diamonds rose, prospectors scoured the countryside for new sources. Each time a new site was discovered, the mining firms exploited it quickly and hurled cartloads of diamonds on to a market driven largely by vanity. When the abundant supply temporarily sated the demand, the price of diamonds sank. Small companies went bankrupt and sold their holdings to big companies, which then tried to restrict supply to shore up the price. Most capitalists knew that only when both the production and the distribution of the gems could be controlled by a single monopoly would the price of diamonds remain permanently high. Until then they took advantage of every surge and tried to weather every drop.

Gold, in contrast, was an economic oddity. Under normal market conditions a rise in demand causes a rise in price, which in turn brings a rise in production. As production grows, supply increases and prices fall.

In some markets, such as pencils, the fluctuations among demand, price, and supply are small and predictable; in others, such as diamonds, they can be wild and cyclical. Throughout much of the nineteenth and twentieth centuries gold did not obey any of these rules because it enjoyed a unique status as the medium of international exchange. As nations bought and sold from one another they settled their accounts in gold at an immovable price, first specified relative to the British pound and later to the U.S. dollar. In other words, the demand for gold was unlimited but the price was fixed.

For the mine owners and mine laborers this abstract peculiarity had a very real consequence. In a normal market, if the price of a commodity rises steadily, lifting profits, workers can usually persuade management to increase their wages. In South African gold mining, however, the only way to maintain or increase profits was to reduce costs, and the largest single cost was labor. Thus, from its inception, the gold mining industry faced an economic conundrum: how to attract huge numbers of workers into a backbreaking, labor-intensive industry while paying them the lowest possible wages. To solve this problem, the mining companies consolidated themselves into a single recruiting unit so that Africans could not shop around among the mines for better-paying jobs. The mining magnates also called intermittently on the power of the state to create a cheap labor pool from which workers could be drawn. Indeed, it was at the mines that key economic elements of South Africa's system of racial domination—workers' compounds, migrant labor at subsistence wages, and punitive controls—originated.

To run profitable mines, however, the mining companies needed more than cheap workers. They also needed capital, particularly in the form of foreign currency, to purchase the machines, vehicles, and other equipment with which to extract and transport the treasure. Since South Africa had a small, relatively impoverished population, the pool of domestic savings from which to draw such investment capital was small. The mining companies had to reach across the globe to the large reserves of capital fermenting in banks or sloshing around Western stock markets. In the nineteenth century the mining company owners turned primarily to London. However, in the twentieth century, as Britain spent its wealth and vigor in two devastating world wars and as another former British colony across the Atlantic emerged as a major industrial power, South Africans increasingly turned for money and technology to the United States.

Because California had experienced a gold rush a generation before the Transvaal, the United States in the late nineteenth century was a leading innovator and world supplier of mining technology. South African mine owners who could not acquire enough of the machines and equipment they needed from the small domestic manufacturing sector eagerly purchased the necessary items from the United States. Eventually American behemoths such as Newmont Mining and American Metal Climax entered into joint ventures and other cooperative arrangements with South African companies to search for and exploit new lodes.

It was this kind of far-flung connection among money, know-how, and resources that produced the most powerful company in South Africa's history. The firm began modestly, the brainchild of a German Jew who had come to South Africa by way of England. Ernest Oppenheimer was born in Friedberg, Germany, in 1880 and went to England to work as a diamond sorter for the firm of Dunkelsbuhler. At the age of twenty-two, soon after he had become a British citizen, he traveled to South Africa to become the Dunkelsbuhler representative. Within ten years he had become the mayor of the town of Kimberley, but he was forced to resign the post in 1915 when anti-German feeling provoked by the First World War triggered riots around his house. As the war dragged on into 1917, Dunkelsbuhler decided to close down its small gold investments and instructed Oppenheimer to make the arrangements.

Oppenheimer was unhappy. He believed that more gold would be found and that new investments would be profitable. He wanted to start his own firm, but wartime South Africa and Europe had little capital to spare. He wrote to an American friend, William Honold, who had just returned to the United States to work with Herbert Hoover, at that time an internationally recognized mining engineer. Honold was enthusiastic about helping to form the company and urged Oppenheimer to appeal directly to Hoover. In April 1917, Oppenheimer wrote to Hoover and implored him to help. "If American capital wishes to obtain a footing in the South African mining business," he told Hoover, "the easiest course will be to acquire an interest in our company." Hoover was persuaded and talked his friends at the New York bank of J. P. Morgan into putting up the money.

After securing the permission of General Smuts, who believed that South Africa would benefit from an infusion of American money, Oppenheimer and Honold volleyed cables across the Atlantic to work out the details. One sticking point was the name for the new company. Oppenheimer felt that the title needed to include "Africa" and Honold believed it had to mention "America." An associate of Oppenheimer's, H. C. Hull, suggested to Honold that the new company be called the African American Corporation Limited. Honold objected strongly, cabling Oppenheimer on July 6, 1917, that "African American would suggest on this side our dark-skinned fellow countrymen and possibly result in ridicule." Oppenheimer suggested then that the firm be known as the

Anglo-American Corporation of South Africa, Limited, and Honold agreed. Within little more than a decade Ernest Oppenheimer had skillfully surrounded and captured the De Beers Mining Company to create an effective monopoly of diamond mining and distribution. Anglo-American soared to become the most powerful financial and mining conglomerate in South Africa.

While World War I killed more than a million young British men and mangled the English economy, the United States emerged from its brief expedition as a new world power. For most of the young republic's history, American companies had been struggling to grow and develop at home in the face of foreign imports, regional competition, and rapid westward expansion. Those companies that had fought off consolidation, adopted methods of mass production, and conquered the huge national market began in the new century to explore possibilities for business beyond America's borders. South Africa, whose mining industry had created a relatively small but unusually affluent collection of white consumers, seemed a promising toehold from which to explore the rest of colonial southern Africa. As early as the 1920s, American firms began to experiment not only with increased trade but with setting up wholly owned subsidiaries thousands of miles from home. One of the earliest firms to do so was the Ford Motor Company, which decided in 1924 to stop shipping whole automobiles and to ship parts instead. Ford built a large assembly plant in Port Elizabeth in the Eastern Cape, not far from where the ships unloaded the components. General Motors followed with an assembly plant of its own in Port Elizabeth two years later. By the end of the 1920s American companies had captured two-thirds of the automobile market in South Africa and, despite the economic depression of the 1930s, within a generation South African whites owned more automobiles per capita than all but a few of the nations of the world.

During the interwar period American investors and firms tentatively stretched their productive capacity from one continent to another. After the Second World War, which again wrecked the European powers, the United States emerged as the global economic dynamo. American companies, invigorated by the huge manufacturing demands of defeating Hitler, expanded rapidly, sometimes into a vacuum left by a European competitor, but mostly into entirely new fields and lands. By 1953 the United States was responsible for fifty-two percent of all capitalist industrial production in the world. United States direct investment abroad—the value of all the plants, machines, and buildings American companies owned in other countries—rose from $2.7 billion in 1914 and $7.3 billion just before World War II to $32.8 billion in 1960, at that time almost half of the world's total.

Though Great Britain still had the largest amount of investment in South Africa, American companies moved in rapidly after 1945. Before the war U.S. direct investment in the country had been valued at only $50.7 million; within five years of the war it nearly tripled to $140 million. Kennecott Copper Corporation channeled more than $21 million into South Africa to open up mines in the Orange Free State. The United States Export-Import Bank offered $130 million in loans to finance the extraction of uranium. About the same time Newmont Mining Corporation purchased a network of copper, lead, and zinc mines in South Africa and South West Africa.

The South African governments both before and after 1948 encouraged such investments. They were particularly keen on using foreign money and technology to spur the growth of domestic manufacturing. In 1941, however, a government commission reported that South Africa's dependence on foreign manufacturing represented a long-term threat to the nation's health. Since the mines were widely expected to peter out, the commissioners believed that South Africa had to develop a domestic manufacturing base or slide into permanent economic decline. They recommended that domestic production be protected to encourage its growth and that incomes in the general population be allowed to rise. These moves, they argued, would create a large market of consumers, stimulate longer production runs, induce greater efficiency, and make South African manufacturers more internationally competitive.

The National Party's attitude toward the manufacturing industry was complex and contradictory. On the one hand, every Afrikaner politician wanted to free the country from dependence on the mining firms, whose sympathies for England and whose antagonism toward white workers had, in their minds, been conclusively demonstrated. Nationalist prime ministers, like the leaders of all developing countries, also wanted to strengthen and diversify their economies in order to diminish the ability of foreign nations to influence their affairs. In addition, various commissions had warned the government that as the mines became more mechanized, they would need fewer workers. With a growing population, the economy would have to rely on manufacturing to provide jobs for the hundreds of thousands of young people who annually left school to look for work.

At the same time, the manufacturing industry posed problems for a government committed to apartheid. As long as factories required only unskilled laborers, manufacturers benefited from the cheap pool of African workers that apartheid created and preserved. As soon as the need for skilled labor rose, company owners pressured the government to permit greater immigration and to allow the members of other races to occupy white jobs. The Nationalists had restricted white immigration at first, fearing that a large influx of English speakers from Europe or Australia would dilute the Afrikaners' political hold. Forced to choose between allowing foreign whites or domestic blacks to fill the new skilled jobs, the government opted for the foreigners.

The growth of the manufacturing industry presented another serious problem for Verwoerd. The earliest manufacturing industries in South Africa had concentrated in the Transvaal to supply the mines with equipment, clothing, tools, and explosives. By the mid-1950s more than half of all the industries in the entire country were located within a relatively tight cluster around Pretoria and Johannesburg known as the Vaal Triangle. This dense concentration strained water supplies and encouraged the migration of millions of Africans from the rural areas, in direct opposition to the government; policies of influx control and separate development. The more manufacturing grew, the more the government would be faced with a large and permanent urban African population who needed housing, utilities, medical care, food, and schooling. This was a future Verwoerd refused to accept.

Nonetheless, from the government's point of view there were three key advantages to a growth in manufacturing fueled by foreign investment: technology, tax revenues, and legitimacy. Foreign companies would import technology superior to that which South Africa could develop on its own; government planners believed that this would strengthen the nation's independence and self-sufficiency in the long run. Moreover, when a foreign company came to conduct business in South Africa, it contributed directly to the government by paying taxes on its profits. And finally, Verwoerd knew that the presence of foreign firms legitimized South Africa's claim of membership in the Western political and economic sphere. Western countries with substantial investments, he reasoned, would be less willing to defy their domestic business interests to challenge the National Party government.

Throughout the 1950s, in the first decade of National Party rule, U.S. trade and investments rose steadily. In 1953 Mobil Corporation, at the time known as Socony-Vacuum, built South Africa's first oil refinery at a cost of more than $20 million dollars; within a few years the facility processed a quarter of the nation's import requirements. General Motors expanded its assembly plant in Port Elizabeth and began to build truck cabs with local materials. By 1960 U.S. direct investment—that is, the asset value of majority-owned subsidiaries—exceeded $475 million.

The surge in American foreign investment coincided with a rush of interest in American culture. Young English-speaking South Africans read American comic books, listened to rock and roll, and eagerly lined up at the local movie theaters to see the latest westerns. White South African families ate Corn Flakes and Rice Krispies for breakfast and subscribed to *Reader's Digest* and *National Geographic.* Young people in Soweto swirled to the tunes of Glenn Miller, Louis Armstrong, and Bing Crosby. Township musicians formed bands with names like the Boston Stars and the Manhattan Brothers, who struggled to master American jazz. Black writers and journalists imitated American literary styles and discussed the Harlem Renaissance. In Sophiatown, before its destruction, a gang of African teenagers donned flashy clothes, dubbed themselves "the Young Americans," and adopted a hotheaded, daring style that provoked both admiration and fear.

Not everyone was happy about such influences on South Africa's culture and economy. Verwoerd's frame of reference was built around Europe; he viewed Americans as brash and sanctimonious. Eight months after Sharpeville, Verwoerd expressed his frustrations with American hypocrisy to a German magazine reporter. "Why should the Afrikaner suffer because our forefathers did not shoot the blacks?" he asked. "The experiences of our ancestors in this country were rather similar to those of the Americans and the Indians. But while the Americans annihilated the Indians as they advanced through the continent, the Boers allowed the blacks to live. Should we now suffer because our ancestors behaved in such a Christian and humane fashion? No, I tell you, this is a white country and any concessions to blacks only means demands for fresh concessions. It would be absurd to turn blacks into imitations of Europeans and force a Western type democracy upon them. We plan to develop them along their own lines using their own traditional communities and tribal chieftains."

Some within the resistance movement hoped that the leaders of the United States, who so frequently broadcast their devotion to equality and democracy, would press South Africa to change. When America did little to help the Defiance Campaign or the ANC's appeals for international pressure in the 1950s, many grew disillusioned. Nelson Mandela articulated such complaints in March 1958, when he wrote an article expressing alarm about the invasion of American money and ideas into Africa in general and South Africa in particular. He warned that the decline in European colonialism had been followed by a rise in American imperialism and pointed to the Marshall Plan, NATO, and the rapid expansion of American military bases around the world as evidence. He agreed that an infusion of foreign capital was necessary for the development of Africa, but "the idea of making quick and high profits, which underlies all the developmental plans launched in Africa by the U.S.A., completely effaces the value of such plans. . . . The big and powerful American trade monopolies that are springing up in various parts of the continent and which are destroying the small trade, the low wages paid the ordinary man, the resulting poverty and misery, his illiteracy and the

squalid tenements in which he dwells, are the simplest and most eloquent exposition of the falsity of the argument that American investments in Africa will raise the standards of the people of this continent."
He complimented the Soviet Union and China for sending delegations
to the recent Cairo conference of Afro-Asian nations and suggested that
America's growing obsession with the apparent advances of Communism in Africa was a "stunt to distract the attention of the people of
Africa from the real issue facing them, namely, American imperialism."

"The peoples of resurgent Africa are perfectly capable of deciding
upon their own future form of government and discovering and themselves dealing with any dangers which may arise," Mandela concluded in
a passage that could almost have been written by Verwoerd. "They do
not require any schooling from the U.S.A. which—to judge from such
events as the Little Rock outrage and the activities of the Un-American
Witch-hunting Committee—should learn to put its own house in order
before trying to teach everyone else."

The massacre at Sharpeville nearly derailed the South African economy.
Even before the crisis, the nation's commercial life had shown signs of
fragility, which had been partially offset by an increase in foreign investment. During Verwoerd's first year as prime minister, business leaders
warned him of the economic dangers of creating an Afrikaner republic
and a constellation of black states. Harry Oppenheimer, the son of Ernest and the chairman of Anglo-American, criticized both of Verwoerd's
goals on the grounds that they would destroy South Africa's relations
with the Commonwealth and the other industrialized nations of the
Western world. So concerned had Oppenheimer been about South Africa's increasingly negative image abroad that in January 1960, two
months before Sharpeville, he and several others, including American
multimillionaire Charles Engelhard, established the South Africa Foundation, an institution designed to burnish the country's image among
American business and political leaders. The foundation set up offices
throughout the United States and began squiring prominent Americans
around South Africa on free "fact-finding" trips.

The immense press coverage of Sharpeville sparked hysteria among
investors. For weeks after the shootings the Johannesburg stock exchange remained buried under an avalanche of sell orders from Europe.
Share prices plummeted so rapidly that only a wave of desperate buying
by South Africa's largest insurance companies, pension funds, and trusts
prevented a complete crash. Property values in Cape Town and Johannesburg slumped dramatically. Capital leaked, then poured out of the
country. By early April, South African newspapers were running special
editions with grim headlines such as RACIAL STRIFE HITS UNION FINANCIALLY;

AMERICAN INVESTORS ARE DUBIOUS. A week after Kgosana's arrest and only
four days before the assassination attempt against Verwoerd, the *Johannesburg Star* announced that certain unnamed but highly prominent
business leaders had asked for an emergency meeting with Verwoerd.
According to the story, the men intended to ask for the elimination of
the current pass system, a steep reduction in influx controls, "continuous
discussion with responsible natives," and a "strong campaign against the
hooligan element among the natives." Though the business leaders' position fell far short of the minimum requirements of the African National Congress, the newspaper declared that the request for an interview amounted to "a demand from the men who run the nation's
economy for a radical change of policy."

The business leaders' request was postponed because of the attempt
on Verwoerd's life. When they did meet, Verwoerd was enjoying a gush
of public support that allowed him to rebuff the men completely. As the
prime minister recovered, criticisms bubbled up again, even from within
his own party. On April 19, Paul Sauer, the author of the Nationalist
Party's 1948 pro-segregation report, announced that the Sharpeville riots had closed a chapter of South African history and that he would try
to persuade Verwoerd to open a new one by softening apartheid. Sauer
announced that he would ask the prime minister to increase urban African wages and relax the pass restrictions and liquor laws. When Verwoerd heard about the speech, he sent a furious message from his sickbed demanding that Sauer "stand firm."

Verwoerd also dispatched his hardline minister of external affairs,
Eric Louw, to represent him publicly. Louw charged out to blame the
disturbances on Communist agitation among otherwise content Africans. He attacked the "distortions" of foreign and domestic correspondents, helped shepherd new press restrictions through parliament, and
approved the jailing or deportation of a host of journalists. Louw also
ordered the South African ambassador to the United States, L. J. du
Plessis, to ask Caltex Corporation, a joint venture of Chevron and Texaco and a major sponsor of NBC television news, to pressure broad-
caster Chet Huntley to "calm down" his commentaries about South
Africa. Finally, Louw traveled to both the United Nations and a meeting
of Commonwealth prime ministers to attack South Africa's critics and to
defend the wisdom of apartheid.

As South Africa entered the winter months of June and July, wealthy
citizens, corporations, and investors continued to send millions of rand a
week abroad, straining the nation's foreign exchange and gold reserves.
On June 16, 1960, the *New York Times* reported that South Africa's
reserves had dropped twenty-five percent, or more than $95 million.
Government economists considered devaluing the rand but decided that

this might increase the rate of financial hemorrhage. To make matters worse, political groups and labor unions in Sweden, Great Britain, West Germany, and other countries were pressing forward with boycotts of South African goods. In the United States several AFL-CIO unions called on Americans not to buy South African goods. In India, Prime Minister Jawaharlal Nehru, incensed about Verwoerd's treatment of South Africans of Indian descent, demanded a united boycott by Commonwealth nations. Kwame Nkrumah of Ghana cut off purchases, closed his country's seaports and airports to South African ships and airplanes, and demanded that any South African citizens entering the country make a formal declaration of opposition to apartheid.

Through all of this Verwoerd remained publicly unperturbed. He summarily dismissed the opinions of African leaders as inferior and ineffectual. While the reports of European and American citizens protesting apartheid in their capitals irritated him, he doubted that their governments would actually do anything. At worst, he thought, the Western countries would pay lip service to the idea of racial integration to win the support of the emerging African nations or of their own liberals; but in the end white pride, commercial necessity, and anti-Communism—not vague humanitarian sentiment—would guide relations with South Africa.

Verwoerd, even before the Sharpeville crisis and the attempt on his life, had made it clear that nothing would prevent him from fulfilling his dream of creating an Afrikaner republic. In January he had announced that he would hold a referendum on the republic; on the actual day of the Sharpeville massacre he had told the House of Assembly that even if the voters rejected the republic in the referendum, he would create it anyway through an act of parliament. In his first speech after the assassination attempt, Verwoerd insisted that the future republic must remain in the hands of whites at all costs. Verwoerd issued orders from his sickbed to muzzle the press and arrest politically active South Africans of all races. To quell his opponents in the United Party, Verwoerd forced parliament to adjourn. And to forestall future disturbances, the prime minister approved the formation of a new internal security force made up of members of national guard and military commando units.

By August Verwoerd felt sufficiently confident to schedule the referendum for early October. A week before the election he wrote a four-page, handwritten appeal and sent copies to a million voters. On October 5, 1960, ninety percent of the 1.8 million eligible white voters went to the polls. The measure, as expected, passed overwhelmingly in the Afrikaner strongholds in the Transvaal, South West Africa, and the Orange Free State; barely squeaked by in the Cape Province; and failed decisively in Natal by almost a hundred thousand votes. Nonetheless, when all the votes were tallied, the measure had passed with a majority of fifty-two percent. The Afrikaner dream of full independence from Britain, nurtured for five generations, had finally come true.

His victory in hand, Verwoerd announced that he would ask the Commonwealth nations to permit South Africa to remain a member even after its transformation into a republic. In March 1961 he flew to London to present South Africa's case himself. The prime ministers of the other Commonwealth countries, with the exception of Macmillan of Britain, peppered Verwoerd for fifteen hours with criticisms of apartheid. Verwoerd refused to budge. When the prime ministers told Verwoerd that they would expel South Africa from the Commonwealth for its racial practices, Verwoerd preempted them by withdrawing his country's application publicly. Verwoerd could barely contain his glee as he made the announcement to television reporters outside Lancaster House. "Our opponents who wanted us out of the Commonwealth have won their wish but they have lost their cause," said Verwoerd with a wide and self-satisfied grin. "Goodbye to you all!" Verwoerd returned to South Africa on the eve of the first anniversary of the Sharpeville killings to an ecstatic welcome. At the airports in Johannesburg and Cape Town, huge crowds of whites gathered to praise the father of the new republic. Verwoerd stood below an immense picture of himself and listened while a host of politicians showered him with compliments. "You are the leader of the white man in South Africa," said one, ". . . and the world!"

The season of Hendrik Verwoerd's political triumph was one of enormous stress for Nelson Mandela. In December 1960, still pinned down by the fourth year of the Treason Trial and the tenth year of his banning by the government, Mandela learned that his son Makgatho was seriously ill in the Transkei. Defying his banning restrictions Mandela secretly left Johannesburg. He drove rapidly, for he had to cover nearly a thousand miles, round trip, in twenty-four hours so that the police would not notice his absence. When Mandela arrived, he found the senior wife of his cousin Kaiser Matanzima nursing the boy. Convinced that his son needed better medical attention, Mandela wrapped the trembling youth in a blanket and roared back to Johannesburg. When he returned he discovered that in his absence Winnie, nearly eight months pregnant, had gone into labor, entered the primitive "non-European" section of the local hospital, and delivered her second daughter, Zindzi. While his wife and son recovered, Mandela dutifully returned to the interminable courtroom maneuvers in Pretoria.

For months the government prosecutors had labored to prove that the members of the African National Congress were guilty of high treason.

Their questioning of Mandela and the other defendants alternated between subtle traps and brazen assaults. Sometimes the judges intervened with their own questions and clarifications. When Mandela spoke about the need for freedom, one judge asked, "Isn't your freedom a direct threat to Europeans?" "We are not anti-white," Mandela responded. "We are against white supremacy, and in struggling against white supremacy we have the support of some sections of the European population. . . . [The African National] Congress has consistently preached a policy of race harmony and we have condemned racialism no matter by whom it is professed."

The prosecutors asked him if he supported the ANC's commitment to nonviolence. Yes, he replied. Did he also support the nationalist movements elsewhere in Africa? Yes, said Mandela. But there must be a contradiction, said the prosecutors, since the other nationalist movements had sometimes used violent methods. This was not necessarily contradictory, said Mandela, since different methods might be required in different settings. The prosecutors tried a different tack. If Mandela didn't believe in violence, why did he encourage his followers to challenge the government, which might become violent? And didn't the increased strength of the ANC amplify the probability of government violence? "Oh yes," said Mandela grimly. "We felt that the government will not hesitate to massacre hundreds of African in order to intimidate them not to oppose its reactionary policy."

When challenged on whether he supported a one-party system of government, Mandela replied that he believed in democracy. When the judges suggested that the majority were too uneducated to vote, Mandela responded indignantly. "This is what happens," he explained to the court. "A man stands up to contest a seat in a particular area. He draws up a manifesto; he says 'These are the things for which I stand.' For example, in a rural area he might say 'I am against stock limitation.' Then listening to the policy of this person, you decide whether this man will advance your interests if you return him to parliament; on that basis you vote for a candidate. It has *nothing* to do with education."

In frustration, the prosecutors finally asked Mandela point-blank: hadn't he repudiated the early ANC position of anti-Communism and become a Communist? "I don't know if I did become a Communist," said Mandela thoughtfully. "If by Communist you mean a member of the Communist Party and a person who believes in the theory of Marx, Engels, Lenin, and Stalin, and who adheres strictly to the discipline of the party, I did not become a Communist." He said that he had been impressed when he had heard that there was no color bar in the Soviet Union. He also had noticed that the Soviet Union had no colonies in Africa and had supported the call for an end to colonialism.

Shortly after Verwoerd's return from London, the Treason Trials came to a surprising end. The prosecution had recently concluded its argument and defense attorney Bram Fischer had just begun laying out the full defense when suddenly the senior judge announced a week's recess. The defense team, which had already succeeded in eliminating charges against all but thirty-one of the original 156 defendants, had felt reasonably confident. The judge's abrupt announcement threw them into turmoil: did this mean that he intended to reach a summary judgment of guilty?

During the week's recess, Mandela's banning order expired; for the first time in a decade he was legally free to speak to a crowd of people. On March 25, he drove to Pietermaritzburg in Natal to attend a huge All-In African conference. Fourteen hundred delegates had assembled from around the country to discuss what should be done about Verwoerd's relentless drive to create a white republic. Mandela's appearance after years of silence electrified the crowd; one man told a reporter that Mandela's speech reminded him of "a State of the Nation address by the American president." The conference decided to demand that Verwoerd call a "National Convention of elected delegates on an equal basis, irrespective of race, color and creed or other limitation" who would have "sovereign powers" to establish a "new, non-racial democratic constitution" for South Africa—in short, the same demand the ANC had made in the Defiance Campaign and the Freedom Charter years before. To communicate the demand and coordinate the actions to support it, the conference elected a National Action Council and chose Mandela as the leader. Four days later, Nelson Mandela, Walter Sisulu, and the other defendants returned to the courtroom in Pretoria to learn the reason for the recess. Judge F. L. Rumpff, the same judge who had overseen the Defiance Campaign trials, asked them all to stand. "You are found not guilty and discharged," he said. "You are free to go." As they emerged from the courtroom, the crowd outside exploded into cheers and then tearfully sang "Nkosi Sikele Afrika."

It was a poignant moment for Mandela, the end of a long and difficult chapter that would soon be followed by one even more arduous. Over the previous week, he and the other leaders of the ANC had reached a painful decision. As they had discussed the possible outcomes of the trial, they had realized that Verwoerd would never accept an acquittal. If they were freed, he would strike again quickly. To protect their challenge to Verwoerd's white republic, they concluded, Mandela would have to abandon his family, leave his home, and go underground to coordinate the campaign. The day before his trip to Pietermaritzburg, Mandela had returned for a few moments to his home in Orlando and asked Winnie to pack a suitcase for him. "I will be going away for a long time," he told his wife. "You are not to worry; my friends will look after you. They'll give you news of me from time to time. Look well after the children. I know you'll have the strength and courage to do so without me." Then he left. Mandela would not be able to visit his own home again legally for thirty years.

The ANC leaders had accurately predicted Verwoerd's reaction. Immediately after the trial the government again sent the police out to find and arrest Mandela. Trying as best he could to disguise his tall frame, Mandela moved from city to city and township to township. He dressed as a chauffeur and drove around in a car that repeatedly broke down. He spent most of the day indoors, venturing out to attend small meetings or to travel at night. He appeared every now and then in Soweto for furtive reunions with Winnie. As he continued to elude the police month after month, the press dubbed him "the Black Pimpernel."

While he moved around the country, Mandela wrote letters to Verwoerd and to the leader of the opposition, United Party head Sir de Villiers Graaff, appealing to them to call a convention to draft a nonracial constitution. Neither man responded, though Verwoerd told the members of parliament that he had received a "threat" from Mandela; he then passed the letter along to the minister of justice as evidence against Mandela. Throughout April Mandela worked hard to organize a national three-day strike to coincide with the declaration of the republic on May 31. Goaded by the government, the newspapers hysterically announced a secret plan by Africans to overrun the cities. Determined to prevent Mandela and the ANC from spoiling the celebration of the new republic, Verwoerd cracked down harshly. On May 3, 1961, police throughout the country arrested thousands of suspected activists of all races; though they didn't catch Mandela, they imprisoned huge numbers of innocent people. Two weeks later the government gave the police the power to detain anyone for twelve days without charge or bail, seized another fourteen hundred people, and summoned army reservists to active duty. "In the country's biggest call-up since the war," wrote a reporter for the *London Observer,* "scores of citizen's force and commando units were mobilized in the big towns. Camps were established at strategic points; heavy army vehicles carrying equipment and supplies moved in a steady stream along the [Witwatersrand] Reef; helicopters hovered over African residential areas and trained searchlights on houses, yards, lands, and unlit areas. Hundreds of white civilians were sworn in as special constables. Hundreds of white women spent weekends shooting at targets. Gun shops sold out of their stocks of revolvers and ammunition. All police leave was cancelled throughout the country. Armed guards were posted to protect power stations and other sources of essential services. Saracen armored cars and troop carriers patrolled townships. Police vans patrolled areas and broadcast statements that Africans who went on strike would be sacked and forced out of town."

Journalists from around the world, anticipating another Sharpeville, flew in to cover the republican celebrations. Early on the morning of Monday, May 29, before anyone had gone to work, police spokesmen announced on the government-controlled radio (South Africa did not yet have television broadcasting) that the strike had failed completely. Newspaper editors, many of whom had been intimidated by Verwoerd's threats of censorship, printed the claims even though some of their own reporters were finding that more than fifty percent of all workers had stayed away from their jobs in Durban and Johannesburg. Mandela fumed at the perfidy of the government, excoriated the press, praised the participants, and then, recognizing the dwindling momentum, called the strike off. "In the light of the steps taken by the government to suppress it," he told reporters at a secret meeting after the strike, "it was a tremendous success."

The inauguration of the republic took place on Wednesday, May 31, 1961. Though rain dampened the official outdoor celebrations in Pretoria's Church Square and the symbolic white pigeon released by Verwoerd fell to the ground like a stone, the Nationalists were elated. Fifty-one years after its formation, the Union of South Africa had come to an end; formal British rule over the nation had ceased; and an independent republic dominated by Afrikaners had come into existence. In the peculiar tradition of South African prime ministers, Verwoerd now selected the personal slogan that was to summarize his policies and purpose. Malan had chosen an exhortation to the nation: "Believe in God. Believe in Your People. Believe in Yourself." Verwoerd, emphasizing the independence of the new republic and the forward-looking nature of apartheid, admonished the nation: "Create Your Own Future."

To create the future, Verwoerd knew that he would have to stifle dissent, restore stability, and regain the confidence of the domestic business community and of foreign investors. When his minister of justice, F. C. Erasmus, moved on to become the ambassador to Italy, Verwoerd looked around for someone who was intelligent, unquestioning, and ironhanded; he found him in the person of a subcabinet minister, Balthazar Johannes Vorster. Born on September 13, 1915, his parents' thirteenth child (hence his lifelong conviction that thirteen was his lucky number), Vorster had been steeped since childhood in the Afrikaner mythology. As children, he and his siblings would sit around before bedtime and read passages from a book about Boer martyrs executed by the British in the war. "After we had bathed and said our prayers," recalled a brother, "we would sit on a big double bed, with the eldest reading until his voice broke with emotion. Then the next one would take over until he could read no further. And the third and so on, until the end when we all sat weeping on the bed. We, all of us, felt very bitter about the injustices of the war, about what the war had done to us Afrikaners. The English were the enemy and the Boers were our heroes." It is not surprising that when a reporter later asked Vorster about the origins of his nationalism, he said that it had come "absolutely naturally" to him, "like breathing fresh air. It was something I simply accepted, something I never questioned."

During the Second World War Vorster's ardor got him into trouble. Like millions of his compatriots he had been swept with emotion during the 1938 centennial of the Great Trek. Soon afterward his loathing for the English empire and his disgust at the betrayal of the Afrikaner cause by former heroes like Smuts and Hertzog propelled him into the Ossewa Brandwag. Within months he had risen to become, at twenty-four, the youngest "general" in the fascist organization, a development that attracted the attention of the Smuts government, who jailed him on September 23, 1942. Vorster later recounted with horror that the authorities had let him take a bath only once a week and deliberately kept him in a cell normally reserved for Africans. After nearly three months and a brief hunger strike, he was transferred to the intern camp at Koffiefontein. Though the internees complained about the severity of their prison conditions, they managed to arrange prison courses in history, zoology, advanced philosophy, private law, and dozens of other topics; they had a regular music series in which the inmates performed Schubert, Liszt, and Strauss on the piano; and they engineered a rash of escapes. Vorster was elected camp leader after six months and organized his fellow internees so efficiently that even the prison camp commander began referring to him as General Vorster.

After his release, Vorster returned and settled in the small town of Brakpan. In 1948, as a candidate of the small Afrikaner Party, he lost his first campaign for a seat in parliament by two votes. Three years later, when the Nationalist Party and Afrikaner Party merged into the National Party, Vorster finally gained a seat in the legislature. When Verwoerd became prime minister and created a new rank of deputy minister, he tapped Vorster to take the post for education, arts, science, and social welfare. Vorster was surprised: though he had been a student of Verwoerd's at Stellenbosch, he had often ridiculed his old professor during his days in the Ossewa Brandwag. Vorster went to Verwoerd and said, "Doctor, I hope you know what you are doing because I know nothing about education, arts, or science. However, my wife is a social worker. I think you are making a mistake." Verwoerd replied characteristically, "It is not for you to judge. I am the one who must judge. The swearing-in is on Wednesday; just see to it that you are there."

Over the next three years the junior cabinet minister supported Verwoerd vigorously, praising his handling of Sharpeville, congratulating him on withdrawing from the Commonwealth, and rebutting his critics in parliament. When, on July 23, 1961, the prime minister named Vorster minister of justice, Vorster was overjoyed. He quickly warned Verwoerd that he "would have to let me deal with the threat of subversion in my own way." As Vorster recalled years later, Verwoerd "agreed with me and said that he would leave me free to do what I had to do—within reason."

In his war on subversion, Vorster began slicing away the remains of the tattered net of laws that still guarded the civil liberties of South Africans. When asked later to describe his thinking, Vorster recalled that he felt the country was drifting, through the laxity of his predecessor, toward chaos. "These were not normal times; the Communists were plotting revolution, bloodshed, violence, and they were certainly not playing the game according to the rules," Vorster told one of his biographers. "I realized that if the security forces had to play according to the rules it would be like fighting an implacable and vicious enemy with one hand tied behind your back. I was not going to send my men into battle with one hand tied behind their backs."

In addition to selecting Vorster, Verwoerd took steps to address another dangerous problem: the continuing instability of the nation's economy. In the year following Sharpeville, the flight of capital and the drain on the country's reserves had continued, though at a slightly slower pace; by March 1961 the reserves of gold and foreign exchange had dwindled to less than half their value in the previous year. In May 1961, fearing that political disturbances might accelerate the flight and cripple the country, Verwoerd raised the bank rate, intensified import controls, and moved to restrict commercial bank loans; a few weeks later he tightened foreign exchange controls even further.

To shore up support among international capitalists and businessmen, Verwoerd encouraged the work of Oppenheimer's South Africa Foundation and sent his own trade mission to the United States and Canada in April 1961. The trade mission, composed of government officials and business leaders and headed by Hendrik J. van Eck, the head of the South African Industrial Development Corporation, attended a lunch at the Waldorf-Astoria in New York City on April 19. Van Eck told the assembled American business leaders that American investment in South Africa was nearly $600 million, or about sixty percent of all American investments on the continent of Africa, and that conditions in

South Africa were highly favorable for increased foreign investment. Six weeks later, on June 4, while thousands of apartheid opponents languished in detention, South African business interests purchased a huge advertisement in the *New York Times*. The lavish insert, designed to resemble a magazine and more than twenty pages long, extolled the virtues of South Africa's "parliamentary democracy," painted an enticing portrait of South Africa's economic future, and quoted the enthusiastic American executives:

> Mr. Dick Hegland, managing director of General Motors South Africa, said GM is increasing its investment in its ultramodern manufacturing plant in Port Elizabeth. "We in General Motors believe this country's economic position will improve shortly. . . . There is every reason to be optimistic about economic growth over the next decade."
>
> The Coca-Cola Export Corp. just launched this year a 3 million dollar development program centered around a bottling plant near Johannesburg. Mr. J. Paul Austin, president, said, "My corporation does not idly play around with this kind of money. We believe in South Africa and the new plant is a demonstration of faith on our side."

Over time Verwoerd's combination of repression at home and seduction abroad began to work its intended effect, squelching protest, containing capital, and luring investors to return. In August 1961 Verwoerd felt confident enough to announce a parliamentary election for the following October. Mandela, still in hiding, wrestled with growing despair. The African National Congress had tried one strategy after another: petitions, partial participation in government structures, national conventions, economic boycotts, general strikes, appeals for foreign assistance, and assiduous nonviolence. Mandela pondered the problem in an essay written shortly after the May 1961 strike, in which he noted that the ANC's traditional policy of nonviolence, to which Albert Luthuli still adhered, was under renewed fire. "The question that is being asked with monotonous regularity up and down the country is this: Is it politically correct to continue preaching peace and non-violence when dealing with a government whose barbaric practices have brought so much suffering and misery to Africans?" His own ambivalence showed up clearly in his response: "These are crucial questions that merit sane and sober reflection," he wrote. "It would be a serious mistake to brush them aside and leave them unanswered."

With an optimism that was beginning to sound hollow, Mandela told his followers that "the strike at the end of May was only the beginning of our campaign. We are now launching a full-scale, countrywide campaign of non-cooperation with the Verwoerd government, until we have won an elected National Convention, representing all the people of this country, with the power to draw up and enforce a new democratic constitution." In his most famous essay, released to the press on June 26, 1961, the ANC's annual Freedom Day, Mandela developed the idea of total noncollaboration. There was considerable irony in this, for only a few years before Mandela had vigorously endorsed the ANC's policy that some voice in government was better than none and had attacked the members of the Unity Movement and the All African Convention for their twenty-year commitment to noncollaboration. Now Mandela announced the "opening of the second phase in the fight against the Verwoerd Republic and for a National Convention. A full and country-wide campaign of non-cooperation with the Government will be launched immediately. The precise form of the contemplated action, its scope and dimensions and duration will be announced to you at the appropriate time. At the present moment it is sufficient to say that we plan to make government impossible."

Even as he wrote these bold words Mandela knew that the chances of a mass movement of nonresistance taking shape while many of the organizers remained in jail were slim. Those chances slipped even more after John Vorster, as justice minister, took control of the police. Mandela and the other ANC leaders sought desperately to find another point of leverage to use against the Nationalist government. The smattering of boycotts around the globe that had followed Sharpeville offered a sliver of hope. Throughout July and August, as Mandela analyzed the events of the past year and observed Verwoerd's steps to quell the fears of international investors, a new possibility emerged. The flight of capital and the loss of foreign investment that had caused so many white South Africans to question Verwoerd's policies had been triggered by Sharpeville. Couldn't other disturbances be set off that would have a similar effect? And if these disturbances consisted of attacks on unmanned economic installations—railroad tracks and power lines, for example—wouldn't this satisfy both those who wanted to use violence and those who objected to the loss of human life?

Mandela, meeting secretly with his confederates, discussed the idea at length. Without a change in tactics, they agreed, Verwoerd's unbending repression might eradicate the fifty-year-old African National Congress. The Communists in the circle argued that to continue to deny the failure of nonviolence in South Africa or the success of armed struggle in independent countries to the north was to cast their commitment to freedom in doubt. After long deliberations, the officers decided to form an independent military organization called Umkhonto We Sizwe (Spear of the Nation). To lead the new entity, the ANC members again selected their most respected organizer, Nelson Mandela.

Over the next few months, Mandela slowly assembled his organization. Hiding out in the suburban home of a white friend, he studied the literature on military strategy urged on him by his Communist colleagues: Mao Zedong, Che Guevara, Clausewitz. To explain the presence of this studious and dignified African to their Zulu cleaning woman, his hosts told her that their friend "David" was a student who was waiting for clearance to go abroad. Sometimes Mandela missed Winnie so much that he ventured out in disguise to surprise her. In October, ANC supporters rented a small farm named Lilliesleaf in the town of Rivonia, just north of Johannesburg. Mandela moved to the farm and over several days his friends spirited Winnie and her children out of Orlando to join him. For a few idyllic weeks, Winnie happily cooked while Nelson took his daughters for walks in the garden; years later Zeni would repeatedly dream of that garden and ask her mother when they could go "home" to Lilliesleaf.

In the evenings the members of the Umkhonto high command gathered to discuss their strategy. They had four forms of violence they could pursue: sabotage, guerrilla warfare, terrorism, and open revolution. They all agreed that in the light of the ANC's tradition and the Verwoerd government's military might, sabotage made the most sense. Because sabotage could be directed at objects rather than people, Mandela observed, it would keep bitterness to a minimum and offer "the most hope for future race relations."

Even sabotage was not an easy course. Since the republican celebrations in May, Verwoerd had posted heavily armed guards at most of the important installations in the country. Moreover, it took technical knowledge to blow things up; since the government barred Africans from combat training, few in Umkhonto knew what to do. They resolved to experiment. On one occasion two would-be saboteurs planted a charge next to an outhouse on a deserted farm. They lit the fuse, watched it burn, and shouted with joy when the outhouse exploded into splinters. "Now we are ready to take over South Africa!" exulted one. "Yes," said his partner, "one outhouse at a time."

The preparations for Umkhonto's campaign were overshadowed when, on October 23, 1961, Albert Luthuli won the Nobel Peace Prize. Luthuli, still under a government ban, learned of the award while cutting sugarcane outside his home in Natal. Ironically, Luthuli was being showered with public recognition for the nonviolent struggle against apartheid at precisely the same time that his colleagues had secretly repudiated his approach. Luthuli's reaction to the news was reflective: he told a reporter, "I have only been thinking of the spiritual importance of the hour and what it means in terms of spiritual encouragement," adding that he wanted "a period of quiet meditation and did not want to see anyone for several hours."

Verwoerd, who only days before had won another crushing parliamentary election by contrasting the National Party, "the party of granite," with the United Party, "the putty party, the party you can squeeze into any form at any time," refused to comment on the award. Later he announced that Luthuli would not be permitted to go to Oslo to receive the prize; then, under pressure from abroad, he reversed himself. On December 11, 1961, Luthuli stood before the Norwegian royal family, Nobel laureates, and international correspondents and delivered a stirring and vigorous attack on the immorality of apartheid. South Africa, he said, "is a museum piece in our time, a hangover from the dark past of mankind, a relic of an age which everywhere else is dying or dead. Here the cult of race superiority and of white supremacy is worshiped like a god. . . . I, as a Christian, have always felt that there is one thing above all about 'apartheid' or 'separate development' that is unforgivable. It seems utterly indifferent to the suffering of individual persons, who have lost their land, their homes, their jobs, in the pursuit of what is surely the most terrible dream in the world. This terrible dream is not held on to by a crack-pot group. It is the deliberate policy of a government, supported actively by a large part of the white population, and tolerated passively by the overwhelming white majority."

Luthuli's speech did not, as he had hoped, open a new chapter in the struggle against apartheid; rather it marked the end of an old one. Five days after Luthuli's speech in Oslo, on the 123rd anniversary of the Battle of Blood River, the members of Umkhonto We Sizwe exploded small bombs at various government office buildings and installations around the country. "The Nationalist government has rejected every peaceable demand by the people for rights and freedom and answered every such demand with force and yet more force," stated leaflets distributed throughout the country. "The time comes in the life of any nation when there remain only two choices: submit or fight."

In late 1961 Mandela learned from Oliver Tambo that the African National Congress had been invited to participate in a Pan-African Freedom Conference in Addis Ababa. Tambo urged Mandela to slip out of the country to attend the event and to travel around Europe and Africa to solicit support for the armed struggle. Mandela left, arrived in Ethiopia in January 1962, and explained the new ANC approach to the delegates. "South Africa is now a land ruled by the gun," he said. "The government is increasing the size of its army, of its navy, of its air force, and the police. . . . Armament factories are being set up. . . . All opportunities for peaceful agitation and struggle have been closed to us. Africans no longer have the freedom even to stay peacefully in their houses in protest against the oppressive policies of the government. During the strike in May last year the police went from house to house, beating up Africans and driving them back to work."

From Ethiopia Mandela toured North and West Africa, looking to set up military training camps for ANC recruits and trying to line up scholarships for young refugees from South Africa. In June he visited London with Tambo and met with the leaders of the British Labour Party. Then he made his way back toward South Africa, stopping in Algeria to take a course in mortar firing and demolition and in East Africa where he met Julius Nyerere, the future president of Tanzania, and Kenneth Kaunda, the future president of Zambia. After he slipped back into South Africa he traveled to Johannesburg for a meeting with the other members of Umkhonto and a brief reunion with Winnie. Afterward he journeyed to Natal and met, on Saturday, August 4, 1962, with Albert Luthuli. The man who drove Mandela to the meeting recalled that they greeted each other with great warmth and dignity, like a leader receiving his commander. Mandela gave Luthuli a full report of his trip, pointing out that many of the Pan-Africanists in other countries had challenged him on the ANC's policies of working with South Africans of other races. Luthuli in turn chided Mandela for deciding to form Umkhonto without consulting him or the "grassroots"; the decision had compromised Luthuli in many ways. Mandela apologized but pointed out that it would have been difficult to organize a guerrilla force if their intention had been announced in public meetings.

During the six months of Mandela's travels to the north, Hendrik Verwoerd and John Vorster were not idle. The Umkhonto explosions had not been the only outbreak of violence. In December 1961 the small but still functioning Pan Africanist Congress had announced the formation of its own military wing, known as Poqo. The sporadic attacks by these organizations had proved a boon to Verwoerd and Vorster, quelling their liberal critics, shifting the focus from apartheid to Communism, and providing evidence for their claims of imminent revolution. In early 1962 Verwoerd announced the construction of three new munitions plants; extended the period of compulsive military training for whites; and nearly doubled the military's budget from $90 million in 1961 to $162 million in 1962. In June, Vorster persuaded parliament to pass the Sabotage Act. The draconian bill defined sabotage broadly as the commission of or intent to commit damage to any property; provided for detention without charge and trial without jury; established a punishment of death even for juveniles; and placed the burden of proof that the offense had not been committed on the accused rather than on the state, a provision sharply denounced by the International Jurists Commission. Vorster also won permission to jail anyone who wrote political graffiti, to punish any journalist who quoted a banned person, and to confine any South African deemed a threat to the state to long-term house arrest, a measure suggested to him while reading the Bible one night.

In addition to expanding the police force, Vorster built up an elaborate network of informers and agents provocateurs to help him track and disrupt his political opponents. In this he was helped by information provided by the intelligence agencies of other countries, particularly the United States and Great Britain. Vorster used these sources to search for Mandela, whose highly publicized underground life and foreign travels had been a persistent embarrassment to the government. In early August 1962, Vorster learned that Mandela had traveled to Durban. Nearly thirty years later an American reporter uncovered evidence indicating that the source of this information was an undercover agent working for the American CIA, who knew where Mandela was having a secret dinner with his ANC colleagues and who provided the South African police with his itinerary for the following day. On Sunday, August 5, the day after his reunion with Luthuli, Mandela drove north out of Durban toward Johannesburg. Just outside the town of Howick Falls, three carloads of police stopped his car, arrested Mandela, and took him to prison to spend the next ten thousand days behind bars.

PART TWO

The Internationalization
of Civil Rights

THREE

John F. Kennedy
and the Politics
of Racial Equality
(1960–1963)

Nothing is more paradoxical than that events [denying civil rights] should take place in the United States at a time when that country is anxious to project its image before the world as the archetype of democracy and the champion of freedom. Mr. President, the ears and eyes of the world are concentrated on Alabama.
—MILTON OBOTE

IN EARLY 1960, as Hendrik Verwoerd stifled rebellion and survived his wounds, racial disturbances also erupted in the United States. On Monday, February 1, 1960, three days before British Prime Minister Harold Macmillan's "wind of change" speech to the South African Parliament, four black college freshmen from the Agricultural and Technical College outside Greensboro, North Carolina, walked into a downtown Woolworth's store, entered the segregated lunch area, and took seats at a whites-only counter. After sitting quietly all afternoon without being served, they left. The next morning they came back with nineteen friends; on Wednesday, with eighty-five. Within the week similar protests had started in other parts of the country. By the end of the month, lunch counter sit-ins had been organized in thirty-one segregated southern cities in eight states, and the oft-suppressed issue of racial equality had flared again in America's political life.

The sit-ins were not the first protests against racial discrimination in the United States. A century earlier, Americans had fought a butchering war after which, during the brief period of Reconstruction, the principles of political unity and racial equality seemed to have been established. Newly enfranchised slaves sent twenty-two blacks to the United

States Congress and elected a black U.S. senator in Mississippi and a black governor in Louisiana. The gains did not last. Embittered white southerners, much like the Afrikaners a generation later, gradually reestablished their control through a mixture of artifice and violence. When blacks appealed to the federal government, the white politicians in Washington studiously ignored them for their own political reasons. Republicans, identified nationally for their abolitionist stance, were bereft of elected officials throughout most of the South and refused to tear at the healing wounds of war. Northern Democrats, eager to pry power from Republicans, did not want to inflame the racial prejudices of their own immigrant supporters. Southern Democrats, elected on increasingly racist platforms, sheltered their bias and privilege under the doctrine of states' rights. This combination of denial, self-interest, and perfidy enabled white southerners over two generations to reverse the gains of Reconstruction and reassert their domination. As in South Africa, city councils and state legislatures passed reams of laws to deny blacks jobs, corral them into specially designated neighborhoods, and bar them from using the water fountains, restaurants, movie theaters, benches, buses, schools, and bathrooms reserved for whites. By mid-century, though blacks were in the majority in many southern areas, every member of every jury was white. Southern registrars used a combination of obfuscation and intimidation to exclude nine out of ten eligible blacks from the voter registry. In thirteen southern counties, white officials succeeded in creating an American form of apartheid by eliminating every single black from the rolls.

Just as the Second World War had brought a loosening of racial stratification in South Africa, so did it begin to erode divisions in the United States. Thousands of black Americans enlisted and fought around the world as members of all-black army companies or air force fighter squadrons. President Franklin Roosevelt, under duress from his wife, Eleanor, ordered an end to racial discrimination in federal agencies in 1941. When the war ended, improvements slowly continued, symbolized by baseball player Jackie Robinson's entry into the previously all-white major leagues in 1947 and President Harry Truman's formal desegregation of the American armed forces in 1948.

Throughout the decades American blacks and their supporters had tried, with mixed results, to use one weapon on which South Africans who opposed Verwoerd could not rely: the United States Constitution. The leaders of the National Association for the Advancement of Colored People (NAACP), which had been founded in 1909, three years before the African National Congress, believed that America's conscience could eventually be pried open with the crowbar of the Bill of Rights. Year after year NAACP lawyers wedged lawsuits into the cracks of official discrimination. In 1954 they obtained a major victory when the Supreme Court declared in *Brown v. Board of Education* that America's widespread system of segregated and grossly unequal public schools could not be reconciled with the principles of the Constitution.

The court had decided, but who would listen? President Dwight D. Eisenhower, when asked whether he had any advice for southern states about the ruling, said he did not, thus signaling the federal government's indifference toward implementing the court order. Later, when asked if he believed in the need for new civil rights legislation, he responded with his famous dictum "You can't legislate morality." Denied the vote, refused the support of the federal executive, and faced with the prospect of interminable inequity, blacks throughout the South tried to exercise their power as consumers. In 1953 a boycott of the segregated bus system in Baton Rouge, Louisiana, resulted in a partial lessening of segregation. In 1955, six months after the passage of the Freedom Charter in South Africa, the arrest of the NAACP's local secretary, Rosa Parks, for sitting in a whites-only seat on a bus, prompted women's groups and churches to organize what became a year-long boycott of the bus system in Montgomery, Alabama. In conjunction with another NAACP lawsuit, the boycott forced an end to segregated seating in that city's public transportation. The campaign also brought its leader, a twenty-six-year-old Baptist minister named Martin Luther King Jr., into the national spotlight for the first time.

As disagreement over race percolated around the country, members of Congress began to consider racial issues. Despite Eisenhower's complacency, Vice President Richard Nixon decided to support a new civil rights bill when it came before Congress in 1957. Nixon had met Martin Luther King for the first time in March of that year in Africa, where both men were attending the celebrations marking the independence of Ghana. Nixon quickly realized that the presence of King abroad—along with that of black labor leader A. Philip Randolph, diplomat and Nobel laureate Ralph Bunche, and U.S. Representative Adam Clayton Powell—signaled that events on the African continent had acquired new domestic political significance for the United States.

In June 1957 Nixon invited King to Washington to discuss how to get the civil rights bill through Congress. Like many American blacks, King and his colleague the Reverend Ralph Abernathy retained an allegiance to the "party of Lincoln" and had voted for the Republican Eisenhower in 1956. They told Nixon that if the civil rights bill, which was designed to force states to restore the franchise to blacks, became law, they would launch a massive voter registration drive. Nixon, tantalized by the possibility of undermining the Democratic monopoly in the South, promised his support. The bill gradually gathered momentum among moderate

Republicans and progressive southern Democrats but was opposed by liberals (who thought the bill too weak) and archconservatives (who considered it too strong). When Democratic Senator Strom Thurmond of South Carolina filibustered for twenty-four hours, Senate majority leader Lyndon B. Johnson of Texas stripped out several of the enforcement provisions and forced the measure to a vote on August 2, 1957. When the bill passed, the editors of the *New York Times* called it "the most significant domestic action of any Congress in this century," though the supporters of the original bill, from the NAACP to Nixon, believed that their opponents had succeeded in castrating the measure.

The lesson to all who had been involved in the passage of the bill was clear: civil rights was a politically precarious field, in which a strong stand in any direction was more likely to be punished than rewarded. In September 1957, a month after the bill passed, Americans learned anew about the volatility of prejudice. When nine black students sought to take their court-ordered places in Central High School in Little Rock, Arkansas, Governor Orval Faubus instructed the national guard to prevent them. Every day for nearly two weeks the students attempted to enter the school and were turned back by the guardsmen and by an unruly mob of whites. President Eisenhower negotiated privately with Faubus, but Faubus wiggled out of every arrangement and publicly denounced the federal government. On September 23, after showering Eisenhower with assurances, Faubus double-crossed the president and withdrew the guardsmen from the vicinity of the school. The white mob smashed school windows and brutally beat several students and reporters. The next morning, Eisenhower grimly ordered General Maxwell Taylor to move the 101st Airborne Division into Little Rock as rapidly as possible. The following day, faced with thousands of soldiers in combat gear, the governor's bravado and the crowd's resistance collapsed.

Even without the showdowns in the Senate and at Little Rock, the political cost of supporting integration had registered in the mind of every American, especially every Democrat, who wanted to become president of the United States. Adlai Stevenson, the Democratic presidential nominee in 1952 and 1956, had remained diffident about civil rights throughout the decade. Senator John F. Kennedy of Massachusetts, who had tried for the vice presidential spot in 1956 and who was widely expected to run for president in 1960, had voted for the weakening amendments to the civil rights bill. Only the most ideological liberals in the party—such as Hubert Humphrey of Minnesota and Chester Bowles of Connecticut—felt strongly about racial equality, but it seemed unlikely that such men could win the nomination of a party with a large southern bloc or the votes of a nation that had twice given its heart to Eisenhower.

John F. Kennedy's caution resulted not only from his ambitions but also from the direction of his vision, which focused more on foreign policy than on domestic issues. From his youth Kennedy had nurtured interests in history and diplomacy; during his father's tenure as the U.S. ambassador to Great Britain before the Second World War, the young man had received front-row lessons in both. Elected to Congress in 1946 at the age of twenty-nine, Kennedy turned his attention to foreign affairs. In 1951 the young congressman traveled to Vietnam to examine the French war against the Communist Viet Minh. Ricocheting around the country, peppering everyone he met with questions, Kennedy reached the conclusion that despite their military achievements the French could not suppress the rebellion unless they promised their colony independence. When he returned to the United States he spoke vividly of the growing force of nationalism in Vietnam and in all of Southeast Asia. The struggle there, he said, was not so much between Communists and capitalists as it was between "civilizations striving to be born and those desperately trying to retain what they have held for so long." He had seen several Asian nations "in which the fires of nationalism so long dormant have been kindled and are now ablaze. . . . Here colonialism is not a topic for tea-talk discussion; it is the daily fare of millions of men." In 1952 Kennedy ran for the Senate from Massachusetts against an incumbent and, despite the effect of Eisenhower's strong victory over Stevenson, captured the seat. In his Senate speeches Kennedy returned repeatedly to the global brushfire of nationalism, which, he often said, he understood because of his Irish ancestors' struggles against British colonialism. On the Senate floor he again warned that the Vietnamese insurgency could not be stopped unless France offered the colony independence in exchange for its opposition to the advance of Communism.

Kennedy's words were either ignored or ridiculed by most of his colleagues and by the new administration. Americans' dread of Communism had risen dramatically since Truman had sent U.S. troops to fight Chinese and North Korean troops in 1950. Senator Joseph McCarthy was still building his reputation on the carcasses of Americans whose careers he had wrecked by his charges of Communism. The new secretary of state, John Foster Dulles, cast every international encounter as a Manichean conflict between the forces of good and evil. To protect the free world from further Communist encroachments, Dulles labored to construct new military alliances around the planet. When India, Indonesia, and other nations tried to steer a middle course between the superpowers, Dulles seethed with angry suspicion. To Dulles, nonalignment masked Communist sympathy, and anticolonial protest sprang from Communist subversion. Though he paid occasional lip service to the right of self-determination, Dulles believed that obligations to the European security pact of NATO required Americans to support Europe's colonial authority.

Kennedy caused another explosion in July 1957 when he rose in the Senate and renewed his criticism of U.S. support for French policy. To suppress an armed rebellion in its North African colony of Algeria, the French government had sent five hundred thousand soldiers across the Mediterranean. In the brutal fighting that had ensued, atrocities had been committed by both sides. In his speech Kennedy assailed Eisenhower and Dulles for refusing to acknowledge the legitimacy of Algerian nationalist feeling because such an acknowledgment might displease the French. Algeria would have to be freed someday, he insisted. Referring to the crushing, ultimate defeat of French forces at Dien Bien Phu in Vietnam in 1954, Kennedy asked: "Did that tragic episode not teach us whether France likes it or not, admits it or not, or has our support or not, that their overseas territories are sooner or later, one by one, going to break free and look with suspicion on the Western nations who impeded their steps to independence?"

In the ensuing days, French politicians and editors attacked the young senator, and many Americans followed suit. Adlai Stevenson said that the speech was "terrible." Dulles commented that Kennedy should be more concerned about Communist colonialism and subversion than the policies of America's allies. Kennedy's office received more mail on the speech than on any other he delivered in his two Senate terms; much of it was unfavorable. Concerned by the sharp reaction, Kennedy discussed the speech with his father. "You lucky mush," said Joseph Kennedy. "You don't know it and neither does anyone else, but within a few months everyone is going to know just how right you were on Algeria." The elder Kennedy was correct: within less than a year the Algerian war had provoked a coup d'état in France and the collapse of the Fourth Republic. France's new head of state, Charles de Gaulle, promptly withdrew the French troops and granted independence to Algeria. Through his prescience Kennedy had established himself as a serious analyst of foreign affairs. Around the world nationalists took note, and from then on a steady stream of diplomats and factional leaders filed eagerly into Kennedy's Senate office to meet the man who understood their cause. They were even more pleased when, in 1958, the Senate Foreign Relations Committee created a subcommittee on Africa and gave the chairmanship to the junior senator from Massachusetts.

As interested as Kennedy was to meet the Africans who claimed him as a friend, his outspoken positions on nationalism had an important domestic target. To obtain the Democratic presidential nomination, Kennedy knew that he would have to turn either to the southern party bosses or to the liberals. He wanted to avoid the former but to gain the latter he needed to win the approval of Adlai Stevenson, Hubert Humphrey, Eleanor Roosevelt, and other liberal leaders. The liberals, in general, were cool to him. Stevenson had told his associates that "Kennedy stands for nothing." Eleanor Roosevelt had said in public that she thought Kennedy was too young and too impatient, a view shared by many who honored her husband's legacy. Though Kennedy's book *Profiles in Courage* earned favorable comment and a Pulitzer Prize in 1957, the prevailing attitude among liberals toward Kennedy before 1960 was "More Courage, Less Profile."

In January 1960, as expected, forty-two-year-old John Kennedy announced that he was running for president. To attract liberal support he immediately appointed Chester Bowles, who had recently written a book called *Africa's Challenge to America,* as his chief foreign policy adviser. Kennedy then began the gauntlet of primaries, winning in New Hampshire in February, winning in Humphrey's backyard of Wisconsin in April, and then overcoming the prejudice against his Catholicism by winning in overwhelmingly Protestant West Virginia in May. Kennedy hoped that his victories would bring an outpouring of liberal support for him, but support came in trickles instead. Kennedy particularly courted Stevenson, hoping for an endorsement, but Stevenson, whose name was being advanced for a third presidential bid, remained studiously neutral.

By late April, members of the Kennedy campaign knew that they might have to do without Stevenson's support and would have to find another way of locking up the liberal vote at the nominating convention. One possibility was to secure the support of the small but critical percentage of black delegates. In early May, Robert F. Kennedy invited a thirty-four-year-old lawyer, Harris Wofford, to join the campaign. Wofford's commitment to racial equality, including his insistence on enrolling as the first white law student at Howard University in Washington, D.C., had caused convulsions in his patrician Alabama family. When he informed his loyal Democratic grandmother of his plans to study civil rights law at Howard, she told him, "You can go there to teach them, to help them, but you can't go and be a student with them." When Wofford said he had made up his mind, she had an emotional collapse. As Wofford and his father carried her upstairs, she shouted, "If God made them equal, I hate God! I hate God! I hate God!"

Wofford was convinced that Gandhian civil disobedience, which he had traveled to India to study, could be of use to American blacks. By the end of the 1950s he was close to Martin Luther King Jr. and had become a staff member for Father Theodore Hesburgh on the newly created Civil Rights Commission, a by-product of the controversial 1957 civil rights bill. On the side, Wofford had helped write several of Kennedy's strongest speeches on nationalism in Africa. The Kennedy team saw Wofford as the perfect choice to talk to American blacks. A purist at heart, Wofford remained suspicious of the Kennedy presidential drive and had rejected an early offer from the campaign to take a position on the faculty of Notre Dame's law school. In 1960 the Kennedy campaign again recruited Wofford and he assented. His moral sensibilities were offended, however, when over lunch Theodore Sorensen, a Kennedy aide, told him the campaign's definitions of good and bad. "Whatever helps the election of John Kennedy is good," Sorenson said crisply. "Whatever hinders it is bad."

Despite his reservations, Wofford went to see Robert Kennedy, the campaign manager, to find out his responsibilities. "We are in trouble with Negroes," Kennedy told him. "We really don't know much about this whole thing. We've been dealing outside the field of the main Negro leadership and have to start from scratch." Kennedy asked Wofford to help Sargent Shriver, a lawyer and a Kennedy brother-in-law, to set up a new civil rights section for the campaign. "We want you to do everything you need to do to deliver every Negro delegate going to the convention," Kennedy told Wofford. "It's up to you."

Within a few weeks, Wofford and Shriver encountered their first major problem. Kennedy desperately needed the support of all the delegates from Michigan to win the nomination. The head of the delegation was Governor G. Mennen Williams, nicknamed "Soapy" because of his family's role in the detergent and cosmetics business. Williams was a tall, exuberant man whose personal trademarks included a crew cut and a polka-dot bow tie. During his twelve years as governor, Williams had earned a national reputation as an enthusiastic supporter of liberal causes, especially civil rights. On the floor of the 1952 Democratic convention he had clashed sharply with the segregationist governor of South Carolina and had angered the other southern delegates by pushing a relatively forceful civil rights plank into the Democratic Party's platform. Though his own presidential chances had been dimmed by the incident, Williams remained a prominent national spokesman; in early May the Michigan state Democratic convention had nominated the governor as a favorite son candidate for president to give him the maximum power to bargain for liberal programs at the convention.

Williams was well disposed toward Kennedy, though he remained concerned about the candidate's liberal credentials. He remembered vividly his first encounter with Kennedy in the Senate dining room in the early 1950s, when Kennedy had congratulated him on some of his initiatives in Michigan. "I wish I could be a liberal like you and Hubert Humphrey," Kennedy confided, "but you can't do that in Massachusetts." Unlike some of his colleagues, however, Williams did not want Stevenson to run a third time. His support for Kennedy had grown when, in the spring of 1960, Kennedy published a new book of essays called *Strategies for Peace* (largely written by Harris Wofford). Williams liked the book enough to send three hundred copies around the state to political leaders who might support Kennedy.

Though Williams applauded Kennedy's stand on international independence movements, he told Wofford and Shriver that the senator's tepid approach to civil rights concerned the black members of his delegation and the powerful United Auto Workers union leaders. Over some objections, Wofford and Shriver talked Kennedy into sending his campaign airplane, the *Caroline,* out to Michigan to bring Williams and a group of major civil rights leaders back to Washington for a candid discussion. Unbeknownst to Wofford and Shriver, other members of the campaign staff had already prepared a briefing paper for Kennedy on Williams's personality. "Williams is a man of strong convictions," said the report. "He takes himself very seriously and believes that he is an instrument of God's will in furthering liberal, humanitarian causes. He is a devout Episcopalian . . . who sees himself as having been tapped to put the Sermon on the Mount into governmental practice. This is not a pose but reflects a sincere, if unusual, conviction. . . . Any approach to him which overlooks this strong religious drive . . . will miss the mark."

On the brilliant morning of June 20, 1960, the delegation from Michigan trooped through Kennedy's Georgetown townhouse into the courtyard where Jacqueline Kennedy had set up an elegant brunch. The mood of the group was uneven; some were openly hostile to the candidate. After a few pleasantries, members of the delegation immediately challenged Kennedy for his position on the Greensboro sit-ins. In February Kennedy had issued a statement that he supported the lunch counter demonstrators as long as "they act peacefully." The black members told the candidate that they took offense at the stipulation; Kennedy responded that he didn't understand why. After a tense discussion, Williams finally broke in and said, "Well, Jack, as I understand my Negro friends, what they are trying to say is that your insisting on including this 'by peaceful means' in your statement, although they indicate that they have no intention of anything except acting peacefully—they feel that it's as if you issued an invitation to them to dinner and said 'Please come to dinner, but wash your hands before you sit down.' Obviously you would expect your guests to wash their hands before you sat down and you would be insulting them if you said that. And by saying this 'by peaceful means' you are doing the same thing." Williams's folksy translation satisfied both the members of the delegation and Kennedy, and the candidate went on to give his pitch. He stated "categorically" that the civil rights issue was "of overwhelming moral significance" to him and that if he were elected president he would "use the full prestige and weight of the office to completely eliminate second-class citizenship in America." The delegation was won over. As they filed out, Kennedy handed each person a commemorative pin. On the front steps the delegation encountered a nest of reporters and microphones; one by one, each person stepped up and backed Kennedy for president. Two weeks later, many of the new converts tried to persuade their skeptical colleagues at the NAACP annual convention that the Massachusetts senator would stand by his word on civil rights.

On July 11, 1960, the Democratic convention opened in Los Angeles. Despite a brief, last-minute rally for Stevenson, Kennedy's forces pushed and pulled the delegations into line behind their candidate. Reluctant liberal delegates queried the Kennedy representatives closely on his likely vice presidential choice. The Kennedy emissaries—men like Robert Kennedy, Sargent Shriver, and Soapy Williams—told them that it would not be a southerner but a midwestern liberal. Reassured, the delegates pledged their support.

On Wednesday, July 13, John Kennedy won the nomination and moved forward to select a vice presidential candidate. Through an intricate series of steps which have been dissected in memoirs and histories ever since, John and Robert Kennedy designed a flirtation that backfired. Kennedy's leading choice for a running mate was Stuart Symington of Missouri, but before he offered the position to Symington he wanted to shore up the backing of his strong-willed Senate colleague Lyndon Johnson. Johnson had taken a stab at the presidential nomination and had been defeated on the floor. Kennedy wanted to smooth over the loss, for he knew that he would need the Texan's vigorous support in the election and beyond. The ploy seemed safe because Johnson had said repeatedly and emphatically that he did not want to be vice president and everyone believed him. Kennedy, particularly, knowing Johnson's love of command, could not imagine that the Senate majority leader would exchange his powerful position for the ghostly role of vice president. The morning after the victory celebration over his own nomination, Kennedy went to Johnson's suite on a mission of political seduction. To his shock, when Kennedy broached the subject, Johnson said he was interested. As Kennedy described it later, "I didn't offer the vice-presidency to him. I just held it out like this"—he simulated taking something out of his pocket and holding it near his body—"and he grabbed it."

While Johnson pondered whether to accept the nomination, the leaders of the Kennedy campaign debated how they could induce Johnson to turn it down. Robert Kennedy was dispatched with the delicate task of counseling Johnson to withdraw, but before he arrived John Kennedy confirmed the offer to Johnson by telephone and Johnson formally accepted. Robert Kennedy's arrival in the Johnson suite and his unwitting attempts to discourage Johnson *after* his brother's final call caused resentment in the Texan toward the younger Kennedy that never completely healed. Johnson's anger, however, was nothing compared with the rage that swept the liberal caucuses when they learned of Kennedy's selection. Ann Williams, Soapy's wife, turned in her Kennedy button. Her husband stormed into the Kennedy headquarters shouting that he would oppose the choice. When the Michigan delegation voted unanimously to fight the nomination on the floor, the Kennedy team had to work furiously to calm the revolt. The next morning, the two candidates made an exhausting tour of the angry delegations to reassure them of their commitment to civil rights. Appearing before the black caucus, Johnson told the delegates that he knew they might not be comfortable with his candidacy because of his previous lack of support for civil rights. Whatever his past record, he wanted to promise them one thing: if they helped elect the Kennedy-Johnson team, the new administration would pass more civil rights laws than ever before in the history of the country.

Departing the convention, the presidential candidate faced a fierce political dilemma. To win the black voters who had supported Eisenhower and to fulfill his convention pledges, Kennedy needed to take a strong stand on civil rights. Yet three southern governors had already told Robert Kennedy bluntly that if his brother supported "Jimmy Hoffa, Nikita Khrushchev, or Martin Luther King" they would throw their traditionally Democratic states to Nixon.

Kennedy found the solution in the central African nation of the Congo. For more than seventy years, this large country—equal in size to all of the United States east of the Mississippi—had been ruled as the personal property of the king of Belgium. The king had permitted a Belgian company, the Union Minière du Haut Katanga, to exploit the rich mineral resources throughout the country, but the brutal treatment of the indigenous peoples by the firm and by the king's representatives had shocked the world when it had come to light in the late 1950s. In early 1960 the king and the Belgian government had announced that the Congo would be granted independence on July 1 of that year. Independence, though, meant confronting a crushing problem that touched many other African nations. After years of denying Africans education, training, and access to positions of authority, the European powers expected those same people to fill and master administrative positions literally overnight. In the Congo, a nation of more than three million Africans, only two dozen had ever attended a university.

To compound the problem, the Europeans remaining in the Congo had little intention of yielding control, no matter what their governments at home might say. As independence approached, the mining companies maneuvered to tighten their grip on the nation's natural resources. The white officer corps of the army remained in place after July 1. When the African troops grumbled about the lack of real change after independence, the Belgian military commander, Emile Janssens, called them together to dispel their illusions. He did so by writing on a large blackboard: BEFORE INDEPENDENCE = AFTER INDEPENDENCE. Stung by the betrayal, the troops rebelled, attacking European persons and property. On July 10, the night before the American Democratic convention began, the Belgian government dropped paratroopers to protect the white residents of the Congo.

As the fighting raged, the Belgians, in cooperation with the executives of the mining companies, encouraged the Congo's largest and richest province, Katanga, to secede. Watching the sudden dismemberment of his newly free country, the prime minister of the Congo, Patrice Lumumba, appealed to the United States for troops to restore order and unity. When President Eisenhower turned him down, Lumumba requested help from both the United Nations and the Soviet Union, touching off cold war alarms throughout Washington. In late July, while his country unraveled, Lumumba traveled to Washington to make a personal bid for American support. His universally acknowledged charisma, combined with his private requests for both a weapon and a white female companion, worried and offended the top American leaders. Eisenhower, deeply concerned about Lumumba's appeal to the Soviet Union for aid, concluded that Lumumba was an irrational and dangerous revolutionary.

Eisenhower had been frustrated over the previous months by a string of global setbacks and stung by John Kennedy's charge that he had allowed the United States to slide into weakness and indolence. Though official American policy supported the United Nations pledge to restore unity to the Congo—by force if necessary—Eisenhower was determined not to allow the Congo to become a Communist pocket in the center of the African continent. Prominent members of Congress were denouncing the United Nations and painting the Katanga secession as a brave pro-Western rebellion against native savagery and Lumumba's leftist tyranny. On August 18 Eisenhower told a National Security Council meeting that to prevent a direct confrontation between the United States and the Soviet Union over control of the Congo, he wanted Lumumba removed. To several of those present, the president seemed to be suggesting an assassination. Acting on this interpretation, the director of the Central Intelligence Agency, Allen Dulles, immediately set in motion a secret plot to kill the Congolese leader.

For candidate John F. Kennedy, the turmoil in Africa offered the chance to solve a host of political problems with a single strategy. For months he had been searching for ways to challenge the foreign policy legacy of the avuncular and popular Eisenhower—a legacy that Republican candidate Nixon was fully claiming as his own. In its policy toward Africa, however, the United States seemed to be asleep. New African countries were being born at the rate of more than one a month, yet the Republican administration seemed unable to shift away from its support of the European colonial powers. Kennedy, zeroing in on the tide of independence and the immediate crisis in the Congo, began to pound on the Republican failure to adjust to the new international realities. During the few months between the nomination and the election, Kennedy mentioned Africa nearly five hundred times in his speeches, stressing that the eruption of nationalist aspirations—and the potential for Communist exploitation of those feelings—required new vision and new leadership in the White House. Kennedy's speeches permitted him to show concern for the rights of Africans in other parts of the world— thus appealing to black American voters—while at the same time avoiding raising the hackles of white southerners.

In September and October, as Hendrik Verwoerd won electoral approval for his beloved republic and the remaining days to the American election dwindled away, tension over civil rights in the United States grew. Kennedy had tried to show his concern by sponsoring a major conference on "constitutional rights" on October 11 in New York, but events in the South soon dragged him in more deeply than he had intended. On Wednesday, October 19, two days before the final Kennedy-Nixon debate and less than three weeks before the election, Martin Luther King Jr. and several dozen students were arrested and jailed for attempting to be seated in white restaurants in Atlanta, Georgia. Over the weekend, while King was still in jail, Harris Wofford called a friend in Atlanta, Morris Abram, to ask him to encourage Mayor William Hartsfield to release King. Soon word got out that Hartsfield had been asked by Kennedy to work for King's release, thus undermining Hartsfield's efforts and endangering the campaign's appeal to white southerners. The Kennedy campaign made a swift disavowal.

On Monday, the jailed activists learned that everyone would be released—except King. Judge Oscar Mitchell had decided to hold King for violating probation on a traffic ticket he had received for driving with an Alabama permit in Georgia. On Tuesday, Mitchell revoked King's probation, denied him bail, and sentenced him to four months on a chain gang, to begin immediately. King's wife, Coretta, now six months pregnant, feared for her husband's life and called Wofford. "They are going to kill him," she said desperately. "I know they are going to kill him." Wofford, despite his knowledge that his influence in the Kennedy campaign had waned after the Hartsfield incident, communicated Coretta King's fears to the top echelons. That evening Kennedy and his staff worked out an arrangement with Georgia Governor Ernest Vandiver to engineer King's release without public association with the campaign. Wofford, still frustrated by the campaign's timidity in the face of what he perceived to be a clear moral test, disconsolately pondered what else could be done. He and Louis Martin, a black member of the Kennedy civil rights staff, decided that if the candidate made a sympathetic call to Mrs. King, they might be able to spread the news throughout the black community without alarming southern whites. Wofford called Shriver, who instantly accepted the idea and sought out Kennedy. Knowing that the members of the civil rights section of the campaign were seen by the other insiders as reckless moralists, Shriver waited until he was alone with the nominee to suggest the call. Kennedy pondered for a moment and said, "What the hell. That's the decent thing to do." Shriver dialed and handed the phone to the tired candidate. Kennedy told Coretta King that he was concerned about her husband, offered his help, and, in less than two minutes, signed off.

When Robert Kennedy heard what had happened, he summoned Wofford and Martin. Telling them they might have thrown away the entire election, he angrily forbade anyone in the civil rights section from doing anything controversial for the rest of the campaign. To defend themselves, the two men drew Kennedy's attention to the gross injustice of a man sentenced to hard labor on a bogus traffic ticket. At first Kennedy seemed to dismiss this explanation, but later, as both his indignation and his desire to divert the press's attention from his brother rose, he called Judge Mitchell himself and chastised him for denying bail on such a flimsy charge. The next morning Mitchell released King on a two-thousand dollar bond. At a mass meeting at the Ebenezer Baptist Church in Atlanta, where King and his father shared the pastorate, the elder King got up and told the crowd that the time had come to shift their political loyalties. "I had expected to vote against Senator Kennedy because of his religion," he said. "But now he can be my President, Catholic or whatever he is. It took courage to call my daughter-in-law at a time like this. He has the moral courage to stand up for what he knows is right. I've got all my votes and I've got a suitcase. I'm going to take them up there and dump them in his lap."

Though the *New York Times* and other national newspapers ran accounts of King's release that included a brief mention of Kennedy's call to Coretta King, the story quickly disappeared from the attention of the white press. Most of the members of the Kennedy campaign staff were grateful. Shriver, Martin, and Wofford, however, knew that the word would have to be widely disseminated among blacks to have an effect on the voting less than two weeks away. Working around Robert Kennedy's restrictions and Martin Luther King's refusal to endorse Kennedy directly, they composed a pamphlet of statements by King's family and clergy friends on John Kennedy's call to Coretta. Jabbing at Richard Nixon's silence, the staff members labeled the pamphlet *"No Comment" Nixon versus a Candidate with a Heart, Senator Kennedy.* On Sunday, November 6, just two days before the election, two million copies of the pamphlet found their way into black churches across the country.

On November 8, 1960, Americans went to the polls and elected John Kennedy the thirty-fifth president of the United States. Kennedy did not learn of the results until early in the morning the next day, when he found that he had outdistanced Nixon by the tiniest of margins. Out of nearly 70 million ballots cast, Kennedy defeated Nixon by less than 113,000 votes—less than two-tenths of one percent. If he had received 5,000 fewer in Illinois or 28,000 fewer in Texas, the Republicans would have held on to the White House. Kennedy did not even earn a majority; he won by 49.7 percent to Nixon's 49.6 percent. As political analysts scoured the returns to discover the secret to the Democratic success, they fixed on the astonishing shift in political allegiance among blacks. In 1956, six black voters out of ten had supported Eisenhower; in 1960, seven out of ten supported Kennedy. In six key states—Michigan, New Jersey, Pennsylvania, Illinois, North Carolina, and South Carolina—the shift in black support had provided more votes than Kennedy's margin of victory.

Throughout his career Kennedy liked to quote Thomas Jefferson's admonition that "great innovations should not be forced on slender majorities." As a man who had promised great innovations in his campaign and who had been elected by the most slender majority in American history, Kennedy had to choose his people and his policies carefully. To staff the new administration, Kennedy asked Shriver and Wofford to search for the most talented persons in the country, regardless of party affiliation, while his aide David Powers screened the multitude of Democrats clamoring for patronage posts. As the suggestions poured in, Kennedy sifted and sorted the names into a kind of coalition administration.

Kennedy's pragmatism—which included an immediate announcement that he would keep both Allen Dulles at the Central Intelligence Agency and J. Edgar Hoover at the Federal Bureau of Investigation—irritated liberals who had wanted a decisive break with the past. Panning the river of names directed to him by his staff, the president-elect pondered how to placate the conservatives in Congress, on Wall Street, and in the government. Kennedy decided on a Republican, Douglas Dillon, as secretary of the treasury. He disregarded Eleanor Roosevelt's advice that he make Adlai Stevenson secretary of state and slated him for the United Nations. He approached another Republican, McGeorge Bundy, the dean of the Harvard faculty, to become his national security adviser. To the consternation of many around him, he intimated that he was considering his thirty-five-year-old brother Robert, whom many viewed as a hothead, for the job of attorney general.

Kennedy also wanted to reward Soapy Williams for his timely support, though he was unsure which spot would suit the governor's enthusiastic idealism. The governor had let it be known that he would like to be secretary for health, education, and welfare, but Kennedy worried that Williams, with his effusive style and reputation as a big-spending liberal, would not be the best one to persuade Congress to increase the department's budget. The president-elect called Williams in and asked him if he would consider a more exotic post, that of assistant secretary of state for African affairs. The position had existed for only a few years and had done little under the restrictions of Eisenhower's European bias. Kennedy told Williams that he considered the position "second to none" in his administration because he wanted to establish a completely new reputation and policy for the United States in Africa. Later in the day, Kennedy told presidential assistant and historian Arthur Schlesinger Jr. that he thought he had mollified Williams. "After all," said Kennedy, "you could hardly ask for a more challenging job." On December 1, 1960, the Kennedy transition team formally released Williams's name, before all others, as the first appointment of the incoming administration.

Williams, with characteristic vigor, hurled himself into the task well before the inauguration. Finding that he could not arrange a visit to Africa until he had actually assumed his new post, he concentrated on staffing. Both Williams and the president-elect believed that African ambassadorships should not be used to reward aging foreign service officers who wanted to serve quietly until their retirement but should be filled with newer, younger men who were excited about the rebirth of the continent. Throughout December and January Williams compiled a list of names of energetic foreign service officers. He decided early on to ask his predecessor, Joseph Satterthwaite, to become the new ambassador to South Africa. He then tracked down a political associate from Michigan, J. Wayne Fredericks, to become his deputy.

Fredericks was an unusually shrewd choice. An engineer and B-17 pilot during the Second World War, he had worked for Kellogg's, the cereal manufacturer, establishing its first Corn Flakes and Rice Krispies plant in South Africa in 1949. During his stay Fredericks had traveled thousands of miles through Northern and Southern Rhodesia, Bechuanaland (later Botswana), and Mozambique. Even before his departure overseas, Fredericks had been interested in race relations and had worked with the Michigan NAACP and with groups of black employees in the Kellogg's plants in Battle Creek. South Africa under Verwoerd came as a shock. The labor color bar caused problems for the plant, preventing Fredericks from hiring Africans for anything but the most menial positions. Fredericks was also astonished by the bigotry of most of the white workers, so he included questions on the job application forms to help him identify the least racist whites. While managing a small baseball team, the Transvaal Yankees, Fredericks engaged the players, most of whom were young American executives, in a discussion of whether American business practices and values could be transported into the South African setting. After all, he pointed out, in America businesses could not implement such an overtly discriminatory policy. He found little comprehension or support among his colleagues for introducing expensive American innovations into highly profitable operations.

Fredericks returned to the United States and continued to work for Kellogg's. He flirted with a possible run for Congress but eventually accepted an offer from the Ford Foundation to move to New York City to help develop an African program. By this time Fredericks, through his extensive travels, knew more about the continent than all but a tiny handful of Americans. His expertise was increasingly valued by the cadre of politicians who wanted America to pay more attention to the area. Fredericks channeled information to Humphrey, Bowles, Stevenson, and eventually Kennedy, for whom he drafted ideas for the 1957 speech on Algeria. Fredericks, through his Michigan allies and his new contacts, urged the Democratic Party to include a new policy toward independent Africa in its platform.

In their pre-inauguration discussions of how to alter American policy, Williams and Fredericks quickly identified four fronts on which they would have to act. First, they had to persuade the newly independent African countries that the United States would no longer allow the European powers to determine American policy. This meant finding ways to show that the United States understood and supported the drive for African freedom and independence. Second, they would have to manage the pique that would arise among the Europeans and their partisans in Washington. Third, the subcabinet Africa Bureau had to establish itself as a force not only within the State Department but within the government; this meant working internally with the Defense Department, the Commerce Department, the Central Intelligence Agency, and all the other departments and agencies that had entrenched positions on Africa. Finally, Williams and Fredericks would have to negotiate the complexities of Capitol Hill, where many senators and representatives were likely to see Africa through the warped prisms of cold war paranoia and Tarzan movies. The task, they both knew, was daunting. Williams decided to show the new American resolve by traveling to Africa personally, forgoing any formal visits to Europe until he had visited every single country on the African continent.

In the winter of 1961 many influential Americans offered their ideas about the proper direction for African policy under the new administration. During the interregnum the president-elect had approved the creation of a string of task forces to advise him on new directions. One of the task forces, under the leadership of former Stevenson supporter George Ball, had taken a comprehensive look at Africa and had urged the president-elect to block Communist expansion by identifying America with the new forces of freedom. Shortly after the election, Senators Frank Church, Gale W. McGee, and Frank E. Moss traveled to sixteen African countries (accompanied by the president-elect's youngest brother, Edward) and came back brimming with supportive recommendations. The press was filled with speculations about the progress of the cold war on the "Dark Continent." *U.S. News and World Report* ran a cover story asking, "Who's Going to Win in Africa?" Columnist Joseph Alsop offered his dire predictions in an article in the *Saturday Evening Post* titled "Will Africa Go Communist?," a piece that Senator Thomas Dodd of Connecticut placed in the *Congressional Record.*

To be sure he fully understood and represented the president's intentions, Williams went to see Kennedy at the White House before his trip. The two men discussed how to phrase the new American approach. "Might I characterize our policy like this?" Williams asked. " 'What we want for Africa is what Africans want for themselves.' It covers in a general way our support for African self-determination, for a better standard of living, and for equal dignity, all of which we endorse." Kennedy agreed and on February 16, 1961, the new assistant secretary of state, toting copies of *Strategies for Peace* autographed for African leaders by the president, accompanied by his wife, a small staff, and a reporter from the *Detroit Free Press,* departed for a month of political barnstorming across the immense African land.

Wherever he touched down, Williams displayed the happy enthusiasm that his supporters found charming and his critics naive. Traveling to a new country every other day, Williams unself-consciously pulled out his own camera and snapped pictures of people and places he liked. When he entered a busy marketplace, Williams plunged into the crowds, smiled, waved, pumped hands, and departed in a flurry, leaving most Africans wondering who this eager white man was. In meetings he usually discarded the long texts prepared by the embassies and lapsed into the pithy political homilies he had mastered in six campaigns for governor. In an audience with the emperor of Ethiopia, he eschewed an interpreter and chatted in midwestern-drenched French. When visiting an agricultural project in the Congo, he took off his coat, rolled up his sleeves, and, to the astonishment and then the cheers of the workers, waded into the river mud to help move a piece of machinery.

Not every stop was a diplomatic triumph. In Nairobi, Kenya, Williams held a press conference. "What is American foreign policy for Africa?" asked a reporter. "What we want for Africans is what Africans want for themselves," replied Williams, using the agreed-upon formula. "What about Europeans?" the reporter asked. Williams instantly realized that he had been using the term "Africans" generically, whereas the reporters had understood it as referring exclusively to blacks. "By Africans," he said, "I mean anyone who lives in Africa, regardless of race or color." The clarification did not help; the next morning the headlines of white newspapers from Rhodesia to South Africa twisted Williams's statement into an endorsement of the central Pan-Africanist slogan: *SOAPY SAYS 'AFRICA FOR THE AFRICANS!'* French, British, and Portuguese diplomats in Washington complained, and Williams's political enemies pounced. At a press conference, President Kennedy was asked whether he agreed with Williams that Africa was for the Africans. "I don't know who else Africa would be for," said Kennedy lightly. The new secretary of state, Dean Rusk, sent Williams a telegram urging him to keep quiet. Several weeks later, the president referred to the incident at the annual Gridiron Club dinner. Kennedy told the members that he had just received a cable from Williams asking if he could stay in Africa for a few more weeks. "I felt I had better send this reply," the president said. " 'No Soapy. Africa is for the Africans.' "

Though some chalked up Williams's comment to diplomatic inexperience, conservatives around the world suspected that he had inadvertently revealed the new administration's true allegiance. The suspicion increased in the light of Kennedy's actions in another international setting, the United Nations. For Europeans and the United States, the UN, formed out of the ashes of World War II, provided for the settlement of disputes under the wise tutelage of the victorious powers. For the young, far-flung states groping for recognition, the international body offered chances to build coalitions and bargain for concessions. The leverage of the emerging nations increased steadily with their numbers. In the five years from 1958 to 1963, thirty-five new countries sent delegations to the UN General Assembly, almost half in the single year 1960 and all but five from the continent of Africa. As the numbers of freshly minted, nonaligned countries grew, each with its own portfolio of problems and opportunities, each with its own special economic resources and needs, the Soviet Union and the United States, supported by their vassals and allies, jockeyed for advantage.

Throughout 1960 Soviet diplomats had seized the initiative and aggressively portrayed the USSR as the defender of the cause of international justice. In September 1960, during the same visit in which he thumped his shoe on the podium of the General Assembly, Soviet Premier Nikita Khrushchev had proposed that the upcoming session include a "declaration on the granting of independence to colonial countries and peoples." The suggestion was adopted and in December 1960, forty-three African and Asian states called for an immediate end to colonialism throughout the world. Though the U.S. representatives had worked to soften the language and believed that the White House would support it, President Eisenhower bowed to British Prime Minister Harold Macmillan's urgent appeal and abruptly instructed the American delegation to abstain. When the resolution passed unanimously, American prestige sank. So great was the dissatisfaction within the American delegation that one black member, Zelma Watson George, broke with her colleagues and rose from her chair in the General Assembly to join the rest of the world in applause.

In January 1961, less than three weeks before the Kennedy inauguration, Khrushchev again turned up the heat. Speaking to the Academy of Social Sciences in Moscow, Khrushchev made a distinction between world wars and wars of national liberation. The former were to be avoided through a policy of peaceful coexistence with the United States, he said, but the latter he considered "just," "sacred," and "inevitable." Khrushchev then promised that wherever Third World peoples were fighting to end colonial domination, they would be supported by the Communist world. In light of the continuing convulsions in the Congo and in Southeast Asia, Khrushchev's words seemed filled with grim portents to John F. Kennedy, who in his inaugural address promised to "pay any price, bear any burden, meet any hardship, support any friend, oppose any foe to assure the survival and the success of liberty."

Kennedy's political challenge at the United Nations started with his new ambassador, Adlai Stevenson, the second most conspicuous voice of American policy after his own. The relationship between the former political rivals was strained. Kennedy, still irked by Stevenson's cool attitude during the campaign, sardonically introduced himself at one private meeting as "the ambassador to the United Nations' special representative at the White House." Nonetheless, the combination of presidential interest, ambassadorial eloquence, and superpower drama brought unprecedented media attention to the operations of the international body.

The representatives of the new African nations, spurred by their growing numbers, clamored for the delegates of the world to focus on the unresolved quandary of colonialism in southern Africa. In their view there were four interrelated problems: white supremacy in the British colony of Rhodesia; South Africa's abuse of its role as a trustee of South West Africa; South Africa's internal policy of apartheid; and the injustices wrought by the Portuguese in their African colonies.

Kennedy had to face the Portuguese dilemma on January 21, the day after his inauguration, when two former Portuguese government officials, Henrique Galavao and Humberto Delgado, hijacked a Portuguese luxury liner off the coast of Venezuela to protest Portugal's policies in Africa. Galavao, a former colonial inspector and deputy for Angola, had thirteen years before written a scathing attack on Portugal's labor practices in which he offered the chilling conclusion that in Angola "only the dead are exempt from forced labor." Delgado, a hugely popular former general in the Portuguese army, had been denied the presidency of Portugal through outright fraud. Both men had taken the drastic step of hijacking to draw international attention to Portuguese abuses in Africa. Kennedy, asked about Portugal at his first press conference, tried to walk a line between support for a traditional ally and sympathy for the hijackers' grievances. His approach irritated both the Portuguese government, which considered the act one of simple piracy, and those who pressed for an end of Portuguese colonial rule.

The Portuguese government's attitudes toward Africa flowed from the country's history and geography. Portugal, a small nation perched on the western rim of the European continent, had no ports in the calm waters of the Mediterranean. For centuries its ships and people had ventured resolutely out onto the broad Atlantic. As a result, despite a tiny population, feudal society, and agrarian economy, Portugal had nurtured twenty generations of intrepid explorers. Where they landed—on the eastern coast of South America, on the Azores in the middle of the Atlantic, on both coasts of southern Africa—they often established settlements that grew into colonies. Though these colonies in Brazil, Mozambique, Angola, and Guinea-Bissau were dozens of times larger than the parent country, Portuguese leaders had always viewed them as the bounty of their Renaissance bravery, as the beneficiaries of Portugal's civilization, and as the primary source of Portugal's limited financial prosperity.

No one believed this myth more fiercely than the prime minister,

Antonio Oliveira Salazar. Born in a small town in central Portugal, trained in the increasingly narrow disciplines of theology, law, and economics, steeped in militant Catholicism, Salazar spent his formative years watching division, intrigue, and violence ravage his country. From 1910 to 1926 Portugal had no less than forty-five separate governments, four of which ended in military coups. In 1926 Salazar was summoned from his books to become the finance minister; he performed so well that in 1932, when John F. Kennedy was only fifteen years old, Salazar became the prime minister. Aided by a new constitution that gave him nearly absolute power, Salazar built an elaborate system of spies, toadies, censors, and thugs to eradicate what he viewed as the destructive impulse to democracy. During the Second World War Portugal officially remained neutral, though Salazar cultivated close relations with the fascist governments in Spain, Italy, and Germany.

In the aftermath of the war, Salazar needed the African colonies more than ever to supplement Portugal's dwindling economy and to provide an object for the nation's eroding imperial pride. Though Portugal was a member of the North Atlantic Treaty Organization (NATO), Salazar viewed the other European states as disorganized and gutless for granting independence to their colonies. Throughout the 1950s Salazar supported the theory of "lusotropicalism," which argued that the Portuguese had a unique responsibility to colonize because they had the physical capacity to adapt to tropical climates, the moral humility to avoid exploitation, and the personal tolerance to create just multiracial societies in Africa. The theory allowed Salazar to defy international pressures and declare that the territories were not colonies at all, but provinces integral to Portugal. Nationalists who desired independence were therefore traitors to Portugal itself. Foreigners who questioned Portugal's role in Africa were meddling in the nation's internal affairs. Barricaded behind his walls and his legions of underlings, seated on his crimson velvet Louis XIV chair, absorbed, as one American put it, "by a time dimension quite different from ours," the prime minister, whose only visit abroad had been a single six-mile foray into Spain, derided the new American president's statements on self-determination as folly.

Events in Africa soon forced Salazar to pay renewed attention to the region. On February 4, 1961, several hundred Angolans armed with machetes and clubs attacked Luanda's prison and police barracks and murdered seven officers. At the funeral the next day, crowds of Europeans turned on innocent African bystanders and killed them in retaliation. The incidents triggered riots and counterattacks on both sides. When the violence spread to other cities, the Portuguese security forces and their vigilante supporters entered the poor sections of towns and slaughtered hundreds. At the United Nations the African delegates asked Stevenson if the United States would permit the Angolan crisis to be brought before the Security Council. Stevenson consulted the president and Kennedy agreed. Stevenson then asked the president if he could support the expected African resolution calling for self-determination in Angola. Kennedy told Stevenson to wait to see what the resolution said.

However much Kennedy might have wanted to make a clean break with Portugal, he was constrained by his competition with Moscow. Khrushchev had been increasing pressure on NATO to cede control of West Berlin, the tiny urban island of democracy buried inside Communist East Germany. Kennedy had vowed that as a matter of principle the United States would never do so. To back up his pledge, the president needed to be able to airlift troops and equipment rapidly across the Atlantic. In 1960, however, military cargo fighters and planes were not yet able to cross the ocean in one hop; they had to set down somewhere to refuel. By far the most advantageous spot was the Portuguese air base on the largest of the Azores, a cluster of islands poking up from the ocean floor about two-thirds of the way across the Atlantic to Europe. In the Second World War Portugal had granted American planes the right to use the Azores base in return for a promise to "respect Portuguese sovereignty in all Portuguese colonies." In 1951 and in 1956 the United States had signed leases in which it paid all of Portugal's NATO fees in lieu of rent. The United States government also promised that if Portugal ever needed to use NATO military equipment in its colonies, the permission would "no doubt . . . be promptly forthcoming." Kennedy knew that the current agreement would expire in 1962. Salazar had sent word that a major shift in the American position on colonialism would make the negotiations for continued use of the base more difficult.

Nonetheless, Kennedy was determined to send a message to the Africans that he was serious about ending colonialism. On March 15, when the resolution condemning Portugal reached the Security Council just as a new and more organized nationalist rebellion exploded in Angola, Kennedy instructed Stevenson to vote with the African states. Stevenson told the council that from then on the guiding principle of U.S. foreign policy would be the American Declaration of Independence, which states that "governments derive their just powers from the consent of the governed." When France and Britain abstained along with four other members, the resolution failed, but the image of the United States voting against Europe and with the Soviet Union sent a jolt through the diplomatic halls of the world.

In the months to come, the American decision to support the resolution for self-determination provided an important counterweight to the negative reaction to two other American problems, one international, the other domestic. In April 1961, a month after the Security Council meeting, President Kennedy had to go on national television and acknowledge the failure of the Bay of Pigs invasion of Cuba. Kennedy's quick acceptance of responsibility mitigated some of the international outcry, but African leaders wondered whether Kennedy's inspiring words about self-determination concealed a frightening preference for force.

The second source of African suspicion of Kennedy's intentions flowed directly from America's continuing domestic friction over race. During their African tour, Senators McGee, Moss, and Church had noticed a sharply increased sensitivity among Africans to the problem of race relations in the United States. In their report to Congress the men commented that "racial discrimination in the United States probably is the most important of all natural barriers to a better understanding between Africa and this country." The senators had told African officials that, unlike the white regimes of southern Africa, the United States government officially opposed discrimination. Nonetheless, they wrote, "even those Africans who understand our problems and respect our efforts quite naturally cannot help but react emotionally to widely advertised instances of racial intolerance or violence in this country."

Some of those instances struck the Africans themselves. As scores of new African diplomats streamed into New York and Washington, they met harassment and humiliation from whites who mistook them for American blacks. The problem had existed for some time, but in 1961 the number of occurrences increased. On the morning after the inauguration, the *Washington Post* reported that young diplomats in the nation's segregated capital had been barred from renting apartments, ignored by taxi drivers, and denied access to restaurants and grocery stores. Irritated, the new attorney general, Robert F. Kennedy, asked Secretary of State Dean Rusk to see what the State Department could do to reduce these incidents. Rusk wrote back advising a cautious approach, beginning with a survey.

Unfortunately for Rusk, the problem increased with each passing month. During the spring, in separate incidents, high-level officials from Sierra Leone, Mali, Niger, Ghana, and Cameroon were denied service in restaurants or threatened by white Americans. Each occasion sent a ripple of affront through the African diplomatic community and their home governments. When the Nigerian ambassador was kicked out of a restaurant in Charlottesville, Virginia, the National Council of Nigeria and the Cameroons issued a formal protest. "It is a matter of great regret that America, self-appointed leader of the Western power blocs and great advocate of racial equality in other peoples' countries, should be a country to practice racial discrimination against Nigeria," they wrote. "A country devoid of respect for human dignity, a country which still lives in the dark ages, has no claim to the leadership of free man."

The crowning incident came in June 1961 when the new ambassador of Chad, driving down from the United Nations in New York to present his credentials to the president of the United States, was not permitted to eat in a roadside restaurant along Route 40, a primary corridor through Maryland. The infuriated ambassador arrived in Washington, drove to the White House, walked straight into the Oval Office, and told Kennedy that he had been "thrown on his rear end as a result of entering the Bonnie Brea restaurant on Route 40." Kennedy turned to his chief of protocol, Angier Biddle Duke, and asked him if there wasn't something he could do about this problem. Thus began one of the more bizarre initiatives of the Kennedy administration: the attempt by the Protocol Office in the State Department—a group normally concerned with the intricacies of diplomatic salutation and ceremony—to dismantle segregation in a string of roadside diners, fast-food joints, and hot dog stands in the name of American national security.

Armed with a specific presidential request, Duke and his staff tackled the problem vigorously. They called together representatives from the White House, the Bureau of African Affairs at the State Department, the Justice Department, the Civil Rights Commission, and the office of the governor of Maryland to discuss how they could reduce segregation along Route 40, where many of the incidents had taken place. Breaking into teams, the representatives journeyed up and down the asphalt strip, stopping to explain to the managers and owners of restaurants how their refusal to feed blacks was harming the international reputation of the United States. They helped to guide a new nondiscriminatory public accommodations bill through the Maryland legislature; they enlisted the support of local newspapers and television stations; and they assisted in the creation of a restaurant owners' association that vowed to take some action. When Kennedy asked in early November how the efforts were progressing, his aide Frederick Dutton wrote back that the governor of Maryland had decided to support the new legislation. "The effort along Route 40 is important not only as an attempt to end segregation in Maryland and tangibly show the African diplomats we are trying to be of assistance to them," Dutton told the president. "It is also the first time the State Department has really recognized that domestic race problems affect our relations with African diplomats."

Though Kennedy had not foreseen that his remark in June would lead to such a massive campaign, he supported it as long as it did not attract too much attention and drain too much energy from other efforts. For him the issue was not so much a moral as a political problem: how to satisfy the most people with the least change. By November, however, the controversy seemed to be growing rather than shrinking. The Congress on Racial Equality (CORE), which had pioneered the use of the sit-in in the 1940s, began to pay attention. CORE and its allies had faced violence during the summer of 1961 as they launched wave after wave of Freedom Riders to challenge the segregated seating and facilities of the major bus lines in the South. Only after Attorney General Robert Kennedy had sent in hundreds of federal marshals to escort the Freedom Riders to safety had the violence subsided. Now James Farmer, director of CORE, and other CORE members decided that Route 40 was another place in which the American government could be forced into acting to protect civil rights. The CORE organizers announced that if the restaurants along the road were not desegregated by November 11, they would begin sit-ins throughout Maryland.

The president and his staff fretted about the impending confrontation. The White House drafted a strong directive to the attorney general and secretary of commerce that Kennedy could release if events turned sour. "It is not enough just to apologize to indignant African diplomats who are refused service or are denied equal facilities in restaurants, stores, gasoline stations, hotels, and motels," said the draft. "If we are to develop a satisfactory relationship with the colored nations which now constitute a majority of the United Nations, we must move quickly to end all racial discrimination at home. We must do this, of course, not just because of our international responsibilities, but above all because it is required by our own first principles." The statement ordered the two departments to end the discrimination, using persuasion and, if necessary, lawsuits. The statement also announced a White House conference at which the president and the secretary of state would explain the international significance of ending restaurant segregation.

After the experience with the Freedom Rides, Kennedy did not want to issue another edict pitting the White House directly against local custom and state law. He pondered whether there wasn't another way to resolve the Route 40 problems. When a new article appeared in the *Washington Post* about an African diplomat who had been denied a drink of water in a restaurant, Kennedy immediately phoned Duke. "Can't you tell them not to do it?" the president asked. Duke, thinking Kennedy was referring to the restaurants, launched into a lengthy account of the steps they had taken and the progress they were making. "That's not what I am calling about," said the president. "Can't you tell these African ambassadors not to drive on Route 40? It's a hell of a road—I used to drive it years ago. But why would anyone drive it today when you can fly? Tell these ambassadors I wouldn't think of driving from New York to Washington. Tell them to fly!"

By the end of the year, all sides, eager to avoid a clash, wrangled out a deal that brought the tempest to a close. Duke's protocol teams persuaded about half of the restaurants in the association to desegregate; CORE agreed to call off the sit-ins and moderate its demands; Kennedy sat on his directive to the attorney general and the secretary of commerce; the public facilities law was passed by the Maryland legislature; and some of the African diplomats decided to take the new airborne shuttle between New York and Washington.

In his first year as president, John F. Kennedy put forward a host of striking innovations such as the Alliance for Progress in Latin America, the Peace Corps, the nuclear test ban, and the new Africa policy, but it was not long before the harsh realities of the struggle with Communism and of his slim domestic margin tempered his enthusiasm. As he faced challenges from Khrushchev in Western Europe, in Southeast Asia, and in Cuba, Kennedy increasingly employed the strict calculus of the cold war, weighing persons and events in terms of their effect on American influence. His caution, especially with regard to domestic matters, he believed, was temporary; reelection in 1964, he felt, would give him the mandate to proceed at a faster rate. As racial issues at home and abroad became more contentious, Kennedy, as he had in the battle of the restaurants, initially preferred to work out an uneasy compromise, to hedge, dodge, and muddle through.

In few areas of the world was his tendency toward equivocation more evident than in southern Africa. In August 1961 a London newspaper reported that the Portuguese had bombarded a village in Angola which they suspected of harboring nationalist guerrillas, leaving behind bomb fragments clearly marked "Made in America." Kennedy, sensing political harm, promptly issued National Security Action Memorandum No. 77 to the secretaries of state and defense. This discovery, he said in the directive, "is going to present problems to us both in Angola and in Portugal. Have we considered 1) whether we can be successful in persuading the Portuguese of this, or 2) whether this will have an adverse effect upon the Azores base? I wonder if we should perhaps content ourselves with a public statement with regard to the matter."

Defense Secretary Robert S. McNamara wrote back that the United States had provided more than $300 million in military assistance and equipment to Portugal. The Portuguese had acknowledged that some of this equipment was being used in Angola. Though McNamara noted that "such diversion of Military Assistance Plan supplied equipment of U.S. origin by Portugal for use in its African territories, without prior U.S. consent, is contrary to our bilateral agreement," he also reminded the president that the United States had secretly promised in 1951 to grant that permission automatically. McNamara outlined his steps for tightening the flow of weapons from the United States to Portugal, but he urged Kennedy not to comment publicly. Kennedy followed his advice and kept silent.

The tension produced by differing opinions about the white regimes of southern Africa was rending the bureaucratic fabric of the State Department. On one side, Soapy Williams and Wayne Fredericks were telling the president and the secretary of state that the appearance of support for the military suppression of nationalist movements would undermine the entire effort to create a new American policy in Africa. On the other side, the powerful European bureau of the State Department, aided by its International Organizations section, insisted on the preeminence of American ties to Europe and to NATO. The Europeanists were joined by the Joint Chiefs of Staff, who pointed to the sudden construction of the Berlin Wall in August 1961 as evidence of malevolent Soviet intent and insisted that Europe could not be defended without the Azores base.

These tensions remained throughout Kennedy's term as the different interests—Africanist, Europeanist, military, and diplomatic—battled for presidential attention and preference. Kennedy relied on his National Security Council staff, especially McGeorge Bundy, to help him sort the torrent of information and opinion that flooded into the White House. Wherever possible Kennedy pressed for reconciliation; when consensus could not be reached, he sometimes granted different parties their wishes in sequence. To satisfy Williams, Bowles, and the liberal-Africanist wing, he welcomed dozens of African heads of state to the White House and directed lesser nationalists to the attorney general. To keep the more conservative Europeanists and the soldiers in the Pentagon happy, Kennedy labored diligently to maintain cordial relations with Portugal. At the United Nations he told Stevenson that he would support some African initiatives but instructed him to work behind the scenes to water down the resolutions as much as possible.

From the beginning the White House knew that South Africa could flare into a major problem with domestic and international consequences. Two months after his inauguration the president issued National Security Memorandum No. 33 ordering a review of U.S. policy toward the country. "The recent action of the prime minister of the Union of South Africa in withdrawing his country from the British Commonwealth and the recent action of the United Nations on Angola have created problems not anticipated in the outstanding national security policy relating to Angola, the Union of South Africa, and the Portuguese possessions of Africa," McGeorge Bundy wrote to the secretary of state. Bundy asked Rusk to "look at the provisions with respect to the encouraging of American private capital to seek investment outlets in South Africa and with respect to the purchase of gold and other raw materials that provide a major source of economic support for the South African economy."

Over the next few months, the White House tried to strike a balance between the opposing forces in South Africa. When South Africa became a republic in May, Kennedy sent a letter of congratulations to the new state president, Charles Swart. When Albert Luthuli won the Nobel Prize in October, Kennedy congratulated him too. Though the South African government refused to allow Soapy Williams to tour the country after his "Africa for the Africans" statement, Kennedy permitted five American navy vessels to visit Cape Town on a goodwill visit just before the end of May, even though Verwoerd demanded that the nearly five hundred black American sailors obey all apartheid laws during their shore leave.

In June, South African Foreign Minister Eric Louw called in U.S. Ambassador Joseph Satterthwaite to ask for a formal indication of the Kennedy administration's attitude toward future cooperation with the South African government. Two months later, after discussions among Williams, Fredericks, and the other branches of the State Department, Secretary Rusk sent his response in the form of an aide-mémoire. The text began with the usual diplomatic flattery, noting the long tradition of cooperation between the two countries, and agreeing with the South African government's contention that "there is much misunderstanding and misrepresentation in the world concerning South Africa's racial problem." Rusk pointed out, however, that "most nations of the world . . . find themselves unable to accept a governmental policy which compels and perpetuates a system which denies fundamental human rights to the vast majority of the country's population only because of the color of their skin." Rusk also refused to accept the South African position that the country's racial policy was an exclusively domestic matter, for "this policy does violence to the human rights provisions of the UN Charter [and] tends to weaken the position of the West in its efforts to resist Communist influence and penetration in newly emerged Afro-Asian nations." Accordingly, he said, the United States "would warmly welcome the beginnings of any steps which the South African government could take to permit non-whites to play a greater role in the life of their country." The United States would move to full cooperation if South Africa promised full future participation to its citizens. Without such measures, however, the United States "could not be expected to cooperate in matters which it believed would lend support to South Africa's present racial policies." To remove the sting, Rusk concluded with what would become a standard assurance: "There are numerous fields in which our two countries can continue to collaborate closely and fruitfully to our mutual benefit and for good of the Free World, especially in the areas of common defense against threats emanating from the Communist bloc" and in "the fields of missile activity and space exploration, atomic energy, and in the entire range of scientific, technical, and research activities." Rusk also promised that the American government would "maintain and strengthen mutually desirable cooperation and exchanges which have existed in cultural, educational, health and welfare and other fields."

Verwoerd, after receiving the message, immediately probed to determine how far Kennedy was willing to go to maintain the ties to which Rusk referred. His overtures set off objections among the Africanists in the State Department. In September, Undersecretary of State Chester Bowles wrote McGeorge Bundy that the South African government was pressing for a host of concessions that would "be costly to us in the United Nations and in our relations with the world generally." The United States could not easily rebuff Verwoerd, he said, because of a preliminary agreement signed by Eisenhower in the last months of his administration to build an air force missile tracking station outside of Pretoria. The American government had already constructed a deep-space tracking station outside Pretoria operated jointly by the National Aeronautic and Space Administration (NASA) and the South African government. The new facility would gather data from medium and long-range ballistic missile tests in the southern Atlantic and Indian Oceans. Bowles told Bundy that Verwoerd now wanted to participate in joint naval maneuvers, purchase $100 million in airplanes from a U.S. corporation, and receive $75 million in loans from the International Monetary Fund.

Without the tracking station, Bowles wrote, the United States would probably deny all of these requests, but because of U.S. military interests the government was being drawn into an appearance of support for the apartheid regime. Bowles pointed out that although Ambassador Satterthwaite had been sent to South Africa with the specific instructions to invite Africans to public gatherings at the embassy, he had not done so for fear of jeopardizing the negotiations. Bowles complained that although the original agreement had stipulated that the United States could back out for political reasons, the Pentagon was now insisting that the military station was of such enormous importance that it must outweigh all other considerations. Bowles did not agree, telling Bundy that "if we are forced to take these actions, most of which will become known to the public in the midst of a highly explosive United Nations session in which the attitudes of the Asians and Africans will be of decisive importance, we will probably have to pay a heavy political price." The disagreement had reached an impasse that only the White House could resolve. Bowles asked Bundy to appoint Jerome Wiesner, the scientific adviser on the staff of the National Security Council, to arbitrate.

Wiesner spent nearly four weeks talking to the different branches of government and forwarded his opinion to Bundy on October 18. The missile program was important, but not at the top of the air force's priorities, he said. Without the South African station the air force could proceed with the tests but would be deprived of some data until another site could be found or a tracking ship constructed. Since the tests could continue, Wiesner wrote, the secretary of the air force had reluctantly agreed that the loss of the site would be painful but not fatal. Accordingly, Wiesner wrote, the White House should instruct State Department officials to walk a diplomatic tightrope: they should "neither be deliberately provocative and thus insure that we will be ordered out nor permit the need for the site to be the reason for compromise on issues which the State Department regards as fundamental in the conduct of its foreign policy." The U.S. government would, in other words, continue to speak with many voices and send many signals to the South Africans, strengthening Verwoerd's conviction that Kennedy's words would never be backed by deeds.

The fundamental inconsistencies that characterized American policy toward southern Africa sufficiently troubled the White House and the State Department that they commissioned multiple policy reviews throughout the Kennedy administration. Though the studies varied widely in sophistication and depth, their authors shared certain questionable assumptions and conclusions. They all, for example, accepted large blocks of Afrikaner political fiction as fact: that whites in general and Afrikaners in particular were highly unified, that they were impervious to pressure, and that any efforts to impose sanctions would only solidify the National Party and undermine its opponents. They held to this assumption even though they had ample evidence of the anxiety and discord that nearly tore apart the Afrikaner community in the economic crisis after Sharpeville. They also believed that an outbreak of violence in South Africa would lead to an interracial bloodbath. In this they drew from the still harrowing experience of the Congo and from the deep psychic fears whites have always harbored about unleashed black rage. These fears were intensified by a widely held concern that a race conflict in South Africa might trigger a similar convulsion in the United States. Finally, as bureaucrats, they dreaded anarchy and worshiped incremental reform. These silent, underlying dispositions steadily warped American analysis in favor of the white regime: the methodical racial brutality of Verwoerd's police was subconsciously excused as a legitimate attempt to maintain order, while the few, haphazard acts of sabotage by Umkhonto We Sizwe were seen as precursors to the savage destruction of civil society.

Primed by Khrushchev's aggressive challenges, the Americans also became convinced that a revolution would open the door for a Communist takeover or a superpower confrontation over the southern sea lanes and the world's largest supply of gold. They read with alarm the CIA reports that Communists had infiltrated the African National Congress. The problem of identifying who was an independent nationalist and who was a covert tool of the "Sino-Soviet bloc" was exacerbated by the widespread use of anticapitalist rhetoric in nationalist pronouncements. The lens of the cold war thus altered—and sometimes distorted—every intelligence or policy analysis, casting suspicion on all acts of resistance against colonialism or apartheid.

Groping for an intelligible policy, the American planners tried to enumerate the points they viewed as incontrovertible: The Afrikaners were politically invulnerable. Open black revolt would lead to massacre and tyranny. The defense of the free world required both continued military cooperation with South Africa and the appeasement of the new African nations' anger about apartheid. In the end, the only policy that could flow from such contradictions was one that embodied them. The United States, the studies concluded, should adopt a "two-pronged approach" that objected to apartheid but continued a normal relationship with the country. Military support and cooperation should be denied to South Africa for use against nationalists but freely offered for the battle with Communists. Public denouncements should be salved with private assurances. To conceal their illogic, the planners piled up fuzzy phrases; one study, in a gem of euphemistic understatement, described the American objective as seeking modification of South Africa's racial policies through "an imaginative combination of firmness and tact."

Verwoerd and Louw deftly exploited the American incongruities, which they viewed as Machiavellian hypocrisy. Nurturing American reveries of reform, they doled out crumbs of hope. In June 1961 President Kennedy met privately with two South African businessmen, who sounded him out about a possible visit by Verwoerd to the White House and assured him that Verwoerd's policies would soon be moderated. One of the businessmen later assured an American diplomat of Verwoerd's good intentions but warned that he could not "move too far ahead of the Afrikaner farmers." The South African ambassador to the United States, W. C. Naudé, also tried to gain American sympathy in several meetings with Dean Rusk, commenting how separate development was misunderstood and would eventually be shown to benefit all the peoples of South Africa. Rusk's responses, as recorded in the department's record of conversations, were tactful but dubious.

Verwoerd, the master of ideological jujitsu, leapt nimbly over the uncertain American boundary between nationalists and Communists. He portrayed all domestic disturbances as the work of the Kremlin, even though this contradicted his simultaneous assertion that South Africa's problems were purely internal. He defended every new weapon, oppressive law, and jailed protester as necessary to the defense of the free world. Some in the American government agreed with his position; others recognized it as a dodge; but until support for South Africa began to impose a cost in the international community, the United States did little to close the loophole. When the American government—through Stevenson, Williams, Rusk, or Kennedy—did denounce apartheid on occasion, Verwoerd and his emissaries struck back in kind, drawing attention to the racial strife in the United States. Foreign Minister Louw, in speeches at the UN and in private conversations from New York to Washington, challenged America's moral authority to call others to account. His message was picked up by some within the American government, who cautioned that the United States should get its own house in order before attempting to correct the behavior of other sovereign governments.

To those in government who longed for a bold moral statement from Kennedy on racial discrimination at home and abroad, the president's caution was deeply frustrating. On the surface, Kennedy was still conveying an aura of concern and interest. Williams pressed on with his trips to Africa, completing four in under eighteen months. Kennedy held a large reception at the State Department on Africa Freedom Day and continued to receive African heads of state at the White House with clockwork regularity—twenty-eight in all, or nearly one a month. In the wrangling over the Congo, Kennedy held off the pro-Katanga lobby in the Senate and supported UN Secretary General Dag Hammarskjöld's efforts to push the Belgian troops out and restore the nation's unity. In Ghana, Kennedy chose to overlook Kwame Nkrumah's leftist rhetoric and decided to devote a substantial piece of American aid to the construction of a dam across the Volta River. Yet on southern Africa, Kennedy's policy was riddled with inconsistency.

Kennedy could steer such a course because at the time there was no organized domestic constituency to reward him for courage or punish him for duplicity. This was due in part to lingering effects of McCarthyism, with its insistence that all Americans demonstrate their undivided loyalty to the United States. American blacks who spoke up and criticized the United States, like the actor Paul Robeson, were harassed or punished. As Europe slowly loosened its colonial grip in the late 1950s,

black interest in Africa quickly resurfaced. And as the struggle for civil
rights took shape, black preachers and politicians grew fond of portraying the movement in America as a single flank in an immense battle for
freedom that stretched across the centuries and the continents. This
growing international perspective raised anew the question of loyalty
and identity for persons both inside and outside the black community.
Black intellectuals debated the nature of their ties to their ancestral and
adopted homes. African garb, music, and artifacts gained popularity.
Ominously, the FBI and other American security agencies, in a manner
reminiscent of Verwoerd, interpreted this revived interest and emerging
militancy as part of a broad plan of subversion that the government had
to control or disrupt.

Kennedy himself was uncomfortable with the perception that he owed
his job to the votes of American blacks and did not want to reinforce it.
He was also affected by the peculiar laws of politics, in which politicians
elected to executive positions often attempt to broaden their base by
moving toward the opposition and away from the coalition that put
them in office. Kennedy worried mostly about the conservatives in his
party and in the Congress. He believed he had paid his debt to American blacks through his clashes with southern segregationists over the
Freedom Rides, the registration of voters, and the admission of blacks
to southern universities. When Martin Luther King Jr. and other civil
rights leaders pressed him for more rapid action, he deflected them to
Harris Wofford, who found his job as the White House buffer increasingly disturbing. Though Kennedy knew from the Route 40 campaign
that racism in America bothered Africans, he doubted that racism in
Africa affected many Americans. On one occasion, traveling aboard *Air
Force One* to speak at Boston College, he engaged his British friend and
informal African adviser Barbara Ward Jackson, on the topic. "The
thing we talked about nearly all the way up," she recalled, "was whether
Africa could become an issue in American politics on the par with the
Israeli issue with the Jewish vote." Jackson told Kennedy that there was
a good possibility that freedom in Africa might someday emerge as a
potent domestic topic. Kennedy agreed but said "he didn't think it
would be soon because he didn't have the impression that the black
leadership at the moment had much time for anything but the internal
American struggle. Of course, it was something that one would have to
bear in mind. And he showed himself very aware of the range of issues
that would come up on southern Africa and, like many other people,
was considerably confused as to how you dealt with them."

The growing black interest in Africa, while central for the later history
of the divestment movement, did not significantly influence Kennedy
because it did not yet determine votes at the ballot box or in the legisla-

tures. The American black community, though nearly ten percent of the population, had only a tiny handful of representatives in the U.S. House, none in the Senate, none in any governor's chair, and none on the Supreme Court. Even in Kennedy's administration, vital departments like Justice and State had a few dozen black employees among thousands of whites. Nor was the problem confined to the federal government. In some state assemblies there were no blacks; in the rest, few. Though blacks had been pouring into American metropolises since the Second World War, the mayors from one sea to the other were exclusively white.

Within the Kennedy administration, Williams, Fredericks, Wofford, and other liberals recognized the problem and attempted to increase the leverage of the black community in other ways. Wofford tried to bring American civil rights leaders together with visiting African dignitaries for private conversations in his home. Not all of these sessions went smoothly. On one occasion, Wofford invited Martin Luther King and the new president of independent Uganda to his home for dinner. Though King tried to engage the president in conversation, the president showed little interest in his dinner partner's role in American life. The dinner took an even more awkward turn when Wofford brought one of his young children to meet the guests. Wofford had primed the boy by telling him that one of the guests was very important, the "George Washington of Uganda." The little boy entered the room, shook hands with the distinguished guest, and then protested aloud to his father, "This can't be George Washington! George Washington wasn't black!"

In early 1962 leaders in the black community formed the American Negro Leadership Conference on Africa (ANLCA). Designed to increase black influence on U.S. foreign policy, the group was governed by a Call Committee composed of six heads of major black organizations: Martin Luther King from the Southern Christian Leadership Conference (SCLC); Whitney Young from the National Urban League; A. Philip Randolph from the Brotherhood of Sleeping Car Porters, AFL-CIO; Dorothy Height from the National Council of Negro Women; Roy Wilkins from the NAACP; and James Farmer from CORE. Though the organization got off to a strong start and held two important conferences, one of which was addressed by the secretary of state, the organization sputtered because its plans were too big, its budget too small, and its leaders too busy.

Soapy Williams and Wayne Fredericks welcomed the formation and support of the ANLCA. Searching for additional ways to advance the Africanist cause within the bureaucratic and political maze, they decided to borrow a technique that had served them well in Michigan and at the Ford Foundation. They invited a broad range of scholars, lawyers, activists, businesspeople, foundation executives, and other institutional leaders to form a State Department Advisory Council on African Affairs. The roster of participants resembles a bibliography of American writers on Africa: Melville Herskovitz and Gwendolyn Carter from Northwestern University; John Marcum of Lincoln University; Vernon McKay of Johns Hopkins; Immanuel Wallerstein from Columbia; Helen Kitchen from *Africa Report;* Frank Ferrari from the African American Institute; and George Houser from the American Committee on Africa, to name a few. Williams and Fredericks used the group in many ways. They called on the members individually to ask them for advice in their areas of expertise. They brought them together in a conference to ponder possible new directions in American policy. They also used them to defend the Africanist position to branches of the foreign service, the press, the other agencies of government, and the legislators on Capitol Hill. Williams and Fredericks assiduously developed their ties to the president's men, coaxing Bundy and his staff to consider the African implications of global problems. They also took advantage of their attendance at Kennedy's many meetings with African heads of state to offer suggestions directly to the president.

African leaders were also rummaging for new ways to change American and Western policies on southern Africa in the United Nations. Finding that their attempts in the Security Council were often blocked by the great powers, they injected the South African question into the General Assembly. In the fall of 1961, South African Foreign Minister Louw flew in to rebut their efforts. "The leaders of the anti-colonial campaign . . . labor under the mistaken impression that the parliamentary system born in Britain and adopted by other Western countries . . . could be grafted on to the traditional customs and practices of the African peoples," Louw explained. "It simply does not work that way." He fiercely attacked Kwame Nkrumah and other African leaders for consorting with China and the Soviet Union and flaunted Verwoerd's successful repression.

Louw defended apartheid with all of Verwoerd's favorite rationalizations and accused the Western powers of gross hypocrisy. "Would the United States of America, Canada, the Latin American countries," he asked, "all countries whose respective early histories of colonization are similar to that of South Africa—would they, if their relative proportions of white to non-white populations were the same as South Africa, be prepared to hand over the control of their countries to Negro or to 'Indian' majorities?" Louw ended with a plea that "we be permitted to carry out our policy of looking after the interests of our Bantu and other non-white peoples without interference from outside."

At the end of the speech, the delegate from Liberia exploded in fury and demanded that the entire speech be expunged from the record. The matter was put to a vote and passed sixty-seven to one, with Great Britain, the United States, and twenty others abstaining. Adlai Stevenson explained that "while we reject the views of the Foreign Minister on the subject of apartheid . . . we resolutely support his right—and the right of every speaker before the General Assembly—to state his views." The UN delegates then spent several weeks debating whether to impose sanctions on South Africa. The African countries put forward a proposal for comprehensive, multilateral economic and material sanctions, but the Western powers blocked the measure, despite an appeal from Albert Luthuli. The delegate from India offered a more moderate proposal calling on individual members to decide on their own sanctions; this passed seventy-four to two, though the United States, Great Britain, and France abstained.

Dissatisfied with the tepid European and American response, the African delegates searched for other means of pressuring South Africa. In February the United Nations Economic Committee on Africa (ECA) voted to recommend the expulsion of South Africa's delegates to the committee because of apartheid. Throughout the spring and fall Africans maneuvered to challenge South Africa's mandate to govern South West Africa on the grounds that South Africa had illegally extended apartheid into the territory. When Verwoerd announced that the 1964 South African Olympic team would be entirely white, the International Olympic Committee, facing rebellion from its Asian and African members, expelled South Africa from the competition.

Through 1962 Kennedy, Rusk, and Stevenson managed to parry or duck most of these challenges. The president had his hands full trying to respond to new Soviet atmospheric nuclear explosions, control the violence accompanying the admission of James Meredith to the University of Mississippi, and navigate through the atomic showdown over Soviet missiles in Cuba. The Pentagon concluded an agreement in June 1962 to supply South Africa with weapons, vehicles, and parts in return for permission to set up the air force missile tracking station. In deference to the "two-pronged approach," the State Department attached a perfunctory stipulation that the weapons could not be used to repress internal dissent but only for defense against Communism.

In the fall of 1962 the UN General Assembly again debated apartheid and Louw again denounced the delegates in a speech. This time he pilfered Kennedy's own vocabulary and described separate development as "the new frontier" in Africa. The American representatives, on instruction from Rusk, opposed even limited economic sanctions and worked to deflect the drive to take the issue of South West Africa to the International Court of Justice. When the Soviet Union charged that the United States was deliberately ignoring human rights because of its half-billion-dollar investments in South Africa, the U.S. ambassador, anticipating a defense that would be used heavily over the next thirty years, responded that "U.S. investments and loans were given in such a way that they went for the improvement of the social and economic conditions of all the people of South Africa."

Though the United States and its allies were able to prevent the expulsion of South Africa from the United Nations, the African bloc surprised the West with its aggressive parliamentary tactics that led to the successful passage of limited sanctions—despite abstentions by more than twenty countries, including the United States—and to the creation of a UN Special Committee on Apartheid to oversee implementation of the sanctions. Foreign Minister Louw dismissed the move, noting smugly that the restrictions would fail because more than three-fifths of South Africa's imports came from countries that had opposed the measure. Kennedy, monitoring events from the White House, expressed frustration at the General Assembly for engaging in what he viewed as ineffectual grandstanding.

As the end of 1962 approached, the Americans increasingly recognized that the Africans were not going to give up. Rusk's advisers told him that the delaying tactics of the fall would hold for a year at best. Undersecretary Chester Bowles, after a month-long trip to Africa, reported that though the United States was in a favorable position in Africa, this position was fragile and could be substantially harmed by continued American involvement with South Africa. Adlai Stevenson, in his year-end summary of events at the United Nations, recounted in depth the battle over apartheid and noted that feeling had grown substantially in favor of "the breaking of diplomatic relations, the closing of ports, the boycotting of all South African goods, refusing of passage to South African airplanes, the application of sanctions and consideration of expulsion from United Nations. . . . The strength of the Afro-Asian feeling is now such that the U.S. will have to review its position on apartheid before the next General Assembly. Otherwise continued opposition to such resolutions on apartheid will be considered by all but a very few of the Afro-Asians as evidence of our tacit approval of the policies of the Government of South Africa."

The Africans had new allies in the American civil rights movement. On December 17, 1962, Martin Luther King Jr. and several other civil rights leaders from the ANLCA went to the White House to talk to the president about Africa. They urged Kennedy to act more boldly, to create a new "Marshall Plan" to aid the fledgling economies. They also voiced their increasing concern about apartheid and pressed him to support sanctions against South Africa. They were particularly incensed about the United States' negative vote on a UN attempt to condemn Portugal's armed suppression of the independence movements sweeping through Angola, Mozambique, and Guinea-Bissau. Kennedy shared his dilemma with the visitors, describing how his commitments to NATO prevented a cutoff of weapons to Portugal, how he didn't trust Portugal, and how he had tried to design mechanisms to prevent American weapons from being used in the colonies. Much to the discomfort of his schedulers, the president listened and expounded to the civil rights leaders for nearly three hours, slipping out only briefly to light the White House Christmas tree. The leaders left in the Kennedy thrall; the black press trumpeted that the meeting was "the longest conference ever held by Negroes with a U.S. president in the White House."

Through the winter of 1962–63, political turmoil around southern Africa steadily increased. The International Court of Justice agreed to decide on the charges brought by Ethiopia and Liberia against Verwoerd's imposition of apartheid in South West Africa. The Third Afro-Asian Peoples Solidarity Conference denounced France and Great Britain for supplying weapons to South Africa and endorsed the use of violence to overthrow Verwoerd. In March, South African police swept through the country in search of saboteurs and imprisoned more than three thousand people. At the same time, a United States senator and prominent leader of the Democratic Party, visiting South Africa, publicly endorsed apartheid.

The senator, Allen J. Ellender, a Democrat from Louisiana, had some years before announced his intention of visiting every country on the planet before he retired from the Senate. After each voyage, he published his travel journals in the *Congressional Record* and lined the walls of his study with the bound copies. In late 1962 Ellender chose to traipse through Africa and ended up in Rhodesia, where he offered his observations at a press conference. It was a great mistake for the European colonialists to have given up control of their territories, said this senior elected official from Kennedy's own party, because black Africans were completely incompetent. Instantly, diplomatic telegram lines to the State Department sizzled with outrage and Kennedy had to publicly reaffirm his support for African nationalism. Edward R. Murrow, the head of the United States Information Agency (USIA), told the White House shortly afterward that "Senator Ellender's remark that Africans do not have the ability to govern themselves has now been so widely disseminated by press and radio in Africa that prolonged damage to US prestige is likely to result."

Unconcerned by the diplomatic wreckage he was producing with his pronouncements, Ellender meandered from African capital to capital, repeating at every stop that if one removed what the Europeans had done, there would be nothing left in Africa. Finding himself barred from visits to Somalia, Uganda, and Tanzania, a disgruntled Ellender made his way to South Africa. There, in March, he held another press conference. This time he told the receptive reporters that the Europeans should always remain in power because majority rule in South Africa would result in "something worse than the Congo." Afrikaner newspapers seized on his remarks and quoted them for months as evidence of the true American attitude toward apartheid.

Though Kennedy and Rusk repudiated Ellender's comments, both men were slowly being drawn into deeper collaboration with Verwoerd. Rusk, hoping that the controversy in the United Nations might stir South Africa to a change in South West Africa, instructed Ambassador Satterthwaite to press Foreign Minister Louw to accept a United Nations presence in the territory. At the same time, on March 16, 1963, the secretary of state wrote to the president to ask him for a decision that Rusk knew would have tremendous consequences. Verwoerd, he told Kennedy, had inquired through a naval attaché whether the United States would be willing to sell two or three attack submarines and provide training to the South African crews. To do so, Rusk told the president, would strengthen military relations between the countries but might entail significant costs. "If South Africa's international position continues to deteriorate," Rusk wrote, "it is probable that delivery of US submarines in 1966 could have highly unfavorable repercussions abroad and at home." At the same time, "in terms of our political relations with South Africa and potential benefits to our balance of payments," Rusk concluded, the U.S. government should be willing at least to discuss the sale. The next week Kennedy sent word through his aide Carl Kaysen authorizing the discussion and noting that "on balance it is desirable to make such a transaction if it can be made on acceptable terms."

Despite John F. Kennedy's attempts to manage the foreign and domestic racial controversies separately, in 1963 they converged. Africans paid new attention to the battle for civil rights in the United States, and Americans, especially American blacks, called on their government to demonstrate the same commitment to equality abroad as they had voiced at home. The confluence of events forced Kennedy to choose between acting decisively or allowing the initiative to slip to others. With speed and skill, Kennedy rose to the occasion and took steps onto the world stage as a champion of racial equality, though behind the scenes he continued to reassure the South African and Portuguese governments of United States support.

Kennedy's problems began in March when Martin Luther King and a team of experienced civil rights organizers decided to force a nonviolent showdown over segregation in Birmingham, Alabama. Their plan called first for small sit-ins and then larger demonstrations and a boycott of downtown businesses. When these had attracted attention and support, the organizers would begin mass marches to strengthen the boycott and to fill the jails. If the white leaders had not succumbed at that point, the civil rights leaders would then call in outsiders from around the country to join the marches and pack the prisons to overflowing.

At the time, the political leaders of Birmingham were paralyzed in a bizarre stalemate. A coalition of white business leaders was trying to eject the crude segregationist Eugene "Bull" Connor, now the police chief, from office by reorganizing the city structure and pitting Connor in a mayoral race against the more moderate Albert Boutwell. The March primary had produced no clear-cut winner, so the two factions were girding for a runoff on April 2. Many told King that this was the worst possible time for massive demonstrations to desegregate the city, that such actions would play into Connor's hands and sink the chance to elect a more thoughtful white executive. King decided to go ahead with the campaign but to begin it the day after the election. On April 2 Boutwell defeated Connor. Connor challenged the victory in court and announced that pending a decision he would not leave office as scheduled on April 15.

The first few days of the desegregation campaign went poorly. When the demonstrators took their seats in white restaurants, the managers simply turned out the lights and closed down. Though a few dozen demonstrators went to jail for picketing city hall, the number of volunteers willing to be arrested by Connor's men dwindled. Moderate black businessmen, pleased with Boutwell's victory, received King coolly. On April 10 Bull Connor obtained a state court injunction barring any further protests or demonstrations.

Martin Luther King and his lieutenants had to decide whether to disobey the injunction, which might overplay their hand, or to back out and risk the collapse of the campaign. The inner circle of advisers could not agree. The white city leaders had just increased the bail fee nearly tenfold and the sputtering desegregation campaign was perilously low on funds. King disappeared into his hotel bedroom to ponder the problem alone. He emerged shortly afterward in his blue jeans and work shirt, signaling his intention to march and go to jail. "I don't know what will happen," he told the somber group. "I don't know where the money will come from. But I have to make a faith act." On Good Friday,

April 12, King marched downtown. As soon as he arrived, Bull Connor's detectives shoved him into a paddy wagon, took him to the jail, and threw him into solitary confinement.

King remained locked up for nine days. When his wife, Coretta, reported that she had received a call from the president inquiring about her husband, the press noted condescendingly that Kennedy was only returning a call placed by her. Support for the Birmingham demonstrations continued to dissipate, even with King behind bars. A group of liberal white clergy from Birmingham criticized King for his timing, saying in a public statement that "we do not believe that these days of new hope are days when extreme measures are justified in Birmingham." When King read their remarks, he was seized by a feverish desire to respond. Writing on miscellaneous scraps of paper, he penned a "letter from the Birmingham jail," in which he attacked their paternalistic attempts to establish "the timetable for another man's freedom." With an ardor that made the letter one of his most famous writings, King spewed out the reasons why he and his followers could no longer wait for justice to be granted piecemeal. Whatever the barriers, he wrote, the future was clear: "We will reach the goal of freedom in Birmingham and all over the nation, because the goal of America is freedom. . . . If the inexpressible cruelties of slavery could not stop us, the opposition we now face will surely fail. We will win our freedom because the sacred heritage of our nation and the eternal will of God are embodied in our echoing demands."

On April 21, King was let out of jail, on bond. Five days later an Alabama judge found King and his associates guilty of criminal contempt and sentenced them to five days' imprisonment. The civil rights leaders applied for permission to hold another protest rally but were turned down by two parallel city governments—Boutwell's and Connor's—that were both claiming to run the city while they waited for a court decision about whose regime was legitimate. Despite a high level of emotion at the evening mass meetings in black churches, few adult volunteers wanted to face Connor's dogs and jails. The passionate nonviolent organizers around King, veterans of similar struggles across the South, turned instead to the hundreds of high school students and children who had been clamoring to participate.

On Thursday, May 2, a large crowd of black children left the Sixteenth Street Baptist Church and headed downtown. When they tried to cross police barricades designed to restrict them to the black sections of town, the police arrested them, loading paddy wagons and school buses with children as young as six. The next day, another thousand poured out of the church and found themselves facing rows of police cars, school buses, and fire engines. Connor, struggling to cope with city jails filled with children, had decided not to arrest any more but to prevent them from marching at all. When the children refused to disperse, he ordered the fire engines to douse them. Most fled, but a small group of soaked demonstrators refused to budge. Connor ordered the firemen to increase the water pressure on the demonstrators, who were now sitting on the ground. The firemen focused on them with their monitor guns, devices that funneled two hoses through a single nozzle with enough power to strip the bark from trees at a hundred feet. The blasting stream pummeled and shoved the young people aside like pieces of crumpled paper. One little girl was rolled down the street like a tin can.

When the crowd responded by throwing bricks and rocks, Connor ordered eight K-9 units to move forward. The snarling dogs chased bystanders and bit three demonstrators badly enough to send them to the hospital. Outside a restaurant, one policeman grabbed the shirt of a black boy with one hand and released his hold on the leash of his dog with the other. The dog leapt up and sank his teeth into the boy's abdomen. Standing a few feet away, a photographer captured the scene on film. The next morning most of the country and much of the world viewed this icon of the American struggle for racial equality on the front page of the morning papers. President Kennedy told visitors to the White House that day that the picture had made him sick.

Over the following weeks, white authority in Birmingham began to crumble. Inspired by their children, thousands of new demonstrators volunteered to march. On one occasion, when again faced with the fire hoses, a large crowd of blacks knelt to pray, and the firemen would not obey Connor's command to fire the monitor guns on them at point-blank range. The campaign to desegregate the city's downtown businesses continued; sporadic violence flared; and King landed back in jail on the contempt charge. Finally the leading businessmen of the city entered into intense negotiations with King's representative Andrew Young. Young and the business leaders carefully patched together an agreement for a phased desegregation of all businesses. The attorney general, represented by Justice Department official Burke Marshall, lent his private support, and the president, facing his first press conference that focused predominantly on racial issues, publicly endorsed the settlement. When King was released, he also spoke in favor of the agreement at a mass meeting. King drew particular attention to the global implications of the actions in Birmingham. "The United States is concerned about its image. When things started happening down here, Mr. Kennedy got disturbed," King proclaimed from the pulpit. "Mr. Kennedy . . . is battling for the minds and the hearts of men in Asia and Africa—some one billion men in the neutralist sector of the world—and they aren't gonna respect the United States of America if she deprives men and women of the basic rights of life because of the color of their skin. Mr. Kennedy knows that."

If Kennedy had not known it before, he could not have disputed it after Birmingham. Newspapers around the world, especially in Africa, reported daily on the tumult in Alabama. From May 14 to May 26, the research and intelligence branch of the State Department counted more than fourteen hundred Soviet radio commentaries beamed worldwide denouncing the violence and racism of American society as the inevitable fruits of capitalism. "If America's rulers can act like slave holders towards millions of their own people," asked one Kremlin broadcast, "what can the nations of Asia, Africa, and Latin America expect of them?" White supremacist editors and government officials in Rhodesia, Mozambique, and South Africa noted smugly that the United States obviously had not found the solution to racial harmony. In the midst of the Birmingham crisis Julius Nyerere, president of Tanganyika, wrote to Kennedy to implore him to take new steps against Portugal and South Africa. At the end of May the heads of state and foreign ministers of Africa's newly independent countries met in Ethiopia at the invitation of Emperor Haile Selassie to form the Organization for African Unity (OAU). While the public agenda focused on the refusal of the Western powers to act decisively against Portugal and South Africa, many private conversations turned on the unfolding racial drama in the United States.

Pressure on Kennedy from inside and outside the United States rose in early June. Since the beginning of April there had been nearly eight hundred racial demonstrations in 186 American cities. In one demonstration, the student body president of North Carolina A&T, Jesse Jackson, led almost three hundred students in a protest in Greensboro, North Carolina. Throughout the nation nearly fifteen thousand people had been arrested. On June 11, when governor George Wallace of Alabama refused to heed a federal court order to admit two blacks to the University of Alabama, Kennedy took control of the Alabama national guard and placed the students under military protection.

That night the president went on national radio and television to explain his actions. Though the speech was thrown together in less than two hours, Kennedy delivered it with conviction and eloquence. "This nation was founded by men of many nations and backgrounds. It was founded on the principle that all men are created equal and the rights of every man are diminished when the rights of one man are threatened," he began. "Today we are committed to a worldwide struggle to promote and protect the rights of all who wish to be free, and when Americans are sent to Vietnam or to West Berlin, we do not ask for whites only. It ought to be possible, therefore, for American students of any color to attend any public institution they select without having to be backed up by troops. It ought to be possible for American consumers of any color to receive equal service in places of public accommodation, such as hotels and restaurants and theaters and retail stores, without being forced to resort to demonstrations in the street, and it ought to be possible for American citizens of any color to register and to vote in a free election without interference or fear of reprisal. . . . But this is not the case."

Kennedy then laid out the crippling barriers facing American blacks in education, voting, housing, medical care, and employment. He dismissed the contention that he was reviving the sectional feud of the Civil War, noting that discrimination existed in the North as well as the South. "We are confronted primarily with a moral issue," said the president. "It is as old as the scriptures and as clear as the American Constitution." In terms reminiscent of King's letter written in the Birmingham jail, Kennedy argued that blacks had been waiting long enough, a full century in fact, for the freedoms promised in Abraham Lincoln's Emancipation Proclamation. Like King, the president also drew the attention of his listeners to the international consequences of the American civil rights struggle. "We preach freedom around the world, and we mean it, and we cherish our freedom here at home, but are we to say to the world, and more importantly, to each other, that this is a land of the free except for the Negroes; that we have no second-class citizens except Negroes; that we have no class or caste system, no ghettos, no master race except with respect to Negroes?

"Now the time has come for this nation to fulfill its promise," Kennedy told his audience. "The events in Birmingham and elsewhere have so increased the cries for equality that no city or state or legislative body can prudently choose to ignore them." Running out of prepared text, Kennedy concluded with a list of legal remedies he would request of Congress and an awkward final appeal for support from all American citizens. King, watching the speech in Atlanta, instantly wrote to Kennedy, praising his speech as "one of the most eloquent profound and unequivocal pleas for Justice and the Freedom of all men ever made by a President. You spoke passionately to the moral issues involved in the integration struggle." Other civil rights leaders around the country felt a similar surge of gratitude and hope. Their enthusiasm was soon snapped when they learned that on the same evening as the president's speech, Medgar Evars, the director of the NAACP in Jackson, Mississippi, had been shot and killed in front of his own home by a white assassin.

Diplomats scattered around the world reported to the White House that the speech had helped them counter growing anti-American sentiment. To assist official American representatives, Dean Rusk forwarded to every embassy copies of the letter the president had sent to Congress in conjunction with his speech and attached lengthy instructions on how to deal with criticisms of American racial policy. "Foreign reaction is the source of great concern," Rusk wrote. "Evidence from all parts of the world indicates that racial incidents have produced extremely negative reactions." Rusk noted the State Department's concern that without a vigorous response "our racial problems will impinge even more seriously upon our policies and objectives." Rusk advised American diplomats to admit the seriousness of the racial problem, draw attention to the steps the government was taking, circulate the USIA film of Kennedy's speech, and generally accentuate the positive.

At the same time, Soapy Williams and Wayne Fredericks had to endure nearly continuous criticism in the press and in Congress from those who thought that African concerns were unimportant and that the United Nations was either so weak that it was irrelevant or so strong that it posed a threat to American sovereignty. In 1962 the attacks had come from powerful Democratic senators like majority leader Mike Mansfield and Henry M. "Scoop" Jackson, raising the possibility that the United States might not issue a hundred-million-dollar bond to keep the United Nations solvent. Without the bond, the institution might go under, taking with it the UN presence in the Congo and the centerpiece of Kennedy's Africa policy. In 1963 the complaints increased. Senator Ellender continued broadcasting his racist views on television and radio; Richard Nixon, while visiting Lisbon, commented that independence was "not necessarily the best thing for Africa or the Africans"; and a committee appointed by the president to defend his expanded foreign aid plans rejected Kennedy's own policy on the grounds that because Africa was not contiguous with the Communist bloc, it was not part of the "frontier of freedom" and did not deserve substantial American assistance.

To shore up their support, Williams and Fredericks brought their case directly to the president whenever they had the opportunity. At the end of May, after Kennedy had concluded a state visit with Ivory Coast President Félix Houphouet-Boigny, he turned to Williams and Fredericks in the Oval Office and said that he enjoyed such meetings. "I have a spot for one more state visit later this year and I think I would like it to be an African," Kennedy said. "Do you have any suggestions?" "Julius Nyerere," blurted out Fredericks. "Fine," said Kennedy. On the way back to the State Department, Williams looked at his colleague quizzically. The president of Tanganyika had already made a state visit to the United States. "I don't disagree with you," said Williams, "I just wonder why you were so sure." Fredericks explained that Nyerere would be the best person to persuade Kennedy of the deep repugnance among leaders of the new African nations for apartheid. Fredericks's nudge encouraged Kennedy to respond to Nyerere's recent plea for sanctions with an invitation to visit the White House in July.

As a former governor who knew how to exploit unanticipated public events to advance his causes, Williams tried to use the turbulence in Birmingham to overcome his bureaucratic opponents in the State Department. The day after Kennedy's speech on civil rights, Williams urgently wrote to Rusk. Citing the reaction of African leaders at the OAU conference in Addis Ababa, Williams told Rusk that "we must now take a more vigorous stand against apartheid. . . . We can no longer rest our case on a condemnation of apartheid. We must be ready to back our condemnation with some meaningful action." Implicitly tying his request to the president's appeal, he told Rusk that "we confront this African pressure for action at a time when powerful forces in our own society are demanding action on racial inequalities at home. The two forces are interrelated and . . . Africans are as aware of the inter-relationship as those who are opposing segregation in the United States." Noting that several countries intended to press the matter before the UN Security Council, Williams warned Rusk that "failure of the United States to take a stand . . . in the same forthcoming fashion as it had handled matters in Alabama and Mississippi would lead to unfortunate domestic, as well as international, repercussions." Williams had a specific recommendation. Since the partial arms embargo was widely viewed as ineffective and hypocritical, he argued, the United States should, if it was not yet willing to support economic sanctions, at least consider a complete arms boycott against South Africa.

Williams's letter brought an immediate shout of protest from the Europeanist branch of the State Department. Deputy Undersecretary U. Alexis Johnson fired off a sharp rebuttal. "South Africa continues to be friendly and cooperative with us in a wide range of defense matters . . . all of which are important to our missile development and to the position of our Navy and Air Force in the South Atlantic and Indian Oceans," wrote Johnson. He reminded Rusk that Kennedy had approved the sale of three submarines to South Africa only three months before and told him that if the United States implemented an arms embargo, it would not satisfy the Africans and "might well lose us whatever advantages exist in our present relationship with South Africa without materially affecting its policy on apartheid."

Faced with such a sharp conflict between two of his most senior officials, Rusk felt compelled to reply immediately. On June 15, 1963, in a memo circulated to all the parties, he formally rebuked Williams. "At the heart of issue is how we relate ourselves to those countries whose internal arrangements and practices are not only foreign to our way of thinking but, in many cases, repugnant to us. . . . We have the strongest objections to apartheid in the Union *[sic]* of South Africa; we have said so repeatedly and have asserted our view to the point where our relations with the Union of South Africa are in a continuing state of tension," Rusk wrote. "But I believe that it is worth reminding ourselves that there are other states where obnoxious practices of one sort or another exist. . . . The question is whether we ourselves precipitate sharp crises in our relations with other states over such issues," lectured Rusk, "or whether we try to maintain the structure of international relations in order to be able to work doggedly and persistently toward the decent world community which is our main objective." Apartheid was bad, he said, but "I would not put it ahead of the violations of human rights within the Communist bloc." Responding directly to Williams's allusion to Birmingham, Rusk insisted that there was "a sharp distinction between our deep concern about racial discrimination in the United States and the way we crusade on that issue outside the United States. The United States is *our* responsibility; our failures are *our* failures; we live under a constitutional system in which *we* can do something about it. But no one has elected us to undertake such responsibilities in other countries. The President has reminded us that we are not interested in a Pax Americana. . . . We are not the self-elected gendarmes for the political problems of other states."

Rusk then strongly endorsed the prevailing policy. Overlooking or unaware of the Nationalists' attitudes before they came to power, Rusk cited South Africa's loyalty in both world wars and its vital role as "part of a total confrontation affecting the life and death of our own nation." Before considering sanctions, he insisted, the United States would have to establish priorities and identify those countries and practices that offended the most. Until then, he would approve only "the most intensive study of apartheid." A few days later, in another attempt to build consensus, Rusk assembled a committee of representatives from the White House, Defense Department, Central Intelligence Agency, Agency for International Development, United States Information Agency, and the different contending parts of the State Department. To placate Williams, Rusk asked him to assume the chairmanship of the committee. The secretary of state also asked Walt Rostow in the Policy Planning Bureau to begin yet another comprehensive review of American policy.

At the same time as Rusk was trying to assuage tempers abroad and calm dissension at home, he faced another problem so potentially explosive that its resolution required the personal involvement of the president. On June 3, as violence rippled through American cities, the secretary of state received a cable from Adlai Stevenson informing him that Martin Luther King had requested an appearance before the United

Nations Special Committee on Apartheid. The committee, formed the previous fall, had spent the winter asking the nations of the world to spell out how each would implement the international body's limited sanctions against South Africa. Beginning in May, the members of the committee had begun three months of hearings on white minority rule in southern Africa.

Rusk feared that an appearance by King would conjoin American domestic and foreign policies toward race as they had never been before. If the nation's leading civil rights activist, only a few weeks after his release from American jails, testified before the international body, he would forge in the minds of the international community the very link between Alabama and Pretoria that Rusk had rejected in his memo to Williams. The consequences would be bad enough if King, in offering his observations about South Africa, seemed to be criticizing American policy toward South Africa; this would, at the very least, offer African leaders new leverage over Kennedy. The consequences would be far worse if King were seen to be asking the United Nations for assistance. If the international press portrayed King as another Albert Luthuli, appealing for international intervention in a internal battle for equality, then the Kremlin's relentless criticism of American racism at home and abroad would gain ground and the hapless two-pronged policy toward southern Africa would collapse.

Rusk, on learning that King's appearance had been scheduled for June 28, instructed Ambassador Stevenson to work behind the scenes to manipulate the event. Stevenson persuaded the acting chairman of the UN special committee, the ambassador from Costa Rica, to ask the individual members of the committee to avoid any questions about the United States. As the date approached, Rusk's concerns rose. When he learned that the president would be meeting with King, Rusk wrote directly to Kennedy, telling him that King's appearance would be highly damaging and urging him to ask King not to go. "Certainly both the Special Committee and his constituency in this country would understand," wrote Rusk, "if he were to back out by pleading the pressure of other duties in connection with the domestic civil rights problem."

King came to the White House on June 22 for a meeting with the president and the top civil rights leaders in the Cabinet Room to discuss the leaders' intentions to organize a massive march on Washington in August to press for new legislation. When King arrived, the president's staff ushered him into the Oval Office, where Kennedy greeted King and asked him to go for a private stroll in the Rose Garden. The appearance at the United Nations was not the only matter on Kennedy's mind. Kennedy had also been receiving a stream of reports from J. Edgar Hoover at the FBI that identified two white associates of King, Jack

O'Dell and Stanley Levison, as Communists. This was not news to King, who knew that for two white men to work so closely with a black organization, they had to hold beliefs that the majority of the white community would view as subversive. Kennedy, however, insisted that as long as the two men worked for King, Kennedy's legislation and the entire civil rights effort were in jeopardy and that, therefore, King would have to fire them. King asked for evidence of the charges and Kennedy promised that it would be provided.

There is no documentary record of whether Kennedy also asked King to withdraw from the United Nations hearings, since the two men spoke alone and neither lived long enough to write a memoir. The circumstantial evidence, however, strongly suggests that Kennedy repeated Rusk's concerns to King. The focus of their conversation that day was on the ways in which King's actions could hurt or help the impending battle in Congress. In Kennedy's political calculations, a request by King for help from the United Nations just as the matter came before the American legislature would smack of a disloyalty as profound as that implied by the association with O'Dell and Levison. Remembering that Kennedy had just gone on national television and tied his political future to civil rights, knowing that the planned march on Washington might cause Kennedy more problems, and wanting to resist Kennedy's demand to dismiss O'Dell and Levison, King was surely looking for something to which he could assent. King entered the White House intending to appear before the United Nations; a few days after his meeting with Kennedy, King abruptly told the special committee that his schedule would not permit him to appear after all.

Kennedy left his meeting with the civil rights leaders to fly to Europe, where he visited the Berlin Wall and delivered his famous "Ich Bin Ein Berliner" speech to the thunderous applause of hundreds of thousands of West Germans. Newspaper editors and television commentators criticized the president's decision to leave the United States during the continuing civil rights turmoil to tour European countries, chat with the pope and miscellaneous heads of states, and visit his family's ancestral home in Ireland. In private, Kennedy predicted that the trip would divert American attention away from race. Kennedy's instincts proved accurate, but only for a short time. When he returned, he faced a new showdown in the United Nations.

Adlai Stevenson laid out the problem in a letter to Kennedy written on June 26. "When the African states bring apartheid and the Portuguese territories before the Security Council starting about July 22, the United States will be under direct fire for the first time," wrote Stevenson. African patience for American indecision had worn thin, he continued, and African leaders now wanted to know whether "we will stand for self-determination and human rights and, therefore, for the mind of Africa, or whether we will give our Azores base and the tracking stations in South Africa priority. Obviously, we want to avoid such a showdown . . . but the Africans have the capability, and I believe the intention, of posing the problem in such a way that important risks will have to be assumed one way or another." Stevenson urged Kennedy to favor the future relations with the people of Africa. America's positive position on the newly independent continent could quickly be reversed by a misstep on "these extremely emotional questions, compounded as they are by our own problems." Stevenson predicted that Kennedy, faced with objections from Western allies, from the Defense Department, and from Congress, would find the decision difficult. "To lose the Azores base . . . may appear to some in Congress and the country like a hard bargain for the uncertain advantage of goodwill in Africa," Stevenson concluded.

Upon his return from Europe, Kennedy ordered his staff to send him information to help him decide. At the Pentagon the heads of the armed services weighed the relative merits of American bases throughout Africa and a junior official named Harold Brown, who would later serve as Secretary of Defense under Jimmy Carter, pondered the value of the tracking stations. White House aide Carl Kaysen collected the exchange of letters among Williams, Johnson, and Rusk and gave them to Kennedy to read. National Security Council staff member Samuel Belk, at the president's request, gathered data on investment and trade with South Africa, authorization of weapons sales, and dependence on strategic metals. Belk also commissioned reports on African reactions to events in the United States. The reports said that most American ambassadors had received an understanding response from African officials; one official wrote that black Africans "were elated over President Kennedy's stance on civil rights, in part because it would now be more difficult for the president to adopt a different standard toward South Africa." Soapy Williams and Wayne Fredericks prepared for Julius Nyerere's visit, hoping that the African leader would tip Kennedy toward stronger action.

American officials also probed the South African and Portuguese governments to find out whether there was any new flexibility. In most cases, they found continued recalcitrance. When Joseph Satterthwaite had paid a courtesy call on Albert Luthuli in May, Verwoerd had sent word that he was strongly displeased. That same month, Satterthwaite had written to Rusk to ask whether the United States should go forward with a multiracial reception on the Fourth of July in light of Verwoerd's fierce opposition, the government law prohibiting serving alcohol to Africans, and the possibility that "non-white guests . . . will be known

to the South African government and might suffer recriminations."
Rusk ruled that the reception should be held, though most of the executives of American companies, despite appeals to their patriotism, refused to attend in order to avoid offending the government.

As the deadline for a decision approached, the recommendations from the different branches of government trickled in. The Joint Chiefs of Staff sat on the fence, writing that while "the US requirements in the Azores are of primary strategic importance," American bases in Ethiopia, Libya, and Morocco were also "of major importance." While America must "deny the African continent to the Sino-Soviet bloc," said the chiefs, "the government must also resist the weakening of NATO through the implementation of measures against Portugal." On South Africa, they expressed the empty opinion that any resolution should be examined on the merits and "harsh and irresponsible castigations" should be avoided. Secretary of Defense Robert McNamara commented in a cover letter to Dean Rusk that unlike the Azores base, the tracking stations in South Africa were "not vital." "We recommend that the United States clearly state its strong objections to apartheid in the Union [sic] of South Africa and its criticism of the policies of Portugal in the Portuguese territories," wrote McNamara. "However, I hope it will be possible to avoid a vote in the United Nations in favor of economic sanctions, arms embargo, or expulsion in the cases of Portugal and South Africa."

The task of pulling the views together into memoranda for the president fell to Undersecretary of State George Ball, who delivered his analysis and recommendations to Kennedy on July 13. After reviewing the situation, Ball told the president that he would have to do something, though Ball counseled against approving a trade embargo or restrictions on investment, because such actions would "establish a precedent that economic and political sanctions could be voted against a country on the ground that its internal policies are wanting or threatening to create problems of international peace and security." It might be extremely difficult to hold the United Nations to a partial arms embargo, Ball argued, and American support of a total UN arms embargo would definitely lead to the loss of all American military facilities.

In a conversation the day before, Kennedy had asked Ball to consider a new stroke. What if the United States, rather than fighting a long battle in the United Nations, suddenly announced a unilateral decision that it would no longer sell weapons to South Africa after the first of the year, as long as apartheid was still in place? Kennedy knew that the cost of this position would be low for both South Africa and the United States. Samuel Belk had collected data showing that less than a million dollars in sales—including revolvers, parachutes, radar, and small aircraft—had been authorized in the first ten months of 1962, though the Defense Department had predicted future South African purchases of up to $75 million a year. Ball, after conferring with Rusk and others, wrote the president that his idea was highly promising. The Africans would be pleased by the apparent tightening of American policy, and the South Africans might still be persuaded to go ahead with the tracking stations. The submarine sales, which could total as much as $120 million, were still in the earliest stages of planning, he wrote, and might not have gone through anyway.

Though Bundy attached a brief memorandum stating that a total loss of the tracking stations would cost only about $50 million and that he was in favor of "the Black African position," Kennedy spent several days pondering and testing the idea of a unilateral arms embargo by the United States. On July 15, he held his state meeting with Julius Nyerere, who again pressed him to take some action against the violent suppression of freedom across southern Africa. During such conversations Kennedy realized that in addition to mollifying African opinion on South Africa, the arms policy could be used to screen a more passive approach toward Portugal. To prepare the South African government, Kennedy instructed Rusk to meet with South African Ambassador W. C. Naudé to inform him of an imminent change in American direction.

Rusk did so on July 17. The South African ambassador, deeply stung, commented on the irony that the United States and South Africa had fought on the same side in the Korean War a decade before and that now South Africa was to be denied arms. Naudé told the secretary of state that the eventual goal of apartheid was the disappearance of all forms of discrimination but that the country needed time. Until then, South Africa required the same help the United States was giving to Israel, since it too was "a little nation which needed support for its survival."

That night at a press conference President Kennedy was asked about the challenge to American policy in the Security Council, which was to begin the next day. Kennedy replied that the United States was opposed to the expulsion of South Africa or any other nation on the grounds that it would set a bad precedent and undermine the functioning of the international body. The next day, July 18, Kennedy convened a final discussion of the matter at the White House with Rusk, Ball, Stevenson, and others. Kennedy told the group that his main priority was Senate ratification of the nuclear test ban treaty, which was being negotiated at that moment by Averell Harriman in Moscow. If the United States pushed Portugal too hard, it might lose the Azores base, which in turn would split NATO, enrage Congress, and jeopardize the treaty. Why should the United States take the lead in pressing for a UN resolution?

Kennedy asked. What if we were instead to hang back and let nature take its course? Then the Portuguese government would have to confront the ire of the Africans directly. The president turned to Stevenson and asked him what the French would do during the debate. Stevenson told him that, as usual, the French would seek the best of both worlds. "Well," said Kennedy, "let us try that this time." To compensate for inaction on Portugal, he concluded, he would proceed with the unilateral American arms embargo against South Africa.

When George Ball wrote a follow-up memo detailing the steps that would have to be taken to implement Kennedy's decision, the president instructed Bundy to respond. "Our discussion with the South Africans should be in the context of our conviction that the course we are adopting represents the minimum changes necessary if we are to be able to assist in preventing much less satisfactory results, from South Africa's own point of view," Bundy told Ball. "It should be emphasized that we intend to oppose [sanctions] and that our own suspension of arms shipments will not be of critical importance to South Africa since we are not a prime source for South Africa in this field at present. . . . The President wishes it made clear," Bundy concluded, "that in our judgment it would be best for both sides to maintain our existing cooperation in other fields."

Stevenson made the announcement at a meeting of the UN Security Council on August 2. "We expect to bring to an end the sale of military equipment to the Government of South Africa by the end of this calendar year," Stevenson declared dramatically, adding that the ban did not cover "existing contracts." He went on to reintroduce, at least implicitly, the distinction between internal and external threats that the new policy had supposedly eliminated. "The United States . . . reserves the right to interpret this policy in the light of future requirements for assuring the maintenance of international peace and security," he told the delegates. "If the interests of the world community require the provision of equipment for use in the common defense effort, we would naturally feel able to do so without violating the spirit and intent of this resolution." Groping back to the high ground, Stevenson concluded that the United States was "taking this step to indicate the deep concern which the Government of the United States feels at the failure of the Republic of South Africa to abandon its policy of apartheid."

The ploy worked. The *New York Times* reported the American action with great fanfare. Great Britain, trying to climb on the bandwagon, adopted the American policy and announced that it would now refuse to sell weapons to enforce apartheid. The African delegates publicly welcomed the change in U.S. policy. Believing he had gained some time, Kennedy continued to probe Portugal and South Africa for concessions.

He sent George Ball to Lisbon to meet with Prime Minister Salazar, who told the American envoy that he did not understand why the United States wanted to interfere with Portugal's "civilizing mission."

Rusk made his own attempt with the South Africans. After their meeting on July 17 the South African ambassador had asked for an additional chance to explain Verwoerd's long-range plans. Rusk agreed and met with Naudé again on July 20. Their conversation, recorded in detail in an aide-mémoire, reveals not only the finesse of South Africa's diplomatic arguments but also a growing willingness by the American government to acquiesce in the logic of separate development. Naudé began by trying to ingratiate himself with Rusk, noting that the two of them had both risen "to the heights" from humble beginnings. From there Naudé moved quickly to his central complaint: separate development had been misunderstood. The world had arrived at a point of regarding all discrimination as bad, said the ambassador, yet everyone still believed in discrimination between men and women. Discrimination in South Africa, he continued, was never meant to oppress the black man; the aim was that he should be enabled to be himself.

Playing subtly on African nationalist themes, Naudé stressed that the aim of Verwoerd's policy was to preserve the black group. Rusk stopped him to ask what, in his opinion, was essentially to be preserved in the black group. Naudé responded that it was the distinctive African personality, the sort of thing Kwame Nkrumah of Ghana talked about. Verwoerd believed that if a black man in South Africa wanted to be a Zulu, let him be a Zulu. This was the essential difference with the racial problem in the United States, said Naudé. In American, the Negro was different because he had lost his African character, except, possibly, for music.

In his presentation Naudé unleashed a barrage of self-serving historical errors that Rusk did not challenge. When his ancestors arrived in South Africa, he said, the nearest blacks were six hundred miles away. Most of South Africa was empty because of Shaka's wars in the early nineteenth century, and "since the whites had occupied empty territory, they had a moral right" to the land. Moreover, earlier in this century the population of South Africa had been almost evenly divided, half white and half black. South African blacks had always lived in tightly defined, highly separatist ethnic communities, "as different as the Finns and the Greeks," and preferred to be ruled by tribal chiefs. The South African government's only desire was to help blacks to stand on their own two feet, and Verwoerd had assisted them by ousting the missionaries and giving blacks the chance to control their own schools through the Bantu Education Act.

When Rusk interrupted Naudé to ask about a timetable for the creation of the new black states he had heard about, Naudé craftily replied that it was hard to say, about as hard as it would be to predict when integration would be achieved in the United States. After listening for a while longer, Rusk stopped Naudé and said that he wanted to ask him a question not as the secretary of state but as an individual. If there were ever any mention of his having brought it up, Rusk cautioned, he would deny it. In political matters, he said, sometimes a broad, breathtaking, imaginative approach had more chance than a creeping, timid one. Suppose one took all of southern Africa—the territories, protectorates, proposed bantustans, and sovereign countries—and redrew the boundaries to create six or eight largely black states and two or three white ones? Suppose these states then joined in a confederation whose central authority would care only about external defense? White and blacks living in each other's states would be resident aliens without rights of participation as citizens.

Naudé could scarcely believe his ears, exclaiming that Rusk had "precisely, almost word for word, expressed the intent of the South African government." Rusk, encouraged, told Naudé that he had studied many different forms of constitution in use in the British Commonwealth and had been impressed how they had been devised to prevent one group from swamping another. If the whites were interested only in preserving themselves as a group, and not in domination, then such an arrangement could surely be devised. Naudé happily agreed. The South African program of developing independent states, the ambassador said, was a revolutionary idea, not a preservation of the status quo. But speaking as the ambassador from South Africa, Naudé warned that such a scheme would have no chance if there was any sort of pressure exerted on South Africa. He agreed with Clarence Randall, the American businessman who had led the president's delegation to Ghana, that voices should be muted about the South African problem. Quieting the debate, said Naudé, was his main goal in Washington. Any small nation in South Africa's situation, alone in Africa, could react in only one way to outside pressure, by resistance. Rusk commented that the world was full of pressures and that the United States was helping to alleviate some of them for South Africa by blocking mandatory sanctions.

Rusk, apparently eager to persuade Naudé that American actions toward South Africa had little to do with civil rights, concluded the meeting by telling the ambassador that the United States was not sentimental about his country. The United States faced a global challenge, he said, deployed a million men in uniform outside its boundaries, and sustained casualties every week. The nation would thus weigh its relationship to South Africa coldly in its own national interest. The United

States was not approaching the matter in a gay mood for the fun of it, he said.

Rusk's interest in partitioning southern Africa into independent states had not sprung into his mind at the moment. Many within the State Department and beyond believed that the traditional formula of one-man, one-vote would never work in South Africa. Ambassador Satterthwaite reported from private conversations with opposition parties that even most liberal whites did not support such a scheme. Adlai Stevenson himself had speculated at times whether the solution to South Africa's problems would require division, as it had in India with the creation of Pakistan. In his conversations with Naudé, Rusk, in keeping with Kennedy's instructions, was trying to paint the arms embargo as a relatively unimportant measure designed to block more serious efforts. The talk of partition was intended, at least in part, to coax some movement out of the South African government. To Naudé, however, it could only have appeared as a private American endorsement of separate development.

Having planted the seed, Rusk and his subordinates waited to see if any initiative would sprout in Pretoria. Within a month they believed they had spotted one. On August 27, Hendrik Verwoerd delivered a major speech in Durban in which he denounced Western pressure for South African concessions. Any lessening of apartheid would only create momentum toward integration, he declared, which would be equivalent to suicide. Only if the Western powers would provide an absolute, ironclad guarantee against future pressures would South Africa even consider any compromise. Because the West could not and would not provide such guarantees, Verwoerd concluded, South Africa had no choice but to stand firm. Besides, said Verwoerd, perhaps thinking of Naudé's conversations with Rusk, "we know that there is far more understanding and sympathy overseas than what many of these nations will admit publicly. We know that there is an increasing conviction abroad of our honorableness and purposefulness."

Verwoerd's Durban speech set off an enthusiastic ripple through the American government. For some, the excitement was enhanced by Verwoerd's announcement a week later that he would be happy to see South Africa take control of the British protectorates of Bechuanaland, Swaziland, and Basutoland to guide them into becoming independent black nations in confederation with South Africa. This seemed, on the face of it, close to what Rusk had proposed to Naudé. Analysts in the Central Intelligence Agency, after reviewing the speech in Durban, got carried away and described it as "a new bid for Western support." Walt Rostow's Policy Planning Bureau, which had been laboring with the African Bureau of the State Department since May to draft another analysis of South African policy, seized on the opening and proposed that the United States, Great Britain, and other countries guarantee to protect the lives of South African nationals from external invasion and to ensure the preservation of the rights of all groups in return for the dismantling of apartheid. Verwoerd's speech strengthened the conviction of those in government who believed that a policy of mild public criticism combined with private cooperation would coax Verwoerd into easing apartheid; in other words, they felt that the two-pronged policy was paying off.

Verwoerd chose the same period to renew his private bid to buy American military equipment. On August 28, the day after Verwoerd's speech, George Ball sent a memorandum to the president asking him to decide what the government should do about the sale of the submarines and about the contract to supply approximately one million dollars a year in spare parts for seven C-130 transport planes sold to South Africa by Lockheed in 1961. Ball noted that the agreement to establish the tracking station in 1962 had included a promise by the United States to give "sympathetic attention" to such requests. At the same time, he cautioned, a decision to sell the equipment might produce serious fall-out in the Security Council. Ball told Kennedy that the South African press had been echoing the Nationalist line that nothing had really changed in U.S. policy toward South Africa. A military sale at this point, he wrote, would confirm this view and undercut whatever sobering influence the arms embargo was having. Ball recommended that the United States proceed with the sale of the airplane parts, because they had been agreed to two years before, and defer the submarine decision until the new year.

When Kennedy learned that the Department of Defense strongly favored selling the submarines as soon as possible, he put Ball's memorandum aside and asked Rusk and McNamara to tell him whether it would be possible to stall the sale until after the fall session of the United Nations General Assembly. Because Kennedy had worried for more than a year about the deterioration of America's balance of payments and its steady drain on the national gold reserves, he also asked Rusk and McNamara to explore the impact of the submarines sales on the trade deficit. Meanwhile, Adlai Stevenson, who had heard about the proposal, fired off an angry protest to Rusk from New York. "To enter now into new contracts even for such strategic materials as submarines would in the eyes of the world directly controvert our announced policy," he argued. "It would put in question the sincerity of our public utterances and the sincerity of our opposition to apartheid. Our influence would accordingly suffer, not only in the eyes of the African nations but in the eyes of other nations as well. I don't believe we should risk these consequences and loss of respect for our good faith."

On September 16, the two secretaries sent over a memorandum reflecting their consensus. The balance of payments benefit, they told Kennedy, would depend on whether South Africa settled in cash, paid in installments, or received a loan from the United States. With regard to stalling, both men believed that the South Africans deserved some sort of answer soon; otherwise, they would likely interpret American silence as a refusal and purchase the submarines from someone else. Moreover, Foreign Minister Louw had recently threatened that because of their new positions the United States and Great Britain might lose the use of the naval facilities at Simonstown. The secretaries offered Kennedy two choices: either to tell the South Africans that the sale was deferred for the time being or to enter into secret negotiations with the South African government with the clear understanding that no decision could be reached until after the end of the year. Rusk indicated no preference; McNamara told the president he wanted to go ahead with the negotiations. In a separate memo, National Security Council staff member William Brubeck repeated Stevenson's fears that a decision to sell would reinforce South African beliefs that the arms embargo was an empty gesture and would be politically embarrassing at the United Nations. Kennedy again hesitated and decided to call in the two secretaries for a discussion. On September 23, he finally decided to go ahead with both the sale of the C-130 parts and the discussions with the South Africans. McGeorge Bundy told the secretaries that the president wanted it "made clear to the South Africans that any informal discussions held during the balance of this year are to be strictly confidential and involve no implied commitment to sell." Moreover, said Bundy, "the US can make no decision before the end of the year regarding sales and any eventual decision will be taken in the light of circumstances at the time."

Having made the decision, the various leaders of the American government turned to a consideration of how to respond to the renewed challenges from African countries in the fall sessions of the United Nations. On the one side, Stevenson, Williams, and others warned the president that the Africans would raise the issue of South Africa and Portugal in every general and special session of the United Nations and that there was danger that the "imminent threat to U.S. leadership in the United Nations and throughout Africa posed by [these] problems . . . [will] be underestimated. Rightly or wrongly, the African nations ascribe predominant importance to the U.S. role in the satisfactory resolution of these problems."

On November 6, Dean Rusk told the president that the United States should hold its course and continue to oppose mandatory sanctions, though he urged Kennedy to expand the arms embargo to include machines used for manufacturing weapons. The next day, Kennedy wrote back that he accepted Rusk's approach. "Having made a major concession in August, we cannot get in the position of having to make substantial changes every few months," said the president. "I think it is important, therefore, that in announcing our willingness to apply the arms embargo to 'materials for the production of military equipment,' we make it very clear that we regard this as merely part of the position we voluntarily took in August and that the August resolution should be given a more reasonable further term to do its work."

As the fall neared an end, Kennedy knew that he could not defer the choice between the African and the South African positions forever. In late October Walt Rostow sent over an intermediate draft of his new South Africa study with the advice that Kennedy take a close look at the recommendations for a Western guarantee in response to Verwoerd's presumed overtures. On Tuesday, November 19, William Brubeck told Kennedy that the navy had persuaded its American supplier to design a smaller, cheaper submarine to suit South Africa's needs; this brought the price down from nearly $100 million to about $38 million and lessened the advantage to the American trade deficit. At the same time, the South Africans had now asked if they could buy a $40 million air defense system for the Simonstown base. "Given its political difficulties and its sharply reduced balance of payments value, should we continue to explore the submarine sale?" Brubeck asked the president. "Or should we not only continue the submarine talks, but also entertain some additional South African requests such as the Simonstown air defense system?" Kennedy never had the chance to answer Brubeck's questions. On Thursday, he left for the first campaign swing of the 1964 presidential election and on Friday the mind that was weighing the decision was shattered by a high-speed rifle bullet in Dallas.

FOUR

The Varieties of Dissent (1964–1966)

I consider myself neither legally nor morally bound to obey laws made by a parliament in which I have no representation.
—NELSON MANDELA

AROUND THE WORLD President Kennedy's murder struck with elemental force. In Africa, thousands grieved at the loss of their new friend. African families posted photographs of the slain president in their public buildings and homes. Julius Nyerere stayed up all night to listen to news bulletins from Dallas. Top African officials flocked to the president's funeral in Washington, D.C. As with all martyrs, Kennedy's failings were swiftly forgotten and his virtues extolled, leaving most unaware that his policies toward Africa in general and South Africa in particular had often been nuanced to the point of contradiction. He had tried to steer a difficult course between the nation's loyalties to Europe and promises to Africa, between acceptable nationalism and repugnant Communism, between angry blacks and fearful whites. Struggling with racial upheavals in his own country, hamstrung by divisions within his own party, and engaged with a global adversary in a competition that risked the incineration of the earth, Kennedy can perhaps be pardoned for viewing Verwoerdian apartheid as secondary. Even when Kennedy focused on the African continent, there were many problems other than white supremacy in southern Africa to consider, such as the potential superpower conflict in the Congo, the politics of foreign aid, and the rising influence of the new African states in the United Nations. No domestic American constituency could compel Kennedy to act on South Africa. Moreover, like many at the time, Kennedy believed that the situation in South Africa could not endure. America did not need to intervene forcefully, he thought, because the tide of history would bring an end to white supremacy with the same swiftness and surety that had freed the African colonies at the end of the Eisenhower presidency.

The ambiguity of his position could be seen at the level of both people and policy. On the one hand, Kennedy raised Africa to a new level of attention in Washington; he installed activists like Soapy Williams and Wayne Fredericks to lead the charge; and he publicly acknowledged the link between the elimination of racial discrimination in the United States and abroad. On the other hand, his administration's "two-pronged" policy toward South Africa was riven with questionable assumptions. In the end, Kennedy tried to eat his cake and have it too, to construct a policy toward South Africa that was commendable in form but empty in substance. In doing so he set a pattern for American presidential dealings with southern Africa that endured with minor variations for the next generation. The pattern combined overt condemnation with covert cooperation, symbolic opposition with substantive support. As the years stretched into decades, America's public words and private deeds steadily slipped farther apart.

Lyndon Johnson, catapulted into the presidency by the assassination in Dallas, initially intended to keep all of Kennedy's advisers and policies in place until the nation had weathered the storm. By early 1964, however, Johnson had already made changes to fit his strategy and style. Unlike Kennedy, who preferred freewheeling debate and enigmatic relationships with his staff, Johnson preferred order, hierarchy, and consensus. While Kennedy viewed domestic politics as a prerequisite for operating on the international stage, Johnson saw it the opposite way, instinctively analyzing foreign policy matters in the light of their effects on domestic constituencies. In such a calculus, Ireland, Italy, and Israel all deserved special attention.

Johnson grasped the political significance of the mutual awareness of Africans and African Americans early on. Less than two months after taking office, he asked Martin Luther King, Roy Wilkins from the NAACP, and Whitney Young from the National Urban League to come to the White House to discuss his plan to launch a "war on poverty" and to promise them that the passage of new civil rights legislation would be the centerpiece of his immediate domestic agenda. He also spoke expansively about what American technology and economic assistance would be able to accomplish in Africa. Though his understanding of the continent was crude, the president, as a man who had grown up in the impoverished hills of east Texas, believed he understood the aspirations of the rural peoples of Africa.

In the spring of 1964 Johnson decided to streamline his administration to tackle a few major challenges, among them the civil rights bill, the growing conflict in Vietnam, and, most important, the presidential election that was less than six months away. The president sent word to his close advisers that "foreigners and foreign affairs were to do nothing, except, where possible, advance the Johnson electoral cause." As the election approached, senior officials in the State and Defense Departments were tapped to respond to archconservative Barry Goldwater's campaign charges. The White House gave control of foreign policy to the State Department, retaining oversight for a handful of major matters. In this atmosphere, the Africa Bureau's prominence rapidly wilted. Soapy Williams did not enjoy the same ties of respect and loyalty with Johnson that had guaranteed him access to Kennedy. Indeed, Johnson still resented Williams for leading the charge against his selection as vice president in 1960—nor had Johnson forgotten that Kennedy's early endorsement of Williams for the post of assistant secretary had been designed to placate party liberals irritated by the choice of Johnson. In addition, Williams had developed over the past three years a reputation as an activist assistant secretary, an irritant who continually tried to bring nettlesome issues like apartheid to the attention of busy superiors. In March 1964, acting on the belief that Williams should, like all other assistant secretaries, transmit his recommendations to the White House through the State Department, Johnson appointed Averell Harriman ambassador at large with special responsibilities for Africa.

Though most saw Harriman's appointment as a slap at Williams, it was the best possible outcome for an assistant secretary whose direct line to the Oval Office had just been severed. While Secretary of State Dean Rusk had little interest in Africa, Harriman believed that diplomatic relations with the new nations on the continent deserved care. With the help of Harriman and of several sympathetic staff members in the White House (including Johnson's press secretary, former Baptist clergyman Bill Moyers), Williams and Fredericks continued to press the Africanist cause. In March, Williams decided to deliver a fierce attack against apartheid in an address at Harvard Law School. When Rusk and Ball learned about Williams's intentions, they forced a reluctant Williams to deliver a bland endorsement of the current policy rather than the major foreign policy statement that he had planned. In April, however, Williams and Fredericks were able to shape an important presidential speech on Africa. "We began a revolt from colonial rule which is now reshaping continents," said Johnson. "Having helped create hopes, we must now help satisfy them or we will witness a rising discontent which may ultimately menace our own welfare." America intended to win the war on poverty both at home and abroad, the president continued, and "the world must not be divided into rich nations and poor nations, or white nations and colored nations. In such division are the seeds of terrible discord and danger in decades to come."

On the other side of the world, Hendrik Verwoerd was doing everything he could to prove that the world both could and should be divided by race. Segregation, the South African prime minister insisted, would bring not discord and danger but cooperation and peace. Though many came to believe him, there remained certain irreducible pockets—in the African community, in parliament, and in the churches —whose dissent he could never completely stifle. Though Nelson Mandela was in prison, most of the other ANC leaders and Umkhonto strategists were still loose. Even from inside his cell, Mandela's national and international influence had increased, in large part because of the trial that followed his arrest in 1962. The government had attempted to convict Mandela on two counts: inciting Africans to strike during the March 1961 protest against the republic and leaving South Africa in early 1962 without a valid travel document. On the first day of the proceedings in October 1962, Mandela had appeared in the old synagogue in Pretoria, now the state courthouse, wearing a traditional Xhosa leopard skin robe given to him by supporters. As he entered the room, the spectators and press instinctively rose to their feet. "Amandla!" he shouted—"Power!" "Ngawethu!" responded the crowd—"To the people!"

Informing the judge that he intended to conduct his own defense with the assistance of a legal colleague, Mandela immediately attacked the racism of the South African courts by asking the judge to recuse himself. "Why is it that this afternoon I face a white magistrate; I am confronted by a white prosecutor; and I am escorted into the dock by a white orderly?" Mandela asked. "Can anyone honestly and seriously suggest that in this type of atmosphere the scales of justice are equally balanced? Why is it that no African in the history of this country has ever had the honor of being tried by his own kith and kin, by his own flesh and blood?

"I feel oppressed by the atmosphere of white domination that lurks all around in the courtroom," Mandela continued. "It reminds me that I am voteless because there is a parliament in this country which is white controlled. I am without land because the white minority has taken a lion's share of my country and forced my people to occupy poverty-stricken reserves, overpopulated and overstocked, in which we are ravaged by starvation and disease."

The magistrate stopped Mandela. "What has that do to do with the case, Mr. Mandela?" he asked. "You must confine yourself to the application and not go beyond it. I don't want to know about starvation. That has got nothing to do with the case at the present moment."

"These courts are not impartial tribunals dispensing justice," Mandela responded, "but instruments used by the white man to punish those who clamor for deliverance from white rule. How should I be expected to believe that this same racial discrimination which has been the cause of so much injustice and suffering right through the years, should now operate to give me a fair trial?" Mandela granted that there were a few whites who approved of greater rights for Africans but said that they "had not succeeded in convincing the vast majority of the rest of the white population that white supremacy leads to danger and disaster. . . . I hate race discrimination most intensely and in all its manifestations," he said. "I have fought it all my life; I fight it now, and will do so until the end of my days. Although I now happen to be tried by one whose opinion I hold in high esteem, I detest most violently the set-up that surrounds me here. . . . I am a black man in a white man's court."

While the prosecutors struggled to keep the proceedings tightly focused on the charges, Mandela sought to broaden them into a debate on the legitimacy of apartheid. The government's attempt required them to reverse some of their earlier positions. Having formerly dismissed the efforts of the ANC as inconsequential, the government prosecutors now emphasized the organization's widespread and threatening influence. Having originally gone to great lengths to portray the 1961 general strike as a total failure, the government now painted it as major disruption for which Mandela was personally responsible.

Though Mandela had led the prosecutors to believe that he would respond with a massive defense, he stunned them by announcing that he would rest his case without calling a single witness. "Through my cross-examination and attempts to force the judge to recuse himself, I had made the statements I wanted about the unfairness of the court," he wrote later. "I saw no advantage in calling witnesses to try to disprove something that was incontrovertible." On October 25, 1962, the magistrate found Mandela guilty and informed him that he would have one more chance to address the court in a plea for mitigation. The next day when Mandela arrived in court the prosecutor came over and spoke to him privately. "For the first time in my career, I despise what I am doing," he told Mandela. "It hurts me that I should be asking the court to send you to prison."

Soon afterward Mandela stood before the judge. "It has not been easy for me to separate myself from my wife and children . . . and to take up the life of a man hunted continuously by the police, living separately from those closest to me, in my own country, facing continually the hazards of detection and arrest," Mandela said, glancing at Winnie, who sat stoically in the visitors' section. "But there comes a time, as it came in my life, when a man is denied the right to live a normal life, when he can only live the life of an outlaw because the government has so decreed to use the law to impose a state of outlawry upon him.

"History shows that penalties do not deter men when their conscience is aroused, nor will they deter my people or the colleagues with whom I have worked," Mandela continued. "More powerful than my fear of the dreadful conditions to which I might be subjected in prison is my hatred for the dreadful conditions to which my people are subjected outside prison throughout this country. . . . I hate the systematic inculcation of children with color prejudice and I am sustained in that hatred by the fact that the overwhelming majority of mankind, here and abroad, are with me in that," he said. "I hate the racial arrogance which decrees that the good things of life shall be retained as the exclusive right of a minority of the population, and which reduces the majority of the population to a position of subservience and inferiority and maintains them as voteless chattel to work where they are told and behave as they are told. Nothing this Court can do will change in any way that hatred in me, which can only be removed by the removal of injustice. . . . I have done my duty to my people and South Africa," Mandela concluded with quiet defiance. "I have no doubt that posterity will pronounce that I was innocent and that the criminals who should have been brought before this court were the members of the Verwoerd government."

Two weeks later the judge sentenced Mandela to five years in prison as the "leader, instigator, figurehead, main mouthpiece, and brains" behind the ANC strike. Since the prisoner had expressed no remorse and had vowed to continue his activities when freed, the judge said, the requirements of law and order demanded a lengthy incarceration. Mandela was immediately transported to Pretoria Local, a gloomy red-brick prison, where he was issued the standard prison uniform for Africans: a pair of short trousers, a rough khaki shirt, sandals, and a canvas jacket. When Mandela protested the shorts, the prison authorities tossed him into solitary confinement. "I had never been in isolation before," he recalled, "and every hour seemed like a year. . . . After a time in solitary, I relished the company even of the insects of my cell and found myself on the verge of initiating a conversation with a cockroach." Eventually Mandela gave in and told the prison warden that he would wear the shorts if he could have some company. Officials put him with the other political prisoners, including Robert Sobukwe, who was still in jail after his arrest on the day of the Sharpeville massacre more than two years before.

In May 1963 prison officials suddenly came to Mandela, shackled him to three other prisoners, and loaded them all into a van. After an all-night drive to the docks in Cape Town, Mandela and his fellow prisoners were placed in the hold of an aging wooden ferry, where the only light and air came from a small porthole through which the warders also occasionally urinated on the prisoners. After the ferry had left the dock the prisoners were allowed on deck to view their destination: a long, green strip of land eighteen miles out in Table Bay known as Robben Island. Over the centuries it had served as a place of banishment for early indigenous resisters, then as a leper colony, insane asylum, and World War II naval base. Only recently had the government built a new facility for political prisoners. There, guarded by legions of white police, separated from his country by the treacherous currents of the southern Atlantic, Mandela was locked inside a small concrete cell with a felt mat for a bed and a bucket for a toilet. His window looked out on a barren courtyard where he spent his days breaking rocks.

Mandela's imprisonment did not stem the acts of sabotage; in the six months following his incarceration they steadily increased. By the middle of 1963 more than two hundred attacks by Umkhonto We Sizwe, Poqo, and others had taken place. In March saboteurs managed to blow up the main railway line between Johannesburg and Durban. In response, Verwoerd and his minister of justice, John Vorster, placed scores of citizens under house arrest and pushed through parliament the so-called Ninety-Day Law, allowing the security police to detain people in solitary confinement without charges, hearings, or trial for up to ninety days. Even when the term was up, detention could be extended— "until this side of eternity," Vorster said—if prisoners did not give satisfactory answers to their interrogators. Freed from restraint, the security police turned to torture, using electric shock, near-suffocation, and savage beatings. It was not long before they went too far and killed a young ANC member from Cape Town. When the death brought no penalties, the police realized that inside the thick-walled prisons they could do whatever they liked.

Vorster, who had promised that he would give his police "the powers to check the forces of destruction," was determined to crush Umkhonto We Sizwe. In July 1963, just as John F. Kennedy was pondering how to respond to the UN Security Council's debate on South Africa, Vorster's forces discovered the precise location of Umkhonto's headquarters. Speeding out to the Lilliesleaf farm in dry cleaner trucks and bakery vans, they surrounded the main building and stormed it. As they rushed in, Walter Sisulu tried to leap through a window but was stopped by a snarling dog. Although the ANC planners always referred to the South African government as fascist, they had never acted as though it really was. The ANC had used the same safe house for years even though dozens knew of its existence. The farmhouse was crammed with incriminating documents, including maps, speeches, detailed plans, and even

Mandela's diary from his trip abroad. The police also found a radio transmitter and a cache of explosives. With the arrests, the government had decapitated the armed resistance of the ANC at a single stroke. The prisoners, including several whites and Indians, all disappeared into the abyss of ninety-day detention. Mandela was roused from his cell on Robben Island, whisked a thousand miles northeast, and jailed with his friends in Pretoria to await trial on new charges. The prisoners whiled away their time in the cells singing African freedom songs. When warders switched off the lights for the evening, a voice would shout "Amandla!" and the prisoners would respond "Ngawethu!"

The government's delight at the arrests could not be concealed. While the prosecutors refused to tell the defense attorneys exactly who had been arrested and what the charges were, officials of the Ministry of Justice crowed to the press about the prisoners' guilt. When the "Rivonia trials" began in October in a high-domed rococo room inside the Palace of Justice in Pretoria, the police jammed the seats and patrolled the doors and corridors with tear gas canisters and machine guns at the ready. They recorded the name and address of everyone who wanted to sit in the public gallery and they photographed everyone leaving the court.

The defense lawyers knew that the government prosecutors, still furious at having lost the Treason Trials, intended not only to convict but to hang the defendants. The head of the defense team, Bram Fischer, a brilliant attorney and Communist whose father had once served as the most senior judge in South Africa, started by attacking the government's indictment. The charges contained so many absurdities, he said, that they could not possibly serve as the basis for a trial. To Fischer's amazement, the judge agreed, quashed the indictments, and abruptly freed the prisoners. Before any of the startled defendants could move, Lieutenant Theunis Swanepoel instantly arrested them all anew on charges of sabotage.

In early December the trial on the new charges opened. The prosecutor, Dr. Percy Yutar, accused Mandela and the others of causing violent insurrections designed to lead to "armed invasion of the country by foreign military powers." Though government and other witnesses later testified that the defendants had instructed anyone planning acts of sabotage to avoid the loss of human life, Yutar repeatedly asserted that the defendants plotted the murder of innocents. Over the weeks of the trials, the government produced the booty from the raid on Lilliesleaf, including Umkhonto maps showing police stations, Bantu Administration buildings, and electric power facilities. They called 173 witnesses, including "Mr. X," a former ANC member named Bruno Mtolo. Mtolo, who appeared in court surrounded by white security police, said that he had agreed to appear as government witness because after joining the ANC he had come to believe that it was controlled by the Communist Party.

The defense team had a difficult job. The government turned over documents so late that the defense lawyers had to analyze thousands of pages in less than a month. The lawyers and defendants also had to cope with innumerable petty harassments and indignities imposed by the security police. The police would not permit the defense lawyers to consult with their clients in the courtroom or at lunchtime. The police also barred Winnie Mandela from attending the trial because she was under a banning order. Winnie appealed directly to Hendrik Verwoerd, who permitted her to attend on the condition that she not wear traditional African dress, as this might "cause an incident." There was considerable irony in this stipulation, since Verwoerd, who normally insisted that people remain faithful to their culture, was insisting that Winnie Mandela appear in *European* clothes. In another peculiar twist, Nelson Mandela requested books and documents in prison to prepare for his defense and included on his list Leo Tolstoy's *War and Peace,* which he had long wanted to read. The prison authorities refused to give it to him because they said he was not permitted to read Communist literature, especially not Communist literature about war.

The relentless pressure and the specter of the gallows took their toll on all the participants. The only hope seemed to be to persuade the judge that the defendants had never intended to lead a real guerrilla war against the government. On April 24, 1964, in the same month that Lyndon Johnson delivered his speech on Africa, Mandela rose in court to make a statement from the dock. For four hours he offered a tightly argued and passionate defense of Umkhonto We Sizwe, citing the complete lack of response of the government to all peaceful measures of protest. Quoting Albert Luthuli, who almost a decade before had concluded sadly that "thirty years of my life have been spent knocking in vain, patiently, moderately and modestly at a closed and barred door," Mandela led the court through a roll call of the ANC's nonviolent efforts. He argued that the only way the ANC could maintain control of the spiraling crisis, prevent civil war, and sustain its dream of racial equality was to institute its own program of sabotage designed to put material pressure on the government without killing people.

To the crucial charge that the ANC had plotted to conduct a war, Mandela responded that preparation for guerrilla warfare was necessary as a defense against the possibility that the government might use military force. To the government's attack that he was a Communist, Mandela responded coolly that this "old allegation" had been a central charge in the Treason Trials and had been conclusively rejected only a few years before. "There has often been close cooperation between the ANC and the Communist Party," he told the court, "but cooperation is merely proof of a common goal—in this case the removal of white supremacy—and is not proof of a complete community of interests." Mandela noted that even though the United States and Great Britain had assisted the Soviet Union during the Second World War, "nobody but Hitler would have dared to suggest that such cooperation turned Churchill or Roosevelt into Communists or Communist tools." When he had first joined the ANC he had feared that working with Communists would water down the commitment to African nationalism, but he had decided later that "theoretical differences amongst those fighting against oppression is a luxury we cannot afford at this stage." Besides, he said, "for many decades Communists were the only political group in South Africa who were prepared to treat Africans as human beings and their equals; who were prepared to eat with us, talk us, live with us and work with us. Because of this, there are many Africans who today tend to equate freedom with Communism. They are supported in this belief by a legislature which brands all exponents of democratic government and African freedom as Communists."

With regard to his own beliefs, said Mandela, "I have always regarded myself, in the first place as an African patriot. . . . I am attracted by the idea of a classless society, an idea which springs in part from Marxist readings and in part from my admiration of the structure and organization of early African societies in this country. The land, the main means of production, belonged to the tribe." He had been influenced by Marxism, he said, but so had Gandhi, Nehru, Nkrumah, and Nasser, all of whom were searching for a brand of democratic socialism that would raise their peoples from poverty. He had also admired and learned from other political institutions and traditions, from the Magna Carta to the Bill of Rights, from the British Parliament to the American Congress.

Mandela then led the court through a searing description of the contrast between South Africa's natural wealth and Africans' crushing deprivation. He recited statistics on overcrowding, malnutrition, disease, and the destruction of family life. He attacked the system of Bantu education, quoting Verwoerd's own words from the 1953 parliamentary debate that his intention was to reform the schools "so that Natives will be taught from childhood to realize that equality with Europeans is not for them." He challenged the industrial color bar, the government's refusal to permit collective bargaining, and the pass laws. The root of all of these restrictions was the elemental distortion of human relations caused by racism, for which the best antidote was democracy, he said: "We want equal political rights, because without them our disabilities will be permanent. I know this sounds revolutionary to the whites in this country, because the majority of the voters will be Africans. This makes the white man fear democracy. But this fear cannot be allowed to stand in the way of the only solution which will guarantee racial harmony and freedom for all."

Reaching the end of his text, Mandela looked up at Justice de Wet. The courtroom was silent. Mandela concluded quietly. "During my lifetime I have dedicated myself to this struggle of the African people," he said. "I have fought against white domination and I have fought against black domination. I have cherished the ideal of a democratic and free society in which all persons live together in harmony and with equal opportunities. It is an ideal which I hope to live for and to achieve. But if needs be, it is an ideal for which I am prepared to die."

Those were the last words Nelson Mandela spoke in public for more than a quarter of a century. Over the next few weeks his colleagues Govan Mbeki, Walter Sisulu, Lionel Bernstein, and others took the stand, defended their positions against Yutar's scornful cross-examination, and articulated their dreams for South Africa. Like Mandela, they did not dispute their roles. At the end, Yutar delivered a summation for the state that lasted four days. On Thursday, June 11, Justice de Wet summoned the defendants to announce his verdict. Mandela and the others had already conceded their participation in the formation of Umkhonto, he said briskly. He accepted their contention that they had not intended the loss of life but believed they should have anticipated that the effort might get out of hand. He thus found all of the defendants, with the exception of Lionel Bernstein, guilty. The sentence, he said, would be passed the next day.

The vigilant Lieutenant Swanepoel immediately rearrested Bernstein, and the other defendants were sent back to jail. That night the defense team visited the prisoners to discuss what Mandela would say if they were sentenced to death. Mandela said that he would tell the judge that if he thought a sentence of death would destroy the liberation movement, he was wrong. The lawyers told Mandela that such a statement would not assist an appeal; Mandela replied that he had no intention of filing one. The next day in court, Fischer produced two distinguished white South Africans to argue against the death penalty: Harold Hanson, a famous attorney, and Alan Paton, the novelist and president of the Liberal Party. When they finished, the judge spoke. The crime of which they had been convicted was in essence that of high treason, he said, but since the state had not charged them in this form, he had decided not to hang them. "The sentence in the case of all of the accused shall be life imprisonment," said de Wet. "Consistent with my duty that is the only leniency I can show." The police herded the prisoners into vans and drove them away; the crowd outside bravely shouted

"Amandla!" Mandela's mother walked dejectedly down the front steps of the courthouse; and Winnie Mandela took her two small daughters back to their little home in Soweto, put them in bed, and wept.

Around the world demonstrators assailed the Rivonia proceedings. In late May, in anticipation of the guilty verdict, thirty-two African nations called on the United States and Great Britain to press South Africa not to impose the death penalty. In early June eleven American civil rights demonstrators held a sit-in at the South African mission to the United Nations. In England forty-eight members of the British Parliament marched down Whitehall to protest the trial. After the sentences had been pronounced on the Rivonia defendants, new demonstrations broke out in England, France, Israel, and the United States. Albert Luthuli called on the Western powers to reconsider their opposition to sanctions. The *New York Times* commented that "to most of the world these men are heroes and freedom fighters. [They are] the George Washingtons and the Ben Franklins of South Africa. . . . The verdict of history will be that the ultimate guilty party is the government in power, and that already is the verdict of world opinion."

Verwoerd and Vorster were characteristically defiant. Vorster vowed to extend the ninety-day detention law, to crack down on violence, and to stifle all forms of revolutionary activity. On the day of Mandela's sentencing, Vorster ordered police and military units to take up positions along the entire forty-mile route from the Witwatersrand to Pretoria. The next day, despite Vorster's precautions, saboteurs blew up the front of a post office building. Verwoerd, for his part, reacted with anger to the objections of foreign governments. "The cables went straight into the wastebasket," he said, insisting that his government was "totally above pressure from anywhere." Those who had been found guilty were Communist criminals, he insisted; if they had succeeded in their plots, they would have established a "tyrannical Communist-orientated regime."

With Mandela, Sisulu, Mbeki, and the other Rivonia defendants safely imprisoned on Robben Island, Vorster turned his attention to crushing the remaining fragments of resistance. Dozens of others of all races were arrested, brought to trial in Pietermaritzburg and Cape Town, and jailed for lengthy terms. Hundreds disappeared into detention and languished for months in solitary confinement. African activists who eluded arrest slipped across the border and made their way north in an attempt to hook up with Oliver Tambo's growing external wing of the African National Congress. Scores of young white radicals, demoralized after a decade of fruitless battles, faced with the likelihood of imprisonment, left for England, Canada, and the United States to pursue new lives as doctors, lawyers, professors, and businesspeople. Some attached themselves to the anti-apartheid movements in Europe and North America, providing a vital link of knowledge and contacts with the dwindling resistance in South Africa. Inside the country, acting with unfettered brutality, Vorster's police slowly and systematically muted the most raucous opponents of apartheid.

As the months passed, Mandela and the other Rivonia defendants faded from public view. Vorster's repression and Verwoerd's bravado erased the sense of imminent collapse that had plagued the country since Sharpeville. As the nation's anxiety eased, the economy surged forward with astonishing power, growing annually by more than six percent to set the highest five-year rate in the country's history. Gold production and reserves soared, trade with Europe blossomed, and the gross national product expanded rapidly. As Verwoerd had predicted, the tide of investment capital that had ebbed so drastically for two years reversed course and flooded into the country. European and American companies sent boatloads of cash and equipment to establish positions in what everyone believed would be the economic powerhouse of Africa.

The United States, the home of the world's most successful international corporations of the time, poured hundreds of millions of dollars of new investment, both direct and indirect, into South Africa in this period. American direct investment doubled, from more than $475 million to nearly $1 billion by the end of the decade. In 1963 General Motors purchased 395 acres in Port Elizabeth to expand its auto assembly plant; when announcing the decision, a GM spokesman said that the company "has not given the racial situation any thought whatsoever, either in its short-term or its long-term planning." That same year, a huge American mining firm, Newmont Corporation, became a major partner in a $104 million copper mining project in the northern Transvaal. When asked about the desirability of such a project in August, just two weeks after the United States had announced the unilateral arms embargo, a Newmont executive told a *New York Times* reporter, "I'd rather invest in South Africa than in any other country in the world, except Canada."

Other American executives were equally enthusiastic about Verwoerd's leadership and South Africa's future. The managing director of Ford Motor Company's operations, the largest American employer in South Africa with more than fifty-five hundred employees, said that his company would expand and improve its manufacturing facility because of "the faith we have in South Africa." Shortly afterward, the chairman of the Norton Company of Worcester, Massachusetts, traveled to South Africa to open a new plant near Johannesburg. At the ceremony he explained his decision to build the plant by declaring, "I think South Africa is going to remain a strong country, led by white people." In February 1965, eight months after the Rivonia trials, the president of the Jeffrey Company, inaugurating a new factory in Germiston, a town ten miles southeast of Johannesburg, stated that he and his board of directors "have complete faith in the soundness of the South African economy, full confidence in the stability of the country, and know that the substantial investments that we have made in the past and further investments we are presently making are all in good care." Not long afterward Caltex erected an immense new refinery, and Weyerhaeuser completed its third new factory in less than four years.

Riding the wave of economic success, Verwoerd dismissed the talk of sanctions in the United Nations and, to cope with the mild restrictions of the arms embargo, moved aggressively to develop South Africa's domestic weapons industry. He laid the foundations to establish a new quasi-governmental corporation, ARMSCOR, and quickly erected a $28 million munitions plant to churn out firearms, artillery, and ammunition. He set the defense budget at $362 million for 1964–1965, far more than the country spent for military purposes at the height of World War II. He announced the construction of numerous military airfields around the country to support the squadrons of new supersonic Mirage III-C jet fighters that he had acquired from France. He arranged the purchase of a fleet of American Boeing 707s, which were intended for the civilian South African airline but which could quickly be shifted to troop transport duty. Working with the foreign automobile companies, particularly those from France and the United States, Verwoerd ordered an increase in the production of armored vehicles and personnel carriers. In 1965 Verwoerd established a new Nuclear Institute, designed to provide the oil-bereft nation with nuclear energy and, though it was not publicly admitted, nuclear weapons. He blamed the increasing militarization of South African society on the Western powers who had imposed the limited arms embargo. If he could not rely on the West to defend against the threat of armed Communist aggression, he told every audience, he would make sure that the whites of South Africa could do it themselves.

Verwoerd's apparent political and economic triumph sapped the already meager will of his parliamentary opposition. The United Party, after more than a decade of uninspired leadership, had continued its slow disintegration, losing seats in every major election. Large numbers of voters from two of the United Party's three traditional blocs—centrist business leaders and conservative rural *plattelanders* loyal to the memory of Jan Smuts—had defected to the Nationalists. When party leaders tried to regain the support of their conservative wing by attacking Verwoerd for giving away white land and by repudiating their traditional support of Coloured and African rights, they ignited a rebellion among the members of the third bloc, that of urban liberals, some of whom broke off to form the small Progressive Party in 1959.

Verwoerd, sensing the United Party's insecurities, masterfully controlled his parliamentary opposition by turning each major bill into a test of patriotism and machismo. Almost every time, United Party leader Sir de Villiers Graaff and his supporters took the bait. After the Sharpeville crisis, Graaff loudly endorsed the Unlawful Organizations Act, which banned the ANC and the PAC. After the march on Cape Town, he refused for nearly a month to use his parliamentary privilege to press the government to comment on the thousands of persons who had been jailed. When the Sabotage Act came before the Assembly in 1962, the opposition was silent until forced, under intense prodding by newspaper editorialists, to criticize the measure. After the Rivonia defendants were sentenced, Graaff told the press that he wished the defendants had been charged with treason and executed. This pattern of meek concession was so well known that after one government victory in parliament a Nationalist newspaper gloated that, as usual, "the United Party lay down like curs."

Of the hundreds of members who sat in the South African Assembly and Senate during the decade after Sharpeville, only one boldly challenged apartheid. Helen Gavronsky was born on November 7, 1917, in Germiston. Her father, Samuel, had emigrated from Lithuania and set up a large butchery and skin business. Samuel's wife, Frieda, died in an influenza epidemic two weeks after giving birth to Helen, so for the first half of their childhood Helen and her sister were raised by their mother's sister. Helen entered Parktown Convent School at the age of ten and, propelled by her exceptional mind, sped through high school and into college at the age of sixteen. She enrolled at the University of the Witwatersrand, studied for a bachelor of commerce, and in 1936, before she had finished, met and married thirty-three-year-old Moses Meyer Suzman, a Johannesburg physician.

Helen Suzman had grown to maturity and settled in an unusual political environment, that of Johannesburg's small Jewish community. Most of the older generation had fled from European persecution and felt gratitude to South Africa for offering them refuge. Though Jews were barred from certain schools, clubs, and jobs, there were few legislated restrictions. The older generation of immigrants wanted, for the most part, to build new lives and stay clear of the bruising struggle between the English and the Afrikaner. The next generations, however, felt less caution: born on South African soil, educated in English-speaking schools, exposed to other races and cultures in South African society, the children of the immigrants realized uncomfortably that their families had evaded prejudice based on religion by taking refuge in a country built on prejudice based on race. For whatever reasons—cultural tradition, higher education, or rebellious idealism—many young Jewish men and women veered toward political activism. Some became reforming liberals, like Suzman; others, romantic Trotskyites; still others, doctrinaire Communists. A few ended up in prison; others left the country; but only Suzman weathered the storm from inside the South African parliament.

Helen Suzman had not intended to pursue a career in electoral politics. In her first decade of marriage she had lived through World War II, given birth to two daughters, and returned to the university to complete a degree in economics and economic history. When a lectureship at the university opened up in 1944, the faculty hired her to fill it. In this post she expanded her research on the history of South Africa's migratory labor policies, prepared documents for the South African Institute of Race Relations, and honed her skills as a public speaker. After the Nationalist Party victory in 1948, she devoted herself increasingly to the revitalization of the United Party, especially among women. As more and more people heard her lucid monthly presentations to the United Party Women's Council, her reputation rose. In 1953 her supporters urged her to try to capture the United Party nomination from the incumbent, a snoozing absentee legislator. To her amazement, she succeeded. Her victory filled her with both exhilaration and distress, since the half-year parliamentary sessions in Cape Town would require her to leave her husband and young daughters behind in Johannesburg. As she left the meeting at which her victory had been confirmed, she told a friend, "My God! I have got a safe seat in my hot little hands, and I don't really want it."

Moses Suzman encouraged his wife to take on the challenge and traveled with her to the opening of parliament in July 1953. Helen looked up from her seat in the House chamber and was relieved to spot her husband squeezed into the wives' gallery, "a lonely little baldhead among all those nodding plumes." Though a junior backbencher, Suzman used her academic training to strike at the assumptions underlying apartheid. The poor white problem had been caused not by excess numbers of Africans, she insisted, but by the worldwide depression; it had been solved not by the industrial color bar but through economic growth. Apartheid was thus not the source of prosperity, as the government insisted, but its enemy. Racial restrictions could only reduce productivity, distort the allocation of resources, and prevent the development of a black consumer market, Suzman insisted. To deny these forces and their outcomes—such as massive African urbanization—would be to consign South Africa to a grim and impoverished future.

She reserved special scorn for Verwoerd, though she found his garrulous parliamentary performances so mesmerizing that she had to remind herself over and over that no matter how logical he sounded, his premises were false. She criticized his bantustan scheme as unworkable, primarily because more than two-thirds of all Africans would have to live outside their supposed homelands. "Strangely enough," she said in one speech, "people like to enjoy rights where they live, not where they do not live." As the United Party skidded steadily to the right, the conflict between Suzman's loyalty and liberalism grew until, in 1959, she joined an exodus of protesters who formed the Progressive Party. Freed from the shackles of United Party discipline, the protesters began to pester Verwoerd with renewed vigor. Verwoerd, irritated by the relentless questioning from the Progressives during the Sharpeville crisis, called a general election for 1961 in part to squash these pests. He nearly succeeded: eleven of the twelve rebels lost their seats. The exception was Helen Suzman, who, by the slim margin of 564 votes, earned the right to be the Nationalist prime minister's sole liberal opponent in parliament for the next thirteen years.

Realizing that she had become the de facto representative of millions of disfranchised South African citizens, Suzman hurled herself into her responsibilities. Working marathon hours, drafting all her own speeches, she fought every major piece of apartheid legislation. In one particularly grueling session of one hundred and four days during which she battled Vorster's security bills, Suzman delivered sixty-six speeches, moved twenty-seven amendments, and asked a hundred and thirty-seven formal questions of the government. Her performance earned her the grudging respect of one pro-Nationalist editor, who wrote in *Die Burger* that "she is putting up a parliamentary performance which is impressing even her enemies. For one person alone to state her party's viewpoint on every major item of legislation is crippling work . . . and she is doing it well."

Inside the chamber, throughout her career, her Nationalist opponents showered her with abuse. When she challenged the government after Sharpeville, one member of parliament condescendingly announced, "I forgive you; you are naive; you are a woman." When she criticized the brutal labor practices on farms, the opposing backbenchers shouted, "Go preach in a synagogue!" and "We don't like your screeching Jewish voice!" When she attacked job reservation for whites, the Nationalists accused her of being simultaneously an avaricious Jewish capitalist and a dangerous Jewish Communist. Often her opponents behaved like children. On one occasion the government proposed a bill to ban all Coloured persons from trade union executives. Suzman stood up in parlia-

ment and ridiculed the government's contention that Coloureds were
"unfit." The minister of labour looked over at her and sneered, "Sez
you." Another time, when Suzman had finished a tightly reasoned
speech, the minister of justice, John Vorster, told his guffawing associates that "my grandmother had a parrot who made much more intelligent remarks."

As Verwoerd's stature grew, he spent less and less time debating in
parliament, preferring to listen "in lofty silence," as Suzman described it
to her constituents. "It was almost as if the father-figure were giving his
offspring the opportunity of demonstrating how well they had learned
their lesson at his knee—or maybe over it." Nonetheless, she still managed on occasion to provoke a reaction. Ignoring the continuous barrage of accusations, insinuations, and insults from Vorster and others,
Suzman hammered at Verwoerd's policies so powerfully that in the middle of one of her speeches the infuriated prime minister rose from his
seat, stomped down to her spot, and bellowed in her face, "You are of
no account!"

Undeterred, Suzman fought on for years, the ultimate outsider, dif-
ferentiated from her political opponents by every feature of her identity:
a mature woman among childish men; a secular Jew among supposedly
devout Christians; an open-minded liberal among right-wing fanatics; an
intelligent independent among dull toadies. Sometimes she was overcome with fatigue and discouragement; other times she recognized de-
spondently that her presence might even be helping the Nationalists. "I
suppose I have my uses," she commented ironically after winning another election. "I do more to improve South Africa's image than the
whole of the Department of Information." Despite her reservations, she
kept going "like a cricket in a thorn tree when it is very dry in the bush
veld," as one opponent put it, whose "chirping makes you deaf but the
tune remains the same year in and year out." She persisted because of
the hundreds of letters she received from the victims of apartheid and
because, as one American reporter said at the time, she represented
"more South Africans than all the other 159 members of parliament put
together."

By his sixth year as prime minister, having mollified business, seduced
the electorate, jailed his enemies, emasculated the United Party, and
deflected world protest, Hendrik Verwoerd believed he had eliminated
the major obstacles that hindered the full implementation of apartheid.
Those that remained were irritating but, in his view, insignificant, such
as the objections of some of the churches. As in all countries, South
Africa's political leaders continually sought to bolster their authority by
obtaining the blessing of the ecclesiastical realm. Such backing is easier

to obtain in a nation with a homogeneous faith, but in countries filled with immigrants, like South Africa and the United States, political quarrels are so deeply intertwined with religious differences that such support is hard to enlist. In South Africa, Christians had been divided along lines of theology, nationality, geography, politics, and, of course, race. The Afrikaner population alone had divided, as the result of nineteenth-century theological and political debates, into three separate Calvinist denominations, all claiming superior fidelity to their country's history and their scripture's faith.

The original Dutch Reformed Church (NGK) retained the loyalty of most Afrikaners and thus exercised the greatest influence on the nation's attitudes toward race. Ironically, the church's commitment to segregation evolved from its desire to convert mixed-race and indigenous peoples. Early in the nineteenth century the Dutch Reformed Church welcomed two clergy of Scottish descent, the brothers John Murray and Andrew Murray Jr., into the fold. Andrew believed that the work of the church was to promote personal conversion to Jesus Christ; his enthusiasm, energy, and piety during six terms as the church's national moderator, the top elected position, sparked a wave of religious revival. The strict Calvinists in the denomination, who believed that the growth and spread of Christianity would be accomplished by God without human intervention, viewed the surge of evangelical fervor with alarm. When they eventually moved off into the more conservative splinter churches—the Nederduitsch Hervormde Kerk (NHK), which was formed in reaction to the NGK's opposition to the Voortrekker expeditions, and the Gereformeerde Kerk (GK)—Murray and his theological heirs were free to promote missions vigorously. They moved with great success into the Afrikaans-speaking Coloured population around the towns, establishing vibrant congregations at a steady clip.

As the new parishes grew, the church faced a theological and practical dilemma: how should the "mother" churches, almost exclusively white, relate to these racially mixed "daughters"? In 1829, before the Great Trek, the Dutch Reformed synod's position was that Holy Communion, the central sacrament of the church, should be administered "simultaneously and to all members without distinction of color or origin" because this was an "unshakable principle based on the infallible word of God." A generation later, as disputes over land, labor, and race swelled, the church retreated. In 1853 church leaders approved racially segregated congregations, though they specified that they had reached the decision only to circumvent the resistance of white bigots and to encourage the propagation of the gospel among other races.

Such profound disagreements over the nature of Christian fellowship were not new. Through the centuries the homogeneity of congregations and communities has generally been viewed as a spiritual failing to be overcome. In the United States and South Africa, however, the successful maintenance of racial segregation depended on the ability of pastors and theologians to transmute this failing into a virtue, to justify exclusivity as beneficial to the excluded. In the United States, for example, antebellum southern clergy took to defending slavery on the grounds that it would permit a more rapid education and evangelization of the "heathen" slaves. South African clerics used similar homiletic inversions. Influenced by German mission theorists, who insisted that people would best accept and adapt to Christianity within their own cultures, the leaders of the Dutch Reformed Church argued that by partitioning the church into racially distinct congregations, they would achieve several results at once: they would quell the noisy supremacists in the white churches, promote speedy evangelization among Coloureds and Africans, and obey the recommendations of the most up-to-date and learned European scholars. By doing so, however, they also created, as one South African theologian later wrote, "an ecclesiological blueprint for the Nationalist policy of separate development."

The transformation of the Dutch Reformed Church into a potent defender of apartheid required more than racial division. It also required a crisis to elevate the survival and success of Afrikaner culture into a prime directive. The crisis came in the two brutal nineteenth-century wars with Great Britain, from which the Dutch Reformed Church emerged a hardened, myopic supporter of Afrikaner nationalism. From then on, like a harmful virus, ardent patriotism entered and infected the cells of the church, releasing its secular code into the theological nucleus. What emerged was a mutant, a fusion of the love of nation with the love of Christ, creating a dangerous strain of Christian nationalism. To the outsider it might appear that such a doctrine simply cloaked ethnic self-interest in religious garb, but to a participant the belief brought an order and harmony to the relentless conflicts of South African life. Many nations have experienced periods of unreflective synonymity between religious values and national goals. South Africa was slightly different: with its strange social structure and warring white elites, the religious identification was not with the country as a whole but with the Afrikaner people, the *volk*.

The Dutch Reformed Church was not the only South African denomination to follow such a troubled course. Throughout the nineteenth century the Anglican Church endured fierce battles between clergy who endorsed British imperialism and clergy who questioned it. As the white population expanded, a new crop of English-speaking churches took root on South African soil. The Presbyterians established urban churches. The Methodists deployed missionaries who fanned out across the vast South African terrain, often bumping into the American Congregationalists, who had built their own network of schools and churches. The Roman Catholic and Baptist Churches sent pastors to tend to the spiritual needs of their small but growing flocks.

For all the religious communities of South Africa, the Nationalist Party victory of 1948 came as a shock. To the Afrikaner churches, it seemed as though God had led them out of the political wilderness and into the Promised Land. For English-speaking clerics and lay leaders, the moment was one of embarrassment. When Verwoerd wheeled out his plans for apartheid, the Afrikaner pastors genuflected while the English-speaking clerics convinced themselves that his policies would be reversed at the next election. When the Nationalists won again in 1953 and started to tear Africans from their homes and schools, some religious leaders murmured. In the Afrikaner churches the dissent was modest. While a few prominent theologians spoke out, most church leaders confined their misgivings to private conversations.

The Dutch Reformed denominations eventually salved their consciences by embracing Verwoerd's claim that separate development was not a symptom of racism—which the church formally denounced—but its solution. The theological justification, they insisted, lay in the distinction between "Christian unity" and "ethnic diversity." Christian unity, said one 1956 church document, was not to be confused with "the general cry for equality and unity in the world today. . . . It is mostly a surrogate unity and brotherhood that men seek to realize without Christ in a world disrupted by sin. It is a futile attempt, because true unity among men can only be realized in Christ." In other words, racial integration was so difficult that it could be achieved only by an act of divine intervention; failing that, segregation was the best choice.

In the English-speaking churches, only a few intrepid bishops, articulate laypeople, and rebellious priests spoke out. Trevor Huddleston, the Anglican priest whose searing description of the destruction of Sophiatown earned him international attention and ejection from South Africa, criticized not only the government but also the church, which, he said, was dormant, "though it occasionally talks in its sleep." Confronted with increasing numbers of white parishioners who supported the government, most bishops relied on a time-honored ecclesial compromise: they said much and did little. Resolutions against apartheid flowed out of religious conferences and conventions but were not matched by concrete actions. Indeed, racial discrimination persisted within the churches themselves: white clergy held all the leading positions and earned much higher salaries than their colleagues of other races.

The shootings at Sharpeville jolted all the churches of South Africa.

As criticism cascaded into the country from around the world, the leaders of the Dutch Reformed Church, including John Vorster's older brother Koot, drafted a shrill response. "We cannot condone the continuous besmirching of our country, people, and church by untrue and slanted information," the ministers wrote. International criticisms of government policy, they said, were "precipitating a clash in our country the end of which is not to be foreseen." The church had endorsed separate development, they continued, with the condition that it be "carried out in a just and honorable way, without impairing or offending human dignity."

The reaction of the Dutch Reformed leaders drew a hot retort from the Anglican archbishop, Joost de Blank, who had arrived in 1957. Though his supporters had hoped that an archbishop with a Dutch name would help build bridges with the Afrikaners, de Blank, a small, intense man, immediately shattered this expectation by writing and preaching passionately—often in Dutch—against apartheid. An autocrat by nature, de Blank demanded that the church endorse his prophetic stand. He pushed through a program to redistribute wealth from the affluent white dioceses to the needy African areas. He posted a large sign outside St. George's Cathedral in Cape Town welcoming "All Races to All Services at All Times." He oversaw the consecration of the country's first African bishop, Alphaeus Zulu, and objected loudly when the government prevented Zulu from spending the night at Bishopscourt, the archbishop's elegant formal residence, because the mansion sat in a manicured white neighborhood of Cape Town.

Outraged by the Dutch Reformed Church's refusal to condemn the Sharpeville massacre, de Blank insisted that the World Council of Churches eject the denomination. "The future of Christianity in this country demands our complete dissociation from the Dutch Reformed attitude," he wrote. "Either they must be expelled or we shall be compelled to withdraw." The national moderator of the Dutch Reformed Church, Dr. A. J. van der Merwe, cut off all ties with the Anglican Church and denounced de Blank as a hypocrite, since the Anglicans maintained all-white schools. The leaders of the World Council of Churches, in turn, worried that a precedent of expulsion would lead to the collapse of the international ecumenical body. De Blank's colleague in Ceylon, Archbishop Ladkasa de Mel, argued that "the expulsion of the Dutch Reformed Church would be in effect a kind of ecclesiastical apartheid adding one more scandal to an already scandalous situation." Instead, they proposed a special "consultation on Christian race relations and social problems in South Africa." The elders of the Dutch Reformed Church, eager to show their reasonable sides, agreed. The World Council sent an associate general secretary, American Robert

Bilheimer, to work with an ecumenical South African team to plan the event. Thus, in December 1961, in the small Johannesburg suburb of Cottesloe, Dr. Franklin Clark Fry, a Lutheran minister from the United States and the chairman of the central committee of the World Council of Churches, convened a week-long meeting of more than eighty representatives from South Africa's many Christian factions. The gathering, though predominantly white, included such prominent Africans as Bishop Zulu and Professor Z. K. Matthews.

Verwoerd viewed the meeting with alarm. If a group of prominent clergy from across denominational and racial lines—including some of the most respected leaders of his own church—criticized apartheid, his proposals and even his position as prime minister might be tainted or jeopardized. Though the proceedings were closed to the public, Verwoerd reportedly received daily briefings from representatives of the archconservative NHK. To his dismay, he learned that the leaders of the Cape and Transvaal synods of the Dutch Reformed Church had agreed to discuss the entire theological and political base of racial segregation and separate development.

To make matters worse, the previously warring factions gradually reconciled over the course of the week. Every morning before the delegates turned to discussion, they shared in common worship and engaged in small-group Bible studies. With each passing day the delegates felt a growing sense of forgiveness and unity, a sense so astonishing that many later testified it could only have been the work of the Holy Spirit. Originally the conference planners had not envisaged a closing statement, but by the middle of the session the delegates spontaneously decided that they should write one. As they worked together to draft the statement, the painful rifts of the past were at least partly healed. Even fiery Archbishop de Blank was touched: on the last day of the conference, he stood up in front of all the delegates, apologized for his temper, and retracted his condemnation of the Dutch Reformed Church. The Dutch Reformed leader, A. J. van der Merwe, replied that the hand of friendship was gladly accepted and that he and his colleagues had been painfully aware of the tensions and controversies that had divided the church. Touched by the unexpected mood of hope, the delegates agreed to meet again, both informally and in future World Council consultations. In the end, only Verwoerd's allies in the NHK refused to support the statement; in a stinging slap to the government, the representatives of all the other churches rejected the religious foundation of apartheid.

When the closing statement was released to the public, Verwoerd discovered that his worst fears had come true. In a decisive repudiation of the most basic principle of apartheid, the church leaders concluded that "all racial groups who permanently inhabit our country are a part of our total population and we regard them as indigenous. Members of all these groups have an equal right to make their contributions towards the enrichment of the life of their country and to share in the ensuing responsibilities, rewards and privileges. No one who believes in Jesus Christ may be excluded from any church on the grounds of his color or race." In the remainder of their statement the delegates explicitly denounced many Nationalist policies. While portraying mixed marriages as inadvisable, the delegates declared them valid. Brushing aside Verwoerd's grand design for the future, the delegates challenged the oppressive systems of migratory labor, job reservation, and low wages. Though for the sake of unity they skirted the question of a franchise for Africans, the delegates rejected the Nationalists' insistence on an all-white parliament and supported the direct representation of Coloureds in the legislature.

Faced with a religious mutiny that might destroy his leadership, Verwoerd leapt to the offensive. Like a stern patriarch, he immediately announced his personal displeasure at the actions of the Dutch Reformed Church delegates. Mobilizing his contacts through Afrikaner society, from the newspapers to the churches to the Broederbond, Verwoerd set out to crush the Cottesloe statement. He enlisted zealots to denounce the Dutch Reformed delegates for betraying their people. For months the editors of *Die Transvaler* printed vituperative attacks. Verwoerd knew that the Cottesloe statement would not be binding until it had secured the ratification of the four provincial synods; his strategy was to orchestrate so much strife that none of the synods would have the courage to pass it. In his 1961 New Year's address, the prime minister told the nation that the Cottesloe statement was reprehensible because it had been imposed on the Dutch Reformed Church delegates by foreigners. Over the next three months, as the more conservative Natal and Free State provinces each rejected the Cottesloe findings and as the Dutch Reformed Church voted to quit the World Council of Churches, pressure built on the church as a whole. At the meeting of the Transvaal synod in April, the delegates who participated in the conference were formally asked to recant. Under the crushing force of Verwoerd's blitz, the church's scorn, and the Broederbond's demands, the participants all backed down. The assembly then formally rejected the Cottesloe statement and withdrew from the World Council of Churches for good.

One of the Dutch Reformed delegates felt such disgust at his own equivocation on the Cottesloe statement that he swore it would be the last time he ever would mute his criticism of apartheid. At the time, C. F. Beyers Naudé was one of the brightest stars in the Afrikaner firmament. His father, Jozua Naudé, had fought in the Boer War with such passion that even in the face of certain defeat and despite the heartfelt personal entreaty of Jan Smuts, he had refused to sign the peace treaty. In the following decade Jozua Naudé became a Dutch Reformed clergyman, whose sole dream was to see unity and justice restored to the Afrikaner people. He tried to advance his cause in every possible way. He banded together with five friends into the original nucleus of the Broederbond. He insisted on preaching in Afrikaans despite the heated objections of his parishioners to the use of such "kitchen Dutch" in the pulpit. He gave his six daughters and two sons peculiar names to commemorate the milestones and martyrs of Boer history. He named his second son, born on May 10, 1915, after his close friend General Christian Frederick Beyers, who had been a hero in the Boer War and had drowned while fleeing the British in the brief World War I rebellion.

With such a patrimony, young Beyers Naudé would, even if he had lacked ability, have been assured of a prominent place in Afrikaner society. The young Naudé was, however, affable and gifted. He grew up in the Cape region and attended the University of Stellenbosch, where he excelled in Verwoerd's sociology class, though he later remembered that he had been frightened by the professor's "ruthlessness of logic." Though Naudé's knowledge of theology was thin, he swiftly qualified for ordination and became, like his father, brother, and two uncles, a clergyman. As a young pastor he was attracted to the Murray tradition of evangelism and mission and deeply angered his mother by marrying Ilse Weder, who was not an Afrikaner but the daughter of German Moravian missionaries. At the age of twenty-five, the earliest possible moment under the organization's rules, Naudé was inducted into the Broederbond at a secret ceremony of Bible reading, hymn singing, and solemn oaths.

By 1960 the forty-five-year-old Naudé had served a string of parishes across the country and was nearing the pinnacle of his vocation and his society. He had recently become the pastor of the Aasvoëlkop church in a suburb just outside of Johannesburg, one of the most important congregations in the country. Week after week he preached fervent evangelical sermons on Christian love of neighbor to cabinet ministers and government officials. He had just been elected the vice chairman of the Transvaal province of the Dutch Reformed Church. His supporters noted that it was only a matter of time before he ascended to the post of national moderator; indeed, with his friendly manner, eloquent style, and impeccable heritage, they speculated that one day he might even become prime minister. When van der Merwe needed to select someone to plan and attend the Cottesloe meeting, he turned naturally to such a prime specimen of Afrikaner virtues.

Unbeknownst to almost everyone, however, Naudé's convictions were in flux. As a youth, Naudé recalled, it simply never entered his mind that blacks could be considered a part of South Africa. Though he displayed flashes of independent thinking in college, it wasn't until he was nearly forty, when he first traveled extensively abroad, that he began to question the received truths of the Afrikaner faith. As Naudé toured Europe and the United States in 1953 to study methods of youth work, church leaders asked him about the Defiance Campaign. Naudé had to reply that he knew little about it. Others asked him about Chief Albert Luthuli and Professor Z. K. Matthews, but Naudé, who for years had read only censored newspapers, had no idea who they were. When people wanted to know his thoughts on Alan Paton's book *Cry the Beloved Country,* Naudé stammered uncomfortably that he had never heard of the book or the author. Even when his questioners stuck to theology, Naudé found that they swiftly demolished the biblical justifications for segregation which he had long accepted at face value.

Stung by his ignorance of his country's policies and his church's doctrines, Naudé returned home and secretly began an intensive program of study. With great care he secured and read the books that the world knew but his government had banned. For months he diligently reviewed his own church's religious justifications for apartheid and concluded, to his horror, that they were without merit. Uncertain of his fortitude and mindful of the consequences of dissent, Naudé tried to stifle his new doubts. In the pulpit and around the family dinner table he remained the same; only in the privacy of his monthly Broederbond meetings did he voice a few veiled questions.

In 1958 he visited, for the first time in his life, an African mining compound. Surveying the cold concrete bunks, reflecting on the aching loneliness, and realizing the devastating effect that eleven months of such privation must have on the physical, emotional, and spiritual lives of the workers and their families, Naudé was horrified. "If this is what apartheid is about, it is evil, it is inhuman," he thought. "It is something which can never be supported." He gathered a few friends who had let slip their own doubts; together they began a small Bible study to weigh the policies of Verwoerd against the word of God. With every passing month, as Verwoerd forcefully buttressed the nation's faith in the virtues of separate development, Naudé watched the moral underpinnings of his life and his people erode. In 1960, when van der Merwe selected Naudé to work on the Cottesloe conference, the national moderator did not realize that he had tapped a man whose interior life was honeycombed with doubt, a man on the verge of an epiphany.

It was not the conference but the reaction to it that set Naudé on his new course. He and the other Dutch Reformed delegates, anticipating discord, had drafted a written explanation of their support for the

Cottesloe statement in which they affirmed Verwoerd's notion of "diversity." The explanation proved ineffective. Naudé was stunned by the fury and duration of the assaults. As every political and ecclesial force he had ever respected lined up against him, as his fellow clergy, national leaders, and Broederbond brothers implored him to change his mind, Naudé waffled. How could he, a single pastor without a doctorate, presume to know more than the most learned and important members of his society? Even as he tried to find a middle ground between his conscience and his colleagues, Naudé realized with a sinking heart that soon he would have to choose. "I asked myself: 'how long are you going to remain silent and fearful?,'" he recalled. "Eventually I came to the point where I said, 'I can't continue to live this way. . . . How can I justify this kind of duplicity?' I realized that to do so I would have to live a life of hypocrisy and deviousness. I felt it was not possible. But I realized, on the other hand, the price one would have to pay."

Because Naudé's own transformation had come through examining scripture, he believed that the best way to lead Afrikaners into a new understanding would be through Bible study. His hopes foundered when most of the pastors he approached told him that in the aftermath of the church's decision to reject Cottesloe they were not willing to explore the theological foundations of racial discrimination. In the age-old tension between forms of authority in the church, the pastors, despite their Protestant heritage, had decided that the synod was more important than scripture. "I simply had to accept," wrote Naudé, "that the power of the synod, the political pressure, the newspapers, the radio, and the Broederbond were so overwhelming that it would be impossible to bring the church to another view for the next five or eight or ten years."

After months of effort Naudé gathered a few supporters and together they decided to publish their theological thoughts and doubts in a new journal, *Pro Veritate.* The conservatives in his congregation lodged a formal complaint against Naudé for his work on *Pro Veritate,* and the Broederbond again asked their wayward member to change his ways. Naudé, who had been wondering for years whether his loyalty to the Broederbond was compatible with his commitment to Christ, finally resigned in March 1963 from the secret organization his father had founded. To his surprise, his decision was supported by the Dutch Reformed clergy who were not Broederbonders and who deeply resented the control the secret organization exerted over the top spots in church and government. When Naudé attended the Transvaal synod meeting a few weeks later to defend the work of *Pro Veritate,* he was startled to find that his name had been put forward as a candidate for moderator of the synod. He was stunned when, after two secret ballots, he was elected.

Naudé faced an extraordinary new temptation. Despite his participation at Cottesloe, his editorials in *Pro Veritate,* and his resignation from the Broederbond, he had been elevated to the second highest position in his denomination, a position from which he could conceivably exercise great influence and even challenge Verwoerd. The price, he quickly came to understand, was that he would have to moderate his views substantially. His antagonists brought a resolution to the floor criticizing *Pro Veritate* and asked him directly to resign from the publication. Naudé realized that if he refused, the denomination would conclude that he did not owe his primary loyalty to them. Naudé, however, having broken free from the Dutch Reformed orbit, decided that he did not want to return under such conditions. In May he announced that he would not resign from *Pro Veritate;* in August he declared that he and a group of others were forming a new organization committed to ecumenism and racial justice called the Christian Institute. Naudé said that he had applied to remain as the pastor at Aasvoëlkop while serving as the director of the new institute. The leaders of the Dutch Reformed Church denied the application and told him that he would have to quit the Christian Institute or be defrocked. In September Naudé announced his decision from the pulpit. Preaching on the text from the fifth chapter of the Book of Acts—"We must obey God, rather than men"—Naudé told his congregation that the denomination had denied him "the God-given right and freedom of the minister and member to witness to the truth of God's word in the spirit of the prophets and the Reformers." The effect of the synod's recent decisions was that "the minister of the gospel in principle no longer enjoys the freedom to declare his deepest Christian convictions. . . . Consequently, the choice facing me is . . . between obedience in faith and subjection to the authority of the church," Naudé told his flock, concluding that he was not willing to "save my face but lose my soul."

With that sermon, Naudé set off like a latter-day prophet across a long desert of ostracism and abuse in search of the promise of a new South Africa. He left his congregation permanently in December 1963 and over the next three years he and his associates endured an avalanche of disapproval. When Albert Geyser, a friend of his who was being tried for heresy by an ecclesial court made up of Broederbond members, asked him for help, Naudé showed him some of the secret documents in which the Broederbond urged its members to squash religious dissenters. Geyser photographed some of the documents and gave them, without Naudé's knowledge, to the *Sunday Times,* which published a huge exposé. John Vorster, a member of the Broederbond, vowed to discover who was behind this breach of security of an ostensibly private organization. He gave the investigation to his former pro-Nazi chief of security police Hendrik van den Bergh, who quickly pinpointed Naudé as the source. When the news came out, Naudé and his family were vilified as traitors. The meager Afrikaner support for the Christian Institute dwindled further. When the police raided the offices of the institute and frisked Naudé in early 1965, Naudé wrote articles comparing the behavior of the South Africans to that of the Nazis and calling for the creation of a "confessing church" to challenge the doctrines of the quiescent state religion. The leaders of the Dutch Reformed Church responded by declaring the Christian Institute heretical and forbidding its members or clergy from belonging. The Christian Institute survived only because support outside South Africa was growing; to the South African church's dismay, the Reformed Churches in America and in Holland sent money and congratulations. For Naudé the new expressions of international interest did not assuage the pain of isolation and rejection by those he loved. One of his sisters would no longer speak to him. When his mother died and Naudé flew to her burial, the members of his family turned their backs, crowded around, and would not permit him to approach her grave.

At the same time, on the other side of the world, another preacher of the gospel was struggling to find his own path to racial harmony through a treacherous political thicket. In mid-1964 Martin Luther King Jr. and his cohorts at the Southern Christian Leadership Conference (SCLC) faced a strategic dilemma. The protests in Alabama and around the country had produced seemingly dramatic changes. The downtown merchants and business leaders of Birmingham had vowed to end desegregation voluntarily. The civil rights movement enjoyed the official, though sometimes clandestine, support of the White House. A major civil rights bill had been sent to Congress backed by such potent domestic enthusiasm and by such massive demonstrations in Washington that it seemed as though the prodigious resistance of the southern senators might finally be crushed.

The death of President Kennedy had extinguished the central star in America's political solar system and provoked a realignment of the remaining bodies. In the year that followed, the distances between the three largest elements—Lyndon Johnson, Robert Kennedy, and Martin Luther King Jr.—changed, and with those changes came a shift in gravity and direction for America's struggle over racial justice. Johnson's relationship with the attorney general, precarious since the vice presidential fiasco at the 1960 convention, soured with each passing month. Robert Kennedy had begrudged Johnson's decision to be sworn in on the airplane in Dallas immediately following the assassination and resented his abrupt arrival in the Oval Office and ejection of President Kennedy's personal secretary first thing the next morning. Johnson, for his part, believed that he had served President Kennedy loyally and patiently, suppressing his desire for the spotlight a thousand times. Now, reasoned the new president, the younger Kennedy should do no less. When Johnson sought to steer the government in new directions, Kennedy indicated to those around him that he believed that the men who had been appointed by his brother—men like McGeorge Bundy, Robert McNamara, and Dean Rusk—owed a higher duty to the past than to the present. Johnson alternated between sympathy for the attorney general's grief, anger at his arrogance, and fear of his power. Kennedy, in turn, viewed Johnson increasingly as a self-centered, deceptive buffoon.

The personal and political problems between the two men were dramatically enhanced by the continuous public speculation throughout the spring of 1964 that Johnson would select Kennedy as his vice president for the fall election, a proposition Johnson found threatening. Johnson knew in his gut that if he put Kennedy on the ticket he would forever be upstaged by his subordinate and plagued by the suspicion that he could not have won the election on his own. On July 29, 1964, the president summoned Kennedy to the White House and told him that he would not be the vice presidential candidate. A month later, Kennedy announced that he was resigning as U.S. attorney general to run for the Senate from New York.

With the presidential election looming, President Johnson also tried to guide the civil rights movement. "I knew that if I didn't get out front on this issue, [the liberals] would get me," Johnson said years later. "I had to produce a civil rights bill that was even stronger than the one they'd have gotten if Kennedy had lived. Without this I'd be dead before I had even begun." Johnson slyly offered to follow Robert F. Kennedy's lead, knowing that if the bill failed, the blame could be shifted from the White House to the Justice Department. As the months passed, Johnson and Kennedy worked closely with liberal Democrats and moderate Republicans to wear down the traditional resistance of the southern senators. In June 1964, the same month that three young civil rights workers, two white and one black, were murdered in Mississippi, Johnson got his bill.

Johnson signed the civil rights bill into law at a White House ceremony on July 2, 1964. Martin Luther King, Roy Wilkins, Walter Fauntroy, and other civil rights leaders attended, but, as Fauntlroy noted later, their enthusiasm "was dampened by the sadness we saw in Bobby's eyes and the coldness with which the president obviously treated him." As the visitors filed out, clutching their commemorative pens, the president asked King, Wilkins, and some of the other black leaders to stay behind for a private talk. Johnson told the men that from then on there had to be "an understanding of the fact that the rights Negroes possessed could now be secured by law, making demonstrations unnecessary and possibly even self-defeating." The true nature of his message was unmistakable: don't give the Republicans anything with which to scare voters before November.

Johnson's veiled admonition opened fissures in the civil rights movement. Several weeks later Roy Wilkins of the NAACP called a meeting of civil rights leaders to ask them to "observe a moratorium of all mass marches, picketing, and demonstrations until after Election Day." Whitney Young of the National Urban League supported the idea; James Farmer of CORE and John Lewis of SNCC opposed it. Martin Luther King was uncertain. He had no desire to increase support for Barry Goldwater, the Republican presidential candidate, nor did he want simply to enlist as a member of Johnson's increasingly potent political legions. He coaxed the two sides to a precarious agreement; the final resolution issued to the press urged "a broad curtailment, if not total moratorium" on mass demonstrations.

Part of King's dubiety, however, came from his growing conviction that the passage of Johnson's bill marked the beginning of a new era for the civil rights movement, an era in which it needed to shift both goals and tactics. While the segregation of public and private facilities was still symbolically important, King believed that a far greater challenge would be to obtain full political and economic rights for American blacks. To gain political power, blacks needed the federal government to help them secure and protect their right to vote. To acquire economic power, blacks needed to force wealthy whites to share more of the nation's resources—jobs, capital, housing, education. One of the most effective means of doing so, King thought, was the boycott.

In Alabama and Georgia, blacks had proven that withholding money from white-owned merchants was an effective, nonviolent way to split the white elite and force them to contend with black demands. In Atlanta a small but growing effort known as Operation Breadbasket—in which specific businesses with poor minority hiring records were targeted for boycott until they entered into a formal agreement to improve—had achieved important successes. As early as the fall of 1963, King had told the leaders of the SCLC that he hoped Operation Breadbasket could expand across the country, involving nationwide boycotts of industries and businesses with poor hiring records. King also believed that boycotts should be used against business leaders in Birmingham who had promised to desegregate but had failed to do so. SCLC Executive Director Wyatt T. Walker had also recommended a broadened use of economic tactics. "A massive refusal to buy on the part of the Negro community and others of good will," Walker told the SCLC board of directors at the time, "would throw the business world into shock" and cause "the nation's financial leaders [to] exert some initiative in eliminating the evils of segregation and discrimination."

In the fall of 1964, in a single three-week period from October to early November, American political astronomy changed again as each of the great bodies—King, Johnson, and Kennedy—entered a new orbit. On October 14, 1964, as King lay exhausted, ill, and depressed at St. John's Infirmary in Atlanta, wire service reporters contacted his wife, Coretta, to tell her that he had just been awarded the 1964 Nobel Peace Prize. King saw the award as a sign of international approval for the civil rights movement, comparable to the support for the anti-apartheid struggle symbolized by Chief Albert Luthuli's winning the prize three years before. Less than three weeks later Lyndon Johnson swamped Barry Goldwater by the largest percentage (sixty-one) in American history. As feared, the civil rights legacy cost Johnson five states in the Deep South—Mississippi, Alabama, Louisiana, South Carolina, and Georgia—but every other state, with the exception of Goldwater's home state of Arizona, swung to the incumbent. That same election officially transported Robert Kennedy out of the executive branch and into his first elective office as the junior United States senator from New York.

The three men now held entirely different positions from which to pursue their goals. Johnson was no longer occupying the presidency by virtue of tragedy but through the overwhelming support of the electorate. King was no longer one spokesperson from one constituency but the internationally recognized voice of America's conscience. Kennedy was no longer a cabinet officer shackled by duties and sorrow but an independent voice in another branch of government and the heir apparent to his party's leadership. From their newly augmented positions of authority, the three men were in a position to work together toward the aims they shared, especially racial justice and an end to poverty. In the early stages, when they kept the focus on domestic problems, they did cooperate, but as each man looked at America's role in the world, especially in South Africa and in Vietnam, the distance and antagonism among them swelled.

King's increasingly global perspective became evident in his December 1965 trip to Europe to accept the Nobel Peace Prize. In London, reporters asked him about apartheid. "More and more I have come to realize that racism is a world problem," he responded. The next night he urged that South Africa be subjected to the same pressures he intended for Alabama, "a massive economic boycott." During his Nobel speech in Oslo, King revealed the new breadth of his vision by linking the nonviolent struggle against racism in the United States to what he hoped would become an international campaign for disarmament and peace.

Shortly after returning to the United States, King plunged into the intensifying conflict over voter registration in Selma, Alabama. On February 1, 1965, King and nearly a thousand demonstrators were arrested for violating parade ordinances. While King sat in his jail cell, the SCLC ran a large advertisement in the *New York Times* on his behalf. The "Letter from Martin Luther King from a Selma, Alabama Jail" noted that "when the King of Norway participated in awarding the Nobel Peace Prize to me he surely did not think that in less than sixty days I would be in jail." King denounced the dozens of petty restrictions that the state registrars had dreamed up to bar black citizens from exercising their right to vote and urged *Times* readers to support his efforts in a place "where there are more Negroes in jail with me than there are on the voting rolls."

President Johnson, sensing that attention to Selma might open a new opportunity for legislation, called King to the White House as soon as he was released and told him that he was about to submit a voting rights proposal to Congress. Over the next few weeks, the battle in Selma grew more violent, leading to a bloody skirmish between state troopers that left several injured and one young black man dead. The death prompted the demonstrators to organize a protest march from Selma to the state capital, Montgomery. On Sunday, March 7, more than five hundred marchers were attacked by state troopers who fired teargas and savagely beat the demonstrators with clubs. Local white residents, observing from the sidelines, cheered wildly.

National television film crews, positioned on rooftops and on the street, recorded the entire event. By nightfall the footage had been broadcast across the country. The ABC network interrupted a movie, *Judgment at Nuremberg,* to show its viewers the contemporary consequences of racial hatred in their own country. An outraged Martin Luther King, who had spent the day in Atlanta, issued a call for civil rights supporters nationwide to converge on Selma for another attempt at a march. Thousands of citizens, including hundreds of white clergy, filled buses and headed south. Robert Kennedy told his friends at the time that he supported the effort but noted mordantly that people from New York City were much more eager to go to Alabama than to Harlem.

On Tuesday, Martin Luther King led a group of several thousand marchers back to the site of the attack, where they knelt in prayer before obeying a temporary judicial restraining order and returning to their point of departure. That night, white vigilantes attacked a minister from Boston, James Reeb, striking him on the head with such force that he died forty-eight hours later. Reeb's death triggered a new wave of national outrage; both the president and the vice president called Reeb's family to offer their condolences. A number of blacks noted caustically that the death of the minister, who was white, had upset the country far more than the death of the black man in Selma.

On Friday, March 12, an edgy Governor George Wallace of Alabama flew to Washington to meet with the president. Wallace tried to blame the violence on the demonstrators and outsiders. Johnson, at his best, brushed aside the excuse. He told the governor bluntly that the real problem was that blacks had been denied a fundamental right and that the state troopers had violated their duty to protect peaceful demonstrators. Outside in the Rose Garden the president informed Wallace and a bevy of reporters that he would submit his voting rights proposal within days and expected it to receive speedy passage. On Monday, Johnson took it to Capitol Hill himself, the first time a president had personally delivered a special message on a domestic issue in nearly twenty years. Selma, he said, was as important a moment in the nation's history as the battles at Lexington and Appomattox; it was an event "where history and fate meet at a single time in a single place to shape a turning point in man's unending search for freedom." America had many continuing problems with race, he said, but these "we shall overcome." When Martin Luther King, watching the speech on television in Selma, heard the president use the central phrase of the civil rights movement, he burst into tears. A president of the United States, ironically one who had been born and bred in the South, had publicly thrown the full prestige of his office and the full might of the federal government behind the dream to which King had devoted his life.

The march from Selma to Montgomery took place over five days, ending on March 25 with an impassioned speech by King in the shadow of the Confederate flag that fluttered on top of the state house. The intense emotions of the march fired the imaginations of the participants, some of whom saw the event as the beginning of a new era. James Bevel, one of the most passionate SCLC organizers, told a group of ministers and nuns that "it is time to start thinking about where the movement is going when we are through in the Alabama Black Belt. . . . We will go to Harlem and do something about housing and income. There are too many people who do not have enough to live on. Then we will go to South Africa and start a movement there. After that we will find a way to use nonviolence instead of war and armaments in international relations."

Some dismissed such talk as fantasy. Martin Luther King was not one of them. Over the previous year, and especially since the Nobel Peace Prize, King, like Bevel, had become convinced the civil rights movement had to break new ground. The decision, in part, was the result of its success. To the surprise of many, thousands of institutions across the

South had voluntarily complied with the 1964 civil rights law. Yet even as the victories unfolded, King was tormented by the idea that, in the end, they were not enough. After touring the Watts section of Los Angeles in 1965, King told Bayard Rustin, "You know, Bayard, I worked to get these people the right to eat hamburgers, and now I've got to do something to help them get the money to buy them." As the year wore on, King's vision expanded along every dimension: from the South to the North, from constitutional rights to what he called "human rights," from political tactics to economic pressure, from a regional to a global commitment. For King, the struggle for racial justice could no longer be regarded or pursued in isolation; it was intimately connected to the fundamental evils of poverty and war.

King's new interests aroused sharp editorial dissent. Newspaper and television commentators objected to his call for increased economic pressures on southern states, portraying it as coercive and arguing, in a phrase that would become common in the divestment movement in the following two decades, that such actions would harm blacks more than whites. Undeterred, King continued to discuss a nationwide boycott of products from Alabama. He explained to the SCLC board that he envisioned three stages, all precursors of measures that would later be taken against South Africa. The first stage would be to secure promises from companies that they would locate no new plants or investments in Alabama and from the United States government that it would provide no federal support for any Alabama business that discriminated. The second stage would urge all private and federal organizations to withdraw their funds and investments from the state. Finally, if these measures had not produced results, the organizers would call on supporters throughout the United States to refuse to buy anything produced in Alabama. As the idea continued to receive negative comment in the press, some of King's advisers counseled him to back off. King refused; in his mind he was simply expanding the technique of the Montgomery bus boycott of 1955 to a national scale.

As King's vision moved beyond the boundaries of the South and roamed across the national horizon, he became more and more unhappy with the behavior of American corporations and of the American government abroad, particularly in South Africa. His thinking had been shaped, in part, by a Methodist minister named George Houser who had been trying to drum up opposition in the United States to apartheid since the Defiance Campaign in the early 1950s. Born in Ohio in 1916 and raised by missionary parents in the Philippines, Houser had been a radical Christian since early adulthood. During the 1930s and 1940s Houser had studied at Union Theological Seminary, joined the Young People's Socialist League, and spent a year in a federal prison in Connecticut for refusing to sign up for the peacetime draft. After his ordination Houser had been appointed the first executive director of the Congress of Racial Equality (CORE) with the charge of bringing Gandhi's methods of nonviolent protest to the struggle for racial justice in the United States. During the Defiance Campaign Houser had organized rallies and protests; after one gathering at Adam Clayton Powell's church in Harlem, Houser had collected three hundred dollars and sent it directly to Walter Sisulu in Johannesburg. During Z. K. Matthews's year as a visiting professor at Union Theological Seminary, Houser had sought him out to learn more about the complexities of South African politics. In 1954 Houser had visited South Africa himself and established close ties with anti-apartheid leaders all over the country. In 1955 Houser had left CORE to become the executive director of a new organization, the American Committee on Africa (ACOA), designed to educate the American public about the importance of ending colonialism and white supremacy in Africa.

By the mid-1960s Houser and the other members of ACOA were more certain than ever that the U.S. government would never press for changes in South Africa, and they had watched with alarm as American investments rose rapidly. In March 1964, the organization's editorial board had devoted the entire issue of its publication *Africa Today* to a condemnation of U.S. policy in South Africa, labeling the government "Partners in Apartheid" and calling for an international boycott. In March 1965, as the nation followed the events in Selma, the American Committee on Africa held a national conference on South Africa, chaired by Episcopal Bishop James A. Pike of California, in which participants explicitly linked the domestic and international problems of race. At the conclusion of the conference, the participants delivered their recommendations for a series of graduated steps against South Africa to McGeorge Bundy and Dean Rusk.

Other groups saw similar connections between the increase in American investment and the growing strength of the Verwoerd regime. On March 19, 1965, the day before the march to Montgomery, a brand-new organization whose youthful members had named it Students for a Democratic Society held a five-hour protest in front of the Chase Manhattan building in lower Manhattan. While more than four hundred students picketed, forty-nine "chanting and singing demonstrators" staged a "sitdown," according to the press reports, in front of the building. When Lawrence C. Marshall, vice chairman of the Chase board of directors, emerged to talk to the students, Paul Potter, president of SDS, tried to engage him in a discussion of the morality of the bank's loans to the South African government. Marshall refused to talk, returned inside, and had the students arrested. Later the bank issued a curt statement that "so long as our own government maintains friendly relations with a country, we believe that we would not be warranted in any attempt to interfere with the flow of international commerce by discriminating against such a country."

A week later at the annual Chase Manhattan shareholders' meeting, the question of the relation of the bank with foreign governments arose again. David Rockefeller, president of the bank, announced that he believed the time had come to expand short-term lending to the Soviet Union but commented that he did not believe long-term lending was in the national interest. He reported that the Arab threat to boycott the bank because of the bank's willingness to lend to Israel—a threat backed by hundreds of millions of petrodollars—had been withdrawn. When a shareholder asked about the moral implications of doing business with South Africa, the chairman of the board, George C. Champion, responded. "We can't be the arbiter of the social affairs of a country," he said. "Where there's commerce and trade, we feel we should take a part in it."

Martin Luther King reacted angrily to such myopia in a speech he delivered on Human Rights Day, December 10, 1965, to a benefit dinner held at Hunter College for the American Committee on Africa. He set the tone quickly by linking poverty and racism. "The large majority of the human race is non-white," said King, "yet it is that large majority which lives in hideous poverty." As an example, King pointed to South Africa, a country where "all opposition to white supremacy is condemned as Communism, and in its name, due process is destroyed, a medieval segregation is organized with twentieth century efficiency and drive, a sophisticated form of slavery is imposed by a minority upon a majority who are kept in grinding poverty, the dignity of human personality is defiled and world opinion is arrogantly defied."

King vigorously rejected the contention by the South African government and by American columnists that South Africa was immune to international pressures. The truth was, he said, that American "protest is so muted . . . that it merely disturbs the sensibilities of the segregationists, while our trade and investments substantially stimulate their economy to greater heights." It is not that the South Africans were so strong, King insisted, but that "the great nations will not sacrifice trade and profit to effectively oppose them. The shame of our nation is that it is objectively an ally of this monstrous government in its grim war with its own black people." Sweeping toward his conclusion, King laid out a vision of the divestment and sanctions movement that was to follow over the next two decades. "Have we the power to be more than peevish with South Africa?" King asked. "To list the extensive economic relations of the great powers with South Africa is to suggest a potent non-violent

path . . . a massive, international boycott." For King the two struggles—for civil rights in the United States and for political freedom—
were intimately connected. "In this period when the American Negro is
giving moral leadership and inspiration to his own nation, he must find
the resources to aid his suffering brothers in his ancestral homeland,"
King insisted. "Nor is this a one-way street. The civil rights movement in
the United States has derived immense inspiration from the successful
struggles of those Africans who have attained freedom in their own
nations."

King concluded, as he usually did, with a beatific vision of a reconciled humanity. "Negro and white have been separated for centuries by
evil men and evil myths. But they have found each other. . . . The
whole human race will benefit when it ends the abomination that has
diminished the stature of man for too long. This is the task to which we
are called by the suffering in South Africa and our response should be
swift and unstinting. Out of this struggle will come the glorious reality of
the family of man."

By 1966, Martin Luther King Jr. and Robert F. Kennedy were among a
small but influential group of persons who were growing disenchanted
with the direction of Lyndon Johnson's foreign policy. Over the previous
two years, the president had shown an alarming fondness for force.
Three weeks after his landslide election, Johnson joined the Belgians
and sent American airplanes and troops to participate in a massive rescue operation in the Congo. Five months after that, in April 1965, Johnson sent twenty-two thousand American soldiers to suppress an uprising
in the Dominican Republic. Throughout the same period the president
dramatically escalated the war in Vietnam. Johnson, spoon-fed optimistic reports by his military, believed that at any moment the North Vietnamese would crack. To slack off, the president believed, would be to
betray the legacy of President Kennedy, the South Vietnamese government, and the men who had already died. Yet as the North Vietnamese
proved unexpectedly resilient and as the human toll mounted on both
sides, Martin Luther King and Robert Kennedy, men who had shared so
many of Johnson's goals, became troubled. They feared, accurately, that
the gargantuan military expense would starve Johnson's domestic programs—that, in effect, the war in Vietnam would strangle the war on
poverty.

The policy toward Vietnam was not the only one that was beginning
to flounder; Johnson was also beginning to lose the initiative in Africa.
The difficulties arose in part from the maturation and cantankerousness
of the new African countries, from suspicion of Western intent across
the continent heightened by the American role in the Congo, and from

In 1938 future Prime Minister Hendrik F. Verwoerd and his wife, wearing nineteenth-century Voortrekker clothes, were among thousands who marked the centennial celebration of Afrikaner settler victories. The nationalist fervor unleashed by the festivities helped to unite Afrikaner factions and build a movement that led to political victory ten years later. (Mrs. Lucie Cloetie, Bloemfontein)

In June 1955 the African National Congress formulated a set of political principles, known as the Freedom Charter, that were read and voted on at a large gathering near Johannesburg. On the second day, the South African police mounted the platform, confiscated all signs and materials, recorded everyone's name, and broke up the meeting. The leaders of the gathering were later tried for treason. (American Committee on Africa)

Overcoming personal and racial obstacles, Nelson Mandela became a lawyer in the 1950s and opened the first African law firm in the country with his friend Oliver Tambo (note the reversed "Mandela & Tambo" sign in the window). The two were immediately swamped defending men and women who had fallen afoul of the National Party's myriad new discriminatory laws. (Mayibuye Center)

Nelson and Winnie Mandela on their wedding day, June 14, 1958. After Nelson's first marriage had failed because of his demanding responsibilities for the ANC, he was delighted to find an energetic new wife who had been trained as a social worker and who, he believed, would be able to understand and share his life. (Mayibuye Center)

On March 21, 1960, as part of national demonstrations against the pass laws, a large crowd gathered at the police station at Sharpeville. Panicky police opened fire, killing 69 people and wounding 186 others. The Sharpeville massacre attracted world attention and caused a flight of capital that nearly forced the apartheid government to change course. (Mayibuye Center)

Prime Minister Hendrik Verwoerd led the apartheid government successfully
through the post-Sharpeville crisis with a combination of skillful politics
and iron will. Here the "man of granite" is shown in March 1961 addressing a welcoming crowd at Jan Smuts Airport in Johannesburg after returning from London, where he had pulled South Africa out of the British
Commonwealth rather than accede to the members' demands that he ease
his white supremacist policies. (South African Ministry of Information)

The only known photograph of ANC leaders Nelson Mandela and Walter Sisulu on Robben Island, taken in the mid-1960s by a British journalist. Mandela spent nineteen years in one of the cells seen in the background. Though conditions on the isolated island in Table Bay were harsh, Mandela and Sisulu helped to maintain good spirits and discipline among prisoners, even organizing a "university" in which the students were assigned to work details with older prisoners who lectured on everything from history and economics to literature. (Mayibuye Center)

After G. Mennen "Soapy" Williams, the Democratic governor of Michigan, helped John F. Kennedy win the presidential nomination by assuring party liberals of the candidate's commitment to civil rights, the new president made him assistant U.S. secretary of state for African affairs. Williams (at left), an energetic idealist, visited dozens of newly independent countries in Africa, as shown on the map he is reviewing at the State Department. (Wayne Fredericks)

John F. Kennedy had the difficult task of trying to persuade the many African leaders who visited the White House that America was more reliable than the Soviet Union while at the same time deflecting their discomfort with his cautious approach toward white racism in southern Africa and the American South. In July 1963 Kennedy welcomed Tanzanian President Julius Nyerere (center), who privately urged his host to take stronger steps against apartheid. On the left is Wayne Fredericks, deputy assistant secretary of state for African affairs, who would later play important roles at both the Ford Foundation and Ford Motor Company in relation to South Africa. (Wayne Fredericks)

In June 1966 New York Senator Robert F. Kennedy and his wife, Ethel, embarked on a tumultuous three-day trip through South Africa. After delivering the greatest speech of his career on June 6 in Cape Town, Kennedy flew by helicopter without the government's approval to visit Albert Luthuli, the winner of the 1960 Nobel Peace Prize and the banned president of the African National Congress. Kennedy was touched by Luthuli's courage and piety, calling him "one of the most impressive men I have ever met." (Africana Museum, Johannesburg)

In the eyes of many activists, the willingness of American companies to supply the South African government and military with strategic products—such as these South African police trucks manufactured by Chrysler—advertised U.S. support for apartheid. (Tim Smith, ICCR)

Prime Minister John Vorster had been sent to jail in South Africa during World War II for his involvement in a pro-Nazi Afrikaner nationalist group. After serving as minister of law and order under Hendrik Verwoerd, the new prime minister brutally suppressed internal dissent while trying to reposition South Africa more favorably with its African neighbors. (Mayibuye Center)

First elected to Congress in 1954, Rep. Charles C. Diggs Jr. of Michigan rose fifteen years later to lead the House Subcommittee on Africa. In the decade that followed he used his authority effectively to put pressure on U.S. commercial and diplomatic ties with the white regimes of southern Africa and even traveled to South Africa to confront American plant managers about their segregated facilities. (Arthur Ashe Foreign Policy Library, TransAfrica)

When forty-year-old Derek Bok moved from the deanship of Harvard Law School to the presidency of Harvard University in 1971, he was immediately confronted with challenges to the university's investment policies toward southern Africa. The controversy was so enduring that at his retirement twenty years later he commented ruefully that his tenure "sometimes seemed like one long debate about divestment." (*Columbia Spectator* photo archive)

the recognition that the lofty promises made by everyone, socialists and capitalists alike, were not going to alleviate the ravaging poverty of the region. Inside the Johnson administration, bureaucratic factions continued to wrangle over the appropriate approach toward American interests in Africa. When white Rhodesian leader Ian Smith suddenly announced a "unilateral declaration of independence" from Great Britain on November 11, 1965—meaning that 250,000 whites were going to exert total political control over nearly 5 million Africans—White House spokesmen immediately announced American support for British Prime Minister Harold Wilson's efforts to quell the rebellion. The question that split the executive branch was how far this support should go. Soapy Williams at the Africa Bureau believed that the United States should consider severe economic penalties and possibly military action to force the whites to grant political rights to the majority. Others wanted to hang far back. Out in the political arena, Martin Luther King delivered a strong denunciation of Ian Smith, while conservative Americans supported the leader and his racist state. After meeting with Prime Minister Wilson at the White House, Johnson decided to follow the British lead and impose sanctions.

From the beginning, however, the British and American effort to impose sanctions on Rhodesia was hamstrung by both countries' trade relations with South Africa. Though officially he did not applaud the rebellion, Verwoerd was prepared to break any sanctions imposed on his northern neighbor. As South African shipments of oil, food, equipment, and weapons flowed by rail across the Zambezi River into Rhodesia, Britain and the United States faced a choice: they could either extend the sanctions to South Africa or they could leave a gaping loophole in the embargo. Wilson, knowing that Britain's trade with South Africa was vital to the English economy, recognized that he could not sustain an embargo on South Africa politically. Members of the American government felt that if the British were not willing to pay the price, the United States had no incentive to take the lead and jeopardize its own interests.

The result was another halfhearted allied effort. Johnson, trying to help a foreign leader whom he viewed as a friend, supported Wilson's announcement of an oil embargo against Rhodesia, even though, in the months following, the United States had to spend four million dollars airlifting oil to the Congo for shipment into Zambia (formerly Northern Rhodesia), whose supply of fuel was cut in revenge by the Smith regime. Over the following years, the United States steadily imposed additional boycotts of Rhodesian products, sparking the rise of a vociferous pro-Rhodesian lobby in Congress.

Turning to the other problem of Western colonialism in southern Africa—Portugal's heavy-handed domination in Angola and Mozam-

bique—Johnson also made little headway. The gradual stifling of the
Africa Bureau and the ascendance of the Europeanists had tilted the
government toward Lisbon and away from the nationalist movements,
which had now assembled armies and launched military campaigns. Portuguese Prime Minister Salazar, still in tight control, had responded to
the military challenge by sending 125,000 Portuguese troops to the colonies. In early 1965, to coax the Portuguese into a new Azores agreement,
the State Department, over Williams's objections, secretly approved the
sale of twenty World War II vintage B-26 bombers for use in the colonies. The sale, known as Operation Sparrow, was uncovered several
months later by the Treasury Department and stopped, but only after
seven planes had already been delivered to the Portuguese. Under the
guidance of U.S. Ambassador George W. Anderson, the obstreperous
pro-Salazar admiral whom John F. Kennedy had shipped off to Lisbon
("I thought they sort of deserved each other," he said at the time), the
Johnson administration made a last private attempt to persuade the
Portuguese to grant independence to their African territories. Salazar,
after listening to the ambassador's ideas in October 1965, told Anderson
that African nationalism was not invincible and that Africans were incompetent. The formal rejection of the Anderson plan by the Portuguese in January 1966 marked the end of the last attempt by the American government to promote independence in the Portuguese colonies
for nearly a decade.

Lyndon Johnson also tried to tighten up the South Africa policy inherited from Kennedy. He barred the sale of three submarines to South
Africa, forcing Verwoerd to purchase them from the French. He broadly
interpreted the unilateral ban on weapons sales to South Africa to include a long list of heavy-duty capital goods such as metalworking machines and precision drills, which Verwoerd wanted for the domestic
arms industry. He cut down on the shipment of "gray area" items, products like Cessna airplanes that could be converted to military use by the
South African Defence Force, and encouraged the U.S. embassies and
consulates in South Africa to hold multiracial receptions. But Johnson
took no position on the rapid rise of American investment, even though
American automotive, petroleum, and computer companies were transferring important technologies to the regime. The official policy, established under President Kennedy, was a nonpolicy: the United States
government would neither encourage nor discourage American investment. In fact, enthusiastic Commerce Department officials could often
be found promoting American business in South Africa as vigorously as
they did in other countries.

The tensions in the American position finally took their toll on Soapy
Williams. The assistant secretary had come to believe that without a

strong, personal commitment from the president and without increased expenditures on Africa—unlikely in the light of Vietnam and with Johnson's domestic commitments—the chances to revitalize the government's African agenda were nil. Long a proponent of more aggressive actions against South Africa, held in check by Rusk, Ball, and many others, Williams found himself forced to argue contradictory positions in public. While testifying before the House subcommittee on Africa in March 1966, Williams said that a suspension of United States investment in South Africa not only would improve American relations with much of the world but might also force the South Africans to reflect seriously on the disadvantages of apartheid. Then, as if chagrined by his own candor, Williams instantly backpedaled and presented the opposite view, the one held by his superiors, that a ban on investment might also harden South African defiance of world opinion, isolate the country from contact with outside views, and damage American economic, scientific, and strategic interests. Within the week, Williams gave up the battle. After more than five years as assistant secretary of state for African affairs he resigned to run for the U.S. Senate from Michigan. The secretary of state, in a final slap, refused to promote Wayne Fredericks, who was viewed as a political appointee, and selected Joseph Palmer, a senior foreign service officer and former U.S. consul in Rhodesia, to become the new assistant secretary of state for Africa.

As Robert F. Kennedy's and Martin Luther King's public criticism of the president's domestic and foreign policies increased, Johnson felt betrayed. In his mind, he had enthusiastically supported both men's goals, breaking with many of his own southern political supporters to promote sweeping changes in America's legal and social life. Now he had moved on to an even more magnificent goal, the construction of the Great Society. King and Kennedy had responded not with allegiance but with strident demands. In such a frame of mind, it was easy for Johnson to view anything King or Kennedy did with paranoia. Johnson, like all presidents before him, believed that domestic and international politics should be disentangled, that foreign policy was the responsibility of the president and not of a clamorous Congress. When King and other civil rights leaders approached the president and asked him to become more involved in African matters, he expressed displeasure. He had been even more appalled when Black Muslim leader Malcolm X had traveled to the annual meeting of the Organization for African Unity in 1964 to appeal to the African states to come to the aid of American blacks. "The president's view," wrote aides to McGeorge Bundy in a White House memorandum in 1965, "is that since he is working to make the American Negro fully a part of American society, he doesn't think it is at all a good idea to encourage a separate point of view on foreign policy. We don't want an integrated domestic policy and a segregated foreign policy. . . . They should be interested in the totality of American policy as Americans."

Despite these assertions, members of the White House staff had been aware for years of the connections between civil rights and Africa. As Bill Moyers wrote in June 1965, "the key to an American president's standing in Africa is his relationship at home to the civil rights movement. Your voting rights speech . . . coming after 98% of the Negro voters cast their ballots for you in the 1964 presidential election, makes you a hero to the Negro at home—and it has spilled over into Africa." The next winter, the staff members muttered uneasily when Martin Luther King received an invitation from a student group to visit South Africa. They grumbled even more loudly when Robert Kennedy received one as well, though privately Wayne Fredericks urged the senator to go.

The South African government denied King a visa and approved one for Kennedy on the same day, March 22, 1966, though they told the senator that "it would not be convenient" for him to arrive at the end of May, during the celebration of the fifth anniversary of the republic. Kennedy's Senate office announced that he would travel to South Africa for several days in early June. Though the White House viewed the trip as pure political grandstanding, some in Johnson's camp realized that the incident could be used to jolt the administration's Africa policy back to life. For more than a year members of the National Security Council had been prodding the State Department to come up with a new African program as sweeping as the Great Society—but with no additional expenditures. In April 1966 the U.S. ambassador to the United Nations, former Supreme Court Justice Arthur Goldberg, bypassed all the squabbling groups and wrote directly to the president, telling him that the time had come for a "Johnson plan" for Africa, comparable to the Marshall Plan two decades earlier. "It is highly desirable," wrote Goldberg, "in light of the international political difficulties we will continue to have over Vietnam, for you to take a new and constructive initiative in foreign policy which will attract those who are most disquieted about Vietnam and who believe we can only act vigorously in 'reaction to a "communist" menace.' " He noted that John Kennedy had tried the same thing in Latin America by creating the Alliance for Progress; Africa is where Johnson could make his mark. Johnson agreed and ordered the State Department to develop a program and write a speech, which he would deliver on May 26, the third anniversary of the founding of the Organization for African Unity. The grinding policy wheels at

State, overseen by the political engineers in the White House, turned furiously to meet the deadline.

At three A.M. on the day of Johnson's speech, Bill Moyers wrote a final memo to the president detailing the political benefit that Johnson would derive from the speech, which, he assured his boss, would be "big news throughout the world." His speech would also be important "for its impact on the civil rights people at home; it is a cheap way to keep them quiet at least on one issue. . . . There is also another reason," wrote Moyers, knowing where the president's interest lay. "Bobby Kennedy goes to South Africa next week. He will try to get ahead of you on the question of political liberty for Negro Africans. Your speech preempts the stage. I think it would be wrong for us simply to offer economic assistance and material aid while Kennedy trots off making hay on the intangible issue of the rights of man."

The speech, which had been heralded by the White House as a major address resulting from months of review, turned out to be an eloquent but insubstantial declaration of American sympathy for the cause of self-determination in Africa. "Across the continent the majority of people prefer self-government with peril to subservience with serenity. This makes all the more repugnant the narrow and outmoded policy which in some parts of Africa permits the few to rule at the expense of the many," Johnson said. He attacked Rhodesia by name but avoided explicit criticisms of South Africa and Portugal. Like King, Johnson drew a direct connection between racial justice at home and abroad. "We will not permit human rights to be restricted in our own country," said Johnson, "and we will not support policies abroad which are based on the rule of minorities or the discredited notion that men are unequal before the law."

Though White House speechwriters were instructed to refer to the address as "the boldest statement on Africa by any Head of State," reaction around the world was mixed. Editorials in American newspapers, noting the absence of any promise for new funds, wondered whether the president was simply setting out general (and well-known) principles or recommending something specific. Some African leaders applauded; others sat back to see whether Johnson would follow through. Their caution was apt, for once again Johnson's foreign policy was being driven more by domestic than by international concerns. The little band of Johnson staffers at the White House, along with their allies at the State Department and the United Nations, has succeeded in focusing Johnson on Africa by persuading him that presidential action would reduce the swelling criticism inside his own party about civil rights and Vietnam. When the maneuver failed, the president's interest waned. American relations with Africa, lobbed briefly to the top of White House priorities, dropped again to the bottom and stayed there.

The irritation of the White House staff toward the mixed reaction to Johnson's speech was heightened by the admiring coverage many American papers gave to Robert Kennedy's trip to South Africa. Kennedy had been invited by the National Union of South African Students (NUSAS), an organization open to all races but led by liberal whites. John Vorster, having smashed all other forms of resistance, had taken a particular interest in this motley group of teenagers, whose "subversive" leaders, he told parliament, had created an "obnoxious and reprehensible organization." On May 11, just before Kennedy's trip, Vorster had slapped the NUSAS president, Ian Robertson, with a five-year banning order. The terms stipulated that Robertson could not leave Cape Town, could not speak to more than one person at a time, could not enter any educational institution except to attend lectures for which he was already registered, could not enter NUSAS offices or participate in any of its activities, and could not assist in the writing of anything for publication. Four thousand students marched through Johannesburg with signs calling on Vorster to charge or release Robertson. While the police watched passively, flowerpots, water bombs, spit, and urine from chamberpots were dropped on the marchers from buildings along the city route. Vorster later met with a student delegation and told them that he found NUSAS repugnant because its views were "diametrically opposed" to his own. When the students asked the minister of justice to charge Robertson formally or to launch a judicial inquiry, Vorster told them that he did not need to do so because Robertson had been banned not as the president of NUSAS but as an individual. After they left, Vorster permanently prohibited all further protest marches.

Robert and Ethel Kennedy and their small entourage arrived at midnight on Saturday, June 4, 1966. More than a thousand students greeted them at Jan Smuts Airport in Johannesburg. When Kennedy delivered his brief opening remarks, students from the pro-government Afrikaner student group heckled him and members of NUSAS cheered. From then on, for four feverish days, details of Kennedy's visit formed the lead headlines of almost every edition of every South African paper. On Sunday morning, as the Kennedys attended mass at the Catholic church in Pretoria, thousands read the moderate *Sunday Times*'s word of caution that the senator "take full account of . . . the big differences that render invalid close comparisons between Negroes and Africans. As a result of his own experience in his late brother's cabinet, Mr. Kennedy knows how hard it is to make rapid race relations advances in the teeth of popular prejudices coupled with old tradition."

Kennedy tried to avoid igniting needless controversy. He told reporters that while he vigorously rejected the idea of apartheid, he did not have any specific solutions to recommend. He said repeatedly that despite Prime Minister Verwoerd's instruction that no member of the cabinet was to see him, he was still willing to meet with any member of the government. As a former attorney general, he said, he had hoped especially that he might be able to meet with his counterpart, John Vorster. When Dr. G. D. Schultz, the editor of *Die Transvaler,* refused to attend a meeting between the senator and a group of Afrikaner editors on the grounds that "Sunday was not a proper day for a political discussion," Kennedy responded graciously. "I quite understand his feelings," he said. "I would be delighted to see him some other time."

Sunday night Kennedy and his wife attended a private dinner held by the South Africa Foundation. The businessmen irked Kennedy by complaining, over cigars and brandy, about their beleaguered existence, though he refused to criticize them in public. The next morning, he and his party flew to Cape Town, stopping at Kimberley for fuel and for a twenty-minute stroll on the tarmac with Bishop Clarence Crowther, an American citizen who served as Anglican bishop of the area and who had been persecuted by Vorster. As the plane swooped in over Cape Town, Kennedy delighted at the sight of the beautiful city, clinging to the side of Table Mountain beside a glittering sea. Then the plane arced over Robben Island, where Nelson Mandela and hundreds of others were spending their days gathering seaweed and digging limestone with hand tools. As Kennedy looked down at the prison, his mood turned somber.

At the D. F. Malan Airport in Cape Town he was mobbed by students again. Ushered to a plush mayoral reception, he slipped out early and went to see Ian Robertson. He stayed for half an hour and gave the student leader a copy of *Profiles in Courage.* That evening Kennedy, at a NUSAS event at the University of Cape Town, delivered what observers and biographers have called the greatest speech of his career. Asserting that freedom of the individual is what distinguished Western democracy from Nazism and Communism, Kennedy outlined the freedoms that had to be preserved—freedom of speech, freedom to participate in government, freedom to worship, freedom to pursue education and employment. "The way of opposition to communism," he continued, "is not to imitate its dictatorship but to enlarge individual human freedom—in our country and around the globe. . . . The denial of communism only strengthens the very communism it claims to oppose."

Kennedy then turned to America's efforts to live up to these principles. "For two centuries my own country has struggled to overcome the self-imposed handicap of prejudice and discrimination based on nationality, social class, or race." He mentioned, for example, the job advertisements in Boston in his father's day which stipulated that "no Irish need apply." "In the last five years," he declared, "the winds of change have blown as fiercely in the United States as anywhere in the world. But they will not—they cannot—abate." He talked of the millions of blacks who could not find jobs, housing, education, and political rights. At the same time, he said, in that same country a black man was training to become an astronaut and another, Martin Luther King, "is the second man of African descent to win the Nobel Peace Prize for his non-violent efforts for social justice between the races."

In a sweeping passage, he portrayed a world rapidly overcoming geographical and historical limits, a world breaking free from "dark and poisoning" superstition and prejudice. He told the students that a South Africa "cleansed of hate and fear and artificial barriers" could lead the world in overcoming poverty and oppression and that it was up to them, to the young, to see that it did. In what later became one of his most frequently quoted remarks, Kennedy set out his own philosophy of social action: "Each time a man stands up for an ideal, or acts to improve the lot of others, or strikes out against injustice, he sends forth a tiny ripple of hope, and crossing each other from a million different centers of energy and daring those ripples build a current which can sweep down the mightiest walls of oppression." Reaching the end, he urged the students to reject timidity. "For every ten men who are willing to face the guns of an enemy there is only one willing to brave the censure of his colleagues, the wrath of his society," concluded Kennedy. "Moral courage is a rarer commodity than bravery in battle or great intelligence. Yet it is the one essential, vital quality for those who seek to change a world which yields most painfully to change."

The speech stunned the students and swept the country. Reprinted in many of the English-speaking papers—some of whom said it was the most important speech since Harold Macmillan's "wind of change" address six years before—it ignited an interest and enthusiasm for Kennedy far beyond the campuses. Over the next two days Kennedy attracted thousands more to his public appearances. Even the Afrikaner papers applauded Kennedy's vision and tact and criticized the government's refusal to meet with him. The day after the speech Kennedy journeyed to the University of Stellenbosch, Verwoerd's alma mater, where the senator's candor and accessibility disarmed many of his most vociferous critics. Kennedy then flew to Durban, on the Indian Ocean, where he addressed twenty thousand people at the University of Natal. Outside, after the speech, Kennedy clambered up on the roof of a car and joined the immense crowd in singing "We Shall Overcome." From there he drove to his beachfront hotel, where he served as host at a large dinner whose guests included Catholic Archbishop Denis Hurley,

Alan Paton, and several Zulu chiefs. "I haven't met with so many people in trouble since I was attorney general," Kennedy quipped. At dawn the next morning, he and his wife boarded a chartered helicopter and flew to the Groutville mission station to meet with Albert Luthuli. Kennedy was moved by Luthuli, calling the former head of the African National Congress "one of the most impressive men I have met in my travels around the world" and a "man of God." After strolling through the soft fields around the chief's tin-roofed home for an hour, Kennedy flew back to Durban and on to Johannesburg, where he spent the afternoon standing on top of a slow-moving car waving to thousands of startled and enthusiastic residents of Soweto. That evening at the University of the Witwatersrand he delivered another major speech, for which students had stayed up through a freezing winter night to obtain tickets. From there he and Ethel went to a fashionable party, where he remained until two o'clock in the morning talking to a cluster of mesmerized South African undergraduates about Martin Luther King's work in the United States.

In the morning he left. As his plane prepared to lift off for Nairobi, Kennedy pondered an editorial titled "Kennedy, Come Back" that had appeared that morning in the *Rand Daily Mail.* "Senator Robert Kennedy's visit is the best thing that has happened to South Africa for years," the editorial said. "It is as if a window has been flung open and a gust of fresh air has swept into a room in which the atmosphere had become stale and fetid. Suddenly it is possible to breathe again without feeling choked." The editors reviewed the whirlwind tour and commented on the invigorating effect it had had on the youth of South Africa. After reading the editorial, Kennedy turned pensive. If he lived in South Africa, he told his companions, "I would gather up everything I have and get out now." Of course, he continued wryly, "if we had stayed another two days, we could have taken over the country." In the days that followed, Kennedy, when asked about American corporate involvement in South Africa, said that he intended to talk to American companies when he got home but that he was opposed to economic sanctions "at the present time." He also announced that he intended to return to South Africa within a year, but Verwoerd's government soon gave notice that he would never be permitted to return. Though Kennedy's speeches were passed from hand to hand and his picture was plastered on walls across the shacks and huts of South Africa's townships, a commentator from the *Cape Argus* articulated the grim truth: "Like a meteor, Mr. Kennedy has flashed across the South African sky and has gone. . . . South Africa remains as it was."

□ □ □ □

Despite the brief passion stirred by Kennedy's trip, Verwoerd continued to strengthen his grip. He now openly defied his opponents at home and abroad. His relations with Great Britain had soured rapidly when Labour Party leader Harold Wilson became prime minister in November 1964. Days after his election, Wilson announced that England would embargo future arms shipments to South Africa. The decision provoked an outcry among British conservatives and English-speaking South Africans, and Verwoerd skillfully fanned the discontent. If South Africa did not receive the Buccaneer bomber and other weapons it wanted, Verwoerd warned, South Africa would have to reconsider whether Britain would be permitted to use the Simonstown naval base in the Western Cape. Wilson struggled to maintain the ban but eventually had to dilute the restrictions.

After years of observing American leaders' insubstantial poses, Verwoerd felt equally certain that the U.S. government had no stomach for a real confrontation. He refused to allow South African government officials to attend the integrated celebrations and receptions held occasionally by American embassies and consular offices. Though for years the United States naval vessels had stopped for refueling and shore leave in Cape Town, such visits became a new source of contention in May 1965, when the Pentagon asked the South African government for permission to bring the U.S. aircraft carrier *Independence* to Cape Town. Word got out that Verwoerd had laid down conditions: all American Negro sailors would have to obey the apartheid laws while in Cape Town and no Negro could be included in the crew of any aircraft landing on South African fields. The Johnson administration, faced with public embarrassment, refused to accept the terms and spent a huge amount of money refueling the aircraft carrier and all future warships en route from Vietnam at sea. When challenged about the shore leave policy in the House of Assembly, Verwoerd said that while his government desired the highest degree of friendship with the United States, South Africa had the right to demand that the South African way of life be respected. Besides, he pointed out, South Africa had always required that no Negro would be stationed at the American missile tracking stations, and the American agencies had accepted this from the beginning. Verwoerd's revelation triggered another flurry of condemnations in the U.S. House of Representatives and vigorous protest from some South African businessmen, but Verwoerd remained unmoved.

While thumbing his nose at the United States, Verwoerd quintupled the defense budget; combined with the security police, it absorbed a third of all government spending. Whenever the ANC managed to commit an act of sabotage, the government responded by tightening control. The police jailed hundreds under the Ninety-Day Law, which was briefly suspended in 1965 and then extended to allow for six months' detention without charges. Showy political trials also continued. John Vorster was delighted when he had gathered enough information from informers to prove that Nelson Mandela's attorney, Bram Fischer, had been active in the secret South African Communist Party. Fischer was arrested in 1964, jumped bail in 1965, and spent a year in hiding until Vorster's men finally tracked him down in February 1966. At his trial, the government tried to use Fischer to incriminate Beyers Naudé and other activists, but to no avail. The prosecutors succeeded in winning a conviction of Fischer under the Suppression of Communism Act, and the judge sentenced the former star attorney to life in prison.

Throughout the middle of the decade, the police arrested more than seven hundred fifty thousand people annually for pass law violations. More and more, terse press reports announced that this or that prisoner had died in detention; the police usually explained that the person had committed suicide, leapt from a tenth-story window, or had been killed trying to escape. Courts around the country swelled with political trials. In 1965 the long-term prison population surged to more than seventy-two thousand. Fifteen thousand people were tied to stakes and given the lash. When queried about the brutality, Verwoerd never flinched. South Africa was, he believed, trying to win a war. Indeed, in words which antithetically echoed Mandela's, Verwoerd announced in speech after speech that white supremacy was a virtue for which "we must be prepared to die." In truth, most of the dying was being done by others.

Verwoerd's rule was not without setbacks. His plan to encourage the industrialization of the areas around the homelands had faltered. Despite onerous influx controls, tens of thousands continued to pour into the Johannesburg area every year in a desperate search for work. While his glib defense of the government's policies had lulled foreign investors and the white electorate of South Africa, most nations of the world showed little sign of accepting apartheid. Not only did the International Olympic Committee ban the South African team from the 1964 Olympics; but as various countries learned of Verwoerd's insistence that any team visiting his country or representing South Africa abroad had to be entirely white, they gradually withdrew from bilateral competition.

One of Verwoerd's most serious dilemmas—and a potentially disastrous crack in the rationale for apartheid—arose out of the government's treatment of the Coloured population. On the one hand, Verwoerd continued his effort to disentangle persons of all races. He ordered the removal of nearly eighty thousand adults and children from District Six, a historic Coloured neighborhood in Cape Town, because the area had been designated white. After the families had been forced out, the government bulldozed hundreds of homes and buildings that had stood for generations, leaving a naked and barren wound near the center of the city. At the same time, Verwoerd had to battle with the continuing question of the political rights of the Coloureds. Politicians from across the white political spectrum—from Progressives to United Party members to Cape Nationalists—challenged the prime minister on how separate development would apply to the Coloured population, who had no geographical homeland to which they could be assigned. As the questioning intensified, Verwoerd acknowledged what many had suspected all along—that apartheid, in the end, was not primarily a territorial concept, but a political one. Verwoerd's insistence that despite their permanent presence in "white" South Africa, Coloureds would never be permitted to participate in parliament but would have to rely on councils and parliaments of their own drew attention to the weakest point in Verwoerd's grand theory. In the end, the distinction that mattered was not culture or geography or capacity, but race.

By 1966, however, it seemed as though Verwoerd's problems would be swept aside by the white population's rising infatuation with their leader. Cabinet ministers, party officials, and sympathetic journalists heaped praise on him, describing him as "the greatest Western leader of our time," "the Joshua who led his people to the promised land," and "the savior of white civilization." Government bureaucrats and town councils stumbled over each other in the rush to name public places after him. During his life, Verwoerd could drive over several Verwoerd Bridges and down numerous Verwoerd Streets. He could stop and speak at Hendrik Verwoerd primary and secondary schools across the country or stroll through the Hendrik Verwoerd Social Science Center at Stellenbosch University. The brand-new post office in central Johannesburg, constructed across from city hall, was named for Verwoerd. The government, as part of the half-billion-dollar Orange River irrigation project, created a huge artificial lake with the aid of the massive Hendrik Verwoerd Dam. In Durban, white teenage boys formed Verwoerd commando groups and marched through town in military formation, beating drums and carrying huge photographs of their hero. After the attempt on his life in 1960, the prime minister's admirers created the Hendrik Verwoerd trust fund. Several years later the trustees of the fund created an annual five-thousand-pound award to be given to someone who had rendered a service of national importance. The first winner of the Hendrik Verwoerd Prize, awarded on the eve of the fifth anniversary of the republic, was Prime Minister Hendrik Verwoerd.

Verwoerd's confidence in his political and personal support was so strong that in early 1966 he called a general election almost a year before he was required to do so. The campaign was swift and his opponents were disorganized. Even Helen Suzman's supporters expected her to lose. Nationalist colleagues approached her regularly in parliament and told her, "I'll miss you, Helen." "Why?" asked Suzman, with her usual pluck. "Aren't you running again?" As election day neared, black newspapers urged whites to support Suzman, and Harry Oppenheimer campaigned for her vigorously, telling gatherings that a vote for her would be a blow struck for all that was best in South Africa. "I think I have a good chance to win," Helen told a reporter. "And what a horrible fate that will be—to have to listen to these characters for another five years! If I win, I'll fall on my sword." In March, Suzman again squeaked by, with a margin of 711 votes.

The election gave the National Party 126 members in parliament, the highest number ever. Verwoerd was elated; separate development could now push forward rapidly. In July, Verwoerd received another boost when the long-standing debate in the United Nations and the World Court over South Africa's mandate in South West Africa sputtered to a ridiculous end. After more than five years of discussion and three thousand pages of written opinion, the World Court, in a tight vote of eight to seven, dismissed the complaint against South Africa for extending apartheid to the mandated territory on the technical grounds that the two original plaintiffs, Ethiopia and Liberia, had lacked sufficient legal standing to bring the charge. The United States government expressed surprise; the African nations were crestfallen and never again fully trusted the World Court as a forum for international justice. When the African nations vowed to bring up the matter of South African control of South West Africa in the United Nations, the South African ambassador announced that as a result of the World Court ruling his country no longer felt bound by any international body in its administration of the vast desert colony.

As Verwoerd approached the September parliamentary session, he turned his attention to the lingering problems facing his country. The first was to increase the nation's economic and military self-sufficiency to shield it from whatever pressures the world community might attempt. The second was to expand South Africa's influence in the region, in part to intimidate neighbors and deny the ANC their support. To that end, he invited Chief Leabua Jonathan, prime minister of Lesotho, the former British protectorate Basutoland, to pay a "state visit" to Pretoria. Verwoerd seemed to hope that relations with this tiny, landlocked state in the middle of South Africa and its counterpart Swaziland, to the northeast, could serve as models for South African relations with the fractured and artificial bantustans. Moreover, Verwoerd intended to warn the chief that he would use economic and military force against Lesotho if the ANC again attempted to use it as a staging area and an escape route for acts of sabotage. Chief Jonathan arrived for his formal visit on Friday, September 2; after two hours of conversation, they issued a joint statement pledging "not to interfere in one another's domestic affairs."

Verwoerd then left for a weekend at the little farm on the banks of the Vaal River—Stokkiesdraai (Playing Hooky)—which his admirers had purchased and given to him as a retreat. He hurried back to his office in Pretoria on Monday to prepare a major parliamentary address on foreign policy. On Tuesday morning, September 6, he and his wife flew to Cape Town. Verwoerd met with his party caucus, had lunch, and then went to the parliamentary building for the two o'clock session. In the lobby outside the chamber, he kissed his wife and gave leave of his two bodyguards as they headed upstairs to the public gallery. As the bells announcing the opening of the session began to ring, the prime minister strolled onto the floor of the chamber with J. E. Potgieter, the National Party whip. Potgieter told him that the opposition party had asked whether the prime minister intended to speak first. No, said Verwoerd, Sir de Villiers Graaff could begin. Potgieter told Verwoerd that because he had to be out of town two days later, he wanted to wish the prime minister a happy sixty-fifth birthday a little early. The prime minister thanked him warmly, shook his hand, and sat down.

At nearly quarter past two, as the deputies took their seats and the press scrambled in from lunch, a tall parliamentary messenger in a black and green uniform moved quickly onto the floor of parliament and crossed to the prime minister's seat. A Nationalist deputy noticed with irritation that the man didn't seem to be fully dressed, that he was fumbling with the buttons of his coat. John Vorster, sitting near Verwoerd, did not observe the messenger because he had forgotten his glasses and, having borrowed those of another cabinet minister, P. W. Botha, was struggling to adjust them in preparation for his own remarks. As the messenger approached the prime minister, Verwoerd looked up and smiled in greeting. The messenger seemed to stumble; the deputies looked over in alarm. But the messenger had not stumbled; with his right hand he had pulled a razor-sharp knife from its sheath and plunged it directly into the carotid artery in the prime minister's neck. Three more lightning strikes pierced Verwoerd's right lung, left lung, and heart.

The deputies, momentarily dazed, hurled themselves on the assailant, who slashed and punched at them with maniacal strength. Mrs. Verwoerd, who had just arrived in the viewing gallery, wondered about the scuffle; she could not see her husband slumped across his desk nor the blood streaming onto the green carpet. The messenger, tackled and pinned to the floor by four men, shouted, "Where's that bastard? I'll get the bastard!" His captors discovered two more hunting knives, one stuck in his belt, the other in his underwear. Botha, blinded by fury, jumped over to Helen Suzman's seat, grabbed her, and screamed, "It's you who did this! It's all you liberals! You incite people! Now we will get you! We will get the lot of you!"

A few deputies who were medical doctors rushed to aid the wounded prime minister, ripping open his clothes, pressing handkerchiefs into his wounds, giving him mouth to mouth resuscitation. Fifteen minutes after the attack, medics had loaded the prime minister onto a stretcher and rushed him to the hospital. When the ambulance arrived at the hospital, ten doctors worked desperately to revive the prime minister. Within minutes, they gave up. Judging from the nature of the wounds, they agreed that Hendrik Verwoerd, the man of granite, had been slain instantly in his seat.

As in America with the murder of John F. Kennedy, the whole country froze, shocked into a stupor. Verwoerd, the brilliant mastermind of white supremacy, the overwhelming voice of Afrikaner nationalism for a generation, and the indomitable force in government for sixteen years, had suddenly been effaced. The nation, launched on the great trek into apartheid, had in a horrible instant lost the only man who seemed to know the directions. Moses had been struck down before reaching the Promised Land.

The attention of the nation, bordering on hysteria, turned immediately to the assassin. John Vorster took personal charge of the investigation. Could this be the work of the African National Congress? everyone wondered. Could this be an act of terrorism by the Communist forces that, Verwoerd had warned, threatened South Africa from inside and out? The truth, as it emerged, was more bizarre and, in a sense, more frustrating. The messenger was not an agent of the ANC; he was a forty-eight-year-old schizophrenic named Dmitri Tsafendas, born in Mozambique to a Greek father and a Portuguese-African mother. Ferried in his childhood among relatives in Greece, Mozambique, and South Africa, Tsafendas had worked as a young man in a South African tank factory and then boarded a U.S. naval convoy, where he worked until the end of World War II. After the war, he tried to enter the United States permanently and was locked up for several weeks in a psychiatric ward in Massachusetts; eventually U.S. immigration officials deported him to Greece. The Greeks soon expelled him and sent him on to Portugal, where the authorities threw him in jail without trial for three years for having originally left Mozambique without a passport. In 1958 he escaped, obtained false documents, and drifted through a dozen countries, including England, the United States, Rhodesia, Germany, and various spots in the Middle East. Local authorities alternated between locking him up in mental institutions (by the time of the assassination he had spent time in eight) and kicking him out of their countries. In December 1965, Tsafendas made his way back to South Africa. The holder of a coveted "white" identity card, he took a variety of odd jobs until he was hired by parliament as a temporary messenger just eight weeks before the murder. Much of the controversy focused on how such an unstable person could have been awarded such a job, and indeed the investigation uncovered multiple files on Tsafendas scattered throughout the government bureaucracy. The commission faulted the lack of cross-referencing; no one mentioned the obvious fact that since the parliament required its messengers to be white, the continual shortage of white labor for such low-paying jobs caused the messenger corps to take virtually anyone who applied.

The commission of inquiry and Vorster's police interviewed dozens of people who had known Tsafendas, trying to unearth an explanation for his act. They heard a few garbled, inconsistent complaints, but nothing decisive. They asked Tsafendas himself and he gave a horrendous answer. His body was inhabited by a huge, serrated tapeworm, he said, which wriggled toward his neck every time he ate delicious food. The tapeworm, which he also called the dragon, the demon, and the snake, had become increasingly demanding, had controlled more and more of his thoughts and actions, and had finally ordered the death of Verwoerd. Why? "I don't know," said Tsafendas. "I can't explain it. It is complex, frustrations, you know." Government officials, furious that they had not found a conspiracy, sentenced Tsafendas to life imprisonment in a psychiatric prison. In the end, the nation had to struggle with a profound irony: the man of unyielding principle had not been killed for his principles; he had been snuffed out by a madman. In hindsight it seems evident that if Verwoerd's murderer had been anyone else—an African, an agent of the African National Congress, a white radical—it would have unleashed a storm of retribution on whole populations of innocents. Instead, left with the news that the assassination had been the work of a single, deranged individual, the nation mourned fitfully.

Verwoerd's funeral required a massive airlift to move hundreds of elected representatives and government officials, who had just migrated south to attend the spring session of parliament in Cape Town, all the way back to Pretoria, where the government sat the rest of the year. On Saturday, September 10, as hundreds of thousands of people filled the streets of Pretoria bearing signs saying, "Ons Treur"—We Mourn—Verwoerd's funeral, attended by ten thousand guests, was held in the huge amphitheater just below the ruddy sandstone Union Building, now decked with purple and black, where Verwoerd had worked for sixteen years. Across the valley and up on the opposite hill, the solid mass of the Voortrekker Monument stood in silhouette against the sky. The Dutch

Reformed minister who preached spoke plaintively of South Africa's eager desire for peace in the midst of "vicious attacks" and an "evil propaganda campaign" inflicted on it by the outside world. Just as King David's message endured in Israel even after his death, so would Verwoerd's in South Africa. Many in the crowd wept.

Afterward soldiers mounted Verwoerd's coffin on a truck-drawn gun carriage and formed a military honor guard to accompany his body through the city to the graveyard at Hero's Acre. Scores of National Party officials fell into line behind. "Die laaste trek," said one burly Afrikaner as he and his family watched the procession go by. The coffin moved slowly along Church Street and through Church Square, where, in sight of the statue of Paul Kruger and of the Supreme Court Building in which Mandela had been sentenced, a thousand more soldiers and police joined the ranks of the honor guard. Minutes later, several squadrons of South Africa's Sabre and Mirage jet fighters screamed overhead in salute. At the graveside, only Verwoerd's family moved forward; borne by five sons and two sons-in-law, the prime minister's coffin came to rest in the plot next to his predecessor, Hans Strijdom.

Three days later, National Party leaders deliberated over a successor, searching for a man with the *kradigheid,* or brute forcefulness, to tighten the vise of white supremacy. They quickly found him in the fifty-year-old minister of justice, John Vorster. After selecting him unanimously, the elders of the National Party herded together behind their new leader as he made his first statement. "I promise you that as far as it is humanly possible I will strive for the security of South Africa," he said, waving his fist in the air for emphasis. "As far as it pleases God Almighty to allow man to work out his own future and decide on his own destiny, the destiny of South Africa will be decided by ourselves." That destiny, he continued, was to walk farther along the road set by Verwoerd and his predecessors. When Vorster finished, the entire National Party caucus spontaneously sang a hymn, "Laat Heer U seen op hom daal"—"O God, let your mercy descend on him." Vorster bowed his head while his wife and daughter beamed with pride.

FIVE

Students and Strategists (1966–1970)

It is nauseating to hear those who have reduced Africans to silence by force now boast of that silence as proof of their happiness and contentment.
—EDGAR BROOKES

"THE APPOINTMENT of Mr. Vorster means that South African Nationalists . . . have turned over the reins of government to the most extreme, most ruthless, and most totalitarian of their party leaders," wrote the editors of the *New York Times* in September 1966. "Mr. Vorster's accession almost certainly means that South Africa will move at an accelerated pace toward complete isolation and eventual collision with most of the rest of the world."

The elevation of Vorster, the brutal enforcer of Verwoerdian apartheid, brought new urgency to the small band of black and liberal anti-apartheid activists in the United States. Their ten-year drive to get the American government or the United Nations to impose sanctions on South Africa had failed. The African nations had won passage of several resolutions favoring sanctions in the UN General Assembly, but each time the Western powers had blocked discussion in the Security Council, the only place where sanctions could be made binding. A few countries announced their own unilateral trade restrictions against South Africa, but the economic price to each nation was high and the cost to South Africa's flourishing commerce low. The leaders of some African nations, succumbing to necessity, expediency, and greed, resumed trade under the table, strengthening the South African government's view that most foreigners were hypocrites who liked to denounce the evil of apartheid publicly while wrestling privately for a piece of South Africa's wealth.

The Security Council did impose sanctions in 1965 on Rhodesia, but as he had done with the British and American embargoes, Ian Smith found numerous ways to elude the restrictions.

Within the United States the activists had also lost faith in the possibilities for presidential initiative. Kennedy and Johnson had made halting attempts, but those had been stalled by domestic, international, and bureaucratic politics. Each department within the American government had an institutional reason to maintain cordial relations with South Africa: the Defense Department valued the overflight rights, the use of South African ports, and the information on Soviet ship movements in the Indian Ocean; the Commerce Department pursued its mandate of seeding and watering American investment around the world and of protecting the American balance of payments; the Treasury Department worried about the destabilizing effect of a disruption in the flow of African gold on the international monetary system; NASA guarded its tracking stations; and the CIA protected its close relationship with the South African intelligence services and police. Even within the State Department, warring factions battled to an uneasy truce that acquired the inertia of tradition the longer it endured. Change was always portrayed as someone else's responsibility: the White House thought that the question of investment in South Africa should be a market judgment for American businessmen at the very time when American businessmen argued that it was a foreign policy decision best left to the White House. At the intersections of Washington's labyrinthine bureaucracy, differing policy recommendations on South Africa would press forward and then stall in hopeless gridlock.

The Congress of the United States, for its part, offered little evidence of imminent boldness on African affairs. The Senate subcommittee on Africa had been moribund since John F. Kennedy's move from the chairmanship to the presidency. The House subcommittee on Africa, chaired by Barrett O'Hara, an amiable liberal Democrat from Illinois, confined its activities to high-speed tours of Africa and inconsequential hearings. In 1966, on the sole occasion when O'Hara decided to quiz American companies on their holdings in South Africa, not a single industry representative deigned to appear. Nor could black elected officials provide the necessary spark. In the mid-1960s there were still only a handful of black representatives; these few chose to husband their limited seniority and influence for use on domestic issues and to ensure their own reelection.

The paralysis of the federal government required American activists to shift away from that target and toward American public opinion and American businesses operating in South Africa. The initial prospects were not promising. Though a growing number of Americans had begun to ask questions about southern Africa, the opinions of the great majority fluctuated between ignorance and apathy. In an effort to correct this, the American Committee on Africa continued to organize conferences and to publish a magazine, *Africa Today,* though its circulation rarely exceeded four thousand. Ted Brown, the executive director of the American Negro Leadership Conference on Africa, tried to promote his organization as a unified front of American blacks, but the leaders on his board and their constituents showed only sporadic enthusiasm for the idea. They were no match for the sleek lobbying and public relations teams assembled by industry groups or hired by the Portuguese, Rhodesians, and South Africans, who routinely spent hundreds of thousands of dollars to court legislators, buy advertisements, mail out mountains of literature, and organize free trips.

If the government would not impose limitations on American investment in South Africa, the activists reasoned, maybe pressure could be brought to bear directly on American businesses. The need for such pressure seemed especially urgent because the Nationalist government had started pointing to foreign investment as a sign of moral support for its vision of the future. Henry P. Van Dusen, the dean of Union Theological Seminary in New York City, had visited South Africa in 1963 and had been shocked by how many South Africans equated American investment with endorsement of apartheid. "Let there be no underestimate of the importance which the ruling minority . . . attaches to American financial support," he wrote in a letter from Johannesburg. "I know from firsthand testimony that it is their strongest single encouragement to pursuit of their present policies. . . . One of the foremost statesmen of South Africa remarked to me in personal conversation: 'So long as United States banks and business back us, we can go ahead.'"

George Houser at the American Committee on Africa, who had been promoting the idea of economic disengagement for several years, had, in 1964 and again in 1966, attacked Charles Engelhard, an American citizen who ran a tangled network of companies with enormous holdings of South African gold, uranium, coal, and chrome. British author Ian Fleming, whose father had assisted Engelhard with legal matters in 1949, had been so struck by the American magnate that he is said to have used him as the model for one of his most famous villains, Goldfinger. Charles Engelhard was deeply involved in the economic life of South Africa, serving as one of the cofounders of the South Africa Foundation and a director of the South African Chamber of Mines (which enforced uniform wages and living conditions for all black miners) as well as twenty-two other South African concerns. In 1958 he had arranged a thirty-million-dollar American bank loan to South Africa and then set up the American–South African Investment Corporation to help shore up the South African economy after the Sharpeville crisis.

Engelhard was also a major contributor to the Democratic Party in the United States. As the result of his largesse, he had almost been picked by Kennedy to serve as ambassador to France. Instead Kennedy and Johnson sent him as the U.S. representative to the celebration of the independence of Gabon in 1962 and the consecration of Pope Paul VI in 1963. Engelhard had also made a brief but unsuccessful pass at the Democratic nomination for governor of New Jersey. In 1964 Lyndon Johnson selected him to serve on the advisory board of the new federal Community Relations Service (created to improve racial harmony in local areas) and sent him to attend the ceremonies marking the independence of Zambia. At a garden party outside the state house in Zambia, Engelhard met George Houser and commented amiably that the American Committee on Africa had criticized him for maintaining directorships and other corporate ties about which he had completely forgotten.

In early 1966, Houser focused on Engelhard again after discovering that the New Jersey regional office of the National Conference of Christians and Jews intended to give Engelhard the group's annual brotherhood award at a special dinner in his honor. Houser protested sharply on the grounds that Engelhard was a major supporter and beneficiary of the apartheid economy. Engelhard refused comment, but reporters covering the controversy dug up a recent speech in which Engelhard had argued that "racial harmony is one of the prerequisites for economic prosperity in South Africa." At the same time, he said, South Africa's "nonwhites enjoy a considerably higher standard of living and better education facilities than the population in any other country in Africa." On the day of the award, five hundred chanting demonstrators from the American Committee on Africa, the NAACP, CORE, the United Auto Workers, the Drug and Hospital Workers Union, and local churches and universities picketed the dinner. Red-faced and angry, Engelhard, surrounded by a police escort, pressed through the barrier of people and received the award for "building human understanding."

The protest against Engelhard produced no real results, however, leaving Houser and the representatives of other anti-apartheid groups— who had formed themselves into a coalition known as the Consultative Council—pondering where to focus. The answer came in the spring of 1966, with the efforts of two students at Union Theological Seminary, Charles W. Powers and David Hornbeck, both of whom had been enrolled in a special one-year intensive program at Columbia's School of International Relations. The two young men, prompted by Van Dusen's writings about the role of American banks, decided to spend part of their year studying U.S. bank lending to the Verwoerd regime. After months of research, they concluded that the two banks that had shown the most initiative in extending financial assistance were Chase Manhattan and First National City Bank (later Citibank), both of which owned and operated their own branches in South Africa. Armed with their study, Powers and Hornbeck visited student groups in nearby schools to enlist their support in a boycott of First National's branches on Morningside Heights near the seminary. Quickly the student cabinet of Union Seminary, the Columbia University Student Council, the executive committee of the government at the Jewish Theological Seminary, and the managing board of the newspaper at Barnard College all signed on. Soon afterward other groups from outside academia offered their support, including the American Committee on Africa and the Southern Africa Council of the National Student Christian Federation (which later became the University Christian Movement).

On March 13, 1966, Powers, Hornbeck, and their supporters announced that because of First National City Bank's support for the "socially and morally abhorrent" policy of apartheid, they were asking the bank to close its South African branches. If the bank did not, the students vowed to move their accounts to other financial institutions on April 20. A spokesman for the bank immediately rejected the students' contentions and request. "The only government whose policies we support is the United States government," he said, adding that he didn't "think it would be appropriate for us to get into any public controversy with these lads." Four days later, Powers and Hornbeck met with Richard S. Perkins, the chairman of the bank's executive committee. They asked him to close the branches and stop lending to the government and to businesses in South Africa. When Perkins refused on all counts, the students pressed forward with their plans.

While feverishly organizing the upcoming events, Powers and Hornbeck wrote to Wendell Foster, one of Houser's assistants, to urge the American Committee on Africa to offer counsel on the future of the drive against the banks. They proposed that the staff of the ACOA work with the members of the Consultative Council to build a citywide drive. Their suggestions produced a favorable response, for soon afterward the ACOA staff developed a preliminary internal plan for a fall campaign against the two banks.

The student protest went off without a hitch. Just after lunch on April 20, scores of students suddenly crowded into First National City Bank's branch office at 111th Street and Broadway. "The branch's integrated teller staff received them pleasantly," wrote a reporter, "and closed out the accounts of about seventy with dispatch." Outside, nearly three hundred students, plus a smattering of faculty, marched in double file and waved signs denouncing the bank. "Most of them were ministerial students," described the reporter, "and the manner of their protest was sober, quiet, courteous, and dignified."

This protest, though brief and tame compared with the antiwar demonstrations that would soon follow, gave birth to a prolonged process of reflection within the bureaucracies of the mainline churches. Confronted with the students' request to various religious boards that church money be withdrawn from the banks, the trustees and members of these boards had to respond—and they had no idea what to say. At first they tried to slough the problem off. At an early meeting with nearly two dozen representatives from the Methodist, Episcopal, Presbyterian, and Lutheran Churches and from the National Council of Churches, the students were told that if the denominations withdrew from First National City they would have to deposit their funds "in some other international bank and would be in much the same situation as we are now." Moreover, "such an action would not really correct the situation in South Africa . . . and would hurt [black South Africans] more than it would help them." The most the church leaders were willing to do, they said, was to discuss the matter within their respective denominations and to form a joint committee to study the question.

Such attempts to deflect the problem succeeded only temporarily. In a strange slow-motion chain reaction, the students' request that churches offer a moral defense for their investments triggered several decades of internal deliberation. Over the next few years the obscure committees that form the cogs of religious bureaucracies gradually and methodically cranked their way through the ethics of bank lending to South Africa. At the beginning the churches confined themselves to statements of concern and promises to search for more information. In June, for example, the members of the Executive Council of the Episcopal Church urged all dioceses and parishes to examine the "moral dilemma" posed by profits earned from investments in South Africa. Soon the very process of deliberation, boosted by events in South Africa, would take on a life and direction of its own, as these lumbering institutions worked out the practical implications of their own commitments.

In the summer, the members of the American Committee on Africa and the National Student Christian Federation joined forces to create the Committee of Conscience against Apartheid, demanding an end to American participation in a consortium of banks that sponsored a revolving loan fund to South Africa. A. Philip Randolph, the chairman of the effort, sent out letters urging that organizations withdraw their money from banks in the consortium on December 9, the day before Human Rights Day. Soon afterward the editorial board of the liberal religious publication *Christianity and Crisis* announced the withdrawal of ten thousand dollars from First National City Bank. Randolph also led two demonstrations, held a summer press conference, and engaged in several negotiations with the banks.

In preparation for the campaign, George Houser drafted a document entitled "Rationale for the Protest against Banks Doing Business with South Africa," which stands as one of the most succinct arguments for economic disengagement from South Africa. Houser made five observations about the current American policy. First, the policy, despite the 1963 arms embargo, could only be said to be one of engagement, since American investments were rapidly rising with the tacit approval of the United States government. Second, as the corporate stake in South Africa grew, the executives of American companies had become less, rather than more, outspoken against apartheid. Third, the economic structure of South Africa could not be significantly reformed as long as hundreds of white supremacist laws were enforced. Fourth, apartheid was not a simple problem of discrimination; it was an entire social and economic system that would not be affected by minor changes within a particular industry. Last, Houser insisted, the argument advanced by Engelhard and others that economic growth by itself would cause dramatic improvements had been disproven over the past five years, when soaring economic growth had been accompanied by increasingly repressive tactics.

Houser then offered four reasons for disinvestment. The first, which he called the "moral argument," was that "South Africa's apartheid policy was unique" and that a failure to resolve apartheid would lead to violence throughout Africa and perhaps beyond. Thus Americans had a moral obligation to act quickly to avert such violence. The second, "the effectiveness argument," noted that unilateral American disinvestment would be a sign of international leadership and might be followed by other countries, thus generating the same result as formal United Nations sanctions. The third reason was that of "prestige"—basically, of America's putting its money where its mouth was. "America's policy towards South Africa is looked upon by the rest of the world as the measure of American sincerity in espousing freedom and equality for all men," Houser wrote. "The policy will be found wanting as long as American capital supports and profits from apartheid." Finally, Houser advanced the "non-necessity argument," in which he pointed out that American trade with and investment in South Africa was such a small portion of total U.S. foreign commerce that the nation could easily afford to forgo it.

Houser advanced a claim that would be hotly debated for the next two decades. If American companies did not withdraw from South Africa, he insisted, American citizens should withdraw from those companies.

His focus was on closing accounts at banks, but in the next decade the notion would be expanded into divestment, that is, purging stock portfolios of the equities of offending companies. In linking *divestment* (the sale of stock) to *disinvestment* (the withdrawal of U.S. firms from South Africa), Houser outlined the argument that would vex policymakers in thousands of American financial institutions, foundations, universities, religious groups, pension funds, city councils, state legislatures, and corporations for the next quarter century. The debate could be simplified into two questions: First, would the disinvestment of American companies lead to the elimination of apartheid? Second, would divestment cause those companies to disinvest? Though Houser acknowledged freely that the bank campaign by itself was not likely to do either, he believed that cumulatively, over time, the answer to both questions would be yes.

On December 9, 1966, three months after Verwoerd's assassination, A. Philip Randolph announced that more than twenty-three million dollars had been withdrawn from the targeted banks as a result of the campaign. Spokespersons for the banks immediately disputed the number and said that less than fifteen thousand dollars had been removed. Houser, noting that his organization had more than two hundred signed documents from persons pledging to withdraw their funds, attributed the discrepancy in part to the failure of the pledgers to notify the banks of the reasons for their withdrawals.

Though the banks made no immediate move to change policy, their public statements revealed that the moral contours of the debate had changed significantly over the previous eighteen months. In a statement to the press, bank executives revealed an interesting shift in their public reasoning. "We believe," they said, "that withdrawal from South Africa would be a move away from the goal that all of us want: the sound development of the continent of Africa for the benefit of all Africans." Though there was no mention of political or human rights, the bank executives could no longer argue that they could lend anywhere in the world. The central question, the spokesmen now felt obliged to say, was what was best—in this case economically—for the Africans.

From then on, the bank campaign continued to expand. In January 1967, thirty-one Protestant leaders announced their support for a drive to block the extension of the revolving loan fund to South Africa. A week later Chicago police arrested twenty-four people for a sit-in at Continental Illinois National Bank. In March, as the *New York Times* reported, "the struggle for civil rights reached the stockholders' meeting of a major New York City bank," when James Farmer of CORE appeared at the annual meeting of Morgan Guaranty and argued that the bank's participation in the loan fund made it complicit in apartheid. A week later a stockholder stood up at the annual meeting of Chase Manhattan to ask the bank to withdraw from South Africa, but he was ruled out of order by the chairman, George Champion.

The burgeoning protest was not limited to banks. In May the chairman of General Motors, Frederic G. Donner, had to fend off a question about the automaker's employment practices at the plant in Port Elizabeth. Donner said that the company ran the plant in the "usual nondiscriminatory manner within the laws of the country." The intrusion of social issues into the normally stodgy annual meetings attracted the notice of some business writers, one of whom remarked presciently that the trend was sure to grow.

In September 1967, the first large religious denomination made its move. Earlier that year, during their annual meeting, the members of the Methodist Board of Missions, the largest agency of the Methodist Church, had backed away from any position on bank lending. "If withdrawal of our funds from banks doing business with the Republic of South Africa would do more than merely make a public gesture of opposition to apartheid, we would immediately do so," they said in a public statement. The issue was "more complex" because it was "a question of national policy." Activists and editors of church publications howled in protest. The statement, said one editor, "reveals how completely the board deluded itself, circumvented the main issue, and shifted the responsibility to someone else. . . . In the first place," the critic continued, "who's to say withdrawing is 'merely a public gesture' and since when have we belittled public gestures? If a public gesture is so inconsequential, it wouldn't have taken much courage to have made it. . . . [In addition], national policy is a reflection of us and is only changed when *we* change it by what *we* do." Faced with such derision, the Methodist board members quickly reversed course. In the fall they announced they would remove ten million dollars from First National City Bank if the bank renewed its credit arrangement with the South African government. When the bank executives went ahead and renewed the loan, the Missions Board, backed by the national church office, yanked its deposits.

In addition to the church efforts, students at various universities across the country began to debate the South African question. Three hundred students from Amherst College, Smith College, and the University of Massachusetts held a rally on Valentine's Day 1968 to protest the presence of recruiters from Dow Chemical, the chief manufacturer of the napalm used in Vietnam, and Chase Manhattan, for its loans to South Africa. Later that spring hundreds of students at Princeton University, Cornell University, and the University of Wisconsin marched to object to their universities' investments in companies operating in South

Africa; university administrators responded soon afterward by forming faculty or trustee committees to look into the matter. At Harvard Law School, fifty students demonstrated against the presence of recruiters from the law firm of Milbank, Tweed, Hadley & McCoy on the grounds that the firm had represented Chase Manhattan bank. At Spelman College, a black school in Atlanta that since 1882 had received the majority of its philanthropic support from the Rockefeller family (and had been named for the family matriarch, Laura Spelman Rockefeller), students heckled her grandson, Republican governor and presidential candidate Nelson Rockefeller, for his brother David's role as the chairman of Chase Manhattan. "Get your money out of South Africa," they shouted, stinging a man who prided himself on his long-standing support for civil rights.

In South Africa, John Vorster struggled to be faithful to the doctrine of his dead master and to bring Verwoerd's gauzy vision of the future into the gritty present. It was a task for which Vorster was poorly equipped. Lacking his predecessor's ideological brilliance, Vorster found himself pressed to respond to the multiplying and unforeseen consequences of Verwoerd's plan. On the surface, Vorster had little cause for concern. The South African economy, though increasingly concentrated in sprawling conglomerates or immense state-owned monopolies, continued to flourish. The annual growth rate reached nearly seven percent, equivalent to the best that any industrialized nation, including Japan, had achieved. The manufacturing industry, though still dependent on the mines, had grown into adolescence, aided by the government's enormous investments in energy, weaponry, and steel. South Africa seemed destined to fulfill the glowing predictions that its public relations teams had seeded in newspapers and magazines around the world. Foreign investments, lured by high profits, low wages, and a tame workforce, flowed in freely. It mattered little that the growth was based on an artificial stimulant—gold—or that the stability was enforced with the truncheon, the machine gun, and the noose. Vorster was able to maintain, for the first few years of his rule, that the fantasy would endure forever.

A closer look, however, told another story. There were, for example, the increasing numbers of bizarre incidents of people caught and crushed in the maw of racial taxonomy. As privileges were taken away from Coloureds and given to whites, more Coloured persons tried to leap over the divide. This prompted the government to tighten the rules annually for qualifications as white. To prevent people from slipping through on the basis of appearance, the government ordered that applicants show proof of their parentage based on the 1951 census, disregarding the slipshod way in which those earlier assignments of race had been made. The intensified genealogical research produced some embarrassing results: one white South African scholar, for example, concluded that the average supposedly pure-bred Afrikaner was actually about seven percent black. Despite the drive to tighten the restrictions, the bureaucrats in the Vorster government proved that they could be flexible when they found it necessary. When Japanese businessmen arrived in South Africa to establish trading and investment links, the South African government, not wishing to offend, decided that the Japanese would be classified as "honorary whites." The nine thousand South Africans of Chinese descent, however, were classified as nonwhites, though, said one department head, they could use white facilities if the whites "did not object."

The tales of individual misery created by the government system of classification piled up steadily in the press. In 1967 Sandra Laing was eleven years old. Though Sandra was the daughter of white parents and had white siblings, she herself had olive skin and tightly curled hair. Observing her appearance, an apartheid bureaucrat reclassified her as Coloured. Her family challenged the ruling, but the superior court upheld it, at which point Sandra was immediately expelled from her all-white school. When her family tried to enroll her in another white school, parents of the other students threatened a boycott. Representatives of the Race Classification Board told the Laings that Sandra, as a Coloured person, could no longer live in the white neighborhood with her family unless they applied for a permit for her to remain as a servant. Just when it seemed that Sandra might be forced out of her home, the members of the Race Classification Board, facing sharp protest, reversed themselves and declared her white.

The wrath of the Race Classification Board was often summoned by vigilant neighbors eager to preserve the racial purity of their communities. Mr. and Mrs. William Walker, who were both in their sixties, had lived abroad for a number of years, returned to South Africa, and moved with seven of their ten children into a neighborhood in Pretoria. The watchful residents around their new home reported to the Department of the Interior that they doubted that Mr. Walker was truly white. The department investigated and found that Mr. Walker and his wife held white identity cards and that three of their daughters had married white South Africans and borne white children. Nonetheless, the department decided to reclassify Mr. Walker as Coloured. Mr. Walker appealed to the Supreme Court, but the case was dismissed. Mr. Walker now was technically in violation of the Mixed Marriages Act, and, as the South African Institute of Race Relations reported laconically, "all the family marriages, including those of relatives, were threatened and the future of all children of these marriages insecure."

Susara Kirk was a young blond woman with blue eyes who lived in the town of Brakpran. She, her parents, and her grandmother had always lived in white communities and held white identity cards. While preparing for her wedding, she misplaced her identity card and was forced to apply for another. The wedding took place, and her new identity card arrived, which showed that she had been reclassified as Coloured. Despite her protests, the board refused to change its mind. Her new husband then filed successfully for an annullment of the marriage and she was fired from her job.

Often such apartheid decisions drifted from tragedy into farce. In 1970 the government banned the use of black mannequins in department store windows. That same year, when four "nonwhite" pianists tried to enter a Beethoven competition, the judges at South African Radio Corporation ejected them on the grounds that "different races perform best in their own idioms." Even though the national government gave Percy Sledge, an American soul singer, a special visa to enable him to perform before white audiences, the city authorities in Bloemfontein nonetheless barred the concert because the municipal rules forbade the presence of Coloureds or Africans in the hall unless they were there to clean up.

Perhaps the most peculiar incident of all took place at the very moment when South Africa captured the world's attention for a reason other than race. On December 3, 1967, South African surgeon Christian N. Barnard of the University of Cape Town performed the first heart transplant in history when he transferred the heart of a young woman into a grocer named Louis Washkansky. Washkansky died after thirteen days, but Barnard quickly performed another transplant on January 2, 1968, on white dentist Philip Blaiberg. The revelation that Blaiberg's heart had come from a Coloured man, Clive Haupt, produced a brief flurry of debate among South Africa's racial purists about whether Blaiberg should be reclassified; they eventually decided that he could remain a white. Haupt, in turn, became a posthumous hero to the members of the Coloured community, six thousand of whom joined Barnard, the mayor, and Blaiberg's wife at a massive funeral in the Coloured section of Cape Town.

The Kafkaesque quality of such incidents, combined with the high visibility of social segregation, tended to conceal a more grandiose and malevolent strategy. Put simply, Vorster, like his predecessor, was determined to create a fiction of political independence for Africans while maintaining economic dominion over them. The vehicle was separate development, Verwoerd's vision that each and every African would be a citizen of an impotent and impoverished statelet surrounded by a well-armed, wealthy, and white South Africa. Such a configuration justified both a refusal to address the economic, educational, or health needs of the little "sovereign" nations and the denial of elemental rights to their "immigrants" who came to South Africa as temporary foreign residents to work.

To create such a neatly separated reality out of the deeply entangled peoples and places of South Africa required the complex system of coercion that Verwoerd had instituted. Vorster's government continued to expand the system of passes. The police stopped thousands of Africans every day and demanded their passes; if they had forgotten them or were in the wrong place, the police sent them to jail. From 1967 to 1971, the police arrested more than three million people for pass law violations, a number equivalent to a quarter of the African population of the country, including children. Every single day of the year for half a decade, the police arrested an average of 1,649 people, virtually all of whom had to give up at least two days of work and wages to go to court. Those who were convicted had to pay a fine or spend time in jail, and they risked harsher punishment the next time. Some emerged from the ordeal to discover that in their absence their job had been given to someone else.

The system of migratory labor and influx control shattered African families, as husbands, desperate for income, continued to leave their families in the reserves for eleven months at a time. When their wives and children tried to join them, they were often arrested, jailed, and deported back to the reserves. Despite the brutality of the system and the toll on their loved ones, thousands of Africans continued to move from the crushing poverty of the reserves to the urban areas, particularly around Johannesburg and Cape Town. To stem this human tide, Vorster promised every year in parliament to invest more in the development of the homelands, but the government, in its feverish desire to improve the lot and might of the white community, never set aside more than a pittance. The authorities also deliberately tried to make life in the urban townships more difficult. The huge township of Soweto, for example, had only one movie theater; the government said that since the residents were there only temporarily to work, they could seek their entertainment at home in the reserves. Using the same logic, Vorster's government refused to grant licenses to African professionals to practice in the townships and commanded them to move back to the homelands. The result was that Soweto, with nearly one million residents, had only one hospital and only two doctors in private practice.

If people could not be pressured or intimidated to move where the government wanted them to go, Vorster's police and army would force them. In an effort to eliminate the "black spots" that contaminated "white areas," the authorities forced tens of thousands of people out of their homes at gunpoint. Persons who objected were beaten, imprisoned, or shot. Large numbers of women and children were simply taken back to the reserves and dumped on the sun-baked ground. The policy of mass removals to the homelands, combined with the natural increase in population, put a strain on the arid land that it could not bear. Ample forests fell before the axes of men and women searching for building materials and firewood. Rich topsoil steadily drained away from fields overworked by hungry farmers. Even under the original assumptions of the Tomlinson Commission, the government had concluded that the homelands could support a limited number of persons at subsistence level. As the populations shipped by Vorster to the reserves exceeded those original limits by two or three times, the rate of malnutrition skyrocketed. By the late 1960s, one of every two children born in the homelands would die before the age of five. In spite of these conditions, the white government continued to ship tens of thousands of women and children to these human dumping grounds, leaving some with the growing conviction that the policy of resettlement was a facade designed to conceal a much more straightforward objective—genocide.

As Lyndon Johnson's elected term in the White House passed the midpoint in 1967, discord between the president and the two other titans of American politics—Martin Luther King Jr. and Robert F. Kennedy—grew. What drove them apart was the Vietnam War. By 1967, when young Americans were dying at the rate of nearly one an hour, 144 every week, those who opposed the war grew in number and volume. Soon the debate spilled anew onto the floor of the United States Senate. On March 2, 1967, against the advice of his political counselors, Robert F. Kennedy rose in the Senate to assail Johnson for his refusal to consider negotiation as a means to end the war. Kennedy bowed briefly in the direction of current American policy, saying that he still believed the United States should fulfill its "commitments" to Vietnam, but then he derided those who had sanitized the war and had refused to acknowledge the volume of destruction it had unleashed. Kennedy asked why the United States should expand the war just when opportunities for peace seemed imminent. He suggested that Johnson test Hanoi's sincerity by stopping the bombing and requesting immediate negotiations.

Though Kennedy was supported by some of his Senate colleagues, the reaction to the speech was strongly negative. The newspapers swelled with irritated letters and editorials. Public opinion polls showed at the time that only twenty-four percent of the American people believed that the heavy bombing of North Vietnam should be halted. Johnson, of course, was furious. He had done everything he could in advance to undermine the speech—from prompting his cabinet to issue preemptive statements against negotiation to making a string of unscheduled appearances to squeeze Kennedy out of the headlines. A man of nearly infinite capacity for guile, Johnson thought that his nemesis had willfully ignored the military evidence in order to garner attention. Indeed, Johnson believed that, at bottom, Kennedy had chosen to denounce the conduct of the war for only one reason: to capture the White House in 1968 himself.

Robert F. Kennedy was not the only person who had been sickened by the destruction. Only weeks before, while waiting in an airport restaurant, Martin Luther King had come across a story in the January issue of *Ramparts* magazine. Titled "The Children of Vietnam," the article carried graphic photographs of the grotesque burns inflicted by napalm, a gelatinous mixture of fatty acids and gasoline that was used in American flamethrowers and dropped from American aircraft. "He saw a picture of a Vietnamese mother holding her dead baby, a baby killed by our military," recalled King's aide Bernard Lee. "Then Martin just pushed the food away from him. I looked up at him and said 'Doesn't it taste good?,' and he answered, 'Nothing will ever taste any good for me until I do everything I can to end that war.' "

For King the war was a twofold source of anguish. First, as a disciple of Gandhi and Jesus, as a winner of the Nobel Peace Prize, and as the leading American proponent of nonviolence as a method of social change, King believed that he had a special obligation to work for international peace, even if it meant challenging his own government. Second, the war, with its voracious appetite for federal dollars, threatened to devour the crusade against poverty. This King could not tolerate. He firmly believed that an alliance between the civil rights movement and the peace movement could be advantageous for both sides. It could reinvigorate the civil rights movement at the very moment when liberal white attention was shifting to the war. At the same time, it could impart new legitimacy to the peace effort, by providing it with the moral language and the political networks that black Americans had developed over the previous decade.

King's fusion of the problems—domestic poverty and foreign war—created an explosion when he brought them together in a sermon at Riverside Church in New York City on April 4, 1967, just one month after Kennedy's Senate speech. From the pulpit King explained that he could no longer remain silent. The war was "an enemy of the poor," depriving them of life both abroad and at home. "I knew that I could never again raise my voice against the violence of the oppressed in the ghetto without having first spoken clearly to the greatest purveyor of violence in the world today—my own government." Moreover, his Christian commitment went deeper than his nationalism and required him to take a global perspective. King demanded that Johnson halt the bombing, declare a unilateral cease-fire, and accept the Viet Cong at the negotiating table. He called on all young American men to declare themselves conscientious objectors. Finally, King urged America to rethink its values. "The war in Vietnam is but a symptom of a far deeper malady within the American spirit," he said, a malady that could be seen in its relentless materialism and, in a veiled reference to South Africa, its refusal to give up the exploitative profits earned in overseas investments. He concluded by urging a "radical revolution of values" that would turn American "from a 'thing-oriented' society to a 'person-oriented' society."

The public reaction to King's speech, as it had been to Robert Kennedy's, was negative. Critics accused him of betraying the cause of civil rights, injecting a newly partisan element into a previously spiritual crusade, and meddling self-righteously into matters he had little knowledge of or jurisdiction over. His longtime enemies, such as J. Edgar Hoover, exulted in the belief that King had finally demonstrated his disloyalty to America and his enthusiasm for socialism in public. King, undeterred, barreled along with new plans for confrontation. After riots had erupted in July throughout America's urban ghettos, King kept to his themes. "Riots are caused by nice, gentle, timid white moderates who are more concerned about order than justice," he said in San Francisco, and "by an administration more concerned about winning the war in Vietnam than the war against poverty right here at home." In the early fall, the SCLC convention, at King's urging, adopted a strong resolution against the war. King himself spoke favorably about possible moderate Republican candidates for president—like Nelson Rockefeller and Illinois Senator Charles Percy—and said that he intended to go "all out" to defeat Lyndon Johnson in the next election.

Throughout the fall King pondered how to launch a more serious challenge to the structures of power that he believed were maintaining poverty. At the end of November, at an SCLC retreat, he and his lieutenants laid the groundwork for a massive march on Washington, a "Poor People's Campaign." In an image strangely reminiscent of the 1938 Voortrekker celebration in South Africa, King envisaged a mule cart procession of the poorest Americans beginning in Mississippi and gathering adherents all along the route to the U.S. Capitol. He also brought Jesse Jackson onto the national staff of the SCLC to enhance the organization's ability to bring economic pressure against corporations and governments. Jackson, who had had great success with Operation Breadbasket in Chicago and Cleveland, had told an audience in

July that if the method of selective boycott could be expanded nationally to bring pressure on huge companies like General Motors, Kellogg's, Kraft, and Del Monte all across the country, it would lead to thousands of new positions for blacks. King, though he was suspicious of Jackson's affinity for capitalism and his talent for self-promotion, decided that Jackson was probably right.

In late January 1968 the North Vietnamese launched a surprise attack on South Vietnam, pounding thirty provincial cities and briefly overrunning the American embassy itself in Saigon. The Tet Offensive made a mockery of Johnson's three-year insistence that victory was imminent. Robert Kennedy, speaking to an audience ten days later, noted that the assault proved the pointlessness of searching for a military solution. Though Johnson continued to insist in public that "We will win the war!" Democratic voters seemed increasingly to disagree. Polls showed that Senator Eugene McCarthy of Minnesota, whose antiwar candidacy against an incumbent president had seemed madness, was rapidly gaining on Johnson. Robert Kennedy's supporters pressed him to enter the race; Kennedy decided that he would do so if McCarthy could be persuaded to withdraw. But McCarthy, now the happy leader of a moral crusade, had no intention of stepping aside and swept through the New Hampshire primary with a strong forty-two percent of the vote. On March 16, Kennedy announced his decision to enter the race anyway, unleashing a bitter internecine fight within the liberal wing of the Democratic Party.

Then, in the space of just ten weeks, as Johnson, Kennedy, and King and their respective forces were hurtling into battle to define the future of America, all three men suddenly disappeared from American politics. On March 31, President Johnson, whose advisers now warned him of the likelihood of military defeat abroad and political mutiny at home, dejectedly announced on national radio and television that he would not run for reelection. Four days later, on April 4, an assassin shot Martin Luther King Jr. as he stood on the balcony of the Lorraine Motel in Memphis. Exactly two months afterward, Robert F. Kennedy slipped out of the delirious celebration of his California primary victory and cut through the hotel kitchen, where a young man stepped up and discharged a revolver bullet into his brain.

Johnson's withdrawal, combined with the deaths of King and Kennedy, removed with shocking swiftness the three American leaders who had, more than any others, shaped the national debate for the previous five years. Though the initial hope for collaboration between them had crumbled under the weight of personality and politics, they had shared a moral vocabulary and a deep inner allegiance to the causes of racial justice and economic equality that would not be replaced when they were gone from the scene. Vice President Hubert Humphrey, who announced his candidacy for the presidency in late April and received his party's nomination, tried to revive their language but could not reconcile the divisive elements within his party. In the closing days of the campaign, Humphrey's ebullience and Johnson's flirtations with peace in Vietnam boosted the Democratic candidate into a neck-and-neck race with his Republican counterpart, Richard Nixon, but to no avail. On November 5, 1968, Richard Nixon fulfilled his lifelong dream and was elected president of the United States.

Nixon immediately set about planning the best manner to bring his Republican convictions to bear on an executive branch that had been ruled by Democrats for twenty-eight of the previous thirty-six years. This would be a problem throughout the government, he believed, but nowhere more difficult than at the State Department. The difficulties with State arose, in part, from a clash of cultures. The staff at the White House orbited around a single individual whose job was to persuade and to command; to them, the warren of diplomats at Foggy Bottom seemed filled with paper-pushing, paramilitary drones whose traditions and regulations stifled the few initiatives that emerged. To the foreign service officers at State, in contrast, the White House staff, particularly those at the National Security Council, seemed a bunch of arrogant amateurs, more devoted to scoring domestic political points than to guiding the ship of state through complex international waters. The political activists in the president's circle often saw the task of government as a hiatus between campaigns; the bureaucrats at State saw campaigns as an unpleasant necessity that threatened to disrupt the smooth execution of American foreign policy. Politicians liked inflammatory partisan slogans; foreign service professionals preferred soothing diplomatic obscurities. Finally, there were suspicions on each side about the other's wisdom and loyalties. To those who enjoyed the flag-waving inanities of domestic electioneering, the denizens at State seemed weakened and compromised by questionable allegiances—to the "client" countries in which they served, to a vision of global polity that fitted poorly with American national interest, or to the foreign policy elite itself. To the diplomats, moralism and nationalism were powerful sentiments that had to be contained to enable the interaction of nations and to avoid war. The differences between the two cultures produced continuous difficulties for the conduct of American foreign policy, requiring diplomatic maneuvers within the government as complex as those with other nations.

Each president developed a system to manage the problem. Dwight Eisenhower, drawing on his military experience, produced an elaborate national security system with formal procedures and reviews. John F.

Kennedy scrapped the formal system and replaced it with a more ambiguous and flexible network built on personal allegiance to the president. Johnson focused on a small number of foreign policy matters that were discussed informally at weekly "Tuesday lunches." Richard Nixon, as president-elect, knew that he did not want to retain the nebulous system of his predecessor—where, as he said in the campaign, decisions were made in "catch-as-catch-can talk-fests"—yet he did not want to return to the rigidity of the Eisenhower years.

Nixon also believed that he would have to exercise direct personal control over foreign policy to produce change. Suspecting that clandestine Democratic loyalists might try to constrain him by limiting the information and range of choices they sent over to the White House, Nixon wanted a system that would allow him to hear as many ideas as possible and then make decisions himself. "I refuse to be confronted with a bureaucratic consensus," he said after he became president, "that leaves me no options but acceptance or rejection and that gives me no way of knowing what alternatives exist." Nixon had few doubts about his competence in the field of foreign affairs. As a congressman he had built his career decrying the global Communist threat; as Eisenhower's vice president and emissary he had traveled throughout the world and tangled with Khrushchev; and as the Republican standard-bearer in two national campaigns he had spoken on hundreds of foreign policy issues. Nixon believed he knew how to exercise control if he could figure out a way to obtain it.

To centralize foreign policy decision making at the White House, Nixon needed a compliant secretary of state and a forceful national security adviser. He found the former in William Rogers, a bland former attorney general. For the latter he turned to Henry Kissinger, a brilliant and temperamental German émigré who had become a professor of government at Harvard. Kissinger had originally attracted President Kennedy's eye and had served briefly and unsuccessfully in the stable of academics to whom Kennedy liked to turn for advice. During the later campaigns, Kissinger had supported Nelson Rockefeller and met Richard Nixon once. Kissinger was thus startled when he was invited to come to New York at the end of November 1968 for an audience with the president-elect at the Hotel Pierre. At the meeting Nixon laid out "his massive organizational program." He told Kissinger that he thought there should be a new decision-making structure, one that bypassed the State Department and the CIA. Kissinger strongly agreed. Despite their differences in background, Nixon and Kissinger shared important assumptions. Both believed that foreign policy was the proper responsibility of the president and should be freed as much as possible from "the violent historical fluctuations between euphoria and panic" that usually characterized the field. Foreign policy, they also agreed, should not be driven by the whims of presidential personality or the caprice of a myopic Congress but by a sound calculation of enduring American interests. Finally, they shared a deep distaste for the limits placed by bureaucracy on statesmanship, which had been one of the central themes of Kissinger's scholarship. From such studies Kissinger had concluded that bureaucracies were always the enemy of active diplomacy, for they were built on routines "designed to execute, not to conceive," and were so driven by their "paralyzing quest for safety" that they could not endure innovation. The great challenge for the statesman was to jolt the inert diplomatic corps out of its reactive concern for operational problems into the consideration and execution of long-term goals.

Though in their first meeting Kissinger had no idea what the president-elect wanted him to do, Nixon recalled in his memoirs that he "had a strong intuition about Henry Kissinger" and "decided on the spot that he should be my National Security Adviser." Two days later Nixon informed Kissinger of his decision and asked him to design a system that would reduce interagency bickering and premature compromise. Within a few weeks, Kissinger and his aides had crafted an administrative structure that was implemented by presidential order on Inauguration Day. The structure, borrowed partly from systems used by Robert McNamara at the Defense Department, was built around the concept of the National Security Study Memorandum (NSSM). The president, through Kissinger, would issue an NSSM asking an interdepartmental study group to examine some piece of American foreign policy and to provide policy options, not recommendations. The purpose was to convert the study group members, who represented diverse government departments and agencies, from advocates into analysts and to free them from rote allegiance to their particular agency's parochial priorities. Only when the debate reached the National Security Council (NSC), which would serve as an advisory forum for the president, would cabinet members be permitted to identify their departmental preferences. The president would then decide alone and communicate his decision to the rest of the government through a National Security Decision Memorandum.

On the surface the system seemed so innocuous that the secretaries of state and defense approved it without objection. In fact, the design represented, in the words of one former NSC staff member, a quiet "coup d'etat" that transferred large portions of the traditional authority of the State and Defense Departments to a supposedly neutral paper sorter in the White House. Henry Kissinger maximized his power in several ways. He placed a member of the NSC staff in each study group to guide the proceedings and to alert him to problems. When finished, the study group sent its report to the Review Group, chaired by Kissinger, from which position he could intercept, cut, amend, or reject a study before it reached the Oval Office. When a set of options was finally ready to go to the president, Kissinger would write a secret cover memo for Nixon analyzing the different positions and setting forth his private recommendation. Thus, at several critical junctures—formulation, revision, and delivery—Kissinger ensured that his perspective prevailed. The result was ironic. On the one hand, the system gave Nixon greater control from the White House while offering the participating agencies the comforting illusion of due process. On the other hand, Nixon's increasing tendency to rely solely on Kissinger for information and advice allowed the president's national security adviser, supposedly a mere manager of information, to amass unprecedented control of foreign affairs.

Such control enabled Nixon and Kissinger to pursue some diplomatic efforts with unusual freedom. Topics that ignited the two men's interest—such as relations with the Soviet Union and China, negotiations with North Vietnam over the war, and the Middle East—received enormous attention during Nixon's first term. Areas that both men viewed as secondary—such as the United Nations, Latin America, and Africa—languished from presidential neglect. Kissinger's imperious disregard for the problems of Africa was such that, on finding a set of cables and memoranda about Africa in his daily reading, he is said to have flung them across the room in disgust, shouting, "Bring me something important!" Members of the National Security Council in charge of such low-priority matters soon learned that it was pointless to try to "educate" Kissinger and found themselves instead trying to obtain just enough of the necessary signatures to permit the other branches of government to conduct their essential business with these overlooked regions.

The weaknesses of the NSSM system were nowhere more evident than in the development of American policy toward southern Africa. Nixon had signaled early on that he believed that the hostility of the Kennedy administration and the "benign neutrality" of Johnson toward the white regimes of southern Africa had been a mistake. Meeting with Portuguese Prime Minister Marcel Caetano, who had come to Washington for Eisenhower's funeral in March 1969, Nixon assured the Portuguese government of his unqualified support. The White House then immediately issued a directive cutting off all American contacts with nationalist groups fighting for independence in Africa. A few weeks later, at a meeting between Nixon, Kissinger, and Portuguese Foreign Minister Franco Nogueira, the president told the Portuguese official that his predecessors had erred in criticizing Portuguese behavior in Angola and Mozambique since Portugal was a highly valued ally. That evening, at a formal White House dinner celebrating the twentieth anniversary of NATO, Nixon physically embraced Nogueira. "Just remember," the president told the foreign minister, "I'll never do to you what Kennedy did."

The new American perspective took formal shape in NSSM 39, a directive sent out by the White House on April 10, 1969, which demanded an articulation of possible options for future relations with the white regimes of southern Africa. The directive had been drafted by Roger P. Morris, an energetic NSC member who had just completed a doctorate in government at Harvard and was eager to attract Kissinger's attention. Morris approached the task with a powerful set of presuppositions. First, he believed that no American president, especially a conservative who lacked interest in Africa, would be willing to jeopardize American investments in southern Africa. In addition, Morris believed that it was a "clear historical lesson" that outside coercion would harden the resolve of whites in Angola, Mozambique, Rhodesia, and South Africa. Morris had been heavily influenced by a June 1968 article by English journalist Norman Macrae in the *Economist*, which argued that in South Africa economic prosperity would translate into political liberalization. Morris's belief that industrialization would lead to liberalization fell on fertile ground at the White House; indeed, the notion that expanded commercial links could be used to tame a hostile regime would later be used to justify the expansion of U.S. investment in the Soviet Union as part of the Nixon-Kissinger policy of détente. For Morris, the correct premises of American policy toward southern Africa were clear: the United States should "accept the expedient American stakes in the tyrannies" and "use that presence wherever possible to encourage racial progress."

Despite their orders to move swiftly and to avoid bureaucratic posturing, the members of the study group spent months struggling with the contradictory impulses of American policy. Morris remembered the process with distaste. "Battled out over verbs and commas, vague intelligence estimates, and nuances of diplomacy that would never be practiced," he wrote, "the conduct of the review was alternately childish, venomous, dull, colossally wasteful of official time, and very much the daily stuff of government in foreign affairs." The members of the group never seriously considered the two extreme options—aligning fully with white states or supporting their military destruction—but haggled over the choices in between. By the end of the summer, the interdepartmental group had come up with five options. The first, known as the "Acheson option" for the former secretary of state who had been Rhodesia's most vocal public defender, reflected the view that American condemnation of white supremacy constituted an excess of moralism in diplomacy and recommended a much closer alignment with, if not outright approval of, white minority regimes as defenders of American interests and bulwarks against Communism. Option Two, while not so eager to embrace the white regimes, assumed bluntly that "the whites are here to stay and the only way that constructive change can come about is through them. There is no hope for the blacks to gain the political rights they seek through violence, which will only lead to chaos and increased opportunity for the Communists." The general posture of the United States under Option Two would be to "maintain public opposition to racial repression but relax political isolation and economic restrictions on the white states. . . . At the same time," the report continued, "we would take diplomatic steps to convince the black states of the area that their current liberation and majority rule aspirations in the south are not attainable by violence and that their only hope for a peaceful and prosperous future lies in closer relations with white dominated states."

The remainder of the options tilted the United States more toward support for black liberation. Option Three tried to place the United States squarely in the middle by openly compensating for involvement with the white regimes with increased assistance to the black states. Option Four suggested calibrated pressures on the white governments combined with decreased contact. Option Five envisaged the severance of all ties with the white regimes and active support of the resistance movements.

From the beginning, Morris, Kennedy, and Kissinger all supported Option Two—improved contacts and softened restrictions. State Department officials caustically labeled the idea the "tar baby option," on the grounds that once the United States moved closer to the white minority governments, it would never be able to abandon the policy. When the study group finally sent its recommendations to the review group in November, the choices had been whittled to four: the two unacceptable extremes, the equally unacceptable leftover Johnson policy of balancing interests of white and African states, and Option Two. Sensing the inevitable, David Newsom, assistant secretary of state for African affairs, made a last-ditch effort to soften the plan, urging that the United States discuss Option Two with African leaders *before* adopting it. Newsom apparently hoped that the vehement opposition Kissinger would encounter among African leaders would cause him to change his mind. In the meeting Kissinger politely agreed to consider the idea; when he returned to his office, he raged at the notion of giving the African states a veto over American policy and at the overall "intellectual squalor" of the State Department.

As Roger Morris noted later, the deliberations about NSSM 39 had unfolded under a persistent "pall of racism" in the corridors of power. When Africa appeared on the agenda of the NSC staff meetings, for example, Alexander Haig, Kissinger's top aide, would amuse his boss and others by pretending to beat drums on the table. Kissinger, for his part, suggested in conversations with Morris that he believed Negroid features to be a sign of lower intelligence. Richard Nixon revealed his own perspective when on one occasion he asked Kissinger, who was completing the first presidential message on foreign policy, to "make sure there's something in it for the jigs." Option Two was thus the result not so much of a careful intellectual process as of a combination of bias, ignorance, and arrogance at the center of the American government.

Nowhere was this more evident than in the peculiar meeting of the full National Security Council on December 17, 1969, at which NSSM 39 and American policy toward southern Africa were formally discussed. Nixon began by reciting the talking points that had been given to him by Kissinger. The subject, he said, was not only a complex foreign policy problem but also a matter of extraordinary moral and political dimensions. In front of the president, bound in a fat briefing book, lay a copy of the completed NSSM study and a summary report by Kissinger. Also included was a report by NSC staff member Winston Lord entitled "Domestic and Moral Factors in Southern Africa," which noted the unique relationship between white supremacy in southern Africa and America's own moral and political sensitivities about race. Lord argued that of all the tyrannies in the world, white supremacy was philosophically the most reprehensible because it depended solely on the random circumstance of birth. Moreover, even though disengagement from the white regimes could not be justified on purely foreign policy grounds, there were other serious risks to consider. Of the U.S. interests in the area, the paper concluded, "none is sufficiently important to run even the potential risks of southern Africa becoming a serious and divisive domestic issue" inside the United States. Lord recommended political, diplomatic, and economic disengagement.

Lord's advice went not only unheeded but undiscussed. In response to Nixon's opening comments about the complexity of the issue, Secretary of State William Rogers remarked that the matter could not be that difficult since so many of them around the table—Attorney General John Mitchell, Vice President Spiro Agnew, Undersecretary of State Elliot Richardson, the president, and Rogers himself—were "lawyers who must have had clients in South Africa. . . . I know I did." CIA Director Richard Helms followed with a presentation on the dangers of black nationalism that was so grotesquely biased by the agency's close relationship with the white security services of the region that Kissinger turned to Morris, sitting in the back, and expressed his private pique.

Not to be outdone, the vice president of the United States, Spiro Agnew, launched into a prepared diatribe that mangled the history and geography of the region with spectacular abandon. Using an argument popular with American right-wing extremists, Agnew insisted that "South African" independence "in 1965" was similar to that of the United States in 1776, when black inhabitants did not have the vote. When Agnew concluded, an embarrassed silence fell over the room until the president said, "You mean Rhodesia, don't you?" While Agnew sat, silent and flushed, Nixon moved on to a discussion of specific decisions relating to southern Africa. From then on, each participant tried to outdo the others in demonstrating his toughness on Communism, his loyalty to "American interests," and his ability to advance his own department's goals. At the end, an NSC aide who had sat through the whole thing told Haig that he had found the meeting "unbelievable." "Not only is it believable," Haig commented, "it sounds like one of the best they've had." Not long afterward, Kissinger sent his recommendations for the acceptance of Option Two to the president. Kissinger suggested that the arms embargo against South Africa be maintained but that the one against Portugal be relaxed, because the Portuguese had "generally" respected the ban on the use of NATO weapons in their colonies and because they were a "NATO ally defending the West on its African flank." Nixon approved the policy shift in early January 1970.

Though the results of NSSM 39 and the president's decision were never announced to the public, the signals to the governments of southern Africa were unmistakable. Over the next year, the United States government approved the sale of Boeing jetliners to Portugal, even though the Portuguese government informed the Americans that they might use the aircraft to transport troops to their African colonies. The Nixon administration maintained the arms embargo against South Africa but substantially reduced the restrictions of so-called dual-use or gray area materials such as Cessna airplanes and permitted the embassies to play a more vigorous role in encouraging the expansion of American trade. Nixon let stand a decision made at the end of the Johnson administration to allow South African Airways to fly directly into Kennedy Airport in New York. The United States government also retained its consulate and CIA connections in Rhodesia until the British government made a formal request that they be withdrawn. Cooperation between the CIA and the South African intelligence service increased.

In short, over the next five years, in the belief that the white regimes of Angola, Mozambique, South Africa, and to some extent Rhodesia were invincible, the White House effectively abandoned a policy of opposition to white minority rule. Though the pro forma verbal statements remained, the combination of moral, diplomatic, economic, and intelligence support provided John Vorster with unequivocal evidence of American confidence. Yet, like the administrations before it, the Nixon administration tried to defuse the domestic political implications by keeping Option Two secret. The secrecy enabled some members of the State Department to pretend for a while that American policy had not changed very much. In the end, however, the inherent contradictions of the policy, the assumption of the invincibility of the whites, the arrogance of the national security adviser, the preoccupation with the hot war in Vietnam and the cold war everywhere else, the residual tensions among the branches of government, and the president's belief that he owed nothing to a black American constituency who had denied him the presidency in 1960 and voted overwhelmingly for his opponent in 1968, all combined to eviscerate an already feeble official opposition to white supremacy. In this there was considerable irony, for having rejected the prior administration's policy as contradictory and unproductive, Nixon and Kissinger ended up with a policy that choked all presidential initiative against racial injustice in southern Africa for the next five years.

While Nixon and Kissinger believed that closer relations between the United States and South Africa might speed the erosion of apartheid, John Vorster believed the reverse. Vorster's foreign policy during the first four years of his rule was straightforward. To the neighboring white Portuguese colonies and to Rhodesia he offered a mix of public and clandestine support. To the Western powers he labored to represent South Africa as a vigorous and devoted ally against Communism. To the black nations of Africa, especially those in the south that depended on South African trade, supply routes, and employment, he presented a carrot and a stick. To those who would agree to squelch their public hostility to apartheid and suppress the meager corps of South African exiles within their borders, Vorster proffered the lure of cordial commercial relations; if they would not accept, he vowed, South Africa would impose a heavy economic and military price. A few of his efforts met with success. In early 1967 the South African government signed a trade agreement and established diplomatic relations with Malawi, the first such pact with an African country since the Nationalist victory in 1948. Still, most African nations resisted the temptations and threats as best they could. Some barred direct flights to South Africa and refused to admit visitors who had South African visas stamped in their passports. Tanzania barred its citizens from making payments to South Africa. Kenneth Kaunda of Zambia continued to provide limited support for both ANC and PAC guerrillas and diplomats.

As he had in the past, Vorster vigorously denounced any opposition to his government's policies as evidence of a Communist plot. Obsessed with national security, he found conspiracies everywhere. Some of his suspicions had a basis in fact. It was true, for example, that an increasing

number of South African exiles, denied moral and material support
from the West, were searching for assistance from Marxist ideologies
and governments. It was also true that the world's Communist governments reflexively condemned South Africa in the United Nations and
other international gatherings. Yet Vorster refused to accept a simple
fact: that while all Communists were opposed to apartheid, not all those
who were opposed to apartheid were Communists. Instead, he seized on
every bit of evidence, real, imagined, or fabricated, to position South
Africa as a Western ally and to distract attention from his domestic
policies. His approach attracted some support in the West. Letters to
American newspapers periodically urged closer cooperation with South
Africa in the war against Communism. During the 1968 campaign,
George Wallace, the segregationist governor of Alabama and an independent candidate for president, said in a speech at the National Press
Club that he considered South Africa a good friend and would, if
elected, end all economic and military sanctions against the nation. In
February 1969, U.S. Senator James O. Eastland of Mississippi said at a
press conference in Johannesburg that he fully supported apartheid, "or
whatever you call it." Even senior statesman George F. Kennan wrote a
strong article denouncing American criticism of apartheid as "purely
emotional and subjective" and arguing that "South Africa's white rulers
know their situation better than any outsider" and should be left to find
their own solution.

At home, Vorster's repression was so complete that by 1968 the South
African Institute of Race Relations, which published an annual yearbook on race relations, could offer no comment at all on the attitudes of
the majority of the country's inhabitants about political events. "Since
the banning of their two political organizations and the imprisonment,
banning, or departure overseas of nearly all the former leaders," said
the yearbook, "it has been impossible to know how Africans have reacted to political events and philosophies." Most of the leaders, except
those who supported the National Party line within the homelands, had
been silenced. When Robert Sobukwe, jailed on the day of Sharpeville,
completed his sentence in 1963, parliament passed a special bill extending his imprisonment indefinitely. Six years later, Sobukwe was finally released, sent to his home in Kimberley, and placed under permanent house arrest. In July 1967 Chief Albert Luthuli died under
mysterious circumstances when he was struck by a train while taking his
daily walk.

In 1968 Nelson Mandela celebrated his fiftieth birthday. By that time
he had been in jail for six years, four on Robben Island, which he described later as "the harshest, most iron-fisted outpost in the South
African penal system. . . . The challenge for every prisoner, particu-

larly every political prisoner, is how to survive prison intact, how to emerge from prison undiminished, how to conserve and even replenish one's beliefs. . . . Our survival depended on understanding what the authorities were attempting to do to us and sharing that understanding with each other." Together Mandela, Walter Sisulu, Govan Mbeki, and the scores of other political prisoners gradually worked out a system of mutually accepted rules, support, and governance that allowed them to survive the warders' attempts to break them. Mandela was eventually chosen to serve on the "High Organ," the committee that made most of the decisions and settled disputes among the political prisoners.

The physical toll on the prisoners, particularly in the early years, was severe. At first the guards put the prisoners to work in the prisoner courtyard smashing stones the size of volleyballs into gravel with hammers. Later they transported the prisoners to excavate lime at a quarry on the island, where the reflected sunlight was so bright that many of the prisoners suffered damage to their eyesight. The unchanging prison diet consisted of cornmeal porridge—known as *milliepap*—and stale vegetables. At night the prisoners were locked behind bars and heavy wooden doors in seven-foot-square cells.

The warders also attempted to control the prisoners by ranking them on the basis of their privileges. All political prisoners were assigned to the lowest group—D Group—and thus were permitted one visitor and one letter every six months. "A letter was like the summer rain that could make the desert bloom," Mandela recalled. "When I did not receive a letter I felt as dry and as barren as the Great Karoo desert." When Mandela did receive letters, they had often been defaced by government censors, who used black markers or razors to excise passages. When Winnie visited she was allowed to speak to her husband through a heavy and smudged window and her trips were restricted to thirty minutes. At one point she was not allowed to return for nearly two years, though the authorities kept Mandela informed by leaving him neat newspaper clippings that maligned Winnie and described her harassment by the police. Despite this psychological pressure, Mandela waged a continuous campaign for the improvement of prison conditions. On one occasion Mandela spoke directly to a member of the American Bar Association who was being given a tour of the island by the commissioner of prisons. As Mandela enumerated the prisoners' grievances the lawyer, a southerner, dismissed them. "When I started to detail the problems with our cells," Mandela recalled, "he interjected that the conditions in backward American prisons were far worse than Robben Island, which was a paradise by comparison. He added that we had been justly convicted and were lucky not have received the death sentence, which we probably deserved."

Eventually the prisoners took advantage of the conversation permitted by their outdoor work to organize courses on a wide array of subjects. Students would select a topic and labor in a circle around the "faculty member," who would lecture or respond to questions as they all cut and loaded lime. The academic curriculum of the "University," as Robben Island was quickly dubbed, led students through courses in everything from English, Afrikaans, and art to geography and mathematics. The political curriculum introduced the participants to a quasi-Marxist analysis of South Africa's economic development and to the history of resistance by the African National Congress and other anti-apartheid groups. Eventually prisoners in the general section—a separate facility on the island where nonpolitical prisoners were held—expressed such interest that the faculty set up clandestine correspondence courses. During his thirteen years of working at the quarry Mandela not only taught a course on political economy but also provided a steady stream of legal advice to prisoners in both the political and the general section, even writing their appeals, though it was illegal for him to do so. Here racism helped them: the information could be passed back and forth wrapped in plastic at the bottom of a bucket of dirty dishes or taped inside the rim of a toilet, two places that the white guards would be too revolted to look.

While one branch of the apartheid government focused on Mandela and his colleagues, others put pressure on Winnie. She had been banned under the Suppression of Communism Act in 1962, banned again for five years under tighter restrictions in 1965, and subjected to innumerable arrests for technical violations. She responded to the harassments feistily, refusing to give her name and scuffling with police when they grabbed her. Her domestic situation, however, was grim. Whenever she tried to get a job, the police would visit her employer and she would be fired. When she enrolled her children in a school, she could not enter the building or meet with their teachers because of her banning order. The children could not stay in any school for long, for the administration and the other parents would become fearful and ask them to withdraw. Eventually Zindzi and Zeni had to be sent to boarding school in Swaziland. At night Winnie worried about the effect on her daughters of the relentless persecution and about what would happen to them if she, too, were arrested.

Her fears came true in May 1969 when the police detained Winnie and twenty-one other men and women under the Terrorism Act. The Security Police locked her up in a death row cell in Pretoria's Central Prison, isolated from everyone else. When she asked to wash herself, they gave her a dirty latrine bucket filled with water. "I had to use my panties to wash my body because there was nothing else," she remembered. She was never provided with clean clothes and she was not permitted to wash the ones she had. During her menstrual period, she asked for sanitary napkins and was told by the female warders to "go and use your big fat hands." At night, beneath the harsh glare of a bare lightbulb, she slept on a thin straw mat under stinking blankets.

During the day she tried to devise ways to pass the time. One day she found two ants and played with them from morning until night. She spent part of a week unbraiding and rebraiding a section of her blanket. The only reading material she had was a Bible given to her by a warder, who opened the door and flung it in, saying, "There is the Bible. Ask your God to release you from jail." Every day she had to endure inspection. Two female warders would walk in and order her in Afrikaans to stand up and remove her clothes. "They start by inspecting your shoes as you stand there stark naked," Winnie remembered. "They go through your panties, your bra, they go through every seam of every garment. They then go through your hair and they inspect your vagina. Of course, they never succeeded with me, but with female prisoners it is common practice. . . . Nothing is more humiliating. And you are all alone in that cell." Her meals, like her husband's, consisted of porridge and vegetables, though the vegetables came caked in dirt from the ground and the porridge was either uncooked, covered in bird excrement, or floating in a pool of blood. Winnie could barely eat. Her complexion became sallow; her gums bled; she suffered from occasional blackouts. When the authorities realized she would have to appear in court to be charged, she was transferred to the prison hospital just long enough to improve her appearance.

After she had been in prison for several months awaiting trial, Winnie was taken out of her cell and interrogated by the infamous Lieutenant Theunis Swanepoel, who, along with his team, questioned her for five days and five nights without interruption. He focused closely on her work with the Anglican Church to raise money for the families of women who had been imprisoned since 1960. When the torture of sleep deprivation caused her to begin urinating blood, Swanepoel stepped up the pressure. "You are going to be broken completely," he told her, "you are finished, you are a shattered woman." Swanepoel let her know that she could be released from prison immediately, she could return to her children, if she agreed to cooperate and use her voice on the radio to call upon ANC supporters to abandon their resistance. If she did so, he said, she would be flown to see her husband; he would be moved to a more comfortable setting; he would suffer less. When it became clear that she would not agree, Swanepoel told her that the police had already told everyone she was cooperating, so the damage to her reputation was already done.

When she and the prisoners were finally brought to trial nearly six months later, they found that they had been accused of "furthering the aims of an unlawful organization"—the ANC—by giving the ANC salute, singing ANC songs, recruiting members, discussing or possessing ANC literature, and "polluting" youth. The state's evidence was so obviously based on confessions exacted under torture that the case collapsed. Winnie, thrilled at the thought of seeing her children after nine months, was heartbroken when she was redetained under the same charges the moment she stepped outside the courtroom. She spent eight more months in prison, during which she fought not only for her own rights but for the women on her cell block who were being physically abused by their interrogators and female warders. Finally, in September 1970, after 491 days of solitary confinement, the court acquitted and released her. The Security Police immediately served her with a new five-year banning order, placed her under house arrest, and forbade her to receive any visitors at all.

Though Vorster's maneuvers at home and abroad earned him some breathing room with some Western governments, not all were as receptive as the Nixon administration. Vorster experienced some of his greatest difficulties with Great Britain under the Labour government of Prime Minister Harold Wilson. Though the economies of Great Britain and South Africa were so intertwined that Wilson found it politically impossible to call for economic withdrawal, he was determined to prevent the Nationalists from using British weapons to enforce apartheid. Wilson faced resistance even within his own cabinet: when he tried to renew the British arms embargo in 1967, he had to go around his appointees and secure the signatures of one hundred and thirty Labour MPs in support of a continuation of the ban. In the end, Wilson had to cut a deal with the Tory members of Parliament, who agreed to maintain the embargo in exchange for a cut in public spending at home. John Vorster denounced the decision and threatened, as usual, to withdraw South Africa's permission for British use of the naval base at Simonstown. A month later Defence Minister P. W. Botha warned that Britain could no longer depend on the use of South Africa's airfields for long-range defense.

In June 1970 Wilson's Labour Party lost the general election and the Conservatives came to power under Prime Minister Edward Heath. Heath, who had long opposed the arms embargo against South Africa and who was reportedly irritated that France had sold more than five hundred million dollars' worth of armaments to South Africa over the previous five years, announced that he would permit Vorster to buy a wide range of British weapons, including artillery, jet fighters, and warships. When the South African foreign minister flew to England to discuss the arrangements, Harold Wilson blasted the idea in the House of Commons. Conceding that the sales might help British industry, Wilson insisted that they should not be permitted because Britain's world standing must be "rooted in morality and idealism." Heath responded that while Great Britain would never condone racism, his government would not follow an unrealistic policy that would harm Great Britain's economy and do no good in Africa.

The storm unleashed by Heath's announced intention gathered strength throughout the summer. U.S. Secretary of State William Rogers, after meeting with British Foreign Secretary Alec Douglas-Home, announced that England and the United States had agreed to disagree about the resumption of sales. "Obviously there will be some unhappiness" about the decision, Rogers said, "but we will understand it." In a later conversation with Heath, Rogers explained that American opposition was due largely to the "increased identification of U.S. Negroes with African causes." Within a week thirty-seven nations, including Yugoslavia, India, Pakistan, and Saudi Arabia and more than two dozen African countries, had petitioned the UN Security Council to hold an urgent meeting. When leaders from the Methodist Church, the Church of England, and the Church of Scotland denounced Heath's plan, some members of his own party began to back away.

In the face of such dissent, Heath tried to duck the charge that the weapons would support apartheid. Though Douglas-Home insisted publicly that the arms would be only for maritime defense, protests erupted around the British Commonwealth. Hundreds of students stoned the British High Command building in Lusaka, Zambia. Thousands took to the streets in Lagos, Nigeria, to object. India's foreign minister said publicly that arming South Africa would increase, rather than decrease, military tensions in the Indian Ocean. New Zealand's prime minister reiterated his government's opposition to any weapons sales. When Wilson made a searing speech in Parliament denouncing Britain's abandonment of international law, Douglas-Home lashed back, calling Wilson the "prime humbug of all time" and insisting "on moral grounds that South Africa ought not to be ostracized" but "opened up to the civilizing influence of the outside world."

In late July 1970 the Security Council voted unanimously to tighten the arms embargo against South Africa, though three of the permanent members—France, the United States, and Britain—abstained. In October Kenneth Kaunda of Zambia traveled in person to London to attempt to dissuade Heath; when Heath said that England had a right to determine its own interests, Kaunda precipitously warned that England might be ejected from the Commonwealth as a result. Kaunda journeyed next to Paris, where French President Georges Pompidou, eager to score points against Britain, promised that he would bar the export of French armored cars, helicopters, and other weapons that could be used to suppress insurrection.

John Vorster, observing the debate from afar, tried to align his government closely with Heath's. "We do not need arms . . . for the purpose of attacking anybody," he said in a speech to the South African assembly. "South Africa does not have any evil intentions." If his government wanted to oppress blacks in his country or in neighboring black states by force of arms, he continued, "we would not need even a tickey's worth" of foreign weapons, since South Africa could manufacture what it needed. "We are only asking for arms because we see the Communist threat unfurling before our eyes in this part of the world . . . and must protect ourselves against onslaughts from outside and [guard] the interests of the free world." P. W. Botha, the defense minister, announced in another speech that the Third World War had actually already begun and that South Africa was one of the few remaining bulwarks against Communist subjugation of the planet.

Throughout the fall and early winter of 1970, Prime Minister Heath stuck to his course, despite the growing reservations of those around him. In January 1971 Heath faced the ire of his peers at a Commonwealth meeting in Singapore. The presidents of Zambia and Tanzania both threatened to quit the organization if the sales went through. Some members of Heath's own cabinet counseled him that a resumption of sales would not only give a boost to Vorster but might hasten disillusionment with England and the penetration of Communism in the rest of Africa. Heath stood by his contention that Great Britain had to fulfill its obligations to supply South Africa in return for the use of the port of Simonstown and that Soviet influence in the Indian Ocean had to be blocked. To support his position, he pointed triumphantly to the nineteen-thousand-ton Russian cruiser *Aleksandr Suvorov* and its escorting destroyer *Blestyashehi,* both of which happened to be steaming through the Strait of Malacca toward the Indian Ocean during the middle of the conference.

For nearly a week the heads of state argued in public, then in secret session, until on January 20 they emerged with a compromise agreement. The results were startling: the members had agreed that Britain could proceed with the arms sales while the Commonwealth nations formed an eight-member "study group" that would include Great Britain and its three most bitter opponents, Uganda, Tanzania, and Zambia. A few days later the heads of state also agreed to condemn racial discrimination but refused to punish countries that aided those who practiced it. Heath, in other words, had gotten exactly what he wanted.

Returning to Great Britain, the prime minister tried to heal the political wounds caused by his persistence. Appearing in the House of Commons, he said that the arms sales to South Africa might turn out to be quite limited, involving three antisubmarine frigates under contract, with a full complement of WASP helicopters, and spare parts for previously sold British ships. He again insisted that his sole purpose was to protect the sea lanes and that this could not be interpreted as support for Vorster's government. Besides, the prime minister said, he had received Vorster's personal assurances that South Africa had no aggressive intentions.

John Vorster, though exultant at Heath's victory, recognized that South Africa could not rely on foreign equipment. Each year he demanded that the South African parliament expand his military, though it was already substantial for a country with a white population of less than four million and a total population of less than twenty-seven million. From 1958 to 1970 South Africa's defense budget multiplied sevenfold to more than $350 million in 1970 dollars. In 1970 South Africa had more than thirteen thousand white troops under arms and the ability to call up an additional seventy thousand soldiers and fifty-eight thousand rural militia. The army possessed two hundred tanks; the navy thirty warships and three submarines; and the air force forty-four British jets, fifty French Mirage fighter-bombers, eighty helicopters, and nearly one hundred other military aircraft. In addition, Vorster had established a sophisticated underground radio communications center, an underground air defense radar station, and five special "anti-terrorist" training centers, some of whose members operated on joint patrols with Rhodesian security forces along the Zambian border. Finally, Vorster told parliament in July 1970 that South Africa had developed a new method for enriching its vast supplies of uranium that, according to one observer, would "lift her into the ranks of the world nuclear powers, with the potential for nuclear weapons." Vorster did not say, though many people suspected, that the South African military was developing atomic weapons at a secret missile site on the Indian Ocean with the assistance of nuclear technicians from Israel.

Having assembled the most massive military in the region, Vorster also took steps to protect his society from within. When allegations surfaced in the press that wardens were neglecting, beating, and torturing people inside South African prisons, the government passed the Prisons Act, which made it illegal to take photographs in a prison, of a prison, near a prison, or of a prisoner. To get around the restrictions,

Benjamin Pogrund of the *Rand Daily Mail* took sworn statements from released prisoners and wrote a series of articles describing the brutal measures to which they had been subjected. Vorster's government prosecuted both the author and his editor, Laurence Gandar. The judge found them guilty, on the grounds that, despite the sworn statements, the author and editor had not taken "reasonable steps" to verify the charges. From then on, the only officially acceptable method for reporting on prisons was to ask the wardens for information. If they denied any allegation, it could not be printed.

By 1969, the combined efforts of the Censorship Board and its successor, the Publications Control Board, which worked with the postal and customs services to restrict the import of subversive and pornographic works, had raised the number of forbidden publications to an estimated thirteen thousand. When the second volume of the Oxford University Press's *History of South Africa,* edited by Leonard Thompson and Monica Wilson, appeared in 1970, the South African edition contained fifty-two blank pages where an article on African nationalism, written by South African professor Leo Kuper, should have appeared. The publishers said that they had omitted the chapter after their lawyers had advised them that Kuper's discussion of the role of South Africa's imprisoned black leaders would lead to the seizure of the book. The 1971 edition of the South African Institute's annual *Survey of Race Relations* appeared with thick black lines obscuring the quotations from various leaders, religious and political, white and black, who had been banned by the government.

Not content with the array of police and military powers at his disposal, Vorster in 1969 established a new and largely secret organization known as the Bureau of State Security, which was immediately nicknamed BOSS. To run the organization, which would not have to answer to parliament, Vorster selected his close friend and former Ossewa Brandwag associate Hendrik van den Bergh. Though Vorster's supporters tried to portray the agency as a South African version of the CIA that would not have police powers and would be used to "extend the hand of friendship to other African states," the law spelling out its powers was explicit about its internal application. According to the language of the bill, any person who had information about military, police, or security matters could be imprisoned for up to seven years. "Security matters" were defined as "relating to the security of the Republic, including any matter dealt with or relating to the Bureau for State Security." The members of the bureau were also exempted, under section 29, from giving testimony in courts of law if the prime minister or anyone appointed by him said that the matter involved the security of the state.

Protest against the "BOSS bill" erupted from all sides. Helen Suzman denounced it in speech after speech; United Party officials maneuvered to try to water it down. English-speaking editors, swiftly perceiving the threat to their few freedoms, penned scathing columns. Even South Africa's jurists emerged from their customary hibernation to object forcefully to section 29. Most surprisingly, the archconservatives in Vorster's own party rallied against it out of fear that the prime minister would use it to extend and perpetuate his personal power. When two right-wing members of parliament, Albert Hertzog and Jaap Marais, attacked the bill, arguing that BOSS would be far more expensive than the prime minister had said, Vorster demanded that they reveal their source of information. When they refused, government attorneys prosecuted them and obtained a conviction against one of them.

Vorster's souring relationship with Hertzog produced the first serious split within the National Party's ranks since it had come to power. Hertzog was the ringleader of a small band of extremist journalists, academics, clergy, and politicians known as the *verkramptes,* or "unenlightened." From their standpoint, Vorster's public commitment to separate development, his willingness to make overtures to black African leaders, and his attempts to woo English-speaking voters all indicated a preference for the view of the *verligte,* or "enlightened," wing of the party. To the *verkramptes,* such coddling violated the Verwoerdian ideal of eternal white supremacy, and they denounced it vociferously. Vorster skillfully forced Hertzog's hand by calling for a general election in early 1970 on the grounds that "we cannot let the world get the idea that we have an unstable government." Hertzog, not wanting to see Vorster's policies affirmed, organized a breakaway party named, after its historical predecessor of the 1930s, the Herstigte ("purified") Nasionale Party. Despite their early threats and bravado, Hertzog's candidates were obliterated at the polls in April. If anything, the voting patterns indicated a faint shift to the left. Many young Afrikaners, dissatisfied with Vorster but unwilling to move to the United Party, simply did not vote. As a result, the United Party picked up 9 seats, to hold 47 against the Nationalists' majority of 118. Helen Suzman continued as the sole Progressive member of parliament but increased her margin of victory from 711 in 1966 to 2,049.

However skillfully Vorster dealt with the Western governments or with his own domestic antagonists, there was one source of relentless irritation that he could not control: the world of international athletics. South Africa's warm climate and self-perception as a rugged, frontier nation nurtured a deep passion for sports. Much of the competitive instinct flowed through British colonial channels into cricket, rugby, and soccer. South Africans also loved tennis and golf; indeed, one South African golfer, Gary Player, had become famous in the United States.

For the average white South African, the ability to compete against other countries' teams was a far more visible, and thus important, indicator of international acceptance than the obscure permutations of foreign capital or the abundance of off-loaded machinery parts in South Africa's ports. Recognizing this, Vorster tried from the beginning to paint South Africa as a benign and eager participant in international tournaments. Within six months of becoming prime minister, he announced that South Africa was on the threshold of "moving out into the world," hinting that he might ease apartheid in sports. Not long afterward he cracked opened the door, saying he might allow foreign teams with nonwhite members to visit South Africa, but then he quickly slammed it shut again when the *verkramptes* protested.

Noting white South Africans' devotion to sports, anti-apartheid activists around the world pressed for the elimination of South Africa from international competition. In early 1968 Jackie Robinson and twenty-three other prominent athletes urged the U.S. Olympic Committee to support the extension of the 1963 ban on South African participation in the Olympics. South Africa's petition to rejoin the games presented a horrendous problem for the International Olympic Committee, whose members detested the intrusion of "politics" into sports but who knew they would be faced with a walkout by many nations if South Africa came back. The committee sent a study group to explore Vorster's promise that he would integrate his teams and then, in February 1968, announced that South Africa could compete in the Olympics. Ten weeks later the committee reversed its decision, again booting South Africa out.

From then on, South African sports were under constant pressure. In 1968 the International Amateur Boxing Association expelled South Africa, and Poland withdrew its tennis players rather than have them compete against South Africans in the second round of the Davis Cup tournament. Vorster, in turn, refused to admit a London cricket club to play in South Africa because one of its members was a "nonwhite" born in South Africa; in 1969 he rejected a plea from the South African tennis players' union and from Gary Player that he admit black American champion Arthur Ashe. U.S. Secretary of State Rogers met with Ashe in Paris and told the tennis player publicly that he would intercede with the South African government to obtain his visa.

Soon the protests against South African athletes turned violent. When the South African national rugby team, the Springboks, toured Great Britain in 1969, thousands of protesters disrupted their matches in England, Wales, and Scotland. Gary Player, the target of anti-apartheid demonstrations in the United States, had to be escorted by armed guards when he played in Miami and at the Masters tournament in Augusta, Georgia. When the Springboks planned a return trip to Great Britain in 1970, Prime Minister Harold Wilson said that he hoped all Britons would "feel free" to demonstrate at their games, and Queen Elizabeth II let it be known that she would neither attend the matches nor invite the team to Buckingham Palace. As a result, the British hosts withdrew the invitation to South Africa.

Though Vorster maintained the public position that South Africa was being victimized by a conspiracy of Communist and Afro-Asian countries that were blackmailing the spineless West, the pressures showed signs of cracking the apartheid wall. In May 1970 a prominent group of South African athletes and fans called for a national conference to discuss the future of sports and to ease the apartheid restrictions to combat South Africa's growing isolation. The government, concerned about the strong support for the idea among the press and the population, put out the word that it was considering a range of concessions. The lesson to be learned, noted American columnist Anthony Lewis, who wrote frequently about South Africa, was that outside pressure, consistently applied, worked.

The lesson was not lost on George Houser and the staff of the American Committee on Africa; the difficulty was to find the best ways to raise public awareness and spur protest. The committee was hampered by its broad mandate, which was to address issues not only in southern Africa but for the continent as a whole. To assist in coordinating the massive amounts of information related to different countries, corporations, and economic questions, Houser had hired a young South African economist, Jennifer Davis, as director of research in 1966. Born Jennifer Heymann on December 15, 1933, into the same prosperous Jewish environment that had nurtured Helen Suzman, she had been since childhood a fierce opponent of apartheid and had moved from handing out peanut butter sandwiches to poor black families as a girl to handing out copies of the radical newspaper the *Torch* as a teenager.

After studying economics at the University of Witwatersrand, she moved to New York in 1966 with her husband and two children. Casting about for a way to use her passion and her skills, she ended up at the American Committee on Africa. There she threw herself into research on all the many topics in which Houser had involved the organization: the struggle for racial justice in Rhodesia; Portuguese colonialism in Mozambique, Guinea-Bissau, and Angola; South African control of Namibia; and, of course, apartheid. She paid special attention to a major exploration for oil taking place both on- and offshore of the Portuguese possession of Cabinda. After several years of searching, Gulf Oil struck a huge pool and entered into a long-term arrangement with the

Portuguese government that not only brought revenues to the regime but also induced American companies to push the Congo to rein in anti-Portuguese rebels. In 1969 she helped bring pressure on the United Nations to stop using Chemical Bank as its primary financial institution because of its loans to South African industry. She also helped Houser plan steps to compel the bank consortium not to renew its forty-million-dollar revolving loan to South Africa. Throughout the summer and fall of 1969, as the White House was putting the finishing touches on NSSM 39, Houser and Davis enlisted the support of the network of anti-apartheid activists to stop the bank loans. The officers of Union Theological Seminary, the Methodist Church, the Episcopal Church, the United Presbyterian Church, and the United Church of Christ all announced officially that they would withdraw church funds from the banks in the consortium if the loans were renewed. A New York State assemblyman called on the controller of the state of New York to pull out all state government accounts. Nine U.S. congressmen wrote to the bank presidents urging no loan renewal. The bank executives hedged. Suddenly, in late November, officials of the South African government announced that they would not renew their request for the loan. Though the South African spokesman insisted that his government had no further need for the loan, Houser, Davis, and the other activists believed that the anti-apartheid forces had scored a significant victory.

Like a great wave whose intensity and volume increases over the open ocean and then smashes with full force against the shore, the turbulence of America's domestic life swelled as the nation moved into the new decade. The frequent disturbances on American campuses, combined with the seemingly intractable national divisions over race, generated a certain smugness within official South African circles. When U.S. national guardsmen shot and killed four students during an antiwar protest at Kent State University in May 1970, the editors of *Die Transvaler* commented that the students had been "silly asses" who had been stirred up by "Red agents." Though the war in Vietnam and the continuation of the military draft were the central focus of student protest, issues of race in general and South Africa in particular were never far removed. As larger numbers of black students appeared on American campuses carrying with them the dress, ideas, and slogans of the Black Power movement, they demanded that the curriculum be broadened to reflect their experience and concerns. The separatist instinct of Black Power, coming so close on the heels of the integrationist impulse of civil rights, confused liberal white academics, who debated whether this was a step forward or backward. Officials at some colleges endorsed major changes, such as the creation of programs in Afro-American studies, while others, fearful that the whole move was a divisive fad, ardently refused.

The tactic most favored by university officials when confronted with student protests was the sidestep. College presidents knew that student protest, while fervent, was notoriously fleeting. It usually flared in March, when the weather warmed, and waned in May with the approach of exams and graduation. If a university could avoid taking any action, many of the protest leaders would be ejected with diplomas at graduation. The next fall the student groups would have to devote their energies to recruiting and reorganizing in order to prepare for the next spring's round of demonstrations. If a college could hold off for a few cycles, the administrators had learned, they would see not only a new set of faces but often a new set of issues.

A classic early example of this protest cycle came at Princeton University. In the aftermath of student demonstrations in the spring of 1968, President William Goheen had established a committee headed by economist Burton Malkiel to investigate the university's ties to corporations doing business in South Africa and to explore what steps the university could take to end racial injustice there. When Princeton members of Students for a Democratic Society announced again in February 1970 that they were launching a drive to force the university to divest, Goheen was ready with the Malkiel report. According to Malkiel and his committee, the university owned more than $127 million in securities of companies doing business in South Africa, or nearly a third of the university's investment portfolio at the time. The committee projected that divestment would cost the university $5 million in one-time brokerage fees, combined with $3.5 million in annual fees, and an additional annual $3.5 million in opportunity costs, that is, money that the university could have earned if it had remained invested in the firms. Though the figures had been arrived at using debatable, worst-case assumptions, the faculty of the university was sufficiently impressed to shy away from divestment. Instead President Goheen recommended—and the faculty approved—a ban on university investments in companies that did a *majority* of their business in South Africa. Since the university held no stock in such companies, the move had little substance, but it was enough to deflate the student effort at Princeton for several years.

Though the intermingled themes of student activism, black power, and corporate investment may have seemed far removed from the core of Americans politics to some observers in the United States, those same themes over the next few years would, in part through American influence, become a major force in South African life. Ironically, one of those who contributed greatly to the transfer of American ideas to South Africa and who played a leadership role in the divestment campaign was not originally from the United States but from Canada. Timothy Smith was born in Winnipeg, Manitoba, in September 1943 and grew up in Toronto. His father was a china salesman who spent much of his time crisscrossing Canada by train on business trips. An idealist in high school, Smith attended a church with an active youth group led by young evangelicals. Their convictions "moved me and got me involved," Smith remembered later, "not just their theology, but their willingness to take the faith seriously. . . . It had an important influence in my life because it connected me so closely to the church and it confirmed that you could be publicly and unashamedly committed to religious and social beliefs."

Smith entered the University of Toronto in the fall of 1962 and quickly got involved in the intricate battles of student government. After spending a summer serving as pastor of two small churches in Saskatchewan, Smith decided at his graduation that he would enroll at Union Theological Seminary in New York City and might eventually seek ordination. Smith spent the summer before his entrance in Kenya, where he built a community center with a racially integrated team of Americans. Every evening the young people talked politics. Some of the black Americans favored the militant tactics of the Black Panthers; many of the whites in the group found this approach disconcerting. For Smith, the experience of discussing basic issues of race while living and working in the Third World ignited a lifelong interest in Africa.

When he arrived at the seminary in New York in the fall of 1966, Smith quickly gravitated toward the Southern Africa Committee of the University Christian Movement. The members of the committee, which had been organized several years before and had just emerged from the campaign against First National City Bank in the spring, served as a nucleus of anti-apartheid activism among seminary students. Many of its members—Gail Hovey, William Minter, Don Morlan, Ruth Minter, Janet Hooper—went on to pursue careers writing and teaching about southern Africa. The committee worked with the American Committee on Africa and with others in New York who had shouldered the anti-apartheid cause. Clergy such as Kenneth Carstens, a Methodist minister from South Africa who had recently testified before Congress, and William Johnston, an American priest who had formed Episcopal Churchmen for Southern Africa, lent their support.

Smith threw himself into the work of the Southern Africa Committee, first as a researcher and then as a delegate to a convention in Cleveland where he met with the members of the South African delegation. In the spring of 1968, he and other members formed an interracial team and applied for visas to attend a University Christian Movement conference in Stutterheim, South Africa. When the Vorster government refused to grant visas to the black members of the group, the students initially decided not to go. Later they changed their minds, sending Smith and co-worker Mary McAnally to South Africa for two months. When Smith and the other delegates arrived at the Stutterheim conference, they walked into the center of a fierce controversy that was to have an important effect on South Africa's future. In South Africa the squashing of virtually all anti-apartheid activism in the political realm had left the National Union of South African Students (NUSAS), which drew most of its members from liberal whites at the English-speaking universities, as one of the only legal organizations opposed to the government's racial policies. Despite its vital role, the student organization had, as the result of government threats and pressure, become steadily more cautious.

When NUSAS president Jonty Driver had called on the organization in 1964 to take more radical steps to oppose the government, he not only had been denounced by the government but had been censured by his own organization. Two years later, at the time of Robert Kennedy's visit, NUSAS president Ian Robertson had been silenced by a government ban. By 1968 NUSAS still had thousands of members, including hundreds of blacks, but it was floundering badly. One problem was hypocrisy. Despite the liberal talk, the pattern of governance within NUSAS followed the old tradition of United Party paternalism. Whites held all the leadership spots, decided what were the biggest problems, selected the strategies to be pursued, and served as spokespersons. By 1968 the student group had restricted its tactics to verbal protests and symbolic interracial gatherings.

Gradually the black members of NUSAS began to question these arrangements. One of the restive black students was a twenty-one-year-old medical student from Durban named Stephen Biko. Born in 1946 in King William's Town in the Eastern Cape, Biko had first been exposed to politics when his older brother was jailed for nine months in 1963 as a suspected Poqo activist. The police, searching for evidence, interrogated Biko and then, for good measure, had him expelled from Lovedale High School. Biko then attended a liberal Catholic boarding school and entered the non-European section of Wentworth Medical School at the University of Natal in Durban. Those who knew Biko at the time recalled how impressive he was, even at twenty-two: a tall man with an incisive mind and a winning smile, a quiet presence in discussions who waited until the end to deliver his opinion, and an electrifying public speaker. Biko was quickly elected to the Student Representative Council of his medical school and attended his first annual NUSAS convention in July 1966 as an observer. The following year he went as a formal delegate. When he arrived in 1967, he learned that the host institution,

Rhodes University, had refused to permit racially mixed eating facilities or accommodations at the conference. The Africans in attendance had to be bused to and from inferior lodgings in the local black township. For Biko and others, the incident outlined sharply the contradictions at the core of NUSAS's identity. During the year before the next conference Biko pondered whether such an organization was really the best forum for developing black leadership and articulating black concerns.

At the July 1968 conference Biko engaged other black students in a debate about their role as second-class citizens in NUSAS. When the NUSAS conference ended, Biko and many of the other delegates traveled directly to the University Christian Movement conference in Stutterheim, where they continued their discussion and encountered Tim Smith and the others from America. The University Christian Movement, led by Protestant pastor Basil Moore and Catholic priest Colin Collins, had been founded nearly two years before and had rapidly attracted black support. This was in part because Moore, an attentive follower of developments in the United States, believed that the American language of Black Power—with its emerging corollary in religion, Black Theology—might have important consequences in South Africa.

In the midst of the UCM conference, Biko, his associate Barney Pityana, and their allies began to assemble support for the formation of an all-black organization that would reject the false integration and persistent paternalism of NUSAS. When his group asked for time to caucus as an all-black group, the whites students at the conference were shocked. Tim Smith, however, urged the white South Africans to accept the idea, arguing that the seizure of political initiative by blacks in the United States had been a healthy development. Biko was impressed by Smith's endorsement and invited him and the Americans to attend one of the sessions of the black caucus. At the end of the conference, Biko, Smith, and several others piled into a car and drove back to King William's Town, where Smith visited Biko's home and talked to his mother. Before Smith left, Biko asked him if he would send all the material he could gather on Black Power in the United States. On his return home, Smith obliged, forwarding a large collection of books and articles.

Meeting again in December, Biko and the other students decided to form the South African Students' Association (SASO). In July 1969 the organization was officially launched at Turfloop and Biko was elected its first president. Initial reaction to the new black organization was mixed. The Vorster government and its mouthpiece newspapers expressed their approval and pointed to SASO as an example of the acceptance of apartheid among Africans. Conversely, white liberals protested that SASO's separatism undermined everything for which they had worked. Black students and intellectuals expressed ambivalence. The young

Marxists and other radicals worried that SASO represented yet another form of obeisance to white supremacy, like the homeland governments. Older blacks, chastened by the savage repression of the movements in the 1950s and 1960s, feared SASO's seeming rejection of integration and wondered whether the group was headed down the self-destructive path of the Pan-Africanist Congress.

The task of publicly clarifying SASO's identity and goals in the midst of such confusion fell to the new president. For this Stephen Biko was well qualified, combining a subtle understanding of human nature with a direct, persuasive style. "Very few of the South African students' organizations have elicited as mixed a response on their establishment as SASO," Biko commented with bemusement in his first presidential address in December 1969. "Cries of 'shame' were heard from the white students who have struggled for years to maintain interracial contact. From some of the black militants' point of view, SASO was far from the answer." Both reactions were mistaken, said Biko, for "not only was the move taken by the non-white students defensible, but it was a long overdue step. . . . It seems sometimes that it is a crime for the non-white students to think for themselves," Biko continued pointedly. "The idea of everything being done for the blacks is an old one and all liberals take pride in it; but once the black students want to do things for themselves suddenly they are regarded as becoming 'militant.' " The goals of SASO, he said, were primarily to serve as an effective lobbying force for "non-white" interests and programs. The creation of a separate black organization was a means, not an end. "What we want is not black visibility," he said, "but real black participation."

Within six months, however, Biko's vision for SASO had greatly expanded. As Biko read more and more widely, searching systematically for analytical tools to use in the development of SASO, his writings began to show the influences of both African and American thought. Biko's attempt to delineate a rationale for an all-black organization took him down the same ideological path that Africanists such as Anton Lembede and Robert Sobukwe had trod over the previous two decades—though it was impossible for him to cite Sobukwe or other members of the PAC because of government restrictions. Biko also drew moral and intellectual support from Pan-Africanist writings from around the continent, such as those of Julius Nyerere.

Some of the strongest influences on Biko's thought, however, came from the United States. American texts such as *Soul on Ice* by Eldridge Cleaver, *The Autobiography of Malcolm X,* and *Black Power* by Stokely Carmichael and Charles Hamilton passed from hand to hand through SASO's top circles. Fascinated by developments in the United States, Biko read as widely as he could. Soon American phrases like "power structure," "relevance," and "black power" and slogans like "Say It Loud; I'm Black and I'm Proud!" appeared regularly in his speech and prose. Discussion of the similarities and differences between the racial situation in the United States and South Africa soon became a favorite exercise in SASO leadership training sessions. Within a year SASO members had dropped the term "nonwhite" and adopted the inclusive American term "black," which SASO members now used to refer to all persons—African, Coloured, or Asian—who were denied privileges on the basis of race.

By the second annual SASO conference in July 1970, Biko, Pityana, and the other leaders promoted SASO not only as a student group but as the vehicle for the rebirth of black pride and activism across the country. During the conference Pityana became the new president and Biko shifted to become the head of SASO Publications. Freed from some of his administrative duties, the twenty-four-year-old Biko turned his skillful pen to writing a column in the monthly SASO newsletter. Called "I Write What I Like" and written under the pseudonym Frank Talk, Biko's first two columns, blistering attacks on the hypocrisy of whites and the cowardice of blacks, ignited controversy and made him famous.

In his first essay, "Black Souls in White Skins?," Biko deftly described the debilitating effect of white liberalism on the black struggle. Only a tiny percentage of whites showed any true concern for blacks, and even those few could not resist the urge to dominate. While liberal whites found it nearly impossible to shake off their patronizing schooling, blacks were crippled by their lifelong self-perception as inferiors. Under such conditions, efforts at integration would be useless until there was "a very strong grassroots build-up of black consciousness such that blacks can learn to assert themselves and stake their rightful claim." Biko did not mince words. "The myth of integration as propounded under the banner of liberal ideology must be cracked and killed," Biko argued, "because it makes people believe that something is being done." Liberal whites, he wrote caustically, liked to demonstrate their solidarity with the majority by arranging tea parties with the black elite. "The more such tea-parties one calls," he said, "the more of a liberal he is and the freer he shall feel from guilt that harnesses and binds his con-science. Hence he moves around his white circles—whites-only hotels, beaches, restaurants, and cinemas—with a lighter load, feeling that he is not like the rest of the others." White liberals could not avoid the reality that "no matter what a white man does, the colour of his skin—his passport to privilege—will always put him miles ahead of the black man." Biko wrote, "Thus, in the ultimate analysis, no white person can escape being part of the oppressor camp." For blacks to recognize this, he insisted, did not make them racists, as some had charged. "One cannot be a racist unless he has the power to subjugate," Biko insisted. "What blacks are doing is merely to respond to a situation in which they find themselves the objects of white racism. We are in the position we are because of our skin."

For NUSAS members, SASO's separatism was a bitter pill, though in belittling Biko's conclusions many white students unwittingly displayed the very contempt for black judgment, opinions, and leadership that Biko acerbically denounced. Liberal whites also argued, with some justification, that Biko had attacked a group that was already under considerable government duress. Biko's white critics drew little solace from the even sharper criticisms he offered of black behavior. In his next essay, "We Blacks," written in the fall of 1970, Biko relentlessly attacked the despair of South African blacks. "Black people under the Smuts government were oppressed but they were still men," Biko wrote. "But the type of black man we have today has lost his manhood. Reduced to an obliging shell, he looks with awe at the white power structure and accepts what he regards as 'the inevitable position.' "

Biko's portrait of the emasculation of the black man was chilling. "All in all the black man has become a shell," he wrote, "a shadow of a man, completely defeated, drowning in his own misery, a slave, an ox bearing the yoke of oppression with sheepish timidity. . . . The first step therefore," Biko continued, "is to make the black man come to himself; to pump back life into his empty shell; to infuse him with pride and dignity; to remind him of his complicity in the crime of allowing himself to be misled and therefore letting evil reign supreme in the country of his birth. This is what we mean by an inward-looking process. This is the definition of Black Consciousness."

Such an effort would require a comprehensive reappraisal of African culture, religion, and especially history, for, as Biko noted, "a people without a positive history is like a vehicle without an engine." Instead of picturing African culture as primitive and European culture as advanced, Biko wrote, blacks should value their own traditions. Finally, turning to a force that had great power in the black community, the black churches, Biko urged the African independent churches and the Africans within the traditional denominations to reexamine their message. Biko personally had developed a strong ambivalence toward Christianity. On the one hand, he detested the way in which Christianity had been used to suppress African beliefs, to enforce African passivity, and to justify apartheid. On the other hand, his close friendship with particular white members of the clergy, such as Anglican priest Aelred Stubbs, had shown him that Christianity could be a powerful force in breaching the barriers of racism. Surveying the hold that Christianity had on the majority of Africans through the African independent churches and the various traditional denominations and reflecting on the role that the black church had played in the American civil rights movement, Biko did not believe that the churches could simply be ignored. Instead he believed that the churches should recognize the revolutionary implications of the Bible.

Biko and his cohorts had been strongly influenced in this line of thought by the U.S. publication the year before of James Cone's landmark treatise *Black Theology and Black Power.* Basil Moore of the University Christian Movement had organized clergy discussion groups, an academic conference at which a taped address by James Cone (who had been denied a visa) was played, and a collection of essays on Black Theology, including contributions by Biko and Pityana, which the Vorster government eventually suppressed. He also hired Stanley Sabelo Ntwasa to become the first director of the Black Theology Project. Ntwasa pursued the task until he was banned by the government, at which point all of his essays had to be deleted from the organization's publications. Biko's awareness of the emerging trends in Black Theology can be seen as early as 1970, when, in the conclusion to his essay "We Blacks," he dealt directly with the question of African Christianity.

"What of the white man's religion—Christianity? It seems that people involved in imparting Christianity to the black people steadfastly refuse to get rid of the rotten foundation which many of the missionaries created when they came," Biko wrote. At the same time, Biko continued pragmatically, "too many people are involved in religion for blacks to ignore. Obviously the only path open for us now is to redefine the message in the Bible and to make it relevant to the struggling masses. The Bible must not be seen to preach that all authority is divinely instituted. It must rather preach that it is a sin to allow oneself to be oppressed. . . . This is the message implicit in black theology."

The more Biko wrote, even under a pseudonym, the more his reputation among Africans grew. Though the organization primarily attracted members who were young, urban, and intellectual, the seeds of Black Consciousness were slowly but steadily carried by the winds of discontent into other communities: into the churches, the factories, the townships, the mining compounds, and the high schools. In less than six years they would sprout and change the landscape of South African politics for good.

For liberal whites, Biko's ideas continued to smack of racism. Biko did his best to walk an intellectual tight rope, trying to trace out a distinctive African culture in which blacks could be proud without falling into the Verwoerdian trap that separate cultures required separate communities. In his passion Biko sometimes stumbled, painting precolonial African culture in romantically pure hues, ignoring the contributions his own missionary education had made to his thought, glossing over important ethnic and cultural differences between indigenous African communities, and stereotyping Africans as uniformly in love with "music and rhythm." Yet anyone who read Biko, including the members of the Security Police, could sense the muscular truth underlying his words, the kind of truth that gave birth to power.

PART THREE

The Challenge to Legitimacy

SIX

Confrontations with General Motors (1971)

For forty-five years General Motors has been a guest in South Africa and, as in all other countries where it operates, it obeys the laws of the host country, although that need not constitute an endorsement of such laws.
—JAMES M. ROCHE

THE FIVE YEARS that followed the passage of the U.S. Voting Rights Act in 1965 saw the rapid enfranchisement of thousands of black voters, who in turn elected hundreds of new black officials. In 1965 there were 280 black elected officials in the United States. By 1970 that number had multiplied more than five times, to 1,469. Eighty-seven percent of the officials were at the local level: members of county governments, city councils, and boards of education. One hundred sixty-nine had been elected to one of the fifty state legislatures and nine had made it to the U.S. House of Representatives. In 1965 there had been only three black mayors in the country; in 1970 there were forty-eight. These advances, combined with the election of Republican Edward Brooke as senator from Massachusetts in 1966 and the confirmation of Thurgood Marshall as an associate justice of the Supreme Court in 1967, appeared to herald a new era of racial equality and recalibrated power in American politics. The nation seemed to be edging steadily away from the segregation of the 1940s and 1950s, when even a congressman like Adam Clayton Powell was not permitted to get a haircut in the whites-only barbershop of the House of Representatives.

One American black who had weathered the difficult climate of the early years and secured political prominence was Charles Coles Diggs Jr. Diggs was born in Michigan in 1922 and came from a long line of public leaders with roguish private lives. His grandfather James had been a Baptist missionary who had journeyed to Liberia for a year, during which he fathered a child out of wedlock. His father, Charles Sr., started the House of Diggs, a funeral home in Detroit, and a real estate business, both of which flourished and made him wealthy. Charles Sr. then ran for a seat in the Michigan state senate and won. From there he hoped he could capture a spot in the United States Congress. His arrest, conviction, and prison sentence for graft squashed those hopes, but his son and apprentice, Charles Jr., fulfilled the dream in 1954 by becoming, at the age of thirty-one, the first black from Michigan ever elected to the U.S. House of Representatives.

Like all rookies in Congress—and especially those from minority communities—Diggs spent his first few terms on the political bench. Though he expressed a strong interest in Africa from the beginning and attended the independence ceremonies for Ghana in 1957, it took five years to persuade the House leadership to place him on the subcommittee on Africa of the Committee on Foreign Relations. Over time he slowly acquired a reputation as a serious legislator. Of medium height, with dark glasses framing a large, balding head, Diggs always spoke in a slow, serious manner, a trait that journalists often associated with his stint as a mortician. White politicians tended to see him as a "responsible" representative of "his people," while blacks upheld him as the sign of their advancement. To all he gave the impression of a man of independence, moderation, and growing clout. During the 1960 presidential campaign, Soapy Williams worked hard to persuade Diggs, one of the leaders of the Michigan Democratic delegation and a supporter of Stuart Symington, to back John F. Kennedy. Diggs, suspicious of Kennedy's strong overtures to southern Democrats, had resisted and believed his suspicions confirmed when Kennedy skipped over Symington and picked Johnson as a running mate. Diggs warmed to the new administration, however, when Kennedy picked Williams to run the Africa Bureau at State.

As the glacial process of seniority carried Diggs to higher and higher seats on the Africa subcommittee, he encouraged his chairman, Barratt O'Hara, to pay more attention to the problems of southern Africa. His prodding helped prevent the House subcommittee from drifting into the paralysis and irrelevance of its Senate counterpart. As long as Soapy Williams was at State and a Democrat was in the White House, however, most of Diggs's colleagues preferred to let the executive branch run this peripheral piece of the nation's foreign policy. In 1969, however, when Richard Nixon became president, Diggs, in his fifteenth year in Congress, finally advanced to the chairmanship of the House subcommittee on Africa.

Diggs had cultivated friends in the State Department during Soapy Williams's tenure, and from them he learned instantly of National Security memo NSSM 39, Kissinger's request for the reconsideration of Africa policy. Diggs even received the secret early drafts of the options under review. Flatly opposed to the administration's "communication policy," as it was being called, Diggs used his new authority as a House subcommittee chairman to hold hearings, organize trips, commission studies, issue press releases, and pepper the departments of the executive branch with queries and requests. When South African Airways started flying into John F. Kennedy International Airport in New York City, Diggs called a hearing—at which George Houser testified—and charged that the airline's advertising urging tourists to come to South Africa never mentioned that the resorts depicted were open only to whites. Six months later, after receiving numerous letters from Diggs, the Civil Aeronautics Board yanked the airline's right to advertise or distribute promotional materials in the United States.

Diggs also tried to strip away the implicit support the different branches of the United States government had been giving to the South African regime. He asked Defense Department officials to spell out the details of the tracking station treaties with South Africa and to defend their placement. He pushed the Justice Department to end the FBI's exchange of fingerprint and other forensic information with Vorster's police. Later, when Diggs learned that John Hurd, the conservative Texas millionaire whom Nixon appointed ambassador to South Africa, had held a segregated reception in honor of the tenth anniversary of the founding the Republic of South Africa, Diggs protested to Secretary of State William Rogers. Quoting the State Department's official statement that it would be "the practice of the American embassy and consular posts in South Africa to invite white and non-white guests, together or separately, as appropriate to the occasion," Diggs asked what criteria the ambassador had used to decide that segregation was "appropriate."

Diggs went beyond symbolism to seek financial leverage. The decision of the Civil Aeronautics Board to bar advertising imposed only a slight cost, for even though South Africa depended each year on a quarter of a million tourists to bring in over a hundred million rand of hard currency, most of them were British. Burrowing through the welter of federal regulations and proclamations, Diggs discovered to his shock that the United States, as part of its price support system for sugar, set an annual quota that allowed the white farmers of Natal to sell sixty thousand tons of sugar in the United States at twice the prevailing world price. For years Diggs denounced this arrangement in his own subcommittee and he and other black members in the House, backed by Massachusetts Senators Edward Kennedy and Edward Brooke, repeatedly sponsored amendments on the floor to cut off what they described as a five-million-dollar-a-year U.S. government subsidy of apartheid. Each time they were defeated.

By the end of 1970, even though the full details of the NSSM 39 policy had not been revealed, it had become clear to Diggs, as it had to George Houser, Tim Smith, and other anti-apartheid activists, that Nixon and Kissinger could not be relied on to put any serious pressure on John Vorster. In the absence of the political, military, and diplomatic levers available only to the White House, the activists' focus increasingly shifted to the American corporation. When they did so, they had to confront two widespread assumptions about the role of American business in South Africa. The first was the thesis that industrialization would automatically bring liberalization. The second was the notion that American executives would, by virtue of their Yankee decency and sense of fair play, provide the liberal leavening that would transform South African racial attitudes.

In truth, the role of the American executive operating a subsidiary in a foreign country was filled with ambiguity, most easily observed in the contradictory images the executives sought to project. When the executives wished to demonstrate their patriotism or defend their economic interests, they portrayed themselves as crusaders on the front lines of freedom and capitalism, willing to challenge governments (usually left-leaning) with the aid (if necessary) of the U.S. armed forces. When they wished to stay clear of controversies or to duck the responsibility that others wished to confer on them, the same executives switched metaphors, arguing that as neutral fingers of the invisible hand, they abstained from disputations over politics and morality.

American managers of overseas offices also had to accept a variety of conflicting duties and roles. They were expected to be both innovators and conformists, leaders and team players, soldiers and diplomats. They had to balance loyalties to their country with duties to their firm. To walk this tightrope inside an immense global bureaucracy, managers needed to learn and to respect the limits imposed by their corporation's culture. Business managers, said the credo of most firms, were not missionaries; they preferred to profit rather than preach; to make money rather than waves. Given this profile, few thought it wise to tackle any government's policies, let alone those of a stubborn regime with a long and violent record.

In addition, the majority of the presidents—or "managing directors," to use the local term—of U.S. subsidiaries were not Americans. In 1972, for example, South Africans managed 171 of the American subsidiaries; British nationals managed another 44; citizens of other countries managed 27. Only 66 companies were actually run by Americans sent from the United States. Such a distribution undercut even the limited possibilities for corporate activism. The managers who were South African citizens, as employees of foreign companies, did not want to cast further suspicions on their national loyalties by challenging the basic structure of their own country. The executives who were United States citizens and who had been posted for a few years to the southern tip of Africa saw their sojourn as a temporary rung on what they hoped would be a ladder to the top. In such a position, a shrewd executive would not waste time or resources trying to accomplish something for which the home office showed disregard or distaste. Such a person would focus on more narrow, acceptable goals: building plants or market share, squeezing out costs and competitors, and settling in to the pampered suburban neighborhoods that resembled those they had left behind in the States and those to which they hoped soon to return.

The result was that American executives in South Africa, as Wayne Fredericks had discovered decades before, had little personal or institutional interest in racial justice. Indeed, rather than observing a liberal chain reaction in which the Americans converted their British colleagues who would then evangelize the Afrikaners, most saw the influences flowing the other way. By the early 1970s, with the slow collapse of the United Party, larger and larger numbers of English speakers were voting for the Nationalists. American executives living in South Africa, through protective coloration, acquired similar sympathies. At the same time that Diggs was stirring up a small corner of the U.S. Congress, the South African Institute of Race Relations published the results of a poll taken among American businessmen in South Africa in 1968. When asked for whom they would vote if they were eligible, thirty-five percent favored John Vorster and the National Party. Another thirty-one percent endorsed the almost equally discriminatory policies of the United Party. Only fifteen percent said that they would have voted for Helen Suzman's Progressives. When asked about Vorster's policy of separate development, the majority responded favorably to its achievements and eighty-one percent described it as "an attempt to develop a solution." When another management consultant surveyed the attitudes of American managers a few years later, he summarized his findings brusquely: "After twenty minutes in South Africa, take any American manager and he's pro–South African and anti-American."

Tim Smith had the chance to explore the attitudes of American managers during his second trip to South Africa, in 1970. He had returned from his first visit two years before deeply pessimistic about the possibilities for peaceful change in South Africa. Opposition to apartheid within South Africa, he believed, was floundering. Though most white liberals clung to the hope that industrialization would inexorably break down racial barriers, he had found little evidence during his visit to support this theory. Moreover, though Smith agreed with the goal of American economic disengagement, he thought the likelihood of it happening was small. "American business will not withdraw from South Africa without a U.S. government mandate," he wrote in a report to church leaders after his 1968 trip, "and that is not in the offing." The central question, therefore, was how to "use American business to humanize this bad situation a little." Smith pondered the levers available to activists. "Perhaps stockholders should state that business should withdraw from South Africa if it is compelled by law or custom to engage in slave labor," he suggested. If American churches wanted to alter corporate policy, they would have to consider their tactics carefully. "The questions to consider," he concluded, outlining the themes of the future divestment debate, "are: how do concerned groups in America convince American business to be a more responsible employer in a situation where there is no union or government regulation to push him? What strategy can be worked out from the domestic front to alter foreign business practices? Is the only way to influence business policy, supervision, or regulation by American government?"

At the time of Smith's first trip and his subsequent memo, American church leaders were beginning to question their churches' own investments in South Africa. But activist church leaders were finding it difficult to act without more data on corporate performance and employment practices in South Africa. Smith's 1970 trip was made to gather such information. Through church connections, he collected letters of introduction from the home offices of American corporations with subsidiaries in South Africa. Starting in July he traveled around the country for two months, visiting nearly two dozen companies and conducting long interviews, most of them tape-recorded, with the managing directors and senior staff. Smith found, to his surprise, that he was received cordially and openly. Some of the businessmen feted him in their executive dining rooms; others gave him personal tours of their plants. He was even more startled by what he found: tight job restrictions barring Africans and Coloureds from many kinds of work; gross pay disparities that awarded whites several times the salary for essentially the same jobs as Africans and Coloureds; segregated toilets, locker rooms, and eating facilities for the different races. But he was most astonished by the attitude of his hosts, most of whom found the situation in South Africa not only normal but desirable.

Over the days he spent chatting with executives, Smith discovered, as had the 1968 opinion poll, a wellspring of support for Vorster's efforts. David Knowles, the head of economics and planning at Esso (later

Exxon), told Smith outright that the policy of separate development was correct. David Brown, a South African managing director of the joint venture of Barlow-Weyerhaeuser, confided that though he had voted against Vorster, he believed that the policy of separate development was a "much more humanitarian concept" than people gave it credit for. In some cases, Smith's American hosts were breathtakingly blunt. "This Bantustan thing, I agree with it one hundred per cent. It is economically and politically sound," said the managing director of International Harvester. "I am sympathetic to what the South African government is trying to do. I don't want hundreds of Africans running around in front of my house."

The only widespread dissatisfaction with government policy focused on job restriction, which, to the executives' way of thinking, forced companies to hire dimwitted and lazy whites at high salaries when intelligent, industrious persons of other races were available at lower cost. The executives explained that they had dealt with these limitations by asking the government privately for waivers, by breaking jobs into pieces and distributing them among Coloureds and Africans, or by concealing a specialized job beneath a menial-sounding name (and a low salary). Despite these efforts, the shortage of skilled labor remained acute; in some occupations, it approached twenty-four percent. When a flu epidemic swept through the ranks of white railway workers the month before Smith arrived, seventy freight trains were canceled every day because there was no one to handle them. Cargo ships stopping in South Africa's ports had to wait three days to be unloaded. Prominent business leaders and English-speaking newspaper editors joined in denouncing the government's devotion to job restrictions for whites. Though the executives with whom Smith met grumbled about the color bar, they did not want to object publicly. The executives at Chrysler, for example, told Smith that it was less trouble to recruit skilled white workers in England and Switzerland and bring them halfway around the world.

Smith also learned that none of the businessmen had any friends who were not white. One executive told him that he occasionally came into contact with Coloured or African people who worshiped at his Anglican church. Another said that he had met a few nonwhites once at an interracial reception hosted by the American consulate. Most told Smith that such exchanges were difficult to arrange; few gave him the impression that they had tried. R. J. Scott, the belligerent managing director at Ford, the largest American employer in South Africa, explained his situation succinctly. When asked about whether he ever had any contact across racial lines, he replied, "I didn't do it when I was back in the United States; I don't want to do it here; and I wouldn't do it if I went back."

About the only regular contact that senior executives had with Africans was with their domestic servants. Given their lack of personal contact, the American managers tended toward bigoted views of South African blacks. "You can't take these people from here to there overnight," the managing director of Deere, who was from Louisiana, told Smith. "They're savage." At General Motors he heard that Africans "lacked reasoning power," "enjoyed repetitive work," and had "no depth perception." They had to be introduced to the most elemental tools, such as a screwdriver (Chrysler) and even then "lacked dexterity with their fingers" (Union Carbide). Africans all looked alike; the men smelled and the women could not keep their genitals clean (Deere). Over and over the executives stressed the great chasms of culture, history, and biology that divided white from black. "Americans often make the mistake that Africans are just like Negroes," Logan Emlet, the managing director of Union Carbide, tried to explain to his visitor, "[but] Negroes have white blood and grow up in pretty much the same culture." "If you saw these Africans on Friday afternoon after payday," concluded another executive at Deere, "you would see that they are not quite human."

Smith was amazed by the common themes that suffused the conversation of his hosts. All of the managers believed that their company's mere presence in South Africa would, without any special effort, inure to the benefit of all the races. All believed that social change had to be slow and incremental in South Africa, lest the country spin into chaos and Communism. All believed that Vorster's talk of reform was sincere and that South Africa was misunderstood abroad. All believed that criticism of South Africa in the United States was unfair, because America still had racial problems of its own and because South Africa was essential to the economy and defense of the West. And, most important, despite their lack of personal contact with people of other races, all of the white executives of American companies believed that they could judge what was best for their Coloured, Asian, and African employees.

This mix of paternalism and economic self-interest allowed the American executives to withhold workplace rights considered essential back in their own country. Executives at Chrysler, for example, told Smith that they did not provide medical insurance for their African workers, as they did for whites, because the government provided free medical care in the townships. The executives at Barlow Tractor, a distributor of Caterpillar machinery and parts, said that they had never instituted a pension plan for Africans because the Africans wouldn't want their pay cut. The men at Mobil said that Africans didn't believe in pensions because Africans intended to return to their tribes where their families would take care of them. Some executives told Smith that it would not be a good idea to raise African wages because they would just waste the money (Chrysler) or because it would cause inflation (Deere). Finally, when Smith asked about creating unions for blacks comparable to those for whites, all of the businessmen said unions were unnecessary because they ran such open and understanding shops and because Africans preferred hierarchy. "The Bantu looks on the employer as his father," a labor relations officer at Chrysler explained to Smith. "The concept that he is going to sit down at a table and bargain with the employer is a very foreign one. He accepts the white man as his guardian." The director of personnel at Ford Motor Company went so far as to insist that his workers were not interested in unions because "over the years, the master-servant relationship has been a good one."

In the middle of his trip Smith visited an American official at the consulate in Durban who was depressed by the behavior of his American compatriots. "You shouldn't allow yourself to be fed a lot of pap by the big companies," he told Smith. The government might be easing job restrictions in a few areas, but it was enforcing its policies more vigorously in others. American firms bent government regulations, he said, only "when pushed to the wall." He had found that the American executives divided into two groups: "expatriates who become virtual South Africans" and "those who try to do the most for the company and get a good promotion." Both groups, he said, did everything they could to please the government. In Port Elizabeth, the executives from the big American auto companies had refused to attend official receptions at the United States consulate, including one on the Fourth of July, because persons of other races had been included. "In all my foreign service," said the official, "I've never seen such intransigence as in these Americans." The American official told Smith that over the years he had lost faith in his compatriots. "I used to hope that we could get the American businesses here to move off their bottoms and do something," he concluded wistfully. "But we are putting pressure at the wrong end. The pressure should be applied in New York or in Detroit."

Less than six weeks after Smith returned from his trip, a brief but important confrontation over South Africa flared on the banks of the Charles River in Cambridge, Massachusetts. In early October 1970, Ken Williams, a black photographer and employee of the Polaroid Corporation, came across the mock-up of a badge for the South African Department of Mines. When Williams asked about it, he learned that the Polaroid Corporation was selling its I.D.-2 system—through which identification cards could be made in a few instants with its patented photographic technology—to various industries in South Africa. Williams, a political radical, hurriedly consulted with his wife, Caroline

Hunter, who was a chemist at Polaroid, and within a few days they had secretly concocted and posted dozens of fliers around the office announcing, "Polaroid Imprisons Black People in 60 Seconds." Describing themselves as the vanguard of the Polaroid Revolutionary Workers Movement, Williams and Hunter threatened to launch a national boycott of Polaroid products unless Polaroid stopped selling all photographic equipment in South Africa and withdrew from the country.

From a distance, the choice of Polaroid as a target might have seemed odd. Of the hundreds of American companies operating in South Africa, Polaroid was one of the smallest, with no plant, no direct investments, and minuscule sales. Moreover, with an eccentric and liberal visionary, Edwin H. Land, as its founder and head, and former Kennedy advisers like Carl Kaysen on its board, the firm seemed far removed from the conservative global behemoths that received most of the criticism. The decision to target Polaroid turned out to be wise, however, because the liberal instincts of the firm prompted it to react swiftly and publicly, thus establishing a precedent for other companies. The day after the fliers appeared, the legal department of the corporation produced a two-page rebuttal denying that the I.D.-2 system was being sold to South African government agencies. The company noted, however, that the I.D.-2 system was being sold to an independent local distributor, Frank and Hersch, for resale to industrial users for their own employees and to the South African army and air force to identify military personnel.

Such reasoning did not persuade Hunter and Williams, who struck back with more strident claims. When the story was picked up in the *Boston Globe* and began circulating around the country, company officials responded aggressively. They announced a temporary ban on the sale of all I.D.-2 systems to South Africa. They took out a full-page advertisement in newspapers throughout the United States asking, "What Is Polaroid Doing in South Africa?" "Why was Polaroid chosen to be the first company to face pressure . . . about business in South Africa?" the advertisement continued. "Perhaps because the revolutionaries thought we would take the subject seriously. They were right. We do." Noting that "the question of South Africa is too important and too complex for a hasty decision" and that they wanted to learn "what is the best solution for the black people of South Africa," they announced that they were sending a team of four employees, two black and two white, to South Africa to investigate.

Within days after the team returned, the executives of Polaroid announced that they had decided not to withdraw all their products from South Africa but would instead impose a strict ban on all sales to the government, military, and police. In addition, they would immediately launch a one-year "experiment" to raise wages, increase job training and other benefits, and establish scholarships for black education and cultural organizations. Polaroid trumpeted its decision in full-page ads in major metropolitan newspapers and in the black press at an estimated cost of more than fifty thousand dollars. The Polaroid experiment became a major story in South African newspapers, some of which blamed the demonic influence of the American Committee on Africa. South Africa's ambassador to the United States wrote stiffly to Polaroid that "we in South Africa are used to the 'holier than thou' approach. We know there are those who like to confess South Africa's 'sins' in public and who hope thereby to save their own souls."

Williams and Hunter believed the Polaroid experiment to be a smoke screen to conceal the firm's continued involvement. In January 1971 they again demanded that Polaroid withdraw and contribute the profits earned in South Africa to the recognized African liberation movements. When Hunter traveled the next month to New York to testify before a United Nations hearing, she returned to find that she had been suspended without pay because of her "public advocacy of a boycott of Polaroid corporation and its products." Her boss wrote in the official letter: "Such conduct is inconsistent with your responsibilities as an employee of the Company. Your persistent activities in fomenting public disapproval of the enterprise which employs you violates elementary principles of propriety and good faith." Hunter told the press that she interpreted the suspension as a firing and offered it as proof of the racism of the firm.

The Polaroid episode, along with the increasing activism of the churches, strengthened Charles Diggs's conviction that he needed to take a much closer look at the question of American investments in South Africa. Diggs also felt pressure from some of the younger, more zealous black congressmen who had banded together in January 1971 to form the Congressional Black Caucus (CBC). Though the thirteen members of this group elected Diggs to the chair because of his seniority, they had to prod him to be more confrontational. As a result of the formation of the CBC, the rift between Richard Nixon and the black members of Congress grew. When Nixon gave his State of the Union address in 1971, the members of the Congressional Black Caucus—including an uncomfortable Diggs—refused to attend. In March the president received the members of the caucus at the White House but did nothing about the sixty-one policy recommendations—including several on South Africa—that they handed him during the meeting. Faced with such inaction, the members encouraged Diggs to direct the attention of the House subcommittee on Africa to American business. Privately the caucus members wondered whether Diggs would be willing to do so, since his district was in Detroit, the center of American automobile manufacturing.

In the spring of 1971, Diggs decided to hold hearings on American business in South Africa. On Tuesday, May 4, Diggs opened the proceedings by noting that "during the past five years in the US there has been an increasing interest in the role of the American corporation in southern Africa, and particularly in South Africa. Questions have come from many quarters: from universities, from church groups, from Peace Corps volunteer returnees, from the sectors of the black community." Diggs drew parallels to other concerns about corporate behavior, commenting that "while pressure on corporations who pollute the environment or have discriminatory hiring practices is often based on hard, detailed data, too often that data has been lacking as we have analyzed specific American companies in South Africa." Noting that the Department of Commerce showed a mean return on investment of seventeen percent in South Africa (compared to a world average of ten percent) and that American companies had made over $120 million dollars in profits the year before, Diggs said that he wanted to find out how the companies could "use their considerable pressure" to "improve conditions for black Africans."

The hearings were just part of a trend toward closer scrutiny of corporate practices, one that was prompted not by politicians but by institutions and activists and that took place not on Capitol Hill but on the corporations' own turf: the annual shareholders meeting. One of the first prominent Americans to employ this tactic was the presiding bishop of the Episcopal Church, John Elbridge Hines. Hines, a former bishop of Texas who had been elected presiding bishop in 1964, had decided from the beginning to push his patrician church into more direct confrontation with racism both at home and abroad. Despite his lofty title and personal energy, the presiding bishop could not rule by decree. The Protestant Episcopal Church in the United States, as the denomination was officially known, was the grandchild of the colonial Church of England. In the eighteenth century, most of its clergy were Englishmen or Tories; after the Declaration of Independence, the majority fled to Great Britain. During the war, the laity had to take charge of their own congregations and afterward they refused to let go. As a result, despite the church's hierarchical name—*episcopal* comes from the Greek word for "bishop"—the denomination had retained from these formative years a sturdily democratic bias. Bishops influence but do not control local church affairs; they exercise leadership through moral suasion, committee appointments, and control of diocesan programs.

The national policies of the church are set by delegates to General Convention, which meets every three years in a bicameral assembly modeled roughly on the U.S. Congress. The larger House of Deputies is comparable to the House of Representatives and is composed of clergy and lay representatives elected by the dioceses. The smaller House of Bishops is made up of all the bishops of the church. Most of the important resolutions originate in the House of Deputies, but every twelve years the House of Bishops exercises the important task of electing one of its number to serve as presiding bishop. In the years between General Conventions, the affairs of the church are handled by the Executive Council of the Domestic and Foreign Missionary Society of the Episcopal Church in the United States, the legal embodiment of the church and the controller of the church's endowment funds. The presiding bishop and the executive officers handle day-to-day tasks and guide the programs and committees of the national church from the Episcopal Church Center in New York City.

Though Episcopal membership has hovered since World War II below the three million mark—far fewer than the big Protestant denominations like the United Methodists (nine million) and the Southern Baptists (fifteen million)—the church's links to colonial times have given it an upper-class reputation and attendant wealth. The Episcopal Church's influence can also be felt through those claiming allegiance to it. Though constituting only 1.2 percent of the population, Episcopalians have usually made up about 15 percent of the U.S. Congress. Corporate leaders have also been disproportionately represented; according to one study in the 1970s, Episcopalians at the time represented 21 percent of all chief executive officers.

The nominal participation of such a high proportion of the American elite has sometimes tempted Episcopal clergy to believe that they should, like their counterparts in England, try to play the role of a national church, one whose ethos is woven into the nation's culture and whose pronouncements should influence the debate on public policy. Such aspirations, however, can also spawn a deep ambivalence of purpose. Each week, as Episcopal clergy around the country climb into their ornately carved pulpits and gaze out over ranks of prominent executives, professionals, and officials, they have to decide whose gospel they are going to preach.

For John Hines in 1971, this was an issue. He was convinced that access to the elite gave the Episcopal Church a special obligation to call for justice for the poor and the oppressed. Keenly aware that the Episcopal Church in the nineteenth century had avoided outspoken criticism of slavery, Hines had pushed and cajoled his denomination forward on the issue of civil rights. In 1967, after touring the ghettos of New York and Detroit, he proposed a radical solution at General Convention in 1967: that three million dollars be set aside in a "special program" to "encourage the use of political and economic power to support justice and self-determination for all." In this manner, he said, "the church can take its place humbly and boldly alongside, and in support of, the dispossessed and oppressed peoples of this country."

After General Convention had approved the proposal, Hines hired a staff that included veterans of many activist and civil rights groups. As this staff began to hand out monies to an assortment of minority groups whose beliefs, culture, and tactics were at variance with the traditions upheld by the church, Hines came under sharp criticism. The hysteria increased when church leaders were subjected in May 1969 to the demands of the Black Manifesto. The document, written by clergyman and Black Power leader James Forman, who interrupted a service at Riverside Church to present it, insisted that white churches pay "reparations" to blacks for supporting slavery in the United States. Hines did not support the manifesto but continued to argue that his church should move more aggressively against racism. Gradually his gaze widened beyond the boundaries of the United States to take in the many other members of the Anglican communion—churches planted around the globe in former British colonies. His attention quickly alighted on the problems of the sister church in South Africa. His instincts told him that there he would find, in one place, an example of many things that bothered him: the persistence of institutional racism, the amorality of American foreign policy, the unthinking greed of big companies, and the special obligations of his church.

The church as a body had already paid brief attention to apartheid. In 1967 the delegates to General Convention, spurred on by the bank campaigns and by the debate over Hines's "special program," passed a resolution asking Hines to look into the question of South African investments. Hines appointed a new committee, whose members recommended eighteen months later that the church should gauge the involvement of particular businesses in the South African economy and then judge whether that involvement was contributing to the development of black family life, improved labor relations, more equitable wage scales, and wider political reforms. The Executive Council approved the recommendation and bounced it over to the Committee on Trust Funds for implementation. The Trust Funds members balked, kicking the proposal back to the Executive Council on the grounds that the criteria were too vague and the information too scant. In May 1970 the members of the Executive Council, realizing that the issue could not be resolved with dispatch, decided to create a special Ad Hoc Committee on Social Criteria in Investments to gather information and to make recommendations on specific companies doing business in South Africa.

When the next General Convention met, in the summer of 1970, activist delegates expressed dissatisfaction with the slow pace of their church's progress and introduced a resolution asking the Executive Council to use its shares of stock in General Motors to pressure the company to withdraw from South Africa. When the vote passed, the members of the Executive Council moved swiftly, sending a fact-finding team to South Africa, establishing a permanent Committee on Social Responsibility in Investments (CSRI), and authorizing Hines to challenge the largest corporation in the United States. "The Episcopal Church has been increasingly concerned in recent years about the stewardship of the economic resources entrusted to her," the members of the committee noted in a document explaining their actions. "That we possess considerable economic power is obvious and undeniable. What has not always been so obvious is the necessity for this Church to use its economic power for Godly purposes in the framing of a more just and equitable society which respects and enhances human dignity while preserving the only inhabitable environment we have. One form of wealth is in our portfolio of stocks and bonds. . . . What we do with our funds for investment must be in accord with the quality of human community to which our pronouncements and resolutions have committed our church."

In the winter of 1971, while the Polaroid controversy raged and Charles Diggs planned his hearings, John Hines dropped a small bombshell. On February 1, he sent a letter directly to the chairman of the board of General Motors, James M. Roche. "We believe that the apartheid policies presently pursued by the Republic of South Africa in its own territories and in South West Africa will lead inextricably to great instability and turmoil in South Africa," he wrote. "We are further convinced that this turmoil will inevitably result in the destruction of foreign capital invested in South Africa." Hines told Roche that the Episcopal Church planned to use its 12,574 shares in GM to offer a shareholder resolution urging the auto company to withdraw. As the *New York Times* noted in its front-page story the next day, "the move is expected to be a forerunner of a large-scale reexamination of investment portfolios by churches and foundations with an eye towards helping relieve social problems." Frank White, the director of resource studies for the National Council of Churches, concurred, pointing out that, in addition to the Episcopal Church, at least five other major Protestant denominations had formed committees to study "the question of how to bring investments into line with stated social and public policies."

Shortly afterwards, the members of the board of General Motors announced that they opposed the church's resolution.

Roche, whose firm had been under attack from several sides, was said to be personally infuriated at the intrusion of the church. He was a Roman Catholic who took his faith so seriously that on his relentless global travels his far-flung minions offered him fish every Friday (even though he disliked seafood) and made arrangements to drive him, sometimes great distances, to attend mass. Roche found the invasion of the ecclesial sphere into the economic deeply troubling, and he struck back. The critics of American corporations, he told the members of the Executive Club of Chicago, "crusade for radical changes in our system of corporate ownership . . . so drastic that they would all but destroy free enterprise as we know it." Roche noted ominously that the critics' views were "antagonistic to our American ideas of private property and individual responsibility." He vigorously endorsed the current system of corporate governance. "Management must be responsive to the wishes of the stockholders," he said. "Management is obliged to inform the stockholders as to the problems and the short-term costs as well as the potential long-range benefits of a greater and more direct involvement in social objectives. Then management must abide by the owner's decisions. Through his proxy, every stockholder has the right to decide and must exercise it."

Roche's strong reaction would have seemed a little bizarre to anyone who looked at the numbers. At the time General Motors had more than 286 million shares outstanding. As a percentage of this immense pool of capital, the Episcopal Church's shares equaled less than one-half of one-hundredth of one percent. But Roche knew—as did Hines—that at stake was something far more important. Despite Roche's dramatic rhetoric, his basic claim was true: At the root, the debate was about the fundamental structure, governance, and legitimacy of America's corporate titans. To comprehend how this could be so, one must refer to the legal and economic theories that undergird American capitalism.

The corporate form was imported from British law and was in limited use in the United States at the time of the Revolutionary War. Most Americans owned and ran businesses as individuals or, if a venture required more capital and participants, as partners. The partnership was an excellent structure for those who intended to be in business together for a long time, but it had certain drawbacks. A person who wished to leave a partnership and withdraw his financial share could do so only with the approval of all the other partners. Moreover, the failure of a partnership could strip its members not only of their business but also of their personal assets. The corporation, in contrast, was an entirely different legal animal. Originally the corporation had been, in essence, a contract awarded by the British monarch to raise money and administer some project as a monopoly. In the early nineteenth century the prevailing judicial opinion in America held that the ability to organize a corporation was not a right a citizen could demand, but a privilege the government could grant. Corporate charters were thus usually specific in intent and limited in duration, designed to build a road or a canal or conduct exclusive trade along a particular route. From the early days, however, both democrats and autocrats worried that corporations might breach their original charters and acquire wealth and power far exceeding that of any individual. As a result, relatively few corporate charters were granted; and those that came into existence were subjected to uneasy scrutiny.

As corporations became more numerous, however, their economic advantages over the partnership grew apparent. In contrast to the partnership, which used the family as a model for governance, the corporation borrowed its structure and legitimacy from democratic theory. "The analogy between state and corporation has been congenial to American lawmakers, legislative and judicial," wrote legal scholar Abram Chayes. "The shareholders were the electorate, the directors, the legislature, enacting general policies and committing to the officers for execution." Persons who bought a financial share thus also acquired the political right—and duty—to vote. The new form proved an enormous boon to the young American economy, creating pools of investment capital that could be tapped to open shops, lay down railroads, launch ships, and erect factories. Those who held equity in companies were not bound for life but could sell their shares on an open market. This feature, combined with limited liability, a legal provision that confined one's financial obligations to the value of one's investment, coaxed the pennies and dollars out of American mattresses, cookie jars, and bank vaults. State governments, eager to attract investment capital and chartering fees, granted corporate charters that were less and less restrictive. Securities markets, in which stock was bought and sold daily, sprouted around the United States.

So from the beginning, ownership of a share in a corporation was an alloy forged from the two most basic American metals: belief in private property and belief in democracy. Yet as businesses grew and proliferated through the end of the nineteenth century, financial inventiveness slid into financial manipulation. Industrial robber barons pulled every lever at their disposal to construct ever more complicated trusts. Whole industries careened away from competition and into monopoly. The market, so effective an instrument of social control when the participants were numerous and equal, seemed incapable of stopping the abuses. Reformers from Teddy Roosevelt to Eugene Debs denounced the excesses and called for their correction. It was not, however, until the collapse of the stock market in 1929—which destroyed the value of half of all the stock issued since World War I and triggered global deflation, depression, unrest, and eventually war—that the American government accepted the need to introduce new checks and balances.

The members of the U.S. Congress were guided in their thinking by the ideas of a young lawyer named Adolph A. Berle and a young economist named Gardiner C. Means. The two men had collaborated on a study of American corporations and concluded that the system had failed because of the growing separation between *ownership* and *control.* In their landmark book *The Modern Corporation and Private Property,* published in 1932, Berle and Means noted that traditionally owners exercised control over their property—be it object, land, or business— directly. Corporate theory was supposed to preserve this control through the mechanism of the election of directors. However, Berle and Means asserted, when the number of shares in a firm increased, the ability of the owners to exercise control over the firm decreased. Managers, supposedly the hired hands, could then turn the institution more and more to their own course, picking directors who supported their views (including subordinate employees, who were known as "inside directors"), benefiting financially from access to private knowledge while restricting the flow of information to the public, and otherwise using corporate assets for whatever business or personal purposes they might fancy.

Spurred by the writings of Berle and Means, the agonies of the Great Depression, and the proddings of the new president, Franklin D. Roosevelt, Congress passed several important laws to tighten control over the stock market, restore confidence in the financial system, and reinvigorate corporate democracy. The centerpieces of the new legislation were the Securities Exchange Acts of 1933 and 1934, which created the Securities and Exchange Commission (SEC) and dramatically expanded the rights of shareholders. Managers were now required, among other things, to disclose large amounts of information on a regular basis; to unveil hidden conflicts of interest; and to permit shareholders who met certain conditions to contact each other. The SEC also eventually added Rule 14a-8, which some scholars have called the "shareholder bill of rights," requiring companies to include resolutions from dissident shareholders in the proxy statements mailed each year for the election of directors. This last measure would prove essential thirty years later in the divestment movement.

While the new regulations accomplished some of their objectives— drawing wary investors back into the stock market and deterring swindlers—they did not usher in the new and golden era of corporate democracy for which some had hoped. Through the 1950s the separation of ownership and control actually increased. Managers exerted a firmer grip over their boards and subordinates, fashioned more tightly hierarchical, quasi-military organizations, and went out to conquer the new postwar national and international markets. The lack of democratic accountability did not mean that American corporations operated without constraints. There were the economic requirements to raise money, build plants, expand market share, and turn a profit. There were the political limits set, with varying degrees of resolve, by the state and federal governments. There were legal boundaries imposed by the precedents of common law and by statute. There were the bewilderingly complex challenges of inducing thousands of people to mesh their skills and aspirations in the pursuit of a common end. Corporations, even very large ones, were not like superpowers; they were more like medieval duchies, doing battle, seeking protection, forming alliances, and exacting tribute as they saw fit.

Yet the irony was inescapable. Though the theory that undergirded corporations was supposedly democratic, the institutions themselves were not. Indeed, the governance of American corporations during the height of the cold war paradoxically came to resemble that of the Soviet Politburo: American managers used democratic rhetoric to disguise the self-perpetuating dictatorship of an elite that was certified by an annual "election" in which an insider-selected slate of officials was chosen unanimously by a passive electorate. As in the style of the Politburo, the fiction also required a few occasional appearances in public to give the illusion of responsiveness, though the corporate managers could control the unpredictable by their choice of an obscure venue, a tight agenda, and a blizzard of propaganda. Small wonder, then, that by the mid-twentieth century more than one scholar had concluded that the quaint concepts at the heart of corporate law had little relevance to the economic realities of the day. "Corporation law, as a field of intellectual effort, is dead in the United States," wrote the prominent legal scholar Bayless Manning. "When American law ceased to take the 'corporation' seriously, the entire body of law that had been built on that intellectual construct slowly perforated and rotted away. We have nothing left but our great empty corporation statutes—towering skyscrapers of rusted girders, internally welded together and containing nothing but wind."

In the post–World War II years the United States economy roared forward at such speed that no one seemed inclined to stop and question the soundness of its chassis—no one, that is, except a few quixotic reformers. One such person was Lewis D. Gilbert, a young newspaper reporter who, after receiving a small inheritance, decided to attend his first annual meeting in 1932. He traveled over to the offices of New York City's Consolidated Gas Company and sat among a handful of other shareholders. The chairman of the board, George Cortelyou, who had served as stenographer for President McKinley, opened the meeting, mumbled through the company's annual report in a "steady, drowsy drone, and then, without calling on any of the shareholders who had their hands in the air, adjourned the meeting. 'And now,' said the chairman happily, 'a delightful collation awaits you in the next room.' " Gilbert was shocked. Soon afterward he decided to leave his newspaper job to "fight this silent dictatorship over other people's money." Enlisting his younger brother John and a few others, Gilbert set out on a sixty-year crusade to transform annual meetings into a "modern extension of the New England town meeting." The Gilberts doggedly attended as many annual meetings as they could, sometimes more than one hundred a year. Over and over they seized on those brief public appearances by the chairman and his board to demand disclosure of more information about the firm, to protest the large sums of money the board members had gratuitously awarded to managers or to themselves, and to promote the rights of smaller shareholders. They battled the widespread tradition of scheduling annual meetings in inconvenient settings—such as distant resort areas—to reduce the already minuscule number of shareholders who attended. Whenever boards of directors cooked up a new scheme to increase their power or line their pockets, the Gilberts filed resolutions and showed up at the annual meeting to object.

Chief executives reacted with indignation and fury. General Douglas MacArthur, a member of the board of Remington Rand, was infuriated by Gilbert's impertinence. George Washington Hill of American Tobacco Company threatened to resign in 1940 rather than see his $423,000 salary cut. One chief executive summed up the feelings of his colleagues when he roared at Gilbert, "I wish you were dead." Initially most managers refused to include the Gilberts' shareholder resolutions in the proxy materials, but after a lawsuit against Hill and American Tobacco in 1940, the Gilberts established the important precedent that managers could not block a resolution simply because they did not like it.

The Gilberts devoted much of their attention to recommending procedural changes to reduce the tyranny of the majority over small shareholders. They did not, however, always limit their queries to such matters. In 1941, Lewis Gilbert embarrassed the chairman of Standard Oil of New Jersey by asking him about the company's oil sales to the Axis powers. That same year he challenged the presiding officer of the Curtis Publishing Company to defend the *Saturday Evening Post*'s "scandalous isolationist policy." Though the Gilberts were always careful to say that the manager's actions would harm shareholder returns, the debate was really not about money but about power.

Throughout the 1950s and 1960s, a few other gadflies emerged to pester chief executives at their annual appearances in public, including two notable women, Wilma Porter Soss, the founder of the Federation of Women Shareholders in American Business, and Evelyn Y. Davis, who followed in Soss's footsteps. Despite getting some attention, the Gilberts, Soss, and Davis were only individuals who might cause a moment's embarrassment but could inflict no long-term damage. The great institutions that channeled capital into American industry—banks, pension funds, insurance companies, foundations, and so on—faithfully backed managers' recommendations and candidates year after year. As long as they received unflinching support from these immense shareholders, the managers continued to profess their undying commitment to the shareholders' interests.

In the mid-1960s, however, the first serious cracks in this mutually supportive edifice appeared. After race riots swept through Rochester, New York, local black clergy invited radical community organizer Saul Alinsky to come to their city and build the ghetto into a potent political force. Alinsky arrived and formed a coalition called FIGHT (Freedom, Integration, God, Honor—Today) out of one hundred black groups. During its first year, the members of FIGHT pushed the city to provide more low-cost housing and to launch new federally funded adult education programs. In 1966 the members of the coalition turned their attention to the hiring practices of the Eastman Kodak Company, which employed approximately thirteen percent of Rochester's workforce and whose employees helped run the community's hospitals, community service programs, and schools. In September 1966, the leaders of FIGHT demanded that Kodak adopt a preferential training and hiring program for six hundred unskilled and unemployed blacks. After several months of wrangling and intense media attention, the president of FIGHT and an assistant vice president of Kodak worked out on agreement. When the top managers learned the details of the agreement, which not only set targets for hiring but also provided for semimonthly meetings between Kodak and FIGHT, they publicly repudiated it. The result, said one observer, was a "colossal public relations blunder" that radicalized FIGHT's members and increased third-party support for its goals. Alinsky and the members of FIGHT, in pondering ways to increase the pressure on Kodak, decided that they would try to embarrass the senior managers at the annual meeting. Alinsky immediately set about writing letters and delivering speeches to urge organizations sympathetic to FIGHT—religious groups, student groups, labor unions, and foundations—to sign over their proxies or to attend the annual meeting and support their efforts. "If you are on the level, then prove it at no cost to yourselves," Alinsky argued. "We are not asking for a penny. Just assign us the proxies of the stock you hold."

The annual meeting in 1967 little resembled the tranquil ritual to which Kodak's directors were accustomed. Buses of demonstrators, white and black, poured in from the slums and suburbs of Rochester, from around New York State, from universities like Cornell, Yale, Princeton, and Dartmouth. On arrival the demonstrators met a phalanx of local police, state troopers, and Kodak security guards. The president of FIGHT, the Reverend Franklin D. Roosevelt Florence, entered the hall, delivered a broadside, and stormed out. The directors spent the rest of the meeting discussing the problems of minority hiring and the FIGHT demands. Two months later, the two sides worked out an agreement with the assistance of the chairman of the President's Council on Urban Affairs, Daniel Patrick Moynihan; one scholar, David Vogel, estimated that as a result the company provided new jobs to between two hundred and six hundred unemployed blacks.

Alinsky, thinking back on the events, believed that an important new tool had been found to mobilize the passive middle class. "Proxies can be the mechanism by which [the middle class] can organize," he wrote in his book *Rules for Radicals*. "Once organized around proxies they will have a reason to examine, to become educated about the various corporate policies, both domestic and foreign, because they can now do something about them." Activist groups of shareholders could, with the help of a national clearinghouse of some kind, enliven annual meetings into edifying dramatic events. "The way of proxy participation," he wrote, "could mean the democratization of corporate America."

In three years the number of activist challenges at annual meetings increased—over South African loans, employment practices, and especially defense contracts for the war in Vietnam. Eventually the activity resulted in a lawsuit filed by the Medical Committee on Human Rights, a group of physicians opposed to the war, against Dow Chemical, charging that the company had improperly blocked the organization's attempt to include a proxy resolution objecting to Dow's manufacture of napalm. The case, which ended up in the federal circuit court of the District of Columbia, was decided in 1970. In his opinion Judge Edward Allen Tamm forcibly affirmed the rights of investor activists. "Congress intended by its enactment of . . . the Securities Exchange Act of 1934 to give true vitality to the concept of corporate democracy," he wrote, [and] "to assure corporate shareholders the ability to exercise their right—some would say their duty—to control the important decisions which affect them in their capacity as stockholders and owners of the corporation." Managers thus could not legitimately prevent one group of owners from asking others whether they wished "to have their assets used in a manner which they believe to be more socially responsible but possibly less profitable than that which is dictated by present company policy." Indeed, Tamm commented, "the management of Dow Chemical Company is repeatedly quoted in sources which include the company's own publications as proclaiming that the decision to continue manufacturing and marketing napalm was made not *because* of business decisions but *in spite* of them; that management in essence had decided to pursue a course of activity which generated little profit for the shareholders and actively impaired the company's public relations and recruitment activities because the management considered this action morally and politically desirable."

In language that would be studied in law schools and quoted thousands of times in the ensuing years, Judge Tamm enunciated the basic right of investors to challenge managerial power: "There is a clear and compelling distinction between management's legitimate need for freedom to apply its expertise in matters of day-to-day business judgment," Tamm declared, "and management's patently illegitimate claim of power to treat modern corporations with their vast resources as personal satrapies implementing personal political or moral predilections. It could scarcely be argued that management is more qualified or more entitled to make these kinds of decisions than the shareholders who are the true beneficial owners of the corporation."

As the new investor activism gained favor with the courts and the federal government, more corporations found themselves answering embarrassing shareholder questions in public—including General Motors, America's largest and most visible company. In 1970, the year before John Hines's proxy announcement, a group of young lawyers, many of whom had worked for consumer advocate Ralph Nader, announced the formation of Campaign GM. The centerpiece of their effort was the filing of shareholder resolutions to promote the expansion of the corporation's board to include women and minorities and the creation of a committee to examine the social impact of the company's policies. When the SEC ordered GM to include the resolutions in their proxy statements, the auto executives spent millions of dollars on a massive public relations effort in retaliation. They mailed out a twenty-one-page booklet defending their record on safety, pollution, and social welfare to all 1.3 million of their shareholders; ran full-page advertisements in 150 daily and college newspapers; and contacted every major institutional investor by telephone "to make sure that the proxies are being returned and that they are being voted the right way." "Aside from feeling occasionally like our one thousand shares is a majority holding in GM," the vice president for finance at Antioch College commented wryly, "there hasn't been any pressure at all." Another bank trust officer grumbled that the effort was "a classic example of corporate overkill."

The intense lobbying around Campaign GM produced some of the public debate for which its organizers had hoped, especially on college campuses. Harvard University polled its students, faculty, and alumni for their thoughts; MIT sponsored a formal debate between representatives of the corporation and of the campaign. A number of colleges, including Williams, Stanford, Swarthmore, Rockefeller, and Yale, were unwilling to back either side and abstained from voting on the shareholder resolutions. Several dozen institutional investors, though deciding to support the managers of General Motors, wrote letters to the board of directors with questions or comments about the issues raised by the campaign.

At General Motors' annual meeting on May 22, 1970, nearly three thousand people showed up, including Leonard Woodcock, president of the United Auto Workers; George Wald, a Nobel laureate and biologist from Harvard; and 130 reporters. Chairman James Roche set the tone by beginning the meeting with a specially produced twenty-five-minute film that lauded GM's record in all fields. In contrast to more raucous sessions that had taken place at the annual meetings of Kodak and Honeywell, the six-and-a-half-hour marathon was marked by civility on both sides. At one point, however, the questioning between the chairman and the shareholders from the floor sharpened. Barbara Williams, a black law student from UCLA, went to the microphone and asked Roche, "Why are there no blacks on the board?"

"Because none of them have been elected," replied Roche.

"I expected better of you," said Williams. "Why are there no blacks on the board?"

"No black has been nominated and no black has been elected."

"Why are there no blacks on the board?" persisted Williams.

"I have answered the question," said Roche.

"You have failed not only the shareholders, but the country," said Williams. "Why are there no women on the board?"

"Our directors are selected on the basis of their ability to make a contribution to the success of General Motors," said Roche.

"You have not adequately answered those questions," Williams concluded. "We will be back with the same question next year and we expect you to have done something about it."

The actual proxy votes turned out to be something of a surprise. Campaign GM's two proposals had garnered approximately seven million votes. Though this formed only two and a half percent of General Motors' outstanding stock, it testified to nascent dissatisfaction among the shareholders. GM executives were even more perturbed by the private concerns that had been expressed by some of the institutional investors. After the meeting, the organizers of Campaign GM said that "round one" had been concluded and that they would be back the next year for "round two." John Connor, a former U.S. secretary of commerce and a member of General Motors' board, expressed his unhappiness with "the nature of the questions and the tone of the questions—as if the board was a public body whose deliberations were a matter of public record." Roche paid the organizers a faint compliment when he told a press conference, "They were very precise. It was obvious that they did a lot of homework. I'm sure there is going to be continued interest."

Having been bloodied in round one, James Roche and the top brass of General Motors tried to preempt round two. They appointed a committee formed of five outside directors to examine all phases of GM operations related to public policy; they established a committee of six distinguished scientists to advise the corporation on environmental matters; they appointed a prominent authority on air pollution as a vice president in charge of environmental affairs; they lent one million dollars to black groups in two cities to support the creation of low-income housing; and they deposited five million dollars into black-controlled banks around the country. While denying that they were responding to public pressure, they also initiated an intensive private search for a black person to put on the board of directors. The challenge, they knew, was to find someone who had sufficient standing in the black community to neutralize criticisms of the corporation yet who could be counted on to understand and support the basic principles of capitalism. They eventually settled on the Reverend Leon H. Sullivan, the forty-nine-year-old pastor of Zion Baptist Church in North Philadelphia and a national advocate of remedial and vocational training for the inner-city poor.

Born in 1922 in an unpainted clapboard house in Charleston, West Virginia, Sullivan had been raised by his deeply religious grandmother. At the age of ten he was thrown out of a drugstore in downtown Charleston after unwittingly trying to buy a Coca-Cola at a whites-only counter. Demonstrating precocious resolve, Sullivan immediately embarked on a personal crusade against racial injustice. Even when he had no money he entered every white drugstore, restaurant, or movie theater he could find and asked for service. For years he persisted without encouragement or success. He was still going at it in the tenth grade when he entered a greasy diner at the intersection of Washington and Capital Streets in downtown Charleston, a spot where he had already been refused several times. Blacks were supposed to enter on one side, purchase their food, and carry it out. Sullivan entered on the other side and sat down at the white counter. When the owner came over to tell him to leave, Sullivan, who had been studying American history in high school, started loudly to recite the Declaration of Independence: "We hold these truths to be self-evident, that all men are created equal; that they are endowed by their creator with certain inalienable rights." The owner and white customers froze in fascination. When Sullivan finished, the owner walked around the counter and put his hand on the teen-ager's shoulder. "Son, you can come in here and sit down and eat any-time you want to," he said. "Anybody who can remember stuff like that deserves to be treated right." He then gave Sullivan a free hamburger and a doughnut and served him without complaint whenever he re-turned.

When he graduated from high school, Sullivan attended West Virginia State College, an all-black institution, on a basketball scholarship. In his sophomore year, his grandmother, whose health was rapidly failing and who could not afford medical care, exhorted him from her sickbed. "Leonie, help your people," she told him. "And don't let this kind of thing happen to anybody else." A few days later, Sullivan decided to become a clergyman. While still in college, he studied the Bible, was ordained, and began serving two congregations on alternate Sundays. In the spring of 1943, his senior year, he persuaded Adam Clayton Powell, who had come to Charleston for an NAACP rally, to preach in his church. Powell liked Sullivan, urged him to go to New York City, and offered to help him when he got there. From then on, Sullivan set his sights on moving to New York. He applied for and received a scholar-ship to Union Theological Seminary and at the end of the summer, at the age of twenty-one, he boarded the northbound train. When he ar-rived at Penn Station he cut a strange figure: a six-foot-five, one-hun-dred-sixty-pound black man with bright blue eyes. Few would have pre-dicted, looking at his wide-brimmed straw hat and his clothes bag tied with twine, that he would have much success in Manhattan. Over the next two years, however, Sullivan rocketed upward.

With Adam Clayton Powell as his patron, Sullivan quickly met the most powerful set in Harlem, including A. Philip Randolph, who, Sulli-van later recalled, "tutored me as a father would in movement tactics and philosophy." Powell also helped Sullivan secure a post with AT&T as the first black coin box collector in the United States—though to get the job Sullivan had to run a gauntlet of interviews with the secretary, treasurer, and vice president of the huge company. "You would have thought I was being considered for president," Sullivan remembered later. He also became the supply minister at the Rendall Presbyterian Church on 137th Street, where he worked to redirect the energies of gang members into athletics. When Sullivan spoke at a rally of community leaders on "What Harlem Must Do about Juvenile Delinquency," Mayor Fiorello H. La Guardia was so impressed that he invited the young minister down to City Hall to discuss what Harlem needed. Sullivan pointed out that though Harlem was almost entirely black, it had an almost entirely white police force. La Guardia gave Sullivan permission immediately to recruit a hundred black men for the New York City police force, which Sullivan did from an office in the precinct building on 135th Street. Not long afterward, Powell asked Sullivan to join him as an assistant minister at the Abyssinian Baptist Church. He then moved on to serve for five years as the pastor of a Baptist church in South Orange, New Jersey. In 1950, at the age of twenty-eight, he was called to lead the Zion Baptist Church in Philadelphia.

Zion Baptist Church was in the northern part of the city, an area undergoing rapid demographic change. Just as Africans from the Transkei had moved north after the war to find work in the Transvaal, so had American blacks migrated in large numbers from southern communities to the northern industrial centers in search of better jobs and a better life. From 1930 to 1950 the black population of Philadelphia more than doubled, to almost 400,000. The influx created fear among whites. As blacks moved into new neighborhoods, entire streets of white residents suddenly put their houses up for sale.

In his early years at Zion, Sullivan concentrated on working with young people and building his church, whose membership soared from six hundred to five thousand. He also became a community activist. After Sullivan helped organize a citywide Citizens Committee to address the problem of gang violence, the national Junior Chamber of Commerce picked him as one of the ten outstanding young Americans of 1955 and Vice President Richard Nixon appeared at the ceremony to give him the award. As the nation skidded through the early civil rights period, Sullivan concentrated more on the "depth causes," as he put it, of his congregation's problems. The most pressing need was for jobs. He started by opening a youth employment office in the basement of his church. Though the office found work for a thousand young people a year, it had to turn thousands more away.

Sullivan became even more disturbed by a clear pattern he noticed in hiring. When Sullivan sent white boys and girls to apply for jobs, they were usually hired; when he sent blacks, they were turned away. One day Sullivan received a phone call from a white personnel worker in a major department store, who told Sullivan in tears that her boss had instructed her to treat black applicants "as nicely as possible. Then, when they leave, forget about it." In 1958 Sullivan decided to appeal directly to the corporate leaders in his community. He wrote personal letters to the chief executives of Philadelphia's three hundred largest companies, asking each of them to permit him to refer "two colored workers for consideration for jobs." Of the three hundred, twelve allowed Sullivan to send applicants, and only five companies hired any of them.

As Sullivan examined the employment trends in his city, he became more and more aware of how deeply entrenched bigotry had become. "Everywhere you went where the jobs were good, you saw whites," Sullivan recalled, "and everywhere you went where the jobs were poor, you saw blacks. And even these 'black jobs' had white bosses, for the most part." One evening in 1960, after Sullivan had returned from a picket against a dime-store chain in support of the civil rights sit-ins, his wife, Grace, asked him why he was working so hard to help people eat lunch in Georgia when blacks could not drive a bread truck in Pennsylvania. That night Sullivan couldn't sleep; flipping through his Bible he came to the passage "Ask, and it shall be given; seek, and you shall find; knock, and it shall be opened to you." Sullivan decided then and there to tackle the problem of the color bar in Philadelphia. The next Sunday he appeared in his pulpit before two thousand congregants and preached a fiery sermon. "The walls of Jericho must come down," he proclaimed. Calling his plan "selective patronage," Sullivan announced a "vast new kind of economic withdrawal campaign." If white businesses would not give their jobs to blacks, he said, then blacks would not give their dollars to whites.

Though Martin Luther King's experience with the bus company in Montgomery had already shown the power of a well-organized boycott, the plan Sullivan had in mind contained some important variations. The program would be targeted at individual consumer product companies, whose image was vulnerable to tarnishing and whose market share was vulnerable to competition. It became the model for Jesse Jackson's Operation Breadbasket and the other economic efforts that swept the country in the ensuing decades.

Over the next few weeks Sullivan enlisted the support of nearly four hundred black preachers in Philadelphia. One of the first campaigns focused on the Tasty Baking Company of Philadelphia. The ministers asked the company to hire a few black drivers for its delivery trucks. The company adamantly refused. The ministers launched a boycott, but after nearly three months the allure of the company's delicious cakes began to erode the congregations' willpower. When the clergy exhorted their flocks more fervently, some of their members complained that they wanted "to hear about Jesus, not about Tastykake." Just when Sullivan thought the whole effort might collapse, Tasty Baking Company suddenly caved in and agreed to hire black workers as salesmen-drivers, office clerks, and production line workers.

Between 1959 and 1963, twenty-nine selective patronage campaigns produced an estimated two thousand new skilled jobs for the black community. For the first three years the effort received no coverage in the white press; then in June 1962, the *New York Times* ran a front-page story. Soon afterward Martin Luther King invited Sullivan to the SCLC convention in Atlanta to lay out the blueprint for similar efforts around the country. In reflecting on his experience, Sullivan decided that the success of the selective patronage campaigns had depended on four elements. Three of them—prayer, maintaining the moral initiative, and unity—had a spiritual dimension. The fourth was far more prosaic. "Nothing influences a company's attitudes or changes its directions more than losing money," he wrote. "In order to hit prejudice where it hurts most, hit it in the pocketbook!" At the time, Sullivan believed that his approach could be used to achieve racial progress not only in the United States, but around the world. "If banking institutions, industrial enterprises, and large money-holding establishments were to focus their attention on . . . South Africa," Sullivan wrote in 1969, "initiating selective investment and patronage against her and the commodities that she produces and sells abroad, within a single year the practice and preaching of apartheid there would begin to disappear."

As the firms in Philadelphia gradually opened their employment rolls to blacks, Sullivan realized that another, potentially disastrous problem loomed. After years of segregated education and limited jobs, a significant number of the applicants were having trouble meeting the mathematical, writing, and technical standards of their new positions. In 1963 Sullivan and his associates rented a decrepit old jailhouse in the center of one of Philadelphia's most burnt-out neighborhoods and renovated it as a vocational training center. In January 1964 they opened the first Opportunities Industrialization Center (OIC), an organization that Sullivan described as "an entirely new direction for black people in America: massive, militant, people-centered, self-help programs initiated by the black community for the black community." The logo for the new organization was a skeleton key, to show that OIC could unlock any door, and the motto, which had a delicious double meaning, was "We Help Ourselves."

Sullivan's organization steadily picked up steam. When the teachers in OIC discovered that many of their students had such low opinions of themselves that they had trouble completing their courses, OIC set up a prevocational "feeder program." Every applicant had to pass through the program, which combined remedial reading and writing with pep talks on everything from black history to personal grooming. Corporate executives from mammoth firms like General Electric, Westinghouse, and IBM donated used equipment for the classes. Money streamed in, as government agencies and private philanthropies like the Ford Foundation sensed that Sullivan had discovered a workable solution. Though companies were initially reluctant to hire OIC graduates, many of whom had never completed high school and had police records from their youth, attitudes gradually changed, and more and more graduates found good jobs.

Politicians from both sides of the spectrum flocked to pay their respects—Democrats because it was an inner-city poverty program, Republicans because it was a self-help effort. In 1967 Lyndon Johnson flew up from Washington on *Air Force One* to tour the facility; the next year, candidate Richard Nixon stopped by. Soon other minority communities were asking how to develop OIC and feeder programs in their cities, so Sullivan and Executive Director Gus Roman set up training seminars and offered technical advice. By 1969, less than five years after the creation of the first project, there were nearly seventy OICs in various stages around the country and the idea had spread to five African countries.

Sullivan, however, did not rest on his laurels. Dreaming of the day when there would be a vocational training center "in every shopping center," as he put it, Sullivan asked George Champion, the chairman of Chase Manhattan Bank, to help him assemble a national industrial advisory council composed of top executives from the nation's largest industrial companies, including Boeing, Coca-Cola, Brown and Root, Rohm and Haas, IBM, and National Cash Register. Sullivan believed that he could persuade these men, as members of an advisory council, to take unprecedented steps toward resolving racial discrimination. The executives preferred Sullivan's pragmatic approach to the fire-breathing militancy of Black Power. For Sullivan, the challenge was to balance his religious commitment to justice with his desire to avoid alienating the white men who held the reins of power. In his discussions with business leaders, Sullivan often attached to his strong demands the self-deprecating preface "I am only a preacher, but . . ." The ploy must have worked. For whatever reasons—moral integrity, tactical silence, or personal charisma—the executives who admitted Sullivan into their midst decided that he was someone with whom they could work. When James Roche let it be known that he needed a black for the board of General Motors, the clubby network of American executives assured him that Sullivan was the man.

In the fall of 1970 James Roche called Leon Sullivan and asked if he would be willing to come to New York to meet him. Sullivan, who had never met Roche, said no, he was too busy with pastoral duties like setting up the church's kindergarten. If Roche were able to come to Philadelphia, Sullivan continued, he would try to squeeze him in. The chastened chairman of General Motors made his pilgrimage to Zion and offered Sullivan a spot on the board. Before accepting, Sullivan asked his aides to stand at Philadelphia's five busiest intersections at rush hour to count the number of Cadillacs driven by blacks who were not chauffeurs. Having estimated, through this crude poll, that blacks in Philadelphia purchased about sixty percent of General Motors' most expensive car, Sullivan decided that he had not only an interest in the company but some leverage. "We buy more Cadillacs than anybody else," Sullivan later told the annual conference of the Urban League. "If we stopped buying them, they would have to stop making them."

Sullivan's acceptance was big news around the country; the editors of both *Jet* magazine and *Business Week* immediately slapped his photograph on their covers. Sullivan told reporters that he did not intend to be a patsy and at his first meeting as a member of the board, on February 1, 1971, he told his new colleagues the same thing. He was a minister of God and not an economic expert, he said, and he was interested in justice. Accordingly, he would be "particularly interested in training programs and in black dealerships and in black and other minority employment opportunities at General Motors plants and among General Motors vendors and producers."

Bishop Hines's letter informing Roche of the Episcopal Church's resolution on South Africa arrived on the same day as Sullivan's first board meeting, and the announcement provided Sullivan with a immediate test of his loyalties. Sullivan decided that he agreed with Hines and told the other board members, much to their consternation, that he intended to vote in favor of the Episcopal Church's resolution at the annual meeting. On May 21, 1971, all of the parties convened in Cobo Hall, in Detroit, for another well-attended annual meeting; indeed, the diversity of persons and topics assembled bore some resemblance to the New England town meeting of which Lewis Gilbert had dreamed forty years before. Among the more than three thousand people present were not only Leon Sullivan, attending his first annual meeting, but also Charles Stewart Mott, the ninety-five-year-old patriarch who had been serving on the board of General Motors since 1913, nine years before Sullivan was born. In the audience were the leaders of Campaign GM, who had brought new proposals urging the corporation to broaden representation on the board of directors; Timothy Smith, who had recently published the report summarizing his interviews with corporate executives in South Africa; the three perennials Lewis Gilbert, Wilma Porter Soss, and Evelyn Y. Davis; and the presiding bishop of the Episcopal Church himself, resplendent in the purple shirt and pectoral cross denoting his position.

The meeting took nearly seven hours. Dozens of persons lined up at the microphone to offer their support for Campaign GM or for the Episcopal Church's resolution. Bishop Hines made history when, as the head of a major religious denomination, he made a personal plea to the board of directors, arguing that by remaining in South Africa General Motors was "increasing the strength and control of the racist dictatorship." James Roche replied that no one favored apartheid; the question was what General Motors should do. The managers had two choices: to withdraw unilaterally or to work "within the framework of existing laws to further the progress of nonwhites. . . . GM is convinced," he said, "that the proper course is not to turn its back on a complex situation but to further the progress already being made and through our operations, work to bring about progressive change." Eager to move the meeting along, Roche cut off several speakers who tried to support Hines. Then, after four hours of running the meeting, a tired Roche stumbled into an embarrassing moment. He told the assembly that they should remember that the corporation was responsible not to the general public, but only to its stockholders. "We are a public corporation owned by free, white . . ." Roche said, suddenly losing his train of thought. Some members of the audience groaned and tittered while Roche struggled for a few milliseconds to recover: ". . . black, and yellow people all over the world."

Toward the end, Leon Sullivan stood up. Simultaneously breaking rank and precedent, Sullivan became the first board member ever to disagree with company policy at an annual meeting. "American industry cannot morally continue to do business," said Sullivan, "in a country that so blatantly and ruthlessly and clearly maintains such dehumanizing practices against such large numbers of people." His voice rising, his hands striking the air, Sullivan told the executives, "I hear voices say to me: 'Things will work out in time. Things are getting better. Let's go slow on this matter.' And I ask: Why does the world always want to go slow when the rights of black men are at stake? . . . I want to go on record, for all to know, that I will continue to pursue my desire to see that American enterprises, including General Motors, withdraw from South Africa until clear changes have been made in the practices, the policies of the government as they pertain to the treatment of blacks and other non-whites. . . . Although I know the position I take will lose today," Sullivan proclaimed, "you can be sure that I shall continue to pursue it tomorrow until black people in South Africa are free."

Three million shares—more than two hundred forty times the original amount held by the Episcopal Church—were voted in favor of withdrawing from South Africa, though this sum represented only 1.29 percent of the votes cast. Even the most popular resolution filed by Campaign GM, one urging the annual disclosure of information relating to pollution control and employment practices, received just 2.36 percent of the vote, far lower than the sponsors had expected. Though the chairman of First Pennsylvania Bank, John Bunting, sent a shock wave through the financial community by making his bank the first for-profit institution to vote against management when he supported Campaign GM's disclosure proposal, most of the large institutional investors on whom Campaign GM had pinned their hopes continued to support the status quo. The absence of a dramatic improvement in the voting threw the Campaign GM leaders into anguished self-examination and by the next year the members of the group had disbanded to pursue other projects.

The summer that followed the annual meeting was difficult for Leon Sullivan. "I was the only one in the world to make such a statement," he recalled years later. "The board was in total disagreement with me. At the meeting, no one spoke to me. When I went to the next [board of directors] meeting, backs were turned on me. I received letters from other board members criticizing what I had done." Even more painful, however, was the silence from those whose support he expected. "I didn't get a single card or call of support from any of the anti-apartheid groups," he recalled with a mixture of anger and sorrow. "Not one." Twenty years later the memory brought forth a deep sigh. "And yet I went through all that fire."

Charles Diggs's hearings in the House subcommittee on Africa stretched intermittently through the spring and summer of 1971 and were a mixed success. Though Thomas Wyman, a vice president of Polaroid, showed up to explain his company's experiment, most of the corporate executives to whom Diggs had sent invitations refused to appear. And despite the skilled questioning of the new staff director, Goler Teal Butcher, a former attorney at the State Department who had quit over NSSM 39, the details about specific corporations proved impossible to collect. In South Africa, however, the newspapers reported on the hearings daily; many editorial writers vilified Diggs as an agitator and a Communist. Toward the end of the hearings, Diggs decided that he would have to send a questionnaire to all the American companies operating in South Africa and to apply, as he had unsuccessfully in the past, to visit the country himself.

The questionnaire, which was mailed out on July 22, 1971, numbered eleven pages and asked, among other things, for an explanation of the company's decision to invest in South Africa; for breakdowns of the hiring, promotion, and payment of employees by race; for the distribution of fringe benefits to each racial group; for a description of the collective bargaining procedures for all employees; for a list of each subsidiary's charitable contributions; and for an assessment of the attitudes and plans of the white executives. Some of the questions were highly specific—"What was the incidence of Kwashiorkhor (a starvation disease) during the year your company opened its plant? What is it today?" Others were sweepingly broad—"Do U.S. executives in southern Africa support majority rule?"

The American executives who received it were apparently not impressed, for of the two hundred forty questionnaires sent out, the subcommittee received only twenty-six responses that it ranked "complete" or "fair." Two hundred four companies did not reply, said that they would not answer the questionnaire, or gave answers that the committee judged "non-responsive." The group vice president of General Motors declined to answer the questionnaire because the firm's South African investments had been "discussed in extensive detail at our annual meeting of stockholders last May 21." Most said they couldn't collect the information because their operations were too decentralized—that, in effect, they had no idea what was going on. Some companies sent public relations notices or histories of the company; others challenged Diggs's right to investigate their operations.

Not long after Diggs sent out the ill-fated questionnaire, he received some unexpected news: His application for a visa to South Africa and its Namibian protectorate had been granted. The South African leaders' sudden shift in policy seemed difficult to explain. Apparently, they were sufficiently concerned about the House hearings and the threat of U.S. corporate withdrawal that they did not wish to antagonize Diggs any longer. Moreover, they had had, through the work of organizations like the South African Foundation, considerable recent success in bringing Americans over to South Africa, exhibiting their showcase projects, confiding their commitment to change with anguished sincerity, and sending them home as advocates for patience. C. L. Sulzberger of the *New York Times* had gone on such trips and returned to write a series of opinion pieces in the *New York Times* in 1967, 1968, and again in 1971 urging Americans to soften their criticism of South Africa. Even more important from the South African point of view, Carl Rowan, a columnist, a former State Department official under John F. Kennedy, and the first black U.S. ambassador to Finland, had visited South Africa in 1970 and returned to counsel forbearance.

Diggs, accompanied by Republican Congressman Guy Vanderjagt and the subcommittee staff director Goler Butcher, arrived at Jan Smuts Airport in Johannesburg on August 11, 1971. As he stepped off the airplane, Diggs was met by Ambassador Hurd, who told him that while Diggs was en route, John Vorster had decided that Diggs would not be able to visit Namibia without an official escort. An enraged Diggs decided to take the next plane home. Since the next plane did not depart for twenty-four hours, the ambassador and political officer Herbert Kaiser persuaded Diggs and Vanderjagt to follow the first part of their itinerary and visit Soweto.

The tour of the sprawling township led off with a visit to a technical training institute for young men. When they reached the class on "advanced technical training," Diggs asked what the students were learning to make. Toys, the tour guide replied. And how much could they be expected to earn making toys? A few dollars a week, he was told. They then moved to a municipal hall where they met with the Urban Bantu Council, the government-approved and -controlled structure for township governance. In conversation with a large group of officials, who Diggs thought would be completely subservient to the Vorster regime, the congressman was surprised to hear criticism of apartheid and enthusiasm for the racial progress that had taken place in the United States. At one point Diggs was asked for his opinion of separate development. "We call separate development discrimination based on race and we take a most dim view of this kind of concept," Diggs replied. "We have been through it. We called it separate but equal, but it was far more separate than equal, and we suspect it will be the same way here—a lot of separate and not much development."

One questioner boldly risked government retaliation by telling Diggs point-blank that American companies must disengage. "It is said in argument to this that we the black people feel that we would be the first people that might suffer," said the young man. "This is nonsense. We are suffering already." However, said the man, though "this might be regarded as contradictory," he also felt that as long as the American companies remained in South Africa they could at least pay a living wage. Diggs responded that "the question of disengagement is perhaps academic, because the amount of U.S. investment is considerable and the amount of profit generated unprecedented anywhere in the world," but he thought that some early progress could be made in employment practices. Many of the questions to Diggs showed great interest in the American experience with race, and Diggs tried to offer practical advice. When one person asked Diggs if it was possible for blacks to work together toward a common identity and goal while at the same time pursuing integration, Diggs said that he thought it was and pointed to the experience of the Congressional Black Caucus.

Diggs left the meeting still dissatisfied and planning a quick departure from South Africa. In front of the municipal hall, however, he encountered a scene that changed his mind. As word had spread through the township that an important American visitor—a black!—had come to Soweto, waves of people had congregated around the municipal building. When Diggs emerged, a large group of young teenagers burst into a song of praise. Diggs stopped to ask for a translation and was told that they were singing:

> Here is a black man who is lionhearted
> And he is here with us today
> Perhaps he'll help us
> With the difficulties we have.
> AMEN.

Diggs, moved nearly to tears, vowed to stay.

Diggs roared through the remainder of his trip with the energy of a crusader. He toured the NASA facility outside Johannesburg and was appalled to find that the building, staffed almost entirely by South Africans, had strictly segregated bathrooms and eating rooms. After meeting labor and student activists—including Steve Biko—in Cape Town, he moved up the coast to the industrial city of Port Elizabeth, home of most of the auto manufacturing and assembly plants. At the Ford Motor Company, he engaged in a heated exchange with managing director R. J. Scott, the man who had told Tim Smith he didn't like to associate with blacks in the United States.

Afterward Diggs visited the General Motors plant and met with the managing director, William G. Slocum. Slocum was a graduate of the University of Michigan and had already held positions with General Motors in Mexico, Peru, Argentina, Venezuela, and Denmark before coming to South Africa in 1965. Several weeks before Diggs's arrival, Slocum had received word from headquarters that he was going to be transferred back to the United States on the first of September. Prior to the congressional visit, Slocum assembled his top staff and told them not to give Diggs any information. He would answer the questions himself, Slocum said, because he was leaving and could take the heat.

As he had told Tim Smith the year before, Slocum believed fervently that his role as a managing director precluded him from becoming involved in politics. At the same time, Slocum had taken steps from the beginning of his tenure to ensure a favorable impression of General Motors at the top of the Nationalist government. Shortly after arriving in South Africa, Slocum had hired a second-tier bureaucrat from Verwoerd's government, Victor Verster, to serve as his special consultant on government affairs. When Verwoerd was assassinated, Slocum was asked to attend the funeral and had been personally invited by John Vorster to ride in one of the government limousines.

Slocum subsequently got to know Vorster well. As president of NAMSA, the South African automobile trade association, Slocum gave dinners twice a year at which the prime minister sat beside him. Slocum also belonged to the most prestigious golf club in Port Elizabeth, which was Vorster's hometown, and saw the prime minister there regularly. Slocum always marveled at how Vorster, who had a reputation as a dour hardliner, could be so engaging in person. The prime minister, Slocum recalled years later, "was absolutely the funniest guy you have ever heard in your life. I heard him give lots of informal talks at one of the golf clubs I was a member of in Port Elizabeth. He would tell these great stories. The first story would be in Afrikaans, and at the punch line the Afrikaners would roll over and be practically in tears and then he would switch; his next story would be in English. . . . If there were men or women it wouldn't have made any difference, because his stories were never off color. But he actually had people, both English and Afrikaans speaking, rolling in the aisles."

During his six years in South Africa Slocum wrestled with a wide range of business problems, including the growing popularity of small Japanese pickup trucks, the government requirement to increase the percentage of locally manufactured parts in GM vehicles, and the continuing labor shortages. Slocum believed he had done an excellent job, implementing small reforms in the workplace without incurring the wrath of the government or the criticism of distant overseers at GM International. The only person who ever criticized what he did, Slocum remembered years later, was Charles Diggs.

Diggs began the meeting by quoting from a corporate document which asserted that the firm had been "actively pursuing easements" of the job reservation restrictions. What was the evidence for this? he asked Slocum. Slocum restively pointed to the company's history. When General Motors had started in the 1920s there had been no nonwhites at all, and now there were both "Bantus" and Coloureds. The Coloureds, moreover, would "soon" be moved into training programs to qualify as foremen, from which positions they would supervise other Coloureds and Africans. Diggs then asked about the questionnaire from the House subcommittee on Africa, which had been sent out three weeks before. They had not received it, said Slocum. What about the regulations requiring separate eating and bathroom facilities? asked Diggs. Are they enforced? Yes, said Slocum, there had been a factory inspector there within the last twenty-four hours.

"Doesn't it turn your stomach that I, as an American, in an American plant, would have to use a segregated facility?" asked Diggs.

"I am not going to reply to that," replied Slocum. "I accepted an assignment out here. . . . Whether my stomach is turned or not is not important. I feel our company, in being out here, is doing a useful service to all persons here. The job opportunities we provide would not be provided without us."

Diggs pressed his advantage. "In view of the contribution this firm is making in the local economy to all the people," he asked, and "in view of the fact that this company has been here for forty-five years, do you really believe that they would put you in jail or close down the plant?"

"The law is enforced, Mr. Diggs," said Slocum.

"Who would they arrest?" asked Diggs.

"Me."

"You really believe that they would arrest you if some black person went into the white restaurant or restroom or vice versa?" asked Diggs.

"I never thought of it in those terms," said Slocum. "I thought of complying with the law. I would be liable for ten years in jail under the Factory Act."

"If you shot someone, you would be liable," said Diggs. "But specifically, if you took a sign down, would a South African official arrest you?"

Slocum, increasingly uncomfortable, did not answer.

"Would *I* be barred," asked Diggs, growing incensed, "if I used the white bathroom?"

"I do not think so," said Slocum.

"Why?"

"Well, Mr. Diggs, you have diplomatic immunity, you are a congressman."

"What about Mrs. Butcher?" Diggs asked, pointing to his staff director.

"I do not know why you are asking me these questions," said Slocum evasively.

Diggs exploded with rage. "General Motors can do a hell of a lot more," he roared. "I will go back and recommend to Roche that he come to South Africa. . . . He has not been here since 1964. . . . I think that if he is as compassionate as I know him to be in the United States, I cannot believe he could keep anything in his stomach. I believe that he would be compelled to maximize the effort for change."

Slocum tried to recoup. "This is a very unique country," he bleated. "We are in the forefront of progressive change." Diggs was not in the mood to listen. He toured the plant quickly and noted that the majority of the workers were white, with a few Coloured workers scattered here and there. Later that day he gave a press conference in which he denounced the American firms he had visited for operating on a "double standard." "I am convinced that there are many more things that these companies can do which are more consistent with fair employment," he said, "things that would aid the people here and set an example that others businesses might follow. I personally believe that United States companies should lead the way."

A few days later, during a press conference held just before his departure, journalists asked Diggs if his views on American investment had changed. "No, I think I have a greater understanding of the problem," said Diggs, who had cooled off since his encounter at General Motors. "I believe we ought to think in terms of the conditions under which American enterprise operates in this country. . . . I think there is an opportunity for American enterprise to permit a sharing in the benefits of its productivity on an equal basis within the law."

A South African journalist then asked Diggs whether Congress would pass a law forcing American companies to leave. Diggs, responding politically, said that he doubted that such a bill could pass. The editors of the newspaper misinterpreted the remark. DIGGS CHANGES HIS TUNE ON US FIRMS IN SOUTH AFRICA, crowed the headline, whose attached story noted that Diggs showed "a significant change in attitude since his departure from the United States when he urged the withdrawal of American investment." The same paper prominently noted the opinion of an obscure professor from Colorado Western College who was in town for a wedding. When asked about the Diggs trip, the professor said that since he had never heard of Diggs, he was sure that the congressman had no real concern for the rights of blacks and was "interested only in his own advancement."

Though Diggs returned to the United States determined to increase the pressure on South Africa, the political opportunities for doing so seemed bleak. Indeed, while Diggs had been in Africa, a long-standing campaign by American conservatives in Congress to lift sanctions against Rhodesia had come to a head. For years, assorted right-wing representatives had introduced bills and resolutions to lend support to the minority regime of Ian Smith, but these had easily been rebuffed. Then in March, the legislators found a new formula, which was encapsulated in Senate bill 1404, introduced by Virginia Senator Harry Byrd. Byrd's bill avoided any mention of either Rhodesia or the United Nations, focusing instead on preventing "the imposition of any prohibition on the importation into the United States of strategic and critical ore from any free world country for so long as the importation of like ore from any Communist country is not prohibited by law."

Like a brilliant bomber pilot, Byrd skillfully guided the bill so low to the political ground that it was not picked up by liberal radar until too late. The only material that would be affected by the legislation, he insisted on the floor of the Senate, was chrome. The only issue was

America's national security, which could not be held hostage to Soviet supplies of chrome when other sources (such as in Rhodesia) were available. Waving reams of paper supplied to him by lobbyists from mining and steel companies, Byrd painted the issue as one of fairness and patriotism, even though the assistant secretary for African affairs, David Newsom, opposed the bill. Maneuvering deftly around liberal opposition, Byrd attached his measure as an amendment to a large military procurement bill that eventually passed. As a result, the United States, which had built its postwar foreign policy on the concept of collective security and international cooperation, officially broke the first mandatory and comprehensive sanctions program ever approved by the United Nations.

The first shipment of twenty-five thousand tons of Rhodesian chromeferrite arrived at Burnside, Louisiana, four months later. Soon afterward, the Office of Emergency Preparedness determined that the definition of metal ore "strategic and critical" to the defense of the States included not only chrome but an additional seventy-one substances, thirteen of which were mined in Rhodesia. Far from permitting the United States to procure a single substance in short supply, the bill allowed large amounts of minerals to flow out of Rhodesia and large amounts of money to flow into its white supremacist government.

Shortly after the passage of the Byrd amendment, John Vorster, perhaps sensing that Western governments were now even less likely to condemn a crackdown, ordered his police to conduct a major sweep. Between four and five A.M. on Sunday, October 24, the police in seven towns raided the homes of more than a hundred people. One target was the handful of clergy who had tried to protest apartheid. Vorster, who throughout his adult life read a chapter from the Bible every night, had a particular revulsion for clergy who "got involved in politics." A decision in September 1970 by the central committee of the World Council of Churches to form the Programme to Combat Racism and to distribute $200,000 among an assortment of African liberation groups, including the African National Congress, had proved to Vorster that the churches were becoming the tools of Communism. He was determined to put a stop to it.

In January 1971 the Security Police had arrested and charged the Very Reverend Gonville A. ffrench-Beytagh, the Anglican dean of Johannesburg, under the Suppression of Communism Act. The government charged ffrench-Beytagh, who was a British citizen, with disseminating literature advocating guerrilla warfare and with receiving and distributing money on behalf of the African National Congress. The dean insisted that the literature had been planted and that the money he had received from supporters was intended for the assistance of persons imprisoned by the South African government and their families. The case went to trial in August, dragged on through the fall, and ended with his conviction on three of the ten original counts. Despite vigorous protest from inside and outside the country, the magistrate sentenced him to five years in prison.

Throughout September and October, Vorster pressed forward with his campaign against the church. In the October raids, nine of the homes into which the police charged belonged to clergy. Roman Catholic priest Cosmas Desmond and black theologian Stanley Ntwasa were both banned and their words and articles were blacked out of books in which they had been published. Beyers Naudé and Dale White, an Anglican minister in charge of the Wilgespruit Fellowship Center near Roodepoort, were subjected to new harassments. Basil Moore of the University Christian Movement was restricted and then banned. For good measure, the security police slashed his children's swimming pool in his backyard and left the skinned body of the family cat on the doorstep of his home.

Another target of the police assault was the small but growing troupe of political activists in the Indian community, especially among the Muslims. Two years earlier a core of Indians had been radicalized by the detention and suspicious death of one of their religious leaders, Imam Abdullah Haron. Haron had been arrested in May 1969 and relentlessly interrogated every day for eight hours for more than ten weeks; then, without warning, the police announced his death. The postmortem found twenty-six separate bruises of varying age, a fractured rib, and a huge hematoma on his back; the police attributed these injuries to a fall down the stairs. The magistrate concluded that the death had resulted from heart trouble brought on by his accidental fall and refused to speculate about the source of the older injuries.

Haron's death prompted protests, including a two-month fast by a white Anglican priest and calls by leaders of the Presbyterian, Anglican, Roman Catholic, and United Congregational Churches, as well as the Christian Institute and the chief rabbi of Johannesburg, for a judicial inquiry. Vorster flatly refused and tightened the surveillance and suppression of dissent among Muslims. In the October 1971 raid, the police picked up several dozen students including Mohammed Essop and Ahmed Timol. Essop, a young doctor, was so savagely beaten that he had to be transferred under guard for emergency treatment at the Hendrik Verwoerd Hospital in Pretoria. The neurosurgeon who examined Essop officially concluded that the student had inflicted the wounds on himself as the result of hysteria. At the same time, the police announced that Timol had committed suicide. Major General C. A. Buys reported that

Timol had been sitting on a chair in a room on the tenth floor of police headquarters in Johannesburg, "in the most relaxed atmosphere one can imagine," and had suddenly made a dash for the door. When he was headed off, Buys reported, Timol had swerved to the window and inexplicably jumped out. Vorster again dismissed the request for a judicial inquiry and would not permit Timol's brother, who had also been jailed, to attend the funeral.

Despite the inauspicious political climate in the United States, Diggs resolutely looked for new ways to push South Africa. He called on the United States government to end discrimination within its own agencies in South Africa, specifically NASA and the State Department, which had never posted a black to the South African embassy or consulates. Diggs said that there were "three prerequisites" to be met by American firms in South Africa: equal pay for equal work, increased training, and refusal to obey racial restrictions inside the plant. He announced that he would urge that fair employment practices in South Africa be made a condition for eligibility of U.S. firms for government contracts and that he would meet with the boards of major American companies to urge them to exert more control over their subsidiaries.

Diggs acted with dispatch. In November, at the same time as the signing of the Byrd amendment into law, Diggs sent out another edition of his questionnaire to try to gather information about employment practices; this also met with a paltry response. In the late fall, while serving as a member of the U.S. delegation to the United Nations, Diggs walked out of the General Assembly chamber rather than cast the Nixon administration's votes against several anti-apartheid resolutions. When he learned that the U.S. mission had been instructed to vote against a resolution condemning arms sale to Portugal for use against the insurgents in Angola and Mozambique, Diggs, ignoring the pleas of U.S. Ambassador George Bush, resigned publicly from the delegation. In December he formally introduced House bill 1287 in Congress to extend the equal opportunity requirements imposed on the domestic operations of firms with government contracts to their foreign—and particularly South African—subsidiaries. Finally, in March 1972, he issued an "action manifesto," consisting of fifty-five recommendations to the president on everything from the sugar quota to the bantustans, from sales of military equipment to Portugal to American investment in South Africa.

Diggs achieved a few successes through his blizzard of proposals. Within the year, the State Department sent its first black foreign service officer to South Africa. Though NASA continued to celebrate its connection to South Africa—even sending its Apollo astronauts in February

1972 to tour the Johannesburg facility and present the government with a flag that had been carried to the moon—the administrators of the space agency started to explore other sites.

Diggs also succeeded in capturing the attention of the American auto-makers. When the executives of Ford Motor Company heard about Diggs's exchange with managing director R. J. Scott, they yanked Scott out of his job. William Slocum left on September 1 at the end of his rotation, but he believed until the end of his days that his argument with Diggs had irreparably damaged his career. Diggs, for his part, did as he had promised: he met personally with James Roche and demanded that General Motors improve its record of hiring, training, and compensation. In response, Roche dispatched Elliott M. Estes, the group vice president for all operations outside the United States and Canada, to South Africa in October. Estes announced to the South African press that the firm was training one hundred eleven non-whites "for ultimate advancement to supervisory positions as foremen." When asked by a reporter whether his visit was related to the "current question of the morality of American corporate involvement in South Africa," Estes insisted that he was only making a "routine operational visit." In defending General Motors' presence, Estes pointed out that the company provided medical benefits, scholarships for children of all races, and free education for employees. "We feel we can do far more to help black South Africans by staying here than by leaving," he said. "We have made very good progress so far . . . but it isn't as fast as we would like. It will take time to bring about full equality." He was careful to state that the employment policy would not bring the company into conflict with the government or with South African custom; nor, said the newspaper article published in the *Eastern Province Herald,* would it lead to the appointment of a black in a position of superiority over a white.

Diggs's victories were few because he could not advance against his opponents in the legislative and executive branches without the covering firepower of popular support. Most Americans had little concern for events in southern Africa; even the members of Congress who supposedly knew and cared about the region rarely ventured forth in parliamentary battle on its behalf. Diggs had to devote much of his effort to winning approval for a few of his proposals from the members of his own committee. Bills outside of his purview, such as the resolution tying employment practices to government contracts, were shipped to the appropriate committees, where they were quietly smothered. On the rare occasion that a bill made it to the floor of the House, it stood no chance. Recommendations, pleas, admonitions, and demands bounced off the White House as easily as rain off a roof. Nonetheless, through his labors, those of his staff, and those of the members of the Congressional Black Caucus, Diggs had introduced an important idea: that when black citizens secured the political power to which they aspired, they would use it tirelessly to bring coherence to America's official positions on race.

SEVEN

The Awakening of the Institutional Investor (1971–1973)

It was surely inevitable that the campaigns for peace, for racial and social justice, for environmental defense and consumer protection should at last assault the classic citadel of political neutrality: the American university.
—JOHN SIMON, CHARLES POWERS, AND JON GUNNEMANN

BY THE EARLY 1970s the South African divestment movement had begun to affect scores of huge institutions throughout the United States. The effects were slow and nearly imperceptible at first, confined to paneled boardrooms and executive suites, legal consultations and committee meetings. However tedious the pace or imperceptible the steps, the process steadily transformed the logic that underlies American corporate governance. Eventually the leaders of hundreds of elite institutions—from pension funds like TIAA-CREF to religious denominations like the United Church of Christ, from philanthropic organizations such as the Ford Foundation to universities like Harvard—would address the morality of investing in companies operating in South Africa. As they did, they found themselves reassessing everything from their organizational mission to the moral legitimacy of American capitalism.

The American economy is a huge flotilla of businesses floating on a restive sea of capital. Some of the capital flows from pension funds, the immense pool of savings siphoned from the salaries of the employed, or from foundations, the reservoirs of past generosity that support everything from science to symphonies. Capital courses across the nation through the intertwined tributaries of banking and insurance and bubbles in the savings accounts and stock portfolios of those whose luck or labor has lifted them into affluence. Every day millions of investment

managers must decide where to direct this capital so that it will reproduce itself. They can send it into manufacturing or service industries
through corporate stock; into shopping malls or office buildings through
commercial mortgages; into urban development through municipal
bonds; or into the federal government through Treasury notes. In making each decision, the investment managers must balance the promise of
return with the risk of default. They must predict how the economy—or
various sectors of it—will perform. They must push through a blizzard
of theories, promises, and data; trace their way along the treacherous
paths of precedents, duties, and laws; and avoid losing their nerve when
they hear the cries of others who have misstepped.

Over the years this daunting environment has bred certain under-
standings about the way the stock market should work. The most important was known as the "Wall Street rule." This widespread convention
dictated that shareholders should hold on to their stock as long as they
were happy with the managers and sell the stock when they became
dissatisfied. Corporate managers liked this understanding because it
equated possession of stock with approval of management. Financial
theorists also loved the Wall Street rule because it meant that the infinite galaxy of differences between industries, companies, managers, and
strategies could be reduced to a single measurement—the stock price. If
people bought the stock, the price went up, and the company was said to
be doing well. If the stock went down, this reflected disapproval. Like an
omniscient deity, the market thus allotted merit and demerit with each
shudder of the ticker tape, and like the high priests of all deities, the
managers and the theorists fervently defended theirs as infallible.

To transform the shareholder resolution system into a mechanism for
influencing corporate policy, Bishop Hines and the organizers of Campaign GM knew they had to argue that dissatisfaction with a corporation's policies should prompt shareholders *not* to sell their stock but to
exercise their democratic rights as owners. Such a repudiation of the
Wall Street rule also meant a rejection of the tradition of blind investor
support for the managers' candidates for director and their positions on
resolutions. Any failure to offer such support, managers insisted, would
be seen as a crippling vote of no confidence. Indeed, signing the proxy
automatically over to managers was more than a matter of custom; it
also, according to some, made rational sense. As economist Herbert
Simon and others have shown, decisions require information; information requires a search; and searches are costly. Given the plethora of
financial data with which investors already had to struggle—return on
investment, market share, risk quotient, stock price, quarterly earnings—few were eager to tackle the contentious arguments and amor-
phous facts about a corporation's social policy. Far better, they thought,

to trust the managers to work it out, and, if the numbers started to look poor, to dump the stock and move on. Such "rational apathy," some scholars have argued, was a natural human response to excess information.

To overcome this resistance, the shareholder activists knew they would have to stir up enough controversy to prevent stockholders from signing their proxies over to management automatically. If public attention could be focused not only on the companies, but on the decisions of the investors, they reasoned, then someone would find it necessary to sit down and read the activists' proposals and the managers' rebuttals. Then, whether they liked it or not, they would have to make a decision. For some individual shareholders, the activists' aspiration came true. Youthful heirs to family fortunes, whose consciences had been pricked by the civil rights and antiwar movements, scrutinized their holdings with new vigor. Such interest created a new niche in the investment market for managers who could design portfolios to reflect the personal moral beliefs of the rich.

Individuals, however, can respond to shareholder challenges far more quickly than institutions. Institutions—the pension funds, foundations, insurance companies, and endowments—make decisions on the basis of *policies,* and those decisions require internal deliberations. Sometimes the deliberation takes place informally: the president or chairman of the board confers privately with a few selected advisers and subordinates before reaching a decision. When public interest in the decision increases and the implications for the future expands, the boldness of most administrators contracts. In the face of greater complexity and pressure, many administrators establish special committees to adjudicate the matter. Such groups serve multiple purposes. They guarantee a more thorough exploration of the problems, alternatives, and consequences. They free the administrators from demands on their time and transfer responsibility for a controversial decision to another party. Finally, they give administrators a legitimate reason to slow down the response of the organization. Sometimes, if the response is slow enough, the pressures dissolve or the problem goes away on its own.

The activists knew that to harness the power of the institutional investor they would have to hack through a thicket of laws, duties, and, especially, precedents. Organizational policies represented years of accrued effort and dozens of delicate internal compromises. There were powerful incentives to avoid changing them. Indeed, some policies had been around for so long that they had become part of the organizational culture, and people feared that change would destroy something essential about the organization. The activists could combat this fear only by offering the reverse argument: that something essential would be destroyed if the organization did *not* respond.

The activists who brought the South African withdrawal resolution and the Campaign GM proposals to the General Motors annual meeting in 1971 had hoped that the moral urgency of their claims, combined with Leon Sullivan's public breach, would produce a stampede of institutional support for their efforts. Their enthusiasm had been dampened when the votes were counted and revealed that most of the institutions had, once again, reflexively backed the GM managers. What the activists could not immediately perceive, however, was the process that their deeds engendered. Inside churches, pension funds, foundations, and universities the moral questions they planted took root and began to grow. At the time, few people would have guessed or believed how abundant would be the fruits.

To comprehend the nature and magnitude of this process, one must peel back the covering of a few representative institutions and explore what happened when morality and policy clashed. In retrospect, one can catch a glimmer of the inner turmoil as early as the shareholder confrontation with General Motors in May 1971. The trustees of the New York City Pension Funds, the Boston City Hospital and Public Library funds, the San Francisco Pension Fund, the Iowa State Pension system, and the Wisconsin State Investment Board all voted for at least one of the dissident shareholder resolutions. Amherst College, Antioch College, Boston University, Brown University, Iowa State, and Tufts University voted for at least one of the Campaign GM proposals; Yale, Stanford, Rockefeller, Swarthmore, and Williams abstained. Even more significantly, the trustees of the $1.5 billion College Retirement Equities Fund (CREF) announced on April 30, 1971, that though they opposed the South African withdrawal resolution, they intended to vote 715,000 shares in support of the Campaign GM proposal that the automaker disclose its progress in minority hiring, auto safety, and air pollution. The decision was significant not only because of its unprecedented challenge to management and the huge number of shares involved, but also because of the magnitude of the organization itself. CREF was part of a much larger conglomerate known as TIAA-CREF. TIAA—the Teachers' Insurance and Annuity Association—had been founded in 1912 as a nonprofit insurance company for college teachers and had most of its investments in fixed-rate loans and mortgages. CREF had been established in 1952 as a stock fund to provide for teacher pensions. In 1971 the two funds served schools and colleges across the United States and had hundreds of thousands of beneficiaries.

The chairman of TIAA-CREF, William Greenough, announced at a press conference on May 1, 1971, that the joint fund had decided to support the Campaign GM disclosure resolution but not the Episcopal Church proposal on South Africa. He would instead inform James Roche that General Motors had, in the fund's view, an obligation to take the lead in improving working conditions for blacks. The next day, in an op-ed piece in the *New York Times,* Greenough assessed the implications of greater investor involvement in corporate decisions. He began by referring to recent events. "Just a year ago, General Motors stated that 'a corporation can only discharge its obligation to society if it continues to be a profitable investment for its stockholders,' " Greenough wrote. "But it is time to rearrange those priorities: a corporation can only continue to be a profitable investment for its stockholders if it discharges its obligations to society."

Greenough then chronicled the rapidly increasing wealth of institutional shareholders, a wealth which, he argued, put the shareholders in "a position of great potential power and responsibility." This wealth had also raised new questions. Could institutions give up short-term earnings in return for long-term gain for themselves or for society? What guidelines could an investor use when reviewing managerial decisions? And, finally, how strict was the fiduciary requirement that institutions maximize their investments?

In addressing the use of the shareholder resolution, Greenough endorsed the move to greater activism, which, he wrote, could take four forms. First, the investor could reject management's attempts to portray shareholder resolutions as a "no-confidence" debate on the overall competence of the managers and consider each resolution on its merits. Second, the investor could abstain in voting as long as the reasons were made clear to the company and the public. Third, the investor could actually initiate shareholder proposals. Greenough commented that this was "an option rarely used. . . . Its potentials for good are great but so also are its dangers of misuse. Institutional investors should not be trying to manage American business, nor to give specific directives through frequent sponsorship of proposals. But there are occasions when such initiatives would be both practical and helpful." The final possibility was to combine the previous suggestions with a letter or meeting with top managers. "Careful use of such a letter can be an effective way for an investor to change prevailing management attitudes," Greenough wrote, "even where the total of all votes on a proposition may be overwhelmingly in favor of management's initiatives."

TIAA-CREF's directors were not the only institutional leaders for whom a new awareness of the responsibilities of stock ownership had been sparked by the clash with General Motors over South Africa and corporate governance. Officials of the United Church of Christ, a coalition of Congregational churches with nearly two million members, had been pondering the South African question for more than six years. In 1965 the denomination had called on the U.S. government to support economic sanctions and had urged corporations to oppose apartheid "effectively." Two years later they focused on the question of their investments. Noting that the church had long refused to hold stock in tobacco, alcohol, and munitions firms, the denomination's central legislative body, known as the General Synod, declared that "social values and social justice ought to be given consideration . . . in the investment of funds held by religious organizations." By 1969, church leaders had connected the two issues of investment and apartheid. They voted to support the ban on bank loans and urged the withdrawal of all investment funds from financial institutions doing business with South Africa. They suggested that the church's Commission on Racial Justice be given "a significant role in the decision-making process in the determination of the use of capital funds and of investment funds."

Despite the wrangling that often takes place at church gatherings, it remains easier to pass a resolution than to ensure its implementation. In the United Church of Christ the problem was compounded by its division into four different branches or "instrumentalities," two of which had been established for the missionary work of the church. The first, known as the United Church Board for World Ministries, traced its roots back to the agency that had sent the first six American missionaries to the Zulus. The World Board used the income from its forty-million-dollar endowment to work on everything from peace and disarmament to infant formula and South Africa. The second was the United Church Board for Homeland Ministries, which used its thirty-million-dollar fund to support health, education, and church development projects within the United States. To coordinate the corporate social responsibility programs of these and other church funds, church leaders hired Howard Schomer, the former president of Chicago Theological Seminary.

Schomer brought both ecclesial and international experience to the job. After graduating from Harvard in 1937, he had traveled to Europe and studied with Martin Heidegger and Jacques Maritain. In 1938 he simultaneously entered the bachelor of divinity program at Chicago Theological Seminary and the Ph.D. program at Harvard. During World War II he defied the exemption of clergy from military service and, classified as a conscientious objector, spent the war smashing rocks, cleaning bedpans, and chopping down trees in a dozen locations around the United States. After the war Schomer went to France, where for ten years he and his wife worked and taught at a little college in

LeChambon. In 1955 the World Council of Churches invited him to become secretary for Europe for inter-church aid. For three years Schomer crisscrossed the continent dispensing church assistance to war-ravaged European communities. In 1958 he returned to the United States to become president of Chicago Theological Seminary. He served in that post for eight years, teaching courses on the world church and ecumenical movement to hundreds of future clergy, including young Jesse Jackson. In 1966 he accepted a position with the National Council of Churches, where he was involved in the effort to end the war in Vietnam, and in 1969 he came to the United Church of Christ.

One of the first projects in which Schomer was involved was a formal study of the question of ethical investment through a newly established Committee on Financial Investments (COFI). In its report of October 1970, titled "Investing Church Funds for Maximum Social Impact," the committee sought to find a middle ground between prophetic fervor and pragmatic reform. In doing so, they articulated policies and principles that endured, to some extent, for the next two decades. In their report the COFI members affirmed that the church *should* seek consistency between its investments and its social programs. They also argued that the church had a duty to "use its prerogatives and influence as an investor" to influence corporations. Differentiating between a large group of legally "restricted funds" and the smaller, more discretionary pool of "unrestricted funds," they argued that if the unrestricted funds were placed in more socially acceptable, lower-yield investments, "the part of the normal yield that is forgone should be considered as equivalent to an expenditure for a social purpose." While supporting an increased role of the United Church of Christ in the investment field, however, they were pessimistic about the potential for a single denomination acting alone. Noting that the church should "strive for effectiveness rather than purity," they specifically rejected the tactics of divestment and litigation. The best tactics, they concluded, were likely to be attending shareholder meetings and initiating discussions with managers. "Since most corporations legally exist for the benefit of the stockholder," they wrote, managers would be likely to respond to the "concerted and informed expression of the views of large institutional shareholders."

Largely because of the South African debate, a new perspective on the proper relation of the large shareholder to corporate managers spread steadily from institution to institution. When students, clergy, or other constituents asked their institutions to sell their stock, most institutions argued that divestment was not the appropriate response. Whenever a president, trustee, administrator, or committee adopted this position, it immediately triggered new questions: What *is* the appropriate response? What *will* this institution do?

As more institutions found these secondary questions difficult to address, they turned to a growing number of academics and intellectuals who were exploring and defining the terms of the debate. One of these was Charles Powers, the student who had organized the protest against Chase Manhattan while he was at Union Theological Seminary. Powers had left Union to pursue a doctorate in theological ethics at Yale Divinity School. Within a few years he was being asked to advise or join committees that had been charged to draft guidelines for various churches; in this manner he made large contributions to both the United Church of Christ's COFI report and to the policies that developed at the Presbyterian church. He also promoted discussion of the topic within Yale University. With the help of another graduate student, Jon Gunnemann, Powers established the South African Study Group, comprising graduate students and undergraduates from different departments. In the spring of 1968 Powers and Gunnemann persuaded the university's treasurer, John C. Ecklund, to meet to discuss the university's South African investments. Their appointment happened to fall on April 4, 1968, the day Martin Luther King Jr. was shot. Gunnemann remembered later how peculiar he felt as he looked through the treasurer's window and saw hundreds of grief-stricken students and townspeople milling about on the New Haven green at the very moment that Ecklund was telling him how racial problems in South Africa were not relevant to the life of the school.

Undeterred, Powers and Gunnemann set about analyzing the governing structure of Yale University. The board of trustees, known as the Yale Corporation, was made up of Ivy League luminaries like William Scranton, the governor of Pennsylvania; William McKenzie Martin, the head of the Federal Reserve; John Lindsay, the mayor of New York City; and Paul Moore, the Episcopal bishop of New York. The chairman was J. Irwin Miller, the founder and chief executive of the Cummins Engine Corporation in Columbus, Indiana. Miller was a business Renaissance man: a Rhodes scholar, a graduate of the Harvard Business School, and the first lay president of the National Council of Churches. Uncertain how to get through to Miller, Charles Powers decided to try to call him in Indiana; to Powers's amazement, Miller himself picked up the phone. After listening to the young man's comments, Miller consented to meet during his next visit to New Haven.

In his meeting with the students, Miller agreed to raise the issue of South African investments with Yale president Kingman Brewster. Powers and Gunnemann decided afterward that they could best encourage a debate among the Yale trustees by setting their argument on paper.

They chose the liberal church publication the *Christian Century* and in a strikingly moderate article insisted that nonprofit institutions should develop mechanisms to adjudicate ethical investments issues as they came up. At universities, they wrote, hoping Miller would take note, "it should be possible to have an advisory committee made up of representatives of students, faculty, administration, and alumni" that could "formulate the consensus of the constituent groups."

The article, combined with Miller's internal support, had the desired effect. In the early spring of 1969, Miller invited Powers and Gunnemann to join him and a select group of Yale trustees at the Century Club in New York City. A few days before the meeting, Gunnemann and Powers received a dense legal brief from the treasurer's office that argued that the idea of considering the ethical implications of investments was flatly illegal. "We took one look and we realized that we were in over our heads," Gunnemann recalled. Desperate for legal advice, the two scrambled to find someone who could provide it. They hit upon John Simon, a professor at Yale Law School who served as president of the Taconic Foundation, a small activist group that had just set aside ten percent of its endowment for investment in minority small business.

When Gunnemann and Powers arrived at the Century Club, they found a phalanx of senior university officials: Yale President Kingman Brewster, investment committee chairman J. Richardson Dilworth (who also managed much of the Rockefeller family's wealth), Governor Scranton, John Ecklund, and Irwin Miller. Just when the two graduate students thought they would have to make the legal case themselves, Simon arrived. Powers and Gunnemann gave their presentation, urging the trustees to think more carefully about the disposition of their investments. Ecklund responded with his objections. Simon then coolly pointed out the deficiencies in the treasurer's arguments and stressed that the law pertaining to investments was actually quite flexible. As the meeting drew to a close, Gunnemann sensed hesitation among the directors. This was new territory. Eventually Kingman Brewster turned to Irwin Miller, who had been sitting quietly, and asked for his opinion.

"When I sit in church on Sunday morning listening to a sermon," Miller said in a relaxed and folksy manner, "I keep thinking that the congregation should have a chance to answer back. And I keep thinking that the clergy should be held accountable for what they say." Where is he going with this? Gunnemann wondered silently. "All these fellows are asking us to do is to be accountable for our decisions," continued Miller. "I think that accountability is a good thing. There is nothing wrong in asking us to explain ourselves."

Instantly, the mood in the room shifted. Miller had transformed the matter of social investment from an institutional threat into a question worthy of reflection. Brewster instantly backed him up. Since Yale was an institution of research and learning, Brewster said, then Yale should take the lead in studying the moral issues in investment. Simon immediately volunteered to teach a course on the matter at the law school if he could find money for research assistants and course development. "I'm going over to see Mac Bundy at the Ford Foundation tomorrow," said Brewster. "I will see what I can do." Brewster returned to New Haven the next day with Bundy's promise of ten thousand dollars.

Simon worked with Gunnemann and Powers to design and teach the new course, which lasted for a full year and included students from many different professional schools. While they did so, they also prepared, at Brewster's request, a report for the university. Simon, Powers, and Gunnemann assembled a prestigious advisory committee—including theological ethicist James Gustafson, political theorist Charles Lindblom, and future Nobel laureate in economics James Tobin—and completed a draft of the report in 1970. Their continued collaboration led to a book entitled *The Ethical Investor.*

The book, which appeared in 1972, broke important ground by distinguishing between negative injunctions and affirmative duties in investment policy. Negative injunctions are those which say human beings should not harm each other. Affirmative duties, conversely, insist that human beings should actively help each other. Whereas negative injunctions create a powerful obligation—a "moral minimum," the authors called it—affirmative duties are more complicated. "We have not succeeded in devising laws that create within our citizens a predisposition to love and kindness," wrote Simon, Powers, and Gunnemann, "but we can devise laws which will minimize the injury that one citizen must suffer at the hands of another. Although the virtue of love may be the possession of a few, justice—in the minimal sense of not injuring others—can be required of all." Still, there remained a problem. How could people be held accountable for something for which they had not *chosen* to be accountable? One could require people to live up to a civic contract into which they had entered freely, but how could a person who acknowledged no obligations to another group (say, blacks in South Africa) be persuaded that he or she has them? *The Ethical Investor* answered that there were four criteria: the degree of need, of proximity, of capability, and of being in a position of last resort.

Having developed moral principles to help define the university's obligations, Simon, Powers, and Gunnemann addressed the law. Yale's treasurer had argued that employing ethical criteria in investment violated the trustees' fiduciary responsibility. The legal section of *The Ethical Investor* demonstrated that this was not necessarily true. The key was the difference in the laws that regulate *trusts* and those that govern *corpora-*

tions. Fiduciaries are persons to whom wealth is entrusted to fulfill the goals of donors after their deaths. To protect the assets of a trust, nineteenth-century common law gradually laid down the specific duties of a trustee. The central principle was that of "exclusive benefit": the trustee could think only of what advanced the interests of the beneficiaries. The law vigorously condemned anyone who used trust assets to pursue his or her own personal goals or gain.

Nineteenth-century common law also spelled out the standard trustees should use in making investments on behalf of the trust. In the 1830 case of *Harvard College v. Amory,* the judge ruled that a trustee was required to "conduct himself faithfully and exercise a sound discretion. He is to observe how men of prudence, discretion, and intelligence manage their own affairs, not in regard to speculation, but in regard to the permanent disposition of their funds, considering probable income, as well as the probable safety of the capital to be invested." Over the following decades other courts borrowed the exclusive benefit principle and the "prudent man rule" from Massachusetts and applied them to trusts in their own states. Eventually legislators incorporated the Massachusetts language into their state codes. As a result, courts, when asked to review the decisions of the fiduciaries of trusts, increasingly held to the strictest possible definition of prudence. Trustees, fearful that they might be held liable for a bad decision, gravitated toward low-risk and low-return investments. To give themselves further protection, they awarded the administration of the funds to the most reputable and conservative bank officers they could find. The officers, in turn, avoided the erratic fluctuations of equity markets and stowed the wealth safely in fixed-return government or corporate bonds.

Under the law of trusts, Simon agreed, it would be difficult to condone taking ethical considerations into account in making investments unless the original donor had specifically requested this. The law of trusts, however, was *not* the only standard that the courts could apply in the judicial oversight of trustees. Indeed, Simon pointed out, most nonprofit or charitable organizations, such as foundations, universities, and churches, had been organized as corporations, which were governed by different rules. As W. L. Cary and C. B. Bright argued in *The Law and the Lore of Endowment Funds,* a 1969 report to the Ford Foundation, "where the issue involves the investment of funds, accounting for their use, or other aspects of administration or housekeeping, the courts [have shown] a marked tendency to apply corporate principles rather than trust principles in order to accord charitable corporations a maximum degree of flexibility."

The most important corporate principle that applied to investments was the "business judgment rule," a standard far more lenient than the law of trusts. The business judgment rule said that unless there was clear evidence of self-dealing or of gross mismanagement, the courts would not second-guess the judgment of presumably well-intentioned and well-informed trustees, directors, and managers of corporations. Under the business judgment rule, investing for social purposes might be considered acceptable if "it contributes sufficiently to the accomplishment of the organization's purposes to justify its cost." In other words, the question of whether divestment was legal depended not on some external attribute of the law but on the institution's self-understanding. An institution could not decide how to vote on a shareholder resolution or whether to divest its stock without evaluating its basic functions and mission. The role of director and fiduciary, the standards of prudence, and finally the core purpose of the organization itself all had to be examined, discussed, and articulated.

In the end, the most important result of *The Ethical Investor* was its direct assault on the Wall Street rule. Institutional investors, argued Simon, Powers, and Gunnemann, could not avoid the obligations of ownership. They had a duty to examine the decisions of corporate managers and to express preferences through private persuasion or public proxy fights. The only rebuttal the book's critics could offer was a return to the status quo: if an institution's trustees were dissatisfied with a company's performance, financial or moral, they should sell the stock. This was a bizarre twist: the conservative critics who objected to what they saw as shareholder meddling were publicly declaring themselves in favor of the principle of divestment.

The controversy over the role of institutional investors in relation to business corporations soon touched another branch of the American elite, the philanthropic foundation. The trustees of the Ford Foundation, for example, had watched Campaign GM with discomfort. If the premier car manufacturer in the nation had been challenged, they reasoned, who was more likely to be the next target than the number two firm? The president of the Ford Foundation, McGeorge Bundy, who had moved from his White House post as national security adviser in March 1966, conferred with his vice president for finance, Roger Kennedy, about Campaign GM; shortly afterward the two urged their board of trustees to launch a broad examination of the responsibilities of large investors.

When the trustees agreed, Kennedy first commissioned Jon Gunnemann to write a report on the moral dimensions of the question. Kennedy then hired two attorneys, Bevis Longstreth and H. David Rosenbloom, to investigate other institutional investors' views on the question of "social investing." Longstreth and Rosenbloom set up a small organization, interviewed Ford Foundation trustees, commissioned briefs on legal precedent, and sent out questionnaires to two hundred major institutional investors. All this was done in great secrecy. "You would have thought we were working on the Pentagon Papers or something," Rosenbloom recalled. "Some of the trustees were so scared of this topic they didn't know what to do. Henry Ford II, particularly. He was out of control."

Ford was apprehensive because his family's conservatism and the foundation's liberalism had long been in tension. Originally founded by Henry Ford as a means of avoiding the crippling inheritance taxes his heirs would face upon his death, the Ford Foundation had become the largest foundation in the country by the late 1940s. The trustees then formed a committee to chart a future course; the committee's 1950 report suggested that the Ford Foundation promote peace, education, allegiance to democracy, and economic well-being. In doing so, the foundation became the target for right-wing attacks. Congress eventually passed a bill to regulate American foundations, prevent their future use as an inheritance tax dodge, and require them to avoid "unreasonable accumulations of capital" by dispersing five percent of their assets each year. Despite his personal conservatism, Henry Ford II grudgingly tolerated the gradual expansion of the foundation into social activism. In 1965, the foundation trustees debated at great length whether to give money to the National Urban League for a large-scale effort to alleviate racism. When they finally decided to do so, Ford said grumpily, "I think it's O.K., but let me know if you ever get ready to make a grant to Martin Luther King."

When McGeorge Bundy became president, he immediately pushed the foundation into new areas of social responsibility. He also hired more former government officials and Kennedy loyalists. Wayne Fredericks left the State Department and returned to the foundation in 1967 as director of the Middle East and Africa program, which funded a string of vigorous development projects around the continent, with the exception of South Africa. Fredericks inquired about the absence and found that his superiors and subordinates all felt that to support programs in South Africa would be to support apartheid. Fredericks repeated this line of reasoning to an African friend during a visit to Lesotho. "That's a convenient position for people to take who are sitting on 42nd Street," the friend challenged, referring to the location of the Ford Foundation's New York headquarters. "I thought the foundation was interested in helping people. Go back and tell them that there are people in South Africa who need help." Fredericks returned to New York and, after vigorous debate with his staff and with Bundy, eventually persuaded the group to make the first grant to the South African Institute of Race

Relations to help it compile its annual yearbook of statistics and information on apartheid.

In his report Jon Gunnemann followed the argument of *The Ethical Investor,* which he and his colleagues were in the process of completing, and concluded that though the trustees of the Ford Foundation might not be morally required to use their investments to promote change, they had a strong duty to avoid harm. With regard to South Africa, therefore, they had an obligation to be sure that the companies in which the foundation invested were not making matters worse. In a separate study Bevis Longstreth and David Rosenbloom reported that their questionnaire had shown, much to everyone's surprise, that 57.4 percent of the respondents were *already* taking social considerations into account in the selection and retention of investments. After several months Kennedy and Bundy set forth their own recommendations to the trustees on the Finance Committee, affirming that "the foundation should now frame a conscious policy under which it will do what it appropriately can to make its actions in the field of investment as constructive as possible in terms of its chartered purpose to advance the public welfare."

Bundy and Kennedy recommended four specific changes. First, the foundation should consider corporate executives' "awareness of their social context" when selecting companies in which to invest. Second, the foundation should "attempt to connect our investment management more directly with our program purposes." Third, it should "explicitly recognize the business corporation as one of the most important elements in our society." Thus, "research on corporate behavior, corporate responsibility, and the ways and means of improving the corporation in American life," they wrote, "should be an explicit and significant part of our work." Finally, "on proxy contests the foundation should move from its current temporary policy of general abstention and adopt a policy of case-by-case decision-making." For the Ford Foundation, as for others, the South African question remained especially troubling. "Since the foundation itself has for many years had a sustained interest with the problems of southern Africa," Bundy and Kennedy wrote, "we see no reasonable alternative but to develop a carefully considered policy on such proxy contests."

The fundamental principle, Kennedy argued in an article published a few years later, was that institutions should adopt an "Integrity Doctrine." "The right hand should know what the left hand is doing," Kennedy wrote. "If a church is preaching against alcohol, it should not own distilleries. If a foundation supports research and information to inform the public of the perils of smoking, it should not draw income from the sale of cigarettes." By the same logic, the trustees of a foundation that had made a major program commitment to improving the lives of black

South Africans under Wayne Fredericks could no longer ignore the challenges being brought to bear on firms in whose ownership and profits they shared.

Despite the initial consternation, most of Bundy's and Kennedy's ideas were implemented with success. Even though most buy and sell decisions were made without consideration of social issues, the investment team, many of whom were employees of the Ford Foundation rather than hired managers, had shied away from tobacco and alcohol stocks for many years. The foundation developed criteria on a few other social issues and refused to invest in corporations that did not meet them. In addition to screening out companies with negative attributes, the Ford Foundation also developed more affirmative sides of social investing, such as making "program related investments" that were designed to further a social purpose rather than make money.

Their last recommendation—to move from a policy of abstention to a more thoughtful exercise of the proxy voting rights—was the most successful of all. The Finance Committee approved the creation of a subcommittee on proxy voting and hired Mary Camper-Titsingh, then the research librarian, to work half-time and later full-time as staff person to the committee. She reviewed upcoming resolutions and materials from advocates and corporate managers and read the independent research documents prepared under contract with the foundation. Then she wrote recommendations for the trustees. "When we started this, I can't tell you how strange it seemed," recalled Camper-Titsingh. "The prevailing opinion was that only kooks and nuts voted proxies; everybody else just signed them. Gradually the managers conceded that since the Ford Foundation had program objectives such as aid for child nutrition or assistance to Native Americans, this might explain our concern and our votes on infant formula or strip mining on reservations. But it still seemed radical." As the trustees considered many of the same issues year after year, policies and precedents emerged. On some questions, mostly governance matters, a formal list was drawn up detailing the official position of the Ford Foundation on a range of common resolution topics; proxies could then be voted automatically without further discussion unless Camper-Titsingh recommended a reconsideration.

As the early divestment debate spread across the country, it also floated up the Charles River to Cambridge, Massachusetts, where it jostled and changed another great American institution, Harvard University, in the hands of a new president, forty-one-year-old Derek Curtis Bok. Bok was born in 1930 into a family of letters and law. His great-grandfather Cyrus Curtis had started the Curtis Publishing Company in Philadelphia, the parent firm of the *Saturday Evening Post* and the *Ladies' Home Journal.* His grandfather had been the first editor of the *Journal* and had written an autobiography entitled *The Americanization of Edward Bok.* One of his grandfather's cousins was W. E. Bok, who traveled to South Africa and helped establish a mining town that eventually bore his name, Boksburg.

When Derek Bok was a young child, his parents divorced. His mother, Margaret Plummer, took him and his two older siblings and moved to Los Angeles, where she eventually remarried a prominent plastic surgeon. In California Bok's life settled into a pleasant rhythm of athletic days and intellectual evenings. His mother gathered around her a coterie of thinkers and artists, including Aldous Huxley, Georgia O'Keeffe, Christopher Isherwood, and Bertrand Russell. She was also an admirer of John Dewey's theories of education and had helped found the Miquon School in Philadelphia and the University Elementary School in Los Angeles, to which she sent her youngest son. When Derek reached high school, he attended Harvard Military School in North Hollywood, where he drilled under the leadership of a student commander named H. R. Haldeman.

In the fall of 1947 Bok traveled north to Palo Alto and entered Stanford University. He played varsity basketball for two years and excelled academically. Those who knew him at the time recall the easy confidence and regal bearing with which he navigated the campus. When he graduated from college in 1951, he told his mother that he wanted to stay at Stanford to go to law school. She objected, telling him that it was time to broaden his experience. Unless he went to law school in some other part of the country, she said, she would not pay for it. Bok sought the advice of the resident adviser in his dormitory, a law student named William Rehnquist, who told Bok to go to Harvard Law School because he would never have to explain to anyone why he had chosen it.

Bok took Rehnquist's advice and went to Cambridge in the fall of 1951. He endured the grueling first year, took his final exams, and left for a summer trip to India convinced that he had done poorly. One afternoon, while sitting in Bombay in the midst of a monsoon, he learned that his first-year grades had been good enough to put him on the *Harvard Law Review.* He went back to Harvard, finished his degree in 1954, and won a Fulbright scholarship to study at the University of Paris. To improve his French, Bok first traveled to Geneva, whose citizens, he had been told, spoke French more slowly. At a student dance he met Sissela Myrdal, the nineteen-year-old daughter of Gunnar and Alva Myrdal. They married the following summer in the little French town of Louviers in a service performed by former French prime minister Pierre Mendès-France.

It is one of the peculiar twists of history that Derek Bok, whose administrative career would be marked by an almost continuous debate about apartheid, had married into a family that had an international reputation for expertise in race relations in both the United States and South Africa. Gunnar Myrdal, a well-known economist in Sweden, was the author of *An American Dilemma: The Negro Problem and Modern Democracy,* a landmark commentary on race relations in the United States published in 1944. His wife, Alva Myrdal, was a diplomat who in the 1960s headed a United Nations special study commission on apartheid which recommended that the Security Council offer to help South Africa develop a new constitution and which recognized the need for economic sanctions if the National Party government refused. She later served as the minister of disarmament—the only such post in the world—and as minister of church affairs in the Swedish cabinet. By the mid-1960s, the Myrdals were so famous for their leadership on race relations that Martin Luther King Jr. made a special visit to greet them when he passed through Stockholm after receiving his Nobel Prize. In the 1970s Gunnar Myrdal received the Nobel Prize in economics and in the 1980s, a few years before her death, Alva Myrdal won the Nobel Peace Prize for her disarmament work, making them the only couple in history to have been awarded separate Nobel Prizes.

Derek Bok, at the time of his wedding, had no inkling that he too would eventually become entangled in many of the same issues as had his parents-in-law. Indeed, he was having enough trouble figuring out what he was going to do with his life. After their wedding, the Boks returned to the United States. Bok spent two years in the military in Washington, D.C., as an army lawyer, during which time he picked up a master's degree in economics. At the end of the stint, Bok was unhappy about the prospect of going into private practice. He consulted with his favorite professor at Harvard Law School, Kingman Brewster, who suggested that he come back to Cambridge and try his hand in the classroom. In the fall of 1958 the twenty-eight-year-old Bok returned to his alma mater as an assistant professor.

Right away Bok showed an affinity for teaching. "Even in the first year he was a talented teacher with very good instincts, warm, outgoing, very open," remembered Michael Dukakis, one of Bok's first students. "His was a class you looked forward to going to. And in the afternoon, he'd be out on the basketball court playing with the students." Bok taught labor law, collective bargaining, and negotiation. He also took a keen interest in pedagogy, sometimes selecting students for his restricted courses from the bottom third of the class rather than the top. Once again, success came quickly: within three years Bok had tenure. As offers for administrative positions started to trickle in from around the country, Gunnar Myrdal exhorted his son-in-law not to accept them, arguing, Sissela remembered, that "administrators are nothing but failed scholars." Bok accepted his advice until 1968, when Harvard President Nathan Pusey asked Bok to become dean of the Harvard Law School.

Pusey himself was nearing the end of his eighteen-year presidency of Harvard. A native Iowan with a patrician demeanor, Pusey had overseen dramatic growth at the university. He had raised total enrollment from ten thousand to fifteen thousand, a third of whom were undergraduates. He had nearly tripled the faculty from three thousand to eight thousand and had quadrupled the endowment to $1.2 billion dollars. Despite these achievements, Pusey's imperious style brought him increasingly into conflict with students and faculty. The most memorable incident took place on April 9, 1969, when fifty Harvard students, brimming with antiwar, anti-institutional rancor, seized control of University Hall, insulted deans in their offices, and ransacked administration filing cabinets. When Pusey learned that the students intended to spend the night, he called in the police. The police, dressed in full riot gear, stormed the building at five A.M. and ejected the students by force. The resulting melee left 45 students injured and 197 students in jail. This brutality galvanized the rest of the campus against Pusey and sparked a week-long student strike. When the ruckus died down, Pusey's effectiveness as president went into sharp decline.

Derek Bok endured similar convulsions over at the law school but handled them differently. When a group of law students occupied the Langdell classroom building, the new dean went there himself to discuss their grievances. When the conversation took them to midnight, Bok sent not for the police but for doughnuts and coffee. Bok always preferred "discourse and dialogue," his friend and colleague John Dunlop remembered. Bok thought "like a labor relations expert," commented James Vorenberg, Bok's successor as dean. "He worked hard to find ways to avoid conflict."

Student protest was not the only new challenge to the university with which Pusey had to contend. The next year he had to face Campaign GM. When Harvard's treasurer, George F. Bennett, heard of the shareholder campaign, he told the president and the five other trustees of the Harvard Corporation—or "Fellows," as they are referred to in Cambridge—that the university should automatically back James Roche. Pusey, wary from his experience the year before, disagreed. He encouraged the students and the faculty to discuss the issue. The debate raged with fierce intensity. On May 1, the faculty of arts and sciences passed a resolution calling on the corporation to support Campaign GM. Two weeks later the trustees voted to support GM management. A report later noted that the whole incident left everyone furious and that "the behavior of none—students, faculty, or Fellows—appeared responsible to the other."

In the fall of 1970, Pusey, recognizing that such challenges would recur, appointed a Committee on University Relations with Corporate Enterprise and asked Harvard business school professor Robert W. Austin to serve as chair. Pusey charged the members to examine whether the essential identity and purpose of the university permitted it to try to influence corporations. The Austin committee pondered the question for six months. Their report, issued in January 1971, set precedents that influenced Harvard's institutional response to South Africa and to other issues for the next two decades. The members concluded that the central purpose of the university was to be "a center of free inquiry" and that this required a basic stance of institutional neutrality, although it did not imply that faculty and students should be barred from expressing their opinions as citizens or that there were no issues on which Harvard might take a position as an institution. The Austin committee members also agreed that ethics should influence investment decisions, by specifically approving the exclusion of tobacco and alcohol stocks on moral grounds and accepting the extension of this principle to other, as yet unnamed categories. In language comparable to that used by the Ford Foundation, the committee members insisted that more consistency had to be introduced between Harvard's principles and its practices. "It will not do to look to the legality of the corporation's activities . . . as the sole criterion of eligibility for investment," the members noted. "If the university would not consider buying stock in gambling houses, even where legal and however attractive financially— as presumably it would not—it cannot close its eyes to the moral factors in [other investments]."

The members also agreed that "the university, like any other institutional investor . . . may properly, and sometimes should, attempt to influence management in directions that are considered to be socially desirable." They did not try to articulate which companies should be influenced on which issues, though. On the question of American companies doing business in South Africa, for instance, the committee noted only that it was a complex question, since there were other repressive countries in which American companies were doing business and it would be difficult to define what level of involvement an investor found unacceptable.

The Austin committee members' conclusions were important for two reasons. First, they did not reject the moral questions raised by investments, and they legitimized future debate. Second, they publicly criticized—although in a characteristically genteel manner—the process through which Harvard's investments and shareholder responsibilities had been managed up to that point. At the time, George Bennett was not only Harvard's treasurer and a Fellow of the Harvard Corporation but also the managing partner of the State Street Research and Management Company, which directed several large subsidiary mutual funds. The committee implied that such an arrangement not only raised problems of conflict of interest but also left the discretion of shareholder voting excessively concentrated in the hands of a single individual.

When Nathan Pusey announced that he would retire in 1972, two years before the mandatory age, many believed that Pusey's repeated confrontations with students had cut his career short. For eleven months a presidential search committee headed by Francis "Hooks" Burr invited more than two hundred thousand alumni, faculty, and others to submit names of candidates. By the middle of December 1971, Derek Bok was one of four finalists, a position he found uncomfortable. He had been dean of the law school for only two years. The burdens of becoming president of Harvard on his wife, two young daughters, and son might be excessive. After years of studying philosophy and ethics at Harvard, Sissela had just received her doctorate and hoped to teach. On the snowy evening of December 13, 1971, Bok sat down at his desk in his Belmont home and penned a letter to Burr. Choosing his words carefully, Bok told Burr that he was very happy at the law school and would not want to leave that post. Bok finished the letter, folded it up, stamped it, and took it downstairs to mail. When he was halfway down the stairs, the telephone rang. "Mr. Burr is on the line," Sissela told him. Bok went to the phone. "I would like to come out and see you immediately," Burr told Bok. He arrived at nine-thirty in a taxi and promptly offered Bok the presidency of Harvard.

With characteristic caution, Bok asked if he could have ten days to think about it. He systematically discussed the idea with all the members of the Harvard Corporation and warned them that he was not a good fundraiser. When Kingman Brewster, who had become president of Yale in 1963, heard that his former protégé was hesitating, he called Bok. "I don't want you to make a final decision without coming to have dinner in New York," he told Bok. Derek and Sissela traveled to New York and had dinner with Kingman and Mary Louise Brewster in their room at the Westbury Hotel. Kingman talked almost entirely to Sissela; both of the Brewsters made it abundantly clear that they enjoyed their tasks in New Haven. After they left, Sissela turned to her husband and said, "Derek, maybe we should do this job."

As soon as the choice was announced, reporters from around the country descended on Bok to ask his views on higher education and to analyze where he would lead Harvard. Most of the news stories mentioned his youth, his liberalism (he was a registered Democrat), and his decision while dean of the law school to oppose President Nixon's nomination of G. Harrold Carswell to the Supreme Court. Some pointed out that his selection seemed to reflect a trend in major universities, since three others (the University of Chicago, the University of Michigan, and Yale) had also selected lawyers with training in conflict resolution as their presidents.

Very few noted that, for all its prestige, the presidency of Harvard carried little day-to-day clout. Harvard is structured as an affiliation of academic and professional schools, each of which is governed by a powerful administrative dean who raises and jealously guards his or her own endowment. The president could shape the direction of the school over the long term through his power to tenure faculty and appoint deans, but his influence on everyday operations was remarkably small. The president, Bok told a reporter from *Newsweek,* "must have a capacity for an enormous amount of patience because his options for exerting influence are so indirect. The president exerts moral authority." When asked by another reporter how he would deal with continued student pressures, Bok replied that "one has to work very hard not to make decisions under the pressure of disturbance. You are apt to reward behavior that you disapprove of and make bad decisions. If you respond to problems only when students are protesting, you are going to have a lot of protests."

Bok soon had the opportunity to test this theory. A few weeks after he moved into the presidential office in Massachusetts Hall in the summer of 1972, he received word that a group of black students wished to meet with him. Among them was a former law student, Randall Robinson, who had established a friendship with Bok when they were both at the law school. Robinson, thirty years old, was born in Richmond, Virginia. His father was a history teacher at one of the two black high schools in the rigidly segregated city; he urged his children to explore the many books on foreign affairs that filled their home. Robinson went from high school into the army, where, he recalled, "I met the first white person in my life." While serving at army posts in South Carolina and Georgia, he read everything he could get his hands on about Africa, including a book by E. R. Braithwaite, whose description of his first trip to Africa in *A Kind of Homecoming,* published in 1962, moved Robinson deeply. After leaving the army, Robinson got his undergraduate degree at Virginia Union in Richmond and then received a scholarship to Harvard Law School.

Robinson quickly moved into the circle of black activists at the law school. He set up funds to gather money for many of the black nationalist movements of southern Africa, including the ANC in South Africa, FRELIMO in Mozambique, and SWAPO in Namibia, and he persuaded Derek Bok to contribute. Bok liked the tall, fervent student; when he became dean of the law school, Bok asked Robinson to travel with him to a Daedalus conference on the governance of historically black colleges. So when Robinson called and asked the new president if he could meet with him, Bok readily accepted. Robinson arrived for the meeting with a group of black law students and presented their case. The massive Cabinda oil find by Gulf Oil off the coast of Angola, Robinson said, had provided the Portuguese colonialist government with windfall profits that it was using to suppress the local population. The United Presbyterian Church had filed a shareholder resolution with Gulf requesting that the firm disclose more information about its operations in Angola. Robinson pointed out that Harvard owned 760,000 shares of Gulf and urged Bok to sell the stock or, at the very least, to support the church resolution. Bok said he would think about it.

Over the next six months the members of the Harvard Corporation declined to act on the Gulf issue, so on February 25, 1972, fifty black students staged a "mill-in" at Massachusetts Hall, demanding that Harvard sell its Gulf stock. Bok again met with the students and issued a statement saying "there is no question in my mind that Portugal has inflicted grave wrongs on black people in Angola and Mozambique. The question for Harvard to consider is the most responsible action for Harvard to take as a shareholder." The members of the Harvard Corporation agreed to consider the issue again. Two months later, however, on April 19, 1972, the Fellows announced that they would neither sell the Gulf stock nor support the church-sponsored resolutions asking Gulf to disclose information. The most they would do was to abstain on the resolution, which they believed would signal to the managers of Gulf that Harvard did not support them unreservedly.

Feeling betrayed, the black students reacted immediately. On April 20, at five-thirty A.M., thirty black students, led by Randall Robinson, Jim Winston, and South African exile Chris Nteta, pried open a window at Massachusetts Hall and entered Bok's office. Within twenty minutes, they had hooked up a loudspeaker to a window and had begun broadcasting their actions and intentions to a sleepy Harvard Yard. By midmorning a large crowd had gathered. When the university cut off the electricity, the students restored power by running a long extension cord from the roof of Massachusetts Hall to a dormitory. The university then cut off the telephones, forcing the students to send notes through sympathizers. Derek Bok set up a temporary office in another building and, against the advice of some members of the corporation, tried to resolve the situation without bringing in the police. Day after day, the thirty-three demonstrators held the attention of the campus and attracted coverage by the national press. Outside, the supporters of the takeover maintained a twenty-four-hour vigil and organized a meal shuttle from area restaurants.

Though some present outside recalled a sense of exhilaration that made the confrontation almost "a spiritual experience," the mood was mostly sober. The students feared being expelled far more than being arrested. "These were some of the best students in the school," Robinson recalled, "and they spent the entire week studying and preparing for finals. Not a room was disturbed and every waking moment was spent in academic preparation. At the same time, they sustained their commitment to the objective." After a few days one parent was so overwrought at the idea that her son, a freshman, would be thrown out of Harvard that she came and pleaded with him through a window, Robinson recalled. The students discussed his dilemma and recommended that he leave.

Bok informed the students through intermediaries that he would not negotiate with them while they were inside the building. As the days wore on, Bok requested and obtained a court order requiring the students to vacate the building. The black students caucused and decided that while they were not afraid of arrest, they were concerned that the violation of a court order might lead them to be expelled. If they stayed much longer, they would also run the risk of being unable to finish papers or attend final exams. After seven days, the longest occupation in Harvard's history, they left. They felt a certain rush of vindication when, on the morning they departed, the *Harvard Crimson* reported that the president of Columbia University, William McGill, had announced to a group of student antiwar protesters in New York City that he would recommend that the Columbia trustees adopt a policy of total divestment. McGill, who had served on many corporate boards of directors and believed that shareholder resolutions had no effect, said that Columbia should sell its shares in the twenty largest defense contractors and in all companies doing business with South Africa as "the strongest expression of dissatisfaction or disapproval of a company's policies."

It remains unclear whether Bok and Robinson reached any specific agreements at the time of the takeover about the university's position on its investments in southern Africa. The members of the Harvard Corporation, like all trustees, vociferously insisted that they were impervious to such public pressure. Nonetheless on May 4, just two weeks after the confrontation, the members of the Harvard Corporation announced that for the first time in the university's history they would cast shareholder votes against management. They also declared themselves in favor of a remarkably activist interpretation of the university's role.

"The trustees believe the university, as an investor, must focus not only on maximum economic return, but also on issues of social responsibility, as produced by the company in which the university holds securities," said the trustees' statement. "Harvard's definition of 'social responsibility' encompasses such areas as a company's position on or involvement in labor relations, racial discrimination, minority employment practices, consumer protection, pollution control, military contracts, and international diplomacy." The trustees subsequently cast 293,000 shares of Ford Motor Company stock (valued at eighteen million dollars) and 265,062 shares of General Motors (valued at twenty-one million dollars) in favor of resolutions urging the companies to make disclosures of their South African operations.

The experiences of the spring of 1972 persuaded Bok that he needed to establish a new mechanism for the ethics of Harvard's investments. "I spent more than a quarter of my time last spring on shareholder resolutions," he grumbled to a student reporter. To cope with these pressures, Bok established not one but two deliberative committees: a Corporation Committee on Shareholder Responsibility (CCSR) made up of four members of the Harvard Corporation in whom the actual decision-making power would be vested and an Advisory Committee on Shareholder Responsibility (ACSR), with five alumni, five faculty, and five students, including two undergraduates, to provide an opportunity for different university constituencies to express themselves.

By the time the proxy season in spring 1973 rolled around, Bok had thus created a mechanism that served the dual purpose of providing a forum for sustained discussion and of diverting pressures that had been focused on him. "If you want to understand Derek Bok," commented his longtime friend Robert Monks, a former administrator in the Department of Labor, "you need to know that as a lawyer he is interested in designing the proper process and as an administrator he is interested in 'boompf.' Boompf is what you need when somebody—student, faculty member, or alumnus—comes in ranting and raving about an issue. The administrator spins around in his chair, picks up a two-inch-thick, unreadable report, turns back, and says, 'I'd be delighted to discuss it when you've read this.' Then he drops the report on his desk with a loud 'BOOMPF.' "

Through the debate on the social responsibility of corporations there was one point on which everyone agreed: information about corporate social performance was scarce. The first institutions to seek out such information were the churches, who formed the Interfaith Center on Corporate Responsibility (ICCR) in 1971 and hired Tim Smith as the director of research. Though the new organization met the information needs of the churches, it did not satisfy the institutional investors, who considered ICCR an advocacy group. Soon other groups stepped forward to fill the gap. One of the most effective was the Council on Economic Priorities, a small research team put together by Alice Tepper Marlin, which raised money from liberal foundations and performed important studies of the pollution records of particular industries. Business professors also took an interest and tried to devise formal ways to measure social performance. Professor Raymond Bauer of the Harvard Business School argued that since financial accountants had been able to find ways of tracking revenues, costs, and internal transactions, new indicators might be found to track social performance. Bauer's interest in the "social audit" led to several important innovations, but the concept never took root on the rocky soil of most management faculties.

Yet another possible source of information could be found among Wall Street securities analysts and mutual fund managers. Though social issues were often dismissed as "soft" in the tough world of number crunchers and pit traders, mutual fund managers, who designed and ran specialized portfolios, periodically sniffed the winds to detect new market opportunities. The managers of mutual funds had already tried to tap into investor preferences by designing portfolios of companies that would grow rapidly, or companies that paid high dividends, or companies in certain industries, such as health care. In 1971 there emerged three new funds—the Dreyfus Third Century Fund, the Pax World Fund, the First Spectrum Fund—whose managers all promised that they would select only socially responsible firms. Conventional brokerage houses greeted the idea with scorn, though later, when they discovered how many institutions were interested in such social investment "screens," the skeptics quickly established their own.

Neither the church center nor the fledgling mutual funds could meet the particular information needs of institutional investors such as the Ford Foundation and Harvard University. They needed someone who could tell them not only whether they should buy or sell stock, but also on what basis they should vote their proxies. After the dispute over the role of Gulf Oil in Angola, Derek Bok had sent his assistant Stephen Farber to the African country to find out what was going on. "I don't know why they sent him all the way over there," Randall Robinson remarked sardonically, "since he could have found everything he needed in Widener Library [at Harvard]." Bok soon realized, however, that Harvard could not send a special assistant into every corporation and country that was the focus of a shareholder dispute. After Farber returned, Bok asked him to explore setting up a joint information center with other institutional investors to assist them in sorting out the charges and rebuttals. Farber spent nearly a year working with the Ford

Foundation and other universities and in 1972 he became the chairman of the board of a new information collection firm known as the Investor Responsibility Research Center (IRRC)—an acronym often confused with Tim Smith's church-based ICCR.

During the period in which the new investment committees at Harvard—the ACSR and the CCSR—began their work, the university's endowment rose from $1.26 billion in 1971 to $1.46 billion in 1977, the largest educational endowment in the country at the time. Throughout this period the university held equities valued at between three and four hundred million dollars in roughly fifty corporations doing business in South Africa. The university also held debt instruments from these corporations and from banks making loans to the South African government. The first few years were a period of gradual mutual adjustment. The students debated the manner in which their representatives would be selected to the ACSR. The committees found by trial and error how frequently and publicly they should meet. The South African issue, though present each year, did not dominate the shareholder agenda; and though some of the students favored outright divestment, the members of both committees agreed that the corporations doing business in South Africa should disclose more information about their operations. Over the opposition of Treasurer George Bennett, the Harvard trustees cast their votes in favor of disclosure resolutions at Caterpillar, General Electric, Union Carbide, and several other corporations. Though refusing to take a direct stance on corporate involvement in South Africa, they endorsed United Nations and United States policies against investment in Namibia and voted in favor of limiting Namibia investment at several oil companies between 1973 and 1976.

Though largely invisible, the trustees of philanthropies like the Ford Foundation, of universities like Harvard, and of many other institutions from churches to pension funds who debated the ethics of investment played a key role in the development of the divestment movement. Standing near the fulcrum that balances political and economic forces in the United States, institutional investors are ponderous beasts, weighed down by their bulk and tradition, instinctively rigid and wary. Under most circumstances, their inertia helps to steady society. Even when surrounded by great turbulence, they alter their positions slowly and incrementally. Yet, like elephants in the hold of a clipper ship, they did not need to move far to give the vessel a new center of gravity. Prodded by their own constituencies, forced to rouse themselves from somnolence and complacency, the institutional investors, when they finally awoke, changed the direction in which America would sail.

EIGHT

The Enigma of Buthelezi (1972–1975)

There can be few countries other than South Africa where dominant elites talk so much about the need for change but do so little to bring it about. Talk of change has indeed become a political tactic in itself, designed on the one hand to keep blacks quiescent and on the other to stave off foreign pressures against apartheid.
—JOHN KANE-BERMAN

Though South Africa's most prominent resistance leaders had been squashed and its African population chastened into resentful silence, an active though largely hidden debate continued between pragmatists and purists, integrationists and separatists, reformers and revolutionaries. In the early 1970s, as the Nationalist government continued to press forward with its Verwoerdian dreams, there emerged a new and enigmatic voice: that of the bantustan leader. Following a strategy well established by the British in the nineteenth century, John Vorster had hoped to cajole and coopt traditional leaders into endorsing the government's policy and thereby become instruments of its implementation. The men who had chosen to accept such semi-autocratic rule—men like Lucas Mangope of Bophuthatswana and Nelson Mandela's cousin Kaiser Matanzima of the Transkei—strove to obey Pretoria's guidelines while employing the rhetoric of liberation. It seemed clear to both their admirers and detractors that the bantustan leaders were double-crossing someone. They differed on whom.

The most enigmatic of these leaders was the gifted, guarded Mangosuthu Gatsha Buthelezi of KwaZulu. Buthelezi's leadership in the Zulu community had been disputed from the moment of his birth.

His mother, Constance Magogo Zulu, was a princess in the bloodline of Shaka. She was the granddaughter of King Cetshwayo, the daughter of King Dinizulu, and the sister of King Solomon. She was also the aunt, through one of her older sisters, of Pixley Seme, one of the founding members of the African National Congress. Despite her prominent lineage, she reached adulthood in the mid-1920s without a marriage proposal. Her brother King Solomon decided that he would arrange a diplomatic marriage between his sister and Chief Mathole, the aged leader of the large and influential Buthelezi clan. Mathole was somewhat reluctant; he already had nine wives, had fathered a flock of children, and knew that the *lobola,* the bride price paid by one family to the other, would be steep for a princess. Magogo also disliked the idea at first. She had heard that Mathole was so old that he could no longer father children and she feared a life of barrenness. The wedding nonetheless went forward in 1925, and Magogo entered her husband's tribe with a somewhat confused status. As the most recent addition to Mathole's consorts, she was the most junior; yet as the sister of the king, she could claim consideration as his "great wife." This distinction later proved important when her son Gatsha claimed a hereditary right to lead the Buthelezi tribe. The tension in the chief's circle eased as months passed without a pregnancy. Magogo began to despair. Then, after nearly three years of marriage, she bore a son on August 27, 1928. Chief Mathole, astonished at the news, declared that the announcement of the birth was a lie concocted by the Usuthu tribe. The exclamation later provided him with a formal name for his new son, Mangosuthu, the "lie of the Usuthu." The child was known by his nickname, Gatsha, which means "twig."

Gatsha's birth sparked jealousy among Mathole's other wives and sons, so much so that King Solomon, fearing for the lives of his sister and nephew, transported them directly from the hospital back to the royal household. Young Gatsha Buthelezi grew up in the king's enclave at Mahashini, the "place of horses," a high, flat-topped hill where humans and beasts could find relief from the steamy humidity of lower Zululand. As a child Buthelezi slept in a rondavel, a circular Zulu hut, and scampered among the king's houses, limousines, and forty wives. As soon as he was old enough, he was sent out to the fields to herd cattle, like all the boys in his community. When Buthelezi had completed primary school, his family decided to send him to Adams College for his secondary education. Shortly before he was to depart, his father, Chief Mathole, died. The fourteen-year-old Buthelezi took part in the funeral, standing stoically in the middle of a ritual *kraal* with his spear pointing to the place where his father would be buried. The thousands of tribesmen who had gathered for the occasion watched with interest, wondering whether this teenager would claim the right to succeed the venerable Mathole.

Buthelezi could not do so immediately because of his youth. His father's brother was chosen to govern the tribe until Buthelezi had received his education and the final decision about succession could be made. His mother's brother Prince Mshiyeni, who had been serving as regent of the Zulu nation since the death of King Solomon in 1933, took him under his wing and escorted young Gatsha to his new boarding school. On their way, the two stopped to visit John Dube, the American-educated first president of the ANC, now a crotchety seventy-one-year-old invalid. Though weakened by age, Dube impressed the young Gatsha, who later would frequently cite his connections to Seme, Dube, and others as evidence that the original ANC had been led by "Zulu patriots." After meeting Dube, the regent and his nephew drove to Durban, where they purchased some formal clothes for school, and then on to Adams College. There they met the principal, Edgar Brookes, a liberal historian, theologian, and senator in the South African parliament. In his years at Adams, Buthelezi perfected his spoken and written English, acted in plays by Shakespeare and Shaw, studied world history, and made a strong personal commitment to the Anglican faith.

In 1948, the year of the Nationalist Party victory, Buthelezi moved on to the University of Fort Hare. He quickly fell into the small, turbulent circle of the African educated elite. Both of his uncles had resisted the idea of sending him to university, but his mother, remembering her husband's deep desire for his son to receive an education, had dug into her small purse and sent him. Despite a stiff warning from the Zulu regent not to get involved in politics, Buthelezi could scarcely avoid doing so. He was surrounded by dynamic leaders, both present and future: Professor Z. K. Matthews and his son Joe; Robert Sobukwe, who was president of the ANC Youth League at the time; and Nthato Motlana, who would become a driving force in Soweto in the 1970s. Buthelezi joined the ANC Youth League in his first year, another association with the ANC to which he would often draw attention in the future.

Over the next two years, Buthelezi increased his involvement in the resistance movement. When deadly riots broke out in 1949 between Africans and Indians, Buthelezi immediately traveled to Durban and helped answer the telephones and coordinate relief efforts at the office of the African National Congress. In 1950, when the governor general came for a visit to Fort Hare, the ANC Youth League at the university called for a boycott. The call was successful: when the governor general arrived, only a dozen students showed up to greet him. The ANC Youth League then began to harass those students, tying their sheets in knots or dousing their beds with water. After one such incident, Buthelezi was spotted carrying a bucket of water from the bathroom. Though Buthelezi insisted he was innocent, the disciplinary committee expelled him from the university.

Buthelezi was devastated. Humiliated and desperate, he appealed to Pixley Seme and to his former principal, Edgar Brookes, who was able to secure a spot for Buthelezi at the University of Natal in exchange for a pledge that the young man would steer clear of politics. Those who knew Buthelezi during his senior year in exile remember his mood of shyness and caution. He had reason to be careful, for his expulsion had also marked him for scrutiny by the South African Security Police. Brookes arranged for Buthelezi to take Fort Hare's final examinations and to return to his original school to graduate.

In retrospect, Buthelezi's expulsion stands out as a critical event, one whose trauma molded his career and his behavior for the rest of his life. In his youth Buthelezi had considered following Seme, Mandela, and Sisulu into the law. By the time he graduated he had decided instead to seek installation as the chief of the Buthelezi tribe. In years to come, Buthelezi would attribute his decision to the example of Albert Luthuli, who had given up a teaching post at Adams College in 1935 and accepted the chieftainship of the Groutville Reserve. After Luthuli's death, Buthelezi would increasingly claim that the ANC leader not only had persuaded him to become a chief but had made him the guardian of the original principles of the ANC. There was, however, a notable difference between the careers of the two men. Luthuli had taken on the chieftainship before the Nationalist Party had come to power. When told by the Nationalists in the early 1950s that he would have to choose between his affiliation with the ANC and his chieftainship, Luthuli had chosen the ANC. A year later, when W. W. M. Eiselen—the very official who had confronted Luthuli—presented Gatsha Buthelezi with the same choice, Buthelezi complied with the government's demands. In their interview Eiselen told Buthelezi he would pay close attention to the young man's behavior. Another blemish on his record, Eiselen said, would destroy his chances of becoming a chief. Buthelezi decided that under such circumstances his best strategy was to position himself directly under the government's nose, so for the next few years he toiled as a clerk in the Department of Native Affairs. Though he bridled at the patronizing behavior of his white supervisors, Buthelezi stoically endured the post in the hope of obtaining their consent to become a chief.

Buthelezi's ambition also compelled him to seek the approval of the Zulu royal family. Since the defeat of Cetshwayo by the British, the Zulu monarchy had fallen on hard times, as successive kings had collapsed into defeatism, depression, and drink. Many Zulu intellectuals, liberals, and democrats had come to believe that hereditary rule by chiefs and kings was a cultural remnant to be discarded, just as it had been by most European nations. In rural communities, however, the monarchy conjured up fragmented memories of the unified Zulu nation that had dominated the region under Shaka's iron grip. Even in the urban areas, respect for the monarchy bloomed in the hellish migrant worker hostels, not so much because the men loved kings but because they loathed capitalism.

Buthelezi worked diligently to align himself with the royal family. Though the title in Zulu culture does not pass down through matriarchal lines, Buthelezi nonetheless encouraged those around him, particularly foreigners, to call him *mntwana,* or "prince." Buthelezi also insisted that his grandfather's service as an adviser to King Cetshwayo had established a hereditary right for the head of the Buthelezi tribe to serve as the king's "prime minister." Buthelezi moved swiftly to position himself as the principal adviser to his cousin Cyprian, who became king of the Zulus in 1951. Buthelezi persuaded the young monarch, with whom he had played as a child at Mahashini, to travel to Fort Hare to attend his graduation. For the next sixteen years, Buthelezi assiduously cultivated his role of councilor, protector, and confidant as the young monarch, like his father, sank into alcoholic incapacity.

From the beginning, Buthelezi revealed a dazzling ability to turn the very ambiguity of his relationships—with the ANC, the South African government, and the Zulu royal family—to his own ends. His early career was littered with apparent contradictions. Buthelezi had claimed to be a leading opponent of Verwoerd's Bantu Authorities Act, yet he sought the government's approval under the act to become a traditional chief. He had touted his commitment to the ANC, dined at Nelson Mandela's home in Soweto, while refusing to identify with the organization's words or deeds. He had proclaimed himself a fierce opponent of apartheid yet threatened *Drum* magazine with a libel suit for describing him in print as a "rebel chief." Even when his wife and mother had joined the women's pass law rebellion in 1956, Buthelezi had declined to participate, for fear that the government would prevent his ascension to the chieftainship. Buthelezi would later defend these moves as tactically necessary: the only reward others ever received for their outspokenness, he pointed out, were bannings, imprisonment, exile, or death.

After six years of waiting, Gatsha finally got his wish on September 6, 1957, when the government formally acknowledged his claim to become chief of the Buthelezi, a tribe that numbered about thirty thousand at the time. From then on, Buthelezi continued to walk a delicate line between collaboration and resistance. In the early years, the government viewed him with suspicion while ANC leaders looked on him with approval. Africans from many quarters thought that Buthelezi, as the only chief in Zululand who had received a university education, would be able to use his position to advance the cause of liberation. Buthelezi was, in their eyes, a kind of double agent, a man who participated in the government's structures without believing in them, who could force the concealed contradictions of the government's policies into the open, who could use his rural base to supply them with information and support. It was far better, they reasoned, to have such an intelligent ally in the bantustans than a genuine government flunky.

Buthelezi shared this view of his role. If the South African government could be forced to implement separate development, rather than simply pay lip service to it, then the bantustans could become vehicles for radical change. If Pretoria could be obliged to invest tens of millions of rand in rural industry, to grant political independence to huge numbers of blacks, to permit the training of African police and soldiers, to relinquish control of black education, and to break the regional grip of white farmers and industrialists, then the bantustans could become potent bases for black economic, political, and military power. If, on the other hand, the South African government refused to do these things, the policy of separate development would be conclusively revealed as a fraud.

Years later, when Buthelezi was challenged about his early strategy, he would angrily describe how the South African government tried to undermine his authority as a leader and chief. In this, Buthelezi was correct: throughout the 1950s and 1960s Nationalist government officials surreptitiously fueled his political opponents in Zululand. As a result Buthelezi gradually came to view all political opposition as a conspiracy from either the right or the left. At the same time, Buthelezi rarely mentioned that he also relied on the white South African government to secure and protect his position. In 1959 Mceleli Buthelezi, the oldest son of Mathole's first wife, challenged Gatsha's claim to the chieftainship in court. Gatsha dismissed the legitimacy of Mceleli's claim, telling everyone who would listen that the dispute had been orchestrated by the South African government to cut him down. Nonetheless, for nearly two years Mceleli enjoyed growing support among the members of the Buthelezi tribe. After two years the case reached the South African Supreme Court, where the justices threw it out, saying that they had no jurisdiction in cases of tribal succession. Buthelezi then turned in a panic to the Department of Bantu Administration. After considerable prodding, the Security Police issued a warrant for Mceleli's arrest. Though Buthelezi vigorously gathered and forwarded intelligence on his half-brother's whereabouts to the police, they repeatedly failed to catch him. When Gatsha learned that Mceleli's supporters had made plans to spirit him to safety in Swaziland, he wrote an angry letter to Major Von Keyserlink, the regional head of the South African police, complaining about the inefficiency of his force. In 1961 the police finally nabbed Mceleli and banished him for six years to a distant town in the Transvaal.

The next serious challenge to Buthelezi's authority came in September 1968 when King Cyprian, having drunk more than two bottles of whiskey in a single day, lapsed into a diabetic coma and died at age forty-four. Because the king's son Prince Goodwill Zwelithini was considered too young to ascend immediately to the throne, power passed to the king's brother Prince Israel Mcwayizeni, as regent. Immediately a rift opened between Israel and Buthelezi. Buthelezi would later say that Israel wanted to ask the South African government to move the homeland to the next stage of separate development—the creation of a Zulustan Territorial Authority—while Buthelezi wanted to wait. The issue also seems to have been personal: Israel allegedly told his inner circle that he distrusted Buthelezi and wanted advice only from his brothers. Over the next few months royal disfavor with Buthelezi increased. Israel removed Buthelezi as a trustee of Prince Goodwill's financial trust and rejected Buthelezi's attempt to continue to serve as "prime minister." Buthelezi, in turn, believed that he had been edged out through the encouragement of the South African secret police.

Despite his claim to have opposed the creation of the Zulustan Territorial Authority, Buthelezi now latched on to the idea as a way to return to power. Buthelezi knew that the person who became leader of the Territorial Authority would draft the region's constitution and design its legislature. To position himself for the job, Buthelezi first accepted appointment by the South African government as the head of Mashonangashoni region. From this post Buthelezi immediately began campaigning to become head of the entire territory. Alarmed, Israel advanced his own candidate for the post, Chief Charles Hlengwa. At the election in June 1970, the commissioner of Bantu affairs counted the ballots and announced that Buthelezi had been elected unanimously. The commissioner then handed Buthelezi a check for 12,200 rand to pay the early expenses of the Territorial Authority.

Buthelezi swiftly appointed his allies to the executive committee and turned to drafting a constitution. The central question was the role of the king. Prince Israel wanted a strong executive monarch, like the one in the neighboring state of Swaziland, and his views enjoyed the support of a potent conservative alliance of traders, small businessmen, Zulu nationalists, and security agents. Though Buthelezi might have been enamored of a powerful monarchy when he was the confidant of Cyprian, he now opposed it. The young heir to the throne, Prince Goodwill, eager to persuade his family to let him become king, lamely pledged his support to whoever would help him. The wild card in the process was John Vorster, who could scuttle the entire constitutional process by cutting off the government's subsidy or refusing to accept the end result.

For months Buthelezi and his opponents struggled for supremacy. Each side claimed the mantle of history and the leadership of the Zulu nation; and each side privately courted the support of the regime in Pretoria. The battle was waged mostly in committee meetings, secret negotiations, legal clauses, and ponderous speeches. In the end, Buthelezi triumphed. In 1972 the members of the Zulu Territorial Authority approved the creation of a new legislature (the KwaZulu Legislative Authority), instituted a strong executive council with Buthelezi as the "chief minister," and established a constitutional monarchy whose king was expressly forbidden to enter into politics. The constitution also pledged allegiance to all laws "applicable in the area," meaning, in effect, that any rules passed by the white parliament in Pretoria would supersede those passed in KwaZulu. When the KwaZulu Legislative Assembly held its first parliamentary session in 1972, the forty-four-year-old chief emerged as a leader of national importance. In two decades of byzantine struggle, Buthelezi had rebuffed every attempt by Zulu and Afrikaner opponents to foil his paradoxical master plan: to use the policy of separate development to advance not only his own career but also the cause of national black liberation.

As controversial as his strategy seemed to some, it was actually quite clear. First, Buthelezi would insist that the South African government consolidate the fragments of KwaZulu into an economically viable whole. Second, he would demand that the Nationalists pour capital into the industrial development of the impoverished region. Third, he would gain control of the schools in KwaZulu and free the students from the crippling inadequacies of Bantu education. Fourth, he would block the attempts of the South African government to divide and rule the homelands by forming alliances with his peers in the Transkei, Ciskei, and Bophuthatswana. Fifth, he would restore Zulu self-confidence—particularly in urban communities—by celebrating ethnic history and achievement in a way that the South African government could not readily oppose. Finally, if the South African government did not live up to its promises, Buthelezi would refuse to accept "independence" for KwaZulu and destroy Pretoria's chances of winning international acceptance for the idea of separate development.

Buthelezi knew that the first component—shaping KwaZulu into a single territory—was going to be difficult. When Kaiser Matanzima had said that he would refuse independence until the Transkei, which was already relatively large and consolidated, received more land, John Vorster had responded that the Transkeian government was "wasting its time." Compared to the Transkei, KwaZulu was in far worse shape. A map of Buthelezi's "homeland" looked like the hide of a giraffe, with more than forty islands of Zulu territory surrounded by and intermingled with blotches of white property. A person driving from Durban to Ulundi could pass in and out of the Zulu homeland a half dozen times without ever seeing a demarcation. The most arable spots between the rolling green hills were occupied by sprawling white plantations, most of which grew sugarcane. Only in the places where the combination of soil, elevation, and temperature produced hundreds of square miles of semiarid scrub was the Zulu right to the land unchallenged.

In a speech in April 1972, Buthelezi announced that he intended to petition the government for more land and a consolidation of territory. John Vorster resisted the idea vigorously, since it would have meant forcing white farmers to sell their properties or live under a Zulu government. About the most he was willing to do, the prime minister said, was to fulfill the intentions of the Native Land and Trust Act, passed three and a half decades earlier under Prime Minister Hertzog. At a meeting between Vorster and the KwaZulu Executive Council, Buthelezi told the prime minister that this would not be enough. When Buthelezi insisted that the arable land, the beaches on the Indian Ocean, and the port at Richards Bay would all have to become part of the Zulu homeland, the South African government bluntly refused. Shortly afterward the Department of Bantu Administration issued "consolidation" plans that left KwaZulu in a dozen fragments and the port in white South Africa. The plan also envisaged the purchase of two hundred fifty white farms, the division of several game reserves into white and black sectors, the reservation of virtually all waterfront property for whites, and the forcible resettlement of hundreds of thousands of Zulus.

Buthelezi was furious. "We cannot see ourselves being used in this way in covering up naked and outright white domination," he fumed to a reporter from the *Johannesburg Star.* "We feel that South Africa should be honest and rule us without any consolidation, instead of giving the world the illusionary impression that we are a black government in the making." In July 1972, Buthelezi and the other members of the KwaZulu Executive Council flatly rejected the proposal. When he and his council traveled to Pretoria to discuss the problem with the minister of Bantu affairs, the meeting collapsed into acrimonious dispute.

Buthelezi's ability and willingness to condemn John Vorster's policies in words sharp enough to have landed almost anyone else in jail earned him support from around the country and around the world. Helen Suzman, Harry Oppenheimer, and other leaders of the Progressive Party increasingly saw Buthelezi as a forceful, educated, and subtle leader with whom they hoped to lay the groundwork for a new political dispensation. A liberal band of intellectuals and clergy who had formed the Study Project on Christianity in Apartheid Society (SPRO-CAS) noted approvingly in 1973 that "Chief Gatsha Buthelezi has led the way among Bantustan leaders in voicing demands that could be satisfied only by a substantial modification . . . or abandonment of separate development." Buthelezi's reputation also grew when he publicly bridled at the indignities of apartheid. In August 1972 Buthelezi invited Father Cosmas Desmond, a Catholic priest under modified house arrest, to join him for lunch at the President Hotel in Johannesburg. When they arrived, the maître d'hotel refused Buthelezi service, prompting the Zulu leader to file a formal complaint with the Hotel Board. The head of the Hotel Board responded that the proper procedure would have been to write a letter to the Department of Community Development asking permission to have lunch, to secure the written approval of the chairman of the Liquor Licensing Board, and finally to take the documents for an official stamp and signature by the local police commander. In December, Buthelezi was again at the center of a frenzy when it was reported in the newspapers that he had attended a dinner of the Cape Town Press Club and danced with a white woman. The deputy minister of police denounced the action at a National Party rally. Connie Mulder, the interior minister and a man widely viewed as a possible successor to Vorster, told an Afrikaner newspaper grimly that such activities might have to be curbed. For a while the controversy centered on the question of who had invited whom to dance. When some journalists insisted that the woman had asked Buthelezi, her husband threatened to sue them for libel. Buthelezi, when queried, said that the very question was undignified.

By the early 1970s Buthelezi's actions and comments were regularly reported in both the Afrikaans and English press, giving credence to his claim that the bantustan system provided a platform for the expression of black views that would otherwise be completely absent. By 1972 his stature was such that the Society of South African journalists selected him Newsmaker of the Year. His name also began to circulate abroad. When the KwaZulu Executive Council refused to adopt the customary loyalty oath to the South African government, Buthelezi received favorable ratings from papers in Europe and the United States. Such coverage triggered invitations from a wide array of foreign organizations and governments, and Buthelezi, capitalizing on the Pretorian government's insistence that he was an "independent African leader," left South Africa with increasing frequency. From 1971 to 1973 alone, he made five trips to Europe or the United States.

With exceptional political artistry, Buthelezi used these trips abroad to enhance his reputation. He boosted his reputation for commitment to nonviolence by attending international church conferences. Though Buthelezi did not approve of the actions of the World Council of Churches against South Africa, he maintained close ties with the organization through his good friend Bishop Alphaeus Zulu, who served as one of the vice presidents of the church body. As an Anglican, Buthelezi also worked diligently to develop ties with others of his denomination in South Africa, England, and the United States. On one of his periodic sweeps to the north, he passed through Rome and secured an audience with Pope Paul VI.

During his travels Buthelezi made sure to touch base with persons from every point on the political spectrum. He toured Africa, stopping to meet with Julius Nyerere, Kenneth Kaunda, and Haile Selassie. In London in 1971, traveling with Kaiser Matanzima of the Transkei and Lucas Mangope of Bophuthatswana, he met with Prince Philip and gave him a traditional Zulu tribal stick. He met with business executives, liberals and conservatives from the British Parliament, and his old colleagues from Fort Hare who had joined the Pan-Africanist Congress and fled South Africa. Despite Pretoria's disapproval, he maintained steady contact with Oliver Tambo and other leaders of the African National Congress in exile. In 1971, for example, the three bantustan leaders made a pilgrimage to see Tambo, who was delighted to see them, especially Mangope, who had been one of Tambo's students in high school. On this occasion, Buthelezi told the ANC leaders that he was doing everything he could to advance the day of national liberation from within KwaZulu. Whenever Buthelezi returned home, his aides organized large rallies to welcome him. Sometimes they took place at the airport, sometimes back in KwaZulu, and, on more than one occasion, in Jabulani stadium in Soweto. The photographs from these events were massively reproduced in official KwaZulu literature. Because the dates were often left unspecified, they generated the impression that each came from a different event, as though thousands appeared every time Buthelezi spoke in public.

Through such political wizardry, Buthelezi tried to win acceptance from everyone. Depending on the context, Buthelezi could present himself as a reforming pragmatist, a black nationalist, a democratic politician, an ANC loyalist, a hereditary autocrat, a nonviolent Christian, a descendant of Shaka the warrior, a pro-capitalist industrialist, an urbane intellectual, or a Zulu traditionalist. Buthelezi's genius arose from his understanding that if he used the right rhetoric, people would come to see what they wanted to see. Even more important, many believed that even when Buthelezi said something contradictory in public he was really, in his heart of hearts, on their side.

□ □ □ □

Despite Buthelezi's apparent success, mistrust of his intentions and anger about apartheid grew steadily among the tiny number of Africans who were enrolled in universities. In April, 1972, one event sparked a chain reaction of explosions across the campuses of the country. During the commencement ceremonies of the University College of the North, the graduation speaker, Onkgopotse Ramothibi Tiro, who had been elected by the students, chose this highly public moment to attack the inequities of Bantu education. Drawing a direct comparison with the struggle for integration in American schools, Tiro, a former mine worker who had spent years to get a college degree, detailed the many examples of discrimination at Turfloop. He pointed to the front rows in the auditorium, which were filled with the white administrators of the school and their guests, and said that the African parents of most of the students, including his own, had been either pushed to the back or forced to wait outside. Tiro urged the students to disassociate themselves from the structures of apartheid and to take greater responsibility for the "liberation of our people."

The day after the ceremony, the all-white disciplinary committee revoked Tiro's degree and expelled him from the university. The students petitioned for Tiro's reinstatement; the administrators refused; and a group of students held a sit-in in the main hall. In response, the university's rector expelled all 1,146 students and called in the riot police to seal off the campus. After vigorous protests from the opposition in parliament and petitions from parents, the head of the university allowed the students to reapply one by one. They would be granted readmission, he announced, only if they each signed a document accepting the expulsion of Tiro, the dismantling of the Student Representative Council, and the banning of all black committees on campus, including the South African Students' Association (SASO).

Over the next month, subsidiary protests spread to other black schools. On May 22 the National Union of South African Students (NUSAS) launched a Free Education campaign. On June 2 police attacked a mostly white student meeting on the steps of St. George's Cathedral in Cape Town. When the students fled into the cathedral for refuge, the police chased them, caught a few, and beat them ferociously. The students called for Helen Suzman, who ran over one block from her office in the parliament building, pushed her way through the encircling ranks of police, and negotiated safe conduct for the fugitives huddled inside. Over the next few days the photographers for the international press eagerly snapped pictures as the police used tear gas, batons, and attack dogs to disperse and arrest student demonstrators around the country. Black observers noted grimly that the global press had paid little attention during the first month of the protest as long as black students were attacked; but when white students were brutalized, the story shot across the world.

Though Helen Suzman and other members of parliament sharply attacked the government, Vorster's cabinet ministers and police officers were unrepentant. Some of them offered their own explanations for the university unrest. Speaking to high school students at a conference organized by the pro-apartheid South African Bureau of Racial Affairs (SABRA), Major General P. J. "Tiny" Venter, head of the Security Police, warned that Russian-invented sensitivity training was being used to undermine South Africa. This "terrorism of the brain" reduced "race-inhibitions," he explained, and led to a questioning of established norms and authority. After his remarks, a Middelburg schoolboy named Jacob Odendaal stood up to pose a question: Why had the police used batons against the students when they could have used machine guns? His schoolmates burst into cheers and applause. The security forces were "peace officials," Venter replied modestly, and should never use more force than was absolutely necessary.

It was against this backdrop of student turmoil that SASO held its third annual conference at St. Peter's Seminary in Hamanskraal during the first week of July. The students had been delighted earlier in the year when C. Eric Lincoln, one of the leading scholars of black religion in the United States, had visited South Africa and put them in touch with the Black Caucus at Union Theological Seminary in New York. The leaders of SASO had then asked one of the members of the caucus, Robert Williams, who was working at the time as a lecturer in the Religion Department at Vassar College, to come to South Africa to be the keynote speaker for their annual meeting. Williams had readily agreed, but the night before his departure, he learned that the South African government had revoked his visa. Williams sent a message anyway, telling the students that "black people in America are watching with pride and interest the work of our black brothers in South Africa. . . . The black hand of togetherness reaches across all geographical boundaries. Power to the People!"

Lacking a keynote speaker, the students asked the current president of SASO, Temba Sono, to deliver the talk. In the words of the SASO newsletter that reported on the event several months later, "the entire conference was expecting an unflinching, unapologetic address." Instead, "without any consultation with the executive committee he delivered a paper that left the committee shocked, dismayed, and angry." The content of Sono's speech, in retrospect, does not seem to have justified such hysteria. He quoted at length from both Aimé Césaire and Eldridge Cleaver, two canonical writers of Black Consciousness. Sono's error, according to his detractors, was his insistence that SASO maintain a dialogue with others and work more closely with bantustan leaders like Buthelezi. To those in the inner circle of SASO—Stephen Biko, Strini Moodley, and Barney Pityana—this was heresy. Declaring that the whole speech "smacked of a sell-out," Pityana and Moodley offered a resolution that Sono be deposed as president. The measure passed and Sono, who had arrived as the head of the organization, was kicked off the executive committee and asked to leave the conference.

Having meted out such a stark penalty, the inner circle of SASO unleashed its full criticism of the bantustan system. Biko warned that the bantustan idea was gaining adherents. "If we don't fight it," Biko declared from the podium, "we will find ourselves clamoring for Zulustans, Xhosastans, and so on." Though in the past they had considered tolerating the system, Biko declared, "I think we should now work against it." Biko appealed directly to Buthelezi to change course and told the audience that Buthelezi is "the one man who has led the entire world to believe in the bantustan policy."

Biko reserved his most skillfully crafted criticism for an article in the September–October 1972 SASO newsletter entitled "Let's Talk about Bantustans." Biko avoided attacking Buthelezi and Matanzima directly; indeed, only a few months before, Biko had edited a book entitled *Black Viewpoints* in which he had included an article by Buthelezi. Biko focused on the idea of using the bantustans as a base for black liberation. The strategy was doomed to failure, Biko argued, because of the gross inequity in the distribution of land between white and black. No system, he insisted, in which twenty percent of the population kept eighty-seven percent of a country's territory and then herded eighty percent of the population on to the remaining thirteen percent of the land could ever be considered fair. Not one of the bantustans, Biko noted, had access to the sea. Not one had retained the rights to its mineral reserves. As a result, no bantustan could ever become economically powerful. The most serious danger of attempting to use the system, however, was not physical but psychological. The notion that bantustans could "be exploited towards the attainment of our overall goals" was wrong, he wrote, because it led to the "subconscious acceptance of the bantustan idea *per se* by the masses who cannot appreciate the nuances of debate surrounding the so-called strategy."

Buthelezi's plan was flawed, Biko wrote fervently, because he and the other bantustan leaders were "aiding and abetting in the total subjugation of the black people in this country." Buthelezi was also playing into the government's hands by reintroducing ethnicity into African politics. "At this stage of our history," Biko commented, "we cannot have our struggle be tribalized through the creation of Zulu, Xhosa, and Tswana politicians by the system." And finally, Biko argued, Buthelezi and the other bantustan leaders, by speaking militantly, "have managed to confuse the blacks sufficiently to believe that something great is about to happen. The picture is also confused by the exaggeration given by the white press to the possibilities open to these leaders." As a result, Biko concluded, "for white South Africa it is extremely important to have a man like Buthelezi speaking and sounding the way he is doing. . . . It has been said that the combination of Buthelezi and the white press make up the finest ambassadors that South Africa has ever had."

By late 1973 South Africa was nearing the end of a decade of vigorous economic growth. Despite the many predictions that apartheid and separate development would lead to economic catastrophe, South Africa's gross domestic product had risen in real terms by an average of six percent a year. Unlike most countries on the developing continents of the world, the bureaucrats in the Ministry of Finance worried little about growth and a lot about controlling inflation. To the extent that the government had an economic plan, it had changed little since the time of Verwoerd. The goals were straightforward: to encourage domestic manufacturing through the imposition of import tariffs and local content laws; to protect choice jobs for whites; to increase state involvement in the economy through the establishment of large quasi-governmental monopolies; and to continue to draw the maximum benefit at the lowest cost from the African labor force. These objectives did not mesh perfectly with the political goals of apartheid. Verwoerd had started off urging the economic development of the segregated homelands while retaining political sovereignty for South Africa; but gradually the emphasis had reversed. By the early 1970s John Vorster's government was promoting the idea of political "independence" of the bantustans while trying to ensure that capital remained in white South Africa.

There were other tensions as well. It made economic sense for the industrial heartland around Johannesburg to continue to grow, thereby concentrating skills and capital and bringing industrial suppliers closer together. Such concentration also acted as a magnet for tens of thousands of unemployed African workers, who, despite influx control, swelled the townships, set up squatter camps, and provided an inexhaustible pool of unskilled and inexpensive labor. The Nationalist government, however, wanted to reverse this trend, to force or lure businesses and their African workers back in the direction of the homelands. The government offered a host of tax credits and other incentives—such as a waiver of the minimum wage and safety regulations—to companies that would resettle to the "border areas." A few did, but most of the jobs remained near the cities.

Even after a decade of accelerated growth, the disparities between the races were stunning. Just ten percent of South Africa's districts produced nearly seventy percent of the country's total economic output. The combined economic output of all nine homelands equaled less than three percent of the national total. Indeed, if one ranked the 263 districts in terms of output per capita, the bantustans occupied nine of the ten bottom spots. In the mid-1970s, the average white person's wage was twelve times greater than his or her African counterpart; during the previous fifteen years the gap between white and black (measured in gross domestic product per capita) had actually widened. In the mines, despite three generations of development, the wage gap between white and black had increased. At the beginning of the twentieth century the average white man was paid ten times more than a black; in 1970 he was paid twenty-one times more. In 1972 the South African economist Francis Wilson released a study of the mines which showed that, in real terms, black miners' wages had not risen since 1911. In 1972 a young black man who spent his life manipulating dangerous machinery in a sweltering tunnel two miles below the surface could look forward to a daily cash wage of forty-two cents.

As these data surfaced, the debate about the mutual dependence of capitalism and apartheid grew. For liberal politicians, churchmen, and business leaders like Helen Suzman, Alan Paton, and Harry Oppenheimer, the enduring disparities of wealth demonstrated that capitalism was being hampered by the restrictions of apartheid. "It's just a plain, obvious truth," Oppenheimer told an American business reporter in 1972, "that a country that refuses to allow something like eighty per cent of its labor force to do the best work of which they are capable cannot progress as it should or hold its place in the world."

Though the liberals agreed with Oppenheimer's diagnosis, they differed on the cure. Some believed that economic growth would, by itself, eventually alter the political community. Industrialization would inexorably lead to liberalization. Others reversed the syllogism: economic growth would not be the cause but the *result* of political reform. Unless South Africa found a way to alter course, they insisted, the black majority would never acquire the education, skills, and purchasing power necessary to carry South Africa into prosperity in the next half century. The other interpretation, held by such disparate persons as the *verkrampte* Afrikaner and the ANC Marxist, was that South Africa had flourished *because* of apartheid. The economic and political systems strengthened each other. Ferocious police repression guaranteed low wages and a compliant workforce, which in turn boosted profits, attracted foreign capital, and raised white living standards. Only through the political mechanisms of white supremacy, insisted these analysts of left and right, could the majority of a country's population be rendered economically dependent on the minority. And only by continuing to abscond with the resources generated by cheap labor could the minority retain power.

These differing interpretations were not quibbling academic disputes. They led to completely different strategic attitudes toward change in South Africa. Those with the former view—that industrialization would liberalize the country—believed that the focus should be on increased foreign investment and incremental reforms. Those who believed that apartheid and capitalism were closely correlated insisted that the only process that would unseat apartheid, short of armed invasion, was the disruption of the economy. For the first half of the 1970s, however, it seemed as though South Africa's bubble of prosperity could not pop. Part of the reason was South Africa's continued reliance on gold. Throughout most of the century South Africa had supplied almost three-quarters of the world's annual gold production; as long as the world's currencies were tied to gold at the fixed price of thirty-five dollars an ounce, South Africa could depend on a healthy balance of payments. When the finance ministers of the Western world agreed in 1968 to create a two-tiered system—an "official" gold price for monetary purposes and a market price for the commercial markets—South Africa again prospered. Even when President Nixon took the United States off the gold standard and devalued the dollar—forcing the rand down as well—South Africa was able to recoup as the market price of gold rose to $187 an ounce, more than five times its original official value. Thus, while most of the world was struggling with the economic shock and recession caused by the first Arab oil embargo of 1973 and while the cost of base metals and other commodities plummeted, squeezing developing nations around the world, South Africa flourished.

As long as the boom continued, so did the enthusiasm of foreign investors. South Africa's ten-year growth had been fueled by a net capital inflow of more than 3.5 billion rand. Part of it was in the form of direct investment, which had been so substantial that foreign companies now controlled large blocks of strategic industries. In banking, for example, foreign firms controlled 73.2 percent of South African commercial bank assets, a number so high that Vorster appointed a commission to examine whether this represented a threat to national security. In oil production, American companies owned the majority of the refineries and the filling stations around the country. American companies similarly controlled nearly 40 percent of all new car sales in the country— and a higher percentage of trucks—though the Japanese were rapidly adding manufacturing capacity. Even in the fields of electronics, computers, and telecommunications, American firms controlled large and critical blocks. Foreign bankers were also lining up to invest in the South

African economy, placing most of their funds into loans to government-owned steel, weapons, and electrical companies. As money poured in, South African executives were able, despite the government's effort to encourage local manufacturing, to purchase increased amounts of capital goods and advanced equipment from abroad. The executives defended the action, saying that it was the only way they could gain access to the most advanced technology and skills and thereby remain competitive.

As capital from Europe and the United States continued to roll in, and as South Africa's policies were discussed more prominently in those countries, attention focused increasingly on the role played by foreign firms in the maintenance or erosion of white supremacy. American corporate executives, conservative columnists, and business reporters all emphasized the changes in South African society, the leadership role of American firms, and the emergence of a new, liberal generation of Afrikaners who were willing to reform apartheid. The members of the Nationalist government, conversely, crowed that the infusion of capital and the growth in trade were vindications of separate development. "Every time a South African product is bought," John Vorster had said in 1972, "it is another brick in the wall of our continued existence."

In the United States, the charges and countercharges were so contradictory that flocks of Americans decided to go see for themselves. Religious leaders, academic researchers, government administrators, corporate executives, foundation officials, and itinerant reporters zoomed into Johannesburg and Cape Town for a few days of intense meetings. Some never even made it off the airport grounds. In 1971 the United States–South Africa Leadership Exchange Program (USSALEP), a new venture launched by moderates in both countries, held a string of highly publicized meetings between white and black delegates from both countries at Johannesburg airport's Holiday Inn. Two years later, when USSALEP brought a group of black and white Americans, the English-speaking press again avidly reported every rumor about the closed-door conference.

In March 1972 the head of the NAACP, Roy Wilkins, arrived with his wife for a week-long visit to deliver several talks on the American civil rights movement at the Universities of the Witwatersrand and Cape Town. The *New York Times* reported in a front-page story that Wilkins, when asked to comment about the role of American businesses in South Africa, had "defended" their involvement. "How many black jobs would be lost if General Motors went back to Detroit, if John Deere and Chase Manhattan pulled out?" he was reported to have asked. Instead of withdrawing, he said, American companies should make dramatic improvements in the wage structures and training of African workers. The stories triggered a bitter outcry against Wilkins from some American blacks. Wilkins instantly responded. "I have not 'defended' United States business involvement in South Africa," he said in Johannesburg. "What I did was pose some questions about American business in this country and leave them undecided. The question to be decided was whether it would be better for United States companies to stay in South Africa or quit."

Executives of corporations who had received shareholder resolutions also paid new attention to South Africa. Only two weeks after Wilkins's visit, James Roche's successor at General Motors, Richard Gerstenberg, flew to South Africa to examine conditions at the firm's plant in Port Elizabeth. After a string of meetings—with GM workers, Port Elizabeth clergy, and John Vorster—Gerstenberg held a press conference. "Our stockholders in America say that we should withdraw from South Africa," he said. "But this would be the wrong thing to do. We have no intention of doing so. I think staying here will be the best way to help the non-white workers." The editors of South Africa's press were thrilled at the announcement. THANK YOU, GM! exclaimed the lead editorial in the *Johannesburg Sunday Times.* "There will be a sigh of relief over General Motors' decision not to pull out of South Africa, but to stay here and do its best to advance its non-White workers," the column continued. "This decision required a good deal of courage because the pressures being brought to bear in America on American companies to boycott South Africa are heavy and they are mounting."

Researchers and reporters were also beginning to nose into the question of American corporate commitment to change. Donald McHenry, a young foreign service officer on leave from the State Department, made several lengthy trips to South Africa in 1971 and 1972 to study American corporate performance. McHenry found his project slow going because of the unwillingness of American companies to disclose data about overseas subsidiaries. Examining the employment practices of the American subsidiaries, he found that, with a few exceptions, the record was not exemplary. Even when it was above average—for example, at IBM—there were other problems. McHenry documented the sale of IBM 360 and other large computers to the South African Defence Ministry, the Ministry of the Interior, the Department of Prisons, South African Airways, the South African Broadcasting Corporation, and other government departments and industries. "Perhaps the most ominous function of computers will be in the new Population Registration System," McHenry wrote, "which will require each South African to carry a comprehensive identity booklet. . . . This would be impossible to implement without the sophisticated technology of computers."

The conduct of American companies was even beginning to receive criticism from its usual boosters, the business press. In July 1972, for example, John Blashill, the Africa correspondent for *Fortune* magazine, wrote an influential article entitled "The Proper Role for U.S. Business in South Africa." In a few sentences Blashill dismissed those who were calling for corporate withdrawal. "Those who cry abandon ship," he said, "have not consulted the passengers. Many of South Africa's blacks, on whose behalf the issue is supposedly being fought, want U.S. business to stay." To support his point, Blashill quoted Lucy Mvubelo, the general secretary of the National Union of Clothing Workers, an African union that was not recognized by the government. "I feel if the Americans withdraw," she said, "it will lower the general standard of living here, and the Africans will be first to suffer." In addition to hurting blacks, Blashill insisted that withdrawal would backfire with the government. "An enforced U.S. retreat," he wrote, "would almost certainly cause a violent reaction among South Africa's whites."

At the same time, Blashill sharply criticized the conduct of some American companies. "The climate is ripe for change . . . [yet] few American subsidiaries in South Africa seem to know it—or want it," he wrote. There were exceptions among the larger firms who had, in response to criticism, implemented some workplace reforms. Until that year, for example, Ford had granted medical coverage to whites who had been employed for three months while nonwhites were covered only after ten years. In January 1972, five months after Charles Diggs's visit, the policy had been switched to three months for all employees, regardless of race. General Motors had increased the number of African, Coloured, and Indian workers in technical training programs; provided a small number of educational scholarships for primary and secondary students; and accepted the formation of an African "works committee," which could take up grievances with management. Despite these efforts, wrote Blashill, "there are probably not more than twenty-five subsidiaries of American corporations that can be considered to be reacting responsibly to the growing pressures for changes. . . . [Most firms]— and there are more than 250 of them—either oppose change or are dragging their feet." American firms, he argued, should stop hiding behind South African laws—which were more flexible than the executives chose to believe—and be more aggressive in improving workplace conditions whether the top brass in the United States issued the order or not.

Back in Washington at the Africa Bureau of the State Department, Assistant Secretary David Newsom agreed. Though hampered by the restrictions of NSSM 39, which was still not public knowledge, Newsom circulated an anonymous memo in 1971 recommending that American firms engage in comprehensive workplace reform. "American firms have found that investment in South Africa is very profitable," the document said. "But political ramifications of these investments have increasingly led to public relations difficulties for firms with interests in South Africa. The situation in southern Africa has become an area of major concern to many Americans, particularly labor unions, church groups, civil rights organizations, and college students, as they have made abundantly clear. Many people predict that within a relatively short time (six months to two years) the issue will replace Vietnam as the issue of the day."

The paper urged an increase in wages, the equalization of pay rates, the awarding of pension, life, health, and disability benefits to non-whites, legal assistance, sick leave, educational counseling and support for both adults and children, and subsidizied housing and transport. Firms should also invest more in the training and promotion of non-whites; if white workers objected to nonwhites doing equivalent jobs, the document suggested, then they could be physically separated from Africans. The paper proposed that American executives support African professionals and businessmen and consider relocating within the homelands rather than in the border areas. Finally, it urged American subsidiaries to enforce standards of mutual courtesy, to desegregate facilities within their plants as much as possible, and to contribute to organizations like USSALEP, the Christian Institute, and the Association for the Educational and Cultural Advancement of the African People of South Africa (ASSECA) "instead of, or at least in addition to, contributing to institutions like the South Africa Foundation whose raison d'être is to justify South Africa and South African society."

These recommendations were nowhere to be found in the February 1973 version of the document released by the Bureau of African Affairs. The explicit references to the profitability of American firms, the domestic debate in the United States over South Africa, and the sensitivities of white South Africa had been stripped out and replaced with the banal standard disclaimer that "the U.S. government neither encourages nor discourages investment in South Africa." Though interested companies could seek government information about the advantages and disadvantages, the "final decision is theirs."

The new document then proceeded to offer evidence of American corporate activism. Working its way through the list of recommendations on wages, benefits, training, and promotion, the document identified specific improvements that American firms had made, ranging from a movie IBM had produced to encourage whites to treat persons of other races with more respect to GE's increase of nonwhite wages by "41% in the past five years" (a rate that just barely exceeded inflation) to a current average salary of "over $96.00 a month." Under job promotions, the document noted that "General Motors currently has 25 Coloured and African supervisors, including one Coloured foreman and nineteen Coloured and African salaried employees. In the past year and a half, although total Coloured and African employment declined by 604, Coloureds and Africans in skilled grades 6 through 9 more than double to over 400."

Though the document ended with no particular recommendations, its overall intent was clear. By accepting the companies' decision to lump Africans and Coloureds together statistically in the category of "non-white," the report obscured the lack of progress being made for most of the Africans working for American companies. By providing concrete examples of scattered improvements, the report strengthened the argument that American companies were in the vanguard of change while goading laggards to hop on the bandwagon. And by refusing to set the workplace reforms in any larger political context—whether in South Africa or in the United States—the report made it seem as though these workplace improvements were spontaneous acts of goodwill on the part of American managers.

From the host of trips, articles, and reports that appeared in the first half of the decade, there emerged a mainstream consensus in the early 1970s. With the exception of a band of ardent religious and political activists in the United States, an uneasy coalition of persons in government, business, foundations, universities, and some religious circles agreed that workplace reforms by American corporations offered the best strategy against apartheid. For American corporate executives, South African liberals, and Republican policymakers, the confidence in workplace reform arose from the poorly examined assumption that disinvestment would hurt blacks and cause a counterproductive reaction among whites. Workplace reforms represented a reasonable, incremental approach to advancing African interests; it would slowly move Africans upward without offending white sensibilities too much.

The religious and political activists saw the matter in a completely different light. In May 1972, the month after GM's Gerstenberg made his trip, Tim Smith and the Corporate Information Center of the National Council of Churches published a detailed attack on General Motors' role in South Africa. General Motors, they wrote, was a huge and influential company by South African standards. Measured in terms of assets, it would be the eleventh largest in the country. Of its five thousand employees, fifty percent were white, forty percent were Coloured, and ten percent were African. Of 1,380 skilled and salaried workers, only 6 were "non-white." In light of these statistics, workplace reforms

As the pastor of Zion Baptist Church in North Philadelphia, the Reverend Leon Sullivan pioneered the use of economic pressures to force local businesses to open up positions for blacks and later founded job training centers that spread around the country and the world. His success led to his selection as the first black director of General Motors, a position he used to establish and promote a set of principles for workplace equality and reform in South Africa. (*Columbia College Today*)

From his post as the executive director of the Interfaith Center on Corporate Responsibility, a national coalition of Protestant denominations and Catholic orders, Tim Smith guided more than two decades of shareholder actions against U.S. companies operating in South Africa. (Fotoburo Thuring)

In the early 1970s President William McGill of Columbia University, when first confronted with church-sponsored shareholder resolutions on southern Africa, supported divestment—the selling off of Columbia's stock— but was blocked by his board of trustees. (*Columbia Spectator*)

Angered by liberal white paternalism and stirred by Black Power literature from the United States, Stephen Biko wrote powerful essays in the 1970s that sparked the creation of the Black Consciousness movement and a new generation of resistance to apartheid. (AP/Wide World Photos)

On June 16, 1976, thousands of children in the Soweto township outside of Johannesburg marched to protest a government edict that they take half of their courses in Afrikaans. "As I drove into their midst," said one black eyewitness, "they made way for me and stood on both sides of the road with their fists raised and shouting 'power' at the top of their voices. They were in an extremely jovial mood. The whole atmosphere was quite a happy one." (Mayibuye Center)

The Soweto riots began when the South African police opened fire on the protesting schoolchildren. Thirteen-year-old Hector Petersen, shown here, was the first to die. The brutality of the following weeks, in which rioters burned government buildings and were killed indiscriminately by South African soldiers, shocked the world. (Mayibuye Center)

In May 1977 Winnie Mandela was evicted from her home by the South African police and driven more than two hundred miles to a township outside of the conservative white stronghold of Brandfort. There she and her possessions were dumped in front of the tiny cinderblock hut without electricity or running water that was to be her home for the next seven years. Barred from receiving visitors, under constant surveillance by the police, and forced to send her daughters Zindzi (left) and Zenani away to school, Mandela (right) became deeply embittered. (Mayibuye Center)

First elected to parliament in 1953, Helen Suzman of the Progressive Party spent thirteen years (1952–1972) as the only liberal voice in the all-white assembly. A constant advocate for the rights of Africans and other disfranchised groups, she in fact represented, in the words of an American reporter, "more South Africans than all the other 159 members of parliament put together." (Mayibuye Center)

In 1979 the Reverend Howard Schomer (left), the director of social responsibility in investments for the United Church of Christ, took his former student from Chicago Theology Seminary the Reverend Jesse Jackson (right) to visit South Africa. During the trip Jackson tried, with little success, to persuade Mangosuthu Gatsha Buthelezi (center) and his rivals to resolve their differences. In the decade that followed, including two campaigns for president, Jackson was a strong advocate of sanctions. (Howard Schomer Collection, Andover Newton Library, Harvard Divinity School)

For more than a decade, sometimes with covert American support, the South African government engaged in a vicious secret war with guerrillas in Namibia and southern Angola. Here the three top leaders—from left, Minister of Foreign Affairs Pik Botha, Prime Minister P. W. Botha, and Minister of Defense Magnus Malan—are shown at a rare military briefing for the press in 1982. (*The Star*)

Allan Boesak, an ordained minister in the "Coloured" branch of the Dutch Reformed Church, carried many of the lessons he learned from writing a master's thesis on Martin Luther King Jr. and Malcolm X into his leadership of the United Democratic Front in the 1980s. (Mayibuye Center)

The apartheid policy of resettlement into arid "homelands" made the plight of millions of rural residents such as this family in Natal largely invisible. Without electricity, water, fuel, food, or employment, many, particularly children, succumbed to disease and early death. (United Nations Photo/151708)

During one of his visits to South Africa in the late 1970s, church activist Tim Smith snapped this photograph inside the Ford automotive assembly plant. Even in American companies apartheid labor laws dictated that supervisory positions be reserved for whites, who received training, salary, and benefits many times greater than those of their African and Coloured counterparts. (Tim Smith, ICCR)

Before returning to South Africa in 1975 to become the dean of the Anglican cathedral in Johannesburg, Desmond Tutu had spent ten years in Europe as a student, priest, and ecumenical officer. Swiftly elected bishop and then chosen as head of the South African Council of Churches in 1978, Tutu used his sparkling personality, global network of friends, and relentless courage to attract renewed attention to the struggle against apartheid. His efforts brought him the Nobel Peace Prize for 1984. (Mayibuye Center)

Chosen by Ronald Reagan in 1981 to become assistant secretary of state for African affairs, Chester A. Crocker designed and implemented the policy of "constructive engagement," which tried to lure the South African government into new configurations with its neighbors while shielding it from the growing demands for economic sanctions. (U.S. Department of State)

were not, as the executives thought, a daring advance into social improvement but a moral *minimum* for remaining in the country.

During the same period, the debate over the relative merits of corporate disinvestment and workplace reform began to divide the activist community in a manner both painful and enduring. Some, like Charles Diggs and eventually Leon Sullivan, who grew tired of watching their proposals for corporate withdrawal fail, made tactical moves to promoting workplace reforms in order to garner more support. Another group, including the American Committee on Africa, viewed such intermediate strategies as ill-conceived or even damaging. A preoccupation with minor improvements inside the factory or with the psychological attitudes of whites towards blacks, they felt, obscured the far more important economic dimension. To them, the most revealing statement in John Blashill's article came not from a pious corporate spokesman but from a plant manager in Natal. When asked about whether he believed in equal pay for equal work, the manager replied, "If New York orders me to pay the rate for the job, I'll pay it. But if I don't have to, I won't. . . . I am here to make profits," he concluded. "If the Bantus don't like it, they can work somewhere else."

For Gatsha Buthelezi, the intensified scrutiny of the role of foreign corporations in South Africa offered new opportunities to build up the economic power of Africans in general and KwaZulu in particular. It also gave him the chance to pressure the South African government to invest more money in his territory. The primary conduit was the budget of the KwaZulu Legislative Authority, which stood at thirty-two million rand in 1972 (about $160 million in 1994 dollars), two-thirds of which came directly from Pretoria. Buthelezi also pushed for more money for the Bantu Investment Corporation (BIC), a white-controlled fund that made loans to African businesses, and he demanded that the homeland governments be given more control of investment decisions. When asked about his reasons for doing so, Buthelezi made two arguments, one moral, the other strategic. He had a moral obligation, he said, to alleviate poverty in whatever way he could. Moreover, given the repressive might of the South African state, the only sound strategic course was to build up the economic power of Africans.

The situation in KwaZulu—and in the homelands in general—was indeed dire. By the early 1970s more than half of all economically active rural males—and virtually all of those between age eighteen and forty—had been driven from the homelands in search of work. Though the men sent back some of their salaries, the majority was spent in the white urban economy where they lived. In the homelands the opportunities for employment were so low that the *average* per capita income was below the international poverty line of two hundred dollars a year. Even when the homelands were situated near economically important sites, they had difficulty capturing the wealth. The mines preferred importing workers from Swaziland, Mozambique, or Lesotho to employing local men. By the mid-1970s, there were twenty-six mines operating within the Tswana homeland of Bophuthatswana, but only one percent of the miners were of Tswana origin. Industrialists who could be enticed out of the urban communities usually established their plants in the border areas just outside the boundaries of the bantustan, where government subsidies provided the roads, electrical power, and other forms of infrastructure that the homelands could not. Nor were Africans allowed to compete in industries considered important by whites. To prevent Africans from digging for minerals on their own, the South African parliament passed a law restricting the homelands' territorial rights to a depth of six feet below the surface. Entrepreneurship, tightly restricted by law in the urban areas, was also hamstrung in the homelands, so that the little money circulating inside tended to migrate outward to white businesses.

Such conditions did more than undermine the chance for economic vitality; they also corroded the social foundations of African communities. Families, fractured by financial pressures and eleven-month absences, collapsed with greater and greater frequency. Rural African agriculture, starved of investment, topsoil, and laborers, continued its decline. Researchers noted with alarm that the system was becoming more ingrained with each passing year. "The prolonged continuation of the migrant labor system has socialized the rural communities into accepting it as a way of life," wrote South African economist Jill Nattrass. "Boys growing up without their fathers take it as inevitable that they too will leave the rural areas."

For these and others reasons, Buthelezi rejected disinvestment. "Those who are contemplating withdrawing from South Africa would do better by remaining involved and improving the conditions of employment of black people here," he said in late 1971. "The agitation for disengagement had been started by black people in the United States. They and the young people supporting that view in this country are under a misconception." Buthelezi eagerly courted contact with both American and South African corporate leaders. In his conversations he seemed willing to use the threat of disinvestment to promote industrial change in the same manner he used concern about potential violence to spur political advances. "If you are going to ask foreign companies to withdraw, as least make it a reasonable exercise," he said in early 1973. "Give the firms a timetable to improve the wages of black workers and if they don't stick to it, then you can ask them to withdraw." Though

Buthelezi's critics were scornful—"You do not challenge your enemy to a duel and then accept the unloaded of the two guns," wrote Stephen Biko—Buthelezi's admirers in the liberal community applauded.

For a while it seemed that Buthelezi might be able to sustain yet another contradictory image, that of wooing corporate investment while pressing for workers' rights. Then, in January 1973, a string of events forced him to make a painful choice. Thousands of workers, most of them Zulu, went on strike for higher wages in the area around Durban. The action was encouraged by a group of students from NUSAS at the University of Natal, many of whom were veterans of previous clashes with Vorster and had helped to set up wage commissions to publicize the gross underpayment of black workers. They also printed newsletters—in which they printed supportive statements by Buthelezi—and more explosive broadsides. In early February police broke up a demonstration of nearly seven thousand workers with tear gas and arrests. When the black municipal workers joined the strike, the mayor told them that they had twenty-four hours to come back to work or be fired; at a huge mass meeting, they decided to return. Nonetheless, more and more workers continued to join; by mid-February the numbers exceeded thirty thousand and affected more than one hundred major white businesses.

Just before Buthelezi left for another trip to the United States, he had been shocked by a decision by the young King Goodwill to address striking workers at Coronation Brick Works. Buthelezi took this as a sign that members of the royal circle wanted the young monarch to develop an independent power base. He immediately brought the king before the KwaZulu Legislative Authority to deny it. As he prepared to go to America, Buthelezi discussed the growing labor unrest with his lieutenant, Barney Dladla, who served as minister of community affairs, lived in Pietermaritzburg, and maintained close contact with the workers. The new wave of strikes caught Buthelezi in the middle of his trip, which had included a prayer breakfast with Richard Nixon. Though Helen Suzman and Colin Eglin, the new leader of the Progressive Party, cabled him in the United States to ask him to return to South Africa immediately, Buthelezi accepted the long-distance assurances from Dladla that the situation was under control. Buthelezi maintained his schedule, but told a press conference in New York City that he hoped the employers would be sympathetic to the workers' appeals.

Nonetheless, a conflict rapidly emerged for Buthelezi. Though Buthelezi and Dladla had agreed in general that the KwaZulu government should not get directly involved in the strike, Dladla made his approval for the workers' wage campaign increasingly public. Dladla said openly that when he heard of the strikes his "heart filled with joy." Striking, he said, "is our only weapon of defeating the whites who are after our energy." Dladla threw his support behind the Trade Union Advisory and Co-ordinating Council, which was attempting to coordinate the effort of the fledgling unions in Natal. He also intervened in the bitter strike at the Alusaf aluminum refinery in Richards Bay, during which white army recruits were brought to keep the critical supplies of aluminum flowing. Dladla made it clear that he supported the demands of the workers for wage increases and told the managers that the KwaZulu government would not permit the industry to recruit scabs from the homelands if the workers' demands were not met. Through such statements Dladla, despite his status as a bantustan official, was rapidly becoming a hero among workers.

Though Dladla's efforts were supported at first by Buthelezi, they produced a hailstorm of complaints from business leaders. The Natal and Federated Chamber of Industries asked the South African government to stop all meddling by bantustan officials in labor disputes. The Trade Union Council of South Africa, an association of segregated unions, joined the call and spurred Buthelezi's suspicions by calling Dladla a "Black power politician . . . trying to find any issue which will gain him the senior position in KwaZulu politics." Buthelezi, when he returned to South Africa, faced a difficult choice. Should he support Dladla and press for the rights of black workers in the Natal region that surrounded and interpenetrated KwaZulu? Or should he pull back to demonstrate that he was a "responsible" black leader who could provide a stable, low-wage environment for South African and foreign investment? The decision, Buthelezi knew, would deeply affect his strategy for KwaZulu and his personal reputation.

Buthelezi's hypersensitivity to political competition had surfaced when he heard rumors that Dladla was considering the establishment of a new labor party in KwaZulu that would challenge Buthelezi with the support of the unions. When Dladla led a march in January 1974 of five thousand workers against a notoriously abusive textile mill and then negotiated on the strikers' behalf, Buthelezi cracked down. First he demanded that his subordinate reaffirm his loyalty, which Dladla did. Then he demanded that Dladla, as proof of his loyalty, give up the post of minister of community affairs and move from Pietermaritzburg to become minister of justice in Nongoma. The choice was untenable: Dladla knew that it would cut him off physically from his base of support and put him in the role of enforcing all KwaZulu (and by extension South African) laws. Dladla maneuvered to try to remain in his old post but, after enormous pressure from Buthelezi, finally resigned from the KwaZulu cabinet in August 1974. From then on, Buthelezi condemned strikes whenever they occurred, because, wrote a sympathetic South African professor, he was "taking into account the effect of strikes on business confidence and willingness to invest." Though Buthelezi continued to threaten the withdrawal of African labor from "industry and commerce if the government did not respond favorably to demands made by homeland leaders," he never again initiated or supported a job action. In years to come, he would bitterly and sometimes violently oppose those who did.

Throughout the early 1970s, even as Buthelezi struggled with the South African government, the labor unions, and rivals such as Dladla, he continued to make frequent travels abroad in an effort to raise his profile and drum up corporate investment; he made three trips to the United States in 1973 alone. On the second one, in June, he went to address the General Synod of the United Church of Christ, staying at Howard Schomer's home in Montclair, New Jersey. Schomer, who had met Buthelezi on an earlier trip to South Africa, had been captivated by his eloquence and conviction. He also agreed with Buthelezi on the question of disinvestment. "When I went out there I believed in the total removal of all foreign investment," Schomer recalled years later. "But as I moved around among the churches and the workers such as the Coloured Labour Party, I found nobody really thinking about this subject. It was not the number one issue for them at all. They cared about detention, pass books, and the vote. . . . They regarded the question of foreign investment as secondary indeed." Schomer's perceptions were reinforced by his strong personal friendships with Buthelezi and with one of the leaders of the Coloured Labour Party, the Reverend Allan Hendrickse. Schomer returned to the United States and "with considerable difficulty" told the four boards of the United Church of Christ that disinvestment was "an American issue," that it was "not what people shout at you when you walk down the street."

As the result of this new perspective, Schomer turned the UCC investment machinery into another proponent of workplace reforms. He encouraged the different branches of the United Church of Christ to vote for and to file dozens of shareholder resolutions asking for corporate disclosure of statistics on hiring, training, and compensation in South Africa. He zigzagged around the nation in the spring to attend annual meetings and pose questions to boards of directors. And he worked diligently behind the scenes to persuade corporate leaders that they had to act.

His confidence in the tactic of private persuasion was bolstered by a number of notable successes. Schomer met repeatedly with Richard Hill, the chairman of the First National Bank of Boston and an active member of the Congregational Church in Marblehead, Massachusetts. Over five years Hill gradually moved the bank from a policy of no restrictions on loans to South Africa to one of "no new loans" to finally closing the loans that had already been made. Schomer also went to see Jim Beré, the chief executive of Borg-Warner, because Beré had been a member of the board of directors of Chicago Theological Seminary when Schomer was president. When Schomer laid out the poor conditions of black workers in the firm's South Africa plant, Beré called in his top industrial relations person and said, "I didn't know a lot of those things, Howard. . . . And as of today we are going to start setting those things right."

Schomer told Beré that the UCC was trying to persuade all the American corporations in South Africa to take a new approach. "Yours is a very recent and relatively small investment," Schomer told Beré. "By far the biggest is Mobil; it's a quarter of the whole. I've got lots of problems there. What should I do about it?" Beré told Schomer to go directly to Rawleigh Warner, the chief executive of Mobil, whom Beré had known in Congregational Sunday school back in Illinois. When Schomer returned to New York he called Warner's office and, to his amazement, instantly obtained an interview. Warner listened carefully to Schomer's pitch and then called in his vice president for corporate affairs, Herbert Schmertz. "Herb, listen to this man," said Warner. Schomer repeated his arguments. At the end, Warner turned to Schmertz and asked him if he had ever been to South Africa. Schmertz said he had not. "Well, why don't you go next week?" said Warner.

To Schomer, Mobil's response seemed exemplary. Not only did Schmertz travel to South Africa, but he then arranged for the entire board of directors of the Mobil Corporation to fly there in late 1972 and hold a set of meetings. In response to the United Church of Christ's request for more information about Mobil's hiring and promotion practices, Mobil released tabulated data on positions held by whites and other races, monthly salary ranges, and benefit plans. Though the document noted that "Mobil's salary and benefit structures in the many countries in which the company has affiliates relate, in varying degree, to local customs and practices," it also affirmed "Mobil's policy worldwide to provide equal pay for equal work in any given area." At the same time, the corporation's directors vigorously opposed withdrawal. "Pulling out of South Africa would not be in the best interest of nonwhites there nor in the interest of our shareholders," stated the Mobil document. "What is most needed . . . is not disinvestment but greater investment."

For Gatsha Buthelezi the disinvestment debate, just like that over the bantustans, offered a means to win more international attention and enhance his position relative to the South African government. In October 1973, while he was struggling with Dladla and turning away from support of the fledgling trade unions, Buthelezi took a decisive step against disinvestment by allowing his name and photograph to be blanketed across American and European newspapers and publications as part of a series of advertisements opposing U.S. corporate withdrawal. The series, which also included the testimonies of Lucas Mangope, the chief of Bophuthatswana, and union official Lucy Mvubelo, was paid for by the Trust Bank of South Africa. "Those who advocate trade sanctions and economic withdrawal to help my people and punish the whites in South Africa may be killing us with kindness," said the quotation appended to a huge picture of Buthelezi's face that appeared in papers across the United States. "What we need is not disengagement, but full foreign participation in South Africa's overall economic development to create more jobs, higher wages, and better training opportunities. I am no apologist for apartheid but a realist who knows that a job may make the difference between living or starving for many black families in South Africa."

Gatsha Buthelezi was not the only person trying to walk a tightrope in South Africa. Throughout the early 1970s John Vorster attempted a similar feat, trying to find a compromise between the commercially prosperous *verligte* wing of the National Party, which wanted to see a slight lessening of the economic strictures of apartheid, and the *verkramptes*, who cared mostly about the maintenance of racial purity. As Vorster felt his way along this delicate political line, he also tried to juggle South Africa's image abroad. To the world he desperately wanted to project the illusion that South Africa was steadily improving, even while he suppressed those who advocated such transformation at home.

To achieve this balance Vorster enacted a policy of "détente," a term borrowed from the efforts of the Nixon administration to lower tensions with the leaders of the Soviet Union. The prime minister sought to improve relations with other African countries—particularly those near South Africa's northern borders, often referred to as the "front line" states—through a judicious alternation of carrot and stick. As carrots, Vorster offered a host of attractive material possibilities, from access to South African resources, technology, and markets to assistance in ending the protracted civil war in Rhodesia. The stick was South Africa's considerable economic power, which could be used coercively, and its crushing military might. South Africa had already shown that it was willing to use its economic and military power to support Ian Smith's attempt to maintain the dominion of 250,000 whites over the remaining ninety-five percent of the Rhodesian population who were Africans. When the chief of the South African Defence Force denied an allegation that four thousand South African troops had crossed into Rhodesia in 1973 to support Ian Smith's troops, few believed him.

Vorster wanted other African countries to soften their criticism of South Africa on the international stage and to reduce their hospitality to South African revolutionaries in exile. He also wanted to improve relations with African countries in order to give greater credence to the policy of separate development. If Vorster could demonstrate that South Africa could deal in a congenial manner with legitimate black states like Zambia and Botswana, then, he thought, the world would see that it could do so with KwaZulu and the Transkei. It would show the world that Vorster was not a racist, but merely the leader of a white country that had been stitched by history into a patchwork of black nations.

Vorster had achieved an early success through the exchange of diplomats and a state visit from the president of Malawi, but he wanted something more: the public support of some of his most visible critics, men like Kenneth Kaunda of Zambia. The Organization for African Unity had continued to attack South Africa, though the ferocity of the members' language seemed to increase in inverse proportion to their effectiveness. Kaunda had tried to combine word and deed. He had made an attack on racism in southern Africa a cornerstone of almost every speech while providing exiled nationalist leaders from both South Africa and Rhodesia refuge and support.

Vorster, determined to advance his policy of détente, instructed one of his most trusted emissaries, Roelof "Pik" Botha, to make secret overtures to the governments of other African countries. Pik Botha, who was not related to Defence Minister P. W. Botha, was South Africa's ambassador to the United Nations and would soon become ambassador to the United States. Vorster backed Botha's efforts with statements in parliament, in which he continuously professed South Africa's interest in improving relations with its neighbors. He also went far out of his way to encourage the international perception that South Africa eventually would eliminate the irritants of petty apartheid. When United Nations General Secretary Kurt Waldheim asked if he could come to South Africa in 1973 to open a dialogue on black-white relations, Vorster responded favorably.

At the same time, Vorster attempted to circumvent the tight international sports boycotts by holding a widely publicized "multinational" competition inside South Africa. This effort backfired when a prominent black American track and field coach, Stan Wright of Sacramento State College, returned from eight days in South Africa and denounced the effort as "a farce." Noting that the teams had been chosen according to race rather than merit and that the seating in the stadium had been segregated, Wright told the *New York Times* that in private conversations

South African officials had been candid about their intent. "The minister of sport admitted to me that multi-racial and multi-national are political terms," he said. "Multi-racial is used when you are talking to the liberals and want to stimulate them, and multi-national is used when you are talking to the conservatives whom you don't want to arouse."

Vorster also sent signals to the Nixon administration that were readily interpreted as evidence of his commitment to reform and of the success of the NSSM 39 strategy of communication. When James Baker became the first black American foreign service officer to be sent to South Africa, Vorster ignored the protests of the extreme right and did not object. He also reversed a long-standing policy and permitted several undersecretaries from his government to attend the interracial Fourth of July reception held at the American embassy in 1973. He encouraged American dignitaries, such as Norman Vincent Peale, to visit South Africa and was pleased when they refused to criticize South Africa to the press. Despite these efforts, though, American blacks still ran into trouble. Charles Diggs was repeatedly denied his visa requests; American editor and diplomat Richard Saunders and his wife were thrown out of a nightclub in Durban; and Eartha Kitt, who was performing before segregated audiences throughout South Africa, was forced by an Indian attendant in a Durban amusement park to get out of a roller-coaster car reserved for whites.

While Vorster was trying to project a conciliatory image abroad, he cracked down hard at home. The Schlebusch Commission, which had been appointed by Vorster to explore the origins of domestic unrest, issued its report in February 1973, attacking the students of NUSAS as subversives acting in support of Communism. "It was not relevant whether the persons concerned were Communists," the report commented, "what had to be considered objectively was whether their actions further the aims of Communism." On February 27, Vorster announced that eight leaders of NUSAS had been banned. For five years their movement would be restricted; they were barred from further study; they could not write or appear in public; they could meet with only one person at a time. Helen Suzman was the only person to denounce the action in parliament.

Vorster dealt even more harshly with those of other races. In early March he issued banning orders against Stephen Biko, Barney Pityana, Saths Cooper, and five other leaders of SASO or the black consciousness coordinating group known as the Black People's Convention. Later in the year he banned the leading black theologian, Manas Buthelezi (no relation to Gatsha), bringing the total number of banned persons to twenty-nine whites and one hundred seventy-two blacks. Hundreds more were harassed, detained, assaulted, and deported back to the reserves. Some, through the work of the Security Police, met fates even more grim. O. R. Tiro, the student who had used his graduation speech at Turfloop to object to Bantu education, had been forced to flee the country. While living in exile in Botswana, he received a package from Geneva. The second he opened it, a bomb blew him to pieces.

The wave of strikes in 1973 brought renewed international and domestic attention to the issue of African wages and unions. In 1973 the *Guardian,* a British newspaper, reported that many of the striking workers in Natal had been employed by British firms who had paid them less than ten dollars a week even though the official starvation level for the area had been calculated at thirty dollars. Indignation shot through church groups, members of parliament, and trade unions in England, and the executives in the companies in question instantly ordered a reexamination. In South Africa, as academic studies of payment schedules in various parts of the country documented that eighty percent of all black workers were receiving less than the official minimum subsistence level, both industrial and government administrators squirmed. The national wage board, which had ignored the problem for years, suddenly conducted a review of salary structures in more than thirty industrial categories and recommended salary increases of thirty to fifty percent in almost all of them. Even such apparently substantial increases, however, did not bring many African workers above the poverty line, let alone to parity with whites.

The gold mining industry, in which Oppenheimer's Anglo-American Corporation was the largest employer, with nearly 118,000 African workers, provides an instructive example of the kinds of changes that were taking place. As gold prices rose, profits at the mines skyrocketed to more than sixty percent of gross revenues. Even after giving half of their net income to the state, the mine companies were still making thirty percent a year. In 1971, the average cash earnings of an African gold miner consisted of 21 rand a month (about $112 in 1994 dollars), compared to 391 rand for the average white ($2,100). In addition to cash earnings, the Chamber of Mines pointed out, African miners received other benefits, including a concrete bed in a hostel, food, and rudimentary health coverage. The quality of the food and the medical care can be deduced from the chamber's calculations that the cost for both benefits for each worker was seventy-seven rand a year, or twenty-three cents a day.

In 1973 the Chamber of Mines, under public and private pressure, increased wages a second time, so that average African pay was now twenty-five percent higher than in 1971. This sounded impressive, though the average inflation rate of nearly nine percent lowered the true total value of the raises to less than seven percent. Moreover, the Chamber of Mines felt that to avoid a confrontation with the white unions, any raises to Africans had to coincide with raises to white workers. The seven thousand white artisans who worked in the gold mines, for example, each received an increase of more than one hundred rand a month, an increment equal to the total monthly earnings of five Africans. As a result, according to the South African Institute of Race Relations, "the 1973 wage bill for Africans, who constitute about 90% of the labor force in the gold and coal mining industry, was increased by roughly the same amount as that of the white force," which had been about 5%. The SAIRR report also noted that even if all of the other "benefits" were added to the cash wages, it would bring the compensation just barely in line with the lowest *cash* wages given to African workers in other sectors of the economy, with the notorious exception of agriculture.

Despite the wage increases, which the South African government trumpeted to the rest of the world as an example of dramatic improvement, tension at the mines over wages continued to build. On September 11, at Anglo-American's Western Deep Levels Mine at Carletonville, a large crowd of workers gathered to protest their conditions. When the manager of the compound could no longer control the group with his black security force, he called in the white police. When they arrived, the mob pelted them with rocks and brandished sticks. During the confrontation, some of the protesters ransacked the company beer hall and kitchen and, according to the official reports, intimidated and abused other workers. The police attempted a baton charge and fired a round of tear gas, but the workers refused to withdraw. The police then opened fire with live ammunition, slaying twelve miners and injuring dozens more.

Reactions around the country and around the world were swift and sharp. Buthelezi commented that the shootings were an indication that "a black life is regarded as very cheap in South Africa." Helen Suzman condemned the government for refusing to train the police in proper riot control methods. In the United States, Timothy Smith wrote a pamphlet describing Carletonville as "a new Sharpeville," though the incident received only a tiny fraction of the international press coverage of the events thirteen years before. Pressure also intensified on Harry Oppenheimer. The morning after the incident, twelve students from the University of the Witswatersrand forced their way into Anglo-American's headquarters to demand a full judicial inquiry. Though Oppenheimer readily agreed, the English-speaking students were speedily turning against him. At a mass meeting at the University of Cape Town a large group of students called on Oppenheimer to resign his ceremonial role as chancellor of the university unless he immediately increased African wages and recognized genuine unions.

The event produced a brief display of public soul-searching by the mining authorities and by the government. The chairman of the Western Deep Levels Mine acknowledged that "we may have made a mistake in our wage structuring . . . maybe in the African mind we have done them an injustice." The prime minister told a gathering of National Party supporters that he deplored the loss of life and extended his sympathy to the next of kin. The violence, he insisted disingenuously, had been the fault of the miners. It was "not a striker's demonstration but a looting mob out to destroy life and property with dangerous and murderous weapons," he said. This echoed the statement by the minister of police. "In an effort to protect the property and other black workers from death and serious injury and in protection of their own lives," he said, "they were forced to fire."

Such events, combined with the numerous, scattered, and uncontrollable strikes that had rocked Natal and spread to other sectors of the country, generated much broader support for African trade unions. "The strikes badly frightened management," said one foreign diplomat, "and one reason was that they had no one to talk to." South African business leaders began conferring among themselves and moving toward the consensus that some structure was better than none. The business leaders were also losing their fear of the power of the white unions to object, and they talked far more openly about the need to move African, Coloured, and Asian workers into positions that had been reserved for whites.

Vorster seemed to agree, signaling that he would not necessarily force companies to maintain a strict color bar. In a speech before the South African Motor Industries Federation on October 6, 1973, less than a month after the Carletonville shootings, Vorster told the auto executives that "there is nothing in government policy to prevent the employers, with the cooperation of trade unions"—a reference to the white unions—"from taking the necessary steps to bring about improvement in the productive use of nonwhite labor." Vorster's willingness to make incremental concessions pleased Helen Suzman and the members of the Progressive Party, who believed that they were now in a position to make some significant political advances. The evidence around them seemed abundant. The United Party was rapidly collapsing under the weight of its contradictions. In addition to Harry Oppenheimer's traditional support, reforms were now being promoted by other business leaders, including a few Afrikaners. At a speech during a dinner to celebrate her twenty-first year in Parliament, Suzman described the change in mood. "Perhaps the most heartening thing of all is to observe that many of the things that we Progs have been proposing over and over again during all these years—the need for a Federal system, for shared power, for compulsory and free education for all our children, for an end to the migratory labor system, for collective bargaining rights for Africans—these things are no longer considered the wild ravings of political extremists."

Suzman's reference to the "Federal system" was important, for it was one of the points that allowed her to extend her personal friendships with several of the bantustan leaders into a political alliance. For some time, Buthelezi, Matanzima, and Mangope (who was the principal speaker at Suzman's anniversary party) had been discussing the idea of a federation. To them, the creation of South African states (in the American sense) linked through some sort of federal agreement seemed to be a fine compromise between the impossibility of a single unitary country under white (or black) rule and the falsity of the separate "nations" of grand apartheid. Buthelezi was particularly devoted to the idea and discussed it with the other homeland leaders at a summit in the Transkei in October 1973. Buthelezi also introduced the concept into a historic agreement which he signed with a young and dynamic member of the United Party, Harry Schwartz, who soon would break away from his affiliation to start a new organization, the Reform Party. The agreement, known as the Mahlabatini Declaration, also stated that change in South Africa must be brought about peacefully and through consultation and that any future arrangement must provide opportunity to all peoples for material and educational advancement. It was hailed by the English-speaking press as a breakthrough in race relations.

Buthelezi's strategy—to pull the homeland leaders together and present Vorster with a set of unified demands—was, however, beginning to fray. Though Buthelezi insisted that he would never legitimize separate development by accepting full "independence" for KwaZulu and wanted the others to do the same, Matanzima was beginning to edge away. Buthelezi's high hopes for moving forward with Vorster were dashed when a highly publicized meeting of the prime minister with all eight of the bantustan leaders in March 1974 came to nothing. Buthelezi fretted to reporters that separate development had come to an impasse and encouraged Vorster to "try a little détente at home."

Vorster may have been especially cautious at this meeting because he had called a general election to take place in seven weeks. On April 24, 1974, white South Africans used their ballots to deliver a mixed message: the National Party increased its membership in parliament by five members (mostly new spots because of population growth) and effectively prevented the Herstigte Party from gaining a single seat; the United Party membership dropped by six to forty-one, signaling that it was in its last stages of decline; and, most surprisingly, the Progressives gained six new seats. Colin Eglin had even defeated David Graaff, the son of the United Party leader, in a hotly contested race in Sea Point, near Cape Town. Helen Suzman, after thirteen years alone in parliament, exulted at the thought of serving with six dynamic colleagues. Together, she hoped, they could work with the bantustan leaders to help speed the drive for reform.

Though John Vorster's attempts to win acceptance for separate development rested on the premise that the South African economy would continue to grow at a vigorous rate, the grounds for that assumption were rapidly eroding. By the mid-1970s the international monetary and trade conditions that had favored South Africa for more than a decade turned decidedly negative. The world economic recession had endured longer than anyone had predicted, slicing South Africa's export earnings, slowing foreign investment, and restricting the country's annual rate of growth to 2.2 percent. In previous recessions the price of gold—the traditional refuge of nervous investors—had risen, giving a countercyclical boost to the South African economy. This time, however, several events combined to depress it. In early 1975 the directors of the International Monetary Fund (IMF) removed gold as the standard for world currencies, replacing it with an artificial medium of exchange known as the special drawing right (SDR). The IMF and the United States then sold some of their reserve gold on the open market. Soon afterward the Soviet Union, needing hard currency to pay for its immense purchases of Western grain, did the same. As truckloads of bullion went on sale, the price of South Africa's recently mined supply dropped. The balloon that had lifted the South African economy for nearly fifteen years finally burst, and from then on the economy fitfully sank.

As in most countries, it would take the South African government a long time to realize what had happened. For years officials had interpreted South Africa's prosperity as evidence of their wisdom and virtue. With military problems brewing on their borders, they continued to pour money into weaponry. Over two years, government expenditures on security and defense doubled, from 597 million rand in 1973 to 1,195 million in 1975. Nor was the economy a model of competitiveness, since the government's commitment to enhancing the economic clout of Afrikaners had prompted it to intervene in almost every sector. By the 1970s the central government was paying for the police and the military; white education from primary to graduate school; the major proportion of health care, pensions, and medical research; the postal and telecommunications networks; the roads and highways; the railways and harbors; all broadcasting; and the generation and transmission of electrical power. In addition, the government dominated or monopolized the production of iron, steel, chemicals, weapons, aircraft, fertilizers, and enriched uranium. By 1975 the government accounted for one-third of the gross domestic product of South Africa. As government spending continued to rise while productivity and real incomes stagnated, the country experienced a painful dose of high inflation—more than seventeen percent—robbing workers of the wage gains they had secured and provoking renewed questioning of the government's wisdom in the country's business circles.

The government's vigor in foreign affairs, combined with the turbulence inside the country, sparked speculation that Vorster would eventually match his international initiatives with comparable domestic reforms. In public, Vorster flatly denied it. He had "made no promises for changes in domestic policy," he said repeatedly, and was "not going to change it because our critics here and elsewhere demand it." Nonetheless, many foreign journalists, eager to spot a trend, continued to predict that South Africa was on the verge of fundamental change. Articles with suggestive headlines appeared regularly in the *New York Times:* "South Africa's Course in Racism Less Certain" (1973), "In South Africa, Tides of Change" (1974), "Vorster Balancing Hints of South African Change with Assurances" (1975). One piece, entitled "Mr. Vorster's Detente," was based on a background interview by a member of the editorial staff of the *New York Times* with the prime minister himself. Vorster, the author predicted, would not only pursue peace in Rhodesia and eventually disengage from Namibia, but would gradually "dismantle the symbols and trappings of apartheid and eliminate some of the glaring practices of racial discrimination—while carefully covering his tracks and making occasional bellicose pronouncements aimed at pacifying the restless *verkrampte* or hardline faction of his Nationalist *[sic]* Party."

For Vorster, the easiest way to buy more time for apartheid was to hint continually at its demise. He knew he could count on a fusion of Western reflexes—facile optimism, commercial self-interest, anti-Communist machismo, and subconscious racism—to award him the benefit of the doubt. But he also knew that the benefit was not eternal. Every promise that change was forthcoming had some sort of half-life and waned in strength with the passage of time. There were only two ways to forestall an eventual expiration. The first was to dribble the reforms out slowly, emphasizing image over substance, heralding even the most minor one as a dramatic improvement. The second was to argue that because external conditions had changed, a new strategy, which deserved a new benefit of the doubt and a new time limit, was needed.

Vorster adeptly used both of these mechanisms. He pressed forward aggressively with the implementation of separate development, the forced relocation of black communities, and the eviction and deportation of urban families. At the same time, he made an occasional concession, such as permitting persons of different races to attend performances at the Nico Malan theater in Cape Town or allowing black nannies to visit white swimming pools (but not swim in them) while caring for their white charges. When both companies and police were forced by necessity to hire black workers to fill spots for which they could not find whites, Vorster painted this as a virtue. When Bram Fischer, Nelson Mandela's imprisoned lawyer, was found to have terminal cancer and had only a few weeks to live, Vorster released him to die at home.

Many business leaders pointed to these developments as significant improvements. A survey in mid-1974 of executives of American companies in South Africa found that only two percent opposed Vorster's version of separate development. Vorster's opponents, however, were not sanguine. Helen Suzman commented that despite the foreign policy initiatives, Vorster's government "adheres grimly to its policy of retaining all meaningful political power in the hands of the Republic's four million white inhabitants. . . . A vote in a homeland several hundred miles away is about as much use to an urbanized black man permanently residing in Johannesburg," she wrote, "as a vote in County Cork would be to an Irishman living in New York."

Gatsha Buthelezi was not fooled either. His efforts to mobilize the other bantustan leaders and pressure Vorster to live up to the promises of separate development had fared poorly. By mid-1975 he had concluded that the only way he could press his case was to amass power that would reach beyond the flimsy parliamentary structures of the KwaZulu Legislative Assembly, mobilize the support of the millions of Zulus in urban and rural areas around the country, and capture the resurgent interest in African culture that had been stimulated by Black Consciousness. His idea was to reestablish an organization that had existed briefly under King Solomon known as Inkatha Ka Zulu as a "national cultural liberation movement," designed to build pride in Zulu tradition. The name itself was a direct appeal to Zulu heritage: the *inkatha* had been a circular ceremonial ring, about as thick as an arm and as wide as a human body, woven of grass and smeared with dust that had been poured over the king. Wrapped in the skin of a python, normally hidden from all but a few courtiers, the inkatha was brought forth only for special occasions. At his coronation, the king stood in the center of the inkatha, while the praise poets sang songs. When the king was ill, the doctors seated him on the inkatha while they treated him. The inkatha was thus a potent symbol of supernatural power, national unity, and royal authority.

The decision to form Inkatha was a characteristically shrewd move by Buthelezi. The South African government could hardly object to an organization that affirmed the importance of ethnic identity; ANC leaders informed Buthelezi through intermediaries that they approved of the creation of what they thought would be a "mass democratic organization"; and the formation of Inkatha would dramatically consolidate his personal power and cut off incipient rivals at the local level. The researchers of the South African Institute of Race Relations, in their description of the structure of Inkatha, clarified this last point. "The aim [of *Inkatha*] was stated to be to promote 'African democracy,' considered to be more suited to the Zulu way of life than Western-type democracy," they wrote in the 1975 annual survey. Though "membership in Inkatha would be open to all Zulus," they continued, "there would only be one political party. Paid-up members would not be precluded from expressing disagreement with courses of action discussed at meetings, decisions being made on the basis of consensus. Members would, however, have to refrain from making public criticism of the movement, its actions, or activities of members in connection with the affairs of the organization."

The intimate connections that Buthelezi sought to forge among the mass movement, the KwaZulu Legislative Assembly, and his personal control can be seen from the requirements built into Inkatha's constitution. Only members of Inkatha would be eligible for election to the Legislative Assembly or to local governing bodies. Inkatha's president would also be the chief minister of KwaZulu. Since the KwaZulu constitution required, in addition, that the chief minister be a hereditary chief, the number of legally eligible rivals for Buthelezi's job was cut to a tiny number. Finally, Buthelezi ensured that potential rivals would find it impossible to build a base in some regional wing of Inkatha by stipulating that "no branch of the movement would be recognized unless it had been formally launched by a member of the central committee on the instructions of the president."

In essence, Buthelezi was doing what had already been done by many African leaders in other countries on the continent: justifying the seizure and retention of centralized personal power by appealing to the necessities of national liberation and the uniqueness of African culture. Since the decolonialization of Africa, a dozen states had been structured as one-party "democracies." The arrangement had a surprising number of defenders: from Marxists who saw it as a prologue to the dictatorship of the proletariat, to liberals whose willingness to condemn dictatorship was hampered by gauzy fantasies about cooperation and community, to

outright racists who saw the phenomenon as proof of African incompetence and thus a justification for continued white supremacy. For
Buthelezi, the centralization of control not only meant the consolidation
of power but also the blurring, in his mind, of the characteristics of the
state with his individual identity. As it has around the world, such a
blurring encouraged the spread of a cult of personality. In years to
come, persons visiting KwaZulu's diminutive capital of Ulundi would
arrive at Prince Mangosuthu Buthelezi Airport and drive along Prince
Mangosuthu Buthelezi Street to reach the local Holiday Inn. Inside,
near the registration desk, the visitor would encounter two large photographs: one of King Goodwill and the other of Prince Mangosuthu
Buthelezi, both in full traditional Zulu regalia. As one strolled past the
Prince Mangosuthu Buthelezi meeting room in the hotel, one encountered a plaque which declared that the hotel had been opened in a
special ceremony by Prince Mangosuthu Buthelezi. And so it went, in
virtually every corner of the town. In such an environment, it was perhaps not surprising that Prince Mangosuthu Buthelezi interpreted criticism of his policies as an attack on his person.

When Inkatha was created, Buthelezi was so determined to make
certain that he would remain unchallenged in KwaZulu—whether by
legitimate opponents or Pretorian stooges—that he wrote to the central
government to ask for its cooperation in the prohibition of all political
parties, with the exception of Inkatha. The director of the Department
of Bantu Administration, eager to retain some mechanism to control
Buthelezi's power, was not enthusiastic. The exchange between the two
men revealed an exquisite irony. Gatsha Buthelezi, the man welcomed
in every Western capital as South Africa's leading advocate of democracy, was demanding the right to create a one-party state controlled
entirely by himself. And it was the South African bureaucrat, the guardian and administrator of the fiercely antidemocratic policy of separate
development, who said no.

NINE

The Opening of New Fronts (1974–1976)

Resistance to Soviet expansion by military means must be a fundamental element of U.S. foreign policy. There must be no question in Angola or elsewhere in the world of American resolve in this regard. The failure of the United States to take a stand would inevitably lead our friends and supporters to conclusions about our steadfastness and resolve.
—GERALD R. FORD

THOUGH JOHN VORSTER described the South African election of April 1974 as heralding a "new era," the era actually lasted less than twenty-four hours. The event that would most dramatically affect South Africa's future did not take place inside its borders, or anywhere in southern Africa, but half a world away. It dislodged whatever fragile commitments Vorster had made to reform and pushed South Africa into another decade of repression and militarism. It also undercut the most basic premise of American foreign policy toward southern Africa—that "the whites were here to stay"—leaving it so awash in contradiction that the U.S. eventually found itself cooperating in one of apartheid's border wars.

It began with a song. Shortly after midnight on April 25, 1974, while the ballots in South Africa were still being counted, a Portuguese radio station near Lisbon began playing "Grandola," a popular anthem of protest chosen as the signal for the beginning of a military coup. As the chords resonated across Portugal, young officers at bases across the country arrested their superiors, roused the troops from their barracks, and led them along darkened roads toward the government's seat of power. The act was one of desperation, a response to problems that had been growing unabatedly for years. Though the fascist head of state Antonio Salazar had been replaced in 1968 by the more moderate professor Marcel Caetano, who had tried to introduce market reforms and to support the growth of capitalism, Caetano's caution had made it difficult for him to lead a government mired in the lethargy of repression. He had also refused to abandon the fantasy that Portugal's African colonies were an integral part of the Portuguese "nation." For this he and Portugal paid a great price: during the 1960s, more than one million Portuguese—nearly eleven percent of the country's population—had emigrated, leaving behind a workforce of 3.5 million and a population of 8.6 million. Most of those who left were young men between age eighteen and thirty-five who were trying to avoid the draft and find better wages in northern Europe. By the early 1970s the second largest Portuguese city, after Lisbon, was Paris.

Despite such indications, Caetano's government pressed on, spending four hundred million dollars a year, nearly half its entire budget, on the military. The draft had scooped up 140,000 men, giving Portugal one of the highest percentages of population under arms in the world. Many of them had been sent to three distant colonies, Mozambique, Angola, and Guinea-Bissau, where for more than a decade they had tried without success to suppress the nationalist rebels. In Angola the Portuguese faced the challenge of fighting three separate nationalist groups, each with its own international patrons. The three thousand troops of the Popular Movement for the Liberation of Angola (MPLA) received weapons and support from the Soviet Union, Cuba, Algeria, and Yugoslavia. The Front for the Liberation of Angola (FNLA) was kept afloat through the support of Mobutu Sese Seko of Zaire (formerly the Congo) and a community of several hundred thousand refugees. Jonas Savimbi, leader of the National Union for the Total Independence of Angola (UNITA), had dug himself into a region in central and southern Angola.

The rebel forces were not only gnawing at Portugal's military strength but also attacking its commitment to colonial rule in the international arena. In June 1971 the leaders of the national liberation movement in Mozambique, known as FRELIMO, pulled off a public relations coup when they received an audience and sympathetic hearing from Pope Paul VI. NATO representatives from Denmark, Holland, and Norway relentlessly attacked Portugal's heavy-handedness in Africa. The West German government announced a ban on arms sales to the Portuguese. Even Marcel Caetano's visit to London to celebrate the six-hundredth anniversary of the Anglo-Portuguese treaty—the oldest continuous pact between any two nations—was marked by protests triggered by reports of a Portuguese massacre of unarmed civilians in northern Mozambique.

In the face of these protests, the Portuguese appealed to the United States for support, pointing to the flow of Eastern bloc weapons into the colonies. Though Nixon and Kissinger were generally sympathetic, Democrats in the Senate kept pressure on the White House to reduce American commitments to Portugal. Caetano tried, as had his predecessor, to threaten the United States government with the withdrawal of the use of the Azores, but in the era of long-distance air transport, this was a much less effective point of leverage than in the past.

Thus, by early 1974, discontent within Portugal's military command was approaching the boiling point. The professional officer corps, smarting from real and imagined indignities, had begun to meet secretly to discuss their grievances. In February, General Antonio de Spinola, the mentor of many of the officers, openly challenged his superiors by publishing a slim volume entitled *Portugal and the Future.* Spinola, a heavily decorated and immensely popular leader and the son of one of Salazar's closest advisers, had tried privately to move the government toward a negotiated settlement with the African nationalist rebels. Having been rebuffed, he repeated his arguments in print. He said that the government should admit that the wars in Africa could not be won through military means and should negotiate a political settlement and referendum in the colonies. He predicted that, given the choice, the populations would choose to remain within Portugal. Though the book was moderate in tone, it electrified the country, selling fifty thousand copies in a matter of days. The prime minister read it until the early hours of the morning and instantly realized that he was facing a possible coup d'état. Trying to head it off, he fired Spinola, dispersed his protégés throughout the country, and extracted an oath of loyalty from the top one hundred generals and admirals. A few weeks later, the army suppressed a spontaneous mutiny by the Fifth Infantry Regiment. Caetano and his advisers told themselves they had survived the worst.

They were wrong. Unbeknownst to them, a group of Spinola loyalists had continued to plot and had already drafted a political program calling for the democratization of Portugal and the decolonialization of the African territories. A few hours after "Grandola" had played on the radio waves, converging regiments surrounded the capital city and encircled the barracks to which Caetano had fled for refuge. That evening, after Caetano capitulated and fled into exile, Spinola entered the capital to public acclaim. At a press conference, the general declared that he was the head of a "junta of national salvation" and promised respect for all of Portugal's international treaties and free elections to the national assembly. Within a few days, the new government had arrested the former security police, lifted the restrictions on the press, and released the country's political prisoners.

The coup caught many of Portugal's former allies by surprise; just a few days before, the South African Broadcasting Corporation had described South Africa and Portugal as the two most stable governments in the world. This was a populist coup committed to what many saw as a leftist agenda. Kissinger, suddenly fearful that socialists and Communists would find a way to seize control of a strategically important country, took new interest in Portugal. As the new Portuguese government made good on its pledge and began negotiating a transfer of power with the rebel groups in all of its colonies, Kissinger realized that two of the biggest pieces of the "white redoubt"—Angola and Mozambique—would shift from white to black control.

No one feared the implications of this more keenly than John Vorster, who watched in astonishment as two bulwarks of white supremacy, one bordering South Africa and the other Namibia, collapsed overnight. Instead of making common cause with other Europeans against black Communists, Vorster realized that South Africa and Rhodesia would now face a host of antagonistic countries, including several whose heads of state had only recently been hunted as terrorists. Several weeks after the Portuguese coup, Rhodesian Prime Minister Ian Smith and his top aides, fearing that Mozambique might cut the rail lines to their land-locked nation, flew to Pretoria to ask Vorster for additional help. Vorster privately promised assistance but remained publicly cautious. South Africa depended on the ports and rail lines in Mozambique to ship goods abroad, on the hundreds of thousands of mine workers who labored in the gold mines, and on power from the massive Cabora Bossa hydroelectric dam. When Marcelino dos Cantos of FRELIMO promised that an independent Mozambique would apply all UN sanctions against "racist, fascist, colonialist" South Africa, his words sent a tremor through Vorster's government.

Looking for some room to maneuver, Vorster tried to persuade the world that South Africa was committed to external peace. In October 1974 he told the South African Senate he would do all he could to promote stability in other African countries through economic means, pledging not to intervene in their affairs and urging them not to meddle in his, and he volunteered to sign a nonaggression pact with any African state. Most surprising, he signaled that he would like to help resolve the Rhodesian civil war that had sparked and flared with savage intensity for more than ten years. He also intimated that change in South Africa would not tarry; the world would be surprised, he said, by the developments in South Africa over the following six months. The next day, the South African ambassador to the United Nations, Pik Botha, facing a threat that South Africa would be expelled from the international body, reiterated Vorster's points. He admitted that South Africa had discriminatory laws and practices and that "unsavory and reprehensible incidents" between whites and blacks did occur. Despite this, he insisted, "my government does not condone discrimination purely on the grounds of race or colour. Discrimination based solely on the colour of a man's skin cannot be defended. And we shall do everything in our power to move away from discrimination based on race and colour." As commentators noted, Botha's seemingly bold statement was undercut by his use of the words *purely* and *solely;* these allowed him, in the same manner as Verwoerd, to retain the position that segregation in South Africa had nothing to do with race but with nationality and culture. Botha concluded with an appeal to the other African countries for understanding. "We have not waged a war against black Africa or against anyone," he said. "We were, in fact, the first African nationalists. . . . Being an African country, we understand African aspirations. We have stolen land from nobody. We have conquered no people. We threaten no one. We have absolutely no designs of aggrandizement."

Vorster's "six months" speech and Botha's pleas did little to dissuade the representatives of the African countries. For them, the destruction of "racism and colonialism" in South Africa had become a superordinate goal that allowed them to conceal some of the fractures in their own ranks and to avoid examining their own monsters, such as Idi Amin of Uganda. Two weeks after Botha's speech the African countries, over the objections of the United States, which insisted that it was a terrible precedent, pushed through a resolution expelling South Africa from the General Assembly. Not long afterward, the Labour government in Great Britain announced that it was canceling its agreement with South Africa over the use of the Simonstown base.

Despite these setbacks, Vorster persisted in his overtures to other African countries. He flew secretly to meet with President William Tolbert of Liberia in early 1975, and then with Félix Houphouet-Boigny of the Ivory Coast. Finally, in his most important gesture, he and Kenneth Kaunda brought the antagonists in the Rhodesian conflict together on August 25, 1975, for a full day of talks inside a train parked on a bridge over the Zambezi River near Victoria Falls. Though the negotiations did not lead to a resolution, they were hailed as an example of the success of Vorster's foreign policy.

In the year after the coup in Lisbon, the Portuguese junta ceased all military operations in Africa, released thousands of political prisoners, and announced that power would be handed over to provisional governments in its colonies. In Mozambique and Guinea-Bissau this posed no problem, for in each of these countries there was only one nationalist force; Angola, with three warring factions, presented a dilemma. The Portuguese government announced it would recognize the FNLA, the MPLA, and UNITA as political parties as soon as they stopped fighting each other. For a short time, they did. During the spring of 1975, they struggled to find common ground, but for several reasons peace was elusive. Ethnic differences kept the sides apart: the MPLA drew its principal support from Luanda's urban intellectuals and among the Kimbundu/Mbundu peoples; the FNLA from the Kikongo/Bakongo of northern Angola; and UNITA from the Ovimbundu of the central and southern regions. Added to those differences was mistrust by the excluded third party whenever the other two made a deal, as the MPLA and the FNLA did in 1972, or as UNITA and the FNLA did in 1974. With no accord, each nationalist group had to continue to scramble for financial and military support in order to increase its internal leverage. This search led inevitably to the superpowers, to whom the civil war inside Angola appeared as a minor regional clash in the global cold war.

At the center of the free-for-all was Jonas Savimbi, a charismatic forty-year-old Angolan with a graduate degree in political science from the University of Lausanne. Savimbi had once been a member of the MPLA and later the FNLA, before founding UNITA. In preparation for his life as a guerrilla leader Savimbi had studied the works of Mao Zedong and debated Che Guevera on the best strategies for rural war. In 1966 Savimbi spent six months in China receiving military training and returned to Angola with a fighting force consisting of eleven men and one pistol. For eight years he steadily built up his force, recruiting peasants, traveling rapidly on foot, and securing weapons through an occasional ambush of Portuguese troops.

The Portuguese coup caught Savimbi by surprise. With the Chinese supplying the FNLA through Zaire, and the Soviets shipping directly to the MPLA, Savimbi at first had no one to turn to. He tried first to align himself with his former enemies, the Portuguese military, by negotiating a truce with them within weeks of the coup. Soon afterward the MPLA and FNLA published letters which, they said, showed that Savimbi had asked the Portuguese not only for peace but also for weapons and other assistance in return for UNITA's promise to attack the MPLA and FNLA. Though Savimbi declared that the letters were forgeries, they ended his flirtation with the Portuguese and forced him to look elsewhere. He found an unlikely ally in Kenneth Kaunda of Zambia, who had been disturbed by the rapid influx of Soviet weapons and repulsed by the factional fighting of the MPLA, some of which had taken place inside Zambia. When he learned that some of the MPLA leaders finished off their captured rivals by slowly cracking their skulls in wooden frames, a disgusted Kaunda finally agreed to meet with Savimbi and to press for a negotiated settlement.

For a few months it seemed as though Savimbi and Kaunda's attempts would work. Then, in March 1975, FNLA and MPLA forces again attacked each other, setting off a new round of civil war. As bloody reprisals rippled across the Angolan countryside, in April matters grew more complicated and strange. Kaunda used a state visit to Washington, D.C., to urge President Gerald Ford and Secretary of State Henry Kissinger to provide covert military support to the nominally Marxist UNITA and the FNLA to counterbalance the growing power of the MPLA. In June the fighting spread when MPLA troops attacked and killed a large group of UNITA recruits. In July MPLA troops gunned down hundreds of UNITA supporters after they had been given safe passage across a river near the town of Dondo.

Within two weeks of the massacre, U.S. weapons and supplies began flowing to UNITA under the supervision of CIA officer John Stockwell, who had recently been transferred from his post in Saigon and was given responsibility for a new Angola task force. Stockwell reported to Kissinger and the members of the "40 Committee," the subsidiary of the National Security Council that oversaw covert actions and had approved aid for the factions opposing the MPLA on July 17. The CIA had already expended most of its covert funds for the year and Kissinger doubted that Congress would approve another hundred million dollars for a foreign military adventure so soon after the collapse of Vietnam. Still, Congress had supported the president's decision to use military force in May to recapture the U.S.S. *Mayagüez* off the coast of Cambodia; perhaps the legislators would be willing, if the news leaked out, to swallow this as well.

Not everyone agreed on the wisdom of the policy. One of the most vigorous opponents was the new assistant secretary of state for African affairs, Nathaniel Davis. Though Davis, a career diplomat, had only recently been confirmed to the post over the objections of Charles Diggs and the members of the Congressional Black Caucus, as well as the Organization for African Unity, he quickly surprised his detractors by arguing that the FNLA and UNITA would not be effective and that the United States should not align itself with South Africa's foreign policy. The United States should instead launch a multinational effort, Davis told Kissinger, to find a diplomatic solution in Angola. Kissinger, relying on CIA intelligence that FNLA forces were strong enough to overcome the MPLA and capture Luanda, overruled Davis and decided that UNITA and the FNLA should receive fourteen million dollars in military supplies. Davis quietly resigned after only five months at his post. It was, wrote one analyst, "the first high level resignation-in-protest in the

State Department in nearly two decades." To keep Davis's objections quiet, Kissinger sent him off to serve as the ambassador to Switzerland.

As head of the Angola task force, John Stockwell had been instructed to use the CIA money to "prevent an easy victory" by the MPLA. By early August, Stockwell had ensured that Savimbi had received sufficient weapons to enter the civil war. The dramatic increase in arms shipments and in fighting were all geared toward the same goal: November 11, 1975, the date on which the Portuguese had promised to grant the formal independence of Angola. The leaders of each warring group wanted to seize enough land, command enough weapons and troops, and do enough damage to their opponents so that they could declare themselves the official government of Angola. By the middle of August, the MPLA controlled twelve of Angola's fifteen provinces. The United States responded by authorizing another ten million dollars in rifles, rocket launchers, and vehicles and by sending eighty-three CIA officers to support the effort throughout southern Africa. In late September, the MPLA received a new burst of support when a thousand well-trained and rested Cuban infantry troops arrived to take up positions to defend the MPLA's hold on Luanda.

As the fighting increased, thousands of Portuguese fled the colony, piling onto boats, driving to the airport, and hurling their car keys into the sewers to prevent Africans from using their vehicles after they had left. On the day of independence, the Portuguese high commissioner, Admiral Leonel Cardoso, buttoned up his formal naval uniform and appeared before the press in Luanda at noon. With artillery fire from a battle on the edge of the city punctuating his remarks, Cardoso read a statement in which he handed over sovereignty to "the Angolan people," none of whose representatives were present. As soon as he had finished, Cardoso grabbed the Portuguese flag, jumped into a heavily guarded motorcade, sped to the city's naval base, clambered aboard a flotilla of frigates, and steamed away. The end of five centuries of Portugal's "civilized rule" could not have been more ignominious.

As the boats departed, Agostinho Neto of the MPLA declared himself president of the "People's Republic of Angola." His regime, despite immediate recognition by Yugoslavia, North Vietnam, the Soviet Union, and a few African states, wobbled on the brink of oblivion. The MPLA had been pushed out of many of Angola's provinces and was now caught in a squeeze by UNITA from the south and the FNLA from the north. On the outskirts of Luanda the FNLA, with American, British, and French military advisers, was preparing a large assault on the MPLA's control of the city. They spent nearly a day bombarding the entrenched Cuban positions before launching an infantry attack across a bridge and a bog. Holden Roberto, the FNLA leader, had little military experience and refused to organize any diversionary or flanking maneuvers, sending his men forward in a single, tightly packed column. As soon as the FNLA soldiers came into the open in the Quifangondo Valley, the MPLA and Cubans unleashed a murderous barrage of artillery fire. Within minutes the FNLA's armored cars and jeeps had been reduced to charred rubble. Two thousand rockets streaked down and exploded into razor-sharp slivers in the middle of the FNLA column. Hundreds died instantly; those who survived fled in primal terror. From then on, the inexperienced troops of the FNLA bolted whenever they faced rocket fire. In a handful of hours, Roberto's military force had been crushed.

While the forces of the MPLA and the FNLA savaged each other in Luanda, Jonas Savimbi was ensconced several hundred miles to the south in the town of Nova Lisboa, which he renamed Huambo. Savimbi was convinced that if the military conflict could be brought to a stalemate, then the parties would have to negotiate a political settlement. This would be followed by an election which he, as a member of the majority Ovimbundu tribe, would be likely to win. For a man with few identifiable patrons, Savimbi's self-assurance seemed peculiar. Indeed, during the weeks leading up to independence, Savimbi's forces had achieved a number of inexplicable successes. They had somehow managed to drive the MPLA out of the great port of Lobito and had freed large portions of the key Benguela railway, over which Zambia shipped its goods to the sea. Foreign correspondents following events in Angola had difficulty accounting for these achievements. The mystery was solved by Fred Bridgland, a British journalist working for Reuters news service. Bridgland had spent time hopping around the country with Savimbi on his executive jet and, on two occasions when the jet made stops at airfields in central Angola, had spotted a cluster of Panhard armored cars occupied by white soldiers. When he approached the soldiers and asked them where they were from, they would not say, though their accents revealed that they were South Africans.

A few days later, the British pilots of Savimbi's jet urged Bridgland and his colleague Mike Nicholson, a British television reporter, to stay on board while they flew without Savimbi to another site to refuel. On November 10, the day before independence, Savimbi's jet flew four hundred miles to the south. As they descended toward the airport, Bridgland was shocked to learn that it was Rundu, a South African military base just across the border between Angola and Namibia. While the pilots chatted with the mechanics outside, Bridgland and his colleague, who had been lying on the floor to avoid discovery, peeked outside the jet. They saw troops, weapons, and a long column of Panhard armored cars waiting to be loaded onto huge Lockheed Hercules C-130 transport planes—and flown into Angola.

When they returned to Angola, Nicholson scrambled to try to get television evidence of the South Africans' involvement in the civil war and managed to catch one of the armored cars in Angola on film. Bridgland, in the meantime, asked Savimbi at a press conference whether the South African army was the secret of his recent successes. "There are no troops committed by the South African government here," lied Savimbi. "I agree that we have some white troops—not soldiers but technicians— working for us." Unaware of the nature of the journalists' proof, however, Savimbi permitted Bridgland to leave Angola. Even after Bridgland had filed his story from Lusaka, his editors refused to accuse South Africa point-blank of invading Angola. It took Bridgland another week to persuade them to name the soldiers' country of origin. On November 23, the news that South African troops had been battling the MPLA and the Cubans on behalf of UNITA appeared on the front page of the *Washington Post.* "The propaganda and political war was lost in that stroke," wrote Stockwell. "There was nothing the Lusaka station could invent that would be as damaging to the other side as our alliance with the hated South Africans was to our cause."

The exact nature of Jonas Savimbi's pact with John Vorster and the South African military is still shrouded in secrecy. It seems that at approximately the same time that the first Cuban troops arrived in September, Savimbi contacted the South Africans through a third party, possibly the United States or the Zambian government. He apparently asked the minister of defense, P. W. Botha, to provide him with the military support to seize and control UNITA's "traditional zone of operations" in southern and central Angola in preparation for independence. Botha had agreed and had ordered three columns of armored cars and about two thousand South African troops to cross the border into Angola and sweep northward. Botha concealed the full dimensions of the invasion from John Vorster, telling the prime minister that the troops were being sent to protect a jointly owned hydroelectric plant just north of the border. In fact, the troops had been instructed to seize as much territory as possible by November 11, hand it over to UNITA, and withdraw.

The officers at the CIA, with the exception of task force head Stockwell, expressed delight at the South African intervention. CIA officers "liked the South Africans," according to Stockwell, and "admired their efficiency." The CIA also enjoyed its close relationship with the South African Bureau of State Security (BOSS). On at least two occasions, Hendrick van dan Bergh, the head of BOSS and John Vorster's old friend from the pro-Nazi internment camp, had met with senior CIA officials to discuss southern Africa. Jim Potts, Stockwell's superior at the CIA, told Stockwell that African blacks were "irrational" about South Africa, and Stockwell noted that this viewpoint was widely shared at the agency. The result of such contacts and opinions became evident in the Angolan adventure. "Without any memos being written at CIA headquarters saying 'Let's coordinate with the South Africans,'" wrote Stockwell two years later, "coordination was effected at all CIA levels and the South Africans escalated their involvement in step with our own." The South Africans were equally pleased. At a confidential meeting with the South African press, P. W. Botha hinted that the operation was sponsored by the United States. "We're not in it alone," he told reporters at a secret briefing. "You'd be surprised to know who's in it with us."

Once the South Africans had crossed the Angolan border in mid-October, a coastal column of fifty armored cars and nearly a thousand troops led by a colonel nicknamed "Rommel," had advanced with amazing speed. By early November the South Africans had pushed hundreds of miles inside Angola and were closing in on the town of Novo Redondo, a port only two hundred miles south of the capital. On November 7, after learning of the South Africans' presence, Fidel Castro launched Operation Carlota, an airlift across the Atlantic that would increase the number of Cuban soldiers and support personnel to more than twelve thousand in two months. The Soviets, for their part, sent new shipments of tanks, trucks, helicopters, and MiG 21 fighters to be flown by Cuban pilots. During the battle for Luanda, South African artillery units had joined the FNLA while three South African Mirage fighters had attempted unsuccessfully to attack the Cuban-MPLA positions. Within a few days after independence, the South Africans had succeeded in taking Novo Redondo, though in the fighting seventeen of their soldiers had been wounded and one killed.

Published reports of South African involvement in Angola instantly changed the shape of the international debate. The Nigerian government was so angered that it instantly cut off its assistance to UNITA and gave twenty million dollars to the MPLA. Kissinger, nervous about the damage to America's international reputation, began seeding the newspapers with comments by a "high and authoritative" figure that the United States had to worry about the Soviet Union's attempts to use Angola as a "springboard" for black guerrilla movements in Rhodesia, Namibia, and South Africa and for the "subversion" of other black states. The CIA, in the meantime, had been paying for two representatives of UNITA to travel around the East Coast (despite an official ban on such CIA propaganda efforts in the United States) to plead their cause. The members of Congress, however, were not persuaded by the UNITA visits or by the bulletins from Kissinger. The recent pictures from the fall of Saigon, the symbol of America's most costly foreign failure, burned vividly in their memories. Most could not see why American weapons and personnel should be involved in beefing up an obscure guerrilla leader in an obscure country on an obscure continent—especially if this brought Americans into direct collaboration with the white supremacists of South Africa. On December 19 the Senate approved an amendment brought by Democratic Senator Dick Clark of Iowa, the chairman of the Senate Foreign Relations Committee, to end all covert aid to the liberation movements in Angola. During the floor debate in the House, Democrat John L. Burton of California summed up the feelings of the majority. "Angola," he said, "does not mean a damn thing to the future of this country."

President Ford was furious that Congress had "pulled the plug" on American involvement in Angola. "How can the United States, the greatest power in the world, take the position that the Soviet Union can operate with impunity many thousands of miles away with Cuban troops and massive amounts of military equipment," Ford asked publicly, "while we refuse any assistance to the majority of the local people who ask only for equipment to defend themselves?" The South Africans were also irate. They thought they had a clear understanding: if the South Africans entered Angola, the Americans would supply them with whatever weapons they needed. The Angolan adventure had already cost South Africa $133 million. Now the United States was refusing to offer any public support for the South Africans' efforts; indeed, the Americans even refused to block a United Nations Security Council measure that called on South Africa to pay war reparations to the MPLA. "If the West does not want to contribute its share for the sake of itself and the free world," said P. W. Botha, "it cannot expect South Africa to do it. . . . South Africa is not prepared to fight the West's battle against Communist penetration on its own." John Vorster gathered his advisers and decided that South Africa would withdraw from Angola within a few weeks. The South African commander in Angola informed Savimbi of the decision on Christmas Day.

From then on, events unfolded rapidly. In early January the OAU met in Addis Ababa and debated the crisis in Angola. The heads of state were deeply torn between their discomfort with the Soviet and Cuban incursion and their loathing of South Africa. When presented with a resolution calling for the withdrawal of foreign troops and the blending of the three movements into a government of national unity, they split their vote, twenty-two to twenty-two, with two abstentions. When given the chance to recognize the MPLA as the legitimate government, they split again. A few weeks later, the two countries that had abstained—Ethiopia and Uganda—recognized the MPLA, triggering a cascade of approvals. By February 10 the MPLA had been recognized by forty-one members of the OAU, and Agostinho Neto's government became its forty-seventh member.

Throughout January and February the MPLA army, with its Soviet advisers, Zairian mercenaries, and Cuban pilots and soldiers, chased the disintegrating FNLA back into Zaire and shoved Savimbi's forces toward the south. As the MPLA overran Huambo and other former UNITA strongholds, both sides bitterly accused the other of atrocities. In the meantime, CIA support vanished. CIA Director William Colby was fired from his post and replaced by George Bush, who spent months fending off congressional attempts to control the agency. Ford and Kissinger, watching the military debacle, tried to offer additional support. Kissinger berated Congress for refusing to authorize the "trivial sums" that the American-backed forces needed in Angola. Though Ford and Kissinger disliked linking progress with the Soviets on arms control to disagreements over human rights or regional conflict, the president spoke sharply to the Soviet ambassador, Anatoly Dobrynin, telling him that there was no question in his mind that "the Cuban troops, with Russian weapons, were acting as proxies for the Soviets."

While Ford and Kissinger were attempting to move the United States closer to South Africa, Charles Diggs and the other members of the Congressional Black Caucus were doing everything they could to pry them apart. This remained difficult. Though the caucus steadily acquired new members and obtained an occasional meeting with the president or the secretary of state, the interests of seventeen junior congressmen did not count heavily. Even Charles Diggs's increasing seniority could not compensate for the numerical disparity. His impact on African legislation in the House was actually weakened when the chairman of the Committee on Foreign Affairs, Thomas E. Morgan, decided in February 1975, as part of the general post-Watergate House reforms, to reorganize his subcommittees completely, giving each subcommittee charge over a particular topic rather than a particular region. Diggs found himself the head of a subcommittee on international resources, food, and energy. Though the problems of southern Africa could still be subsumed under these categories, Diggs's responsibilities for famine and problems in other countries limited how much he could get done.

As Diggs and his colleagues in the Congressional Black Caucus tried to influence American foreign and investment policy toward southern Africa, they faced the enduring problem of potentially conflicting loyalties. It was the same problem that the civil rights leaders had faced the decade before, when the Johnson White House had lectured American blacks about the dangers of developing a "segregated" foreign policy. It was a dilemma that black intellectuals pondered relentlessly. The problem could be at least partly concealed under a guise of partisanship: the Black Caucus, all Democrats, could oppose a Republican foreign policy without appearing to be motivated by race. The broader problem of articulating the nature and extent of the responsibility of black Americans for African affairs, however, remained. Many relied on the domestic argument that if American foreign policy aligned itself too closely with white supremacy, it might have negative effects on race relations in the United States. In the absence of a full-scale South African conflagration, however, such warnings rang somewhat hollow.

In an interview with *Africa* magazine in the fall of 1975, Diggs defended the record of the Black Caucus with regard to Africa but admitted that even for the members of the caucus, foreign concerns ranked third, behind the needs of their congressional districts and the push for domestic legislation for American blacks. He noted that the caucus, to be effective, had to be linked to external groups that could mobilize support for specific pieces of legislation, "a network of like-minded Americans," as Diggs put it, who could create "a massive groundswell of support." Even more important, he said, was to encourage education about Africa among American blacks. "What is required," wrote another black analyst, "is a mechanism for informing blacks as to what their true interests are on various international issues, and for translating the perhaps unformulated but nonetheless intense feelings which U.S. blacks are certain to have over some issues into a voice which cannot be ignored with impunity."

But what was this mechanism? The small but influential community of black intellectuals who were interested in foreign policy had been considering this question for some time. Three years earlier, in February 1972, more than two dozen black leaders and intellectuals had traveled to Baranquitas in Puerto Rico to discuss how they could find an intellectual focus for their diverse efforts. The group had included Tilden LeMelle of Hunter College, Walter Carrington of the African American Institute, Karen Whittemore of the American Committee on Africa, Asa Davis from Hunter College, and Willard Johnson, a professor of politics at MIT and one of the founders of the African Heritage Studies Center, an all-black counterpart to the more conventional (and predominantly white) African Studies Association. After intense debate the group had decided to focus on American support for Portuguese colonialism in Africa. Several months later, in the spring of 1972, some of the participants also joined an effort to repeal the pro-Rhodesian Byrd amendment. The attempt ended in farce. The protesters chose to march at the State Department (which supported the repeal) instead of the Capitol, where the Rhodesian government's paid representatives just barely succeeded, in the absence of any counterpressure, in stopping the bill that would have achieved the protester's goals.

By the fall of 1975 Charles Diggs, Goler Butcher, Willard Johnson, and other members of the network of blacks interested in foreign policy decided that the time had come to consider forming a new organization. Reasoning that the white establishment developed its leaders, formulated its foreign policy ideas, and propagated its conclusions through various think tanks, they discussed the possibility of forming a similar group to focus on African issues. At the first organizational meeting, held in September 1975, the participants debated whether they should model the new organization on the elite New York–based Council on Foreign Relations. Some felt that the adoption of similar goals—the dissemination of information, the exchange of ideas, and the analysis of international problems—was just what the black community needed. Others felt that it should be more of a lobbying group that could tap a network to rally against things like the Davis nomination. When someone suggested that the organization should be restricted to blacks, Butcher pointed out that an attempt to restrict the membership by race would cause legal problems. They finally agreed that if the organization focused on African problems and included "black" in the title, it would not attract a large number of whites, so the possibility of losing the black focus was minimal. They eventually decided to call the new group the Black Forum on Foreign Policy.

Leon Sullivan was also looking for a new strategy. Every spring for five years, beginning with his dramatic remarks at the 1971 General Motors annual meeting, Leon Sullivan had faithfully advocated GM's withdrawal from South Africa. The other directors tolerated his apostasy but refused to act. By June 1975, Sullivan was ready to consider another approach, which he developed on his sixth trip to visit offshoots of his Opportunities Industrialization Centers in Africa. Sullivan, his wife, Grace, and three of their children, accompanied by the international director of OIC, hopped from Kenya, Tanzania, Zaire, and Ghana to Botswana, Zambia, and Lesotho. During a transit stop at the airport in Johannesburg, Sullivan met with a host of moderate community leaders and business representatives, including Lucy Mvubelo of the National Union of Clothing Workers and Adam Klein, the general secretary of the Garment Workers Union of South Africa. Mvubelo, Klein, and others with whom Sullivan met told him that he should concentrate on workplace reforms. Disinvestment, Klein told Sullivan, was a bad idea because it "would not have 100% success and is therefore a meaningless gesture." "Rather than encourage the withdrawal of American capital from South Africa," Klein wrote in a follow-up letter to Sullivan in which he reiterated the points of the meeting, "you could take a positive stance and call for American companies in South Africa to recognize the same working conditions they employ in America."

Sullivan was already sympathetic to such an approach. It fit perfectly with his past experience with OIC, which had been designed to use capital investment and business practices to alter patterns of segregation in the United States. He was also well aware of Charles Diggs's attempts to pressure American companies to hold to the same standards in South Africa that were customary in America. Finally, Sullivan desperately wanted to find a new point of leverage. "If you could get companies involved in change, it had to make an impact, it had to alter things," Sullivan recalled years later. "There was nothing else I could think of to get a handle on it. The churches couldn't do it. The schools couldn't do it, because they were part of apartheid. The government couldn't do it, because they *were* apartheid." Nor, said Sullivan, had international pressure been successful. "I had to get my hand on something that could begin the process of change."

Ironically, it was a member of the South African customs police who did more than anyone to launch Sullivan on his new course. After Sullivan had finished meeting with his visitors at the airport, the Security Police, suspicious that an illegal document might have been passed to Sullivan, took him to a separate room and ordered him to strip. As Sullivan, angry and humiliated, removed his garments, he turned to one of the officers and said, "Why do you do it?" "I do what I have to do," the officer replied, "and you do what you have to do." While the police rifled through the pockets and peeked into the seams of his clothes, Sullivan made a vow. "I was standing there stripped and I thought to myself, when I leave, I *will* do what I have to do."

Upon his return to the United States, Sullivan persuaded the board of Zion Baptist Church to launch a South African program with the same themes as the selective patronage campaign. Over the summer, in the same manner as he had tackled the issue of discrimination in the employment of blacks in Philadelphia sixteen years before, Sullivan announced his new effort from the pulpit. Sullivan's preliminary idea closely followed that of Charles Diggs, of using the U.S. government's immense purchasing power to force American businesses to implement the same employment standards in South Africa as at home. In the earliest incarnation, published in September 1975, Sullivan called for a "concerted double-directed effort on the part of the government of the United States and American-based businesses operating in the Union *[sic]* of South Africa." The government portion consisted primarily of an appeal to the Ford administration to put more pressure on Pretoria. The appeal to business, however, contained all the building blocks of Sullivan's emerging strategy: a commitment to fair employment practices; equal pay; recognition of black labor committees to bargain collectively; and support of external programs for African health, education, and housing. To capture the attention of American business, Sullivan turned to his corporate contacts. The two men who responded most eagerly were Tom Murphy, the chairman of General Motors, and Frank Cary, the chairman of IBM, who jointly agreed to convene a small committee of top executives to discuss the notion. They chose a date in January 1976 and Cary agreed to serve as host at the IBM Development Center at Sands Point, New York.

On December 17, 1975, Sullivan sent out a letter of invitation to twenty-one top executives. "As a senior executive of a United States firm doing business in South Africa, you are well aware of the attention which is being devoted to the presence of major companies such as yours in South Africa," Sullivan began. Though Sullivan acknowledged that "the tide of criticism . . . has subsided," he said that "a useful purpose would be served by companies such as yours getting together to exchange information about their operations and programs." This was somewhat disingenuous: Sullivan already knew that he wanted the executives to commit to a particular program. The hypersensitivity of the executives on this issue, however, required diplomacy. The discussion, wrote Sullivan, would be informal, unpublicized, open only to the chairman or president, and "completely non-political."

The Sands Point meeting took place on January 29, 1976, and had mixed results. Though Sullivan had managed, with the help of Murphy and Cary, to gather eighteen of America's top business leaders for a discussion lasting nearly five hours on a very small part of their global business, the executives responded with little enthusiasm to Sullivan's suggestion that they make a public commitment to a "statement of principles." Sullivan found this reluctance deeply frustrating, since his original principles had already been diluted in an effort to win corporate support. Sullivan had, however, won two important concessions. The first was a commitment to meet again "in nine months or so to once again exchange experiences and information." The second was an agreement that Sullivan should send all the American companies in South Africa "a simple questionnaire to get a comprehensive picture of what our companies are doing."

Before they broke up, the senior executives decided to appoint a committee of subordinates to refine the statement of principles and coordinate its implementation over the next six months. One of the committee members was Wayne Fredericks, who was now working for the Ford Motor Company. Fredericks had moved first from the Ford Foundation to the Chase Manhattan Bank to help David Rockefeller establish the bank's new Middle East and Africa offices. Shortly afterward, Henry Ford came to Fredericks and asked him to become, in Fredericks's words, "a kind of secretary of state for the Ford Motor Company. . . . Ford wanted someone to travel around the world a great deal, someone who had experience both in business and government because he realized that government policy and social movements were having greater and greater impact on the management of the corporation. He wanted me to bring the outside environment to the attention of the managers. So he wasn't offering me a position to design cars, make cars, or sell cars, but to try to describe this external world."

From his new post, Fredericks helped to negotiate the construction of a massive new Ford plant in Spain and organized the first Ford overtures to China and the Soviet Union. He told Henry Ford that he should endorse majority rule in Rhodesia, and as a result Ford, despite resistance from some of his own executives, sent letters to Charles Diggs supporting the repeal of the Byrd amendment and the end of white supremacy. In his contacts with Leon Sullivan, Wayne Fredericks labored to persuade him that he should start with what was politically possible. He convinced Sullivan that they could afford to drop the union recognition clause in order to draw in IBM because, Fredericks confided, the Ford Motor Company was about to recognize a black union in South Africa, a move that would put pressure on the other signatories to do the same. For Fredericks, the critical purpose of the statement of principles was as a vehicle for educating American executives. "I remember saying this had to be a living document, so it could bring people in who have not thought about it before," Fredericks said later. He told Sullivan that "as people begin working with this, they will learn more about the black community, housing problems, education, medical. We ought not to conceive of this document as the end of all thought. As we go along, we will define other fields, the situation will change, new things will become possible, and people will gain more courage from [these] efforts."

Leon Sullivan was not the only person who had decided by 1976 that a new initiative in southern Africa was necessary. Convinced that southern Africa had become an important piece of the geopolitical game but barred from covert military operations by the Clark amendment, Henry Kissinger decided to try his hand at resolving the problem of white minority rule in Rhodesia. Kissinger launched his campaign to broker a settlement with a tour around Africa in April 1976. Gerald Ford approved the trip over the objections of his campaign staff, who believed that Ford's challenger for the Republican nomination, former California governor Ronald Reagan, would exploit the effort politically. "Political stability in Africa was crumbling everywhere," Ford recalled in his memoirs, "and it was imperative to send Henry Kissinger to the continent to see if he could head off a race war. . . . My political advisers warned me that the timing of the trip was poor. We were about to contest Reagan in several key Southern states. Did we have to remind voters— as Henry's mission would do—that we favored majority rule where whites were in the minority?" Ford decided to send Kissinger anyway. On April 22, the day before Kissinger departed for Africa, the editors of the *New York Times* commented on the difficulty of his task. "He is not in a position to say convincingly what black African leaders most want to hear from the United States," they wrote. "Africans know that he is concerned above all to check Soviet and Cuban intervention on the continent, while they are concerned above all to bring majority rule in Rhodesia and Namibia and the dismantling of apartheid in South Africa."

Kissinger's problems started even before he left. Though the governments of Tanzania, Zambia, and five other countries had extended invitations, three others—Ghana, Mozambique, and Nigeria—indicated that they did not wish to receive him. As soon as he arrived in Africa, Kissinger moved to modify America's reputation as a supporter of white supremacy. In Lusaka, on April 27, in a major statement on U.S. policy, he acknowledged America's neglect of Africa and then surprised everyone by laying out a new set of commitments that seemed to repudiate the seven-year-old policy of NSSM 39. The United States, he said, wanted to see a comprehensive solution to the problems of southern Africa. The Ford administration was "wholly committed to help bring about a rapid, just, and African solution" in Rhodesia; it would urge South Africa to fix a timetable for self-determination in Namibia; and it would press for the end of "the institutionalized separation of the races" in South Africa itself. Most significantly, he did not try to terrify the African countries with the horrors of Soviet intervention or to recast the region's conflicts as a clash between ideological spheres—as both he and John Vorster had done only a few months before with regard to Angola.

The reaction to the speech in many quarters was positive. The British, in particular, were delighted to see the world's preeminent diplomat join the effort for a negotiated settlement in Rhodesia. African leaders responded with cautious approval. Conservatives from the Transvaal to California, on the other hand, howled. "When Henry said our policy toward continued white minority rule in Rhodesia would be one of 'unrelenting opposition,' " Gerald Ford remembered, "conservatives hit the ceiling." Increasingly Ford and Reagan wrangled in public over Kissinger's policies, with Reagan accusing Ford of "losing" Angola and of selling out the Rhodesians but then overstepping himself by telling a reporter that as president he would consider sending the United States army to defend the white minority in Rhodesia. Ford pounced on the remark as evidence of Reagan's irresponsibility. Once again, foreign policy became a political tool for domestic positioning as both candidates used the problems of southern Africa to demonstrate their mettle to American conservatives.

For Kissinger, however, the resolution to all these problems lay not in London, Lusaka, or Los Angeles but in Pretoria. In his view, only the prime minister of South Africa could release Namibia, alter apartheid, and pressure the recalcitrant white Rhodesians into an agreement. Kissinger believed, moreover, that Vorster was willing to move on all of these fronts, especially the last. Despite the public outcry against the American collaboration with South Africa in Angola, Kissinger sent a stream of signals to Vorster indicating that he would like to meet. In May the president himself told a group of reporters at the White House that he would be happy to sit down with the South African leader, though the White House press office quickly tempered his comment with assurances that no such meeting was being planned.

Vorster had his own reasons for wanting to see a settlement in Rhodesia. Though his gamble in Angola had backfired, Vorster still wanted to continue with détente. He had concluded that Ian Smith's strident defenses of white supremacy were contaminating South Africa's attempts to win acceptance of separate development and to improve relations with other African countries. Moreover, Vorster distrusted Smith. After Vorster's efforts at the Victoria Falls bridge had failed to produce a settlement, Smith had criticized him in public. Vorster had demanded—and received—a public apology, but he remained wary of the Rhodesian. Both Kissinger and Vorster, however, knew that South Africa could bring enormous pressure to bear on the Rhodesian government. In March 1976 the FRELIMO government in Mozambique had closed its borders with Rhodesia; now virtually all goods to and from Smith's country had to flow through South Africa. The South Africans had supplied financial credit and an assortment of planes, helicopters, and armored vehicles. South African police and army also supported and participated in military operations against the guerrillas in the regions near the South African border.

Though the members of the two governments shared a commitment to minority rule, the members of Vorster's cabinet viewed many of their Rhodesian counterparts as incompetents or louts. The Afrikaners disliked the culturally English Rhodesians; occasionally, their prodigious capacity to hold historical grudges erupted into view. In one such instance the South African minister of police and prisons, Jimmy Kruger, asked the Rhodesians to release a white South African police officer who had been arrested for slitting the throat of an African infant in broad daylight in front of a host of witnesses. When the Rhodesians refused, Kruger exploded in anger. "You bastards," he shouted at a senior Rhodesian official, "you started the Boer War with the Jameson raid!"

Given the leverage South Africa held in the region, Kissinger could afford to be encouraged when he obtained an agreement from Vorster to meet in Germany in June. Little could Kissinger have guessed that when he finally met with Vorster, it would be during the worst domestic crisis of Vorster's reign. In most of South Africa's townships conditions had worsened steadily. Outside Johannesburg, the population of Soweto was rising into the millions while jobs and housing remained scarce. Existing shelter was primitive: out of every ten houses, six had no running water, seven had no ceilings, eight had no electricity, and nine had no toilets. New immigrants to the township piled into the cramped abodes of family or friends or settled in squatters' camps, where they fashioned hovels out of corrugated tin, packing crates, and the other flotsam of industry.

Obtaining food was also a constant problem. Supplies inside the townships were limited because the government wanted blacks to buy from stores in the white areas. In addition, forty-three percent of the residents of Soweto lived below the "poverty datum line" (PDL), the official starvation level of 130 rand per month for a family of six. Some scholars insisted that the PDL was too low and that a realistic measure of the minimum standard for survival was the "effective minimum level," a figure fifty percent higher. The government rejected this standard because research showed that four out of every five residents of Soweto fell below it.

The compression of human bodies in Soweto bred litter, disease, and crime. The labyrinth of government regulations, designed by distant theorists and imposed by capricious bureaucrats, sapped the will of those it ensnared. Employment officials, for example, refused to allow Africans to register for work until they obtained authorized accommodation, and housing officials refused to authorize accommodation until the Africans had registered for work. Similarly, though all Africans over age sixteen were required under pain of arrest to carry their passbooks, the government made it arduous to obtain them.

Most persons living in Soweto lived under the constant threat of deportation back to a homeland. In 1972 the deputy minister of Bantu administration made it clear that one of his department's functions was to transfer to the bantustans all "unproductive people—those who because of age, weak health, unfitness, or other reasons are no longer able to work." In 1975 the chairman of a regional government board reiterated the policy. "We must curb the flow to white areas and attempt to create a counter-flow to the homelands," he said. "In our prescribed areas we have room for productive elements but not for superfluous people who are parasitic on us and especially on their own friends and relations. Such people we will, where possible, repatriate to the homelands." The primary legal weapon for such "repatriation" was a provision known as Section 10. Under this law no African could remain in a proclaimed area for more than seventy-two hours unless he had fulfilled certain strict requirements, including lawful residence in the same area for fifteen years, service with the same employer for ten years, or special permission from a labor bureau. Section 10 gave white employers tremendous power over their African employees, for both knew that a dismissal for the African meant not only the loss of income but also the loss of home.

Additional anxiety surged through the township when the government announced that at the end of 1976 the Transkei would become the first bantustan to achieve "independence." This meant that the 1.6 million Xhosas living in the rural territory would instantly lose their South African citizenship and become citizens of the new "country." The additional 1.3 million urban Xhosas who resided in the townships felt acutely uneasy about what would happen to them. Despite the government's concerted attempts to force township residents to live in tribal enclaves, ethnic identity had continued to erode under the force of urbanization. Many of the residents who would be classified as Transkeian had been born in the Transvaal, had never been to their "homeland," and had no intention of going. The leader of the Transkei, Kaiser Matanzima, announced that he had reassurances that urban residents would not be forced to choose Transkeian citizenship. Later when independence arrived, the Nationalist government used a spectacular piece of sophistry to renege on that promise. Officials announced that urban Xhosas did not have to *choose* Transkeian citizenship because they had been Transkeian citizens *all along*.

By the mid-1970s more than half the population of Soweto was under age twenty-five and nearly two-thirds were under thirty. Though the older residents of Soweto had bowed to the daily demands of survival and of the state, the younger ones bridled at such acquiescence. Month by month, they grew more and more frustrated with the wretched conditions in their homes and schools. The Nationalist government, as part of its attempt to "curb the flow," had carefully limited the number of schools in the townships. Though some primary education was provided, secondary schooling was restricted in order to prompt children to leave their parents and return to the homelands to be educated. One newspaper estimated in 1975 that more than thirty-five thousand Soweto children were receiving no schooling at all and that to accommodate them forty new schools with seven hundred new classrooms would have to be built immediately. For those who were in school, the conditions were odious. Only twelve percent of the *teachers* had successfully completed high school. Classrooms were abysmally underequipped and over-crowded. In 1976 each teacher had an average of forty-eight students—and in some periods the number bubbled up to sixty. As a result, teachers in most African schools had been forced to split their classes into shorter shifts, with some children coming for a morning session and others for the afternoon.

Such conditions offered fecund soil for the seeds of Black Consciousness. Though the South African Students' Association (SASO) had been organized for university students, its leaders formed a counterpart for high school students known as the South African Student Movement (SASM). Black Consciousness leaders like Stephen Biko, Barney Pityana, and the martyred O. R. Tiro (who had been a high school teacher in Soweto) were admired as much as the silenced figures of Mandela and Sobukwe. Indeed, the theoretical Pan-Africanism and the strategic energy of SASO were very much in continuity with both the ANC and the PAC of sixteen years before. Just as the PAC had drawn strength from the tide of anticolonial, Pan-Africanist feeling sweeping the continent, so did Black Consciousness appeal to the enthusiasm created by the liberation of Angola and Mozambique from Portuguese rule. Just as the impatience of the ANC Youth League with the compromises and failures of the earlier ANC members had reinvigorated the resistance movement, so did SASO identify and exploit the generation gap between the vibrant aspirations of the young and the bitter experience of the old. "There has been a lull in black political activity since the banning of the African National Congress," one black teacher told a white investigative reporter in May 1976, "but its ideas have lived on. We see them embodied today in SASO and the Black People's Convention. Black Consciousness is germinating. It is spreading among youth and young adults, and has filtered through to their younger brothers and sisters."

The students' pent-up frustration coalesced in the issue of language. Since 1958, the Nationalist government had continued its drive to put Afrikaans on an equal footing with English by requiring that whatever courses were not taught in an indigenous African tongue had to be split between the two European languages. This "fifty-fifty" rule had proved difficult to enforce, largely because there were insufficient textbooks in

Afrikaans and few teachers competent in both languages. In early 1976, however, the officials of the Department of Bantu Education, worried that so many Africans had switched exclusively to English, announced that they intended to enforce the provision. Students objected to being forced to study their academic subjects in three different languages. They also worried when they learned that the government intended to administer a portion of the next year's national examinations in Afrikaans, of which most pupils had only a rudimentary grasp. In addition to these practical considerations, most of the children hated Afrikaans as the "language of the conqueror," the tongue of the police who harassed and brutalized their families.

The first visible resistance to the language policy appeared on May 17, 1976, when sixteen hundred students walked out of Orlando West Junior Secondary School in Soweto and announced they would not return to school until the fifty-fifty rule was abandoned. The next day, pupils in two more schools joined the strike. The white inspector of the West Rand Education Council expressed puzzlement. "Have you ever heard of thirteen year olds striking?" he asked a newspaper reporter. "The public does not realize that there are many who want to spread unrest in South Africa. I don't know who is behind this—but it is not the children." Manie Mulder, the head of the West Rand Administration Board, a government entity that controlled the entire township, was interviewed by a reporter from the *Rand Daily Mail* in the middle of May about the growing problems. "The broad masses of Soweto are perfectly content, perfectly happy," said Mulder. "Black-white relations are as healthy as they can be." Was there any danger of some kind of "blow-up" in the townships? asked the reporter. "None whatever," Mulder replied.

Over the next month, antagonism toward the use of Afrikaans swelled. Pupils out on strike clamored for their friends to join them. The Black Parents' Association implored the children to go back to school and let the parents deal with the problem, but their pleas had little effect. On June 8, young people threw stones at police and set a police car afire on the grounds of Naledi High School. On Tuesday, June 15, a committee of students announced a walk-out and a mass rally at the stadium in Orlando West for the next day. Early in the morning on Wednesday, June 16, thousands of high school students and primary school children emerged from their homes and streamed toward the stadium. Some were carrying signs made from notebook covers reading "Afrikaans is a tribal language," "50-50 Zulu for Vorster." Soon a whole segment of Soweto was blanketed with exuberant youngsters. "As I drove into their midst," said one black eyewitness, "they made way for me and stood on both sides of the road with their fists raised and shouting 'power' at the top of their voices. They were in an extremely jovial mood. The whole atmosphere was quite a happy one."

When reports came that the police were on their way, one of the students appealed to those around him. "Keep calm and cool," he said. "Don't taunt them, don't do anything to them. We are not fighting." The police—both black and white officers—pulled up in vans loaded with batons, tear gas, automatic rifles, and submachine guns. They quickly filed out and formed a line in front of the children. The students hesitated, expecting an announcement. Instead, the police lobbed several tear gas canisters into the crowd. The children held their ground. Then a white policeman pulled out his revolver and aimed it at short range at the row of young boys and girls. As some of them turned to flee, he fired. The bullet struck thirteen-year-old Hector Petersen in the back and killed him.

At the sound of gunfire, the situation exploded. The students hurled rocks. The police fired again. Within an hour, news of the shootings had flashed across Soweto, igniting violence from other young people. Administrative buildings, post offices, liquor stores, magistrates' offices, and beer halls—all property of the Bantu Administration and sources of its income—were attacked and burned. The police, in turn, set up roadblocks and unleashed a fury of small-weapons fire on the darting children. In one place, "the children began stoning the police," reported Alf Kumalo of the *Sunday Times,* "and shots were fired. I remember looking at the children in their school uniforms and wondering how long they would stand up to the police. What frightened me more than anything was the attitude of the children. Many seemed oblivious to the danger. They continued running towards the police, dodging and ducking. Suddenly a small boy dropped to the ground next to me. Blood poured from his mouth and some children knelt next to him and tried to stop the flow of blood."

By the afternoon, police reinforcements had poured in from around the region. One unit of fifty-five men was led by Theunis Swanepoel, the same lieutenant who had harassed Nelson Mandela in the Rivonia trials in 1963 and interrogated Winnie Mandela in 1969. Swanepoel, now a colonel, described the turmoil as the "most *waansinnig* [demented] I have come across in my life." He ordered his officers to identify the leaders of the mob and to shoot to kill. The introduction of white military units, filled with inexperienced draftees toting automatic weapons, inflamed the riots even more. While authorities insisted that few people had been killed, residents described hundreds of casualties. When the parents of the children returned to the township on the evening of June 16 after a long day of work, they were met by the sights and sounds of war—rumbling armored vehicles, thumping helicopters, billowing smoke, and crackling small-arms fire. As darkness fell, more fires illuminated the sky as young men attacked black policemen's homes, government buildings, and the buses that drove their parents to and from the white city on the horizon.

Over the next few days, the brutality in Soweto increased. When the pupils set their schools ablaze, the police responded by shooting at them indiscriminately. Students in Alexandra township, on the northern side of Johannesburg, organized marches and then also erupted into frenzy. Several people were killed by rioters, including two whites, one of whom was a liberal sociologist who ironically had been studying the depth of African discontent. When the buses stopped running, thousands of stranded workers swelled the ranks of the protesters. The medical personnel at Baragwanath Hospital, the only major facility in Soweto, struggled to cope with the flood of gunshot victims, including dozens of children under age ten. By Thursday night, the official police report counted 58 dead and 788 wounded.

In the weeks following the Soweto riots, spasms of violence continued to jolt the township. On June 26, Jimmy Kruger, the minister of police and prisons, set the official death toll at 176, though most residents and reporters believed the true number to be much higher. The Black Parents' Association—of which Winnie Mandela was a prominent member—had to call a special meeting just to discuss how to hold funerals and bury the numerous young who had died. The parents also agonized helplessly about the scores of teenagers and children who disappeared daily into the maw of police detention.

Reaction in the white community ranged from fear and horror to relief that the situation, thanks to strict currency controls, had not caused a financial panic comparable to that during the Sharpeville crisis. "One should be careful not to place too much emphasis on the riots," said Wally Reed, the financial director of Tongaat, a large group of companies, two weeks after the outbreak of violence. "The stock market has been relatively unaffected and there has been no loss of confidence." Not everyone felt so reassured. In the weeks after the riots, purchases of firearms by whites skyrocketed six hundred percent. In the meantime, the government, stung by the avalanche of editorial and official condemnation from abroad, made a few swift concessions. Despite Deputy Minister Andries Treurnicht's objection that "it was for the Bantu's own good that he learn in Afrikaans," the head of the Department of Bantu Education formally lifted the language requirement in early July. Because most government officials continued to believe the unrest had been an anomaly, the result of outside agitation, the students returned to their schools at the end of July to find that nothing important had changed.

One group of high school students, unwilling to give up, came together to form the most remarkable organization of the period, the Soweto Students Representative Council (SSRC). Led by a nineteen-year-old student from Morris Isaacson Secondary School named Tsietsi Mashinini, the teenagers believed that the riots had not been successful in causing change because the disturbances had been confined to the townships. If students could hold their demonstrations in the central business district of Johannesburg, whites would have to pay attention. If they could persuade their parents and the other workers of Soweto to stay home from work, the whole South African economy would shudder. Mashinini believed that a stay-away, if sustained, would prompt white business leaders to press the government for concessions such as the release of the detainees.

Working feverishly, the members of the SSRC planned a huge march and work boycott. Their parents were torn; they wanted to support the students but feared losing their jobs. On August 4, in response to the call of the SSRC, thousands of adults decided not to go to work. Those who tried to leave the township encountered scattered bands of intimidating teenagers. The march into the business district ended, once again, in bloodshed. Twenty thousand students left the township, broke through one police roadblock, and then ran into a phalanx of paramilitary forces farther down the road. The students retreated when the police opened fire, wounding twelve and killing three.

The students' mobilization of the township filled an important vacuum of leadership. The government-created Urban Bantu Council had lost all credibility. Other organizations—such as the Black Parents' Association—still held sway but had been decimated by arrests. When the townships outside Cape Town erupted on August 11, leaving more than thirty people dead, the police in the Transvaal stepped up their campaign to jail every identifiable leader. On August 15, the police arrested Winnie Mandela and dozens of other parents. They conducted a furious search for Mashinini, who was now forced to move from house to house around the township. "The blacks are always saying 'We Shall Overcome,' " Kruger said two days later to a laughing Afrikaner crowd, "but I tell you it is we who shall overcome."

Despite Kruger's threats, Mashinini and his associates, encouraged by the ANC underground, refused to stop. On Saturday, August 21, leaflets written by the SSRC, printed secretly by black officeworkers and bearing the name of the African National Congress, appeared under the door of every home in the twenty-eight-square-mile area of Soweto. The flier called for a three-day general strike to begin on Monday. Major General M. Geldenhuys warned that if such a strike were attempted there would be a violent "backlash" from the "law-abiding citizens." On Monday, when the first hours of the morning showed that the strike might be successful, the police stepped up their threats. That same day, Tsietsi Mashinini, whose daring escapes from arrest were now being covered by the newspapers, finally fled to Botswana. His tenure as president of the student organization had lasted only three weeks.

During the following weeks many Soweto residents spotted packs of white men who had taken to shooting African children at random. Beginning in late August and continuing for several weeks, residents saw a white Valiant and a green Chevrolet, each loaded with men in camouflage uniforms, cruising the streets of Soweto. When the men came across clusters of African boys, they opened fire. The Valiant appeared on August 21 in Orlando West and shot six boys who were playing soccer, killing two of them. The mother of one of the wounded managed to get the license plate, which a newspaper checked out. The vehicle was owned by the police department.

The police exploited the friction that existed between the families of Soweto and the lonely workers who were crammed into concrete mining hostels for eleven months of the year. On Tuesday morning, August 24, black newspapers carried a printed warning from the police: "Go to work and disregard the groups of young intimidators telling people not to go to work. People must go to work and just thrash the children stopping them." A few hours later, the "backlash" the police had been predicting finally materialized. That afternoon, provoked by real or imagined affronts, a thousand men from the Mzimholpe hostel, armed with sticks, knives, and spears, burst out of their compound and conducted a murderous house-to-house search for "cheeky" children. As news of the marauders shot through the townships, residents tried to set up barricades. The police shoved the barriers aside with their "Hippos," rumbling armored personnel carriers. "Men carrying butcher knives, pangas, tomahawks, kieries and stones started chasing people around," wrote a reporter for the *Star*. "What amazed me was that as they assaulted people, heavily armed police stood by and did nothing to protect the residents." Indeed, evidence swiftly accumulated that the police had planned and assisted in the mayhem. One reporter overheard the police instructing the hostel dwellers on what buildings and groups they should attack; another saw a line of armed men leaving the hostels by night under the protection of police Hippos; a third saw police deliver a young man into the hands of the hostel dwellers and watch calmly as they chopped him to pieces with axes.

Though the press reports described the attackers as "Zulu impis," some historians of the riots, such as John Kane-Berman of the South African Institute of Race Relations, insisted that only a minority of the hostel dwellers were Zulu. Nor was the violence completely one-sided.

Inflamed by rumors of the abduction and rape of township women by the hostel dwellers, hundreds of young men attacked Mzimholpe at one point to liberate the women. In an attempt to calm the situation, Gatsha Buthelezi rushed to Johannesburg on August 26 and announced that he had tape recordings proving that the police had instigated the fighting. Buthelezi also asked the forgiveness of the residents for the behavior of the Zulus who had been involved in the killings. When Buthelezi tried to go to Soweto himself, Minister of Police Kruger ordered him not to interfere. The next day Buthelezi defied Kruger, entered the township, and demanded that the hostel dwellers stop the rampage and unite with the residents of Soweto. Despite Buthelezi's efforts at reconciliation, the events of Mzimholpe only strengthened the sentiment among Soweto's residents that Buthelezi, Inkatha, and the Zulu urban hostel dwellers, for whatever reasons, were allowing themselves to become the tools of government violence.

The Soweto riots exploded a week before Kissinger left to meet John Vorster. Charles Diggs urged the secretary to cancel the meeting, but Kissinger decided that the events in South Africa might make Vorster even more willing to negotiate. During their meeting in the Bavarian resort town of Grafenau, Kissinger indeed found Vorster, smarting from the international outcry over Soweto, more prepared than ever to push Ian Smith to settle. Afterward, Kissinger sent emissaries to the British and to Julius Nyerere of Tanzania, Kenneth Kaunda of Zambia, and Samora Machel of Mozambique, suggesting that if Smith could be persuaded to step down, an interim government could then be formed which could work out the constitutional details. The African leaders ruminated separately, then together, then with the nationalist leaders they supported, but they found it difficult to agree whether to trust Kissinger.

In early August the prospects for peace in Rhodesia nearly disappeared completely when a detachment of the Rhodesian army attacked the refugee camp at Nyadzonia. Rhodesian soldiers swept in and gunned down more than a thousand men, women, and children. A captured member of the Selous Scouts, the unit of the Rhodesian army made up of African soldiers, said that they had been told before the raid that Nyadzonia was a guerrilla camp containing thousands of unarmed refugees who would be recruited to join the guerrillas. "They said it would be easier if we went in and wiped them out while they were unarmed," he told his captors, "rather than waiting for the possibility of them being trained and sent back armed to Rhodesia." His superiors, he said, had been delighted with the results. Afterward the soldiers had received bonuses for their high kill rate and a formal blessing from the unit's white chaplain.

By early September, Kissinger believed that he had the support of the key African countries and from the nationalist factions to work out a Rhodesian agreement through John Vorster. While the African leaders caucused in Dar Es Salaam, Kissinger met Vorster again on September 4 and 5 in Zurich. Kissinger persuaded the South African that the time had come for a face-to-face meeting with Smith. On September 17, Kissinger flew directly to Pretoria, ostensibly to see Vorster, but in fact to persuade the Rhodesian prime minister and his cabinet to abandon the white community's century-old grip on power. The announcement of Kissinger's impending visit set off another cycle of violent protest in some of South Africa's townships.

After Kissinger arrived, Smith and his compatriots drove to the American ambassador's luxurious residence in the suburb of Water-kloof. There they received the full Kissinger treatment. "Kissinger was disarming," one of Smith's aides told two historians shortly after the meeting. "He knew his subject, he was forthright, and he kept saying that he had no mandate for negotiations, he was only trying to help." While maintaining a tone of congeniality, he bluntly laid out his conviction that this was the best possible time for them to make a deal. The proposals he had, he said, were British proposals that he would be willing to support to the fullest as long as he was in power, which might only be until the November U.S. presidential election. If Jimmy Carter came in, he told them, there would be "no possibility" of a settlement. Kissinger also tried to dissuade them from thinking they could fight on forever. Kissinger dazzled his listeners with a tour through the world's diplomatic problems, in which, according to the aide, he reduced Rhodesia "to a microscopic point near the end." Then he suggested that if Smith wanted to settle the conflict, he must make a public commitment to majority rule and establish an interracial executive council as an interim government. Though Smith yanked, pulled, and wiggled, Kissinger had landed him. In return for accepting majority rule within two years, Smith demanded that the chairman of the interim executive council, the minister of defense, and the minister of law and order all remain white. Kissinger told Smith that these were details that could be worked out later, a point on which he would turn out to be wrong.

Shortly afterward, as he was flying to consult with the African leaders, Kissinger discussed the negotiations off the record with several American reporters. Why did he think he had secured an agreement this time, they asked, when Smith had wriggled out of every other such settlement? "It is one thing to double-cross Kaunda," Kissinger said grimly, "and quite another to double-cross South Africa and the United States jointly." Ian Smith made a public address to his country on September 24 in which he announced his acceptance of the five-point plan that Kissinger had offered. The pilot of Kissinger's plane picked up the BBC broadcast over Newfoundland and piped it into the secretary's cabin. Kissinger, attired in baggy pants, a rumpled shirt, and slippers, listened intently. "Kissinger's face," wrote a reporter who was with him, "was impassive, almost like a scowling Buddha," as he listened to Smith's public promise to dismantle white supremacy in Rhodesia.

There was only one problem. Kissinger had not received permission in advance from the African countries to concede control of defense and of law and order to whites in the interim government. Kissinger had not objected to Smith's idea because he apparently thought Smith's terms were an acceptable price for a public commitment to majority rule. When Kissinger briefed the African leaders immediately afterward, he glossed the point. Kissinger also overestimated the influence the African leaders had over the nationalist groups they were supporting. Instead of enthusiasm for Kissinger's triumph, the African leaders and the nationalist guerrillas were infuriated that the interim government would not only retain Smith—whom they loathed—but would preserve the weaponry in the hands of whites. In their public statement they hailed Smith's commitment to majority rule but rejected "the proposals as outlined by the illegal and racist regime which if accepted would be tantamount to legalizing the colonialist and racist structures of power."

With this pronouncement, the chances for settlement evaporated and Rhodesia plunged into three more years of vicious civil war. Ironically, the failure revealed both the strengths and weaknesses of the NSSM 39 policy. Because of America's tacit cooperation with the white regimes, Kissinger had succeeded in using South Africa as a crowbar to pry loose the white supremacists of Rhodesia. At the same time, the long legacy of African anger at Kissinger, Smith, and Vorster—provoked by the same American rapprochement—eventually drowned that achievement in distrust. For Kissinger, the failure seemed temporary. He had, after all, succeeded on the most important point: that of getting Smith to agree to majority rule within two years. With England, South Africa, and the United States all breathing down his neck, Smith could never retreat from that commitment. With this promise as a foundation, Kissinger knew he could, over the next few years, press for additional concessions, iron out the glitches in the interim government, and help the leaders reach a new settlement. Yet Kissinger did not have any years left. On the first Tuesday in November, just six weeks after the Rhodesian negotiations, Jimmy Carter defeated Gerald Ford, and Kissinger's long reign over American foreign policy came to an abrupt end.

TEN

Points of Pressure
(1976–1977)

Whilst it is illegal for us to call for trade boycotts, arms embargoes, and the withdrawal of investments, America herself is quite free to decide what price South Africa must pay for maintaining its obnoxious policies.
—STEPHEN BIKO

THE ELECTION of Jimmy Carter delighted Charles Diggs and the other members of the Congressional Black Caucus, who believed that the new Democratic administration would offer black Americans unprecedented opportunities to influence U.S. policy on southern Africa. To be effective, however, they knew they would have to transform the Black Forum on Foreign Policy into a serious organization. By the fall of 1976 they had been struggling for a year to clarify the group's purpose. A steering committee had selected a group of prominent "convenors," identified potential members, written by-laws, established a dues structure, and sent out a letter of invitation over Charles Diggs's signature. The committee members had continued to debate whether the organization should be a dispassionate educational forum or an active lobbying group. By the time of Carter's election, the infant council had already entered several public debates. In February 1976, for example, when Kissinger and Ford were still trying to bolster Savimbi in Angola, the forum opposed attempts by the CIA to recruit black Vietnam veterans to fight for UNITA as mercenaries.

As the organization took shape, the need to choose an executive director increased. The leading candidate was a talented foreign policy expert named Herschelle Challenor, a graduate of Spelman College, the Sorbonne, and Johns Hopkins, who had then gone on to obtain a Ph.D.

in international relations from Columbia in 1970. After two years as a program officer for the Ford Foundation, she had come to Washington to serve as the staff director of the House subcommittee on Africa. She had been intensively involved in the planning of the Black Forum on Foreign Policy, keeping Diggs, who was too busy to attend the meetings, informed through a stream of memos. Many people thought at the time that she was the natural choice, until another candidate emerged: Randall Robinson.

In the four years since his confrontation with Derek Bok at Harvard over Gulf's investments in Angola, Robinson had hopped among five jobs. While working with the Boston Legal Assistance Project, he had objected to his superiors that all of the managers of the project were white. When they ignored him, Robinson organized a letter writing campaign. When his superiors asked Robinson to retract the letter and he refused, they fired him. He then took a job at the Roxbury Multiservice Center, until Congressman William L. Clay of Missouri offered him a job in Washington. Robinson stayed with Clay for only six months and then moved to the Lawyers' Committee for Civil Rights under Law until early 1976, when Charles Diggs asked him to become his administrative assistant.

It was in Diggs's office, Robinson recalled, that he fully came to understand the importance of "the link between what was happening in Congress and what was happening on the campuses. You couldn't get anything going legislatively unless you had built a base." Robinson, who had his hands full straightening out administrative problems in Diggs's office during the first stage of discussion of the Black Forum, sided with those who at the time favored the creation of an active lobbying group that could stir up enough trouble in the field to capture the attention of the representatives in Washington. Organizers of the Black Forum continued to refine the organization's purpose and design, steadily turning away from the original notion of a detached study group. As the participants discovered the similarity of their reactions to the Clark amendment, the civil war in Angola, the Soweto riots, and Kissinger's sudden decision to involve himself in the Rhodesian conflict, the numbers of those who favored a nonpartisan clearinghouse dwindled. The differences in approach crystallized when the steering committee had to select either Challenor or Robinson for executive director. Challenor was a foreign policy expert, schooled in global analysis. Robinson was a lawyer who was keenly focused on the dynamics of domestic politics. Challenor favored reflection; Robinson strongly endorsed activism. Challenor had wanted to start the group and have it grow steadily; Robinson preferred to wait, raise a full year's budget in advance, and have a big-bang launch. Challenor believed in building an association guided by discussion and consensus; Robinson believed that effectiveness demanded that the group be tightly organized around a strong director. Whatever the reason, as Robinson's position waxed, Challenor's waned.

Robinson's increased influence over the new organization and his view that the critical participants had to raise a large amount of money slowed down its establishment. In September 1976, a year after the original discussion, the members of the Congressional Black Caucus again held a conference to discuss foreign policy, during which they criticized Kissinger's involvement with Vorster and Smith. At the same conference, they approved the formation of the new lobbying group. The official announcement of the organization—which had been renamed TransAfrica—and of Randall Robinson's selection as executive director came the following July, six months after Carter's inauguration. Robinson and the fledgling staff of TransAfrica didn't actually open up shop—assisted by significant grants from several church groups—until the spring of 1978, two and a half years after the initial discussions. Despite this slow beginning, the new organization would soon emerge as one of the most powerful forces in the transformation of America's relationship with South Africa.

Outside Washington, the growing community of activist investors had responded to the Soweto riots with a new burst of support for South African resolutions of various kinds. Corporate executives also began feeling more pressure to articulate a plausible policy with which to respond to public inquiries. The surge of interest induced some executives to back Leon Sullivan's efforts to draft a statement of principles. Most decided to wait. During the summer of 1976, as the media debated the role of the American government and business in South Africa, calls for decisive action increased. Tim Smith and the Interfaith Center on Corporate Responsibility stung General Motors by publicizing a full-page advertisement that had been purchased by General Motors dealers in South Africa declaring their support for the South African Defence Force. In August 1976, Vernon Jordan of the National Urban League publicly demanded that U.S. corporations in South Africa declare a moratorium on all new investments and become more active in ending apartheid. By the fall, the external pressure on corporations had eased, and Sullivan's efforts to advance the principles faltered. Sullivan's campaign received a boost with the election of Jimmy Carter, who indicated his intention to redirect American foreign policy. The president-elect picked liberal lawyer Cyrus Vance as the new secretary of state and former Martin Luther King aide and Georgia Congressman Andrew Young as ambassador to the United Nations.

Because of Young's leadership in the Southern Christian Leadership Conference and the civil rights movement, everyone expected him to take a strong stand against apartheid. Few knew that he had an even more personal reason for doing so, as the result of the friendship he had formed with Robert Sobukwe, the founder of the Pan-Africanist Congress, during a trip to South Africa with tennis star Arthur Ashe in the early 1970s. Young had asked Sobukwe whether there was anything he could do to help. Sobukwe had said no, the South Africans had to wage their own struggle. Young politely disagreed and said he was sure there were some ways that Americans could be of assistance. Sobukwe, impressed by Young's determination, asked if Young could help him provide a decent education for his teenage son and daughter. Young returned to the United States, arranged for visas, and secured spots in a remedial program at Atlanta Junior College, where Young's wife, Jean, taught. In May 1975 Miliswa and Dinilesizwe Sobukwe arrived in Atlanta and moved into Young's home. In November 1976, Miliswa was studying biology at Spelman College and Dinilesizwe was an engineering student at Morehouse College when their host was tapped by Carter for the UN post.

President Carter's new foreign policy team faced the gargantuan task of altering the tangle of policies, practices, and personnel established over eight years by Henry Kissinger. The new president had announced that the cornerstone of his foreign policy would be a commitment to human rights, a commitment that forced a reevaluation of the official American relationships with dozens of countries, especially the Soviet Union. Young was quick to extend the new approach to southern Africa. In January 1977, even before he had assumed his post, he told reporters that he thought the new administration would have "a very aggressive policy to move towards majority rule in southern Africa. . . . I don't see sanctions," Young continued, "because sanctions very seldom have worked. I think what we have got to do is find ways to use the tremendous influence we have to move towards majority rule."

The new president and secretary of state, while agreeing with Young's sentiments, spent the first months searching for a balance between the tacit cooperation of the past and an outright break with Pretoria. Within weeks after the inauguration, the United States began proposing that the members of the UN Security Council approve a Declaration of Principles opposing racism in southern Africa, a move which attracted enough support from the nationalist groups and African nations that the Soviets reportedly had to scramble to block it. The State Department then drew up a secret list of additional steps—from withdrawing U.S. military attachés in Pretoria and ending the exchange of intelligence information to reducing Export-Import Bank loan guarantees and refusing visas to South Africans—that the U.S. government could take. Leon Sullivan's effort—a privately sponsored, religiously guided effort to induce change within key sectors of the South African economy—seemed the perfect corollary.

Vance and Young worked actively to shape and promote the endorsement of the corporate statement of principles. Within weeks of becoming secretary of state, Vance invited the chief executives of the major companies who were considering becoming signatories to come to his office at the State Department. Wayne Fredericks accompanied them. As he and the chief executives stood outside the secretary's office, some began to get cold feet. Despite the many statements they had made about their commitment to equality, the riots in Soweto, and a full year of private discussions, several of the executives were still uncertain whether they should sign Sullivan's statement. "One of them spoke up and said, 'Don't you think we should go over and talk to the South African ambassador first?'" Fredericks recalled. "And the others seemed to agree, saying, 'We really should do that.' Although my rank and status did not really permit me to make the comment, I spoke up. 'We cannot appear to be seeking the approval of the South Africa ambassador before embarking on this,' I told them. 'We worked on this, we are ready, the only thing is to go in and do it.' I was concerned that even at this late stage, people were fearful of moving forward on it."

On the first of March 1977, after eighteen months of private pushing, debating, and cajoling, Sullivan finally announced the "Statement of Principles of U.S. Firms with Affiliates in the Republic of South Africa," which called for

1. Non-segregation of the races in all eating, comfort, and work facilities
2. Equal and fair employment practices for all employees
3. Equal pay for all employees doing equal or comparable work for the same period of time
4. Initiation of and development of training programs that will prepare, in substantial numbers, Blacks and other non-whites for supervisory, administrative, clerical and technical jobs
5. Increasing the number of Blacks and other non-whites in management and supervisory positions
6. Improving the quality of employees' lives outside the work environment in such areas as housing, transportation, schooling, recreation, and health facilities.

"We agree to further implement these principles," said the document. "Where implementation requires a modification of existing South Africa working conditions, we will seek such modification through appropriate channels. We believe that the implementation of the foregoing principles is consistent with respect for human dignity and will contribute directly to the general economic welfare of all the people of the Republic of South Africa." After months of effort, Sullivan had succeeded in persuading a dozen companies to sign on: American Cyanamid, Burroughs, Caltex, Citicorp, Ford, General Motors, IBM, International Harvester, Minnesota Mining and Manufacturing, Otis Elevator, and Union Carbide. Reaction to the "Sullivan Principles," as they were quickly dubbed in British and then American newspapers, was uneven. The South African government responded with cautious approval. "This . . . is a very laudable stand to take as opposed to the one you first advocated," wrote the South African consul to Sullivan. Anti-apartheid groups were less enthusiastic. George Houser and Jennifer Davis at the American Committee on Africa instantly attacked the principles as "an exercise in triviality." They argued that the workplace reforms, even if implemented, could not make up for the massive material, financial, and psychological support American corporations provided to the South African government. "There is no demand for any change in the fundamental structure of apartheid, no demand for black political rights, and, closer to home, no commitment to negotiating with black trade unions or demands for their recognition by the government," wrote Davis a month after the announcement. As a result, she concluded, "there is no way that a continued U.S. corporate presence in South Africa can serve any purpose except to reinforce white rule."

Timothy Smith and the members of the Interfaith Center on Corporate Responsibility substantially agreed with Davis and Houser. Smith realized, however, that the differences between ICCR and Sullivan could be used to increase pressure on corporate executives. In March 1977, Sullivan and Smith met to discuss the relationship between their strategies. Smith assured Sullivan that the churches would do what they could to push corporations to sign and implement the principles. Sullivan in turn agreed to raise broader questions—bank loans, sales to the military and police, and transfer of nuclear technology—with the top executives of the companies with which he was in contact.

While the church community debated the acceptability and effectiveness of the Sullivan Principles, the Carter administration moved forward with its plans to increase the pressure on Vorster. On May 5, 1977, Vance announced that Vice President Walter Mondale would be meeting with John Vorster in Vienna and that Mondale would formally ask Vorster to describe how South Africa planned to end apartheid. Shortly afterward Andrew Young said that he had accepted an invitation to pass through Johannesburg on his way back from a UN conference in Mozambique. The meetings were preceded by a flurry of controversy in the press about remarks made by Young. In April he had told a British television team that economic sanctions might be a legitimate nonviolent method to use against South Africa, comparable to Martin Luther King's use of sit-ins in the American South. "At some point we've got to come to the conclusion that we're no longer going to finance apartheid," he said. "When we come to that conclusion, it's amazing how quickly the South Africans will come to their senses."

Such outspokenness about South Africa and other sensitive diplomatic issues often got Young into trouble, sometimes forcing Cyrus Vance to issue a stream of retractions or corrections. When Young said that South Africa could force Rhodesia to negotiate, Vance had to respond, "I don't think it's quite that simple." When Young asserted that "there's a sense in which the Cubans bring a certain stability and order to Angola," Vance had to correct him by saying that "the presence of any outside forces is not helpful to a peaceful solution." In mid-April, Young touched off another round of debate when a reporter asked him if he considered the South African government "illegitimate." Young, who had been discussing the philosophical principle of majority rule, said "Yeah." Since the U.S. government's official position was that the National Party leaders were the legitimate rulers of South Africa, both the State Department and the White House had to issue formal retractions of Young's remarks.

Young tried to explain himself in his first major speech eleven weeks after taking office. "All my life, everything I have done has been controversial and naive and people have advised me against it," he said to the United Nations Association on April 19. "You know that protocol has never been part of my style." He acted, he told the group, out of optimism about what could happen between human beings. As a civil rights worker, he noted, he had been beaten and jailed on several occasions. Then, a few days later, his jailers had apologized for their behavior. "I have faith that the same kind of thing can happen between blacks and whites in South Africa," he continued. "Everybody tells me that's ridiculous, that the situation is just not the same . . . [but] if we ever believe things are impossible then we've got nothing to live for. The impossible dreams make life worthwhile and I wouldn't trade them for any amount of realism, caution, and protocol in the world."

Young's explicit linkage of the civil rights movement with American policy toward South Africa helped to frame the debate in a way that previous administrations had tried to avoid. The connection had been pointed out for years by religious and political activists, and it was gaining ground on American campuses, but Young was the first American government official since Soapy Williams to link the two directly and publicly. The danger of such a fusion had long been apparent to the South African government, whose representatives vigorously rejected the comparison. Civil rights for blacks could be achieved in the United States at relatively low cost, argued Pik Botha, South Africa's new foreign minister, because whites were in the overwhelming majority. In South Africa such rights would lead to white "self-annihilation." "We have been here for as long as the Americans have been in America," Botha told a *New York Times* reporter shortly before the meeting between Mondale and Vorster. "Would they do it? Would the Americans do it if the whole world insisted that they ought to follow a policy which inevitably would lead to their destruction?"

On Monday, May 16, 1977, three days before the meeting between Mondale and Vorster, Winnie Mandela was awakened at four in the morning by loud pounding on her doors and windows. She opened the front door and found a detachment of heavily armed members of the Security Branch, who told her nothing and took her to the Protea police station. Six hours later she was informed that she and her daughter Zindzi were being banished permanently from Soweto. The police took her briefly back to her home, where she watched them rip the sheets from the bed, throw them on the floor, and hurl her worldly possessions—her dishes, Nelson's books, her personal items and clothes—into indiscriminate piles in the center. The men then threw the bundles into the back of one military truck while Zindzi and Winnie were loaded into another. The column started up, moved out of town, turned southwest, and drove two hundred sixty miles into the Orange Free State. Winnie and Zindzi spent the trip in the back of the truck, encircled by armed white police. The truck transported them into the town of Brandfort, the same rural, heavily Afrikaner enclave in which Hendrik Verwoerd had spent his childhood. There the security officers delivered the Mandelas and their bundles to the local police, who were waiting for them in full battle gear. The local police took the mother and daughter to the African community on the outskirts of town and dropped them and their bundles in front of their new house, a small cinderblock structure filled with trash. Inside, Winnie found three tiny rooms, which together made up barely more than a hundred square feet. The doors were so narrow that none of her furniture could be brought inside, so the police took it and stored it at the station. There was no electricity, no stove, and no water. The police finally left, after warning Winnie's new neighbors not to speak to her. Winnie and Zindzi shoveled the dirt out of one of the rooms, stretched out a mattress, and huddled together on it, trying to shut out the brutality of the day and the biting winter wind that whistled all night through the dark house.

□ □ □ □

In his meeting with John Vorster, Vice President Mondale did the best he could to make it clear that the official American attitude toward South Africa had changed. From now on the United States would not rely solely on anti-apartheid rhetoric, but would back up its words with actions. Unless South Africa was willing to commit to a "progressive transformation," Mondale said, President Carter would be forced to take diplomatic steps against the country. Nor was the United States willing to trade progress in Rhodesia and Namibia for inaction on apartheid, as Kissinger had done. Vorster responded equally bluntly. South Africa was not a multiracial country, he told Mondale, but a multinational one, whose design would guarantee the maintenance of distinctive forms of culture. Even when Mondale asked him about the banishment of Winnie Mandela, Vorster offered no concession. Mrs. Mandela was free to emigrate from the country whenever she wished.

Mondale did not believe that he had changed Vorster's mind, but he left the meeting feeling he had done his job. In the past, the pattern had been, as a member of Mondale's staff put it, one of "saying these things to Vorster and then winking." "I think most Americans feel very good about having come clean on this issue," Mondale told reporters at a press conference in London immediately after the encounter. He had told Vorster that the United States would not intervene to save South Africa from the consequences of its policies. If Vorster persisted, "our paths will diverge and our policies will come into conflict. . . . In that event we would take steps true to our beliefs and values." At his press conference, Mondale went further than any American official had ever gone. A South African journalist asked him if he could "go into slightly more detail on the concept of full participation as opposed to one-man-one-vote? Do you see some kind of compromise?" Mondale refused to hedge. "No, no, it's the same thing," he said, embracing the greatest heresy of white South African politics. "Every citizen should have the right to vote and every vote should be equally weighted."

Vorster was convinced that the Carter administration's rhetorical stance was driven by American domestic politics rather than a genuine desire to change South Africa. Public posturing by American officials, he felt, could not erase the reality of South Africa's might or America's own economic interests. "I think sound judgment will prevail," Vorster told reporters. There was always a difference between theory and practice, he continued, and "we'll see in six or nine months how it works out." Against this backdrop, Andrew Young arrived in South Africa one day after the Vorster-Mondale conversations had concluded. When his U.S. air force jet touched down in Johannesburg, the South African customs police escorted it to a distant part of the airport. Young stepped off the plane, greeted the white customs officials, and then shook hands—in the double clutch black power handshake—with all the black chauffeurs. He was driven around town in a convoy surrounded by a dozen motorcycle police. Shortly after his arrival he spoke to a group of two hundred business leaders and again drew a direct comparison between apartheid and the experience in the American South. Just as business leaders had played a vital role in ending the segregated rule of Bull Connor in Birmingham, he said, so could they exercise powerful leadership in South Africa. He strongly endorsed the concept of free enterprise, telling them that if Africans at the bottom of the system were given an economic stake in the society, they would not want revolution. "People will vote their interest, not their ideology," he said. "One of the good things about South Africa is that nobody has anywhere to go and you have no choice but to work it out or to fight it out. I hope you work it out." During the question and answer period, Lionel Leon, a leader of the Labour Party, asked Young, "How long must we talk to people who have gone deaf?" "I think you have to find a way to make them hear," Young responded. "We used to say in the civil rights movement that there were only two things white people would listen to: votes and dollars. Since we didn't have the votes, we used the dollars." Young stopped himself and smiled. "I'm not advocating [a boycott] because to do so would be to interfere in your internal affairs. I'm a sophisticated diplomat and I wouldn't want to do that."

The next day, however, Young again brought up the role of boycotts. He had originally intended to visit Soweto but changed his mind because he did not want to antagonize the government further. Instead, he met with several black delegations and student groups. Though the meetings were ostensibly private, they were widely reported in the black press. Young told the delegations that he thought they should use economic boycotts against apartheid. He also told them that he thought it would be hypocritical for the United States to condemn violence by blacks seeking freedom when Americans had themselves fought a revolutionary war of independence. Such deliberate linkage of American and South African history again infuriated the government and many of its supporters. "Who does he think he is, coming here and telling us how to run our country?" asked a middle-aged Afrikaner woman as she watched the ambassador walk into his hotel. "He may know something about racial questions in America, but he doesn't know anything about us."

In early July, Secretary Vance kept up the pressure on South Africa. In a major speech to the NAACP, Vance rejected his predecessor's policy of ignoring apartheid for the sake of Rhodesia and Namibia, insisted that America had a direct stake in progress inside South Africa, and issued a warning. If South Africa was not willing to play a "progressive role" in these areas, "our relations will inevitably suffer. We cannot defend a system that is based on racial domination and remain true to ourselves." Foreign Minister Pik Botha struck back shortly afterward, telling an American reporter in South Africa that Vorster was interested in reform but that the Carter administration's position was already producing a "backlash" among the Afrikaners. "They're making it impossible for us," he said. "All they're doing is encouraging violence and confrontation." Botha's own rhetoric had also sharpened as he denounced the "selective morality" and "hypocrisy" of the Carter approach, which, he said, did not try to hold other African states to the same standards.

In August 1977, John Vorster himself retaliated even more fiercely, claiming that Carter was acting solely for domestic motives. "It is true that the bulk of Negroes in the United States voted for the Carter Administration," said Vorster at an event marking the fiftieth anniversary of South Africa's Department of Foreign Affairs, "and it is accepted in the United States and elsewhere that the Carter Administration is at present under pressure from the Black Caucus and other organizations." Such influence had forced Carter to adopt a policy that would lead to "chaos and anarchy in South Africa," Vorster continued. If Carter persisted, the end result would be exactly the same as if South Africa had been subverted by Marxism. "In one case, it will come about as a result of brute force," said Vorster, "and in the other it will be strangulation with finesse."

Since his 1973 banning and restriction to King William's Town, Stephen Biko had continued to promote Black Consciousness and self-help through local "Black Community Programs." With Dr. Mamphela Ramphele, one of a handful of female black physicians in South Africa and a longtime companion, Biko helped set up the Zanempilo Clinic on a small hill outside of town. The clinic provided operating facilities, maternity wards, nutrition classes, and health instruction for thousands of rural Africans who could not travel to the city hospital. It also served as a clearinghouse of information for the kinds of community efforts that Biko was trying to promote.

During this period Biko, Ramphele, and their colleagues were exasperated by articles in the white press attacking Black Consciousness and praising Buthelezi, Mangope, Matanzima, and the other bantustan leaders. One of those who bothered them most was Donald Woods, the liberal editor of the East London *Daily Dispatch,* who wrote a stream of columns accusing SASO of racism. The forty-year-old Woods was fiercely proud of his liberal convictions. He was born on December 15, 1933—the same day as Jennifer Davis—and grew up on a farm in the

Transkei among the Bomvana people, from whom he learned to speak fluent Xhosa. After studying law at the University of Cape Town and flirting with politics, he moved into journalism. He spent a few years as a junior reporter and then traveled to Britain and Canada in 1958, wrote for several papers there, and even made a trip through the southern United States, where he had a chance to observe examples of American racism firsthand. When Woods arrived in Little Rock, Arkansas, for example, he checked into a hotel and then visited its bar. Suddenly, a state trooper ran into the room and announced that the Ku Klux Klan had "dynamited a nigger's house on the edge of town. There were whoops of approval by the bar from customers who ordered more drinks to celebrate," Woods wrote later.

Woods returned to South Africa in 1960 and remained in journalism, rising over the next thirteen years to become the editor of the *Daily Dispatch.* In his regular columns he fiercely attacked National Party policies, defended nonracialism, promoted the work of white liberal organizations like NUSAS, and advocated integration. When Black Consciousness emerged and led to the formation of SASO, Woods felt it was "a betrayal of the white liberal commitment. . . . I felt the same way about the other Black Consciousness groups Biko had founded, such as the Black Community Programs, and all-black sports bodies and trust funds for maintenance of the families of political prisoners," Woods wrote a few years later. "They seemed to me to be inversions of the apartheid mentality—racism in reverse." After one such column Biko dispatched Ramphele to invite Woods to King William's Town. When Woods heard that a "Dr. Ramphele" was waiting to see him, he pictured an "elderly, gray-haired medico with an Uncle Tom diffidence." Instead, a small woman in blue jeans and white sweater burst through his office door, planted herself in front of his desk, put her hands on her hips, and dressed him down. "Why do you give all the headlines to sell-outs like Buthelezi and Matanzima?" she asked. "Why don't you get to know the real black leaders? When are you coming to talk to Steve Biko? You know he is banned and can't come to you, so why don't you come to him? What's the matter with you?"

Woods was so startled that he instantly accepted. A few days later he drove to King William's Town and found the office of the Black Community Programs in a converted church on Leopold Street. Woods was led out to the backyard and introduced to Biko. "My first impression was of his size," Woods remembered. "He stood a couple of inches over me and had the bulky build of a heavyweight boxer." Within minutes the two men had launched into a verbal tussle over white liberalism and Black Consciousness. After several hours, Woods realized that his facile dismissal of Black Consciousness had been overcome by Biko's impassioned explanation of the necessity of restoring black self-confidence. By the time they parted, Woods had agreed to hire a columnist for his paper to report on Black Consciousness and Biko felt comfortable enough to tease the liberal editor about his Mercedes. "My God," he said, "how can a champion of the people be driving around in such a thing!" "Look," Woods replied, "the days of white privilege are numbered and I am enjoying it while I can." Biko laughed.

Over the next few months, Woods, his wife, Wendy, and their children made many pilgrimages to King William's Town. Knowing of Biko's love of American music, the Woodses brought tunes by Scott Joplin, Fats Waller, and Duke Ellington to play on the piano for their new friend. Soon they became a part of Biko's circle. They were not the only whites in this group; Biko also enjoyed close relationships with Anglican clergy such as Aelrud Stubbs and David Russell, with whom he frequently discussed theology, and with economist Francis Wilson. For Biko, however, Woods represented a special challenge. If he could convince this disputatious liberal editor of the merits of the Black Consciousness movement, then there was hope. Woods, for his part, was drawn, first through argument and then through experience, into deeper and deeper respect and affection for the young leader.

One of the things about which Biko and Woods argued regularly was the policy of the United States government toward South Africa. Biko, though wary of Soviet Communism, pointed out that the Eastern bloc had been far more willing to censure South Africa in the United Nations and to impose sanctions. "There was much about American ideals that he liked," Woods recalled, "but he was cynical about Western capitalism and the West's protective attitude towards its investments in South Africa. He explained that the young blacks of South Africa were becoming increasingly anti-West because the Western countries merely slapped the wrist of the Vorster government when they felt an anti-apartheid gesture was called for, but maintained their diplomatic and economic links which helped to bolster the regime."

Biko's opinion about Western investment fit closely with the official position of SASO and the Black People's Convention, which had condemned foreign investment in South Africa at their earliest meetings. In 1976, despite his banning, Biko was able to present his opinion on foreign investment publicly during the lengthy trial of a group of his colleagues. Six months after a pro-FRELIMO rally in the fall of 1974, the Nationalist government had arrested and prosecuted nine young blacks for alleged "subversion by intent." The charge included the accusation that they had conspired to "create and foster feelings of racial hatred, hostility, and antipathy by the Blacks towards the White Population . . . [and] to denigrate the Whites and to represent them as inhuman oppressors, and to induce, persuade, and pressure the Blacks to totally reject the White man and his way of life and to defy him." The state's argument, in effect, was that the opinions of the defendants were so dangerous that they caused a severe threat to public safety. Black Consciousness, said the prosecutor, would eventually lead to the mobilization of black opinion against the white establishment and thus to "racial confrontation." The defendants—and those like Biko who were called as witnesses for the defense—were placed in the difficult position of having to defend themselves against charges of treason without renouncing their philosophy.

The prosecution's case took much of 1975 to establish; then, in early 1976, the defense lawyers carefully constructed their rebuttal. Biko was called to offer public testimony in May. His lengthy exchanges provided an extraordinary view of the speed and subtlety of his mind as he attempted to persuade the court of the legitimacy of Black Consciousness without providing ammunition to the prosecution. Throughout this intellectual high-wire act, which took place before an evidently biased judge, Biko displayed both wit and insight. At one point, during questioning by defense attorney David Soggott, Biko explained his use of the American black power phrase "Black is beautiful."

SOGGOTT: The use of the word "black," what does black signify and how is it used in language?

JUDGE BOSHOFF: Is it a comprehensive term?

BIKO: If I understand you correctly, the reference I think of common literature to the term black is normally associated with negative aspects. You speak of the black market, you speak of the black sheep of the family, you speak of—you know, anything which is supposed to be bad is also considered to be black.

THE JUDGE: Now the word, black there, surely it has nothing to do with the black man. Isn't it just idiom over the years because darkness usually, the night, was a mystery for the primitive man—I mean, I include the whites when I talk about "primitive man." So when he talks about "dark forces" or he refers to "black magic," isn't that the reason for this?

BIKO: That certainly is the reason, but I think there has been through history and through common reference the attitude where exactly that kind of association is perpetuated even for the black man. The black man sees this as being said of black magic, of the black market, precisely because, like him, it is an inferior thing; it is an unwanted thing; it is a thing rejected by society. And of course, typically, and in the face of this logic, whiteness goes with angels, God, and beauty. I think this tends to help in creating this kind of feeling of self-censure within

the black man. . . . When you say "black is beautiful," what you are
in fact saying is: "Man, you are okay as you are. Begin to look upon
yourself as a human being."

THE JUDGE: Mr. Biko, why do you people then pick on the word "black"?
I mean "black" is really an innocent reference which has been arrived
at over the years, the same as white. Snow is regarded as white, and
snow is regarded as the purest form of water, and so it symbolizes
purity. So "white" there has got nothing to do with the white man?

BIKO: Right.

THE JUDGE: But now, why do you refer to your people as blacks? Why
not brown people? I mean, you people are more brown than black.

BIKO: In the same way as I think white people are more pink than white.

On May 3, 1976, Biko was quizzed extensively about SASO's position
on foreign investment. Since the defendants had also been formally
charged with conspiracy "to discourage, hamper, deter, or prevent foreign investment in the economy of the Republic of South Africa, and to
call upon investors to disengage themselves from the said economy,"
Biko again had to walk an extremely delicate line. "We believe South
Africa is particularly sensitive to criticism by the world of its policies,"
Biko told the court. "We believe that part of our political campaign is to
make sure that as many people as possible criticize South Africa. Putting pressure on foreign companies about their participation in this immoral setup was also calculated to make sure that foreign governments
began to feel unhappy about the participation of their firms in this
country and to assist generally in building up pressure to make South
Africa shift its attitudes gradually to a more acceptable stance."

Judge Boshoff again intervened. "Were there any pushers of the
antiforeign investment line whose aim was to achieve a weakening of the
South Africa economy?" he asked. No, said Biko disingenuously. "Or
the creation of widespread unemployment?" "Certainly not," replied
Biko. Did the leaders of SASO believe that the foreign companies would
actually leave? asked the defense attorney. No, said Biko. "We never,
for a moment, believed that foreign firms would, as a result of this kind
of stance, withdraw." Since Sharpeville, Biko pointed out, the government had made it extremely difficult for foreign investors to withdraw
their funds. Nonetheless, there was still value in urging withdrawal. "We
believe that if we are to move toward a peaceful solution, our efforts
must be coupled with support from other people, from other governments," Biko told the court, "and we see this whole foreign investment
question as a vehicle for generating pressure to sympathize with our
point of view." Biko explicitly rejected the argument that investment
created jobs and thus helped blacks. "This is like the attitude taken by

Polaroid to say they are going to be involved in the future problems of the black man by donating part of their profits to welfare programs," Biko said. "We felt this was paternalistic. We felt that the point of application of foreign investors must be the humanity of the men they employ rather than pandering to considerations of materialism, like giving him a token increment here or giving him token assistance at the social welfare level.

"There is no way in which established industry which has been set up with foreign capital in this country is going to be killed just because one proprietor pulls out," Biko continued, "because there is always going to be another who takes over. So from the point of view of jobs and job situations, those blacks who are employed in firms by direct foreign investment are going to continue in employment. What we attack is precisely the fact that when these people have got a point of leverage, because they are not South Africans, because they are subject back at home, probably, to more liberal attitudes, they don't make use of this. This is what we attack."

Biko's remarks, which were reported every day for a week in the *Rand Daily Mail,* dramatically increased his reputation in townships and spread the doctrine of Black Consciousness more widely than ever before. Less than ten days later, the children of Soweto began their strike against the teaching of Afrikaans. Biko believed that the ideas were catching on and hoped that this would mark the beginning of significant change. The police also thought that Biko's ideas were responsible for some of the unrest. During one of the national police sweeps in August, they arrested and imprisoned him without charges for a hundred and one days. "On the day of his detention, he seemed sure he would be back soon and did not appear unduly worried," recalled his wife, Ntsiki, ". . . but we became extremely worried and his mother actually feared for his life."

Biko emerged from jail to find the South African government determined to squash resistance in the townships once and for all. In late September, the police had opened fire during a funeral for a twenty-year-old man and had killed seven mourners. The Soweto Student Representative Council, still the dominant political force in the township, had managed to organize a third stay-away, this time with the assistance of the hostel dwellers, but a fourth one in early November had failed. The SSRC members had then tried to redirect their attention to problems within the township. They launched campaigns to clean up the mountains of garbage that had piled up since the government had stopped collecting it in June; they demanded that the hundreds of *shebeens,* or private township saloons, shut down for sapping the strength and money from the population; and they organized a partially successful Christmas boycott of white stores by black consumers. A few months later, at the height of their power, the SSRC successfully fought a large rent increase for all of Soweto.

Nonetheless, the students faced insurmountable problems. They were fundamentally split over the question of education. Should they boycott the Bantu schools until the schools were improved, or should they continue to get an education, no matter how inferior it might be? Rifts in opinion on this question stymied the organizers for months. The students also worried because they knew they were slowly losing the support of their parents, who, after three stay-aways, legitimately feared that any future job actions would leave them unemployed. And they suffered from the constant assaults by the government on their leaders and supporters. In eleven months, the SSRC went through no less than four presidents; one was arrested, and three fled to Botswana. Thousands of the most active black youth left the country to join the guerrilla wings of the ANC and PAC.

In January 1977, Biko wrote a memorandum on American foreign policy in preparation for a meeting with U.S. Senator Dick Clark. "America's choice is narrowed down to either entrenching the existing minority white regime," Biko wrote, "or alternatively assisting, in a very definite way, the attainment of the aspirations of millions of the black population as well as those of whites of good will." Though "many words and statements to this effect have been made by politicians in America," Biko noted, "very little by way of constructive action has been taken to apply concerted pressure on the minority white South African regime to the detriment of the interests of black people."

On the contrary, Biko argued, American involvement with South Africa had actually increased and he called on the Carter administration to take a harder line. "Where American firms do not withdraw," Biko continued, "the least that can be expected is for their government to set rigid rules on questions like remuneration, rate for the job, job reservations, and trade unions, to make completely sure that American companies are not involved in the exploitation of blacks." Biko's strategy—that the American *government* should "set rigid rules"—resembled that of Charles Diggs more than that of Leon Sullivan, whose private initiative was not publicly announced until two months after Biko's memo. When the Carter administration endorsed the voluntary Sullivan approach, Biko reacted with irritation. In a private interview in July 1977, Biko, unfettered by the strictures of the courtroom, rebutted the most common argument about the need for American investment. "The argument is often made that loss of foreign investment would hurt blacks most," he said. "It would undoubtedly hurt blacks in the short run, because many of them would stand to lose their jobs, but it should be understood in Europe and North America that foreign investment supports the present economic system and thus indirectly the present system of political injustice. We blacks are therefore not interested in foreign investment. If Washington wants to contribute to the development of a just society in South Africa, it must discourage investment in South Africa. We blacks are perfectly willing to suffer the consequences. We are quite accustomed to suffering."

Despite the new rhetorical tone, the Carter administration's incrementalist policy toward South Africa seems to have embittered Biko toward the United States. When the leaders of the U.S.–South African Leadership Exchange Program (USSALEP) urged Biko to accept a scholarship to visit the United States for several months, Biko declined, saying that he would not do so until the United States had given proof of a radically changed policy toward South Africa. When Andrew Young visited in May, Biko refused to meet him because he felt that Young should try to see Mandela first. Biko doubted that the American efforts would accomplish much and worried that President Carter's personal piety and choice of Andrew Young would shield American policy from legitimate criticism. "Carter uses Andrew Young's color as a special passport to the Third World," Biko complained. "But Young has no program except the furtherance of the American system."

For months, official harassment of Biko by the Security Police increased steadily. They arrested him in March 1977 and then released him. They arrested him again in July, charged him under the Suppression of Communism Act, and let him out on bail until his trial. On August 18, a police roadblock captured Biko and a friend near Grahamstown in the Eastern Cape, far outside the limits of his banning restriction. The officers transported Biko to the police headquarters in Port Elizabeth, stripped him naked, and threw him in a cell. For the next two and a half weeks, his guards would not let him out, either to exercise, to contact his family, or to wash. He was fed only bread and water and was denied clothes. On September 2, a magistrate toured the facility and came upon Biko, sitting huddled under a prison blanket. "Is it compulsory that I have to be naked?" Biko asked him. "I have been naked since I came here."

On Tuesday morning, September 6, after nearly three weeks in his cell, the guards brought Biko to an interrogation room, where they permitted him to dress in undershorts. For eight hours, they confronted him with pamphlets obtained from informants that they wished him to acknowledge as his own. Receiving an unsatisfactory response, they left him for the night team, whose traditional role was to inflict sufficient physical and mental pain on the prisoner to secure compliance. Biko had received such treatment before and had vowed never to suffer physical abuse without trying to strike back. At some point in the early hours of the morning of Wednesday, September 7, 1977, Biko's white tormentors, enraged by him and by everything he stood for, unleashed their full fury on their defiant captive.

When the morning team returned, they found a bruised and unresponsive Biko shackled to a grille and lying on the floor. Unable to rouse him, they left him for several hours. When they came back, they found that Biko had not moved, and they summoned a doctor, who revived him. Though he found that Biko slurred his words and had difficulty moving his limbs, the doctor concluded that there was nothing wrong. The Security Police kept Biko shackled in the interrogation room for another twenty-four hours, during which they noticed that he neither ate nor urinated. Colonel Pieter Goosen, the head of the Port Elizabeth Security Police, said later that he was not alarmed by this because he believed that Biko, a medical student, was capable of faking these symptoms through the use of yoga. The next day, when Biko's condition had not changed, the police called in a specialist who discovered that Biko had lost the extensor planar reflex in his foot, an unmistakable sign of neurological damage.

At this point Colonel Goosen acknowledged that Biko needed medical attention but would not permit him to be transferred to a hospital because of the lack of security. Goosen sent him instead to the Sydenham prison infirmary, where technicians performed a spinal tap to determine whether there was cerebral bleeding. Though the tap came back full of red cells, the authorities concluded that the sample had been contaminated during the procedure and could not be interpreted as proof of injury to the brain. For the next two days Biko, only partially conscious, neither ate nor drank. On Sunday, September 11, when the police moved Biko back to his cell, he was breathing hurriedly and foaming around the lips. The doctors again informed Colonel Goosen that Biko needed to be transferred to a hospital, and the police commander repeated his refusal to allow a transfer to a local facility. Instead, Goosen ordered that Biko be transported to the fortified police hospital outside of Pretoria, more than seven hundred miles north. Two police officers loaded Biko's inert body, still naked, into the back of a Land Rover, chained him inside, and drove through the night. When they arrived in Pretoria, they carried him in and dropped him on the concrete floor of a filthy cell. The doctor who examined Biko on his arrival was given no information about his prior history and only administered a shot of vitamins. A few hours later, battered, naked, and alone, Stephen Biko died.

The police made the terse announcement the following day. Though the English newspapers and international wire services sizzled with the news of Biko's death, the state-controlled radio and television stations did not mention it. Biko's widow, Ntsiki, was not contacted by the police directly but heard the news through her sister. Donald Woods received word at his office. At first he didn't believe it—the Nationalists aren't *that* crazy, he thought. When the truth was confirmed, Woods's whole world changed. "South Africa became a different place for me," he recalled. "The Nationalists were no longer simply disastrously misguided racists—they were now the mortal enemy, who stopped at nothing."

Police Minister Kruger's first public reaction was to suggest that Biko had died of a hunger strike. On hearing this, Woods instantly recalled the many conversations he had had with Biko about death in detention. Biko had known that it might happen and had said that if the police said that he had died by suffocation, hanging, bleeding, or starvation, Woods should recognize it as a lie. When Kruger was asked about Biko's death at the Transvaal congress of the Nationalist Party, which was taking place at the time, the minister of police flaunted his toughness. "Biko's death," he said to the applauding delegates, "leaves me cold."

Within a few days, as an avalanche of questions and criticisms engulfed Pretoria, Kruger retracted his early explanations. Biko had not died *because* of a hunger strike, he said, but simply *after* one. Kruger also launched his own offensive, appearing on television to accuse Biko of plotting and advocating violence. Woods, infuriated by Kruger's lies, challenged the minister of police to a public wager. If an independent team of pathologists agreed that Biko had died of a hunger strike, Woods not only would resign but would never write again. If they found that the cause of death was due to something else, Kruger would resign. Kruger declined to respond.

When the police pathologists finally did release Biko to the family for burial, Woods took Ntsiki to the mortuary. They found the body bruised but not emaciated. Both Wendy and Donald Woods wanted to attend Biko's interment on September 25, though they worried what would happen to a handful of whites in the midst of thousands of grief-stricken and enraged Africans. When they arrived, they were astonished by what they saw: hundreds of young whites, jammed together with more than twenty thousand Africans. Thousands more Africans from the Transvaal had tried to come by bus, but they had been prevented when black policemen had stopped the vehicles from departing and had beaten the occupants with truncheons. At the center of the sea of Africans sat a cluster of dignitaries from around the country and around the world. Nthato Motlana, the head of the Committee of Ten, a coordinating group for the many grassroots organizations in Soweto that had sprung up to fill the leadership vacuum, sat near Helen Suzman. Around them were distributed the official representatives of thirteen foreign countries. The United States government was represented not only by the U.S. ambassador but also by Donald McHenry, now deputy ambassador to the United Nations, who had been sent personally by President Carter.

John Vorster, sensing that he might be able to turn the panicky mood of the country to his advantage, announced a general election campaign shortly after Biko's funeral. In the preceding months, the United Party, succumbing to years of internal contradictions, had collapsed and broken into several bickering factions. Vorster himself had to contend with the factional tensions within his own party between pragmatists and apartheid hardliners. Vorster tried to split the difference and blame South Africa's problems on the outside world. South Africa would be "tested in the coming months and years as never before," he warned in his campaign speeches. "Internally and externally, pressure will be applied against us."

In the midst of the campaign, Vorster demonstrated his resolve to suppress dissent on one spectacularly repressive day. On October 19, 1977, Donald Woods was on his way to the United States to attend a conference of the African American Institute in Virginia with his friend Percy Qoboza, the editor of the leading black South African newspaper, the *World.* Security Police officers intercepted Woods at Jan Smuts Airport in Johannesburg, took him aside, and served him with banning orders preventing him from speaking in public, leaving East London, or writing anything for publication for five years. Woods soon found out that Qoboza had been "dragged away as if he had killed somebody," in the words of Qoboza's secretary, and that the *World* had been shut down. At the same moment, in Soweto, the police picked up Nthato Motlana and threw him in prison. Across town, other officers swept into the Christian Institute, seized its files, and served Beyers Naudé with a banning order similar to that given to Woods. Around the country, security officials closed the remnants of SASO, the Black People's Convention, the Black Women's Federation, and other black organizations. Though the forms of Vorster's repressions were not new, the depth and breadth of them were. By striking not only at Africans but also at well-known whites, Vorster had made it clear that the wrath of apartheid was far from spent.

Though the Nationalist government declined to initiate any criminal proceedings in the Biko case, the public outcry had been sufficiently loud to force the government to order an official inquest into the cause of his death. The proceedings began on Monday, November 14, 1977, in the same Old Synagogue Building in which Nelson Mandela had been tried. Though Woods had been the leader of the call for the inquest, his banning orders prevented him from attending; Wendy, however, faithfully sat through the entire proceedings along with Biko's mother, his wife, and his extended family. For three weeks, the police from Port Elizabeth testified in Afrikaans about the last month of Biko's life. Bit by bit, the official version of the events came out: how the police had collected proof (including columns by Donald Woods) that Biko was involved in a plot to link Black Consciousness to the ANC and PAC and was planning violent demonstrations for Port Elizabeth; how Biko had been arrested to expose him as a revolutionary; how Biko had been kept naked and chained for almost his entire incarceration; how he had grown violent when confronted with the evidence of his treason and had attacked the interrogators—first three and then, in later versions, five; how during the prodigious struggle he had fallen and hit his head against the wall; how they had not noticed there was anything wrong with him for some time; and then, when they had, how they had sought prompt and appropriate medical attention.

Through it all, the attorney for the Biko family, Sidney Kentridge, assiduously pieced together the details of Biko's treatment, pouncing on the inconsistencies in the story presented by the Security Police. The police, for example, said that Biko had freely admitted his complicity in a plot to promote violence but that the police had not used physical pressure to get him to do so. Kentridge reminded them that the year before, Biko had spent two and a half months in detention without changing his mind about anything. What methods had the police used, he asked, to secure success this time? Major Harold Snyman insisted that the police officers who had visited Biko at night had merely come to "watch" the shackled prisoner while he slept. If that was so, Kentridge asked, why had the major referred to them as the "night interrogation team"? In response to the official police claim that Biko had fallen and hit the back of his head, Kentridge put a pathologist on the stand who said, on the basis of the autopsy, that the damage to the brain had been caused by at least three and perhaps four blows to the head, the principal one coming to the left forehead. Finally, when Colonel Goosen said that Biko had been kept in chains to prevent him from committing suicide, Kentridge asked him for a piece of paper showing that he had the right to subject prisoners to such treatment. "We have full authority," Goosen replied. "It is left to my sound discretion." "Under what statutory authority?" queried Kentridge. "We don't work under statutory authority," Goosen answered. "You don't work under statutory authority?" Kentridge asked. "Thank you very much, Colonel. That's what we have always suspected."

On November 30, as the inquest was drawing to a close, white South Africans went to the polls for the general election. The next day, as

Sidney Kentridge was delivering his closing arguments in the Biko inquest, the radio and television blared that Vorster had won a landslide. Seventy percent of the 1.2 million white South African voters had supported Nationalist Party candidates, giving the Nationalists 134 of the 165 seats in the assembly, eighteen more than before. Those who had hoped that Vorster might use his enhanced authority to lead the country toward reform were instantly disappointed. "Hardly had the polls closed in the general election," wrote one South African observer, "when Vorster once again made it clear that there was to be no deviation from the fundamentals of apartheid." As if to confirm the grim future, the judge in the Biko inquest announced his findings the next morning. In less than two minutes the judge declared, in English and in Afrikaans, that Biko's head injuries "were probably sustained on September 7 in a scuffle in the Security Police offices in Port Elizabeth" and that "on the available evidence the death cannot be attributed to any act or omission . . . on the part of any person."

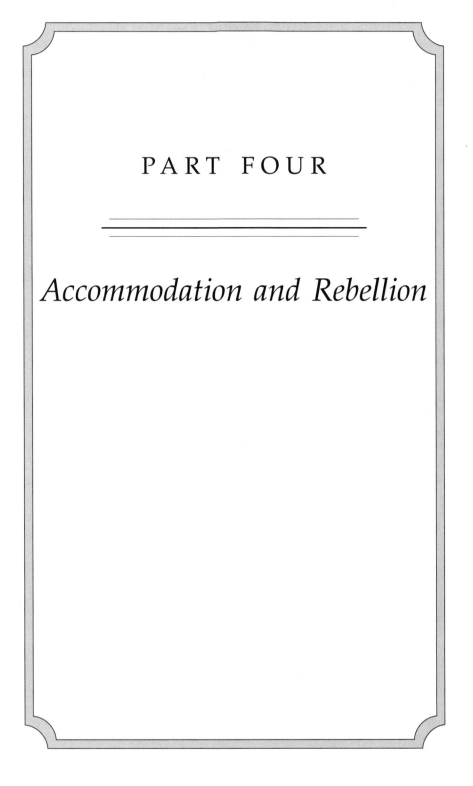

PART FOUR

Accommodation and Rebellion

ELEVEN

Definition from Below (1978–1980)

There is nothing unusual or deplorable about the definition of public values from below. Our standards of conduct are often framed first by the protests of private citizens and institutions.
—Editorial, *New York Times*

THE BIKO VERDICT did not surprise Donald Woods, who had secretly begun writing an account of the life and death of his friend. "The more I wrote, detailing the crimes against humanity by the apartheid system, . . . the more I realized that my family and I would have to leave South Africa," Woods recalled. "The main reason was that I was calling in print for economic sanctions against the Pretoria regime. . . . Under the new Terrorism Act, this was classified as an act of terrorism meriting the death penalty." Two incidents—the injury of his five-year-old daughter by an acid-laced T-shirt secretly mailed by the Security Police and the firing of five bullets into the front of their house—convinced Woods and his wife that they had to leave South Africa immediately. On December 29, 1977, two weeks after his forty-third birthday, Woods, disguised as a priest, left home lying on the floor of the family car. He arrived at the river that borders Lesotho, swam across, and met up with his wife and children, who had traveled separately to Maseru, Lesotho's capital. From there they flew to Zambia, where Kenneth Kaunda received them as guests of the state, and on to England, where they were greeted at the airport by an army of reporters.

Soon afterward Woods arrived in the United States, where he used his new celebrity to denounce the South African government before Charles Diggs and the reconstituted House subcommittee on Africa and before the UN Security Council. Woods also spoke to the executive council of the AFL-CIO, whose members were so moved they immediately adopted a resolution urging U.S. corporate withdrawal from South Africa. In his speeches and articles, Woods brushed aside calls for incremental change and demanded that the international community impose economic sanctions. Things in South Africa, he said, "have never been worse . . . from every point of view." The National Party government now viewed anyone who supported racial equality as a direct threat to the state. In one piece Woods described a young Security Police officer in South Africa who had been asked whom he was fighting. "Communists," the man had answered. And what was a Communist? "A Communist," replied the officer, "is a person who wants whites and blacks to mix." Having adopted such a sweeping view of subversion, Woods warned, the police were now prepared to take any steps to suppress it. As if to confirm his claim, newspapers around the world reported the next day on the fate of Richard Turner, a thirty-six-year-old white professor of politics at the University of Natal who had studied and supported Black Consciousness and who had been languishing for nearly five years under a banning order that was about to expire. His wife had left the house when Turner heard the doorbell ring. He had gone to the front door, found no one outside, and then walked into his two young daughters' bedroom to look out the window. As he peered out, a powerful gun blast had shattered the glass. Turner's teenage daughter rushed forward and cradled her father's head in her lap as he died.

On February 3, in Washington, D.C., Woods brought his message directly to the White House, where he met with Vice President Mondale, who introduced him briefly to President Carter. That night, Woods traveled to Yale University, where he called publicly for the withdrawal of U.S. firms from South Africa, a measure that not only would have economic effect but would "deal a firm psychological blow against the structure of the system of apartheid. The white government in South Africa is terribly conscious of world opinion," said Woods. "It affects not to be, but it is extremely conscious of it."

Woods's strong message—which contrasted sharply with the proposals for gradual workplace reform that businesses were favoring—found a receptive audience among university students. The debate over university investments in South Africa, having waned at the beginning of the 1970s, had been growing again on American campuses for nearly two years. There were several reasons. First, the increased numbers of minority students who had been admitted to elite colleges were now raising new political issues—including South Africa—on the campuses. Second, there was a desire by many young white students to emulate their older brothers, sisters, and friends. The generation that had gone to college in the mid-1960s had, in the minds of these younger students, played a vital role in the civil rights movement. The generation in the early 1970s had, in turn, led the country in opposing the war in Vietnam. The students who were seniors in the spring of 1978 had arrived on campus as freshmen just in time to hear the stories of the antiwar marches and strikes from those who had participated in them several years before. Surrounded by earnest graduate students, junior faculty, and chaplains who had cut their political teeth in either the civil rights or antiwar movement, growing numbers of young students around the country, especially in elite private schools, saw in the South African issue a powerful confluence of these two traditions: like the civil rights movement, it was a struggle for racial justice, and like the protests over Vietnam, it was a debate over the direction of United States foreign policy and the role of large corporations in society.

Until the late 1970s, the debate about Western involvement in the politics of southern Africa had simmered on campus for years as a rarefied cause championed by a few liberals, leftists, Pan-Africanists, and Marxists. To raise campus awareness, student anti-apartheid activists came to believe that they would have to link the issue to something closer to home. They took a few whacks at the federal government but met with little success. They then shifted attention to the role of American corporations in the South African economy. While this stimulated some interest, the connection between American corporate investment in South Africa and the daily lives of universities remained, to the average student, obscure. As the result of both strategic analysis and frustrated trial and error, student activists in the late 1970s again focused on the investment practices of their universities.

Their reasoning and rhetoric were simple: apartheid was evil, they insisted, and represented the antithesis of all the principles to which American universities were publicly committed. American companies were supporting this evil materially and psychologically through their investments. American companies were also profiting through the low wages that apartheid forced Africans to accept. American universities—one of the institutions responsible for upholding, embodying, and teaching the country's principles—were in turn benefiting from these arrangements through the ownership of stock. Therefore, universities that retained such investments were betraying their core principles and purpose. Going beyond calls for voting one way or another on shareholder resolutions, students of the late 1970s affirmed the more direct strategy of selling off the shares of any company operating in South Africa.

At first most university presidents, chief counsels, and trustees dismissed this line of argument as incoherent, unrealistic, or even dishonest. The problem was not with the premise—every statement on South Africa by administrators began with a ritualistic profession of abhorrence for apartheid—but with the subsequent reasoning. The problem was not even with the students' logic, although many administrators felt that the students' syllogisms refused to acknowledge the complexities in South Africa. The critical question for administrators was that of effectiveness. What was the chance that any action by a single university—from divesting to voting for shareholder resolutions—would actually produce the desired result? And what costs, in the near and distant future, would be incurred as the result of such actions? In the minds of many administrators and trustees, the probabilities of success were low because the chain of causality linking campus to township was too long and fragile. A university owning only a tiny fraction of a company's stock could not tell the company what to do; American firms had only limited control of what their subsidiaries and competitors did in foreign countries; American companies, even as a block, could not compel South African firms to act. Finally, business leaders in South Africa, whether foreign or domestic, had rarely been able to persuade the National Party to move one way or the other. The students who thought otherwise were, in the administrators' opinions, being carried away by youthful overestimations of the power of the older generation.

The conflict between the administrators and the students was, in some ways, a classic ethical debate: the administrators emphasized the importance of assessing consequences while the students insisted on fulfilling duties. In many cases, whether they were aware of it or not, the students were employing two of the arguments raised by John Simon, Charles Powers, and Jon Gunnemann in *The Ethical Investor:* that investment policies can reflect an institution's mission and that the ownership implied by holding stock carries with it certain duties. If shareholders, including universities, were the actual owners of firms, with all the rights and responsibilities implied by the concept of property, then they had a moral and legal duty to scrutinize the actions of American companies in South Africa. Over a period of twenty years, the syllogism would prove sufficiently powerful to compel, over stubborn resistance, hundreds of colleges and universities to institute new forms of oversight for their investments.

By 1978 thousands of students across the United States, inflamed by idealism and unencumbered by experience, believed that university administrators should act to oppose U.S. investment in South Africa. The moral obligations were clear: either the administrators took steps to urge companies to depart from South Africa, or they exposed the institution's commitment to principle as a rhetorical facade concealing unvarnished materialism. The frequent reference made by administrators to the lengthy, flimsy chain of causality was, in the student view, simply an attempt to evade responsibility. The connections between America and apartheid, argued the students, were not long and tenuous; they were tight and intimate. They could be seen in the enduring inequalities of American society, in the racism and the rapacious appetite of American business, and in the self-satisfied elitism of American education. For years students painted signs and banners that read "Princeton Supports Apartheid" or "Stanford Backs Racism." Those who carried them believed such statements to be provocative and self-evident; those who read them from their university offices found them simplistic and offensive.

Over several years a predictable pattern emerged for the debate. Those who started with the conviction that an incrementalist approach was the most reasonable gradually became impatient when it did not secure the results they expected. They then would argue for bolder action and perhaps later for direct confrontation. As more and more people were drawn into the argument, those who had been involved for a long time found themselves on committees or in debate with people who were brand new and who felt that an incrementalist approach was worth a try.

Despite the life cycle of attitudes and the turnover in membership, university committees around the country were slowly expanding their policies in response to events in South Africa, pressures from students, and the relentless stream of shareholder resolutions filed by Tim Smith and the member churches of ICCR. The voting records of scores of universities and other institutional investors reveal a progression, sometimes steady, sometimes abrupt, through a series of increments. It is useful to think of the increments in terms of distinct stages that can be numbered from 0 to 10 and to track how different organizations moved through this progression over time. At the starting point, stage 0, the institutional investor had never considered the South African issue or had no formal mechanism for deciding it. At stage 1, the investor had started to ponder the question but had not yet taken a position. By stage 2, the investor might have been willing to vote for resolutions restricting Namibian oil exploration (because South African control of Namibia violated UN and U.S. policy) but would not have wanted to interfere with the operations of U.S. subsidiaries abroad. The investor, feeling ill informed about what was happening in South Africa, might also have voted for a company to disclose its employment practices.

By stage 3, the investor believed more firmly that corporations were a positive force for change in South Africa. Some investors distinguished between participation in the South African economy and direct support—such as bank loans or military supplies—to the South African government. At this stage most investors thought that influence was best exercised through reasonable personal discussions with corporate executives or with the political leaders of South Africa. Stage 4 investors, doubting the corporate reassurances, took the position that they, as shareholders, had the right to ask corporations to accept minimum employment standards and external standardized verification. By stage 5, investors had come to feel that employment practices were not the only relevant issue in South Africa, that discussions with managers were not necessarily the most effective approach, and that a broader range of economic ties—for example, loans, sales to the military or police, or sales of African products in the United States—had to be considered and limited by corporate executives. At stages 6 and 7, investors were looking for strong evidence of corporate commitment to implementing the Sullivan Principles and to challenging the government, possibly linked to a specific deadline for the ending of apartheid. At stages 8 and 9, investors believed that American companies should withdraw from South Africa and were willing to use the divestment of stock, either in large blocks or in a phased program of selling, to express that opinion. At stage 10 the investor favored using all methods of economic pressure simultaneously—disinvestment, divestment, selective purchasing, and international sanctions—against South Africa and its economic partners.*

Using these measurements, one can detect important trends in the investment policies and shareholder voting of America's largest institutional investors throughout the 1970s and beyond. Between 1971 and 1976, scores of large nonprofit institutional investors around the United States worked their way from the starting point of 0 to voting for shareholder resolutions between stages 2 (more information) and 4 (improve employment practices). In 1977 and 1978, the two proxy seasons following the Soweto riots and Stephen Biko's death, the institutional shareholders, on average, increased by two stages. In other words, the members of the committees who were making the decisions on how to vote were steadily becoming more sophisticated about apartheid and about the distinctions one should make between forms of involvement in the South African economy. They also were less tolerant of pleas from corporate executives for more time. After several years of asking privately for information to no avail, some committees began voting publicly for disclosure resolutions. Throughout the country, as the images from South Africa prompted more and more students to protest, the members of the committees scrambled to discover new incremental strategies. Thus, in a strange way, the institutional investors, the American

* For a closer examination of the voting patterns at several large institutional investors in the 1970s and 1980s, see Appendix C.

corporate executives, and the members of Vorster's government were all playing the same game: searching for small steps they could take to persuade external critics of their commitment to reform and thereby to fend off pressures for more rapid and fundamental change.

In response to calls from students, a few institutions—such as the University of Massachusetts at Amherst in September 1977—simply decided to divest outright. Others struggled more intensively with the controversy with each passing month. By 1978 a coalition of students at Princeton University, for example, had been fighting the administration of President William G. Bowen for more than two years. In April the students staged a twenty-seven-hour sit-in at Nassau Hall, the university's chief administration building. Their efforts, on the surface, changed little. The university charged the students with disobeying university rules, but the committee that heard the charges let them all off with a warning. The student activists continued to attack the president, particularly when they discovered that he was moonlighting as one of the principal financial advisers to the Rockefeller fortune, whose holdings included more than $550 million—sixty-three percent of the total—in companies invested in South Africa. The students also filled several buses and drove into New York to hear Adhimu Chunga, leader of the student coalition, testify before the UN Special Committee on Apartheid and to hold a rally in front of the New York Stock Exchange. The senior class, in a surprise move, voted for Adhimu Chunga to receive the annual award for the greatest contribution to the life of the school. The university, however, did not divest.

Despite this failure, the sit-in had a pronounced effect in some initially imperceptible ways. The stories about it, appearing in the midst of accounts of other actions at other schools, added to the impression that the time had come for nonprofit institutions to take new steps on South Africa. The running debate between college students and administrators around the country was recorded and analyzed in many newspapers. In a lengthy piece, the editors of the *New York Times* acknowledged the complexity of the dilemma facing university trustees and corporate executives but came down in favor of the students. "If the nation's heart responds to the agitation, as we hope it will," they wrote, "the head will find a way."

The spring of 1978 thus represented a critical transition in the South Africa debate in the United States. More and more institutions came to view the question of investment in South Africa not as something the U.S. government should decide but as a topic that could and should be discussed by the thousands of universities and other nonprofit institutions around the country. It also proved a cathartic moment for some of the students who participated in the protests. Many of the students involved in the divestment debate came to see that their education was not only about courses and teachers, but about the structure of the institution itself, about its goals and values, its purpose and principles. Education, in other words, went beyond acquiring skills for personal advancement and encompassed understanding and creating a moral community.

To the skeptical, such student outbursts seemed both childish and hypocritical, because the students vented untempered emotions and refused to acknowledge the moral ambiguities of life. To the students at Princeton and elsewhere, however, such events offered a brief moment of political purity, when one could rise above the demands of academic competition and act collectively out of principle. When derided by critics, who pointed out that such virtue was cheap, the students believed that this was all the more reason for them to embrace it. By trying, however imperfectly, to transform theory into practice, they, like the much younger high school students of Soweto who were paying a far higher price, unleashed unexpected energies not only in themselves but in the society whose leaders they would become.

The Princeton sit-in was but one of several major disturbances on American campuses in the spring of 1978. In March, students in Tennessee protested Vanderbilt University's decision to serve as the host for the Davis Cup tennis matches between the United States and South Africa. Members of the Ku Klux Klan organized a counterdemonstration and offered their services to the local police to help keep order, though the police declined. At Hampshire College, Smith College, Stanford University, Wesleyan University, Cornell University, and many others, students signed petitions, organized rallies, testified before investment committees, and demanded responses from the presidents and trustees of their institutions. At Columbia University, President William McGill took advantage of the turbulence to press for trustee approval of a statement of ethical guidelines for investments. McGill, a former professor of psychology, had served as the chancellor of the University of California at San Diego during the campus battles between radicals guided by Herbert Marcuse and Angela Davis and the police under the control of Governor Ronald Reagan. After the convulsive Columbia strike of 1968, the trustees chose McGill as president because they thought he knew how to cope with student unrest.

From the beginning of his tenure, McGill believed that the university's investments—which consisted mostly of real estate, including Rockefeller Center and more than six thousand apartments in New York City—would remain controversial, at least until the institution had formulated a defensible policy. He decided to try his hand at drafting one himself and submitted the document, entitled "Ethical Guidelines for Business Dealings, Investments, and Relations with Foreign Governments," to the board of trustees in 1973. The chairman and treasurer of the board, alarmed by its implications, blocked its approval. In 1977, as student agitation increased and as the chairmanship of the board of trustees passed to Arthur Krim, a prominent liberal, McGill resubmitted the document. In his essay McGill set out his understanding of the core purpose of a university as an institution devoted to "human betterment and intellectual integrity." As a result, he asserted, the university had to establish guidelines of what to do when the legitimacy of the institution conflicted with its economic pursuits. "I do not believe it to be proper for the University to own a racetrack or a liquor store," McGill wrote. "These activities conflict with our conception of ourselves as an institution with a special place in society and special dignity required by that place. . . . We should also avoid dealings that exploit the university's name, real estate investment in slum areas, and business conducted without regard for the natural environment."

McGill suggested that "where good reason is found for believing that an investment might be directed away from the humane values which the University exists to sustain, then we shall refuse to become involved." He boldly advocated divestment over shareholder activism through the proxy system because the latter was often a "charade" that did not affect managers. He recognized that the sale of stock might entail some financial cost to the university but he reasoned that *not* to create and follow such guidelines would also impose costs on the institution. "Adherence to such standards may occasionally lose us the benefits of windfall income," he continued, but "observance of these guidelines will work in the long run to benefit Columbia by attracting support dependent upon continuance of the University's excellent reputation. The University risks losing much more through the disillusionment of potential admirers and supporters via certain questionable business ventures than it stands to gain in new income from such investments."

Though the trustees gave closer scrutiny to the idea than they had before, they remained cautious. In September 1977, after hundreds of students signed a petition and demonstrated at Columbia in support of divestment, the trustees created a special committee to determine "whether the university's divestment of such securities would be legally permissible and if so whether such divestment would help or hinder those . . . who seek to abolish apartheid." The committee, made up of four faculty, one alumnus, and one undergraduate, labored for six months. On April 14, 1978, the same day as the Princeton sit-in, the *Columbia Spectator* reported that the committee would not recommend divestment. On April 20, several hundred students who had gone to hear a panel discussion on the student uprising of 1968 marched on President McGill's house to protest the university's refusal. One week later, the committee members, as predicted, issued their report rejecting divestment as financially unsound. The committee recommended that the university exercise its shareholder voting rights, correspond with managers about embracing the Sullivan Principles, divest itself of stock in banks that made loans to the South African government and of firms "which by act or omission manifest indifference to repressive racial policies prevailing in South Africa." One member, Professor Alexander Erlich, submitted a minority report calling for a timetable for both divestment and disinvestment.

The report triggered a sit-in on May 1 by 275 people at the business school and a rally of more than seven hundred in front of the library. Speaking to the crowd, student leader Wayne Brody said, "Every day this university picks up a dividend check, every day the trustees sit on the boards of corporations who do business in South Africa, we participate in apartheid. We will no longer be complicit in corporate crimes. This university is ours and the responsibility is ours." Two days later, on May 3, McGill wrote a letter to the community criticizing the recent "slogans, banners, and public shouting matches." He encouraged the students to read the committee report carefully and asked them bluntly whether they would be willing to accept cuts in financial aid as the price of divestment. Later that day, the University Senate—a joint legislative body made up of students, faculty, and staff—debated the investment committee's report and Erlich's minority recommendations. "When the provost and his associates discovered that the vote on divestment was going to be close," recalled President McGill, "we all spent a lot of time on the telephone rounding up every senator from the medical school and from other parts of the university who were not, in our judgment, prone to act foolishly. We tried to make sure they would be there and that they understood the issues. If the vote had been against us that time, there would have been a very serious problem. If we had just ignored the thing, I think we would have been defeated."

The resolution supporting Erlich's minority position was narrowly rejected, twenty-six to twenty-four. The senate then recommended that the trustees adopt the policy of selective divestment proposed by the committee. On June 5, after graduation, the trustees announced that they would dump their stock in banks making loans to South Africa and institute step-by-step pressures, including public opposition to the expansion of American firms' investments, divestment of "companies expressing indifference," and a case-by-case support for shareholder resolutions. Several bank executives vented their fury directly at McGill. "Gabriel Hauge, the chairman of Manufacturers Hanover, asked me to come down to his office to see him," McGill remembered. "When I went into his office, he chewed me up and down for half an hour over this pernicious new policy. He told me the bank would never give another gift to Columbia, and he would not do anything to help. We ended up divesting two banks who told us to go to hell."

The shock waves of Soweto, combined with the protests at universities in the Ivy League and beyond, were also felt in Cambridge. The dual committee system that President Derek Bok had designed at Harvard to review questions of shareholder responsibility was beginning to show signs of strain. Over the course of the system's six years of existence, committee members had slowly advanced through the incremental policy stages in their shareholder voting, moving from requesting information to casting their first vote in favor of limiting corporate expansion in South Africa with Union Carbide in 1977. That same year, the committee members abstained on a vote urging General Electric to withdraw from South Africa, an indication that they had considered approving it and wanted to send a message to GE's executives to that effect. The fall of the academic year 1977–78 began ominously with the death of Biko and the arrest in South Africa of former Harvard Nieman fellow Percy Qoboza. President Bok immediately cabled Prime Minister Vorster urging Qoboza's release. In November the chairman of the powerful Harvard Corporation Committee on Shareholder Responsibility, Hugh Calkins, wrote to fifty-seven corporations in Harvard's portfolio and asked them to increase their minimum wages and "adopt a policy which permits nonwhite workers to bargain collectively."

Bok also had to contend with a new campus organization founded by Neva Seidman, an undergraduate who had become a student activist because of a remarkable connection to the African National Congress. Seidman was the daughter of activist parents who had helped create a multiracial suburb in Connecticut in the 1950s and who had taught in Ghana, Nigeria, and Tanzania in the 1960s. After graduating from high school in 1973, Seidman had traveled to Zambia, where she worked for the African National Congress at the Liberation Center, a shoddy one-story compound in which Zambian President Kenneth Kaunda housed a cluster of southern African nationalist movements. Seidman typed letters and other documents for Zephania Makgetla, with whom she fell in love. Over time Seidman became friends with all the other ANC leaders in exile such as Oliver Tambo and Max Sisulu, the son of Walter and Albertina. "The exiles were very close," Seidman recalled. "I didn't feel like a foreigner. . . . We all were like a family."

One afternoon during her months in Zambia, Seidman decided to drive home for lunch; when she came back to the office an hour later, she found the street cordoned off by police. Pushing her way through the line, she discovered that her office had been destroyed by a letter bomb. Max Sisulu had been struck so hard by the blast that he had been hurled through a plate glass window and literally had his shoes and socks knocked off his feet. Another ANC worker had been blown to pieces. As the police poked around for evidence, Seidman and her friends began to clean up. "There were papers everywhere," she recalled, "things that were supposed to be secret. At one point this sad little policeman came up with a plastic bag that contained a human finger. 'What should I do with this?' he asked. Nobody knew, so I took it and Zeph buried it that night."

In the fall of 1974 Seidman returned from Africa to enroll as a freshman at Harvard. While in Africa she had discussed with the senior ANC staff the possibility of doing research into U.S. corporate involvement in South Africa; when she got to Cambridge she hurled herself into the task. Night after night she traveled across the Charles River to Baker Library at Harvard Business School to sift through corporate annual reports. By the end of her first term in college she had produced a hundred-page paper that she later expanded, with her mother's help, into a book published several years later. By the time she was a senior, in the fall of 1977, Seidman had not only become an expert on South African economics but had married Zeph Makgetla in a ceremony in Cambridge. Seidman and her student supporters were determined to bring pressure to bear on Harvard's portfolio companies through a new organization they named the South African Solidarity Committee (SASC). The organization's activities were well covered in the *Harvard Crimson,* in part because Neva's twin sister, Gay, had been elected president of the newspaper.

The new student group demanded that the university examine its stock in banks making direct loans to the South African government and that it sell nearly $600,000 of its stock in Manufacturers Hanover. In response, the Advisory Committee on Shareholder Responsibility, chaired by Professor Henry F. Reiling of Harvard Business School, decided to engage in a full review of the university's South Africa policy and issue a report with results and recommendations. Reiling's committee met to discuss the issue on more than two dozen occasions, including several raucous public hearings. At one such committee meeting, on February 16, 1978, Citibank official George Vojta defended his bank's policy of lending to the South African government on the grounds that Citibank "will make loans anywhere in the world as long as they are profitable." In response, the SASC planted hundreds of black crosses in Harvard Yard to symbolize the martyrs of apartheid.

The Advisory Committee's recommendations, published in March

1978, sought an uneasy balance between the competing positions. The committee members agreed with the students that "U.S. economic interests . . . have been pivotal in assisting the South African Government during its worst economic difficulties in the past"; that Harvard had obligations of "good citizenship" that should sometimes "supersede economic calculation"; and that "portfolio companies have an obligation to operate both here and abroad within the bounds of widely held moral principles." They also agreed that the university should not own stock in banks that made loans to the South African government because "the aggregate effect [of such loans] is one of permitting the government to continue to develop an economic and political system based on apartheid." At the same time, the committee members agreed with Bok and the trustees that divestment was not the right solution, except on "those occasions where management and shareholders have shown by their actions or statements an intransigence in adopting policies advocated by Harvard or on those occasions where management policy has demonstrated direct and substantial support of apartheid, as we found in the case of the banks." They recommended that Harvard continue its activist role as a shareholder and consider not only voting more aggressively but actually sponsoring its own shareholder resolutions if companies refused to comply.

The committee members' negative conclusions about divestment hinged on two assumptions: that the effect of divestment on corporations would be low and that the cost to Harvard would be high. They spelled out their reasoning in an appendix, which divided divestment costs into short-term expenses (commissions and effect of transactions on market prices) and long-term opportunity costs (donations and long-run investment costs). The report estimated that the commission costs for Harvard were between one and one and a half million dollars; the short-run price effects, which rested on the assumption that a sale by Harvard would cause the price of the stock to fall, were estimated at between one and a half and five percent of the market value of the stock, or between $4.7 and $15.7 million. Under donations, the ACSR judged that since thirty to thirty-five percent of all security gifts were in the stocks of companies with South African operations, Harvard would not receive such gifts in the future and thus would forgo about three million dollars in revenues per year. They also figured the long-run lost return at between $1.8 and $6.8 million. The total estimated one-time costs thus ranged from $5.7 to $16.5 million and the total annual costs from $4.8 to $9.8 million.

The committee soberly reminded readers that "the estimated maximum one-time cost of $16.5 million is roughly equivalent to the cost of Harvard constructing the entire new athletic facilities project and

greater than the cost of the Kennedy School [of Government] by 50%.
. . . The annual costs is approximately equivalent to the annual operating expenses of the Graduate School of Education and the Divinity
School." As a result of these calculations, the committee recommended
against general divestment because it provided "inadequate proportionality between cost and effectiveness."

A few months later, Professor Kenneth Arrow, a Nobel laureate in
economics, challenged these cost figures as far too high; in retrospect,
Arrow seems to have been correct. As many large institutional investors
later discovered, one-time costs could be minimized if the sale of stock
was phased in over a year or more. In such cases, the commissions
became roughly equivalent to what would have been spent for normal
market transactions (unless the fund was indexed) and the market-price
effects were essentially reduced to zero. The opportunity costs also may
be considerably smaller since many divested funds subsequently found
that their move into smaller, domestic, high-growth firms had higher risk
but gave higher returns than the blue chips. In addition, a serious flaw in
the 1978 Harvard opportunity cost estimates can be traced to their reliance on the Princeton report done ten years earlier, a study drawn from
data collected from 1953 to 1968, a period of significantly different market environments. Finally, the donation cost assumed that if Harvard
alumni could not bequeath South Africa stock, they would bequeath
nothing, when instead they might find alternative gifts to make. Because
the assumptions were buried in the appendix, most people, including
some on the committee, did not realize they were making a recommendation based on worst-case assumptions in every category.

On April 10, 1978, shortly after the ACSR issued its report, the Fellows of the Harvard Corporation held an open meeting in which Bok
and CCSR chair Calkins listened to angry student speeches about the
essential role and obligations of a university. For the next few weeks,
tension on campus rose as local newspapers reported on student protests around the country. When the corporation issued a statement on
April 24 that the announcement of its decision would be postponed, a
thousand students descended on the president's office at Massachusetts
Hall. Derek Bok's departure that evening was delayed while security
officers cleared a path through the bodies of students who had thrown
themselves in front of his automobile's wheels. On April 27, the president and Fellows issued their response. "Having considered these conflicting arguments, we must be honest in acknowledging frankly that we
cannot tell whether remaining or withdrawing will eventually prove most
effective in bringing an end to apartheid," they wrote. "We find ourselves in the unenviable position of groping for a responsible, ethical
position in the face of extreme uncertainty." Harvard's trustees an-

nounced that they had decided to agree with the ACSR and support shareholder resolutions for withdrawal when companies refused to disclose information or to implement the ACSR's employment recommendations or when they did not show progress in making workplace reforms. They also promised to support resolutions calling for an end to bank loans to South Africa but deferred for future discussion the proposal that Harvard file its own shareholder resolutions. They would not, however, support divestment.

The new positions of the Advisory and Corporation Committees did not mollify the student activists, who viewed shareholder voting and workplace reform as a diversion from the real issue: the gain both Harvard and the South African government received from American firms. Shortly after the corporation issued its statement in April 1978, thirty-five hundred students held a demonstration that shut down University Hall for a day. As at Princeton and Columbia, the unrest on the Harvard campus continued until June. Then, as administrators around the country breathed a sigh of relief, many of the student ringleaders accepted their diplomas and left town. Neva Seidman, now Neva Makgetla, followed her husband to East Germany and enrolled in a Ph.D. program in economics and development studies. Gay Seidman went to work at the United Nations and then moved to Swaziland to teach junior high school.

Despite the summer break, Derek Bok again found himself pressed about South Africa in the fall of 1978. This time Bok was challenged to debates on divestment not only by the student South Africa Solidarity Committee but also by such leading professors as Stanley Hoffmann, Michael Walzer, Joseph Nye, and Duncan Kennedy, who, along with others, questioned the president in faculty meetings and signed a petition calling for divestment. The junior U.S. senator from Massachusetts, Democrat Paul Tsongas, who had traveled to South Africa, publicly invited Bok to debate the ethics of the university's investments. Bok, who had repeatedly said that it was not the size of crowds but the cogency of arguments that swayed him, could not refuse such public expositions of his reasoning without offering some alternative. He chose instead to write several "open letters to the Harvard community" that set forth his understanding of the balance between moral reasoning, university policy, and investment decisions.

In his first letter, "Reflections on the Ethical Responsibilities of the University in Society," issued in March 1979, Bok expressed a view of the essential purpose of the university different from that proposed by McGill at Columbia. Universities, he wrote, were institutions designed to discover and transmit knowledge, not to reform society. "Society respects the freedom of academic institutions only because it assumes that they will devote themselves to the academic pursuits for which that freedom was extended." Even if Harvard were to try to influence other institutions, the impact would be small. "Neither as stockholders nor as purchasers nor as contractors of services," Bok commented, "do universities possess sufficient leverage to move large corporations, let alone entire governments." In "Reflections on the Divestment of Stock," released several weeks later, Bok argued that Harvard could not sever every link to South Africa, as this would mean refusing to accept donations, purchase products, or admit South African students. Nor, he insisted, was corporate disinvestment from South Africa a worthy goal, since Africans were divided on its merits and American corporations could have a positive effect through remaining and implementing employment principles. Even if disinvestment were desirable, Bok wrote, divestment was an expensive and ineffective way of achieving it. It would be far better, he insisted, for the university to vote for shareholder resolutions and to make Harvard's displeasure known directly to management. Only rarely, when protracted efforts to persuade a company to change its ways had proven ineffective, might Harvard sell its stock, "not because it believes that such action will force the company to alter its behavior but simply because the University will have lost confidence in the management of the company and will not wish to maintain an association with the firm."

Though Bok and Corporation Committee chair Calkins agreed on most points, they used strikingly different interpretations of the effect of divestment on corporate policies. Bok repeatedly stressed the extremely *limited* effect of any divestment on a firm's behavior. Calkins, writing for the *Harvard Crimson* commencement issue a few years later, insisted that "a primary objection to a divestment policy is its *coercive* nature." With regard to the corporate impact on Harvard's independence, however, they agreed. "Harvard gets lots of money from the business community and is very dependent on it," he said. "It would be easy for someone in the business community to say, 'Look, Harvard is trying to pressure us to change our policy in South Africa, even though our actions there are reasonable. They are not buying our stocks and bonds and products. Why shouldn't we refuse to give to Harvard?' "

As universities and other institutional investors struggled to design and defend incremental investment policies that would satisfy their constituencies, the anti-apartheid groups in the United States stepped up their campaign for corporate withdrawal. The American Committee on Africa, which had teamed up with the antiwar group Clergy and Laity Concerned to press its bank campaign, was beginning to see some results as Chase Manhattan, Citibank, and Continental promised publicly in 1978 that they would make no new loans to South African parastatal corporations. Though Jennifer Davis and her colleagues at the ACOA dismissed the Sullivan Principles as "too little, too late," they worried that American companies would nonetheless use them as a means of deflecting attention from substantive questions like loans, strategic industries, and weapons shipments. At the Interfaith Center on Corporate Responsibility, Timothy Smith now coordinated shareholder resolutions by member churches with nearly seventy American companies. The resolutions in the 1977 proxy season touched on a wide range of topics, including international weapons sales, infant formula marketing, women's rights, labor practices in Guatemala, strip mining, and sponsorship of violence on television. Resolutions urging withdrawal from South Africa or an end to bank loans were second in number only to those urging a revision of corporate rules for political contributions.

The members of the board of the ICCR, like those at the ACOA, worried that the new Sullivan Principles would seriously detract from their campaign for corporate withdrawal from South Africa. On November 7, 1977, three weeks after Vorster's mass crackdown, Sister Regina Murphy, a member of the Sisters of Mercy and the chair of the ICCR, sent letters to several dozen chief executive officers of American companies, including the Sullivan signatories, in which she called for withdrawal. The replies of the American executives, which trickled in over the next four months, sounded remarkably similar. They all declared their profound opposition to apartheid and rejected Murphy's requests. Unaware or unconcerned that South Africans were not permitted by law to advocate corporate withdrawal, the executives cited positive statements about investment and workplace reforms made by Gatsha Buthelezi, the U.S. Chamber of Commerce, and the South African Council of Churches. They also criticized the ICCR churches' focus. "I question your concentrating on South Africa," wrote the chairman of Rockwell, "to the exclusion of dozens of other countries where repression and lack of civil rights are well-known problems." "In my opinion it is time that U.S. citizens afford themselves the luxury of indulging in a bit of national self-interest," wrote the head of Dresser, "rather than to continue to moralize ourselves into increasingly less competitive economic and political positions."

Some of the corporate executives discovered that the church organizations refused to be dismissed. The 1978 proxy season included thirty-three shareholder resolutions on South Africa—a seventy percent increase from the year before—all of which enjoyed more support from investors than they ever had in the past. In 1977 not a single one of the resolutions urging an end to bank loans or corporate withdrawal had been able to muster the 3 percent vote necessary for automatic resubmission. Twelve months later, the *average* for all of the votes had nearly doubled to 5.41 percent. Though far short of a majority, the rapid increase in voting margins signaled strong shareholder dissatisfaction. The 1978 proxy season also represented the first appearance of resolutions urging the adoption of the Sullivan Principles. These resolutions, which had been filed not by ICCR but the University of Minnesota, fared spectacularly well. Of the eleven filed by the university, ten had been omitted or withdrawn before a final vote because the corporations had agreed to sign the principles. The eleventh, with Motorola Corporation, had been endorsed by management and had passed with 99.34 percent of the vote.

In the wake of the Soweto student riots, U.S. business began to have doubts about stability in South Africa. A confidential survey conducted in the spring of 1977 pointed up this uncertainty. Of the five hundred top U.S. executives polled, twenty-six percent believed that they should withdraw or cut back; eleven percent felt that they should expand cautiously; and the majority—sixty-two percent—believed that they should stay in South Africa but limit their expansion for a while. At about the same time, the South African Reserve Bank noticed with alarm that, despite currency controls, foreign capital had stopped flowing into the country and had started flowing out, as foreign companies that had traditionally reinvested their South African profits began sending them home. In late 1976 Professor Meyer Feldberg, director of the Graduate School of Business at the University of Cape Town, published a report comparing the changes in attitudes among the executives of U.S. subsidiaries (many of whom were not U.S. citizens) since 1974. He found that in the aftermath of Soweto, the number of those who rejected the policy of separate development had risen from only two percent just two years before to twenty-two percent, though the majority remained neutral. The executives showed some concern about the pressures in the United States but worried far more about whether the National Party would be able to maintain political and economic stability in the years ahead.

Skittish American executives, facing demands for improvements from many sides, sought safety in numbers by signing up for the Sullivan Principles at a record rate. By June 1977, three months after Leon Sullivan had announced the original twelve signatories, he had signed up twenty-one more. In October, when he presided over the first annual dinner for signatory executives at the Pierre Hotel in New York City, Sullivan had collected a total of fifty-three. At that dinner, Secretary of State Cyrus Vance told the executives that Sullivan's attempt to create a common employment code had prompted others around the world to do the same. For the next eight months, Sullivan invested most of his time signing up new companies. By July 1978, the number had nearly doubled again, to one hundred three. At this point, however, Sullivan ran into two difficult problems, one with General Motors, the other with the implementation of the principles themselves.

In the spring of 1978 George Houser and Jennifer Davis at the American Committee on Africa obtained and released two memoranda written by the top GM executives in South Africa to their boss in the United States. The memos discussed the contingency plans the executives had made in case of organized protest and rebellion against apartheid, but they reassured their boss that they thought this reaction was unlikely. "No doubt the type of civil unrest experienced in the U.S. comes to mind in this context," wrote director Louis H. Wilking, "but as you are aware, the free mobility of dissidents and the ability to organize large numbers of non-whites and generate action is not the same in South Africa as it is in the U.S." However, since unrest, if it occurred, could threaten the operations of the plant, Wilking had arranged for security to be worked out in collaboration with the South African military and police. Wilking doubted that the unrest could ever spread, because Africans traditionally "lacked purpose." If it did, he wrote, the plant, which had been designated a "National Key Point" under South African legislation, would be placed under military control.

Anti-apartheid activists around the country pounced on the memos as evidence of General Motors' covert support for the apartheid state. For Leon Sullivan, who was still serving on the automaker's board of directors, the revelations were profoundly embarrassing. South Africa's conservative newspaper editors had already gone out of their way to applaud General Motors' rejection of what they inaccurately referred to as the "Carter-backed campaign for corporate disinvestment." Sullivan found himself in an even more uncomfortable position when Timothy Smith wrote to him directly asking for his views on the contingency plans and urging him to raise the matter with the board of General Motors. Soon after the disclosure of the memo, Sullivan reiterated forcefully that the corporations would have to do more than sign their names to his principles. "The signatory companies are expected to be a positive force for change in South Africa by implementing the Principles to the fullest possible extent," said the press release in which Sullivan announced that he had "amplified" the principles, "or they have no justification for continuing their business operations in that country." By the fall of 1978, he was privately telling David Russell and other activists that he eventually intended to expand the principles to address the issues of housing, health, and education for black workers.

The reporting and public accountability of the existing principles, however, were raising serious administrative problems. The moral credibility of the principles hinged on Sullivan's supervision, but Sullivan, who was still overseeing the vast OIC network and preaching every Sunday in a church with thousands of members, could not provide this himself. For more than a year the Industry Steering Committee which had been formed after the Sands Point meeting—and which now included Sullivan's close associate Gus Roman, Jim Rawlings of Union Carbide, and Wayne Fredericks of Ford—had grappled with these administrative problems. In April 1978 the committee announced that separate task groups, made up of executives from the signatory companies, would be formed to plan and oversee the implementation of the individual principles. In August, the steering committee traveled to South Africa to evaluate the attitudes of different groups toward the principles.

One of the participants in the trip was Sal Marzullo, a vice president for international government relations at Mobil Oil. Marzullo seemed to be an anomaly—an ardent idealist who in his youth had lived in an ashram in the Philippines, studied the works of Gandhi, gone to work for the YMCA, and ended up as a spokesman for a huge multinational oil company. In truth, he was not alone: many corporations used either black employees or liberal whites to defend their policies in South Africa. Those who were hired into such positions were often lured with the promise that they could serve as the corporation's conscience. Marzullo's belief that the Sullivan Principles were of vital importance deepened during his first trip to South Africa, when at one point during a meeting with young black clergy he was so overwhelmed by their tales of suffering that he excused himself, went to the men's room, and wept. It was also during that first trip of the Industry Steering Committee to South Africa that Marzullo struck up what would become a close friendship with Gatsha Buthelezi, who had already announced that Inkatha would help monitor the activities of foreign multinationals. Buthelezi met with the American visitors shortly before he was to travel to the United States to promote investment in South Africa and to meet with Leon Sullivan, Congressman Stephen Solarz, and Vice President Mondale. "What was your name again?" asked Buthelezi when he was introduced to the representative from Mobil. "Mar-ZULL-o," he replied. "Well, I must say," laughed Buthelezi, looking at the stocky Italian American executive, "you are the funniest looking Zulu I ever saw in my life."

After the Industry Steering Committee had returned from South Africa, its members continued to wrangle during the fall of 1978 with the problem of control and funding. Sullivan had made it clear that he wanted the administrative support unit to be located in Philadelphia, staffed by noncorporate personnel, and headed by a minister chosen by

Sullivan to serve as executive director and as his alter ego. He also insisted that the organization should be a nonprofit, charitable entity that could receive corporate contributions but also be free to raise money from foundations. He even told the committee that he had already selected the name for his group, the International Council for Equality of Opportunity Principles, or ICEOP. Jim Rawlings of Union Carbide had originally proposed that the support group be set up as a foundation with a board of trustees made up of both public and corporate representatives, but Sullivan rejected this idea because it would impinge on his independence. By December the committee had agreed with Sullivan that two organizations would be formed: ICEOP, to be controlled by Sullivan, and an Industry Support Unit, made up of representatives of the signatory companies, whose primary responsibility was to kick in the annual dues that would pay for the cost of monitoring compliance and supporting ICEOP.

It was soon recognized that ICEOP, based in Philadelphia with a small staff, would not have the resources to gather and interpret the compliance records of scores of companies, so Sullivan announced in October 1978 that he had hired the Cambridge, Massachusetts, accounting firm of Arthur D. Little (ADL) to design, distribute, collect, and analyze a corporate questionnaire. In January 1979, D. Reid Weedon, the senior vice president at ADL in charge of the project, persuaded Sullivan and the newly established Industry Support Unit that an effective program would require not only a more comprehensive system of measurement but an examination of each corporation's plans for implementation and site visits in South Africa.

Though the members of the Industry Support Unit fretted about the price tag, they worried far more about Sullivan's plan to issue an annual evaluation of each company's success at implementing the principles. The original proposal suggested by the staff of Arthur D. Little envisaged classifying the companies into one of three ratings: "Making Acceptable Progress," "Cooperating/Maintaining Status Quo," and "Non-Respondent," plus a fourth group of "Endorsers"—firms that supported the principles but had no employees in South Africa. Sullivan considered these categories too weak; the industry representatives thought them too strong. Indeed, the notion of any sort of public assessment alarmed the members of the Industry Steering Committee so much that they urged Sullivan to keep the grades private. When Sullivan refused, they called a special meeting in Sal Marzullo's office at Mobil on February 22, 1979. The tone of the encounter is captured by the panicky message sent by one of the participants, Tom Krzesinski, to Robert J. McCabe at General Motors, late that night:

Steering committee again tried to get suspension of grading system or even collapse of first two categories (Making progress and cooperating/ Status Quo) into one. LHS [Sullivan] would not! would not! even consider. Must have grading system in place and public announcements of categories and each company placement . . . with release of latest report results (March 1979). With backs up against wall and no, none, absolutely no choice, steering committee will propose compromise [to Sullivan]. . . . GM will be graded in top category for now. . . . Getting extremely hot.

Indeed, the pressure had infuriated Sullivan, so much so that he had stood up in the meeting, told the executives that he might publicly repudiate the principles, and stormed out. The next day, with Reid Weedon serving as mediator, Sullivan and the corporate executives agreed to accept the original proposal.

By the spring of 1979, nearly four years after Sullivan's trip to South Africa and more than three years after the Sands Point meeting, Sullivan could finally point to concrete successes. He had persuaded 116 companies to commit themselves publicly to desegregating their workplaces, establish equal wage scales, and train and promote black workers. Journalists in South Africa regularly reported on the disappearance of some of the more visible signs of apartheid at American plants. Members of the Carter administration continuously expressed their support for Sullivan's work; Cyrus Vance even played host at the State Department to the third annual signatory dinner, attended by more than a hundred top executives. In South Africa, the same National Party politicians who originally had praised Sullivan's effort now grumbled that he had become a nuisance. "Go back and tell your Rev. Sullivan this," the minister of labour and mines reportedly told Gus Roman. "Tell him we don't want him interfering in the matters of South Africa. Tell him to go to other countries in Africa. Tell him to stay in his church . . . we don't need him here." Even more important, Sullivan had resisted the systematic effort of American corporate executives to use the Sullivan Principles as an excuse to do nothing, as had happened with the European and South African employment codes. The principles would not become "camouflage for business to hide behind," Sullivan told a conference on South Africa attended by black American clergy in April 1979. "All of the signatory companies are expected to *implement* the plans, *abide* by the guidelines, and *report* progress on a regular basis." By the fall of 1979, seven different task groups (Fair Employment Practice, Equal Pay, Education, Training, Management Development, Health Care and Housing, and Economic Development), staffed by executives of American companies with subsidiaries in South Africa, were busily gathering information, setting goals and timetables, and ordering changes.

The grading system was also beginning to bite. Dozens of executives phoned Reid Weedon to find out what the requirements were for obtaining a high rating and complained sharply when they did not achieve one. Ironically, the executives from companies like General Motors who had originally fought to collapse the two top ratings into one discovered that they disliked being grouped with more lax firms and asked for a new, higher rating for those who were making an "extra effort." Trustees of universities and other institutional investors immediately took to using the Sullivan ratings in their deliberations about whether companies were acting in good faith. In addition, to the executives' consistent irritation, Sullivan continuously put forward new requirements for the corporations to meet. By the spring of 1979 Sullivan had added to the list of corporate goals the rights of migrant workers to bring their families and of unions to organize; that fall he publicly demanded that all American banks stop making any loans to the South African government or any of its parastatal corporations. Whenever he gathered the representatives of the signatory companies together—usually about twice a year—Sullivan reminded them that his support for the principles was not immutable. "At any point that I believe meaningful movement toward the complete implementation of the Principles and Amplified Guidelines is not happening," he told the executives in November 1979, "I will call you together and I will tell you I have gone as far as I can."

Despite his momentum and moral authority, Sullivan still faced some extremely difficult obstacles. Two years after the principles had been announced, 164 American companies operating in South Africa still had not signed. Sullivan had said openly that he hoped the U.S. Congress would make the implementation of the principles mandatory, but there was little support for this on Capitol Hill. Sullivan had wanted to establish a monitoring group in South Africa, but the companies refused to pay for it. Even routine funding was not easily won; many of the signatory corporations stalled for months before paying their sliding-scale assessments to support the monitoring of the principles. To make matters worse, expenses were skyrocketing. In six months, Reid Weedon's team ran up a bill of nearly $100,000. Members of the Industry Support Unit grumbled that the work had not been sufficiently itemized. Weedon replied that he had not anticipated how much work was required to review so many questionnaires or to field so many phone calls from distressed executives. Though they finally settled the bill in the fall of 1979, the two sides continuously haggled over money. By early 1980, Arthur D. Little's charges exceeded $18,000 a month.

Despite the problems, however, Sullivan remained convinced that

American corporations could be cajoled or coerced into making a difference in South Africa. "You, probably better than any audience, can understand the forces in me that keep me going on this difficult mission," Sullivan told a conference of black clergy in April 1979. "It is my belief that God is guiding me in what I am doing. It is this belief and faith that keeps me going. I believe that God is using this effort to start a chain reaction that will spread throughout South Africa and that, along with other forces, it will lead to the end of racial discrimination . . . and apartheid."

Though the South African government publicly professed to be uninterested in the Sullivan Principles or the threat of sanctions, its actions suggested otherwise. Despite the success experienced by the state-run electric utilities, railways, steel company, and television network in their efforts to borrow money in Europe and the United States, John Vorster conceded in early 1978 that South Africa would probably no longer be able to raise the necessary international capital to keep the national growth rate above three percent. At a national conference on investment that same year, Professor Arnt Spandau of the University of the Witwatersrand warned that unless foreign investor confidence could be maintained, the South African economy would soon find itself in deep trouble.

Vorster, surveying the effect of the Soweto riots on his country's reputation and on foreign investment, quickly took the offensive. He dispatched cabinet officials to business meetings and conferences around the world to defend National Party policies. The minister of economic affairs, J. Christiaan Heunis, publicly appealed to the executives of foreign companies in South Africa to use their power to persuade policymakers at home that sanctions or disinvestment would be counterproductive. In June 1977 Foreign Minister Pik Botha flew to Rye, New York, to argue for increased investment before an audience of 350 leading American business executives.

The conference had been the joint brainchild of the South African Foreign Trade Organization and the South African Reserve Bank. To attract the requisite political and business leaders, Eschel Rhoodie, the director of South Africa's Department of Information, had hired the American public relations firm of Sydney D. Baron for an annual fee of $365,000. The vice president in charge of the South African account at Baron was Andrew Hatcher, an American black who had served for a time as an adviser to President Kennedy. Hatcher appeared on South Africa's behalf before a variety of black groups in the United States, including the association of businessmen known as 100 Black Men. He also helped organize the Rye conference, at which former U.S. Treasury

Secretary William Simon and other American conservatives extolled the social and financial virtues of investing in South Africa.

Eschel Rhoodie and the South African Department of Information pursued other avenues of influence in the United States. To balance their affiliation with Sydney Baron, which had close ties to the Democratic Party, they also hired the Washington law firm of Collier, Shannon, Rill, and Edwards. One of the law firm's employees, Donald Kieffer, served as the principal lobbyist, spending thousands of dollars on entertainment for corporate and congressional staff members, writing "fact sheets" to counter a House resolution criticizing the independence of the Transkei, and pushing for an end to Export-Import Bank restrictions. The South African Foreign Trade Organization also continued to organize business conferences including one in Houston in 1978 at which former President Ford spoke in defense of investment in South Africa for a reported honorarium of ten thousand dollars.

One of the most persistent of South Africa's defenders was publisher John McGoff, a U.S. citizen who owned more than fifty American newspapers as well as a London-based television network. In 1975 McGoff had fought hard but unsuccessfully to purchase the *Washington Star,* in part, he said at the time, to bring a more balanced perspective on South Africa to the nation's capital. That same year he also joined with a German publisher and an Afrikaner millionaire in a failed attempt to purchase the South African Associated Newspaper chain, which owned and operated the *Rand Daily Mail,* a paper usually critical of John Vorster.

McGoff made no secret of his strong sympathies for the National Party and insisted that his editors make ample room for his views. He regularly published columns by Lester Kinsolving, an Episcopal priest who was paid by Collier, Shannon, Rill, and Edwards to attend the annual meetings of corporations in order to attack Tim Smith and the resolutions filed by ICCR. After the arrests and bannings of October 1977, McGoff printed articles by J. Van Zyl Alberts, a South African editor who defended the actions as necessary for the maintenance of law and order. McGoff and Van Zyl Alberts also teamed up for a peculiar escapade. In 1976 the two men started a comic book series about "Mighty Man," a black hero modeled on Superman, who lived in a South African township and defended the status quo by defeating an assortment of muggers, agitators, and Communists. McGoff printed seventy-five thousand copies of the first edition and shipped them to Soweto. "The blacks are going to lap this up," predicted one of the executives of the South African distributor. He was mistaken. The young people tore the comics up or, in some cases, burned the newsstands to the ground.

In an effort to revive the perception that he was committed to reform, John Vorster made a few cosmetic changes at home. When his old friend Hendrick van den Bergh retired as the director of the Bureau of State Security, Vorster dropped the name, with its authoritarian acronym of BOSS, and replaced it with Department of National Security (DONS). When M. C. Botha, the minister of Bantu affairs, left his post, Vorster installed Connie Mulder, the former minister of information and the man who most people thought would be the next prime minister, and changed the name to the Department of Plural Relations. This produced a stream of derision among Africans, who had become used to the semantic shell games of Nationalist politicians. An African from the homelands, they joked, would now be known as a "rural plural."

By the end of 1978, however, Vorster's rule was grinding to a halt. Though he was only sixty-two, his lifelong habit of consuming eggs and bacon at every breakfast, combined with a lack of exercise and the pressure of serving as prime minister for twelve years, had begun to take a toll on his health. In September 1978 Vorster was hospitalized in Cape Town for ten days with reported cases of bronchitis and exhaustion. At the end of the month, he announced that he would retire and accept the ceremonial role of South African state president. The National Party immediately sprung to life, as supporters of the various candidates to succeed Vorster moved to secure the parliamentary votes necessary to become prime minister. Connie Mulder had been weakened by a brewing financial scandal at the Department of Information. The auditor general's office had announced in May that there had been significant unauthorized expenditures in Mulder's department during his tenure. Shortly afterward, Vorster fired Eschel Rhoodie, disbanded the department, and asked Hendrik van den Bergh to investigate. Though the reports of the investigation had not been made public that September, rumors and allegations were cutting into Mulder's support in the party.

The other major aspirant was P. W. Botha, the minister of defense. Botha knew that his candidacy faced long odds. The party had traditionally promoted the leader of the National Party in the conservative Transvaal—in this case Mulder—rather than someone from the Cape Province like Botha. Moreover, despite the scandal, Mulder was still popular among the Nationalist members of parliament. When straw polls taken by newspapers around the country revealed that most whites strongly preferred Foreign Minister Pik Botha (who, despite his vigorous defense of apartheid overseas, was considered a "reformist" in South Africa), P. W. Botha saw his chance. He pressed the foreign minister to throw his name into the ring, hoping to draw votes away from Mulder. The ruse worked: on the first round of voting P. W. Botha won seventy-eight votes, Connie Mulder seventy-two, and Pik Botha twenty-two. Pik Botha then withdrew and backed the minister of defense, who carried the next ballot by eighteen votes.

Within days of becoming prime minister, Botha moved to crush his opposition within the National Party by expanding the investigation in the Department of Information. He tried to keep the evidence secret but failed when Judge Anton Mostert, refusing to be intimidated, released some of the findings to the press. From late 1978 through the first half of 1979, the country reeled under a hurricane of damaging revelations in a crisis that came to be known as the Information Scandal or Muldergate. Tens of millions of dollars, the public learned, had flowed directly from the South African treasury into 134 secret efforts to influence opinion about apartheid inside South Africa and around the world. John McGoff's attempts to purchase the *Washington Star* and the *Rand Daily Mail,* for example, turned out to have been financed with millions of government rand. Even more egregious, from the South Africans' point of view, was the discovery that the *Citizen,* the most avid English-language defender of government policy, had been launched and maintained with huge amounts of public money. The collapse of Mulder and his circle came swiftly. Eschel Rhoodie fled to France, where he threatened to reveal even more damaging information about South Africa's international network, until he was arrested, extradited to South Africa, and imprisoned. P. W. Botha forced Mulder to resign from the cabinet, then from the leadership of the Transvaal congress, and finally from parliament altogether. It was later reported that Hendrik van den Bergh, far from investigating the claims, had done everything he could to cover them up. There were even allegations in the press that the murder of a prominent National Party politician and his wife, Robert and Cora Smit, could be linked to Smit's discovery of the Department of Information foreign exchange violations. Though the investigating judge formally recommended that van den Bergh be prosecuted on a variety of criminal charges, the attorney general of the Transvaal refused on the grounds that van den Bergh could reveal too many state secrets. Finally, less than eight months after he had become state president, John Vorster, insisting that he was innocent, resigned his post in disgrace.

After trouncing his political rivals, Botha could now steer the South African state in the direction he had long desired. During his many years as the minister of defense, Botha had acquired a military man's perspective on politics: it was a messy, duplicitous business in need of order, planning, precision, and discipline. From within his predecessor's cabinet, Botha had watched in dismay as Vorster had tried to run the cumbersome government like a political party. Vorster had, for example, allowed the government departments to grow and proliferate so much that the only way he could control them was by filling them with cronies or pitting them against each other. P. W. Botha had particularly resented the way in which Hendrik van den Bergh and his minions at BOSS had, in the name of national security, continuously meddled in military matters.

In Botha's opinion, John Vorster and his cabinet had refused to accept the severity and breadth of the crisis facing South Africa, despite Botha's attempts to persuade them. Every year, for nearly a decade, in his annual Defence White Papers to parliament, Botha had warned that South Africa faced a "total onslaught" from Marxist forces led by the Kremlin. The threat, he insisted, could be identified at every level of society: from the takeover of neighboring Angola and Mozambique by Communist regimes, to the willingness of the border states to tolerate ANC guerrilla training camps, to the subversion that bubbled up in the nation's classrooms, factories, newspapers, and pulpits. The proper response, as Botha argued in the white paper of 1977, was a "total national strategy," which would entail "interdependent and co-ordinated action in all fields: military, psychological, economic, political, sociological, technological, diplomatic, ideological, and cultural, etc."

As minister of defense, Botha had surrounded himself with relatively young officers who believed themselves to be a new breed—more realistic, more efficient, and, if necessary, more aggressive than the earlier cadre. They assiduously studied the military concepts of the French theorist André Beaufre and of Lieutenant Colonel John McCuen of the United States army, both of whom advocated supplementing military force with a program to win the "hearts and minds" of the population. One of the most ardent supporters of this comprehensive approach was the chief of the South African Defence Force, General Magnus Malan. Malan, the son of an Afrikaner banker, had been attached to the French forces in Algeria and had gone on to study counterinsurgency techniques intensively at the U.S. Army Command and General Staff College.

Botha had been impressed by the loyalty, efficiency, and rationality of his military subordinates. With such men, he believed, he could centralize control and eliminate the bickering and stupidity that sapped the national will to resist. Botha had already taken steps in 1972 to align the departments of government with the military's objectives through the creation of a State Security Council. As prime minister he went even further. He imported military and business leaders to help run the bureaucracy more efficiently; he chopped up and consolidated government departments to reduce their number and extend his clout; and he gradually expanded the power of the State Security Council until its members made most of the government's major decisions.

Despite the similarities in their rhetoric, John Vorster and P. W. Botha defined South Africa's problems in profoundly different ways. Both men, struggling to strike a balance between preserving the old and introducing the new, said they would pursue reforms while retaining apartheid, but they differed in their approaches to South Africa's international and domestic strategies. In essence, Vorster was conciliatory abroad and brutal at home, while Botha, in his early years, tried to be the reverse. Vorster offered détente to his African neighbors, while Botha repeatedly used military force. Vorster said that there would never be any change in apartheid, while Botha told his Afrikaner constituency early on that they would have to "adapt or die." Vorster had built his foreign policy around the alignment of South Africa with NATO's battle against Communism and had been bitterly disappointed by the unwillingness of the United States and its allies to intervene sufficiently to crush the MPLA in Angola. Botha, despite the implacable anti-Communism of both his analysis and his strategy, made it clear that South Africa could no longer be counted on to support the West automatically.

Though both Vorster and Botha were ardent defenders of the concept of separate development, Vorster had stubbornly refused to address the theory's most glaring shortcomings: the absence of a "homeland" for South Africa's Indian and Coloured populations and the permanent and economically mandatory presence of millions of African residents around South Africa's white cities. Vorster, like his predecessor, Verwoerd, had preferred to say that these problems would work themselves out in some mythical future. Botha, priding himself on his realistic outlook, resolved to tackle them head on. He continued the lethargic but highly visible desegregation of some public facilities and of some aspects of South Africa sport. He and his cabinet formally accepted the findings of the Rieckert Commission, which, in its report on influx control, had admitted that the African residents in the townships should be considered permanent. He also accepted the Wiehahn Commission's recommendation that in order to reduce labor unrest and give African workers a stake in the economy, the government should recognize African trade unions.

In addition, Botha, who had served under Vorster as the head of a committee reviewing alternative constitutions for South Africa, continued his search for a formula that would permit limited participation by other racial groups, appease the international community, and yet retain white dominance. In November 1979 the prime minister convened a closed meeting of the cabinet, senior members of the civil service, and business leaders at the Carlton Hotel in Johannesburg to discuss the possible formation of a "constellation of states" in southern Africa. This idea was the latest in a long line of political locutions that South African politicians hoped would solve their problems. For years, members of parliament had debated the differences between federations, confederations, cantonal systems, and commonwealths. Botha's "constellation" called for the gathering of all the little regional territories, including the homelands and the independent nations of Swaziland and Lesotho, into a formal economic, military, and political alliance led by South Africa. After his private consultations, the prime minister presented his idea to parliament as a dramatic innovation. Once they studied the details of the plan, however, members of the opposition denounced it as a repackaged version of separate development.

Botha had hoped that these attempts at innovation would persuade the Western governments, particularly the Carter administration, to ease their pressure on South Africa. When Secretary of State Vance traveled to South Africa soon after Botha's elevation, carrying with him a personal letter from President Carter, the press reported that the meeting had ended on a positive note. Relations soon soured, however, over the issue of South Africa's continued control of Namibia. The United States insisted that South Africa abide by UN Security Resolution 435, which called for a military cease-fire and internationally supervised elections. Botha, fearful that such elections would lead to the installation of the leftist Southwest African People's Organization (SWAPO), announced that South Africa would organize its own elections, without SWAPO, among the officially approved parties known collectively as the Democratic Turnhalle Alliance. The United States formally objected to the idea through UN Ambassador Donald McHenry, prompting Foreign Minister Pik Botha to assail McHenry as a "friend of SWAPO." When the National Party learned that Colin Eglin, the leader of the Progressive Federal Party, had been talking to McHenry, Pik Botha excoriated Eglin for "trafficking with the enemy." The accusations proved sufficiently damaging that Eglin was replaced by Frederick van Zyl Slabbert as party leader.

The United States also expressed concern about South Africa's continued refusal to sign the Nuclear Non-Proliferation Treaty. For some years American and European intelligence services had tracked South Africa's secret efforts to develop its own atomic weapons. When the Stockholm International Peace Research Institute announced in 1978 that the South Africans had constructed a nuclear test site in the Kalahari Desert, international pressure had forced John Vorster to dismantle the facility. P. W. Botha, however, was determined to secure the ultimate weapon. In early 1979 he expelled two United States embassy personnel for photographing sensitive South African military installations from the air. Eight months later, in September, an American Vela spy satellite picked up a bright flash over the South Atlantic, and the United States accused South Africa of exploding its first nuclear bomb.

Though a team of American scientists assembled by the White House later found the evidence inconclusive, a second flash the following year raised the question again.

The continued disapproval of the Western leaders exasperated the South African government, which had to devote substantial amounts of time and money to circumventing the web of international restrictions on weapons, oil, money, and machinery. In years to come, this drain on the economy would take a severe toll and force the government to reconsider its choices. It would have done so earlier, had it not been for three unexpected developments early in P. W. Botha's tenure. Margaret Thatcher, the new Conservative prime minister of Great Britain, who before her election had often spoken in favor of a rapprochement with Pretoria, announced that South Africa would be permitted to purchase oil from the British fields in the North Sea. Thatcher also removed an ongoing problem for the South Africans by finally forcing the parties in the Rhodesian conflict to the negotiating table at Lancaster House. There, after months of discussion under the guidance of the British foreign secretary, Ian Smith's government finally ceded control, under a fresh constitution, to the majority population of the new nation of Zimbabwe.

Jimmy Carter's declining political strength also gave Botha a boost. The Soviet invasion of Afghanistan, the renewed oil shock, and the seizure of the American hostages in Iran, all of which took place in 1979, distracted the attention of the White House and State Department away from the problems of southern Africa. Moreover, as the doubling of petroleum prices ravaged the American economy, Carter's popularity and influence sank. The final unexpected advantage, which provided P. W. Botha with the resources to pursue his expensive military adventures and domestic programs without raising taxes, was a dramatic surge in the market value of gold. Prompted by the oil-induced fears of instability and inflation, international investors bid the price to spectacular new heights. In one ten-month period in 1979, for example, gold shot from $165 to $501 an ounce. This allowed South Africa, which had continued to experience a serious outflow of short-term capital, to end the year nonetheless with a large surplus in its current account balance. Once again, the world's passion for bullion led the defenders of apartheid to believe that their dream could be pursued without cost.

Though Botha talked about unifying the population groups of South Africa into a total strategy, his real intent was to split his opposition. He pursued this goal in several ways. He loosened the restrictions on entrepreneurship among blacks in an effort to foster a more prosperous and conservative middle class. He increased the central government's subsidies of the bantustans in order to strengthen the grip of the homeland leaders on their subjects. He recruited thousands more Africans into the police and army, where, under white command, they fought on behalf of the government from Soweto to Namibia. Botha also tried to strengthen the government's ties to the Indian and Coloured communities. He announced that he was forming separate "advisory councils" for Indians and Coloureds and tried, with minimal success, to lure prominent politicians from these communities into participating. Despite these efforts, the early years of Botha's rule saw an explosion of groups organized to oppose the apartheid state. Some were reconfigurations of old groups that had been banned, such as the Azanian People's Organization (AZAPO), which was built out of the pieces of the Black Consciousness movement, and the Congress of South African Students (COSAS), a national group of high school and other students formed out of the ashes of the Soweto Students Representative Council (SSRC). Other groups were new in form and function. In Soweto, Nthato Motlana and the Committee of Ten organized a conference of six hundred people which in turn created the Soweto Civic Association. A similar group, the Port Elizabeth Black Civic Organization (PEBCO), was formed to the south. Both groups immediately began organizing streets and neighborhoods in the townships and building ties to the fledgling unions popping up around the industrial landscape. The unions themselves tried to increase their leverage by forming, in April 1979, an alliance known as the Federation of South African Trade Unions (FOSATU). Though these new groups spent an enormous amount of energy arguing about ideology and strategy, wrestling with the arduous logistics of organizing large numbers of people without the benefit of communications technology, and trying to keep ahead of the battery of bureaucrats, spies, stooges, and police inflicted on them by the white government, they exhibited a flexibility and vitality that would soon spell serious trouble for the Botha government.

During this period some of Botha's most irritating and persistent opponents arose from the churches. Though the majority of clergy remained preoccupied with pastoral duties and the majority of parishioners, even in the more liberal English-speaking churches, limited themselves to occasional pronouncements on the evils of discrimination, there continued to emerge courageous men and women from church circles who opposed apartheid as a matter of Christian conscience—and in doing so courted retaliation by the state. These men and women quickly became the target of state repression. By the end of the 1970s, dozens of clergy had been banned, deported, or intimidated. During Muldergate it was revealed that the government had funneled hundreds of thousands of rand to Dutch Reformed Church leaders to help them attack the Programme to Combat Racism of the World Council of Churches. Secret funds had also been passed to the Christian League, an organization dedicated primarily to attacking the South Africa Council of Churches. After the payments were revealed, Dr. J. D. Vorster, the moderator of the Cape Province of the church and the brother of the former prime minister, defended the payments because they were intended for use against "the enemies of our volk." Not everyone agreed. Several prominent Reformed Church theologians said publicly that the church had been morally wrong to accept the money. Hundreds of unsolicited donations from church members flooded in to the General Synod, over Vorster's objections, to help the church repay the money to the government.

Despite the government's attempts to manipulate or suppress religious opposition, the question of the morality and scriptural legitimacy of apartheid gnawed at every branch of the church. In 1979 the Dutch Reformed Church released a new report called "Race, People, and Nation," which once again tried to find an ethical and biblical justification for a segregated society. The Coloured "daughter" churches continued to debate whether it was preferable to sever or maintain their links to their white counterparts. Most important, the English-speaking churches provided a haven for black theologians and clergy, who, after many years in subordinate roles, were slowly rising into positions of genuine leadership and power. As they did so, they carried their ardor with them and set the stage for an explosive challenge to the government.

Three persons played a particularly important role in this process: Manas Buthelezi, Allan Boesak, and Desmond Tutu. During the long and difficult period of the mid-1970s, Manas Buthelezi (who was not related to Gatsha Buthelezi), a Lutheran clergyman with a doctorate in theology, had led the way in exploring the links between the themes of human identity and liberation in Black Consciousness and Black Theology. The official use of the term "non-white" to refer to Africans, Indians, and Coloureds, Buthelezi wrote in 1973, "suggests that they have the identity of non-persons who exist only as negative shadows of whites. In a theological sense, this means that they were created in the image of the white man and not of God." In another place Buthelezi wrote, "It is imperative for the black man to reflect upon the Gospel out of his experience as a black man in order to discover its power as a liberating factor for him as well as for the white man."

While Manas Buthelezi explored the relationship between Black Theology and Black Consciousness, another minister mined the American experience with race for ethical and strategic insights. Allan Boesak was born in Kakamas, a town on the border of the Kalahari Desert, on

February 23, 1946. Boesak's father was a relatively privileged member of the Coloured community, serving as the principal of a local school run by the Dutch Reformed Sendingkerk (or "Mission Church"), a segregated Coloured offshoot of the white Dutch Reformed Church. When Allan was six, his father died, leaving a wife with eight children and no income. "My mother had to work as a seamstress making clothes for others at the meager wage of three rands a week," Boesak recalled. "She was a very religious person and through her I got my love of the church. . . . Her eight children all became ministers or teachers or married them." Though Boesak learned to love the church, the combination of poverty and apartheid bred in him a deep hatred of whites. In 1964 he went to study theology at the Sendingkerk seminary attached to the University of the Western Cape near Cape Town. "I remember wanting revenge more than anything else in the world," Boesak told an English reporter, "until I met Beyers Naudé." Boesak first met Naudé when Naudé came to speak to a group of church people in Somerset West. At the time, Boesak said, "I hated all whites. And Dr. Naudé was the perfect person to hate. He was white. He was in the Broederbond. He was an Afrikaner." Despite Boesak's predisposition to hate Naudé, Boesak found himself moved by Naudé's deep and vibrant Christian faith. "Beyers cannot hate anybody—it's not in him," Boesak recalled. "He doesn't compromise on his beliefs. But he cannot hate. . . . You cannot mix with somebody like that without it rubbing off on you."

In 1966 Dr. James McCord, the president of Princeton Theological Seminary, visited South Africa and invited Boesak to come study theology in New Jersey. Boesak was ready to go but found himself blocked by a white South African professor who felt that Boesak was a troublemaker and had no business, as a man of color, pursuing foreign degrees. Boesak took a small church instead, married, and wrote a series of open letters attacking the mediocre quality of theological education for those who were not white. In 1970 Boesak was invited to study in Holland. Again the same white professor tried to block him, but Boesak managed to get around the restrictions and departed with his wife for Europe. Over the next several years Boesak worked toward a doctorate in theology. In the early 1970s he obtained a scholarship from the United Presbyterian Church to travel to the United States. Boesak came to the United States, where he met with leaders in the field of Black Theology such as Gayraud Wilmore, and gradually wrote a thesis comparing Martin Luther King Jr. and Malcolm X.

In this work Boesak compared the theology, ethics, and strategies of the two Americans. In some ways, Boesak noted, the two could not have been more different. King believed that all human beings had potential for good, while Malcolm X preached that all white people were devils.

King wanted integration, while Malcolm X desired separation. King advocated nonviolence, while Malcolm X insisted on retaliation. Yet, Boesak noted, as the two men matured they began to converge in interesting ways. After King's Nobel Prize and experience in Chicago, he became more radical, more willing to attack capitalism. After his trip to Mecca, conversely, Malcolm X shifted his views to accept the idea that racial barriers could be overcome through the sharing of a common faith. Boesak's study allowed him to examine the central problems of race relations in a new light. He tapped the ideas of the two men on the relationship between race and class; revolution and reform; and the roles of the church, black radicals, and white liberals. Boesak also gained insight from exploring the strategy of nonviolent civil disobedience, insight he soon would bring to bear directly on South Africa.

In terms of South Africa's future relations with the United States, the single most important religious leader was a member of the Anglican Church named Desmond Mpilo Tutu, who was born on October 10, 1931, in the little town of Klerksdorp in the western Transvaal. His father was Xhosa, had been educated at a mission school, and served as the headmaster of a Methodist primary school. His mother, a domestic servant, was part Motswana and part Mosotho. Desmond would later use himself as a vivid example of the foolishness of trying to divide Africans into ethnic communities. Since he spoke Xhosa, Tswana, and Sotho as a boy, he asked a government commission, to which group did he belong?

While growing up, Tutu at first accepted the gross disparities between black and white, as did most of those in his neighborhood. One of the worst things about apartheid, he wrote later, was that "you are brainwashed into an acquiescence in your oppression and exploitation. You come to believe what others have determined about you, filling you with self-disgust, self-contempt, and self-hatred." Looking back on his youth, Tutu remembered a combination of incidents that altered his awareness. One was the discovery, when he was a teenager, of a tattered copy of *Ebony* magazine describing Jackie Robinson's entry into previously all-white American baseball. Though he "didn't know baseball from ping-pong," he was thrilled. "I grew inches that day and I puffed out my chest," he later told an audience of American blacks, "as I drank in . . . this account of how my soul brothers and sisters were making it against untold odds those many thousands of miles across the seas."

In the early 1940s, the Tutu family moved to Roodepoort, another town in the Transvaal. His mother took a job at the first black school for the blind. One day, when Desmond was about eleven, he and his mother were standing outside the school when they noticed a white Anglican priest, wearing a black cassock and a large black hat, walking toward them along the street. As the priest passed them, he turned, smiled, and raised his hat to Mrs. Tutu. Tutu was stunned—what folly could have come over this white man to prompt such an inconceivable act of courtesy to a black woman? The priest, Tutu later learned, was Trevor Huddleston, the bold Englishman who had served in the Johannesburg township of Sophiatown and later chronicled its destruction by Hendrik Verwoerd.

Soon Huddleston met Tutu again. Tutu, whose frailty as an infant had prompted his grandmother to give him the African middle name Mpilo, meaning "life," contracted tuberculosis at age fourteen. He was taken to Rietfontein Hospital, a grim state sanatorium filled with advanced tubercular and syphilitic patients. For the next twenty months Desmond was confined to the institution, where he had to endure painful treatments thought to aid his tuberculosis. On a chance visit to the hospital, Huddleston came across Tutu in one of the wards, and from then on the priest visited him every week. Huddleston returned in part because he enjoyed the company of this exceptionally intelligent, optimistic, and alert boy. Tutu was equally thrilled, remembering Huddleston as "full of laughter and caring." After Tutu emerged from the hospital, he attached himself to Huddleston's parish. There he marveled at the priest's openness. "His white cassock became grubby quickly as he walked around the streets of Sophiatown, because he attracted children so naturally and they all wanted to grab him," Tutu remembered. "At one time his office would be filled with urchins playing marbles on the floor and the very next moment, it held some very important personage, an ambassador or an influential businessman."

Though Tutu's experience with Huddleston affected him so deeply that he named his first son Trevor, he did not immediately decide to enter the priesthood. He first wanted to become a doctor. Though he was admitted to medical school at the University of the Witwatersrand, there were not enough scholarships and he couldn't afford the tuition. Tutu then decided to follow his father into teaching. He completed a bachelor's degree by correspondence from the University of South Africa and then studied for a teacher's diploma at the Bantu Normal College, one of the first institutions of Bantu education. When he emerged, he took a job teaching high school in Munsieville, next to the school where his father served as headmaster. On July 2, 1955, he married Leah Shenxane, a fellow teacher and formerly one of his father's brightest students.

After three successful years, Tutu, at age twenty-seven, decided to seek ordination, to the dismay of his father and friends, who viewed the ministry as a step down on the social ladder and the waste of a good brain. Nonetheless, in 1958 he and Leah moved to St. Peter's College, the Anglican theological school run by the Community of the Resurrection. Tutu's photographic memory and academic brilliance rocketed him to the top of his class and into the most difficult degree program, the licentiate in theology. Tutu not only thrived academically; he eagerly embraced the theology and practice of the Community of the Resurrection, with its monastic cycle of meditations, matins, Bible study, and daily Eucharist. Though he was not particularly politically aware, he recalled being profoundly affected when Albert Luthuli and Z. K. Matthews visited the school after their release from the Treason Trials and spoke to the students. After his graduation in 1960, Tutu was ordained a deacon and then a priest and served for eighteen months as curate in a parish in Benoni township. In the meantime, the rector of his former seminary, Father Aelred Stubbs, lobbied King's College at the University of London to offer Tutu a scholarship for Desmond to pursue additional theological study in England. Eventually he succeeded. On September 14, 1962, the thirty-one-year-old Tutu and his family—which by then included four children—arrived in England.

The Tutus resided in South Africa for only three of the next thirteen years. On his first sojourn abroad, from 1962 to 1967, Tutu completed British bachelor's and master's degrees in theology and served as the part-time curate at St. Mary's in the town Bletchingly in Surrey. Tutu's experiences in England slowly but steadily restored his sense of self-worth and broadened his vision of human relations. It took many months for him and Leah to stop worrying about whether they were carrying their passbook; to overcome their surprise at seeing mixed-race couples openly holding hands; and to grow accustomed to the amazing freedom "to just walk around and use any exit. . . . It's difficult to describe the sense of exhilaration, of liberation, of being made to feel human," Tutu remembered.

In 1967 Tutu and his family returned to South Africa, where he taught at the Federal Theological Seminary at Alice, an ecumenical facility that brought together Presbyterian, Methodist, Congregational, and Anglican students and teachers whose facilities had been seized by the South Africa government. While at the seminary, Tutu also served as the chaplain for the University of Fort Hare. After one student protest against Bantu education, the university's administrators announced that all the students would be permanently expelled. When the students refused to leave the campus, police surrounded them with armored cars and attack dogs. Tutu rushed over from the seminary and approached the phalanx of police. The officers tried to prevent him from crossing the line. "Don't stop me," Tutu said, "because if you are arresting the students you can count on arresting me, as their chaplain, with them." Barney Pityana, a friend of Stephen Biko's and the future president of SASO, was so moved by Tutu's courage and leadership that he decided then and there to seek ordination as an Anglican priest.

After two years at the Federal Theological Seminary, Tutu accepted a lectureship at the University of Roma in the mountainous kingdom of Lesotho; then in January 1972 he and his family returned to England, where he joined the staff of the Theological Education Fund. In his capacity as associate director of the ecumenical agency, Tutu traveled extensively, especially around Africa, acquiring a pan-African and global perspective that would profoundly shape his responses to South Africa's problems. In 1975 Tutu's supporters in South Africa nominated him to become the first black bishop of Johannesburg. Aelred Stubbs was so eager for his protégé to be chosen that when his own name was also advanced, he withdrew it. After multiple ballots, the multiracial convention gradually shied away from Tutu and elected Timothy Bavin, the white dean of St. Mary's Cathedral in Johannesburg. Bavin immediately invited Tutu to return to South Africa and serve under him as the new dean.

While a bishop tends to the spiritual and administrative health of an entire diocese, a dean serves as the rector of the bishop's cathedral. Some of the previous deans in Johannesburg, most notably Gonville ffrench-Beytagh, had used their posts to lead an ecclesial challenge to apartheid. Tutu, as the first black dean, was determined to expand on their example and turn the cathedral into the incarnation of an alternative South African society. He labored to bring more people from Soweto to worship at the cathedral. He preached relentlessly on the power of the Christian gospel to break down barriers between human beings. On occasion he was rewarded with a glimpse of God's kingdom. "As I knelt in the Dean's stall at the superb 9:30 high mass," Tutu recalled, "with incense, bells and everything, watching a multiracial crowd file up to the altar rails to be communicated, the one bread and the one cup given by a mixed team of clergy and lay ministers, with multiracial choir, servers, and sidemen—all this in apartheid-mad South Africa—then tears sometimes streamed down my cheeks, tears of joy that it could be that indeed Jesus Christ had broken down the wall of partition."

Tutu had been dean of Johannesburg for less than a year when, in early 1976, he was elected bishop of Lesotho. In May, shortly before his departure, Tutu went on a three-day silent retreat, during which he wrote a lengthy and eloquent letter to John Vorster. He began by appealing to the prime minister as a fellow human and a fellow Christian. "I am writing to you, Sir, because I know you to be a loving and caring father and husband, a doting grandfather who has experienced the joys and anguish of family life, its laughter and gaiety, its sorrows and pangs," he wrote. "I am writing to you as one human person to another human person, gloriously created in the image of the self-same God, redeemed by the self-same Son of God who for all our sakes died on the cross." After complimenting him on the policy of détente, Tutu reminded Vorster of the violent consequences that had befallen other countries when they refused to address their internal divisions and pleaded with him to alter his course. "Please may God inspire you to hear us before it is too late," Tutu concluded, "and may he bless you and your government now and always." John Vorster wrote back in three weeks, dismissing his appeal as political propaganda. Less than two weeks later, Hector Petersen was shot and the Soweto riots exploded.

Tutu was consecrated bishop of Lesotho in July 1976. Though retaining his South African citizenship, he moved to Lesotho and immediately launched into the exhausting cycle of ordinations, confirmations, and other religious services that mark the life of any diocesan bishop. In some instances he spent days traveling to and from distant mountain villages by pony, though he was always thrilled when he arrived to find the whole community singing in welcome and praise. Tutu believed firmly that a pastor, even a bishop, had to spend most of his time visiting his charges. "You can sit all day in your house and not visit your people, not bring communion to the sick, to the aged, and nobody will usually complain to you, but your church will grow emptier," he explained in 1977 to a group of deacons preparing for ordination to the priesthood. "You can't love people and not visit them. You can't love them unless you know them, and you can't know them unless you visit them regularly."

Despite Tutu's devotion to his episcopal responsibilities, he continued to be drawn back into South African politics. Since his return to South Africa in 1975, he had increasingly identified himself with the Black Consciousness movement, Black Theology, and their leaders. This had been partly the result of the urging of Aelred Stubbs, who had become the close confidant of Stephen Biko, and who urged his two friends to meet each other. The meeting never came to pass because of Biko's lengthy detentions, but Tutu did spend several days at the Zanempilo Clinic with Mamphela Ramphele. When Biko was killed, his friends asked Bishop Tutu to deliver the funeral oration for the man he had never met.

Desmond Tutu's intellectual and personal affiliation with the Black Consciousness movement strengthened his commitment to Black Theology and its themes of liberation. Tutu had at one point wanted to pursue a doctorate in Old Testament theology and had for years harbored a keen interest in Islam. His studies had persuaded him that the Hebrew scriptures depicted a God who not only cared about human injustice but was willing to act to assist those who suffered under it. Tutu saw evidence for this everywhere, but most especially in the story of the exodus from slavery in Egypt, the same text from which the early Boers had also drawn some solace in their struggles against the British. In this event and throughout the Bible, Tutu said, "God did not just talk—he acted. He showed himself to be a doing God. . . . And He takes sides. He is not a neutral God. He took the sides of the slaves, the oppressed, the victims. He is still the same even today: he sides with the poor, the hungry, the oppressed, the victims of injustice."

The theme of God actively pursuing justice meshed well with the other central motif of Tutu's preaching, that of the infinite value of every human being. In this, Tutu was doing theologically what Biko had done politically: to restore to all South African blacks their sense of self-worth. "The most horrible aspect of apartheid, a blasphemous aspect," Tutu said, "is that it can make a child of God doubt that they are a child of God. [It can make] you ask yourself in the middle of the night, 'God, am I only your stepchild?' " The Christian gospel, Tutu declared from pulpits in township churches and ornate cathedrals, declared that all humans were equally loved and cherished by God, no matter what their race, ethnicity, or abilities.

Soon after his elevation as bishop, Tutu's academic training, international experience, and moral eloquence once again attracted the attention of a group of Christians seeking to fill a difficult job. Shortly after he had gone to Lesotho, the board of the South African Council of Churches (SACC) asked him to become their general secretary. Tutu consulted his fellow bishops in the region, who advised him not to accept. The board then selected someone else, who resigned after three months. The board again approached Tutu and he again referred the matter to the synod of bishops. This time they unanimously urged him to accept. Tutu returned to South Africa in one of the most visible and difficult positions in the country. Since so many of the country's political black leaders had been suppressed, jailed, exiled, or killed, and since alternative forces, such as the labor unions, were still weak, the South African Council of Churches, whose membership was eighty percent black, was for a time the most significant legal institution representing the black majority. Tutu's predecessor, John Rees, a white Methodist layman, had helped to push the SACC to the forefront of change by removing the vestiges of apartheid from inside the ecumenical organization, establishing a large fund to help defend political prisoners and support their families, and leading the member churches through discussions of their attitudes toward economic sanctions or violence.

Tutu, however, brought new gifts and vision to the position. There was, to begin with, his exceptional personality. Tutu could evince a startling range of styles and moods over a single day. On the one hand, he believed fervently in the dignity and authority of his office and would sputter with rage when white officials refused to acknowledge them. He also loved the formality, precision, and pomp of the Anglican liturgy and would adorn himself in cope and mitre even for small celebrations of the Eucharist. On the other hand, Tutu could also be humble, informal, and spontaneous. Though Anglican bishops are usually addressed throughout the former British colonies as "My Lord," Tutu insisted on "Father" or "Bishop." Later, when he had the opportunity to move into a mansion in a white suburb, he and Leah remained in their little home in Soweto.

Tutu could also endure regular attacks by South African journalists—some of whom vilified him as a Marxist, a traitor, and an "insect in dark glasses"—and yet be profoundly wounded if a friend overlooked his birthday. He alternated between his African roots and his European training so regularly that his two secretaries, one a black Seventh-Day Adventist, the other a white Methodist, would alert each other to whether he was using a "white" or a "black" mode that day. He could attack the National Party as perpetuating the worst system since Nazism and Communism and yet insist that his staff pray for P. W. Botha every day at the morning prayer meeting. He allowed himself to express his emotions most freely in religious services. Many persons have seen him break down in prayer and weep openly. At the same time, those around him speak of the peculiar lightheartedness and inexplicable joy that bubble forth in his speech, his gestures, and his actions. One friend remembered spotting Tutu in a church garden while he was still in England: Tutu had emerged from a late Christmas Eve service and was dancing and swirling alone under the stars in silent elation.

In his speeches Tutu often turned this sense of irony and whimsy into biting wit. When criticizing the system of migrant labor, Tutu commented that "this is the only country in the world where it is illegal to sleep with your own wife." Describing the role of the church in South Africa, Tutu said that when the settlers first arrived, "we had the land and they had the Bible. Then they said 'Let us pray' and we closed our eyes. When we opened them again, they had the land and we had the Bible." He often made joking references to his color. "One of the great advantages of a black skin," he often said after receiving a compliment from a white, "is that when you blush, no one notices."

The SACC of which Tutu took control in 1978 had fifty-eight staff members drawn from the different denominations and divided into an array of programs. Many of these programs had been running autonomously, with little coordination from the center. Financial oversight was poor, in part because funds were channeled through a separate organization, whose chief accountant was later convicted of falsifying invoices and embezzling funds. Though not a skilled manager of money, Tutu proved himself a good delegator and a superb fundraiser. He also launched several new initiatives. He invited Black Sash, the liberal anti-apartheid group made up mostly of white women, to join the churches in setting up advice centers to help Africans through the labyrinth of government rules and regulations. He expanded the programs that sent young South Africans overseas for academic and leadership training. He used the monies in the Asingeni Fund, a discretionary account established by John Rees, to assist a wide variety of apartheid's victims, including legal defense and family support for political prisoners.

Tutu also lashed out at P. W. Botha's continued program of forced removals, in which tens of thousands of Africans in the cities were rounded up and deported to "resettlement" camps. In 1979 Tutu visited a camp in Zweledinga, near Queenstown. In one shack he met a small girl, her widowed mother, and her little sister. He asked whether the mother received any pension or money from anyone. No, he was told.

"Then what do you do for food?" he asked the small girl.

"We borrow food," she answered.

"Have you ever returned any of the food you have borrowed?"

"No."

"What do you do when you can't borrow food?"

"We drink water to fill our stomachs."

This encounter, and others like it, filled Tutu with a holy fury. "People are starving in most of these resettlement camps," Tutu said several months later. "I know, for I have seen it. They are starving not because of an accident or misfortune. No, they are starving because of deliberate government policy made in the name of white Christian civilization."

Tutu's eloquence, his affinity for the Black Consciousness movement, and his willingness to use the resources of the South African Council of Churches did not go unnoticed by the government. P. W. Botha warned Tutu that he would not tolerate the involvement of church people in politics. Tutu immediately responded by pointing out that Botha had never objected when clergy of the Dutch Reformed Church had offered theological justifications and political support for the government. Though trying to avoid deliberate provocation, Tutu encouraged the staff of the SACC to organize conferences and write articles on the most sensitive issues in South African politics, including whether it was moral for Christians to serve in the South African Defence Force, whether it was legitimate for Christians to use violence to overturn a violent regime, and whether the churches of South Africa, in defiance of government penalties, should call for economic sanctions. Tutu also steadfastly refused to endorse the system of bantustans and publicly excoriated the homeland leaders as "largely corrupt men looking after their own interests." Such statements enraged Gatsha Buthelezi, who, though an Anglican himself, watched with alarm as Tutu's influence grew, both in South Africa and abroad.

Buthelezi, for his part, was still avidly seeking recognition as the leader of the anti-apartheid struggle. Though in contrast to the leaders of the Transkei and the Ciskei, he had steadfastly refused to accept independence for KwaZulu, he was having difficulty transforming Inkatha into the national movement he had originally envisioned. Part of the problem was his insistence that Inkatha could be everything at once. He asserted, for example, that Inkatha was primarily a vehicle for promoting Zulu culture, demanded that the teachings of Inkatha be made a compulsory subject in all KwaZulu schools, and threatened to fire any teacher or principal who refused to comply. Then, to everyone's surprise, he announced that Inkatha would be opened to all blacks and amended its constitution to remove references to KwaZulu. When African workers began to organize themselves into trade unions, Buthelezi announced that Inkatha was a workers' organization. When there was unrest in rural areas, Buthelezi insisted that Inkatha was a peasant movement. When he was talking to supporters of the ANC, Inkatha was an instrument of liberation; when he spoke to foreigners, it was a conventional political party. Though all of these claims had a small element of truth, by the end of the 1970s Inkatha was becoming, more than anything, the vehicle through which Buthelezi intended to claim leadership of every segment of black society.

Buthelezi's frustration over his lack of national acceptance quickly became focused on two individuals. The first was Desmond Tutu. Buthelezi had been furious at Tutu since early 1978 because of what he believed was the bishop's complicity in Buthelezi's public humiliation at the funeral of Robert Sobukwe, the founder of the PAC, who died not long after being released from prison. Buthelezi had not been invited but had come anyway to demonstrate his loyalty and connections to this mythic hero of South African politics. When he arrived in his limousine, young members of the crowd began singing songs denouncing Buthelezi as a traitor. Buthelezi's sudden appearance on the platform produced a wave of catcalls and forced the funeral to a halt. When one of the clergy asked Buthelezi if he would consider departing, Buthelezi refused. Then Tutu, who was leading the service, approached and asked the Zulu chief to reconsider. This time Buthelezi agreed but pointed out to Tutu that his departure might prove difficult since the platform was now surrounded by hostile crowds. Tutu and the other clergy formed a ring around Buthelezi and his party and launched into the crowd. Suddenly some of the mourners tried to break through the line of clerics and attack the Zulu chief. Stones flew, knives flashed, and Buthelezi's bodyguards fired a shot, forcing the crowd to retreat. Buthelezi escaped unharmed, though only because one of his aides had deflected a knife aimed at his back.

In a furious speech a few weeks later, Buthelezi bitterly accused Tutu of having allowed a few "thugs" to take control of the funeral. He failed to mention that Tutu and the other clergy had protected him or that one archdeacon had been seriously injured in his defense. Instead he told his audience that Tutu and the others had run away "as fast as their legs could carry them." Buthelezi was also offended that Tutu, in later statements to the press, had not denounced the crowd but had chosen to describe them instead as a "new breed of blacks" who, in their fierce opposition to separate development, were displaying "the iron in their souls."

Buthelezi was even more enraged by Nthato Motlana, the head of Soweto's Committee of Ten, whose prominence and clout had made it difficult for Inkatha to expand its base in the urban townships. When Motlana was in detention, the members of Inkatha had refused government offers to participate in elections for the community councils, but when Motlana was released Buthelezi backed away from that commitment. Motlana and the other leaders of the Committee of Ten opposed participation by any black groups in the elections and attacked Buthelezi for considering it. In April 1978 Buthelezi tried to wiggle away from the accusation by announcing that Inkatha had officially voted not to participate in the elections. The question of individual participation, he added slyly, would be "left to the people of Soweto themselves." Motlana formally refused to participate in the community councils in May. Buthelezi then announced that he had authorized Inkatha members to serve because their presence would block the implementation of apartheid and keep other "sellouts" from misleading the people of Soweto. Motlana and his colleagues viewed the move as another government-sponsored power grab by the Zulu chief.

In July 1979 the relationship between Buthelezi, on the one hand, and Motlana and Tutu, on the other, deteriorated even further as the result of the annual conference of the South African Council of Churches. At this gathering, Allan Boesak delivered a thunderous call for the churches to throw off their timidity and challenge the state directly. He proposed a massive program of civil disobedience, conscientious objection, and economic boycotts. The speech, which meant a rejection of Buthelezi's strategy of incremental reform, propelled Boesak to the forefront of the anti-apartheid struggle and prompted the South African Council of Churches to pass an aggressive resolution. "The South African churches are under an obligation to withdraw," the resolution said, "as far as that is possible, from co-operation with the State in all those areas . . . where the law violates the justice of God."

Another speaker at the conference was Jesse Jackson, who had managed to obtain a visa and was touring South Africa for two weeks with his friend and former professor Howard Schomer. Schomer had warned Jackson that he might not be as well known in South Africa as he was in the United States and was surprised when the two men arrived at Crossroads, a township outside of Cape Town, to be greeted with an immense banner reading "Welcome Rev. Jackson, Noble Son of Mother Africa." Jackson's seventeen-day visit was so controversial that the U.S. ambassador arranged for several American firms to provide him with a security detail. During those two weeks, Jackson, accompanied by Schomer, visited the offices of American companies and queried the executives closely about what they were doing to eradicate apartheid in their workplace and communities, delivered speeches that were broadcast on South African television, and preached at Regina Mundi Catholic Church in Soweto. During these talks, Jackson accepted that American companies had made a small amount of progress but continued to insist that this was outweighed by the support they gave to the system of apartheid.

At the conference of the South African Council of Churches, Jackson made a speech in which he argued that the key to black power was black unity. He then tried to manufacture that unity himself by asking Gatsha Buthelezi, Desmond Tutu, and Nthato Motlana to come to his hotel to meet him. When they balked, Jackson announced that he would not leave the hotel until they complied. Finally, the three of them appeared, though Buthelezi brought with him an entourage of nearly a dozen men whom he insisted on bringing into the meeting. All through the evening the four men argued about the matters that divided them. After many hours of tense discussion, Jackson crafted an ambiguous statement about the need for black unity and persuaded his three guests to sign it. Though Jackson left South Africa believing that he had made a significant contribution by bringing the three men together, the agreement collapsed almost instantly.

From then on the gulf between Motlana and Buthelezi—and the factions they represented in black politics—widened. When Buthelezi announced in October that Inkatha representatives had been meeting regularly overseas with members of the ANC, Motlana said that he doubted this was true, since the ANC would not "collaborate with traitors." The reaction of Inkatha was swift and violent. In Durban, a group of seventy Inkatha members stormed into a meeting, seized a man they mistook for Motlana, and tarred and feathered him. Though Oscar

Dhlomo, the secretary general of Inkatha, disavowed the attack, the active involvement of a leading Inkatha official, Winnington Sabelo, in the assault, raised doubts about the disclaimer.

With his attempts to unify black groups under Inkatha's banner meeting opposition, Buthelezi tried to make common cause with the African National Congress. In October, not long after Motlana's statement about "meeting with traitors," Buthelezi and seventeen members of Inkatha, including the leaders of the Youth and Women's Brigades, met with Oliver Tambo and a delegation from the exiled African National Congress in London. Buthelezi proposed that the ANC and Inkatha form a united front of opposition to apartheid. The ANC members, who believed that the meeting was a private one, seem to have agreed that different strategies could be pursued simultaneously and that KwaZulu might prove a useful base for building a national assault on apartheid. They were appalled when Buthelezi, upon returning to South Africa, trumpeted many of the details of the meeting and claimed that the ANC had approved of Inkatha's role—a ploy that only strengthened the suspicion of the more radical and Communist members of the ANC that Buthelezi was dangerous and that they never should have met him in the first place.

Within days of returning from the meeting, Buthelezi visited Soweto and delivered one of his lengthy speeches at the Jubalani stadium. In the speech he read from a history of the ANC, described his early role in the Youth League, and claimed that Inkatha was now the true heir to this tradition. He then launched into a ferocious hour-long verbal attack on Nthato Motlana, excoriating him for falling away from the cause of liberation and denouncing him as a "political skunk." Soon afterward, Buthelezi's lieutenants warned that Inkatha would now become far less tolerant of dissent. David Thebehali, the head of the government-sponsored Soweto Community Council and a member of Inkatha, said that Inkatha would make a concerted effort to take control of the immense African township away from Motlana and the unofficial Soweto Civic Association. Oscar Dhlomo, speaking in December, said that the success of the black liberation struggle required the elimination of the Black Consciousness movement, which produced division among blacks. By mid-1980, Buthelezi himself was saying that "the emergence of Inkatha must be seen as the people's challenge to the deviation of the ANC's leadership." Having realized that he was unlikely to secure the formal approval of the ANC or capture the hearts of the Black Consciousness leaders, Buthelezi seemed ready, in laying claim to the leadership of South African blacks, to resort to force.

TWELVE

The Limits of Engagement and Reform (1980–1983)

The land of apartheid operates as a magnet for one-dimensional minds.
—CHESTER A. CROCKER

AS JIMMY CARTER struggled to free the American hostages in Tehe-ran and to win a second term, the United States government's focus on southern Africa dwindled. When Carter attempted a military rescue of the hostages in April 1980, Secretary of State Cyrus Vance abruptly resigned, slowing U.S. diplomatic efforts around the world, including efforts to resolve the problems in Namibia. Around the United States, investor support for shareholder resolutions on corporate withdrawal slackened, as the trustees of major institutions decided to wait and see whether P. W. Botha's promises of reform or the adoption of the Sulli-van Principles by American firms bore fruit. U.S. anti-apartheid activists who had been strengthened by the wave of post-Soweto protests found themselves once again facing strategic problems, particularly in Con-gress. On the positive side, a growing number of congressional represen-tatives had publicly stepped forward to embrace the anti-apartheid movement. At the same time, congressional leadership on southern Af-rica had been seriously undermined by the disappearance of the activist chairs of both the House and Senate subcommittees on Africa. Senator Dick Clark of Iowa, a liberal Democrat who had held extensive hearings on U.S. business in South Africa, had been defeated in the fall of 1978 by Republican Roger Jepsen, a businessman whose campaign was said to have received contributions from the South African Department of Information slush fund. In addition, Charles Diggs, the most senior member of the Congressional Black Caucus, with more than a quarter century of seniority in the House of Representatives, had lost his chairmanship as the result of a scandal.

In March 1978, while Diggs was visiting Mozambique, he learned that he had been charged by a federal grand jury with diverting more than $100,000 in congressional funds to his personal use. The thirty-five-count indictment alleged that in 1973 and 1974 Diggs had paid the salaries of three employees who worked at the House of Diggs, his Detroit funeral home, with federal monies and that he had given his employees pay raises and then asked them to pay his personal bills. Newspaper accounts speculated that Diggs's financial problems had arisen from the gradual decline of the House of Diggs, once the state's largest funeral home, and from the burden of alimony from two divorces and support payments for his six children. Appearing before the judge on April 7, Diggs pleaded not guilty. The trial in U.S. district court lasted throughout the summer. Diggs admitted that the facts of the case were correct but insisted that his employees had paid his bills voluntarily. Jesse Jackson, Andrew Young, and Coretta Scott King all took the stand as character witnesses and told the jury of eleven blacks and one white that though they had no knowledge of Diggs's personal financial dealings, they had always found him to be a man of honesty and integrity. Their testimony proved insufficient. On October 7, 1978, the jury convicted Diggs on twenty-nine counts of mail fraud and lying.

Diggs, emboldened by polls which showed that his constituents thought his conviction had been engineered by whites because he had become too powerful, announced that he would appeal. Though under House rules he was required to relinquish the chair of both the House District of Columbia subcommittee and the subcommittee on Africa, he announced that he would not resign from Congress and would instead stand for reelection. A month later, in November 1978, Diggs won eighty percent of the vote and a thirteenth term in the House of Representatives. Less than three weeks later, on November 20, 1978, U.S. district court judge Oliver Gasch sentenced Diggs to three years in prison for mail fraud. Diggs continued to serve in Congress and submitted his appeal to the United States Supreme Court. On June 2, 1980, the Supreme Court announced that it would not hear the case. The next day Diggs resigned from Congress and, in July, entered a federal penitentiary in Montgomery, Alabama. Seven months later, Diggs earned his parole, moved into a halfway house, and took a job as a legislative aide on the staff of the Congressional Black Caucus, the organization that he had helped found.

When Diggs relinquished his committees, the chairmanship of the subcommittee on Africa passed to Stephen Solarz, a Democrat from Brooklyn. Solarz, who served in the position for a little more than a year, took a keen interest in South Africa and visited the country in August 1980. He also held hearings on a bill to make the Sullivan Principles mandatory for all U.S. firms. Randall Robinson and Leon Sullivan came up to the Capitol to testify in favor of it. The National Council of Churches also supported the bill through its affiliate, the Washington Office on Africa. The corporate representatives who appeared were uniformly opposed. William Broderick, an associate of Wayne Fredericks's at Ford Motor Company, told the committee that in his view the principles would be more likely to be implemented if they were voluntary.

The most interesting initiatives of the period, however, unfolded not in Washington but around the country, in many cases through the work of prominent American blacks. One emerged at the Ford Foundation. In 1979, upon the retirement of McGeorge Bundy, the trustees of the foundation considered more than three hundred candidates, including several heads of Ivy League universities, and finally settled on one of their own members, Franklin Thomas, to be the new president. Vernon Jordan, president of the National Urban League and a close friend of Thomas's, exuberantly called it "the most significant black appointment in my time . . . the first real example of a case where whites have turned meaningful power over to a black."

Thomas had already had a remarkable career. Born to Anglican parents from the West Indies who settled in Brooklyn's Bedford-Stuyvesant section, Thomas was raised by his mother, Viola, after his father, a laborer, died when his son was eleven. In high school Franklin grew to six foot four, played brilliant basketball, and then turned down a flood of athletic scholarships to attend Columbia University on an academic grant. He continued to play basketball, though, and became the first black captain of an Ivy League team. After graduation in 1956, Thomas spent four years as a navigator for the Strategic Air Command, winging between the ice and stars of the North Pole. He then returned to Columbia for a law degree, awarded in 1963, and eventually became assistant U.S. attorney for the southern district of New York and deputy police commissioner in charge of legal matters. There he came to the attention of Robert Kennedy, who persuaded Thomas to head a new redevelopment project in Bedford-Stuyvesant that was being supported in part by the Ford Foundation. During his ten years as president of the Bedford-Stuyvesant Corporation, Thomas raised sixty-three million dollars in public and private funds that helped establish 116 new businesses and provided 3,300 jobs, renovated the exteriors of 3,000 homes, built more than 650 new or rehabilitated housing units, and secured a twenty-one-million-dollar mortgage pool for local residents. He acquired the reputation as an honest, tenacious manager who got tough things done.

In the Ford Foundation, Thomas inherited an organization that touched almost every part of global society. In forty-three years the foundation had dispensed five billion dollars to 7,300 institutions and 100,000 individuals in ninety-six countries. The foundation had succeeded in bolstering mental health research, developing the National Merit Scholarships, improving opportunities for minorities in higher education, upgrading agricultural methods in developing countries, encouraging the development of birth control, conserving natural wildlife, studying coal and other energy usage, creating housing in urban ghetto areas, and assisting the arts.

When he took over from McGeorge Bundy, Thomas found some serious problems. Inflation had cut into the foundation's endowments so much that it had had to dip into its principal to meet its grant obligations. Because of its generous salaries, benevolent goals, and relaxed atmosphere, employee turnover had dropped nearly to zero. Thomas spent his first nine months reviewing the procedures of the foundation in detail and then began tightening the grant-making process. All proposals—no matter how long they had received foundation support—would have to be explained and justified in detail. In addition, in early 1981 he announced that thirty of forty-five senior program officers would not have their contracts renewed. For these and other austerity decisions he endured months of criticism and litigation.

Thomas also shifted the emphasis of the grant making to local organizations that attempted to craft hands-on, practical solutions to the thorny problems of poverty. He regrouped the areas of interest into six: urban poverty, rural poverty and resources, human rights and social justice, governance and public policy, education and culture, and international affairs. He also increased the numbers of minorities and women throughout the organizations, appointed a black and a woman to vice presidencies, and increased the diversity of the board of directors, adding three white women, three black men, and a black woman out of a total of twenty.

Thomas also found himself increasingly involved in America's relations with South Africa. In 1976 he had traveled around South Africa for several weeks with Vernon Jordan and William Spencer, the president of Citibank. When the group traveled to the Transkei and met with Kaiser Matanzima, Thomas, in an uncharacteristic burst of emotion, got into such an argument with Matanzima about separate development that Jordan had to kick him under the table to shut him up. In August 1979, just before his selection as president of the Ford Foundation, Thomas had been asked by the Rockefeller Foundation—on whose board Vernon Jordan sat—to become the chairman of a commission to review the goals of U.S. government policy toward southern Africa. Over two years the Rockefeller Commission and its research staff interviewed dozens of persons and representatives of organizations, ordered up special studies, and traveled to South Africa as a group in 1980. During their trip they met with Gatsha Buthelezi, who passionately insisted that South African blacks did not support corporate withdrawal.

The commission published its findings in 1981 in a massive report called *Time Running Out.* The report sounded a note of urgency, insisting that "if genuine progress toward meeting the grievances of South Africa's blacks is not made soon, [conflict] will intensify and spread." The major premises of the report were that apartheid could not and would not remain; that South Africa was moving toward change; that this change could be evolutionary or revolutionary; and that the U.S. corporations in South Africa were more likely to contribute to evolutionary change by remaining than by withdrawing. "Although the commission ruled against disinvestment," Thomas wrote several years later, "no recommendation in the entire report underwent more careful scrutiny or produced greater soul-searching." To be effective, the group believed, sanctions or disinvestment would have to be imposed by all the Western nations at once. "We found no likelihood of such a multilateral withdrawal," he continued. "If U.S. companies were to pull out, the vacuum would be filled by foreign and South African firms eager to expand market shares. The influence exercised by American companies would be lost, and their replacements might be less inclined toward the black labor force and less likely to press the South African government for progressive change. To the commission, this last argument proved decisive."

Thomas recalled later that while they were writing the final report, in the last months of the Carter administration, the commission members expected it to be attacked as too conservative. By the time the report appeared, however, the mood of the country had shifted enough to the right that its recommendations were seen as liberal. The commission recommended, for example, that though corporations should not withdraw, neither should they expand; that corporations should continue to improve working conditions and press the South African government for change; that the United States government should create an interdepartmental agency to coordinate South Africa policy; and that banks should stop making loans to the South African government.

After his experience with the Rockefeller Commission, Thomas resolved to bring the resources of the Ford Foundation to bear on educational, community health, and developmental programs throughout southern Africa. Thomas made frequent trips to South Africa himself to learn about the programs and the problems of the country and spoke privately about his views to the directors and corporate managers with whom he met. Indeed, it was the combination of factors—Thomas's exceptional access to the top ranks of the American business, academic, and political elite; his authoritative exploration of policy through the Rockefeller Foundation; his close connections to other prominent establishment blacks like Vernon Jordan and Donald McHenry; and his willingness to avoid public pronouncements in order to maximize his private impact—that made him so effective.

The great institutions in America slowly altered their policies toward South Africa in part because of the external pressures they felt from shareholders, reporters, and protesters, but also because there were, throughout the country, insiders like Thomas who could advocate and legitimize incremental change. Thomas, for example, urged the companies on whose boards he sat to adopt the Sullivan Principles. He was also reported to have used his position as the only black on Citicorp's board of directors to speak against making loans to the South African government. The effect of these private discussions was amplified by the Ford Foundation trustees' willingness to vote against management on an array of social issues. In 1979 the foundation voted for shareholder resolutions asking BankAmerica to stop lending to South Africa and Phillips Petroleum to withdraw from South Africa because of its poor performance as measured by the Sullivan Principles. In 1980 the trustees asked J. P. Morgan to set up a special committee to review its loans to South Africa, pushed Coca-Cola to sign the Sullivan Principles, and rejected a measure urging IBM to withdraw because it had a record as a progressive employer.

The careful explanations offered by the Ford Foundation trustees for their shareholder votes represented the fulfillment of McGeorge Bundy's aspirations a decade earlier as well as those of the original supporters of the Securities Exchange Acts. Under the pressure of these South African resolutions, institutions gradually found themselves compelled to do two things: examine their stock portfolios in the light of their institutional purpose; and weigh the arguments offered by opposing sides, evaluate their ethical implications, and, in some manner, adjudicate between them. The confrontation between the churches that filed resolutions and the corporations that opposed them thus sparked sustained moral deliberation inside the investing institutions. Those deliberations in turn led to decisions that had to be defended publicly. As a result, after decades of delay, by the early 1980s the proxy mechanism was finally beginning to fulfill its original intention, that of creating a national, nongovernmental debate over the economic, political, and moral implications of the decisions of American managers.

Throughout this period corporate executives, when asked, strenuously denied that proxies had any effect on their decisions. Behind the scenes, however, these same managers often worked hard to persuade institu-

tional investors like the Ford Foundation not to support dissident resolutions. "I was always amazed at how terrified corporate managers were
of shareholders voting against them," said Mary Camper-Titsingh, the
staff officer who worked for the shareholder responsibility committee at
the Ford Foundation. "I have been astonished at the lengths they would
go to prevent such voting. At one point one group of managers called
the members of our board of trustees to urge them to reconsider on a
social issue. Of course, they were rebuffed. But I have seen managers
spend enormous amounts of time on some occasions and issues."

The election of 1980, which brought Ronald Reagan to the presidency
and a Republican majority to the United States Senate, changed the
terrain of the domestic anti-apartheid movement overnight. With the
executive branch and half of the legislature firmly in the control of
conservatives, hopes for federal action on South Africa disappeared. In
the aftermath of the election, the activist leaders concluded that they
needed to close ranks and shift attention from the federal to the state
and local legislatures. They had been particularly encouraged by the
April 1979 victory of a referendum in Berkeley, California, which required the city council to withdraw more than $4.5 million in funds from
banks involved in South Africa and by other bills that had been filed and
were awaiting action in Massachusetts and Connecticut.

The new regional focus led to greater cooperation among the anti-
apartheid groups. For years, the groups had maintained contact and had
even met for a time in a series of informal "coherence meetings" designed to bring greater unity and focus to the overall anti-apartheid
campaign. In late 1980 they created the Campaign against Investment in
South Africa, a joint project of the American Committee on Africa
(ACOA), the American Friends Service Committee, Clergy and Laity
Concerned, the Connecticut Anti-Apartheid Committee, the Interfaith
Center on Corporate Responsibility (ICCR), TransAfrica, the United
Methodist Church office, and the Washington Office on Africa. They
quickly decided to hold a national conference on public investment in
South Africa for the spring of 1981 and agreed that Dumisani Kumalo, a
South African journalist who had fled the country in 1978 and had
joined the staff of ACOA, would be the conference coordinator. In
addition, Randall Robinson and his staff at TransAfrica began contact-
ing black state and local legislators around the country to urge them to
file divestment bills.

At the United Church of Christ, the change in strategy was also a
function of a change in leadership. Howard Schomer, who had been one
of the most ardent advocates of the use of the shareholder resolution as
a means of promoting corporate reform in South Africa, had retired

from his position as world issues secretary and become a consultant for some of the corporations he had been lobbying the year before. In March 1981, to replace Schomer, the church hired Audrey Chapman, an ordained minister with a Ph.D. in political science and African studies who had spent almost ten years teaching and researching in Nigeria, Kenya, and Ghana. From the outset, Chapman's leadership style and focus differed from Schomer's. "Howard had a lot of experience in Europe and a basically East-West, European orientation," she commented later. "I came with a more North-South perspective and a special concern for Africa. Howard had a more focused interest in shareholder activism; I saw corporate responsibility in the larger framework of the peace and justice responsibilities of the Board for World Ministries."

The relationship between Schomer and Chapman was strained from the beginning. Chapman felt uncomfortable discussing her actions with someone who was actively soliciting corporate business. In addition, Chapman believed that Schomer's preference for filing and voting shareholder resolutions had been too narrow a strategy. Through shareholder voting "we only worked with corporations that were in our portfolio, trying to correct their abuses," said Chapman. "That seemed too focused on specific firms and too negative. I thought it might be better to look at whole sectors and industries, since many corporations used the argument that they could not respond to us because it would put them at a disadvantage to their competitors." Chapman also wanted to strengthen the church's ties to Timothy Smith and the Interfaith Center on Corporate Responsibility, ties that had weakened in the last few years of Schomer's work. Chapman went about making connections within and between organizations and soon found herself the chair of an unusual church-sponsored symposium. The conference, which was held on September 28, 1981, and moderated by Donald McHenry, brought together the representatives of twenty-nine corporations and thirty church agencies to discuss South Africa in a nonadversarial way. Chapman, encouraged by the results of the gathering, helped set up an ongoing Agricultural Chemicals Dialogue Group made up of representatives of the chemical industries and of the churches who were concerned about the abuse and health hazards of pesticides in the Third World. Chapman tried repeatedly to duplicate this collaborative model of discussion with regard to South Africa, but after extensive discussions with General Motors and Ford the automakers finally declined to participate.

In 1981 there was also a change of leadership at the American Committee on Africa, when George Houser retired after nearly thirty years as executive director. The board selected Jennifer Davis, who had served for fifteen years as research director, to replace him. Davis and

Dumisani Kumalo were convinced that the state and local strategy could succeed because of their experience the previous year with the Nebraska state legislature. In the fall of 1980 state Senator Ernie Chambers had discovered that someone had donated several thousand dollars' worth of South African gold Krugerrands to the University of Nebraska. Chambers immediately filed a bill in the Nebraska senate to reduce the state's contribution to the university for that year by an amount equivalent to the donation. When the bill went into hearings, Chambers contacted Kumalo for advice; Kumalo flew out to Omaha and testified; not long afterward, to everyone's amazement, the bill passed.

Kumalo and the other anti-apartheid activists spent the winter and early spring of 1981 organizing the public investment conference, which was paid for by small grants from various churches and individuals and by a five-thousand-dollar matching grant from the Programme to Combat Racism of the World Council of Churches. The letter of invitation, signed by Julian Bond of Georgia, Jack Backman of Massachusetts, Perry Bullard of Michigan, and Carol Mosely Braun of Illinois went out to more than eight hundred of their state legislator colleagues in March. Nearly two hundred union leaders, anti-apartheid activists, city officials, financial experts, and state legislators came together for a conference that began on Friday, June 12. A press conference at the United Nations sponsored by B. Akporode Clark, the ambassador from Nigeria and head of the UN Special Committee against Apartheid, featured twelve state legislators from nine states reporting on the bills they had already filed. In a speech at the Church Center, Julian Bond criticized the Reagan administration and called on the participants to "end American investment in evil." The speech, combined with the workshops the next day and the final plenary session in which the participants vowed to act when they got home, had the intended effect; according to Richard Knight of the American Committee on Africa, the legislators who attended were so fired up by the experience that when they returned home every single one filed a divestment bill.

In Washington the new man chosen by Ronald Reagan to steer United States policy toward Africa was Chester Arthur Crocker, a thirty-nine-year-old foreign policy scholar from Georgetown University. Named for his great-grandfather, U.S. President Chester A. Arthur, Crocker grew up in a liberal East Coast family, attended the elite Phillips Andover Academy, and dropped out of high school before graduation. After wandering around for a while, Crocker eventually enrolled at Ohio State University, which was willing to admit him without a high school diploma. In college Crocker roomed with Henry F. Jackson, who hailed from a poor black farming family in Georgia and who later also became an expert on U.S. relations with Africa. The two young men, Crocker wrote in his memoirs, "took every course and attended every lecture we could find on imperial history, comparative politics, African and Arab nationalism, and the struggle against apartheid in South Africa." Crocker fell in love with history, wrote an undergraduate thesis on European colonial policies in Africa, and decided to do graduate work at the School of Advanced International Studies (SAIS) at Johns Hopkins.

Crocker arrived at SAIS in the fall of 1964 with a grab bag of liberal views. In his first months he joined his classmates in boycotting lectures by South African officials. In 1965 Crocker married Shone Baron, the daughter of a prominent Rhodesian lawyer and a recent graduate of the University of Cape Town. Over time Crocker discovered that the field of African studies was riven by ideological antagonisms and that most Africanists were, in his words, "to the left of Trotsky." The same contrarian instincts that had propelled Crocker out of prep school were prompting him to stake out an increasingly conservative viewpoint in the midst of his liberal friends.

By the end of the 1960s, Crocker was finishing his dissertation on the military relationship between Europe and Africa, serving as the news editor of the magazine *Africa Report,* and trying to decide what to do next. He did not particularly support the Nixon administration; indeed, on one occasion he had marched in an antiwar protest at the Pentagon. In the spring of 1970, however, Crocker received a phone call from a friend who informed him of a vacancy on the National Security Council staff. Crocker applied for the job, got it in July, and went to work for Henry Kissinger in the Planning and Coordination Department of the NSC. For months, Crocker carefully examined the intricacies of formulating policy in an immense bureaucracy like the United States government. Crocker later summarized his findings in a brilliant article on Kissinger's system at the National Security Council. While Crocker never worked directly on Africa policy while at the White House, he paid close attention to it. He concluded that Kissinger had failed because he did not formulate a genuine policy until after the collapse of Portuguese colonialism and that when he finally did, he never bothered to make the case for that policy to the American people.

After leaving the National Security Council, Crocker moved to Georgetown University to direct the master of science in foreign service program. He taught courses on Africa and on the role of military power in foreign policy, became the director of African studies, and, after 1976, began writing articles attacking the Democratic administration's policy toward the African continent, arguing for less piety and more realism in the pursuit of American objectives abroad. In a piece for the *Washington Post,* Crocker fiercely attacked Carter, Vance, and Young for pursuing a "runaway ethnic policy" driven by domestic politics and "a popularity contest in which success is measured by having the best possible relations with the maximum number of governments. . . . In the end, the goals and ideologies we identify with are those of the people who scream the loudest—and all screamers are given equal time."

Crocker expanded his criticisms in an essay that appeared in *Foreign Policy* in 1979. "Washington's preoccupation with rhetorical principles only reduces its freedom of maneuver in dealing with both black and white-ruled states," wrote Crocker and his coauthor, William Lewis. The Carter policy, they continued, was riddled with inconsistencies. The State Department paid lip service to the idea that multinational corporations were agents of positive change, but it did nothing to assist American companies. Similarly, the American government paternalistically assumed that development, rather than security, was the primary question for Africans, but then would not back this up with a decent amount of foreign aid. With regard to South Africa, the Carter administration's policy had actually backfired. "The South African government's response to the new administration's tougher rhetoric," they wrote, "was to use it as a stepping stone to an unprecedented landslide while continuing repressive actions at home and dragging its feet over cooperation with Western initiatives in Namibia and Rhodesia."

Crocker developed his thinking on South Africa in a piece for *Foreign Affairs* that appeared shortly after the 1980 election. In it he portrayed P. W. Botha and his cabinet as cautious reformers who had accepted the failure of the Verwoerdian scheme. "The modernizers who are taking over Afrikaner nationalist politics, unlike Verwoerd, do not have an ideological blueprint," Crocker wrote. "They have a set of attitudes—pragmatic, flexible, determined, and a concept of strategy defined as a continuing process of matching means and ends." As in most arguments about South African policy, Crocker's premises were important. Since change was both likely and necessary, "a basic U.S. objective should be to support change, recognizing the need to minimize the damage to our interests in the process but also recognizing that American interests will suffer inevitably if such change does not occur." Economic pressures to encourage change, however, would not be effective. "The option of U.S. disengagement hardly exists in practice. . . . By its nature and history South Africa is a part of the Western experience and an integral part of the Western economic system," he wrote. "In addition, the exigencies of U.S. domestic politics rule out disengagement."

If denied the tool of economic pressure, how then could America support the process of change? Through a policy of "constructive engagement," Crocker argued, which would position the United States as a broker between the different parties in southern Africa. Crocker was careful to distinguish that policy from the Nixon policy of "communication." The latter policy, he wrote, had failed because of "White House unwillingness to push the policy publicly and energetically. What had emerged was a two-track policy—public abhorrence combined with a willingness to work confidentially over the Angolan, Namibian, and Rhodesian conflicts." Though that particular approach had not yielded results, Crocker wrote, it did not invalidate the original idea because true constructive engagement had never really been tried. Above all, Crocker stressed the importance of the United States acting like a superpower. "The real choice we will face in southern Africa in the 1980s," he wrote, "concerns our readiness to compete with our global adversary in the politics of a changing region whose future depends on those who participate in shaping it."

Crocker's analysis of what was likely to take place in South Africa hinged, more than anything, on his respect for the South African military. In 1979 Crocker had traveled to South Africa for several months to conduct research on the country's military strategy and strength. He had interviewed dozens of top officials, studied defense budgets and documents, and published his findings in a short book published by Georgetown's Center for Strategic and International Studies (CSIS). Noting that through most of the 1970s South Africa was responsible for one-third of all military spending on the entire continent, excluding Egypt, and for one-half of all the arms imports, Crocker painted a portrait of a well-organized, well-supplied, and well-trained force that could strike at will at any of the countries in the south. Though the South African Defence Force suffered from chronic personnel shortages and though the government had to pay a premium for weapons produced domestically by ARMSCOR, South Africa could suppress any military challenge short of a massive assault by soldiers imported from East Germany, Cuba, and the Soviet Union. Attacks by SWAPO guerrillas in Namibia or ANC guerrillas entering from the frontline states would cost time and money to suppress, Crocker argued, but there was no danger of South Africa being overwhelmed from outside. Similarly, efficient and brutal repression by the internal police, he asserted, meant that internal black resistance could never become sufficiently organized to pose a serious threat. His argument, in essence, was the same as the one at the core of NSSM 39. Despite the reversals of white power in Rhodesia, Mozambique, and Angola, in South Africa at least the whites were really there to stay.

It was not just South Africa's firepower that impressed Crocker. His months of interviews had persuaded him that the military, instead of being a "rogue elephant," might actually be the secret key to reform. Botha's "total strategy," for example, was built on the premise that all members of South African society—particularly the Coloured and Indian communities—could be persuaded to see themselves as citizens of South Africa and to defend it against Communist aggression. The South African Defence Force, Crocker noted, had also stepped up its efforts to recruit Coloured and African men, thus eroding the policy of apartheid from within. In his assessment, Crocker was following an argument that had privately been voiced by South Africa's elite since Botha took power: that the prime minister, by surrounding himself with military men and centralizing control, was secretly pursuing a "de Gaulle option," that is, using the power of the military to suppress the left and contain right-wing resistance to change.

Crocker wrote his steady stream of articles in the hope that a Republican president would pick him to become the assistant secretary of state for African affairs. To increase the possibility, Crocker signed on as a foreign policy adviser with Republican candidate George Bush. When Bush lost the nomination to Reagan and then was picked for the vice presidential slot, Crocker, like scores of other Bush supporters, loyally trudged into the Reagan camp. After Reagan won, the transition team, at the suggestion of national security adviser Richard Allen, offered Crocker the Africa job at State, which he accepted, pending confirmation by the Senate.

Over the previous two decades the Bureau of African Affairs had grown from modest beginnings into a significant diplomatic fiefdom. In his new post Crocker would have control over forty-four embassies, a staff of 135 in Washington and 3,400 abroad, and an operating budget of approximately $100 million. With responsibility for U.S. policy toward an entire continent, Crocker faced a withering combination of wars, dictatorships, famines, and other economic disasters. He could not expect much help from above: most Reagan officials thought of Africa only as a terrain on which Soviet expansionism must be checked. With regard to southern Africa, Crocker recognized that his new boss had only the most superficial understanding. "All Reagan knows about southern Africa," Crocker told a South African reporter in October 1980, "is that he's on the side of the whites." Reagan confirmed this perception within weeks of his inauguration. On March 4 the president told a television reporter that the United States would try to be "helpful" as long as South Africa was making "a sincere and honest effort" to reform apartheid. One should not forget, Reagan said, that South Africa was an important ally in the international battle against Communism. "Can we abandon a country that has stood by us in every war we have fought?" Reagan asked the interviewer. "A country that, strategically, is essential to the free world in its production of minerals that we all must have? . . . If we're going to sit down at a table and negotiate with the

Russians, surely we can keep the door open and continue to negotiate with a friendly nation like South Africa."

Crocker, in his memoirs, remembered his shock when he heard the president of the United States "repeating verbatim the theme song in press handouts of every South African embassy in the Western world." The South African government and the Afrikaner press, understandably, expressed delight at Reagan's remarks. Subsequently, the United States continued to take steps that were interpreted as favorable to Pretoria. Two weeks after Reagan's remark, the State Department allowed top South African military officials, including Lieutenant General Pieter W. van der Westhuizen, the chief of South African military intelligence, to travel around the United States and meet with government officials, including Jeane Kirkpatrick, the new U.S. ambassador to the United Nations. The South Africans also conferred quietly with a host of American conservatives in the hope of blocking Crocker's nomination. When news of Westhuizen's presence in the United States leaked, the State Department insisted that the visitors' military rank had not been indicated on the visa applications. The visas were a mistake, the State Department spokesman said, and the South African team would be asked to leave immediately. Not everyone was satisfied. "The military officers met in Washington with a Cabinet member, an official of the U.S. Defense Intelligence Agency, a staff officer at the National Security Council and members and staff in Congress," wrote Gail Morlan, the new research director for the American Committee on Africa, in a letter to the *New York Times*. "For the Reagan administration to argue that it had no advance knowledge of the trip stretches credulity to the breaking point."

Over the next few months, the United States government made more conciliatory gestures. In April U.S. officials suggested that South Africa be readmitted to the International Labor Organization, from which it had been expelled in the early 1960s. Shortly afterward Ambassador Kirkpatrick, assisted by Great Britain and France, vetoed four Security Council resolutions brought by Uganda and supported by Spain, Mexico, the Soviet Union, and China, to cease all trade with South Africa until it complied with the United Nations directive on Namibia. In July, despite a wave of objections, the State Department admitted the South African national rugby team, the Springboks, to play in the United States.

When it became clear that Crocker's nomination might take time to work its way through the Senate, Secretary of State Alexander Haig asked Crocker to start overseeing the work of the bureau anyway. The main piece of leftover business from the Carter administration was the negotiation over the status of Namibia. In the last year of Carter's term,

Kurt Waldheim, secretary general of the United Nations, had invited both SWAPO and the South Africans to a "pre-implementation multi-party meeting." For a time the parties fought over who should participate. The South African government, angry that the United Nations had deemed SWAPO the "sole legitimate representative" of the Namibian people, insisted that the South African puppet government, the Democratic Turnhalle Alliance, negotiate directly with SWAPO. Sam Nujoma, the leader of SWAPO, insisted that he wanted to negotiate directly with South Africa. In January 1981 the parties went to Geneva and spent several days arguing about whether or not the United Nations had to revoke the recognition of SWAPO before it would supervise free and fair elections. The South Africans, who believed that the election of Reagan had improved their bargaining position, dug in their heels and refused to budge.

Most of the Reagan team charged with reviewing southern African policy did not consider Namibia a priority; from their point of view, the most serious problem was the continued presence of Cuban combat troops in Angola. Nor did they want to go slowly. "It was not in the character of the early Reagan period to identify safe, predictable outcomes around the world," Crocker wrote later. "There was an ornery quality to our approach, an eagerness to take on the odds." Crocker wanted to solve the Namibian problem; the resolution of this seventy-year-old dilemma was one of the most elusive prizes of international diplomacy. To do so, however, he had to neutralize the swarms of ultra-right-wing lobbyists, both foreign and domestic, who were urging the Reagan administration into an overt anti-Communist alliance with South Africa.

By early January 1981 Crocker believed that he had devised a way to address the problem without falling into an endorsement of Pretoria. The previous administration, he believed, had made an error by trying to separate the major problems of southern Africa—Rhodesia, Angola, Namibia, and South Africa. Instead, Crocker decided, the United States should try to "play one intractable problem off against the other." What did the South Africans want so badly that they would be willing to let go of Namibia? To Crocker the answer seemed clear: the withdrawal of Cuban troops from Angola. And what did the Angolans want so badly that they would be willing to let the Cubans leave? Again, the answer seemed evident: an end to South African and UNITA attacks from bases in Namibia. "By expanding the agenda and defining a new settlement formula," Crocker wrote, "the Reagan team was seeking to acquire the leverage previously lacking. . . . It would offer a major visible, strategic quid pro quo for agreeing to implement the Namibian decolonization plan: the reversal of South Africa's lonely humiliation;

the removal of the SADF's [South African Defence Force's] only conventional equal; the likely reduction of Communist influence in the region; a serious constraint on SWAPO; and a likely boost for UNITA."

Though the merits of such "linkage" were not obvious to all, Crocker saw it as the best means of obtaining a firm South African commitment to settle. The South Africans, for their part, were generally in no rush. If they waited, they might win a decisive military victory over SWAPO and not ever be forced to the table. If they didn't crush SWAPO, they might now be able to obtain the elimination of the Cuban threat by doing something they might eventually have been forced to do anyway.

Much of Crocker's writing about this decision takes on the macho tone characteristic of the Reagan period. The administration had to move away from the "limp and indecisive stance of our predecessors," he wrote, and embrace "tough-minded leadership." Similarly, the policy of linkage was "based on cold realism and careful analysis" that matched "the hardball, geopolitical instincts and conceptual style of the new administration." In his memoirs, Crocker repeatedly insisted on the "logic" of constructive engagement, though he rarely paused to query the assumptions that underlay his reasoning. For example, the Carter administration had believed that improvement in South Africa's domestic policies and an end to apartheid would lead to greater stability in the region. Under Crocker, the position reversed: only when the regional tensions were solved would the South African government feel sufficiently secure to reform apartheid. This inversion also allowed Crocker to ignore South African domestic politics for years, limit most of his exchanges to the National Party, and focus his energies on Namibia with the clear conscience born of his untested conviction that regional diplomacy was the fastest and best way to undermine apartheid.

So convinced were Crocker and his associates of the merits of their approach that they predicted to each other that the Namibian problem would take less than two years to settle. Eager to get started, Crocker left the United States in April 1981 for a three-week trip to introduce himself to the main players in Africa and to consult with representatives of the other members of the "Western Five"—Germany, Britain, France, and Canada—who were trying to broker the Namibian agreement. The trip was not without bumps. Passing through Angola, Crocker told MPLA government officials that whether they liked it or not, the questions of Namibian independence and Cuban withdrawal would have to be resolved simultaneously. When he arrived in South Africa he found that P. W. Botha, who was only days away from a general election, would not meet him. Botha told a South African newspaper that he had refused because he believed that Crocker had been responsible for ejecting the military team from the United States the month before. In addition, said Botha, "I don't like the way he referred to SWAPO. . . . He's trying to create an atmosphere in which he can talk to SWAPO's friends," the prime minister continued. "This doesn't suit us. We know that SWAPO is Communist-controlled and that they have one idea and one idea only: to subordinate South-West Africa by brutal force."

Though the prime minister would not see Crocker, Foreign Minister Pik Botha and Defence Minister Magnus Malan met with the assistant secretary for two days of discussions. The official notes from the private talks recorded an unusually blunt exchange. Pik Botha immediately put Crocker on the defensive by telling him in great detail that the South African government had no reason to trust the United States. Reagan's rhetoric during the campaign had been encouraging, Botha said, but the South Africans doubted that the new administration could resist the pressure from domestic constituencies or African countries. Crocker reassured his host that the present administration would have "more backbone" than the previous one. The U.S. objective, he said, was to increase South Africa's confidence.

Having secured Crocker's pledge of cooperation, Botha explained that the South Africa government's goal was to preserve white values, not white privileges. He launched into an appeal for the United States to accept the "constellation of states" and exhorted Crocker not to repeat Mondale's blunder of urging "one-man, one-vote." Defence Minister Malan interjected that South Africa had never understood why the Carter administration refused to acknowledge that SWAPO was a virulently Communist group controlled directly by Moscow. If SWAPO came to power, the Soviet Union would have control over the key Namibian port of Walvis Bay, something that South Africa would never accept. Crocker agreed that this would be a source of concern for the United States. Crocker suggested that the time might be ripe for an official visit by Foreign Minister Botha to the United States, though he warned Botha not to come unless the South African government had decided to take positive, concrete steps toward resolving the Namibian question.

When Crocker returned to Washington, he found that Senator Jesse Helms, the archconservative senator from North Carolina who sat on the Foreign Relations Committee, had put a hold on his nomination. "Some senior players in Pretoria had apparently concluded that I was not their candidate for the job," Crocker commented later. Botha's rebuff of "Reagan's first emissary would," he wrote, "create the impression that my mission had 'failed.' I could be portrayed as an 'obstacle' to constructive relations, providing ammunition to right-wing conservatives in Washington who hoped to string out the Senate confirmation process." In addition to highlighting disagreement about how to treat Pretoria, the dispute between Crocker and Helms reflected an enduring rift within the Republican Party: on one side were the moderate internationalists, men like Ford, Kissinger, and Bush, the men to whom Crocker had originally been attracted; on the other were the conservative true believers, men like Reagan and Helms, for whom the only important international question was the battle against Communism. Helms vowed to prevent the internationalists from flooding into the State Department and subverting the glorious victory that Reagan had won. The new president himself "didn't know one thing about these people who had been nominated," said the senator, so Helms himself would have to be the guardian. For the next six weeks, Helms poked and prodded Crocker. "I'm sure your wife loves you, your children love you, and your dog wags his tail when you come home," Helms told Crocker at the first hearing, "but I want to know where you stand." When Crocker returned for the second round of hearings on April 27, Helms socked him with 107 written questions, some of which, Crocker noted ironically, "appeared to have been inspired by people on the right fringe of the National Party who distrusted P. W. Botha's own reformist agenda!"

Though moderate Republicans like Senate Foreign Relations Committee chair Charles Percy of Illinois and Nancy Landon Kassebaum of Kansas expressed displeasure with Helms's decision to hold up the nomination, the senator from North Carolina was determined to make sure that Crocker would be sufficiently sympathetic to the South African government. "It would be wrong to assume that the doctrine of apartheid was conceived in bad faith or rooted in racial hatred," Helms said in one of his opening statements at the hearings. Helms commended the "deeply religious nature of the Afrikaner spirit, which was untainted by modernist philosophy. . . . To condemn apartheid as an inequitable practical failure is one thing," continued Helms, "but to demand 'purposeful evolutionary change towards a nonracial system' is to impose secular values that would destabilize both white communities and the contending black nations." The problems at his confirmation hearings arose, Crocker later recalled, because "I was from the wrong side of the street for Jesse. Jesse represented the hairy back wing of the Reagan coalition—the social movement, aligned with fundamentalist Christianity and anti-Communism. . . . Helms's ideal model for assistant secretary would be an agronomist or a retired dentist, someone who had been to South Africa's game preserves and liked the quality of service in the hotels. I had the wrong kind of degrees and I knew too much."

Another tricky matter Crocker had to face in the Senate was whether the United States intended to support Jonas Savimbi and UNITA. The administration had been forbidden by Congress from doing so. During the confirmation hearings, Massachusetts Senator Paul Tsongas told Crocker that he supported the efforts to find an agreement in Namibia but that he was absolutely opposed to any change in the current law. At the same time, in one of the more bizarre twists of political fortune, Savimbi, despite his history as a Maoist, had emerged as a darling of the American right. Whenever he traveled to Washington, Savimbi found himself feted by anti-Communists as a hero of democracy. Helms and the other right-wing supporters believed that Savimbi should be treated with the same enthusiasm as the insurgents in Nicaragua and Afghanistan who were being supported under the emerging "Reagan doctrine," which promised American material support for those rebelling against Communist regimes.

Trying to preserve his chance of being approved, Crocker sought the pragmatic middle ground. The United States, he privately told the senators and the African leaders on his trip, had not yet made a decision about whether to support Savimbi. The conflicting claims that Savimbi was a creation of the South African military or that he was the "George Washington of Africa," as an article in *Reader's Digest* put it, were both false. Savimbi was a resilient and often brutal leader of one portion of Angola's population. As such he would have to be party to any eventual solution. Crocker also said he supported the provision of military equipment to Savimbi because this would increase both the American influence over Savimbi and the likelihood that the Angolan government would move to settle.

In May 1981, while his nomination was still being debated, Crocker threw himself into preparing Secretary of State Haig for the official visit by Pik Botha that was scheduled for the middle of the month. Crocker was pleased that the South African government had accepted the invitation and believed that a mixture of intellectual candor and material inducements could overcome Botha's resistance. In a briefing memo to Haig, Crocker urged the secretary of state to tell Botha that the main obstacle to an improvement in relations was the situation in Namibia. There was little mention of apartheid, except for Crocker's brief comment that Haig should tell Botha the United States could not "condone a system of institutionalized racial differentiation," but "we can cooperate with a society undergoing constructive change." Crocker suggested that the secretary should be candid about how American and South African interests aligned and diverged, for example telling Botha that "a Russian flag in Windhoek is as unacceptable to us as it is to you." Crocker also said that Haig should explicitly link the Namibian and Angolan problems. A Namibian settlement, he wrote, would "contribute to the leverage we need to produce a withdrawal of Soviet/Cuban military forces from Angola."

By early June, Crocker's plans almost crashed when secret documents from the Africa Bureau began showing up in the *Washington Post* and the *New York Times*. On June 4, the *Wall Street Journal* reported that the State Department and White House were suddenly blaming Crocker's woes on each other. Helms, in the meantime, hammered away at the breach of confidence on the Senate floor. He then let it be known that he might consider approving Crocker if Crocker hired Clifford Kiracofe, an archconservative researcher from the Fletcher School of Law and International Diplomacy at Tufts University. Crocker, convinced that Kiracofe had close ties to the South African intelligence services, refused. Crocker's nomination was rescued when the Senate moderates appealed to Majority Leader Howard Baker of Tennessee, who blocked Helms's attempt to extend the hold. Crocker was confirmed on June 9, five months after he had started his job, by a vote of eighty-four to seven.

The next few months brought more turbulence for Crocker. In August, Randall Robinson obtained and published the secret memoranda Crocker had prepared for Haig's meeting with Botha. The documents provoked accusations that Crocker was actively pursuing a rapprochement with South Africa. Crocker tried to rebut this in his first major speech on southern Africa, which he delivered to the American Legion in Honolulu on August 29. After outlining the economic and geopolitical importance of southern Africa, Crocker addressed the question of apartheid. "In South Africa, it is not our task to choose between black and white," he said. "In this rich land of talented and diverse people, important Western economic, strategic, moral, and political interests are at stake. . . . The Reagan administration has no intention of destabilizing South Africa in order to curry favor elsewhere. Neither will we align ourselves with apartheid policies that are abhorrent to our multiracial democracy. . . . We will not support the severing of [economic] ties," Crocker concluded. "It does not serve our interests to walk away from South Africa any more than it does to play down the seriousness of domestic and regional problems it faces."

The policy of constructive engagement offered P. W. Botha more military and political maneuvering room than he had ever enjoyed. When National Security Adviser William Clark visited South Africa in June 1981, Botha did his best to get Clark to promise that the United States would guarantee the removal of Cubans from Angola. Clark, though sympathetic to the South Africans, balked at the ham-handed treatment. Nonetheless the new American attentiveness to Pretoria gave Botha additional room to try to pound his regional neighbors into submission. Though Crocker had identified the ending of cross-border raids as one of the central goals of his policy, attacks by nationalist guerrillas and the South African Defence Force actually increased after he took office.

However much Botha complained about the leftist regimes on his borders, his strategy was not primarily aimed at them. Without massive intervention by the Warsaw Pact, Botha knew, no state in the region could ever challenge his government on the open battlefield. Similarly, despite the frontline states' attempts to curb their reliance on South African products, railroads, and ports, the results had been meager. The diatribes erupting from Lusaka and Harare and Maputo could not eliminate the economic dependence that Botha could count on to keep his neighbors in line. The real focus, therefore, was not the governments of the Frontline states but Umkhonto We Sizwe, the armed wing of the African National Congress, which had emerged after more than a decade in hibernation to embarrass and harass the Nationalist government.

The blow that the South African police struck against the ANC leadership in 1963 had nearly proved fatal. As one historian wrote, it would have required "a titanic leap of faith . . . in 1963 to believe in the ultimate resurrection of the ANC." In the ANC's own assessment, the destruction had been almost complete. "Internal organization was shattered," said one report, "grass roots activity was limited, communication links were broken, and a gap was evident between the rank and file." While Hendrik Verwoerd and John Vorster presided over their burgeoning apartheid state, Oliver Tambo, operating with a small number of assistants from an office in London, cut off from supporters and funds inside South Africa, strained to control a fractious, dwindling movement in exile. The twenty-three-member ANC Executive Committee, the group that made all of the decisions, spent six years squabbling over the direction of the movement. Umkhonto We Sizwe had shrunk to a tiny band capable of only an occasional ineffective act of sabotage. It was not until 1969, when the ANC held its Third Consultative Conference in Morogoro, Tanzania, that the organization began to show signs of unity and coordination.

The new structure and rhetoric of the ANC reflected the growing influence of members of the South African Communist Party within the organization. With the earlier strategies of protest and boycott discredited, the Communists in the ANC seemed vindicated. The Western nations offered only words, they pointed out, while the Soviet Union and East Germany provided money, weapons, and training. The Western countries spurned even mild economic pressures while the Eastern bloc attacked capitalist exploitation and proclaimed the necessity of class struggle. The Western countries stalled, waiting for change to come from the top down, through the gradual enlightenment of the Afrikaner, while the Eastern countries spoke urgently of people seizing power from the bottom up by overcoming a determined oppressor. For those who had devoted their lives to the ANC, each additional year the National Party remained in power lent credence to both the Communists' critique and their recommended course of action.

Despite the renewed commitment to armed struggle, the few hundred ANC guerrillas under Umkhonto's command could not easily penetrate South Africa as long as the country was surrounded by white-minority regimes in Mozambique, Rhodesia, and Angola. From 1969 to 1974, even though ANC couriers slipped into the country from Lesotho and Swaziland, the organization found it impossible to establish the national network of internal cells and support systems that would make it possible to strike against economic and military targets. As a result, when the Black Consciousness movement emerged, the ANC could do little but applaud from the sidelines. Indeed, the movement, despite the vigor it was imparting to African students and intellectuals, posed ideological and tactical problems for the ANC. The movement's emphasis on the importance of African identity was closer to the exclusivist tradition of the Pan-Africanist Congress than to the multiracialism of the ANC. Moreover, the ANC's revolutionary strategy viewed the self-help projects promoted by Black Consciousness as bourgeois and counterproductive. "We . . . oppose such efforts as the building of clinics, work camps, and home industries no matter how well meant," said one ANC statement. "That energy and enthusiasm of the youth must be directed in efforts to destroy the one and only source of our misery and oppression, namely white domination." The tensions simmered inside the ANC until 1975, when a group of eight dissidents launched an internal attack on the ANC's decision to open its ranks to whites and on the increased influence of the South African Communist Party. The party, they argued, was controlled by whites and was increasingly dictating the direction of the ANC. After a raucous debate, during which the Communists argued that nonracialism was not only in the oldest tradition of the ANC but also helped maintain the focus on the root cause of apartheid, which was class oppression, the dissidents lost ground and eventually were expelled.

In the wake of the Soweto riots, the ANC faced the difficult task of feeding, clothing, educating, training, and deploying the thousands of young people who were streaming out of South Africa. To cope, the ANC set up new headquarters in Lusaka, Zambia, where it employed several hundred people in eleven departments and organized a large refugee camp and educational facility outside of Dar Es Salaam, Tanzania. Joe Modise, the commander of Umkhonto We Sizwe, and his chief of staff, Joe Slovo, who was also head of the Communist Party and the only white member of the ANC Executive Committee, established military camps in Tanzania, Mozambique, and Angola. Using surplus Czech and Soviet equipment, Umkhonto volunteers learned how to conduct reconnaissance missions, place explosives, throw grenades, fire rocket launchers, and set limpet mines. Whereas in 1976 Umkhonto commanded only about three hundred guerrillas, five years later its force was an estimated eight thousand.

Though some harbored the hope that this small army could tackle the military power of Pretoria, Umkhonto's top planners knew that the best they could do was to demoralize the white population, discredit P. W. Botha's claim to control the country, and give encouragement to the black majority. Umkhonto strategists viewed guerrilla missions as "armed propaganda" that could be classified into three types. "Linkage" missions were designed to show support for an action being taken by another group, such as an attack on a plant at which black workers had launched a strike. "Retaliation" missions were organized to extract a price for military actions by the South African Defence Force and police. "Challenge" missions were intended to demonstrate that even South Africa's most precious economic and military facilities could not be shielded from attack. Relying on espionage from both whites and blacks, the leaders of Umkhonto drew up a long list of potential targets to sabotage; dispatched guerrillas, some of them with limpet mines and other weapons strapped to their bodies under their clothes, through Botswana, Zimbabwe, Mozambique, and Swaziland—and then hoped for the best.

The "challenge" missions were the most spectacular. In June 1980 the ANC attacked the large Natref oil refinery near Durban and blew up portions of SASOL I and SASOL II, South Africa's prized multibillion-dollar coal-to-oil conversion plants that had been built by the American construction firm Fluor. Throughout 1981 Umkhonto guerrillas destroyed more than a dozen small power stations and railroad segments to protest the celebration of the twentieth anniversary of the republic. In December 1982, using documents stolen by a white spy, they evaded tight security and set off explosions at the Koeberg nuclear power plant near Cape Town, hundreds of miles from the nearest border, causing more than forty million dollars' worth of damage and delaying the commissioning of the plant for more than a year.

In addition to these high-profile attacks, the ANC slowly expanded its network of supporters and carried out an increasing number of small-scale missions. Examining the period from 1977 to 1983, the University of Cape Town's Centre for Intergroup Studies recorded more than two hundred acts of political violence that they attributed to the ANC. Since South African television and newspapers had been ordered by the Botha government not to emphasize such attacks in their reporting, many believed the true number to be much higher. Because the South African government did not officially count the many unexploded mines, bombs, or weapons caches they discovered; or include incidents that they could classify as "criminal" (such as the assassination of black informants by Umkhonto operatives); or publicize attacks that the government believed would disrupt public opinion, "the actual number of missions traceable to insurgents," wrote one scholar, "could be as much as three times the reported figure."

At the end of 1981, Foreign Minister Pik Botha informed Chester Crocker that Pretoria had decided to accept the provisions of Security Council Resolution 435 on the independence of Namibia. Crocker was elated. After less than a year, the policy of constructive engagement seemed to be bearing fruit. If the Americans could now persuade the Angolan government, both the Angolan civil war and the lingering Namibian ordeal could be brought to a close. In the meantime, however, Reagan, Haig, and Crocker tried to encourage the new spirit of cooperation that had emerged from Pretoria. During the first six months of 1982, the administration loosened a range of financial, military, and technological constraints on South Africa. In February President Reagan eased the restriction on the sale of nonmilitary items—food, clothing, building materials, and the like—to the South African police and military. Less than two months later, the Commerce Department, acting under the new policy, issued export licenses for the sale of twenty-five hundred high-voltage cattle prods to the South African police, a move the Reagan administration disallowed six months later when it was pointed out that the police would use the electrical batons on people. The Commerce Department approved applications from four U.S. airplane manufacturers to sell light aircraft to the police and South African Defence Force. Soon afterward the department agreed that U.S. computer firms could supply the South African military and various homeland administrations. In March, when Control Data asked for permission to sell a particularly powerful mainframe to the South African government, the Commerce Department referred the request to the White House. Though the Defense Department and the Nuclear Regulatory Commission opposed the sale because it would "greatly aid Pretoria's nuclear weapons program," Reagan said yes.

The president also signaled his support for P. W. Botha by nominating Herman W. Nickel to serve as U.S. ambassador to South Africa. Born in Germany in 1928, Nickel had come to the United States as a scholarship student after the war and had eventually become a journalist for *Time* magazine, serving as a correspondent in South Africa in 1962.

When he managed to secure an interview with Nelson Mandela shortly before Mandela's arrest, the South African government kicked Nickel out. Nickel subsequently served as *Time* bureau chief in London, Bonn, and Tokyo before shifting to *Fortune* in 1977 to write about the relationship between politics and business. In 1978 Nickel wrote a lengthy article entitled "The Case for Doing Business in South Africa," in which he argued that U.S. multinationals, through their promotion of economic growth and the Sullivan Principles, were leading the corporate battle against apartheid. In 1980, in an article entitled "The Corporation Haters," Nickel penned a blistering attack on Timothy Smith and the member churches of the Interfaith Center on Corporate Responsibility for their efforts to use the proxy resolution system to bring issues like investment in South Africa or the marketing of infant formula before managers and shareholders. Nickel's nomination as U.S. ambassador two years later infuriated the anti-apartheid community, as did his comments about his new role. "All we can do is to lend encouragement to moderate forces across the spectrum, black and white, to help this process along," Nickel told a reporter. "I don't think we can do this by public lecturing or hectoring." Though Randall Robinson of Trans-Africa, Jean Sindab of the Washington Office on Africa, and Herbert Hill, the national labor director of the NAACP, all traveled to Capitol Hill to testify against Nickel, the U.S. Senate confirmed him on March 29, 1982.

In November 1982, the United States again intervened to support a South African application for a $1.1 billion loan from the International Monetary Fund. Botha needed the loan because of the decline in the price of gold, and the Reagan administration actively support the measure. When thirty-five members of the U.S. House of Representatives wrote to U.S. Treasury Secretary Donald Regan to object, Regan replied that the United States should not "introduce political considerations in the IMF." Congressman William H. Gray III, a clergyman and leading member of the Congressional Black Caucus, responded that "the Reagan Administration had already politicized the IMF by opposing loans to Nicaragua, Vietnam, and Grenada and by insisting on a loan to El Salvador in spite of opposition from Western Europe and the IMF staff." Though the United Nations General Assembly voted 121 to 3 to ask the IMF not to make the loan, the directors of the fund approved it two weeks later.

In Congress, those who wanted to pass additional anti-apartheid legislation found themselves stymied, in part because moderates, such as Senator Nancy Kassebaum, had decided to wait and see whether the policy of constructive engagement would live up to its promise. Kassebaum, the new chair of the Senate subcommittee on Africa, had never been sympathetic to South Africa. In mid-1981 she had written a news-paper column in which she argued that every principle dear to Republicans—the rights of property, self-expression, and freedom—was violated by apartheid. She had vigorously defended Crocker's nomination against Jesse Helms and, now that Crocker was in office, she thought that he should be given some breathing room. Democratic Senator Paul Tsongas agreed that constructive engagement should be given a chance, so long as it did not "degenerate into what is in essence a pro-South Africa policy."

In the House of Representatives, the members of the Congressional Black Caucus and their white allies continued to write and file bills that would make the Sullivan Principles mandatory, eliminate the deductibility of corporate taxes paid to the South African government, and restrict new investment. These measures emerged regularly from the subcommittee on Africa but died when the full committee failed to vote them out onto the House floor. Two such bills—one filed by Stephen Solarz and the other by William Gray—died in late 1982 when the 97th Congress adjourned before the Committee on Foreign Affairs had voted on them. The problem, said many congressional staff members, was that the representatives felt no pressure from their constituents to act. Other representatives reported the same. Phil Christensen, the conservative staff director of the Senate subcommittee on Africa, told investigators from the Investor Responsibility Research Center that this was unlikely to change because there was "no significant lobby" on the South African question. When asked about the efforts of the activist community to influence the debate, Christensen was blunt. "Their impact," he said, "is nil."

To P. W. Botha and the "secureaucrats" who sat on the State Security Council, the rising incidents of sabotage by Umkhonto We Sizwe were both an affront to their pride and a vindication of their strategy. Poring over maps, the generals plotted how to put a stop to the attacks. They began by building fences, laying mines, planting dense rows of sharp sisal plants, and beefing up patrols along the borders. Noting with alarm that many white farmers had left the border areas, the government tried to lure them back by offering low-cost loans to discharged soldiers and setting up a military radio network. To increase the mobility of the South African Defence Force, the government improved rural roads, straightening and widening some stretches so they could be used as emergency runways. The combination of efforts, they hoped, would create a "ring of steel" to deter Africans from leaving the country and guerrillas from attempting to return.

Such methods, they knew, would only slow the flow across South

Africa's borders. To stanch it completely would require the dismantling of ANC bases and transit points in the frontline states. Since Vorster's attempts to achieve détente with his neighbors had failed, the next best method, Botha believed, was to threaten to destabilize the neighboring governments in order to force them to expel the ANC. The first tool at his disposal was South Africa's economic power, which was especially effective against landlocked countries like Lesotho, Swaziland, and Zambia. The second was to train, supply, and support surrogate military forces. During the Rhodesian civil war, South Africa and Rhodesia had formed a covert military group called the Mozambique National Resistance (RENAMO), set up bases for them in the eastern Transvaal, provided them with weapons, and unleashed them. RENAMO troops crossed into Mozambique at will and wreaked havoc with the economy by blowing up roads, bridges, power lines, and railways and by terrorizing tens of thousands of rural residents. South Africa tried the same tactic with Lesotho, establishing and maintaining the tiny Lesotho Liberation Army whose guerrillas attacked points throughout the mountain kingdom. In August 1981, in a bizarre escapade, a group of mercenaries disguised as rugby players flew to the Seychelles Islands and attempted to seize control of the government. When their coup attempt failed, they commandeered a plane and flew back to Durban, where they were arrested. During their trial, several members asserted that the National Intelligence Service had known about the coup and that the South African Defence Force had supplied the weapons. The judge accepted their testimony but ruled that there was not enough evidence to prove that the South African government had been formally involved.

The South African army and air force also struck directly at ANC facilities within the neighboring countries. In 1981 South African commandos darted over the border and attacked several ANC houses in Matola, Mozambique, killing twelve people. In December of the following year, Defence Forces swept into Lesotho's capital of Maseru, burst into twelve homes and apartments, and shot forty-two people dead, eight of them citizens of Lesotho and the rest South African refugees. Such incidents traumatized the neighboring governments. Delegates to a summit meeting of the frontline states in March 1982 accused South Africa of "waging a non-declared war against the free and independent states of the region." Foreign Minister Botha responded by assuring the members of the South African parliament that the principle of noninterference remained a cornerstone of the government's policy. The prime minister himself, however, made it abundantly clear that neighboring countries could expect more of the same. In his New Year's address in 1983, P. W. Botha said that he would not allow neighboring states to be used as springboards for attacks on South Africa. Botha then offered to sign nonaggression pacts with any frontline state that would prohibit each side from permitting attacks on the other. Elaborating on the prime minister's point a few days later, General Magnus Malan warned that countries that did not sign such an agreement would face increased military pressures from South Africa and its surrogates.

To make good on their threat, Botha and his cabinet continued the general militarization of South African society. The publicly revealed portion of the defense budget increased steadily every year, from 1.6 billion rand in 1978 to 3 billion in 1983. ARMSCOR, the huge government-controlled corporation that manufactured everything from bullets to helicopters, ballooned up to more than a hundred thousand employees and dispatched emissaries around the world looking for export customers. National Party members in parliament voted through one law after another increasing the military responsibilities of the citizenry. By 1983 a white man in South Africa could expect to spend most of his life attached to a military unit of some kind. As a boy he would train in a school military club. At age eighteen he would be drafted into the military for two years. After his discharge, he was required to put in an additional twenty-four months spread out over the next fourteen years. As he reached middle age, he was required to contribute twelve days a year to the Citizen Force, whose units could be sent on border patrol, or in the paramilitary commandos. When he reached age fifty-five, he was transferred to the National Reserve, from which he could still be called to active duty for the next ten years. In addition to this heavy demand on white males, the South African Defence Force also established several battalions of Africans—grouped by ethnic background—and vigorously recruited Coloured men and white women to supplement their ranks.

The encroachment of the military on the private lives of so many citizens produced resistance. Businessmen complained that the government was soaking up the time and talents of their most skilled workers. The South African Council of Churches demanded that the government permit young men to list themselves as conscientious objectors, a position that attracted support from clergy in the different branches of the Dutch Reformed Church. Students and parents banded together in an End Conscription Campaign that won increasing support until the government made it illegal to criticize the draft. The average man in the street grumbled when he learned that the government, in an attempt to increase white immigration to South Africa, had exempted newcomers from the onerous demands of military service. Even critics to the right of the government, men like Andries Treurnicht who believed that Botha was too soft, worried aloud that the process of militarization was gathering too much power in the hands of too few.

The continuous emphasis on the terrorist threats that faced South

Africa; the endless stream of official posters, advertisements, and pronouncements on the dangers of Communism and the successes of the South African forces; the intrusion of military responsibilities and concerns into all aspects of civilian life all generated a psychological climate of polarization and fear. The idea that the country was already involved in a war had a particularly strong effect on the police and intelligence services, which were charged with discovering and suppressing dissent. The first years of the Reagan administration and the policy of constructive engagement corresponded with a significant increase in the brutality of the methods the police and military used against individuals. Mindful of the eventual failure of the Rhodesian police to crack and infiltrate the guerrilla movement, the Security Branch police routinely detained and tortured individuals until they produced some sort of testimony.

On October 26, 1981, a heavily bandaged man walked into a black police station at Sibasa, a small town in the northern homeland of Venda. As he complained to the three officers about his injuries, the man, an ANC guerrilla in disguise, suddenly withdrew a hand grenade from his clothes and lobbed it toward them. As he fled, bullets and rockets streaked into the police station, destroying the building and killing two of the policemen. Newspapers throughout the country played up the attack. Chief Mphephu of Venda, embarrassed and enraged, ordered a massive crackdown on many of the church, student, and political leaders in his territory and called on the white Security Police to assist him. One of the men they picked up was Isaac Tshifhiwa Muofe, who died suddenly after three weeks in detention. When his friend and pastor, Dean Tshenuwani Simon Farisani, visited and consoled the dead man's widow, the police came and arrested him too.

As a theological student, Farisani had become enamored of Black Theology, had met Stephen Biko, had joined SASO, and eventually had risen to serve as the head of the Black People's Convention from 1973 to 1975. Ordained in the Lutheran Church, Farisani had already survived two lengthy detentions in the late 1970s. During his third detention, the police tortured him relentlessly to get him to sign a false confession that he had participated in the attack on the police station. On one occasion, Farisani was forced to lie on his back with his legs spread apart while a police captain kicked his genitals. "I am determined to destroy your manhood," the captain told him, "those dirty testicles that make you feel like a small bull." The policemen beat him savagely for hours, pausing only to force the clergyman to wipe his own blood from the floor. Later they tortured him with electricity. "From morning until noon . . . I cried like a baby and begged for mercy," Farisani wrote in a detailed account of his experience. "In response the police sang, led by their captain, 'Hallelujah, let us praise the Lord.' " The captain mocked the pastor between electrocutions: " 'Dean, you are a man of God. Call God! He will help you!' " A broken Farisani poured out false details about the ANC raid which the police happily gathered and used as evidence against others. Because of his torture, Farisani suffered two nearly fatal heart attacks. After his release, Farisani eventually was treated at the Center for Torture Victims in Saint Paul, Minnesota.

Not everyone survived. The widespread use of such techniques in police stations across South Africa caused a dramatic surge in the number of deaths in detention. By 1982 at least twenty-eight people had died of suspicious causes while under the care of the police. The police almost always said that death was the result of suicide, and they were never contradicted by the courts. When Mapetla Mohapi died in 1980, for example, the police claimed that he had killed himself, and they produced a suicide note to prove it. His widow sued the police for damages. During the court case, the defense produced a witness, Thenjiwa Mtintso, who had been tortured by the police. At one point the police had drawn a wet towel tightly across her face until she nearly suffocated. When they removed the towel, a policeman leered and told her, "Now you know how Mohapi died." Despite this evidence, and the opinion of two international experts that the suicide note was a forgery, the judge ruled in favor of the police.

Union leaders were a special target for police detention in the urban areas and in the homelands. Scores were arrested in the homeland of the Ciskei, where Lennox Sebe, a pro-apartheid tyrant who had declared himself president for life, ruled with an iron fist. In September 1981, in anticipation of opposition to the forthcoming Ciskeian "independence," homeland Security Police arrested more than two hundred labor leaders from the South Africa Allied Workers' Union, the African Food and Canning Workers' Union, and other unions. In November South African police picked up several dozen more union leaders, including Dr. Neil Aggett, a twenty-eight-year-old white medical doctor who served as the Transvaal regional secretary of the Food and Canning Workers' Union. According to reliable accounts, Aggett was so severely tortured that he became mentally unhinged.

On February 5, the police released a statement that Neil Aggett had committed suicide by hanging himself with the sash of his bathrobe in his cell. The announcement triggered an outcry across South Africa and around the world. More than ten thousand people of all races showed up for his funeral. The Food and Canning Workers' Union called for a half-hour nationwide strike on February 11 to honor him. The Australian Council of Trade Unions announced a week-long ban on South African shipping and air travel to protest his death. Several union leaders who had been trying to work out a unity agreement for more than a year, a move which Aggett strongly favored, promised to renew their efforts. In the United States, the AFL-CIO paid tribute to Aggett by posthumously awarding him the George Meany Human Rights Award, a gesture which offended many unionists in South Africa because the award was given jointly with Gatsha Buthelezi. At the time of the inquest, Louis Le Grange, the minister of law and order, felt sufficiently uncomfortable that he allowed the press to tour the cell in John Vorster Square where Aggett had died. In a meeting with foreign journalists Le Grange later tried to justify police behavior on the grounds that "you won't get much information if you keep a detainee in a five star hotel or with a friend." The police who had interrogated the young doctor testified at the inquest that he had not been mistreated in any way. In December the judge rejected the eyewitness testimony of Aggett's fellow detainees and ruled that the police had not been responsible.

The sharp rise in arrests, abuse, and death in detention was matched by an increase in the number of suspicious accidents and outright assassinations that took the lives of National Party opponents both in South Africa and abroad. In August 1981 Joe Gqabi, the ANC representative in Zimbabwe, was murdered in Harare. In June 1982 a car bomb killed ANC officials Petrus and Abu Nzima in Swaziland. Two months later, Ruth First, the wife of ANC leader Joe Slovo and the author of a harrowing account of her detention in the 1960s and another work urging sanctions against South Africa, was blown to pieces in her university office in Mozambique by a letter bomb. The package carried the imprint of the African Bibliographic Center in Washington, D.C., and bore an American postmark.

Anti-apartheid activists within South Africa were also dying at an abnormally high rate. In February 1979, Winnie Mandela, who had been languishing for nearly two years in Brandfort, was delighted that she had finally received the authorization to go to work for an Afrikaner physician named Chris Hattingh. "I battled to get permission to work for him from October last year," wrote Winnie. "Brigadier Coetzee told me permission was granted and I could start but had to wait for it in writing. In the meantime Hattingh told me he was regularly being trailed by a car with four men. On the first of March—the day I was supposed to start work—he came to find out about the permit. Six kilometers from me, at 8 p.m., his car mysteriously overturned. He died on the spot. After his death, permission was promptly granted in writing." Winnie was heartsick. "They killed him and have got away with it, like the Steve Bikos," she wrote a friend several months later, "but this one is worse as the world will never know. . . . I never knew I could grieve so much for someone other than my own kind."

During the early years of constructive engagement, the number of these incidents rose dramatically. On November 20, 1981, Griffiths Mxenge, a Durban lawyer and a former prisoner on Robben Island, died under violent and suspicious circumstances. Though the investigation never identified Mxenge's assailants, his wife, Victoria, publicly claimed that both her husband and Professor Richard Turner had been killed by a "right-wing death squad." Later that year Joe Mavi, the president of the Black Municipal Workers' Union, the Reverend James Gawe, rector of St. Gregory's Anglican Church, and several other union leaders and churchmen died in car wrecks. One casualty was Frikkie Conradie, a young Dutch Reformed clergyman who had refused ordination in the white branch of the church and had chosen instead to be ordained and to work in the black church; he perished in an automobile accident. The turning point in Conradie's life had come when he traveled to Holland in the 1970s and met Allan Boesak, who had asked Conradie what he thought of apartheid. Conradie had given the standard guarded answer, which Boesak challenged. Boesak and Conradie had then stayed up the entire night while Boesak detailed the repeated forced removals that his family had suffered in the Cape Province. "I met Allan, and that's where the whole story started," he explained to American reporter Joseph Lelyveld in an interview a week before his death. When asked whether he considered himself a missionary to the Africans in whose township he served, he said no, that his parishioners were ministering to him. "They take you as a racist and a paternalist," Conradie said, "and they turn you into a human being."

Conradie died in March 1982 at age thirty-five, just twelve hours before his wife gave birth to their first child. The members of Conradie's family, many of whom had shunned him in life, traveled to his church in the township of Alexandra and sat as hundreds of Africans filled the pews and surrounded the building. Desmond Tutu and Allan Boesak both delivered eulogies in which they noted that Conradie's widow had asked that her husband be buried in the township's cemetery, becoming the first white in the area and possibly in the country who had done so. "Can you imagine an Afrikaner, a DRC dominee of all people, leaving his own community to identify himself so closely with the downtrodden, the poor, and the suffering, a white man giving himself and his family to a black community, to be their servant and to work for justice and reconciliation and to work under a black minister?" asked Tutu. "It is unbelievable, and yet we saw this miracle of God's grace working here in Alexandra Township here in South Africa." "I do not come to praise Frikkie Conradie," declared Boesak forcefully, "but I come to praise God for this man. For Frikkie Conradie lived and died a free man."

□ □ □ □

However great the violence that marked the army's battle with ANC guerrillas or the police's campaign against the opponents in apartheid, it was no match for the brutality and carnage that were unfolding during the same period in the "operational areas" of Namibia and Angola. Ever since the invasion of Angola in 1975 and the alliance with Jonas Savimbi, the South African Defence Force had attempted to crush SWAPO. The SADF developed a variety of methods for pursuing the mobile SWAPO guerrillas, ranging from helicopters and rapid personnel carriers to teams of soldiers with dogs or on dirt bikes. Sometimes they struck directly at encampments inside Angola. In May 1978, two hundred South African commandos had descended on a refugee camp and shot twelve hundred unarmed men, women, and children, killing half of them.

Starting in June 1980, the military launched large-scale penetrations into Angola. They began with Operation Smokeshell, which swept through southern Angola in an attempt to clean out SWAPO staging areas. The SWAPO guerrillas, armed with Soviet bloc weapons and supported by the MPLA, managed to survive and struck back. In keeping with their policy of surrogacy, South Africa continued to support Jonas Savimbi and to conduct joint operations with UNITA. Indeed, the South African government was so eager to make Savimbi look effective that South African commandos put on UNITA uniforms and carried out several daring raids in Angola, leaving behind evidence to suggest that the strike had been the work of Savimbi's men.

In 1981, as Chester Crocker was pushing South Africa to come to terms on Namibia, Botha decided to put the Reagan administration's professions of friendship to the test. In July 1981 the SADF launched a small offensive known as Operation Carnation. On August 23, less than a week before Crocker's Honolulu speech, South African fighter planes streaked northward and destroyed Angola's early warning system. The next day, more than ten thousand South African troops in armored car and tank columns thundered across the border in Operation Protea. The Angolan army, despite its Soviet weaponry, withdrew under the fierce ground and air attack, leaving the South Africans in control of half a dozen towns, including the provincial capital, and over forty thousand square miles of Angolan territory. After the offensive the South Africans consolidated their control of Cunene province. In an attempt to establish a cordon sanitaire in which SWAPO could no longer operate, the South African soldiers burned villages, destroyed livestock, and mined roads. In late 1981 and in early 1982, during the same period that Alexander Haig was announcing that the Botha government had formally accepted Security Council Resolution 435, South African units struck twice more in Operations Daisy and Super.

The doctrine embraced by the South African high command was not purely military. They understood that for SWAPO to fail, the local peoples would have to be persuaded that it was in their best interests to support the South African occupation. They organized a civic action program designed to capture the "hearts and minds" of the citizenry by launching development projects and stationing national servicemen at schools and medical facilities. They touted the existence of the 201 Battalion, a force of eight hundred black men stationed with their wives and children at a base in the western Caprivi and controlled by an officer corps of more than two hundred whites, as evidence of the population's support. In the sparsely populated Kavango bantustan just south of the border with Angola, the South Africans constructed many facilities, especially roads, which they said were for the benefit of the local population but also had important military applications. Despite these efforts, social services throughout Namibia deteriorated rapidly, in part because of the war and in part because of the duplication and waste from having separate health and educational departments for each of the eleven officially designated "population groups" in Namibia.

Whatever goodwill the South African military might have earned through its civic programs was negated by its reputation for brutality. The most notorious group was a counterinsurgency unit known as Koevoet (the Afrikaans word for "crowbar") whose mission was to destroy SWAPO in whatever way it could. The black and white soldiers in the unit were rigorously trained to be, in the words of an official statement, "cold, calculating . . . and very ruthless." A Koevoet commander asserted that his men were selected, drilled, and fashioned into "killing machines" and had a policy of never taking prisoners. Reports of Koevoet members' brutality accumulated throughout the decade. In 1980, SWAPO obtained and published a list of fifty people whom Koevoet had targeted for assassination. When many of them later died, the military blamed their murders on SWAPO. To increase both blame and fear of SWAPO, the members of Koevoet would sometimes disguise themselves as rebel guerrillas, arm themselves with captured AK-47 assault rifles, and enter a village requesting food, shelter, and assistance. If the villagers responded, the soldiers shot them dead. Such behavior was encouraged by an official military bounty or *kopgeld* (literally "head money") which offered payment for every killing.

Koevoet atrocities proved difficult to document because the South African Defence Force barred most South African and international journalists from the operational areas in Namibia, the Caprivi strip, and southern Angola. Only church leaders managed to circumvent the restrictions. In 1981 a British Council of Churches delegation to Namibia described the military presence as a "reign of terror." Shortly afterward, the Catholic archbishop of South Africa, Denis Hurley, personally led a group from the Southern African Catholic Bishops Conference to Namibia. The participants interviewed nearly two hundred people and came back with an immense list of tortures, hangings, beatings, and other atrocities. In early 1982 Desmond Tutu and Methodist bishop Peter Storey, representing the South African Council of Churches, made a similar trip and released a catalog of specific incidents of savagery. A few months later a fourth religious delegation, sent by the archbishop of Canterbury and accompanied by his special assistant, Terry Waite, visited Anglicans in Namibia and reported on abuse.

The South African clerics went to great lengths to publicize their findings. When Archbishop Hurley returned, he instantly called a press conference to denounce Koevoet. The bishop's report, which was later banned by the South African government, was scathing. "The Security Forces stop at nothing to force information out of people," the report stated. "They break into homes, beat up residents, shoot people, steal and kill cattle, and often pillage stores and tea rooms. Wherever the tracks of SWAPO guerrillas are discovered by the Security Forces the local people are in danger. . . . People are blindfolded, taken from their homes, and left beaten up and dead by the roadside. . . . It is not unknown for a detachment to break into a home and while black soldiers keep watch over the family, white soldiers select the best-looking girls and take them into the *veld* to rape them."

The government responded by charging Hurley under a law that made it a crime to publish "any untrue matter in relation to any action by the South African Defence Force." When international objections cascaded into Pretoria and Hurley said that he would be happy to stand trial so that he could reveal additional details, government prosecutors reversed themselves and dropped the charges. Soon afterward, the government arrested and tried several Koevoet members, two of whom were convicted and imprisoned for an extended rape, robbery, and murder spree while dressed as SWAPO guerrillas. Another soldier, who killed a woman for refusing to have sex with him, received a four-year sentence. If the victim did not die, however, the soldiers were usually let off lightly. A white soldier, who raped an eighty-year-old black woman and sent her to the hospital for two weeks with profuse bleeding, was acquitted when the court accepted his testimony that she had consented. In 1983 two soldiers who had taken a sixty-three-year-old man and roasted him alive, burning his right arm off at the elbow, were fined fifty rand—or about forty dollars—each.

For all his faith in the merit of military force and the necessity of police repression, P. W. Botha understood that these measures, even if successful, could only buy time. Botha, like both of his predecessors, continued to believe that if the policy of separate development could somehow be redesigned, repackaged, and properly sold, it would finally attract the domestic and international support it deserved. Like an alchemist, Botha tried and abandoned different constitutional formulas, first as the head of a constitutional review committee in 1977, then in his advocacy of the "constellation of states" at the Carlton conference in 1979, and again the next year through the Schlebusch Commission. In 1980 Botha formed a President's Council and asked its members to solve the problem of Coloured representation. In early 1981, Botha told parliament that he would soon propose a third chamber of parliament that would include Coloured representatives elected by the Coloured citizens of South Africa.

Botha's actions galled the extreme right-wing members of his party, who perceived, accurately, that the prime minister was veering away from the vision of Verwoerd. Cracks steadily appeared throughout the National Party. Archconservatives openly challenged the Broederbond and the State Security Council. The traditionally dominant and conservative Transvaal wing grumbled loudly about Botha's irresponsible supporters from the Cape. Skirmishes broke out during elections for regional party positions. When Piet Koornhof, the minister of cooperation and development, had attempted in 1980 to become the vice chair of the party in the Transvaal, he was blocked so decisively that the delegates eventually had to turn to a compromise candidate, the minister of mineral and energy affairs, F. W. de Klerk.

The battles were not limited to political caucuses. Debate simmered in the Afrikaner universities and churches, where intellectuals like André du Toit and Herman Gilliomee and theologians like David Bosch were beginning to gather support for their challenges to the intellectual, historical, and biblical underpinnings of apartheid. Discontent bubbled in the halls of commerce, where Afrikaner businessmen watched with alarm as a global slide in the price of gold squashed the economy's growth rate. Nor had the general election of April 1981 given the prime minister the mandate he had sought. The extreme right-wing Herstigte National Party, which had received only 3.3 percent of the vote in 1977, had grabbed 14 percent. Helen Suzman's Progressive Federal Party also garnered more support than ever before. In the face of rising economic, political, and social pressures, South African whites were not pulling into a *laager,* as everyone had predicted, but were breaking up into small, bitterly contentious factions.

By mid-February 1982, Botha decided that the time had come to squelch his opponents and called for a show of confidence within his parliamentary caucus. Botha won, one hundred votes to twenty-two. The prime minister then told Andries Treurnicht and the other dissenters that they had a week to decide whether they would pledge their loyalty and remain members of the party or be booted out. Several days later, Botha's supporters in the Transvaal increased the pressure by ousting Treurnicht as the regional party leader. On March 15 Treurnicht and sixteen other members of parliament stormed out and announced they would form a new entity, the Conservative Party. At its organizing rally in March, which was attended by seven thousand people, Treurnicht promised that his new party would accept the Bible as the norm in the regulation of community life, uphold the principles of Christian nationalism, protect the spiritual, cultural, and political viability of the Afrikaner *volk,* and implement Hendrik Verwoerd's original constitutional proposals from 1966. Within days of its formation, the Conservative Party was endorsed by Connie Mulder, former Minister of Police Jimmy Kruger, and Verwoerd's elderly widow, Betsie.

There was also new activity on the left. Local civic groups like the Port Elizabeth Black Civic Organization (PEBCO) had achieved incremental successes in their hometowns and were reaching out to try to form coalitions with each other. Union leaders had banded together into two large federations, the Federation of South African Trade Unions (FOSATU) and the Council of Unions of South Africa (CUSA). While resisting the requests of various leaders to align themselves formally with a particular political movement, the union representatives had continued to win recognition and concessions at the plant level and to discuss how to increase their unity and political clout.

Much of the attention focused on Nelson and Winnie Mandela. Though Nelson had been banned and imprisoned for nearly two decades, the sixty-three-year-old ANC leader's popularity at home and abroad had grown steadily since the Soweto riots. In 1981, when thirteen United States congressmen had visited South Africa, they had requested permission to see Mandela on Robben Island and had been turned down. In 1982 Winnie Mandela was awarded an honorary doctorate by Haverford College in the United States and Nelson was nominated to be chancellor of the University of the Witwatersrand. That same year a national campaign and petition drive was launched inside South Africa to release Mandela, a move publicly supported by newly installed UN Secretary General Javier Pérez de Cuellar and by fourteen hundred mayors from around the world. In April 1982, in part because of this increased attention, the South African government transferred Nelson Mandela, Walter Sisulu, and two other prominent political prisoners from Robben Island to Pollsmoor Prison.

In May 1982, Botha's President's Council finally unveiled its new constitutional plan. On the surface the changes appeared sweeping. The white Senate would be abolished. The white House of Assembly would remain. In addition, a House of Representatives would be established for Coloureds and a House of Delegates for Indians. The number of representatives in each house would be roughly proportional to the racial distribution in the country: 178 whites, 85 Coloureds, and 45 Indians. To allow the different racial groups to retain control over their daily lives without interference, each assembly would handle its "own" affairs and administer a budget providing for separate ministries of education, health, and so on. Foreign policy, defense, and sports were classified as "general affairs" and would be handled by an "interracial" council composed predominantly of whites. Power in the system centered in the state president, a strong executive who would replace the prime minister, be chosen by an electoral college composed mostly of whites, and appoint nearly half the members of the interracial cabinet. The state president would also have the right to classify policy questions as "own" or "general," thereby controlling the debate. The state president would also be the arbiter of disagreements within the tricameral parliament. If bills passed by the different chambers disagreed with one another, they would be referred to the state president and the President's Council, whose decisions on how to reconcile them would be final.

For nearly two years—from early 1982 until the end of 1983—South African politics was dominated by the furious debate over the tricameral proposal. The National Party, guided tightly by Botha, invested enormous energy and resources in trying to persuade white voters that they should endorse the move. Botha dispatched his lieutenants to spread the word that the change was necessary but not precipitous. F. W. de Klerk, the minister of internal affairs, told the Transvaal Party Congress that while the voters might not agree with every clause in the provision, they would have to decide whether to move South Africa forward or throw it back into deadlock. He appealed for party unity, arguing that those who shared the views of the National Party had to stand fast in order to withstand the onslaught facing the country. Gerrit Viljoen, the minister of national education, attempted to calm right-wing jitters by insisting that "separation, differentiation, and self-determination" were not in jeopardy but would be maintained by the distinction between "own" and "general" affairs.

P. W. Botha found a few political allies outside the National Party. Lennox Sebe, the ruler of the Ciskei, endorsed the new constitution because, he said, it would eventually lead to more political rights for Africans. The minuscule New Republic Party backed the government, as did a large group of business leaders who argued that a no vote would adversely affect foreign investment. The most important boost came from the Labour Party, the dominant political organization among

Coloureds. When P. W. Botha first formed the President's Council, the Labour Party had refused to participate. When Botha offered elected representation, however, those favoring participation gained the upper hand. The Reverend Allan Hendrickse, the leader of the Labour Party, told the public that while the members of his party rejected the tricameral formula as a permanent solution, they also thought that they could use the system to advance the goal of a "democratic and progressive South Africa."

Opposition to the tricameral proposal created strange partners: the African National Congress and the Conservative Party both called on the white electorate to reject the constitution, the first because it did too little, the second because it did too much. One Conservative Party leader even argued that he opposed the new constitution because it would destroy the equality of separate development and lead to white supremacy. Jaap Marais, the leader of the extreme right-wing Herstigte National Party, in an exceptional flight of fancy even for the bizarre world of South African politics, accused Botha of becoming "the tool of the United States," predicted that South Africa would soon become an American colony, and charged that the Reagan administration and the National Party were engaged in a conspiracy to promote the spread of Communism.

The proposal also forged new bonds of allegiance between Buthelezi and the Progressive Federal Party. Buthelezi had been trying for months to win greater acceptance for the findings of the Buthelezi Commission, which had rejected the concept of universal franchise in a unitary state but had urged the creation of an experimental joint regional government in Natal. In 1982 Buthelezi and the leader of the Progressive Federal Party, Frederick van Zyl Slabbert, began to organize joint rallies and share podiums, a move attacked in speeches by F. W. de Klerk. Whites could fight each other, said de Klerk, but they should not enter into partnerships with people "who ought not to be present in the white political arena." P. W. Botha, for his part, was delighted that his proposal had stolen the initiative from his opposition and split them asunder. Those who had long been arguing in favor of incremental change now seemed to be opposing it. The ultra-extremists who had been urging a return to an idyllic Verwoerdian world had been isolated and undercut. His strategy of titillating liberals with the prospect of change while reassuring conservatives that nothing substantial would be lost seemed to be working. He was able to succeed in this apparent contradiction because the two messages were delivered in separate ways. While Pik Botha and other *verligte* lieutenants were privately assuring foreign diplomats that this was just the tip of the iceberg of change, the prime minister was vigorously denouncing those who argued that it would lead to majority rule. The ruse worked beautifully. In June 1983 the U.S. undersecretary of state, Lawrence Eagleburger, gave a speech on in which he predicted that striking changes would soon be seen in South Africa. He discounted Botha's conservative rhetoric on the grounds that one could not expect "South Africa's would-be reformers to announce their game plan and their bottom line to the world at large." In response, Botha publicly denied that there was a hidden agenda, telling a National Party youth congress that an integrated parliament with a fourth chamber for Africans was an impossibility not only in his lifetime but in his children's lifetime. Nonetheless, many business leaders reported that they intended to support the new constitution because they had been assured privately that the government would then take steps to solve the African problem.

One group that continued to pester P. W. Botha was the South African Council of Churches, whose members relentlessly criticized his government's behavior in the homelands, schools, townships, prisons, and military areas. Botha was particularly infuriated that Desmond Tutu had succeeded in increasing international financial, political, and ecclesiastical support for the South African Council of Churches. Through his travels around the world, the bishop had focused attention on aspects of apartheid that Botha most wanted to conceal. Moreover, Tutu, in defiance of the law against economic sabotage, was edging closer and closer to an open call for sanctions. In September 1979, during a trip to Denmark, a journalist asked Tutu why the SACC opposed foreign investment. Tutu replied that it was because the churches believed that investment supported apartheid. The Sullivan Principles, he continued, could not be effective because they were only "shifting the furniture around the room, instead of changing the furniture." Should Denmark then continue to buy South African coal? the interviewer asked. "I find it rather disgraceful that Denmark is buying South African coal and increasing a dependence on South Africa," said Tutu bluntly, "whereas one would hope that we could get South Africa to have a weaker position in bargaining, so that we could get this change as soon as possible." But wouldn't blacks suffer, the interviewer continued, if the coal were not purchased? Yes, said the bishop, but "it would be suffering with a purpose. We would not be doing what is happening now, where blacks are suffering and it seems to be a suffering that is going on and on and on." Tutu's remarks set off such an avalanche of white outrage in South Africa that the board of the SACC had to stop to decide whether they would permit the general secretary to make such statements in the future without prior approval. Tutu defended his views, telling board members that economic sanctions were one of the few nonviolent forms

In 1979 Franklin Thomas, the former head of the Bedford-Stuyvesant Corporation, was chosen as president of the Ford Foundation. A member of several boards of companies with operations in South Africa, he publicly opposed corporate withdrawal but used his authority at the foundation and his connections to support less visible forms of anti-apartheid activism. (*Columbia Spectator*)

In the year following the death of Stephen Biko, university campuses and other institutions were rocked by anti-apartheid sit-ins and demonstrations. This protest against U.S. bank loans to South Africa was held on Wall Street on June 16, 1978, the second anniversary of the Soweto riots. (American Committee on Africa, South Africa Protest File)

Dismayed by the jubilant reaction of the apartheid government to Ronald Reagan's landslide reelection in 1984, Randall Robinson (center) invited U.S. Human Rights Commission member Mary Frances Berry (left) and U.S. Representative of the District of Columbia Walter Fauntroy (right) to join him in a sit-in at the South African embassy. (TransAfrica)

The embassy protests helped to connect the U.S. civil rights struggle with the movement against apartheid as hundreds of prominent American citizens were arrested outside the embassy, including, for the first time in her life, Martin Luther King Jr.'s widow, Coretta. (TransAfrica)

In 1985 a new wave of protests against apartheid swept across American campuses. At Columbia University a blockade of Hamilton Hall (renamed "Mandela Hall" in this photo) in April lasted for nearly three weeks and received international attention. A few months later the trustees of Columbia decided to sell off their stock in companies operating in South Africa. (Nick Romanenko, through *Columbia College Today*)

Nineteen years after his brother Robert's visit, Senator Edward M. Kennedy's stormy 1985 trip included protests by Black Consciousness groups, a snub by the American ambassador, and outdoor speeches such as this one in Cape Town (UDF leader Allan Boesak is in the white suit on the left). After returning to Washington, Kennedy redoubled his efforts to force changes in Reagan and Crocker's policies. (*The Argus*)

Though operating from cramped headquarters above a camera store in Manhattan, South African–born Jennifer Davis exerted enormous influence on the U.S. anti-apartheid movement. As executive director of the American Committee  on Africa, she along with other members of her staff testified all over the United States, prompting scores of state and local governments to impose stiff investment and purchasing restrictions on companies with subsidiaries in South Africa. (Rick Reinhard—American Committee on Africa)

George Houser, the former civil rights leader and first executive director of the American Committee on Africa, attends a rally with his successor, Jennifer Davis. (American Committee on Africa)

Though the South African government insisted throughout the 1970s that segregationist practices of "petty apartheid" were coming to an end, signs such as this one at a Cape Town beach, put up in 1981, still flourished. (American Committee on Africa)

The frequent juxtaposition of the symbols of Western capitalism and of apartheid, such as the notices on the back of this segregated Johannesburg bus in 1982, strengthened the impression that American and European companies at best ignored and at worst profited from racial discrimination. (United Nations Photo)

Union Theological Seminary Professor James Cone's landmark treatise
Black Theology and Black Power, first published in 1969, had a powerful
effect on the development of Black Consciousness and Black Theology in
South Africa. Here Cone (center) is shown at a Howard University conference in 1985 with another leader in the field, Professor Gayraud Wilmore
(right), and with Dumisani Kumalo of the American Committee on Africa
(left), whose relentless work to promote divestment legislation was
beginning to bear fruit in states around the country. (American Committee
on Africa)

Having been led to believe that Prime Minister P. W. Botha would announce major reforms in apartheid, international television stations carried his August 1985 "Rubicon" speech live around the world. His finger-wagging belligerence shocked the Reagan White House, deepened South Africa's crisis with international banks, and led directly to the imposition of the first phase of U.S. economic sanctions. (Mayibuye Center)

of pressure to which they could turn. In the end, the board fully endorsed Tutu's "prophetic calling" to say whatever he felt was necessary. From then on Tutu spoke more openly and adamantly than ever.

The secret to Tutu's growing impact lay not only in the power of his public rhetoric but also in the vast network of private friendships that he had steadily established around the world since his days as an ecumenical officer. Through his repeated trips to the United States, Tutu had built strong ties of affection with many American clerics, particularly those in the Episcopal Church. In May 1979, for example, Desmond and Leah Tutu had traveled for a month to Newark, New Jersey, so that Desmond could work as an assistant to John Spong, a bishop who had participated in Tutu's consecration. Tutu had journeyed throughout the diocese, preaching, conducting confirmations, making pastoral visits, and speaking about apartheid. He also became close friends with Hays Rockwell, the rector of St. James Episcopal Church on Madison Avenue in Manhattan, often staying with the Rockwells when he was in the city. Rockwell made sure that Tutu had ample opportunity to meet his many prominent parishioners. "He was just extraordinary," recalled one woman who met Tutu. "None of us had any contact with the issue [apartheid]. . . . Not everyone believed him at first, but slowly and surely they were converted." When the Botha government temporarily withdrew Tutu's passport in 1980, the whole congregation responded. "I was overwhelmed by messages of support from all over the world," Tutu recalled, "but nothing touched me more than to get from the Sunday School children at Saint James . . . what the children called passports of love, which I pasted up on the walls of my office. How can anyone range himself against this international, global fellowship?"

Tutu also angered Botha by visiting with international officials to urge them to act against apartheid. In March 1981 Tutu met with UN General Secretary Kurt Waldheim and with U.S. Ambassador Jeane Kirkpatrick at the United Nations, the same week she met with the South African military officials. On his way home he delivered a sermon in Westminster Abbey in which he attacked certain Western countries and corporations for maintaining "a conspiracy to keep South African blacks in bondage." His words—and the tumultuous welcome he received when he returned to South Africa in April—so enraged the prime minister that he again yanked the bishop's passport. Several months later P. W. Botha established the Eloff Commission to trace the foreign sources and domestic uses of the funds of the South African Council of Churches. If the commission found that the council was an "affected" organization, Botha knew, it would be subject to the provisions of the Fund-Raising Act, which would bar it from receiving any contributions from abroad. Since the SACC drew ninety-six percent of its budget from foreign religious groups, such a finding would be a fatal blow. To defend the organization Tutu hired Sydney Kentridge, the attorney who had represented the Biko family at the official inquest. Tutu also announced that the SACC would cooperate fully, providing whatever documentation the state requested.

The investigators took ten months to gather evidence and even sent a team to the United States in an attempt to uncover damaging information on the bishop's activities. They finally called Tutu to testify in person on September 1, 1982. The courtroom was filled not only with South African journalists but also with church representatives from Norway, Denmark, Holland, Germany, and other countries that had strongly supported the South African Council of Churches. "They were intending to separate us off from our friends, to discredit us to such an extent that our friends would not want to touch us," Tutu recalled. "They ended up being hoisted on their own petard. It was an incredible experience of ecclesiology. I picked up my telephone in Johannesburg and called the archbishop of Canterbury and said, 'This is what the government is trying to do. Could you send someone to be in solidarity with us?' We called our friends at the National Council of Churches in the United States and our friends at the World Council of Churches in Geneva. The government probably never recovered from the shock to their system from this expression of solidarity and support of the international church. We were over the moon with joy because our friends were ready to drop everything and come, even though it was Holy Week, one of the busiest times of the year. I don't think we could ever repay them for that." The archbishop of Canterbury, Robert Runcie, sent a five-person delegation, including the primus of the Scottish Episcopal Church, senior members of the Anglican Churches in the United States and Canada, the archbishop of New Zealand, and Runcie's personal assistant, Terry Waite. Runcie said that he had sent the delegation to say "that you are not simply dealing with a domestic matter. If you touch Desmond Tutu, you touch a world family of Christians."

On the day of his testimony, Tutu delivered what journalist Allister Sparks called the "greatest sermon of the bishop's life." "He sat bouncing and twisting in a carved chair, his hands shaping the outlines of his ideas with vivid gestures," wrote Sparks. "It was like a mime show with voice accompaniment. When he spoke of the resurrection of the body, his arms folded around his own body in a hug. The voice was the other instrument in this concert performance. Sometimes it would be sonorous, playing with the cadences of his African accent, and sometimes it would break into a high-pitched chuckle as he would hit on some pertinent insight. It would be somber, joyful, impatient, humorous, reflective, switching rapidly in response to a quicksilver spirit. And all the while the white commissioners watched expressionless."

Tutu stressed that his argument was essentially theological rather than political. "My purpose is to demonstrate from the scriptures and from hallowed Christian tradition and teaching that what we are as the South African Council of Churches, what we say and what we do, all of these are not determined by politics or any other ideology," Tutu told the magistrates. "We are what we are in obedience to God and in response to the gracious gospel of His son, Our Lord and Saviour Jesus Christ. Ultimately we owe loyalty not to any human authority. . . . We must obey the divine imperative and word whatever the cost." Drawing on both black and liberation theologies, Tutu described God as a creator who would not sit impassively while humanity suffered. "Our God cares that children starve in resettlement camps, the somewhat respectable name for apartheid's dumping grounds for the pathetic casualties of this vicious and evil system. The God we worship does care that people die in detention. . . . If God did not care about these and similar matters, I would not worship him, for he would be a totally useless God."

Since Christianity was fundamentally a religion of reconciliation, in which barriers were broken down and humans were reconciled with God and each other, apartheid, built as it was on separation, was anathema. "If anyone were to show me that apartheid is biblical or Christian," said Tutu dramatically, "I would burn my Bible and cease to be a Christian." Though Tutu freely acknowledged that the South African Council of Churches, like any human organization, had made mistakes, he criticized Botha for trying to squelch dissent. "I want the government to know now and always that I do not fear them," Tutu said. "They are trying to defend the utterly indefensible. Apartheid is as evil as Nazism and Communism. The government will fail completely for it is ranging itself on the side of evil, injustice, and oppression. The government is not God, they are just ordinary human beings who very soon—like all tyrants before them—will bite the dust."

"There is nothing the government can do to me that will stop me from being involved in what I believe is what God wants me to do," Tutu concluded. "I do not do it because I like doing it. I do it because I am under what I believe to be the influence of God's hand. I cannot help it. I cannot help it when I see injustice. I cannot keep quiet. I will not keep quiet, for, as Jeremiah says, when I try to keep quiet God's word burns like a fire in my breast. But what is it that they can ultimately do? The most awful thing they can do is to kill me, and death is not the worst thing that can happen to a Christian."

□   □   □   □

Though Tutu's tone was confrontational, his tactics remained conciliatory. His colleagues and supporters warned him that his desire to engage in dialogue with his opponents would encourage them to take advantage of him. In June 1980, when South Africa was being convulsed by strikes and boycotts, Tutu asked for an audience with P. W. Botha. The prime minister replied that he would meet with the SACC delegation on the condition that the group publicly "reject Communism for South Africa, disassociate themselves from undermining national service, denounce any organization connected with violence, and denounce the attempts by the ANC to overthrow orderly government in the republic." Tutu and the council agreed to the conditions, and the meeting was held in August. Botha refused to budge on any of the council's concerns and instead took advantage of the occasion to lecture the clerics about their disloyalty. Allan Boesak criticized the council's decision to confer with Botha. "It is the old game of talking and talking," he said, "while the government retains all the instruments of power to continue executing its policies."

Boesak had a different strategy for attacking apartheid, which focused on forcing to the surface the inconsistencies and contradictions implicit in the Dutch Reformed Church's position on apartheid and thereby undermining the legitimacy of the entire state. Boesak pressed his campaign in a variety of ways. He formed the Broederkring, a liberal ecclesial counterpart to the Broederbond, and set up the Alliance of Black Reformed Christians in Southern Africa. The Dutch Reformed parent church responded by calling a multilateral church conference in 1981, during which it tried to reaffirm both the unity of faith and the diversity of political positions on apartheid. In August 1982, Boesak traveled to Ottawa for ten days to attend the meeting of the World Alliance of Reformed Churches, an assembly of one hundred and fifty Calvinist churches in seventy-six countries representing more than seventy million members. There he introduced a motion that apartheid be declared a heresy contrary to the gospel and inconsistent with Reformed tradition. "Not only is South Africa the most blatantly racist country in the world," wrote Boesak in a document to support his motion, "it is also the country where the church is most openly identified with the racism and oppression that exists in society." During the floor debate, a white theologian from the University of Pretoria, Johan Heyns, tried to rebut Boesak. While admitting that apartheid was a sin "if understood in a certain sense and a certain connotation," he insisted that there was "only one NGK [Dutch Reformed] church, organized in four cultural dimensions. The NGK is not a closed church. The doors of the white church are open to blacks, while the communion service is open to all races." Boesak responded that this was not true. An investigation the previous month had shown that out of all the churches in the area of Pretoria, only one permitted black worshipers to enter. Another eight allowed blacks to use the sanctuary when whites were not present. When Boesak concluded his remarks, the six hundred delegates gave him a lengthy ovation.

The leaders of the Dutch Reformed Church, acting moderator Kobus Potgieter and chief executive Pierre Roussow, sealed the outcome of the deliberations by affirming that "a political system based on separate development of various population groups can be justified by the Bible" as long as it was implemented in accordance with Christian principles of love and justice. The outraged delegates promptly voted for the suspension of two of South Africa's white Reformed churches, the Dutch Reformed (NGK) and the Nederduitsch Hervormde Kerk (NHK). They formally declared that apartheid was a heresy and voted a special commendation for Beyers Naudé, who was completing his fifth year of enforced silence. Finally, for good measure, they elected Allan Boesak president of the World Alliance, making him the religious leader of all the Reformed churches in the world. In an ironic twist, the firebrand black preacher had become, at least technically, the spiritual authority over all the white Reformed churches in South Africa.

Suspension from the World Alliance threw the white churches into disarray. At the meeting of the General Synod in October, delegates furiously debated whether they should accede to the World Alliance's conditions for readmission, including the open participation of blacks and a public rejection of apartheid. A few moderates like Heyns suggested that the World Alliance's criticisms might be valid. Conservatives argued that the church should just resign from the World Alliance and be done with it. The resignation motion passed 234 to 230, but since it required a two-thirds vote to take effect, it was tabled. The conservatives, struggling with dissent from within, ejected Heyns and other moderates from positions of leadership and tightened their control.

Boesak, for his part, returned to South Africa in a position of far greater authority than when he had left. Though he failed in his attempt to become the moderator of the Coloured church, he used his new stature as head of the World Alliance to attack the government's constitutional proposals at every turn. In late 1982 he publicly suggested that all groups opposed to the tricameral proposals should band together in a United Democratic Front, and by January 1983 a steering committee had been formed for that purpose. He bitterly attacked the decision of Allan Hendrickse, another Coloured minister and the leader of the Labour Party, for being willing to participate in the new arrangement. The Labour Party's decision, said Boesak, meant that "apartheid would no longer have a white face."

□   □   □   □

Throughout 1983, the debate over the new constitutional proposal coincided with a sharp rise in violence and turmoil. On May 20, in a rare deviation from their official policy of minimizing the loss of human life, ANC guerrillas detonated a huge car bomb directly in front of the South African air force headquarters in Pretoria, killing 19 people and injuring 217, many of them black. Three days later, seven fighters from the South African air force retaliated, bombing a section of the port city of Maputo in Mozambique, where they believed the ANC had a base. When the smoke cleared, Mozambican authorities discovered that in addition to hitting one ANC residence, the South Africans had destroyed a jam factory, a preschool, two private homes, and a hut. A correspondent for a British newspaper reported that of the twenty-five people who died, only one had a connection with the ANC. The South African government also stepped up its domestic campaign against the ANC, choking off Lesotho's border crossings and executing three captured ANC guerrillas despite international pleas for clemency.

In August the prime minister, frustrated that after months of debate the members of parliament had worked their way through only one-third of the constitution's clauses, cut off all further debate and announced that the constitution would be submitted to the white electorate in a referendum in November. For the next ten weeks, virtually every prominent person and political group in South Africa came out with a position for or against the new constitution. National Party representatives fanned out to defend the proposal in every city and town, skillfully matching their descriptions to the fears and aspirations of their audiences. They lined up as many allies as they could. In addition to Allan Hendrickse and the Labour Party, the Nationalists pointed to a group of two hundred academics from Afrikaans universities who supported the new constitution and to more than one hundred prominent business leaders who argued that a no vote would adversely affect foreign investment while a yes vote would enable the process of reform to continue. Even though Harry Oppenheimer of Anglo-American opposed the constitution, Gavin Relly, the chair of Anglo-American's board, favored it, arguing that a rejection of the constitution would be interpreted by foreigners as a lack of commitment to reform and offer South Africa's enemies new chances to "smear" the country. To encourage this line of reasoning, Foreign Minister Pik Botha brought three of South Africa's most important ambassadors—Brand Fourie from Washington, Marais Steyn from London, and Neil van Heerden from West Germany—back to the country in order to argue, on television, that the outside world was looking for a yes vote.

The opponents of the constitution, though numerous, found it difficult to work together. Buthelezi organized rallies and demonstrations in which his rhetoric became far more threatening than ever. He attacked the President's Council as a "forum for racism" and said that the constitutional proposals were designed to turn Indians and Coloured people into a buffer between whites and Africans. He berated Hendrickse, the Labour Party, and the South African Indian Council, saying that from the moment they joined the parliament they would become the enemies of Africans. A member of the Indian Council responded that Buthelezi was hardly in a position to make this criticism, since he was "working for the South African government himself." Buthelezi banded together with five other homeland leaders to denounce the constitution. In speech after speech he warned darkly that if the new constitution was approved, Inkatha might be forced to organize strikes and boycotts, to abandon its "pragmatic" commitment to nonviolence, and to join with the African National Congress in a "marriage of convenience." He also declared that approval would mean he would have to reconsider his support of foreign investment.

Buthelezi's biggest and most infuriating problem, however, was not the government but the millions of South African blacks who refused to acknowledge him as their leader. In August 1983 the United Democratic Front was formally launched as a national organization during a rally of seven thousand people in Cape Town, the largest such gathering in twenty-two years. A thousand delegates representing 575 civic groups, trade unions, sporting bodies, and women's and youth groups met at Mitchells Plain near Cape Town to vote on various resolutions and establish its structure. Though the UDF was set up as a coordinating group that could not make policy for its members, the delegates passed resolutions condemning British and American imperialism, calling for the repeal of the Group Areas Act, and vowing to create a united and democratic South African free of bantustans. They also elected a host of "patrons," including Nelson Mandela, Martha Mahlangu (the mother of an executed ANC guerrilla), Helen Joseph, Beyers Naudé, and Allan Boesak. The delegates elected three presidents: Archie Gumede, the chair of the Release Mandela Campaign, Albertina Sisulu, a prominent activist in the Federation of South African Women and the wife of ANC leader Walter Sisulu, and Oscar Mpetha of the African Food and Canning Workers' Union. The general secretary was Popo Molefe, a member of the Soweto Committee of Ten.

The United Democratic Front not only brought together an exceptional range of South Africans from many ideological, racial, and economic categories but also combined two powerful traditions in the history of South African resistance. The choice of Nelson Mandela as patron and Albertina Sisulu as president indicated a strong commitment to the goals of the African National Congress. At the same time, the UDF's strategy—that of boycotting all government structures, including elections—was in direct line with the tradition of the Non-European Unity Movement of the 1950s and all the other "noncollaborationists" who had emerged in the previous two generations. For Buthelezi, who had built his career through a strategy of participation, these developments, just at the moment when he was threatening the government and building common cause with the Progressives, seemed disastrous. His public condemnations of the UDF started immediately, and rapidly became harsh. It would have been better for the UDF, Buthelezi said publicly, to join with groups like his own recently formed South African Black Alliance than to try to become "Johnny-come-lately heroes." The UDF "will come to naught without Inkatha support," Buthelezi insisted, because "Inkatha is the largest black political constituency ever created in the history of this country."

As the months passed, the UDF did not turn into the "paper organization" Buthelezi had predicted but grew in strength and appeal. The Labour Party noticed that its support among Coloureds was leaking away to the UDF throughout the Cape. Buthelezi, to his alarm, found the same thing among young urban Zulus, especially in Natal. Buthelezi's panic at this development flared into violence in a terrible incident in October at the University of Zululand. Though the University of Zululand was located inside KwaZulu in the town of Ngoye, was the source of most of the civil servants and professionals for the homeland, and had Buthelezi as its chancellor, most of the students disliked Inkatha. When the students learned that Buthelezi was planning to hold a rally on campus to commemorate the centennial of King Cetshwayo's death and that his lieutenants had asked local Inkatha headmen to bring armed supporters to campus, they protested. The students formed a crisis committee, sent a lawyer to Durban to try to obtain a court injunction against Buthelezi's visit, boycotted classes, and finally made a "desperate plea" to Buthelezi to call off the rally because it might degenerate into violence. On Friday, October 28, they staged a protest march, during which the rector of the university called in the police, who dispersed the students with tear gas and batons.

The next day Buthelezi's men responded. "The early morning mist had hardly lifted when Zulu warriors armed with spears, cowhide shields, *knobkerries,* and battle-axes slipped onto campus chanting and singing," wrote one reporter. Some of the students responded by shouting insults and hurling stones. The Inkatha men then attacked the students, who ran into their dormitories and barricaded themselves inside. The Inkatha irregulars surrounded the women's dormitory and forced the women to come out and sing praises to Buthelezi; any who refused were beaten. They broke the windows of the men's dormitories, smashed down the doors, tore up clothes and bedding, wrecked furniture, ripped up UDF posters, and went room to room in search of specific student leaders. One student leader, Fumane Marivate, was selected because he had helped disrupt an Inkatha meeting two months before. The Inkatha warriors beat him unconscious in his room, dragged his limp body outside, suspended him upside down from a tree, and bludgeoned him to death. By the time they departed, the Inkatha men had killed four other students and wounded dozens.

The rampage attracted intense press commentary, much of it critical of Buthelezi. Buthelezi, smarting from the reaction, gave his version of the events at Ngoye a few days later in a speech before the KwaZulu state legislature, arguing that the display of force was only the natural outgrowth of the Zulu people's military spirit. Though Inkatha had held its peace during years of "terrible provocation," its members' refusal to "put into practice the political philosophy of an eye for an eye and a tooth for a tooth" had been misinterpreted as cowardice. Ngoye had proven that Inkatha "warriors" would respond when necessary. Buthelezi then tried to steer the blame to other ethnic groups. "We as Zulus think it despicable that people from other parts of the country with different ethnic origins see fit to desecrate the memory of our king by the kind of campaigns we saw in evidence on Friday and Saturday," Buthelezi said, ignoring the reality that virtually all of the students enrolled at Ngoye were Zulu. "We are not a rootless rabble; we are people with a heritage and dignity. We will not tolerate people from other ethnic backgrounds who . . . carry out a campaign of denigration and vilification against me, whilst I fight the apartheid regime single-handed every day of the week, which they would never try in areas from which they originally came." To the leaders of the United Democratic Front who heard these words, Buthelezi's intention seemed clear: if he personally could not dominate an interracial anti-apartheid alliance, he would use ethnicity to undermine it.

On Wednesday, November 2, 1983, less than two weeks after the violence at Ngoye, two million white voters—nearly seventy-five percent of all eligible white voters—went to the polls. When the returns came in, Botha learned that the new constitution had received a two-thirds majority. Even more important, the government had carried every town in the country, except small, conservative Pietersburg. Even in Pretoria, where the Conservative Party was particularly strong, voters approved the new constitution by nearly sixty percent. Postelection analysis revealed that nearly half of the supporters of the Progressive Party had gone against their leaders' recommendations and backed the new constitution. Various reactions poured in from around the country and around the world. The U.S. State Department formally welcomed the outcome, as did a large number of South African businessmen, who felt that it would dispel uncertainty among foreign investors. Gatsha Buthelezi said that in view of the election, the members of KwaZulu and Inkatha would have to review their commitment to nonviolence. The leaders of the United Democratic Front dismissed the whole referendum because it did not address the major problems of the country.

P. W. Botha, however, expressed delight, telling reporters that the vote had exceeded his "wildest expectations." Though the government now felt strengthened to "go ahead with proper and evolutionary reform," he again denied that he could ever foresee bringing Africans into the central government in any way. Had the new constitution thus succeeded in enshrining apartheid? a reporter asked the prime minister. "I do not know what you mean by the word," said Botha passionately. "If it means oppression, I reject it. If it means positive development, I accept it."

THIRTEEN

The Spread of the Divestment Movement (1982–1984)

The international community must make up its mind whether it wants to see a peaceful resolution to the South African crisis or not.
—DESMOND TUTU

THE EARLY YEARS of constructive engagement coincided with a serious effort by Leon Sullivan to turn his principles from pious abstractions to measurable realities. It was a difficult task. National interest in South Africa ebbed during Reagan's first term as politicians, the public, and the press waited to see whether constructive engagement and the Sullivan Principles had any effect. The waning of interest meant a drop in external pressure on American companies, which, in turn, made it more difficult for Sullivan to capture and hold the attention of top corporate leaders. In the early years Sullivan had been able to assemble a hundred chief executive officers at the drop of a hat. In the fall of 1982, however, he had to cancel the annual meeting of chief executives when it became clear that very few were going to show up.

In the face of such slackened pressure, Sullivan spent several years flogging the corporate task groups to establish timetables, set goals, and meet targets. Every four months Sullivan summoned second-tier managers from the signatory companies to a plenary meeting to hear reports from the task group leaders. When companies stalled or balked, Sullivan reverted to his preacher style and administered a potent brew of exhortation and warning. If they did not make progress fast enough, Sullivan reminded almost every corporate audience, he would withdraw his support for the whole venture.

Despite Sullivan's clout, many in the task groups resisted his demands for numerical targets. Some believed it impossible to set uniform standards across scores of firms in different industries; others objected to being told what to do by an outsider. The members of Task Group 4, who were charged with setting up worker training programs, argued that the absence of skilled labor in South Africa was sufficient incentive for American companies to initiate training programs and that each firm would best know how to do so. Task Group 5, which focused on managerial education for blacks under the leadership of Sal Marzullo of Mobil, decided to aim to have 400 blacks in management training. They then did an inventory and found, to their surprise, that the Sullivan signatories already had 566 black management trainees. Though they had exceeded their goal, they did not revise the target upward for fear that a higher level could not be met.

Sometimes, when task groups resisted, Sullivan simply set the goals himself. When Task Group 3, which handled education, announced that it would create an Adopt-a-School program, Sullivan declared that the companies would assist 500 schools by 1980 and 1,000 by 1983. By June 1982, however, American firms in South Africa had adopted only 159 schools; in many cases their support amounted to just a few thousand dollars a year. There were a few showcase projects, like the vocational high school in Soweto know as PACE Commercial College, which opened in February 1982. PACE had been a project of the U.S. Chamber of Commerce in South Africa, was supported by big companies like IBM, and received extensive coverage in corporate annual reports and in the American business press. Such high-profile efforts masked the continuing resentment of many executives about being pushed to support ventures outside of the plant. Some feared that in the aftermath of the black student boycotts, support for the apartheid schools was actually a bad idea. "There is great dissatisfaction among blacks on the quality of the black educational system," one manager wrote to Reid Weedon. "Adopting a school can be seen as supporting a system which is not accepted by blacks . . . and [thus as] counter-productive."

By 1983, six years after the principles had been announced, Sullivan could point to a few important successes. He had signed up 146 firms, slightly more than half of the American companies operating in the country. According to Weedon's seventh report, released in the fall of 1983, the great majority of U.S. subsidiaries were now fully complying with the first three principles on desegregation, equal employment practices, and equal pay for all employees. Even more important, Sullivan had managed to fulfill Wayne Fredericks's aspiration that the principles be dynamic. Not only had Sullivan amplified the principles three times, goading companies into areas like housing and union rights, he had also drawn up a list of nine "basic requirements." The requirements insisted that companies give black workers pay and benefits equal to those given to their white counterparts; grant equivalent rights to organize and bargain collectively; inform all employees of the company's Sullivan ratings and review the plans for implementation with worker committees; and submit their reports to an outside accounting firm for verification. If a company did not comply with any one of these requirements, Weedon automatically assigned it to the lowest grade.

The basic requirements caused widespread grumbling. In one instance, the companies forced Sullivan to reverse himself and eliminate the basic requirement that all U.S. firms become dues-paying members of the National African Federated Chambers of Commerce (NAFCOC), the primary association of black businessmen and entrepreneurs. In general, despite complaints that Sullivan was continually "moving the goalposts," most executives swallowed hard and followed the Philadelphia preacher. They knew that without Sullivan, their problems would be worse. If Sullivan dropped out, commented Robert Corp, international labor affairs manager at Ford Motor Company, there would be simply "no other credible person or movement around which the companies can rally." Without him, echoed James Rawlings, chair of Union Carbide Southern Africa, "the critics would really have something to sink their teeth into." "If Leon wants it," George Schroll of Colgate-Palmolive told the IRRC, "you try to deliver."

In addition to these limited successes, Sullivan also experienced serious difficulties, delays, and outright failures. After a flurry in the first three years, Sullivan had found it increasingly difficult to sign up new companies; even those who had agreed were not enthusiastic. "My calculation is that twenty percent of the signatory companies are pulling hard, fifty percent are just pulling, and the rest are simply being pulled along," said Sullivan in January 1983. Reid Weedon's yearly reports supported this view. In 1982, for example, thirty-eight companies—less than a third of the signatories—had done enough to place them in category 1, "making good progress," and by the next year the number had dropped to twenty-nine. Ten companies that received low grades in 1981 simply refused to submit reports the next year.

Though for some companies the problem was bad faith, for others it was economics. As the South African economy sank into recession in 1982 and 1983, managers struggling with soft demand, excess plant capacity, and dwindling profits shied away from making any new expenditures. In 1983 the group vice president of Masonite noted that his wood plantation and fiberboard mill were far more labor-intensive than plants in the United States. Though Masonite paid well by rural standards, the wages were still lower than the minimum Sullivan had set. With Masonite's plant operating at fifty percent of capacity, the only way the executive could raise wages would be to fire part of his workforce. "I filled out the sixth report [1982], but by God I didn't file it," the executive commented. "I knew that despite all we've done, all I'm going to get is a big fat 'Needs to Become More Active' at a time we just can't afford to do any more."

The combination of the recession and the fluctuating number of signatories made it difficult for Weedon and his staff to track progress from year to year. In 1980, for example, Weedon reported that Sullivan signatory companies employed nearly 2,000 black managers and supervisors. The next year the number had swelled to 2,500; the following year it dropped again to 1,950. Sal Marzullo attributed the decrease to the drop in the number of reporting companies and to the South African recession. However, a number of critics pointed out that the way Weedon and his staff reported the data made it difficult to assess what was really going on. In some key charts and graphs they lumped black, Asian, and Coloured workers into a single category. They also aggregated the data across all companies, making it impossible for anyone other than themselves to assess developments within particular companies or industries.

Even so, there was enough data to suggest that in some areas the progress had been painfully slow. According to the seventh report (1983), the reporting signatories employed a total of 66,175 workers—a tiny portion of South Africa's active workforce. Though only a third of the employees were white, they dominated the hierarchy, occupying two-thirds of all supervisory positions and ninety-six percent of all managerial jobs. More disturbing, these trends were not changing rapidly. Half of all supervisory vacancies and ninety-four percent of all managerial openings were being filled by whites. In 1983 whites filled sixty percent of all the supervisory training programs and eighty-six percent of all management training programs, higher proportions than the years before. Though average pay increases for blacks, Coloureds, and Asians exceeded those of whites (nineteen versus fifteen percent in 1983), the wage gaps between different levels of the hierarchy meant that in most cases whites received far more in absolute terms. Finally, the recession had cut deeply into corporate philanthropy. In 1982 the total contribution of American corporations to community projects had been 11,130,000 rand, an average that worked out to 168 rand per employee. In 1983 that number fell by more than half, to 5,200,000 rand. Compared to the tens of millions of rand that American corporations paid in South African taxes, this figure was not a cause for celebration.

Despite the problems of implementation, the Sullivan Principles—and the grading system that went with them—quickly became a standard by which hundreds of institutional investors across the United States judged corporate behavior. At Harvard, for example, though Derek Bok continued publicly to resist divestment, he and the other members of the Harvard Corporation found it increasingly difficult to retain stock in banks that lent to the South African government and to companies that had a low Sullivan rating. In the fall of 1978 both Harvard and Yale had decided to dump the stock of Morgan Guaranty when the bank officers announced that they would be making direct loans to the South African government. A Morgan vice president had traveled to both campuses to explain to the advisory committees that the money would be used for housing in the townships and other humanitarian purposes, but the committees had been unmoved. The issue reemerged in 1981 when Citibank officials announced that they would participate in a $250 million loan to Pretoria. Harvard representative Lawrence Stevens met with bank officials and urged them to change their policy. When the bank refused, Harvard withdrew $5 million in certificates of deposit and $45 million in floating rate bonds at a substantial loss. "They sold well under their value," said Michael Thonis, a partner in the Harvard Management Company (the part of the university that managed the portfolio). "You'd measure the loss in millions of dollars, not in hundreds of thousands."

This sale did more than cost Harvard money; it also elicited vehement protest from Harvard alumni on Wall Street. The Citibank loan had been solicited by the South African government to help in the building of schools and hospitals in black townships, and Citibank felt that even though the loan would be a direct infusion of capital to the regime, the purpose warranted it. "The Citibank sale made a lot of the financial community in New York furious," commented Harvard treasurer George C. Putnam. "They thought we hadn't considered it carefully enough." The unexpectedly fierce response, Putnam suggested, made Harvard officials much more cautious. The next year, the Corporation Committee on Shareholder Responsibility (CCSR) asked the Advisory Committee (ACSR) to reconsider the bank restriction, since a blanket ban made "no allowance for the use of discretion" in "making humanitarian loans to South Africa." The ACSR briefly did so, but it met with such instantaneous and vigorous student opposition that it quickly recommended that the Corporation Committee not change its mind. The Corporation Committee considered overriding the ACSR but then let the policy stand.

By 1983 the Harvard policy was beginning to show cracks and strain. Under chair Walter J. Salmon of the Harvard Business School, members of the ACSR again began a comprehensive review of the university's South African position. They were propelled in part by a week-long hunger strike by thirty students and one faculty member and by the public outcry over a statement by CCSR chair Hugh Calkins that Harvard purchased stock for purely financial reasons and in fact continued to hold thousands of shares in non-Sullivan signatories. Many activists felt this was a violation of the intention of the 1978 policy, and Salmon seemed to agree. "Ethically there is something incongruous," Salmon said, "about our current policy of commencing a dialogue with a company which is not a Sullivan signatory in good standing after we buy the stock rather than before." Committee members recommended that Harvard screen its investments in advance and refuse to purchase any non-Sullivan signatories. They also pressed for an increased interchange with companies to urge them to sign the principles and for a policy of divestment if a company had not obliged within eighteen months. In response, the Corporation Committee rejected the timetable and the purchase screen but agreed to step up exchanges with companies through a policy of "intensive dialogue." Through the fall of 1983 and the winter of 1984, chair Hugh Calkins and university secretary Michael Blumenfeld met with the chief executives of half a dozen companies. Executives at Dun and Bradstreet first rebuffed Calkins and Blumenfeld, saying that they did not need or want any outside monitoring because their practices were as good as the Sullivan Principles required. Eventually they changed their minds and signed the principles. A similar process took place at Pepsico, which signed the principles in March 1984. A series of meetings with the president of Joy Manufacturing led not only to the president's willingness to sign the principles but also to a visit by the chief executive to South Africa and to permission for the IRRC to inspect the company's facilities. In other cases, Calkins and Blumenfeld had less success. After seven years of promises from Carnation's managers that they would improve their low Sullivan rating, Calkins and the Corporation Committee finally decided to dispose of the stock that same spring.

At the same time that Calkins was pursuing his discussions, the Advisory Committee continued to widen the gap between the committees. On May 10, 1984, the ACSR, under chair Richard B. Stewart of the Harvard Law School, voted six to five with one abstention in favor of *total* divestment. In their report, published on May 18, the committee members specifically rejected Calkins's principal argument, saying "the argument that divestiture is a coercive tactic which abrogates free speech seems to us to have no merit." The committee also attacked Bok's consequentialist reasoning. "President Bok on June 9, 1983 argued that divestiture would be 'ineffective,' " wrote the members of the committee. "If we were to insist on 'getting results' from each responsible action of conscience, then who would ever write a letter to a senator? We act in the faith and the hope that others will join us, that we can contribute in our own small way to the arousal of public conscience. We cannot expect—or bargain in advance—to see the precise results of our commitment before we make them. We must do what we believe is right and hope that what we do will contribute to the eventual success of what we believe is right."

The committee also rejected its 1978 report, under chair Henry Reiling, which had characterized the cost of divestment as excessive. The committee even questioned the economic imperatives as significant criteria in the decision. "Even if the cost were great," the committee report asked, "would it be too great for this University—which exists to serve the pursuit of Truth—to pay in order to separate itself from support of a regime which denies the truth to which this university has always been dedicated: that all people are created equal?" The committee concluded its report with an indictment of the Corporation Committee's conduct. "Since 1978 Harvard has failed to enforce its existing policies with sufficient vigor. . . . Not a single divestment has been made despite continued or intermittent Harvard ownership over several years of companies who have not demonstrated compliance with the Sullivan Principles."

Such a break with earlier policy called for a careful response, which the corporation and president waited until the next fall to release. The corporation defended its contention that divestment was ineffective, rejected a timetable for signing the principles, and refused to expand the requirement to the Tutu Principles, a stronger set of corporate guidelines that the South African bishop had recently promulgated. Derek Bok issued his own statement, which was similar to his open letter on divestment in 1979. He again pointed to the potential threat to the independence of the university, to the ineffectiveness of divestment, to the impossibility of cutting all links, and to Harvard's limited national influence. Bok exhorted the students and faculty to get more involved, as he had, in trying to influence federal policy. He concluded on a surprisingly personal note in which he drew attention to the tension between his own values and those that had to inform his institutional decisions. "It is never a pleasant task to disagree with others who care deeply about injustice," he wrote. "In the case of South Africa, the injustice is so monstrous that the heart aches for some opportunity to resist effectively. Nevertheless, such feelings cannot bring me to support a course of action that would force this University to deviate from its proper role, jeopardize its independence, and risk resources in behalf of a dubious strategy that has no realistic prospect of success."

Such squabbles between institutional investors and their constituencies over whether to endorse the Sullivan Principles gradually reshaped the structure of corporate responsibility in the United States. Endorsing the principles—originally seen as a radical move—became accepted as a reasonable middle ground between doing nothing and actively divesting. The Sullivan Principles were also having an effect on state politics. State elected officials from both parties found themselves struggling with a cloud of new divestment proposals filed by their liberal white and African American colleagues. Though the advocates of divestment and disinvestment complained—accurately—that discussion of the Sullivan Principles diverted attention from more fundamental problems in South Africa, the discussion about the measures had two salutary effects. First, it shifted the debate from the narrow confines of Washington, D.C., to much broader and more diverse arenas around the nation. Second, it introduced regional political elites—elected representatives, government officials, business executives, clergy, lobbyists, educators, and so on—to the grim realities of apartheid, prompting them to act.

This process, in which regional representatives found themselves debating the merits of foreign investment, sanctions, and international diplomacy, was, for Ronald Reagan, painfully ironic. The doctrine that state governments should take more initiative in what normally had been considered federal policy areas had been an essential feature of Reagan's conservative ideology. At the same time, this seizure of the initiative had arisen from the perception that Reagan's own foreign policy was inadequate. There was also, everyone knew, a partisan component to the devolution of the anti-apartheid debate to the local states. Democrats knew that they could not get these initiatives through a federal government ruled by a Republican Senate and president, so they acted at the state level, where Democratic majorities and governors were still in abundance.

One of the first states to grapple with the domestic politics of apartheid was Connecticut. In August 1978 several recent college graduates who had been spurred by divestment protests on their campuses formed the Connecticut Anti-Apartheid Committee (CAAC) and set about educating and organizing a coalition of labor unions, churches, and community groups throughout the state. A nucleus of six to ten people, working from their own homes in their spare time, with an infinitesimal budget of fifteen hundred dollars, labored diligently for more than two years to inform the people of Connecticut about apartheid. They printed and distributed fliers; wrote newspaper columns; held social and cultural events; spoke at meetings around the state; and sponsored speaking engagements and conferences. In June 1980, for example, the committee organized a dinner for a hundred people to commemorate the fourth anniversary of the Soweto uprising and invited Dumisani Kumalo of the American Committee on Africa to come up from New York City to speak. Kumalo, as he did everywhere he traveled, urged the attendees to find ways to force American companies to withdraw.

At the same time that the CAAC was building a statewide network, the first ripples of activity were surfacing in the state assembly building. In 1979 and 1980, unbeknownst to the CAAC, two bills were filed calling for divestment of state monies in companies doing business in South Africa. The first had been introduced by Representative Boyd Hinds, a white activist from Hartford, and the second by Representative William Dyson, a black schoolteacher from New Haven. When the legislation met opposition in committee, Senator Sanford Cloud, a lawyer from Hartford and the only black in the Senate, amended it to require divestment from all corporations that had not adopted the Sullivan Principles. The amended bill made it to the floor of the Senate and passed, but it ran into problems in the House. Dyson, after consulting with the CAAC, tried to strip out the Sullivan provisions on the grounds that the principles were ineffective. Conservative representatives successfully attached a provision requiring the divestment of companies doing business with Iran (which was still holding American hostages). When the bill finally passed, Connecticut state treasurer Henry Parker, the first black politician elected to statewide office, sent official letters to the nonsignatory companies urging them to enroll. At least one company, Dresser Industries, sent back an angry refusal. Eventually the state sold off the stock of seven nonsignatory corporations: Baxter Laboratories, Dresser Industries, IMS International, Lubrizol, Owens Corning, Pepsico, and Tenneco.

In September 1980, Connecticut General Life Insurance Company and the state Treasury Department sponsored a conference on corporate social responsibility to which they invited government officials, corporate managers, and academics. The insurance company had long played an active shareholder role under the leadership of Vice President Allan Nelson, a committed Lutheran layperson and former chair of the Investor Responsibility Research Center, who had visited South Africa several times and done volunteer work in Namibia. The keynote speaker at the conference was Leon Sullivan who, instead of speaking in soothing boardroom terms, delivered a barn-burning sermon. American affiliates in South Africa, he declared loudly, "must either shape up or ship out." The tone and content of the speech shocked many of those present, who realized that if a supposedly moderate corporate director felt so passionately about this problem, it was not going to go away.

In the winter of 1981, anti-apartheid state legislators tried again, introducing two new bills requiring the sale of all state investments in corporations or banks doing business in South Africa. This time the CAAC organized a substantial lobbying campaign, bringing the leaders of community groups, black organizations, labor union locals, and religious institutions to the capital. Business leaders were caught off guard and either were not fully aware of the legislation or believed it couldn't pass. When some representatives objected that the state might lose money, supporters accepted an amendment stipulating that the state could not be forced to incur a financial loss. With that, to everyone's amazement, the bill sailed through both houses with more than a two-thirds majority.

The passage of the bill shocked the business community into action. Business leaders from Connecticut's biggest banks, manufacturers, insurance companies, and law firms streaked into Hartford and arrived at Governor William O'Neill and Treasurer Parker's offices, clamoring for a reconsideration. The bill, they said, had been decided too quickly, was too sweeping and too vague, would hurt business in Connecticut, and wouldn't accomplish its own objectives. Moreover, it would require the sale of stock in companies that maintained large facilities or headquarters in Connecticut, firms like Chesebrough-Pond, Loctite, Olin Corporation, Perkin-Elmer, Union Carbide, United Technologies, Xerox, and General Electric.

On July 1, two weeks after the Connecticut Anti-Apartheid Coalition had held its second annual Soweto dinner to celebrate its victory, Governor O'Neill vetoed the divestment bill. The activists were momentarily stunned; then it was their turn to spring into action. They dropped a blizzard of letters on the assembly; they brought in Jesse Jackson's Operation PUSH and the Hartford Black Ministerial Alliance to lobby; and they attacked the governor for sabotaging the will of the people in a backroom deal with corporate lobbyists. The business campaign, however, had weakened legislative support for the measure, and many Democratic legislators were reluctant to embarrass a governor of their own party. The attempt to override O'Neill's veto failed.

In October, in an effort to educate the state's leaders about conditions in South Africa, the Episcopal diocese held a conference, cosponsored by the governor, on business and government responses to apartheid. Organizers invited twelve South African religious leaders, including Desmond Tutu, who could not come because Pretoria was still denying him a passport. A broad assortment of government officials, elected representatives, business executives, CAAC members, union leaders, and local pastors gathered to hear what the remaining eleven had to say. The South Africans delivered a stinging condemnation of the Sullivan Principles and, though barred by South African law from calling for disinvestment, expressed a deep skepticism that foreign investment would ever do anything other than prop up the Botha government.

To cope with the discontent, Governor O'Neill appointed a Task

Force on South African Investment Policy in December 1981. The task force consisted of two bankers, two corporate managers (one from General Electric, the other from United Technologies), two lawyers, two investment executives (one from Connecticut General Life Insurance), two labor officials (one the head of the CAAC), two legislators, and Edythe Gaines, a public utilities commissioner. Despite the great diversity of backgrounds and opinions, the committee, under the skilled leadership of Treasurer Parker, completed its task in just over two months. During those weeks the members spent dozens of hours arguing over the meaning of key words. What, exactly, did it mean for a company to be "doing business" in South Africa? Owning an affiliate? A manufacturing plant? What if the company owned less than half of the affiliate or plant? Did "doing business" also mean selling products, even if they were sold through third-party vendors? Some wanted to limit the sale of "strategic" products, but what exactly did this mean? Was selling toothpaste to the South African government "strategic"? How about lightbulbs, boots, replacement parts, and so on? Everyone on the committee knew that under certain definitions of "strategic," the state of Connecticut would be barred from investing in General Electric, which maintained its headquarters in southern Connecticut, and in United Technologies, the largest employer in the state. When it became clear that the GE and United Technologies representatives on the committee would block any agreement unless their firms were exempted, Christy Hoffman of the CAAC agreed.

The task force members also wrangled about the potential financial dangers of divestment. To the business executives, attempts to look at anything other than risk and return when making an investment were dangerous, both for corporate managers and for investors. If cut free from purely financial considerations, the reasoning went, corporate managers would not know what goals to pursue, what policies to adopt, or which constituencies to try to please. Similarly, investors would be more confused and earn less money, since the theory of efficient capital markets suggested that all necessary information was available in the stock price and that any attempt to limit the "universe" of possible investments on social grounds would result in lower returns. For a person, this was simply foolish. For a fiduciary charged with administering someone else's money, it was also potentially illegal.

With this in mind, the Connecticut task force wrote to nine separate investment companies and asked them to evaluate what would happen to Connecticut state monies if the state was to divest from companies with subsidiaries in South Africa. Some wrote back that they did not like the restrictions but could manage the money within the constraints. One objected to the whole idea. At least three of the firms analyzed the different outcomes statistically. They all concluded that if they threw out the companies operating in South Africa—many of whom were big multinational, blue chip firms—the remaining stock portfolio would have more volatility and risk. At the same time, they could expect to earn more money. The reason for this was that when investors moved out of huge, mature, highly capitalized international companies, they had to invest in smaller, less capitalized, domestically oriented companies. In the late 1970s and early 1980s, despite a serious recession in the United States, the latter companies had, on average, grown faster and earned higher profits than the big blue chips. As a result, when task forces and commissions throughout the United States decided to look into the financial cost of divestment, expecting that it would be so expensive that the idea would be dropped, they sometimes found, to their embarrassment, that South Africa–free portfolios were making more money rather than less. Thus the studies prepared for the task force all agreed that a South Africa–free portfolio would have higher risk and higher returns than an unrestricted portfolio.

If the business executives who had opposed the divestment legislation had hoped that financial analyses would strike a decisive blow against divestment, they were severely disappointed. More than anything, the studies showed how vulnerable financial analysis was to the premises and prejudices of the analysts. The answer of what would happen to a portfolio, for example, could only be constructed out of a web of assumptions about what was held fixed and what was allowed to vary, about what was being measured and what standard it was being measured against, about the appropriate balance of risk and return, and other objectives. The closer one looked at the sea of numbers flowing from the computers of econometricians and analysts, the more it became clear that the numbers did not capture a hard and immutable reality. All the charts, tables, graphs, statistics, and formulas that filled the financial reports were in fact a frantic attempt to impose order on that most mercurial of phenomena, human perceptions. The numbers, framed by the economic and legal concepts that gave them life, were indeed a kind of language based on both reason and faith. If one spoke the language and shared the faith, events could be made to sound not only rational, but inevitable. The trick for persons seeking to justify a new direction in investments, therefore, was not to change the reality, but to find new words to describe it.

On April 21, 1982, the Connecticut task force submitted a report recommending that the state divest all companies that were not in the top two Sullivan categories; all companies that made strategic sales (defined as "arms, ammunitions, and implements of war" and "computers sold for military or police use or for use in connection with the pass system"); and all companies that refused to recognize the right of South African employees to organize and strike. A bill reflecting the recommendations breezed through both houses and was signed into law by Governor O'Neill on June 9, 1982.

The bill had a number of important implications. Though it was not the sweeping divestment bill the activists had sought, it was the first time that a state pension system—in this case, one with $2.7 billion in assets—tied its investment decisions directly to a company's behavior in South Africa. By making a high Sullivan grade the determining factor in investment, the law accomplished at the state level what Sullivan had urged unsuccessfully on the U.S. Congress. As soon as the law was passed, Parker began to implement it, sending off letters to all the corporations and banks in Connecticut's portfolio advising them of the new law and asking them if they were in compliance. "Our approach is to be persuasive," said Parker at the time, "not punitive." In February 1983 Parker created the position of social compliance investment officer and hired Barbara Reid, an experienced analyst, to fill it. By early 1984 a comprehensive system for monitoring and grading corporate performance had been established and had begun to have an effect. Though United Technologies had two subsidiaries in South Africa, only one was in compliance with the law, so Parker sold off the state's United Technologies securities. When the second subsidiary finally met the standard, Parker readmitted the company to the acceptable list. The effect on General Electric was even more pronounced. Executives at the huge American conglomerate had planned to participate in a new anthracite mining operation inside KwaZulu through a GE subsidiary, Utah International. In late 1982, in the aftermath of the Connecticut legislation, the GE executives, apparently believing it would be imprudent suddenly to become one of the largest U.S. investors in South Africa, canceled the deal. Embarrassed executives in Pretoria told the South African press that the foreign parent had backed out because of "press publicity and political pressures" in the United States.

The divestment battle in Connecticut attracted the attention of government representatives around the country. Henry Parker received requests for information from dozens of state and municipal officials who were trying to cope with similar demands from activists in their own areas. For more than two years liberal state legislators and city councilors had been filing divestment bills, holding public hearings, educating their colleagues, and marshaling support. By the end of 1982, three cities (Philadelphia, Wilmington, and Grand Rapids) and three states (Connecticut, Michigan, and Massachusetts) had approved the divestment of more than $250 million in public monies. Similar bills had been filed in the state legislatures of Alabama, California, Colorado, Delaware, Florida, Georgia, Illinois, Indiana, Iowa, Kansas, Maryland, Minnesota, Nebraska, Nevada, New Jersey, New York, Oregon, Ohio, Pennsylvania, Rhode Island, Texas, Washington, and Wisconsin.

Many states adopted an incremental strategy, moving progressively from the sale of bank stock or non-Sullivan signatories to broader divestment. In Michigan, Representative Perry Bullard, the chair of the Judiciary Committee and a member of the state's Black Caucus, adopted this approach with great success. In the summer of 1980 Bullard filed a bill preventing any state government monies from being deposited in a bank that made loans to the South African government. When the state assembly approved the bill and the governor signed it into law, more than 250 Michigan banks had to file affidavits with the treasurer's office certifying that they had not made such loans. Two years later, Bullard invited Dumisani Kumalo and Gail Hovey of the American Committee on Africa to testify on a second bill requiring the state's universities to divest. Despite sustained lobbying efforts by representatives from Michigan-based Ford and General Motors, the trustees of the University of Michigan, and the South African consulate, the Michigan assembly approved the bill in late 1982 and the governor signed it into law on his last day in office. The regents of the university later watered the measure down by excluding companies that had their headquarters or a "substantial number" of employees in Michigan. They also limited divestment to stocks and approved the retention of large amounts of bonds in companies with subsidiaries in South Africa.

The Michigan strategy of filing successive bills targeting banks, state universities, and public pension funds and asking them to take increasingly strict steps—from voting their shares to selling their stock—was being duplicated around the country as other anti-apartheid activists labored to find a political formula that would appeal to their local legislators. The biggest prize, from the activists' standpoint, was the huge piles of public pension money, the accrued savings of millions of teachers, firefighters, police, civil servants, and other public workers. These funds were immense, often stretching into tens of billions of dollars, sums hundreds of times larger than what churches or other nonprofits could bring to bear on the capital markets. At the same time, their funds had, by legal design, been carefully insulated from political influence. The monies were often invested by professional portfolio managers under the general supervision of a comptroller (usually an elected official) and a board of trustees. In addition, most trustees considered themselves bound by the tight fiduciary standards of the federal Employee Retirement Income Security Act (ERISA), although this was not strictly true since the actual ERISA standards covered only private pension plans, not state or federal pension programs. ERISA, which had become law in 1974, federalized the common law language on exclusive benefits and prudence; established accountability by designating "named fiduciaries" who were allowed to share some decision making with investment managers; required that pensions be adequately funded; and set standards so that workers could not unreasonably be denied access to their benefits. The enforcement of the law was split between the Internal Revenue Service at the Treasury Department and a new Pension and Welfare Benefits Administration in the Labor Department, though by 1979 an agreement between the departments moved enforcement authority entirely to Labor.

The ERISA statute had many far-reaching consequences, some of them unintended. Though the law did not require any organization to establish a pension plan, the tax-deductibility of funds devoted to plans soon made them the largest tax deduction of all, as tens of billions of dollars in potential tax revenue flowed away from the government and into private retirement funds. This, combined with the tighter funding provisions and an aging population, caused an explosion in plan assets. In 1975 private plans had $485 billion in constant 1984 dollar assets, whereas public plans (those of state and local governments not covered by ERISA) had $173 billion. Over the next five years that amount increased nearly fifty percent to $1 trillion in combined assets. By the year 2000 combined public and private pension assets are conservatively estimated to hit $3 trillion. By contrast, the total value of all publicly traded stock in the United States by the mid-1980s was estimated to be about $2 trillion. Some individual funds grew fabulously large. By the mid-1980s the assets of New York City's plans exceeded $30 billion, New York State's $33 billion, TIAA-CREF's $50 billion, and the combined California pension system's $60 billion. Together these four had held assets equivalent in simple dollar terms to the total of *all* public and private pension funds in the United States in 1960.

Because ERISA regulations were murky and changing, virtually every committee in every large institution asked for a legal analysis of divestment. Each committee received a wide variety of opinions. The attorneys for the Episcopal Church Pension Fund, the United Church of Christ Pension Board, and New York State, for example, concluded that divestment was improper. The attorneys employed by New York City, the United Church of Christ, the Episcopal Church, and Columbia University concluded that if the choice was between a portfolio that included corporations doing business in South Africa and one that excluded them, state corporate law would have no objection to divestment if the costs were insubstantial and the directors believed that such costs were justified to fulfill an organizational purpose. "As long as the directors act in good faith and can demonstrate at least some rational basis for their conclusion," said one study, "a court applying the business judgment rule is highly unlikely to challenge their judgment."

Such opinions had the effect of shifting the decisive criterion to an economic judgment about the performance of different sorts of investment portfolios, and since on this, too, there was considerable disagreement, the fiduciaries of some funds were left to make their own decisions. Though ERISA applied directly only to some institutional investors, it still had significant bearing on the South Africa issue. First of all, it provided the managers of roughly $500 billion that was invested in the pension funds of large corporations with a convenient excuse for not becoming involved in any social shareholder questions. Second, the exclusive benefit and prudence standards of ERISA were making themselves felt, through a process called "creeping ERISA," even in those funds that did not fall under its statutory authority. This phenomenon grew out of the increasing willingness of the Internal Revenue Service to apply Labor Department standards developed for ERISA to a wider variety of charitable funds that wanted to maintain their tax-deductible and tax-exempt status.

The implications of ERISA for social activism through the capital markets were thus mixed. Some believed that the statute discouraged divestment but required active participation in shareholder proxy contacts. Others believed that trustees were free to do what they wanted as long as they upheld the interests of the plan beneficiaries and had an economic rationale for their behavior. The law was interpreted as barring the use of pension monies for "social investment" projects that earned a lower than market rate (like setting aside pension money for abnormally cheap mortgages), and it also was generally accepted that social criteria could be used in selecting between several economically comparable investments. "We have never said that a plan requires the highest possible return for all its investments at all times," said one administrator in the Labor Department. "What ERISA requires is a rational thought process. . . . Social criteria can be brought into the mix only after the economic merits of a particular course of action have been decided." Similarly, trustees of a pension fund could legitimize divestment if they phrased their social concerns in economic terms. Robert Monks, a former head of the Pension and Welfare Benefits Administration, put this bluntly. "Can you justify social investing for a lower return under ERISA or divestment on the grounds that it affects a small portion of a large fund? The answer is no. Can you recast divestment as an economic question and arrive at the same answer as when you viewed it as a social question? The answer is yes. You might, for example, say that contempt for the Sullivan principles was an indication of a management so woefully out of touch as to cast doubt on their capacity to manage such a large enterprise." In other words, ERISA required that every institution show evidence of a rational, internal deliberation, since the acceptability of the decision hinged not so much on the *outcome,* but on the *type of reasons* that had been marshaled to make it.

The discovery made by Henry Parker's task force in Connecticut—that the divestment of stocks might shift funds into a portfolio that yielded higher returns—became an even more significant factor as the American economy moved out of the recession of 1982 and into a boom which was to double the value of the stock market in just six years. The debate over the cost of divestment shifted from how much money one would lose if one divested to which portfolio—the old one or the new one—would rise faster in a bull market. As once staid investors like Harvard and TIAA-CREF found themselves branching out into all kinds of new investments—everything from direct venture capital projects to leveraged buyouts with "high-yield" (junk) bonds—the older reservations on what could and should be done with large pools of capital began to erode.

These factors, in combination with the tenacity of anti-apartheid activists at the state and local levels and the increasingly visible turmoil in South Africa, meant that the attempts to force state pension funds to divest began to succeed. The first full divestment of a state pension plan was passed in Massachusetts. Representative Mel King of Boston, a leading black politician and a member of the state's Black Caucus, had been holding hearings to push the state to do something about its investments since the Soweto riots. In 1979, after a commission study showed that the state had more money invested in companies doing business in South Africa than in companies doing business in Massachusetts, King joined a white liberal senator, Jack Backman, to file a divestment bill. Though the bill failed, King and Backman were able to push through another provision that barred the state from making any *new* purchases of stock in companies doing business in South Africa.

The next year they tried again. Despite a lengthy and supportive series in the *Boston Globe* and the testimony of Dumisani Kumalo, the bill failed a second time. In late 1980, King and Backman called a meeting of representatives of the Black Ecumenical Council, the Catholic archdiocese of Boston, the Massachusetts Council of Churches, the Massachusetts Teachers Association, the local chapter of TransAfrica (headed by Willard Johnson of MIT), the American Federation of State, County, and Municipal Employees, and other sympathetic groups. Together they formed an anti-apartheid umbrella coalition called MassDivest, which was committed to seeking a policy of total divestment—selling all stocks and bonds from every company and bank doing business in South Africa. As in the effort in Connecticut, the activists wrote articles, created a slide show, and traveled around the state urging more investment in the state and less in a distant and cruel South African economy. To press the point, MassDivest workers printed up thousands of bumper stickers and pamphlets with the slogan "Make It in Massachusetts, Not in South Africa." They also visited key state legislators, pointing out that the divestment bill had the support not only of all the major religious leaders in the state but also of the union officials who represented the pension beneficiaries. To their delight, the divestment bill passed the Senate in late 1981, but since there was no time left in the legislative season, it was never considered by the House. For the third time, the bill died.

At the beginning of 1982 the organizers of MassDivest studied their mistakes and went back to the State House again. They smothered legislators with information about South Africa; they anticipated and responded to all of their objections; and they were able to defeat an amendment, first suggested by a Ford Motor Company lobbyist, that the state follow Connecticut and limit its divestment to those who would not sign the Sullivan Principles. At the end of 1982 both the House and Senate passed the bill and sent it to Governor Edward King, a conservative Democrat who had just been defeated by his predecessor and archrival, Michael Dukakis. The governor amended the bill, watering down the key provisions, and bounced it back to the legislature. Representatives King and Backman then had to decide whether to accept the weakened version or to send their original version back to the governor, where it would almost certainly be vetoed. They decided to stick with the original version and the governor, as expected, vetoed the bill. On January 4, 1983, just before the legislature adjourned, Mel King and Jack Backman pushed through a stunning veto override in both houses, the only one of that legislative session. Despite the opposition of the governor, the full divestment bill, affecting $91 million in state investments, became law.

The new governor, Michael Dukakis, announced that he supported the law and would seek its rapid implementation. Within nine months, $68 million in investments in companies doing business in South Africa had been sold off. Jennifer Davis and Dumisani Kumalo were so pleased by the developments in Massachusetts that they immediately scheduled a second national Conference on Public Investment and South Africa in Boston. The gathering, which took place in April 1983, brought together two hundred activists, legislators, financial consultants, union leaders, and treasury officials from around the country. Governor Dukakis welcomed the participants to the opening session, which was held at the State House. In the aftermath of the Boston conference, Davis, Kumalo, and other staff members of the American Committee on Africa zipped like bees around the country, cross-pollinating state capitals with ideas about divestment. In 1983, for example, Kumalo traveled to Nebraska, Rhode Island, and Nevada; Gail Hovey testified before the Illinois House of Representatives; and Davis spoke to the annual conference of the National Association of State Treasurers. They also began publishing a national newsletter called *Public Investment and South Africa,* which reached more than six hundred legislators and divestment activists around the country.

Sensing that the tide might be turning in their favor, Davis and the others hammered away at the rationale for employment codes and constructive engagement. "Face It: The Sullivan Principles Haven't Worked" was the headline of an op-ed piece Davis wrote for the *Washington Post* on May 21, 1983. "Whatever the original intention of Leon Sullivan, the author of the principles, the principles have been an extremely useful tool for the South African government and the corporations," wrote Davis. "Instead of discussing the role that the corporations play in supplying the government with vital products and technology, the debate focuses on the working conditions . . . of workers who represent fewer than one per cent of the black labor force. . . . What the [South African] state fears is not a code of conduct that makes it easier for foreign corporations to stay," she concluded, "but pressure on them to pull out."

To score one of ACOA's biggest victories, Davis, Kumalo, and the others did not need to fly to a distant state; all they had to do was leave their offices above a discount camera store at 198 Broadway in Manhattan, turn north, and walk a few blocks up to the massive and ornate office building that housed many of New York City's municipal departments. There they provided important information and advice to different parties in a lengthy dispute between Mayor Edward Koch, City Council President Carol Bellamy, and City Comptroller Harrison Goldin over the divestment of hundreds of millions of dollars of municipal money and pension funds. The dispute started slowly, when Goldin agreed to a suggestion from Steven Newman, the deputy assistant comptroller, that the city start voting its shareholder proxies on issues like South Africa and infant formula marketing rather than simply endorsing them over to management.

Goldin liked the idea in part because he had a long interest in racial justice, having started his career as a junior litigator in the Civil Rights Division of the U.S. Department of Justice under Robert F. Kennedy. When Newman suggested to Goldin that they take a closer look at the shareholder resolutions on South Africa that were pouring across their desks, Goldin authorized his assistant to review the issues and begin voting the shares. Newman cast tens of millions of shareholder votes in favor of disclosure of more information about South African affiliates, review committees, and the Sullivan Principles. In 1980 Goldin and Newman began supporting resolutions urging companies to adopt the Sullivan Principles or withdraw resolutions and to end computer sales to the police and military resolutions.

Though they were in steady conversation with Jennifer Davis and others at the American Committee on Africa and were aware of the divestment drives in other cities and states, Goldin and Newman chose to exercise the city's shareholder voting power quietly. This approach changed in the spring of 1983, shortly after the second ACOA conference. On June 20, 1983, a labor newspaper, the *Unionist,* reported that two brands of pineapple desserts from the Republic of South Africa were being served to homeless men at the Park Avenue Armory shelter. Four days later, City Council President Carol Bellamy sent a formal letter to Joseph Barkan, the president of the Board of Education, asking him to find out whether South African products were being served in New York City schools, whether the board had a policy against such use, and, if not, whether the board would be willing to adopt one. Two weeks later, on July 7, she wrote to Mayor Ed Koch. "The City of New York should not be in the business of economically supporting South Africa until . . . it eliminates apartheid," she said. "Accordingly, I urge you to issue an Executive Order mandating that all City contracts prohibit the use of any product grown, produced, or manufactured in the Republic of South Africa."

When Koch stalled, Bellamy shifted her attention to the city's massive pension funds. New York City's pension system is organized into five separate funds: the New York City Employees' Retirement System (NYCERS); the Fire Department Pension Fund (known by its authorizing legislation as F1B); the Police Pension Fund (similarly referred to as PA2); the Teachers' Retirement System (TRS); and the Board of Education Fund. As a citywide elected official, Comptroller Goldin served as a trustee on all five boards. The largest of the funds, NYCERS, had seven trustees. Six were individuals: three citywide officials (Koch, Bellamy, and Goldin) and three union leaders. The seventh "trustee" was the collective vote of the five New York borough presidents. The constitutional rules for this group stipulated that a resolution could pass only if the majority vote included at least one union or citywide elected official.

During the fall, Carol Bellamy and her staff gradually persuaded the union leaders, all of whom were white, that this was an issue that their predominantly black membership would care deeply about. In December, when Bellamy was confident she had secured a voting majority of the trustees, she wrote on NYCERS stationery to Comptroller Goldin soliciting his support. Bellamy knew that without Goldin, the mayor might be able to turn the political tide and reverse the majority she had pieced together. Her staff negotiated with Goldin's, settling on a phased program that would go after the worst offenders first. The negotiating team produced a draft resolution that Goldin agreed to cosponsor.

Bellamy then refocused her attention on Koch. By this time Koch had publicly denounced the effort to impose any economic boycotts such as selective purchasing or divestment unless it included all of the world's "pariah nations," which he listed as South Africa, the Soviet Union, Iran, Libya, and Syria. Bellamy and Goldin in their public testimony to the NYCERS trustees and the City Council's Government Operations Committee stressed that the explicit racism of South Africa's policies made it unique. Koch also questioned the introduction of moral issues into investment decisions. Goldin and Bellamy publicly (and somewhat disingenuously) responded that their concern was not primarily moral but represented their informed judgment as fiduciaries. Goldin told the *New York Times* that he had written to dozens of corporate chief executives to determine their position on South Africa and to ask them to "work actively to improve conditions there." One executive scrawled a note at the bottom of Goldin's letter and sent it back to him. "Our mission is to return a profit for our shareholders by serving our customers," he told the comptroller. "If your philosophy does not agree with ours, perhaps you should invest your funds elsewhere." Goldin agreed. "A company which says, 'We don't care how people are treated—our work could be done by slaves and we'd be thrilled,' is a company with which I don't think we should do business," the comptroller told a reporter from the *New York Times*. "Those are dangerous people with that attitude, foolish people. As an investment, it is a highly risky place to have money. Since I take no risks with pension money, I don't want to be involved with such a company."

To deflect the charge that they were being imprudent, Bellamy, Goldin, and the others released their divestment resolution and pointed out that it provided for divestment in three phases: phase one would drop all non-Sullivan signatories within fifteen months; phase two would drop all firms that did not submit to outside review within twenty-four months; and phase three would drop all signatories who did not achieve a high Sullivan rating within three years. They also built in a financial safety valve. "If during the process of divestiture, the Trustees determine that completion of divestiture within the five year limit will significantly reduce the overall rate of return to the Retirement System in violation of the Trustees' fiduciary obligations," the proposal read, "then the Trustees shall authorize an extension of time within which to complete the divestiture." With five of the seven NYCERS trustees opposed to him, Koch realized that the chance of his opinion prevailing had disappeared. On May 30, he announced that he was abandoning his position that restrictions should be broadened to other countries. Bellamy was delighted. "To the extent that the Mayor has changed his mind," she told the press, "I welcome it. He ought to do it more often."

Koch tried one final maneuver to regain the political initiative: he announced that he was appointing his own internal deliberative body—the Mayor's Panel on City Policy with Respect to South Africa—to study the NYCERS and City Council proposals and to recommend a course of action. The panel was headed by New York City counsel Frederick A. O. Schwarz, several other Koch aides, and Ford Foundation president Franklin Thomas. On July 12, 1984, the panel released its report recommending that the city not only divest its pension fund but also ban the purchase of South African products. Koch tried to put the best face on his new policy, telling reporters that "the city has a moral responsibility to lead the fight against discrimination here and abroad."

With Koch effectively beaten, the trustees toughened the draft resolution to include a phase four: all firms who were not actively pursuing the dismantling of apartheid outside the workplace were to be divested by the fifth anniversary of the enactment of the resolution. The resolution also instructed the comptroller to write to all companies under consideration and "give them notice of the actions they should take in order to avoid divestiture." The comptroller was also to "seek out and persuade other shareholders to act in a concerted manner to change corporate political, social, and economic activities in the Republic of South Africa and Namibia." The resolution was submitted to the trustees formally on August 3, 1984, and passed unanimously.

Within six months, Harrison Goldin had hired two lawyers, Eric Wollman and Kenneth Sylvester, and established the South African Investment Responsibility Unit (SAIRU). Wollman and Sylvester began by determining how many companies with subsidiaries in South Africa were in the city's portfolio (156) and how many of these would be subject to divestment under phase one (44). They then drafted letters to all of these companies asking them about their practices and warning them of the city's intention to divest their stock; when the companies replied, the city made their answers public. Goldin also wrote to 323 major institutional investors and 95 colleges around the country asking them to join the New York City effort. "A few public pension funds replied favorably; many of the other funds expressed no interest in this type of policy," recalled Wollman. "The reply from corporate pension funds was particularly negative: we never do *anything* like this." Wollman and Sylvester turned to Tim Smith and Audrey Chapman of the Interfaith Center on Corporate Responsibility for guidance on how to file shareholder resolutions.

The following spring, Harrison Goldin, on behalf of the NYCERS fund, began filing shareholder resolutions pressing for the Sullivan Principles. The corporate response to the New York City actions was swift. NYCERS filed resolutions with twenty firms, all of whom had been resisting the Sullivan Principles for more than eight years. Ten of them—including American Hospital Supply, Manufacturers Hanover, Martin Marietta, Phibro-Salomon, Revlon, G. D. Searle, and Singer— agreed to sign the principles immediately. By the end of the spring the number had risen to seventeen. Of the resolutions that actually came to a vote, all easily passed the SEC's five percent threshold for automatic resubmission the following year. One resolution, at Chesebrough-Pond, earned an unprecedented twenty-three percent of all the proxies voted.

The proxy actions and divestment letters were not the only pressures the city exerted on corporations, for the debate quickly spilled over into city purchasing policies and its relationships with banks. In 1985 Goldin wrote to members of banks with which New York City kept more than $3 billion in deposits, asked whether they made loans to the South African government, and warned them that the City Council was likely to pass a bill restricting the placement of city funds in any bank that held such loans. The banks, including Citibank, Manufacturers Hanover, J. P. Morgan, and North Carolina National Bank, all responded quickly and told the comptroller that they had established policies barring loans to the government. The next year Goldin argued, over Mayor Koch's objections, that if the city did not deposit its money in banks that lent to South Africa, then the city's pension funds should not own stock in those banks. Though Koch was still uncomfortable about the use of city monies, by early 1985 the South African issue had become such a political hot potato that both he and Carol Bellamy found it necessary to announce that they were selling off portions of their personal portfolios.

Once the city had established a policy of voting shares and pursuing selective divestment, it was a short jump to restricting the purchase of products from firms doing business in South Africa. In late 1984 the mayor's office and the City Council worked out a resolution that would be legally and politically acceptable. On February 26, 1985, the City Council passed a law restricting bank deposits and barring purchases from firms that did not meet certain standards in their South African operations. Within months, two major New York suppliers, Eastman Kodak and Motorola, announced that they were ceasing sales to the South African military and police. Shortly afterward the same firms told the city that they would sell their South Africa subsidiaries in order to comply with the New York City law.

□   □   □   □

Throughout 1984, as larger and larger institutions in the United States gave their attention to South Africa, P. W. Botha labored mightily to attract international support for his policies. Diplomats from around the world, including the United States, had repeatedly reminded the South African foreign ministry that Western approval depended on three developments: progress in the Namibian-Angolan negotiations, the cessation of cross-border attacks, and legitimate domestic reform. As he had in the past, Botha worked to give Western governments the impression that he was complying, while framing his actions in a manner that favored the continuation of South Africa's regional dominance and of white supremacy within its borders.

By late 1983 Chester Crocker had spent more than two years trying to persuade Angolan officials that it would be in their best interest to ask Castro's troops to leave. The MPLA government, noticing the enthusiasm with which Reagan's most conservative supporters embraced both Jonas Savimbi and the South African government, doubted Crocker's good faith. In April 1983 Crocker arranged for a high-level Angolan delegation to visit Washington and escorted them to meetings with National Security Adviser Robert McFarlane, Secretary of State George Shultz, and Vice President George Bush. The visit produced some movement in the Angolan position; a tentative timetable for Cuban troop withdrawal had been drawn up and sent back to Luanda for discussion. A delighted Crocker told Shultz that a substantive response from the MPLA would probably be forthcoming by the end of June.

The prediction proved tragically wrong. With South African support, Savimbi's UNITA movement had doubled their strength in two years and had made serious inroads into MPLA control. Conservatives in Washington chortled that no negotiations with MPLA were really necessary since it was about to be defeated. The MPLA leaders, their government rife with inner tension and uncertainty, sent a message saying that while they accepted the withdrawal of Cuban troops "in principle," they demanded that the United States recognize their government and stop trying to link the South African release of Namibia with an explicit schedule for the Cubans.

For Crocker, it was as though the carefully assembled pieces of his puzzle had come to life and were actively scurrying away from each other. Though he had given the South Africans a strict warning about the need for restraint, their fondness for military action had grown. The Angolan government showed less inclination to respond to the American proposals. The Frontline states continued to oppose linkage publicly. On October 28, 1983, the UN Security Council passed Resolution 538, affirming that Resolution 435 was the exclusive basis for Namibia's independence and attacking South Africa's insistence on "irrelevant and extraneous issues" like Cuban troop withdrawal. Three days later, Crocker received a memo informing him that the State Department's Policy Planning Staff was conducting a comprehensive review of constructive engagement and would report its findings to Undersecretary Lawrence Eagleburger. The group's task was specifically to evaluate where Crocker's policy stood, whether the goals of the policy were still valid, and whether other methods might achieve them.

After three years of effort, Crocker's whole scheme seemed on the verge of falling apart. In an attempt to breathe new life into it, he traveled to Rome to meet with Pik Botha for the first time in a year. Crocker told Botha that for U.S. officials to extract additional concessions from the Angolans, they needed a "significant military gesture" from South Africa. The next day, December 6, Crocker got the opposite of what he intended when the South African Defence Force launched Operation Askari, a month-long series of air strikes and infantry sweeps designed to eliminate SWAPO guerrillas from within a hundred miles of the Namibian border. The renewed fighting led to a flurry of diplomatic initiatives. By the third week in January Crocker's deputy, Frank Wisner, after meeting with Angolan representatives in Cape Verde, had reached an agreement. If the South Africans would withdraw their troops, the Angolans would from then on restrain SWAPO's guerrillas.

A week later, on Thursday, January 26, P. W. Botha summoned Namibia's splinter parties to Cape Town for a lecture. The interests of South Africa and of Namibia were not identical, he said. South Africa could not afford much longer to protect Namibians nor could it accept the costs of full-fledged economic sanctions. The Namibian factions could settle on any constitution or form of government they liked, he continued, as long as it did not include something "unacceptable to the South African electorate" such as the inclusion of SWAPO. The next morning Crocker and his assistants arrived in Cape Town for an extended series of meetings with Pik Botha and Magnus Malan at an elegant Cape Dutch estate known as Fleur du Cap. Eventually the South Africans agreed to disengage their troops and to send a delegation to a three-way meeting between the United States, South Africa, and Angola. A few weeks later representatives of the three countries met in Lusaka and, goaded by Crocker, agreed to form a Joint Monitoring Commission composed of representatives of both the Angolan and South African governments to supervise the pull-out and resolve disputes as they came up.

Though Magnus Malan and the chiefs of South African security remained skeptical about such diplomatic arrangements, they understood their objectives clearly. "Our target was not and is not the state of

Angola," Malan told parliament later. "Our target was and is the ANC and SWAPO." The Defense Force had demonstrated the capacity and willingness to strike at the ANC anywhere in the region, but the secureaucrats quickly realized that it would be even better if the border states could be compelled to evict or control the guerrillas. One by one the Frontline states had been bullied into submission. Indeed, the move had been so successful that the South Africans toyed with the idea of pitting guerrilla groups against each other. Shortly after the Fleur du Cap negotiations, P. W. Botha had sent Pieter van der Westhuizen, his chief of military intelligence, for clandestine discussions with Sam Nujoma of SWAPO to determine whether Nujoma, if he should ever take control of Namibia, would refuse to host Umkhonto We Sizwe.

Having succeeded on their western border, the South Africans explored using the same approach in the east, with Mozambique. Mozambique's economy had been so pulverized by RENAMO rebels that President Samora Machel had started sending steady diplomatic signals that he was willing to talk. The Americans repeatedly reminded the South Africans that their international standing would improve if they stopped supporting the RENAMO forces, whose penchant for atrocities was provoking global disgust. Some of the secureaucrats remained dubious about the wisdom of cutting a deal with a Marxist government. According to one account, it was not until the Americans persuaded South Africa's commissioner of police that the eviction of ANC guerrillas from Mozambique would reduce incursions and sabotage that the State Security Council finally agreed.

Negotiations between Mozambique and South Africa proceeded secretly until early March 1984, when the two governments suddenly announced that they had concluded a pact of "non-aggression and good neighborliness." The South Africans, in an effort to seize the initiative, also proposed a regional peace conference to extend such arrangements to the entire region. On March 16 Machel and Botha appeared together on the banks of the crocodile-filled Nkomati River, which separates their countries. Protected by helicopters, patrol boats, and sharpshooters, the two men described their intentions to more than a thousand guests, including the ambassadors from most of the Frontline states. Botha declared that the pact demonstrated South Africa's belief that countries with different economic and political systems could coexist in peace as "a veritable constellation of states working together for the benefit of all." Machel, noting realistically that "one cannot pick one's neighbors," said he hoped the agreement would end the cycle of violence that had laid hold of southern Africa. Reaction to the accord poured in from around the region and the world. The United States, West Germany, and Great Britain sent telegrams; most of the Frontline states sent their ambassadors. Anti-apartheid groups both inside and outside South Africa expressed dismay. Alan Boesak of the United Democratic Front dismissed the whole exercise as "peace out of the barrel of a gun."

For the African National Congress, the Nkomati accord was a disaster. Though Samora Machel had refused to ban the ANC inside Mozambique, he had pledged to evict all but a handful of officials and to cease military support for Umkhonto We Sizwe. The day after the accord was signed, Mozambican police searched the homes of ANC officials around the country. Within four months most ANC and Umkhonto operatives had left, including Joe Slovo. Some fled immediately to Swaziland, only to learn, at the end of March, that the South Africans had secretly signed a similar nonaggression agreement with the Swazi government two years before. In addition to the disruptions caused by the new arrangements, it became increasingly clear that South Africa's intelligence services had penetrated large parts of Umkhonto's structure. In response to the internal and external pressures, Umkhonto's leaders became more ruthless. Suspected informants were sent to prison camps, where ANC security personnel sometimes extracted confessions under torture. Two hundred and fifty Umkhonto guerrillas stationed at a camp in Angola mutinied and demanded to meet with the ANC leadership. Angolan troops were brought in to disarm them; ten representatives were chosen to bring their grievances forward; and none was ever heard from again.

By the end of March 1984, P. W. Botha's strategy of militarization and gradual reform seemed to be paying off. His neighbors were crumbling under South Africa's military and economic pressure; the concept of a regional "consociation" of independent states seemed closer to reality than ever before; the ANC was on the defensive; Botha's rightwing opponents had been expelled from the National Party; he had pushed through a new constitution that gave him power to control the pace of change; he had avoided international economic sanctions; and he had fulfilled many of the conditions that foreign governments had laid down for international acceptance. He even offered Nelson Mandela freedom, conditional on Mandela's renunciation of the armed struggle and agreement to live within the boundaries of the Transkei. "Mr. Mandela is, of course, a Transkei citizen," explained the minister of law and order, Louis Le Grange. Mandela, through his lawyer, refused the offer.

As Botha pressed forward with the implementation of the new constitution, he continued to drive a deeper and deeper wedge into the heart of Afrikaner politics. Disagreements over the direction of government policy flared within Afrikaner institutions, including the Broederbond.

Three out of five former Broederbond chairmen, including Hendrik Verwoerd's son-in-law Professor Carel Boshoff, joined together in 1984 to launch a rival cultural organization known as the Afrikaner Volkswag. The group attracted instant support from Eugene Terreblanche, the leader of the neo-Nazi Afrikaner Weerstandbeweging (AWB), and from Betsie Verwoerd. Botha's lieutenants quickly responded. The minister of national education, Gerrit Viljoen, denounced the Volkswag as an attempt to divide Afrikaners and politicize their cultural life. Professor J. P. de Lange, the current chair of the Broederbond and another Botha supporter, officially distanced himself from the past when he told an American reporter that "apartheid was a simplistic solution based on extremely naive political assumptions." The policy of separate development, he insisted, was "as dead as a dodo."

To prove the point, Botha continued to press for improvements at the margins. The government officially acknowledged the permanence of urban Africans and promised to increase the number of ninety-nine-year lease holdings available in townships. Botha also gradually became more vocal in his opposition to the Prohibition of Mixed Marriages Act and the Immorality Act, which, he told an audience in November, had created problems and enemies for the country. A nation that required such laws to maintain itself, he continued, was not worth maintaining. Besides, "there has been racial mixing since Jan van Riebeeck arrived," he said, "and these laws were introduced in 1927. So what happened between 1652 and 1927?" Early in 1985, at Botha's urging, parliament formally rescinded both acts. The move was quickly embraced by the Reagan administration as a sign of improvement, but Botha's domestic opponents were unimpressed. "We are not interested in the repeal of these laws," said Nthato Motlana. "We want effective participation in the running of our country."

The leaders of the United Democratic Front, the unions, the South African Council of Churches, and other anti-apartheid groups within South Africa dismissed Botha's limited reforms as window dressing designed to obscure the reality that the new constitution denied any political role for Africans and that all of the main legislative pillars of apartheid—the Group Areas Act, the Population Registration Act, the influx control laws, and the homeland structures—remained in place. The functionaries of the government showed no sign of easing up in their enforcement. In the two-year period 1983–1984 the police arrested more than five hundred thousand Africans for pass law violations. Forced removals of African families from areas that had been classified as "black spots" continued; even the three hundred families from the village of Mogopa in the western Transvaal, whose plight had attracted international religious and diplomatic attention, were compelled to relocate to another site a hundred miles away.

Grotesque distortions also continued throughout all parts of South African life, including, for example, medical care. In January the *Rand Daily Mail* reported that South African hospitals considered it acceptable to give blood drawn from whites to Africans, but they refused to give blood drawn from Africans to whites. In April, South African newspapers reported that a Coloured television announcer who had been injured in a car crash had died because H. F. Verwoerd Hospital in Pretoria had delayed treating him while they tried to determine his color. In late 1983 an American dancer named Barry Martin and a South African friend were both seriously hurt in a car accident near Rustenberg. When the ambulance came, the attendants took the South African, who was white, to the hospital but left Martin, who was black, by the side of the road. An African passerby loaded Martin into his car and drove him to a local hospital, where he was left unattended, with a broken spine, for several hours. An American doctor later testified that the failure to treat him properly at the beginning was the probable cause of the severing of Martin's spinal cord, which left the dancer permanently paralyzed from the waist down.

For P. W. Botha, such incidents were irritating aberrations that unfairly weakened international support for his new constitution and his achievements as a regional peacemaker. In May and June he made a new bid to secure Western endorsement when he became the first South African prime minister to visit Europe officially since Hendrik Verwoerd's trip to the Commonwealth meeting in London nearly a quarter century before. The willingness of Western leaders to receive Botha at all was touted in the South African press as evidence of the country's new respectability. Moving through eight countries in two weeks, Botha received, at best, a cool welcome. The French government allowed him to come but dispatched a junior member of the foreign ministry to meet him. Pope John Paul II greeted him at the Vatican but instantly issued a sharp statement denouncing apartheid. Moments before Botha arrived, West German Chancellor Helmut Kohl had a large sofa removed from his office so that he would not have to be photographed sitting next to the South African. While fourteen thousand anti-apartheid protesters snarled traffic in central London, Prime Minister Margaret Thatcher received Botha at Chequers, her official residence in Buckinghamshire. During their five-hour conversation, Botha told Thatcher that South Africa would relinquish control of Namibia to the Contact Group—the United States, Canada, Great Britain, France, and West Germany—if Cuban troops left Angola and if the five Western countries would pick up the costs. Thatcher, in turn, urged Botha to release Nelson Mandela and read aloud an appeal Queen Elizabeth had received from the blacks at KwaNgema, who were about to be forcibly removed. International approval would never be fully forthcoming, she told him, unless such removals stopped. Soon after his return to South Africa, Botha announced publicly that his government would have to heed the growing international and local sensitivity to large-scale removals; six months after Botha's meeting with Thatcher the South African government announced that they had been suspended.

South Africa's new constitution formally took effect on September 3, 1984. The night before, shortly before midnight, P. W. Botha resigned the office of prime minister just before it legally ceased to exist. A few moments later he was unanimously chosen state president by an eighty-eight-member electoral college composed of whites, Coloureds, and Indians. Two weeks later the new state president told the first session of the tricameral parliament that he recognized that the new constitution did not provide fully for the diversity of the South African population. Negotiations with the homeland leaders would continue, Botha said, and "means would be found" to enable Africans living outside the homelands to participate in political decision making.

By early October 1984, Botha's future seemed bright. He had coaxed and nudged his white constituents into accepting a parliament that included members of other races. He had led South Africa to the brink of both regional and global acceptance. He had gathered all the reins of legislative power through his standing as leader of the National Party and the veto authority of the new President's Council, which he chaired. As the head of the State Security Council and of the cabinet, Botha held absolute executive authority over the entire government, all the way down to the local level. He could now, he believed, lead South Africa toward the constellation of states, which would permit permanent white dominion.

There was only one catch. Throughout 1984, unrest had steadily been growing throughout the country. Through the early months of the year students in increasing numbers refused to attend classes to protest expulsion of activist students and teachers. The boycott of classes spread from the Transvaal to the Eastern Cape and eventually to the Orange Free State. Student protests led to clashes with police; in one incident near Pretoria a fifteen-year-old girl was killed and one hundred and two students were injured. Though the demonstrations and boycotts never affected more than seven percent of the total black student population at any given time, they continued throughout the year and eventually attracted the support of more than six hundred thousand Coloured students, a group that had previously been cautious about politics. In August new violence broke out, as police used tear gas, leather truncheons known as *sjamboks,* and rubber bullets against demonstrators protesting the election of Indian and Coloured representatives to the tricameral parliament. In the same period, township residents responded to a government announcement of increased rents with street demonstrations and a massive rent boycott. Tensions rose within the townships as different political groups impulsively announced work stay-aways and tried on occasion to enforce them through intimidation.

P. W. Botha, determined that these demonstrations would not get out of hand, instructed the minister of law and order, the commissioner of police, and the commanders of the South African Defence Force to work together and do whatever they had to do to put a stop to them. On October 23, seven thousand heavily armed South African police and soldiers sealed off the townships of Sebokeng, Sharpeville, and Boipatong in the Vaal Triangle. The purpose of Operation Palmiet, explained Louis Le Grange, minister of law and order, was to "restore law and order" to the area by ridding it of "criminal and revolutionary elements." After searching every shack and dwelling, the soldiers arrested more than four hundred people. A week later, on October 31, the soldiers returned and conducted the entire operation a second time.

Despite the turbulence in South Africa, concern in the United States was lackluster. Newspaper and television reporters were busy covering Ronald Reagan's reelection battle against his Democratic challenger, former Vice President Walter Mondale. Most business leaders, politicians, and journalists continued to believe that the four-year-old policy of constructive engagement should be allowed time to bear fruit. This tranquil indifference was soon to be disrupted by three major developments: the rise in violent unrest in South Africa, the outburst of new public protests in the United States, and the elevation of Desmond Tutu by the American media to the position of most visible and credible spokesperson for South African blacks.

As general secretary of the South African Council of Churches, which received the majority of its funds from abroad, Tutu considered it part of his job to cultivate a network of international friends and supporters. He gave particular attention to the United States, from which he was receiving a growing number of requests to speak. In September 1982, in the middle of the Eloff Commission hearings, Tutu left South Africa to attend the triennial General Convention of the Episcopal Church in New Orleans. At first the South African government had denied him permission to travel, but when the presiding bishop, John Allin, asked fellow Episcopalian George Bush to intervene, the South African government relented and gave Tutu a short-term travel document.

When Tutu arrived at the convention hall in New Orleans, he overwhelmed his audience. In his address he not only showed a complete absence of fear of government officials, but he urged the delegates to feel some compassion for them. "The people who are perpetrators of injury in our land are not sprouting horns or tails," Tutu told the lay and clergy delegates from around the country. "They're just ordinary people like you and me . . . ordinary people who are scared. Wouldn't you be scared if you were outnumbered five to one?" Using his gift for ironic humor, he pointed out the peculiarities of a system that permitted a pimply, semiliterate white teenager to make choices at the ballot box while denying the opportunity to a fifty-year-old bishop with numerous academic degrees. The delegates listened with rapt attention and, when he finished, they gave him a fifteen-minute standing ovation. "I think that even if I had stood and said 'Rub a dub dub' they would have given me a standing ovation," Tutu recalled later, shaking his head with amazement. "They had made up their minds that they were going to like me; they really adopted me." After this experience, records one of his biographers, Tutu decided that "the Episcopal Church of the United States was firmly on his side. He could say anything, do anything, and they would support him."

Because of his eloquence and prominence, Tutu also attracted the attention of an increasing number of American universities. Caught between the accusation of indifference and the demand to divest, many university presidents seized on the idea of demonstrating opposition to apartheid by awarding an honorary degree to a black South African. Desmond Tutu was one of the most popular candidates. In 1979 Tutu was awarded an honorary doctor of laws by Derek Bok at Harvard and in 1982 by Michael Sovern at Columbia. When the South African government refused to give Tutu a passport to attend the Columbia graduation, Sovern set out an empty chair at the ceremony. In August, Sovern and two trustees traveled all the way to South Africa to confer the degree on Tutu.

In the last half of 1984, Desmond Tutu was invited by his friend James Fenhagen, the dean of General Theological Seminary in New York City, to come and spend three months as theologian in residence. Tutu happily accepted, for it offered him a respite from the relentless pressure of his responsibilities at the South African Council of Churches and would give him and his wife the chance to see their daughter Naomi, who had married an American and now lived in the United States. Tutu spent several months attending classes, preaching, making pastoral calls, and celebrating the Eucharist. He generally kept a low profile, though he continued to speak privately to prominent Americans about the growing unrest in South Africa. On October 4, 1984, for example, he joined Allan Boesak at a lunch with Senator Edward Kennedy and his foreign aide, Gregory Craig. Both Tutu and Boesak spoke passionately about the increased suffering of South African blacks. When Kennedy asked what he could do, they invited him to visit. Kennedy immediately accepted.

Within weeks of his arrival, however, Tutu's desire for a peaceful sabbatical was shattered. At nine o'clock in the morning on October 15, 1984, a large limousine arrived and delivered Norway's UN ambassador to the Tutus' front door. Handing Leah a huge bunch of yellow lilies, blue irises, and red zinnias, the ambassador informed Tutu that he had won the Nobel Peace Prize. Together they walked across the seminary campus to the chapel, where the entire community—students, faculty, maintenance workers, and administrators—had gathered for a service of celebration. As Tutu stepped into the chapel he was met by a wave of applause and the rolling cadences of "Now Thank We All Our God."

As thousands of congratulatory phone calls, letters, and telegrams flooded in to General Seminary and reporters from around the world clamored for his attention, Tutu emphasized that he did not view the prize as a personal award. It was, he said, recognition of the patient suffering and just aspirations of his people, a "tremendous political statement," and "a kind of sacrament, a wonderful symbol." He announced that the majority of the prize money would be placed in a scholarship fund for black students. Within forty-eight hours Tutu had gathered his wife and his two daughters and made arrangements to return to Johannesburg. At Jan Smuts Airport, hundreds of friends and supporters greeted the Tutus with songs, dancing, and banners. When the police warned that unless people stop singing they would release the dogs, one of Tutu's associates pointed to the international television cameras and said "Please feel free!"

The South African government and its state-run news services tried first to ignore the award and then to belittle it. The South African Broadcasting Corporation, which governed all television, prepared a brief documentary arguing that the award had become corrupted and that Tutu could not possibly be a symbol of peace because he supported violence. To support its claim the network broadcast a few carefully edited sound bites in which Tutu, who frequently warned his audiences of what might happen in South Africa if a peaceful solution were not found, seemed to be predicting a bloodbath. Though some Afrikaner newspapers chided P. W. Botha for refusing to congratulate Tutu on the award, other editors attacked the bishop.

However much the National Party leaders would have liked to ignore or suppress Tutu, the Nobel Prize meant that they no longer could do so. The prize transformed Tutu into a figure of international reputation and importance, someone who could instantly command the attention of the world's media. From then on, Tutu saturated the news, especially in the United States. "Whether Americans liked him or not," commented Frank Ferrari of the African-American Institute, "they saw him when they got up on the morning talk shows, they saw him on the evening talk shows, and they went to bed with him on the late night news." Doors that had been shut to him now opened; people who had responded to him with mild interest now clamored for him to speak to their groups.

Tutu's prominence in American newspapers and on American television was not solely due to the Nobel Peace Prize. It also represented a critical transition in American thinking about South Africa. Though American reporters had struggled for years to explain the contours of South Africa's political life to their readers, it was still, for many, a distant and incomprehensible problem. No single spokesperson had ever emerged to capture the imagination of American viewers and interpret the meaning of events. Oliver Tambo had been prevented from taking this role because he was by nature a quiet man and could too easily be discredited from the right because of the ANC's commitment to armed struggle and its affiliations with the Soviet Union. Gatsha Buthelezi had tried for years to become the spokesperson for South African blacks in the United States and for a time he almost succeeded, but then his pro-investment stand alienated the American anti-apartheid movement, which then discredited him from the left. Desmond Tutu, however, was not vulnerable. He advocated both nonviolence (like Buthelezi) and sanctions (like Tambo)—in fact, he urged sanctions as the most effective nonviolent way to promote change in apartheid.

Most important, Tutu fit into a preexisting American archetype created and hallowed by Martin Luther King Jr. Though Tutu himself repeatedly and emphatically denied the connection, pointing out differences between the South African struggle and the American civil rights movement and between himself and King, the American press—and the American population—chose to see him differently. There were a number of striking similarities—both men of deep and evident faith, advocates of nonviolence, at the forefront of a major struggle for racial freedom, both spellbinding orators, attacked from the right as Communists and from the left as sellouts. Both advocated the use of economic weapons—boycotts, selective purchasing, and investments—to add muscle to their campaigns for rights. Now they were both recipients of the Nobel Peace Prize—exactly twenty years apart—an award they received in the middle of their campaigns that catapulted them to even greater prominence.

The first person to draw the connection was Jesse Jackson, who knew both men and who returned from his 1979 trip declaring that he had "met the Martin Luther King of South Africa." The comparison did not become common currency, however, until after Tutu's peace prize. In an article written two days after the announcement, columnist Flora Lewis directly connected Tutu to King, "another black preacher struggling for the rights of his people." As Tutu's prominence rose, with coverage of his actions in New York jumping to seven times the level of 1982, more journalists turned to the King analogy as a kind of descriptive shorthand. Even when the connection was not drawn explicitly, it remained, shaping Americans' emotional and intellectual responses to the energetic bishop, casting his words in a new, if reflected, light of legitimacy. In the past, senior members of the Reagan administration had been able to brush Tutu off; "whatever his moral splendor," said one State Department official, "the bishop is a political ignoramus." As Tutu's importance as a figure in American domestic politics rose, they could no longer do so publicly.

When Tutu traveled to Oslo in December to claim his prize, he, like Albert Luthuli in 1960 and Martin Luther King in 1964, vigorously defended the role of the church as a nonviolent peacemaker. "Let us work to be peacemakers, as those given a wonderful share in our Lord's ministry of reconciliation," he told the audience. "And if we want peace, so we have been told, let us work for justice. Let us beat our swords into ploughshares." During the gala dinner, at which Tutu received the gold medal, the police suddenly cleared the hall because of a bomb threat. As the king of Norway, the other Nobel prizewinners, and all their guests shivered on the steps outside, Tutu restored their spirits by inviting them all to sing "We Shall Overcome."

FOURTEEN

The Explosion
(1985–1986)

If you want politicians to lead, just form a parade and they will find their way to the front.
—RANDALL ROBINSON

ON TUESDAY, November 6, 1984, the day after a massive worker stay-away in South Africa, Ronald Reagan was reelected in a landslide. While the South African government was "plainly delighted," as one reporter in the *Cape Times* wrote, American activists reacted with dismay. After six years of organizing, testifying, and letter writing, Randall Robinson at TransAfrica simmered with frustration. Congress had refused to take any major steps. Proposals to make the Sullivan Principles mandatory had failed. A sense of gloom settled on the anti-apartheid community. "We heard from black South Africans that when Reagan was reelected whites were dancing in the streets," recalled Cecilie Counts, a TransAfrica staff member. "They were saying 'We're safe for four more years.'"

In response, Robinson decided to return to the tactics of his youth. The time had come, he felt, for a boldly defiant gesture that would tell the Pretoria government that the American activists did not plan to give up. As South African police continued with a crackdown on unions and political leaders, including the mass arrest of twenty-three hundred people in one township, Robinson phoned two friends, District of Columbia Representative Walter Fauntroy and U.S. Civil Rights Commission member Mary Frances Berry. On November 21, 1984, the day before Thanksgiving, Robinson, Fauntroy, and Berry visited the South African ambassador, Bernardus G. Fourie, in his embassy office. They asked for the immediate release of more than one hundred United Democratic Front leaders who had been detained. Fourie said that he would see what he could do. At the end of the discussion, the three visitors told the ambassador that they would not leave the premises until their demands had been met. Fourie, dumbfounded, ducked out of his office to phone Pik Botha in Pretoria. What should I do? he asked the foreign minister. Call the police, Botha replied. The police arrived, arrested Robinson and his companions, and hauled them away. Because Fauntroy waived his congressional immunity and Robinson and Berry refused bail, all three spent the night in jail.

After his release the next morning Fauntroy said that he had participated in the protest as "an act of moral witness" and announced that he, Robinson, and others intended to launch a new "national campaign" to oppose South Africa. Three days later, Representative Charles Hayes of Illinois and the Reverend Joseph E. Lowery of the Southern Christian Leadership Conference appeared at the embassy and were arrested. "The moral conscience of Americans should be pricked," said Lowery. "Through our government and our businesses, we have become participants in apartheid." Over the next two days, as hundreds of demonstrators gathered outside the embassies, two more members of Congress, Ronald V. Dellums and John Conyers, as well as a member of the D.C. City Council, entered the embassy and were arrested.

Randall Robinson and the leaders of the new campaign, dubbed the Free South Africa Movement, decided that they would stretch out the demonstrations and arrests for as long as possible. "We are in for the long haul," Robinson told reporters a week after his arrest. "We already have enough willing people committed to being arrested to let us continue these protests indefinitely here in Washington and around the United States." Robinson maintained the supply by limiting the number of people to be arrested to three a day and put Cecilie Counts in charge of scheduling them. Dozens, then scores, then hundreds of people began asking to be put on the calendar. "After a week or two," Counts said, "we were antagonizing people by limiting it to three a day."

As December unfolded into January, more and more people clamored to participate. Satellite demonstrations popped up at South African consular offices in other cities. For those who had marched in the civil rights movement, the gatherings at the embassy offered a chance for reunion and revival. For liberal politicians frazzled by Republican triumphalism, the demonstrations provided an opportunity for a public display of their convictions. Union leaders, college students, congressional representatives, musicians, professors, mayors, movie stars, and clergy, most of whom had never been arrested before, flocked to the sidewalks outside the embassy only to be carted away by the police. For some participants—like Jimmy Carter's daughter, Amy, Martin Luther King's children, and a large flock of youthful Kennedys, all of whom had been too young to participate actively in the civil rights and antiwar movements—the demonstrations and arrests served as a rite of passage. Coretta Scott King, who had been obliged to remain with her four children when her husband was in jail, presented herself for arrest for the first time in her life.

Newspaper editors, tired after a year of reporting conventional politics, faced with a tedious inauguration and a slow news season, gave the demonstrations good coverage, which brought out more volunteers and complicated the task of scheduling who was to be arrested when. On one occasion, Counts had slated a group of professors from around the country who belonged to Academics against Apartheid. "We thought this was an important group because we knew that they would go back with a commitment," recalled Counts. "Then suddenly we got a phone call saying that Stevie Wonder wanted to come, so we stuck him in with them. The next day the press reported that Stevie Wonder had been arrested at the embassy. They forgot to mention that it was Stevie Wonder and fifty-seven professors. That happened a lot, and so the impression developed that you had to be a celebrity to participate. But that wasn't true."

The size of the demonstrations, the number of arrests, and the rapid diffusion to other cities captured the attention of Congress and threw the Reagan administration on the defensive. Even before the demonstrations had started, the editors of the *New York Times* had asked why, after four full years, constructive engagement had not shown more results. "One early fruit of engagement was to have been to end South Africa's illegal occupation of neighboring Namibia," they wrote, "yet the great prize of a regional bargain—independence for Namibia and the departure of Cuban troops from Angola—continues to elude Washington's grasp." As the protests swelled, the belief that constructive engagement had not lived up to its promise grew among prominent groups of moderate Republicans. The newly elected chair of the Senate Foreign Relations Committee, Senator Richard Lugar of Indiana, told reporters after a meeting with Jesse Jackson in early December that he thought the administration should adopt a stronger policy against apartheid. Shortly afterward he wrote a letter to Reagan, cosigned by the chair of the Senate subcommittee on Africa, Nancy Kassebaum of Kansas. The two midwestern Republicans asked the president to take a personal interest in the problems of southern Africa. The White House staff slighted the senators by forwarding the letter to the State Department without immediate reply.

Another sign of dissent within the Republican Party appeared soon afterward when the most ardent conservatives in the House of Representatives fired a warning shot of their own at the South African embassy. On December 4, Newt Gingrich, Robert Walker, Vin Weber, and thirty-two others signed a formal letter cautioning Ambassador Fourie not to take their support for granted. "Events of recent weeks in South Africa have raised serious questions about your government's willingness to move more progressively and aggressively toward real human rights reforms," they wrote. They had supported constructive engagement in the past, they said, but would not allow the South African government to use the policy as "an excuse for maintaining the unacceptable status quo." If the South African government did not display a "demonstrated sense of urgency in ending apartheid," the representatives would recommend the implementation of restrictions on investment and of other "international diplomatic and economic sanctions against South Africa."

Public protest, combined with a budding mutiny within his own party, prompted Reagan to act. On Monday, December 3, Reagan consulted with Chester Crocker at the White House. After briefing the president, Crocker emerged to defend his policies to reporters. "Constructive engagement is not an embracing of any status quo," he insisted. The accusation that the policy had been ineffective, he said, was "rubbish. . . . There's a considerable lack of information as to what we stand for. Many things we are doing in the region are not things we can talk about at press conferences." Crocker, who had long argued that predecessors had failed because they could not muster domestic political support, now felt the foundation of his own policies eroding. The process even touched his family. When students at his daughter's high school decided to stage a vigil outside the embassy, Crocker interrupted his schedule to visit her social studies class and defend his diplomacy to her classmates.

President Reagan also had to contend with Desmond Tutu's new authority, which had been augmented not only by the Nobel Peace Prize in October but by his selection in November as the first black Anglican bishop of Johannesburg. As Tutu bounced around the United States, he drew larger crowds and more attention than ever before. He testified before the UN Security Council and the House subcommittee on Africa, where he received a standing ovation from the representatives and audience in the packed hearing room. In every appearance Tutu shredded the rosy picture of reform that the South Africans had promoted through their lobbyists and friends. Tutu told a group of senior corporate executives at St. Luke's Episcopal Church in Darien, Connecticut, that whether they liked it or not their subsidiaries were "buttressing a vicious system." Before the House subcommittee Tutu insisted that constructive engagement without economic sanctions was "giving democracy a bad name" and had only led to "escalating intransigence and repression" on the part of the Botha government. The South African system remained "immoral, evil, and totally un-Christian," he told Congress. It could not be reformed; it had to be destroyed. "We don't want our chains made more comfortable," said Tutu bluntly. "We want them removed."

Tutu's prominence soon reached the point that even Reagan could no longer politically afford to shun the bishop. On December 7, Tutu received an "audience," as the South African newspapers put it, with Reagan and other government officials in the Oval Office. "It was early in the morning," Tutu remembered. "I was his first appointment. I was impressed with the president, who was very much in charge. Throughout the whole hour-long meeting, only he spoke." Tutu told Reagan that the situation in South Africa was rapidly deteriorating. Reagan disagreed, telling the bishop that he had heard much progress had been made. Though the bishop later reported that the president had seemed "shaken" when Tutu mentioned that he did not have a South African passport and that his nationality was officially listed as "undetermined at present," Tutu left feeling disheartened that he had not changed Reagan's thinking at all. Tutu knew that the major achievement was the visit itself; in South Africa this would be seen as a blow to Botha—who fervently hoped to come to the White House someday himself—and a boost to anti-apartheid activists. Reagan defended his administration's approach at a press conference immediately after the meeting. "We have made sizable progress in expressing our repugnance for apartheid," Reagan said, "and in persuading the South African government to make changes. And we are going to continue that policy." Would the administration now encourage the withdrawal of U.S. firms? asked a reporter. No, Reagan responded. "The simple truth is that most black tribal leaders there have openly expressed their support for American business investment there."

On Monday, December 10, only hours before Tutu received the Nobel Prize in Oslo, the South African government abruptly announced that the detention orders for fourteen of the UDF leaders had been nullified, though six of the fourteen were later arrested and formally charged with treason. Simultaneously, during a ceremony marking International Human Rights Day, President Reagan broke with his tradition of quiet diplomacy. In the midst of a litany of criticism of the Soviet Union and Afghanistan, Reagan suddenly rebuked P. W. Botha for his use of forced removals and detentions without trial. Botha's brusque reply came three days later. "No quiet diplomacy or hard shouting," the South African prime minister told students at a graduation ceremony at the University of Stellenbosch, "will keep us from seeking the road of justice with the retention of civilized values for our country and our people."

Rejuvenated interest in the South African struggle among many people across the United States inspired a string of new visits by prominent Americans to see the situation for themselves. Two visits in particular— by Edward Kennedy in January and Ted Koppel in March—had a lasting impact on U.S.–South African relations. The Massachusetts Democrat, remembering his brother's trip nineteen years before, planned his visit carefully. After arriving in Johannesburg, Kennedy intended to spend his first night in Desmond Tutu's modest home in Soweto; a few days later he would travel to Brandfort to see Winnie Mandela; and finally he would travel to Cape Town where, he hoped, he would obtain the government's permission to visit Nelson Mandela at Pollsmoor Prison.

Kennedy arrived at Jan Smuts Airport in Johannesburg on Saturday, January 5, and immediately found himself at the center of a dispute between the Black Consciousness and Charterist factions within the anti-apartheid movement. The Charterists—represented by the African National Congress and the United Democratic Front—were seeking to isolate the National Party government by building as many allies as possible to the left and right, subordinating ideological positions to the larger strategic goal of eliminating apartheid. For the smaller, more strident Black Consciousness forces, who saw ideology as the central binding force, consorting with contaminated third parties meant the evisceration of their convictions and the demise of the struggle. Kennedy's visit became a symbol and a focus of the increasingly bitter dispute. Because of their ideological breadth and inclusiveness, the Charterists could understand and exploit a U.S. senator's opposition to his own president's policy. For the Azanian People's Organization (AZAPO) and other Black Consciousness groups, however, Kennedy and Reagan represented the same U.S. government that had, in their view, contributed to the success of apartheid.

The leaders of AZAPO and their allies in the National Forum Committee (a Black Consciousness umbrella group) set out to spoil Kennedy's visit. They sent forty activists to the airport to protest his arrival. Chanting "Kennedy, go home!" the demonstrators scuffled with white security police and embarrassed Tutu, Boesak, and Beyers Naudé, who had come to welcome Kennedy to South Africa. "We do not need Kennedy to choose our leaders for us," an AZAPO activist told a reporter at the airport. "He is a capitalist and an imperialist." Ironically, the AZAPO activists had latched on to the same accusation as P. W. Botha and National Party leaders: the only reason Kennedy, or any other American politician, came to South Africa was to boost his standing among blacks at home. That night an unhappy Tutu tried to make up for the airport incident. More than five hundred people gathered around the bishop's Soweto home, held candles, and sang songs for Kennedy. "We cannot give you the freedom of Soweto," Tutu told his guest, "but we can give you our hearts."

Kennedy also encountered resistance from the U.S. ambassador. During his two and a half years in South Africa, Herman Nickel had assiduously courted the friendship of National Party politicians and other white leaders and avoided contact with anyone controversial in the black community. Though Nickel disliked P. W. Botha, he believed that economic growth had forced the government into significant reforms. When pressure increased on American companies to withdraw, Nickel rushed to their defense. As American executives streamed through his office each week, complaining that their firms' problems with South Africa were too time-consuming, Nickel pleaded with them to stay. The more Nickel voiced his opposition to corporate disinvestment, the more he sounded like a spokesman for the South African foreign ministry.

Nickel displayed a particularly memorable lack of diplomacy during Kennedy's visit. When asked to introduce Kennedy at a lunch at the American Chamber of Commerce in Johannesburg, Nickel delivered a pugnacious forty-five-minute tirade that sought to rebut Kennedy's speech before the senator had delivered it. When Kennedy finally reached the podium, he tried to make light of the incident. "I thought I was being asked to give an after-lunch speech," Kennedy said, "but now I think we should call it a pre-dinner speech." Nickel's harangue rankled Kennedy for months, however, and made him all the more determined to put a stop to constructive engagement.

From Johannesburg Kennedy traveled to Brandfort, where he met Winnie Mandela, who was in her seventh year of near-total isolation. On his way to her tiny dwelling, the Massachusetts senator passed graffiti that read "Kennedy Go Home—and Take Tutu With You." From Winnie's home he traveled to a six-year-old resettlement camp at Onverwacht, where he got into an argument with a white South African official about African infant mortality rates. At many of his destinations, Kennedy had to endure interference from more AZAPO demonstrators and from the omnipresent South African Broadcasting crews eager to record the sight of an American liberal being jeered by Africans. In Cape Town Kennedy was not allowed to see Nelson Mandela but paid a visit to the Crossroads squatter camp. In Durban he held meetings with Gatsha Buthelezi, who attacked Desmond Tutu bitterly for his support of sanctions. On Kennedy's last day in South Africa he returned to Johannesburg for a final rally at Regina Mundi Catholic Church in Soweto. Four thousand people came out to hear him, along with a hundred AZAPO demonstrators with placards reading "Away with the CIA, Kennedy, Oppression, and Capitalism." When some of them pushed toward the altar shouting "No More Kennedy!" Tutu intervened. He asked the crowd if it was their will that Kennedy should address the meeting. Yes! shouted the majority. No! shouted the demonstrators. As tempers flared inside and outside the building, the armed riot police and SADF troops on the periphery tensed. After caucusing with Kennedy and his aides, Tutu advised him to withdraw. Kennedy left the church and drove to the airport.

From that point on, Desmond Tutu's enthusiasm and support for Black Consciousness groups in South Africa dropped sharply. Until the Kennedy visit, Tutu had tried to straddle the divide between the Black Consciousness and Charterist traditions. He had published articles on Black Theology; had supported and attended the creation of the National Forum; and had publicly protested when AZAPO officials were detained. AZAPO's behavior during the Kennedy visit had humiliated the bishop in front of an important American friend. It displayed, he felt, an appalling lack of political awareness. "It seemed such a silly time to decide to turn away from the concentration on the real enemy," Tutu commented later, "to exploit this particular incident in the way that they did. They should have asked themselves why the pro-government media suddenly gave them so much coverage which they hadn't had in a very long while." Tutu's irritation with AZAPO proved to be a boon for the United Democratic Front. Two months later, when the UDF leaders asked Tutu to become a patron of the Charterist organization, he accepted.

The next important American visit came two months later, in March 1985, when Ted Koppel and the staff of *Nightline* flew to South Africa to conduct an entire week of live broadcasts from South Africa. *Nightline,* a staple in the daily news diet of American government officials, businesspeople, academics, and politically active voters, had pioneered the art of organizing live broadcasts from different parts of the world, a practice that would later be mastered by global networks like CNN. The producers of *Nightline,* prompted by the ongoing demonstrations at the South African embassy and by the awareness that March 21, 1985, would be the twenty-fifth anniversary of the Sharpeville massacre, applied for permission to go to South Africa and use the state-run television facilities to conduct live broadcasts back to the United States. To their amazement the South African government agreed.

The *Nightline* broadcasts, conducted live for five consecutive nights from South Africa, proved to be a watershed in the relations between the two countries. Despite the hurried pace and the superficiality of the taped segments, which often caricatured South African history and politics, the broadcasting team managed to distill the debate into an accessible form. Over the succession of nights, some of South Africa's most visible political figures had the opportunity to speak directly not only to each other but to a huge audience of influential Americans. On March 18, for example, viewers heard Pik Botha gripe about the "selective morality and selective indignation" that had focused apartheid. A few minutes later they watched Desmond Tutu put Botha on the spot by asking him why it was that a fifty-three-year-old bishop was not permitted to vote. The next evening viewers heard a debate about the South African government's forced removals of black families from areas that had been designated white. On Wednesday, March 20, Harry Oppenheimer demonstrated the intricacies of the liberal position by simultaneously opposing apartheid yet defending the reforms of the National Party, supporting strong unions yet rejecting the unions' belief in sanctions. Louis Wilking, the managing director of General Motors, appeared on camera to insist that his firm, along with other American companies, were "in the vanguard of enticing South Africa to make many of the political changes you see today." In the same broadcast Arries Paulus, the head of the white Mineworkers' Union, attacked Cyril Ramaphosa of the black National Union of Mineworkers for wanting blacks to suffer under sanctions. "It is true that if there is disinvestment people would suffer," said Ramaphosa coolly, "but black people in this country have suffered for well over three hundred years, and the suffering they will go through is not much more than what they are going through now."

The next day—Thursday, March 21—was the twenty-fifth anniversary of Sharpeville. Koppel and his team drove to Soweto to tape an illegal interview with Winnie Mandela, who was still under a ban. As Koppel and Mandela sat down to talk, they received word that police had shot and killed a group of demonstrators in a township outside of Uitenhague. The emerging details proved horrific. The crowd had gathered to attend the funerals of two young "comrades" who had been killed two weeks before. Originally the funeral had been scheduled for Sunday, but the local police commander had decided to move the date forward to Thursday to cut down on the attendance. Only the night before did someone inform him that the funeral would fall on the anniversary of Sharpeville, at which point he immediately obtained another ban, which was announced in the wrong township. While the people who gathered for the funeral did not know that their assembly had been declared unlawful, the police saw the crowd as deliberately defying an official order. The police had also received general orders from Pretoria to use greater force in putting down protests and had been given explicit permission to shoot "selected and properly specified targets" with the intention to kill. On March 21 the police therefore had no riot gear, but only high-powered automatic rifles and heavy-gauge shotguns. When the crowd tried to enter buses to take them to the funeral, the police ordered them off. The leaders in the crowd then tried to organize the group to start walking, but two Hippos, the police armored vehicles, drove up and blocked their path. As a young boy tried to pass the Hippos on his bicycle, the police opened fire. Within a few minutes the police had killed twenty people and wounded twenty-seven more, making it the single worst police massacre since Sharpeville.

In her interview with Koppel, taped only moments after she learned of the killings, Winnie Mandela voiced her emotions. "This is what our leaders went to prison for," she said with quiet rage. "This confirms what we've been saying all along: that there has been no change in this government, no change whatsoever." Later that evening, on the same program, Beyers Naudé reinforced her claim. "What happened in Uitenhague today was not an isolated incident," Naudé said. "It is not purely something which came about by mistake." The most effective proof of the distortions of apartheid came not from Naudé or Mandela but from the government's defenders, who justified the government's actions in a chillingly blithe manner. In the broadcast that took place on the night of the shootings, Otto Krause, a conservative white journalist, casually dismissed Percy Qoboza's fury. "Percy," Krause exclaimed, "stop complaining, complaining, complaining!" When Koppel flew to Cape Town the next day and taped an interview with P. W. Botha, the state president accused Koppel of deliberately distorting the truth. On camera South Africa's president freely vented his paranoia. "You Americans are fighting your elections in America on South African soil," said Botha. "Your Senator Kennedy came here to show his sympathy with the poor blacks. But what happened to him? The blacks in South Africa united with us to tell him to go back." Botha defended the police in Uitenhague and warned Koppel that there would be more such violence. "I'm going to keep order in South Africa," Botha said with grim determination, "and nobody in the world is going to stop me."

On March 22, the final evening of broadcast, Koppel scored a coup by bringing Oliver Tambo, Gatsha Buthelezi, Allan Boesak, and Connie Mulder together electronically from three cities for a live debate. When Mulder defended the banning of the ANC for its commitment to violence, Tambo reminded him that the ANC had been banned a year *before* Umkhonto We Sizwe had been formed. In the same program Boesak attacked Buthelezi for reinforcing ethnic nationalism, a charge Buthelezi vigorously denied. Boesak persisted, arguing that in his view Buthelezi's approach would "cause us tremendous problems as we go ahead to the future." When Koppel pressed Boesak about whether the

UDF was controlled by Communists, Boesak found himself on the defensive. "My opposition to apartheid is based on my Christian beliefs," said Boesak. "I do not believe in any form of Communism. . . . but if there is anyone in this country who is actually furthering the aims of Communism and making people believe that Communism ought to be looked at as a viable alternative, it is the government."

Though some criticized the format as forced and artificial, the *Nightline* broadcasts captured the attention of millions of Americans, introduced them to the complexities of the debate inside South Africa, ripped holes in the South African government's explanations, and brought new energy to divestment advocates in hundreds of institutions around the United States. Only a week later, on March 29, the South African government reinforced its repressive image by outlawing meetings of the United Democratic Front, AZAPO, COSAS, and twenty-six other opposition groups. The increased pace of violence in South Africa—combined with the ongoing demonstrations at the South African embassy—strengthened the sentiment in many organizations that in the absence of federal leadership some sort of response had to be made. Fierce debates among students, administrators, faculty, alumni, and staff erupted at universities across the nation. Students from the University of Wisconsin held a weeklong protest at the state capitol. Students at the University of California at Los Angeles and Rutgers University in New Jersey organized large sit-ins. Undergraduates at the University of Louisville in Kentucky, Oberlin College in Ohio, San Jose State University in California, and many others held rallies and demonstrations. To dramatize living conditions and forced removals in South Africa, students at Cornell University constructed a miniature shantytown, which fire marshals immediately condemned as unsafe.

At Columbia University, the violence in South Africa brought a sense of urgency to the student anti-apartheid organizers, who had been trying to provoke a response from the university trustees for nearly two years. In March 1983 a black undergraduate named Barbara Ransby had delivered such a stirring oration before the University Senate that the group had passed a divestment resolution on the spot. That summer, while the students were away, the university trustees rejected the resolution as "precipitous" and referred the matter to yet another committee, this one chaired by the dean of the college, Robert Pollack. After a year of testimony the committee remained deadlocked and could only recommend to the trustees that they freeze the university's South Africa–related holdings at thirty-nine million dollars. The undergraduates scoffed at their reasoning. "If the university's investments help South African blacks, why freeze?" asked one senior. "Why not increase the investments?"

To the students the endless ping-ponging between the senate and the trustees (five iterations in six years) proved a basic unwillingness to address the moral problem: the support American firms were giving to the Pretoria government and the apartheid economy. In March 1985, in an effort to raise the issue again, the leaders of the Coalition for a Free South Africa asked to meet with President Michael Sovern and several members of the board of trustees during their next meeting on March 30. When the activists were rebuffed, members of the steering committee announced that they would hold a hunger strike to obtain the meeting and to focus the trustees' attention. By Monday, April 1, the activist students were in a rage: not only had the trustees refused to meet with them, but reportedly one trustee had mocked their effort with the words "Let them go ahead and fast."

The steering committee planned a rally to support the fasters and to denounce the university on April 4, which was both Maundy Thursday and the anniversary of the assassination of Martin Luther King. The students also prepared a small act of civil disobedience: they would march a few hundred yards from the rally at the Sundial, the center of the campus, to the steps of Hamilton Hall and chain one of the entrances shut. On April 4, 1985, the student leaders were not surprised when more than five hundred students showed up. Their astonishment came later, when they marched to Hamilton Hall, chained the doors, sat down on the steps, and found more than a hundred fifty students sitting with them. All those on the steps pledged to stay until the university divested or arrested them. Their consternation deepened when the police did not show up. Whether Sovern and his colleagues were reluctant to have photographs of policemen clubbing Columbia students beamed across the nation, as they had been in 1968, or because they thought the students were not likely to stay very long, they decided to try to resolve the problem through a combination of negotiation, legal maneuvers, and threatened academic penalties.

By suppertime the students realized that they were likely to be there all night and possibly for several days. They immediately created a network to supply sleeping bags, food, and rain gear. Within forty-eight hours the students had posted a large banner renaming the building "Mandela Hall" and erected a huge tarpaulin that could be unfurled rapidly in the event of rain. The steering committee established a press office in a dorm room overlooking the small plaza where the students were encamped. With the help of a Kaypro-2 computer, printer, and multiple phone lines, the students began notifying reporters, churning out press releases, and publishing a daily newsletter. One student gained electronic access to the alumni lists on the university mainframe; within days the coalition had printed and mailed hundreds of personalized appeals for support. Down the hall another room was converted into the blockade's kitchen, where vats of coffee, tea, chili, and black bean soup bubbled on every available burner and emitted rich odors that filled the hallways.

On Easter Sunday, April 7, a rumor swept the blockaders that the university was about to call in the police. Leaders hurriedly repeated instructions about proper nonviolent civil disobedience. In fact, the university had been seeking a restraining order from the state supreme court in Manhattan barring the students from continuing to barricade the hall, which Justice Harold Baer Jr. granted that evening. In the past their dispute had been with the university; if they continued their blockade, they would now be defying New York State's judicial system. After intense discussions, the students decided to stay put. As soon as the students defied the court order, the *New York Times* began daily coverage of the blockade. The story had lots of attractive angles: the resurgence of activism at Columbia, the alma mater of student rebellion; the connection to the events in South Africa; and the symbolic tie to Martin Luther King. Moreover, as Columbia's administrators grumbled, it was easy for reporters to get up to the campus, cover the event, and be back to their Midtown offices in the same morning. The *New York Times* coverage in turn attracted reporters from wider and wider areas. As television crews and foreign journalists swung by, the university came under greater pressure not to call the police. Instead, university security officials started videotaping the demonstrators in order to identify them for disciplinary proceedings.

On Thursday, April 11, Columbia's students awoke to find a letter from President Sovern that had been slipped under their bedroom doors before dawn. The "Toothpaste Manifesto," as it was quickly dubbed, argued that the blockaders' actions were undermining their own goals. "The offenders are hurting not only Columbia but the struggle against apartheid itself," wrote Sovern. "The disrupters have, unfortunately, made it seem to many that we support South Africa's racist regime." He warned that the punishment for their behavior might be severe: the university had the right to suspend or expel them, and the state might find them in contempt of court.

Shortly after Sovern's letter appeared, the leaders of the student committee received letters threatening them with expulsion. Until that moment, most of the participants had believed that the only penalty they faced was symbolic arrest; the threat of expulsion, especially for juniors and seniors, was much more frightening. According to sociologist Eric L. Hirsch, an assistant professor at Columbia who studied the blockaders, the short-term effect of the threat was to strengthen their commitment and to polarize the students against the administration even more.

As the blockade entered its second week, it attracted international attention. Desmond Tutu sent a supportive cable noting, "We seek to change the vicious, unjust system peacefully and welcome your effort to have economic decisions be based on moral principles." The blockaders received endorsements from the hospital workers', autoworkers', teachers', and public employees' unions; from singers Peter Yarrow of Peter, Paul, and Mary, Pete Seeger, and Bono of U-2; and from the National Organization for Women, TransAfrica, and assorted literary celebrities. Students from other universities sent banners and flags decorated with supportive messages that were hung from the statues and windows of Hamilton Hall. Former student leaders from Columbia and other protests came and taught the blockaders their vintage chants. Local and national politicians including Ruth Messenger of the New York City Council and Jesse Jackson made pilgrimages to the Upper East Side to speak to the students. Phil Donahue invited several students and faculty on both sides of the issue to appear on his program on April 22.

As the days wore on, the blockading students developed a strong bond that broke down racial suspicions and barriers. "It was like you'd like it to be all the time," said one student, "black, white, everyone together; everyone shared." When students living in nearby dorms complained of nighttime noise, the blockaders agreed to impose a "quiet time" every night. When some students began to suffer from missing classes, others offered to serve as tutors. As the blockade reached the end of the third week, however, the students' persistence was waning. Throughout the blockade persons had joined the students for a night here and a night there, but now more and more were drifting away at dusk to seek the comfort of a warm bed and to prepare for rapidly approaching exams. The crisis atmosphere eroded and the university's refusal to negotiate while the blockade continued seemed insurmountable.

On Monday, April 22, Judge Burton S. Sherman of the New York State Supreme Court ordered the students to remove the chains and designated an area nearby where they could continue their protest if they wanted. "While the evil policy of apartheid is an affront to human rights, the narrow issue here is one of public safety," he wrote in his opinion. "The First Amendment does not permit the padlocking of a building which could result in endangering innocent lives." After consultation and debate, the students ended the blockade on April 25 by cutting the chains and marching with more than a thousand supporters for a rally at the Canaan Baptist Church in Harlem, where the pastor, former Martin Luther King associate Wyatt T. Walker, welcomed them as companions in the global battle for racial justice.

Three months after the blockade, in July 1985, the trustee Ad Hoc

Committee Regarding Investments in Companies with Operations in South Africa finally issued its report. Once again the trustees rejected total divestment, reiterating their faith in the power of economic growth to change South Africa. Instead they recommended a new series of reports, committees, panels, and public statements of opposition to apartheid. The trustees also endorsed federal sanctions legislation and a closer tie with the teacher pension fund, TIAA-CREF, for the first time. They noted that the fund had not divested but actively used its shareholder influence and that Columbia would be pouring over $100 million into the fund in the ensuing five years.

As the television crackled with pictures of township violence and student protests, university administrators across the country found themselves under increased pressure to act. After a visit to Harvard University in early 1985 by Desmond Tutu, in which he urged the university to divest, the call was taken up by a group of black faculty. The spring 1985 edition of a guide to American colleges published for black students criticized Harvard for its reluctance to address the South African question. Activist Harvard students announced the formation of an independent endowment fund, the Endowment for Divestment. Under the scheme students would place all future contributions to Harvard in the "E4D" escrow fund until the trustees divested. At the same time, a group of Harvard graduates announced that they were forming Harvard/ Radcliffe Alumni against Apartheid (HRAAA) and would sponsor their own candidates for election to the Harvard board of overseers, a thirty-member advisory body elected by the alumni. Though the president of the board of overseers, Joan T. Bok (no relation to Derek), publicly opposed the HRAAA candidates and included a mailing against their candidacy with the ballot to the alumni, one of them, Gay Seidman, was elected the next year.

On the anniversary of Martin Luther King's birthday, the same day as the launch of the Columbia blockade, more than five thousand students and faculty gathered in front of Memorial Church in Harvard Yard for an anti-apartheid protest. The principal speaker was Jesse Jackson, who excoriated the university. "South Africa is the economic prostitute of the Western world!" shouted Jackson. "Our churches, our universities, our government jump into bed with South Africa and make cheap love and cheap profits off of slave labor. They preach morality by day but reap economic gratification by night." Derek Bok reacted with indignation. "Jesse Jackson comes to a Harvard rally in a big black car that was made by a company doing business in South Africa," he grumbled to a reporter. "Jesse Jackson isn't divesting."

The continued pressure by all the activists from different constituencies at Harvard did not achieve the policy of divestment that they hoped for, but it was a factor in the selected divestments that did take place during that period. On February 14, 1985, Harvard announced that it was selling $1 million of stock in Baker International because of the firm's refusal to provide information on employment practices. Harvard also later sold $1.8 million in the Echlin Corporation because it refused to provide similar information (the chairman of Echlin commented afterward that he had not known that Harvard wanted information or that the university was planning to divest). The following year, the advisory committee voted to recommend the sale of $74.7 million in stocks and $84 million in bonds in Mobil, Texaco, Chevron, Exxon, and Ford because these companies refused to release information on whether they sold to the military and police. The companies, when informed of the move, objected that they were not permitted to release this information under South African law. Members of the Corporation Committee for Shareholder Responsibility reviewed the recommendation and the companies' objections and announced that they had decided to sell the stock. The legislation posed a "difficult dilemma," they noted in their semiannual report. "The university, however, cannot allow the South African government to succeed in thwarting the exercise of our ethical obligations as a shareholder."

Around the country, religious denominations and other groups also viewed the developments in South Africa with alarm. At the United Church of Christ, Audrey Chapman had been working for more than two years as both the elected chair of the Interfaith Center on Corporate Responsibility and the director of her denomination's social responsibility unit. After months of engaging corporate executives in discussion, she had achieved some important successes. In September 1983, after many years of refusal, BankAmerica announced that it would no longer make loans to the government of South Africa or to government corporations. In the two years after that achievement, however, Chapman held repeated meetings with representatives of twenty-two corporations and positive results were becoming more scarce. Though the church continued to file and vote for proxy resolutions, Chapman had a growing sense that the strategies of shareholder activism and dialogue with executives might have run their course. Corporations that were likely to respond to such actions had already done so. Chapman was also influenced by her contact with Desmond Tutu and with the representatives of the United Congregational Churches of Southern Africa, who were all pleading for American churches to take more forceful action.

A partial shift in favor of disinvestment and divestment took place at the fourteenth General Synod in 1983. The church delegates, Chapman later recalled, were gradually coming to believe that the issue was "not particular instances of corporate malpractice but a systemic problem." Corporations had no choice but to provide essential support to the state, she pointed out: they had to pay taxes; they had to obey the "national key points," laws which gave the state control over industrial facilities in the event of an emergency. "It was a whole web of relationships from which they could not escape. Once those of us within the church looked at it this way," she continued, "disinvestment and divestment began to make good sense."

In 1984 several interest groups within the United Church of Christ began to press more vigorously for the church to dump its stock. In October, the Commission on Racial Justice voted unanimously to recommend total divestment. The following month the eighth biennial convention of United Black Christians issued a similar call. A few weeks later the directors of the United Church Board for World Ministries voted to implement a program of selective divestment, which they later expanded to total divestment. By the time the delegates to the fifteenth General Synod met in July 1985, the South African government had declared a state of emergency and the nightly television news shows were filled with pictures of burning black townships.

In late June 1985, Allan Boesak flew from South Africa to Ames, Iowa, to attend the fifteenth General Synod of the United Church of Christ. Though the South African preacher's political and moral authority had been tarnished by his recent admission that he had had an affair with a white church worker, Boesak retained his ability to fire up a crowd. Appearing before the church delegates on July 1, Boesak read a statement calling for sanctions and disinvestment that had been approved by the South African Council of Churches only a few days before; then he put down his text and spoke directly to the delegates. "You will surely ask whether your action will make us suffer," he said. "But you will begin to understand if you learn, as a woman said on Friday in Johannesburg, that there is a difference between suffering in hopelessness and suffering with hope. You will begin to understand that the vision that we have is of a land of peace and justice." The next day, July 2, the delegates responded to Boesak's summons by voting to divest all United Church of Christ monies—more than half a billion dollars—from companies doing business in South Africa. They also approved the creation of an implementation committee to be formed of the representatives of all the different agencies who would oversee the completion of the divestment and would report back to the sixteenth General Synod in two years.

Two months later, the Episcopal Church took a similar step during its triennial General Convention. Pro-divestment activists, irritated that the

Committee on Social Responsibility in Investments had not forwarded a divestment resolution to the conference, bypassed the committee and brought their own resolution in favor of total divestment of all church monies—including the billion-dollar pension fund—directly to the floor of the House of Deputies. Opponents of the measure desperately maneuvered to water it down. The chairs of both the Executive Council and the Pension Committee pointed out that divestment of their stock would impede the use of shareholder resolutions. The pro-divestment activists argued that the time for discussions was over and that their most respected South African colleague, Desmond Tutu, whose address to the 1982 General Convention still rang in their ears, now supported disinvestment. They found a responsive audience among the delegates, who, according to one church administrator, were "frustrated by the resistance of corporations to engender serious change, by the deafness of the Reagan government, and by the intransigence of Pretoria. The national office had proposed an institutional maintenance resolution— let's just keep doing what we have been doing. But the deputies, many of whom were from the West, rose up and said no. They were completely unequivocal, saying 'You will divest. Period.' " With marching orders in hand, the Executive Council of the national church moved quickly to comply with the resolution. Within six months, the national church— though not the pension fund—had completely divested. As the chairs of the committees had predicted, proxy resolution activity shifted to other social issues and to seeking out alternative social investments.

The pension fund trustees, however, proved far more reluctant to act on what they viewed as a precipitous judgment by the delegates. The Pension Committee moved cautiously until, on February 19, 1986, Tutu's close friend Bishop John Spong of Newark, New Jersey, wrote to the trustees that unless they complied with the resolution of the General Convention, he would organize a separate escrow fund and encourage his clergy to deposit their retirement monies into it. Stung by the threat, the trustees met for two days in April before issuing a statement that seemed to announce changes but in fact affirmed their de facto policy. They declared that they would not hold the stock of any company that refused to sign the Sullivan Principles or that held a rating of less than 2; of any bank that made loans to the South African government; or in any firm "whose actions support that government, its military and police."

Though by the spring of 1985 dozens of universities, religious denominations, and foundations had decided to divest, sending the total value of divested stock into the hundreds of millions of dollars, these remained paltry sums in comparison to the monies controlled by cities and states in their regular and pension accounts, whose combined assets reached into hundreds of billions of dollars. Throughout the year, however, state and local government officials found themselves forced by events in Washington and Pretoria to articulate a South Africa policy. Dozens of bills, resolutions, and ordinances barring South African investments rippled through legislative committees and pension boards around the nation. In May the San Francisco City Retirement Board voted for gradual divestment of $335 million of securities in companies operating in South Africa; the following week the Florida Senate's Governmental Operations Committee voted to divest $1.8 billion in state investments over five years. A few months later the trustees of the $4 billion United Nations employee pension fund also voted to dump its South Africa–related stock.

In the state of New York, the battle over divestment had turned into a major partisan contest. The state comptroller, Edward V. Regan, was a second-term Republican, while the New York City comptroller, Harrison Goldin, was a third-term Democrat. The two had long been political opponents and had actually opposed each other in 1978 in the race for state comptroller, which Regan had won. Goldin's constituency in New York City included many African American voters. Edward Regan's constituency was the entire state, including millions of upstate conservatives. Goldin had a powerful ally in the Democratic governor, Mario Cuomo; Regan had equally powerful support from the Republican-controlled state Senate.

As comptroller for the state of New York, Regan's responsibilities included oversight of the governor's budget, control of state construction and service contracts, and the investment of public funds. Regan also had unusual power over the retirement system, for under state law he was also the sole trustee for the New York State Common Retirement Fund, a huge pension fund with nearly $23 billion in 1985. One of his first steps after taking office in 1979 was to create a broadly representative proxy committee to advise him how to vote on the shareholder resolutions that were pouring across his desk. At first, the proxy committee discussed every shareholder resolution separately, a process that required twenty-three meetings. The next year they streamlined their procedures, reaching agreement on overall policies and then discussing only those that represented changes or deviations.

The committee's deliberations demonstrated from the beginning that the members believed it appropriate for the comptroller to express his opinion on corporate behavior. In 1980, their first year of operation, they voted in favor of seventeen out of nineteen South African resolutions presented to them, including several nonexpansion proposals. The only two they rejected called for American firms to withdraw. For more than five years, Regan relied heavily on the determinations of the committee. If the committee had not yet discussed an issue before it came to a vote, Regan issued an order to abstain. He also rarely deviated from the recommendations he received: of 2,236 resolutions the committee reviewed from 1980 to 1988, Regan voted differently from the committee only six times.

In March 1984 New York State Senator Franz S. Leichter, a Democrat from Manhattan, announced that he would file a bill in the state legislature to require Regan's pension funds to divest. "I see no difference between what our companies are doing in South Africa and someone who, in 1930, would have said, 'I'm going to sell ovens to the Germans or invest in Krupp because they make such good armaments,'" Leichter told the *New York Times.* Regan objected. "The United Nations handles South Africa, not the retirement fund for a $12,000-a-year clerk," the state comptroller said. "You're talking about people . . . whose share in the retirement system is probably their number-one asset. I just don't think you use that, jeopardize that, to attempt to resolve a problem that is completely extraneous."

Regan's resistance deflected the problem for a year, during which the New York City pension fund resolution passed. In May 1985, the pressure on Regan intensified when Governor Cuomo and the Democratic speaker of the assembly announced their support for strong state divestment bills. Only a week before, Cuomo had shared the podium with Desmond Tutu at the graduation ceremony of the University of Rochester, where both men spoke and received honorary degrees. Tutu had thanked Americans in general and undergraduates in particular for the national wave of anti-apartheid protests and urged everyone present to apply more pressures to the Pretoria government. One week later Cuomo announced that he supported the divestment of all state monies. "I have concluded that New York State should adopt a comprehensive and responsible strategy," said Cuomo, "to demonstrate the abhorrence of our residents to the pernicious system of apartheid." Anticipating the comptroller's objection that he was not free to divest under the law, Cuomo added that "the comptroller's public responsibility for these investments appropriately can and should be described by the legislature by statute." Regan, on an official overseas trip, denounced the idea during a phone interview the next day from Tokyo. "We are not in the foreign policy business," he said. "Our main purpose is to keep the taxpayer costs as low as possible and to keep the fund as secure as possible. That's the purpose of a pension fund. Not to have the trustees decide what's current and in vogue."

As more large institutions, municipal governments, and state legislators passed measures restricting the stock they could own and the products they could buy, American firms with South African subsidiaries scrambled to respond. Faced with a souring South African economy and the potential loss of their largest customers in the United States, several companies opted to change course swiftly and quietly. Both the Bank of Boston and Morgan Guaranty announced bans on loans to South Africa rather than lose the business of the cities in which they were based. Perkin-Elmer, a manufacturer of specialized optical and electronic equipment, sold off its South African subsidiary. Pan American Airways suspended its flight service to South Africa. Motorola announced it would stop selling radios to the South African police. Ford Motor Company, citing the depressed South African automobile market, announced plans to merge with another firm into the South African Motor Corporation (SAMCOR).

Other companies looked for ways to become—or at least to appear to become—more active in supporting reform. In December 1984, representatives of one hundred and twenty Sullivan signatories met in New York at Leon Sullivan's request and agreed to expand the principles. Instead of focusing on changes within the workplace, the new goal would be to press the South African government to repeal all apartheid laws. In March the American Chamber of Commerce in South Africa publicly urged the South African government to end influx control and forced removals and to negotiate with those who were currently outlawed or banned. "I think South Africa has underestimated the disinvestment issue," said Franklin Lubke, chair of the Chamber of Commerce. "The time has come—and it may be too late—for the business community in the country to take a stand on discriminatory legislation." As the debate became more turbulent, the language used by corporations and their critics grew more confusing. While religious activists marshaled economic arguments about why companies should leave, executives increasingly used moral reasoning to defend their decisions to stay. Moreover, the pro-Sullivan and the pro-withdrawal camps often found it necessary to contradict not just each other but themselves. The proponents of disinvestment, for example, had to argue that if American companies remained in South Africa they would have little influence, but if they departed it would be a major blow. American executives argued the exact opposite: if the firms stayed, their influence would be great but if they departed the impact would be insignificant.

In an effort to demonstrate their sensitivity and commitment, American corporations announced a new burst of corporate philanthropy. Honeywell said that it would donate 250,000 rand a year for African education; Firestone promised to give a million. General Motors gave four million rand to the centrist, pro-business Urban Foundation, more than half of which was reserved for education. In April 1985 IBM, which had already given several million dollars for programs in various high schools, announced a five-year, twenty-million-rand program to enhance literacy among African children. The company said that it would provide 250 South African schools with computer-assisted education programs that would reach an estimated 37,000 elementary-age children each year. John Akers of IBM also set himself up as a leading proponent of remaining in South Africa. At the end of March, one week after the *Nightline* broadcasts, Akers published an opinion piece in the *New York Times.* "The debate over whether American companies should do business in South Africa has taken on new urgency," Akers wrote. "Some individuals say American firms there must now oppose apartheid more directly and publicly; others are pressuring them to withdraw fully." IBM's leaders had reviewed their policies, he said, and had decided to stay. Those who favor disinvestment "overestimate the economic and political impact such action would have on the government." Though "business people are not social reformers in disguise," Akers continued, "business activity does have profound social effects, direct and indirect, that enhance the climate for change."

Despite the efforts by Akers and the American Chamber of Commerce, pressure on U.S. firms grew month by month. On May 7, 1985, Leon Sullivan suddenly announced that he favored a moratorium on all economic expansion by U.S. corporations in South Africa. "A timetable is needed for conclusive action in South Africa. Lives are being lost daily and the nation is on the threshold of a revolution," he declared at a press conference. As a result, he no longer favored an open-ended corporate commitment to change. "If apartheid is not legally and actually ended within twenty-four months," Sullivan said, "there should be a total U.S. economic embargo against South Africa, including the withdrawal of all U.S. companies." Two weeks later, on May 20, the Interfaith Center on Corporate Responsibility responded to the call from the South African Council of Churches for increased economic pressures. At a press conference in New York City, Tim Smith, Audrey Chapman, and a host of other church leaders announced that fifty-four religious denominations and groups had banded together to push twelve key companies—Burroughs, Chevron, Citicorp, Control Data, Fluor, Ford, General Electric, IBM, Mobil, Newmont Mining, and Texaco—to quit South Africa. At the press conference, Randolph Nugent, general secretary of the General Board of Global Ministries of the United Methodist Church, told reporters that dialogue with most companies had failed. He then ran through the list of corporate targets: Mobil, Texaco, and Chevron had sold to the South African police and military and other government agencies; Burroughs, IBM, and Control Data computers had been purchased by many South African government agencies, helping them to "computerize apartheid"; Fluor had built South Africa's strategic oil-from-coal plant; Citibank made a range of public- and private-sector loans "indicating their faith in the future of a white ruled South Africa."

"Many of these companies will immediately defend their record by pointing to their reforms in the plant under the Sullivan principles," Nugent concluded. "That is increasingly an argument of convenience." Stepping to the microphone, Audrey Chapman amplified his point. "It is true that many of these twelve corporations have admirable workplace conditions and have made worthwhile educational and charitable contributions in South Africa," she said. "Such measures, however, cannot compensate for the major structural support and assistance these corporations either inadvertently or advertently have rendered to the apartheid system."

In South Africa, events continued to deteriorate as the state security machinery attempted once again to crush its enemies. The government banned meetings of the United Democratic Front, detained hundreds of its members, and finally charged dozens of top officials with treason. In April four local UDF leaders in the town of Cradock disappeared minutes after their release from a local police station; their charred bodies, with bullet holes in the back of their skulls, were found shortly afterward. A few months later, Victoria Mxenge, the lawyer and UDF official whose husband had been murdered a few years before, was shot to death in her home by an unknown assailant. As boycotts, demonstrations, and other disturbances rippled across the country, the South African police, bolstered by thousands of white soldiers from the SADF, rumbled repeatedly into the townships to suppress the unrest.

The violence across South Africa was not purely the result of police and military actions; conflict was also growing between the UDF and other African groups. Clashes between the UDF and AZAPO led to the deaths of several AZAPO members in May. Confrontations between members of the UDF and of Inkatha were even more severe. As the UDF grew in numbers and attacked Gatsha Buthelezi as a government stooge, the KwaZulu leader shoved back, arguing to everyone who would listen that Inkatha represented the logical middle ground between the brutality of the National Party and the radicalism of the African National Congress. Though Buthelezi searingly denounced Botha's new constitution, he also rejected the ANC's demand for one man, one vote in a unitary state. "No matter how much I deeply cherish this ideal," he told the KwaZulu legislature in May, "I know that at this point in our history whites will be driven to grave acts of desperation if we tried to ram this solution down their throats." The verbal sparring between Inkatha and the UDF quickly turned murderous at the local level. Inkatha toughs repeatedly struck at UDF gatherings; in one particularly bloody incident during a memorial service for Victoria Mxenge, hundreds of Inkatha men armed with clubs and spears attacked the mourners and killed seventeen people.

Week by week more townships rose in rebellion. A complex system of street committees sprang up, each of which elected representatives to a wider body, giving township civic associations rapid access to the grassroots. Some associations encouraged residents to stop paying their rents, forcing the government to cover the cost of all basic government services. Others organized boycotts of white stores. One boycott in the Eastern Cape, led by the Port Elizabeth Black Civic Organization (PEBCO), was so effective that it eliminated more than eighty percent of white store owners' revenue. After lengthy negotiations with PEBCO to end the boycott, the heads of the white Chamber of Commerce issued a public manifesto calling for common citizenship, the removal of discriminatory legislation, and the participation of blacks in government and business. Though the boycotts were widely supported, bands of "comrades"—teenage boys who saw themselves as enforcers—took to roaming through some urban areas, beating and intimidating citizens into compliance. The comrades also saw themselves as the guardians of revolutionary justice. As alternative "people's courts" popped up in the townships, the comrades played bailiff and administered punishments. Sometimes they also acted as judge and jury. In some areas their undisciplined zeal triggered a response by older and more conservative vigilante groups.

Oliver Tambo and the other ANC leaders in exile watched the growing rebellion with a mixture of delight and incredulity: finally, after more than thirty years, it seemed as though the African population had decided to overturn apartheid themselves. Meeting at a rare consultative conference in Kabwe, Zambia, in June 1985, the ANC leaders decided that if they wanted to avoid being overtaken by events, they needed to impose their leadership swiftly on this incipient revolution. At the end of the conference, Joe Modise, the commander of Umkhonto, announced a change in military strategy. Instead of pursuing selected targets as a form of "armed propaganda," the ANC would broaden its attacks into a "people's war." This meant shifting to softer targets, including facilities used by white civilians, and training large numbers of people to use hand grenades and homemade petrol bombs. Oliver Tambo, speaking several weeks later, explained that the military effort was only one piece of a larger strategy that included diplomatic efforts, economic sanctions, and other pressures, whose goal was to make apartheid unworkable and the country ungovernable.

One aspect of the strategy that quickly led to violence was the effort to persuade municipal officials and employees in the townships to resign. Throughout the year, local councilors were denounced, harassed, and attacked. Five hundred black policemen, who were widely despised as collaborators, saw their houses bombed or burned. In March the home of the Reverend Sam Buti, a minister in the Coloured Sendingkerk and the mayor of Alexandra township, was firebombed. After the massacre at Uitenhague, a township mob invaded the home of a town councilor named T. B. Kinikini and hacked him, his son, and two nephews to death; seconds before he died, Kinikini shot and killed another son to prevent him from suffering a similar fate. Soon the vengeful gangs found a new, more gruesome tool of execution. They would fill the inner rim of an automobile tire with gasoline, place the "necklace" over the head of a victim, and set the tire afire. During the funeral for Victoria Mxenge, a hapless soldier from the Ciskeian army happened to drive his pickup truck into the funeral crowd. Angry youths forced him from the vehicle, chased him down, stoned him to death, and necklaced his corpse.

Such killings horrified many people, especially Desmond Tutu, whose pastoral duties in 1985 consisted primarily of conducting township funerals. On one occasion mourners grabbed a black onlooker and announced that he was a police informer. As they prepared to burn the man on top of his car, Tutu rushed forward and saved him. The scene was captured by an Associated Press photographer, and the next day millions of Americans saw on the front page of the *New York Times* the image of Tutu grappling with the crowd. Ten days later in the township of Duduza, on the eastern Rand, an enraged mob attacked a young mother in full view of several television cameras. When they accused her of being an informer, she took flight. A group of men chased her down, tore her clothes off, stoned her into unconsciousness, rammed a broken bottle up her vagina, and set her body afire. When Tutu learned of the murder, he exploded with indignation. Speaking a few days later to a crowd of thirty thousand at yet another burial, Tutu implored the crowd to avoid violence. "I condemn in the strongest possible terms what happened in Duduza," he said. "Our cause is just and noble. That is why it will prevail and bring victory to us." If such a thing ever happened again, he warned, "I will find it difficult to speak for the cause of liberation. If the violence continues, I will pack my bags, collect my family, and leave this beautiful country that I love so passionately."

As violence spread through South Africa and divestment measures piled up across the United States, Republicans in Congress scrambled to find an effective response to the more than twenty bills that had been filed against South Africa. Efforts to persuade the White House to change course had failed. Though the president had made a few more noises about his discontent with apartheid and had met with Gatsha Buthelezi at the White House in February, neither he nor Secretary of State George Shultz showed any sign of altering their policy. Military actions by the South African government almost immediately undermined their faith. In May the Angolan army captured two South African soldiers who had been sent, disguised as members of UNITA, to sabotage Angola's oil facilities in the Cabinda enclave, a tiny patch of land on the northern border of the country. Three weeks later South African Defence Force commandos struck at an ANC house in Gabarone, the capital of Botswana, killing twelve people, including two domestic workers and a six-year-old-child. An irritated Shultz instantly recalled Ambassador Herman Nickel in protest.

By the middle of the spring Richard Lugar and Nancy Kassebaum had come to doubt that the administration's calm assurances would be enough politically to sustain Republican support in the Senate—and that they had better offer an alternative or risk being overtaken by events. On April 24 the two Republicans, joined by Senator Robert Dole of Kansas and Charles Matthias of Maryland, filed their own bill, which would impose sanctions on South Africa if apartheid did not disappear within two years. The bill was designed to block a much stronger measure filed by Senators Edward Kennedy and Lowell Weicker that would instantly impose restrictions on new investment, computer sales, and the import of Krugerrands. Lugar and Kassebaum pushed their bill through the Senate Foreign Relations Committee in early June. The next day, despite a strongly worded letter of opposition from George Shultz, the House version of the Kennedy-Weicker bill passed the House of Representatives in a vote of 295 to 127. "It is time for us as a nation to put our beliefs into action," said Representative William H. Gray III, the chief sponsor of the House bill, during the floor debate. "Do we stand with the victims or do we stand with the aggressors?"

At the State Department, Chester Crocker watched the growing controversy over his policies with dismay. For four years he had built and nurtured his strategy on the premise that political reform could not come to South Africa until *after* the regional conflicts in southern Africa had been resolved. His critics had ignored the progress he had made toward regional peace and were now unfairly demanding that constructive engagement be judged exclusively in terms of its effect on ending apartheid. South Africa's leaders detected the shift and complained. For years they had believed that the primary focus of the Reagan administration was on eliminating the Cubans from Angola and bringing an end to the Namibian occupation. Botha's internal reforms had all been met with diplomatic purring from the United States. The priorities were now apparently being reversed. As Crocker noted in his memoirs, he and his assistants "gradually lost the ability to tell South African officials with a straight face that their cooperation on Namibia, Angola, or Mozambique would make any difference to the domestic debate over sanctions."

Resistant to the idea that his strategy had failed, Crocker deprecated the motives and reasoning of his critics. South Africa became, in his biting words, "the last remaining land of white hats and black hats, a Manichean playground for underemployed Western activists on the right and left . . . a mother lode of icons and symbols. . . . American politicians, officials, pundits, businessmen, journalists, church leaders, and trade unionists found themselves dealing with something white hot." Their actions were an exercise in sanctimony, he thought, because they could establish the purity of their credentials on racial questions without incurring any costs to themselves. It was, Crocker said at the time, "the moral equivalent of a free lunch."

Whatever Crocker's view, the protests against his policies showed no signs of abating. After eight months there were still daily pickets and arrests in front of the South African embassy. As of July 1985 there had been more than twenty-nine hundred arrests, including twenty-three members of Congress. On July 11 the Senate crushed a filibuster attempt by Jesse Helms and passed a sanctions bill. While weaker than the version already approved by the House, the Senate version banned bank loans and made the Sullivan Principles mandatory. Crocker bristled at the congressional intrusion, which he felt would only weaken his hand. Nor had the South African government been much help. "Pretoria's ministers of brutality, perversity, stupidity, and bad-timing . . . actively facilitated foreign media coverage of township unrest," Crocker later wrote, "imagining that the TV footage would help their cause by focusing on the 'terrorists and hoodlums' causing the violence, and not on the police and defense forces conducting their heavy-handed township sweeps."

On July 20 P. W. Botha and his security officials took an even more heavy-handed step: they declared a state of emergency in thirty-six magisterial districts and conferred almost unlimited powers on the police and military to establish curfews; to search any vehicle or home; and to detain and interrogate anyone without charges or trial. The regulations decreed that no civil or criminal proceedings could be brought against the state, or any person acting in the service of the state, as the result of the regulations. Within a few days General P. J. Coetzee, the commissioner of police, used his new authority to squash the mass funerals which had become a rallying point for resistance. Funerals could not be held for more than one person at a time, he declared, and must be conducted indoors. Only ordained ministers of religion could speak; they could not use a public address system; and they must not "defend, attack, criticize, propagate, or discuss any form of government, any principle or policy of a government of a state; any boycott action; the existence of a state of emergency; or any action of a force or member of a force."

Within four days of the emergency, the South African government announced that it had used its new authority to detain 665 people. The declaration of the state of emergency destroyed the illusion that conditions in South Africa were improving. Senate majority leader Howard Baker and Senator Robert Dole reported to the White House that anti–South Africa sentiment was so strong in both houses of Congress that sanctions legislation, if vetoed, might draw enough support for an override. The administration would have to do something different or else risk losing control of American policy toward the region. The White House tried to respond with symbolic gestures. "We are very disturbed by the violence that is occurring in South Africa," said White House spokesperson Larry Speakes three days after Botha's announcement, adding that the South African government "bears a considerable responsibility at this time" for the disturbances. Shortly afterward the United States departed from its usual support for South Africa in the United Nations by abstaining on a French Security Council resolution calling for an end to the state of emergency.

Shultz and Crocker recognized that these gestures could be dismissed by the South African government as gestures of appeasement for the administration's domestic critics. A stronger communication would be needed. The opportunity came on August 2, when Shultz received an urgent request from Pik Botha for a meeting to discuss what lay ahead. The foreign minister told Shultz that P. W. Botha was considering making a dramatic speech in mid-August at the annual meeting of the National Party in Natal; it would be helpful, the foreign minister intimated, if he had some strong words from the United States to help counteract the hardliners in the South African cabinet. Crocker and Shultz conferred with Robert McFarlane, the president's national security adviser, and persuaded him to lead the delegation.

On April 8, 1985, McFarlane, Nickel, and Crocker met with Pik Botha in Vienna. McFarlane, whose father had been a member of Congress and who understood the passion that was building on Capitol Hill, laid out the domestic political situation bluntly. Sanctions would pass through Congress no matter what Reagan did, he said, unless the South Africans offered some "substantial concessions," such as ending the state of emergency and releasing Nelson Mandela. "I don't think Pik really expected me to present as bleak a picture as I did on the inevitability of sanctions," McFarlane commented later. "He thought I was Ronald Reagan's soulmate, and so he expected me to be a little less severe and more forgiving." Botha responded by reassuring the Americans that the reform program was on track and that the August 15 speech would carry immensely important news. Botha sketched a glowing image of what his president might say: the creation of an elected advisory body for Africans, the end of influx control, perhaps even the release of Mandela. While Nickel and Crocker stayed on for further discussions, McFarlane returned to the White House and reported to Reagan that the prospects for dramatic change were good. Over the next week an amazing process of magnification took place, as more and more diplomats and politicians whispered excitedly about what was going to happen. The process was augmented by the press. Journalists wrote stories about the imminent change in South African policy. *Newsweek* said that Botha would announce a program of power sharing with blacks; *Time* breathlessly predicted that Botha would make "the most important statement since Dutch settlers arrived at the Cape three hundred years ago." Though U.S. Representative Stephen Solarz emerged from a meeting with P. W. Botha on August 12 unimpressed by what the state president had told him, the drumbeat of expectation drowned him out. When Botha finally stepped to the microphone in front of a huge sign reading "Suid Afrika Eerst" (South Africa First), his words and image were transmitted live via American television from Durban directly into the homes and offices of corporate executives, trustees, bishops, members of Congress, governors, and other leaders around the United States and across the world. Unbeknownst to him, he commanded at that moment the largest and most important audience of his life, most of whom were eager for him to seize the initiative and lift South Africa into a new era.

Instead, the speech was a complete disaster. Though Botha began with a few hopeful-sounding phrases, including the assertion that the government had "crossed the Rubicon of reform" by accepting the permanence of Africans in the urban areas, he quickly ruled out any major changes. The homelands would remain; a fourth chamber of parliament for Africans would not be "practical"; and Mandela would not be released unless he agreed to a set of restrictive conditions. Warming to his conservative audience, Botha turned his moderate text into a finger-wagging harangue. "I am not prepared to lead white South Africans and other minority groups on a road to abdication and suicide!" he said. "Listen, my friends. Destroy white South Africa and our influence in this subcontinent of southern Africa and this country will drift into factions, strife, chaos and poverty!" The only alternative to the policy he had advanced, argued Botha, was "bloodshed, turmoil, and murder." Referring to the months of unrest and the declaration of the state of emergency, Botha complimented himself on his restraint. "I have applied much self-discipline during the past few weeks and months," he said to the world. "I have been lenient and patient. Don't push us too far." He thumbed his nose at the United States and all others who were considering sanctions. "We have never given in to outside demands, and we are not going to do so now. South Africa's problems will be solved by South Africans and not by foreigners." He concluded with a warning. "Those who prefer revolution to reform will not succeed. They will not succeed. If necessary we will use stronger measures. But they will not succeed!"

McFarlane, watching Botha's "Rubicon" speech from the president's home in Santa Barbara, recoiled in disgust. "I was less affected by the substance than by the delivery," he commented later. "I don't know when I have been more moved by such blatant hypocrisy." McFarlane immediately arranged a conference call with the secretary of state, who was at his home in Palo Alto, and with Chester Crocker.

"Did you have the same reaction that I did?" asked McFarlane.

"Yeah, it was pretty bad," replied Shultz.

McFarlane told the two men that Botha had reminded him more than anything of Bull Connor in Birmingham. "Apart from the substance of the speech," asked McFarlane, "were you struck that he didn't mean a thing he was saying?"

"Yes," said Shultz. "I got the same impression."

The men concluded that Botha was, in McFarlane's words, a "mean-spirited son of a bitch" and that the South African government had deliberately deceived the Americans in Vienna. "The visual expression of hypocrisy was what turned me around on the question of sanctions," McFarlane recalled. "Whenever you engage in a negotiation with any country and you are being deceived . . . you can't tolerate that. You have to send a shot across the bow. You have to make it clear that you are dealing with the United States and we don't tolerate deception and hypocrisy. . . . It was insulting." Shultz and McFarlane agreed that some sort of congressional sanctions were now inevitable; the only possible alternative was for the president to seize the initiative by implementing his own. After he hung up, McFarlane called his deputy John Poindexter back at the White House and asked him to help Crocker and NSC staff member Fred Wettering draw up a list of sanctions Reagan might be able to impose by executive order right after Labor Day.

McFarlane was not the only one who had been shocked by Botha's speech. Richard Lugar predicted immediately afterward that a compromise would be reached on the House and Senate legislation and that sanctions against South Africa would soon be passed. Governor Thomas Kean of New Jersey, a Republican who had long opposed the divestment bills that had been passed by his legislature, was so disgusted by the speech that he announced he had changed his mind and would now approve a law requiring divestment of the state's ten-billion-dollar public employee pension fund. "There are instances in human history," said Kean, "when the gravity of an evil is so clear, and the cost of its continuance so great, that governments—at every level—must use every tool at their disposal to combat it."

The speech had a similar effect on thousands of city council members, state legislators, and other elected officials. The trustees of Columbia University, after rejecting divestment in the aftermath of the student blockade, suddenly reversed themselves and announced that they would sell all their stock. "The recommendation comes in the wake of the dramatic change in the situation in South Africa," read a statement issued by the trustees. "After raising hopes for significant reforms in the apartheid structure, the South African Government has dashed them. It has moved ruthlessly to buttress the existing system." After the motion passed, President Sovern issued his own statement: "Divestment strengthens our condemnation of apartheid," he said. "It is the right course for us at this time and so we are taking it." In the next few months, another dozen cities and states passed divestment or selective purchasing ordinances. The State University of New York announced its intention to divest on September 24. When Rutgers followed suit, James Burke, the chairman of Johnson & Johnson, resigned his seat on the Rutgers board of trustees because his firm had a large subsidiary in South Africa. Even the South African ambassador to the United States was taken aback by the "firestorm" of negative reaction to Botha's speech. Chester Crocker was characteristically blunt: the Rubicon speech, he told reporters a few weeks later, had been "a public relations disaster."

Not everyone was willing to abandon Pretoria. The leaders of the American right wing, prompted by Jesse Helms in the Senate and by White House communications director Patrick Buchanan, struggled to launch a counterattack. Their main target was Desmond Tutu, who predicted shortly after the speech that South Africa "was on the brink of a catastrophe" and who refused to join an Anglican delegation that met with P. W. Botha on the grounds that Botha would use the meeting as evidence that Tutu supported his reforms. The Reverend Jerry Falwell, the head of the right-wing Moral Majority lobbying group, was leading a nine-person tour of South Africa at the time of the Rubicon speech. After meeting with P. W. Botha on August 19, Falwell announced his support for the South African president's policies. South Africa was "a country that is making progress and is a friend of the West," Falwell told a news conference in Pretoria. Americans did not understand the truth about South Africa's "tribal system" and did not realize what a reformer P. W. Botha was, he insisted. When he returned to the United States, Falwell promised, he would throw the resources of the Moral Majority into opposing sanctions and disinvestment. Falwell promised to lobby against sanctions legislation in Congress, to urge "millions of Christians to buy Krugerrands," and "to go into a million homes . . . to present our cause."

Though Falwell and conservative activist Richard Viguerie both promised to "move heaven and earth" to persuade Congress to support a presidential veto, their effort floundered as soon as Falwell returned to the United States. In his daily cartoon strip *Doonesbury,* Garry Trudeau skewered Falwell's plans for a campaign to promote investment in South Africa by showing the portly clergyman leading a fictional pro–South African concert called "Apart-Aid." Falwell also got scorched when he challenged the moral authority of Desmond Tutu. Within twenty-four hours of his meeting with P. W. Botha, Falwell was back in Washington, D.C., where he told American reporters that during his five-day visit to South Africa he had not met a single South African who favored sanctions. What about Bishop Tutu? one journalist asked. "If Bishop Tutu maintains that he speaks for the black people of South Africa," Falwell sniffed, "he is a phony." An avalanche of criticism engulfed Falwell, and within three days he had issued a public apology.

A few days later, President Reagan, who was still on vacation at his mountaintop ranch in California, gave an interview with an Atlanta radio station in which he was asked about South Africa. Reagan's response could have been written by the South African embassy. South Africa faced serious problems, the president said, because "the black majority of South Africa is a combination of minorities." The National Party government was "reformist" and had produced important results. "They have eliminated the segregation that we once had in our own country, the type of thing where hotels and restaurants and places of entertainment and so forth were segregated," Reagan said blithely. "That has all been eliminated." Blacks could join trade unions, buy property in white areas, and operate businesses in downtown communities, Reagan insisted. When asked about the internal unrest in South Africa, the president said that "for us to believe that the Soviet Union is not, in its usual style, stirring up the pot . . . [would] be very innocent and naive." When asked about Jerry Falwell's comments on Bishop Tutu, Reagan said that Falwell had been trying to point out that Tutu was not universally supported and had simply chosen the wrong word.

Within minutes of the president's interview the White House press office churned out a ream of clarifications. The president did not really believe that all segregation had been eliminated; he knew that it still existed for buses, restrooms, schools, parks, beaches, and housing; his reference to the Soviet Union concerned Mozambique and Angola, not South Africa; and so on. Even Reagan later publicly retracted his statement and apologized for being "careless" in his language. The damage, however, had been done. The South African pro-government press instantly interpreted Reagan's remarks as support for Botha's policies, including the state of emergency.

To Chester Crocker, the turn of events could not have been more frustrating. In addition to battling the sanctions moves in Congress, he had to work to undo the effect of right-wing ideologues at the top of the American government. In an attempt to clear up the growing contradictions in the American position, Crocker called reporters in for a special background briefing. Pretoria's reforms were welcome, he said, but they were not adequate, and they had contributed to the violence and polarization that swept the country. P. W. Botha's efforts to defuse tension had not only failed, they had made matters worse. The government needed to commit itself to negotiation and to ending apartheid.

By this time, however, control of American policy toward South Africa had been temporarily removed from Crocker's hands. On Thursday, September 5, Secretary of State George Shultz met with Republican leaders in Congress, who told him that the sanctions bill, which was scheduled for a vote the following week, would pass with such overwhelming margins that it could not be vetoed. The only way the president could avoid this, they told Shultz, would be to introduce his own administrative sanctions. This might give them the margin they needed to sustain a veto and kill the legislation. Shultz carried their message back to the White House, where he and McFarlane laid out the political realities for Reagan at a formal meeting of the National Security Council. Showing him the vote counts, they urged him to reverse course and impose some sort of sanctions on Pretoria. Reluctantly, the president agreed. On September 9 Reagan announced from the Oval Office that by executive order he was banning the sale of computers to South Africa and implementing most of the other sanctions in the Lugar bill.

Within hours of the president's statement, Senate Republicans pushed through a measure to postpone consideration of all sanctions legislation for several months. Democratic senators argued vigorously that they should go ahead and pass the Lugar bill to ensure that Reagan did what he said he was going to do. When all forty-seven Democrats in the Senate tried to force consideration of the conference report, Robert Dole walked to the front of the Senate chamber and quietly asked the parliamentarian to return the report to Senator Lugar. Lugar stuck the bill in his coat pocket and left the floor. When the Democrats demanded again to consider the bill, Dole replied that since the document was no longer on the clerk's desk, it could not be discussed. Ted Kennedy, sputtering with fury, denounced Dole and Lugar for "trickery beneath the dignity of the Senate."

In their conversations with reporters, administration officials worked hard to insist that their reversal was not a rejection of the policy of constructive engagement. Reagan explained at one point that his new policy should be thought of as "active constructive engagement." Shultz said that the policy was designed to return control of foreign policy to the executive branch and send "a single message to the government of South Africa and the people of South Africa on behalf of all Americans." Chester Crocker gamely went along. "I'm smiling ear to ear," Crocker told reporters on the day of Reagan's announcement. "I'm hoping that we can now lance the misperception about the Administration's policy."

Despite the verbal fireworks that followed the Rubicon speech, its most dramatic effect was not political but economic. The South African economy had been struggling for months: inflation was running high, the prime interest rate had bounced up to twenty-four percent, military expenditures were busting the budget, consumer markets remained sluggish, export sales had slumped, and the overall annual growth rate had slipped to −1 percent. The outburst of violence had forced business confidence into a tailspin, deterring foreign investors from sending money in and prompting domestic investors to ship it out. To counteract these effects, the chairman of the South African Reserve Bank, Gerhard de Kock, had encouraged South African corporations and parastatals to borrow money on the international capital markets. On the surface, this made sense: South Africans could borrow abroad at much lower interest rates than were available at home. The South Africans did not seem to notice or care that the international bankers were steadily shortening the terms of the loans. When the rioting broke out, South African executives and government officials suddenly found themselves trapped. They had borrowed billions of rand short-term and invested the money in long-term projects. By 1985 South Africa had accumulated thirty-four billion rand in short-term obligations, making up fifty-seven percent of its total foreign debt. No one in South Africa had worried about this. Whenever such loans had come due in the past, the South Africans had applied for and received more, enabling them to pay off the old loans with new funds. Everything had worked beautifully as long as the international banks continued rolling over the debt, which they had, year after year, through every upheaval since the National Party had taken power.

Two weeks before the Rubicon speech, however, one bank balked. On July 31, Willard Butcher, the chairman of Chase Manhattan, a bank under increasing pressure from New York City and other institutional investors, announced that his firm would not roll over its $500 million loan to South Africa; when the loan came due, the bank would ask to be repaid. The reason for the bank's decision was not political, Butcher said, but part of a normal cycle of assessing its international debt. Butcher's action triggered the global equivalent of a bank run. Executives at Bankers Trust, Manufacturers Hanover, Security Pacific, and other American banks that had been willing to lend to South Africa suddenly announced that they were now reluctant to do so. One major bank dropped South Africa's credit rating overnight from B to D, only one up from the bottom. Only Citibank, the largest lender to South Africa, said that it would continue to extend credit. Citibank president John Reed was reported to be furious at Butcher. "They got their money," said one Citibank official, "but it was at our expense."

The severity of the crisis became apparent when Barclays Bank announced that according to its calculations South Africa was being asked to repay more than South Africa had in its gold and foreign exchange reserves. The South African Reserve Bank, faced with an immediate bill of more than $400 million, began desperately buying dollars. The more dollars it bought, the more the rand skidded in value. This process was already two weeks old when Botha delivered the Rubicon speech; within twenty-four hours of the speech, the value of South Africa's currency plummeted, wiping out a huge percentage of the dollar value of the shares on the Johannesburg stock exchange. Capital flooded out of the country at an uncontrollable rate. De Kock got on the phone and pleaded with bankers around the world, but he found that only the West Germans and the Swiss were willing to keep their loans steady.

Their support was not enough. By the end of August, the rand had fallen to thirty-four cents to the dollar—its lowest point ever. Even at such a sharp discount, money continued to flood out of the country. Nor could the government hope that the unrest throughout the country would tail off. Despite the efforts of the police and military to suppress dissent, boycotts, demonstrations, and other disturbances continued. In the last week of August the newspapers detailed plans for a UDF march on Pollsmoor Prison, where Allan Boesak and others intended to call for the release of Mandela. On Tuesday, August 27, the day before the march, plainclothes police arrested Boesak at a roadblock and took him to jail. That evening, after the stock markets had closed, Finance Minister Barend du Plessis announced that he had suspended trading on the stock and currency markets for five days. "These steps have been taken so that South Africa can continue to meet all international obligations," du Plessis announced. The move had been made necessary by "abnormal pressure that has arisen over the past week on the capital account of South Africa's balance of payments as a result of reasons unrelated to the healthy underlying conditions in the country."

To attempt to reverse the decisions by foreign banks, du Plessis dispatched Gerard de Kock to Europe and the United States to plead South Africa's cause. Though de Kock had global experience and had been well regarded by international bankers during his term as a director of the International Monetary Fund, the South African was shocked by what he found. Over thirteen days he visited nineteen private banks, four central banks, the International Monetary Fund, and the U.S. State Department. In each place he pleaded for an emergency loan to help tide South Africa through its financial crisis. Instead of the understanding he expected, de Kock found only cold discomfort. Facing their own rising political pressures, South Africa's former financial allies wished to have nothing to do with the pariah state. The year before, complained du Plessis, he could have borrowed a billion dollars overnight; now he could not get a cent.

South Africa's sudden and unexpected fragility in the face of its international credit crisis changed many people's assumptions about the power of economic measures to affect apartheid. Newspaper stories popped up suggesting that the South African economy might indeed be "the Achilles' heel of apartheid." Anti-apartheid activists in the United States expressed their delight at the collapse of the notion of South African invulnerability. "The spectacle of the central banker rushing around Western capitals with cap in hand," wrote British journalist Anthony Sampson, "hardly accorded with the proud Afrikaner legend of defying foreign critics by retreating 'back into the *laager.*'" Even South African business writers recognized the bitter irony of what had happened. "Those whom the far Left would call apartheid's best friends," wrote Nigel Bruce, the editor of the conservative newspaper *Business Day,* "have hit us where it hurts most."

After de Kock's return to South Africa he, du Plessis, and P. W. Botha had to face the grim truth: without more money they would not be able to pay back the loans as they came due. On September 1, du Plessis announced that "the large scale withdrawal of existing credit lines has in the short term placed in jeopardy our ability as a country to repay all these foreign loans." As a result, his government had decided to freeze the repayment of all loans for four months. Under the "standstill" arrangement, banks would continue to receive their interest, but the repayment of principal would have to be negotiated. The finance minister also said that he was reinstating a dual exchange system for South Africa's currency. Persons who wished to import or export capital could do so only through the "financial rand," which would be traded at a value lower than the regular or "commercial" rand. This would increase the incentives for people to bring investment money into South Africa and the impediments for those wanting to take it out.

Having defaulted on the terms of its loans, the South African government now had to contend with a herd of skittish, angry bankers. For assistance the South Africans turned to Fritz Leutwiler, the former president of the Swiss National Bank, and asked him to mediate between Pretoria and its creditors. Leutwiler checked with the president of Switzerland, who approved his involvement, in part because Switzerland's largest banks had outstanding loans to South Africa. Leutwiler discovered that before he could resolve the problems with South Africa he had to contend with arguments among the banks. "The Europeans were furious with Chase and other Americans for beginning the panic," wrote one observer. "The Swiss and Germans criticized the British for political bias; while the Swiss were blamed as usual for making money out of the crisis." Leutwiler announced that the first general meeting with the twenty-nine principal creditor banks would take place in London on October 23. The South Africans arrived and said that they simply could not be expected to pay $14.3 billion within a single year. Moreover, they argued, as they were now increasingly inclined to do on the international stage, that unless the West supported South Africa it would be blacks, not whites, who would suffer. Finance Minister du Plessis stressed South Africa's vital and benevolent effect on the entire region; if the South African economy crumbled, he argued, it would take the entire region down with it.

The central question that faced Leutwiler and his unruly crowd was whether and to what extent the bankers would impose political conditions on the South African government as part of the debt agreement. Traditionally bankers insist that they would never do so, but when billions of dollars in loans have been jeopardized by the political decisions of a particular government, the lines between economic and political decisions disappear. Regardless of political ideology, a country that can maintain a stable domestic climate, a steady currency, and a good credit rating will find the international banking community ready to lend. When those factors slip, the international financial community— whether through private banking consortia or mechanisms like the World Bank or the International Monetary Fund—imposes both political and economic conditions. South American countries that had run up large international debts in the early 1980s were already beginning to discover the painful truth that national sovereignty required solvency.

Though the bankers were reluctant to impose political conditions on South Africa, they found that they could not escape the uncomfortable global spotlight. Trevor Huddleston, the president of the British anti-apartheid movement, wrote to the bankers asking them not to attend the meeting. Beyers Naudé, who since his release from his banning order had been serving as general secretary of the South African Council of Churches, wrote a letter with Desmond Tutu asking the banks to "make rescheduling of South Africa's debt conditional upon the resignation of the present regime and its replacement by an interim government responsive to the needs of all South Africa's people." Robert McNamara, former president of the World Bank, urged the bankers to point out how much easier it would be to lend money to a country that was in the process of negotiating a stable future with the black majority. Even the South Africans realized that the economic and political were inextricably linked. When the October meeting of the bankers broke up without an agreement, the chairman of the South African Reserve Bank blamed it on politics. "Looking at this as an economist you would say there was no problem," de Kock said the following week in Pretoria, "but because of political considerations it was a very difficult meeting to handle. The banks can't be seen as helping South Africa because it would be seen as propping up apartheid."

Throughout the fall of 1985 and into the first months of 1986, a perception grew across the United States that the tools of economic persuasion—selective purchasing, divestment, disinvestment, and credit restrictions—were having an effect on South Africa. The American stock markets, fueled by a frenzy of mergers, takeovers, and leveraged buyouts, boomed. The assets of many institutional investors rocketed up by twenty or more percent a year. Funds that divested their stock from companies doing business in South Africa seemed to grow as rapidly as those that didn't. In this heady financial environment, the debate over South Africa shifted from whether divestment would cause a fund to lose money to whether it would cause one to forgo some ineffable extra profit. This mollified trustees who worried about their legal vulnerability; few investors were likely to sue because their large gains were not larger. Moreover, every institution that joined the divestment bandwagon established another precedent and reduced the barriers for the next one to follow suit.

Despite the president's attempt to recapture the initiative on South Africa through his administrative sanctions, divestment bills rapidly piled up in city councils and state legislatures all over the nation. In New York State, comptroller Edward Regan came under intense and rising pressure from both the governor and the legislature to do something about the billions of dollars of pension investments he controlled. With the support of his Republican counterparts in the New York State Senate, Regan had been able to stop several divestment bills, but he knew that the political dike would not hold forever. In the weeks before the Rubicon speech, Regan had traveled to Washington to encourage the White House to remove the heat from Republican state officials by acting more firmly against South Africa. Only days before the imposition of the president's administrative sanctions, Regan again called for stronger leadership from the White House. "There is a perceived vacuum in our nation's policy . . . created by the failure of Washington to assume its proper responsibility of formulating an effective anti-apartheid policy," Regan told a meeting of the World Affairs Council in Southhampton, Long Island, on September 5, 1985. "States and cities should not be conducting foreign policy, but that is precisely what is happening." If Washington did not move against South Africa, he said, pressure would continue to build for cities and states to end their dealings with the country and with companies that do business there.

Even as he was promoting greater federal involvement, Regan was also considering the steps he might be able to take as trustee to deflect the campaign to divest. In August 1985 Regan watched an NBC television news program called "The Biggest Lump of Money in the World" that vividly described the dramatic increase in pension assets and suggested that those who controlled these assets could have a decisive say in guiding the policies of corporate America. "The comptroller came in the next day," recalled Thomas Pandick, the counsel to the New York State Common Retirement Fund. "He was very enthusiastic about what he had seen and told me that he had made a decision. He said he wanted to create an office that would be dedicated to investor relations and would take a more active stance on corporate issues. He said that he wanted an attorney to serve as the director. He then asked me if I would do it."

During the fall of 1985, Democratic legislators in New York State drafted a flock of new divestment bills that flew through the Assembly but were shot down in the Senate by a grim study from the Senate Finance Committee. The Senate report drew heavily on a contract study provided by Wilshire Associates, analysts whose pessimism about divestment was well known. In addition to the transaction, market effect, and opportunity costs that divestment would impose, the study identified a particularly vexing problem for the huge fund. Because of its enormity and diversity, the New York State Common Retirement Fund had been managed as an index fund whose buy and sell decisions were pegged to movements in the S&P 500. Divestment would force the fund out of certain industries and back into active management, with all the added risks and costs of employing an army of brokers.

Though Regan continued to hold fast against divestment, his genuine opposition to apartheid, his frustration with the lack of leadership in Washington, his belief in the moral responsibility that flowed from ownership, and his desire to respond to the wishes of the electorate all propelled him to search for some set of actions he could take. He began by talking with senior corporate executives about their involvement in South Africa. At one private meeting in October, Regan urged a group of top executives to be more active in opposing apartheid. To refuse to do so, he told them, would inevitably lead to new punitive actions against them within the United States. "What's the difference between boycotting your stock and boycotting your product?" he asked them. "This movement may not just stop at stock."

Regan was not content to limit his efforts to private jawboning, and throughout the fall of 1985 he and Pandick planned a new strategy, which he announced in a speech to a group of institutional investors in New York City on January 9, 1986. Regan started by noting that the fund had often been asked to make unsound economic investments for the public good. "In the 1950's the fund was asked to subsidize low income housing," he said. "In the 1960's it was financing for the Albany Mall. In the 1970's a prolonged attempt was made in the State Assembly to limit the fund's investment in the nation's largest corporations because they were expanding in the south while New York State was temporarily having difficulty retaining industry. In the high-interest rate climate of the early 1980's, the Governor requested pension funds at below market rates for the State's infrastructure program." All of these proposals had been rejected, he said, because they were not in the long-term financial interests of the pension beneficiaries. The pension fund, however, was not immune to social concerns. "The New York State Common Retirement Fund has long recognized," Regan continued, "that as a publicly funded, large institutional investor it has special responsibilities." He then dropped a bombshell. Sweeping away six years of commitment to the incremental approach of the Sullivan Principles, Regan announced that he now agreed with Leon Sullivan's most recent declaration: if apartheid were not dismantled by May 1987, American companies should depart. "If nine months from now, it becomes apparent that the system of apartheid is still so entrenched that it is impossible for it to be dismantled by May 1987," Regan continued, "then we will ask the corporations involved to draw up contingency disinvestment plans. We will draft shareholder resolutions requiring the company's withdrawal. And we will take other appropriate shareholder activities." Though he was opposed to divestment, Regan said, he intended to "use our clout as shareholders . . . to impel the corporate community to institute change for the better."

Within weeks Regan had written letters to more than a hundred corporate executives and dispatched Pandick to several dozen annual meetings. At each Pandick stood up and announced that if the corporation did not have a disinvestment plan in place by the end of the summer of 1986, the New York State Common Retirement Fund would use its millions of dollars in shares to file a shareholder resolution against management in the next season. For many corporate board members, the threat by a Republican state comptroller of one of the country's most populous states to use his billions in pension clout to press for change was the most disturbing development they had yet seen.

The last part of 1985 brought many new forces to bear on P. W. Botha. In addition to the debt standstill, the collapse of the rand, the imposition of partial American sanctions, and the increase in violence, the state president also had to contend with strengthened internal opposition. Some of his long-standing critics showed new vigor. Several of South Africa's labor unions, after years of unity talks, finally banded together into a single federation known as the Congress of South African Trade Unions, COSATU. Representing thirty-three unions and more than four hundred sixty thousand workers, the new organization held its first national conference at the University of Natal in November. After intensive discussions, the leaders decided to broaden their focus to include not only factory but also national political reform. "The struggle of workers on the shop floor cannot be separated from the wider struggle for liberation," said Cyril Ramaphosa. "A giant has risen and will confront all that stand in its way."

From the beginning the member unions of COSATU adopted positions in favor of nonracialism, the Freedom Charter, and the United Democratic Front, and had refused to align themselves with all-black, pro-AZAPO unions. COSATU even endorsed the UDF's position on sanctions, despite the potential cost to union members. "All forms of international pressure on the South African government—including disinvestment or the threat of disinvestment—are an essential and effective form of pressure on the South African regime," read one statement approved at the congress. Gatsha Buthelezi, who continued to fight any mention of sanctions, attacked COSATU bitterly. "Those who have supported sanctions so far from inside," Buthelezi said in December, "have done so as surrogates for the ANC." Several months later Buthelezi announced that Inkatha had formed a new union, the United Workers Union of South Africa (UWUSA) to oppose sanctions and to counter the growth of COSATU.

P. W. Botha also encountered new resistance from opponents. Hundreds of young white men were leaving the country rather than be drafted into the South African Defence Force. Once the government started using soldiers in its efforts to suppress township unrest, the number of young men who refused to report for duty had jumped. The End Conscription Campaign (EEC), an organization formed in 1983 of young people and parents opposed to the draft, grew in strength. The deputy minister of defense, Adriaan Vlok, attacked the EEC for allowing itself to be used by the ANC to achieve "its evil goals." The leaders of the EEC rejected the claim, saying the "EEC has never had, nor will have, links with the ANC."

Opposition grew in religious communities inside and outside South Africa. In June, to mark the anniversary of the Soweto shootings, the South African Council of Churches had called for a massive Day of Prayer for Unjust Rule, which included open calls for the government's removal. In September a group of 151 clergy and lay people released a statement announcing that the church in South Africa had reached a moment of truth—or *kairos*—that called for new actions by Christians. The Kairos Document, as it was called, provided theological reflection on such thorny questions as civil disobedience, armed resistance, and illegitimate government. That same month another group of nearly four hundred Christian leaders announced the formation of a National Initiative for Reconciliation and took out a large advertisement calling for a work stay-away that would allow a time of "repentance, mourning, and prayer for those sinful aspects of our national life which have led us to the present crisis." Since the unions did not support the call, the stay-away failed in all but one section of the country. In early December the World Council of Churches organized a meeting for international church leaders to meet with the South African Council of Churches and members of the African National Congress in Harare. Several prominent American church leaders attended, including Avery Post, president of the United Church of Christ; Bishop James M. Ault, president of the United Methodist General Board of Global Ministries; and Bishop John M. Allin, the presiding bishop of the Episcopal Church. The delegates listened to a stirring oration by Desmond Tutu, spent three days in intense discussion, and then approved the Harare Declaration, a document that called on the international community to "prevent the extension . . . or renewal of bank loans" and urged the application of "immediate and comprehensive sanctions." On returning home, the American church representatives immediately disseminated the document through their religious networks. Some, like Bishop Ault, took the declaration with them to Capitol Hill when they lobbied members of Congress to support stronger sanctions.

The state president also faced new resistance within the Afrikaner community. More than two dozen Afrikaner faculty members from the University of Stellenbosch, alarmed by the Rubicon speech and by what they believed was a looming economic catastrophe, pulled together and drafted a document decrying the government's "inaccurate perceptions" of South Africa's problems. During the annual Cape National Party congress—the heart of P. W. Botha's power base—two party delegates proposed that the government repeal the Group Areas Act. On the opposite side of the spectrum, right-wing Afrikaners denounced Botha with increasing stridency. Andries Treurnicht said publicly that the fatherland was being torn from the white man's hands; that the debt crisis was a direct result of Botha's incompetence; that the state of emergency was "a clumsy admission of defeat," and that the government had erred in restricting the police to birdshot and rubber bullets when greater force was obviously needed to restore law and order. Eugene Terreblanche of the neo-Nazi Afrikaner Weerstandbeweging (AWB) announced that if the police failed to maintain law and order, the AWB would take the law into its own hands.

It was a strange sight for those both inside and outside South Africa who had believed in the myth of Afrikaner unity, for the Afrikaners were rapidly breaking up into small squabbling factions. The National Party still commanded the majority, but the increasing pressure on the economy had produced a crisis of political faith. Fewer people believed Botha's assurances that all was proceeding as planned. Nowhere was the crisis of confidence more pronounced than in the business community, whose leaders began to feel that Botha was mismanaging the process so badly that it might lead to the destruction of their firms. Everywhere Botha looked, normally reticent business leaders were banding together and calling on him to change his policies. Some of the most active executives were from the American companies under fire in the United States. In September, ten of the largest American companies in South Africa formed the U.S. Corporate Council on South Africa and announced that under the leadership of former U.S. Treasury Secretary and Burroughs chair W. Michael Blumenthal, they would lobby the government to end apartheid. In November, after a special meeting of chief executives of U.S. companies, executives from 186 American firms signed a letter to P. W. Botha asking him to act promptly to resolve the crisis in black education.

South African executives were also acting more boldly than at any time in history. Shortly after the Rubicon speech South African grocery store magnate Raymond Ackerman announced that he was forming a special "committee of ten" to demonstrate to the world that South African business did not agree with apartheid. The next month, several of

South Africa's most prominent business leaders—including Gavin Relly, the chairman of Anglo-American, and Tony Bloom, the chairman of the Premier Group—did the unthinkable: they traveled to Lusaka to meet with Oliver Tambo and his principal lieutenants of the African National Congress.

The encounter had been proposed by Zambian president Kenneth Kaunda and took place at his private game lodge. Kaunda exhorted the participants to discover how much they had in common. "The things that men have in common are God-made," Kaunda told the participants, "whereas the things that divide men are man-made." Despite this encouragement, the meeting began awkwardly. Each side had come dressed in the garb of the other: the ANC delegation all wore business suits, the executives wore khakis and sports clothes. "If anyone had been asked who looked like the guerrilla fighters," noted Tony Bloom afterward, "the answer might easily have turned out to be the South African delegation." Gathered under the shade of a large tree, they started off seated opposite one another until Oliver Tambo commented that the seating arrangement was divisive and asked that they rearrange themselves into a mixed group. The South African business leaders were impressed. "I was surprised, almost overwhelmed, by the cordiality of the meeting," Bloom wrote later. "A more attractive and congenial group would be hard to imagine. There was a total lack of aggression, animosity, or hostility toward us."

Despite the personal chemistry, the differences between the men remained acute. Though the executives stressed their belief in a common citizenship, they said that negotiations about universal adult suffrage didn't "seem possible at this time." They criticized the ANC for pursuing a violent strategy, for its economic policies, and for its alliance with the South African Communist Party. When Tony Bloom asked whether there wasn't a role for people who rejected "extremes," Thabo Mbeki, who directed the ANC's Foreign Relations Department, responded that the ANC members considered themselves the moderates of South Africa, in comparison to the Marxists and Africanists, whose solutions were far more severe.

Over lunch and throughout the afternoon the group's discussion ranged over everything from the role of Gatsha Buthelezi to the merits of industrial nationalization. Despite disagreements, the session ended on a positive note. The business leaders were amazed that the ANC delegation was willing to pose for a group photograph, but the ANC men joked that all of their pictures were already on file with the Security Police. "The departure was a strangely poignant one," Tony Bloom recalled a few days later. "We were returning to South Africa and they were staying behind. There was almost an air of sadness." Bloom also noticed the ANC delegations' "overwhelming nostalgia to come back to South Africa. . . . They love to talk about parts of South Africa in detail, to remember people, places, and events in South Africa." Their passion touched Bloom and the other businessmen. "The life of someone who has been in exile for twenty-three years cannot be attractive," Bloom concluded, "particularly as most of them live in fairly abject circumstances."

Relly, Bloom, and the others returned to South Africa convinced that the ANC did not hate whites, were not hardline Marxists, and were not committed to reducing South Africa to anarchy to seize power. "I believe that they are people with whom serious negotiation can be undertaken," wrote Bloom in his summary of the meeting, "and with whom a certain amount of common ground could be found." P. W. Botha, for his part, was furious at what they had done. "I do not know what the businessmen achieved, except to show signs of weakness towards the enemies of South Africa," he said. "The government will not talk to any organization or person who promotes violence."

Despite the criticisms, such runs across the border increased. The next month a delegation of members of parliament from the Progressive Federal Party traveled to Lusaka for similar discussion. They were followed, soon afterward, by a group of Afrikaner theologians. Botha denounced the trips and in some cases was able to intimidate the participants into canceling them. Oliver Tambo, however, actively encouraged such visits because, in his view, they not only isolated the Botha regime but demonstrated to the participants and to the world that the ANC was reasonable. In the United States, civil rights activists, remembering how the willingness of business leaders to negotiate in Birmingham had brought an end to segregation, were elated by the development. "I think it's the beginning of the end," said Joseph Lowery of the Southern Christian Leadership Conference. "I really do."

In Pretoria, P. W. Botha remained confident that his strategy of suppressing dissent while granting limited reforms would succeed. As 1985 rolled into 1986, however, neither piece of the strategy seemed to be working. In October, Botha banned the United Democratic Front and more than one hundred other organizations. In November he imposed draconian regulations on the domestic and international press. Fritz Leutwiler, who was still desperately trying to bring the bankers to an agreement, said that the bannings were "the very opposite of what I had hoped for" and called the press restrictions "the most stupid thing the government could have done." Nor did Botha's actions have any effect on casualties in the black community. By the end of 1985, hundreds of people had been killed in clashes with police. In one instance, a delivery truck rumbled through a township with a load of crates on the back.

When several teenagers threw stones at the truck, police with shotguns popped out of the crates and fired, killing three boys. The "Trojan horse" killings drew new international attention to the military occupation of the townships just at the point when Botha was hoping it would die down.

Both P. W. Botha and Chester Crocker continued to believe that everything would work out beautifully if the other party would just follow his script. For Botha, the script said that Ronald Reagan should stay on the anti-Communist track and allow the National Party to contain its enemies with its blend of military strikes and piecemeal reforms. For Crocker, the South African government was continuously missing the opportunities for change which he thought U.S. diplomacy was making possible. In order to gain leverage over the other, Botha and Crocker fervently encouraged their supporters in the opposite government. Crocker continued to build his alliance and friendship with Foreign Minister Pik Botha, while P. W. Botha dispatched emissaries like Pieter van der Westhuizen to drum up support among the American right wing. For several months, intensive maneuvering between the two governments took place around the possibility of a summit meeting between Reagan and Botha. Botha desperately wanted the meeting to shore up domestic and international support for his program. Van der Westhuizen suggested the idea to CIA director William Casey in late 1985. Shortly afterward William Clark, the president's new national security adviser, told Crocker about the suggestion, saying the president thought that if he and Botha could meet, Reagan might be able to "talk sense" to him. The critical issue was whether the meeting would carry any preconditions. The South Africans wanted none; the State Department insisted that such a meeting would be a political disaster unless the South Africans coughed up huge concessions.

In January 1986 Crocker flew to Cape Town with a letter to P. W. Botha from Reagan. The letter urged Botha to make 1986 a year of "decisive accomplishment" and said that if there were a proper "context," a meeting between Reagan and Botha could take place. Though the foreign minister received Crocker warmly, the state president was frosty. "Why are you here?" Botha asked Crocker bluntly when the American entered his office. He told Crocker that he had been let down by two Republican administrations: first Ford in 1975, now Reagan a decade later. Crocker left the meeting doubtful that anything would come of it; nor was he surprised when he returned to the United States to see van der Westhuizen eagerly urging Casey, Clark, Buchanan, and Poindexter to adopt a more helpful strategy toward South Africa.

Botha was sufficiently desperate for the meeting that he offered a few positive responses. In his private written reply to Reagan's letter he urged the president to have more patience; he said that he would support matching commitments to end violence; and he said he was willing to release Nelson Mandela if the ANC leader would not "personally" be involved in violence. Botha also responded publicly. On January 31, 1986, at the opening of parliament in Cape Town, P. W. Botha gave the address he should have given instead of the Rubicon speech, announcing the end of influx control, the rescision of the pass laws, the elimination of whites-only immigration rules, and the release of all pass law violators. He again offered to release Nelson Mandela, though this time he proposed that the ANC leader would be freed in exchange for the freedom of Soviet dissident Andrei Sakharov and several South African soldiers who had been captured in Angola. South African government officials pointed happily to the speech as evidence that their government was seriously committed to reform, but for most of the world Botha had offered too little, too late.

Still, Botha's willingness to rescind some of apartheid's central pieces of legislation, combined with his decision to remove the state of emergency, raised hopes among European leaders that he could be persuaded, under the right circumstances, to begin negotiating with the African National Congress. For months the members of the British Commonwealth had been locked in a bitter struggle with British Prime Minister Margaret Thatcher. Most of the Commonwealth members had been urging the imposition of economic sanctions against South Africa; Thatcher had stubbornly refused, insisting that such measures would be "immoral." Without Britain's participation, the other prime ministers knew, any opposition of sanctions would be largely meaningless. Thatcher, in the meantime, had been sending steady signals to Botha through various emissaries that the South African leader should release Mandela and speed up the process of reform.

In October 1985, after a turbulent meeting in the Bahamas, Thatcher and her Commonwealth counterparts agreed on a compromise. Before imposing sanctions, she had suggested, the leaders should send a delegation to explore the government's openness to genuine reform and perhaps to help launch quiet negotiations between the government and the ANC. In February 1986 the delegation, known as the Eminent Persons Group, arrived in South Africa under the leadership of Prime Minister Malcolm Fraser of Australia and General Olusegun Obasanjo of Nigeria. Obasanjo was an unusual man; after serving as the military ruler of Nigeria, he handed power back to civilian authorities in 1979 and had largely withdrawn from politics. In South Africa, he pushed himself to find out what was really going on, even traveling to Alexandra township in the midst of the rioting to talk to the residents and interview the police. Over the next few months, Fraser and Obasanjo took their task seriously. They met with P. W. Botha in his presidential palace; with Nelson Mandela at Pollsmoor prison; with the leaders of the United Democratic Front; and with dozens of others inside and outside the country. Finding widespread eagerness for some kind of negotiated settlement in the government, the ANC, and the general population, they shuttled back and forth between Lusaka and Pretoria in an attempt to identify common ground. In the end, they developed a "possible negotiating concept." The government would make an unambiguous declaration of its intentions to eliminate apartheid completely and would engage in various "confidence-building steps" such as releasing Nelson Mandela, lifting the ban on the ANC, and allowing free political activity. The ANC, in turn, would publicly promise to negotiate and would abandon the armed struggle.

After several months of conversation, the ANC seemed ready to accept. When both Mandela and Tambo gave their provisional approval to the "possible negotiating concept," the ball shifted into the Botha government's court. "For years the government had claimed it was only the ANC's commitment to violent struggle that had led to its banning, and that if it would renounce that Mandela could go free and talks begin," wrote South African journalist Allister Sparks. When the Eminent Persons Group returned for another set of discussions in May, Botha and his cabinet realized that they would have to reach a decision: were they really willing to negotiate with the ANC or not? On Tuesday, May 13, 1986, Botha met with his cabinet. Some urged acceptance of the proposal, but the secureaucrats were vehemently opposed. What was needed, they insisted, was not the weakness of negotiation, but more muscle applied with more will.

The South Africans did not immediately inform the Commonwealth team of their decision; the answer came the following Monday, May 19. The Commonwealth leaders, who were visiting the ANC in Lusaka, awoke to learn that South African Defence Forces had again swept into Zimbabwe and Botswana to attack "ANC bases." The South African air force had even bombed a site in Lusaka, though their target turned out to be not a guerrilla camp but a United Nations facility for Angolan and Namibian refugees. The Eminent Persons Group left Lusaka that evening. A few days later the Commonwealth leaders issued a unanimous call for mandatory economic sanctions against South Africa. Though the military effect was limited, the strikes accomplished their purpose: they had destroyed all confidence in Botha's reform program and all hope of a mediated settlement. The police commissioner, the generals of the SADF, the intelligence services, and the other security officials now had the free hand to crush dissent for which they had long aspired.

Reaction poured in from around the world. Though the Reagan administration expressed "outrage" and expelled a military attaché, observers inside and outside South Africa argued that Botha had taken his cue from Reagan himself, who only a month before had ordered a bombing strike against targets in Libya to punish Muammar Qaddafi for supporting terrorism. Other countries responded quickly: within days Canada had recalled its ambassador; Argentina had broken off diplomatic relations; and Denmark had banned all commercial links with South Africa. Only Margaret Thatcher remained unmoved; while condemning the raids, she again rejected the call for economic sanctions.

In the United States, despite the press restrictions, media attention again focused on South Africa. Coverage of South Africa in the *New York Times* continued to swell, building toward a record 1,100 articles in 1986, or an average of 2.3 articles per day. Two days after the raid, members of a bipartisan coalition in the U.S. Congress announced that they would seek a stiffer set of sanctions against South Africa. "To those who see faint signs of progress and ask us to hold off," said Edward Kennedy, "we say: read the morning headlines; talk to anyone in South Africa; open your eyes to the truth that the progress is too little and it may soon be too late." Within a week of the raid, General Motors had announced that it would no longer sell cars and trucks to South Africa's police and military agencies.

Inside South Africa, tensions skyrocketed. Fighting in the Crossroads township between youthful "comrades" and government-supported vigilantes known as the *witdoeke* burst into an urban civil war that left scores of people dead and more than seventy thousand homeless. Afrikaner extremists mobilized, ejecting Pik Botha from one party rally and organizing a mass meeting for more than eight thousand people at which speakers denounced the government and called for complete racial separation. From Lusaka, Oliver Tambo called on South African blacks to pursue "total civil disobedience." The U.S. Chamber of Commerce published a large advertisement signed by eighty American firms urging the legalization of the African National Congress. From inside the country the leaders of COSATU announced that on June 16 they would organize a one-day general strike to mark the tenth anniversary of the beginning of the Soweto uprising. Only five weeks earlier COSATU had led a million and a half workers off their jobs on the first of May, the largest one-day strike in South African history. When the government banned all commemorations of Soweto, Desmond Tutu publicly urged the churches to defy the order. On June 11, the leaders of the United Democratic Front joined Tutu and said that they would hold demonstrations and commemorative events on June 16 no matter what the government said.

The next day Botha struck back. He first tried to push a new slate of security regulations through the tricameral parliament but found himself blocked by the refusal of the Indian and Coloured chambers to grant their approval. In response, Botha declared a nationwide state of emergency, which gave the police and military sweeping rights to order whatever actions they desired and to apply "such force as . . . under the circumstance [they] may deem necessary." The action was required, Botha explained, because ordinary laws were "inadequate to enable the government to insure the security of the public and to maintain public order." Once again his police fanned out across the country, arresting more than a thousand people and searching for hundreds of community organizers and union leaders who had instantly gone into hiding. One Johannesburg police team raided Khotso House, the headquarters of the South African Council of Churches, seizing papers and documents.

Botha's words to parliament and to the nation were defiant. His government, he said, was "well aware that stricter security action will elicit strong criticism and even punitive measures from the outside world. The implications and the price of these have also been taken into account." That night, appearing on national television, Botha waved away the threat of economic reprisal. "South Africans will not allow themselves to be humiliated in order to prevent sanctions," he said. "We are not a nation of weaklings. We do not desire it and we do not seek it, but if we are forced to go it alone, then so be it." He would not allow "our heritage of more than three hundred years to be placed needlessly on the altar of chaos and decay."

The morning after the state of emergency had been declared, Senator Nancy Kassebaum phoned Chester Crocker. "The senator's message was stark, her tone anxious," wrote Crocker later. "She did not know what more she could do to warn us that the president had to 'get out front' on the South African issue or the Republican-controlled Senate would march off in its own direction." She, Richard Lugar, and other senators wanted to meet with Reagan to urge him to adopt several steps, including a radio address professing his disgust over the South African government's behavior and the sending of a special presidential envoy to convey his sentiment directly to P. W. Botha. Later that day, the White House announced that Reagan had dispatched Herman Nickel to P. W. Botha to deliver a personal presidential message urging "massive restraint." Reagan himself undercut the message when he publicly expressed sympathy for Botha's predicament. To understand what was happening in South Africa was "awfully hard when you are not involved," Reagan told a group of out-of-town broadcasters. "What we are seeing now is an outright civil war. . . . It's no longer a context between the black population and the white population. It is black fighting against blacks, because there is still a tribal situation there."

Reagan's lack of understanding and concern, combined with the feverish newspaper coverage of the violence in South Africa, produced a new burst of support for sanctions. A few days before the state of emergency, a strong sanctions bill sponsored by Representative William Gray had sailed effortlessly through the House Committee on Foreign Affairs. On Thursday, June 12, on the same day as the imposition of the state of emergency, the Eminent Persons Group had released a report favoring sanctions; Obasanjo and Fraser were in the middle of their press conference on the report when an assistant brought them news of Botha's actions. By June 17, BankAmerica had decided to stop lending to any South African borrowers; millions of South African workers had gone on strike to commemorate Soweto; and P. W. Botha had responded to Reagan's plea for restraint by telling him, in the words of a White House official, to "bug off."

The next day the U.S. House of Representatives acted decisively. House members spent several hours debating the merits of the sanctions bill that had been forwarded to them by the Committee on Foreign Affairs. At the last minute, Ronald V. Dellums of California proposed his own bill as a substitute. The Dellums bill was much stricter, requiring the president to implement a full trade embargo and immediate disinvestment by U.S. firms. To everyone's amazement, the substitution was approved by a voice vote. Stunned Republicans huddled and decided not to ask for a roll call vote, on the assumption that Dellums's bill was so extreme it would be easy for Reagan to veto. Without opposition from the Republicans, the Dellums bill passed the House of Representatives. This was "the American answer" to the state of emergency, said Representative Stephen Solarz. "It sends the strongest possible signal." After the vote, Dellums was euphoric. "This will be a tremendous boost to the anti-apartheid movement in this country," he said, adding, "I'm still shocked that it happened."

While politicians, ideologues, militarists, diplomats, moralists, and lobbyists wrangled with each other in Washington and in Pretoria, the divestment movement continued to build up steam around the United States. On dozens of college campuses anti-apartheid students built shantytowns, sparking ferocious disputes about whether such practices were coercive and disruptive, as some conservatives argued, or part of the exercise of free speech. At Dartmouth College in Hanover, New Hampshire, the shantytown debate dominated the winter and spring of 1986. When the president had the shanties knocked down, two hundred activist students and faculty held a sit-in and later rebuilt the structures on another site. Shortly afterward, twelve students from the conservative *Dartmouth Review* destroyed the new shanties with sledgehammers, an action for which they were temporarily suspended. The sledgehammer attack became the focus of an impassioned quarrel on the status of blacks, females, homosexuals, Native Americans, and others who did not fit Dartmouth's white male culture. Shantytowns at other colleges also became the focal point of such debates. In April police arrested sixty-one protesters at the University of California at Berkeley who were living in a shantytown in front of the chancellor's office. At Yale University police arrested seventy-eight people in April for passively resisting the destruction of their ten-day-old shantytown. After a teach-in that attracted hundreds of faculty and students, the university relented and allowed the structures to be rebuilt. Yale president Benno Schmidt also announced that he would send a special investigating team, composed of Yale trustees, to South Africa to investigate the companies in which the university owned nearly four hundred million dollars in stock.

Yale's strategy of sending its delegation to South Africa to see for themselves what was going on had become popular at many large institutions, from religious denominations to universities, from pension funds to industrial firms. Harvard University trustee Hugh Calkins visited the president of Joy Manufacturing, a supplier of mining equipment to South African gold and coal mines, and told him that Harvard would sell off its stock unless his firm showed more concern. The chief executive discussed the matter with his board and then flew to South Africa himself. When he returned, he phoned Calkins and told him that he would sign the Sullivan Principles, permit the Investor Responsibility Research Center to conduct on-site interviews, and begin improving worker conditions immediately, starting with the purchase of two vans to help black schoolchildren get to and from school.

One of the most significant trips taken on behalf of an institutional investor were those made by Albert Wilson, general counsel of the teachers' insurance and pension company TIAA-CREF. Wilson, an African American, made his first trip in 1982 to examine the homelands policy. Though he came back disturbed by what he had seen, he believed that American companies could still become a force for change. In early 1986 Wilson went back. He traveled extensively, meeting with business leaders and politicians from the National Party, the Progressive Federal Party, and the Conservative Party. Many of those with whom he spoke were shocked at his appearance and behavior. "One man looked at me and said in amazement, 'My God, Mr. Wilson, you sound and talk like we do,' " Wilson recalled later. "Some could not believe that there was such a large pension fund in the United States or that such a pension fund would send a black man to represent it." At one luncheon organized by the Urban Foundation, Wilson found himself sitting with the senior executives from twelve of South Africa's largest corporations. "I was the only black," Wilson remembered, "except for the silent black waiters who moved in and out of the room." Wilson asked the executives whether it was good business for them to neglect the enormous black consumer market. They told him that Americans did not understand that business had no political role in South Africa. Wilson suggested that it would be easy for any of them to get a government official on the phone. "We talk, but there's only so much we can do," said one executive. "Are you suggesting," another asked in a shocked tone, "that we break the law?"

Later Wilson found himself at a meal with the head of the Johannesburg Stock Exchange, who took his guest to an elite Victorian club. Wilson looked around at the stuffed Victorian upholstery and at the white businessmen being waited on by blacks and realized that whole building smelled like a locker room. "The black servants came from the townships and could not take baths very often," Wilson said later. "It would have been the easiest thing in the world for the club to install showers in the basement and require the waiters to wash when they arrived for work. But they didn't. Why not? Because I think that the smell of the waiters somehow justified the white men's sense of superiority and prejudice, and thus the segregation and the whole system."

Wilson found the country ready to explode. Everyone he spoke to "believed that the National Party would hold on to power even if divestment and disinvestment continues to increase," Wilson wrote in his report. "They will hold on to power despite strikes, boycotts, stay-aways, and increased violence. And they will hold on even if they must unleash their military and police power to do so. Obviously, they are hoping that time will not come, but if they read the face and the words of the majority community correctly, it must come." In mid-March, Allan Boesak insisted that Wilson join him in a trip to Uitenhague to attend a memorial service for those who had been killed the year before. On their way to the service, their car was stopped by a motorcycle policeman. In minutes, two other police vehicles converged on the point. Boesak, Wilson, and the other occupants were ordered out. The men stood in the dusty road while the officers carefully searched their car. When the police realized that they had Allan Boesak and a U.S. citizen, they radioed for instructions and eventually released the passengers. "The others in the car indicated that this was a common occurrence in the majority community," Wilson wrote to his board. "For the first time, as an American, I was exposed to the powerlessness of the majority community."

When Wilson returned, he told the board that American companies could no longer play a positive role in South Africa. TIAA-CREF should urge them to withdraw. The trustees of the immense fund—in

1986 it approached fifty billion dollars in total assets—immediately voted their shares in favor of a resolution urging companies to warn the South African government that they would leave unless apartheid disappeared rapidly. By the next season the policy had become even tougher: TIAA-CREF publicly called for the complete withdrawal of all U.S. companies. In private conversations, Wilson and other TIAA-CREF officials urged the executives to do their own cost-benefit analysis. "We told them that it did not make sense to jeopardize the reputation of ninety-nine percent of their business because of what is happening with one percent," Wilson said, "and they began to listen."

The process that took place at TIAA-CREF—in which the avalanche of contradictory claims about South Africa caused a large institution to send its own representative to make an independent judgment—was repeated in the mid-1980s at scores of institutions around the country. At issue were two questions: first, would disinvestment and sanctions be effective in changing the government's mind? And second, what did the black citizens of South Africa want the outside community to do? Though the South African government continuously denied that sanctions had an effect, the very fervency of those denials—combined with the obvious impact of the bank crisis—revived faith in the use of disinvestment and sanctions as a tool of influence.

One index of the growing impact of the threat of sanctions was the sudden fascination among whites in both countries with black public opinion in South Africa. In the mid-1980s, a burst of polling took place as proponents and opponents of disinvestment sought to ground their positions in the will of the black majority. The process contained considerable irony. After years of ignoring black sentiment, white leaders from all sectors of society—government, business, and academia—were suddenly eager to claim their support. Professor Lawrence Schlemmer of the University of Natal, who was sympathetic to Gatsha Buthelezi and Inkatha, conducted two studies in 1984 which found that blacks favored investment over disinvestment by a margin of three to one. U.S. Secretary of State George Shultz, Ambassador Herman Nickel, Gatsha Buthelezi, and many others used the Schlemmer study to argue against sanctions and disinvestment. A second study, paid for by the South African Council of Churches and conducted by the liberal Community Agency for Social Enquiry (CASE) in late 1985, found the opposite: seventy-three percent of metropolitan blacks favored one or another form of disinvestment. Polls taken in August 1985 and 1986 by Markinor, a Gallup-affiliated organization, showed more than three-quarters of the respondents favoring sanctions and disinvestment, even though half of them thought they would personally be harmed by such actions.

The wide variation between the Schlemmer study and the others produced a feverish dispute about samples, questions, and organizational bias.

In the United States, however, polls ceded prominence to personality. Though support for Buthelezi remained strong among American conservatives, Desmond Tutu's voice continued to grow in power and legitimacy throughout the year. In January 1986, Tutu had come to the United States to visit his daughter Naomi Tutu Seavers, who lived in Hartford, Connecticut, and to receive the Martin Luther King Prize. During a three-week barnstorming tour of the United States to raise money and support for the South African Council of Churches, he delivered four or five speeches a day, met with hundreds of students, religious leaders, politicians, university trustees, and corporate executives, including the chairmen of General Motors and Burroughs. In most of his conversations and speeches he criticized the sudden concern for black suffering and openly called for economic sanctions. "When did white people suddenly become so altruistic and suddenly become so concerned about black suffering," he asked a press conference at the Cathedral of St. John the Divine in New York City, "when over a long time those who have invested have benefited from cheap labor supplied by blacks?" In Washington, D.C., Randall Robinson presented Tutu with a letter of support signed by a million Americans. In Baltimore, speaking before eight hundred hospital employees, Tutu explained how the achievements of Jackie Robinson, Martin Luther King, and Jesse Jackson had inspired South African blacks. In New Jersey Tutu received the keys to the city of Newark, praised the governor for his decision to divest the state pension fund, and criticized Reagan for ignoring the deaths of hundreds of blacks. "If those who died were white," Tutu asked, "would those in the White House be sitting there with equanimity and talking about constructive engagement?"

Whenever Tutu returned to South Africa after such trips, he endured a hailstorm of criticism. "Bishop Tutu's actions and statements in any other country would be construed as treason," growled Andries Treurnicht of the Conservative Party. "He should be dealt with immediately." "There is no greater thorn in South Africa's side," wrote the editors of the pro-government newspaper the *Citizen,* "than this man of the cloth who strides through the world like a religious pop star." Despite the controversy, Tutu found himself propelled into an even more prominent role when, in April 1986, he was elected the first black archbishop of Cape Town. Before, he had served as one bishop among many; now he would become the spiritual head of all Anglicans, white and black, in the Church of the Province of Southern Africa, an area that included Lesotho, Botswana, Namibia, and Mozambique. The Afrikaner press grumbled at the election. The *Pretoria News* expressed hope that the bishop would "learn humility and greater understanding," the *Citizen* that he would "moderate his political activities and viewpoints."

Tutu's commitment to building support for the anti-apartheid movement in the United States remained unwavering. In April he issued a new call for American firms to divest. In May he returned to the United States to deliver several commencement speeches. In June, just two days before the House approved the Dellums bill, Tutu wrote an impassioned plea in favor of sanctions that was published on the op-ed page of the *New York Times* and was read by millions of Americans. "If sanctions don't work, why did Margaret Thatcher apply them to Argentina during the Falklands War?" Tutu asked. "Why did the United States apply them to Poland and Nicaragua? Why was Ronald Reagan so annoyed that his European allies did not want to impose sanctions on Libya?" Sanctions, he insisted, "are the last nonviolent option left. . . . There is no room for neutrality. . . . Are you on the side of oppression or liberation? Are you on the side of death or life? Are you on the side of goodness or of evil?"

In early July 1986 the Reagan administration faced, for the second time in twelve months, a Congress poised to snatch control of foreign policy from the executive branch. Richard Lugar and Nancy Kassebaum, nervous that a failure of White House initiative might contribute to the Republican Party losing control of the Senate in the 1986 elections, pushed again for Reagan to act. At a State Department meeting on July 1, George Shultz and Chester Crocker listened glumly as John Akers of IBM, Roger Smith of General Motors, and James Burke of Johnson & Johnson explained the pressures they were under. According to Crocker's memoirs, the chief executives complained that "the protests, shareholder proposals, public and employee relations problems, restrictive local and state ordinances were all having an effect. . . . They were wasting the time, money, and energy of leadership in boardrooms across the country." The managers said that they could no longer "justify spending twenty-five percent of their time on debates over their activity in a country that accounted for perhaps one half to one percent of their business." Since the "flak factor" had gotten "completely out of hand," they told Shultz, "an immediate and forceful expression of presidential leadership on the issue was imperative."

The signals coming from the administration were mixed. Crocker criticized the South African government sharply at the end of June. Later he insisted that although sanctions had never been "ruled out," the key to changing South Africa was in ending the "siege mentality" of the white leaders. Soon afterward Shultz announced that the entire South

Africa policy would be reviewed to find a way to end apartheid without damaging the economy and that he would go to Capitol Hill to testify about the new policy before Lugar's committee at the end of July. When asked by a reporter traveling on his plane whether this meant that the administration was abandoning constructive engagement, the secretary of state bristled. "The counsel of disengagement is the wrong counsel," Shultz snapped, "but just how to engage and just what is constructive—those are the questions."

Signals that the policy was being changed dribbled steadily out of the White House. On July 3, Vice President George Bush appeared before the seventy-seventh annual convention of the NAACP and declared that "apartheid must end." Soon afterward an unnamed senior White House official told reporters that under the new policy much more effort would be made to build contacts with black opposition groups, including the African National Congress. On July 13 the White House summoned Herman Nickel for consultations. Over the next week, as part of their effort to recapture the initiative from Congress, White House officials leaked the information that Reagan might appoint an African American businessman, Robert J. Brown, as the next U.S. ambassador to South Africa. Brown was an interesting choice: a Republican from North Carolina, Brown had supported Robert F. Kennedy in 1968 and then worked for the Nixon White House; he had accumulated friends all along the political spectrum, including Andrew Young and Jesse Jackson. Richard Lugar told the president that if he did not act decisively, a large majority of the Senate would vote for increased sanctions. In response, the White House told reporters that the secretary of state would testify on July 23 and the president would make a speech on South Africa policy the day before in which he would announce, among other things, the appointment of Brown.

Inside the White House, moderates and conservatives battled furiously for control of the administration's South Africa policy. On July 8, Crocker forwarded a draft of the president's speech for White House review. In that version the president would announce an expansion of the U.S. assistance program for black South Africans, an extension or mild increase of the executive order sanctions from the previous year, a prohibition on new investment by firms that did not adhere to the Sullivan Principles, and a ban on computer sales to government agencies. Five days later Crocker reported to Shultz that the White House had replaced the State Department draft with a speech written by archconservative Patrick Buchanan. Crocker was furious. "Permitting Communications Director Buchanan to mess with the basics of American foreign policy was to me almost obscene," Crocker wrote later. Buchanan's version spent three lines criticizing Pretoria and more than a page on

ANC terrorism and necklacing in the townships. The central goal of U.S. policy, according to the speech, was to keep South Africa's ports, minerals, and other resources out of Soviet hands. A few days later, White House chief of staff Donald Regan indicated his support for this line of reasoning. Without South African minerals, Regan asked, "where are you going to get your chrome for your bathroom fixtures, for hardening steels, for your bumpers and autos and the like? . . . Are the women of American prepared to give up their jewelry?"

While Donald Regan's remarks provoked a new storm of protest, Chester Crocker and George Shultz wrangled with White House conservatives for ten days over the content of the speech. The relentless tinkering with phrases and paragraphs brought to the surface the contradictions in the administration's policy. Crocker had believed that constructive engagement was a policy of graduated pressure, while rightwing ideologues viewed it as domestic cover for an anti-Communist, pro-Botha policy. For four years the policy's skirt had been wide enough to cover its competing offspring. As the fierce national debate over apartheid snipped away at the policy's ambiguity and breadth, the partisans of its different interpretations battled for what remained. Ironically, Crocker now found himself in a similar position to his external critics: pushing the administration to be more bold in its condemnation of apartheid.

Three days before Reagan's speech, Crocker received yet another version. "Alongside our vibrant language on apartheid," Crocker wrote later, "we found formulations that sounded as if they had come from the editors of the South African Broadcasting system." Angered by the clouds of "vintage Afrikaner-speak," Crocker and Shultz again did emergency repairs and fretted that they could not prevent more tinkering by White House ideologues. Even Lugar was alarmed by the dynamics around Reagan. After he and Kassebaum discussed South Africa policy with the president in the Oval Office on July 21, Lugar wrote that it was "clear that Africa policy issues were not getting the attention at the presidential level they needed in light of events in South Africa."

On July 22, the day of the speech, the two men went over to the White House to brief the press and to listen to Reagan deliver his talk. As they passed by John Poindexter's office, the door opened. Out came "the president's own South Africa lobby," as Crocker caustically put it: CIA director William Casey, Pat Buchanan, and several others. "Shultz growled that they would be well advised to keep their hands off the latest draft we had seen," Crocker recalled, "but the crime had already been committed." Crocker and Shultz watched in stoic dismay as Reagan stepped to the podium in the East Room of the White House. Reagan began on a State Department tack. "The root cause of South

Africa's disorder is apartheid," Reagan said, a system he described as "morally wrong and politically unacceptable." The president then launched into an attack on disinvestment, citing Margaret Thatcher and Alan Paton for support. "The primary victims of an economic boycott of South Africa," Reagan said, "would be the very people we seek to help." As the speech progressed, the archconservative voice emerged more and more. Reagan attacked the African National Congress for its program of "calculated terror . . . designed to bring about further repression, the imposition of martial law, and eventually creating the conditions for racial war."

Crocker was appalled at this "abuse of logic," as he described it in his memoirs. "South Africa's state of emergency was now the fault of the ANC." From there the speech got worse. Instead of speaking about the denial of basic human rights, Reagan vigorously defended the "dramatic change" that had taken place under P. W. Botha. Instead of acknowledging black despair, Reagan eloquently described the need for "the social, economic, and physical security of the white people in this land they love and have sacrificed so much to build." Instead of encouraging the South African government to find common ground with its opponents, Reagan exonerated the National Party. "The South African government," said the president, "is under no obligation to negotiate the future of the country with any organization that proclaims a goal of creating a Communist state and uses terrorist tactics to achieve it."

Though Buchanan and his staff were thrilled by Reagan's performance, the speech unleashed a gale of criticism. The next day's newspapers described the speech as a "rebuff" to Congress; the *New York Times* also chose the day to reveal that the U.S. government had been cooperating closely for years with South Africa's intelligence services. "I had hoped the president would take the occasion for an extraordinary message to the world," said Richard Lugar. "He did not do so." Desmond Tutu told an Associated Press reporter that he found the speech "nauseating." Reagan, said the archbishop, "sits there like the great big, white chief of old to tell us black people that we don't know what is good for us." "I am quite angry," Tutu told another reporter in a remark that triggered its own controversy in South Africa. "I think the West, for my part, can go to hell."

The next day George Shultz journeyed to Capitol Hill and attempted to repair the damage. Testifying for more than four hours before the Senate Foreign Relations Committee, Shultz delivered the message he had hoped Reagan would offer. The secretary of state called for the elimination of all apartheid laws, the release of Nelson Mandela, the lifting of the ban on political movements, and the end to the state of emergency. He said that there was no need for additional sanctions because "the market is speaking clearly about where the hardening positions of the South African government and its violent opponents are taking South Africa." The country, he insisted, was already "under siege by self-imposed economic sanctions." Shultz criticized both the South African government's cross-border raids and ANC guerrilla strikes. At the same time, he insisted that the African National Congress was "an important part of the political equation," promised to meet with Oliver Tambo, and went out of his way to praise Nelson Mandela's character. The secretary of state said that he was even prepared to change "the mix of pressures"—that is, approve sanctions—if such a move were coordinated with Allied efforts to restart the Eminent Persons Group process.

The senators were not mollified. The day before Reagan's speech, the president had met with key Republican senators and assured them that he would provide new leadership on the issue. Instead, Crocker wrote, the president's "strident pro-Pretoria tilt" had given them "no ground on which to stand against the pro-sanctions crusade." In Crocker's view, the July 22 speech transformed the "great communicator" into the "great polarizer," splitting his own party on a key foreign policy issue just three months from a critical midterm election. Senators began abandoning the Reagan ship in droves. Nancy Kassebaum introduced new legislation banning new investment; Robert Dole called again for a special envoy; and Richard Lugar pressed forward with his own bill increasing sanctions against South Africa. On Tuesday, August 12, Reagan denounced sanctions again at a press conference, citing Buthelezi as his authority. Three days later, the editors of the *New York Times* urged passage of Lugar's bill. "If the Senate needed any more reason to approve sanctions against South Africa today," they wrote in the lead editorial, "the president provided it with his dreadful message of mumbling indifference in his news conference." That afternoon, Lugar's bill arrived on the floor of the Senate and passed, eighty-four to fourteen. In the vote, thirty-seven Republicans crossed the aisle to vote against their president.

Watching from the House side, the leaders of the Congressional Black Caucus and other supporters of sanctions legislation now faced a tricky choice. Two bills had passed: the strict Dellums bill in the House and the more moderate Lugar bill in the Senate. Under the normal legislative procedure, the two measures would be sent to a joint House-Senate conference where a compromise version would be drafted and resubmitted for a vote in both chambers of Congress. This could take weeks, at which point Reagan would be able to exercise a "pocket veto." (The president is obliged to sign a bill within sixty days of its passage, but if fewer than sixty days remain before Congress adjourns, a president can kill a bill simply by refusing to sign and waiting for Congress to depart.)

The alternative strategy, the House activists realized, would be to jettison their own bill, accept the moderate Senate version, force Reagan to exercise his veto directly, and press for an override by both houses of Congress.

Over the previous year a strong network had arisen between the pro-sanctions forces in Congress. Staff members from the offices of Senators Edward Kennedy, Alan Cranston, Paul Sarbanes, and Lowell Weicker set up a South Africa working group that met every Monday to discuss strategy and policy. The senators themselves conferred frequently not only with each other but with their counterparts in the House—William Gray, Ronald Dellums, Howard Wolpe, and Stephen Solarz. Buzzing in and around all of these proceedings was Randall Robinson, who relentlessly encouraged, coaxed, and prodded the lawmakers forward. Though all of the participants in the coalition supported the stronger sanctions of the Dellums package, they finally decided, after intense discussion, that they should accept the Lugar bill and force a direct confrontation with the president of the United States.

In the following weeks, congressional Republicans again implored Reagan to change his mind and take the lead on the sanctions question. Eleven conservative members of the House of Representatives wrote Reagan an urgent letter asking the president to "propose a constitutional plan in order to begin the process of negotiations." "There is no reason to insist on the principle of one-person one-vote instantly," wrote the representatives, among them James Courter of New Jersey, Robert Dornan of California, and Newt Gingrich of Georgia, "which few on any side of the debate think is realistic in the current context." On August 24, Senator Lugar wrote an op-ed piece in the *New York Times* again asking the president to act.

The White House remained unmoved, choosing only to proceed with plans to nominate a black ambassador to South Africa. Robert Brown had withdrawn after allegations appeared in the press that one of his businesses had been used as front by white backers to gain access to funds and contracts reserved for minorities. The White House poked through the State Department roster and came up with the names of Terrence Todman, the U.S. ambassador to Denmark, and Edward J. Perkins, the U.S. ambassador to Liberia. On September 4, in a last-ditch effort to forestall action by Congress, Reagan announced that he would extend his limited executive order sanctions for one more year. A week later, the full House formally approved the Lugar bill—now known as the Comprehensive Anti-Apartheid Act (CAAA)—and sent it directly to Reagan's desk. Lugar told the press that if the president chose to veto it, he would personally lead the override fight. On September 18, Lugar met with Donald Regan and Robert Dole, who had said that he would back the president. Regan asked Lugar if the president could take any more executive steps that would forestall action; Lugar replied that the White House had had an entire year to exercise leadership and should not try to jump on board just days before a vote.

On September 26, Reagan vetoed Lugar's bill. The White House had picked a Friday to announce the veto in order to have the weekend to line up enough votes to sustain it. In five years as president, Reagan had never lost such a challenge on a question of foreign policy. Nonetheless, on Monday, the House of Representatives overturned his veto and passed the Comprehensive Anti-Apartheid Act by a margin of forty-nine votes. Attention instantly shifted to the Senate. State Department and White House officials scrambled to the phones. George Shultz told Republican senators that it would be dangerous to undercut the president's foreign policy question shortly before the upcoming summit with Mikhail Gorbachev. White House officials formally announced the appointment of Edward Perkins as the U.S. ambassador to Pretoria and promised senators that they were preparing a last-minute set of executive orders as an alternative to the Lugar bill. Most of the senators who heard the proposal rejected it as "a day late and a dollar short," said Mark Helmke, a key member of Lugar's staff. "It's too bad the White House didn't want to discuss this with us three months ago."

The South African lobby also swung into action, working the extensive channels it had developed over the years. On October 1, Jesse Helms summoned two of his farm belt colleagues into the Republican cloakroom just off the Senate floor and handed them the telephone. To their surprise, each found himself talking to South African Foreign Minister Pik Botha nine thousand miles away in Pretoria. Botha told the senators that if the Senate approved the sanctions passage, South Africa would cancel its order for 250,000 metric tons of American grain and would bar grain transhipment to neighboring African states. When Lugar learned of the phone calls, he exploded. Botha's attempts at "intimidation and bribery," he said in a voice trembling with anger, "were an affront to the decency of the American people. . . . I find this entire action—a foreign minister of a foreign country calling senators off the floor—to be despicable," Lugar told reporters. Jesse Helms shrugged off the criticism. "It's all right for a friend to call a friend," Helms said.

The next day, Thursday, October 2, the Senate voted. The Botha effort had actually backfired: thirty-one senators abandoned the president, overriding Reagan's veto with twelve votes to spare. When the outcome became clear, Representative Mickey Leland grabbed Randall Robinson in a bear hug. More than twenty-six years after Sharpeville, the goal of congressional sanctions against South Africa had finally been achieved.

FIFTEEN

The Effect of Sanctions

Once the taps of international capital investment and loans had been turned off, apartheid began to stare the spectre of bankruptcy in the face.
—WILLEM DE KLERK

THE PASSAGE of the Comprehensive Anti-Apartheid Act (CAAA) demonstrated to both American companies and the South African government that apartheid had become a dominant political issue in the United States. Despite the historical differences between the United States and South Africa, the racial struggles in the two countries had become ideologically fused. Just as opposition to Soviet Communism had served as the main measure of American patriotism, so did opposition to apartheid evolve into an index of commitment to racial justice in the United States. The Comprehensive Anti-Apartheid Act had passed, complained Robert Dole, because it had "become a domestic civil rights issue."

In comparison to the original Dellums bill in the House, the provisions of the CAAA were actually rather mild. The law halted the domestic sale of Krugerrands; ended all flights between South Africa and the United States; banned the import of iron, steel, uranium, coal, textiles, and agricultural products; and barred American firms from making any new investments in South Africa. The law also stipulated that the president could not remove sanctions until the South African government met several conditions: lifting the state of emergency; releasing Nelson Mandela and all other political prisoners; unbanned political parties; repealing all apartheid laws; and beginning negotiations with the African National Congress and others about the future form of government.

Foreign Minister Pik Botha immediately attacked the U.S. Congress. "No reason or argument could have stemmed this emotional tide," Botha told reporters in Pretoria. Rebuffing criticisms of his phone calls to the Senate, Botha issued another veiled threat against South Africa's neighboring states. "If we import cotton from Zimbabwe and other African countries and manufacture cloth out of it, can we still export that cloth?" he asked. "If not, must I tell Zimbabwe that I cannot import their cotton?"

After the bill's passage, most academics, journalists, and economists predicted that its measures would have little effect on the South African or American economy because the volume of trade between the two countries was relatively small. The total 1985 value of U.S. imports of South African iron, uranium, agricultural products, and textiles, for example, was just over $400 million dollars. Trade experts predicted that South Africa would easily find other markets for its products. Business leaders in South Africa tried to sound defiant. "There is no question of South Africa being seriously affected," said Franklin Lubke of the American Chamber of Commerce in Johannesburg the day after the bill passed. Despite the bravado, many foreign business executives privately worried. External pressures were on the rise. In early August, under duress from her Commonwealth partners, Margaret Thatcher had agreed to a set of nonbinding sanctions including a ban on new investment and on imports from South Africa. In September the foreign ministers of the European Economic Community had announced a set of measures to curb new investment. Many feared that the American action would trigger a wave of measures by the Europeans and the Japanese.

The act of Congress represented only part of what was happening in the United States. At the time of the passage of the Comprehensive Anti-Apartheid Act, 19 states, 68 cities, and 119 colleges and universities had already approved restrictions of various sorts, and the numbers were increasing. On July 18, 1986, the regents of the University of California system voted to sell $3.1 billion in stock and bonds in twenty-nine major companies with South African subsidiaries. On August 26, the California Senate approved divestment of South Africa–related stock from the state's three major public pension plans, whose total asset value at the time exceeded $65 billion—a sum equal to roughly two-thirds of South Africa's entire national economic output. More than $11 billion in securities were affected, including $500 million in IBM stock and bonds alone. The California Senate action sent shock waves through the financial community. Analysts predicted, for the first time, that divestment might force down the stock price of even America's most mammoth companies.

For some firms the Comprehensive Anti-Apartheid Act was simply the last straw. On Tuesday, October 21, anti-apartheid activists across the country awoke to an astonishing headline: GENERAL MOTORS TO SELL SOUTH AFRICA UNIT TO LOCAL GROUP. The board of General Motors had made the decision to withdraw on October 6, four days after Congress had overridden Reagan's veto. "This was a reluctant decision," said Robert White, the managing director of General Motors in South Africa, "but it is the right decision when you consider the pressure the U.S. company has been under and the pressure we have been under." In a statement from Detroit, chair Roger Smith did not refer to such pressures. "GMSA has been losing money for several years in a very difficult South African business climate," Smith explained, "[and] we have been disappointed in the pace of change in ending apartheid in South Africa." Leon Sullivan, still a member of the GM board, expressed his support for the move, telling reporters that he hoped it would be a "watershed for change." Anti-apartheid groups in the United States were thrilled. "This is a tremendously significant decision," said Tim Smith of ICCR. "Business will understand the significance of the action. We expect the trickle of companies leaving South Africa to turn into a flood."

The very same day, while the GM headline was still fresh, another titan fell when IBM suddenly announced that, after a lengthy internal review, it too was quitting South Africa. The previous April, CEO John Akers had triggered another melee when he hinted that IBM might leave but that, if it did, its decision would have no ethical import. "If we elect to leave, it will be a business decision," Akers had said. "We are not in business to conduct moral activism, we are not in business to conduct socially responsible action. We are in business to conduct business." His remarks were seized upon by activists as evidence of IBM's indifference to South African blacks. On the day of the IBM withdrawal, Akers said that the company had acted not only because of the deteriorating conditions in South Africa, but also because of economic pressure from within the United States. The decision by the two mammoth corporations to withdraw sent the business community in South Africa reeling. "This isn't a buyout, it's a walk-away," said Pierre Renfret, a prominent South African management consultant. "It's mind-boggling in its implications, two of the biggest companies in the world pulling out of South Africa."

The passage of the Comprehensive Anti-Apartheid Act and the withdrawal of General Motors and IBM, though important, did not trigger instant capitulation by the Pretorian government. The American law was too moderate and the Reagan administration's commitment too feeble for the effects to be instantly noticeable. P. W. Botha responded with characteristic defiance. "We dare not yield to the irresponsible and often superficial demands which will destroy everything created over so many decades by so many generations," Botha said in his address on January 1, 1987. "The actions taken us against us have been totally counterproductive." In the same speech, Botha tried to use America's racial history to rebut the Comprehensive Anti-Apartheid Act. Americans did not have a leg to stand on, Botha argued, since it had taken from 1776 to 1870 "to complete their Constitution and grant civil liberties to its black minority and another century and a fierce civil rights struggle to insure that those rights were more than theoretical."

As Vorster had done in 1977, P. W. Botha tried to turn foreign pressures to his advantage by calling for early elections. The election, which took place in May, showed that the National Party retained considerable clout: South Africa's two million white voters increased its parliamentary margin by 7 seats, up to 133. The South African economy also seemed to rally. As companies adjusted to the restrictions, South Africa experienced a brief import substitution boom, leading conservative analysts to claim that sanctions had failed. In fact, the opposite was true: the South African economy was slowly and steadily sinking. Like a small boat trying to cross an ocean, the South African economy could stay afloat only as long as the sea was calm and the vessel did not leak. As the waves of unrest grew larger and the sanctions poked more holes through the hull, the craft became harder to navigate. Just as the crew of a sinking ship would at first bail and row with renewed energy, so did the economy show a false vitality for a short period. Over time, the relentless intake of water, the sudden appearance of unexpected problems, the failure of attempted repairs, and the cumulative effect of crisis and exhaustion would sap the crew's faith that the ship could be saved. With each passing month, waves of dissent crashed more violently and the breaches caused by financial, trade, and investment restrictions forced the South African economy lower into the water. It would not be long before the top officers began to wonder aloud whether their irascible captain could lead them safely to his imagined destination.

South Africa's economy faltered not because of any single action by a company or a country, but because of the combined repercussions on an economy which, even at its best, had serious structural flaws. The restrictions imposed by the outside world fell into four categories that can be ranked in ascending order of their severity of impact on the South African psyche and economy. The first category was that of *trade sanctions,* in which the outside world put limits on what it would buy from or sell to South Africa. The second was *corporate disinvestment,* by which foreign companies, under pressure from home, decided to withdraw their subsidiaries. The third was *psychological or cultural restrictions,* in which South Africans were barred from participating in international events or receiving the benefits of world knowledge and culture. The final, and most ruinous, restrictions were the *financial sanctions* that gradually compelled the South African government to change course.

Even though the first form, trade sanctions, did not bring the South African economy to its knees, it still proved more effective than anyone had predicted. Before sanctions were passed, the South African government had insisted that trade restrictions would not hurt because the economy was largely self-sufficient and because the West was dependent on South Africa's products. There was some truth to this. Despite years of industrialization, South Africa's economy still resembled that of a Third World country: it extracted resources out of the ground and sold them on the international market in exchange for machinery and other capital goods. To get out of this rut, the South African government had for decades imposed tariffs and tried to stimulate domestic manufacturing. The hope was that by selling to a protected domestic market South African manufacturers would soon achieve the economies of scale necessary to compete in a global economy. Ironically, this governmental strategy was undermined by apartheid, which stunted the growth of black incomes and purchasing power. In the automobile industry, for example, the maldistribution of income prevented annual new passenger car sales from ever rising much above three hundred thousand, even though the total South African population was nearly thirty-five million. Blacks simply couldn't afford most South African products. Whites, in general, didn't want them, preferring to pay a premium for foreign electronics and appliances. Despite South Africa's sixty-year campaign to increase its manufacturing base, eighty percent of its annual imports still consisted of machinery, electrical equipment, and other advanced products.

Thus, during the late 1980s, the greatest restrictions of foreign purchases came not from other countries but from the South African government itself. Governments measure their balance of payments with other countries through two accounts. The capital account records investment in a country; the current account measures trade. Most growing countries are receiving enough foreign investment (which creates a capital account surplus) that they can afford to buy more abroad than they are selling (which generates a current account deficit). Because of the debt crisis, South African treasury officials suddenly had to reverse this flow. Paying back billions in bank loans would create a capital account deficit that the government could finance only through a current account surplus, in other words, by forcing South Africa to sell more than it bought.

The result was supremely ironic. The bank crisis not only cut off the flow of money; it forced South Africa to impose import restrictions far more severe than any country could have established. In the mid-1980s the government slapped higher import tariffs on many products, from cars to electronics. In addition, it found that it could not afford to carry out its threat to stop selling strategic metals like chrome, platinum, vanadium, and manganese to the West—indeed, the government had to do everything it could to promote their sale. Maintaining foreign markets for its commodities like coal proved even more difficult. Denmark, which had purchased $135 million worth of coal in 1985, refused to buy any more in 1986. The United States dropped its purchases of uranium, iron, steel, and coal from 351 million rand in 1986 to zero in the first half of 1987. In the same period, total U.S. purchases of South African goods dropped by almost half, from 2.6 billion rand in 1986 to 1.4 billion in 1987. Even though South Africa vigorously slashed the prices of its metals and ores, the United States, Australia, Denmark, Finland, Ireland, New Zealand, Norway, and Sweden collectively cut their imports by more than a third. Despite new purchases by Japan ($748 million in 1986, 44 percent more than in 1985) and Taiwan ($303 million, an increase of 146 percent), South Africa's overall exports still slipped a painful 7 percent in a single year.

Sanctions thus did not actually cut off trade with South Africa; they just made trade much more difficult. South Africa could sell abroad, but it had to do so at a steep "sanctions discount." Advanced Western technology and weaponry continued to flow in, but South Africa had to pay a premium and bring the products in through a maze of deception. Products flowed through shell businesses to exotic ports, were relabeled, and shipped to South Africa. To help businesses make these complicated arrangements, the South African government set up several sanction-busting offices, one of which was led by a former director of the Rhodesian Reserve Bank. Despite its best efforts, the South African government could not avoid a painful reality. Every transaction took extra time. Every middleman demanded an extra fee. Each link in the chain required money, and every cent spent busting sanctions was a cent that could not be spent elsewhere—not on security, not on the citizenry, and not on industrial investment. By the end of the decade, trade sanctions were imposing an estimated 5 billion rand annual penalty ($3.4 billion in 1994 dollars) on the South African economy. For a country with an annual GDP that hovered around $100 billion, the impact was immense.

The area in which trade restrictions had by far the greatest impact was oil, which constituted roughly one-fifth of South Africa's intermediate imports. Though Pretoria had made it a criminal offense to disclose information about the oil industry, the Shipping Research Bureau, a

Dutch anti-apartheid group launched in 1980, succeeded in documenting South Africa's secret oil traffic. By meticulously tracking the movements of the world's tankers, the bureau identified a steady flow of millions of tons of oil, usually carried from the Persian Gulf to Durban by Norwegian ships. Though these shipments were enormously expensive, they formed only part of what South Africa had to pay to protect its access to oil. The Pretorian government also constructed massive storage facilities, stockpiled hundreds of millions of barrels of oil, and built the MOSSGAS natural gas–to–oil conversion plant at Mossel Bay, near the southernmost tip of the African continent. The MOSSGAS plant became a boondoggle whose cost, due in part to the restrictions on foreign technology, ballooned to more than 12 billion rand and could only produce oil at more than double the global price. Combining the cost of circumventing sanctions, the Shipping Research Bureau estimated that South Africa paid about $2 billion a year, or more than $25 billion in cumulative costs, from 1979 to 1989. P. W. Botha himself confirmed the magnitude of the expense when, in an unguarded moment, he told a domestic audience that oil sanctions between 1974 and 1984 had forced South Africa to pay out an extra 22 billion rand. If true, this meant that the oil sanctions alone cut the country's annual growth by more than two percent.

Added to the difficulties of importing and exporting was the cascade of corporate disinvestments. From January 1, 1986, to April 30, 1988, one hundred fourteen U.S. companies pulled out, including major firms like Control Data, Dow Chemical, Eastman Kodak, Exxon, Ford, General Electric, Goodyear, Johnson Controls, Merck, Newmont Mining, and Unisys. In their public statements, some of the chief executives tried to deflect attention from the U.S. anti-apartheid campaign by insisting that their decisions were based on the faltering South African economy. Each time they did so, they sent a shock wave through the Johannesburg Stock Exchange and through the halls of government.

Other executives attributed their decisions to a mix of internal and external pressures. John Bryan, the chairman of Sara Lee, told the *Wall Street Journal* that he had made his decision after being "barraged" by shareholder protests at the 1986 annual meeting. After fielding questions on South Africa for more than an hour, Bryan said, he realized that not a single person had advocated remaining. "You can debate the moral question of whether it's better to stay or go, but the shareholder is the one who owns us," Bryan told a reporter. "If he says 'Get out,' and it can be done without penalizing the company, that's what you do." The rapid spread of selective purchasing ordinances by American cities and states was also blamed. Donald Frey, the president of Bell and Howell, a maker of educational products, told *Business Week* that $12 million in annual sales to South Africa was not worth "the potential negative impact . . . on other Bell and Howell businesses." Though Frey personally rejected the divestment campaign as "wrong-headed," he said that because of the company's dependence on large sales to American public institutions it simply could not risk a product boycott.

The speed and extent of the many American firms' departures took the members of the U.S. anti-apartheid movement by surprise, as did the methods the companies used to transfer the ownership of their assets. Only ten percent of the firms actually shut down. The most prominent of these was Eastman Kodak, which had more than 450 South African employees. In November 1986 Kodak's senior executives, eager to comply with New York City's selective purchasing law, sold the subsidiary and attempted, with limited success, to ban all Kodak products in South Africa. Other companies tried to find ways that would allow them simultaneously to satisfy political demands in the United States, recoup their investment, and maintain as much of a presence in the South African market as possible. The fastest and most popular method was to sell the subsidiary to a South African company or to a group of former managers and to include financing, licensing, and other provisions in the terms of sale that would maintain a relationship with the former parent. IBM, for example, sold its subsidiary on March 1, 1987, to an independent trust headed by two of its former managers. The executives of the new company, now known as ISM, immediately took out large print advertisements reassuring their customers that the full IBM product line would remain available in South Africa. "We are absolutely committed to continuing the supply of IBM products," one manager told South African television. Soon afterward the new managing director of ISM, Brian Mehl, revealed that the former parent had given ISM "a very favorable contract with a minimum three year guarantee for product supply and a minimum five year guarantee for parts supply." Such arrangements provoked dismay in the U.S. anti-apartheid community. "It's not doing what we want, which is to cut off the technology," said Richard Knight of the American Committee on Africa. "IBM might have gone much farther," grumbled Randall Robinson.

For most firms, the process of disinvestment was heavily influenced by the structural problems of the industry. This was particularly true of the auto manufacturers, who had been battling a severe slump since 1983. As more and more companies had built plants and scrambled to sell cars to the small, affluent white population, profit margins had drastically eroded. Faced with a saturated white market and no export demand, South African auto executives had watched their total industry sales plummet from a high of 301,000 in 1981 to 174,500 in 1986. At the same time, rapid inflation and the declining value of the rand caused operating costs to jump by more than two-thirds. The automakers tried to restore profitability by doubling the price of their cars and cutting their workforce from fifty thousand in 1982 to twenty-nine thousand in 1986, but the measures did not eliminate the excess capacity and the abysmal returns. Everyone recognized that some rationalization needed to take place, either through the collapse of the weakest firms or through the merger of competitors. The first major move came in late 1984 when Ford combined its operations with Amcar, the automaking division of Anglo-American. The two companies already had an indirect manufacturing link through Mazda, of which Amcar was the local licensee and Ford was a large shareholder. The Ford-Amcar agreement created the South African Motor Corporation (SAMCOR), in which Ford held forty-two percent and Anglo-American fifty-eight percent. To cut costs, the new company shut down almost all of its facilities in Port Elizabeth, eliminating four thousand jobs.

By 1986, therefore, the economic picture for foreign automakers in South Africa was not rosy. Under normal circumstances, the executives of a multinational firm faced with such conditions do not disinvest. Instead, they trim operations and hope that, with their deeper financial pockets, they will be able to preserve market share, ride out the business cycle, and emerge stronger in a pared-down field. In the South African case, the economics were poor, the prospects for rapid improvement slim, and the pressures at home large and increasing. The withdrawal decision by General Motors in 1986 and Ford Motor Company in 1987 sparked resistance from South Africa's black unions. Despite years of professing concern for their employees, General Motors' managers chose a particularly harsh method of disinvestment. When GM chair Roger Smith said in early October 1986 that his firm was reviewing its presence in South Africa, shop stewards from the local union pressed GM managers about what he meant and were told that the chairman had been misquoted. The union leaders, still suspicious, called a general meeting and drafted several demands, including severance pay, a payout of pension contributions, and the right to appoint two workers to the board of any new company. They also asked for a meeting with management. When they were refused, they staged a sit-in, which ended after two weeks when the company fired 570 of the employees and summoned the police to evict them. In the middle of the strike, GM's executives announced the terms of the disinvestment. General Motors would sell the subsidiary to a group of local managers, who would rename the company Delta Motors. The American parent would assist the new firm by liquidating the accumulated debt of the subsidiary, approximately $40 million, thus freeing the South African executives to raise money on the local capital markets. GM would also continue to supply technology, components, and spare parts through Adam Opel, its wholly owned German subsidiary, and Isuzu of Japan, in which GM held a minority position. Shortly afterward the new managing director announced that Delta would abandon General Motors' ban on sales to the military and police and would vigorously pursue government business. By undercutting the unions, slashing labor costs, curtailing philanthropy, and luring military and government orders, Delta's managers restored the firm to profitability within two years.

In contrast to General Motors' approach, Ford's executives negotiated the terms of their withdrawal directly with the local unions and COSATU. The decision to do so was made by Wayne Fredericks, who at the time was still the director of foreign public affairs for Ford Motor Company. Fredericks worked for half a year with his associate William Broderick on the details of the withdrawal agreement. "Nineteen eighty-seven was the year when Broderick and I seemed to be commuting to South Africa," Fredericks said later. He found the discussions fascinating because "they dealt not only with Ford's departure but also with what Ford would leave behind." Fredericks and Broderick conferred privately with the unions for the first six months of 1987; in June, Ford announced its decision to withdraw. Under the agreement, Ford would split its holdings between Anglo-American and a new worker trust in such a way that the trust would have a twenty-four percent holding in SAMCOR. Ford would continue to market its products through more than 140 Ford dealerships; and sales to the military and police would continue.

Though the offer was exceptional in granting equity participation to unions, it also avoided the twenty-five percent threshold that would, under South Africa law, have given the trust veto power over certain kinds of company decisions. At first, Fredericks and his associates had proposed to the National Automobile and Allied Workers Union (NAAWU) that the shares be placed in a trust and that the dividends be distributed on an individual basis to the workers. The union leaders held a meeting with some of the rank and file at which this was discussed and then said that such an arrangement would co-opt the workers and the workers would prefer individual lump sum payments equal to the value of the shares. The Ford negotiators refused and gave the union three choices: Ford would leave South Africa without setting up a trust; it would set up a trust and distribute the dividends to individual workers; or it would set up a trust and direct the trustees to use the income for community development projects.

When the NAAWU eventually accepted the third option, a rival union ran to the Ford workers in Pretoria, told them that the NAAWU leaders had prevented each of them from receiving a cash payment of

49,000 rand for their shares, and promised to get the money for them if the workers gave their support. The workers repudiated the NAAWU agreement, rejected the shop stewards who supported it, and elected a new "anti-trust" committee. The new committee made a host of threats, which Ford ignored. In April 1988, only days before the agreement was to take effect, the workers went out on a wildcat strike. The strike eventually failed and Ford set up the major trust with the community development provision, as well as two smaller community trusts, one in Mamelodi and the other in Port Elizabeth. When the dividends for 1988 were announced, however, the trustees offered to award them on an individual basis to those who wanted them.

The disinvestment of Coca-Cola also caused controversy. In keeping with its international strategy, the company manufactured syrup in South Africa through a wholly owned subsidiary and then sold it to licensed bottling franchises. At the time of its decision to withdraw, Coca-Cola had a concentrate factory in Durban, a fruit juice company, the majority share of a canning company, and a minority position in a bottling firm. Throughout the early 1980s pressure on Coca-Cola to withdraw had steadily increased. The company, in part because it was based in Atlanta, Georgia, had become a target of prominent civil rights activists, who threatened to launch a national boycott if the company didn't get out of South Africa. Though Coca-Cola endorsed the Sullivan Principles, the refusal of its South African juice business to increase the wages of its farmworkers meant that it never achieved the highest rating.

In part because Donald McHenry, the former ambassador to the UN, was on Coca-Cola's board and had studied U.S. corporate involvement in South Africa in the early 1970s, Coca-Cola planned its disinvestment carefully. In the withdrawal announcement in November 1986, company officials said that although they were still making good profits, they were getting out because of the political situation. They then shut down their Durban plant and moved it to Swaziland; closed all of their corporate offices; sold most of their remaining assets to a new South African company put together by their former managers; arranged for ten percent of the shares in the new company to be made available at below market price to their 3,500 former employees and 8,000 small retailers; persuaded an independent franchiser in East London to sell one of its bottling plants to Kilimanjaro Investments, a group of black South African investors; and promised that it would transfer $10 million to the Equal Opportunity Foundation, a charitable organization established by Coca-Cola in 1986 whose board was made up of prominent South African blacks, including both Allan Boesak and Desmond Tutu.

Almost every component of this arrangement was criticized. South African labor leaders said that Coca-Cola had neither provided enough advance warning nor consulted with the unions about the terms of the withdrawal and that the new company and its former parent were still passing the buck to each other whenever someone asked a question. U.S. anti-apartheid activists charged that Coca-Cola was not really disinvesting by moving its factory a few hundred miles into Swaziland, which was surrounded by South African territory and relied on South Africa for its trade. Though sixty percent of both the workers and the retailers took advantage of the share offer, union leaders from the Food and Allied Workers Union warned that the shares would not really increase their incomes and would distract workers from the more important goals of obtaining higher wages and a genuine role in company decision making. Others debated whether it was right for any anti-apartheid leader to sit on the board of the Equal Opportunity Foundation and whether it was proper for community organizations to accept the foundation's money.

The ingenuity and complexity of the corporate arrangements sparked new debates within both South Africa and the United States. For anti-apartheid activists like Jennifer Davis and Randall Robinson, the decision by American executives to rearrange their ownership patterns so as to comply with the letter of the local, state, and federal laws while simultaneously continuing to supply their full product line to the South African economy was further proof of corporate duplicity and bad faith. For many corporate executives, however, the activists' requirements had been very specific. They had called for disinvestment—that is, the sale of direct investments—not for a unilateral refusal by American companies to sell their products in South Africa. For the activists to achieve their stated goal, and then suddenly demand something else was a form of "moving the goalposts," and proof of *their* duplicity and bad faith.

Tim Smith, Jennifer Davis, and Randall Robinson, however, were determined not to let IBM and other US firms get away with telling American cities, states, and institutional investors that they were no longer doing business with South Africa. In January 1987 the leading U.S. anti-apartheid groups—including the American Committee on Africa, the Interfaith Center on Corporate Responsibility, and Trans-Africa—issued a joint statement that spelled out a broad interpretation of disinvestment. "We support an end to all corporate involvement in or with South Africa and Namibia," they said. A corporation was "involved" if it had "direct investments in South Africa or Namibia . . . or has entered into franchise, licensing or management agreements . . . or is a financial institution that has not prohibited new investments, loans, credits, or related services . . . or has more than 5% of their common stock beneficially owned or controlled by a South African entity." They then devoted considerable effort to ensuring that all of the institutions that had divestment or selective purchasing policies used this broad definition for "doing business" in South Africa rather than the more narrow one that executives were promoting around the country.

By early 1988 the anti-apartheid activists realized that disinvestment by American companies had, in the short term, produced some unintended consequences. Though a few firms made an effort to distribute equity shares to workers, most of the financial benefit of disinvestment went to whites. In the case of the management buyouts, the ability of white managers to use borrowed corporate funds to purchase large companies at low prices produced an instant new generation of paper millionaires. As at Delta Motors, the new owners usually abandoned the Sullivan Principles, jettisoned restrictions on sales to the government, slashed philanthropic support for scholarships, health care, housing, and other community projects, and took a more combative line toward unions.

When the U.S. subsidiaries were purchased by South African conglomerates, increased concentration of South African industry often resulted. By the end of 1987, for example, Anglo-American had taken over the South African portions of the Ford Motor Company, Barclays Bank, and Citicorp, pushing the proportion of the shares it controlled on the Johannesburg Stock Exchange from fifty-four to sixty percent. Ironically, in some cases, the process of disinvestment actually *increased* investment in South Africa. In order to retire their subsidiary's debt, Ford Motor Company gave $61 million to SAMCOR, a move that American anti-apartheid activists criticized as a violation of the Comprehensive Anti-Apartheid Act's ban on new investment.

Another form of sanctions, one that proved more jarring to white South Africans than most outsiders were aware, were the psychological and cultural sanctions. These measures grew rapidly throughout the 1980s and steadily undercut white South Africans' faith in their own government's legitimacy. Though Pretoria's strict media controls drastically reduced the coverage on American network television, South Africa's image as a land of brutal repression continued to grow in the American public mind through portrayals of apartheid in music, theater, films, and alternative television. To protest the attempt by the managers of Sun City, a $90 million resort in Bophuthatswana, to lure American performers for high fees, guitarist Little Steven brought together Pat Benatar, Bono, Jimmy Cliff, Miles Davis, Herbie Hancock, Bruce Springsteen, Ringo Starr, Bob Dylan, and four dozen other musicians from six continents to form Artists United against Apartheid and record a hit single, "I Ain't Gonna Play Sun City," in late 1985. In 1987 Paul Simon hooked up with Ladysmith Black Mombaza, a black South African vocal group; their musical collaboration on Simon's *Graceland* proved widely successful and introduced millions of Americans to the beauty and vitality of black South African culture.

The South African drama quickly moved into other cultural forms. *Sarafina,* a powerful musical about the life of a young girl in Soweto, first appeared on Broadway in 1988. In June 1988 a daylong rock concert, broadcast around the world by satellite, took place at Wembley Stadium outside of London to honor Nelson Mandela's seventieth birthday. Three months later Home Box Office aired *Mandela,* a heroic portrayal of the ANC leader starring Danny Glover. Winnie Mandela and Jerry Falwell both tried to block the broadcast, Mandela arguing that the film invaded her privacy and Falwell that it glorified a Communist. A weekly half-hour television program on events, *South Africa Now,* which used South African exiles as announcers and broadcast illegal footage, started appearing on cable networks in April 1988. About the same time, *Frontline* broadcast a five-part series on the history of apartheid.

Soon Hollywood was paying attention. Athol Fugard's hit play *Master Harold . . . And the Boys* became a movie starring Matthew Broderick. In November 1987, Donald Woods's books about his friendship with Stephen Biko and his escape from South Africa came to the screen as *Cry, Freedom,* directed by Richard Attenborough, who had also treated racial segregation in South Africa in his Oscar-winning film *Gandhi.* Seven months later the film arrived in South Africa but was seized by the police on the first day of its release. The life and death of Joe Slovo's wife, Ruth First, as seen through the eyes of their daughter, appeared in June 1988 as *A World Apart.* Over the next five years films about the struggle against apartheid—including *A Dry White Season, The Power of One,* the movie version of *Sarafina,* and *Bopa*—became, in effect, a cinematic genre, tapping deep into the American impulse to understand and to caricature racial conflict.

The occasional wave of films floated on a rising tide of books in almost every category. Historians like Leonard Thompson and George Frederickson traced the origins of apartheid, while novelists like Nadine Gordimer sketched vivid pictures of South African life in the minds of their readers. South Africans like Janet Levine, Rian Malan, and Winnie Mandela published recollections and memoirs. Reporters such as Joseph Lelyveld, Anthony Sampson, Allister Sparks, and Richard Stengel chronicled their experiences inside the country. Social scientists like Heribert Adam, Robert Edgar, Francis Wilson, and Mamphela Ramphele published searing critiques of what it was like to live under apartheid or of what the Western countries had done. To cope with the volume of new works, some bookstores set up special sections on South

Africa next to their books on the American civil rights movement and the problems of race.

By the end of the 1980s, the amount of material—written, spoken, sung, and performed—about the evils of apartheid was so vast that it finally swept away the excuses that South Africa's publicists and apologists had promoted for years. The South African government continued to send out press releases, tourist packets, and gaudy videos that reminded Americans of the complexity of South Africa's problems and of P. W. Botha's sincere intentions to solve them, but the tone of these pieces became increasingly plaintive.

For most white South Africans, the rising tone of condemnation came as a shock. They discovered it whenever they went abroad, as they were forced to endure innumerable small humiliations and delays because of the passports they carried. The several hundred thousand South African whites who still held British passports took to using them. White South African students formed organizations to help them circumvent foreign travel restrictions; when they finally made it to Europe or the United States, they often pretended they were from somewhere else. South African scholars who traveled abroad found that the opinions that made them sound like liberals at home earned nothing but opprobrium and scorn overseas. Even more irritating, the cultural and academic boycotts promoted by the African National Congress were blocking everything from textbooks to plays from being used in South Africa. The results were uneven: although some books could not be sold in South Africa, certain television programs continued to be broadcast, with bizarre results. In the late 1980s, for example, the most popular program in Soweto was *Dallas;* among whites, it was *The Cosby Show.*

Despite the efforts of South African officials to circumvent trade sanctions, ignore corporate disinvestment, and scoff at the cultural and sports boycotts, they could not ignore the effects of their gradual rejection by the world's capital markets. In March 1987 the original debt standstill agreement negotiated by Fritz Leutwiler was reviewed and extended for three more years. South Africa's difficulties with foreign banks were highlighted shortly afterward when two of the largest foreign banks operating in South Africa decided to pull their subsidiaries. The first was Citibank, which announced in June 1987 that it was withdrawing from South Africa. "We thought we were on strong moral grounds being there and we haven't changed our minds about that," said a bank spokesperson. The bank was making a "business decision," he continued, which had nothing to do with the threat by major American depositors to withdraw their accounts. The reaction from South Africa was glum. "This is really bad news," said Adrian Botha (no relation to Pik or

P. W.) of the American Chamber of Commerce. "I really didn't expect Citibank to go."

The next blow came from England, when Barclays Bank, one of South Africa's largest and most visible financial institutions, announced that it was quitting. Though the Barclays statement also claimed that external pressure had not been a factor, it soon became clear that it had in fact been decisive. For months the British anti-apartheid movement had been gathering pledges from British students that they would not open accounts with Barclays Bank; the campaign had been so effective that Barclays's share of the student market had fallen dramatically, pointing to severe long-term harm for the British bank. Like the American firms that did not want to sacrifice their business with cities and states, the executives at Barclays decided that the bank's presence in South Africa was not worth a loss of position in England.

In addition to the departure of such huge banks, South Africa continued to be strapped for international credit. The debt agreements with foreign banks required South Africa to pay out billions of dollars in both interest and principal each year, putting tremendous pressure on its balance of payments. Also, the capital outflow and slow economy had steadily forced the value of the rand downward against the dollar, making it even more expensive to repay the foreign debts. Normally countries under such pressure can turn for relief to the International Monetary Fund, but a congressional amendment passed in 1988 barred the IMF from making such loans. Though South Africa continued to raise some money from international banks, it had to pay a higher interest cost equal, according to one estimate, to 400 million rand a year.

In desperation, the South African finance ministry pressed businesses to make maximum use of foreign trade credits—short-term loans extended by other governments to enable the purchase of goods from their countries—which were rapidly becoming the only form of foreign finance available to South Africa. Such use of trade credits was akin to borrowing on one's credit cards to pay the mortgage and signaled to everyone that South Africa was struggling. In late 1987, Finance Minister Barend du Plessis admitted that the outflow of capital and the deteriorating current account meant that South Africa's foreign reserves had come under severe pressure. His judgment was echoed in 1988 by the head of the South African Reserve Bank, Gerhard de Kock. "In the present international climate," he said, "the capital account remains the Achilles heel of South Africa's balance of payments."

The combined effect of these four kinds of sanctions severely damaged the South African economy. In September 1988, South Africa's electric utility, ESKOM, announced that it was mothballing thirteen power stations because sanctions had slowed the economy and cut the demand for energy. The same month, P. W. Botha announced that sanctions and boycotts would force his government to eliminate 9.5 billion rand ($5.13 billion in 1994 dollars) in funds set aside for black "upliftment." By late 1989 one senior government official had calculated that sanctions, through various multiplier effects, had cost the South African economy more than 100 billion rand ($48.6 billion). A World Bank study reported in 1988 that South Africa's economy was in the most severe slump since the Second World War and had recently chalked up one of the poorest economic records in the world. Statistics published inside South Africa confirmed this, showing that the country had grown by an average annual rate of only 1.3 percent for most of the 1980s, and had actually *deflated* in the period following sanctions. During the same period, the domestic fixed investment rate had declined by −4 percent. Under these combined pressures, the per capita share of the gross domestic product had, by 1989, fallen back to the level it had been in 1973.

Though the opponents of sanctions had warned that African unemployment would skyrocket, the direct effects of sanctions on African employment proved difficult to gauge. Pretoria's statisticians had refused for many years to measure unemployment in the four "independent" homelands, so there was little reliable data. Nor was it clear whether businesses, faced with declining profits, would fire black workers or their more highly paid white counterparts. The confusion about unemployment produced some tension inside the South African antiapartheid movement. Unions found themselves caught between "workerists" who focused on the interests of their members and "populists" who represented the wider concerns of the liberation struggle. Some union leaders found themselves calling for sanctions and then battling with managers about the terms of disinvestment; or demanding more jobs for unemployed Africans while simultaneously pressing for increases in wages and benefits for their members. Conversely, many South African business leaders, who had spent years either benefiting from or dismissing the problem of large-scale African unemployment, suddenly seized on it as the principal argument against sanctions. As the magnitude of the problems facing Africans became more visible, and as unemployment pushed into previously untouched racial communities, the notion that South Africa's economic structure was grossly distorted suddenly burst from the left-wing academic centers into the mainstream of South African business thinking.

To make matters worse, there was no end in sight to South Africa's economic tribulations. By 1988, twenty-five industrialized democracies had imposed sanctions on South Africa; of these, nine refused to make any loans, seventeen banned the purchase of steel, and twenty barred any new investments. Inside each of these countries were well-organized domestic groups demanding that their governments take even more aggressive steps. Even South Africa's traditional friends were finding it more and more difficult to sustain a relationship: in late 1988, the Israeli cabinet, under pressure from the United States, announced a cutback on the economic, political, and military cooperation between the Israel and South Africa, though the cabinet refused to give the measures the force of law. In the same period the Japanese Ministry of International Trade and Industry sent instructions to its export companies urging them to scale back their trade with South Africa. The United Nations, the Organization for African Unity, the Commonwealth, and the rest of the international community seemed more determined than ever to increase external pressure on South Africa at precisely the moment when all of its trends seemed to be deteriorating. Indeed, by the end of the 1980s South Africa had sunk into a self-reinforcing spiral. Banks balked, capital fled, and the rand fell, making it harder to repay foreign loans. The economic growth rate could not keep pace with the increase in population, and the nation's unemployment and poverty soared to new heights. South Africa's war in Angola and Namibia sucked enormous sums of the national budget, denying P. W. Botha the funds he had promised for new spending on black education and other incremental reforms. As each piece of economic bad news fell, like splashes of cold water, on the somnolent custodians of white government, more and more of them awoke from their apartheid dreams to realize that something, something dramatic, would have to be done to avert the disaster that loomed.

Despite mounting evidence that sanctions were having an effect, the members of the Reagan administration resolutely refused to endorse them. At the same time, constructive engagement appeared completely dead. After six years of diplomacy, Crocker's adamant linkage of the independence of Namibia to Cuban withdrawal from Angola had produced nothing. The South African government seemed more determined than ever to solve its internal and external problems with force. Jonas Savimbi, encouraged by the repeal of the Clark amendment and the Reagan administration's 1986 decision to restore covert funding to UNITA, was not eager to see an immediate settlement. The MPLA government in Luanda, furious about the repeal of the Clark amendment, had refused for months to talk to the Americans. U.S. relations with Mozambique were set back by the death of Samora Machel, its president, in a mysterious plane crash which almost everyone blamed on the South Africans.

The Reagan administration seemed to have run out of options. In February a special blue ribbon commission that had been appointed by

George Shultz and included Leon Sullivan, Franklin Thomas, General Motors chair Roger Smith, former U.S. Secretary of Transportation William Coleman, and former IBM chair Frank Cary announced that "constructive engagement has failed to achieve its objectives." In early June, Leon Sullivan turned up the heat when he called a press conference in Washington, D.C., to announce that the two-year deadline he had established was up and that he now supported total U.S. corporate withdrawal from South Africa, a breaking of diplomatic ties, and a U.S. trade embargo. Sixteen long years after his first speech at the General Motors annual meeting in which he urged the firm to disinvest, Leon Sullivan had returned to where he had started.

The American anti-apartheid groups were delighted by Sullivan's announcement. "U.S. companies remaining in South Africa are really standing in a morally exposed position right now," said Tim Smith at ICCR. Jennifer Davis at the American Committee on Africa agreed. "The last fig leaf has now been stripped from United States corporations," she wrote a few days later. Executives of American companies stepped gingerly around the new development. "We owe a great debt to Leon Sullivan," said Allen Murray, chief executive of Mobil Corporation and the cochair of the United States Corporate Council on South Africa, "but we will now have to carry out the Sullivan Principles without him." Would the principles be maintained without Sullivan? a columnist asked Murray. "Well," said Murray, "they kept the Ten Commandments without Moses." To make up for the loss, Sal Marzullo and the other executives from the Industry Support Unit quickly created a new organization, hired Sullivan's associate Daniel Purnell to run it, and assembled an assortment of unknown black clergy to serve on the board of directors. Without Sullivan, however, the new organization failed to provide much moral cover.

The passage of the Comprehensive Anti-Apartheid Act, the release of the State Department study, and the decision by Sullivan to endorse corporate withdrawal all seemed to confirm that the policy of constructive engagement had been permanently repudiated. Over the following year, however, a strange combination of circumstances brought the policy back to life. The Iran-Contra scandal, which exploded in the fall of 1986, dislodged many of Crocker's opponents. Donald Regan, John Poindexter, and Pat Buchanan all left the government, while William Casey contracted a brain tumor, lapsed into a coma, and died. They were replaced by men who were both more knowledgeable about Africa and more sympathetic to Crocker's views. Frank Carlucci, who had served three tours in Africa and as U.S. ambassador to Portugal, became the national security adviser to the president. Former Senator majority leader Howard Baker became Ronald Reagan's chief of staff. The new team, combined with the continued presence of George Shultz at the State Department, provided Crocker with steady support.

The African National Congress was also beginning to change. Though they used the rhetoric of armed struggle and people's revolution, ANC leaders were slowly accepting the idea that scattered sabotage and assassination was about all the military force they would be able to bring to bear on Pretoria. What could not be won on the battlefield, they decided, could still be achieved through diplomacy. In early 1987 the ANC launched a series of successful initiatives, led by its soft-spoken foreign minister, Thabo Mbeki, designed to paint the South African government as the unreasonable party. In late January, Mbeki brought his boss, Oliver Tambo, to Washington, D.C. The men talked to Citibank chair John Reed and Burroughs chief executive Michael Blumenthal; delivered a speech at Riverside Church in New York; and, to the outrage of American conservatives, met with George Shultz at the State Department. The ANC also encouraged South Africans to defy the government's laws and hold consultations with them abroad. Desmond Tutu went to Lusaka in March 1987. In July a group of liberal Afrikaners, including doctors, university professors, and clergy, spent several days with an ANC delegation in Dakaar; the whites came away moved and impressed. After returning to South Africa, many of them received death threats, and the codirector of IDASA, one of the sponsoring organizations, was shot dead in his car.

Changes were also taking place inside the Angolan and Cuban camps. The Angolans, who had hoped that the American domestic debate over South Africa might compel the administration to drop the Cuban issue, heard otherwise from a succession of American visitors such as Jesse Jackson, Andrew Young, and Howard Wolpe. In April and July 1987 the Angolans met again with Crocker and his team, though they continued to insist that the Cuban troops could not be withdrawn as long as the United States provided support to UNITA. Fidel Castro, however, was beginning to have other thoughts. The Cuban presence in Angola was expensive; the Angolans were finding it difficult to pay their portion; and the Soviet government under Mikhail Gorbachev was looking for an exit. Castro was also disdainful of how little the Soviets had been able to achieve militarily: even with the support of Soviet advisers and billions of dollars in hardware, the periodic dry season offensives against UNITA had achieved nothing. In late July 1987, Castro sent a secret message to the White House asking whether the Americans would allow Cuba to join the negotiations. A few days later Castro met with Angolan President Jose Eduardo dos Santos in Havana and broached the topic with him. Dos Santos returned from Havana with a proposal that shortened the Cuban withdrawal timetable.

The negotiations had not advanced in part because both sides still hoped they could win on the battlefield. In September and October 1987, eighteen thousand Angolan soldiers, backed up by a thousand Soviet advisers and thirty thousand Cuban troops in support roles, launched a major offensive against UNITA. A combined force of eight thousand UNITA and four thousand South African soldiers retaliated, destroying one Angolan brigade and ravaging several others. The UNITA/South African troops then pushed their opponents back to the town of Cuito Cuanavale, two hundred miles north of the Namibian border. The fighting around the town continued fitfully for months; even though the UNITA/South African troops destroyed the local airfield and pinned down thousands of Angolan troops, they could not win an outright victory. The Angolans, for their part, used a combination of Soviet MiG-23 fighters and surface-to-air missiles to batter South Africa's aging Mirage fighters.

In early November, Castro met dos Santos in Moscow and promised him fifteen thousand of his best troops. Chester Crocker, in his memoirs, insists that Castro's motivations were diplomatic: the Cuban leader wanted not only to put a stop to the UNITA/SADF drive but to create the conditions for Cuban withdrawal. "Castro's decision in late 1987 was to design an honorable exit from southern Africa," Crocker wrote. "But this strategy could only work if both his military and political options appeared to be credible." Indeed, Crocker noted ironically, the key to Castro's strategy was "the much maligned concept of linkage": Cubans could leave with honor if they "obtained" the independence of Namibia.

For the next six months the two sides at Cuito Cuanavale continue to reinforce their positions and spar. In January 1988 the UNITA/South African forces tried to drive the Angolans and Cubans back to the western side of the Cuito River; when this failed, the Cubans crowed that they had won a major victory. By February the Cubans sent an advance force of thirty-five hundred men to outflank the South African forces on the west. By May 1988, the Cubans, backed up by SWAPO units, had established a new southern front with more than eleven thousand of their best troops and two hundred tanks. In response, South Africa moved its heaviest armored units into northern Namibia and announced a call-up of the hundred-and-forty-thousand-member reserve known as the Citizen Force. For years the Angolan war had been primarily a game of cat and mouse in which armored units chased guerrillas through hundreds of mile of scrub; in 1988 it metamorphosed into a standoff between two small armies with heavy artillery and modern weapons. "The risk of hairtrigger reactions and miscalculations was substantial," Crocker wrote later. "No matter what Castro's true objectives were, his bold moves risked being misperceived, triggering a major confrontation.

In addition to pressure brought by some of America's largest institutional investors, American companies and Wall Street traders had to contend with regular public protests in New York's financial district, such as this one from 1986. (© David Vita)

Though the government deployed thousands of troops in the mid-1980s to impose military control on the townships, resistance remained high. This woman's gesture of defiance, captured by a photographer in Tsakane township, was a dangerous act, since many had been shot dead for less.
(Mayibuye Center)

When students demonstrated in the streets of Johannesburg against the continued state of emergency, the police attacked with batons and dogs. Despite tight government restrictions on the media, such images of police brutality were still captured and transmitted to the world, leading to increased public pressure on governments and institutions for sanctions. (Noel Watson—Mayibuye Center)

After he spent the first half of his career as a prominent clergyman in the pro-government Dutch Reformed Church, the Reverend C. F. Beyers Naudé's conscience led him to reject National Party policies. Reviled by his family and fellow churchmen as a traitor, Naudé persisted in denouncing the evils of apartheid and eventually became the general secretary of the South African Council of Churches. He is shown here in 1986 on his way to a service in Soweto during the state of emergency. (Mayibuye Center)

Seen by some as a moderate pro-democratic leader and by others as a collaborator and tyrant, Mangosuthu Gatsha Buthelezi deftly used his position as chief minister of a government homeland and president of one of the ANC's rival resistance groups to increase his control over the predominantly Zulu population in KwaZulu-Natal. Though his opposition to disinvestment earned him the praise of business leaders on both sides of the Atlantic, his dictatorial style and exploitation of ethnic grievances undermined his popular support and raised troubling questions about his true motives. (Mayibuye Center)

The descendant of an elite Afrikaner political family, President F. W. de Klerk became convinced that Verwoerd's vision of apartheid could never be implemented, and he helped move the National Party toward a negotiated settlement. (Mayibuye Center)

The image carried live around the world: the release of Nelson Mandela on
February 11, 1990, after 10,052 days in prison. (Mayibuye Center)

The release of Mandela marked the beginning of complex negotiations as formerly mortal enemies sat down to discuss the end of the armed struggle, the transfer of political power, and the constitutional shape of the future nation. Here a tense Mandela and de Klerk, surrounded by their respective delegations, announce an agreement in front of Groot Schuur, a mansion originally constructed by Cecil Rhodes and used as the residence of South Africa's prime ministers when they were in Cape Town. (*The Argus*)

As the first black president of South Africa, Nelson Mandela maintained a relentless focus on reconciliation between the races that quelled white fears and earned him the admiration of the world. (Mayibuye Center)

. . . A small spark . . . could have ignited a cycle of bigger clashes engaging the honor and pride of Fidel Castro and P. W. Botha, two high-strung men."

As the perception grew that the military situation would either remain stalemated or escalate into something far more severe, the opposing governments reevaluated the possibilities for diplomacy. For P. W. Botha, the war in Angola had begun to impose a daunting financial and political cost. The deaths of sixty young white conscripts had produced a rumble of dissatisfaction from Afrikaner churches and other organizations. Castro's decision to send thousands more troops, combined with Western unwillingness to back up South Africa on the battlefield, implied that the military campaign could become enormously expensive just at the point when South Africa was being forced to economize because of sanctions. In addition, there were constraints on the supply of machinery and people. The arms embargo made it difficult to purchase replacement parts for SADF aircraft and weapons; the continued civil unrest inside South Africa meant that white soldiers were needed at home; and the steady rise in white casualties on the battlefield was eroding support for the war not only among young people and English speakers but even in P. W. Botha's Afrikaner base.

Since the South Africans had formally agreed to the timetables and conditions of Resolution 435 in return for a withdrawal of Cuban troops, the main point of the negotiations had remained the timing of that withdrawal. When the Cubans became a formal part of the negotiating process, the possibility that an agreement could be reached on this point became clear. Even as the United States was moving forward with its proposals, some inside South Africa continued to believe that they could cut a better deal with their opponents on the side. In early March, for example, Defence Minister Magnus Malan publicly suggested that South Africa—in its own perception, the great bulwark against Communism—should form a strategic alliance with the Soviet Union. Crocker was contemptuous of the idea, which elite South African circles discussed for months. "In the wishful thinking that often passed for policy analysis," Crocker wrote, "South Africa dreamed of a new Pretoria-Moscow axis sitting astride world markets for gold, diamonds, and strategic minerals." By mid-March, however, Crocker had received indications from all the parties that they were willing to engage in new discussions. The next nine months—from March to December 1988—produced a frenzy of activity. Diplomats representing five different parties—the United States, the Soviet Union, Angola, South Africa, and Cuba—as well as officials from the United Nations, leaders of UNITA, SWAPO, and the ANC, and representatives from the Frontline states engaged in a mammoth square dance of negotiation. In twelve rounds of talks in Geneva, Brazzaville, Cape Verde, and New York, the negotiators unraveled the diplomatic knots.

On the surface, the South Africans, Angolans, and Cubans were not far apart. The South Africans remained committed to grant independence to Namibia under Resolution 435. The Angolans had relinquished their insistence that some Cuban troops remain in northern Angola to protect the MPLA government and the Cubans had offered, in principle, to withdraw completely. Only two sticking points remained, both involving UNITA. The MPLA representatives wanted the Cubans to remain as long as possible to prevent UNITA, even without its South African fighting partners, from winning a military victory against their government. The South Africans, on the other hand, wanted to ensure that the withdrawal of SADF forces would not leave UNITA sandwiched between a Namibia controlled by SWAPO and an Angola dominated by the MPLA.

The American team's ability to offer leadership on this question was fundamentally hampered by the U.S. government's rhetorical and substantive support for Jonas Savimbi. Though Crocker insisted in public and private that the United States was simply a mediator in a complicated dispute, the American role with regard to Savimbi was one of overt advocacy. The Soviets picked up on this quickly and challenged Crocker repeatedly about American intentions. America's true objective, they said, was not Namibian independence and Cuban withdrawal but the overthrow of the MPLA government. Crocker, for his part, was not about to let the negotiations destroy Savimbi. As they continued the discussion, the Soviets complained that the United States and South Africa had developed a second form of linkage: the Cuban-Namibian agreement would not go forward without some promises to Savimbi.

After months of wrangling, the two sides finally reached an uneasy compromise. The Soviets and the Angolans dropped their condition that the United States stop its aid to UNITA, while the United States agreed that the details of the internal Angolan agreement between the MPLA and UNITA would be negotiated after the withdrawal of the Cubans and South Africa. With this tacit understanding in place, the negotiations moved forward rapidly. The parties reaffirmed their commitment to the principles of military withdrawal; the military commanders negotiated a detailed set of incremental measures to disengage; and the diplomats worked on how to match the withdrawal of Cuban troops with the United Nations timetable for South Africans to leave Namibia. This last problem was the most devilish: the South Africans wanted the Cubans to leave within months; the Angolans wanted them to depart over a period of years. When an overall time frame was accepted, the South Africans wanted to front-load the schedule; the Angolans wanted it back-loaded. On November 15, after weeks of poring over charts, tables, graphs, and proposals, the Americans suggested a compromise: two-thirds of the Cubans would leave in the first year; then the rate of departure would slow for six months; then the final twelve thousand troops would leave in the final nine months. With this formula, Crocker wrote exultantly, "we had broken the back of the settlement. This was the deal that would end Africa's Thirty Years War . . . cap an eight year odyssey and validate a concept that been the object of abuse and ridicule." The final pieces then came swiftly. The United Nations would create a verification team backed up by international troops; the signing was set for late December in New York City. The South Africans pushed hard to have P. W. Botha come to the United States and meet Reagan at the time of the ceremony, but they finally backed down when Shultz called Pik Botha and told him that it would not be possible. On December 22, 1988, the foreign ministers of South Africa, Cuba, and Angola came to the United Nations headquarters to sign their tripartite agreement under the watchful eyes of George Shultz and UN General Secretary Pérez de Cuellar.

Crocker's success, after nearly eight years, was filled with little ironies. On the one hand, his original intuition—that the parties would eventually accept linkage as the formula for agreement—turned out to be correct. At the same time, many of his other predictions had misfired. The Reagan administration's hope that a display of greater sympathy toward the South African government would lead to a diminution of cross-border violence had produced a wave of new SADF attacks carried out with impunity. The reframing of the area's problems as a geopolitical struggle between the East and the West—something Crocker had encouraged in his academic writing—had prevented Crocker from focusing on the SADF's real target, the African National Congress, and had exposed Crocker to endless skirmishes with American ideologues who thought Crocker had gone soft on Communism. His personal identification with South African "reformers" like Pik Botha—men who, like him, were caught between the unreasonable domestic demands of both right and left—led him to trust their good faith for longer than was wise.

Crocker had also been wrong about the anti-apartheid movement in the United States and South Africa. His fascination with and deference to South Africa's military establishment had prevented him from believing that internal protest could ever sap the will of the state. His lack of interest in trade and finance caused him to discount the possible effect of sanctions and uncritically to accept the notion that economic pressures would not work. Instead of producing permanent defiance, as he had predicted, the sanctions imposed by the West limited South Africa's military ambitions and redirected its strategic thinking. Indeed, despite his bitter attacks on the folly of the U.S. anti-apartheid movement, Crocker ended up using these domestic pressures as an important lever during the final stages of the negotiations, arguing that if the parties didn't reach an agreement from him, they might have to contend with far less sympathetic parties in the future. One of the most serious failings in Crocker's analysis was his refusal to acknowledge that any other force besides his diplomacy deserved significant credit for the agreement. The Gorbachev-induced changes in the Soviet Union, the explosion of violent opposition in South Africa, the flash flood of domestic protest in the United States, the tightening tourniquet of sanctions, and the limited but tenacious strikes by Umkhonto We Sizwe guerrillas were all dismissed as irrelevant. Even after his resignation from the State Department in April 1989, by which point he had become the longest-serving assistant secretary of state in American history, Crocker continued to insist that during his eight-year tenure the mistakes had largely been the fault of others, while the successes could be traced to his ideas and to those who had had the intelligence to share them.

Though P. W. Botha seemed to be making progress on the diplomatic front, his actions inside South Africa continued to provoke discontent. He released imprisoned ANC leader Govan Mbeki, the father of Thabo Mbeki, in November 1987, then turned around four months later and banned the United Democratic Front, COSATU, and sixteen other major organizations. An infuriated Desmond Tutu led protest marches and called on his international network of supporters to urge their governments to cut diplomatic ties with South Africa. Though Senator Nancy Kassebaum described Botha's actions as "a major disappointment," the Reagan administration, as usual, spoke with more than one voice. Even as Chester Crocker was calling in ambassador Piet Koornhof to express American "shock and distress" at the bannings, Reagan was telling reporters at a press conference that South Africa's problems were caused by "tribal differences" and outsiders who were "stirring up and encouraging trouble."

Despite Botha's aggressive actions, protests in South Africa continued to grow. Strikes increased dramatically in number. In 1987, there were 1,148 job actions—more than three a day. One strike, in August 1987, involved nearly three hundred thousand coal and gold miners from the National Union of Mineworkers who walked off their jobs for three weeks, costing the mines approximately $200 million in lost production. Overall, the strikes resulted in the loss of 5.8 million worker-days—a blow to an already strained economy—and demonstrated the growing discipline and power of the unions. In March and again in June 1988 unions issued strike calls to which more than a million workers responded.

Boycotts also flourished. As in the American South during the civil rights movement, community groups discovered that refusing to pay for goods and services had a powerful effect on the white authorities. In Soweto tens of thousands of residents stopped paying their rent to protest their living conditions and lack of representation. When Desmond Tutu, who now lived in Cape Town, supported the rent strike, the white authorities threatened to evict him from the small home he had retained in Soweto. Rather than cut the township off completely and provoke an explosion, however, the government decided to reach into its own pockets for $100 million to cover garbage collection and other municipal services. When the Conservative Party captured the town council in Boksburg and immediately reimposed strict racial segregation, the local African and Coloured communities responded with a massive consumer boycott. The boycott caused a fifty-nine percent drop in local business sales, pushed nine white businesses into bankruptcy, and forced the town authorities to abandon their economic development plans.

As activism and protest increased across South Africa, Gatsha Buthelezi found himself increasingly ignored or denounced by black leaders around the country. The Zulu leader had hoped that his opposition to sanctions and his advocacy of a joint KwaZulu-Natal executive authority would eventually propel him to national leadership; instead, the power and influence of the United Democratic Front and COSATU—both of which endorsed the Freedom Charter and thus implicitly the ANC—had continued to rise, despite the government's restrictions and crackdown. Buthelezi responded by claiming that the UDF was a tool of the "ANC mission in exile" and that Inkatha was the only true guardian of the ANC's original principles, though he was always careful to express his support for Nelson Mandela and to call for his release. Buthelezi also took steps to tighten his control on KwaZulu by sending Inkatha recruiters into urban areas in Natal. The recruiters, who often used intimidation, ran smack into the growing ranks of young UDF supporters, who were trying to establish their own networks and pursue the ANC's strategy of making South Africa "ungovernable." When the two forces met, they clashed violently. Such conflict simmered during the mid-1980s but boiled over dramatically in 1987 and 1988. In January 1987 thirteen members of a family were massacred in their home by men using UK-47 rifles. At first police said that it was the work of ANC terrorists, and then it became clear that the target of the attack had been a UDF activist who had not been home at the time. In commenting on the incident Buthelezi warned darkly that such strife would end only "if the president of the external mission of the ANC, Mr.

Oliver Tambo, called off the vendetta which his organization and the UDF are waging against me and Inkatha."

From then on the conflict escalated steadily, with each side accusing the other of terrorism and proclaiming its own commitment to peace. Both sides had plenty of blood on their hands. The determination of ANC extremists and others to eliminate black town councilors, policemen, and other "collaborators" (some of whom were members of Inkatha) had resulted in a string of shootings, firebombings, and necklacings. Buthelezi proclaimed publicly that he would seek "an eye for an eye and a tooth for a tooth." His words to his own circle were even more apocalyptic. "The UDF and COSATU are not worthy of reconciliation," he told Inkatha's central committee in December 1987. "We are talking about a life and death struggle; we are talking about all-or-nothing victories; we are talking about the final triumph of good over evil." With such words flowing from their leader, Inkatha thugs aggressively attempted to seize control of neighborhoods by beating or killing anyone who might object. Reports poured into human rights offices that the police had either done nothing to stop Inkatha's attacks or had actively encouraged them.

By the end of 1988 political violence in Natal and across the rest of South Africa had claimed more than thirty-one hundred lives. The international press tended to explain such "black on black" violence as the result of "tribal differences," a claim that reinforced racist perceptions about black savagery and ignored the reality that most of the Natal combatants on both sides were Zulus. Unrest among Africans was matched by rising discontent on the right. To shore up support for his reforms, Botha had called a general election in 1987. Though the National Party had retained its majority, the Conservative Party gained enough to become the official opposition. Other right-wing extremist groups emerged. Hendrik Verwoerd's son-in-law Carel Boshoff, the head of the archconservative Afrikaner Volkswag, announced that he intended to create an Afrikaner *volkstaat*, a homeland carved out of existing South African territory and transformed into an exclusively white state. Eugene Terreblanche, leader of the Afrikaner Weerstandbeweging (AWB), continued to spew violent rhetoric and warned that if the government "was going to capitulate, the AWB will take power by force." When National Party officials suggested that they might ban the AWB's triple-7 swastika, Terreblanche denounced them as blasphemers. The swastika, he said, was a Christian symbol; to ban it "would be like banning Christ himself." In November 1988 former policeman Barend Hendrik Strydom, an AWB member and the leader of a shadowy group called the Wit Wolwe (White Wolves) strolled into a lunchtime crowd in Pretoria, pulled out a pistol, and began firing. According to evidence at his trial, Strydom had prepared for his attack the week earlier by driving to a squatter camp and shooting two women "to see if I was physically capable of killing people." On the day of the Pretoria attack, he had driven to the courthouse at Church Square. When he found the courthouse area overpopulated with police, he drove two blocks away, parked his car, paid the parking meter, and shot his first few victims: an eighty-year-old African woman, an Indian shopkeeper, and another woman waiting for a bus. By the time he had finished, he had shot twenty people, killing seven of them. Shortly afterward Terreblanche publicly warned the ANC not to retaliate and said that he could understand how a man like Strydom was not willing to "stand back to allow a tyrant to take his country from him."

In September 1988, Khotso House, the headquarters of the South African Council of Churches, was destroyed by a bomb that injured twenty-three people, an attack for which the Wit Wolwe later claimed responsibility. When asked to comment, a police spokesman speculated that the blast might have been caused by explosives stored in the basement of the building. In the next eight months two more buildings, one belonging to the South African Bishops Conference, the other to the National Union of South African Students, were destroyed by arson. Attacks also continued on anti-apartheid activists and ANC members both inside and outside South Africa. In March 1988, ANC lawyer Albie Sachs, one of a handful of whites who had participated in the Defiance Campaign and who was living in Mozambique, lost his right arm but miraculously escaped death when a bomb exploded in his car. In the same month, the ANC's representative in Paris, Dulcie September, was shot dead as she was unlocking the door of her office. In 1989 unknown assailants killed two white anti-apartheid activists, Professor David Webster of South Africa and Anton Lubowksi of Namibia, in separate attacks. The murders brought the number of reported external assassination attempts on ANC members to forty-six and the number of unsolved murders of activists inside the country to nearly a hundred.

Despite the resolution of the Namibian conflict and the announcement in January 1989 that the African National Congress would close its Angolan bases, many in government were steadily losing confidence in P. W. Botha's ability to lead South Africa forward. None of his actions—the suppression of anti-apartheid organizations, the restrictions on the press, the piecemeal reforms, the crafting of a precarious constitution, the combination of tough and conciliatory talk, the heavy-handed use of the security forces—had seemed to work. As sanctions and violence dragged the country downward, the National Party elite quarreled privately about what should be done. At the root of the conflict lay the growing doubts among leading Afrikaners. For forty years National Party officials had clung to the Verwoerdian hope that all would someday be well. Disruptive means had been justified by the idyllic end that lay ahead. Each successive formulation—from *basskap* and apartheid to separate development and the constellation of states—had been presented as the key to the future, a future that would be achieved once subversives had finally been suppressed and the international community had been persuaded of Afrikaner goodwill. By the late 1980s, however, many National Party politicians could see that this image of the future was a mirage. The moment the government suppressed one organization, another would spring up in its place. The insertion of soldiers into the townships had not brought peace but had led to an ugly, low-level civil war. The international community, despite decades of flirtation or disregard, had not accepted National Party reforms and had slapped on the sanctions that were steadily strangling the economy.

Indeed, projected outward into the next decade and century, every trend spelled trouble for white rule. The government called in scenario planners like Clem Sunter of the Anglo-American Corporation to anticipate the future of the South African economy and found, as one South African reporter put it, that the "short-term predictions piled abyss on abyss." The black population would increase more rapidly than whites; the number of black urban residents would skyrocket, carrying the problems of crime and housing into unimagined reaches; the South African economy would fall further behind; the homelands would remain captive recipients of stupendous amounts of government cash; racial disparities in health and education would deepen; white emigration would rise; and political murders on all sides would increase. One by one the National Party's top politicians swallowed the bitter pill that apartheid not only was but always would be a failure.

The process, ironically, showed that in at least one way both Chester Crocker and Randall Robinson had been correct. Crocker had insisted that if change were to come in South Africa, it must come through a change of heart in the white population, particularly in the white government. As Mikhail Gorbachev led the Soviet Union out of regional conflicts and paved the way for the collapse of Communism in Eastern Europe and the Soviet Union, National Party mythology about the South African role in the global anti-Communist struggle deflated. The resolution of the Cuban–South African war in Angola and the independence of Namibia allowed the Botha government's attention to focus more fully on South Africa's domestic situation. At the same time, as Randall Robinson had predicted, the change of heart had come not from a sudden moral awakening but from the harsh realization that the world community would never accept apartheid, no matter how it was dressed up. This firm international refusal to confer moral legitimacy on National Party reforms, combined with the imposition of real financial penalties, had caused a collapse of confidence within South Africa's ruling elite. The change in mood was noticeable in the tone and content of the Afrikaner press, whose editors began to suggest bold and previously unthinkable steps. "Is a discussion between the government and a delegation of the African National Congress under leadership of a free Nelson Mandela really so unthinkable?" asked the editors of *Beeld,* a leading pro-government newspaper on January 16, 1989. "Just think what dividends, both political and economic, such a discussion could deliver for our country and its whole population."

Despite the misgivings in the top ranks of the National Party, there seemed little anyone could do as long as P. W. Botha held on to the reins of power. Botha had become irascibly intractable. Hurt and angry that his achievements had gone unrecognized, suspicious of almost everyone, the seventy-three-year-old politician treated those around him with curt disdain or flat rage. The Great Crocodile, as Botha was known, clung fiercely to his conviction that he offered the only alternative between the tyrannies of right and left. In the middle of January 1989, Botha was in Cape Town to prepare for the opening of parliament, at which, it was widely rumored, he would announce more initiatives to reform apartheid. On Wednesday, January 18, the South African government news service broadcast a terse statement: the prime minister had suffered a mild stroke. Though Botha suffered only a minor loss of motion in his left arm and leg and was talking and drinking tea within hours of the incident, his doctors insisted that he remain in the hospital and temporarily relinquish his executive duties.

Newspaper editors across the country immediately speculated whether this was the end of the Botha reign and, if so, who might become his successor. Attention focused on four men: Foreign Minister Pik Botha, whose domestic stature had increased because of the Namibia agreement; Finance Minister Barend du Plessis; Education Minister F. W. de Klerk; and Minister of Constitutional Development J. Christian Heunis. Heunis's prospects seemed to rise when, thirty-six hours after the stroke, he was sworn in as acting president of South Africa. P. W. Botha, who returned to his home after six days in the hospital, let it be known that he did not intend to relinquish the presidency so easily. On February 2, 1989, the state president dropped a bombshell on the National Party delegates who had assembled for a regular party caucus at Tuynhuys, the state president's office in the center of Cape Town. As they arrived, each representative received a formal letter from Botha in which he explained that he intended to remain state president but would resign as leader of the National Party. This would enable him, he said, to focus on his national responsibilities and allow his presidency to become the "binding power in our country."

The stunned National Party delegates broke into four provincial caucuses to discuss what they should do next. When they reconvened, they agreed that they should immediately elect a new head of the party. The four candidates were, as expected, Pik Botha, Heunis, de Klerk, and du Plessis. On the first ballot, Pik Botha earned only sixteen votes and dropped out. On the second ballot Heunis received only twenty-six votes and withdrew. The race had come down to two men: Barend du Plessis, the urbane *verligte* finance minister who had guided the country through the storm of sanctions, and F. W. de Klerk, a party insider widely viewed as a *verkrampte* conservative. On the third round, the one hundred thirty delegates cast their votes knowing that the winner would become the party leader and probably the president of South Africa. De Klerk beat du Plessis by eight votes, sixty-nine to sixty-one.

The new fifty-two-year-old party leader was not well known to the public. Born on March 18, 1936, the youngest of two sons, Frederik Willem de Klerk had been groomed for political life since birth. He had an impeccable Afrikaner lineage. One of his ancestors, Tunis de Klerk, had been among the men hanged by the British for the nineteenth-century rebellion at Slagtersnek. His great-grandfather, a member of the conservative Dopper branch of the Dutch Reformed tradition, had fought to preserve church practice from hymns and other evangelical contaminants brought by Andrew Murray. His grandfather W. J. de Klerk had been a pastor and politician, running unsuccessfully for National Party seats on several occasions. His aunt was married to Prime Minister Johannes Strijdom. His father, Jan de Klerk, had served as a militantly pro-apartheid cabinet minister under Strijdom, Verwoerd, and Vorster and in 1969 had been elected president of the South African Senate. Jan de Klerk exerted a powerful conservative force on those around him. "Don't be afraid to be regarded as narrow-minded or old-fashioned," he once told a group of Afrikaner youth. "By participating in all that is new, we as a nation are forsaking our identity." F. W. de Klerk's older brother, Willem, who was himself a Dopper clergyman and a successor of Hendrik Verwoerd as editor of *Die Transvaler,* recalled the intensely partisan atmosphere in which his brother had grown up. "We often talked politics at home; political public figures were regular guests," he wrote. "Even as children and students, we, and particularly he, were involved in the organization of election campaigns; as a young man he attended dozens of political meetings with our father. . . . In a manner of speaking, he was predestined for politics by his collective subconscious, via his lineage, and honed for the task by his political parentage."

F. W. de Klerk attended Potchefstroom University, a Dopper institution, and studied law. He also embraced the university's dictum that biblical principles should underlie every academic and practical discipline. "People keep calling me a pragmatist," F. W. de Klerk told an American visitor years later, "but that's not right. If anything I have to struggle with not being a fundamentalist. I belong to a church which takes the Bible very seriously. I am always looking, always searching, for the basic foundation, the underlying principle, from which one can build an idea of the future, from which one can construct a plan of action. As a Christian I have always been preoccupied with the question of principle, of what is the *right* thing to do."

For years F. W. de Klerk was convinced that the right thing was apartheid. In 1959, at the age of twenty-three, he married Marike Willemse; at the time he was so impoverished from his years of study that his new bride not only paid for her own wedding ring and the couple's honeymoon but covered their living expenses for the next two years. For the next thirteen years de Klerk practiced law in Klerksdorp, Pretoria, and Vereeniging. In 1972 he was offered a professorship on the law faculty of his alma mater, the University of Potchefstroom. Shortly afterward, National Party officials asked him to run for a seat that had just opened in the House of Assembly. De Klerk turned down the offer from the university, ran for the office, and won. His first year in parliament coincided with his father's last.

De Klerk spent his first years as a loyal backbencher. He delivered carefully reasoned speeches, worked his party from the inside, and quickly became the information officer of the Transvaal National Party. In 1976 he was invited to visit the United States by the U.S. Information Service, which at the time was bringing several dozen South Africans to America each year for exposure tours. De Klerk's visit to the United States and to Western European countries reportedly had a profound effect on his thinking about many matters, including race relations. By 1976 de Klerk had also attracted the attention of John Vorster, who told Willem de Klerk that F. W. would one day become prime minister. Vorster tried to promote de Klerk to deputy minister in his cabinet, but at the last minute he gave the spot to Andries Treurnicht in the hope that it would placate the troublesome archconservative.

De Klerk finally entered the cabinet as minister of social welfare and pensions in April 1978, at the age of forty-two. For the next eleven years de Klerk bounced around the cabinet, serving as minister of sport, of post and telecommunications, of mining, and of the interior, as well as assuming the leadership of the Transvaal wing of the National Party. When P. W. Botha proposed his new constitution, de Klerk defended it against critics from both the right and the left. As the debate developed, de Klerk emerged as the National Party's chief defender against the Conservative Party's attacks. As such, de Klerk became, in his brother's words, the Conservative Party's "most hated political adversary."

The explosions of 1985 and 1986 jarred de Klerk and other National Party insiders to the core. The network of discussion groups within the Broederbond buzzed with controversy as members debated whether the separatist dream that had given them purpose for so long could be revived. De Klerk's thinking about apartheid started to shift when he realized that the neat divisions it had envisaged could not be achieved. He spent hours in intense conversation with Chris Heunis, the minister of constitutional development, and Gerrit Viljoen, the chairman of the Broederbond, and with his brother, Willem de Klerk, who had become a liberal voice in Afrikaner politics and the press. As F. W. de Klerk explained to a British interviewer several years later, such conversations persuaded him that if apartheid could never be implemented practically, it could no longer be defended morally.

Whatever internal changes might have been taking place, F. W. de Klerk continued to cultivate a reputation as a conservative. When Pik Botha had stated publicly that South Africa might one day have a black president, P. W. Botha dressed him down in public; rumors spread swiftly that F. W. de Klerk had been central in urging the reprimand. His wife, Marike, was said to be an ultraconservative who objected even to P. W. Botha's modest reforms. The most tenacious rumor focused on de Klerk's role in Botha's infamous 1985 Rubicon speech. The allegation was that an earlier draft filled with sweeping reforms had been torpedoed by de Klerk, who, it was said, worried that it would boost the Conservative Party to victory over National Party candidates in the Transvaal. De Klerk vehemently denied the charge, arguing that he had helped prepare the original draft and that P. W. Botha had changed the speech himself at the last minute. He blamed the catastrophic consequences of the speech on Pik Botha. "It had been leaked abroad that P. W. was going to announce far-reaching reforms, which had aroused feverish expectations," de Klerk told his brother. "If that had not happened, the speech would have been well received abroad."

De Klerk's elevation to party leader provoked a spirited debate in the domestic and international press about where he would lead South Africa. After de Klerk declared publicly that he would oppose "domination by a majority," most liberal journalists and politicians considered it unlikely that he would act boldly. "I can't see him removing the foundation stones of apartheid," said Helen Suzman shortly after his selection. A few foreign observers were more optimistic. "Just as President Nixon was able to go to China," wrote American scholar Robert Rotberg, "so

Mr. de Klerk could be the leader to go, metaphorically, to Soweto or Lusaka."

Everyone agreed that de Klerk's experience and style differed sharply from those of his predecessors. Unlike earlier leaders, de Klerk had not held the ministries of blunt power; instead of justice (Vorster) or defense (Botha), the new party leader had spent much of his time on sport and education, two areas where the international and domestic penalties of apartheid had been heavy. His approach to politics was also more refined. "I am basically a team man," de Klerk told a press conference shortly after his selection, "and my style will be that of a team man." As one South African journalist wrote, "Where President Botha is rough, de Klerk is smooth; where Botha smashes, he leads; where Botha confronts and rages, he yields and mollifies. De Klerk's career is a tale of compromises, making the best of bad situations, and of smoothing over difficulties."

The need for de Klerk to display his diplomatic skills came quickly. P. W. Botha's decision to step down as party leader created an unprecedented situation of shared executive power. De Klerk and Botha quickly tangled over the date of the next elections and the propriety of de Klerk traveling abroad to represent South Africa. In March 1989, just five weeks after de Klerk's selection, Botha announced that not only would he resume the presidency in late March but he might run for another term. The National Party delegates were appalled. The pro-government newspaper *Beeld* urged Botha to reread a speech by D. F. Malan which argued that good leaders know when to retire. The parliamentary caucus of the National Party, joined by the federal council of the party, passed quick resolutions urging Botha to resign. Botha bluntly refused and went on television to promise that he would stay in his post until the next election, which would be at least a year away. The next day the parliamentary caucus unanimously voted for Botha to quit. Botha again refused, though after extended negotiations he grudgingly agreed to advance the national elections from 1990 to September 1989.

Though de Klerk had been able to patch up his party's relations with P. W. Botha, the demands on him to take more dramatic steps were increasing. In April 1989, South Africa's white liberals formed a new political entity known as the Democratic Party, which brought together the members of the Progressive Federal Party, other smaller groups, and a host of Afrikaners including a former National Party member of parliament, a former South African ambassador to Great Britain, and F. W. de Klerk's older brother, Willem. There were also new pressures from outside South Africa. The outflow of American corporations had continued unbroken for more than two years. On April 28, 1989, South African business leaders were shocked to learn that Mobil Corporation, one of the largest and most powerful firms operating in South Africa, had decided to sell out to Gencor, South Africa's second largest mining corporation. The Mobil decision had come after months of international anti-apartheid activity focused on oil companies. The Royal Dutch Shell Corporation, for example, had been the focus of a broad disinvestment campaign in the United States involving not only the customary anti-apartheid groups but the vigorous participation of several American labor unions. In Shell's home country of Holland and in other European countries, the protests had taken a violent turn when some activists began blowing up gas stations. The effort to push Mobil out of South Africa had found several allies among elected officials. Several states and municipalities had barred the purchase of Mobil products as long as the company was selling in South Africa, and New York City comptroller Harrison Goldin had filed a series of shareholder resolutions on behalf of city's pension funds urging Mobil to stop its sales to the South African government. The single most potent measure was a 1988 congressional amendment by Representative Charles Rangel eliminating the deductibility of South African taxes from U.S. corporate income taxes. This meant that any profit Mobil made in South Africa would, in effect, be taxed twice, first by South Africa and then by the United States—an effective tax rate of 72.5 percent. Allen E. Murray, the chair of Mobil Corporation, announced that the decision to withdraw had been made because of the "very foolish laws that had been passed in the United States."

For the National Party leadership, the Mobil pullout, coupled with Desmond Tutu's renewed call for sanctions and his continued access to the highest reaches of American political power—demonstrated by an Oval Office session with President George Bush in May—underscored the failure of Botha's attempts to win international approval. In an effort to make progress, F. W. de Klerk himself traveled abroad in June. Though denied a visit with Bush at the last minute, de Klerk made the tour of several European capitals. From Margaret Thatcher, Helmut Kohl, and every other leader he met, de Klerk heard the same thing: the time had come for the South African government to release Nelson Mandela and begin negotiating with the ANC. The British, in particular, were pushing hard behind the scenes through Ambassador Robin Renwick to boost de Klerk's resolve and ability. As Prime Minister Margaret Thatcher explained to the British Parliament, if Mandela were released, "the atmosphere would change completely and it would be possible to get negotiations started between the government of South Africa and black South Africans."

De Klerk's trip infuriated P. W. Botha. Such foreign tours, he felt, should be reserved for the head of state. For de Klerk to go abroad at such a time was an act bordering on insubordination. Botha, sensing that his control over the party and government was rapidly eroding, tried to recapture the political initiative through what would have been unthinkable only a few months before: on July 5, 1989, he invited Nelson Mandela to his office at Tuynhuys for a cup of tea. Several of Botha's lieutenants—including Niel Barnard, the head of the National Intelligence Service, and Hendrik Coetsee, the minister of law and order—had been secretly meeting with Mandela since May 1988; on one occasion Botha's team had even met with several members of the ANC leadership abroad. Mandela, for his part, had entered into the conversation with the South African government on his own authority and had even written Botha a lengthy brief on how they could remove the obstacles to negotiation.

The secret meeting of the two leaders was a remarkable moment in history: the man who had spent his career attempting to destroy the ANC was receiving the ANC's greatest hero at his official government office. Mandela, who had been smuggled in by two of Botha's lieutenants, was amazed when he met Botha. He had approached the meeting with anxiety, expecting Botha to confront him with the rage for which he was known; instead, Botha treated Mandela in a relaxed and friendly manner. "What really impressed me," Mandela said later, "was that he even poured the tea." The two leaders discussed the release of Walter Sisulu and the other ANC leaders who remained in prison; Mandela was then smuggled out of the president's office and returned to his cell.

A few days later Botha announced publicly that he and Mandela had met. His action momentarily stunned the nation and fueled speculation about Mandela's release, but it did not restore Botha's authority. Within a month the state president was battling de Klerk over another proposed foreign trip. De Klerk wanted to fly to Zambia to confer with President Kenneth Kaunda, who continued to press publicly and privately for negotiations between the South Africans and the ANC. Botha furiously opposed the trip, arguing that the leader of the National Party could not travel to the city in which the ANC kept its headquarters. Botha, to his despair, found that he could not muster the support of a single cabinet official. At a showdown cabinet meeting, de Klerk urged Botha to resign graciously. "We believe that the least painful solution for you, for the National Party, and for all us," de Klerk told his former boss, "would be that you move to [the town of] Wilderness and say that you have decided to appoint an acting state president from now until after the election." On August 14, 1989, P. W. Botha, still raging and resentful, bowed to the inevitable. "After all the years of my best efforts for the National Party and for the government . . . and security of this country, I am being ignored by ministers in my cabinet," Botha said in a cranky and rambling address on national television. "Consequently I have no choice but to announce my resignation."

The next day F. W. de Klerk was sworn in as the acting president of South Africa. With barely three weeks before the general election, he immediately launched into an aggressive campaign for his party. De Klerk proclaimed that the National Party was committed to a "five-year action plan" which promised to allow every South African citizen the right to participate at all levels of government and to prevent domination by any groups over another. He and the other National Party speakers attacked the Conservative Party for trying to revive the crude racism of the past and the Democratic Party for its treasonous flirtations with the ANC and other "terrorists."

South Africa's anti-apartheid groups, now loosely affiliated under the umbrella known as the Mass Democratic Movement, announced that they would launch a new defiance campaign aimed not only at the all-white elections but at all of the most visible symbols of apartheid. They sent more than two hundred ailing Africans to whites-only hospitals to request treatment. Crowds of demonstrators tried to cross into the whites-only beaches on the Cape, but they were stopped by barbed wire, blasted by sand and wind from hovering helicopters, and attacked by policemen with dogs and clubs. The police also raided the home and office of Richard Kraft, an American priest who had lived in South Africa for twenty years and had become the Anglican bishop of Pretoria. On September 2, four days before the election, police viciously attacked demonstrators in the center of Cape Town with batons, rubber whips, and a water cannon that fired purple dye, marking demonstrators for future arrest. One of the protesters, a young white veteran of the South African Defence Forces, clambered on top of the armored vehicle, disabled the cannon, and scampered away. A few days later graffiti appeared around town which declared, in a twist on the opening sentence of the Freedom Charter, that "the Purple Shall Govern."

On September 6, 1989, as protests and police brutality left dozens dead, just over a million white voters cast their ballots for the National Party, giving the party ninety-three seats in the white House of Assembly. Both of the opposition groups made gains at the National Party's expense. The Conservative Party stole seventeen seats and ended up with a total of thirty-nine, making the Conservatives the official opposition in parliament. The Democratic Party grabbed twelve National Party seats, for a total of thirty-three. Pollsters and other political analysts, noting the significant numbers of Afrikaners who gravitated toward the Democratic Party, interpreted the results as a general shift to the left. F. W. de Klerk did likewise, arguing that the combined votes for the

Democratic Party and National Party demonstrated massive support for change.

In the weeks that followed the election, de Klerk surprised everyone around him by introducing a mix of symbolic and substantive reforms. In the first week, de Klerk ordered the police to stop using whips on protesters, granted the first legal permission in decades for a large outdoor protest, and confined the remnants of the Koevoet brigade to their barracks. The next month he released Walter Sisulu and all the remaining Rivonia trial prisoners, with the exception of Mandela. De Klerk then permitted ANC supporters to hold a huge welcome-home rally for Sisulu and the others in a soccer stadium in Soweto; the participants openly and ecstatically waved black-green-and-gold ANC flags and sang the ANC anthem even though the organization was still banned by the South African government. In November, as South Africans of all races prepared for their summer holidays, de Klerk announced that the thirty-six-year-old Separate Amenities Act, which had enforced segregation on the beaches and in parks, theaters, restaurants, and other public facilities, would be scrapped. Two weeks later he shut down the National Security Management System and restored political control to civilians in the National Party. On December 13, de Klerk himself met with Nelson Mandela to discuss South Africa's future.

The range and speed of de Klerk's actions left observers breathless and created a sense of unstoppable momentum. In the traditional New Year's speech, de Klerk spoke movingly about his desire to unite all South Africans and to lead them into what he called South Africa's "new dispensation," an era that would mark a radical break with the past. Speculation about what de Klerk would do next dominated the country; most attention focused on the possible release of Nelson Mandela. Every third or fourth day a rumor swept the nation that Mandela might appear in a matter of hours. Newspaper editors, whose most recent photographs of Mandela had been taken nearly thirty years before, printed artists' renditions of what the enigmatic prisoner might look like after his years of incarceration. Eugene Terreblanche and other right-wing extremists threatened that Mandela's release would lead to war. Mandela's release became such a dominant theme in articles and conversations that it gradually shifted from an impossibility to a likelihood. Delegations from the United Democratic Front and other organizations streamed in and out of Victor Verster prison, to which Mandela had been transferred in December 1988, to consult with the ANC leader, who was living in a small warder's bungalow with its own swimming pool. "Who would have thought," asked Pieter-Dirk Uys, one of South Africa's leading comedians, "that a faceless man with a fax could run the country from a prison?"

When Mandela's release did not take place in January, attention focused on what de Klerk would say in his opening speech to parliament. The opening speech had traditionally been used by de Klerk's predecessors to articulate the direction of government policy for the next parliamentary season. P. W. Botha had also used the occasion to display some of South Africa's military might, treating onlookers to an array of marching soldiers and aerial salutes. On this opening day, February 2, 1990, exactly one year after his elevation to party leader, F. W. de Klerk had ordered that only the traditional president's guard and a small military band be present. At nine in the morning advance copies of the president's speech were distributed to the international press; as the reporters flipped through it, some of them gasped with astonishment. When de Klerk stepped to the podium in parliament at eleven A.M., he looked out over a chamber packed with attentive listeners. At that moment, he later told his brother, "I had no doubts, because I was convinced that we were doing the right thing. I was about to say what was right. But I was a bit more tense than usual, because I realized that the implications were enormous, and that South Africa would never again be the same after that address." De Klerk started by painting the election of the previous September as a mandate for "drastic change" and as an indicator of the "growing realization . . . that only a negotiated understanding among the representative leaders of the entire population is able to ensure lasting peace." In the year to come, he said, his government would make negotiation "the highest priority" with the goal of creating a "totally new and just constitutional dispensation in which every inhabitant will enjoy equal rights, treatment, and opportunity in every sphere of endeavor—constitutional, social, and economic."

Impressive as his words might sound, most listeners still discounted them: such high-minded rhetoric had come from South African leaders before. De Klerk turned swiftly to the international realm. Instead of insisting that South Africa could go it alone, de Klerk said that he and his colleagues understood "the important part the world at large has to play in the realization of our country's national interests. . . . Without contact and cooperation with the rest of the world," de Klerk said, suddenly reversing the *laager* mentality, "we cannot promote the well-being and security of our citizens." De Klerk then reeled off a list of startling commitments. He opened the door to the reincorporation of the independent homelands; he promised to recognize and protect "the fundamental individual rights which form the constitutional basis of most western democracies"; he promised to create a truly independent judiciary; he suspended the death penalty; and he vowed to end the state of emergency "as soon as circumstances justify it." He saved his most momentous announcements for the end. To enable the country to move forward to negotiations, he had decided to lift the thirty-year-old ban on the African National Congress and the South African Community Party; end all media restrictions; and rescind all restrictions on the United Democratic Front, COSATU, and thirty-one other organizations. Finally, he reached the topic for which everyone was waiting. "The government," de Klerk declared, "has taken a firm decision to release Nelson Mandela unconditionally," a decision which would be "brought to finality without delay."

Allan Boesak, who had just led a march onto the parade ground in front of Cape Town's city hall, was momentarily speechless when he heard the news. "Unbelievable," he finally told reporters. "I admire the courage of F. W." Desmond Tutu, who was also at the protest, said that the state president had "taken my breath away." Eugene Terreblanche reacted with horror. "No, oh no," he said. "It can't be true." Around the country men and women rushed into the streets to express their emotions. In Cape Town a young man scrambled up onto a statue of Jan Smuts and put a woolen green, gold, and black cap on the statue's head. Elsewhere women danced and waved signs proclaiming "Are you ready? Mandela is coming!" In Johannesburg, young men and women punched the air, shouting "Viva Comrade Nelson Mandela!" Soon afterward Johannesburg police attacked the demonstration, which had grown to a thousand people, with tear gas and nightsticks.

The leaders of the African National Congress, who had just held a major conference in Lusaka that Walter Sisulu and other recently released prisoners had attended, responded cautiously. Foreign Minister Thabo Mbeki welcomed the development but called on de Klerk to rein in his police and military before the ANC could agree to end the armed struggle. To many it seemed that the ANC had been caught off guard; they had expected to use Mandela's release to launch a wave of protests to force de Klerk to unban the ANC. Now, suddenly, they had what they wanted, and a host of new problems flourished. The unprecedented realities created by de Klerk's speech had to be analyzed and debated. New priorities had to be established. The leaders of the UDF and other groups faced the challenge of rebuilding their organizations after years of assault by the state. The ANC leaders in Lusaka realized they would have to transform themselves swiftly from an illegal nationalist movement operating abroad to an effective force inside South Africa. Men and women who had been in exile and had not seen their families for decades realized that they might soon be able to go home. As the internal and external parts of the liberation movement came together, long-overlooked differences in age, ideology, gender, and experience bubbled up. The process of coordination also suffered from the absence of Oliver Tambo, who was confined to a Swedish hospital by a stroke. Though

Tambo would slowly recover, the incapacitation of the man who had served as the president of the ANC for twenty-three years made the process of planning in such tumultuous times even more complex and further heightened the expectations for Nelson Mandela.

Hundreds of print and television journalists flew in from around the world to cover the impending release of the world's most famous prisoner. The American networks sent their anchors and crews to broadcast live from Cape Town. Jesse Jackson arrived on his first visit to South Africa in eleven years, hoping to visit Mandela in prison or to greet him on his release. The South African government, irritated by Jackson's presence and worried about his safety, threatened to delay Mandela's release until after Jackson's eight-day visa had expired. For more than a week after de Klerk's speech nothing happened, prompting the editors of the *New York Times* to ask, on February 10, "Why Isn't Nelson Mandela Free?" While government and ANC representatives negotiated in private and made mutual accusations in public, the nation swung between euphoria and apprehension. Andries Treurnicht promised that his Conservative Party would force the National Party to hold a general election, win, and immediately divide the country to create an Afrikaner homeland. At the same time, the Johannesburg Stock Exchange, buoyed by the hope that sanctions would immediately be lifted, shot up two hundred points, or 7.2 percent, in two days.

On Sunday morning, February 11, South Africans awoke to a spectacular sight. There, on the front page of their newspapers, below a huge headline reading HERE HE IS!, was a full-color photograph of the man whose picture had been banned for thirty years. The image showed a tall, thin, gray-haired Mandela in a well-tailored suit standing next to F. W. de Klerk; taken at a meeting at which the two men had finalized the details of Mandela's release, the photograph suggested a summit meeting between two heads of state. Later that morning, de Klerk appeared at a press conference before hundreds of domestic and international reporters and announced that Mandela would be released from Victor Verster prison at three P.M. Instantly all attention shifted to the town of Paarl, where hundreds of people had gathered outside the prison gates. Inside, Mandela finished having a meal with his family and said goodbye to Warrant Officer Gregory, who for twenty-two years had grown from being Mandela's jailer to his friend.

Outside the prison, as ANC flags fluttered in the summer wind, South African Broadcasting Corporation television cameras transmitted live images around South Africa and across the planet. For several hours millions of people around the world waited impatiently in front of their televisions watching for something to happen. Then the cameras spotted several automobiles making their way from the inside of the prison grounds toward the gate. Just inside the gate, the cars stopped. A crowd congregated; for a moment confusion reigned. Then suddenly the crowd parted and Mandela appeared, walking slowly, dressed in the same gray suit, hand in hand with Winnie, who wore a somber black outfit with a white collar. The crowd roared as Mandela crossed the threshold of the prison gates, lifted his fist, and saluted them. Ted Koppel, who had been offering steady commentary from his post in Cape Town, was momentarily speechless. The stunned South African television commentator only managed to say, "There is a very nice picture of Mr. Mandela and his wife." Then, as Cyril Ramaphosa and other UDF leaders helped to keep the crowd back, the Mandelas quickly stepped into a waiting limousine and sped off.

The moment of Mandela's release electrified viewers from Australia to Europe, from Japan to America. In snow-locked Massachusetts, Mandela's daughter Makaziwe Mandela-Amuah cried aloud with joy as she showed her three children the first live image they had ever seen of their grandfather. In New York, Betty Shabazz, the widow of Malcolm X, heard the news while she was driving in her car; she threw her hands up and shouted. At his home in Cape Town, Desmond Tutu jumped up and did a spontaneous dance. In front of Mandela's home in Soweto, hundreds of people shouted as a young man carefully painted the tiny garage in ANC colors. From Paarl, the Mandelas were driven back to Cape Town in a motorcade led by six white policemen on motorcycles. Along the route, to Mandela's amazement and delight, they passed clusters of white South Africans along the road or on overpasses, some of whom were holding signs which read "Welcome Home, Mandela" and "Mandela, Our Leader."

Their destination was Cape Town's Victorian city hall, where a crowd of fifty thousand had gathered to hear Mandela speak. When Jesse Jackson's car appeared, the crowd thought it belonged to Mandela and nearly tore the doors off the hinges. Jackson made it to the front of the crowd and clambered over several barricades in the vain hope of standing beside Mandela when he appeared. When Mandela arrived, he kept the crowd waiting while he met with various delegations inside the building. Impatient youths on the fringes of the crowd smashed the windows of automobiles and shops on the periphery of the parade ground, leading to running skirmishes with police and UDF marshals.

As he was about to go out onto the balcony, Mandela discovered that he had left both his reading glasses and the text of his speech back at the prison. He quickly reconstructed the speech as best he could. As the sun set over the Atlantic Ocean, Mandela finally stepped out onto the balcony. Speaking with a strong voice into a microphone held by Cyril Ramaphosa, Mandela uttered his first public words since 1964. "Amandla!" he shouted. "Ngawethu!" the crowd responded. Mandela launched into a vigorous call to action. "We have waited too long for our freedom," Mandela told the crowd. "We can wait no longer. Now is the time to intensify the struggle on all fronts. To relax our efforts now would be a mistake which generations to come will not be able to forgive." He concluded with the same words he had used in the Pretoria courtroom twenty-six years before. "During my lifetime I have dedicated myself to this struggle of the African people. I have fought against white domination and I have fought against black domination. I have cherished the ideal of a democratic and free society in which all persons live together in harmony and with equal opportunities. It is an ideal which I hope to live for and to achieve. But if needs be, it is an ideal for which I am prepared to die."

As soon as Mandela finished, the limousine drove him around the base of Table Mountain to the archbishop's residence in Bishopscourt, where Desmond Tutu greeted Mandela for the first time in his life. Tucked away in Tutu's study, Mandela spent several hours taking calls from world leaders, including George Bush, who invited him to visit the White House. At the end of the evening Tutu and Mandela gathered with Walter and Albertina Sisulu and other ANC leaders in a large study. It was an extraordinary event: a group of aging African politicians, imprisoned or hunted for decades as terrorists, greeting one another in what had been the center of white ecclesial authority constructed on the very site of Jan van Riebeeck's first farm. Tutu turned to his visitors and asked them to sing, and together they reeled off hymn after hymn of praise. "We sang '*Masi Wu*'—Let us thank Jesus," Tutu recalled. "The chorus is 'Have mercy, Lord, have mercy.' And we sang another one of my favorites, in which there is a beautiful verse: 'Let white and black fall before him in adoration.' That was a wonderful thing to sing with someone who had been in jail for twenty-seven years." At the end Tutu, Mandela, Sisulu, and the others sang the Lord's Prayer in Xhosa, and then the archbishop left his visitors so that they could discuss what, after nearly three decades, they should do next.

Over the next few weeks, Nelson Mandela rocketed into the forefront of South Africa's public life. On the morning after his release, he gave his first press conference and reached out to whites. "Whites are fellow South Africans," he said, "and we want them to feel safe." By the end of the session his calm and gracious answers had so beguiled the reporters that they rewarded him with a burst of applause. From Cape Town he and his party flew to Johannesburg by private jet and made their way back to his tiny home at 8115 Vilakazi Street in Soweto. Over the next twenty-four hours more than a thousand interview requests came in by telephone, telex, fax, or shouts over the garden wall. Camera crews jostled for position in the tiny garden behind his house as Mandela spent ten minutes each with Dan Rather, Ted Koppel, Tom Brokaw, and a dozen other interviewers. To each he repeated several basic points: that he was a disciplined member of the African National Congress who would accept whatever role the organization gave him; that sanctions would have to be kept in force until South Africa had made the transition to a nonracial society; that he continued to support the ANC's position on nationalizing the country's banks and mines. He also answered questions about his years in prison. Though he had never been personally assaulted, he said, he saw such brutality each day. The most poignant moment came when Mandela responded to a question by Allister Sparks, the South African journalist. Sparks asked Mandela what had been the most vivid moment of his first days of freedom. "The most pleasant memory when a man returns to his home after almost twenty-eight years," Mandela said carefully, "is when I closed the bedroom door and I tried to assure my wife that I am back and that her problems will now be shared."

Over the next months Mandela endured a bruising schedule of meetings, appearances, and foreign trips. Not long after a tumultuous welcome-home rally at Orlando Stadium in Soweto, Mandela flew to Durban and urged his followers to stop the factional warfare that had killed more than thirty-five hundred people. Soon afterward he went to Lusaka for an emotional reunion with his old friends, who officially bestowed on him the title of deputy president of the African National Congress. Mandela then stopped off in three other African countries, including Tanzania, where he visited the ANC's Simon Mahlangu College and other exile centers. From there Mandela flew directly to Stockholm to see his old law partner Oliver Tambo in the hospital. Mandela then flew back to South Africa for a few days, before jetting up to Windhoek to attend the formal granting of independence to Namibia on March 21, 1990.

Though in early 1989 SWAPO had initially tried unsuccessfully to sneak hundreds of its troops across the border from Angola, the remainder of the agreement had been implemented without incident. The international community had been particularly interested to see how swiftly SWAPO and the other parties inside the country had agreed to a liberal democratic constitution guaranteed by an independent judiciary and a bill of rights. At the ceremony Mandela found himself sitting with a strange assemblage of foreign leaders: SWAPO leader and new Namibian president Sam Nujoma, U.S. Secretary of State James Baker, Soviet Foreign Minister Eduard Shevardnadze, Libyan dictator Muammar Qaddafi, PLO leader Yassir Arafat, Fidel Castro, and F. W. de

Klerk. Seated in the American delegation was the new assistant secretary of state for African affairs, Henry Cohen, and his predecessor, Chester Crocker, who had been dreaming about the moment for twenty-five years.

In and around the ceremony the foreign leaders held scores of bilateral meetings to promote their agendas. For Baker the goal was to persuade the Angolans and the Soviets to settle with Jonas Savimbi and UNITA. F. W. de Klerk tried to persuade various leaders of the sincerity and irrevocability of his commitment to reform. Nelson Mandela, conversely, used the occasion to thank the nations who had been friendly to the ANC through its years of exile and to remind everyone that the actual dismantling of apartheid had not yet taken place. Mandela's willingness to greet and even to defend some of the West's current archenemies—Castro, Qaddafi, and Arafat—set off warning bells in Washington and triggered protests from Jewish organizations that took several months for the ANC to assuage.

The intimate intertwining of domestic and international politics can be seen from the minuet that Mandela and de Klerk performed with each other and with their international allies over the next few months. The ANC agreed to hold talks with the National Party and then suspended them after a massacre in the township of Sobokeng in which the ANC leaders believed the security forces had been involved. After a three-hour meeting between Mandela and de Klerk, in which de Klerk agreed to investigate the killings, the talks were rescheduled for early May. Before the talks opened, however, Mandela flew up to London to attend a rally for seventy thousand people at Wembley Stadium. Mandela turned down an invitation to meet with Margaret Thatcher because she had suggested that sanctions should be removed. "Do not listen to anyone who says that you must give up the struggle against apartheid," Mandela told the cheering crowd. "Reject any suggestion that the campaign to isolate the apartheid regime should be wound down." Two weeks later Mandela was back in South Africa to lead the ANC team in its negotiations with de Klerk and the National Party. The meetings were held at Groote Schuur, the former home of Cecil Rhodes and the traditional residence of South Africa's white leaders. Standing in front of his large delegation—which included Walter Sisulu, Thabo Mbeki, Alfred Nzo, Joe Slovo, and, to everyone's amazement, Beyers Naudé—Mandela commented with emotion that this was "the first time in seventy-eight years that a truly serious meeting takes place between delegations of the African National Congress and the succession of white governments that have ruled our country for generations." Within a few weeks of the Groote Schuur talks, both men had again jumped on airplanes to shore up international support for their positions. De Klerk hopped around nine European countries over eighteen days, reassuring one leader after another of his plan to eliminate apartheid. Mandela, for his part, flew to Egypt for a meeting with president Hosni Mubarak and another brief but friendly encounter with Arafat, and then back to South Africa for surgery on a benign cyst in his bladder.

The real prize for both men was a trip to the United States. De Klerk, like his predecessors, eagerly wanted to be received at the White House as proof of American acceptance of his policy, and he planned a trip for early June. When Randall Robinson and Jesse Jackson learned that Bush might receive de Klerk before he had welcomed Mandela, they exploded and began dialing their friends on Capitol Hill. Soon the South African Foreign Ministry received word that many American legislators would not be willing to meet with de Klerk if he were to come first. Shortly afterward, the South African government announced that it was postponing the trip.

On Monday, June 4, Nelson and Winnie Mandela, along with a large entourage of ANC leaders, left for a month-long world tour that would take them to Botswana, Zambia, France, Sweden, Switzerland, West Germany, Italy, Canada, Ireland, and the United States. Mandela had three purposes in mind for this lengthy trip: to thank his supporters, to urge them to keep sanctions in place, and to raise money for the ANC's difficult transition back into South African politics. Across Africa and Europe they received a warm welcome from large crowds, but when they arrived in New York City on Wednesday, June 20, it was clear that something unprecedented was unfolding. Mandela was met at the airport by Governor Mario Cuomo, Mayor David Dinkins, Jesse Jackson, and Randall Robinson, who had been one of the principal organizers of Mandela's itinerary in the United States. From there Mandela and his party were whisked away for a huge rally at Boys and Girls High School, an overwhelmingly black school in the Bedford-Stuyvesant section of Brooklyn. When Mandela spoke to the crowd of teenagers, his South African accent seemed out of place, a voice from another world. Mandela beamed with delight. "To enjoy the support of the youth, the future leaders of this country," Mandela said with a large smile, "cuts down my age by at least twenty-five years." Afterward Winnie stepped to the microphone and taught the New Yorkers some chants. "In South Africa, when we see you," she said, "we see the young lions in the struggle of the South African people . . . and we usually greet you by shouting Amandla!" A few voices shouted back "Ngawethu!" Over the next few days, New Yorkers joined enthusiastically in the exchange, though many had no idea what the words meant. One black radio announcer held a phone-in contest to see if any of his listeners could guess. On another occasion, a policeman who was listening turned to a reporter and asked, "And who is this Amanda person anyway?"

From Brooklyn, Winnie and Nelson Mandela roared into Manhattan, where they soon found themselves encased with Dinkins and Cuomo inside a compartment made of light-green bulletproof glass mounted on a flatbed truck. The "Mandelamobile," as it was quickly dubbed, was the centerpiece of a forty-car motorcade that snaked through Manhattan for an old-fashioned ticker tape parade. The practice was so old-fashioned, in fact, that no ticker tape could be found anywhere on Wall Street, whose firms had converted completely to electronics. The parade organizers solved the problem by importing truckloads of ticker tape from out of state and supplementing the supply with thousands of shredded computer printouts. Three-quarters of a million people turned out to see the Mandelas at some point during the day, four hundred thousand along the parade route alone. The entire city seemed electrified. Desmond Tutu's daughter Mpho Tutu told a reporter of her amazement at the "feeling of joy and warmth . . . that has been shown to the Mandelas and seems to be spreading. People are reacting to one another with warmth. People actually greet you on the streets of New York and say 'Good morning, Hi!' " *Time* magazine's editors were so astonished by the reaction to Mandela that they put his picture on their cover with the headline A HERO IN AMERICA. Noting that while Mandela was only a mortal being and a dedicated revolutionary, the magazine noted that "on a more transcendent plane, where history is made and myths are forged, Mandela is a hero, a man like those described by author Joseph Campbell, who has emerged from a symbolic grave 'reborn, made great, and filled with creative power.' "

Mandela plowed through one exhilarating and grueling event after another: a celebration at Riverside Church, at which Jesse Jackson preached; a group interview with eleven reporters from the *New York Times;* a speech before the General Assembly of the United Nations; and a rally at Yankee Stadium, where he was presented with a Yankees cap and jacket. At a meeting in Harlem, Nelson and Winnie Mandela further cemented the symbolic unification of the American and the South African struggles over race when they were introduced to a huge crowd by Betty Shabazz, Malcolm X's widow, who declared that the two struggles were really one and the same. After embracing Shabazz while the crowd roared, Winnie took her place at the microphone and agreed. "I identify myself so directly with her," she said, speaking of Shabazz. "I identify directly with the ideals Malcolm X stood for. And in her I saw an incarnation of Malcolm X himself."

To each group, Mandela repeated his basic message that the West should not lift sanctions until majority rule had been achieved. Though he refused to back down on the question of nationalization, Mandela told reporters and business leaders that foreign investors would have nothing to fear in an ANC-dominated South Africa. "The form of economy will be decided solely by our determination to make the economy perform fully from the point of insuring full employment and the development of a social consciousness," Mandela told prominent business leaders during a meeting on Wall Street. "Any formula, any option which will enable us to do this, we will adopt." At the same time, he continued, "we are sensitive that as investors in a post-apartheid South Africa, you will need to be confident about the security of your investments, and adequate and equitable return on capital, and a general climate of peace and stability."

Mandela also took time to hobnob with celebrities and to raise money for the ANC. On Friday, June 22, he attended a $2,500-a-head cocktail party at the Manhattan home of Arthur Krim, the chief of Orion pictures and the man who had served as chair of Columbia University's board of trustees during much of the divestment debate. He then went downtown to a star-studded dinner at Robert De Niro's TriBeCa loft apartment, where he greeted a long line of dazzled African American celebrities. As Mandela approached, comedian Eddie Murphy, who had donated twenty thousand dollars to the ANC, fidgeted with uncharacteristic nervousness. When Mandela caught sight of Murphy, his eyes widened and he shouted, "Eddie! Good God! How are you?!" Murphy beamed, still speechless. "It is unbelievable that I am meeting you here," Mandela continued, bubbling with enthusiasm. "You kept us very much entertained in prison." Still tongue-tied, Murphy shyly leaned forward and hugged Mandela. Mandela, the former boxer, was also delighted to meet one of his heroes, Jolting Joe Frazier, so much so that he asked Frazier to stand beside him when he delivered his speech.

The pace proved so hectic that Mandela's aides regularly had to cancel meetings and events to provide their leader—who was nearly seventy-two years old, only four months out of prison, and still recovering from surgery—with a few pockets of rest. Even with such cutbacks, the trip exceeded everyone's expectations. As Mandela moved across eight American cities in eleven days, he wove the struggles for racial justice in the United States and South Africa together in new and powerful ways. "The struggle against racial oppression is worldwide," he told Robin MacNeil of the *MacNeil-Lehrer News Hour.* "It is not only confined to South Africa." Appearing on the *Phil Donahue Show,* Winnie Mandela was even more explicit. Her visit to Harlem, she said, had confirmed her "complete identity with the peoples of this country. Throughout the years we have learned to understand . . . that racialism is an international cancer and includes the pains of the black Americans here." In

Atlanta Mandela tightened the connection when he received a doctorate from Spelman College and two dozen other black colleges, met with Leon Sullivan, Rosa Parks, and other historic figures, and laid a green, gold, and black wreath at the tomb of Martin Luther King Jr.

For eleven days, every moment Nelson Mandela appeared in public became suffused with symbolic importance. Six of the cities he visited had black mayors, each of whom used the occasion to make lengthy public statements about democracy and race. After years of frustration about race relations, the visit offered many Americans a moment of celebration and catharsis. Civil rights leaders who had fought for ten years against White House apathy experienced a kind of political ecstasy as Mandela attracted unprecedented attention to the cause. For other American anti-apartheid activists—from the students who had participated in a few demonstrations to the professionals who had been toiling for decades—Mandela's presence was not only a dream come true, but a massive vindication of everything for which they had fought. Politicians, movie stars, sports heroes, and other celebrities jockeyed to shake Mandela's hand, to be seen with him, to have their pictures taken with him. Only in Miami, where a few hundred Cuban Americans demonstrated against Mandela's favorable comments about Castro, was the reception anything less than ecstatic. For many millions of Americans, Mandela's presence and his words offered a desperately desired burst of hope, the hope that a real reconciliation between black and white might someday be possible. If it could happen in South Africa, it might also happen in the United States.

Fueled by such deep desire and experience, the rhetoric sometimes slid into excess. "Mr. Mandela is a George Washington, a Bolivar, a King, a Herzel," said David Dinkins in his official welcoming speech at New York's City Hall. "He is like a modern-day Moses leading the people of South Africa from enslavement at the hands of the Pharoahs." "Never in this history of humankind," Harry Belafonte told the thousands at Yankee Stadium, "has there ever been a voice that has more clearly caught the imagination and the spirit and fired the hope of freedom than the voice of the deputy president of South Africa, Nelson Mandela." For Mandela himself, the adulation came as a surprise. "I couldn't imagine that I could attract such support," he told an interviewer. "It is something which hit me flush in the face." Though it was a "nice feeling" to be referred to as a hero, Mandela continued, "this is not really directed at me. I am used as a peg on which to hang the adulation of the African National Congress." At the same time, Mandela quickly embraced the tactics of a politician on the stump. Before tens of thousands of cheering New Yorkers at Yankee Stadium, he put on a baseball jacket and cap and exclaimed, "You know who I am. I am a Yankee!" He told thousands of UAW workers at a plant outside Detroit, whom he addressed as "comrades," that they should consider him "a member of the UAW." And in Boston, addressing a luncheon hosted by Ted Kennedy at the John F. Kennedy Presidential Library, Mandela looked around the room and said, "Right now, I consider myself an honorary Irishman from Soweto."

As a man of iron discipline, Mandela did not allow the excitement to distract him from his objectives. Day after day he repeated his thanks to those who had helped him and the African National Congress; he relentlessly urged Americans to "keep the pressure on" through the maintenance of sanctions; and he asked his supporters to provide financial support to the ANC. He succeeded in all three goals. By the time Mandela returned to South Africa he had collected seven million dollars in contributions, a huge amount when translated into rand. President Bush greeted him at the White House with a formal South Lawn reception, an honor normally reserved for heads of state. After the president used his remarks to "call elements in South African society to renounce violence and armed struggle," Mandela took his turn at the podium to defend the ANC's view that the armed struggle could be called off only if the South African police and military were reined in. He politely but firmly rejected the implied criticism of the ANC, suggesting that Bush had misspoken because he had not "as yet received a proper briefing from us." Mandela and Bush then entered the White House for a three-hour conversation, including a working lunch. Afterward, Mandela was in a much better mood. "I think that we came out of the meeting understanding each other's positions and much closer to each other," he told one reporter. A few days later, he was even more positive. "Even at the White House," he said, "our mission succeeded beyond our wildest expectations."

The political high point of Mandela's trip came on June 26, 1990, when he became the first African and only the third private citizen in the history of the United States to speak before a joint session of Congress. Appearing in the chamber where America's part in supporting apartheid had been debated for three decades, standing before the officials who for years had either vilified him as a Communist or extolled him as a democrat, the son of a Xhosa chief received a three-minute standing ovation. And then the man who had been silenced for twenty-seven years began to speak. "We have come to Washington . . . and into these hallowed chambers not as pretenders to greatness," he said, "but as a particle of a people whom we know to be noble and heroic, enduring, multiplying, permanent, rejoicing in the expectation and knowledge that their humanity will be reaffirmed and enlarged by open and unfettered communion with the nations of the world.

"Our people demand democracy," Mandela continued. "Our country, which continues to bleed and suffer pain, needs democracy. . . . We fight for and visualize a future in which all shall, without regard to race, color, creed, and sex, have the right to vote and to be voted into all elective offices." For a few moments Mandela sketched the "dehumanization" and the "wretched life of hunger and deprivation" which had been the "terrible fate of all black persons in our country under the system of apartheid." He tried to convey to the American leaders the unjust "opulence of our white compatriots and the deliberate distortion of the economy to feed that opulence," arguing that the reconstruction of South African society would also mean a reshaping of the economy. He said that South Africa needed American capital, technology, expertise, and markets, but he wanted to see a relationship not of subservient dependency and fawning gratitude but of mutual benefit. One benefit for Americans would be to observe how "this complex African society, which has known nothing but racism for three centuries, should be transformed into an oasis of good race relations where the black shall be to the white sister and brother, a fellow South African, and equal human being, both citizens of the world."

Nearing his conclusion, Mandela returned to the history of the struggle in his country. "We went to jail," he said, "because it was impossible to sit still while the obscenity of the apartheid system was being imposed on our people . . . while a racist tyranny sought to reduce an entire people to a status worse than that of beasts of the forest." Mandela deftly turned to the pantheon of American heroes, both black and white, to support his argument. "We could not have made an acquaintance through literature with such human giants as George Washington, Abraham Lincoln, and Thomas Jefferson and not been moved to act. We could not have heard of and admired John Brown, Sojourner Truth, Frederick Douglass, W. E. B. DuBois, Marcus Garvey, Martin Luther King Jr., and others . . . and not be moved to act as they were moved to act. We could not have known of your Declaration of Independence and not elected to join in the struggle to guarantee the people's life, liberty, and the pursuit of happiness." Moving from past to present, Mandela offered an almost personal thanks. "We are glad that you merged with our own people to make it possible for us to emerge from the darkness of the prison cell and join the contemporary process of the renewal of the world . . . and we count on you to persist in your noble endeavor to free the rest of our political prisoners and to emancipate our people from the larger prison that is apartheid South Africa." Mandela looked out over his audience, pausing before his final words. "The day may not be far," he said, "when we will borrow the words of Thomas Jefferson and speak of the will of the South African nation. In

the exercise of that will by this united nation of black and white people
. . . there will be born a country on the southern tip of Africa which
you will be proud to call a friend and an ally because of its contribution
to the universal striving towards liberty, human rights, prosperity, and
peace among all people."

When he finished, the representatives and senators leapt to their feet.
Mandela beamed the widest smile of his life and stretched out his arms
in a gesture of exhilarated embrace. It was moment of dreams. In that
moment, Nelson Mandela received the acclaim of the American people
in a manner which his enemies had craved and been denied and which
no one, not even Mandela himself, had ever imagined. In that moment,
the brute cynicism of politics, the endless calculation of interests, the
relentless struggle for dominance melted into a warm celebration of
hope. And in that moment, however briefly, the two great struggles for
justice that had dominated so much of the history of the United States
and South Africa finally, before the eyes of all the world, became one.

EPILOGUE

Legacy and Future

If such things can happen in this crazy country, who says we should feel gloom and despair? Is the sun not shining behind our clouds?
—DESMOND TUTU

PRIOR TO Nelson Mandela's release, the anti-apartheid struggle had remained roughly balanced between internal and external pressures, but when he walked out of prison the center of gravity shifted back inside the country's borders. Activists like Randall Robinson and Desmond Tutu announced that with the reemergence of South Africa's "true political leaders," their role would become one of support. Legislators around the world who had been prepared to pass additional sanctions paused to see what would happen next. Thousands of exiled South Africans who had helped to fuel the overseas movements hurried back to take part in the historic transformation of their country.

Inside South Africa, the newly legal ANC faced a tangle of problems. Its leaders had to convert it from a revolutionary group scattered across a dozen countries to a political organization inside a nation-state. ANC leaders labored to consolidate the many groups that had fought apartheid, arguing, as they had in the 1950s, that only the African National Congress was broad enough to unite all factions and bring democracy to South Africa. Though the PAC, AZAPO, and Inkatha bitterly resisted this approach, other activists jumped from their posts in unions, church groups, and other organizations into positions in the ANC. Civic groups and street committees in some townships metamorphosed into field extensions of the reemerging organization. Gradually the ANC refashioned itself into what its aging leaders had always wanted it to be:

an organization capable of negotiating the end of white supremacy in South Africa.

For months after Mandela's release the South African airwaves and newspapers were filled with words and images that only a short time before would have been preposterous. Mandela himself, vilified for decades as a Communist demon, was steadily recast as a moderate senior statesman, an image he reinforced with his gracious manner and lack of bitterness. Other former villains such as Oliver Tambo, Chris Hani, and Joe Slovo were met on their return to South Africa not with soldiers and handcuffs but with cameras and flowers. Tambo, in failing health, became an amiable figurehead. Slovo freely admitted in appearances on South African television that the Communist Party had not always been correct and that he now favored small business and a mixed economy. Hani, the popular general secretary of the South African Communist Party and the former chief of staff of Umkhonto We Sizwe, continued to deliver fiery speeches in the townships but moved into a comfortable ranch house in the white suburb of Boksburg through whose streets he regularly went jogging. Newspaper commentary about these men shifted from shrill invective to edgy speculation about whether they could really be trusted.

Most peculiar was the relationship between Nelson Mandela and F. W. de Klerk, which shuttled between partnership and pique. An early period of enthusiasm—in which de Klerk spoke glowingly of Mandela's intelligence and Mandela called the state president a "man of integrity"—was followed by months of mutual suspicion and recrimination. They aired most of their complaints to each other in private, but occasionally raw anger pushed the arguments into public view. Despite their squabbles, the two men steadily maneuvered their supporters to accept a political reality that only shortly before would have been unthinkable. Mandela and de Klerk both understood that to reach a negotiated settlement the African National Congress and the National Party would have to occupy the political center. Only the ANC could hold together the divergent camps within the majority population; only the National Party could foil the terror and fury of the Afrikaner right.

Tethered by history, the two men lurched through a succession of clashes and accords. In August 1990 they negotiated the ANC's agreement to set aside armed struggle. In February 1991 de Klerk, in response to the ANC's long-standing demand, announced that he was scrapping the linchpin of racial discrimination, the Population Registration Act. Five months later the first national ANC conference in more than thirty years ratified support for a negotiated settlement, followed soon afterward by a National Party federal congress that laid out the white group's proposals for power sharing and voting rights. At the end of December 1991 the National Party and the ANC met with sixteen other parties to discuss the new constitution. This negotiation—known as the Congress for Democratic South Africa (CODESA)—ended on a note of hope. That optimism nearly disappeared shortly afterward when the Conservative Party decisively defeated the National Party in a local by-election. The Conservatives claimed that this was proof that de Klerk had exceeded his mandate from the election of 1989 and no longer enjoyed the support of the white population. De Klerk, in a brilliant move, took back the initiative by calling an immediate whites-only referendum on whether he should proceed with the constitutional negotiations. If the referendum question was defeated, de Klerk said, he would quit and leave the nation to its fate. On March 17, 1992, more than two-thirds of the white electorate cast their ballots in support of de Klerk, leaving him again free to move forward with the ANC.

The negotiations were fiendishly complex. At one point, the ANC representatives insisted that the CODESA participants did not have the authority to design a constitution because only a democratically elected constituent assembly could do that. Others—such as those representing the National Party, the Democratic Party, and Inkatha—wanted to be certain that such an assembly, which they expected would be dominated by the ANC, would honor prior binding agreements. The Democratic Party specifically demanded a bill of rights. The National Party called for "power sharing," a move that others rejected as giving a veto to whites. Gatsha Buthelezi pushed hard for the creation of a federal system in which each region would be granted significant autonomy. Adding to the din, a gaggle of international experts—diplomats, lawyers, professors, and negotiation trainers—jetted into Johannesburg and fanned out across the country to offer their counsel.

At the same time, violence was mounting relentlessly. According to the South African Institute of Race Relations, more than ten thousand people died in political violence between January 1989 and December 1992. The killings often seemed random, ignoring race, age, and political affiliation. By the early 1990s the murder rate grew to ten times that of the United States, a statistic fueled by thousands of UK-47 assault rifles, available for less than fifty dollars each, that were flowing in from Mozambique. The worst violence took place in Natal, where clashes between ANC and Inkatha loyalists claimed thousands of lives.

The rhythm of attacks outraged Mandela, but there seemed little he could do. In addition to the ongoing threat to his personal safety—a right-wing assassination plot was uncovered at the time he returned from the United States—he had to contend with the ANC's loss of control of some of its most radical units and the apparent emergence of the anarchy that apartheid's defenders had long predicted. Mandela demanded that de Klerk rein in his police, root out those who might be off-duty murderers, and crack down on the Inkatha forces who were terrorizing large blocks of the country. De Klerk repeatedly promised that he would act, but the continued crackle of midnight gunfire raised questions about his good faith. Mandela also appealed to Buthelezi; in January 1991 the two men signed a peace agreement that was almost instantly invalidated by more fighting. In September 1991 Mandela, de Klerk, and Buthelezi, coaxed by religious and business groups, signed the National Peace Accord, a document that not only secured their promises to work for peace but set up an organization—the national peace secretariat—to implement the agreement.

No matter how much the principals pledged peace, their supporters continued to fight. In March 1992, just six months after the National Peace Accord, Inkatha forces in Alexandra attacked another section of the township; in the ensuing battle, eleven more people died. Mandela and the other leaders of the ANC viewed the government and Buthelezi with growing suspicion and alarm. Most of them agreed with the speculation, rippling daily through the press, that South Africa was being tormented by a network of secret death squads known as the "third force." Mandela pleaded and threatened de Klerk in private, asking him to take firmer control of his police and military, from whose ranks the killers were thought to come. Though de Klerk admitted that there might be a "hidden hand" at work in some of the violence, he seemed unwilling or unable to locate the culpable. In ensuing months, press revelations about the existence of a secret assassination department— blandly named the Civil Cooperation Bureau—and about its role in the murders of activists around the country further undermined de Klerk's credibility.

Mandela was also furious with Buthelezi, who, having lost his bid to become the recognized leader of South Africa's black population, was now acting like a petty tyrant. Gone were Buthelezi's professions of loyalty to the ideals of the ANC, of black solidarity, of South Africa as a unitary democracy; instead, Buthelezi exploited Zulu ethnic pride and fear with a fervor that would have pleased Verwoerd. To the ANC leaders it also seemed that the white government was encouraging Inkatha by refusing to control Inkatha's violent factions. Many inside the ANC insisted that the government and Inkatha were actively in collusion. At one level this was obvious: the government of KwaZulu continued to receive the major portion of its annual budget from the South African treasury. What the ANC leaders suspected was more direct and threatening: that the South African government funded, supported, and encouraged the violent Inkatha campaign against the ANC. Buthelezi vigorously denied such collusion, but over time a scattering of revelations in the press gradually shaped such a picture. In July 1991 it was revealed that Inkatha had received hundreds of thousands of dollars of government money to help organize antidisinvestment rallies. The so-called Inkathagate scandal offered the first direct proof of covert support by the white government of Inkatha's political activities. Over the months to come, more troubling evidence of government collaboration with Inkatha emerged. In March 1992, for example, a former Inkatha official publicly accused the organization of receiving more than one million dollars in government funds and other assistance to train more than two hundred Inkatha paramilitary loyalists.

In 1992 the negotiations foundered again. De Klerk, struggling under revelations of financial corruption in some of his departments and of the complicity of the military in the 1985 murder of four UDF activists in the town of Cradock, only barely restored some of his authority by winning the referendum. Momentum seemed to pick up briefly when the negotiating parties met again in May and collapsed in a new incident of slaughter in June. On the morning of June 17 more than three hundred Inkatha supporters from a hostel in Vanderbiljpark, armed with spears and *panga* machetes, swept down on the adjoining shack settlement of Boipatong and killed forty-eight people. Though the police later arrested seventy-five of the hostel dwellers, the strong suspicion that security forces had assisted in the attack led to an explosive reaction from the ANC. The ANC leadership suspended negotiations with the government. ANC Secretary General Cyril Ramaphosa demanded that the government terminate all covert operations, confine forces to their barracks, prosecute security personnel involved in violence, and stop persecution by homeland leaders.

For Nelson Mandela the tense period of negotiation coincided with the final collapse of his marriage to Winnie. Of all the pains he had suffered in prison, none had been worse than the guilt he felt at not being able to protect his wife and children. "I have wondered," he wrote to Winnie in 1985, "whether any commitment can ever be sufficient cause for abandoning a young and inexperienced woman in a pitiless desert." Despite her early strength in confronting the South African police, Winnie's emotional world had steadily crumbled throughout the early 1980s. Years of confinement, bannings, exile, and persecution finally took their toll. Lost in rage and loneliness, she turned to alcohol and to younger men for comfort. Throughout the 1980s her actions regularly embarrassed the ANC and its allies inside South Africa: her ferocious and unpredictable temper, her secret shopping indulgences, and her use of foreign money to build a hillside mansion in Soweto quickly dubbed "Winnie's Folly" caused resentment and anger among her circle of friends and supporters. In 1986, just when the ANC was trying to moderate its international image, Winnie had offered a horrifying defense of mob violence. "With our boxes of matches and our necklaces," she told one crowd, "we will liberate this country." By the end of the decade, Winnie's behavior had veered out of control. After her return to Soweto she surrounded herself with a troop of aggressive bodyguards who called themselves the Mandela Football Club. The young men wore warm-up suits in ANC colors, played an occasional game of soccer, kept constant watch over her house (which had been firebombed), and provided her with an impressive entourage when she went out into the community to speak. Inflated with their own sense of importance, the members of the Mandela Football Club grew more brazen; eventually several were indicted for murder. Though Winnie may have known nothing of these crimes, she proved unable or unwilling to control the young men who acted in her name, even after some of her closest political allies formed a "crisis committee" and asked her to rein them in.

Winnie's authority within the anti-apartheid movement eroded swiftly after another incident involving the Football Club in February 1989: members held hostage and beat several boys falsely believed to have been molested by a local Methodist pastor, and one of the boys died. The crisis committee met repeatedly and eventually sent a report to Oliver Tambo suggesting that Winnie herself might have been involved in beating the boys. Winnie, learning of the report, threatened in turn to call a press conference and resign from the ANC. The threat did not work: on February 16 the leaders of the UDF and of COSATU, with the knowledge and consent of the ANC in Lusaka, called a press conference to announce that Winnie had been banished from the anti-apartheid movement. "We are not prepared," they said, "to remain silent where those who are violating human rights claim to be doing so in the name of the struggle against apartheid."

For the next year Winnie Mandela receded from view; after her husband emerged from prison, she returned to public life as her husband's companion. When the government charged Winnie with complicity in murder and put her on trial in February 1991, Nelson offered his unstinting support: he cajoled top ANC and Communist Party leaders into showing up as a gesture of support. Within three weeks, however, the ANC leaders told Nelson that they would no longer support Winnie. In May 1991 the judge found Winnie guilty of kidnapping charges and of serving as an accessory to the assault on the group of boys; her final sentence did not come for another two years and was eventually reduced to a steep fine and a suspended prison term. Not long afterward, Nelson's confidence in his wife finally collapsed, and in April 1992 he called a press conference, praised Winnie for her years of loyalty, and announced that his marriage was over. From then on, Winnie took an increasingly combative approach toward the leaders of the ANC. Her reputation among the residents of squatter camps and townships remained vibrant; she could draw a crowd of thousands even when she appeared unannounced. She steadily allied herself with Chris Hani of the Communist Party, appeared at rallies in battle fatigues, and accused the ANC leaders who were negotiating with the government—including Nelson—of betraying the revolutionary principles that had guided them. Though the ANC leaders viewed her with growing discomfort, Nelson Mandela refused to criticize her in public. Though others blamed her, he blamed himself.

Blood continued to be shed in late 1992 and early 1993, but the government and the ANC announced in February 1993 that they had agreed in principle on the creation of a government of national unity, in which, after the elections, both the ANC and the National Party would serve for a period of five years. The people's hopes rose even more when the negotiations of CODESA II began in March, only to be dashed again in early April with the assassination of Chris Hani. Hani, who had been immensely popular among township youth, had strongly backed the negotiations; his murder raised, once again, the specter of national collapse. The crisis was resolved with the speedy apprehension of the white assassin and a Conservative member of parliament who had participated in the conspiracy.

While South Africa again teetered on the brink, de Klerk and Mandela wrangled over the lifting of the international sanctions that continued to hamstring the South African economy and the National Party government. Over the previous decade twenty-five industrial democracies had imposed sanctions on South Africa. Though U.S. President George Bush had eased the restrictions over which he had discretion after Mandela's release, the de Klerk government had been startled to discover that most of the American constraints were beyond the reach of the federal government. State and local divestment and selective purchasing restrictions were in force in thirty states, thirty-nine counties, and one hundred nine cities, including eight of the ten largest U.S. cities. In April 1993 the South African ambassador to the United States, Harry Schwarz, gloomily reported that the more than two hundred American firms that had withdrawn from South Africa were not going to return, nor would funding from the World Bank or International Monetary Fund be released until the African National Congress had given the word. When legislators in New York, Oregon, and Massachusetts, chafing at the slow pace of negotiations, filed new sanctions measures, the news triggered instant panicky headlines across South Africa.

For Mandela and others, the critical question about sanctions was whether the transition to democracy had reached a point of irreversibility. He and the other ANC leaders had been sobered by conversations with international economics experts who had explained the severity of South Africa's economic crisis and the difficulties the nation was likely to face as it sought to become part of a globally competitive world. The ANC, seeking to reassure business leaders at home and abroad, wanted to call for the lifting of sanctions as soon as possible, but not until a fixed date was established for the elections and a Transitional Executive Council was created to oversee the actions of government and promote a climate in which people could "participate freely in politics." In June 1993 the negotiators met the first condition by announcing that South Africa's first democratic elections would take place the following April. The National Party pushed again for the removal of sanctions, but Mandela held firm, insisting that nothing could happen until de Klerk was willing to put his government under the scrutiny of the transitional council. The two men were still arguing about the matter when they arrived in Philadelphia in July 1993 to receive the Medal of Liberty from newly elected President Bill Clinton.

By September, with the formal launch of the Transitional Executive Council only weeks away, Mandela went before the United Nations with the formal request that all nonmilitary sanctions be lifted. Two days later a massive delegation of more than 150 ANC representatives, South African government officials, and business leaders converged on Washington, D.C., for discussions with the World Bank about how to lift their country up from what the South African press was now calling the "lunacy" of apartheid. Shortly afterward, in recognition of the arduous delicacy of their efforts, Nelson Mandela and F. W. de Klerk were jointly awarded the 1993 Nobel Peace Prize.

While Mandela and de Klerk jockeyed for position and fidgeted in the awkward spotlight of international acclaim, thousands of less-well-known South Africans were wrestling with the urgent and precarious task of rebuilding civil society from the ground up. Like all poisonous ideologies, apartheid had contaminated everything it had touched. Every institution on which citizens normally rely for some measure of independence and impartiality—the police, the judiciary, the universities, the churches—had been tainted by the National Party's agenda. The question facing the citizens of South Africa was how, after forty years of systematic distortion, they could reverse the process; how they could cleanse and rebuild these institutions to be once again worthy of public trust. In the midst of the intensely political debates about the constitution and elections, the challenge was, in essence, to depoliticize large parts of South African society.

South Africans of divergent political views recognized the problem early and tackled it head on. In January 1990, shortly before Nelson Mandela's release, several hundred intellectuals had gathered at the University of Cape Town to ponder the problem, which they described as "building a culture of democratic accountability." Throughout the constitutional negotiations, the parties had vied for the right to claim the mantle of procedural and substantive fairness. By 1993 this desire had led to the creation of a half dozen new organizations designed to restore independence and impartiality to civil society. The Commission of Inquiry on the Prevention of Public Violence and Intimidation, chaired by Justice Richard Goldstone, relentlessly unearthed evidence linking South African security forces and Inkatha to the death squads that had been ravaging some parts of the country, and then investigated terrorism by the armed wing of the PAC. The Independent Media Commission and Independent Broadcasting Authority were created to remove the government's control of radio and television. When F. W. de Klerk appointed a panel of jurists to select the new members of the board of the powerful South African Broadcasting Corporation, the jurists conducted their interviews with prospective members on live television.

The largest and most vital political task fell to the Independent Electoral Commission (IEC), created in late 1993 to oversee the first national elections in South Africa's history. The commission consisted of eleven South Africans, including Helen Suzman, and five foreigners, including Gay MacDougall of the Lawyer's Committee for Civil Rights under Law in Washington, D.C. The commissioners had to establish more than ten thousand voting sites for more than twenty million voters, most of whom had never voted before and many of whom could not read. The voting process had to be simple enough to be set up quickly at each site in townships and rural areas without electricity, but rigorous enough to prevent fraud. The IEC had to recruit, train, and identify thousands of election monitors, whose job it would be to resolve conflict at the sites, and thousands more foreign observers, who would be flying in to serve as the eyes and ears of the world. The commission had to organize a massive voter education effort; figure out which people and parties would be allowed to appear on the ballot; design the ballots in a way that was easily understandable; and provide security for those precious pieces of paper from printing to counting. Recognizing that the true test of democracy is not just the holding of elections but the willingness of the population—including the losers—to accept the outcome, the IEC commissioners had to do everything efficiently, fairly, and in the minuscule time span of four months.

Several parties, unhappy with their prospects, threatened to boycott the elections, including the Afrikaner Volksfront under the command of former general Constand Viljoen, and the Inkatha Freedom Party, led by Buthelezi. Buthelezi in particular was frustrated by the strong cooperation between the ANC and the National Party at the negotiating table and tried innumerable tactics to increase his bargaining power. At one point he even insisted that Inkatha, the KwaZulu homeland, and King Goodwill Zwelithini all be given separate seats at the negotiations—the equivalent of asking for three seats at the table for himself. As the elections approached and it became clear that the ANC's popular strength reached well into Natal, Buthelezi launched a frightening game of brinkmanship by announcing that he was withdrawing Inkatha from the elections. He then demanded that the ANC and the National Party arrange for international mediation, which they did. The mediation team, chaired by Henry Kissinger, arrived only days before the election. When Kissinger learned that Buthelezi was trying to use the talks to postpone the elections, he brought the mediation to an abrupt close and left the country. Less than a week before the elections, a frustrated F. W. de Klerk denounced Buthelezi publicly as "erratic, fickle, obstructionist, inconsistent, two-faced, and intolerant." Meanwhile, Nelson Mandela was skillfully undermining Buthelezi's power base by demonstrating his respect to King Goodwill Zwelithini and reassuring him about his position in the new South Africa. Buthelezi, squeezed from all sides, backed down and agreed to participate in the elections.

Buthelezi's abrupt decision added to the IEC's logistical nightmares. The organization had printed millions of ballots with spaces for eighteen parties. The order of appearance on the ballot had been determined by lottery; next to the name and symbol of each party a small photograph of the party's leader had been printed to help those who could not read. Because of Buthelezi's machinations, Inkatha did not have a space on the ballot, so millions of stickers that could be affixed at the bottom of the ballots had to be printed. These and other materials had to be airlifted by SADF helicopters and airplanes to thousands of voting sites around the country.

As the elections approached, tension mounted. Parties held tumultuous rallies; volunteers attached pictures and slogans to every vertical surface; reporters speculated endlessly on the outcome. International observers, arriving to take up their positions around the country, were astonished to find the once-banned likeness of Nelson Mandela grinning from the top of every lamppost, framed by the words "Mandela for

President." Beneath the fervor of a normal presidential campaign lay a universal sense of amazement, even bewilderment, as people watched the lightning transformation of unattainable fantasies into routine realities. There was also a strain of fear, as acts of political terrorism continued. Most South Africans responded with a mixture of outrage and resolve. All that such attacks would achieve, said F. W. de Klerk, would be to "add to the unnecessary suffering of innocent citizens who have already suffered enough." The editors of the *Johannesburg Star* similarly condemned the tragedies as "last ditch attempts by fanatics to sabotage the transition to which the overwhelming majority of South Africans are committed."

The voting, which was intended to stretch over three days, began at seven in the morning on Tuesday, April 26, 1994. On the first day the voting was limited to the elderly and the infirm, in part to give officials at each voting site a chance to iron out their procedures. At Groote Schuur Hospital in Cape Town, women in labor and patients who were about to go into surgery insisted on first casting their ballots at the hospital's polling site. At South African consulates and other polling stations around the world, an estimated quarter of a million overseas South Africans began to cast their ballots. As the first hours of South Africa's democratic miracle passed, the country held its breath, waiting for the expected reports of violence at polling sites, particularly in Natal. Though the IEC struggled with hundreds of administrative glitches, the day passed largely without incident.

The next morning, the first day of voting open to all citizens, people began arriving as early as four A.M. at the polls. Everywhere—from elegant town halls in Afrikaner towns, to Coloured townships, to urban squatters, to rural enclaves—the lines grew longer and longer, until they stretched, in some places, to more than a kilometer. "One of the most poignant and extraordinary sights," wrote a reporter from the *Sowetan,* "was to see blacks and whites in the same queues. In the days of apartheid, blacks and whites used different queues for everything. . . . On April 27, black and white, young and old, men and women stood with eagerness, even when the technical arrangements faltered, waiting with great patience to vote." In the Western Cape, though people were repeatedly soaked by the autumnal cloudbursts characteristic of the province, they refused to give up their places in line. When they reached the entrance to the polling station, they were greeted by a strange assembly of policemen, foreign observers, peace monitors, party representatives, and IEC officials. They moved quickly past a succession of tables as their identity books were examined and marked with invisible ink, their fingernails checked and then sprayed with long-lasting dye that showed up under ultraviolet light. They were then handed a national ballot and escorted to a standing booth where they could mark their ballots in secret. If they had any difficulties, a throng of officials from different organizations would surround them and make sure that the advice they were given was impartial. After depositing their ballots in a sealed box, they collected a second ballot, for provincial government, and voted again. Minutes later they were back outside, their faces bearing a range of emotions from sober dignity to tear-stained joy.

Though the voting was taking place smoothly at the majority of sites around the country, administrative problems ranging from late openings to misplaced ballots were driving IEC officials to near despair. Their mood was lifted a bit at midnight on Tuesday, when South Africa formally abandoned its old blue, white, and orange flag in favor of a jazzy mix of the ANC's green, black, and gold with red, white, and blue. At the nationally televised ceremony, a racially mixed choir of young people sang the country's two new national anthems: "Die Stem" and "Nkosi Sikele Afrika." The next morning thousands of new flags were hoisted all across the country, from post offices to military ships to parliament itself.

In most parts of the country the final day of voting unfolded smoothly, with fewer crowds, more efficient operations, and, most amazingly, no violence. Only in Natal did the system remain so snarled that the IEC decided to extend the voting there for another twenty-four hours. For most people the polls closed at seven P.M. on Thursday, April 28. When the moment came, relief washed across the country. In Langa township near Cape Town, beneath a robust moon and the towering impassivity of Table Mountain, people came out of their homes to laugh and sing in the streets, and the sounds of their burbling joy were carried a great distance by the warm breeze.

For the officials of the Independent Election Commission the vexations were by no means over. Because of an earlier fear that people would be intimidated if they thought the votes would be counted at each polling station, the IEC had organized regional counting stations to which the ballots could be transported to ensure anonymity. The system was designed with innumerable checklists and tallies to show that the officers of each polling station were returning the same number of ballots they had been issued. This elaborate system quickly collapsed, and ballot boxes began arriving at the counting stations in a weird assortment of vehicles, with and without their proper guards and papers. Each ballot had to be examined and counted by several persons representing the IEC and different parties, a process that was maddeningly slow. Dozens of broadcast correspondents from South African and international media, garrisoned at the cavernous central counting station, had to twiddle their thumbs on the air for days. While they waited, the IEC

feverishly tried to collect and verify results; at one point the whole system was jeopardized when officials discovered that someone had broken
into the secure central computer system and doctored the outcome by
inflating the National Party and the Inkatha Freedom Party numbers by
more than five percent. After comparison with the original tallies, the
commissioners announced on Monday, May 2, that the African National
Congress had won a decisive majority. At a reception at the Carlton
Hotel in Johannesburg that night, standing with Coretta Scott King at
his side, Nelson Mandela promised to go to work the next morning to
bring reconciliation to the country.

The IEC took until May 6, a full week after the elections, to release
the final numbers. The African National Congress had captured
12,237,000 votes, or 63.7 percent of the national total, giving it 252 seats
in the new 400-seat parliament. The National Party had received 20.6
percent, the Inkatha Freedom Party 9.1 percent, and the remaining parties had split the last 6.6 percent. In the nine new provinces of South
Africa (into which all the former homelands had been absorbed), the
story was somewhat different. In KwaZulu-Natal, Inkatha had garnered
48.4 percent, compared with the ANC's 31.2 percent, giving Inkatha
control of the provincial legislature and the right to select the "premier," the elected provincial leader. In the Western Cape, despite a
major campaign by the ANC, the National Party had won a surprising
56.2 percent of the vote, leaving the ANC with only 33.6 percent. As a
result, Allan Boesak, the ANC leader in the Western Cape, lost his bid
to become premier to Hernus Kriel, formerly the National Party's minister of law and order. The reason turned out to be a massive shift by tens
of thousands of Coloured voters who, despite decades of discrimination,
had apparently decided that they trusted their fellow Afrikaans speakers
in the National Party more than the predominantly African leaders of
the ANC.

On May 10, in a carnival atmosphere at the Union Buildings in Pretoria, just across the valley from the Voortrekker Monument and directly
in front of the building from which Hendrik Verwoerd had issued so
many of his oppressive decrees, Nelson Mandela was inaugurated the
first black president of South Africa. Before him sat more than forty
heads of state, the representatives of another 120 countries, and tens of
thousands of his exuberant fellow citizens. In his address Mandela again
pledged reconciliation. "The moment to bridge the chasms that divide
us has come," he told the world. "The time to build is upon us." He
paused to pay tribute to his predecessor, F. W. de Klerk, who was giving
up his post as state president to become one of Mandela's two deputy
presidents. The most moving moment came when the top military officials of the South African Defense Force, the most powerful arm of the

security forces that had kept him in prison for twenty-seven years and had done everything possible to destroy the African National Congress, formally pledged their loyalty. Shortly afterward a squadron of South Africa's best fighters screeched overhead in tribute to their new commander in chief.

Over the next few weeks newspaper and television commentators exhausted themselves in praise of Mandela's conciliatory attitudes toward the past and his plans for the future. The *Citizen,* formerly an aggressively pro-government mouthpiece, extolled Mandela as a "president of the people, for the people . . . who emerged from his years of incarceration with no hatred, no bitterness, with compassion for his jailers, yet with a steely will to take his people out of the bondage of apartheid." "Mandela has expressed an inspired, positive, and attainable vision of the future that together we can create for ourselves," commented the normally skeptical editors of *Business Day.* "His vision of our country's future displays an idealism for which we all should strive."

Gradually, as the euphoria of the elections and inauguration subsided, the magnitude of the challenge came into focus. One of Mandela's first and most difficult tasks was to craft a government of national unity which, under the terms of the interim constitution, was supposed to include members of every party that had achieved more than five percent of the vote: Mandela would have to select a certain number of his thirty cabinet ministers from the ranks of the National Party and Inkatha. In addition to appointing F. W. de Klerk deputy president, he made former National Party negotiator Roelf Meyer the minister of constitutional development, Abe Williams the minister of welfare, former Springbok captain Dawie de Villiers the minister of environmental affairs, and, in a move that greatly pleased the South African business community, retained Derek Keys as the minister of finance. In a surprising act of political durability, Pik Botha, who had served as the old regime's primary international mouthpiece in his capacity as ambassador to the United States and then for seventeen years as foreign minister, reemerged as the minister of mineral and energy affairs. Mandela filled out the National Party's presence with three additional deputy ministerships in the ministries of justice, land affairs, and education. After intense negotiations, Gatsha Buthelezi agreed to join the government as the minister of home affairs and received three other posts for Inkatha. In all, Mandela wisely moved to calm criticism of the government by giving the minority parties fifty percent more positions than the constitution required. Mandela also minimized internal sabotage of his efforts by reassuring the army of jittery white bureaucrats within government, many of them Afrikaners, that despite the calls to reduce government spending he was not going to clean them out.

The ANC cabinet appointments represented a mix of formerly internal and external leaders and a blend of generations. Thabo Mbeki, the diplomat who had skillfully assisted Oliver Tambo during many years of exile, became F. W. de Klerk's counterpart as deputy president. Joe Modise, the former head of Umkhonto We Sizwe, was selected as minister of defense. Dullah Omar, an attorney who had spent most of his career defending PAC and ANC prisoners, had served two stints in detention, and had once been targeted by a government death squad, became the minister of justice. Mandela's longtime Robben Island companion Mac Maharaj became the minister of transport, while Joe Slovo, the irrepressible Communist, became minister of housing. Mandela also used the dozen deputy ministerships at his disposal to coax potential antagonists into cooperating with the government. General Bantu Holomisa, the former military leader of the Transkei homeland, was rewarded for his early support of the ANC with the post of deputy minister of the environment. Joe Matthews, a former ANC member who was the son of the late Z. K. Matthews and who had ended up supporting Inkatha, became deputy minister of safety and security. Finally, in a move that raised a few eyebrows, Mandela tried to assuage his estranged wife, Winnie, and her zealous followers by giving her the post of deputy minister of arts, culture, science, and technology.

In addition to presiding over a cabinet that included many formerly mortal enemies, Mandela also had to contend with a national political map that had been completely redrawn. Over the previous months every homeland leader had either given up power or been forced out of office, and every one of the "independent" homelands—those precious fantasy countries into which the white government had poured untold aspirations and money—had been reabsorbed back into South Africa. The former homeland of the Transkei disappeared into the new Eastern Cape; Bophuthatswana merged into the Northwest; and the highly populated region around Johannesburg was named Gauteng, a word drawn from the composite dialect of gold miners. Of the nine provinces, seven had elected leaders from the ANC.

Whatever the oddities and tensions that flowed from the new configuration of power, all those in government knew that the problems they faced were enormous. More than half of all South Africans were living in severe poverty; when one looked at Africans alone, the number was two-thirds. Because of the policies of the National Party government, fifty-three percent of the rural poor had received no education at all. Even in the urban areas, most Africans had to do without sanitation, electricity, and telephone service. The inequalities were even more pronounced between races. Unemployment among whites in 1994 was six percent, for Africans forty-one percent—or, by some estimates, even higher. While most whites had health insurance, ninety-one percent of Africans did not. The poorest forty percent of its households—almost entirely black—received less than one-twentieth of the nation's income, while the richest ten percent—virtually all white—controlled more than half. Relative to countries in the world with similar per capita incomes, South Africa had the lowest life expectancy and the highest infant mortality rates, numbers that were dramatically worse for the African population alone. According to the Gini coefficient, an international measurement of inequality within a nation, South Africa had the second greatest disparity of wealth between rich and poor of any country in the world, just a fraction ahead of Brazil.

The solution, everyone agreed, was to redirect the budget to address the needs of the poor while stimulating new economic growth. Where to locate the proper balance between these two goals was the topic of acrimonious debate. For the first three years after Mandela's release, the economy had remained trapped in a recession, contracting in both 1991 and 1992 and gaining by a tiny fraction in 1993. Part of the problem was the squeeze of sanctions, which had denied South Africa access to international capital markets and choked off the flow of new investment. The country was also laboring under an extended drought that had slashed farming revenues. Fledgling efforts toward growth were also undermined by the anxiety felt by the business community about South Africa's future. At the same time that business leaders were pleading for foreign firms to make new investments, capital continued to pour out of the country.

For Nelson Mandela and his cabinet, the question was how to respond to the high expectations of the population and the crushing social problems they faced in a manner that would not push up the budget deficit, squash domestic savings, and scare away foreign investment. To make the decision, they had to slog through a mud slide of advice from well-meaning financial experts, scenario planners, World Bank technocrats, international trade gurus, senior business executives, impassioned university professors, and economists of every school. Some insisted that the problem was South Africa's relatively high manufacturing wages, which were prompting foreign firms to look first at Latin America, Asia, and the former Soviet states. Some pointed to excess government spending, which, as the result of the National Party's penchant for bureaucrat control and patronage, accounted for more than thirty percent of the GDP. When executives criticized the flaws of government, many in government and the press responded by questioning the structure and behavior of South African business. Despite South Africa's noisy commitment to the rhetoric of free enterprise, the country's business sector had grown into a stodgy, uncompetitive, highly interlocked network of pyramid structures and quasi monopolies. While some executives complained loudly about government waste and corruption, their colleagues were regularly colluding with competitors on everything from price to distribution. Almost every day the business press chronicled some new example of business fraud, including regular tales of senior executives who had embezzled large sums and fled to foreign countries.

Trying to steer a middle course between laissez-faire and overcontrol, the ANC had released a comprehensive economic proposal just before the elections. Known as the Reconstruction and Development Program, or RDP, it became the guiding force for the party's policies in office. The RDP unequivocally emphasized the new government's commitment to attacking everything—contaminated water, illiteracy, substandard housing, pollution, and inadequate health care. It was a tall order, but one consistent with the proposals that had been set forth by the Freedom Charter thirty-nine years before. Mandela signaled his intention to push the program forward vigorously by putting the RDP office inside the presidential office. Though the specific recommendations of the RDP came under intense debate, even the grumpiest business leaders recognized that the euphoria of the election could turn into explosive discontent unless the new government made real progress on the country's most basic needs.

One piece of the Freedom Charter that Mandela and the government of National Unity did not embrace was the nationalization of industry. They vowed to open the country up to regional and international trade, to make it easier for companies to invest, to restructure the capital markets to reduce the number of pyramid holding companies, and to promote entrepreneurship, especially in the tiny township businesses that blossomed in the "informal sector." They also pushed businesses to train black managers and put them in positions of responsibility as quickly as possible, steps that created a running debate in the newspapers and academic journals about affirmative action and its potentially debilitating effects on "standards."

The government's moves to change the status quo and open up South African business practices provoked a rumbling chorus of criticism from all sides of the political spectrum. The leftists within the ANC alliance saw the actions as proof that the ANC had caved in to the capitalist class. Some dubious columnists complained that the ANC's efforts to establish investment companies led by blacks were an attempt to use the government's power to enrich ANC members. Some business leaders, long shielded from competition, complained that the government was meddling in arrangements that had worked well in the past. Most international observers, however, encouraged the reforms. The World Bank stepped in with advice and funding; the International Monetary Fund approved nearly a billion dollars in funds for drought relief and economic support. Trade with South Africa's former adversaries the Frontline states jumped sharply. Foreign investors, who had steadily bolstered their presence in South Africa as the elections approached, dramatically increased their commitments after Mandela took office. South Africa's transactions with Germany, Great Britain, Japan, and the other industrial powerhouses all rose.

In the United States, the Clinton administration stepped in with increased foreign aid, investment assistance from OPIC, regular visits by cabinet members, and eventually a binational commission led by Thabo Mbeki and Vice President Al Gore. A few large American investors, including some of the same pension and mutual funds that had led the divestment movement, became South Africa enthusiasts, forming a variety of financial instruments through which they could put their money into the redevelopment of the country. American name brands flooded the shelves of South African stores, while legions of American executives and state politicians streamed through trade fairs and shop floors around the country in search of potential commerce.

The most striking feature of America's new enthusiasm for South Africa was the complete reversal of the ten-year trend toward disinvestment. According to U.S. embassy figures, pressure on American companies had caused the number of U.S. firms operating in South Africa to drop from 360 to 110, of which only a handful were large companies like Johnson & Johnson. Starting in 1993, scores of American firms began moving back into the country. While many of the smaller and more cautious firms did so through nonequity ventures with South African firms, the bigger companies, particularly those who had been there before, bought or established subsidiaries. Before the elections, companies like Digital and Microsoft carefully worked out with the ANC the timing and nature of their investments; after Mandela took office, other companies jumped even more readily. Some firms simply exercised the buyback rights they had built into their disinvestment agreements, while others negotiated new arrangements and joint ventures. By the end of 1994 Ford, IBM, Honeywell, Polaroid, General Electric, Sara Lee, and Citibank had all reestablished their presence in South Africa. Coca-Cola and Pepsi zoomed into the country in full force in yet another attempt to outflank each other in the global cola war. When Chase Manhattan returned, the new managing director made the implausible statement that the bank's earlier decision to withdraw had not been due to public pressure but because the management had simply redefined its global strategy away from commercial banking. By early 1996, according to South African government statistics, the number of American companies operating in South Africa had risen from 184 to more than 500, with a total asset value of $3.5 billion and more than 45,000 employees.

The new influx of companies prompted a rolling national debate about whether the investing companies should follow a code of conduct. The principles formulated by Leon Sullivan that had been limping along without his approval since 1987 formally closed down after the elections, and several organizations moved in to try to fill the gap. South Africa's trade unions, through COSATU, wary that the new government might overlook their concerns in the rush for new investment, sponsored a code of conduct in 1992; the South African Council of Churches, after consulting with ICCR in New York, issued a code in 1993; and Leon Sullivan drafted and released his own just before the elections. Though institutional investors continued to file shareholder resolutions in support of such measures, the proponents found themselves struggling against resistance from both the U.S. and South African governments. The United States, while open to a code, did not want it to apply only to U.S. firms, lest that hinder them unfairly in their competition with other countries. Mandela's lieutenants in charge of the economy, for their part, were confident that an ANC government would adequately protect the interests of workers and were nervous about anything that might cause foreign businesses to shy away from South Africa in favor of more lenient countries.

Freed from the strife and anxiety of apartheid and challenged by Mandela's call to build a nation, the country's citizens tackled problems with a vigor that surprised even themselves. The huge electric utility ESKOM announced an aggressive policy to bring electricity to the twenty-three million South Africans who did not have it. Telephone usage exploded when it was discovered that cellular phones could help the country bring phone service to millions without installing thousands of miles of phone lines. Hundreds of thousands of construction workers went to work trying to fill the backlog of housing. Township citizens, encouraged by Mandela to take part in reconstruction in their own areas, started rebuilding their communities and fighting crime. To combat disease and infant mortality, the government announced that primary health care would be free for every South African citizen, regardless of income or race. African students, long alienated from the system of education, flooded into schools at all levels, transforming formerly white universities almost overnight.

The country also established organizations that directly challenged the divisions of apartheid. The military, renamed the South African National Defence Force, recruited ANC and PAC guerrillas into its forces, in many cases putting former Umkhonto We Sizwe officers in command of men who previously had tried to kill them. The South

African legion announced that it was opening its ranks to any veteran on either side. To resolve the bitter disputes about white seizure of black property, the government established land courts to hear and adjudicate the complex cases. Most striking of all, parliament established a Truth and Reconciliation Commission modeled on a similar effort that had flourished in Chile. The commission, led by chairman Desmond Tutu, was deeply controversial, for it operated on the premise that knowledge of the truth of what had happened under apartheid was more important than punishment of those who had committed crimes on either side. Rejecting the advice of those who wanted to gloss over the past and those who sought Nuremberg-style trials, parliament gave the commission power not only to hear the horrendous stories of thousands of citizens but also to grant amnesty for any perpetrators who came forward to confess. The amnesty was limited—it applied only to the deeds that a person explicitly detailed—but it still angered the families of some activists who felt that the criminals should be punished.

Though the government promoted many symbolic changes to signal the creation of a new nation, Mandela went out of his way to make sure that these were not provocative. D. F. Malan Airport in Cape Town was renamed simply Cape Town International. When South Africa entered the world rugby cup finals, Nelson Mandela put on a Springbok shirt— once a symbol of apartheid in sports—and went down on the field to congratulate the team, who went on to win the world championship. When Hendrik Verwoerd's grandson Wilhelm joined the African National Congress, when Wilhelm's wife became an ANC member of parliament, and when the citizens of Verwoerdburg voted to change the name of their town, Mandela did not gloat; instead he paid a courteous visit to Hendrik Verwoerd's widow, Betsie.

Through these and other small healing actions, after decades of misery and fear, South Africa gradually began to return to the conventional family of nations. Instead of a divisive tableau against which the world could gauge its moral inclinations, instead of the sharp contours of the rhetoric of struggle, debate inside the country steadily evolved toward the endlessly necessary bickering of any industrial democracy. Politicians jockeyed for position; newspapers reported their stories of scandal, commerce, and crime; the wealthy justified their gains over tea; and the poor struggled and dreamed of a better life. There were still abundant anxieties: Would South Africa be able to weather the transition that would follow Nelson Mandela's rule? Would its citizens be able to reach over the divide of race and history to make progress not only on determining matters of public policy but on healing the deeper wounds of the heart? Would South Africa, having rejected the logic of racial and cultural division, be able to build the nonracial democracy that Mandela and his colleagues had described for more than fifty years? There were many pessimists, but there were even more who were convinced that, given how far the citizens of South Africa had come from their horrendous past, the future was not far from their grasp.

As the rolling wheel of time steadily transformed deeds into memories, those who had fought apartheid on both sides of the Atlantic moved on. Mandela's old friend Oliver Tambo died in 1993, a year before the elections, and Joe Slovo, who had been minister of housing, succumbed to cancer in January 1995 after barely six months in office. Helen Suzman gave up her parliamentary seat and offered trenchant commentary from the sidelines. Neva Seidman Makgetla, the young woman from Harvard who had helped stir up the divestment movement there, took a job as an economist in South Africa's ministry of labor in Pretoria. Beyers Naudé settled into a quieter life in Johannesburg, while Desmond Tutu, after ten years as archbishop of Cape Town, retired from that position to focus on the work of the Truth and Reconciliation Commission. Allan Boesak, after wading through a swamp of marital scandal, found himself sinking further under allegations that he had taken large sums from a relief fund for his personal use.

Back in the United States, Leon Sullivan, though aging and in poor health, continued to exhort companies to be a force for change in South Africa. Charles Diggs lived quietly in suburban Maryland and told visitors that someday he might reenter politics at the local level. Chester Crocker went back to teaching at Georgetown University. Wayne Fredericks accepted a senior position at the Institute for International Education in New York and traveled regularly to South Africa to participate in seminars, promote investment, and visit old friends. Derek Bok completed two decades as president of Harvard University and continued his written exploration of the interplay among morality, education, and leadership. At his retirement Bok told a reporter ruefully that his twenty years in office had "sometimes seemed like one long debate about divestment." In March 1996 Franklin Thomas formally handed over the reins of the Ford Foundation to his successor at a board meeting that took place, at his request, in Johannesburg.

Some continued in their positions but worked to refocus their organizations. Jennifer Davis and her colleagues at the American Committee on Africa worked to expand the interest of their large network of state and local legislators to other countries in southern Africa and on the continent. At TransAfrica, the collapse of apartheid allowed Randall Robinson to focus on the other African and Caribbean nations to which the organization had also been dedicated. He missed the South African elections and inauguration of Nelson Mandela in 1994 because he was in the midst of a twenty-seven-day hunger strike to pressure President Clinton into reversing the policy of turning back Haitian boat people. He spoke out against the extermination of nearly five hundred thousand southern Sudanese Christians by the northern Islamic government, and he called for a U.S. oil embargo against Nigeria to pressure its military government to restore democracy. With the help of Bill Cosby, Sugar Ray Leonard, and the estate of Arthur Ashe, Robinson established a beautiful new headquarters in a small mansion in Washington, D.C., that had once been the German embassy. The headquarters now includes a six-thousand-volume library on African American involvement in foreign policy, a key resource, as Robinson put it, "as we look to pass the baton of leadership to a new generation for the twenty-first century."

Timothy Smith, having spent more than twenty-five years at ICCR and survived a bout with cancer, plunged into the new era with characteristic vigor. The system of shareholder activism that he had helped to establish had, by the end of the 1990s, become a mainstay of American economic life, creating a mechanism through which issues of corporate governance and social policy were regularly brought to the attention of America's largest corporations. In the 1996 shareholder season, more than six hundred shareholder resolutions were filed, many by ICCR members, focusing on tobacco sales, employment practices, environmental standards, and military production. Drawing on the experience of the Sullivan Principles, ICCR also promoted two other codes of conduct—the first, known as the MacBride Principles, focused on employment practices in Northern Ireland; the second, known first as the Valdez and then the CERES Principles, pushed companies to improve their environmental performance.

Through Smith's hard work—and that of thousands of people who were part of his network—the United States spawned a remarkable nongovernmental system during the apartheid years through which disputes about moral, political, and economic issues could be adjudicated within the capital markets. The aspirations of the 1930s members of Congress to foster democratic disclosure, discussion, and decision for America's corporations had, through the South African debate, succeeded more than they had anticipated. Moving into the twenty-first century, America had developed a rare—one might say unique—method that allowed huge pools of capital to respond to criteria other than immediate financial return and to questions about the longer horizon and deeper values by which an economy should be guided.

The nearly fifty-year debate over the United States' relationship with South Africa changed how American institutions thought about their responsibilities because, in large part, it reached deeply into the Ameri-

can psyche. It stirred up some of our most painful insecurities and rever-
berated throughout the thousands of institutions that make up civil society. The protracted debate about America's relationship with a distant
country took on such an enduring structure that it, in effect, became
another chapter in the racial struggle that has defined America's national character. It asked, as other historic moments have asked,
whether Americans have the courage to turn their noble words about
equality into deeds, whether they are really willing to practice the principles they have preached.

Though apartheid has ended, this process of self-assessment will go
on. The more Americans express devotion to democratic rule, commitment to individual rights, aspirations for an equal and prosperous society, confidence that America has a special destiny and duty, the more
they are compelled to explore and correct their failures. Race in America is the hidden theme behind our national mythology and imagery, an
abiding source of anger, mistrust, and pain. Since the great civil war that
soaked the land of promise with blood, since the subsequent decades of
quiet treachery in which the rights secured in battle were slowly stolen,
since the long, arduous march to regain those rights from an indifferent
majority, Americans have been compelled to confront their imperfections and hypocrisies. It has not been easy. Too often the response has
been either to retreat into self-flagellation or to blame errors on others.

Sentiments about the nature and extent of racism in America perme-
ated the country's relationship with South Africa. Advocates on both the
left and the right, drawing from what they had learned at home, confidently offered predictions and advice. For many on the left, the crimes
of the apartheid government were so abundant that one could not risk
being distracted by human rights violations in other African countries
and under totalitarian regimes. For those on the right, the democratic
longings of the South African majority were outweighed by the need to
promote commerce and combat Communism. When blacks attacked
each other in regional struggles for power, closet bigots leapt to argue,
with varying degrees of nuance, that such uncontrollable "tribal" impulses of African people and the outbreak of "black on black" violence
justified the need for white rule. That smug excuse disappeared when
some of the most sadistic human acts of this century were revealed to
have been committed by white people against other white people in
Bosnia, a reality which, however horrifying, did not cause whites anywhere in the world to doubt their own capacity for the virtuous exercise
of power.

For the United States, the struggle over South Africa was part of a
much larger challenge of whether a nation "conceived in liberty and
dedicated to the proposition that all men are created equal," as Lincoln

put it at Gettysburg, could be sustained. Every time Americans have come close to complacency, every time they have thought that their self-inflicted injuries have healed, they learn that the wounds have only scabbed over, waiting for a traumatic event to rip off the cover and expose the gash again. Whether it is the Los Angeles riots, the confirmation hearings of Clarence Thomas, the trial of O. J. Simpson, or any one of a hundred more local controversies, they continuously rediscover the fault line of race.

However constant is the struggle, however profoundly its tendrils reach into the American spirit, there are also reasons for renewed confidence. The South Africa story shows that one does not need to be famous or powerful or wealthy to participate in a historic transformation. Though it took a long time to emerge, the sequence of steps through which average Americans contributed to South Africa's shift to freedom is now clear and incontrovertible. It was an unlikely chain reaction, to be sure, in which thousands of small acts of commitment and protest—from demonstrations to letter writing to voting shares of stock—many of them derided at the time as inconsequential, steadily accumulated into a force that altered history and brought forth justice. The process was slow and incremental, unfolding over great distances and many years. As students, church groups, unions, and civil rights activists and others forced hundreds of American institutions to wrestle with the ethics of their investments, these institutions steadily increased the pressure on American companies either to reform or to withdraw. Eventually state and local legislators joined the effort, passing more than a hundred laws that forced their treasuries to sell off stock or bypass the products of corporations with South African subsidiaries. These measures, in addition to the violent repression of dissent by the South African government, led directly to the refusal of banks to roll over South Africa's foreign debt in 1985; to the passage of a sanctions bill in 1986 over Ronald Reagan's veto; and to a crippling flight of capital. Faced with a deflating economy, plummeting tax revenues, a huge surge in both black and white unemployment, a powerful internal resistance that defied the army's attempts to impose order, and a collapse of business confidence, the South African government finally acknowledged the failure of its policy and agreed to negotiate a transition to majority rule.

In the end, the most striking aspect of this story is that our seemingly rigid and material world is so influenced by ideas. The practice of subjugating people with darker skins began with an idea about difference. The brutally enforced separation of peoples in South Africa was rooted in an idea about culture. Today we swim in an ocean of ideas that influence our decisions. Our lives as citizens are directly affected by such apparent abstractions as the depiction of the modern corporation as a quasi-democracy or the assertion that market forces always accrue benevolently. Our most important human institutions—armies and churches, corporations and governments—are defined and driven by clusters of ideas. These ideas have no existence other than in the minds of living human beings, and it is human beings alone who have the capacity to preserve, revise, transmit, or reject them.

Because the twentieth century saw some ideas mutate into ideologies that caused immense human suffering, many remain wary of being captured by transformative beliefs. Yet in the absence of such beliefs, the institutions through which we live our collective lives become rigid; they turn, almost imperceptibly, from serving a larger human purpose to pursuing their own perpetuation. In America such rigidity has sometimes bred an almost medieval sense of futility, a postmodern fatalism that says we are born into a world we cannot change. Ironically, this fatalism has taken hold in the United States at the very moment when belief in transformative ideas like democracy has rocketed through other nations.

In such a context, this narrative offers a word of hope. It demonstrates that acts of protest and conscience, so often dismissed as pointless, can gradually accumulate into an irresistible force for change. It suggests, in an era when people feel overwhelmed by the power of elites, that social transformation can take place "from below." It outlines the circumstances under which economic calculations about institutional self-interest can give way to a broader concern for human well-being. It counters our sense of futility by reminding us that amazing changes can and do take place in history—and that they depend not only on the evolution of impersonal forces but also on human imagination and commitment. We have control over our ideas, our ideas have material consequences, and, in the end, as a people, we become what we believe.

APPENDIX A

The Freedom Charter

Preamble

We, the people of South Africa, declare for all our country and the
world to know:

That South Africa belongs to all who live in it, black and white, and that
no government can justly claim authority unless it is based on the will
of the people;

That our people have been robbed of their birthright to land, liberty,
and peace by a form of government founded on injustice and inequality;

That our country will never be prosperous or free until all our people
live in brotherhood, enjoying equal rights and opportunities;

That only a democratic state, based on the will of the people, can secure
to all their birthright without distinction of color, race, sex, or belief;

And therefore, we, the people of South Africa, black and white together—equals, countrymen, and brothers—adopt this Freedom
Charter. And we pledge ourselves to strive together, sparing nothing
of our strength, and courage, until the democratic changes here set
out have been won.

The People Shall Govern!

Every man and woman shall have the right to vote for and stand as a
candidate for all bodies which make laws.

All the people shall be entitled to take part in administration of the
country.

The rights of the people shall be the same regardless of race, color, or sex.

All bodies of minority rule, advisory boards, councils, and authorities shall be replaced by democratic organs of self-government.

All National Groups Shall Have Equal Rights!

There shall be equal status in the bodies of state, in the courts, and in the school for all national groups and races;

All national groups shall be protected by law against insults to their race and national pride;

All people shall have equal rights to use their own language and to develop their own folk culture and customs;

The preaching and practice of national, race, or color discrimination and contempt shall be a punishable crime;

All apartheid laws and practices shall be set aside.

The People Shall Share in the Country's Wealth!

The national wealth of our country, the heritage of all South Africans, shall be restored to the people;

The mineral wealth beneath the soil, the banks, and the monopoly industry shall be transferred to the ownership of the people as a whole;

All other industries and trade shall be controlled to assist the well-being of the people;

All people shall have equal rights to trade where they choose, to manufacture and to enter all trades, crafts, and professions.

The Land Shall Be Shared Among Those Who Work It!

Restriction of land ownership on a racial basis shall be ended and all the land redivided amongst those who work it, to banish famine and land hunger;

The state shall help the peasants with implements, seed, tractors, and dams to save the soil and assist the tillers;

Freedom of movement shall be guaranteed to all who work the land;

All shall have the right to occupy the land wherever they choose;

People shall not be robbed of their cattle, and forced labor and farm prisons shall be abolished.

All Shall Be Equal Before the Law!

No one shall be imprisoned, deported, or restricted without a fair trial;

No one shall be condemned by the order of any Government official;

The courts shall be representative of all the people;

Imprisonment shall be only for serious crimes against the people and shall aim at reeducation, not vengeance;

The police force and army shall be open to all on an equal basis and shall be the helpers and protectors of the people;

All laws which discriminate on grounds of race, color, or belief shall be repealed.

All Shall Enjoy Equal Human Rights!

The law shall guarantee to all their right to speak, to organize, to meet together, to publish, to preach, to worship, and to educate their children;

The privacy of the house from police raids shall be protected by law;

All shall be free to travel without restriction from countryside to town, from province to province, and from South Africa abroad;

Pass laws, permits, and all other laws restricting these freedoms shall be abolished.

There Shall Be Work and Security!

All who work shall be free to form trade unions, to elect their officers, and to make wage agreements with their employers;

The state shall recognize the right and duty of all to work and to draw full unemployment benefits;

Men and women of all races shall receive equal pay for equal work;

There shall be a forty-hour working week, a national minimum wage, paid annual leave and sick leave for workers, and maternity leave on full pay for all working mothers;

Miners, domestic workers, farm workers, and civil servants shall have the same rights as all others who work;

Child labor, compound labor, the tot system, and contract labor shall be abolished.

The Doors of Learning and of Culture Shall Be Opened!

The government shall discover, develop, and encourage national talent for the enhancement of our cultural life;

All the cultural treasures of mankind shall be open to all, by free exchange of books, ideas, and contact with other lands;

The aim of education shall be to teach the youth to love their people and their culture, to honor human brotherhood, liberty, and peace;

Education shall be free, compulsory, universal, and equal for all children;

Higher education and technical training shall be opened to all by means of state allowances and scholarships awarded on the basis of merit;

Adult illiteracy shall be ended by a mass state education plan;

Teachers shall have all the rights of other citizens;

The color bar in cultural life, in sport, and in education shall be abolished.

There Shall Be Houses, Security, and Comfort!

All people shall have the right to live where they choose, to be decently housed, and to bring up their families in comfort and security;

Unused housing space will be made available to the people;

Rent and prices shall be lowered, food plentiful, and no one shall go hungry;

A preventive health scheme shall be run by the state;

Free medical care and hospitalization shall be provided for all, with special care for mothers and young children.

Slums shall be demolished and new suburbs built where all have transport, roads, lighting, playing fields, creches, and social centers;

The aged, the orphans, the disabled, and the sick shall be cared for by the state;

Rest, leisure, and recreation shall be the right of all;

Fenced locations and ghettos shall be abolished, and laws which break up families shall be repealed.

There Shall Be Peace and Friendship!

South Africa shall be a fully independent state, which respects the rights and sovereignty of all nations;

South Africa shall strive to maintain world peace and the settlement of all international disputes by negotiation—not war;

Peace and friendship amongst all our people shall be secured by upholding the equal rights, opportunities, and status of all;

The people of the protectorates—Basutoland, Bechuanaland, and Swaziland—shall be free to decide for themselves their own future;

The right of all the people of Africa to independence and self-government shall be recognized and shall be the basis of close cooperation.

Let all who love their people and country now say, as we say here:

"These Freedoms We Will Fight For, Side by Side, Throughout Our Lives, Until We Have Won Our Liberty."

APPENDIX B

The Sullivan Principles

Principle 1: Nonsegregation of the races in all eating, comfort, locker rooms, and work facilities

Principle 2: Fair and equal employment practices for all employees

Principle 3: Equal pay for all employees doing equal or comparable work for the same period of time

Principle 4: Initiation and development of training programs that will prepare blacks, coloureds, and Asians in substantial numbers for supervisory, administrative, clerical, and technical jobs

Principle 5: Increasing the number of blacks, coloureds, and Asians in management and supervisory positions

Principle 6: Improving the quality of employees' lives outside the work environment in such areas as housing, transportation, schooling, recreation, and health facilities.

APPENDIX C

Moral Deliberation and Policy Formulation

The Results of an Empirical Study of Shareholder Voting Trends in Eight Large Institutional Investors from 1971 to 1986

AS PART of the preliminary research for this book, a comparative study of the voting patterns of eight institutional investors was conducted by the author in 1989. The study concluded that the investment behavior of certain investors toward companies operating in South Africa could not be accounted for by traditional financial risk/return models. Instead, the research brought to light a complex process that blended moral deliberation and policy formulation through the medium of an "internal deliberative group." Such groups were generally created by senior managers to adjudicate activists' claims and to formulate policy by balancing five organizational imperatives: survival, efficiency, growth, consistency, and legitimacy. The study concluded that because the first four imperatives all pressed against taking any costly actions on South Africa, the policy changes arose from the overriding need to maintain organizational legitimacy.

The eight institutional investors chosen for the study were two religious denominations (the United Church of Christ and the Episcopal Church); two universities (Harvard and Columbia); two private funds (the Ford Foundation and the teacher's pension fund TIAA-CREF); and two public pension funds (New York City and New York State). The research consisted of two or more site visits to each investor, an exploration of the files and minutes of the relevant deliberative groups, and an intensive analysis of the shareholder voting record on South

Africa of each investor from 1971 to 1987 as collected by the Investor Responsibility Research Center.

The first step in the analysis was to recognize that an organization could embrace a wide range of possible policy responses to the South African question. From an examination of the voting patterns of these and other investors, it became apparent that certain kinds of votes clustered so that eleven clear stages could be distinguished. These stages can be summarized as follows (also see Table 1).

Stage 0: The investor has never considered the issue.

Stage 1: The investor believes that considering social issues will harm profits.

Stage 2: The investor believes that American firms are a positive force in South Africa but is willing to vote for resolutions that request information.

Stage 3: The investor votes against resolutions recommending the withdrawal of manufacturing firms but for resolutions urging banks to restrict their loans to the South African government.

Stage 4: The investor now believes that shareholders have the right to ask corporations to accept and implement minimum employment standards such as the Sullivan Principles.

Stage 5: The investor feels that a broader range of economic ties must be considered and votes to restrict sales of American products to the military and police. Many institutions also organize an independent staff or trustee evaluation of the situation in South Africa.

Stage 6: The investor believes that the Sullivan Principles *must* be signed to justify continued corporate investment and now votes in favor of "no expansion" resolutions.

Stage 7: By this stage the investor accepts that social change is more important than profitability or employment practices and insists that firms have a *duty* to oppose apartheid beyond the workplace. Investors at stage 7 vote for the implementation of the amplified Sullivan Principles.

Stage 8: The investor concludes that corporations do not have the power or will to affect apartheid substantially and votes in favor of resolutions urging companies to withdraw. The investor does not yet accept full portfolio divestment because of the belief that stock can be used to pressure corporations.

Stage 9: The investor believes that firms should sell their subsidiaries and that investors should sell their stock to promote withdrawal. Some investors may impose selective purchasing restrictions.

Stage 10: The investor expands the definition of "doing business in South Africa" to include nonequity ties and foreign firms, thus broadening the ban on stock and products.

One analytical problem posed by the shareholder voting data was that of comparability. Some of the institutional investors had large, highly diversified portfolios and voted on virtually every resolution; others had smaller portfolios or more random voting procedures. Many portfolios had substantial turnover from year to year so that one year an institution might be in a position to vote for a resolution and the next it would not. Moreover, activists tried to circumvent SEC proxy limitations by filing different resolutions each year. How could one use such diverse voting data to capture an institution's overall position on South Africa and compare it consistently with others over time?

The solution was to assign to every South Africa resolution a numerical score based on its stage. Thus, a resolution filed by any organization with any firm that called for disclosure received a score of 2; a Sullivan resolution got 4; a "no expansion" resolution equaled 6; and a withdrawal resolution counted as 8. With each resolution classified, the next step was to analyze the voting records of the institutional investors in the study. The method chosen for this study calculated the policy stages for each institution by taking the average of the top three affirmative votes each year. A careful effort was made to corroborate the policy scores with the minutes and statements of the institutions; the scoring method was found to provide a consistently reliable index of an organization's position.

The results of this scoring procedure can be seen in Table 2, which gives the score and policy position of each institutional investor in each year from 1971 to 1987. Figure 1 shows the same data in a line graph.

Though the sample is small, the results are striking. For example, we note that the religious denominations generally led with the highest score in almost every year except at the beginning of the 1980s. We also note a general relationship between the activities of the investors and the larger political environment. The greatest rate of policy change in all eight investors takes place between 1975 and 1979 and then again between 1983 and 1987—both periods of violent turmoil in South Africa, student activism on American campuses, and intensive coverage in the American press. Similarly, the only period in which the policy stages slipped backward is the early 1980s, when many people were waiting to see if the Sullivan Principles (first introduced in 1977) and the Reagan policy of constructive engagement (which began in 1981) would have any effect.

Now that we have a record of the policy changes of these eight institutional investors over sixteen years, we can consider the central question: Why did the institutional investors gradually move through the stages and, in many cases, choose to accept the cost of shareholder activism and divestment? Some have suggested that the shift can be explained by a heightened notion of risk, an expanded notion of return, or a recognition of nonfinancial costs, though the empirical evidence suggests that none of these was perceived by the participants to be decisive. Instead, when the institutional investors were challenged by activists, directly or through shareholder resolutions, each of the investors created at least one deliberative group whose task was to recommend and justify a new South Africa policy. Our attention is thus drawn to the nature and content of those deliberations.

From a careful reading of the minutes, statements, and studies produced by the deliberative groups over sixteen years, and after scores of interviews with the participants, it seemed that the deliberations could best be characterized as attempts to resolve conflict between five organizational obligations or imperatives: survival, efficiency, growth, consistency, and legitimacy.

1. *The Survival Imperative:* "Thou shalt not cause or allow the destruction of the organization." There are many arguments for the existence of the survival imperative in organizations. First, organizations are often compared to organisms, and among organisms the survival instinct is elemental. Second, under normal circumstances, organizational patterns that lead to self-destruction are not likely to be emulated.

2. *The Efficiency Imperative:* "Thou shalt not needlessly waste resources." The efficiency imperative is one that economists assume drives business firms and, to a lesser extent, all organizations. Intuitively, we would all agree that if we wish to accomplish some purpose it is likely to be easier with more resources, and therefore it is foolish to waste resources needlessly. The study found that though the efficiency imperative is important, it is often overridden when the legitimacy of the organization is perceived to be at stake. For example, all of the investors spent substantial time and money developing systems to evaluate shareholder resolutions, even though the probability that even a large investor would have an effect on corporate policy was not great. All of the investors eventually instituted some form of divestment or stock purchase screen, despite warnings from analysts that such moves might be costly.

3. *The Growth Imperative:* "Thou shalt maintain or expand the power and discretion of the organization." The growth imperative may seem obvious to the point of banality, yet when it comes to the internal deliberation of an organization, it exerts a powerful and often overlooked constraint on discourse. Members of internal deliberative bodies are under strong injunction not to suggest the diminution of the organization's size, power, range, or number of activities, especially if the overall organization is thriving.

4. *The Consistency Imperative:* "Thou shalt be consistent across examples, times, and places." The consistency imperative asserts that (1) one must be logically consistent in one's deliberations, (2) one must apply similar policies to similar cases over short spans of time, and (3) one must apply similar policies to similar cases across space. Such constraints are necessary not only for rational discussion but also to secure the voluntary participation of the organization's members, who will be more inclined to exit if they perceive arrangements to be arbitrary.

The consistency imperative affects policy deliberations strongly. The deliberative group must be confident that its conclusions will not expose the organization to attacks of inconsistency with past decisions. The deliberative group must also consider the implications of its decisions on future actions. They must consider what other cases might be brought to bear citing their decision as precedent and how this would constrain the discretion of the organization and its executives.

5. *The Legitimacy Imperative:* "Thou shalt fulfill the central purpose for which the organization was created." When human beings join or form groups voluntarily, they do so to accomplish some set of "self-centered" purposes which presumably the individual members desire to achieve but could not alone. However, early in the refinement of the organization's identity, "other-centered" purposes emerge, because organizations must articulate more widely beneficial purposes for their existence in order to earn the toleration (if not approval) of the larger group or society. Such a process of defining and articulating the publicly sanctioned purpose and core values of an organization can be deemed the organization's search for legitimacy.

The concept of legitimacy has its intellectual and historical roots in social contract theory and was first applied to governments. Recently the concept was broadened to refer to the implied public consent to an organization's social function, particularly with regard to corporations. There are two forms of legitimacy: *formal,* which is the public acceptance of an organization's role as articulated and protected by law, and *informal,* which is the public perception that an organization is fulfilling its proper purpose. Such public acceptance is measured in part by the absence of outcry, which in turn implies that citizens have the opportunity to object to social arrangements. The concept of organizational legitimacy is thus in an important sense contingent on the existence of a democratic polity. The perceived need to remain faithful to the stated purpose and core values (or to develop new ones) is the legitimacy imperative.

When an organization is perceived to be fulfilling its core purpose, the legitimacy imperative recedes and attention is turned to encouraging growth and efficiency. However, when the organization is under stress—such as a public demand for justification—the legitimacy imperative can reemerge and trump all the other imperatives. This is precisely what happened in each of the institutional investors in the South Africa debate. We know this in two ways: from the weight of the field research and from the process of elimination. The cumulative propensity of all the other organizational imperatives is toward rejecting any action on South Africa.

The survival imperative did not cause the organizations to vote their shares or divest, for none of the institutional investors in the study was seriously threatened with dissolution if it failed to act on the South Africa question. The efficiency and growth imperatives both press forcefully against unnecessary costs. The consistency imperative impels deliberative groups to avoid decisions that could be used as restrictive precedents, and the historical record shows that many members feared opening what they saw as a Pandora's box of social issues in investment. Even the formal dimension of the legitimacy imperative—the state and federal legal constraints on the actions of trustees, directors, and fiduciaries—kept the obligations tightly focused on the needs of the beneficiaries and constituents of the organization. The only imperative that remains is the legitimacy imperative, which, logically, must have dominated all the others in order to produce the change of policy.

The implications of this are broad and point to new avenues of research. Under what conditions might the legitimacy imperative again acquire the force it had in the South Africa debate? How are the five imperatives blended by other organizations, such as firms, in their deliberations and policy formulations? Under what conditions is a participant in a deliberative group allowed to introduce personal values? Are personal values usually cloaked in the language of organizational imperatives to lend them more weight? Through the exploration of such questions, the manner in which the interaction of these five imperatives form a distinctively organizational pattern of moral deliberation will be more fully illumined.

Table 1. Summary of South Africa Policy Stages

Stage 0   No position

Stage 1   Social issues not relevant to profit maximization

Stage 2   Information seeking

Stage 3   Restrictions on bank loans to government

Stage 4   Sullivan Principles

Stage 5   Restrict sales of U.S. products in South Africa

Stage 6   No expansion

Stage 7   Amplified Sullivan Principles or divestment

Stage 8   Disinvestment and partial divestment

Stage 9   Total divestment and selective purchasing

Stage 10   No nonequity ties or foreign firms

TABLE 2. South Africa Policy Stages for Eight Institutional Investors

Year	Episcopal Church	United Church of Christ	Harvard	Columbia	Ford Foundation	TIAA-CREF	New York City Pension	New York State Pension	Average
1971	4.0	8.0	0.0	0.0	0.0	0.0	0.0	0.0	1.5
1972	2.5	3.0	1.0	0.0	2.0	0.0	0.0	0.0	1.1
1973	2.0	3.0	2.0	0.0	2.0	2.0	0.0	0.0	1.4
1974	3.0	4.0	2.0	0.0	4.0	3.0	0.0	0.0	2.0
1975	4.0	4.0	2.0	0.0	4.7	3.0	0.0	0.0	2.2
1976	4.8	5.7	2.0	0.0	4.7	3.0	0.0	0.0	2.5
1977	5.8	6.7	3.7	0.0	5.0	5.7	0.0	0.0	3.4
1978	5.5	6.7	5.0	4.0	5.0	6.0	0.0	0.0	4.0
1979	6.5	7.0	6.0	5.7	6.0	6.7	4.0	0.0	5.2
1980	6.5	6.3	5.3	5.7	5.3	5.0	5.0	6.0	5.6
1981	5.0	5.7	5.3	4.0	4.7	5.3	6.0	6.0	5.3
1982	5.3	5.7	5.3	4.0	4.7	6.3	6.0	5.7	5.4
1983	5.5	6.0	5.3	4.0	4.7	6.3	5.0	5.7	5.3
1984	6.8	7.0	7.0	5.3	7.0	6.0	7.0	6.0	6.5
1985	8.0	9.0	6.3	7.0	6.7	7.0	9.0	6.7	7.5
1986	8.5	9.0	7.0	9.0	6.7	8.0	9.0	8.0	8.2
1987	8.5	10.0	8.0	10.0	6.7	8.0	9.0	8.0	8.5

Average Stage by Type of Investor

Year	Churches	Universities	Private	Public
1971	6.0	0.0	0.0	0.0
1972	2.8	0.5	1.0	0.0
1973	2.5	1.0	2.0	0.0
1974	3.5	1.0	3.5	0.0
1975	4.0	1.0	3.9	0.0
1976	5.3	1.0	3.9	0.0
1977	6.3	1.9	5.4	0.0
1978	6.1	4.5	5.5	0.0
1979	6.8	5.9	6.4	2.0
1980	6.4	5.5	5.2	5.5
1981	5.4	4.7	5.0	6.0
1982	5.5	4.7	5.5	5.9
1983	5.8	4.7	5.5	5.4
1984	6.9	6.2	6.5	6.5
1985	8.5	6.7	6.9	7.9
1986	8.8	8.0	7.4	8.5
1987	9.3	9.0	7.4	8.5

South Africa Policy Stages for Eight Institutional Investors

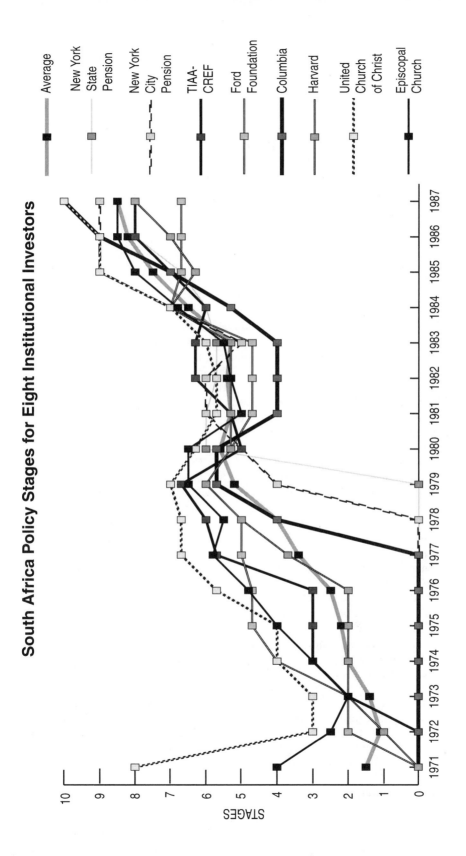

Legend:
- Average
- New York State Pension
- New York City Pension
- TIAA-CREF
- Ford Foundation
- Columbia
- Harvard
- United Church of Christ
- Episcopal Church

STAGES

10 9 8 7 6 5 4 3 2 1 0

1971 1972 1973 1974 1975 1976 1977 1978 1979 1980 1981 1982 1983 1984 1985 1986 1987

Notes

Short titles are used for books and articles cited in the notes. Complete publishing information can be found in the bibliography.

INTRODUCTION: The Mottled Mirror

p. xi: "I come here today": For the full text of Robert Kennedy's speech on the Day of Affirmation in Cape Town, June 6, 1966, see *Robert F. Kennedy in South Africa,* a souvenir booklet compiled by the *Rand Daily Mail.* The printed text differs slightly from Kennedy's spoken words, which can be heard in the Apartheid series on *Frontline,* tape 2, WGBH, Boston, 1988. This opening does not appear in the text of the speech provided to the author by the Robert F. Kennedy Center for Human Rights, suggesting that Kennedy added it during his trip.

p. xi: continually invited comparison: For example, see Frederickson, *White Supremacy,* and Cell, *Highest Stage.*

p. xii: the landing of Jan van Riebeeck: See Thompson, *History of South Africa,* 33ff; see also Readers' Digest Association, *Illustrated Guide,* 26.

p. xii: "where the forest is first to be destroyed": Quoted in Rosenthal, *Stars and Stripes,* 9.

p. xii: early conflict with the Khoikhoi: In March 1658 a Dutch vessel, the *Amersfoort,* intercepted a Portuguese slave ship and seized half of its cargo of five hundred Angolans. Most died on board; a few were sent elsewhere; and seventy-five became the property of the Cape settlers. See Thompson, *History of South Africa,* chap. 2.

p. xii: When the Khoikhoi refused: See Davenport, *South Africa, 4th ed.,* 19.

p. xiii: By the end of the eighteenth century: See Rosenthal, *Stars and Stripes,* chap. 10, and Booth, *United States Experience,* 33–40.

p. xiii: Yankee merchants: Month after month ships set sail from Boston and Salem jammed to the floorboards with hams, butter, chocolate, cheese, salmon, lobster, and fine flour; with household items like pins, lace, saddles, shoes, soup tureens, mugs, and playing cards; and with beautifully crafted violins, desks, sofas, and beds. See Booth, *United States Experience,* 29. The Yankee traders would depart for two or three years, selling and buying in many ports in Africa and India until their inventories had turned over several times and they had acquired enough goods and profit to return to Massachusetts.

p. xiv: "a race of unoffending mortals": Quoted in Rosenthal, *Stars and Stripes,* 36.

p. xiv: "hunting these unfortunate Natives": Ibid.

p. xv: Jacob Glen Cuyler: Ibid., 25.

p. xv: The incident horrified the spectators: For a discussion of the ideological uses to which an embellished version of this story was put, see Thompson, *Political Mythology,* chap. 4.

p. xv: In response to a letter: For descriptions of the origins of the American Board's mission, see du Plessis, *History of Christian Missions,* esp. chap. 23; Lancaster, "Champion among the Heathen"; Booth, *Journal.*

p. xvi: the leadership of Shaka: See Thompson, *History of South Africa,* chap. 3.

p. xvi: "It is not so much their freedom": Ibid., 88.

p. xvii: the death of Jane Wilson: Booth, *United States Experience,* 55; see also Lelyveld, *Move Your Shadow,* 217.

p. xvii: "the thought would rush on our minds": Booth, *United States Experience,* 56.

p. xvii: Dingane . . . gave his visitors the impression: Scholars continue to debate whether Dingane signed a paper ceding the territory, as the Afrikaners later alleged; the most recent research suggests that he did not or that, if he did, he did not understand its contents until later. The idea of Dingane's treachery played an important part in the mythology that developed, as one sees from the iconography of the Voortrekker monument built in 1938 in Pretoria, which shows Dingane signing the paper. For discussions of the incident, see Davenport, *South Africa,* 4th ed., 59; Thompson, *History of South Africa,* 90–91; Reader's Digest Association, *Illustrated History,* 121.

p. xvii: crushed their skulls: Wilson and Thompson, *Oxford History,* 1:360.

p. xvii: Place of Weeping: Thompson, *History of South Africa,* 91.

p. xviii: George Champion agonized for days: Lancaster, "Champion among the Heathen"; Booth, *Journal.*

p. xviii: "we might in some way be counted of abettors": Booth, *Journal,* 133.

p. xviii: Aldin Grout . . . went back: du Plessis, *History of Christian Missions,* chap. 23.

p. xviii: "Unless they come under religious instruction": Quoted in Lelyveld, *Move Your Shadow,* 220.

p. xviii: "The cheapest, speediest, easiest way": Ibid.

p. xix: In gratitude for his efforts: Ibid., 219.

p. xix: leading importer of Cape hides: Booth, *United States Experience,* 88.

p. xix: Farmers on the eastern frontier: Ibid., 96.

p. xix: ice cubes cut from New England lakes: Ibid., 97.

p. xix: many Union soldiers wore boots: Ibid., 93.

p. xix: the story of the *Alabama:* See ibid., 144–50. The capture of the clipper ship *Conrad* and the treatment of the *Alabama* prompted the United States to file a protest with the Geneva Arbitration Commission in 1872. The commission eventually concluded that Great Britain had erred in allowing the Confederate ships to use its facilities and awarded $15 million in damages to the United States.

p. xx: The colonial authorities in Cape Town: See Thompson, *History of South Africa,* chap. 3.

p. xx: Cecil Rhodes and other flamboyant capitalists: For a detailed study of Rhodes, see Rotberg, *Founder.*

p. xx: the battle of Isandlwana and the crushing of Zulu resistance: For a description of the battle, see Reader's Digest Association, *Illustrated History,* 185–87; for a discussion of Cetshwayo's role, see Marks, *Ambiguities of Dependence,* passim.

p. xx: In every military encounter: For a perceptive description of the mismatched military maneuvers, see Mark Twain, *More Tramps Abroad,* 2:284–88.

p. xxi: William P. McKinley: Rosenthal, *Stars and Stripes,* 133.

p. xxi: Samuel Height and the first hotel: Ibid.

p. xxi: small army of pimps and prostitutes: Lelyveld, *Move Your Shadow,* 222.

p. xxi: "The importance of the services": W. P. Taylor, quoted in Rosenthal, *Stars and Stripes,* 135.

p. xxi: "South Africa seems to be the heaven": Twain, *More Tramps Abroad,* op. cit., 296.

p. xxi: Gardner F. Williams: Rosenthal, *Stars and Stripes,* 125–27.

p. xxii: Hammond persuaded Rhodes: Hammond, *Autobiography,* 1:211–14.

p. xxii: President Paul Kruger . . . literally believed: Slocum, *Sailing Alone.* The incident is also reported by Hammond, *Autobiography,* 1:311, and Lelyveld, *Move Your Shadow.*

p. xxii: Twain's visit to prison: Hammond, *Autobiography,* 2:399. For a full account of Twain's trip, see Coleman O. Parson, "Mark Twain: Traveler in South Africa," *Mississippi Quarterly* 29.1 (1975–76): 3–41.

p. xxiii: the Boer War: For a discussion of the tensions between Germany and England that erupted after Kaiser William sent Kruger a letter of congratulations, see Massie, "Jameson Raid."

p. xxiii: Nearly three thousand schoolboys: Davis, *With Both Armies,* 148. According to Davis, "the message set forth that it was fitting that the children of the city which had first declared for independence against Great Britain should send a greeting of sympathy to the leader of the people who were in their turn fighting for their independence against the same nation" (152).

p. xxiii: A specially formed Irish-American brigade: Ibid., 141–43.

p. xxiii: "to transport to the United States": From Robert F. Kennedy's speech on his arrival at Jan Smuts Airport in Johannesburg, June 4, 1966. See *Robert F. Kennedy in South Africa,* op. cit., 5.

p. xxiii: Paul Kruger told a visiting American: For Davis's record of his encounters with Kruger, see Davis, *With Both Armies,* 145; also mentioned in Lelyveld, *Move Your Shadow,* 235.

p. xxiii: They invaded and burned: Davenport, *South Africa,* 140.

p. xxiii: left many Afrikaners filled with bitterness: Ibid., 145–46.

p. xxiv: the Treaty of Vereeniging: The clash between the English and Afrikaners bore some resemblances to the civil war that had torn the United States in half. Both were battles between regional governments that led to more unified national states. The Boer War was also a rebellion against a colonial power, something the United States had finished in the eighteenth century. But as historian George Frederickson *(White Supremacy)* and others have pointed out, these structural similarities obscure vital ideological differences. The American citizens who had fought for independence and for the preservation of their union had justified their actions with appeals to universalistic concepts of freedom and equality. To legitimate the struggle, the Americans had incorporated their appeals into their founding political documents, from the Declaration of Independence and the United States Constitution to the Bill of Rights and the Fourteenth Amendment, which banned slavery. In South Africa, the conflict was between two transplanted European tribes battling for territorial dominance. Though each side glossed its participation with a thin layer of political and religious significance, the end result, geographically and constitutionally, was an uneasy compromise between disparate ethnic cultures.

p. xxiv: Through raw persistence: For a vivid description of missionary life among the Zulus from the 1850s through the 1880s, see Tyler, *Forty Years among the Zulus.*

p. xxiv: When Shaka's regiments killed Dube: Marks, *Ambiguities of Dependence,* 45.

p. xxiv: American blacks treated as honorary whites: For a discussion of this practice, see Clement T. Keto, "Black Americans and South Africa, 1890–1910," *Current Bibliography on African Affairs,* ser. 2, 1972, 5:383–406.

p. xxvi: the influence of Booker T. Washington: See Milfred C. Fierce, "Selected Black American Leaders and Organizations and South Africa, 1900–1977: Some Notes," *Journal of Black Studies* 17, 3 (1987): 305–26.

p. xxvi: the founders of both Afrikaner nationalism: Joseph Lelyveld writes elegantly about this amazing coincidence in *Move Your Shadow,* chap. 8.

CHAPTER ONE: **Rival Dreams of Nationhood**

p. 3: "The problem of the twentieth century": W. E. B. Du Bois, "Of the Dawn of Freedom," in *The Souls of Black Folk* (1903; New York: New American Library, 1969), 54.

p. 3: grocer who longed to become an overseas missionary: Grobbelaar, *This Was a Man,* 9; Hepple, *Verwoerd,* 13. For other biographies of Verwoerd, see Scholtz, *Dr. Hendrik Frensch Verwoerd,* and Kenney, *Architect of Apartheid.*

p. 4: "ever since I was in short pants": Grobbelaar, *This Was a Man,* 14.

p. 4: evicting black sharecroppers: Sol Plaatje, *Native Life in South Africa* (Johannesburg: Ravan Press, 1916), cited in Davenport, *South Africa,* 235.

p. 5: lack of a nationalist patrimony: Verwoerd became the head of the Students' Union and created its first Speakers' Bureau, whose purpose, he wrote at the time, was to prod the faculty to "take part in the cultural uplift of our *volk* and . . . to bring about a closer contact between the *volk* themselves and the higher educational institutions, which are the bearers of their culture" (Hepple, *Verwoerd,* 38–39).

p. 5: changed his course of study: The Reverend Iain Maclean, a Presbyterian minister from South Africa, told the author that Mrs. Alida Daniels, whose grandfather served on the committee that reviewed Verwoerd's application for ordination, had been told by her grandfather that Verwoerd was actually rejected for ordination by the committee. This raises interesting questions about Verwoerd's religious beliefs, his intellectual career, and his future rage at religious figures when they crossed him.

p. 5: accepted a much smaller grant: For a discussion of Verwoerd's decision to go to Germany, see Miller, "Science and Society," 3–4.

p. 5: *Porgy and Bess:* For a brief description of the trip to the United States, see Boshoff, *Betsie Verwoerd.*

p. 6: declaration by the British Crown: Davenport, *South Africa,* 4th ed., 259, 508.

p. 6: the legislative authority to control black labor: Ibid., 266.

p. 6: published one of his earliest articles: H. F. Verwoerd, "A Method for the Experimental Production of Emotions," *American Journal of Psychology* 37 (1926): 357–71, cited in Miller, "Science and Society."

p. 6: "The Arab is fatalist": Quoted in Miller, "Science and Society," 18.

p. 7: Verwoerd's lecturing style: This description comes from a conversation by the author with C. F. Beyers Naudé, who was one of Verwoerd's students.

p. 7: sending the country into depression: For the political developments at the time, see Karis and Carter, *From Protest to Challenge,* 3:3, and Davenport, *South Africa,* 2nd ed., 215.

p. 7: The double burden: O'Meara, 36–37.

p. 7: the Carnegie Commission sponsored a study: Carnegie Commission of Investigation of the Poor White Question in South Africa, *The Poor White Problem in South Africa: A Report of the Carnegie Commission,* 5 vols. (Stellenbosch: Pro Ecclesia-Drukkery, 1932).

p. 7: percentage of the Afrikaner population: Grobbelaar, *This Was a Man,* 29.

p. 7: white farm girls moving to the city: Author interview with André du Toit, May 1989.

p. 7: he became a member of . . . the Broederbond: The exact date of Verwoerd's initiation is unknown. The dating of 1934 is from Hepple, *Verwoerd,* 38.

p. 8: "Where a particular privilege": Ibid., 30, 31. Verwoerd's remarks were delivered to a politically restless Afrikaner community. Only a few months before, Daniel Malan and several other members of Hertzog's Nationalist Party had broken away to form the Purified Nationalist Party. In his address to the Volkscongres Malan, an aging and portly Dutch Reformed clergyman, laid out his increasingly anticapitalist and neofascist views. Speculating on whether Adolf Hitler would provoke a new war in Europe, Malan told the delegates that "if war should come, it will mean, in my opinion, the end of the capitalism system, not only in Europe but also in America. But whether this happens with or without war, by revolution or evolution, the capitalist system which is based on self-interest and the right of the strongest, is in any case doomed" (D. F. Malan, quoted in Hepple, *Verwoerd,* 28). For a discussion of the relationship between Afrikaner religious and political ideas and for a discussion of D. F. Malan's views, see Moodie, *Rise of Afrikanerdom.*

p. 8: "the feather in the hat": Cited in Miller, "Science and Society," 27.

p. 8: five hundred German Jewish refugees: When the English newspapers criticized his speech, Verwoerd attacked the editors as tools of the Jews. Shortly after the ship incident, Verwoerd strongly supported a decision by the Transvaal Congress of the Purified Nationalist Party to exclude all Jews from membership. See Hepple, *Verwoerd,* 223.

p. 9: Jews compete with Afrikaners: Ibid., 221; see also Lelyveld, *Move Your Shadow,* 15.

p. 9: campaign of "open warfare": Hepple, *Verwoerd,* 46, 223.

p. 9: to combat white poverty: For a discussion of the economic position of Afrikaners at the time, see Moodie, *Rise of Afrikanerdom,* chap. 10.

p. 9: economic *volkscongres*: O'Meara, 107.

p. 9: promotion of Afrikaner business: Davenport, *South Africa,* 4th ed., 293; O'Meara, 107–15.

p. 10: Smuts saw Hitler . . . Hertzog viewed him: Davenport, *South Africa,* 4th ed., 230.

p. 10: South African participation in World War II: Thompson, *History of South Africa,* 177.

p. 10: emotional rally at the Voortrekker monument: Grobbelaar, *This Was a Man,* 39.

p. 10: "Britain has lost the war": Botha, *Verwoerd Is Dead,* 11.

p. 11: Verwoerd refused to condemn them: Hepple, *Verwoerd,* 52.

p. 11: "In obedience to God Almighty": Ibid., 170.

p. 11: van Rensburg . . . became commandant general: For a candid and chilling account of van Rensburg's sympathies, see his autobiography, *Their Paths Crossed Mine.*

p. 12: Smuts had already been sufficiently concerned: Hepple, *Verwoerd,* 88.

p. 12: "un-Afrikaans" and . . . "anti-volk": O'Meara, 132–33.

p. 12: system of national segregation began to decay: Davenport, *South Africa,* 4th ed., 241.

p. 13: "a village of women and children": Mandela, *Long Walk,* 7; see also Benson, *Mandela,* 16.

p. 13: "I must have been a comical sight": Mandela, *Long Walk,* 12.

p. 14: stories about African leaders: Benson, *Mandela,* 16.

p. 14: Mandela's notion of leadership: For the description of the regent's policy discussions and their influence on Mandela, see Mandela, *Long Walk,* 18–19. For a less accurate but still vivid picture, see Benson, *Mandela,* 18.

p. 14: "a leader is like a shepherd": Mandela, *Long Walk,* 19.

p. 14: the traditional Xhosa circumcision ceremony: For a description of the lengthy period of preparation and recovery, see Mandela, *Long Walk,* 22–25.

p. 14: Clarkebury Boarding Institute: Ibid., 27–31.

p. 14: Healdtown: For a description of Mandela's education at Healdtown, see ibid., 31–37.

p. 14: "for young black South Africans": Ibid., 37.

p. 15: "I cared more": Ibid., 42.

p. 15: "He loved me very much": Benson, *Mandela,* 21.

p. 16: Mandela as a night watchman: Mandela, *Long Walk,* 56.

p. 16: white law firm: Benson, *Mandela,* 23; Meli, *South Africa Belongs,* 141; Mandela, *Long Walk,* 61ff.

p. 16: Mandela's marriage to Evelyn Mase: Benson, *Mandela,* 24; Mandela, *Long Walk,* 88.

p. 16: "I was not inclined": Mandela, *Long Walk,* 65.

p. 17: "Nelson, . . . please go out and get me": Benson, *Mandela,* 24; Mandela, *Long Walk,* 63.

p. 17: Xuma launched a search: Campbell, *Songs of Zion,* 276.

p. 17: a million-member drive: Davenport, *South Africa,* 4th ed., 246; Karis and Carter, *From Protest to Challenge,* 2:16.

p. 17: the ANC never had more than a few thousand dollars: Davenport, *South Africa,* 4th ed., 246.

p. 18: a list of proposals: See Meli, *South Africa Belongs,* 95ff.

p. 18: Many had been teachers: See author interview with Nthato Motlana, April 6, 1989.

p. 18: "We were never really young": Benson, *Mandela,* 28.

p. 18: Many pointed to the vital role: Karis and Carter, *From Protest to Struggle,* 2:102.

p. 18: The purpose . . . would be to galvanize: Benson, *Mandela,* 28. For discussions of the formation of the ANC Youth League, see Gerhart, *Black Power,* esp. chap. 3; Lodge, *Black Politics,* 21ff.

p. 18: "Programme of Action": Lodge, *Black Politics,* 33–36; Gerhart, *Black Power,* 82ff.

p. 19: When they went to Xuma: Karis and Carter, *From Protest to Struggle,* 2:101.

p. 19: dictate where Indians could work: Meli, *South Africa Belongs,* 96.

p. 19: miners went on strike: Lodge, *Black Politics,* 19–20.

p. 20: the presence of certain visitors: Grobbelaar, *This Was a Man,* 39.

p. 20: the electoral success of 1948: For a discussion of the ways in which the victory of 1948 was integrated into the Afrikaner civil religion, see Moodie, *Rise of Afrikanerdom*, esp. chap. 12.

p. 21: six newly created seats in the House of Assembly: Hepple, *Verwoerd*, 103.

p. 21: designed to halt the miscegenation: For Daniel F. Malan, and probably for most of the other members of parliament, there was unwitting irony in the attempt. A century and a half earlier the prime minister's direct ancestor Dawid Malan had caused a major scandal when he fell in love with a black servant named Sara and fathered a child by her. When Dawid Malan was confronted by his white wife, he took Sara and fled on horseback to the northern frontier. Thus all of Daniel Malan's segregationist efforts were almost certainly directed at some of his own cousins. See Malan, *My Traitor Heart*, 7–11.

p. 21: the "pencil in the hair" test: du Boulay, *Tutu*, 34.

p. 21: The primary target of the legislation: For the history of the South African Communist Party, see Ellis and Sechaba, *Comrades against Apartheid*, esp. chap. 1.

p. 22: guilty of high treason: Strangwayes-Booth, *Cricket in the Thorn Tree*, 50.

p. 22: "Today it is the Communist Party": Meli, *South Africa Belongs*, 119.

p. 22: Verwoerd . . . had lost his 1948 bid: For a discussion of the reasons for Verwoerd's loss, see Moodie, *Rise of Afrikanerdom*, 255.

p. 23: "My dear wife": Hepple, *Verwoerd*, 104.

p. 23: "a vast black empire": Strangwayes-Booth, *Cricket in the Thorn Tree*, 119.

p. 23: "like a giant unchained": Hepple, *Verwoerd*, 107.

p. 23: "I do not have the nagging doubt": Hepple, *Verwoerd*, 237; also quoted in Botha, *Verwoerd Is Dead*, 49.

p. 24: German anthropologists and mission theorists: Verwoerd's precise relationship with this body of ideas, framed by men like Gustav Warnek and Bruno Gutmann, with which he would have been familiar from his original interest in theology and his studies in Germany, is unclear. He may have absorbed and articulated their ideas in a newly political context, or he may have developed them concurrently. Whatever the relationship, the connections between Verwoerdian notions of apartheid and the core concepts of *volk* missiology as developed by Gutmann and Christian Keysser are striking. Even more disturbing is the way in which ideas developed by Keysser, who was a member of the Nazi Party, have been embraced by some modern evangelical missiologists who use the concept of "people groups" as a key component of their strategy to introduce "unreached peoples" to the Christian gospel. See, for example, Christian Keysser, *A People Reborn*, trans. Alfred Allin and John Kuder (Pasadena, Calif.: William Carey Library, 1980), with its adulatory preface by church growth advocate Donald McGavran.

p. 25: "patient schoolmaster" . . . "a professor reaching down": Grobbelaar, *This Was a Man*, 47; Hepple, *Verwoerd*, 108.

p. 25: he droned in a reedy, inflectionless voice: Grobbelaar, *This Was a Man*, 47.

p. 25: Verwoerd replied for half a day: Botha, *Verwoerd Is Dead*, 19.

p. 25: "Long political speeches are wearisome": Hepple, *Verwoerd*, 108.

p. 26: Verwoerd put them on the government payroll: Ibid., 117.

p. 26: Whenever he visited an African community: Ibid., 117.

p. 26: Verwoerd would garrulously instruct: See also Botha, *Verwoerd Is Dead*, 15.

p. 26: Africans responded well: See Grobbelaar's comment in *This Was a Man*, that Verwoerd "had a deep sympathy for the backwardness of the Bantu" (96).

p. 27: "Must the future development": Quoted in Botha, *Verwoerd Is Dead*, 15.

p. 27: They would want the same condition: The quotations and paraphrases are from ibid., 16.

p. 27: "The only possible way out": Hepple, *Verwoerd,* 119. Also *Die Transvaler,* December 6, 1950.

p. 28: network of territorial "zoos": Botha, *Verwoerd Is Dead,* 17.

p. 28: "not an effective body": Ibid., see also Hepple, *Verwoerd,* 119.

p. 28: "The Nationalist Afrikaner is not an oppressor": Botha, *Verwoerd Is Dead,* 14.

p. 28: languages are close cognates: The African languages of South Africa are divided into two main groups, the Nguni and Sotho. The Nguni group includes, among others, Xhosa, Thembu, Mpnodo, and Zulu. Sotho includes northern, southern, and western Sotho. There is also Venda and Tsonga.

p. 29: a race riot in Durban: See Benson, *Mandela,* 36; Meli, *South Africa Belongs,* 99.

p. 29: the Indian and African congresses urgently met: Meli, *South Africa Belongs,* 100.

p. 29: Lembede . . . died that same night: Mandela, *Long Walk,* 93. For a thorough and illuminating discussion of Anton Lembede's role in the formation of Africanist ideology and the formation of the ANC Youth League, see Gerhart, *Black Power,* esp. chap. 3.

p. 29: the officers of the Youth League went to Xuma: Mandela, *Long Walk,* 99.

p. 29: African National "Council": Ibid., 100.

p. 30: a decisive position within the ANC: Benson, *Mandela,* 37. See also Gerhart, *Black Power,* 87; Lodge, *Black Politics,* 26–27.

p. 30: "in the apparent hope": Benson, *Mandela,* 38.

p. 30: All African Convention: See Lodge, *Black Politics,* 86–87; Gerhart, *Black Power,* 126ff. For Ralph Bunche's illuminating eyewitness reflections about the relationship between the ANC and the AAC during his 1937–1938 trip, see Edgar, *African American in South Africa,* 265–71.

p. 30: The tension between the ANC and NEUM: For a discussion of NEUM, see Karis and Carter, *From Protest to Challenge,* 2:98–119; also see Lodge, *Black Politics,* 39; Gerhart, *Black Power,* 131. I am grateful to Professor Seymour Papert of MIT, a former member of NEUM, for our helpful discussions about the group's disagreement with the ANC.

p. 31: Communists were committed not to "true socialism": See also Meli, *South Africa Belongs,* 83.

p. 31: a last marathon negotiation in April 1949: Karis and Carter, *From Protest to Struggle,* 2:108.

p. 31: Mandela and others feverishly rushed around: Benson, *Mandela,* 38.

p. 31: "That day . . . was a turning point": Benson, Ibid., 39.

p. 31: National Day of Mourning and Protest: Davenport, *South Africa,* 4th ed., 265.

p. 32: Though employers in Durban fired a thousand workers: Benson, *Mandela,* 41.

p. 32: "Sailor" Malan: Davenport, *South Africa,* 4th ed., 260.

p. 32: Black Sash: For a discussion of the history and beliefs of the Black Sash, see Denise Mary Ackermann, "Liberating Praxis and the Black Sash: A Feminist Theological Perspective," unpublished doctoral dissertation, University of South Africa, Pretoria, June 1990.

p. 32: How would they find, train, organize: See Kuper, *Passive Resistance.*

p. 33: Mandela was selected: Benson, *Mandela,* 44.

p. 33: "life and death to the people": Ibid., 45.

p. 33: Having just obtained his driver's license: Mandela, *Long Walk,* 108.

p. 33: he would have to walk miles: Benson, *Mandela,* 44.

p. 34: "we can now say unity": Ibid., 46.

p. 34: "The state was far more powerful": Mandela, *Long Walk,* 111.

p. 34: "squalid, dark, and dingy": Mandela, *Long Walk,* 115; Benson, *Mandela,* 47.

p. 34: "Asked whether he thought": Mandela, *Long Walk,* 120.

p. 34: Moroka's lawyer pleaded for leniency: Meli, *South Africa Belongs,* 122.

p. 35: Police had jailed more than eight thousand protesters: Ibid., 121.

p. 35: the government also reintroduced flogging: Benson, *Mandela,* 52; Mandela, *Struggle,* 35.

p. 36: The number of official members of the ANC: Stephen Davis points out that among the new members were a large number of police informants. See Davis, *Apartheid's Rebels,* 6.

p. 36: "The ANC emerged": Mandela, *Long Walk,* 121.

p. 36: Albert Luthuli: For an autobiographical account of Luthuli's life, see Luthuli, *Let My People Go.*

p. 36: Eiselen . . . summoned Luthuli for an audience: Ibid., 121. See also Luthuli's comments in *Advance,* November 20, 1962, quoted in Mzala, *Buthelezi,* 55.

p. 36: Verwoerd immediately deposed him: Luthuli, *Let My People Go,* 123.

p. 36: they asked the local native commissioner: Mzala, *Buthelezi,* 56.

p. 36: Luthuli's refusal to bow: Meli, *South Africa Belongs,* 122. For the relationship between Luthuli's decision not to comply with the Bantu Authorities Act and other Nationalist requirements and the different decision by Gatsha Buthelezi, see Maré and Hamilton, *Appetite for Power,* 33ff.

p. 36: Luthuli was a devout Christian who believed: Lodge makes a similar point, *Black Politics,* 68.

p. 37: a small number of white politicians: See Davenport, *South Africa,* 4th ed., 279–80.

p. 37: the M plan: For Mandela's comments on the strengths and weaknesses of the plan, see Mandela, *Long Walk,* 126–27.

p. 38: time, resources, and energy: As one ANC organizer noted, "Most people were so busy with their ordinary work that they could not find time for Congress duties." *SAIRR, Survey, 1950,* 68, quoted in Lodge, *Black Politics,* 75. Lodge also discusses the origin and design of the M plan in this section.

p. 38: "To reach our desks each morning": Benson, *Mandela,* 55–56.

p. 38: "which did not conform to the standards": Mandela, *Long Walk,* 141–42.

p. 39: "In the courts we were treated": Benson, *Mandela,* 56.

p. 39: "Where does Daddy live?": Mandela, *Long Walk,* 104.

p. 39: "I tried to persuade her": Ibid., 179.

p. 39: it planted a permanent seed of self-doubt: Ibid., 523.

p. 39: Eventually Evelyn returned to the Transkei: See the article on Evelyn in the *Sunday Times* (Johannesburg), February 4, 1990.

p. 39: Even after the Defiance Campaign: Lodge, *Black Politics,* 53.

p. 40: Matthews had just returned: For his description of the time in New York, see Matthews, *Freedom for My People,* chap. 8. Mandela suggests in his autobiography that the idea for the Freedom Charter occurred to Matthews in the United States: "Professor Z. K. Matthews returned to South Africa after a year as a visiting professor in the U.S. armed with an idea that would reshape the liberation struggle" (*Long Walk,* 148).

p. 40: the meetings be open to all races: Karis and Carter, *From Protest to Challenge,* 3:57.

p. 40: Congress of Democrats: Ibid., 3:58–59; Lodge, *Black Politics,* 72.

p. 40: "If you could make the laws": Benson, *Mandela,* 64.

p. 41: some people scribbled on small pieces of paper: See Karis and Carter, *From Protest to Challenge,* 3:59ff.

p. 41: As Albert Luthuli noted with satisfaction: Ibid., 3:61.

p. 41: "large African grandmothers": Ibid.

p. 41: Dozens of plainclothes security police: Ibid.; Mandela, *Long Walk,* 150.

p. 41: "We, the people of South Africa": The full text of the Freedom Charter has been reproduced in hundreds of books. I have drawn from Merlmelstein, *Anti-Apartheid Reader,* 208–11.

p. 42: "It is true that in demanding": See Mandela, *Struggle,* 55; see also Lodge, *Black Politics,* 73.

p. 43: Sten guns: A Sten gun is a light machine gun, similar to the tommy gun used in the United States.

p. 43: Mounted police galloped off: Karis and Carter, *From Protest to Challenge,* 3:62.

p. 44: "Soup with Meat": Benson, *Mandela,* 67.

p. 44: representative of all South Africans: At the same time, the Congress of the People also exacerbated political tensions that would soon cost the movement dearly. Africanists within the ANC grumbled that their leaders had sacrificed the original commitments of the ANC Youth League and its Programme of Action in a needless and dangerous accommodation with other races and ideologies. Moderate whites fretted about the increasing influence of individual Marxists on the analysis, language, and direction of the ANC. The new ideological clarity which the Freedom Charter afforded the African National Congress also brought to life disagreements that had lain dormant in the earlier era of fuzzy purpose. These disagreements prevented the African National Congress from obtaining formal approval at its regular annual conference in December 1955; its leaders had to schedule a special gathering for March 1956, at which the Freedom Charter finally won approval. See Luthuli, *Let My People Go,* 160; Lodge, *Black Politics,* 73–74.

p. 44: From the beginning it had been a thriving center: For a description of life in Sophiatown, see Huddleston, *Naught for Your Comfort,* chap. 7.

p. 45: "gone singing": Strangwayes-Booth, *Cricket in the Thorn Tree,* 95.

p. 45: white suburb known as Triomf: Reader's Digest Association, *Illustrated Guide,* 419, 427.

p. 46: the Eiselen commission: This paragraph is drawn from Lodge, *Black Politics,* 116; however, the quotation "there is no place for him," which Lodge attributes to Eiselen, is credited to Verwoerd by Hepple from the Senate debates on June 16, 1954 (Hepple, *Verwoerd,* 125). For Verwoerd's own exposition of his plans, see Hendrik F. Verwoerd, "Bantu Education: Policy for the Immediate Future," statement to the Senate of the Parliament of the Union of South Africa, June 7, 1954.

p. 46: "black Englishmen": Grobbelaar, *This Was a Man,* 25. "It is not at all the function of good education," Verwoerd also insisted, "to wean the students from the ways of their own people and to free them from their community" (ibid., 51).

p. 46: "Natives will be taught from childhood": House of Assembly debates, September 17, 1953; quoted in Hepple, *Verwoerd,* 124.

p. 47: permanently subservient position: "We do not want Africans in the same university as the young European students of today, who are the leaders of tomorrow," Verwoerd explained to a group of white college students. "We do not want the Europeans to become so accustomed to the Native that they feel there is no difference between them and the Native" (Botha, *Verwoerd Is Dead*, 30).

p. 47: local parent advisory committees: Ibid., 22; Lodge, *Black Politics*, 117.

p. 47: nearly seven thousand children were still out of school: See Lodge, *Black Politics*, 121.

p. 48: "It is essential, as far as the African is concerned": Verwoerd in parliament, September 13, 1961, quoted in Hepple, *Verwoerd* 115.

p. 48: "Reduced to its simplest form": House of Assembly, January 25, 1963, quoted in United Nations, "Apartheid in South Africa," 11.

p. 49: the Tomlinson Commission: Botha, *Verwoerd Is Dead*, 23; Davenport, *South Africa*, 4th ed., 270–72.

p. 50: Verwoerd extended the pass laws: See Benson, *Mandela*, 69.

p. 50: the leaders of the Anglican, Presbyterian: For a discussion of the churches' reactions, see de Gruchy, *Church Struggle*, and Villa-Vicencio, *Trapped in Apartheid*. The full text of Anglican Archbishop Geoffrey Clayton's letter to the prime minister can be found in Peart-Binns, *Archbishop Joost de Blank*, 86–87. Clayton died on March 7, 1957, the morning after Ash Wednesday, only a few hours after signing the letter.

p. 50: "any further participation" . . . **"we will use an iron hand":** Botha, *Verwoerd Is Dead*, 24, 25.

p. 51: potato boycott: See the interview with Joseph Thloloe, assistant editor of the *Sowetan*, May 15, 1989.

p. 51: Tambo . . . had only recently been approved: Benson, *Mandela*, 74; see also David Bonbright, "On the Wrong Side, Again," unpublished manuscript, 93.

p. 52: "I was struck by her beauty": Mandela, *Long Walk*, 185, 186. Winnie Mandela gives a different version of their first encounter; see Mandela, *Part of My Soul*, 57.

p. 52: "one who undergoes trials": Mandela, *Part of My Soul*, 49–50; Benson, *Mandela*, 75; Mandela, *Long Walk*, 186.

p. 52: first black female social worker: Benson, *Mandela*, 74; Mandela, *Long Walk*, 186.

p. 52: wedding of Winnie and Nelson: Mandela, *Long Walk*, 188; Mandela, *Part of My Soul*, 60.

p. 53: "poor and white than rich and mixed" . . . **"A republic in South Africa":** Botha, *Verwoerd Is Dead*, 31.

p. 53: Oswald Pirow: Just two years before, Pirow had written the foreword for van Rensburg's memoirs and had been described by van Rensburg as a close friend and supporter. For Mandela's assessment of Pirow, see Mandela, *Long Walk*, 185, 196.

p. 53: delegation of observers from the International Commission: Benson, *Mandela*, 77.

p. 54: The decision took slightly more than two hours: Grobbelaar, *This Was a Man*, 52–53; Botha, *Verwoerd Is Dead*, 32; Hepple, *Verwoerd*, 130. For another description of the selection of Verwoerd, see Hepple, *Verwoerd*, 133.

CHAPTER TWO: **Crisis and Recovery**

p. 55: "Politics, as a practice": Henry Adams, *The Education of Henry Adams* (New York: Modern Library, 1931), 7.

p. 55: "the will of God" . . . **"No one need doubt":** Hepple, *Verwoerd*, 133, 134.

p. 56: Ultraconservatives screeched: The popular slogan was that the Nationalists would "Steal Oom Piet Van der Merwe's farm"; see Strangwayes-Booth, *Cricket in the Thorn Tree*, 137.

p. 56: Verwoerd adopted a simpler formula: Hepple, *Verwoerd*, 146–47.

p. 56: "Separation, whether it be residential": Verwoerd speech, reprinted in the *Star*, September 4, 1958 quoted in Botha, *Verwoerd Is Dead*, 36; see also Hepple, *Verwoerd*, 134.

p. 57: separate development offered the chance: Verwoerd was, of course, not the only person to defend apartheid and separate development. For an example of the contemporary debate about apartheid ideology, see Pienaar and Sampson, *South Africa*.

p. 57: "man of steel": The papers included *Dagbreek en Sondagnuus, Die Transvaler,* and *Die Volksblad;* quoted in Hepple, *Verwoerd*, 136.

p. 57: "the important thing is that I was elected": *Cape Times*, September 18, 1958; quoted in Hepple, *Verwoerd*, 135.

p. 57: While Betsie served tea: Hepple, *Verwoerd*, 139. For a description of Groote Schuur, see the booklet prepared by the South African Historical Society.

p. 57: "a superman, infallible, austere": Hepple, *Verwoerd*, 139.

p. 58: "is never a tyrant": August 31, 1958; quoted in ibid., 140.

p. 58: "reached its high-water mark": Meredith, *In the Name of Apartheid*, 69.

p. 59: There were still some: For a discussion of African political activists' commitment to gradual reform, see Luthuli, *Let My People Go;* Matthews, *Freedom for My People;* and Lodge, *Black Politics*.

p. 59: They continued to believe: See Lodge, *Black Politics*, 77, for further discussion of the desire to influence the white population; see also Ballinger, *From Union to Apartheid*.

p. 59: Robert became a Methodist lay preacher: Karis and Carter, *From Protest to Challenge*, 4:148; see also Gerhart, *Black Power*, 182ff.

p. 59: "the Prof ": Karis and Carter, *From Protest to Challenge*, 4:149. For a description of Leballo, see 4:54.

p. 60: the "right wing" of the ANC movement: Luthuli wrote that "during the second half of 1958, I addressed a meeting of . . . the Congress of Democrats . . . although I recognized that this activity would draw the criticism of right-wing Africans, particularly of members of the Pan-African[ist] Congress" (Luthuli, *Let My People Go*, 211).

p. 60: the strikers had shouted "Ghana!": Anthony Sampson, "The Bantu Listens to a Louder Drum," *New York Times Magazine*, April 24, 1960, 95. Sampson also found a young messenger boy gazing at a map of Africa that showed the new nations to the north. "Why should all those guys up there be free," he asked the reporter, "while we are still in chains?" (92).

p. 60: This was not the time: For a more detailed discussion of the Africanist position, see Lodge, *Black Politics*, chap. 3. Gerhart argues in her excellent treatment of the origins of the Pan-Africanist Congress (PAC) that the Africanist view was the political expression of pre-industrial peasant outlook; see *Black Power*, esp.

chap. 6. For one ANC historian's view, see Meli, *South Africa Belongs,* 137. For a contemporary description, see *Africa Today,* May 1960, 8.

p. 60: "fanatical African racialism": Meli, *South Africa Belongs,* 137.

p. 60: To make matters worse: Sobukwe, like the leaders of the Unity Movement and other groups, urged a policy of noncollaboration and boycott. Mandela, in turn, argued that these groups had mistakenly elevated a tactic to a principle. See Mandela, *Struggle,* 69–70.

p. 61: When this failed: For a detailed description of the formation of the PAC, see Gerhart, *Black Power,* chap. 6.

p. 61: "Africa for Africans": Ibid., 181; see also Karis and Carter, *From Protest to Challenge,* 3:307ff.

p. 61: "We aim politically": Ibid., 3:516.

p. 61: "United States of Africa": Lodge, *Black Politics,* 85.

p. 61: South Africa would be free from white domination by 1963: An editorial in *Africa Today* reported that "Robert Sobukwe of the Pan-Africanist Congress predicts that Africans will rule South Africa by 1963" and agreed with his assessment *(Africa Today,* May 1960, 2).

p. 62: "Revolution . . . is obviously coming": Kirkpatrick Sales, quoted by dispatch from South Africa to the *Chicago Tribune,* cited in Christopher Cerf and Victor Navasky, *The Experts Speak* (New York: Pantheon, 1984); also quoted in Davis, *Apartheid's Rebels,* 205. The prevalence of this view among journalists is confirmed by Robert K. Massie, the author's father, who was the United Nations correspondent for *Newsweek* at the time. This belief was also widespread among liberals in South Africa. See the comments by representatives of the Christian Institute to Representative Charles C. Diggs Jr. during his trip to South Africa in 1971. "In 1959 and 1960," they told him, "one thought things would be changed by 1963" (Diggs Trip Report, Chron File, September 20, 1971, Box 224, 104, Diggs Collection).

p. 62: "The wind of change": Grobbelaar, *This Was a Man,* 70.

p. 62: individual merit was the only criterion: Ibid., 66; Meredith, *In the Name of Apartheid,* 85.

p. 62: "As a fellow member of the Commonwealth": Grobbelaar, *This Was a Man,* 70.

p. 63: "If our policies were rightly understood": Ibid., 66, 70.

p. 63: "It was only during these days": Macmillan, *Pointing the Way,* 152, 153.

p. 64: In Sharpeville, however: For accounts of the Sharpeville massacre, see Mermelstein, *Anti-Apartheid Reader,* 214; Meredith, *In the Name of Apartheid,* 81; Davenport, *South Africa,* 4th ed., 395; *New York Times,* March 22, 1960; and Botha, *Verwoerd Is Dead,* 69.

p. 64: Though the government later claimed: See, for example, Grobbelaar, who said "the shooting lasted for three seconds at the most" *(This Was a Man,* 71). For the eyewitness reports, see *New York Times,* March 22, 1960.

p. 64: "in a wide arc from his hip": Tyler's account was printed in the United States in *Africa Today,* May 1960, 5. It also appeared in the *Observer* in London and *Contact* in Cape Town.

p. 64: Wounded men and women screamed in pain: *New York Times,* March 22, 1960.

p. 64: "When the shooting started": Tyler, *Africa Today,* May 1960, 5.

p. 64: "I don't know how many we've shot": *New York Times,* March 22, 1960.

p. 64: The editors of *Newsweek:* This edition was dated April 11 and published during the week of April 4.

p. 65: Republicans in the Eisenhower administration: For a discussion of the bureaucratic and political considerations that led to the American statement, see Ronald W. Walters, "The Formulation of United States Policy toward Africa, 1958–1963," unpublished doctoral dissertation, American University, Washington, D.C., 1971.

p. 65: Satterthwaite wrote an unusually strong statement: Satterthwaite interview, JFKL. Just before Sharpeville, however, Satterthwaite had "asked the Senate Committee on Foreign Relations whether it was sensible for the US to express its opposition to National party policies when the government of South Africa offered such unqualified support in the overriding issue of the day: the containment of the Soviet Union" (Coker, *United States and South Africa,* 4).

p. 65: He said that ANC and PAC propaganda: Botha, *Verwoerd Is Dead,* 58.

p. 65: the violent tactics of the ANC and the PAC: Ibid., 58; the South African ambassador to the United Nations repeated this accusation in his speech to the Security Council later that month.

p. 65: "the riots in which law-abiding Bantu are dragged in": House of Assembly debates, May 20, 1960; quoted in Hepple, *Verwoerd,* 155.

p. 65: "the police were attacked": See Fourie's comments reprinted in *Africa Today,* May 1960, 6. For a critique of the UN's behavior and a defense of South African policy, see Heunis, *United Nations versus South Africa.*

p. 65: U.S. ambassador Henry Cabot Lodge: *Newsweek,* April 11, 1960, 26.

p. 66: failed "to see how local police action": Botha, *Verwoerd Is Dead,* 60.

p. 66: Only when Verwoerd received the communication: For comments on Verwoerd and the judicial inquiry, see ibid., 59. South African scholar Barbara Harmel, the daughter of prominent South African Communist Michael Harmel, also referred to the incident in her introduction to the presentation of Herman Cohen, assistant secretary of state for African affairs, to the Seminar on Non-Violent Sanctions, Center for International Affairs, Harvard University, October 30, 1990.

p. 66: Within days he had slapped a ban on public meetings: Davenport, *South Africa,* 4th ed., 396.

p. 66: "We will see to it": House of Assembly debates, March 23, 1960; quoted in Hepple, *Verwoerd,* 153.

p. 66: In Johannesburg, Treason Trial defendants: Benson, *Mandela,* 84.

p. 66: the police would temporarily suspend arrests: Davenport, *South Africa,* 4th ed., 396.

p. 67: Two days later: Lodge, *Black Politics,* 119–21.

p. 67: Philip Kgosana: The best description of Kgosana and the events in Cape Town can be found in Lelyveld, *Move Your Shadow,* chap. 11. See also *Newsweek,* April 11, 1960, 26, and Meredith, *In the Name of Apartheid,* 82.

p. 68: Kgosana . . . had simply disappeared: Some years later Terblanche expressed deep regret about this incident, which he viewed as a breach of honor. See his interview with Granada Television, which aired in the United States in a five-part series on apartheid on *Frontline* in 1988.

p. 69: teach himself Afrikaans: Benson, *Mandela,* 86.

p. 69: As Verwoerd turned to speak to him: For descriptions of the assassination attempt, see Botha, *Verwoerd Is Dead,* 65; Grobbelaar, *This Was a Man,* 80; and Hepple, *Verwoerd,* 154.

p. 70: "a violent urge to shoot at apartheid": Botha, *Verwoerd Is Dead,* 66.

p. 70: The government issued a terse statement: Ibid., 67; Grobbelaar, *This Was a Man,* 80.

p. 70: "that the protection of Divine Providence": Grobbelaar, *This Was a Man,* 96.

p. 70: "I cannot withdraw it": Botha, *Verwoerd Is Dead,* 44.

p. 71: "up and down at every step": Quoted in Sparks, *Mind of South Africa,* 122.

p. 71: Kimberley's Deep Hole: For a vivid description of the early mining years, see Sparks, *Mind of South Africa,* 120–25; see also Reader's Digest Association, *Illustrated Guide.*

pp. 71–72: "imagine a solid mass of rock": Originally quoted in Wilson, *Labour;* also quoted in Pallister, *South Africa Inc.,* 146.

p. 72: as small as a few grains of rice: The average yield was fifteen grams of gold per ton of rock. For a description of the science and technology of gold mining, see Reader's Digest Association, *Illustrated Guide,* 210–13.

p. 72: gold differed dramatically from diamonds: For a discussion of the peculiarities of the markets for diamonds and gold, see Gregory, *Ernest Oppenheimer,* 19, 32ff.

p. 73: To solve this problem: For discussions of the monopsony created by the mining companies with regard to mining labor, see Nattrass, *South African Economy;* Ann Seidman, *The Roots of Crisis in Southern Africa* (Trenton, N.J.: Africa World Press, 1985), chap. 2; Merle Lipton, *Capitalism and Apartheid,* 110–37; and Wilson, *Labour.*

p. 74: Ernest Oppenheimer: For biographies of Oppenheimer and descriptions of the formation of Anglo-American, see Gregory, *Ernest Oppenheimer,* esp. chap. 2; Minter, *King Solomon's Mines,* esp. chap. 2; and Pallister, *South Africa Inc.*

p. 74: "If American capital wishes": Gregory, *Ernest Oppenheimer,* 85.

p. 74: "African American would suggest": Ibid., 88.

p. 75: Ford Motor Company's assembly plant: Minter, *King Solomon's Mines,* 81; Houghton, *South African Economy,* 139.

p. 75: South African whites owned more automobiles: Minter, *King Solomon's Mines,* 81.

p. 75: fifty-two percent of all capitalist industrial production: John H. Dunning, "Changes in the Level and Structure of International Production: The Last One Hundred Years," in Mark Casson, ed., *The Growth of International Business* (London: Allen and Unwin, 1983); cited in ibid.

p. 76: nearly tripled to $140 million: Minter, *King Solomon's Mines,* 82.

p. 76: Newmont Mining Corporation purchased: Ibid., 77.

p. 76: These moves, they argued: For a discussion of the growth of manufacturing and the relevance of the small domestic market, see Houghton, *South African Economy,* 134–39, 171ff.

p. 77: South Africa's first oil refinery: Minter, *King Solomon's Mines,* 82.

p. 78: Township musicians formed bands: Reader's Digest Association, *Illustrated Guide,* 416.

p. 78: "the Young Americans": "Gangsters—known as *tsotsis*—carrying flick-knives or switchblades were plentiful and prominent," wrote Nelson Mandela about life in Alexandra township in the 1940s. "In those days they emulated American movie stars and wore fedoras and double-breasted suits and wide, colorful ties." See Mandela, *Long Walk,* 66. See also the author's May 1989 interview with South African journalist Joe Thloloe, who grew up in Sophiatown.

p. 78: "Why should the Afrikaner suffer": Botha, *Verwoerd Is Dead,* 63 n.

p. 78: "the idea of making quick and high profits": Mandela, *Liberation*, March 1978; quoted in Mandela, *Struggle*, 75–76.

p. 79: "The peoples of resurgent Africa": Ibid., 76.

p. 79: The foundation set up offices: *New York Times*, January 7, 1960.

p. 79: Share prices plummeted so rapidly: *New York Times*, March 31, 1960; *Johannesburg Star*, April 2, 1960, and "Institutional Support Saved the Day Impressively," April 4, 1960.

p. 79: Capital . . . poured out of the country: See Hepple, *Verwoerd*, 153.

p. 79: RACIAL STRIFE HITS UNION: *Johannesburg Star*, April 4, 1960. Some South African business leaders tried to restore morale; the president of the Pretoria Chamber of Commerce, T. O. Weir, for example, lamely told his members at their annual meeting on April 5, 1960, that the government should organize special festivals for tourists so that the world could "get to know the Union as a gay, happy land of sunshine" *(Johannesburg Star*, April 6, 1960). If present trends continued, Weir noted dejectedly, "even the most optimistic of us must view the future with certain doubts."

p. 80: the men intended to ask: *Johannesburg Star*, April 6, 1960. Also see *New York Times*, April 6, 1960. Other business groups, such as the Federated Chamber of Industries, also expressed a desire for an alteration in apartheid; see *New York Times*, May 3, 1960.

p. 80: When Verwoerd heard about the speech: Botha, *Verwoerd Is Dead*, 69; John Kane-Berman contrasts the reaction of South African businessmen at the time of Sharpeville with their reaction sixteen years later during the Soweto riots in *South Africa*, chap. 11, esp. 160–62. See the description in Strangwayes-Booth, *Cricket in the Thorn Tree*, 184–85.

p. 80: Louw also ordered the South African ambassador: *New York Times*, April 22, 1960.

p. 80: Government economists considered: For a discussion of the 1960 capital outflow, see Nattrass, *South African Economy*, 266, and Houghton, *South African Economy*, 180ff.

p. 81: boycotts of South African goods: The number and diversity of boycott efforts, some of which preceded the Sharpeville massacre, reported in 1960 in the *New York Times* are impressive. A selection includes the following: Liverpool, England, Municipal Council votes to boycott Union goods to protest apartheid (January 7, 1960); London rally to back one-month economic boycott of South Africa (January 28, 1960); Swedish labor leaders back plans for massive international boycott against South African goods to protest apartheid (February 2, 1960); AFL-CIO executive council urges boycott of South African exports to US (February 14, 1960); West German Trade Union Federation backs boycott of South Africa (March 12, 1960); ICFTU sets 2 month boycott of South African goods (April 6, 1960); ILWU urges boycott on all trade with South Africa (April 11, 1960); U.S. economic boycott of South Africa urged at Africa Freedom Day (April 14, 1960); Survey shows various boycotts of Union caused $1 million loss to exporters in last 2 months (June 30, 1960); Ghana sets total boycott of South African goods as protest to apartheid; orders its seaports and airports closed to South African traffic; will bar entry of all South Africans who do not declare opposition to apartheid (July 30, 1960); Kenya leader Tom Mboya urges all African states to join boycott (August 4, 1960).

p. 81: white pride, commercial necessity, and anticommunism: Hepple makes this point, *Verwoerd*, 193.

p. 81: even if the voters rejected: *New York Times*, March 22, 1960.

p. 81: formation of a new internal security force: *New York Times,* August 5, 1960.

p. 81: On October 5, 1960: Karis and Carter, *From Protest to Challenge,* 3:804.

p. 81: The measure, as expected: Davenport, *South Africa,* 399; see also Hepple, *Verwoerd,* 170ff; Grobbelaar, *This Was a Man,* 81.

p. 82: Verwoerd refused to budge: "What shocked the conference was that the policy of the present government appeared to set up what we regarded as an unhappy practice . . . as a philosophy of action of the future," recalled one participant. "But the prime minister of South Africa, with an honesty one must recognize, made it abundantly clear, beyond all doubt, that he would not think it right to relax in any form the extreme rigidity of his dogma, either now or in the future" (Hepple, *Verwoerd,* 180).

p. 82: "Our opponents who wanted us out": The quotation and description are taken from a contemporary film clip used in *Frontline*'s documentary on apartheid (1988), episode 3.

p. 82: "You are the leader": Hepple, *Verwoerd,* 8.

p. 82: When he returned he discovered: Benson, *Mandela,* 93; Meer, *Higher than Hope,* 150.

p. 83: Their questioning of Mandela: Mandela's responses to the questioning are from Benson, *Mandela,* 89–92.

p. 84: "a State of the Nation address": Meer, *Higher than Hope,* 162.

p. 84: The conference decided: Benson, *Mandela,* 98.

p. 84: "You are found not guilty": Ibid., 96.

p. 84: "I will be going away": Ibid., 95; Mandela, *Part of My Soul,* 71.

p. 85: "the Black Pimpernel": After the title character in the novel *The Scarlet Pimpernel* by Emmuska Orczy.

p. 85: Neither man responded: Benson, *Mandela,* 101; see court testimony of Verwoerd's private secretary concerning the disposition of Mandela's letter in Mandela, *Struggle,* 132–35.

p. 85: they imprisoned huge numbers: *New York Times,* May 4, 1961; Benson, *Mandela,* 101.

p. 85: the government gave the police: *New York Times,* May 20, 1961; May 23, 1961. The detention law was part of General Law Amendment Act 39 of 1961, passed on May 5, 1961.

p. 85: "In the country's biggest call-up": Quoted in Benson, *Mandela,* 103; see also Mandela, *Struggle,* 119.

p. 86: Journalists from around the world: Benson, 103.

p. 86: more than fifty percent of all workers: Ibid.; Meer, *Higher than Hope,* 166.

p. 86: Mandela fumed: For a longer contemporary assessment by Mandela of the strike, see *Struggle,* 103ff.

p. 86: "In the light of the steps taken": Benson, *Mandela,* 104.

p. 86: "Believe in God": Grobbelaar, *This Was a Man,* 62. For an example of Malan speeches on these and other Nationalist themes, see Pienaar, *Glo in U Volk.*

p. 86: "Create Your Own Future": Grobbelaar, *This Was a Man,* 96.

p. 86: "After we had bathed": D'Oliveira, *Vorster,* 22.

p. 87: "absolutely naturally": Ibid., 9.

p. 87: Vorster later recounted with horror: Ibid., 65.

p. 87: Though the internees complained: Ibid., 75–76 and passim.

p. 87: General Vorster: D'Oliveira, *Vorster,* 101.

p. 87: he lost his first campaign: Ibid., 110.

p. 87: "Doctor, I hope you know what you are doing": Ibid., 115.

p. 88: rebutting his critics in parliament: When in May 1961 members of the United Party challenged Verwoerd over the detentions in May, Vorster defended the action with a long, plaintive recitation of his own imprisonment. "I was an attorney when I was arrested, and I was not even permitted to see my own partners to discuss the cases I was busy on," recounted Vorster. "The people [in detention now] are living in a palace compared to the place where we had to live. The privileges they have cannot even be compared to the privileges we had. . . . Under a Nationalist government," Vorster concluded bitterly, "a Communist has more privileges than an Afrikaner had under the [Smuts] regime!" (ibid., 69).

p. 88: "would have to let me deal": Ibid., 125.

p. 88: "These were not normal times": Ibid., 130.

p. 88: By March 1961 the reserves of gold: Houghton, *South African Economy,* 180; see also Davenport, *South Africa.*

p. 88: In May 1961: Nattrass, *South African Economy,* 266; Houghton, *South African Economy,* 187.

p. 89: "Mr. Dick Hegland": *New York Times,* June 4, 1961. "This Is South Africa," special advertising supplement sponsored and paid for "by South African and American business interests in South Africa."

p. 89: "The question that is being asked": Mandela, *Struggle,* 112.

p. 90: "opening of the second phase": Mandela, *Struggle,* 113.

p. 90: Couldn't other disturbances: Benson, *Mandela,* 108.

p. 90: The formation of Umkhonto We Sizwe: For discussions of the formation of Umkhonto, see Lodge, *Black Politics,* 233; Gerhart, *Black Power,* 252; Meli, *South Africa Belongs,* chap. 6; and Ellis and Sechaba, *Comrades against Apartheid,* chap. 2.

p. 91: To explain the presence: Benson, *Mandela,* 107.

p. 91: he ventured out in disguise . . . go "home" to Lilliesleaf: Mandela, *Part of My Soul,* 74.

p. 91: "the most hope for future race relations": Benson, *Mandela,* 108.

p. 91: "Now we are ready": The story was related to Andries du Toit during his graduate research on the Armed Resistance Movement.

p. 91: "I have only been thinking": *New York Times,* October 24, 1961.

p. 92: "the putty party": Botha, *Verwoerd Is Dead,* 91.

p. 92: "is a museum piece": Ibid.

p. 92: the members of Umkhonto We Sizwe exploded small bombs: "The attempt to blow up the Bantu Administration Department's Office in Durban failed, but the next day a Fordsburg post office, the Resettlement Board headquarters in Meadowlands, and the Bantu Affairs Commission's office in Johannesburg were damaged. Similar offices and an electrical transformer were attacked in Port Elizabeth" (Lodge, *Black Politics,* 235).

p. 92: "The Nationalist government has rejected": Benson, *Mandela,* 75.

p. 92: "South Africa is now a land ruled by the gun": Ibid., 113.

p. 93: they greeted each other with great warmth: Ibid., 116.

p. 93: Mandela apologized: Ibid.

p. 93: formation of . . . Poqo: See Lodge, *Black Politics,* 241–46, 250–51.

p. 93: Vorster persuaded parliament: For discussions of Vorster and the Sabotage Act, see Davenport, *South Africa,* 4th ed., 404. The passage in the Bible referred to by Vorster is the story of Solomon and Shimei in 1 Kings 2.36–46; see D'Oliveira, *Vorster,* 132–33.

p. 94: the intelligence agencies of other countries: For a contemporary assessment of Mandela and other political activists by the Central Intelligence Agency, see CIA,

Office of Current Intelligence, "Subversive Movements in South Africa," May 10, 1963, NSF, JFKL.

p. 94: an American reporter uncovered evidence: *Atlanta Journal and Constitution,* June 10, 1990; see also "C.I.A. Tie Reported in Mandela Arrest," *New York Times,* June 10, 1990; also mentioned in the *Johannesburg Star,* July 14, 1986; cited in Ellis and Sechaba, *Comrades against Apartheid,* 34.

p. 94: On Sunday, August 5: Benson, *Mandela,* 117; Mandela, *Long Walk,* 273.

CHAPTER THREE: **John F. Kennedy and
the Politics of Racial Equality**

p. 97: "Nothing is more paradoxical": Milton Obote, prime minister of Uganda, to John F. Kennedy, May 23, 1963, NSF, Box 3, JFKL.

p. 97: On Monday, February 1, 1960: See Branch, *Parting the Waters,* 271ff.

p. 97: Newly enfranchised slaves: Cited by Clifton Wharton in his unpublished speech to the Michigan State NAACP Martin Luther King banquet, 1971, Box 312, Diggs Collection.

p. 98: by eliminating every single black: Schlesinger, *Thousand Days,* 935.

p. 98: The National Association for the Advancement of Colored People: On the origin and role of the NAACP, see Morris, *Origins,* esp. chap. 1.

p. 99: "You can't legislate morality": Branch, *Parting the Waters,* 213.

p. 99: Baton Rouge bus boycott: Morris, *Origins,* 17–25.

p. 99: Mongomery bus boycott: See Branch, *Parting the Waters;* Harvard Sitkoff, *Struggle,* 37–56; Fairclough, *To Redeem,* 15–18, 53–54.

p. 99: Nixon had met Martin Luther King: For Nixon's public observations about his trip to Africa in 1957, see "The Vice President's Report to the President on Trip to Africa, Feb 28–March 21, 1957," Box 334, Diggs Collection. Nixon's primary interest was in the role of Africa in the East-West competition. He said, for example, that "no one can travel in Africa, even as briefly as I did, without realizing the tremendous potentialities of this great continent. Africa is the most rapidly changing area in the world today. The course of its development, as its people continue to emerge from a colonial status and assume the responsibilities of independence and self-government, could well prove to be the decisive factor in the conflict between the forces of freedom and international communism." For an account the Nixon-King meeting in Ghana, see Branch, *Parting the Waters,* 214; Garrow, *Bearing the Cross,* 90–91.

p. 99: In June 1957 Nixon invited King: Branch, *Parting the Waters,* 218–21.

p. 101: "civilizations striving to be born": Mahoney, *JFK,* 14.

p. 102: "Did that tragic episode": Ibid., 20.

p. 102: "You lucky mush": Ibid., 21.

p. 103: "Kennedy stands for nothing": Ibid., 27.

p. 103: "More Courage, Less Profile": Ibid., 25.

p. 103: the gauntlet of primaries: For the best contemporary account of the 1960 campaign, see White, *Making, 1960.*

p. 103: "You can go there to teach them": Wofford, *Of Kennedys,* 110.

p. 104: "Whatever helps the election": Ibid., 44.

p. 104: "We are in trouble with Negroes": Ibid., 47.

p. 104: G. Mennen Williams: For Williams's account, see his memoir *Africa for the Africans.*

p. 104: On the floor of the 1952 Democratic convention: See Judd Arnett, *Detroit Free Press,* February 16, 1961.

p. 104: "I wish I could be a liberal": G. Mennen Williams, OH, 1, JFKL.

p. 105: "Williams is a man of strong convictions": Wofford, *Of Kennedys,* 48; see also White, *Making, 1960,* 138, which dates the memo in January 1960.

p. 105: "Well, Jack, as I understand my Negro friends": G. Mennen Williams, OH, 14–15, JFKL.

p. 106: "of overwhelming moral significance": Wofford, *Of Kennedys,* 48.

p. 106: each person stepped up: G. Mennen Williams, OH, 15, JFKL.

p. 106: "I didn't offer the vice-presidency": Schlesinger, *Thousand Days,* 48.

p. 107: resentment . . . toward the younger Kennedy: See ibid., chap. 2.

p. 107: more civil rights laws: Author interview with Charles Diggs Jr., May 24, 1990.

p. 107: Yet three southern governors: Robert Kennedy to Harris Wofford, quoted in Wofford, *Of Kennedys,* 19.

p. 108: only two dozen had ever attended a university: Williams, *Africa for the Africans,* 18.

p. 109: a secret plot to kill the Congolese leader: For an extended discussion of American policy toward Lumumba, see Mahoney, *JFK.*

p. 109: Kennedy mentioned Africa nearly five hundred times: Arthur M. Schlesinger Jr. wrote that "in 1960, for the first time in American history, Africa figured prominently in a presidential election. Kennedy charged repeatedly (there are 479 references to Africa in the index of his 1960 campaign speeches) that 'we have lost ground in Africa because we have neglected and ignored the needs and aspirations of the African people' " (*Thousand Days,* 554).

p. 109: a swift disavowal: See Branch, *Parting the Waters,* 354ff. See also Fairclough, *To Redeem,* 74–75.

p. 110: "They are going to kill him": Garrow, *Bearing the Cross,* 146.

p. 110: Mitchell released King: Branch, *Parting the Waters,* 366.

p. 110: "I had expected to vote": Ibid.

p. 111: Out of nearly 70 million ballots: For the exact figures, see White, *Making, 1960,* 350. Arthur Schlesinger Jr. notes that "had only whites gone to the polls in 1960, Nixon would have taken 52 percent of the vote" (*Thousand Days,* 930).

p. 111: "great innovations should not be forced": Schlesinger, *Thousand Days,* 709.

p. 112: "second to none": To allay Williams's fears, Kennedy also skillfully cited historical examples of subcabinet officials who had enjoyed a special relationship with past presidents. See G. Mennen Williams, OH, 35, JFKL.

p. 112: "After all," said Kennedy: Schlesinger, *Thousand Days,* 127.

pp. 112–13: An engineer and B-17 pilot: For Wayne Fredericks's background, see author interview with Fredericks, April 19, 1990.

p. 113: In their pre-inauguration discussions: Ibid.

p. 114: supportive recommendations: Church, McGee, and Moss, *Study Mission to Africa.*

p. 114: "Who' Going to Win in Africa?": *U.S. News and World Report,* March 3, 1961.

p. 114: "Will Africa Go Communist?": Joseph Alsop, *Saturday Evening Post,* February 18, 1961. Dodd placed it in the *Congressional Record* that same week.

p. 114: "Might I characterize": Williams, *Africa for the Africans,* 159.

p. 114: Williams's trip to Africa: The description of Williams's first trip comes from several sources. Judd Arnett's long series of columns on the Williams trips appeared in the *Detroit Free Press* in February and March 1961. Other newspapers also covered the trip. See, for example, "Natives Cheer Williams as He Braves Congo Mud," *Washington Post,* March 2, 1961. Mrs. Williams also described the trip comprehensively in a collection of letters to her children that she shared privately with a few persons, including Representative Charles C. Diggs Jr. of Michigan. See Box 329, Diggs Collection. Though Williams also wrote lengthy State Department memoranda on his trips that were communicated to the White House and can be found in the National Security files at the Kennedy Library, this researcher never located a report from his first trip.

p. 115: "By Africans," he said: Williams, *Africa for the Africans,* 159.

p. 115: Williams's political enemies pounced: William S. White, writing in the *Detroit News,* sniffed that the new assistant secretary had "offended our major allies, notably Britain, by passing harsh, off-the-cuff judgments on matters neither his business nor remotely within his competence. . . . This sort of conduct was predictable," White continued, denouncing Williams as "a special, and happily rare kind of politician—an automatic reactor to pressure-group interest." Fortunately, wrote White, there seemed to be a few cooler heads in the new administration, men like [senior foreign policy adviser] Walt Rostow, who, unlike Soapy Williams, was "no knee-jerk professional liberal, no eager dogmatic saver of the world by tomorrow morning at 10:32" (*Detroit News,* March 3, 1961; Box 329, Diggs Collection).

p. 115: Dean Rusk . . . sent Williams a telegram: Cable, Rusk to Williams, February 23, 1961, NSF, Box 2, JFKL, see also Williams's reply to Rusk via Duggan from Dar Es Salaam, February 26, 1961. "Though I wish it had happened otherwise, believe no real friends lost and new friends encouraged," Williams cabled.

p. 115: "I felt I had better send": Schlesinger, *Thousand Days,* 556.

p. 116: So great was the dissatisfaction: Schneidman, *American Foreign Policy,* 34; see also Walters, *South Africa and the Bomb.*

p. 116: "just", "sacred," and "inevitable": Schneidman, *American Foreign Policy,* 35.

pp. 116–17: "the ambassador to the United Nations' special representative": There are many discussions of the strained relationship between Kennedy and Stevenson. See, for example, Schlesinger, *Thousand Days,* passim.

p. 117: "only the dead are exempt": Schneidman, *American Foreign Policy,* 56.

p. 118: "by a time dimension quite different": The description is George Ball's from his visit in August 1963. See ibid., 130.

p. 118: February uprisings in Angola: See Bridgland, *Jonas Savimbi,* 51.

p. 119: Kennedy told Stevenson to wait: Schneidman, *American Foreign Policy,* 58–59.

p. 119: "no doubt . . . be promptly forthcoming": Ibid., 48.

p. 120: President Kennedy had to go on national television: For an account of the internal deliberations that led to the Bay of Pigs, see Schlesinger, *Thousand Days,* chap. 10.

p. 120: "racial discrimination in the United States": Church, McGee, and Moss, *Study Mission to Africa,* 3.

p. 120: The problem had existed for some time: In 1957, for example, an official from Ghana had been threatened with lynching while driving along the streets of Washington, D.C. On election day in 1960 a Ghanaian official, observing a voting station in Georgia at the invitation of President Eisenhower, was thrown out by local officials because he was black. In New York, African visitors and diplomats were

denied haircuts, meals, and other services in the vicinity of the United Nations. For
an account of these and other incidents, see E. M. Debrah, "The Effect of the
Existence of Segregation in the U.S. on the American Image in Africa," memorandum prepared at the United Nations Educational, Scientific, and Cultural Organization, October 25, 1961, POF, Box 2, JFKL.

p. 120: Rusk wrote back advising: "During my years with the Rockefeller boards,"
Rusk wrote to Kennedy, "we followed the segregation problem very closely because
of our long interest in the situation of Negroes. I am quite sure that the most
constructive efforts were those which were made without fanfare and in a reasonable atmosphere not inflamed by violent public controversy" (Dean Rusk to Robert
F. Kennedy, January 31, 1961, POF, Box 2, JFKL). Rusk also obviously queried his
staff because he attached a memo from Woodruff Wallner of the Bureau for International Organizations detailing the UN delegation's efforts to speak to hotel managers and city officials about curbing discrimination against African diplomats.

p. 120: During the spring, in separate incidents: On March 9 the chargé d'affaires
of Sierra Leone, Dr. W. H. Fitzjohn, left Washington in a chauffeured car to drive to
Pittsburgh to deliver a speech. At seven P.M. he and his driver stopped for supper at
a Howard Johnson's restaurant in Hagerstown, Maryland. When he entered, the
other patrons scowled; when he sat down, the waitress told him he would not be
served; and when he identified himself as a diplomat, she told him to get out (Pedro
Sanjuan to Angier Biddle Duke, April 18, 1961, POF, Box 2, JFKL). In early May
the director of the Civil Aeronautics Commission of Mali, who had been invited by
the American government to attend a conference on international aviation in Okla-
homa City, was vilified and manhandled by a white woman and her companion in his
hotel (Pedro Sanjuan to Frederick Dutton, May 13, 1961, POF, Box 2, JFKL.) Later
that month the education attaché in the Ghanaian embassy received an anonymous
phone call demanding that he and his family move out of the neighborhood or face
violent reprisal. On June 14, the ambassador of Niger was expelled from a bar in
Aberdeen, Maryland. On June 21, the ambassador of Cameroon reported that he
had been refused service in one restaurant and that his chauffeur had been forcibly
ejected from another. (Relevant documents can be found in various files at the John
F. Kennedy Library. See especially module 2 of "United States Policies on
Apartheid and Civil Rights," a curriculum prepared in 1977 by Joan A. Anderson,
Community College of Baltimore, Baltimore, Maryland.)

p. 120: "It is a matter of great regret": For an account of these and other incidents, see Debrah, "Effect of the Existence of Segregation," op. cit.

p. 121: "thrown on his rear end": Wofford, *Of Kennedys,* 127.

p. 121: something he could do about this problem: Even before the president's
request, Duke and his assistant Pedro Sanjuan had tried to cushion the shock of
American racism on the diplomatic corps. They had written letters to all governors
asking them to ensure that African diplomats would be accorded the proper respect
when they traveled through their state. The southern governors wrote back testily.
Orval Faubus, the Arkansas governor who had fought with Eisenhower over the
Little Rock school integration, said that he would oblige in the case of legitimate
diplomatic visits. "However," he cautioned, "if some of these people, prompted by
their Communist advisers, deliberately seek to create situations which will bring
about incidents then, of course, it will be very difficult to prevent them from doing
so (Orval Faubus to Angier Biddle Duke, April 25, 1961, module 2 of "United States
Policies on Apartheid and Civil Rights," op. cit.). The governor of Mississippi, John
Patterson, told Duke sanctimoniously that "we have the right to expect all visitors

who come to Alabama to obey our laws and respect our customs and I am sure that as long as visitors do this, they will have no difficulty in traveling to Alabama and our citizens will certainly extend to them the real genuine hospitality which southerners are noted for" (John Patterson to Angier Biddle Duke, September 7, 1961, module 2 of "United States Policies on Apartheid and Civil Rights," op. cit.).

p. 121: the attempt by the Protocol Office: See Harris Wofford, OH, JFKL.

p. 121: They called together representatives: See Sanjuan to Duke, "Background on the Route 40 Campaign," November 9, 1961, POF, Box 2, JFKL.

p. 121: "The effort along Route 40": See JFK to Duke, November 1, 1961; Dutton to JFK, November 3, 1961, POF, Box 2, JFKL.

p. 122: The president and his staff fretted: See Dutton to JFK: "CORE intends to stage a sit-in . . . this blatant action will undoubtedly set back the efforts at persuasion" (November 3, 1961, POF, Box 2, JFKL). Sanjuan did not share this negative opinion. See Sanjuan to Duke: "The efforts of CORE . . . should not be overlooked in recounting the efforts that eventually led to a partial solution" ("Background on the Route 40 Campaign," November 9, 1961, POF, Box 2, JFKL).

p. 122: "It is not enough just to apologize": Memorandum to the Secretary of Commerce and the Attorney General, POF, JFKL. The precise origin of this document is uncertain. Though undated, it bears a stamp that reads "received November 30, 1961," suggesting that it was drafted outside the White House and mailed to the president. There is also a penciled indication: "Nothing in file to indicate this was sent, May 12, 1962." In an interview with the author, Harris Wofford said that he could not remember this document specifically but that it sounded like something in which he had been involved.

p. 122: "Can't you tell them not to do it?": Wofford, *Of Kennedys,* 127. See also Harris Wofford, OH, JFKL.

p. 123: "is going to present problems": National Security Memorandum No. 77, NSF, JFKL.

p. 124: he urged Kennedy not to comment publicly: "I believe that a quiet, persistent, but unpublicized campaign appealing to the Portuguese understanding of our position might in time be successful," wrote McNamara. "The critical military importance of our rights and continued use of our facilities in the Azores and of securing extension of our rights in negotiations which must be undertaken in 1962 are such that any further public pressure on the Portuguese regarding the use of U.S. military material should be avoided" (McNamara to JFK, Memorandum for the President, "Portuguese Use of Military Equipment in Angola," NSF, Box 2, JFKL).

p. 124: Kennedy followed his advice: The resulting policy formulation—that American weapons could be used for defense against communism but not against nationalists—encouraged colonial and white supremacist governments to do exactly what Kennedy had wanted to avoid: insist that all nationalist upheavals and aspirations were inspired and controlled by Moscow.

p. 124: "The recent action of the prime minister": Bundy to Rusk, National Security Action Memorandum No. 33, "Review of U.S. Policy Toward South Africa," NSF, JFKL.

p. 125: Kennedy permitted five American navy vessels: *New York Times,* May 12, 1961.

p. 125: "there is much misunderstanding and misrepresentation": Rusk to Satterthwaite, August 25, 1961, NSF, JFKL.

p. 126: "be costly to us in the United Nations": Bowles to Bundy, September 21, 1961, NSF, JFKL.

p. 126: "if we are forced to take these actions": Ibid.

p. 127: "neither be deliberatively provocative": Wiesner to Bundy, October 18, 1961, NSF, JFKL.

p. 127: multiple policy reviews: The studies included the initial Ball task force study; the original policy statement on South Africa (to which cables refer but which the author never discovered in the archives); the May 1962 State Department "Guidelines for Policy and Operations, Republic of South Africa"; the July 1962 Planning Group working paper called "The White Redoubt"; and the group's May 1963 revision, "Problems of Southern Africa." There were also the many letters and reports written about the effect of the situation in southern Africa on the rest of Africa by Stevenson at the United Nations, Williams and Fredericks at the Africa Bureau, as well as an array of lower-level assessments such as the report by the U.S. embassy in Pretoria, "U.S. Overseas Internal Defense Policy," drafted in December 1962.

p. 128: "an imaginative combination of firmness and tact": See the Planning Group paper "The White Redoubt," July 22, 1962, NSF, JFKL.

p. 128: "move too far ahead": Satterthwaite to Fredericks, June 21, 1962, POF, JFKL.

p. 130: "The thing we talked about": Interview with Barbara Ward Jackson, oral history recorded by Walter and Elspeth Rostow, June 28, 1964, Washington, D.C., OH, 24–25, JFKL.

p. 131: "George Washington of Uganda": Harris Wofford, OH, JFKL.

p. 131: American Negro Leadership Conference on Africa: For a discussion of the ANLCA, see Philip V. White, "The Black American Constituency for Southern Africa, 1940–80," in Hero and Barratt, *American People,* 86ff. See also Houser, *No One Can Stop,* 266, and Milfred C. Fierce, "Selected Black American Leaders and Organizations and South Africa, 1900–1977: Some Notes," *Journal of Black Studies* 17.3 (March 1987): 305–26.

p. 132: State Department Advisory Council on African Affairs: For the full list and minutes of the meeting, see Fredericks to Bundy, Advisory Council on African Affairs, minutes of the first meeting, June 13–14, 1962, POF, JFKL. See also a list provided by Wayne Fredericks to the author and author interview with Wayne Fredericks, September 10, 1990.

p. 132: They also used them to defend: Ibid.

p. 132: "The leaders of the anti-colonial campaign": "While there has been unrest and turmoil in several other African countries," he said, "quiet conditions prevail in South Africa in spite of strenuous efforts by subversive elements in London, New York, Accra, and Cairo, acting in concert with Bantu subversive organizations, to stir up trouble in the republic." For the text of Louw's speech and substantial commentary on the reaction in the United Nations, see *New York Times,* October 12, 1961.

p. 132: Verwoerd's favorite rationalizations: Separate development, Louw insisted, "is equally in the interests of the white and the Bantu population. It is intended to safeguard what has been built up over three centuries by the whites. . . . [It] also provides for progressively increased legislative, judicial, and administrative powers for the Bantu authorities in their own territories . . . The territories, mostly situated in the most fertile areas in South Africa, were voluntarily occupied by the Bantu tribes, which at the time of the arrival of the first Dutch immigrants, were themselves migrating from Central and East Africa."

p. 133: "while we reject the views": *New York Times,* October 12, 1961.

p. 133: "the new frontier" in Africa: *New York Times,* September 25, 1962.

p. 134: worked to deflect the drive: See, for example, Cleveland and Williams to Rusk, "Policy of South Africa and the South West Africa Problem—Approval Requested," October 3, 1962, NSF, JFKL. The assistant secretaries asked Rusk to authorize the delegation to seek an advisory opinion from the International Court of Justice whether the United Nations could unilaterally revoke the mandate. Even this, they argued, would put a "very great" strain on the "bilateral prong of our present two-pronged policy toward South Africa."

p. 134: When the Soviet Union charged: See *New York Times,* October 12, 1962. The quotation from the ambassador is actually a paraphrase of Stevenson's. See Stevenson to Department of State, "Africans at the Seventeenth General Assembly, 1962," part 1, "The Africans and the Problem of Apartheid," January 23, 1963, NSF, 5, JFKL.

p. 134: the creation of a UN Special Committee on Apartheid: See the *New York Times* stories on Resolution 1761 and other votes, November 6 and 7, 1962.

p. 134: more than three-fifths of South Africa's imports: *New York Times,* November 9, 1962.

p. 134: Rusk's advisers told him: See, for example, Cleveland and Williams to Rusk, "Policy of South Africa," op. cit. The writers note that this was "at best a stopgap measure of one year's duration."

p. 134: Undersecretary Chester Bowles: Bowles report, November 13, 1962, NSF, JFKL. The document in the archives has been sanitized, and the actual reference to South Africa is blacked out, but no other country makes sense in the context of the paragraph.

p. 134: "the breaking of diplomatic relations": Stevenson to Department of State, "Africans at the Seventeenth General Assembly," op. cit., 6.

p. 135: "the longest conference ever held by Negroes": Quoted in Branch, *Parting the Waters,* 684.

p. 135: diplomatic telephone lines to the State Department: See the many cables on the issue from December 1962, NSF, Box 3, JFKL.

p. 135: "Senator Ellender's remark that Africans do not have": Morrow to Bundy, December 5, 1962, NSF, Box 3, JFKL.

p. 136: "something worse than the Congo": *New York Times,* March 8, 1963.

p. 136: Rusk . . . instructed Ambassador Satterthwaite: Rusk to Satterthwaite, February 11, 1963; see also Satterthwaite to Rusk, March 12, 1963, NSF, Box 3, JFKL.

p. 136: "If South Africa's international position": Rusk to JFK, March 16, 1963, NSF, JFKL.

p. 136: "on balance it is desirable": Kaysen to Rusk, March 22, 1963, NSF, Box 3, JFKL.

p. 137: "I don't know what will happen": Branch, *Parting the Waters,* 729.

p. 138: "we do not believe that these days": Ibid., 738.

p. 138: "We will reach the goal of freedom": Ibid., 743.

p. 138: enough power to strip the bark from trees: The description is from ibid., 759.

p. 139: "Mr. Kennedy . . . is battling for the minds": Quoted in ibid., 823.

p. 140: more than fourteen hundred Soviet radio commentaries: See Thomas L. Hughes, Bureau of Intelligence and Research, to Dean Rusk, June 14, 1963, NSF, Box 3, JFKL.

p. 140: "If America's rulers can act": Ibid., 3.

p. 140: "This nation was founded": "Remarks of the President on Nationwide Radio and Television," Office of the White House Press Secretary, June 11, 1963, NSF, Box 3, JFKL.

p. 141: "one of the most eloquent": Branch, *Parting the Waters,* 824.

p. 141: Diplomats scattered around the world: See, for example, one cable from the U.S. representative at a meeting of the International Labor Organization (ILO) in Geneva, where Africans had been trying to oust the South African delegates. The ambassador thanked the president for his "great and heart-warming speech," noting that it was "most helpful at the difficult ILO conference where we need all the African support we can get" (Tubby to Kennedy, June 12, 1963, NSF, Box 3, JFKL).

p. 142: "Foreign reaction is the source of great concern": Dean Rusk to all embassies, June 19, 1963, NSF, Box 3, JFKL.

p. 142: "not necessarily the best thing": Schneidman, *American Foreign Policy,* 279.

p. 142: a committee appointed by the president: Ibid., 124.

p. 142: "I have a spot for one more state visit": See author interview with Wayne Fredericks, April 19, 1990.

p. 143: an invitation to visit the White House: John F. Kennedy to Julius K. Nyerere, President of the Republic of Tanganyika, June 14, 1963, NSF, JFKL.

p. 143: "we must now take a more vigorous stand": G. Mennen Williams to the Secretary of State via Mr. Averell Harriman, June 12, 1963, NSF, JFKL. The letter has been sanitized, presumably to delete references to the American military relationship to South Africa.

p. 143: "South Africa continues to be friendly": Deputy Undersecretary U. Alexis Johnson to the Secretary of State, June 14, 1963, NSF, JFKL.

p. 143: "At the heart of the issue": Memorandum from Secretary of State Dean Rusk to Harriman, Johnson, Williams, Tyler, and Rostow, June 15, 1963, NSF, Box 1, JFKL.

p. 144: Rusk assembled a committee: Dean Rusk to McGeorge Bundy, June 20, 1963, NSF, JFKL.

p. 144: Martin Luther King had requested an appearance: Adlai Stevenson to Dean Rusk, June 3, 1963, NSF, Box 159, JFKL.

p. 145: "Certainly both the Special Committee": Memorandum for the President from Secretary of State Dean Rusk, Subject: Appearance of Martin Luther King before the United Nations Special Committee, June 21, 1963, NSF, Box 159, JFKL.

p. 146: King asked for evidence: Branch, *Parting the Waters,* 837.

p. 146: King abruptly told the special committee: Author interview with George Houser, September 10, 1990. It is possible that the correspondence from the period which is stored at the Martin Luther King Center in Atlanta, Georgia, and which has not yet been opened up for scholarly review will eventually shed light on this.

p. 146: Newspaper editors and television commentators: See, for example, *Washington Report,* CBS News, June 16, 1963.

p. 146: "When the African states bring apartheid": Adlai Stevenson to John F. Kennedy, June 26, 1963, NSF, JFKL.

p. 147: a junior official named Harold Brown: Brown's document noted that "our primary interest in the Republic of South Africa is because of its geographical location. All U.S. satellites launched from the east coast on inclined orbits and from the west coast on polar orbits pass over the republic of South Africa and the Indian Ocean area on the first and most critical orbit. This region is of particular importance because of the critical events in the trajectory which must be recorded from these locations" (Harold Brown, Memorandum for the Deputy Assistant Secretary of Defense for International Security Affairs, June 8, 1963, NSF, JFKL).

p. 147: Carl Kaysen collected the exchange of letters: Carl Kaysen to John F. Kennedy, Memorandum to the President, July 4, 1963, NSF, JFKL.

p. 147: black Africans "were elated": See Benjamin Read to McGeorge Bundy, July 7, 1963, and its attachment, "Status Report of African Reactions to Civil Rights in the United States," July 6, 1963. See a similar report for the week ending July 12, 1963. NSF, JFKL.

p. 147: When Joseph Satterthwaite had paid a courtesy call: Satterthwaite to Rusk, May 7, 1963, NSF, JFKL.

p. 147: "non-white guests . . . will be known": Joseph Satterthwaite to Dean Rusk, May 16, 1963, NSF, JFKL.

p. 148: despite appeals to their patriotism: See William Brubeck to McGeorge Bundy, July 12, 1963, NSF, JFKL.

p. 148: "the US requirements in the Azores": Memorandum from the Joint Chiefs of Staff for the Secretary of Defense, July 10, 1963, NSF, JFKL.

p. 148: "We recommend that the United States": Secretary of Defense Robert S. McNamara to Secretary of State Dean Rusk, July 10, 1963, NSF, JFKL.

p. 148: "establish a precedent": George Ball to John F. Kennedy, "US Policy Regarding Portuguese Territories and Apartheid in South Africa," July 13, 1963. This memo was not in the Kennedy archives but was made available to the author by a researcher who had obtained it from a private collection. Another memorandum, "US Strategy in UN Security Council re Portuguese Territories" (NSF, JFKL), does not identify its author, but based on its voice, content (which overlaps little with the first memo), date (July 13), and physical appearance (it seems to have been written on the same typewriter and in the same manner as the first), it is likely that the author was also Ball, especially since Bundy attached his own comments to the earlier Ball memo.

p. 149: Kennedy spent several days pondering: Kennedy's primary concern remained the consequences of American or United Nations actions on U.S. use of the Azores. See the record, declassified at the author's request, of the National Security Council meeting on July 15, "Memorandum for the Record: Meeting with the President on African Problems, Monday July 15, 1963," NSF, JFKL. The meeting was attended by Ball, Williams, McNamara, Bundy, and Schlesinger, among others.

p. 149: "a little nation which needed support": See U.S. Department of State, Memorandum of Conversation between Secretary of State Dean Rusk and W. C. Naudé, Ambassador of the Republic of South Africa, July 17, 1963, NSF, 3, JFKL.

p. 150: "let us try that this time": Schneidman, *American Foreign Policy,* 125.

p. 150: "Our discussion with the South Africans": McGeorge Bundy to the Secretary of State, July 17, 1963, NSF, Box 159, JFKL.

p. 150: "We expect to bring to an end": Rusk to Stevenson, NSF, Box 159, JFKL.

p. 150: The *New York Times* reported: *New York Times,* August 3, 1963.

p. 150: Great Britain, trying to climb on the bandwagon: *New York Times,* August 4, 1963.

p. 151: "civilizing mission": Schneidman, *American Foreign Policy,* 131.

p. 151: Conversation between Rusk and Naudé: Memorandum of conversation between the Secretary of State and the South African Ambassador, "The South African Program of Grouping Independent Bantu States," July 20, 1963, NSF, JFKL.

p. 153: even most liberal whites did not support such a scheme: See, for example, Joseph Satterthwaite to Dean Rusk, Telegram 416, September 30, 1963, concerning a meeting with Jan Steytler, the head of the Progressive Party. NSF, JFKL.

p. 153: whether the solution to South Africa's problems: See, for example, Adlai Stevenson to Dean Rusk, Telegram 522, August 21, 1963, NSF, JFKL.

p. 153: "we know that there is far more understanding": U.S. Embassy Pretoria to Secretary of State, Telegram 266, August 28, 1963, NSF, JFKL.

p. 153: "a new bid for Western support": Central Intelligence Agency, Special Report, "New South Africa Bid for Western Support," September 13, 1963, NSF, Box 159, JFKL.

p. 153: Walt Rostow's Policy Planning Bureau: Department of State, National Strategy Series, South Africa (intermediate draft), dated October 28, 1963, 212–16, NSF, JFKL.

p. 154: George Ball sent a memorandum: George Ball to John F. Kennedy, Memorandum for the President, "Sale to South Africa of Submarines and of Spare Parts for C-130's," August 28, 1963, NSF, Box 159, JFKL.

p. 154: "To enter now into new contracts": Adlai Stevenson to Dean Rusk, September 12, 1963, NSF, Box 159, JFKL.

p. 154: the two secretaries sent over a memorandum: Dean Rusk and Robert McNamara to John F. Kennedy, Memorandum for the President, "Sale of Submarines to South Africa," September 16, 1963, NSF, Box 159, JFKL.

p. 155: Kennedy again hesitated: Benjamin Read to McGeorge Bundy, September 16, 1963, NSF, Box 159, JFKL.

p. 155: "made clear to the South Africans": McGeorge Bundy to Dean Rusk and Robert McNamara, September 23, 1963, NSF, Box 159, JFKL.

p. 155: "imminent threat to U.S. leadership": See, for example, Adlai Stevenson to Dean Rusk, Telegram 522, August 21, 1963, NSF, JFKL.

p. 155: he urged Kennedy to expand the arms embargo: Dean Rusk to John F. Kennedy, Memorandum for the President, November 6, 1963, NSF, Box 159, JFKL.

p. 156: "Having made a major concession": John F. Kennedy to the Secretary of State, November 7, 1963, NSF, Box 159, JFKL.

p. 156: "Given its political difficulties": William H. Brubeck to John F. Kennedy, Memorandum for the President, "South African Submarine Sales," November 19, 1963, NSF, Box 159, JFKL.

CHAPTER FOUR: **The Varieties of Dissent**

p. 157: "I consider myself neither legally nor morally bound": Mandela made this statement at his 1962 trial. For descriptions and slightly different versions of Mandela's statement, see Benson, *Mandela,* 188ff; Woods, *Biko,* 22ff; Mandela, *Struggle,* 125ff.

p. 158: Ireland, Italy, and Israel all deserved: See Schneidman, *American Foreign Policy,* 185.

p. 159: "foreigners and foreign affairs": Ibid., 174.

p. 159: senior officials in the State and Defense Departments: For a complete account of the 1964 presidential campaign, see White, *Making, 1964.* Johnson freely used government agencies such as Defense, State, and the Federal Bureau of Investigation to provide information and counter Republican charges. White describes, for example, how Barry Goldwater's charge that American missiles were "undependable" produced an immediate response from McNamara's staff at the Pentagon (103).

p. 159: Johnson appointed Averell Harriman: For a description of these events, see Nielsen, *Great Powers,* 307; Schneidman, *American Foreign Policy,* 163.

p. 159: When Rusk and Ball learned about Williams's intentions: Schneidman, *American Foreign Policy,* 164.

p. 159: "We began a revolt from colonial rule": Nielsen, *Great Powers,* 306.

p. 160: On the first day of the proceedings: For accounts of the 1962 trial, see Benson, *Mandela,* 188ff; Woods, *Biko,* 22ff; Mandela, *Struggle,* 125ff; Mandela, *Long Walk,* 277, 282.

p. 161: "Through my cross-examination": Mandela, *Long Walk,* 286.

p. 161: "For the first time in my career": Ibid.

p. 161: "It has not been easy": Mandela, *Struggle,* 150–52.

p. 162: "I had never been in isolation": Mandela, *Long Walk,* 291.

p. 162: After an all-night drive: Ibid., 296.

p. 163: There, guarded by legions of white police: Benson, *Mandela,* 132; Mandela, *Long Walk,* 296.

p. 163: By the middle of 1963: For a discussion of sabotage in this period, see Lodge, *Black Politics,* chap. 10.

p. 163: saboteurs managed to blow up: *New York Times,* March 22, 1963.

p. 163: "until this side of eternity": Benson, *Mandela,* 133.

p. 163: killed a young ANC member: Ibid.

p. 163: Walter Sisulu tried to leap: Meer, *Higher than Hope,* 161.

p. 163: Although the ANC planners: Benson makes this point, *Mandela,* 135.

p. 164: "Mr. X": For Mtolo's account of the events before, during, and after the Rivonia trial and his impassioned plea for Zulus to accept apartheid, see Mtolo, *Umkhonto,* esp. chaps. 19, 25.

p. 165: Winnie appealed directly: Meer, *Higher than Hope,* 162.

p. 165: he was not permitted to read: Benson, *Mandela,* 145.

p. 165: "thirty years of my life have been spent": Ibid., 147.

p. 165: Mandela led the court: Mandela, *Struggle,* 160.

p. 165: To the crucial charge: Ibid., 163.

p. 166: "There has often been close cooperation": Ibid., 169.

p. 167: "The sentence in the case of all of the accused": Benson, *Mandela,* 162–63.

p. 168: In late May: *New York Times,* May 31, 1964.

p. 168: In early June: "Eleven Stage Rights Sit-in at South Africa U.N. Mission," *New York Times,* June 5, 1964. The article does not specify who participated in this sit-in.

p. 168: "to most of the world": *New York Times,* June 14, 1964.

p. 168: "The cables went straight into the wastebasket": Botha, *Verwoerd Is Dead,* 113.

p. 169: Gold production and reserves soared: Hepple, *Verwoerd,* 184.

p. 169: American direct investment doubled: For information on U.S. investment, see Department of Commerce, "Survey of Current Business," as well as Clark, *U.S. Corporate Interests.*

p. 169: "has not given the racial situation": *New York Times,* August 18, 1963.

p. 169: "I'd rather invest in South Africa": *New York Times,* August 18, 1963.

p. 169: "the faith we have in South Africa": Mackler, *Pattern for Profit,* 28.

p. 170: "I think South Africa is going to remain": Ibid.

p. 170: "have complete faith in the soundness": Ibid., 27.

p. 170: Caltex and Weyerhauser: See the notes from the meetings between Timothy Smith and the managing directors of these firms' South African subsidiaries in the summer of 1970, ICCR Active Files.

p. 170: He set up a quasi-governmental corporation: See Cawthra, *Brutal Force,* 16.

p. 170: He announced the construction of numerous military airfields: See "Airfields Built by South Africa," *New York Times,* June 4, 1964.

p. 170: a fleet of American Boeing 707s: Botha, *Verwoerd Is Dead,* 137.

p. 170: Verwoerd established a new Nuclear Institute: Ibid.

p. 171: "the United Party lay down like curs": Strangwayes-Booth, *Cricket in the Thorn Tree,* 214.

p. 172: "My God! I have got a safe seat": Ibid., 62.

p. 172: "a lonely little baldhead": Ibid., 69.

p. 173: "Strangely enough . . . people like to enjoy": Ibid., 202.

p. 173: "she is putting up a parliamentary performance": Ibid., 218.

p. 173: "I forgive you": Ibid., 182.

p. 173: "Go preach in a synagogue": Ibid., 144.

p. 174: "my grandmother had a parrot": Ibid., 121.

p. 174: "It was almost as if the father-figure": Ibid., 211.

p. 174: "You are of no account!": Ibid., 215.

p. 174: "I suppose I have my uses": Ibid., 226.

p. 174: "like a cricket in a thorn tree": Ibid., 218; see also Joseph Lelyveld, "Minority of One in South Africa's Parliament," *New York Times Magazine,* March 20, 1966, 35.

p. 174: "more South Africans": Lelyveld, "Minority of One," op. cit., 94.

p. 175: "simultaneously and to all members": de Gruchy, *Church Struggle,* 7–8.

p. 175: In 1853 church leaders approved: "The synod considers it desirable and scriptural that our members from the Heathen be received and absorbed into our existing congregations wherever possible," said the final resolution, "but where this measure, as a result of the weakness of some, impedes the furtherance of the cause of Christ among the Heathen, the congregation from the Heathen, already to be founded or still to be founded, shall enjoy its Christian privilege in a separate building or institution" (ibid., 8).

p. 176: antebellum southern clergy took to defending slavery: Branch, *Parting the Waters,* 741. Frederickson also discusses the same phenomenon in *White Supremacy.*

p. 176: "an ecclesiological blueprint": de Gruchy, *Church Struggle,* 9.

p. 176: Christian nationalism: See de Gruchy, *Church Struggle,* x.

p. 176: The Anglican Church endured fierce battles: See Reader's Digest Association, *Illustrated Guide,* 156. The Anglican Church also had disputes about its relationship with the indigenous peoples of South Africa. In the 1860s, the Anglican bishop of Natal, John Colenso, was charged with heresy for expressing liberal reservations about the historical accuracy of the Book of Genesis; an important component of the official attack on Colenso was the bishop's record as an advocate for the Zulus against British rapacity.

p. 177: "the general cry for equality": Dutch Reformed Churches of South Africa, *Statements on Race Relations* (Johannesburg: Information Bureau of the Dutch Reformed Church, November 1960), 7.

p. 177: "though it occasionally talks in its sleep": de Gruchy, *Church Struggle,* vii; see also Huddleston, *Naught for Your Comfort,* 107.

p. 177: white clergy held all the leading positions: For detailed discussions of the failure of the white churches to live up to their own principles, see Cochrane, *Servants of Power,* and Villa-Vicencio, *Trapped in Apartheid.*

p. 178: "We cannot condone the continuous besmirching": Dutch Reformed Churches of South Africa, *Statements on Race Relations,* op. cit., 13.

p. 178: Joost de Blank: For a biography, see Peart-Binns, *Archbishop Joost de Blank,* esp. chaps. 8–13. For a contemporary description, see Edwin S. Munger, *Christians and Race Relations in South Africa—the Anglican Church"* (New York: American Universities Field Staff Reports Service, 1961); see also de Gruchy, *Church Struggle,* 63ff, and contemporary press accounts.

p. 178: de Blank insisted that the World Council of Churches: *New York Times,* April 8, 1960; see also Munger, *Christians and Race Relations,* op. cit., 21, and Peart-Binns, *Archbishop Joost de Blank,* chap. 13.

p. 178: "The future of Christianity in this country": de Gruchy, *Church Struggle,* 63.

p. 178: denounced de Blank as a hypocrite: *New York Times,* April 10, 1960. De Blank had been taunted with this claim by the Nationalists since his arrival in South Africa.

p. 178: "the expulsion of the Dutch Reformed Church": de Gruchy, *Church Struggle,* 64; also quoted in Peart-Binns, *Archbishop Joost de Blank,* 167. The view was echoed by the archbishop of Canterbury, Geoffrey Fisher, who privately repeated the comment of Michael Ramsay, the archbishop of York: "You do not cure one form of apartheid by inventing another" (see Peart-Binns, *Archbishop Joost de Blank,* 167).

p. 179: "all racial groups who permanently inhabit": de Gruchy, *Church Struggle,* 66.

p. 181: "ruthlessness of logic": Ryan, *Beyers Naudé,* 20. Naudé confirmed this impression in a conversation with the author in 1991.

p. 181: Naudé was inducted into the Broederbond: Ryan, *Beyers Naudé,* 33.

p. 182: As a youth, Naudé recalled: Lelyveld, *Move Your Shadow,* 304.

p. 182: his thoughts on Alan Paton's book: Ibid., 306.

p. 182: "If this is what apartheid is about": Ryan, *Beyers Naudé,* 48.

p. 183: "I asked myself": Ibid., 62.

p. 183: "I simply had to accept": Ibid., 67.

p. 184: "the God-given right and freedom": Ibid., 81.

p. 185: When his mother died: Ibid., 118.

p. 185: Johnson's relationship with the attorney general: Schlesinger, *Robert Kennedy,* passim.

p. 186: Johnson knew in his gut: Ibid., 657.

p. 186: "I knew that if I didn't get out front": Quoted in ibid., 644.

p. 186: "was dampened by the sadness": Ibid., 645.

p. 186: "an understanding of the fact": Garrow, *Bearing the Cross,* 338.

p. 187: "observe a moratorium": Garrow, Ibid., 343.

p. 187: One of the most effective means: For a general discussion of the history of boycotts, see Smith, *Morality.*

p. 187: King had told the leaders: Garrow, *Bearing the Cross,* 297.

p. 187: "A massive refusal to buy": Garrow, *Bearing the Cross,* 297.

p. 188: largest percentage: For the precise figures, see White, *Making, 1964,* 381, 405.

p. 188: King's . . . December 1965 trip: During his visit to Scandinavia, King stopped in Stockholm and met with the renowned social scientists Gunnar and Alva

Myrdal. Two decades before, Gunnar Myrdal had written a highly influential book on racism in America called *The American Dilemma;* his wife had served as Swedish ambassador to India and then as the chair of a special United Nations study commission on apartheid. Their daughter Sissela was married to Derek Bok, who six years later became president of Harvard University, a position from which he had to struggle with the apartheid question, as described in later chapters.

p. 188: "More and more I have come to realize": Garrow, *Bearing the Cross,* 364.

p. 189: "when the King of Norway": Garrow, *Bearing the Cross,* 386.

p. 189: Robert Kennedy told his friends: Schlesinger, *Robert Kennedy,* 780.

p. 190: He told the governor bluntly: Garrow, *Bearing the Cross,* 407.

p. 190: "when history and fate meet": Ibid., 408.

p. 190: in the shadow of the Confederate flag: *New York Times,* March 26, 1965.

p. 190: "it is time to start thinking": *New York Times,* March 28, 1965.

p. 191: "You know, Bayard": Garrow, *Bearing the Cross,* 439.

p. 191: harm blacks more than whites: This is an example of what Albert Hirschman calls the "perversity thesis" *(Rhetoric of Reaction).*

p. 191: nationwide boycott of products: For example, he raised the idea immediately after the march to Montgomery, on March 28 on the television program *Meet the Press.* See Garrow, *Bearing the Cross,* 414.

p. 191: Born in Ohio in 1916: Houser, *No One Can Stop.*

p. 192: Houser had collected three hundred dollars: Ibid., 14.

p. 192: While more than four hundred students: "49 Arrested at Chase Building in Protest on South Africa Loans," *New York Times,* March 20, 1965. According to Arthur Waskow, a member of SDS and one of the people arrested, "a number of students who took part in the Chase demonstration reported that on their campuses, some faculty and students responded to information about American business support of apartheid with an even deeper sense of moral outrage than they ordinarily gave either racial inequality within the United States or the war in Vietnam" (see *Liberation,* February 1966, quoted by Hauck and Voorhes, *Two Decades,* 9).

p. 193: "so long as our own government": "49 Arrested at Chase Building," op. cit.

p. 193: "We can't be the arbiter of social affairs": "Chase Manhattan Chief Predicts No Antitrust Suit against Bank," *New York Times,* March 31, 1965.

p. 193: "The large majority of the human race": Manuscript copy, "Address of Dr. Martin Luther King on December 10, 1965, for the South Africa Benefit of the American Committee on Africa, Hunter College," Martin Luther King Jr. Library and Archives, Atlanta, Georgia.

p. 194: Johnson sent twenty-two thousand: See Schlesinger, *Robert Kennedy,* 690.

p. 195: "unilateral declaration of independence": For a comprehensive treatment of American policy decisions at the time of the declaration, see Lake, *Tar Baby,* esp. chap. 3.

p. 195: United States had to spend four million dollars: Ibid., 90.

p. 196: Operation Sparrow: Schneidman, *American Foreign Policy,* 178.

p. 196: the last attempt by the American government: Ibid., 183.

p. 196: forcing Verwoerd to purchase them: The French submarines were formally ordered by Vorster in 1967; the first one was delivered in July 1970. See *New York Times,* June 21, 1971, and December 12, 1971.

p. 196: The official policy . . . was a nonpolicy: See, for example, U.S. Department of Commerce, Special Report on Africa, "Sales Frontier for US Business," March 1963.

p. 197: While testifying before the House subcommittee: See the statement of G. Mennen Williams, assistant secretary of state for African affairs, House Committee on Foreign Affairs, Subcommittee on Africa, *United States–South Africa Relations*, 89th Cong., 2nd sess., 1966. During the hearings Williams commented: "It is frequently said that in the last analysis the people of South Africa must work out their own destiny. But how is this to take place when the internal forces for change are so effectively repressed? It is also pointed out that in South Africa economic forces are breaking down segregationist practices and isolationist patterns of thought. But how are such changes to be translated into the political and social fields? How long will it take? And what can outside forces do to accelerate the process?" For additional commentary, see "Williams Backs Apartheid Fight, Calls Race Issue Key to U.S. Thinking on South Africa," *New York Times,* March 2, 1966.

p. 197: "The president's view": McGeorge Bundy from R. W. Komer and Rick Haynes, March 10, 1965, Lyndon Johnson Presidential Library, National Security Files, Africa, Box 76, quoted in Schneidman, *American Foreign Policy,* 189. Ironically, Johnson—and some civil rights leaders—reversed the argument when King began to denounce the Vietnam War. Then, they said, blacks should stick to the particular cause of securing their own civil rights and not get involved with broader national issues like the war. See, for example, the debate at the SCLC annual convention in 1965, Garrow, *Bearing the Cross,* 437.

p. 198: "the key to an American president's standing": Memorandum for the President from Bill Moyers, June 14, 1965, LBJ Papers, 1963–1969, Box 6, Lyndon Johnson Presidential Library, quoted in Schneidman, *American Foreign Policy,* 196.

p. 198: King's and Kennedy's invitations to South Africa: Schlesinger, *Robert Kennedy,* 743. There is a small inconsistency about these invitations. Janet Levine writes that King was invited first by the National Union of South African Students and then, when his visa was denied, Kennedy was invited (*Inside Apartheid,* 81). Yet Kennedy and King were denied visas at the same time. This suggests that the organization invited the men simultaneously.

p. 198: "it would not be convenient": "Robert Kennedy Gets Visa to Visit South Africa," *New York Times,* March 23, 1966.

p. 198: For more than a year: Schneidman, *American Foreign Policy,* 194.

p. 198: "It is highly desirable": Schneidman, *American Foreign Policy,* 220.

p. 199: "big news throughout the world": Memo from Moyers to the President, May 26, 1966, NSF, National Security Council History, Box 14, Lyndon Johnson Presidential Library, quoted in Schneidman, *American Foreign Policy,* 225.

p. 199: "Across the continent the majority of people": Schneidman, *American Foreign Policy,* 226.

p. 199: "We will not permit human rights": This quotation is from the *New York Times,* "America and Apartheid," editorial, June 8, 1966. Schneidman also uses part of it (*American Foreign Policy,* 226).

p. 199: "the boldest statement on Africa": Schneidman, *American Foreign Policy,* 228.

p. 200: "obnoxious and reprehensible organization": Levine, *Inside Apartheid,* 80.

p. 200: The terms stipulated that Robertson: Ibid., 82.

p. 200: "take full account of": "Mr. Kennedy's Visit," *Sunday Times* (South Africa), June 5, 1966.

p. 201: despite Prime Minister Verwoerd's instruction: "Kennedy Still Wants to See Verwoerd," *Sunday Times* (South Africa), June 5, 1966. "I Got Cold Shoulder from Govt.—Kennedy," *Rand Daily Mail,* June 6, 1966.

p. 201: "I quite understand his feelings": *Rand Daily Mail,* June 6, 1966.

p. 201: The businessmen irked Kennedy: Schlesinger, *Robert Kennedy,* 745.

p. 201: the greatest speech of his career: Schlesinger says simply, "It was Kennedy's greatest speech" (*Robert Kennedy,* 746).

p. 201: "The way of opposition to communism": For the full text of Robert Kennedy's speech on the Day of Affirmation in Cape Town, June 6, 1966, see *Robert F. Kennedy in South Africa,* a souvenir booklet compiled by the *Rand Daily Mail.* The printed text differs slightly from Kennedy's spoken words, which can be heard in the Apartheid series on *Frontline,* tape 2, WGBH, Boston, 1988.

p. 202: Kennedy journeyed to the University of Stellenbosch: In his speech, Kennedy made an indirect reference to the work of Martin Luther King. "A pattern of unity is woven into every aspect of the society of man," said Kennedy. "We are protected from tetanus by the work of Japanese scientists, from typhoid by the work of a Russian, an Austrian taught us to transfuse blood and an Italian to protect ourselves from malaria, and an Indian and a grandson of a Negro slave taught us to achieve major social changes without violence." For a detailed analysis of Kennedy's speech at Stellenbosch, see Harriet J. Rudolph, "Robert F. Kennedy at Stellenbosch University," *Communication Quarterly* 31.3 (Summer 1983).

On leaving Stellenbosch Kennedy was informed that a few hours after his speech in Cape Town, James Meredith, the black student who had been at the center of the confrontation at the University of Mississippi in 1962, had been wounded by a blast from a 16-gauge shotgun as he began a two-hundred-mile solo "walk against fear" in Mississippi. Civil rights leaders, including Martin Luther King, descended on the site of the ambush and vowed to finish the march, though the increasingly bitter arguments between the radical SNCC and the more moderate NAACP and Urban League leaders finally drove the moderates away. Kennedy, when asked about the shooting, told the press that he was shocked. "I walked with Meredith during difficult days," he said, "and I know he is dedicated to his country and to human equality" (*Rand Daily Mail,* June 8, 1966).

p. 203: "I haven't met with so many people": "Kennedy Invited Back to South Africa," *New York Times,* June 8, 1966.

p. 203: "one of the most impressive men": "Kennedy Meets Luthuli and Finds Him Impressive," *New York Times,* June 9, 1966.

p. 203: where he remained until two o'clock in the morning: Levine, *Inside Apartheid,* 94.

p. 203: "Senator Robert Kennedy's visit": *Rand Daily Mail,* June 9, 1966; also quoted in Schlesinger, *Robert Kennedy,* 748.

p. 203: "I would gather up everything": Schlesinger, *Robert Kennedy,* 748.

p. 203: "at the present time": "Kennedy Warns on Racial Issue," *New York Times,* June 10, 1966.

p. 203: "Like a meteor": Schlesinger, *Robert Kennedy,* 749. Shortly after his return, Kennedy wrote a provocative article for *Look* magazine entitled "What if God Is Black?" (*Look,* August 23, 1966). Also about this time, Kennedy sent a questionnaire to American companies inquiring about their South African operations. Hauck and Voorhes suggest that this was in 1965 (*Two Decades of Debate* '95), but it would fit better in 1966, given Kennedy's remarks about corporate responsibility that followed his trip.

p. 204: England would embargo future arms shipments: *New York Times,* November 18, 1964; see also, Botha, *Verwoerd Is Dead,* 119.

p. 204: Wilson struggled to maintain the ban: Wilson engaged in a second major battle over extending the South African embargo in December 1967; see *New York Times,* December 17, 1967.

p. 204: all American Negro sailors: *New York Times,* May 14, 1965; Botha, *Verwoerd Is Dead,* 125; Hepple, *Verwoerd,* 200–201.

p. 204: South Africa had always required: See Joseph Lelyveld, "Verwoerd Race Bar Challenges US at Space Tracking Stations, *New York Times,* June 28, 1965. The American agencies denied that there were any specific racial provisions in the agreement but noted that most of those working at the facilities were South African. See Douglas MacArthur II, Assistant Secretary of State for Congressional Relations, to Rep. Charles C. Diggs Jr., July 15, 1965, and James E. Webb, Administrator of NASA, to Charles C. Diggs Jr., July 10, 1965, Box 194, Diggs Collection.

p. 204: vigorous protest from some South African businessmen: According to both South African and American press reports, South African business leader Major General Sir Francis de Guingand, the chairman of the board of Rothmans Cigarettes, and others communicated their strong objections to Verwoerd directly. See "Business Protest at Attacks on U.S. Reported," *East Province Herald,* July 20, 1965; "Americans Feel Verwoerd Harms US-SA Relations," *East London Daily Dispatch,* July 21, 1965.

p. 204: The police jailed hundreds: For examples of its application, see *New York Times,* April 22, May 5, June 11, July 4, July 10, July 12, July 28, and August 24, 1964.

p. 205: Fischer's arrest and trial: For foreign coverage of the arrest and trial, see *New York Times,* July 10, July 11, September 24, October 3, November 17, and November 27, 1964; January 26, 1965; January 29, February 3, March 29, May 5, May 10, May 15, August 14, and August 16, 1966. See also D'Oliveira, *Vorster,* 166–67. In his autobiography, Mandela twice describes his admiration for Fischer: "As an Afrikaner whose conscience forced him to reject his own heritage and be ostracized by his own people he showed a level of courage and sacrifice that was in a class by itself"; "I fought only against injustice, not my own people" (Mandela, *Long Walk,* 340, 411).

p. 205: Fifteen thousand people: See Hepple, *Verwoerd,* 116.

p. 205: "we must be prepared to die": Ibid., 201.

p. 205: the government's treatment of the Coloured population: For an interesting contemporary discussion of the Coloured population under apartheid, see Joseph Lelyveld, *New York Times Magazine,* May 15, 1966.

p. 205: He ordered the removal: District Six was declared a white area in 1966 and gradually cleared over the next fifteen years.

p. 206: not primarily a territorial concept: See Botha, *Verwoerd Is Dead,* 74, 116, 146ff.

p. 206: The first winner: For information on the cult of personality surrounding Hendrik Verwoerd, see Hepple, *Verwoerd,* 199ff. See also Grobbelaar, *This Was a Man,* 146.

p. 207: "I'll miss you, Helen": "One Woman Opposition Charms South Africa," *New York Times,* January 25, 1966.

p. 207: "I think I have a good chance": Ibid.

p. 207: Suzman again squeaked by: Strangwayes-Booth, *Cricket in the Thorn Tree,* 226.

p. 207: Verwoerd was elated: Verwoerd's enthusiasm can be seen from his comments at the time. In a radio address he told the country that "the negative approaches of white rule forever over territories belonging to the black man, or of ultimate black supremacy over the country of the white have been clearly rejected. A mandate has been given for the positive approach of developing the different national groups of South Africa separately. In its own territory, each nation will increasingly determine its own future as it becomes more capable of ruling itself." Not long afterward he told a banquet audience that South Africa's future was bright for everyone except those who dreamed of a multiracial South Africa (Grobbelaar, *This Was a Man,* 146). "To those few who seek to change all this into something wholly new which would bring us to disaster and chaos as elsewhere in Africa—for them I have no word to say, and with them I have no patience" (ibid.; see also Strangwayes-Booth, *Cricket in the Thorn Tree,* 223).

p. 207: the World Court . . . dismissed the complaint: See the extensive international press coverage given this issue beginning on July 19, 1966.

p. 207: the South African ambassador announced: *New York Times,* August 18, 1966.

p. 208: "not to interfere": Grobbelaar, *This Was a Man,* 155.

p. 208: On Tuesday morning, September 6: For the description of the events of September 6, see Botha, *Verwoerd Is Dead,* 3ff; Hepple, *Verwoerd,* 201ff; Grobbelaar, *This Was a Man,* 157ff.

p. 208: Vorster . . . had forgotten his glasses: D'Oliveira, *Vorster,* 178.

p. 208: "Where's that bastard?": Botha, *Verwoerd Is Dead,* 5.

p. 209: Botha, blinded by fury: See Suzman, *In No Uncertain Terms,* 69; Strangwayes-Booth, *Cricket in the Thorn Tree,* 228. Helen Suzman's daughter Dr. Patricia Suzman told the author that Botha seized her mother "by the throat," though Suzman's memoir records only that he shook his finger at her. Patricia Suzman also reported that Helen Suzman's family felt the attack was so violent that she should have sued Botha, though Suzman eventually decided against it.

p. 209: As in America: There are many descriptions of the assassination. The major South African newspapers were filled with speculative articles for days afterward. Verwoerd's death was also front-page news around the world. See, for example, "Verwoerd Is Slain by an Assassin," *New York Times,* September 7, 1966.

p. 210: His body was inhabited: See Hepple, *Verwoerd,* 203; Botha, *Verwoerd Is Dead,* 160.

p. 210: "I don't know": Hepple, *Verwoerd,* 203.

p. 211: Afterward soldiers mounted: Descriptions of the funeral come from Grobbelaar, *This Was a Man,* and from various contemporary news accounts. See, for example, "Verwoerd Rites to Be Held Today," *New York Times,* September 10, 1966, and "10,000 Attend Funeral Service for Verwoerd in Pretoria Ampitheater," *New York Times,* September 11, 1966.

p. 211: National Party leaders deliberated: For a description of the inner politicking that took place between Verwoerd's death and Vorster's selection, see D'Oliveira, *Vorster,* chap. 10.

p. 211: "I promise you": "South African Party Picks Vorster as Prime Minister," *New York Times,* September 14, 1966.

p. 211: Vorster bowed his head: D'Oliveira, *Vorster,* 199.

CHAPTER FIVE: **Students and Strategists**

p. 212: "It is nauseating to hear": Quoted in David Bonbright, "On the Wrong Side Again: The West and Apartheid," unpublished manuscript, 1988, 15. Bonbright was the South Africa program officer for the Ford Foundation.

p. 212: "The appointment of Mr. Vorster": "South Africa Chooses," *New York Times,* September 14, 1966. For additional commentary, see *New York Times,* September 14, September 15, and September 18, 1966.

p. 213: Change was always portrayed: George Houser noted this irony in some of his contemporary material. See, for example, George M. Houser, "A Rationale for the Protest against Banks Doing Business with South Africa," Deats material, author's collection; also Box 100, ACOA Amistad.

p. 214: "Let there be no underestimate": Henry P. Van Dusen originally wrote the letter from Johannesburg to the *New York Times* in response to the Kennedy administration's announcement of a partial arms embargo and to the headlines in South African newspapers that U.S. banks were encouraging investment in South Africa. See *New York Times,* September 6, 1963. Van Dusen's remarks were reprinted many times. See, for example, the "Partners in Apartheid" edition of *Africa Today,* March 1964, in which the entire letter appears as Appendix 1; *Christianity and Crisis,* November 28, 1966, 261, 265.

p. 214: Engelhard as Goldfinger: *Forbes,* August 1, 1965, quoted in *Africa Today,* January 1966, 29.

p. 214: In 1958 he had arranged: For material on Engelhard's connections and contributions, see *Africa Today,* March 1964, 7–8 and Appendix 7; *Africa Today,* January 1966, 27–29; Houser, *No One Stops,* 272–73; and Minter, *King Solomon's Mines,* 75.

p. 215: In early 1966: On the controversy over the brotherhood award, see "Panel Questions Award in New Jersey," *New York Times,* January 27, 1966; Houser, *No One Can Stop,* 272. See also the minutes of the meeting of the Consultative Council on South Africa, February 8, 1966, Box 101, ACOA Amistad.

p. 216: On March 13, 1966: "Students Urge Boycott of Bank over Branches in South Africa," *New York Times,* March 14, 1966.

p. 216: Four days later: "City Bank Unmoved by Student Demand," *New York Times,* March 19, 1966.

p. 216: Powers and Hornbeck wrote to Wendell Foster: Letter dated March 28, 1966, Box 100, File 46, ACOA Amistad.

p. 216: the ACOA staff developed: See an undated two-page action plan titled "Disengagement of American Finance from Support of South African Apartheid; Pilot Project: New York City Campaign on Two Giant Banks Most Closely Involved in the South African Economy" (pencil markings indicate that it is a "Robinson draft"), attached to a copy of the Hornbeck-Powers letter, Box 100, File 46, ACOA Amistad.

p. 216: "The branch's integrated teller staff": "Students Here Stage Bank Run to Protest 'Apartheid Support,'" *New York Times,* April 21, 1966.

p. 217: At an early meeting: Consultation on First National City Bank and Request of Union Theological Seminary Students Regarding South Africa, September 28, 1966, Box 100, File 47, ACOA Amistad.

p. 217: the Executive Council of the Episcopal Church: "Interfaith Community Agency Backed By Episcopal Church," *New York Times,* June 27, 1966.

p. 217: Committee of Conscience against Apartheid: There are many documents on the bank campaign in ACOA Amistad. See, for example, the press release of September 22, 1966; the brochure entitled *An Appeal to the People of New York Not to Bank at First National City and Chase Manhattan to Protest Their Involvement with Racism in South Africa;* and other materials dispersed through Boxes 100 and 101. Randolph received 123 cosponsors, including Dorothy Day, Ed Koch, Theodore

Bikel, Thomas Merton, Daniel Berrigan, Reinhold Niebuhr, and black Representative Charles C. Diggs Jr.

p. 217: Christianity and Crisis announced the withdrawal: For a public explanation of the decision, see "Toward Disengagement from South Africa," editorial, *Christianity and Crisis,* November 28, 1966. See also, in the same edition, the article by Wall Street attorney Frederick A. O. Schwarz Jr. in favor of disinvestment, entitled "The United States and South Africa" (265).

p. 218: Houser drafted a document: Houser, "A Rationale," op. cit. There were at least two slightly different versions of the document. The first, printed on white paper, has no date and seems to have been written in the summer of 1966 (Deats material, 1966, author's collection). The second, printed on bright yellow paper, is dated "Fall 1966" (Broin, ACOA Amistad).

p. 219: A. Philip Randolph announced: Press Release: Committee of Conscience against Apartheid, December 9, 1966, Box 101, File 20, ACOA Amistad. The original figure in the release is fifteen million dollars and was hand-corrected. See also Lake, *Caution and Concern,* 222.

p. 219: Houser . . . attributed the discrepancy: See "Report on the Campaign for the Withdrawal of Accounts from Chase Manhattan and First National City Banks," January 1967, 2, ACOA Amistad.

p. 219: "We believe . . . that withdrawal": "300 Here Protest South African Loans," *New York Times,* December 10, 1966.

p. 219: "the struggle for civil rights": "Morgan Bank Scored at Meeting on Share in South African Loan," *New York Times,* March 16, 1967.

p. 220: In May the chairman of General Motors: "GM Says Auto Prices Will Go Up in 1968," *New York Times,* May 20, 1967.

p. 220: "If withdrawal of our funds": "The Editor's Pulpit: "Mission Board Backs Away from a Tough Decision," *Michigan Christian Advocate,* February 2, 1967, 5.

p. 220: In the fall they announced: See American Committee on Africa, "A Report on the Campaign to Withdraw Funds from US Banks Loaning to South Africa," October 1967, Deats material, 1967, author's collection; see also "Church Leaving Bank As a Protest," *New York Times,* February 10, 1968. In announcing the decision, Porter Brown, the general secretary of the committee, said that "even the most enthusiastic supporters of the board's decisions recognize that the mere transfer of a portfolio amounting to a little more than $10 million would probably not bring radical changes in the policies of either the bank or the government involved. . . . On the other hand," she continued, "it is a moral obligation of the churches to throw whatever light they can upon the dark wounds of suffering in our world."

p. 220: Three hundred students from Amherst College: " 'Napalm Valentine' Is Sent at Amherst," *New York Times,* February 15, 1968.

p. 220: hundreds of students at Princeton: See *New York Times,* April 21, 1968; May 18, 1968.

p. 221: "Get your money out of South Africa": For the story of the heckling, see *New York Times,* May 24, 1968. For the relationship of the Rockefellers to Spelman College, see Branch, *Parting the Waters,* chap. 2. For more on Nelson Rockefeller on civil rights, see White, *Making, 1964.*

p. 222: one white South African scholar: J. A. Heese made the "scientific" claim based on his research into the origins of the Afrikaner people. See Heese, *Die Herkoms,* 17.

p. 222: Japanese and Chinese status in South Africa: See *New York Times,* June 28, 1970; July 23, 1970; August 20, 1970.

p. 222: The story of Sandra Laing: See SAIRR, *Survey, 1967; New York Times,* May 3 and October 2, 1967; see also the transcript of *Africa: South Africa and the United States,* University of Michigan Television Center, May 29, 1968, File: South Africa—General, Box 201, Diggs Collection. The story of Sandra Laing was also told in a public television documentary, *The Search for Sandra Laing,* broadcast on WNET, New York, on April 6, 1978.

p. 222: The case of Mr. and Mrs. Walker: SAIRR, *Survey, 1968,* 35.

p. 223: The case of Susara Kirk: *SAIRR, 1969,* 25.

p. 223: the government banned the use of black mannequins: *New York Times,* February 22, 1970.

p. 223: "different races perform best": *New York Times,* July 12, 1970.

p. 223: Percy Sledge: *New York Times,* July 14, 1970.

p. 223: The revelation that Blaiberg's heart: See *New York Times,* January 3, 4, 7, 9, 1968.

p. 225: the policy of resettlement was a facade: For a description of how a white liberal came to this conclusion, see Levine, *Inside Apartheid,* 11.

p. 225: nearly one an hour: This is based on a total casualty figure of 7,482 for the year 1967, as provided by Schlesinger in *Robert Kennedy,* 822.

p. 225: Robert F. Kennedy rose in the Senate: For a description of and quotations from the speech, see Schlesinger, *Robert Kennedy,* 772ff.

p. 226: Martin Luther King had come across a story: Interview by David Garrow with Bernard Lee, quoted in Garrow, *Bearing the Cross,* 543.

p. 226: From the pulpit King explained: The quotations and paraphrases are from Garrow, *Bearing the Cross,* 553. See the text of the speech in Washington, *Testament of Hope,* 231–44. King again addressed the issue of South Africa in 1967, saying, "The tragedy of South Africa is not simply its policy; it is the fact that the facist government of South Africa is virtually made possible by the economic policies of the United States and Great Britain, two countries which profess to be the moral bastions of our western world" (King, *Where Do We Go,* 173–74); also Hauck and Voorhes, *Two Decades,* 9.

p. 227: Critics accused him: One of the fiercest attacks came several months later from black columnist Carl T. Rowan. See "Martin Luther King's Tragic Decisions," *Reader's Digest,* September 1967, 37–42; also see Garrow, *Bearing the Cross,* 576.

p. 227: "Riots are caused": Garrow, *Bearing the Cross,* 572.

p. 227: the SCLC convention, at King's Urging: Ibid., 575.

p. 227: "Poor People's Campaign": According to Marion Wright Edelman, one of the earliest suggestions for this idea came from Robert Kennedy. Kennedy told Edelman in that summer of 1967 that King should "bring the poor people to Washington." When she passed the idea along to King, Edelman recalls, "he treated me as if I were an emissary of grace here, or something that brought him some light. Out of that, the Poor People's Campaign was born" (Hampton and Fayer, *Voices of Freedom,* 453–54).

p. 228: mule cart procession: Garrow, *Bearing the Cross,* 598.

p. 228: the assault proved the pointlessness of searching: "Half a million soldiers, with seven hundred thousand Vietnamese allies, with total command of the air, total command of the seas, backed by huge resources and the most modern weapons, are unable to secure a single city from the attacks of an enemy whose total strength is about two hundred fifty thousand," Kennedy said with disgust, calling on Johnson again to move toward a settlement (Schlesinger, *Robert Kennedy,* 842).

p. 228: "We will win the war": Johnson made the remark in Minneapolis on

March 17, the day after Robert Kennedy announced his candidacy for president and only two weeks before Johnson himself withdrew from the race. See Schlesinger, *Robert Kennedy,* 860.

p. 230: "I refuse to be confronted": Nixon message to Congress, quoted in Chester Crocker, "Nixon-Kissinger System."

p. 230: Kissinger was thus startled: "[Nixon] had very little confidence in the State Department," Kissinger recalled in his memoirs. "Its personnel had no loyalty to him; the Foreign Service had disdained him as Vice-President and ignored him the moment he was out of office. He was determined to run foreign policy from the White House. . . . He felt it was imperative to exclude the CIA from the formulation of policy; it was staffed by Ivy League liberals who behind the facade of analytical objectivity were usually pushing their own preferences" (Kissinger, *White House Years,* 10ff). For Nixon's perspective, see Nixon, 340ff. For a perceptive and biting commentary on the transformation of American foreign policy by Nixon and Kissinger, see Morris, *Uncertain Greatness,* esp. chap. 2.

p. 231: central themes of Kissinger's scholarship: In his book on early-nineteenth-century diplomacy, *A World Restored* (Boston: Houghton Mifflin, 1979), Kissinger had written that "in 1821 Metternich had greater difficulty with the Austrian than with the Russian ministers, and that in every negotiation Castlereagh had to fight a more desperate battle with his Cabinet than with his foreign colleagues." See Morris, *Uncertain Greatness,* 54.

p. 231: "designed to execute": Morris, *Uncertain Greatness,* 54.

p. 231: "had a strong intuition": Nixon, *Memoirs,* 341.

p. 231: the NSSM system: For a comprehensive assessment written by a former NSC staff member, see Crocker, "Nixon-Kissinger System." See also Morris, *Uncertain Greatness,* esp. chaps. 2 and 3. I am especially indebted to the lucid exposition in Schneidman, *American Foreign Policy,* 282–88.

p. 231: "coup d'etat": Morris, *Uncertain Greatness,* 46.

p. 232: "Bring me something important!": Author interview with Wayne Fredericks, April 19, 1990.

p. 232: Members of the National Security Council: Crocker, "Nixon-Kissinger System," 97.

p. 232: Nixon's reassurances to Portuguese officials: Franco Nogueira, *Dialagos Interditos* (Lisbon: Intervencao, 1979), quoted in Schneidman, *American Foreign Policy,* 279. See also Mahoney, *JFK,* 243.

p. 233: First, he believed: See Morris's candid and somewhat apologetic account of his own involvement in NSSM 39 in *Uncertain Greatness,* 109–10. See also Schneidman, *American Foreign Policy,* 289.

p. 233: Morris had been heavily influenced: "South Africa," Macrae had written, "is a country where richer and securer generally means lefter; which is one reason why efforts to make it less rightist by boycotting it into greater insecurity and poverty would not seem to make any very evident sort of progressive sense" Norman Macrae, "The Green Bay Tree: A Survey by the *Economist* of Why South Africa Is Getting Richer So Quickly and of Why It Is Almost Certainly to Everybody's Advantage That It Should Continue to Do So," *Economist,* June 29, 196, x; also quoted in Lake, *Tar Baby,* 127. Macrae included in his evidence the repeated election of Helen Suzman, whose constituency was one of the wealthiest in the country.

p. 233: the notion that expanded commercial links: This point is made by Coker, *United States and South Africa.* Coker wrote that "we should not be surprised that in 1969 the NSC believed implicitly that contact would produce change, inasmuch as this was to become the very rationale and justification for detente on the much more vital issue of relations between the United States and the Soviet Union" (18).

p. 233: "accept the expedient American stakes": Morris, *Uncertain Greatness,* 110.

p. 233: "Battled out over verbs": Morris, *Uncertain Greatness,* 112.

p. 233: By the end of the summer: The full text of the NSSM 39 study was leaked and published in 1975 with an introduction by Barry Cohen and Mohamed A. El-Khawas *(Kissinger Study).*

p. 234: "the whites are here to stay": See ibid., 66; also quoted in Minter, *King Solomon's Mines,* 220.

p. 234: "maintain public opposition": Cohen and El-Khawas, *Kissinger Study,* 67.

p. 234: "tar baby option": The "tar baby" story is from the collection of Uncle Remus stories, written in the late 1800s. Brer Fox, seeking to catch Brer Rabbit, mixes tar and turpentine and forms it into a tar baby. Brer Rabbit comes along, greets the tar baby in the middle of the road, but the tar baby does not reply. This infuriates Brer Rabbit, so he strikes the tar baby with one paw, which sticks to the tar, then with the other, which sticks also, then with his feet and head. When Brer Rabbit is completely immobilized, Brer Fox emerges from his hiding place. For the original story, see Joel Chandler Harris, *Uncle Remus: His Songs and Sayings* (1880; New York: Appleton, 1901), chap. 2. It is an interesting wrinkle that a story used to condemn a policy favoring white regimes was written by a white and is now considered racist.

p. 234: "intellectual squalor": Morris, *Uncertain Greatness,* 112.

p. 235: Alexander Haig . . . would amuse his boss . . . "something in it for the jigs": For these and other allegations of racism in the White House, see Morris, *Uncertain Greatness,* 131.

p. 235: "Domestic and Moral Factors": On Lord's NSC report, see Morris, *Uncertain Greatness,* 114–15.

p. 235: William Rogers remarked: These and the rest of the descriptions of the NSC meeting come from eyewitness Morris, *Uncertain Greatness,* 114–19.

p. 236: Kissinger suggested: Quoted by Schneidman, *American Foreign Policy,* 298.

p. 236: sale of Boeing jetliners: See the author interview with former U.S. Ambassador to the United Nations Donald McHenry, September 6, 1990.

p. 237: The secrecy enabled: For an interesting assessment of the different public statements emanating from the White House and the State Department at this time, see Jennifer Stoos, "David Newsom and the Africa Bureau at the Department of State, 1969–1973," unpublished master's paper, Harvard Divinity School, 1991.

p. 237: To the neighboring white Portuguese colonies: See, for example, the meeting between John Vorster and Prime Minister Ian Smith of Rhodesia, reported in *New York Times,* July 27, 1967.

p. 237: To the Western powers: For a general discussion of Vorster's foreign policy from 1966 to 1970, see *New York Times,* October 13, 1970.

p. 237: signed a trade agreement: *New York Times,* March 14, 1967; September 11, 1967; February 6, 1968.

p. 238: he seized on every bit of evidence: Whenever Soviet ships appeared in the Indian Ocean, the South African government alerted the American and British militaries. On several occasions, South African diplomats said publicly that they would like to become members of NATO. And when, in 1967, the South Africans actually caught a KGB spy, Y. N. Loginov, who had been trying to learn more about South Africa's role in resupplying Rhodesia and in developing an atomic bomb, Vorster crowed about the discovery for two years until Loginov was swapped for ten

West German agents who had been sitting in East German jails. See *New York Times*, September 13 and 17, 1967; August 23, 24, and 25, 1969.

p. 238: Letters to American newspapers: See, for example, *New York Times*, February 2, 1968.

p. 238: Wallace's speech at the National Press Club: *New York Times*, October 8, 1968.

p. 238: Eastland's press conference: *New York Times*, February 12, 1969.

p. 238: Kennan's article on apartheid: *New York Times*, December 18, 1970.

p. 238: "Since the banning": SAIRR, *Survey, 1967*, 8.

p. 238: When Robert Sobukwe . . . completed his sentence: Karis and Carter, *From Protest to Challenge*, 147–49; see also *New York Times*, June 13, 1967; April 26 and May 14, 1969.

p. 238: Luthuli died under mysterious circumstances: *New York Times*, July 22, 1967.

p. 238: "the harshest, most iron-fisted outpost": Mandela, *Long Walk*, 338, 340.

p. 239: "A letter was like the summer rain": Ibid., 349.

p. 239: the authorities kept Mandela informed: Ibid., 370.

p. 239: "When I started to detail the problems": Ibid., 347. Mandela identifies the lawyer only as "Mr. Hynning."

p. 240: the "University": Ibid., 406. For a fascinating discussion between three participants in this venture, see the 1988 South African documentary film by Lindy Wilson *Robben Island, My University*.

pp. 240–41: "I had to use my panties": Mandela, *Part of My Soul*, 98.

p. 241: Every day she had to endure inspection: Ibid., 100.

p. 241: interrogated by . . . Swanepoel: Ibid., 100–102.

p. 242: Wilson found it politically impossible: See *New York Times*, December 17 and 19, 1967.

p. 242: Vorster denounced the decision: *New York Times*, January 1, 1968.

p. 242: P. W. Botha warned: *New York Times*, February 21, 1968.

pp. 242–43: Heath . . . announced that he would permit: See *New York Times*, June 23 and 25, 1970; July 3, 5, 7, 11, and 13, 1970.

p. 243: "Obviously there will be": *New York Times*, July 13, 1970.

p. 243: "increased identification of U.S. Negroes": Ibid.

p. 243: When Wilson made a searing speech: See *New York Times*, July 23, 1970.

p. 244: "We do not need arms": SAIRR, *Survey, 1970*, 32.

p. 244: P. W. Botha . . . announced: *Johannesburg Star*, June 13, 1970; also cited in SAIRR, *Survey, 1970*, 33.

p. 244: Russian cruiser *Aleksander Suvorov*: *New York Times*, January 16, 1971.

p. 244: The results were startling: *New York Times*, January 21, 1971.

p. 244: the heads of state also agreed: *New York Times*, January 23, 1971.

p. 245: Appearing in the House of Commons: *New York Times*, January 27, 1971.

p. 245: he had received Vorster's personal assurances: Heath had also made this point publicly at the end of the Commonwealth meeting. *New York Times*, January 21, 1971.

p. 245: a country with a white population: Figures from SAIRR, *Survey, 1970*, 24.

p. 245: South Africa's defense budget multiplied sevenfold: *New York Times*, July 27, 1970. See also the sections on defense policy in SAIRR, *Survey, 1969* and *Survey, 1970*.

p. 245: In 1970 South Africa had: Defense statistics from SAIRR, *Survey, 1969*, 31–33.

p. 245: "lift her into the ranks": SAIRR, *Survey, 1970,* 34.

p. 245: the South African military was developing: See, for example, C. L. Sulzberger's series of articles in the *New York Times* in April 1971.

p. 245: Prisons Act: SAIRR, *Survey, 1969,* 57ff.

p. 246: Pogrund and Gandar trials: See the sections on prison conditions in the SAIRR annual race relations surveys from 1965 to 1970, particularly 1969, 57–58; also see *New York Times,* March 30, June 17, July 11, 1969; February 26, 1971. See also author interview with South African journalist Joe Thloloe, May 15, 1989.

p. 246: By 1969, the combined efforts: SAIRR, *Survey, 1969,* 39.

p. 246: *History of South Africa:* SAIRR, *Survey, 1970,* 35; SAIRR, *Survey, 1971,* 66.

p. 246: The 1971 edition: SAIRR, *Survey, 1971,* 42, 43, 50.

p. 246: "extend the hand of friendship": This is the opinion of John D'Oliveira, Vorster's biographer, in *Vorster,* 241.

p. 247: English-speaking editors. . . . Even South Africa's jurists: SAIRR, *Survey, 1969,* 35–36; see also *New York Times,* June 15, 17, and 29, 1969.

p. 247: When they refused: SAIRR, *Survey, 1969,* 37; SAIRR, *Survey, 1970,* 37.

p. 247: "we cannot let the world get the idea": SAIRR, *Survey, 1970,* 1.

p. 247: voting results in the 1970 election: SAIRR, *Survey, 1970,* 1–8.

p. 247: Gary Player: For descriptions of Player's golfing career, see the articles in *Sports Illustrated,* July 20, 1987; July 30, 1990; Feb 25, 1991.

p. 248: Jackie Robinson and twenty-three other prominent athletes: *New York Times,* February 9, 1968.

p. 248: the International Olympic Committee: *New York Times,* February 16, 1968; April 24, 1968.

p. 248: in 1969 he rejected a plea: *New York Times,* December 4 and 21, 1969. Player, to make amends for his government's refusal to admit Ashe, offered in March 1970 to play a series of exhibition matches with American black golf pros for the benefit of the United Negro College Fund; though two black players accepted, the fund turned Player down.

p. 248: U.S. Secretary of State Rogers met with Ashe: *New York Times,* December 12, 1968; see also January 9, 1968.

p. 248: disruption of Springboks tour: *New York Times,* November 9, 13, 16, 23, and December 7, 1969.

p. 248: Player . . . had to be escorted by armed guards: *New York Times,* March 26 and April 10, 1970.

p. 249: all Britons would "feel free": *New York Times,* April 28, 1970.

p. 249: South African athletes and fans called for a national conference: *New York Times,* May 25, June 2, and July 25, 1970.

p. 249: The lesson to be learned: *New York Times,* May 1, 1970.

p. 249: After several years of searching: See Jennifer Davis, "Occupied Africa: Facts the U.S. Needs to Know," *Africa Fund Bulletin,* December 1969.

p. 250: In 1969 she helped bring pressure: "Memorandum on Chemical Bank at the United Nations," August 1969, Box 101, ACOA Amistad.

p. 250: "silly asses": *New York Times,* May 7, 1970.

p. 250: debatable, worst-case assumptions: The Malkiel report, for example, assumed that divestment would take place suddenly, causing extra brokerage fees, rather than over time, when the brokerage fees would be much closer to the normal transaction costs of a university. The Malkiel report also specifically recommended *against* the practice known as the Wall Street rule, which encouraged disgruntled shareholders to sell their stocks, arguing that the best way to change corporate policies was through persuasion and shareholder mechanisms rather than divestment. For more on the Malkiel report, see Hauck and Voorhes, *Two Decades,* and Longstreth and Rosenbloom, *Corporate Social Responsibility.* For a discussion of the Wall Street Rule, see chap. 7 of this book.

p. 252: "moved me and got me involved": Author interview with Timothy Smith, March 19, 1990.

p. 252: Kenneth Carstens: See Carstens's notes for his testimony before the House subcommittee on Africa, Deats files, 1966, author's collection.

p. 253: sending Smith and co-worker Mary McAnally: For Smith's account of the trip, see "Reflections and Comments on a Two-Month Stint in South Africa—Tim Smith, Field Aide for Africa Affairs, United Church of Christ," December 1968. These and other materials about Smith's trips were provided by Timothy Smith or collected by research assistant Elizabeth Grossman from the ICCR Active Files.

p. 254: the formation of an all-black organization: See Gerhart, *Black Power,* 260–62.

p. 254: When his group asked for time: For Stephen Biko's description of the events at the UCM conference, see Biko, *I Write What I Like,* 11.

p. 254: Smith's encounter with Biko at Stutterheim: See author interview with Timothy Smith, March 29, 1990. Even six months later, Smith did not seem aware that the discussion at the UCM conference would lead to a new black student group; he makes no mention of Biko or the possible emergence of SASO in his trip report written in December 1968.

pp. 254–55: The Young Marxists and other radicals: I am indebted to Gail Gerhart's lucid exposition of historical trends in black ideology, particularly her comparison of black consciousness with the Africanism of Anton Lembede and Robert Sobukwe and her typology of "rebels" and "realists." See Gerhart, *Black Power,* esp. chap. 8.

p. 255: "Very few of the South African": Biko, *I Write What I Like,* 4–5.

p. 255: Some of the strongest influences: See Gerhart, *Black Power,* 275.

p. 255: Soon American phrases: See Gerhart, *Black Power,* 277; Biko, *I Write What I Like,* 46.

p. 256: Discussion of the similarities: Gerhart, *Black Power,* 275.

p. 256: "Black Souls in White Skins?": See Biko, *I Write What I Like,* 19–26.

p. 257: "Black people under the Smuts government": Ibid., 27–32. *I Write What I Like.*

p. 257: his close friendship with particular white members: For Stubbs's description of his friendship and his assessment of Biko's personal religious views, see Aelred Stubbs, C.R., "Martyr of Hope: A Personal Memoir," which appears at the conclusion of Biko, *I Write What I Like.*

p. 258: "What of the white man's religion": Biko, *I Write What I Like,* 31.

CHAPTER SIX: **Confrontations with General Motors**

p. 263: "For forty-five years General Motors": Report of the 63rd General Motors stockholders' meeting, May 1971.

p. 263: By 1970 that number had multiplied: From *Black Elected Officials* (Washington, D.C.: Joint Center for Political Studies Press, 1989), table 1. See also Cornell Peterson Horton and Jessie Carney Smith, eds., *Statistical Record of Americans* (Detroit: Gale Research, 1990).

p. 264: child out of wedlock: Author interview with Charles C. Diggs Jr., May 24, 1990.

p. 264: Charles Diggs Sr.: "Soft Spoken Black Congressman: Charles Coles Diggs, Jr.," *New York Times,* December 18, 1971.

p. 264: it took five years: Author interview with Charles C. Diggs Jr., May 24, 1990.

p. 264: a trait that journalists often associated: See, for example, Ken Owen, *Johannesburg Star,* July 7, 1971.

p. 264: suspicious of Kennedy's strong overtures: Author interview with Charles C. Diggs Jr., May 24, 1990.

p. 265: Diggs even received: In the Diggs Collection, one can find documents dated April 1969, marked "secret" and named "Option Alpha" and "Option Beta," that read like early versions of the NSSM review. See File: South Africa—Pol, Box 310, Diggs Collection.

p. 265: When South African Airways started flying: See House Committee on Foreign Relations, Subcommittee on Africa, hearings, April 2, 1969. For this and other material, including much correspondence relating to SAA and the CAB, see File: South African Airways, Box 201, Diggs Collection. See also *New York Times,* April 3, 1969.

p. 265: He asked Defense Department officials: Williams E. Laang, Deputy Assistant Secretary of Defense, to Charles C. Diggs Jr., June 13, 1969. File: South Africa—Pol, Box 310, Diggs Collection.

p. 265: He pushed the Justice Department: Thomas E. Kauper, Acting Assistant Attorney General, Office of Legal Counsel to Diggs, July 2, 1969, File: South Africa—Pol, Box 310, Diggs Collection.

p. 265: Quoting the State Department's: Diggs to Williams Rogers, press release dated July 2, 1971, Active People Files: Charles C. Diggs Jr., ACOA Armistad.

p. 265: even though South Africa depended: See an article from an unidentified South African journal from April 1969 called "The Economics of Tourism," File: South Africa—Pol, Box 310, Diggs Collection.

p. 265: For years Diggs denounced: For a general overview of Diggs's efforts to end the sugar quota, see the study prepared under the direction of Ronald V. Dellums, chair of the Congressional Black Caucus, "The Congressional Black Caucus: Selected Efforts to Influence U.S. Policy towards South Africa, 1971–1989," 8–12. See also the early hearings held on this topic, House Committee on Foreign Relations, Subcommittee on Africa, hearings, April 15, 1969; and the material in File: South Africa—Sugar Quota, Box 357, and File: South Africa—Sugar Quota, Box 410, Diggs Collection. For contemporary press accounts, see *New York Times,* April 19 and 21, 1970; an editorial on June 8, 1971, agreeing with the Kennedy-Diggs position; and the articles on June 11, July 28, July 29, and October 6, 1971, describing the legislative battle that led to the extension of the sugar bill for three more years. In 1974 the issue finally evaporated when the House and Senate—in a move unrelated to South Africa—refused to renew the legislation protecting sugar and restored the setting of its price to the world commodity markets.

p. 266: Only 66 companies: Desaix Myers, *Labor Practices,* 50.

p. 267: "an attempt to develop a solution": *Sunday Express* (South Africa), December 1, 1968; quoted in Dudley Horner, "United States Corporate Investment and Social Change in South Africa" (Johannesburg: SAIRR, undated [probably mid-1971]), 4; see File: South Africa—6, Box 357, Diggs Collection. The author also obtained a copy from the African Studies Library at the University of Cape Town. For a U.S. press account of the Horner study, see *New York Times,* June 28, 1971.

p. 267: "After twenty minutes": Management consultant Charles St. Thomas in Myers, *Labor Practices,* 50.

p. 268: "American business will not withdraw": "I am completely convinced that within five to ten years South Africa will be involved in a major racial war not within her own borders but in southern Africa," Smith wrote in a report that was circulated to church leaders in December 1968, "and that this situation urgently requires interpretation in North America." These observations are drawn from a memorandum "for limited confidential circulation," entitled "Reflections and Comments on a Two-Month Stint in South Africa—Tim Smith, Field Aide for Africa Affairs, United Church of Christ," December 1968, ICCR Active Files.

p. 268: "compelled by law or custom to engage in slave labor": Smith's argument here is reminiscent of the provisions of Section 307 of the Smoot-Hawley Act (1930), which barred the importation of all goods produced by forced labor, convict labor, or indentured labor. Charles Diggs unsuccessfully tried to use this provision to bar South African goods. See File—South Africa 3, Box 357, Diggs Collection.

p. 268: But he was most astonished: When Smith asked about their attitudes toward the Nationalist government's racial and labor policies, the executives stressed that they stayed out of politics. Marshall Smith, the managing director of Caltex, said, "We couldn't live here if we weren't good citizens; therefore we are very law abiding. . . . In order to keep a healthy environment, we have to watch our step." (Timothy Smith interview with Marshall Smith, managing director of Caltex, August 7, 1970. These and all other company verbatim quotations are drawn from ICCR Active File transcriptions and summaries of the tape recordings or notes that Smith made during his visits to the American firms in South Africa. These provided the raw material for Smith's later report, "The American Corporation in South Africa: An Analysis, a Foundation for Action," 1970.) The executives at Chrysler gave Smith a statement from their department of International Public Relations. "Chrysler does not believe that it is its mission to oppose laws and customs in host countries because they differ from ours," the document said. Besides, the paper stated, the moral choice of where to do business was not Chrysler's. "However desirable a business climate a country might have," the document insisted, "Chrysler has not undertaken to do business in it, if doing so had not the support of the United States Government" (Chrysler Corporation, International Public Relations Department, "Statement on Chrysler in South Africa," no date; given to Smith during his interview). "I am no more political or less political here than anywhere else," William G. Slocum, the managing director of General Motors, told Smith. "It is company policy that we don't mix in political matters. . . . I don't consider it appropriate to publicly work for changes in laws" (Timothy Smith interview with William P. Slocum Jr., managing director of General Motors, July 31, 1970, ICCR Active Files). This professed aversion to politics, Smith discovered, did not prevent the companies from contributing large sums of money to the South Africa Foundation, whose role was to polish South Africa's international image.

p. 268: David Knowles: Timothy Smith interview with David Knowles, no date, ICCR Active Files.

p. 269: "much more humanitarian concept": Timothy Smith interview with David Brown, managing director of Barlow-Weyerhaeuser, July 7, 1970, 3–4, ICCR Active Files.

p. 269: "This Bantustan thing": Smith, "American Corporation in South Africa," op. cit., 24; also see File: South Africa—6, Box 357, Diggs Collection.

p. 269: Though the executives with whom Smith met: Ibid., 29ff.

p. 269: The executives at Chrysler: Timothy Smith interview at Chrysler, no date, ICCR Active Files, 2.

p. 269: "I didn't do it": Timothy Smith interview with R. J. Scott, managing director, Ford South Africa, July 30, 1970, ICCR Active Files, 3.

p. 270: "You can't take these people": Timothy Smith interview with Martin Zaunbrecker, managing director of Deere, South Africa, August 1970, ICCR Active Files, 2.

p. 270: At General Motors: The quotations in this paragraph are from Tim Smith's files and from his final report.

p. 270: "If you saw these Africans": Timothy Smith interview with Mr. Martin, first name and position unspecified, at the headquarters of Deere, South Africa, August 1970, ICCR Active Files, 2.

p. 270: All of the managers believed: For Smith's assessment of the common themes in his interviews, see "American Corporation in South Africa."

p. 271: "The Bantu looks on the employer": Timothy Smith interview with Mr. LeRoux (no first name specified), labor relations officer, Chrysler, no date, ICCR Active Files, 2.

p. 271: "over the years, the master-servant relationship": Timothy Smith interview with Fred Ferreira, director of personnel, Ford South Africa, July 30, 1970, ICCR Active Files.

p. 271: "You shouldn't allow yourself": Timothy Smith interview with "Red" Duggan, United States Consul General in Durban, July 24, 1970, ICCR Active Files.

p. 272: Polaroid Revolutionary Workers Movement: See "Polaroid Blacks Ask Worldwide Boycott," *Boston Globe,* October 27, 1970; "Pioneers Recall Divestment Battle," *Boston Globe,* February 16, 1990; Hauck and Voorhes, *Two Decades,* 95–97.

p. 272: two-page rebuttal: "As a matter of corporate policy, Polaroid has consistently refused to sell the Polaroid I.D.-2 System directly or indirectly to the government of South Africa or any agency thereof for use in implementing the apartheid program," the document stated. "Examination of company records indicates that this policy has been fully implemented in practice." Memorandum of Legal Matters from G. R. Dicker, Assistant Legal Secretary to All Polaroid Members, Subject: Polaroid I.D. Sales Practices in South Africa, October 6, 1970, author's files.

p. 272: "What Is Polaroid Doing in South Africa?": *Boston Globe* and other newspapers, November 25, 1971, author's files.

p. 273: full-page ads: For the advertisement and related article, see *New York Times,* January 13, 1971. The fifty-thousand-dollar estimate is George Houser's in "Polaroid's Dramatic Withdrawal from South Africa," *Christian Century,* April 12, 1978.

p. 273: major story in South African newspapers: See, for example, *Johannesburg Star,* January 13, 15, and 20, 1971.

p. 273: "we in South Africa": *Polaroid and South Africa,* pamphlet prepared by Africa Research Group in collaboration with the Polaroid Revolutionary Workers Movement, published March 21, 1971. File: Polaroid, Box 127, Diggs Collection.

p. 273: In January 1971 they again demanded: Leaflet of the Polaroid Revolutionary Workers Movement, January 12, 1971.

p. 273: she had been suspended without pay: For the account of the testimony before the United Nations committee, see *New York Times,* February 7, 1971. For the letter of dismissal, see Terry Mulligan, Laboratory Manager, to Caroline Hunter, February 10, 1971, in *Polaroid and South Africa,* op. cit.

p. 273: Hunter told the press: *New York Times,* February 25, 1971.

p. 273: the president received the members of the caucus: Dellums, "Congressional Black Caucus," op. cit.

p. 274: "during the past five years": House Committee on Foreign Affairs, Subcommittee on Africa, *U.S. Business Involvement in Southern Africa,* opening statement by Charles Diggs, 92nd Cong., 1st sess., 1971. See also a draft of that statement, ACOA Active Files.

p. 274: history of the Episcopal Church: See Manross, *History;* Raymond W. Albright, *A History of the Protestant Episcopal Church* (New York: Macmillan, 1964); and James Thayer Addison, *A Concise History of the Episcopal Church, 1789–1931* (New York: Archon Books, 1969). A portion of the material in this chapter was originally presented in a case study in the author's doctoral dissertation. See Robert K. Massie Jr., "Moral Deliberation and Policy Formulation: A Study of Eight Institutional Investors' Approaches to South African Disinvestment," unpublished doctoral dissertation, Harvard University Graduate School of Business Administration, 1989, esp. chap. 4.

p. 275: according to one study in the 1970s: Vogel, *Lobbying,* 175.

p. 275: try to play the role of a national church: For an examination of this theme, with particular regard to the convolutions in the church's attitudes toward mission, see the Reverend Ian Douglas, "Fling Out the Banner: The National Church Ideal and the Foreign Mission of the Episcopal Church," unpublished doctoral dissertation, Boston University, 1993. I am indebted to the Reverend Dr. Douglas, now on the faculty of the Episcopal Divinity School in Cambridge, Massachusetts, for our conversations about Bishop Hines and the church in this period.

p. 276: "special program" to "encourage the use": Quoted in David E. Sumner, *The Episcopal Church's History, 1945–1985* (Wilton, Conn.: Morehouse-Barlow, 1987), esp. chap. 5.

p. 276: Black Manifesto: See "The Black Manifesto," in Wilmore and Cone, *Black Theology.*

p. 276: Gradually his gaze widened: The author is grateful to the Reverend Charles Cesaretti of the national office of the Episcopal Church, for his insights into John Hines's interests and motivations. Cesaretti commented during an interview in June 1988 that the South Africa effort "grew out of Bishop Hines's increasing recognition of the greater institutional dimensions of racism. He saw the racism of apartheid through the Anglican communion, then readily made the jump to the presence of American corporations and then to our investments."

p. 276: In 1967 the delegates to General Convention: The resolution asked "the officials of this church at all levels to review the church's economic involvement in banks and corporations which do business in the Republic of South Africa, Rhodesia, Mozambique, Angola, and South West Africa; and urge the above-mentioned officials and the Executive Council . . . to exercise responsible stewardship over the funds entrusted to their care" (see *Journal of General Convention,* 1967).

p. 276: special committee's recommendations: See the minutes of the Executive Council, December 1968.

p. 276: The Trust Funds members balked: See the Executive Council Resolution, September 1969.

p. 277: "The Episcopal Church has been increasingly concerned": Resolution of

Executive Council, quoted in Committee on Social Responsibility in Investments Report to General Convention, 1976, 9.

p. 277: "We believe that the apartheid policies": "Episcopal Church Urges G.M. to Close Plants in South Africa," *New York Times,* February 2, 1971.

p. 277: "the move is expected to be": Ibid.

p. 277: "the question of how to bring investments": Ibid.

p. 278: the members of the board: Noting that more than half of its six thousand workers in South Africa were "non-white," they commented that "while General Motors recognizes the complex issues that result from race restrictions in South Africa, its employment record is an indication of the progressive change which has occurred over the years. The corporation is convinced that its operations in South Africa are helping build a climate in which desired social changes can be further implemented" *(New York Times,* April 9, 1971).

p. 278: took his faith so seriously: Author interviews with William G. Slocum, September 20 and 21, 1991.

p. 278: "crusade for radical changes": *New York Times,* April 11, 1971.

p. 279: a privilege the government could grant: Chief Justice John Marshall ruled in 1819 that "a corporation is an artificial being, invisible, intangible, existing only in contemplation of law. Being the mere creature of law, it possesses only those properties which the charter of its creation confers upon it, either expressly, or as incidental to its very existence" *(Trustees of Dartmouth College v. Woodward,* 4 Wheaton 518, 636 [U.S. 1819]; quoted also in James Willard Hurst, *The Legitimacy of the Business Corporation* [Charlottesville: University Press of Virginia, 1970], 9).

p. 279: "The analogy between state and corporation": Vogel, *Lobbying,* 75.

p. 280: guided in their thinking: Berle and Means, *Modern Corporation.* Berle and Means were but two contributors to a fierce legal and theoretical debate fueled by the Great Depression and the apparent successes of communism over the capitalist system of corporate governance. See, for example, E. Merrick Dodd Jr., "For Whom Are Corporate Managers Trustees?" *Harvard Law Review* 45 (1932): 1145, and the response by A. A. Berle Jr., *Harvard Law Review* 45 (1932): 1365; see also William O. Douglas, "Directors Who Do Not Direct," *Harvard Law Review* 47 (1934): 1305.

p. 280: when the number of shares: Berle and Means refer to this as the "centrifugal" and "centripetal" forces *(Modern Corporation,* 9).

p. 281: "Corporation law, as a field": Bayless Manning, "The Shareholder's Appraisal Remedy," *Yale Law Journal* 72 (1962): 245; also cited in Hurst, *Legitimacy,* 10.

p. 282: He traveled over to the offices: For an early account by Gilbert of his own early activities, see Gilbert, *Dividends,* esp. chap. 2; for a summary, see Lauren Talner, *Origins,* 2.

p. 282: "steady, drowsy drone": Gilbert, *Dividends,* 20.

p. 282: "fight this silent dictatorship": Quoted in Talner, *Origins,* 2.

p. 282: "modern extension of the New England town meeting": Gilbert, *Dividends,* 16. Gilbert presciently suggested that participation in the meetings could be expanded through the use of closed-circuit television linking the main annual meeting to regional shareholder gatherings.

p. 282: Chief executives reacted: Gilbert, *Dividends,* 66ff, 6, 9.

p. 282: "scandalous isolationist policy": Talner, *Origins,* 3.

p. 283: Wilma Porter Soss: Soss was prone to theatrics and sailed into the 1949 annual meeting of United States Steel in a late Victorian costume—a two-piece gray suit, lace blouse, and large purple hat. Her attire, she told reporters, "represents management's thinking on stockholder relations." Her mission, she said, was to point out to corporate executives that they were not working for themselves or the company, but rather for the shareholders, many of whom were women and who wanted a woman on the board. "The truth is that we shareholders own the corporation," she said. See her obituary, *New York Times,* October 16, 1986.

p. 283: Evelyn Y. Davis: Davis also occasionally resorted to eccentric displays to make her points. On one occasion she marched up to May Department Stores chairman David Farrell, handed him a $1,600 check for her drapes, and lectured him on how tardy his employees had been in hanging them. On another occasion she nominated soft-porn actress Koo Stark to the board of ITT because, she said, Stark was dating Prince Andrew and the appointment would provide "some much-needed influence with the British royal family" (see "Corporate Chiefs Listen to Heckler with Clout," AP feature story, *Lexington [Kentucky] Herald-Leader,* April 15, 1990).

p. 283: In 1966 the members of the coalition: For a thorough discussion of the Kodak-FIGHT controversy, see Vogel, *Lobbying,* 31ff. Talner also has included an abbreviated treatment drawn from Vogel *(Origins,* 4–8). See also Sethi, *Business Corporations,* and Sethi, *Up Against.*

p. 283: "colossal public relations blunder": Quoted in Sethi, *Business Corporations,* 37; cited in Vogel, *Lobbying,* 33.

p. 284: "If you are on the level": Talner, *Origins,* 6.

p. 284: The annual meeting in 1967: Quoted in Talner, *Origins,* 6. See also Vogel, *Lobbying,* 35.

p. 284: between two hundred and six hundred unemployed blacks: Vogel, *Lobbying,* 35.

p. 284: "Proxies can be the mechanism": Quoted in Talner, *Origins,* 8.

p. 284: "Congress intended by its enactment": "It seems fair to infer that Congress desired to make proxy solicitations a vehicle for *corporate* democracy rather than an all-purpose forum for malcontented shareholders to vent their spleen about irrelevant matters," wrote Tamm, "and also realized that management cannot exercise its specialized talents effectively if corporate investors assert the power to dictate the minutiae of daily business decisions. . . . However, it is also apparent that the two exceptions which these rules carve out of the general requirement of inclusion can be construed so as to permit the exclusion of practically any shareholder proposal on the grounds that it is either 'too general' or 'too specific.' " Tamm zeroed in on the heart of the dispute: "Indeed, in the present case Dow Chemical Company attempted to impale the Medical Committee's proposal on both horns of the dilemma: in its memorandum of counsel it argued that the Medical Committee's proposal was a matter of ordinary business operations properly within the sphere of management expertise and, at the same time, that the proposal clearly had been submitted primarily for the purpose of promoting general political or social causes. The Division of Corporation Finance [of the SEC] made no attempt to choose between these potentially conflicting arguments."

p. 285: General Motors public relations campaign: Vogel, *Lobbying,* 83.

p. 287: "the nature of the questions": Ibid., 85.

p. 287: "They were very precise": Ibid.

p. 287: Born in 1922: For an account of Leon Sullivan's life prior to his appointment to the board of General Motors, see his autobiography, *Build Brother Build.*

p. 288: Sullivan's success in the Charleston diner: Ibid., 38. Sullivan misidentifies the passage from the Declaration of Independence as the preamble of the Constitution.

p. 288: he persuaded Adam Clayton Powell: Ibid., 44.

p. 288: "tutored me as a father would": Ibid., 46.

p. 289: her boss had instructed her: Ibid., 66.

p. 290: "Everywhere you went where the jobs were good": Ibid., 67.

p. 290: "to hear about Jesus, not about Tastykake": Ibid., 83.

p. 291: "Nothing influences a company's attitudes": Ibid., 79.

p. 291: "If banking institutions": Ibid., 81. In the same book, Sullivan echoed the point with regard to diamonds: "If black people of America were to refuse to purchase diamonds until some changes are made in the segregationalist practices of South Africa diamond mines—and hold out for only a single year—their action would have unbelievable impact on employment conditions for black people all over the African continent" (82).

pp. 292–93: Sullivan . . . said no: See "Negro on G.M. Board Ready for Challenge," *New York Times,* January 9, 1971; see also *New Yorker,* May 14, 1979.

p. 293: "We buy more Cadillacs": *New Yorker,* May 14, 1979.

p. 293: "particularly interested in training programs": "The Unorthodox Ministry of Leon H. Sullivan," *Ebony,* May 1971.

p. 294: "increasing the strength and control": *New York Times,* May 22, 1971.

p. 294: "within the framework of existing laws": "Report of the 63rd General Motors Stockholders Meeting," 1971, 9–10.

p. 294: "American industry cannot morally continue": *New Yorker,* May 14, 1979; see also *New York Times,* May 22, 1971.

p. 295: "I was the only one in the world": Author interview with Leon H. Sullivan, August 26, 1991.

p. 295: the newspapers reported on the hearings daily: See, for example, *Argus,* June 5, 1971, which complimented Butcher's skill in the midst of the "interminable inquiries."

p. 295: The questionnaire, which was mailed out on July 22: Box 223, Diggs Archives.

p. 296: The group vice president of General Motors: E. M. Estes to Charles C. Diggs, July 22, 1971, File IV—Poor Response to Questionnaire, Box 223, Diggs Collection.

p. 296: Most said they couldn't collect the information: The correspondent from National Cash Register, noting that the head of the subsidiary was a South African, explained that "day to day operation of all our company operations is the complete responsibility of our local management" (File I: Refusal to Reply, Box 223, Diggs Collection). The reply from Bristol-Myers was similar: "In view of the highly decentralized nature of our international organization, much of the information sought by your questionnaire is only known to local management" who couldn't be bothered because they were involved with budgeting and forecasting.

p. 296: they did not wish to antagonize: Ken Owen, the influential Washington correspondent for the *Johannesburg Star,* had pointed out in print that the South African government's 1969 refusal to admit Diggs unless he promised not to deliver any speeches had been offensive to many American politicians (see *New York Times,* August 2, 6, 9, 17, and 19, 1969). Even though the "park benches, the separate lifts, the multitude of prohibitions, and regulations are all calculated to affront a visitor, even one as light-skinned as Mr. Diggs," Owen argued that it would be far better to admit a moderate than to wait until "a very angry, truly radical Negro bent on mischief joins the queue for visas" (see Ken Owen, "Charles Diggs Not Such Ogre," *Johannesburg Star,* August 7, 1971).

p. 296: C. L. Sulzberger . . . had gone: See *New York Times,* December 3, 6, 8, 10, and 15, 1967; January 5, 1968.

p. 296: Carl Rowan: See *New York Times,* September 7, 1970.

p. 296: Diggs's arrival in South Africa: For Herbert Kaiser's recollections of the trip, see author interview with Kaiser, April 13, 1989.

p. 297: "We call separate development": For verbatim quotations and details of Diggs's trip to South Africa, see the extraordinarily complete record of each meeting kept by someone on Diggs's staff, probably Goler Butcher (Chron File: Sept 20, 1971, Box 224, Diggs Collection, hereafter cited as Diggs Trip Report).

p. 297: "It is said in argument": See Ibid., 68.

p. 298: "Here is a black man who is lionhearted": Ibid., 65; author interview with Herbert Kaiser, April 13, 1989; "Congressman Jolts Along on African Visit," *Christian Science Monitor,* August 14, 1971; see also Diggs press statement, September 16, 1971, Active People Files, ACOA Amistad. For a contemporary South African account, see "Diggs Decides to See Out 9-Day Visit to South Africa," *Cape Times,* August 13, 1971.

p. 298: He toured the NASA facility: Diggs press release, September 16, 1971, Active People Files, ACOA Amistad.

p. 299: "was absolutely the funniest guy": Author interviews with William G. Slocum, September 20 and 21, 1991.

p. 299: Diggs began the meeting: For a detailed description of the meeting, including the verbatim quotations that follow, see "Discussion at General Motors Plant—August 16," 1–9, Diggs Trip Report. For additional perspectives on the encounter at General Motors, see author interview with Charles C. Diggs Jr., May 24, 1990, and author interview with Goler T. Butcher, May 24, 1990.

p. 299: "Doesn't it turn your stomach": The phrasing comes from Diggs Trip Report. Slocum, twenty years later, recalled Diggs's words as even more blunt: "Doesn't it make you want to vomit?" (author interview with William G. Slocum, September 18, 1991).

p. 300: Diggs exploded with rage: Slocum remembered years later that Diggs had become "mad as a hornet" (author interview with William G. Slocum, September 18, 1991).

p. 300: "I am convinced": "Diggs Accuses US Companies," *Cape Times,* August 17, 1971.

p. 301: "No, I think I have a greater understanding": Press release, House Subcommittee on Africa—August 1971, Diggs Trip Report.

**p. 301: *Diggs Changes His Tune: Cape Times,* August 19, 1971. See also the editorial in the *Cape Times* on August 20, 1971, which noted, with only slightly greater accuracy, "Mr. Diggs leaves the Republic convinced that pressures on American investors to withdraw from this country are unrealistic."

p. 301: "interested only in his own advancement": Professor Lucien Pichette also said that Diggs's intention in visiting South Africa had been to cause an incident. "If I were to meet him," said the suddenly famous Pichette, "I would ask him one question, 'How much have you done for blacks in your own country?' " *(Cape Times,* August 20, 1971).

p. 301: Senate bill 1404: For a thorough description of the politics of the Byrd amendment, see Lake, *Tar Baby,* esp. chap. 6.

p. 302: Programme to Combat Racism: For a discussion of the WCC program, see Mbali, *Churches and Racism,* esp. chap. 2.

pp. 302–3: the arrest, trial, and conviction of ffrench-Beytagh: See coverage in

New York Times, January 25, 26, 29, July 1, 3, 4, August 3, 8, 14, 29, September 15, 16, 18, October 16, November 2 and 7, 1971. See also SAIRR, *Survey, 1971,* 87ff.

p. 303: Beyers Naudé and Dale White: See author interview with Dale White, February 1993.

p. 303: For good measure: SAIRR, *Survey, 1972,* 79.

p. 303: Mohammed Essop and Ahmed Timol: See SAIRR, *Survey, 1971,* 91–92, and *New York Times,* October 29 and November 7, 1971.

p. 304: which had never posted a black: According to political officer Herbert Kaiser, this was a much debated topic inside the embassy at the time. Some, such as Kaiser, believed that it would send an important signal to the South African government. Others, like Ambassador Hurd, believed that it would be contrary to the policy of "communication" because it would irritate John Vorster. Moreover, thought Hurd, it would be unfair to the black officer to put him in such an awkward setting (author interview with Herbert Kaiser, April 13, 1989).

p. 304: another edition of his questionnaire: For copies of the second questionnaire, dated November 27, 1972, see Box 223, Diggs Collection.

p. 304: Diggs walked out of the General Assembly: See the study prepared under the direction of Ronald V. Dellums, chair of the Congressional Black Caucus, "The Congressional Black Caucus: Selected Efforts to Influence U.S. Policy towards South Africa, 1971–1989"; also see *New York Times,* December 18, 1971.

p. 304: "action manifesto": Charles C. Diggs Jr., "Action Manifesto as a Result of My Trip to South Africa, Guinea-Bissau, and Cape Verde." There is some disagreement about when this was actually released. The Congressional Black Caucus history places it in December 1971; a press release from the Diggs Archives dates it in March 1972. See File: African Statements—Diggs, Box 416, Diggs Collection.

p. 305: Slocum . . . believed until the end of his days: Author interview with William G. Slocum, September 18, 1991. Slocum is also the source of the information that Scott of Ford Motor Company was fired.

p. 305: he met personally with James Roche: Author interview with Charles C. Diggs Jr., September 18, 1991.

p. 305: "for ultimate advancement": "GM Trains Non-Whites," *Evening Post* (South Africa) October 13, 1971.

p. 305: South African press accounts of Estes's trip: "GM Trains Non-Whites," *Evening Post,* October 13, 1971; "GM Pledge on Treatment of Africans," *Eastern Province Herald,* October 16, 1971; "Critics of GM Are 'Unjust,'" *Argus,* October 15, 1971.

CHAPTER SEVEN: **The Awakening of the Institutional Investor**

p. 307: "It was surely inevitable": Simon, Powers, and Gunnemann, *Ethical Investor,* 1.

p. 307: savings accounts and stock portfolios: In 1952 there were only 6.5 million direct share owners in the United States, or 4.2 percent of a population of 156.2 million. Eighteen years later the number had increased nearly fivefold, to 30.9 million, though the percentage rose to only 15.1 percent. In other words, 85 percent of the American population owned no stock directly; whatever equity ownership they may have had was in the form of pensions. See Jacoby, "Myth of Corporate Economy."

p. 308: dissatisfaction with a corporation's policies: For a discussion of such decisions to exercise "voice" rather than to "exit," see Hirschman, *Exit, Voice, Loyalty.*

p. 308: Herbert Simon and others: See, for example, March and Simon, *Organizations,* and Cyert and Marsh, *Behavioral Theory.*

p. 309: The activists could combat this fear: The shape of this debate very much followed the contours of the "jeopardy thesis" described by Albert Hirschman in his illuminating book *The Rhetoric of Reaction.*

p. 310: Inside churches, pension funds: For an interesting contemporary description of the turmoil over these questions, see Peter Landau, "Do Institutional Investors," 25ff.

p. 310: though they opposed the South African withdrawal: *New York Times,* May 18, 1971.

p. 311: "Just a year ago": William C. Greenough, "The Power of Institutions," *New York Times,* May 2, 1971.

p. 312: "social values and social justice": "Investing Church Funds for Maximum Social Impact," General Synod Committee on Financial Investments (COFI) report to Executive Council of United Church of Christ, October 1970. Hereafter cited as COFI Report.

p. 312: "a significant role": Ibid., 21.

p. 312: United Church Board for World Ministries: The agency, known originally as the American Board of Commissioners for Foreign Mission, was formed in 1810. For a discussion of the role of these missionaries, see du Plessis, *History of Christian Missions,* esp. chap. 23.

p. 312: After graduating from Harvard: Author interview with Howard Schomer, March 1988.

p. 313: the committee sought to find a middle ground: COFI Report, op. cit.

p. 314: how peculiar he felt: See author interview with Jon Gunnemann, November 6, 1991.

p. 314: Miller consented to meet: Author interview with Charles Powers, December 2, 1991.

p. 315: a strikingly moderate article: Charles W. Powers and Jon P. Gunnemann, "Institutions, Investment, and Integrity," *Christian Century,* January 29, 1969, 144.

p. 315: "We took one look and we realized": Author interview with Jon Gunnemann, November 6, 1991.

p. 315: "When I sit in church": Ibid.

p. 316: "We have not succeeded": Simon, Powers, and Gunnemann, *Ethical Investor,* 17.

p. 316: four criteria: Gunnemann proposed the criteria after reflecting on a grotesque crime that had taken place in New York City in the early 1960s. A young woman named Kitty Genovese had been stalked and stabbed by an assailant in the Kew Gardens section of Brooklyn. Though she had screamed for help, not one of the thirty-eight people who admitted to police that they had heard her had done anything to help. Her attacker had fled, then returned, and killed her. The public reaction to the witnesses' failure to assist Genovese had been powerful and negative. Why was that? wondered Gunnemann. What were the moral intuitions that led everyone to agree that the neighbors should have acted on Genovese's behalf? After more reflection, Gunnemann and his coauthors, Simon and Powers, decided there were four components. The first was *need:* when a person's need increases, so does the responsibility to meet it. The second is *proximity:* the closer one is to a problem, the more responsible one is to solve it. Proximity was not purely a function of physical distance, argued the authors, but also of awareness. "We hold a person blameworthy if he knows of imperilment and does not do what he reasonably can do to remedy the situation," they wrote. Thus, "when we become aware of a wrongdoing or a social injury, we take on obligations that we did not have while ignorant." Third, they pointed to *capability*. Grounding their argument in Immanuel Kant's observation that *"ought* implies *can,"* the authors noted that we do not hold persons responsible for actions which would be impossible. Finally, they said, the duty to help is heightened when a situation is one of *last resort:* "one becomes more responsible the less likely it is that someone else will be able to aid." Taken together, the four intuitions formed the "Kew Garden Principle." The Kew Garden Principle offered a critical bridge between negative injunctions (which were imposed on people) and affirmative duties (which were voluntary) by defining terms under which persons or institutions are morally required to help someone else. The Kew Garden Principle thus provided a vital intellectual piece in helping Yale's trustees—and those of other universities—define their moral duties as investors (ibid., 22).

p. 316–17: Fiduciaries are persons: Fiduciaries and trustees who serve on deliberative bodies represent a perplexing group for the conceptual scheme known as agency theory. Fiduciaries are the continuing agents of the deceased principals who originally constituted the organization but who now face insurmountable monitoring costs. They also often consider themselves the agents of unborn generations whose assets they must preserve. At the same time, trustees are also the principals on whose behalf administrators act. For this and other reasons, scholars such as Robert C. Clark at Harvard Law School have argued that agency theory does not apply to fiduciaries and trustees. See Clark, "Agency Costs versus Fiduciary Duties," in Pratt and Zeckhauser, *Principals and Agents,* 55–80.

p. 317: "conduct himself faithfully": *Harvard College v. Amory,* 26 Mass. 446, 9 Pick. 446 (1830).

p. 317: "prudent man rule": This principle states that "where money is given to charitable organization for its general purposes, it may make such investments as a prudent man would make of his own property having in view the preservation of the endowment and the amount and regularity of the income to be derived" (Restatement [Second] of Trusts, American Law Institute, Paragraph 227).

p. 317: legislators incorporated the Massachusetts language: See, for example, Section 2261(1), Civil Code of the State of California.

p. 317: Under the law of trusts: Simon, Powers, and Gunnemann, *Ethical Investor,* 142.

p. 317: "where the issue involves the investment": W. L. Cary and C. B. Bright, *The Law and the Lore of Endowment Funds,* report to the Ford Foundation (New York, 1969), 27; also cited in Simon, Powers, and Gunnemann, *Ethical Investor,* 143, and COFI Report, op. cit.

p. 318: The business judgment rule said: For an excellent discussion of the application of the trust law and corporate law standards, including a confirmation of the Cary and Bright observation that courts are steadily moving toward using corporate law, see Thomas Troyer and Robert A. Boisture, "Divestment of South Africa Investments: A Legal Analysis for Foundations, Other Charitable Institutions, and Pension Funds: A Report to the New World Foundation," brief prepared by attorneys at Caplin and Drysdale, Washington, D.C., April 15, 1985.

p. 318: "it contributes sufficiently": Troyer et al., "Divestment of South Africa Investments: The Legal Implications for Foundations, Other Charitable Institutions, and Pension Funds," *Georgetown Law Journal* 74.1.

p. 318: The only rebuttal: A vigorous conservative criticism of *The Ethical Investor* and an endorsement of the concept of divestment can be found in Eli Goldston, "A Review of *The Ethical Investor," Foundation News,* July/August 1972, 30; see also the reply by John Simon, Charles Powers, and Jon Gunnemann, "A Prophylactic Portfolio?," *Foundation News,* September/October 1972.

p. 318: Kennedy first commissioned Jon Gunnemann: Author interview with Jon Gunnemann, November 7, 1991.

p. 319: "You would have thought": Author interview with H. David Rosenbloom, May 1988.

p. 319: "I think it's O.K.": Ibid.

p. 319: "That's a convenient position": Author interview with Wayne Fredericks, October 15, 1991.

p. 320: In a separate study: The Longstreth and Rosenbloom study went through many drafts (the major ones were June 16, 1971, November 11, 1971, and April 15, 1972) before it was approved by the foundation board. The board also deleted several chapters before permitting public distribution, which appeared as Longstreth and Rosenbloom, *Corporate Social Responsibility.* Because the report includes only anonymous comments by the participants in the study, the author spent two days reviewing the archival files at Debevoise and Plimpton in New York and Caplin and Drysdale in Washington, D.C., searching for the original responses. Unfortunately, despite that search and subsequent efforts by the staffs of both attorneys, the file containing all of the original responses to the letter mailed in the fall of 1971 has been lost.

p. 320: "the foundation should now frame": Memorandum to the members of the Finance Committee, March 17, 1972.

p. 320: The fundamental principle: Roger G. Kennedy, "Portfolio Decisions and Social Responsibility," in Backman, *Social Responsibility.*

p. 321: "program related investments": As early as 1968 the Ford Foundation embarked on a policy of deliberately blurring the line between its programs and investments. Since that year, the foundation has annually set aside a tiny percentage of the portfolio ($15.2 million in 1987) for "Program Related Investments" (PRIs)— "loans, guarantees of loans, or equity investments in projects that serve social purposes." "PRI's are an example of . . . balance sheet philanthropy," states a recent foundation document. They are "social investments that appear on the balance sheets as assets rather than as contributions" ("Program Related Investments," Ford Foundation, March 1983). By 1983, the foundation had made more than 130 PRI loans, providing from $200,000 to $2 million to organizations such as the Spanish Speaking Unity Council of Oakland, California; the Studio Museum of Harlem; the National Rural Development and Finance Corporation; the Industrial Cooperative Association in Somerville, Massachusetts; the National Housing Law Project; and scores of others. The loans were used to construct buildings, establish new programs, and capitalize financial intermediaries for depressed communities. Virtually all of the PRI loans were made in the United States because of difficulties monitoring overseas loans.

p. 321: "When we started this": Author interview with Mary Camper-Titsingh, July 11, 1988. See also the interview of Camper-Titsingh by Heidi Welsh in the September 1988 IRRC publication *News for Investors.*

p. 321: unless Camper-Titsingh recommended a reconsideration: On a few occasions the trustees reversed themselves completely. For example, in the 1980s the trustees originally opposed all poison pill measures (an antitakeover practice that made target companies less attractive to potential buyers) and then switched to approving them in the belief that the takeover movement had gotten out of hand and had become bad for the American economy.

p. 322: Boksburg: Rosenthal, *Stars and Stripes,* 133.

p. 322: In California Bok's life settled: Craig Lambert, "DB: The Public Figure and the Private Man," *Harvard Magazine,* July–August 1991, 28.

p. 322: had helped found the Miquon School: See Bok, *Alva Myrdal,* 131.

p. 322: a law student named William Rehnquist: Lambert, "DB," op. cit., 31.

p. 322: his first-year grades had been good enough: "Harvard's Quiet Man," *Time,* January 25, 1971.

p. 323: His wife, Alva Myrdal: I am grateful to Sissela Myrdal Bok for her willingness to share the unpublished portions of her manuscript for *Alva Myrdal* that dealt with her mother's role on the UN committee and her appointment as Swedish minister of church affairs. For contemporary press accounts, see *New York Times,* January 14, 23, April 21, and May 30, 1964. For a discussion of the life and work of Alva Myrdal, see Bok, *Alva Myrdal.*

p. 323: "Even in the first year": Lambert, "DB," op. cit., 32.

p. 324: "administrators are nothing but failed scholars": Quote is from Bok, *Alva Myrdal;* quoted in Lambert, "DB," op. cit., 33.

p. 324: The most memorable incident: *Newsweek,* January 18, 1971, 72.

p. 324: Dunlop and Vorenberg observations: Lambert, "DB," op. cit., 33.

p. 324: the faculty of arts and sciences passed a resolution: For a description of student and faculty attitudes at that time, see David Ignatius, "Some Notes on the Harvard Experience," *Institutional Investor,* July 1970, 64ff.

p. 325: "the behavior of none": Report of the Committee on University Relations with Corporate Enterprise (the Austin Report), January 1971.

p. 325: "a center of free inquiry": Ibid.

p. 326: He arrived at nine-thirty: For Bok's account, see Lambert, "DB," op. cit., 34; see also *Time,* January 25, 1971, 60.

p. 326: When Kingman Brewster . . . heard that his former protégé: Lambert, "DB," op. cit., 34.

p. 327: three others . . . had also selected lawyers: The three presidents were Edward Levi at the University of Chicago, Robben Fleming at Michigan, and Kingman Brewster at Yale. See "Harvard Picks a President," *Newsweek,* January 18, 1971, 70.

p. 327: "must have a capacity": Ibid., 71.

p. 327: "one has to work very hard": *Time,* January 25, 1971, 61.

p. 327: Robinson . . . was born in Richmond: Details of Robinson's life from author interview with Randall Robinson, August 28, 1991.

p. 327: *A Kind of Homecoming:* E. R. Braithwaite, *A Kind of Homecoming* (Englewood Cliffs, N.J.: Prentice-Hall, 1962). Braithwaite was also the author of the 1959 book *To Sir with Love.*

p. 328: Bok liked the tall, fervent student: See author interview with Derek Bok, September 13, 1988; and author interview with Randall Robinson, August 28, 1991.

p. 328: The massive Cabinda oil find by Gulf Oil: See, for example, the estimates provided in Marcum, *Angolan Revolution,* vol. 2. Marcum writes that by 1973 the Cabinda find was "pumping over $60 million a year into the Portuguese-Angolan treasury. In [the] absence of a constraining public policy, by 1973 American private sector contributions to the Portuguese economy . . . totaled nearly $400 million a year, at a time when Portugal's military-security budget was $400 million a year.

With the rise in oil prices stemming from the Arab-Israeli war of 1973, Cabindan oil revenues alone soared to over $400 million a year. And American capital poured into new extractive, capital-intensive projects to exploit Angolan petroleum, diamonds, and phosphates" (237).

p. 328: Bok said he would think about it: Author interview with Derek Bok, September 1988.

p. 328: "there is no question in my mind": *Harvard Crimson,* February 25, 1972.

p. 329: "a spiritual experience": Author conversation with Hubert Jessup, who was a Harvard undergraduate at the time.

p. 329: "These were some of the best students": Author interview with Randall Robinson, August 28, 1991.

p. 329: believed that shareholder resolutions had no effect: Author interview with William McGill, November 1988.

p. 329: Columbia should sell its shares: Originally reported in the *Columbia Spectator;* reported again in the *Harvard Crimson,* April 27, 1972, the day that Massachusetts Hall protesters departed. There is also a reference to McGill's promise in an editorial in the *Spectator* on November 13, 1972. For a full case study of the Columbia divestment story under William McGill and Michael Sovern and a comparison to that of Harvard University, see Robert K. Massie Jr., "Moral Deliberation and Policy Formulation," unpublished doctoral dissertation, Harvard Graduate School of Business Administration, 1989, chap. 5.

p. 330: "The trustees believe the university": Adapted from a statement by the president and Fellows of Harvard College made on May 4, 1972. Quoted in Goldston, "Review of *Ethical Investor,"* op. cit., 33.

p. 330: "I spent more than a quarter of my time": *Harvard Crimson,* October 11, 1972.

p. 330: Advisory Committee: All of the representatives—except for the two undergraduates—were to be selected by Bok or by the deans of the university or graduate schools. The undergraduates were elected by the Undergraduate Council.

p. 330: "If you want to understand Derek Bok": Author interview with Robert Monks, July 1988.

p. 331: "I don't know why they sent him": Author interview with Randall Robinson, August 28, 1991.

p. 332: the members of both committees agreed: See the statement by the president and Fellows of Harvard College made on May 4, 1972. Quoted in Goldston, "Review of *Ethical Investor,"* op. cit., 33.

p. 332: changed the direction in which America would sail: See, for example, the comment by Phillip I. Blumberg in 1971 that the shareholder resolution campaigns "had shattered for all time the pattern of institutional neutrality under which the institutional shareholder, particularly the non-profit institution, automatically votes its shares for management. As a result . . . American corporate electoral processes have become fundamentally changed" (quoted in Longstreth and Rosenbloom, *Corporate Social Responsibility).*

CHAPTER EIGHT: **The Enigma of Buthelezi**

p. 333: "There can be few countries": Kane-Berman, *South Africa,* 230.

p. 333: Following a strategy well established: The Dutch, the British, and the Afrikaners had all sought to domesticate the indigenous kings first with guns, then with gold, and finally with an appeal to royal government. It was Theophilus Shepstone, a British official who spoke Zulu, who persuaded King Mpande in the 1840s that his best interests lay in transforming his chiefs into the salaried servants of the empire. Chiefs who refused to cooperate were swiftly deposed in favor of jealous and compliant half-brothers. Hendrik Verwoerd had expanded this system and, in his inimitable way, sprayed it with a coating of cultural virtue. He also appealed directly to the chiefs' self-interest, telling them that though modern society, urbanization, and industrialization had eroded the authority of the chiefs, he and the National Party would ensure that they retained their rightful place in Zulu society. (For differing accounts of Verwoerd's comments, which took place at a meeting in Nongoma in October 1955, see Mzala, *Buthelezi,* 57ff, and Temkin, *Buthelezi,* 50–54.) By the time Vorster took power, the principle was well established.

p. 333: Buthelezi's leadership: For summary information about Buthelezi's career, see Gastrow, *Who's Who,* 41; for a poorly organized, biased, but still interesting "official" biography, see Temkin, *Buthelezi.*

p. 334: the aunt . . . of Pixley Seme: Magogo's older sister was Princess Phikisile, the mother of Seme. See Mzala, *Buthelezi,* 104.

p. 334: feared a life of barrenness: Temkin, *Buthelezi,* 19.

p. 334: This distinction later proved important: The dispute is carried into the scholarship on Buthelezi. Biographical works supportive of Buthelezi, such as that by Temkin, stress Mathole's status as a princess and as chief wife; those that are critical, such as Mzala's, insist that the oldest son of the first wife holds the strongest claim. See the discussion in Temkin, *Buthelezi,* chap. 1, and in Mzala, *Buthelezi,* chap. 6.

p. 334: the "lie of the Usuthu": Temkin, *Buthelezi,* 20.

p. 334: fearing for the lives of his sister and nephew: Ibid., 20–21.

p. 334: Buthelezi grew up in the king's enclave: Ibid., 22–23.

p. 334: Buthelezi took part in the funeral: Ibid., 26.

p. 335: the two stopped to visit John Dube: Ibid., for information on John Dube's later career, see Marks, *Ambiguities of Dependence,* 42–73.

p. 335: ANC had been led by "Zulu patriots": This claim of Buthelezi's has been a mainstay of his speeches. He also made it during an interview with the author in Ulundi, KwaZulu, January 25, 1990.

p. 335: There they met the principal: Temkin, *Buthelezi,* 27; see also the biographical entry in Gerhart and Karis, *From Protest to Challenge,* 4:11.

p. 335: Despite a stiff warning: Temkin, *Buthelezi,* 30–31.

p. 335: Over the next two years, Buthelezi increased: Ibid., 34, 36.

p. 336: University of Natal: Ibid., 37.

p. 336: Buthelezi would attribute his decision: See ibid., 39.

p. 336: In their interview Eiselen told Buthelezi: Ibid.

p. 337: Buthelezi nonetheless encouraged: For a justification of this practice, on the grounds that Buthelezi is the "direct descendant of a Zulu king," see the appendix by Dr. Zami Conco in ibid., 404.

p. 337: a hereditary right . . . to serve as the king's "prime minister": For a scathing attack on that claim, see Mzala, *Buthelezi,* chap. 6.

p. 337: Buthelezi persuaded the young monarch: Temkin, *Buthelezi,* 38–40.

p. 337: He had . . . dined at Nelson Mandela's home: Ibid., 56.

p. 337: threatened *Drum* magazine: Ibid., 50. Another example of Buthelezi's desire to avoid a public snub of the government took place around the ceremonial inauguration of the Bantu Authorities Act in 1952. Newspapers noticed that Buthelezi did not attend and interpreted this as a boycott of the proceedings.

Buthelezi indignantly protested that he had wanted to come but had not been invited. See ibid., 73.

p. 338: Mceleli enjoyed growing support: Even Gatsha Buthelezi's most sympathetic biographer concedes this point. See ibid., 73.

p. 339: he wrote an angry letter: Ibid., 78.

p. 339: the police finally nabbed Mceleli: Ibid., 82.

p. 339: Buthelezi . . . believed that he had been edged out: Ibid., 118.

p. 339: Buthelezi now latched on to this idea: Maré and Hamilton state bluntly that through the Zulustan Territorial Authority, "apartheid saved the chief from possible obscurity" *(Appetite for Power,* 37).

p. 339: At the election in June 1970: See SAIRR, *Survey, 1970,* 141–43.

p. 339: Buthelezi had been elected unanimously: None of the available works on Buthelezi lists the margin of his victory; Temkin says that the Bantu affairs commissioner simply announced Buthelezi's victory and notes *afterward* that Buthelezi had been "elected unanimously by acclamation." Temkin is obviously sensitive to the accusation that the election might have been fixed and so goes out of his way to emphasize the government's unhappiness with Buthelezi and therefore lack of enthusiasm for his election. But this event, like so many in bantustan politics, has many conflicting and uncertain aspects. See Temkin, *Buthelezi,* 125.

p. 339: a potent conservative alliance: The influence and conservativism of this alliance was felt in the politics of Zululand during most of the twentieth century. See Marks, *Ambiguities of Dependence,* passim, and Maré and Hamilton, *Appetite for Power,* passim.

p. 341: "wasting its time": For the interchanges between Matanzima and Vorster, see SAIRR, *Survey, 1972,* 33–35. For additional material on Matanzima, see Laurence, *Transkei;* Streek and Wicksteed, *Render under Kaiser;* and Campton, *New Transkei.* For his own account of the path to "independence," see Matanzima, *Independence;* for Nelson Mandela's views, see Mandela, *Long Walk to Freedom,* 156–60, 441.

p. 341: In a speech in April 1972: SAIRR, *Survey, 1972,* 36.

p. 341: At a meeting between Vorster and the KwaZulu Executive Council: Temkin, *Buthelezi,* 170.

p. 341: "We cannot see ourselves": SAIRR, *Survey, 1972,* 36–37.

p. 341: acrimonious dispute: Temkin, *Buthelezi,* 170–72. For additional comment, see *New York Times,* November 27, 1972, and SAIRR, *Survey, 1972,* 84.

p. 341: Helen Suzman, Harry Oppenheimer: For example, in 1971 Buthelezi was welcomed into a discussion group called "Synthesis" led by Progressive leader F. Van Zyl Slabbert and attended by some liberal Afrikaners. See *New York Times,* November 8, 1971.

p. 342: "Chief Gatsha Buthelezi has led the way": Study Project on Christianity in Apartheid Society [SPRO-CAS], *South Africa's Political Alternatives, 1973,* 39; quoted in Maré and Hamilton, *Appetite,* 38.

p. 342: The head of the Hotel Board responded: SAIRR, *Survey, 1972.* The same volume describes the Department of Bantu Administration and Development "protocol guide" to homeland administrators, issued two years earlier, which stated that African leaders should not leave the homelands for political liaison—even to visit individuals—without written authority of the government. "When leaders receive invitations to address members of private institutions outside their areas," the *Survey* notes, summarizing the rules, "the advisability of accepting should be discussed with the Commissioner General. Communications with private White institutions

772 *Notes to Pages 342–46*

must take place with the Department's help, as should liaison with other homelands. Three months before any firm arrangement for visits are made, a tour itinerary should be sent to the department" (176).

p. 342: it was reported in the newspapers: See *New York Times,* December 3, 1972.

p. 342: Newsmaker of the Year: Temkin, *Buthelezi,* 147, 286–87.

p. 342: Buthelezi received favorable ratings: See, for example, the editorial in the *New York Times* on January 30, 1972, praising Buthelezi and warning that his activism, coupled with that of Kaiser Matanzima, spelled trouble for separate development; see also the flattering op-ed piece by Graham Hovey, a member of the *Times* editorial board, February 7, 1972.

p. 343: his old colleagues . . . who had joined the Pan-Africanist Congress: The author encountered an early example of the sympathetic links between Buthelezi and the PAC when, in Paris in 1972, he met Nana Mahomo, the PAC representative whom Robert Sobukwe had sent abroad on the day of the Sharpeville massacre. Mahomo was working on a documentary film about the horrendous conditions in the bantustans that later aired in the United States as *The Last Grave at Dimbaza* and won an Emmy award. Despite his abhorrence for the bantustans, Mahomo at the time named Buthelezi as one of the most important black proponents of change.

p. 343: they generated the impression: Temkin, for example, includes several such pictures from Jabulani, noting in one caption that such a welcome was "typical" *(Buthelezi,* photos after 178).

p. 344: Tiro . . . chose this highly public moment: The text of the speech can be found in the April 1974 issue of the ANC document *Sechaba.* The ANC article and other news account often give Tiro's first name as Abraham or Abram.

p. 344: The day after the ceremony: SAIRR, *Survey, 1972,* 387–88; see also Ruth First, "Student Revolt," *African Survey—Africa,* no. 11, July 1972, 58.

p. 344: The students called for Helen Suzman: Strangwayes-Booth, *Cricket in the Thorn Tree,* 247.

p. 344: Over the next few days: SAIRR, *Survey, 1972,* 392ff.

p. 344: Black observers noted grimly: There were even complaints about this in the black press in the United States. "Africans Started Apartheid Protest, Not Whites," *Muhammad Speaks,* July 7, 1972.

p. 345: Speaking to high school students: See SAIRR, *Survey, 1972,* 56; For Odendaal's question, see "Spiritual Terrorists: A Warning," *Argus,* July 5, 1972. For similar reactions at white universities, see "Protests Split Afrikaner Student Bodies," *Times,* June 24, 1972.

p. 345: C. Eric Lincoln . . . had visited: See "Reports Presented at the 3rd General Students' Council," 17, Reel 2, Gerhart BCM Collection.

p. 345: "black people in America are watching with pride": "Memorandum, Report on the Conference, 1972," 2, Reel 2, Gerhart BCM Collection.

p. 345: "the entire conference was expecting": For these and other comments on the conference, see the SASO newsletter, September–October 1972, 14ff, Reel 2, Gerhart BCM Collection.

p. 346: "If we don't fight it": See *Argus* news reports, July 1972, Reel 2, Gerhart BCM Collection.

p. 346: "the one man who has led the entire world": See "Black-Solidarity Is Our Aim—SASO," *Anti-Apartheid News,* September 1972, 3, Reel 2, Gerhart BCM Collection.

p. 346: "Let's Talk about Bantustans": See "I Write What I Like" column by "Frank Talk" in the September–October issue of the SASO newsletter, 18ff, Reel 2,

Gerhart BCM Collection. The article is reprinted in Biko, *I Write What I Like,* 80–86.

p. 346: Biko had edited a book: Ironically, the book was reviewed in the same newsletter in which Biko published his attack on the bantustan system. See SASO newsletter, September–October, 1972, 15, Reel 2, Gerhart BCM Collection.

p. 347: worried . . . about controlling inflation: South Africa actually had three serious bouts with inflation during the decade in question, the first from mid-1962 to mid-1964, the second from 1966 to 1968, and the third in 1970.

p. 348: comparisons of district output: Nattrass, *South African Economy,* 28, 196.

p. 348: black miners' wages had not risen since 1911: Wilson, *Labour;* also cited in SIARR, *Survey, 1972,* 292, and Nattrass, *South African Economy,* 160.

p. 348: a daily cash wage of forty-two cents: SAIRR, *Survey, 1972,* 293.

p. 348: the debate about the mutual dependence of capitalism and apartheid: For an excellent assessment of this question, see Lipton, *Capitalism and Apartheid.*

p. 348: "It's just a plain, obvious truth": Harry Oppenheimer, quoted in John Blashill, "Proper Role," 50.

p. 348: South Africa had flourished *because* of apartheid: For the Marxist interpretation, see Wolpe, *Race, Class.*

p. 349: 3.5 billion rand: In 1994 constant dollar value this would be approximately $18 billion.

p. 349: American presence in the South African economy (1970–1975): For detailed analyses of U.S. corporate involvement in the South African economy, see Myers, *Labor Practices;* Myers et al., *U.S. Business;* Interfaith Center on Corporate Responsibility, *Church Investments.* For relevant congressional hearings, see House Committee on Foreign Affairs, Subcommittee on Africa, *Hearings, 1971–1973;* House Committee on International Relations, Subcommittees on Africa and International Economic Policy and Trade, *United States Private Investment in South Africa,* 95th Cong., 2nd sess., 1978 (Washington, D.C.: GPO, 1978); House Committee on Foreign Affairs, Subcommittee on International Economic Policy and Trade, *U.S. Corporate Activities in South Africa* (Washington, D.C.: GPO, 1983); Senate Committee on Foreign Relations, Subcommittee on African Affairs, *U.S. Corporate Interests;* Clark, *U.S. Corporate Interests.*

p. 350: "Every time a South African product is bought": *Johannesburg Star,* August 26, 1972; quoted in "U.S. Corporate Expansion in South Africa," Corporate Information Center brief, reprinted by the Africa Fund, April 1976.

p. 350: the English-speaking press avidly reported: The level of interest can be seen from the kinds of headlines that peppered the papers. See, for example, *Rand Daily Mail:* "Multiracial Conference on Labour," July 18, 1973, July 20, 1973; *Daily News:* "Black Visitor in Apartheid Protest," August 8, 1973; "Peaceful Change Possible—American," August 10, 1973; "Worthwhile Conference" (editorial), August 10, 1973; *Natal Mercury:* "The Future Won't Be Dictated," August 10, 1973; *Johannesburg Star:* "A Time for Timetables" (editorial), August 7, 1973; *Sunday Tribune:* "All Part of the Changing Scene," August 12, 1973; *Sunday Times:* "Vorster Gets Restive over Racial Dialogue," September 2, 1973.

p. 350: "How many black jobs would be lost": See "Wilkins Defends U.S. Jobs in Africa," *New York Times,* March 28, 1972. For the South African coverage, see *Rand Daily Mail,* March 29, 1972; *Johannesburg Star,* March 29 and April 3, 1972; and the summary of the trip in SAIRR, *Survey, 1972,* 227.

p. 351: "I have not 'defended' United States business involvement": "Wilkins Denies Defending Plants in South Africa," *New York Times,* March 31, 1972.

p. 351: After a string of meetings: "GM Chiefs to See Buthelezi," *Natal Mercury,* April 13, 1972; "GM Chief Meets Vorster, Graaff" and "Churchmen Put Views Forward," *Eastern Province Herald,* April 13, 1972.

p. 351: "Our stockholders in America": "Pressure to Quit Rejected by GM," *Eastern Province Herald,* April 12, 1972.

p. 351: "Thank you, GM!": *Johannesburg Sunday Times,* April 16, 1972. The editorial continued with an argument that would become more prevalent: "A withdrawal by American industry would mean more unemployment and hardship for non-Whites here and a sharp increase in bitterness in general."

p. 351: Examining the employment practices: Donald McHenry, *United States Firms in South Africa* (Study Project on External Investment in South Africa and Namibia; published by the African Studies Program, Indiana University, 1975).

p. 351: "Perhaps the most ominous function": McHenry, *United States Firms,* 33–34.

p. 352: withdrawal would backfire with the government: The notion that a particular reform or strategy will produce the exact opposite of its intended effect is called "the perversity thesis" by Albert O. Hirschman in his book *The Rhetoric of Reaction.* Ronald Reagan used a compressed form of it in the 1980s when he said that sanctions would "hurt those we want to help."

p. 353: an anonymous memo: After reviewing the economic situation in South Africa, the document suggested that with regard to workplace reforms Vorster's bark was much worse than his bite. "The South African leadership and the white population in general are sensitive about the country's racial policies, and particularly to what they consider outside interference. At the same time they are not inflexible; a number of South Africa firms have been able to engage in efforts to improve the material well-being of non-white South Africans and widen the opportunities open to them. The Polaroid experience suggests that this flexibility extends to the activities of foreign firms.

"In this situation it seems that the best way to defend our economic interests in South Africa against attack," continued the document, "is to act toward non-whites there as nearly as possible as one would act in the United States." Though "it would be clearly worse than useless to break generally observed South African laws in this effort," a wide range of improvement would still be permitted under South African law. The memo urged extreme caution in publicizing the changes, because "anything which gives the South Africans the impression that United States firms were engaged in a coordinated effort to 'change the South Africa way of life' would almost certainly engender harmful reactions." To avoid the impression that American companies were being progressive, the document suggested, the companies could hide behind the example of the few South African firms that had taken the lead in improving working conditions. (Anonymous Department of State paper, "Apartheid and U.S. Firms in South Africa," File: South Africa—3, Box 357, Diggs Collection. The document is undated but refers to "last October [1970]" which puts it somewhere in 1971; it may have been a State Department response to Diggs's visit in August. The paper was apparently sent to Diggs, who forwarded it for review to Goler Butcher.)

p. 353: February 1973 version of the document: U.S. Department of State, Bureau of African Affairs, "Employment Practices of U.S. Firms in South Africa," February 1973.

p. 354: detailed attack on General Motors' role: *General Motors: Apartheid and*

Business in Southern Africa: A CIC Brief for Information and Action (New York: Corporate Information Center of the National Council of Churches, May 1972).

p. 355: "If New York orders me": Blashill, "Proper Role," 90.

p. 355: the budget of the KwaZulu Legislative Authority: Temkin, *Buthelezi*, 184. Economist Jill Nattrass estimated that an even higher percentage (eighty percent) of KwaZulu's money came from the South African government *(South African Economy,* 216).

p. 355: *average* per capita income: Nattrass, *South African Economy,* 208. In 1971, Father David Russell, a white Anglican priest and friend of Stephen Biko's, and Jean Sinclair, the president of the leading liberal women's anti-apartheid group, Black Sash, protested homeland conditions by trying to survive on five rand a month (about $26 in 1994 terms), the pension the government gave to a few retired workers. Every month Russell wrote a letter to the government describing his reaction, and the letters were published in the press. Both Russell and Sinclair described how continuously cold, lethargic, and depressed they felt while trying to survive on this diet (SAIRR, *Survey, 1972,* 207).

p. 356: "The prolonged continuation": Nattrass, *South African Economy,* 117.

p. 356: "Those who are contemplating withdrawing": SAIRR, *Survey, 1972,* 221.

p. 356: "If you are going to ask foreign companies to withdraw": Buthelezi, quoted in *New York Times,* April 8, 1973.

p. 357: more explosive broadsides: One such circular announced a "Black Workers Project." "There is a sure necessity for Blacks to organize themselves to make their demands loudly heard and to be appreciated," the pamphlet said. "There is just too much malnutrition, slum conditions, enforced removals, and pass problems." (quoted in SAIRR, *Survey, 1973,* 282).

p. 357: strikes in Durban: See *New York Times,* February 8 and 9, 1973.

p. 357: Though Helen Suzman and Colin Eglin: Temkin, *Buthelezi*, 201.

p. 357: "heart filled with joy": KwaZulu Legislative Assembly Debates, vol. 2, 44; quoted in Maré and Hamilton, *Appetite for Power,* 121.

p. 358: "Black power politician": SAIRR, *Survey, 1974,* 320–21; also quoted in Maré and Hamilton, *Appetite for Power,* 121.

p. 358: Dladla . . . finally resigned: For Temkin (and thus Buthelezi's) version of the story, see Temkin, *Buthelezi*, 229–37.

p. 358: "taking into account the effect of strikes": Lawrence Schlemmer and Tim Muil, "Social and Political Change in the African Areas: A Case Study of KwaZulu," in Leonard Thompson and Jeffey Butler, eds., *Change in Contemporary South Africa* (Berkeley: University of California Press, 1975), 114; also quoted in Maré and Hamilton, *Appetite for Power,* 123.

p. 359: "When I went out there": Author interview with Howard Schomer, March 1988.

p. 360: Mobil released tabulated data: "Mobil in South Africa," published July 1972 by Mobil Oil Corporation.

p. 361: a series of advertisements: See SAIRR, *Survey, 1973,* 1986–87; the *New York Times* article on the campaign directed by J. Marais, November 13, 1973; and Jennifer Davis, *A New Face for Apartheid,* (New York: Africa Fund, October 1973). Over the years, many of the bantustans ran similar advertisements. In March 1975 one for Gazankulu appeared in the *Financial Mail* with the headline "In the grand design for my homeland, I see many white capitalists making vast amounts of money." The advertisement went on to promise low leases for land and buildings;

tax concessions; low-interest loans for equipment; and 2½ percent mortgages for white managers.

p. 362: "Pik" Botha's career: For a brief summary, see the entry in Gastrow, *Who's Who.* Botha presented his credentials as ambassador to the United States to President Ford on September 3, 1975. He served as ambassador until April 1977.

p. 362: Kurt Waldheim asked if he could come to South Africa: For a critique of the visit, see Joel Carlson, "Walking to Pretoria," *New York Times,* March 31, 1973.

p. 363: "The minister of sport admitted to me": See "Wright Says South African Games 'Distorted' Facts," *New York Times,* April 20, 1973.

p. 363: When James Baker became: See *New York Times* February 12, 1973; for commentary by Donald McHenry, a black former foreign service officer, on Baker's selection, see "On to South Africa," *New York Times,* February 3, 1973.

p. 363: permitted several undersecretaries . . . to attend: *New York Times,* July 29, 1973.

p. 363: Norman Vincent Peale: *New York Times,* January 9, 1974.

p. 363: problems encountered by Diggs, Saunders, and Kitt: *New York Times,* March 20 and 21, 1974.

p. 363: The Schlebusch Commission . . . issued its report: SAIRR, *Survey, 1973.*

p. 363: Helen Suzman was the only person to denounce the action: "I think it is most appalling that the official opposition should have given *carte blanche* to the government to take any action it sees fit against these young people who have not committed any unlawful act" (Strangwayes-Booth, *Cricket in the Thorn Tree,* 255). When several university principals petitioned Vorster in person to soften the punishment, he stood firm, telling them that the bannings were not punitive but preventive (SAIRR, *Survey, 1973,* 343). The new student leaders impetuously predicted that there would be protests throughout the country. Vorster warned sternly that the government "will not in any circumstances tolerate unrest from any quarters" *(New York Times,* March 4, 1973).

p. 363: In early March he issued banning orders: For press reaction in South Africa and abroad, see "Witch Hunt Is On in South Africa," *Sunday Times,* March 4, 1973, and "Vorster's Witch Hunt" (reprint of *New York Times* editorial), *International Herald Tribune,* March 21, 1973.

p. 363: the total number of banned persons: This number is from July 1973; whether it was exactly the same in December when Manas Buthelezi was banned is uncertain. See SAIRR, *Survey, 1973,* 58. For the banning of Manas Buthelezi, see *New York Times,* December 15, 1973; also see material in the SASO collection; and various editions of *Pro Veritate.*

p. 364: The second he opened it: See the April 1974 edition of *Sechaba;* see also *World,* December 6 and 23, 1974.

p. 364: the *Guardian* . . . reported: "South Africa Ties Troubling British," *New York Times,* April 8, 1973.

p. 364: As gold prices rose: See Houghton, *South African Economy,* 107–8.

p. 364: average inflation rate of nearly nine percent: See Nattrass, *South African Economy,* 256.

p. 365: "the 1973 wage bill for Africans": See SAIRR, *Survey, 1973,* 240.

p. 365: shootings at the Carletonville mine and aftermath: SAIRR, *Survey, 1973,* 242–43.

p. 366: In a speech before the South African Motor Industries Federation: "Vorster Pushes Jobs for Blacks," *New York Times,* October 7, 1973.

p. 366: "Perhaps the most heartening thing": *New York Times,* October 10, 1973.

p. 367: Mahlabatini Declaration: SAIRR, *Survey, 1974,* 3; see also "South Africa Party and Zulu in Accord," *New York Times,* January 7, 1974.

p. 368: the price of South Africa's recently mined supply: See Houghton, *South African Economy,* 234–35.

p. 368: government expenditures on security and defense doubled: For a further breakdown of the figures, see SAIRR, *Survey, 1974,* 56, and *Survey, 1975,* 41.

p. 369: the government accounted for one-third: See Nattrass, *South African Economy,* 233 and table 10-1, 234.

p. 369: more than seventeen percent: *New York Times,* October 8, 1975.

p. 369: "dismantle the symbols and trappings of apartheid": Graham Hovey, "Mr. Vorster's Detente," *New York Times,* March 25, 1975. Six months later Hovey repeated his argument, though with a more pessimistic slant, in "Heading Off Racial War in Southern Africa," *Saturday Review,* September 20, 1975.

p. 370: occasional concession: See *New York Times,* October 19, 1975.

p. 370: only two percent opposed: Seventy-six percent held a "neutral view" and twenty-two percent—nearly a quarter—said that they approved of it. The survey, which was followed up in 1976, was conducted and written up by Professor Meyer Feldberg, director, Graduate School of Business Administration, University of Cape Town.

p. 370: "adheres grimly to its policy": *New York Times,* November 9, 1974.

p. 370: His efforts to mobilize: In 1975, as they had the year before, Buthelezi and the other bantustan leaders made a pilgrimage to Pretoria to press their demands for more land, more resources, and more freedoms. They also pushed for the rights of urban Africans, particularly for the right to own property and to open businesses. Vorster responded by asking them to form a committee to help solve the problem of illegal African immigration to the cities. "Only one homeland leader—Chief Buthelezi—said he was not prepared to cooperate in this regard," Vorster told parliament a month later, "because, as he said, this was a white man's law and he had not had a part in the making of that law. . . . The other seven homeland leaders adopted the standpoint that . . . they would cooperate with the department [of Bantu Administration and Development]" (SAIRR, *Survey, 1975,* 103). Buthelezi, for his part, was deeply nettled by Vorster's inflexibility. In the midst of the meeting he pulled out and read a statement warning that unless the homelands were enlarged and consolidated and the rights of urban Africans were enhanced, the only alternative was for Africans to be represented in the central parliament (the paraphrase is from SAIRR, *Survey, 1975,* 27). In a story in the *New York Times* that quoted from Buthelezi's statement, his threat was more indirect: unless separate development were made more attractive, Africans would want to "share power with their white countrymen in a new and meaningful way" (February 2, 1975). Vorster, confident of his strength, ignored the statement.

p. 370: Inkatha Ka Zulu: Buthelezi had already tried this once before, in the 1950s. Though he later insisted that his first attempt to form Inkatha had been in response to "many older Zulu, including a number of ministers of religion," other observers, including King Cyprian, had seen it as a move by Buthelezi to increase his clout (Temkin, *Buthelezi,* 75). Cyprian squelched the idea, though Buthelezi would always insist that the king had done so under duress from the South African government (see ibid., 75).

p. 370: the *inkatha* had been a circular ceremonial ring: See Mzala, *Buthelezi,* 117.

p. 371: "mass democratic organization": For the role of the ANC in the formation of Inkatha, see the discussion by Mzala, who worked in the ANC's research department in Lusaka *(Buthelezi,* 122ff). More details emerged at the ANC conference in 1985 (see Maré and Hamilton, *Appetite for Power,* 145). The debate over the proper role of traditional chiefs was a source of contention on Robben Island. Nelson Mandela took the most inclusive, pragmatic view. "There is no contradiction between being a traditional leader and a member of the ANC," Mandela wrote in his autobiography. "This spurred one of the longest and most delicate debates we had on the island: whether or not the ANC should participate in government-sponsored institutions. Many of the men considered this collaborationist. Once again, I thought it necessary to draw a distinction between principle and tactics. . . . Will our organization emerge stronger through participating in these organizations or by boycotting them?" (Mandela, *Long Walk,* 441).

p. 371: "The aim [of *Inkatha*] was stated to be": SAIRR, *Survey, 1975,* 130ff.

p. 372: he wrote to the central government: Ibid., 132.

CHAPTER NINE: **The Opening of New Fronts**

p. 373: "Resistance to Soviet expansion by military means": Ford, *Time to Heal,* 358.

p. 373: It began with a song: Sparks, *Mind of South Africa,* 298.

p. 374: an integral part of the Portuguese "nation": There is considerable irony here: even as South Africa was trying to portray internal territories as foreign countries, Portugal was painting countries several thousand miles away as part of its political corpus.

p. 374: one million Portuguese . . . had emigrated: Schneidman, *American Foreign Policy,* 270. For the population figures, see Marcum, *Angolan Revolution,* 2:241.

p. 374: In Angola the Portuguese faced the challenge: See Marcum, *Angolan Revolution,* vol. 2; see also Bridgland, *Jonas Savimbi,* chaps. 7–10.

p. 376: Several weeks after the Portuguese coup: "Rhodesia's Prime Minister Off for Talks in South Africa," *New York Times,* May 29, 1974.

p. 376: remained publicly cautious: See SAIRR, *Survey, 1974,* 135ff.

p. 377: "my government does not condone discrimination": Quoted by Kane-Berman, *South Africa,* 98. Kane-Berman also points out the significance of Botha's use of "purely" and "solely."

p. 377: "We have not waged a war": SAIRR, *Survey, 1974,* 120–21.

p. 377: Great Britain announced that it was canceling: See *New York Times,* November 3 and December 3, 1974; and June 17, 1975.

p. 377: He . . . flew secretly: *New York Times,* February 18, 1975.

p. 377: a full day of talks inside a train: *New York Times,* August 26, 1975.

p. 378: Ethnic differences kept the sides apart: For a discussion of ethnicity in the Angolan conflict, see Marcum, *Angolan Revolution,* 2:46–48, 263–64, and passim.

p. 378: He tried first to align himself with . . . the Portuguese military: For a discussion of this point, which remains controversial, see Marcum, *Angolan Revolution,* 2:218; see also Bridgland, *Jonas Savimbi,* 105–6.

p. 379: In July MPLA troops gunned down: Bridgland, *Jonas Savimbi,* 125–26.

p. 379: CIA Officer John Stockwell: For Stockwell's description of the origins of the covert Angolan program and of his role in it, see *In Search of Enemies,* chaps. 2 and 3.

p. 379: Still, Congress had supported the president's decision: For the effect of the *Mayagüez* incident on the decision of the 40 Committee, see Roger Morris,

"Pathology of a Blunder: The Proxy War in Angola," *New Republic,* January 31, 1976, 19ff.

p. 379: over the objections of Charles Diggs: Charles Diggs and the Congressional Black Caucus opposed the nomination on the grounds that Davis had served during the CIA's overthrow of leftist Chilean president Salvador Allende (Statement of the Congressional Black Caucus on the Nomination of Nathaniel Davis to Be Assistant Secretary for African Affairs, February 26, 1975, Box 221, Diggs Collection. See also Willard R. Johnson, "America's Stake in Southern Africa: We Need a Fresh Start," *Black World,* January 1976, 17 n). When the Organization for African Unity protested the nomination, Kissinger responded angrily. "The selection of senior American officials for posts in the U.S. government," Kissinger wrote to the secretary general of the OAU, "is a function of American sovereignty . . . [and] a purely, internal, domestic concern." The South African government, conversely, expressed pleasure with the nomination. Noting that under previous assistant secretaries like Soapy Williams, South Africa had been regarded as a "disruptive influence," progovernment radio commentators welcomed the selection of Davis as a "clear indication of Washington's attitude towards us." South Africa, they insisted, was now recognized by Washington as "a stabilizing influence." "The purpose of the American administration is to strengthen forces for stability in this part of the world," the commentators concluded. "The purpose of the detractors of Mr. Davis was to weaken them" ("South Africa Supports Davis for State Department Post," *New York Times,* February 22, 1975. The South African government later vehemently denied that the radio commentators' comments represented an official viewpoint; see *New York Times,* March 1, 1975).

pp. 379–80: "the first high level resignation-in-protest": Roger Morris, "A Rare Resignation in Protest: Nat Davis and Angola," *Washington Monthly,* February 1976, 23. See also Stockwell, *In Search of Enemies,* 53, and *New York Times,* December 14 and December 19, 1975.

p. 380: "prevent an easy victory": Stockwell, *In Search of Enemies,* 45.

p. 380: the MPLA controlled twelve of Angola's fifteen provinces: Chester Crocker insists that the MPLA's success was the result of unofficial Portuguese policy. "The Soviets and Cubans, with the active connivance of pro-Communist elements of the Portuguese government, effectively installed the MPLA regime," he wrote. "Admiral Rosa Coutinho . . . has publicly declared that he did not consider elections to be a viable option and he favored transferring power to the MPLA as 'the only force capable of directing Angola.' To that end, he actively facilitated the insertion of hundreds of Cuban advisors to set up training camps for the MPLA. His actions began as early as January 1975." See Crocker, *High Noon,* 47.

p. 380: the MPLA received a new burst of support: "In the face of scandalous interference of imperialists, colonialists, and racists," said Ricardo Alarcon De Quesada, the Cuban ambassador to the United Nations, on October 8, "it is an elementary duty for Cuba to offer the Angolan people the effective assistance that may be required for that country to ensure its true independence and full sovereignty" (Stockwell, *In Search of Enemies,* 171).

pp. 380–81: Holden Roberto . . . refused to organize: Marcum, *Angolan Revolution,* 2:274.

p. 381: Bridgland's flight to Rundu: Bridgland, *Jonas Savimbi,* 138–39. For additional information on the South African air force and its Western components, see Jennifer Davis, "The U.S. Role in South Africa's Military Build-Up," Testimony before the Senate Foreign Relations Committee, July 1975 (reprinted by the Africa Fund).

p. 382: On November 23, the news that South African troops: Bridgland, *Jonas Savimbi*, 142.

p. 382: "The propaganda and political war was lost": Stockwell, *In Search of Enemies*, 202.

p. 382: still shrouded in secrecy: For John Marcum's careful discussion of the evidence, see Marcum, *Angolan Revolution*, 2:271ff.

p. 382: Botha concealed the full dimensions: The allegation was made by Hendrik van den Bergh to Allister Sparks. See Sparks, *Mind of South Africa*, 304. Some observers insist that John Vorster and his close associates were never enthusiastic about the venture and that Vorster himself limited the size of the incursion to minimize the international repercussions. See, for example, Richard Leonard's discussion in *South Africa at War*, 76–79.

p. 382: On at least two occasions: Stockwell, *In Search of Enemies*, 187.

p. 383: "Without any memos being written": Ibid., 188.

p. 383: "We're not in it alone": Sparks, *Mind of South Africa*, 306.

p. 383: The Nigerian government was so angered: Bridgland, *Jonas Savimbi*, 142.

p. 383: Kissinger, nervous about the damage: See, for example, *New York Times*, December 14 and December 17, 1975.

p. 384: "Angola does not mean a damn thing": Bridgland, *Jonas Savimbi*, 170.

p. 384: President Ford was furious: Ford, *Time to Heal*, 345, 346.

p. 384: They thought they had a clear understanding: Allister Sparks writes that at the confidential press briefing, "Botha told us South Africa had been given assurances at the highest level by the other parties involved in the operation, but it was absolutely vital to keep a low profile because they could not be seen associating with South Africa in an operation like this" (*Mind of South Africa*, 306).

p. 384: "If the West does not want to contribute": Quoted in Bridgland, *Jonas Savimbi*, 159.

p. 385: George Bush, who spent months fending off: According to John Marcum, George Bush in February 1976 refused to rule out the possibility that American intelligence forces would continue to provide aid to anti-MPLA forces. See Marcum, *Angolan Revolution*, 2:445 n. 289.

p. 385: "the Cuban troops, with Russian weapons": Ford, *Time to Heal*, 358.

p. 385: Morgan's reorganization of the Committee on Foreign Affairs: See the announcement by Morgan, dated February 3, 1975, File: Subcommittee on Africa, Box 221, Diggs Collection. This arrangement did not last very long; eventually the subcommittees reverted to a more geographical base.

p. 385: Diggs's responsibilities for famine: For Diggs's reaction to the reorganization, see his statement at a press conference on Africa, February 25, 1975. From his position Diggs continued to stir up as much trouble as he could for South Africa. He wrote an open letter to Frank Cary of IBM, signed by eighteen other representatives, asking him to support the shareholder resolutions that urged the company to stop selling or leasing computers to the South African government (An Open Letter to IBM Corporation Re: South Africa, April 28, 1975, Box 221, Diggs Collection). When the White House approved the sale of enriched uranium to Pretoria, Diggs filed a bill to prohibit the sale or exchange of nuclear materials or technology to any country that had not ratified the Nuclear Non-Proliferation Treaty. Since South Africa had not done so, this would have cut off the lucrative contracts into which Westinghouse and other American corporations had entered to construct nuclear reactors (see the letter from Diggs, "Dear Friend, I have introduced a bill to prohibit the sale," May 12, 1975, Box 221, Diggs Collection). He asked the Congressional Research Service to investigate the growing trade ties between South Africa and Japan (see Note to the Files Re Japanese South Africa Relations, May 27, 1975, Box 221, Diggs Collection; see also "Japan in South Africa: A New Look at an Important Partner in Apartheid: An Interview with Yoko Kitazawa," *Southern Africa,* March 1975, 5). As chair of the House Subcommittee on the District of Columbia, in June 1975 Diggs encouraged the members of the D.C. School when they debated a resolution about ending school purchases from corporations doing business with South Africa—one of the earliest examples of a local elected body debating such a boycott (for material on this controversy, see "DC School System Contracts—Corporations Invested in South Africa," File: South Africa—3, Box 357, Diggs Collection; also File: South Africa Boycott—DC School Board, Box 410, Diggs Collection).

p. 386: It was a dilemma: "How valid is the argument that the foreign policy interests of black and white Americans do not coincide?" asked Robert Browne, the director of the Black Economic Research Center in New York City, in a speech delivered to the Congressional Black Caucus in September 1975. "Although as Americans, blacks have interests similar to those of our white compatriots, as blacks they are members of the Third World, whose interests are sometimes in conflict with America's." To make his point, Browne asked what would happen if a race war exploded in South Africa and the United States aligned itself with the white community. At that point, "the divergence in interests between black Americans and official policy would become unmistakably apparent in this situation," he wrote, "and a domestic racial confrontation over foreign policy would be virtually inevitable" (Robert S. Browne, "The Black Stake in Global Interdependence," paper presented at the Congressional Black Caucus Workshop, Friday, September 26, 1975, provided to the author by Charles C. Diggs Jr. from his personal files. After reviewing these and other papers provided by Diggs on the founding of TransAfrica, the author forwarded them for cataloging to the Diggs Collection at the Moorland-Spingarn Research Center).

p. 386: it might have negative effects on race relations: Willard Johnson, for example, in testimony before the Senate Foreign Relations Committee in the summer of 1975 argued that "if we insist on joining with the racists and colonialists in their wars of suppression in Africa, ultimately we may have to fight some of the battles of those wars right here."

p. 386: "a network of like-minded Americans": "The Afro-American Stake in Africa," interview with Charles C. Diggs Jr., *Africa,* November 1975, 57.

p. 386: "What is required": Browne, "Black Stake in Global Interdependence," op. cit.

p. 386: the meeting in Baranquitas: See author interview with Willard Johnson, November 21, 1989, and the two-page list of conference participants, provided by Johnson, in the author's files.

p. 386: an effort to repeal the pro-Rhodesian Byrd amendment: Anthony Lake, *Tar Baby,* 220; for a discussion of the repeated efforts to repeal the Byrd amendment, see chaps. 6–8; see also Ross K. Baker, "Towards a New Constituency for a More Active American Foreign Policy for Africa," *Issue,* Spring 1973, 18, quoted in Lake, *Tar Baby,* 232.

p. 387: Black Forum on Foreign Policy: The original title was the Black Council on Foreign Policy, but this had been changed by October 9, 1975. See the materials provided by Charles Diggs to the author.

p. 387: During a transit stop: For a description of the trip, see "Rev. Leon H. Sullivan's June 1975 Africa Trip," File 29, Box 13, OIC Archives.

p. 387: Mvubelo, Klein, and others: For Mvubelo's comments, see author interview with Leon Sullivan, August 26, 1991. For Klein's position, see his letter to Sullivan, August 15, 1971, and author interview with Klein in Johannesburg, January 1993.

p. 388: "Rather than encourage": Adam Klein to Leon Sullivan, August 21, 1975, OIC Archives.

p. 388: "If you could get companies involved": Author interview with Leon Sullivan, August 26, 1991.

p. 388: "I was standing there stripped": Ibid.

p. 388: Sullivan persuaded the board: Ibid.

p. 388: Sullivan announced his new effort from the pulpit: See Sullivan's statement in a press release, April 6, 1978: "Fully conscious of the odds against succeeding, I made the announcement one Sunday morning to members of my congregation of the attempt I was about to initiate and asked for their support and their prayers" (ICEOP Collection).

p. 388: "concerted double-directed effort": See "Sullivan's United States Government and American Business South African Requests," September 1975, Box 1, ICEOP Collection. In the document, Sullivan gives explicit support to Diggs's most recent attempt, in April 1975, to link U.S. government contracts to employment practices in South Africa.

p. 389: "As a senior executive": See Sullivan to Donald Procknow of Westinghouse Electric, December 17, 1975, File 25, Box 1, ICEOP Collection. The letter was sent to executives at American Cyanamid, Burroughs Corporation, Caltex, Chrysler, Firestone, Ford Motor Company, General Electric, General Motors, Goodyear Tire, Honeywell, Ingersoll-Rand, IBM, International Harvester, International Telephone and Telegraph, Joy Manufacturing, Mobil Oil, Motorola, Otis Elevator, 3M, Westinghouse, and Xerox.

p. 389: his original principles had already been diluted: See the letter from Thomas McDaniel to Gus Roman, January 7, 1976, in which McDaniel, working to prepare for Sands Point, tells Roman that "some revision of the 'Statement of Principles' is going to be necessary if we are to get the agreement of any substantial number of companies." McDaniel refers to attached revisions, but these were not in the archival file. Box 1, ICEOP Collection.

p. 389: "in nine months or so": Letter from Leon Sullivan to I. Thompson, president of Goodyear Tire and Rubber Company, February 10, 1976, Sullivan ICEOP Collection.

p. 390: "a kind of secretary of state": Author interview with Wayne Fredericks, October 15, 1991.

p. 390: that he should endorse majority rule in Rhodesia: Ibid.

p. 390: "I remember saying": Ibid.

p. 391: "Political stability in Africa was crumbling": Ford says that he told his advisers: " 'I cannot judge whether the political impact will be good or bad. . . . But we must do this because it is the right thing to do.' " Ford, *Time to Heal*, 380.

p. 391: he acknowledged America's neglect of Africa: Martin and Johnson, *Struggle for Zimbabwe*, 233.

p. 391: "When Henry said our policy": Ford, *Time to Heal*, 380.

p. 391: Increasingly Ford and Reagan wrangled: Ibid., 388.

p. 392: Once again, foreign policy became a political tool: This tendency for American politicians to speak about South Africa for domestic political reasons was derided by South African government leaders who, in turn, often made the mistake of thinking that all pronouncements by Americans were therefore insincere.

p. 392: the president himself told a group of reporters: *New York Times,* May 22, 1976.

p. 393: "You bastards": Martin and Johnson, *Struggle for Zimbabwe,* 239.

p. 393: out of every ten houses: The figures are from Kane-Berman, *South Africa,* 52ff.

p. 393: forty-three percent . . . lived below the "poverty datum line": Ibid., 54.

p. 393: Employment officials . . . refused to allow: Ibid., 89.

p. 394: "unproductive people": Ibid., 79.

p. 394: "We must curb the flow": Ibid.

p. 395: more than thirty-five thousand Soweto children: Quoted in Kane-Berman, *South Africa,* 185.

p. 395: Only twelve percent of the *teachers:* Kane-Berman says that "only 12.3% had matriculated" (*South Africa,* 186).

p. 395: "There has been a lull": Margaret Smith, "Black Anger Starts Young," *Sunday Times,* June 13, 1976.

p. 396: "Have you ever heard of thirteen year olds striking?": Institute for Policy Studies, *Black South Africa Explodes* (Washington, D.C.: Transnational Institute, 1977), 7. Such attitudes were widespread; see, for example, the letter from Desmond Tutu, then the Anglican dean of Johannesburg, to Prime Minister John Vorster, May 8, 1976. EcuNews Bulletin, May 26, 1976. See Reel 3, Gerhart BCM Collection. Kane-Berman also reports that Tutu warned the government that the homelands policy was "highly explosive" the month before (*South Africa,* 52).

p. 396: "The broad masses of Soweto are perfectly content": *Rand Daily Mail,* May 12 and May 13, 1976; quoted in Kane-Berman, *South Africa,* 67.

p. 396: "As I drove into their midst": Institute for Policy Studies, *Black South Africa,* 7. The description of the events of June 16–18 draws on several materials, primarily the day-by-day account compiled by the Transnational Institute in *Black South Africa Explodes.* Other sources include the contemporary accounts in the *Rand Daily Mail,* the *New York Times,* and the *Weekly World.* See also Kane-Berman's descriptions of the events in *South Africa,* passim.

p. 397: "the children began stoning the police": Institute for Policy Studies, *Black South Africa,* 8.

p. 398: The Black Parents' Association . . . had to call: Ibid., 13.

p. 398: "One should be careful not to place": Kane-Berman, *South Africa,* 160.

p. 398: purchases of firearms by whites: Ibid., 153. See also the reprint of an advertisement by a South African gun dealer in Institute for Policy Studies, *Black South Africa Explodes.*

p. 399: "The blacks are always saying": Reel 3, Gerhart BCM Collection.

p. 399: encouraged by the ANC underground: For a discussion of the relationship between the SSRC and the ANC, see Davis, *Apartheid's Rebels,* chap. 1.

p. 400: a white Valiant and a green Chevrolet: Kane-Berman, *South Africa,* 35.

p. 400: "Men carrying butcher knives": Institute for Policy Studies, *Black South Africa Explodes,* 14.

p. 400: only a minority of the hostel dwellers were Zulu: Kane-Berman, *South Africa,* 113.

p. 401: a week before Kissinger left: "The question I want to explore with the Prime Minister," Kissinger had told the House Foreign Affairs Committee on Tuesday, June 14, two days before Hector Petersen was shot, "is whether South Africa is prepared to separate its own future from that of Rhodesia and Namibia." Martin and Johnson, *Struggle for Zimbabwe*, 239.

p. 401: the massacre at Nyadzonia: Ibid., 240–42.

p. 402: "Kissinger was disarming": Ibid., 250.

p. 402: "It is one thing to double-cross Kaunda": Ibid., 252.

p. 403: "Kissinger's face": Ibid., 255.

p. 403: "the proposals as outlined": Ibid.

CHAPTER TEN: Points of Pressure

p. 404: "Whilst it is illegal for us": Biko, *I Write What I Like*, 139; see the original ("American Policy towards Azania," January 12, 1977) in Reel 4, Gerhart BCM Collection.

p. 404: Herschelle Challenor: See Challenor's curriculum vitae, Diggs Collection.

p. 405: "the link between what was happening": Author interview with Randall Robinson, August 28, 1991.

p. 405: straightening out administrative problems: These problems included financial mismanagement and improprieties, for which Diggs was eventually indicted and convicted in federal court (see chap. 12). To date, Robinson has refused to discuss what he discovered when he became Diggs's aide. It is clear from the indictments that improprieties took place in the years before Robinson arrived; Robinson may have been the one who put an end to them. See author interview with Randall Robinson, August 28, 1991.

p. 406: differences between Challenor and Robinson: See author interview with Willard Johnson, December 19, 1989.

p. 406: a full-page advertisement . . . purchased by General Motors dealers: For General Motors' defense, which argued that the company could not control the actions of independent dealers, see the letter from Thomas Pond to Timothy Smith, August 31, 1976, ICEOP Files.

p. 406: Vernon Jordan . . . publicly demanded: *New York Times*, August 2, 1976.

p. 407: Miliswa and Dinilesizwe Sobukwe: *New York Times*, December 18, 1976.

p. 407: "a very aggressive policy": *New York Times*, January 4, 1977.

p. 407: the United States began proposing: *New York Times*, April 4, 1977.

p. 407: The State Department then drew up a secret list: *New York Times*, May 15, 1977.

p. 408: "One of them spoke up": Author interview with Wayne Fredericks, October 15, 1991.

p. 408: "Statement of Principles": This version comes from an undated copy in the ICEOP Collection.

p. 409: Sullivan had succeeded in persuading: This list comes from File 34, Box 3, ICEOP Collection.

p. 409: "This . . . is a very laudable stand": Letter from the South African consul to Leon Sullivan, September 29, 1976, ICEOP Collection. Though this letter actually predates Sullivan's formal announcement, it indicates that Sullivan's plans were well known and tolerated by the South African government.

p. 409: "an exercise in triviality": Jennifer Davis, "Too Little, Too Late: The U.S. Corporation Employment Manifesto for South Africa," in *Southern Africa Perspec-*

tives (New York: Africa Fund, April 1977). George Houser was also sharply critical of Andrew Young's contention that business could play a role in South Africa comparable to that in Birmingham; for an extended critique, see George Houser, "U.S. Policy in Southern Africa: Preaching Freedom, Investing in Oppression," *Christianity and Crisis*, September 19, 1977.

p. 409: Sullivan and Smith met: In later correspondence, Smith and Sullivan made clear that they understood their respective roles as insider and outsider. "We would be pleased to raise [the question of signing the Sullivan Principles] with any other companies you may wish, arguing that it is a minimum standard of decency that should be applied," Smith wrote to Sullivan after the meeting. "However, it is also the consensus of most of the churches that have been working on this problem that such changes in the workplace will not lead to the basic social change that is vitally necessary in South Africa" (Timothy Smith to Leon Sullivan, March 29, 1977, ICEOP Collection).

p. 409: Walter Mondale would be meeting with John Vorster: *New York Times*, May 5, 1977.

p. 409: Andrew Young said that he had accepted an invitation: *New York Times*, May 7, 1977.

p. 410: economic sanctions might be a legitimate nonviolent method: *New York Times*, April 7, 1977.

p. 410: sometimes forcing Cyrus Vance: "Young Stirs Furor; President Backs Him," *New York Times*, April 16, 1977.

p. 410: Young touched off another round of debate: *New York Times*, April 16, 1977.

p. 410: "All my life, everything I have done": *New York Times*, April 20, 1977.

p. 411: "We have been here for as long as the Americans": *New York Times*, May 15, 1977.

p. 411: Winnie Mandela's arrest: For her own description, see *Part of My Soul*, 24–25. See also *New York Times*, May 19, 1977, and " 'First Lady' of Black South Africa Talks about Curbs on Her Freedom," *New York Times*, June 4, 1977. For additional press reaction, see "Mr. Vorster and Mrs. Mandela," editorial, *New York Times*, May 23, 1977.

p. 412: Vorster offered no concession: Vorster emerged from the meeting pleased with his performance. "I'm prepared to hang for what I am," Vorster told a press conference shortly after the meeting, "but I'm damned if I am going to hang for what I am not" (*New York Times*, May 21, 1977).

p. 412: "I think most Americans feel very good": *New York Times*, May 23, 1977.

p. 412: "our paths will diverge": *New York Times*, May 29, 1977.

p. 412: "No, no, it's the same thing": Ibid.

p. 412: "I think sound judgment will prevail": *New York Times*, May 22, 1977.

pp. 412–13: shook hands . . . with all the black chauffeurs: *New York Times*, May 22, 1977.

p. 413: "People will vote their interest": *New York Times*, May 23, 1977.

p. 413: "Who does he think he is": *New York Times*, May 22, 1977. The visit provoked a similar reaction among some Americans; see, for example, the column by James Reston, *New York Times*, May 22, 1977.

p. 413: In a major speech to the NAACP: *New York Times*, July 2, 1977.

p. 414: "They're making it impossible for us": *New York Times*, July 7, 1977.

p. 414: "It is true that the bulk of Negroes": *New York Times*, August 7, 1977.

pp. 414–15: grew up on a farm in the Transkei: For a description of Donald Woods's childhood, see Woods, *Asking for Trouble,* chap. 1.

p. 415: "dynamited a nigger's house": Ibid., 112.

p. 415: "a betrayal of the white liberal commitment": Woods, *Biko,* 48. Woods was one of many white liberals to take this position. For additional discussion, see Richard Turner, "Black Consciousness and White Liberals," *Reality,* July 1972.

p. 415: "elderly, gray-haired medico": Woods, *Biko,* 47.

p. 415: "My first impression was of his size": Ibid., 54–56.

p. 416: Knowing of Biko's love of American music: Ibid., 63.

p. 416: "There was much about American ideals": Ibid., 106.

p. 416: the official position of SASO and the Black People's Convention: SASO passed its first resolution rejecting foreign investment in 1971, the same year as the Polaroid experiment. The Black People's Convention, similarly, resolved at their first national congress in 1972 "1) to reject the involvement of foreign investors in this exploitative economic system and 2) to call upon foreign investors to disengage themselves from this white controlled exploitative system." See Black People's Convention, SASO/BPC Trial Doc, Reel 3, Gerhart BCM Collection.

p. 416: the Nationalist government had arrested and prosecuted: For a detailed chronology of the so-called Terror Trials, see *Detention and Detente in Southern Africa,* a report published by the Christian Institute in April 20, 1976; Reel 3, Gerhart BCM Collection.

p. 416: "create and foster feelings of racial hatred": *Drum,* April 22, 1975.

p. 417: placed in the difficult position: Woods makes this point in *Biko,* 114.

p. 417: "Black is beautiful" exchange: See ibid., 126–27.

p. 418: "We believe South Africa is particularly sensitive": Quoted in ibid., 135. For additional descriptions of Biko's testimony, see "SASO Leader Hits at British Exploitation," *World,* May 4, 1976; "SASO Call 'Just a Stunt,' " *Rand Daily Mail,* May 4, 1976. For a similar claim by Absolom Cindi, former general secretary of the BPC, see "BPC Man Denies Investment Claim," *Rand Daily Mail,* May 8, 1976.

p. 419: "On the day of his detention": "Steve Biko Released after 101 Days," *Rand Daily Mail,* November 30, 1976.

p. 420: meeting with U.S. Senator Dick Clark: Biko had first met Clark the previous August. See author interview with Dick Clark, April 5, 1993.

p. 420: "America's choice is narrowed down": Biko, January 12, 1977, "American Policy towards Azania," in *I Write What I Like,* 139; see the original ("American Policy towards Azania," January 12, 1977) in Reel 4, Gerhart BCM Collection. For Clark's recollections of his meeting with Biko, see author interview with Dick Clark, April 1993.

p. 420: "The argument's often made": See Reel 4, Gerhart SASO Collection.

p. 421: seems to have embittered Biko: This reaction was not restricted to Biko. On October 23, 1977, Mokgethi Motlhabi delivered a paper in the United States entitled "The Problem of Human Rights in South Africa, U.S. Policy, and the Churches" in which he made a similar point. "In view of the United States' position . . . one would expect President Carter to be greatly applauded," he said. "[Instead] he is probably being viewed with skepticism. . . . Rather than being praised, he is probably receiving more criticism than either President Ford or even Nixon, for all their cooperation with South Africa. . . . [Carter's] good words have been heard. But let him go a step further and transform them into action. Only this will prove he means business" (1977 File, Deats Collection).

p. 421: a scholarship to visit the United States: See the recollections of Father

Aelred Stubbs in Biko, *I Write What I Like,* 206. Biko's refusal caused consternation in the State Department, which viewed it as evidence of the radicalization of black politics in South Africa. See Reel 4, Gerhart BCM Collection.

p. 421: "Carter uses Andrew Young's color": Woods, *Biko,* 99–100.

p. 421: "Is it compulsory that I have to be naked?": Ibid., 184.

pp. 421–22: Biko . . . had vowed never to suffer . . . without trying to strike back: At the inquest into Biko's death, this point was stressed by the police, who brought forth an officer to testify that Biko had tried to strike him during an earlier interrogation. Ibid., 196.

p. 422: English newspapers and international wire services sizzled: For descriptions of Biko's interrogation and imprisonment, see ibid., 181–260, and Bernstein, *No. 46,* 19–114. Many international newspapers not only reported on Biko's death but supplied editorial comment. See, for example, "One More Death in South Africa," *New York Times,* September 15, 1977.

p. 423: "South Africa became a different place for me": Woods, *Biko,* 160.

p. 423: Biko had known that it might happen: Ibid., 166.

p. 423: "Biko's death leaves me cold": Ibid.

p. 424: broken into several bickering factions: For a description of the realignments and their electoral successes, see SAIRR, *Survey, 1977,* 14–19.

p. 424: Vorster himself had to contend: Pik Botha had campaigned in his district on the principle of change. "I am prepared to war over our right to exist," Botha said on the stump, "but I am not prepared to die for discriminatory signs on a lift." (ibid., 6). Andries Treurnicht, on the other hand, was touring the country demanding a return to the Verwoerdian ideal.

p. 424: "tested in the coming months": Ibid., 2. Vorster had specifically complained about U.S. "meddling" in South Africa's internal affairs in an interview published in the *New York Times* on September 17, 1997, just five days after Biko's death. See also, Kane-Berman, *South Africa,* 154.

p. 424: Security Police officers intercepted Woods: Woods, *Asking for Trouble,* 313.

p. 424: an official inquest: See Woods, *Biko,* 181–261. See also Bernstein, *No. 46,* chaps. 6–11.

p. 425: "night interrogation team": Bernstein, *No. 46,* 40.

p. 425: pathologist's testimony: Ibid., 66ff. One theory discussed in Bernstein's book is that Biko had received the fatal blows from the night interrogation team and that these had caused a period of unconsciousness followed by the wild behavior that the next team encountered. Under this interpretation, the day team could be telling the truth about Biko's sudden attempt to assault five men, since erratic behaviors are one outcome of brain trauma. At the time of the printing of this book, several of those who were involved in the death had stepped forward to confess their guilt before the Truth and Reconciliation Commission.

p. 425: exchange between Kentridge and Goosen: Quoted in Woods, *Biko,* 199.

p. 426: "Hardly had the polls closed": Kane-Berman, *South Africa,* 180.

p. 426: Biko's head injuries "were probably sustained": Woods, *Biko,* 261; Bernstein, *No. 46,* 115.

CHAPTER ELEVEN: **Definition from Below**

p. 427: "There is nothing unusual": *New York Times,* April 2, 1978.

p. 427: "The more I wrote": Woods, *Asking for Trouble,* 332.

p. 427: On December 29, 1977: The full story of the flight of the Woods family from South Africa is told in several places. The most abbreviated version is in Woods, *Biko*. Woods revealed more details of the experience in *Asking for Trouble*, which then formed the basis for the film version of the escape in *Cry Freedom*.

p. 427: greeted at the airport by an army of reporters: Woods, *Asking for Trouble*, 360. The story of Woods's escape had been front-page news around the world. See *New York Times*, January 1, 1978.

pp. 427–28: before the House subcommittee . . . and . . . UN Security Council: SAIRR, *Survey, 1978*, 104. Woods also "was granted a special visiting fellowship and provision for his family by the Nieman Foundation [at] Harvard University" (ibid.). For Woods's visit to the AFL-CIO executive council, see Hauck and Voorhes, *Two Decades*, 18.

p. 428: In his speeches and articles: For example, see Donald Woods, "Apartheid on Collision Course with Black Anger," *New York Times*, January 8, 1978.

p. 428: "A Communist is a person who wants whites and blacks to mix": *New York Times*, January 8, 1978, 8.

p. 428: the fate of Richard Turner: *New York Times*, January 9, 1978. See also the letter to the editor from John Seiler, January 18, 1978.

p. 428: "deal a firm psychological blow": Donald Woods, quoted in "U.S. Business in South Africa: Voices for Withdrawal," *Southern Africa Perspectives*, no. 1 (New York: Africa Fund, 1978), 4.

p. 429: confluence of these two traditions: The linkage of Vietnam and South Africa was often explicit. "Not so long ago, the reality of bloodshed in Vietnam obliged people to take stands on a whole range of moral and political issues," wrote Jonathan Fox on March 14, 1977, in the *Daily Princetonian*. "Today in Southern Africa, Princeton continues to support a war effort. . . ."

p. 430: a classic ethical debate: The technical terms for these differing approaches are *teleological* (from *telos*, meaning "goal") and *deontological* (from *deon*, meaning "duty"). As many philosophers have pointed out, there is some overlap between the two approaches. In most cases, especially the debate over divestment, opposing groups appeal to both forms of reasoning to make their arguments. Administrators and trustees, for example, defended their decisions on the basis of their duties to past donors and future students; anti-apartheid students tried to sway people with predictions of the dire consequences of failing to act.

p. 431: series of increments: For an extended discussion of the notion of policy stages and the shareholder voting record of eight large institutional investors with regard to South Africa, see Massie, *Moral Deliberation*.

p. 433: University of Massachusetts at Amherst: See *New York Times*, September 16, 1977.

p. 433: By 1978 a coalition of students: "Princeton University holds 87,429 shares of stock with a market value of $1,639,294 in the Firestone Tire and Rubber Corporation which pays African workers as little as 35 cents an hour," student leader Adhimu Chunga had declared at a rally in May 1976. "Is this not enough evidence to show that Princeton supports apartheid?" (*Daily Princetonian*, May 5, 1976). Some of the clippings were gathered by the author; others were included in *DIVEST! Princeton's Sit-in Ten Years Later*, a compendium of documents organized and printed by David Addams and distributed at the tenth reunion of the Princeton Class of 1978. Addams also made a video out of home movie footage of the sit-in.

p. 433: the committee that heard the charges: See "University Policy Statement Concerning Student Demonstration in Nassau Hall, April 14, 1978," author's files.

p. 433: one of the principal financial advisers: See the special issue of *Forerunner*,

April 22, 1978 (*Forerunner* was a short-lived leftist student publication at Princeton); also included in *Divest!*, op. cit. The holdings included $186 million in Exxon, $114 million in Standard Oil of California, and $75 million in IBM.

p. 433: "If the nation's heart responds": "Heading for the Exit in South Africa," *New York Times,* April 2, 1978.

p. 434: students in Tennessee protested: "South Africa Is New Social Issue for College Activists," *New York Times,* March 15, 1978.

p. 434: Ku Klux Klan organized a counterdemonstration: "Klan Offer Is Rejected," *New York Times,* March 15, 1978.

p. 434: At Hampshire College, Smith College: *New York Times,* March 15, 1978.

p. 434: At Columbia University: The material for this segment is drawn from a longer case study. See Massie, *Moral Deliberation.*

p. 435: "human betterment and intellectual integrity": William J. McGill, "Ethical Guidelines for Business Dealings, Investments, and Relations with Foreign Governments," report to the Trustees Committee on Finance, March 23, 1977, author's files.

p. 435: the proxy system as "charade": This comment did not make it into the later text but it is quoted, along with other leaked passages, in "President Recommends Divestiture of Controversial Stock Investments," *Columbia Spectator,* February 16, 1973.

p. 435: "Adherence to such standards": McGill, "Ethical Guidelines," op. cit., 6.

p. 435: "whether the university's divestment": See "Petitioners Demanding CU Divest Itself of 'Unethical' Stock It Owns," *Columbia Spectator,* September 15, 1977; also see *Columbia Spectator,* September 22, 1977, and Resolution of the Board of Trustees of Columbia University, October 3, 1977, author's files. See also "Krim Wants Review of S. Africa Stock," *Columbia Spectator,* September 28, 1977, and "Trustee Board Asks South African Review," October 4, 1977.

p. 435: On April 20, several hundred students: "300 Protesters Hit South Africa; March Sparked by '68 Panel," *Columbia Spectator,* April 21, 1978.

p. 436: "which by act or omission manifest indifference": Report of the Standby Committee on University Investments in Corporate Securities, April 28, 1978.

p. 436: "Every day this university": *Columbia Spectator,* May 2, 1978.

p. 436: McGill wrote a letter to the community: Letter from President William J. McGill to members of the Columbia University Community, May 3, 1978.

p. 436: "When the provost and his associates": Author interview with William McGill, November 1988.

pp. 436–37: "Gabriel Hauge . . . asked me to come down": Author interview with William McGill, November 1988.

p. 437: the committee members abstained: Though there was little evidence that an abstention was perceived by GE's managers as a warning, shareholder committees often used the device to lessen the internal trauma of deciding to vote against management. An institutional investor that had voted to abstain was highly likely to vote against management the next year.

p. 437: Hugh Calkins wrote a letter: Harvard CCSR Report, January 1978.

p. 437: Seidman was the daughter of activist parents: See author interviews with Neva Seidman Makgetla, June 1993; and Gay Seidman, March 1993.

p. 437: "The exiles were very close": Author interview with Neva Seidman Makgetla, June 12, 1993.

p. 438: "There were papers everywhere": Ibid.

p. 438: a book published two years later: Makgetla and Seidman, *Outposts of Monopoly Capitalism.*

p. 438: The organization's activities were well covered: Gay Seidman tried to stay as removed as possible from the activities of her sister in order to be seen as an objective editor. "They had pretty easy access to the media," she recalled years later. "Anything that SASC did got covered. Five people would stand with signs outside the corporation meetings and we'd run a story. One person even told me directly: 'I go to SASC meetings because I am sure to get covered in the *Crimson.*' " See author interview with Gay Seidman, March 1993.

p. 438: Citibank "will make loans": *Harvard Crimson,* February 17, 1978.

p. 439: "U.S. economic interests": Harvard ACSR Report, March 1978.

p. 439: The report estimated: ACSR Report, 1978, app. B.

p. 439: "the estimated maximum one-time cost": Ibid., 46.

p. 440: "inadequate proportionality between cost and effectiveness": Ibid.

p. 440: Professor Kenneth Arrow . . . challenged these cost figures: *Harvard Crimson,* March 15, 1979.

p. 440: a thousand students descended: For accounts of the turmoil of these few days, see *Harvard Crimson,* April 25–April 28, 1978.

p. 440: "Having considered these conflicting arguments": Statement of the president and Fellows of Harvard College, April 27, 1978, 4.

p. 441: Bok was challenged to debates on divestment: See the transcript of the faculty meeting on March 13, 1979, in the *Harvard Crimson,* March 14, 1979.

pp. 441–42: "Society respects the freedom": Derek Bok, "Reflections on the Ethical Responsibilities of the University in Society: An Open Letter to the Harvard Community," March 9, 1979.

p. 442: Bok argued that Harvard could not sever every link: Derek Bok, "Reflections on the Divestment of Stock: An Open Letter to the Harvard Community," April 6, 1979. In May, Bok wrote a third and final open letter in which he discussed whether universities should ever engage in product boycotts. See "Reflections on Boycotts: An Open Letter to the Harvard Community," May 18, 1979. For additional comments on the process that led Bok to write these letters, see author interview with Derek Bok, September 1988.

p. 442: "a primary objection to a divestment policy": *Harvard Crimson,* May 18, 1983.

p. 442: "Harvard gets lots of money": Author interview with Hugh Calkins, September 1988.

pp. 442–43: The American Committee on Africa . . . was beginning to see some results: See various documents from the Committee to Oppose Bank Loans to South Africa, in both the ACOA Active Files, New York, and in ACOA Amistad. ACOA was also intensively involved in the campaign against the sale of Kruger-rands. See "The Krugerrand: Facts about South Africa's Gold Coin," *Southern Africa Perspectives,* no. 7, October 1977. The ICCR also tried to press its member organizations to battle bank loans. See the letter from Tim Smith in June 1977, which began "Dear friends: In recent months the pressure from groups opposing bank loans to South Africa has begun to obtain results," File 34, Box 3, ICEOP Collection.

p. 443: The resolutions in the 1977 proxy season: For the text of the shareholder resolutions filed by member churches of ICCR, see *Church Proxy Resolutions—1977* (New York: Interfaith Center on Corporate Responsibility, January 1977). For information on all social shareholder resolutions filed in 1977 and the votes they received, see Martha Cooper and Jamie Heard, *The 1977 Proxy Season: How Institutions Voted on Shareholder Resolutions and Management Proposals* (Washington, D.C.: Investor Responsibility Research Center, August 1977). The author is grateful to the directors of both ICCR and IRRC for making a complete set of their respective annual reports available for research.

p. 443: Sister Regina Murphy . . . sent letters: "Over the last decade we have repeatedly heard from representatives of U.S. corporations that their presence in South Africa has a positive effect by improving the lives and welfare of South Africa's black majority," Murphy wrote. Instead, she argued, "while U.S. investment had increased, repression against opponents of apartheid has escalated." The recent events, she continued, had demonstrated that the Sullivan Principles were "irrelevant" because the South African government was "not going to allow the good intentions of foreign investors to frustrate their commitment to continued white minority rule." Accordingly, she said, American corporate leaders should stop any expansion of their subsidiaries, gradually terminate their operations, and "put an end to any publicity or statements promoting the idea that U.S. investment is a catalyst for basic social change" (letter from Sister Regina Murphy, Social Concerns Coordinator, Sisters of Charity, New York; Sister Mary Catherine Babbitt, Catholic Coalition for Responsible Investment, Sisters of Loretto; Sister Joan Michalik, Immaculate Heart of Mary Sisters; Kenneth Staubinger, Society of Mary; Sister Agnes Hoormann, Religious of the Sacred Heart; and Patricia Young, Council on Women and the Church, United Presbyterian Church, to William Sneath, Union Carbide Corporation, November 7, 1977, Box 3, ICEOP Collection).

p. 443: corporate responses to the ICCR letter: See Tim Smith, "Summary of Corporate Responses to Church Letter in Light of October 1977 Bannings," ICCR, TNC Task Force, May 15, 1978, ICCR Active File: 1978 ICCR Letter to US Firms in SA. The file also contains the original responses from General Motors, General Electric, Deere, Caterpillar, IBM, and many others.

p. 444: the *average* for all of the votes: The IRRC Annual Survey for 1978, which includes lengthy excerpts from the questionnaires in which institutional investors discussed the *reasons* for their votes, demonstrates that while many investors still believed that American investment would have a positive effect on the lives of South African blacks, they no longer felt the same about loans.

p. 444: strong shareholder dissatisfaction: An interesting question that could be answered with some empirical data is What percentage of shareholder votes do managers view as serious enough to change policies? For example, at one percent of the vote, managers usually ignore shareholder recommendations. At twenty-five percent, they usually change policies to placate the unhappy shareholders. What, over time, has been the critical threshold? The author's hypothesis is that it may be around ten percent because of the psychological effect of double digits. Another related question that could be examined empirically is whether this threshold has changed over time—whether, for example, companies are now more or less sensitive to shareholder voting than they were twenty years ago.

p. 444: The 1978 proxy season: For the text of the shareholder resolutions filed by member churches of ICCR, see *Church Proxy Resolutions—1978* (New York: Interfaith Center on Corporate Responsibility, January 1977). For information on all social shareholder resolutions filed in 1978, including those submitted by the University of Minnesota, see Mary O'Connor, *The 1978 Proxy Season: How Institutions Voted on Shareholder Resolutions and Management Proposals* (Washington, D.C.: Investor Responsibility Research Center, August 1978).

p. 444: A confidential survey: Management Profiled: Risks and Rewards, Opinion Research Council, Early Fall 1977, ICCR Active File: Management Attitudes of US Firms Involved in South Africa. The study makes clear that not every executive who was surveyed actually had a subsidiary in South Africa. Those who did not were asked to imagine that they did and to specify what they would do.

p. 444: foreign companies that had traditionally reinvested: See SAIRR, *Survey 1978,* 138ff.

p. 444: In late 1976 Professor Meyer Feldberg: See the manuscripts in the author's files by Meyer Feldberg, director of the Graduate School of Business at the University of Cape Town, entitled "Business Involvement in South Africa" (c. 1974) and "American Corporations Increasingly Negative on South African Investments" (c. 1976). Feldberg publicized his poll findings in a variety of settings, including the South African press.

p. 444: additional signatories to Sullivan Principles: See "U.S. Companies Operating in South Africa Affirm Commitment to Racial Equality," ICEOP press release, June 20, 1977, and "Black Minister Gets 53 American Companies to Sign Racial Equality Pact for Businesses in the Republic of South Africa," press release, File 26, Box 13, ICEOP Collection.

p. 444: Cyrus Vance told the executives: See "Secretary Vance Gives Unprecedented Support to Black Preacher's Initiatives," October 11, 1977, File 26, Box 1, ICEOP Collection. In August 1977 Frank Cary of IBM had written to Vance personally asking him to come to the dinner. See Frank T. Cary to Cyrus Vance, August 3, 1977, Correspondence Files, ICEOP Collection.

p. 445: the number had nearly doubled again: "Amplified Guidelines to South African Statement of Principles Announced by Reverend Leon Sullivan; 19 Additional Companies Bring Total to 103," ICEOP press release, July 6, 1978, File 26, Box 13, ICEOP Collection.

p. 445: The memos discussed the contingency plans: See Jennifer Davis, "General Motors in South Africa: Secret Contingency Plans 'in the Event of Civil Unrest,' " *Southern Africa Perspectives* (New York: Africa Fund, May 1978).

p. 445: Anti-apartheid activists around the country: See, for example, Timothy Smith, "Comment on the Significance of GM's South Africa Contingency Plan," Interfaith Center on Corporate Responsibility, May 17, 1978. See also Timothy Smith's letter to Tom Murphy at General Motors on the same topic, August 14, 1978; Murphy's lengthy reply, September 21, 1978; and Smith's response, October 10, 1978. All can be found in the File 34, Box 3, ICEOP Collection.

"The documents make a mockery of GM's claim to act as a force for change in South Africa," wrote Jennifer Davis at the time. "GM's white South African managers see the interests of the company as identical to those of the South African government. Not the least sympathy is expressed for black demands." The memos also demonstrated, she wrote, that "the struggle in South Africa is a struggle for political power" and that "the South African government views the presence of companies such as GM and Ford as strategic."

p. 445: "Carter-backed campaign": See "Top Firms Fight Back on SA," *Citizen,* April 3, 1978.

p. 445: Sullivan found himself: See Timothy Smith to Leon Sullivan, July 6, 1978, and October 11, 1978, File 34, Box 3, ICEOP Collection. For Sullivan's reaction to other anti-apartheid activists, see author interview with Leon Sullivan, August 26, 1991. See also "Sticky Issue of Apartheid Haunts Automakers," *Detroit Free Press,* April 23, 1978.

p. 445: "The signatory companies are expected to be": "Amplified Guidelines to South African Statement of Principles Announced by Reverend Sullivan; 19 Additional Companies Announced Bringing Total to 103," news release from Leon Sullivan, July 6, 1978, ICEOP Collection. See also *New York Times,* July 6, 1978.

p. 445: he was privately telling David Russell: See, for example, Sullivan's letter to Stephen Biko's friend David Russell, September 18, 1978.

p. 446: Sullivan, who was still overseeing the vast OIC network: For a description of Sullivan's work with OIC at the time, see the five-part series in the *Philadelphia Inquirer,* December 24–December 28, 1978.

p. 446: Inkatha would help monitor the activities: See SAIRR, *Survey, 1978,* 29.

p. 446: "you are the funniest looking Zulu": Author interview with Sal Marzullo, April 27, 1991.

p. 446: Sullivan had made it clear: For a detailed discussion of the administrative issues relating to the formation of ICEOP, see the minutes of the meetings of the Industry Steering Committee, Subcommittee on Staffing and Funding, October 25, 1978, and November 2, 1978, File 29, Box 3, ICEOP Collection.

p. 447: two organizations would be formed: Minutes of the meeting of the Industry Steering Committee, Subcommittee on Staffing and Funding, November 2, 1978, File 29, Box 3, ICEOP Collection.

p. 447: D. Reid Weedon . . . persuaded Sullivan: For ADL's early approach to Sullivan monitoring, see the original contract letter from Weedon to Sullivan, November 2, 1978, File 11, Box 2, ICEOP Collection, and the letter from Weedon to Gus Roman, December 28, 1978, File 10, Box 2, ICEOP Collection.

p. 448: "Steering committee again tried": Tom K., Datafax, to RJM, February 23, 1979, "late, late at night." Box 3, ICEOP Collection.

p. 448: the pressure had infuriated Sullivan: Tom S. Krzesinski, Dr. L. H. Sullivan's Statement of Principles Meeting, February 22–23, 1979, ICEOP Collection.

p. 448: "Go back and tell your Rev. Sullivan": The minister's reaction is described by Sullivan in "Speech Given by Reverend Leon H. Sullivan to the Summit Conference of Black Religious Leaders of [*sic*] Apartheid, Wednesday, April 18, 1979," 9, File 24, Box 24, OIC Collection, Temple University, Urban Archives.

p. 448: "camouflage for business": Ibid., 4.

p. 449: complained sharply when they did not achieve one: See the letter from Kennecott to Reid Weedon, ICEOP Collection.

p. 449: "At any point that I believe": "Reverend Leon H. Sullivan's Meeting with Representatives of Signatory Companies to Discuss the Status and Future Activity Regarding the Statement of Principles," November 13, 1979, 4, File 6, Box 2, ICEOP Collection.

p. 450: "You, probably better than any audience": "Speech Given by Reverend Leon H. Sullivan, April 18, 1979," op. cit., 1.

p. 450: John Vorster conceded in early 1978: SAIRR, *Survey, 1978,* 140.

p. 450: At a national conference on investment: Arnt Spandau, "The Consequences of a Hypothetical Economic Boycott of South Africa," mimeo document published by the African Studies Institute, 1978; cited in SAIRR, *Survey, 1978,* 140, 556.

p. 450: Heunis . . . publicly appealed: *Cape Times,* April 28, 1978; cited in SAIRR, *Survey, 1978,* 139.

p. 450: The conference had been the joint brainchild: Shelly Pitterman, "A Fine Face for Apartheid," *Southern Africa Update,* September 1977; reprinted by the Africa Fund.

p. 451: spending thousands of dollars: Ibid., 1.

p. 451: former President Ford spoke: The report appeared in the *Sunday Express* in Johannesburg along with unsubstantiated allegations that the Ford reelection campaign had received $3.9 million from the South African government. See *New York Times,* March 25, 1979.

p. 451: McGoff's attempts to buy newspapers: Steve Weissman, "American Publisher Peddles South Africa," *Southern Africa,* January–February 1978.

p. 451: Lester Kinsolving . . . was paid . . . to attend: Ibid.

p. 451: "Mighty Man": "Dealing with Propaganda—Soweto Style," *Southern Africa,* January–February 1978.

p. 451: The young people tore the comics up: Ibid.

p. 452: "rural plural": du Boulay, *Tutu,* 34.

p. 452: eggs and bacon at every breakfast: "My breakfast has been the same, year in and year out," Vorster told biographer John D'Oliveira, "a plate of mealiemeal porridge, a plate of eggs and bacon, or sausage, a slice of home-made bread, and black coffee. It does not vary. It has never varied and it never will vary" (D'Oliveira, *Vorster,* 279).

p. 452: voting for prime minister: See SAIRR, *Survey, 1978,* 3.

p. 453: Muldergate: For a full account, see Rees and Day, *Muldergate.* For summaries of the scandal and its effect on the National Party, see SAIRR, *Survey, 1978,* 3–5; SAIRR, *Survey, 1979,* 7–9.

p. 453: *Washington Star, Rand Daily Mail,* the *Citizen:* For extensive discussion of the information released by Judge Anton Mostert, see the supplementary material available from the New York Times News Service and the Associated Press for the first week of November 1978. See also Rees and Day, *Muldergate,* chap. 12.

p. 453: the murder of . . . Robert and Cora Smit: See *New York Times,* November 6, 1978.

p. 454: P. W. Botha had particularly resented: Cawthra, *Brutal Force,* 27.

p. 454: "total national strategy": Quoted in ibid., 29.

p. 454: supplementing military force: For more on Beaufre, see Davis, *Apartheid's Rebels,* 159. Beaufre "argued that a state may succeed in defeating a guerrilla movement only if it mobilizes all aspects of a power structure, not merely the military, in a sophisticated drive to starve the enemy of psychological resources. The battleground that will determine who the victor is lies in the hearts and minds of the populace. If a government can correctly identify the course of discontent and undermine them with convincing reforms, then, with a two-pronged campaign of politics and force, it can win sufficient public trust to shrink the popular base upon which guerrilla warfare is built."

p. 454: Malan . . . had gone on to study at the U.S. Army Command and General Staff College: Cawthra, *Brutal Force,* 28.

p. 455: the findings of the Rieckert Commission: SAIRR, *Survey, 1979,* 50, 211ff.

p. 455: the Wiehahn Commission's recommendation: See SAIRR, *Survey, 1979,* 274.

p. 455: In November 1979 the prime minister convened a closed meeting: Ibid., 2.

p. 456: the flap over Eglin and McHenry: See ibid., 12, 651.

p. 456: nuclear testing site in the Kalahari Desert: SAIRR, *Survey, 1978,* 58.

p. 456: the United States accused South Africa of exploding its first nuclear bomb: SAIRR, *Survey, 1979,* 86; see also Davis, *Apartheid's Rebels,* 198. For a thorough analysis of the Vela incident and its aftermath, see Walters, *South Africa and the Bomb,* chap. 3. In the spring of 1993, State President F. W. de Klerk announced that South Africa had succeeded in constructing six atomic bombs but emphatically denied that one had ever been tested in the South Atlantic.

p. 457: South Africa would be permitted to purchase oil: SAIRR, *Survey, 1979,* 651.

p. 457: Lancaster House negotiations: SAIRR, *Survey, 1979,* 615.

p. 458: "advisory councils": For the chronology of the complex disputes over the formation of the South African Indian Council (SAIC) and the Coloured Representatives Council (CRC), see the annual sections of the SAIRR's *Survey of Race Relations in South Africa* for this period. Though most observers viewed Botha's desire to provide a voice for the Coloured population as raw political calculation, others believed that Botha had a personal interest in its success. According to one report, a Coloured family had protected P. W. Botha's mother in the early part of the century when she had fled from British repression. She had later, it was said, exacted a promise from her son that if he were ever in a position to assist the Coloured community, he would do so.

p. 458: of AZAPO and COSAS: See SAIRR, *Survey, 1979,* 50, 500.

p. 458: building ties to the fledgling unions: One of the most significant early linkages between a civic organization and a union took place in November 1979 in Port Elizabeth, when seven hundred workers went on strike after Thozamile Botha, a worker at the Ford Struandale plant and a leader of PEBCO, was fired. Though the union, known as the United Auto Workers, was not registered with the government, it was recognized by Ford. After several days of negotiations, Ford reinstated Botha and agreed to pay the workers' salaries for the period during which they were on strike.

p. 458: FOSATU: For discussions of the formation of FOSATU, see MacShane, *Power!,* as well as Baskin, *Striking Back,* esp. chap. 1. Also see Hauck and Voorhes, *Two Decades,* 13. The unions gradually overcame the assertions from both right and left that they had been created to give the government the ability to control workers and soon began applying coordinated pressure, through negotiations and strikes, on different sectors of the South African economy. In this they received the advice and occasionally the support of unions from other countries. The AFL-CIO, for example, established a small program to train South African labor leaders and educate American locals about conditions in South Africa. The effort was funded by the Agency for International Development and directed by a former member of the PAC, Nana Mahomo (see author interview with Nana Mahomo, January 30, 1990). The effectiveness of this program was seriously undercut by the allegation, widely believed in South African labor union circles, that both the program and its director, Mahomo, had received funds from the CIA. The allegations were repeated in a book on the South Africa Security Police. Mahomo sued for defamation of character and eventually won a settlement.

p. 458: the more liberal English-speaking churches: For discussions of the role of the English-speaking churches, see Villa-Vicencio, *Trapped in Apartheid,* and Peter Walshe, *Church versus State.*

p. 459: "the enemies of our volk": SAIRR, *Survey, 1979,* 63.

p. 459: "suggests that they have the identity of non-persons": "The practical consequences of this 'non-white theology,' " Buthelezi wrote, "has been the belief that 'non-whites' can be satisfied with the shadows of things that the white men take for granted when it comes to their needs. . . . There is therefore a need for the substitution of a 'non-white' theology with a 'black theology' or a theology of the image of God in order to put the perspective of human identity in a proper theological perspective," (Manas Buthelezi, "The Relevance of Black Theology," mimeographed booklet, Christian Academy of South Africa, Johannesburg, 1974; also quoted in de Gruchy, *Church Struggle,* 158).

p. 459: "It is imperative for the black man": Buthelezi, "Six Theses," 55, quoted in de Gruchy, *Church Struggle,* 162.

p. 460: "My mother had to work": *Cape Times,* August 31, 1982.

p. 460: "I remember wanting revenge": BBC interview with Allan Boesak, November 1, 1982.

p. 460: "I hated all whites" . . . **"Beyers cannot hate anybody":** *Weekend Argus,* September 25, 1982.

p. 460: Boesak's thesis on King and Malcolm: See Allan Boesak, "Coming in out of the Wilderness: A Comparative Interpretation of the Ethics of Martin Luther King Jr. and Malcolm X," in Garrow, *Martin Luther King Jr.* Boesak later revised and expanded his work and published it as *A Farewell to Innocence.*

p. 461: "I grew inches that day": "A Vision for Humanity," address given on the award of the Martin Luther King Peace Prize, January 1986.

p. 462: Huddleston's visits to Tutu: du Boulay, *Tutu,* 30.

p. 462: "full of laughter and caring": Tutu, evidence to Eloff Commission, quoted by du Boulay, *Tutu,* 31.

p. 462: "His white cassock became grubby": Ibid.

p. 463: "to just walk around and use any exit": Ibid., 58.

pp. 463–64: Barney Pityana . . . was so moved by Tutu's courage: Ibid., 79. See also author interview with Barney Pityana, April 26, 1993.

p. 464: "As I knelt in the Dean's stall": Tutu, *Hope and Suffering,* 135.

p. 464: "I am writing to you, Sir": Ibid., 1–7.

p. 465: "You can sit all day in your house": Ibid., 73.

p. 466: "God did not just talk": Quoted in du Boulay, *Tutu,* 86.

p. 467: Tutu's decision to become general secretary: Ibid., 120.

p. 467: "white" or "black" mode that day: Ibid., 132.

p. 467: dancing and swirling: Ibid., 68.

p. 467: "we had the land and they had the Bible": Quoted in ibid., 133.

p. 467: "One of the great advantages of a black skin": Quoted in ibid., 65.

p. 468: chief accountant was later convicted: Ibid., 147.

p. 468: "People are starving": Tutu, *Hope and Suffering,* 97. Tutu went on in that speech to describe the girl in Zweledinga.

p. 469: "largely corrupt men": *Citizen,* June 30, 1982; quoted in du Boulay, *Tutu,* 168.

p. 469: the funeral of Robert Sobukwe: For Buthelezi's account of the funeral of Robert Sobukwe, see "Heartache and Treachery," the speech he delivered on April 9, 1978, in *Power Is Ours: The Collected Speeches of South African Statesman Gatsha Buthelezi* (New York: Books in Focus, 1979). See also du Boulay, *Tutu,* 240.

p. 470: "as fast as their legs could carry them": Buthelezi, "Heartache and Treachery," op. cit., 123.

p. 470: "new breed of blacks": *Sunday Express,* March 19, 1978; quoted by Buthelezi in ibid., 123.

pp. 470–71: "The South African churches are under an obligation": du Boulay, *Tutu,* 159.

p. 471: Jackson . . . had managed to obtain a visa: According to South African press accounts at the time, the visa was granted through combined pressure from the

U.S. State Department and Gatsha Buthelezi. See "Jackson's Words of Wisdom," *Sunday Times,* August 19, 1979.

p. 471: "Welcome Rev. Jackson": Author interview with Howard Schomer, March 1988.

p. 471: Jackson . . . continued to insist: See, for example, "Jackson May Think Again on Sanctions," *Argus,* July 20, 1979; "Dollars and Dignity: An Interview with Jesse Jackson," *Financial Mail,* July 22, 1979; "I'll Ask Carter to Sever Ties," *Star,* July 30, 1979; "Cyclone Jessie Hits Country," *Voice,* July 29, 1979; "Jackson May Give a New Boost to US Disinvestment," *Rand Daily Mail,* August 3, 1979; and "Fresh Protests on US Cash Expected," *Daily Dispatch,* August 3, 1979.

p. 471: Jackson made a speech: SAIRR, *Survey, 1979,* 44–45.

p. 471: All through the evening: SAIRR, *Survey, 1979,* 44–45. See also author interviews with Howard Schomer, March 1988; with Nthato Motlana, February 1993; and with Desmond Tutu, March 1993.

p. 471: the agreement collapsed almost instantly: Two weeks later, after consulting with the Soweto Committee of Ten, Motlana announced that he could not cooperate with Buthelezi.

p. 471: the ANC would not "collaborate with traitors": SAIRR, *Survey, 1979,* 43; also see Maré and Hamilton, *Appetite for Power,* 143.

p. 471: a group of seventy Inkatha members: SAIRR, *Survey, 1979,* 45.

p. 472: a ploy that only strengthened the suspicion: For a discussion of the Buthelezi-ANC visit, see Davis, *Apartheid's Rebels,* 108.

p. 472: "the emergence of Inkatha must be seen": Maré and Hamilton, *Appetite for Power,* 144.

CHAPTER TWELVE: **The Limits of Engagement and Reform**

p. 473: "The land of apartheid": Chester Crocker, "South Africa," 323.

p. 473: a growing number of congressional representatives: One effort was known as the Congressional Ad Hoc Monitoring Group on South Africa.

p. 474: Diggs . . . had been charged by a federal grand jury: "Rep. Diggs Indicated for Alleged Illegal Payroll Fund Use," *Washington Post,* March 24, 1978; "Rep. Diggs of Michigan Indicted on 35 Counts in Kickback Case," *New York Times,* March 24, 1978.

p. 474: Diggs resigned from Congress: "Rep. Diggs Quits after 25 Years; Faces Jail Term," *New York Times,* June 4, 1980.

p. 475: "the most significant black appointment": Quoted in Janice Simpson, "Our Man at Ford," *Black Enterprise,* September 1980, 40.

p. 476: Jordan had to kick him under the table: Author interview with Franklin Thomas, April 19, 1990.

p. 476: Thomas had been asked by the Rockefeller Foundation: "Ford Foundation Chief to Direct Study Panel on Southern Africa," *New York Times,* August 15, 1979.

p. 477: they met with Gatsha Buthelezi: See SAIRR, *Survey, 1980,* 77.

p. 477: "if genuine progress toward meeting the grievances": Commission on U.S. Policy toward Southern Africa, *South Africa,* xxii.

p. 477: "Although the commission ruled against disinvestment": Thomas, "South Africa: Time Running Out," speech to the Commonwealth Club of California, May 31, 1985, reprinted by the Ford Foundation.

p. 478: used his position as the only black: "New Wheel at Ford," *Black Enterprise,* April 1979, 19.

p. 478: the foundation voted for shareholder resolutions: IRRC, *How Institutions Voted, 1979* (Washington, D.C.: IRRC, 1979).

p. 478: rejected a measure urging IBM to withdraw: The foundation trustees also faced the delicate problem of explaining why, having voted on occasion for withdrawal from South Africa, they did not support a similar policy toward the Soviet Union. "The foundation has generally been willing to recognize a company's right to operate wherever it wishes so long as it conforms to the laws of its host country and those of the U.S.," the trustees wrote to the Investor Responsibility Research Center, which tracked both the outcome and the reasoning behind shareholder voting. "Only a clear causal connection (or strong possibility of one) between a company and substantial social harm from state-organized political or other oppression (as in the case of South Africa) has moved the foundation to depart from its long-standing policy not to support boycotts of other societies simply because of the offensive or adversary character of their current regimes. . . . The foundation has generally been willing" (IRRC, *How Institutions Voted, 1980* [Washington, D.C.: IRRC, 1980]).

p. 479: "I was always amazed": Author interview with Mary Camper-Titsingh, July 1988.

p. 479: the activist leaders concluded: Hauck and Voorhes, *Two Decades,* 7: "The election of Ronald Reagan threw many activist groups on the defensive. Activists are now attempting to unify the anti-apartheid community and substantially broaden their base of support to regain momentum."

p. 479: April 1979 . . . referendum in Berkeley: See Dumisani Kumalo, "Statement Prepared for the Human Rights Seminar to Discuss Measures to Prevent Transnational Corporations from Collaborating with South Africa," Spring 1981, 5, ACOA Active Files, ACOA Campaign to Oppose Investment—National Conference.

p. 479: "coherence meetings": Hauck and Voorhes, *Two Decades,* 25.

p. 479: Campaign against Investment in South Africa: Ibid., 49.

p. 479: Randall Robinson and his staff at TransAfrica: Ibid.

p. 480: the church hired Audrey Chapman: She was known at the time as Audrey Chapman Smock.

p. 480: "Howard had a lot of experience": Author interview with Audrey Chapman, October 1988.

p. 480: The conference, which was held on September 28: See *New York Times,* September 30, 1981.

pp. 480–81: Davis and Dumisani Kumalo were convinced: For South African commentary on their efforts, see SAIRR, *Survey, 1978,* 104.

p. 481: five-thousand-dollar matching grant: See the proposal letter from Randall Robinson and Jean Sindab to Prexy Nesbitt at the Programme to Combat Racism, January 19, 1981. For a sample of the other fundraising letters that were sent out, see George Houser to Canon Robert Powell, March 30, 1981. The ACOA Active Files also include the minutes of the planning meetings held on March 30, April 27, and May 18, 1981, by the representatives of the member groups. See ACOA Active Files, ACOA Campaign to Oppose Investment—National Conference.

p. 481: The letter of invitation: See "Dear Colleague, We invite you to a unique national conference on Public Investment," March 1981, ACOA Active Files, ACOA Campaign to Oppose Investment—National Conference.

p. 481: Nearly two hundred union leaders: See "Attendants at the Conference on Public Investment and South Africa," ACOA Active Files, ACOA Campaign to Oppose Investment—National Conference.

p. 481: "end American investment in evil": For the text of Bond's speech, see a typewritten transcript as well as a printed version in *ACOA Action News,* no. 10, Fall 1981; both can be found in ACOA Active Files, ACOA Campaign to Oppose Investment—National Conference.

p. 481: the legislators who attended: Author interview with Richard Knight, July 1988.

p. 481: Chester Crocker's background: For information on Chester Crocker's childhood and academic career, see author interview with Chester Crocker, May 23, 1990, and the curriculum vitae he provided at that time, author's files.

p. 482: "took every course": Crocker, *High Noon,* 25.

p. 482: "to the left of Trotsky": Author interview with Chester Crocker, May 23, 1990.

p. 482: By the end of the 1960s: See Chester Crocker's curriculm vitae, author's files. See also his entries in various editions of *Who's Who.*

p. 482: brilliant article: See Chester A. Crocker, "Nixon-Kissinger System," 79–99.

p. 483: "runaway ethnic policy": See Chester A. Crocker, "Andy Young: A Runaway Ethnic Rafshooning the World," *Washington Post,* August 26, 1979. The article was summarized in *SA Foundation News,* October 1979, and in *Johannesburg Star,* October 9, 1979.

p. 483: "Washington's preoccupation with rhetorical principles": Crocker and Lewis, "Missing Opportunities," 145.

p. 483: "The modernizers who are taking over": Chester A. Crocker, "South Africa," 337.

p. 484: "White House unwillingness": Ibid., 325.

p. 484: "The real choice we will face": Ibid., 345.

p. 484: short book: *South Africa's Defense Posture: Coping with Vulnerability* (Washington, D.C.: Center for Strategic and International Studies, 1979).

p. 484: instead of being a "rogue elephant": Crocker alluded to this in the *Foreign Affairs* article, but he states it more emphatically in the CSIS book.

p. 485: "de Gaulle option": See Leonard, *South Africa at War,* 13.

p. 485: steady stream of articles: In addition to those cited in preceding notes, see Chester A. Crocker, with Mario Greznes and Robert Henderson, "A U.S. Policy for the 80s," *Africa Report,* January–February 1981.

p. 485: Crocker would have control over: Crocker, *High Noon,* 28.

p. 485: "All Reagan knows about southern Africa": From an interview by Kevin Danaher with Chester Crocker, quoted in Kevin Danaher, "The U.S. Struggle over Sanctions against South Africa," in Orkin, *Sanctions,* 134.

p. 485: "Can we abandon a country": "Reagan's Views on South Africa Praised by Botha," *New York Times,* March 5, 1981; also quoted in Crocker, *High Noon,* 81.

p. 486: "repeating verbatim": Crocker, *High Noon,* 81.

p. 486: The South African government and the Afrikaner press: P. W. Botha praised Reagan for recognizing that South Africa's strategic value depended on "the maintenance of civilized standards." The editors of *Die Vaderland* applauded the new direction with banner headlines. "Not only is it virtually opposite of that adopted by the Carter government," the story read, "but it is even more friendly than the policy of Richard Nixon" ("Reagan's View on South Africa Praised by Botha," *New York Times,* March 5, 1981).

p. 486: "The military officers met in Washington": Gail Morlan letter, *New York*

Times, March 29, 1981. For Chester Crocker's views on van der Westhuizen, see Crocker, *High Noon,* 116–17.

p. 486: Ambassador Kirkpatrick . . . vetoed four Security Council resolutions: "U.S. Africa Ties Face Test over Sanctions," *New York Times,* April 19, 1981; "U.S. Joins in U.N. Veto on South African Trade Ban," *New York Times,* May 1, 1981.

p. 486: South African national rugby team: "Sports-Apartheid Moves Build," *New York Times,* April 26, 1981; see also *New York Times,* July 14 and July 18, 1981.

p. 487: "It was not in the character of the early Reagan period": Crocker, *High Noon,* 73.

p. 487: "play one intractable problem": Presentation by Chester Crocker, Africa Seminar, Harvard University Center for International Affairs, December 12, 1989. It seems that the original linkage, under the Carter administration, was between the withdrawal of Cuban troops and formal American recognition of the Angolan government. Under Reagan, recognition was out of the question, so the linkage shifted. See "Haig's Crocker Enhances African Policy," *Washington Star,* January 30, 1981.

p. 487: "By expanding the agenda": Crocker, *High Noon,* 67.

p. 488: not obvious to all: "There is no legal link between the question of South Africa's occupation of Namibia and the presence of Cuban forces in Angola," wrote one liberal commentator. "South Africa is under legal obligation to end its occupation of Namibia with no preconditions. . . . The Cubans, on the other hand, are in Angola at the invitation of a sovereign government" (Leonard, *South Africa at War,* 76).

p. 488: "limp and indecisive stance": Crocker, *High Noon,* 63.

p. 488: Crocker told MPLA government officials: "U.S. Said to Tie Namibian Freedom to a Cuban Pullout from Angola," *New York Times,* April 30, 1981.

p. 489: "I don't like the way he referred": "Botha Holds Reagan Aid Liable for South Africans' Cancelled U.S. Visit," *New York Times,* April 17, 1981.

p. 489: Botha immediately put Crocker on the defensive: The record of this conversation was preserved in a memorandum of conversation written by State Department official Alan Keyes, who attended the meeting with Crocker. See "Memorandum of Pretoria Meeting, April 15/16, 1981," published in Pauline H. Baker, *United States and South Africa,* 106.

p. 489: Malan interjected: Malan made the same points in an election rally speech in the Transvaal shortly before Crocker departed. See "South Africa Remains Steadfastly Vague on Namibia," *New York Times,* April 21, 1981.

p. 489: "Some senior players in Pretoria": Crocker, *High Noon,* 91.

p. 490: "didn't know one thing": Jesse Helms, quoted in "Showdown Set on Confirmation of State Department Aides," *Washington Post,* April 28, 1981.

p. 490: "I'm sure your wife loves you": "Confirmation Delays Criticized by Senate Democratic Liberal," *Washington Star,* April 7, 1981.

p. 490: "appeared to have been inspired": Crocker, *High Noon,* 91.

p. 490: Nancy Landon Kassebaum: Kassebaum did not share Helms's sympathy for the South African government. On June 10, 1981, several days after Crocker's confirmation, she wrote an opinion piece, "Pretoria Offends Everything Republicans Stand For," in the *Washington Star.* "The euphoria in Pretoria and the despair in black African capitals about the conservative turn in American government originates in a false but widespread belief that the election signalled an American acquiescence to [apartheid]. . . . It is ironic that those in South Africa who sound the most like Republicans by demanding the right to private property, the right to be considered for jobs without regard to race, and freedom from government regulation and interference at home, in the schools, and at work are described as 'radical left' and even Marxists."

p. 490: "It would be wrong to assume": Senate Committee on Foreign Relations, Executive Report on the Nomination of Chester Crocker, May 4, 1981, 21.

p. 490: "I was from the wrong side of the street": Author interview with Chester Crocker, May 23, 1990.

p. 491: In a briefing memo: "The political relationship between the United States and South Africa has now arrived at a crossroads of perhaps historic significance," Crocker wrote in the memo. "The possibility may exist for a more positive and reciprocal arrangement between the two countries based on shared strategic concerns in southern Africa, [and] our recognition that the government of P. W. Botha represents a unique opportunity for domestic change" (see "Crocker's Scope Paper for Haig," in Baker, *United States and South Africa,* 115).

p. 491: could not "condone a system": Ibid., 118.

p. 491: "a Russian flag": Ibid., 120.

p. 492: blaming Crocker's woes on each other: "Haig Is Probing Leaks from Office," *Wall Street Journal,* June 4, 1981. For Crocker's discussion of the leaks, see *High Noon,* 91.

p. 492: if Crocker hired Clifford Kiracofe: See "Helms Offers Nomination Swap," *Washington Post,* June 3, 1981; "Senator Helms to Allow Votes on State Department Nominees," *Washington Post,* June 9, 1981; see also *Congressional Quarterly,* May 2, May 9, June 6, and June 13, 1981; and *New York Times,* June 5, 1981.

p. 492: close ties to the South African intelligence services: Crocker, *High Noon,* 91.

p. 492: Crocker's confirmation: See *Congressional Quarterly's Weekly Report,* June 13, 1981.

p. 492: "In South Africa, it is not our task": Chester A. Crocker, "Regional Strategy for Southern Africa," August 29, 1981, current policy no. 308, United States Department of State.

p. 493: "a titanic leap of faith": Davis, *Apartheid's Rebels,* 22.

p. 493: "Internal organization was shattered": Sheridan Johns, "Obstacles to Guerrilla Warfare: A South African Case Study," *Journal of Modern African Studies* 2.2 (1973): 285; quoted in Davis, *Apartheid's Rebels,* 22.

p. 493: Third Consultative Conference: For discussions of the Morogoro conference, see Ellis and Sechaba, *Comrades against Apartheid,* esp. chap. 3; Meli, *South Africa Belongs,* 163–70. See also Davis, *Apartheid's Rebels,* 23, and Leonard, *South Africa at War,* 34ff. The delegates to the Morogoro conference voted to reduce the National Executive to nine members; reaffirm the strategy of armed struggle; and establish a separate multiracial Revolutionary Council to command Umkhonto We Sizwe.

p. 493: The new structure and rhetoric: For example, the ANC at Morogoro formally adopted two statements, "The Revolutionary Programme of the ANC" and "Strategy and Tactics of the ANC," which emphasized the central role of the "large and growing working class" in South Africa in the overthrow of white minority rule. See Leonard, *South Africa at War,* 35ff.

p. 494: closer to the exclusivist tradition of the Pan-Africanist Congress: For discussions of the ideological links between black consciousness, the ANC, and the PAC, see ibid., 36ff.

p. 494: "We . . . oppose such efforts": Baruch Hirson, *Year of Fire, Year of Ash* (London: Zep Press, 1979), 200; quoted in Davis, *Apartheid's Rebels,* 31.

p. 494: the dissidents . . . were expelled: See Leonard, *South Africa at War,* 41.

p. 495: its force was an estimated eight thousand: In 1980 the South African deputy minister of defense estimated formally estimated the number of guerrillas in Mozambique alone at two thousand; see SAIRR, *Survey, 1980,* 61.

p. 495: blew up portions of SASOL I and SASOL II: See ibid., 61; Davis, *Apartheid's Rebels,* 141.

p. 495: Throughout 1981 Umkhonto guerrillas destroyed: See SAIRR, *Survey, 1981,* 78.

p. 495: set off explosions at the Koeberg plant: Davis, *Apartheid's Rebels,* 142.

p. 495: more than two hundred acts of political violence: SAIRR, *Survey, 1983,* 45.

p. 496: "the actual number of missions": Davis, *Apartheid's Rebels,* 146.

p. 496: the Reagan administration disallowed: *New York Times,* September 21, 1982.

p. 496: licenses for airplanes and computers: Hauck and Voorhes, *Two Decades,* 33–34.

p. 496: when Control Data asked for permission: Ibid., 34.

p. 496: Herman Nickel's background: See "Reagan's Choice for Pretoria," *New York Times,* March 24, 1982. See also author interview with Herman Nickel, April 13, 1989.

p. 497: he argued that U.S. multinationals: Herman Nickel, "The Case for Doing Business in South Africa," *Fortune,* June 19, 1978.

p. 497: Nickel penned a blistering attack: "The Corporation Haters," *Fortune,* 1980. Nickel did not mention that his article had been commissioned by Ernest Lefever, the executive director of the Center for Ethics and Public Policy in Washington, D.C. Lefever had himself been nominated by Reagan to serve as U.S. assistant secretary of state for human rights. The Senate had rejected Lefever after senators learned that his center had received fifty thousand dollars from the Nestlé Corporation, the primary target of the infant formula campaign, to commission an article on the church groups. Lefever had then offered Nickel five thousand dollars to write the piece. "I never would have touched this if I had known Lefever had been taking money from the manufacturers," Nickel said later. Nonetheless, Nickel's article, an unmeasured broadside that characterized Nestlé's religious critics as "Marxists marching under the banner of Christ," had its desired effect, putting ICCR on the defensive for several years.

p. 497: "All we can do is to lend encouragement": "Reagan Choice Urges Care on South Africa," *New York Times,* February 26, 1982.

p. 497: the U.S. Senate confirmed him: *New York Times,* March 30, 1982. For the testimony against him, see "Nominee for Pretoria Post Backs 'Peaceful Change,' " *New York Times,* March 20, 1982.

p. 497: the debate over the IMF: Hauck and Voorhes, *Two Decades,* 38; see also *New York Times,* October 15, 20, 21, 22, 25, 26, 1982; November 1 and 4, 1982.

p. 497: had decided to wait and see: "In order to persuade South Africa to heed American representations on such subjects as an internationally recognized settlement on Namibia, acceptance of the nuclear non-proliferation treaty, and domestic political reforms in South Africa itself," Kassebaum said, ". . . the greatest possible level of public unity must be shown by those responsible for American foreign policy" (Hauck and Voorhes, *Two Decades,* 46).

p. 498: "degenerate into what is in essence": Ibid., 46.

p. 498: the representatives felt no pressure: "There is not much pressure to act on South Africa," said an aide to Solarz at the time, "and the few letters we receive commenting on Solarz's position on South Africa usually come from business interests outside the district" (ibid., 44).

p. 498: "Their impact is nil": Ibid., 45.

p. 499: the formation and support of RENAMO: See SAIRR, *Survey, 1981,* 57ff; SAIRR, *Survey, 1983,* 585ff.

p. 499: the formation of the Lesotho Liberation Army: SAIRR, *Survey, 1981,* 58.

p. 499: The judge accepted their testimony: SAIRR, *Survey, 1982,* 233.

p. 499: attacked several ANC houses in Matola: SAIRR, *Survey, 1981,* 25.

p. 499: Defence Forces swept into Lesotho's capital: SAIRR, *Survey, 1982,* 195; SAIRR, *Survey, 1983,* 590.

p. 499: "waging a non-declared war": SAIRR, *Survey, 1982,* 193.

p. 499: noninterference remained a cornerstone: Ibid.

p. 499: In his New Year's address: SAIRR, *Survey, 1983,* 585.

p. 500: General Magnus Malan warned: Ibid.

p. 500: The publicly revealed portion of the defense budget: See SAIRR, *Survey, 1978,* 53; SAIRR, *Survey, 1983,* 583.

p. 500: ARMSCOR . . . ballooned up to more than a hundred thousand employees: SAIRR, *Survey, 1982,* 199ff.

p. 500: the military life of the white male: See Davis, *Apartheid's Rebels,* 185.

p. 501: the attack in Sibasa: Ibid., 154.

p. 501: the arrest of Dean Farisani: For the full account of this and Farisani's other detentions, see Farisani, *Diary.*

p. 501: "I am determined to destroy": Ibid., 69–70.

p. 502: at least twenty-eight people had died: See *Torture in South Africa: Recent Documents* (London: Catholic Institute for International Relations, International Commission of Jurists, 1982).

p. 502: "Now you know how Mohapi died": SAIRR, *Survey, 1980,* 1975.

p. 502: Lennox Sebe . . . ruled with an iron fist: Sebe had given the job of director general of state security to his brother Charles. Charles had promoted himself to the rank of major general and vowed that he would keep close tabs on subversion anywhere in the Ciskei. Charles Sebe told an interviewer that he intended to especially monitor artists and would henceforth require poets and playwrights to apply to him before they put pen to paper. "During the time of black consciousness they had a method of putting across their ideology through poems and plays," said Sebe. "I have taken it upon myself to insist that any person who has a gift as a poet or playwright should be scrutinized" (supplement to *Daily Dispatch,* December 2, 1981; quoted in SAIRR, *Survey, 1981,* 302). Two years later, Charles Sebe found himself in prison when his brother accused him of fomenting a plot to overthrow him (SAIRR, *Survey, 1983,* 333).

p. 502: South African police picked up: SAIRR, *Survey, 1981,* 89.

p. 502: Aggett was so severely tortured: On January 19, after he had been in detention for nearly two months, Aggett told a visiting magistrate that he had been subjected to assault and torture (SAIRR, *Survey, 1982,* 255). Two magistrates and the new inspector of detainees then made several attempts to visit Aggett but were told by the police that he was "unavailable." On January 28, 1982, Aggett was taken from his cell and interrogated around the clock for nearly three days (SAIRR, *Survey, 1982,* 255). One detainee later reported having seen Aggett doing strenuous physical exercise and being beaten while naked. Auret van Heerden, the prisoner in the cell next to Aggett's, testified that on February 1, Aggett had been returned briefly and had told him that he had been tortured by electric shock to his testicles.

"They forced me to say that I am a Communist," said Aggett, weeping uncontrollably. "They just must not ask me any more questions" (affidavit of Auret van Heerden in *Torture in South,* op. cit., 23). Van Heerden noticed that over the next few days Aggett became "very depressed, tearful, a totally different person from the one I had known. . . . He had undergone a progressive deterioration . . . a kind of disintegration which was making him into a zombie." Another prisoner said that he had seen the police escort Aggett back to his cell on February 4 and had observed that Aggett had been in considerable pain, had blood on his forehead, and could barely walk (SAIRR, *Survey, 1982,* 256).

p. 502: More than ten thousand people: SAIRR, *Survey, 1982,* 254.

p. 502: strikes and bans in response to Aggett's death: SAIRR, *Survey, 1983,* 175.

p. 503: promised to renew their efforts: SAIRR, *Survey, 1982,* 175.

p. 503: George Meany Human Rights Award: Ibid., 160.

p. 503: allowed the press to tour the cell: Ibid., 216.

p. 503: "you won't get much information": *Johannesburg Star,* May 17, 1982; quoted in SAIRR, *Survey, 1982,* 216.

p. 503: the judge rejected the eyewitness testimony: Ibid., 257.

p. 503: Joe Gqabi . . . was murdered: See Leonard, *South Africa at War,* 55, 88.

p. 503: a car bomb killed . . . Petrus and Abu Nzima: SAIRR, *Survey, 1982,* 33; Leonard lists them as "Petros Nyawose and his wife" *(South Africa at War,* 91).

p. 503: Ruth First . . . was blown to pieces: See Leonard, *South Africa at War,* 125; Davis, *Apartheid's Rebels,* 177; SAIRR, *Survey, 1982,* 34. First was the author of *117 Days* and, with Jonathan Steele and Christabel Gurney, of *The South African Connection: Western Investment in Apartheid* (London: Temple Smith, 1972). A memoir by her daughter was later made into the movie *A World Apart.*

p. 503: The package carried the imprint: Leonard, *South Africa at War,* 90.

p. 503: "I battled to get permission": Winnie Mandela, *Part of My Soul,* 45.

p. 504: Griffiths Mxenge . . . died: SAIRR, *Survey, 1982,* 232.

p. 504: "right-wing death squad": SAIRR, *Survey, 1983,* 572.

p. 504: deaths of Mavi and Gawe: Ibid.

p. 504: The turning point in Conradie's life: *New York Times,* March 8, 1982.

p. 504: "Can you imagine": Tutu, *Hope and Suffering,* 132.

p. 504: "I do not come to praise": *New York Times,* March 8, 1982. In 1983 new incidents of sabotage occurred. The general secretary of the Food and Canning Workers' Union—the same union for which Aggett had worked—found that his tires had been drastically overinflated, increasing the possibility of a high-speed blowout. Desmond Tutu reported that the cars of several prominent clergy, including Allan Boesak, had been tampered with. In March the Very Reverend Edward King, dean of St. George's Cathedral in Cape Town, discovered a powerful bomb beneath his car. That same month, two organizers of the National Union of Mineworkers died in an accident near Welkom, not far from where Chris Hattingh had been killed (SAIRR, *Survey, 1983,* 571).

p. 505: In May 1978 two hundred South African commandos: Cawthra, *Brutal Force,* 149.

p. 505: Operation Protea: For descriptions and discussions of this offensive, see ibid., 151.

p. 506: They touted the existence: Ibid., 205.

p. 506: social services throughout Namibia deteriorated: Ibid., 209.

p. 506: "cold, calculating": *Armed Forces,* December–January 1984, quoted in ibid., 124.

p. 506: "killing machines": *Windhoek Observer,* October 17, 1983; quoted in Cawthra, *Brutal Force,* 210. The phrase was used during the trial of two Koevoet members in September 1983; see SAIRR, *Survey, 1983,* 608.

p. 506: the members of Koevoet would sometimes disguise themselves: Cawthra, *Brutal Force,* 210.

p. 507: Denis Hurley . . . led a group: See SAIRR, *Survey, 1982,* 621.

p. 507: Desmond Tutu and Peter Storey: Cawthra, *Brutal Force,* 212.

p. 507: a fourth religious delegation: SAIRR, *Survey, 1983,* 609.

p. 507: "The Security Forces stop at nothing": Southern African Catholic Bishops Conference report, 1982, 20–21; quoted in Cawthra, *Brutal Force,* 212.

p. 507: charging Hurley under a law: Cawthra, *Brutal Force,* 213.

p. 507: two of whom were convicted: See SAIRR, *Survey, 1983,* 608.

p. 507: A white soldier who raped: Cawthra, *Brutal Force,* 245.

p. 507: In 1983 two soldiers: *Windhoek Advertiser,* November 29, 1983; quoted in Cawthra, *Brutal Force,* 211.

p. 508: Koornhof defeated by de Klerk: SAIRR, *Survey, 1980,* 13.

p. 509: the Conservative Party was endorsed: SAIRR, *Survey, 1982,* 11–12.

p. 509: Union leaders had banded together: For a contemporary leftist assessment of the role and power of unions in the early 1980s, see MacShane et al., *Power!,* esp. chap. 3. For the most detailed discussions of current union events, see the issues of *South African Labour Bulletin* from this period.

p. 509: Winnie Mandela was awarded an honorary doctorate: SAIRR, *Survey, 1982,* 34.

p. 509: Nelson was nominated to be chancellor: Ibid., 218.

p. 509: Mandela and Sisulu transferred: Ibid.

p. 509: President's Council finally unveiled: For a careful outline of the new constitutional proposals, see SAIRR, *Survey, 1983,* 71–73.

p. 510: F. W. de Klerk . . . told the Transvaal Party Congress: Ibid., 12.

p. 510: Gerrit Viljoen . . . attempted to calm: Ibid., 11.

p. 510: Lennox Sebe . . . endorsed the new constitution: Ibid., 79.

p. 510: New Republic Party and business leaders: Ibid.

p. 511: Allan Hendrickse, the leader of the Labour Party: Ibid.

p. 511: the Conservative Party . . . called on the white electorate: Conservative Party leader Andries Treurnicht argued that the new constitution would abandon the policy of separate development, destroy white self-determination, and lead to a dictatorship. He warned that Botha and Hendrickse were already "bedfellows" and that there were secret plans to unite the National Party with the Progressives. Parodying P. W. Botha's rhetoric, Treurnicht said that the prime minister was now urging Afrikaners to "adapt *and* die" (ibid., 23).

p. 511: it would destroy the equality: *New York Times,* October 9, 1983.

p. 511: Jaap Marais: SAIRR, *Survey, 1983,* 25.

p. 511: Buthelezi Commission: See SAIRR, *Survey, 1982,* 303, 398ff. The South African Institute of Race Relations selected the Buthelezi Commission for the topic of its annual conference in 1982. See ibid., 578.

p. 511: "who ought not to be present": SAIRR, *Survey, 1983,* 12.

p. 512: "South Africa's would-be reformers": Ibid., 92.

p. 512: Botha publicly denied: Ibid., 93.

p. 512: many business leaders reported: Ted Pavitt, the executive chairman of the General Mining Union Corporation, said that he would support the constitution because he was "taking the government on trust that it intends making some constitutional provision for blacks at a later stage." Members of the government, he said, had privately promised him that the constitution would not "lower the guillotine on future inclusion of blacks" (ibid., 95). The Progressives who argued against the constitution faced the politically difficult task of asserting that Botha's proposals were either insignificant or would not lead to anything further. To make his case, van Zyl Slabbert found himself in the peculiar position of urging people to believe Botha's denial of a "hidden agenda." "It is only those who read their own desires and fancies into the Nationalist plan," said van Zyl Slabbert, "who harbor the fond illusion that somehow blacks will inevitably be included" (ibid., 93).

p. 512: **In September 1979 . . . a journalist asked Tutu:** du Boulay, *Tutu,* 160.

p. 513: **Desmond and Leah Tutu had traveled for a month:** Ibid., 186.

p. 513: **"He was just extraordinary":** Ibid., 196.

p. 513: **"I was overwhelmed":** Tutu, "The Divine Intention," a presentation to the Eloff Commission, September 1, 1982, in *Hope and Suffering,* 183.

p. 513: **"a conspiracy to keep South African blacks":** du Boulay, *Tutu,* 190.

p. 514: **"They were intending to separate us":** Author interview with Desmond Tutu, March 3, 1993.

p. 514: **"that you are not simply dealing":** du Boulay, *Tutu,* 176.

p. 514: **"greatest sermon":** Sparks, *Mind of South Africa,* 290; also quoted in du Boulay, *Tutu,* 173.

p. 515: **"My purpose is to demonstrate":** Tutu, *Hope and Suffering,* 153–55.

p. 515: **"If anyone were to show me":** Ibid., 155. Tutu had made the same statement during a service at Regina Mundi Church in Soweto the previous June.

p. 515: **"I want the government to know":** Tutu, *Hope and Suffering,* 158.

p. 515: **"There is nothing the government can do":** du Boulay, *Tutu,* 174.

p. 516: **"reject communism for South Africa":** SAIRR, *Survey, 1980,* 615.

p. 516: **"It is the old game":** Ibid., 616.

p. 516: **"Not only is South Africa":** SAIRR, *Survey, 1982,* 565.

p. 517: **"a political system based on separate development":** Ibid.

p. 517: **elected Allan Boesak president:** Ibid., 566.

p. 517: **"apartheid would no longer have a white face":** SAIRR, *Survey, 1983,* 31.

p. 518: **detonated a huge car bomb:** See ibid., 43–44, and Davis, *Apartheid's Rebels,* 149. For American commentary, see *New York Times,* May 21–May 24, 1983.

p. 518: **South African air force retaliated:** SAIRR, *Survey, 1983,* 569; Davis, *Apartheid's Rebels,* 177.

p. 518: **of the twenty-five people who died:** *Manchester Guardian,* May 24, 1983; *London Times,* May 25, 1983; quoted in Davis, *Apartheid's Rebels,* 177.

p. 518: **executing three captured ANC guerrillas:** See *New York Times,* June 7, June 9, and June 10, 1983.

p. 518: **more than one hundred prominent business leaders:** See SAIRR, *Survey, 1983,* 79–80.

p. 518: **new chances to "smear" the country:** Ibid., 80.

p. 518: **Botha brought three of South Africa's most important ambassadors:** Ibid., 14.

p. 519: **"forum for racism":** SAIRR, *Survey, 1982,* 397.

p. 519: **"working for the South African government himself":** SAIRR, *Survey, 1983,* 36.

p. 519: **"marriage of convenience":** Ibid., 33.

p. 519: **approval would mean:** Ibid., 52, 82.

p. 519: **the United Democratic Front was formally launched:** Ibid., 58.

p. 520: "Johnny-come-lately heroes": Ibid., 53.

p. 520: "will come to naught": Ibid.

p. 520: "The early morning mist had hardly lifted": *Sunday Times,* November 6, 1983. Quoted in Mzala, *Buthelezi,* 18. Though Mzala, who was a senior researcher for the ANC, might be considered biased, the reports of events at Ngoye have been corroborated by numerous other press accounts and observers.

p. 520: shouting insults and hurling stones: Though the ANC version insists that the students at Ngoye did nothing to trigger the fighting (see the first chapter of Mzala), Maré and Hamilton, whose work is highly critical of Buthelezi, write that "the Inkatha supporters were not unprovoked in their attack on the Ngoye students. The evidence of the Middleton report suggests that Ngoye students were the first to throw stones" *(Appetite for Power,* 197).

p. 521: Though Inkatha had held its peace: Buthelezi speech, quoted in Mzala, *Buthelezi,* 20–21.

p. 522: The U.S. State Department formally welcomed the outcome: *New York Times,* November 4, 1983.

p. 522: "wildest expectations": SAIRR, *Survey, 1983,* 88.

p. 522: "I do not know what you mean": *New York Times,* November 8, 1983.

CHAPTER THIRTEEN: **The Spread of the Divestment Movement**

p. 523: "The international community must make up its mind": Desmond Tutu, "The Role of White Opposition in South Africa," July 1981, in *Hope and Suffering,* 129.

p. 523: he had to cancel the annual meeting: Hauck and Voorhes, *Two Decades,* 110.

p. 524: each firm would best know: Ibid.

p. 524: PACE Commercial College: See Arthur D. Little, Inc. (ADL), Sixth Report to the Sullivan Signatories, November 1, 1982, 1.

p. 524: "There is great dissatisfaction among blacks": Ibid.; also quoted in Hauck and Voorhes, *Two Decades,* 115–16.

p. 524: signed up 146 firms, slightly more than half: The exact number of U.S. companies in South Africa was always open to interpretation, depending on how one counted the subsidiaries of conglomerates, minority ownerships, and so on. These figures come from ADL, Sixth Report, op. cit., 10–11. For a general assessment of the Sullivan performance, see D. Reid Weedon Jr., "The Evolution of Sullivan Principle Compliance," in Sethi, *South African Quagmire,* 393–402.

p. 524: nine "basic requirements": ADL, Sixth Report, op. cit., 5–6; Hauck and Voorhes, *Two Decades,* 113.

p. 525: the companies forced Sullivan to reverse himself: See ADL, Sixth Report, op. cit., 4; Hauck and Voorhes, *Two Decades,* 115.

p. 525: "no other credible person": Corp's, Rawlings's, and Schroll's comments are from Hauck and Voorhes, *Two Decades,* 99.

p. 525: "My calculation": Ibid., 100. For another contemporary assessment, see Daniel Purnell's article on the Sullivan Principles in Hoffmann, *Corporate Governance.*

p. 525: the number had dropped to twenty-nine: Arthur D. Little, Inc. (ADL), Seventh Report to the Sullivan Signatories, October 25, 1983, 1.

p. 525: Ten companies that received low grades: ADL, Sixth Report, op. cit., 3.

p. 526: "I filled out the sixth report": Hauck and Voorhes, *Two Decades,* 117.

p. 526: fluctuating numbers from 1980 to 1982: Ibid., 111.

p. 526: a number of critics pointed out: See, for example, Karen Paul, "The Inadequacy of Sullivan Reporting," *Business and Society Review* (Spring 1986); reprinted in Sethi, *South African Quagmire,* chap. 37.

p. 526: a total of 66,175 workers: ADL, Seventh Report, op. cit., 35 (table 4), 39 (table 16). The other statistics in this paragraph are also from this source.

p. 526: the total contribution of American corporations: ADL, Sixth Report, op. cit., 40 (table 21).

p. 526: In 1983 that number fell: ADL, Seventh Report, op. cit., 41 (table 22).

p. 526: Compared to the tens of millions of rand: For a general critique of the Sullivan Principles as a strategy for change, see Schmidt, *Decoding Corporate Camouflage.*

p. 527: both Harvard and Yale had decided to dump the stock: For a discussion of the controversy at Yale, see Robert K. Massie Jr., "The South African Dilemma," *Connecticut,* October 1979.

p. 527: "They sold well under their value": *Harvard Crimson,* February 18, 1981.

p. 527: "The Citibank sale made a lot of the financial community": *Harvard Crimson,* May 18, 1983.

p. 527: "no allowance for the use of discretion": Hauck and Voorhes, *Two Decades,* 73.

p. 527: The ACSR briefly did so: See "Shareholder Committee Hears Views on South Africa Loan Policy," *Harvard Gazette,* March 5, 1982; "ACSR Unanimously Rejects Bank Loans to South Africa," *Harvard Crimson,* March 12, 1982. See also Hauck and Voorhes, *Two Decades,* 73.

p. 527: The Corporation Committee considered overriding the ACSR: "Corporation Rejects South Africa Loans," *Harvard Crimson,* March 16, 1982.

p. 528: "Ethically there is something incongruous": "Committee Urges Changes in Investment Policy," *Harvard Crimson,* May 6, 1983.

p. 528: meetings with the president of Joy Manufacturing: Author interview with Hugh Calkins, September 1988.

p. 528: After seven years of promises from Carnation's managers: Corporation Committee on Shareholder Responsibility, Annual Report, 1983–1984.

p. 528: "the argument that divestiture": Shareholder Advisory Committee, Report on Investment Policy, May 18, 1984.

p. 529: The corporation defended its contention: Corporation Committee on Shareholder Responsibility, Response to the Report of the Advisory Committee on Shareholder Responsibility, October 1, 1984.

p. 529: "It is never a pleasant task": Derek Bok, "The Problem with Divestment," 13.

p. 530: formation of the CAAC: Much of the material for the section on Connecticut comes from Janice Love, *U.S. Anti-Apartheid Movement,* chap. 4. She describes the formation of the CAAC on pages 101ff. See also American Committee on Africa, "Legislative Action against Apartheid: A Case Study of the Connecticut Divestment Campaign," January 1982, author's files.

p. 531: two bills were filed calling for divestment: Love, *U.S. Anti-Apartheid Movement,* 100, 102.

p. 531: Eventually the state sold off the stock: Ibid., 104. The Dresser, IMS, and Lubrizol shares were worth $6.5 million; see Hauck and Voorhes, *Two Decades,* 86.

p. 531: Allan Nelson: See author interview with Allan Nelson, December 19, 1986.

p. 531: "must either shape up or ship out": *Boston Globe,* September 28, 1980; quoted in Love, *U.S. Anti-Apartheid Movement,* 105.

p. 532: more than a two-thirds majority: The exact vote was 101 to 35 in the House and 25 to 10 in the Senate. See Love, *U.S. Anti-Apartheid Movement,* 109.

p. 532: Business leaders from Connecticut's biggest banks: Ibid., 109ff.

p. 532: companies that maintained large facilities: See ibid., 111 (table 4-3).

p. 533: Christy Hoffman of the CAAC agreed: Ibid., 123.

p. 533: One objected: Robert Schonbrunn, senior vice president, Bernstein-Macaulay, to Lee Van Metter, deputy treasurer, March 30, 1982, in "Report of the Governor's Task Force on South African Investment Policy," April 21, 1982, 47ff, author's files.

p. 534: Thus the studies . . . all agreed: The study by the U.S. Trust Company noted that more than eighty percent of the S&P 500 companies involved in aerospace, autos, chemicals, drugs, hospital supplies, office and business equipment, and international oil would have to be excluded from a South Africa–free portfolio. However, they wrote, the 380 South Africa–free companies they had picked as an alternative universe "produced a total return in excess of the entire index." Though the companies were smaller, making up less than half of the market capitalizations of the S&P 500, their overall "beta," a statistical measurement of risk, was the same as the whole S&P (ibid., 39ff). "The beta, estimated against the entire index from quarterly data," wrote the analysts, "is exactly one with a very small standard error." For the full text of the letter from U.S. Trust to the task force, see Fantu Cheru, *The Financial Implications of Divestment: A Review of the Evidence* (New York: Interfaith Center on Corporate Responsibility, June 1984), app. D.

A second study, by Capital Management Sciences, also concluded that the risk and return were higher for a South Africa–free portfolio. The limitation of the universe "substantially increases the balance sheet risks over the S&P and the actual portfolio by increasing financial leverage; increasing earnings variance; increasing beta; reducing the activity to diversify the portfolio; focusing on lower market capitalization," the report states. "However, it also increases exposure to historically higher growth companies, with higher dividend and earnings growth and higher reinvestment rates" ("Report of the Governor's Task Force," op. cit., 31; see also Cheru, *Financial Implications,* app. B; and the IRRC divestment study [1985], 12). The Capital study was flawed, however, by its decision to analyze the performance of the Connecticut portfolio by excluding the South Africa–related stocks without adding any substitutions. A third study, by Daniels and Bell Management, also reluctantly concluded that "the exclusion of the unacceptable companies from the mutual equity fund will not have any negative impact. In fact, the study has shown the 'sanitized' portfolio to outperform both the original portfolio and the market" ("Report of the Governor's Task Force," op. cit., 34; see also Cheru, *Financial Implications,* app. C; and IRRC Divestment Study, op. cit., 11). Like the Capital study, Daniels and Bell arrived at this judgment simply by removing the South Africa stocks and seeing how the remaining portfolio did without substitutions.

p. 534: the task force submitted a report: See "Report of the Governor's Task Force," op. cit., 125.

p. 535: signed into law: See Public Act No. 82-324.

p. 535: "Our approach is to be persuasive": Hauck and Voorhes, *Two Decades,* 86.

p. 535: comprehensive system for monitoring: See Henry E. Parket, "Progress Report—South Africa Investment Policy," January 25, 1984, author's files.

p. 535: the GE executives . . . canceled the deal: See Hauck and Voorhes, *Two Decades,* 20.

p. 535: "press publicity": See SAIRR, *Survey, 1983,* 387. See also "GE Quits KwaZulu venture," *Rand Daily Mail,* October 15, 1982, which said that "company officials in Johannesburg said the decision by Southern Sphere Mining . . . to sell its stake in a planned R160 million anthracite mine in kwaZulu was influenced by anti-apartheid pressure in Connecticut where GE has its headquarters."

p. 535: three cities . . . and three states had approved the divestment: See Sandy Boyer, *Divesting from Apartheid: A Summary of State and Municipal Legislative Action on South Africa* (New York: American Committee on Africa, March 1983).

p. 536: In the summer of 1980 Bullard filed: See Love, *U.S. Anti-Apartheid Movement,* 179–83.

p. 536: a second bill requiring the state's universities: Ibid., 184–90. On January 13, 1983, Bullard wrote to the American Committee on Africa. "I wanted to take this opportunity to tell you how much I appreciated your expertise and plain hard work—particularly Dumisani Kumalo, for his visits, excellent persuasive talents, patience and stamina. I also want to thank Gail Hovey, for her visit and excellent testimony. . . . We couldn't have done it without you" (Perry Bullard to the American Committee on Africa, January 19, 1983, ACOA Active Files).

p. 536: ERISA: The sensitivity of most trustees to the ERISA provisions can be traced to the history of abuses of pension monies. By the early 1960s, most companies and nonprofit organizations, eager to improve employee benefits, had set up their own private employee pension plans. These plans, however, did not have to meet any particular standards and were not overseen by any government body. In 1962, after the Studebaker Company had collapsed, leaving its workers with worthless pensions, and after officials of the Teamsters Union had been discovered with their hands in the pension till, John F. Kennedy formed a commission to study the problem and to consider whether federal pension legislation was needed to control the pensions of firms whose national operations had exceeded the ability of state law to monitor and control. The commission submitted its report to President Johnson in January 1965, recommending that a federal statute be passed to preempt state law and set national standards for participation, vesting, benefit accrual, funding, survival, and termination insurance for every private pension funds in the country (see President's Commission on Corporate Pension Funds, "Public Policy and Private Pension Programs"). The bill took nine more years to make its way through Congress, but the measure finally passed and was signed into law by President Ford in 1974.

p. 537: ERISA . . . federalized the common law language: Senate Subcommittee on Labor of the Committee on Labor and Public Welfare, *Legislative History of the ERISA of 1974* (Public Law 93-406) (Washington, D.C.: GPO, 1975).

p. 537: The enforcement of the law: After ERISA was passed, numerous persons expressed concern over whether the prudence standard would be interpreted so narrowly that small firms would be denied access to pension fund capital. Without federal guidance, "courts were free to interpret along common law principles which were quite strict. This would have discouraged investment innovation," explained Alan D. Lebowitz, deputy assistant secretary at the Pension Welfare Administration Board. "The concern was that plan fiduciaries faced with this new set of obligations and liabilities would opt for the investment strategy that provided the least personal risk to them of being subject to lawsuits" (author interview with Alan D. Lebowitz, November 1988). The Labor Department spent five years soliciting advice on how to interpret the prudence standard. In 1979 the department promulgated a regulation that changed the focus of the standard from the prudence of *specific* investments to the prudence of an *overall* balanced portfolio which could have higher-return, riskier components as long as they were balanced by more conservative holdings (Ian Lanoff, "ERISA's Prudence Rule and Pension Plan Investments," statement of June 20, 1979, Department of Labor; see also Department of Labor, Labor-Management Services Administration, Office of Employee Benefits Security, "Fiduciary Standards: Employee Retirement Income Security Act," 1976).

p. 537: By the year 2000: For the most comprehensive study of pension economics, see Ippolito, *Pensions.*

p. 537: these four had held assets equivalent: ERISA had another unintended consequence: despite the congressional goal to increase the accountability of fiduciaries, in practice the law threatened to diminish it. Common law decisions had never accepted the delegation of fiduciary responsibility to others; but the new statute had tried to take into account the need of the fiduciaries of huge funds to rely on a diverse group of outside investment managers. The problem was that the outside managers insisted on being held accountable only for their piece, not for the plan as a whole; and the named fiduciaries did not want to be held accountable for actions by individual managers.

pp. 537–38: "As long as the directors act in good faith": Thomas Troyer and Robert A. Boisture, "Divestment of South Africa Investments: A Legal Analysis for Foundations, Other Charitable Institutions, and Pension Funds, a Report to the New World Foundation," brief prepared by attorneys at Caplin and Drysdale, Washington, D.C., April 15, 1985, 4.

p. 538: "creeping ERISA": Institutional Shareholder Services, Inc., newsletter, August 1988.

p. 538: "We have never said": Author interview with Alan D. Lebowitz, November 1988.

p. 538: "Can you justify social investing": Author interview with Robert Monks, October 1988.

p. 539: The first full divestment of a state pension plan: For a description of the Massachusetts campaign, see MassDivest, "Make It in Massachusetts"; see also Hauck and Voorhes, *Two Decades,* 51.

p. 540: stunning veto override: See *New York Times,* January 5, 1983.

p. 540: second national Conference on Public Investment: For a description of the second conference, see the American Committee on Africa, Annual Report, 1983. Also see other documents, including the agenda and the printed remarks of several of the presenters, ACOA Active Files.

p. 541: Kumalo traveled to Nebraska: See American Committee on Africa, Annual Report, 1983.

p. 541: national newsletter: Ibid., 2.

p. 541: "Whatever the original intention": Jennifer Davis, "Face It: The Sullivan Principles Haven't Worked," *Washington Post,* May 21, 1983.

p. 541: having started his career as a junior litigator: Harrison Goldin, "Rooming with James Meredith at Ole Miss," *Princeton Alumni Weekly,* September 16, 1992, 54–55.

p. 542: Goldin and Newman began supporting resolutions: Since the NYCERS trustees and comptroller's office did not respond to the IRRC annual survey prior to 1983, the information on proxy voting from 1979 to 1983 comes from Eric Wollman, project manager, Investment Responsibility Unit, in the New York City comptroller's office, who did an internal analysis of the NYCERS shareholder votes and summarized his findings in an interview with the author in February 1989.

p. 542: two brands of pineapple desserts: "The Fruits of Racism: Why Does New York City Buy South Africa Products?," *Unionist,* June 20, 1983, 4.

p. 542: Carol Bellamy sent a formal letter: New York City Council President Carol Bellamy to Joseph Barkan, president, Board of Education, June 24, 1983.

p. 542: "The City of New York should not be in the business": New York City Council President Carol Bellamy to New York Mayor Edward Koch, July 7, 1983.

p. 543: she wrote on NYCERS stationery: "Several NYCERS trustees have agreed to co-sponsor the attached resolution," wrote Bellamy, ". . . which would begin an orderly divestiture of pension funds from firms which do business in South Africa. I would like your support as well. . . . Public funds should not be used to subsidize South African apartheid. On behalf of our municipal employees and retirees, NYCERS should join the growing number of investors who are saying 'no' to institutional racism through divestiture. I believe we can accomplish this goal with violating our duty as fiduciary trustees to protect pension fund assets" (letter from Carol Bellamy to Harrison J. Goldin, December 9, 1983).

p. 543: the explicit racism of South Africa's policies: See, for example, testimony by New York City Council President Carol Bellamy before the City Council Government Operation Committee, June 28, 1984, in favor of Intro. 619, a resolution prohibiting municipal agencies from purchasing products made in the Republic of South Africa.

p. 543: "Our mission is to return a profit": "Some Trustees Want City Pension Funds to Cut Pretoria Ties," *New York Times,* March 7, 1984.

p. 543: released their divestment resolution: The early NYCERS proposal is interesting because it linked divestment to the movement of *firms* through the South Africa policy stages; phase one paired to stage 4, phase two to stage 5, and phase three to stage 7.

p. 543: "If during the process of divestiture": Draft divestment resolution to the NYCERS board of trustees, April 4, 1984, author's files.

p. 544: "To the extent that the Mayor": *New York Times,* May 31, 1984.

p. 544: "the city has a moral responsibility": Bellamy, Goldin, Gotbaum, and Feinstein issued a statement that "the Mayor has in the past few months come a long way on this issue and that is helpful" (statement by City Council President Carol Bellamy; Comptroller Harrison Goldin; Victor Gotbaum, executive director, D.C. 37; and Barry Feinstein, president of Local 237, the International Brotherhood of Teamsters, released by the New York City Employee Retirement System, July 13, 1984).

p. 544: "give them notice of the actions": New York City Employees Retirement System, Divestment Resolution, CAL No. R-110.

p. 544: "A few public pension funds replied favorably": Author interview with Eric Wollman, February 1989. These were not the only pressures faced by pension fund fiduciaries, who also found themselves under pressure from corporate executives to use these pools of capital to defend companies against the takeovers that had become popular in the mid-1980s. To clarify the proxy voting responsibilities of fiduciaries, the Department of Labor eventually issued a letter in 1988 which specified that named fiduciaries could either retain voting rights (and obligations) for themselves or delegate them formally to someone else (who would be held accountable to the fiduciary standards), but if delegated they could *not* seek to reclaim the voting rights or try to influence those responsible for voting the stock. Moreover, the department announced, all fiduciaries must in the future show evidence of rational deliberation about proxy voting and must keep satisfactory records of their votes on all shareholder resolutions (letter from Alan D. Lebowitz, deputy assistant secretary, Pension Welfare Benefits Administration, U.S. Department of Labor, to Helmuth Fandl, chairman of the Retirement Board of Avon Products, Inc., February 13, 1988, [referred to in the industry as the "Avon letter"], author's files). As Eric Wollman commented, "Now we know that things have changed even for the corporate funds. The Department of Labor said in the 'Avon letter' that under ERISA proxy votes have economic value and must be voted through some rational process. But since back then corporate funds never did anything but vote with management, we learned that we should focus on public pension funds."

p. 545: Ten of them . . . agreed to sign: Report of the Comptroller, "Interim Report on Implementation of the New York City Employees' Retirement System South Africa Resolution," South Africa Investment Responsibility Unit, March 31, 1985, 9.

p. 545: The banks . . . all responded quickly: For references to the bank restrictions, see the SAIRU implementation reports of March and August 1985; the testimony of Harrison Goldin before the New York City Council Committee on Government Operations, February 22, 1985; "City Leadership Urging Pressure on South Africa; Bill to Restrict Deposits in Banks Is Introduced," *New York Times,* February 8, 1985; "Anti-Apartheid Code Wins N.Y. Adherents; Banks Ban Loans," *Crain's New York Business,* February 18, 1985; and "The Screws Are Tightening on U.S. Companies," *Business Week,* February 11, 1985.

p. 545: the city's pension funds should not own stock: See "Pension Fund Divestiture Plan Deepens Rift between Koch and Comptroller," *New York Times,* October 19, 1986. The controversy over the nature of bank involvement continued for several years. In 1989 Eric Wollman spotted an announcement in the *Financial Times* that Chemical Bank was participating in a $2.45 billion loan to finance South Africa–controlled Minorco's hostile bid for Consolidated Gold Fields. The comptroller informed Walter Shipley, the chairman of Chemical, which has had a long-standing no–South African–loan policy, that the bank was in violation of the NYCERS provisions (see "Chemical Bank's Financing Role in Minorco Could Backfire," *Wall Street Journal,* February 22, 1989).

p. 545: he and Carol Bellamy found it necessary: *New York Times,* April 17, 1985. Koch announced that he was selling $38,600 in three firms that did not subscribe to the Sullivan Principles, and Bellamy said that she would sell $4,500 in Xerox because the firm still had a subsidiary in South Africa.

p. 545: Eastman Kodak and Motorola: "Trade with South Africa: When City Hall Turns Up the Heat," *Business Week,* March 17, 1986.

p. 546: Crocker arranged for a high-level Angolan delegation: Crocker, *High Noon,* 162.

p. 546: a substantive response from the MPLA: Ibid., 167. Crocker refers to this in his memoirs as the "worst forecast I ever made."

p. 547: to evaluate where Crocker's policy stood: Ibid., 179.

p. 547: "significant military gesture": Ibid., 187.

p. 547: Operation Askari: Ibid., 190; SAIRR, *Survey, 1983,* 598, 612.

p. 547: South Africa could not afford: SAIRR, *Survey, 1984,* 842.

p. 547: the South Africans agreed to disengage: As P. W. Botha told the House of Assembly on January 31, 1984, "On the basis of assurances received from the US government during the latest round of discussion in Cape Town on 27 and 28 January, I wish now to confirm the RSA's decision to begin disengaging its forces in Angola with effect from today" (SAIRR, *Survey, 1984,* 852).

pp. 547–48: "Our target was not and is not the state of Angola": SAIRR, *Survey, 1985,* 6.

p. 548: Botha had sent Pieter van der Westhuizen: SAIRR, *Survey, 1984,* 844.

p. 548: The Americans repeatedly reminded the South Africans: Ibid., 832.

p. 548: it was not until the Americans persuaded: Ibid.

p. 548: proposed a regional peace conference: The proposal caught the Americans somewhat off guard. See "Pretoria's Plan Takes U.S. by Surprise," *New York Times,* March 13, 1984. For Crocker's discussion, see *High Noon,* 243–44.

p. 548: "a veritable constellation of states": SAIRR, *Survey, 1984,* 48.

p. 549: "peace out of the barrel of a gun": Ibid., 21.

p. 549: including Joe Slovo: Ibid., 833.

p. 549: intelligence services had penetrated: The extensive counterintelligence and espionage effort mounted by the South Africans occasionally came into public view. See "Pretoria Says Apartheid Foe Worked As Its Spy Since 1981," *New York Times,* February 4, 1989.

p. 549: none was ever heard from again: SAIRR, *Survey, 1984,* 94. This report comes from a notorious South African spy, Major Craig Williamson, who himself had penetrated an anti-apartheid organization in London. The claims of abuse and torture in ANC camps later became a hot topic in South Africa; in 1993 the African National Congress appointed a commission composed of South African businessman Sam Motsueyane and American jurist Margaret Burnham to investigate and report on the claims.

p. 549: "Mr. Mandela is . . . a Transkei citizen": SAIRR, *Survey, 1984,* 544.

p. 549: Mandela . . . refused the offer: Ibid., 804.

p. 550: Afrikaner Volkswag: Ibid., 41–42.

p. 550: Viljoen denounced the Volkswag: Ibid., 42. F. W. de Klerk also denounced the Communist Party at the same time, referring to its "hate, fear, and gossip politics." Although the National Party stood unashamedly for white interests, he said, white security could not be built on the domination of others (ibid., 51).

p. 550: "apartheid was a simplistic solution": Ibid., 41.

p. 550: "there has been racial mixing": Ibid., 187.

p. 550: "We are not interested": SAIRR, *Survey, 1985,* 4.

p. 550: arrested more than five hundred thousand: The official figures for 1983 were 262,904 (SAIRR, *Survey, 1984,* 348); for 1984, they were 238, 894 (SAIRR, *Survey, 1985,* 208).

p. 550: Forced removals of African families: SAIRR, *Survey, 1984,* xix.

p. 551: blood drawn from . . . whites: Ibid., 709.

p. 551: a Coloured television announcer . . . had died: Ibid., 368.

p. 551: Barry Martin: Ibid. When Martin announced his plans to sue, a government official named Daan Kirstein insisted that both patients had arrived at the hospital in Rustenberg at the same time.

p. 551: he made a new bid to secure Western endorsement: "South Africa's Stubborn Statesmen," *New York Times,* May 30, 1984.

p. 551: The willingness of Western leaders: "South African Seeks Supports in Europe," *New York Times,* May 29, 1984.

p. 551: meeting between Thatcher and Botha: SAIRR, *Survey, 1984,* 443, 869; see also "Pretoria Leader Has British Talks," *New York Times,* June 3, 1984; and June 2 (for story of KwaNgema community), 10, and 15, 1984. The view that forced removals was the most objectionable aspect of the South African government's policies was widely held by political and business leaders. In an interview in *Leadership* (Second Quarter 1984), David Rockefeller said it was the "greatest irritant" in the disinvestment question. "Each example of this strengthens the forces favoring disinvestment," said Rockefeller, "and undermines those who favor a more constructive course of action."

p. 552: his government would have to heed: SAIRR, *Survey, 1984,* xix. Gerrit Viljoen announced the suspension of such removals in February 1985. See SAIRR, *Survey, 1985,* xxxi.

p. 552: "means would be found": SAIRR, *Survey, 1984,* 50.

p. 552: in one incident near Pretoria: The incident took place in February at Atteridgeville, where the first protests had started the month before. See ibid., 69.

p. 552: new violence broke out: Ibid., 70.

p. 553: a massive rent boycott: Ibid., 71.

p. 553: Operation Palmiet: Ibid., 75.

p. 553: asked . . . George Bush to intervene: du Boulay, *Tutu,* 191.

p. 554: "The people who are perpetrators": Ibid.

p. 554: "I think that even if I had stood": Author interview with Desmond Tutu, March 3, 1993.

p. 554: "the Episcopal Church of the United States": du Boulay, *Tutu,* 192.

p. 554: Sovern and two trustees traveled: This was only the third time in the history of Columbia University that a degree had been awarded at another venue. The first time was to confer a degree on Abraham Lincoln, the second on William O. Douglas.

p. 554: he joined Allan Boesak at a lunch with Senator Edward Kennedy: du Boulay, *Tutu,* 217. The meeting was arranged by Frank Ferrari of the African-American Institute.

p. 555: Nobel Peace Prize: The description of the events on October 15 comes from du Boulay, *Tutu,* 200ff. For local press reaction, see *New York Times,* October 17, 19, and 22, 1984.

p. 555: "tremendous political statement": du Boulay, *Tutu,* 201.

p. 556: "Whether Americans liked him or not": Ibid., 206.

p. 556: preexisting American archetype: For a discussion of the connection, see ibid., 198. See also Elizabeth Holstine, "Tutu As King? The Symbolic Connections between Desmond Tutu and Martin Luther King Jr.," unpublished essay for the author's course America and Apartheid, Harvard Divinity School, 1990.

p. 556: Tutu himself repeatedly . . . denied the connection: Desmond Tutu insists that unlike King he is neither a creative theologian nor a complete pacifist. See author interview with Desmond Tutu, March 25, 1993; also see du Boulay, *Tutu,* 198.

p. 557: "met the Martin Luther King of South Africa": du Boulay, *Tutu,* 198.

p. 557: "another black preacher": *New York Times,* October 19, 1984.

p. 557: "whatever his moral splendor": du Boulay, *Tutu,* 196.

p. 557: "Let us work to be peacemakers": Ibid., 209. Du Boulay also describes the scene outside the hall during the bomb threat.

CHAPTER FOURTEEN: **The Explosion**

p. 558: "If you want politicians to lead": Randall Robinson used this adage in a speech to black students at Harvard Business School in the spring of 1988.

p. 558: "plainly delighted": "Disinvestment Is Still a Threat to SA's Euphoria over Reagan," *Cape Times,* November 10, 1984.

p. 558: After six years of organizing: An interesting contemporary assessment of the difficulties faced by U.S. activists who were trying to attract African American support for Africa in general and southern Africa in particular is offered by Cecilie Counts, a member of the TransAfrica staff, in Cecilie Counts, Sylvia Hill, and Sandra Hill, "Notes on Building Solidarity in the United States," *Black Scholar,* November–December 1984, 44–52.

p. 558: "We heard from black South Africans": Author interview with Cecilie Counts, October 31, 1988.

p. 558: The time had come: For Randall Robinson's account of the objectives of the campaign, see Clarence Lusane, "The State of the U.S. Anti-Apartheid Movement: An Interview with Randall Robinson," *Black Scholar,* November–December 1985, 40–42.

p. 559: the three activists who remained: SAIRR, *Survey, 1984,* 860; *New York Times,* December 12, 1984.

p. 559: they would not leave: See *New York Times,* November 22 and 23, 1984. The three were accompanied by Eleanor Holmes Norton, former head of the Federal Equal Employment Opportunity Commission, who served as spokesperson.

p. 559: "an act of moral witness": "Delegate Who Was Jailed Calls Sit-in 'Moral' Act," *New York Times,* November 23, 1984; see also "U.S. Drive Opposes South African Racial Policies," *New York Times,* November 24, 1993.

p. 559: "The moral conscience of Americans": "Congressman and Rights Leader Arrested at South African Embassy," *New York Times,* November 27, 1984.

p. 559: two more members of Congress: "Conyers Arrested in Racial Protest," *New York Times,* November 28; "Dellums Arrested in Ongoing South African Protest," November 29, 1984.

p. 559: "We are in for the long haul": "Apartheid Protests Takes Page from 60s History," *New York Times,* November 30, 1984.

p. 559: "After a week or two": Author interview with Cecilie Counts, October 31, 1988.

p. 560: The size of the demonstrations: See John Felton, "Capitol Hill Taking a New Look at Apartheid," *Congressional Quarterly,* March 9, 1985. See also "Sanctions: From the Symbolic to the Economic," *Congressional Quarterly,* March 9, 1985, 445ff.

p. 560: "One early fruit of engagement": "The Nightsticks of South Africa," *New York Times,* November 18, 1993.

p. 560: Senator Richard Lugar: For Lugar's account of his developing position on South Africa, see Richard G. Lugar, "Making Foreign Policy: the Congress and Apartheid," *Africa Report,* vol. 31, no. 5 (1986); 33.

p. 560: The White House staff: Author interview with Phil Christiansen, May 24, 1990. Christiansen is a former staff member of the Senate Foreign Relations Committee and the author of the Lugar-Kassebuam letter.

p. 561: "Events of recent weeks": For the full text of the letter, see Baker, *United States and South Africa,* appendix B.

p. 561: "Constructive engagement is not an embracing": "Administration Defends Its Policy on South Africa As Protests Grow," *New York Times,* December 4, 1984.

p. 561: Crocker interrupted his schedule: *New York Times,* December 4, 1984.

p. 561: first black Anglican bishop of Johannesburg: Tutu's selection was not without controversy. During the synod to elect a bishop to replace Timothy Bavin, the diocese split down the middle. White conservative clergy steadily blocked Tutu's election, while Tutu's black clerical supporters barred the selection of alternative white candidates. The situation became deadlocked and was finally thrown over to the Synod of Bishops, who, three weeks later, announced that they had selected Tutu. For a detailed description, see du Boulay, *Tutu,* chap. 16.

p. 561: "buttressing a vicious system": *New York Times,* October 29, 1984.

pp. 561–62: "giving democracy a bad name": "Protests Spreading in U.S. against South Africa Policy," *New York Times,* December 5, 1984.

p. 562: "immoral, evil, and totally unChristian": *New York Times,* December 6, 1984.

p. 562: Reagan disagreed: Both the White House and Senate Republicans were receiving a steady stream of optimistic diplomatic and intelligence reports about developments in South Africa. Foreign Relations staff member Phil Christiansen described them as "endless reports coming in saying that things are moving forward, yet [after a while] it didn't seem that they really were" (author interview with Phil Christiansen, May 24, 1990).

p. 562: the major achievement was the visit: Author interview with Desmond Tutu, March 25, 1993.

p. 562: "We have made sizable progress": *New York Times,* December 8, 1984.

p. 562: "The simple truth": du Boulay, *Tutu,* 208.

p. 562: the South African government abruptly announced: "12 Released by South Africa, Then 6 of Them Are Arrested," *New York Times,* December 11, 1984; "African Dissidents Quit British Mission," *New York Times,* December 13, 1984.

p. 562: Reagan suddenly rebuked: "Reagan Attacks Soviet and South Africa on Rights," *New York Times,* December 11, 1984.

p. 562: "No quiet diplomacy": "South African Leader Denies U.S. Won Release of Jailed Dissidents," *New York Times,* December 14, 1984.

p. 563: a dispute between the black consciousness and Charterist factions: For a compelling discussion of the tensions between these groups and between the "materialist" and "idealist" philosophies they represented, see Marx, *Lessons of Struggle.*

p. 563: "We do not need Kennedy": "Kennedy Is Jeered in Johannesburg," *New York Times,* January 6, 1985.

p. 564: "We cannot give you": Ibid.

p. 564: Herman Nickel: Nickel's distaste for communicating with anyone of whom the government might disapprove strengthened the internal perception that U.S. policy was primarily designed to support the National Party and its reforms. When, during an interview with the author in April 1989, he was asked to name "the most remarkable black leaders he had met," he could name only two: Cyril Ramaphosa of the National Union of Mineworkers and Freddie Sauls, the Coloured union leader in Port Elizabeth whom Nickel had quoted extensively in his 1978 article in favor of U.S. investment in South Africa. The question of whether Nickel had made any serious contacts with black leaders in South Africa came into public view when Anthony Lewis and Herman Nickel exchanged heated views on the matter in December 1985. See Anthony Lewis, "Alienating the Future," *New York Times,* December 30, 1985.

p. 564: Though Nickel disliked P. W. Botha: See author interview with Herman Nickel, April 1989.

p. 564: Nickel's harangue . . . made him all the more determined: Kennedy had made his intentions clear shortly before the trip at a meeting of the African-American Institute when he accepted a posthumous award for Robert F. Kennedy. The official presenter at the ceremony in New York was Desmond Tutu; see *New York Times,* November 28, 1984. For a description of Kennedy's irritation after the trip, see the account of his meeting with Chester Crocker in *High Noon,* 259.

p. 564: Brandfort, where he met Winnie Mandela: "Pretoria Bars Kennedy Visit with Black," *New York Times,* January 10, 1985.

p. 564: graffiti: du Boulay, *Tutu,* 218.

p. 564: resettlement camp at Onverwacht: SAIRR, *Survey, 1985,* 341.

p. 564: paid a visit to the Crossroads squatter camp: During his visit to Cape Town, Kennedy was picketed by the Cape Action League; see ibid., 13.

p. 564: Gatsha Buthelezi: Ibid., 18.

p. 565: He . . . had supported . . . the National Forum: du Boulay, *Tutu,* 219.

p. 565: "It seemed such a silly time": Author interview with Desmond Tutu, March 25, 1993.

p. 565: when the UDF leaders asked Tutu: du Boulay, *Tutu,* 219.

p. 565: *Nightline* broadcasts: For material and quotations from the *Nightline* broadcasts, see transcripts 996–1000, March 18–March 22, 1985.

p. 566: The emerging details proved horrific: For a lengthy description of the Uitenhague massacre, see Sparks, *Mind of South Africa,* 344–46.

p. 567: "This is what our leaders went to prison for": The *Nightline* transcript for March 21, 1985, is number 999, "South Africa: Has Anything Changed?"

p. 568: Though some criticized the format: See, for example, Michael Maren, "A Video Version of Constructive Engagement," *Africa Report,* May–June 1985, 78–80.

p. 568: outlawing meetings of the United Democratic Front: "South Africa Bars 29 Groups of Foes from Any Meeting," *New York Times,* March 30, 1985.

p. 568: student protests at Wisconsin, UCLA, and Rutgers: "Activism at Schools Seems to Be Stirring as Protests Continue," *New York Times,* April 25, 1985, May 1, 1985.

p. 568: constructed a miniature shantytown: *New York Times,* May 12, 1985.

p. 568: After a year of testimony: See the Pollack report, which refers to the committee as "striving for but unable to achieve unanimity" in the spring of 1984; see also an undated piece in *Columbia College Today* that refers to a "stalemate" within the Pollack committee.

p. 568: "If the university's investment": Laird Townsend, *Acta Columbiana* (student publication); quoted in Tom Matthews, "A Morality Play Catches Columbia's Conscience," *Columbia College Today,* Summer 1985, 19.

p. 569: small act of civil disobedience: The students selected Hamilton Hall because of the large number of students and faculty who had to enter or pass by the building and because the building had an alternative entrance through a basement tunnel. Since the students would not be blocking all access to the building, officials could not have the students arrested for obstructing the functioning of the university; instead, the students calculated, the administration would be forced to call in the police to arrest the students for the protest itself.

p. 569: reluctant to have photographs: On April 10, 1985, Judge Burton S. Sherman of the state Supreme Court asked Floyd Abrams, the lawyer for Columbia, why the university was seeking a restraining order against the students instead of calling in the police to end the demonstration. "Columbia could call in the police," said Abrams. "But Columbia had a bad experience in 1968 when it called the police and it has tried hard not to do that" *(New York Times,* April 11, 1985).

p. 569: descriptions of the blockade: For detailed descriptions of the blockade, including articles by the participants, see William Bastone, "Inside the Columbia Blockade," *Village Voice,* April 23, 1985; see also the special "Apartheid Issue" newspaper put out by the Columbia Coalition for a Free South Africa during the blockade as well as the summer 1985 and winter 1985–86 editions of *Columbia College Today.*

p. 570: the university had been seeking a restraining order: "Columbia Moves to Halt Protest," *New York Times,* April 8, 1985.

p. 570: "The offenders are hurting not only Columbia": Letter from President Michael J. Sovern to the Columbia University community, April 11, 1985. In *The Rhetoric of Reaction,* Albert O. Hirschman refers to this form of argumentation— that someone's goals are worthy but that his or her actions are counterproductive— as the "perversity thesis."

p. 570: the short-term effect: Eric L. Hirsch, assistant professor of sociology, Columbia University, "Circling the Wagons: Polarization and Movement Mobilization," unpublished study of the April 1985 divestment blockade by Columbia University students, author's files.

p. 571: "We seek to change": Coalition for a Free South Africa, press release, April 12, 1985.

p. 571: "While the evil policy": *New York Times,* April 23, 1985.

p. 572: the trustees rejected total divestment: "Recent analyses have suggested that apartheid's most powerful enemy is an advancing economy, one that requires ever increasing numbers of well prepared workers," said the report. "On this hypothesis . . . divestiture works to brake the engine of change and thus to prolong apartheid" (Report to the Trustees of the Ad Hoc Committee Regarding Investment in Companies with Operations in South Africa, July 17, 1985).

p. 572: Gay Seidman was elected: See *New York Times,* June 6, 1986.

p. 572: "South Africa is the economic prostitute": See articles in the *New York Times* and the *Harvard Crimson,* April 5, 1985.

p. 572: "Jesse Jackson comes to a Harvard rally": *Harvard Crimson,* April 12, 1985. The exchanges between Jackson and Bok were not always so contentious. Shortly afterward Jackson was invited to attend a meeting of Ivy League presidents at which he, Bok, Sovern, and others discussed the divestment question for three hours. See author interview with Derek Bok, September 13, 1988.

p. 573: "The university, however, cannot allow": See the semiannual report of the Corporation Committee on Shareholder Responsibility, summer 1986; "University Is Divesting from 5 Oil Firms, Ford," *Harvard University Gazette,* October 3, 1986; and "Harvard Cuts South Africa–Linked Holdings," *New York Times,* October 3, 1986.

p. 573: A partial shift: See the Report to the 15th General Synod of the United Church of Christ.

p. 574: "not particular instances": Author interview with Audrey Chapman, October 1988.

p. 574: his recent admission that he had had an affair: "An Apartheid Foe Confirms Rumors," *New York Times,* February 10, 1985.

p. 574: Boesak read a statement: "We ask our partner churches in other countries," he read, "to continue with their efforts to identify and promote effective economic pressures to influence the situation in South Africa" (Chavis and Smock, *Implementation*).

p. 574: the creation of an implementation committee: One of the most important participants in the UCC implementation committee was the Reverend Benjamin

Chavis, the denominational officer in charge of racial justice, who later briefly became the head of the NAACP.

p. 574: Pro-divestment activists: See *Journal of the General Convention of the Protestant Episcopal Church,* 1985, 495.

p. 575: "frustrated by the resistance": See author interview with Charles Cesaretti, June 1988.

p. 575: seeking out alternative investments: Some individual parishes also moved to comply; the most notable of them was Trinity Church, Wall Street. Trinity Church formed a Corporate Divestment Roundtable, which included former U.S. Secretary of State Cyrus Vance, Union Theological Seminary president Donald Shriver, and Trinity Center for Ethics and Corporate Policy director Charles McCoy and which recommended divestment. The vestry agreed and voted on February 5, 1986, to sell the ten percent of its $200 million endowment which was invested in South African–related firms. The rector of Trinity, Robert Ray Parks, said at the time that "the divestment movement all over the United States has long since moved beyond simple economics. It is a primary way for individuals and institutions to make a moral statement with the commitment of their resources" *(Episcopalian,* March 1986, 7).

p. 575: precipitous judgment: "It is difficult to tell what the exact purpose of this resolution is," Craig Casey, the executive vice president of the pension fund, wrote in an October 1985 memo to the Social and Fiduciary Committee. "There is no general agreement . . . as to whether divestment by investors and disinvestment by American corporations will help the situation in South Africa." However, he noted, "there is a strong feeling of support for the Anglican Church in South Africa as personalized by Bishop Tutu. . . . Many bodies within the church have taken to divesting as a symbolic gesture of support whether or not that does help or hurt the church's efforts for a peaceful settlement of the social and political issues in South Africa." (Craig W. Casey to the members of the Social and Fiduciary Committee on Investments, October 30, 1985, author's files).

p. 575: They declared that they would not: Public Letter by Robert A. Robinson, president, Church Pension Fund, April 28, 1986. For a later statement, see the Annual Report of the Church Pension Fund, 1987, 3.

p. 575: the total value of divested stock: In 1985 the value of stock that had been divested by colleges and universities since 1976 was $292 million. See "U.S. Companies Cut Back on Operations," *New York Times,* April 29, 1985.

p. 576: Florida Senate's Governmental Operations Committee: "Florida Panel Moves to Drop Investments in South Africa," *New York Times,* May 7, 1985. Many other cities and states had such legislation under consideration by committees at the time, including Pittsburgh, Cincinatti, and the state of California.

p. 576: $4 billion United Nations employee pension fund: *New York Times,* August 8, 1985.

p. 576: a broadly representative proxy committee: The committee was made up of nine persons: one representative each from the retirees, private industry, and public employers; two legislative representatives; and four union employees.

p. 576: required twenty-three meetings: New York State Common Retirement Fund, Annual Report, 1986, 39.

p. 576: they voted in favor of seventeen: In terms of the policy stages articulated earlier (see pages 431–32), they were at stage 6. See Massie, *Moral Deliberation.*

p. 576: The only two they rejected: Investor Responsibility Research Center, Response to 1980 Survey, 3. See also the section on the Proxy Committee from the 1981 *Annual Analysis of Common Retirement Fund Investments,* 17–18.

p. 577: Regan voted differently: New York State and Local Retirement Systems, supplement to the 1988 Annual Report, 75. See also author interview with Tom Pandick, New York State comptroller's office, February 1989.

p. 577: "I see no difference": *New York Times,* March 7, 1984.

p. 577: "The United Nations handles South Africa": *New York Times,* March 7, 1984.

p. 577: Cuomo had shared the podium with Desmond Tutu: "Cuomo Tells Graduates to Be Politically Active," *New York Times,* May 13, 1985. Tutu had been invited to appear at the graduation by the Reverend Hays Rockwell, his close friend from St. James and a trustee of the university.

p. 577: "I have concluded that New York State": *New York Times,* May 20, 1985.

p. 577: "We are not in the foreign policy business": *New York Times,* May 21, 1985.

p. 578: Bank of Boston and Morgan Guaranty: "Morgan Sets Pretoria Curb," *New York Times,* April 1, 1985.

p. 578: Actions by U.S. corporations: See "U.S. Companies Cut Some South Africa Links," *New York Times,* April 29, 1985.

p. 578: the new goal would be to press: "U.S. Companies Bolster Anti-Apartheid Code," *New York Times,* December 13, 1984.

p. 578: "I think South Africa has underestimated": "US Group in South Africa Urges Changes," *New York Times,* March 20, 1985.

p. 578: new burst of corporate philanthropy: SAIRR, *Survey, 1985,* 369.

p. 579: "The debate over whether American companies": John Akers, "IBM, on South Africa," *New York Times,* March 27, 1985.

p. 579: "A timetable is needed": Statement of the Reverend Leon Sullivan, May 7, 1985, ICEOP Collection. For Sullivan's memories of that event, see the author interview with Leon Sullivan, August 29, 1991.

p. 579: the Interfaith Center on Corporate Responsibility responded to the call: For a more detailed description of the motivation and strategic considerations behind the new campaign, see Robert K. Massie, 164, "The Interfaith Center on Corporate Responsibility and the Debate over South African Disinvesment," Harvard Business School Case 9-387-164. See also author interview with Timothy Smith, July 1985.

p. 579: fifty-four religious denominations and groups: For quotations from the press conference and an expanded discussion, see Massie, "Interfaith Center and Corporate Responsibility," op. cit.

p. 580: charged dozens of top officials with treason: The two main trials were the Pietermaritzburg trial, in which the government accused sixteen members of the UDF, including the Rev. Frank Chikane, of furthering the aims of a "revolutionary alliance"; and the Vaal Triangle trials in June, which included Popo Molefe and Patrick Lekota and twenty others. For a discussion of these trials, see SAIRR, *Survey, 1985,* 41, 511ff.

p. 580: local UDF leaders in the town of Cradock: Ibid., 548; "Death Squads Attacking Blacks, South Africa Opposition Charges," *New York Times,* July 5, 1985. "The South African government takes the strongest possible exception to the callous insinuations which have been made regarding the recent tragic death of Messrs. Matthew Goniwe, Fort Calata, Sparrow Mkhonto, and Didelo Mlhawuli," said a South African government statement issued in denial. Later investigations would show that the men had been killed on government orders.

p. 580: the murder of Victoria Mxenge: SAIRR, *Survey, 1985,* 21, 538.

p. 580: "No matter how much": Ibid., 20.

p. 581: hundreds of Inkatha men armed with clubs: Ibid., 21, 538.

p. 581: Some associations stopped paying their rents: Ibid., 560.

p. 581: After lengthy negotiations with PEBCO: Ibid., 557.

p. 581: In some areas their undisciplined zeal: For a detailed history of conflict in the Crossroads squatter camp, see Cole, *Crossroads.*

p. 581: Meeting at a rare consultative conference: SAIRR, *Survey, 1985,* 540.

p. 581: "people's war": Ibid., 532.

p. 582: The homes of five hundred black policemen: Ibid., xxxiii.

p. 582: the murder of T. B. Kinikini: Ibid., 546.

p. 582: a hapless soldier: For a vivid eyewitness description of the death of the soldier at Mxenge's funeral, see Sparks, *Mind of South Africa,* 264–66. The *New York Times* carried a photo of the burning corpse the next day. See also "Violence Erupts at Black's Rites in a "Homeland," *New York Times,* August 12, 1985.

p. 582: the front page of the *New York Times:* "Bishop Tutu Saves Man from Crowd," *New York Times,* July 11, 1985.

p. 582: an enraged mob attacked a young mother: du Boulay, *Tutu,* 222–23.

p. 582: "I condemn in the strongest possible terms": du Boulay, *Tutu,* 223.

p. 583: neither he nor Secretary of State George Shultz: Indeed, Shultz had gone out of his way to defend constructive engagement. "The only course that is consistent with American values is to engage ourselves as a force for constructive, peaceful change," he told the National Press Club in April 1985. The approach, he insisted, had paid off: cross-border violence had dropped and the pace of reform within South Africa had increased. Withdrawal and disinvestment would be counterproductive. "It is not our business to cheer on, from the sidelines, the forces of polarization that could erupt in a race war; it is not our job to exacerbate hardship, which could lead to the same result" ("Shultz Wary of Anti-Apartheid Moves," *New York Times,* April 17, 1985).

p. 583: Defence Force commandos struck at an ANC house: SAIRR, *Survey, 1985,* xxxiii, 7, 430; *New York Times,* June 15, 1985.

p. 583: "It is time for us as a nation": "House Votes Sanctions against South Africa," *New York Times,* June 6, 1985.

p. 584: "gradually lost the ability to tell South African officials": Crocker, *High Noon,* 263.

p. 584: "the last remaining land": Ibid., 255–56.

p. 584: twenty-nine hundred arrests: "Preparing for Arrest on South Africa's Steps," *New York Times,* July 10, 1985.

p. 584: the Senate version banned bank loans: "Senate Approves Economic Moves against South Africa," *New York Times,* July 12, 1985.

p. 584: "Pretoria's ministers of brutality": Crocker, *High Noon,* 259.

p. 585: they must not "defend, attack": SAIRR, *Survey, 1985,* 455.

p. 585: it had used its new authority: "South Africa Denounces 2 Clerics; Puts Number of Detainees at 665," *New York Times,* July 25, 1985.

p. 585: "We are very disturbed": "Apartheid Blamed by U.S. for Unrest in South Africa," *New York Times,* July 23, 1985.

pp. 585–86: "I don't think Pik really expected": Author interview with Robert McFarlane, May 23, 1990.

p. 586: amazing process of magnification: Allister Sparks described the process aptly. It was, he wrote, "like one of those whispering games played at children's parties, where the message whispered to the first player gets slightly skewed as it is passed to the next until the hilariously distorted version emerges at the end of the line" *(Mind of South Africa,* 349). Exactly what Pik Botha whispered to McFarlane we do not know, though Senator Richard Lugar gives a hearsay summary of the meeting in his book *Letters to the Next President.* He said that Botha had outlined four concepts: (1) there would be no new homelands, (2) that there would be some kind of common citizenship for all South Africans, (3) each person would be able to influence the policies under which he or she was governed, and (4) the entire governmental structure would seek to be responsive to each person. Since these proposals did not represent any significant advances over previous National Party policy, it is hard to see what the Americans at the meeting became excited about. The most likely explanation is that Pik Botha tried to force the situation by embellishing what he knew of the state president's intentions.

p. 586: "the most important statement": Quoted by Sparks, *The Mind of South Africa,* 350.

p. 586: Stephen Solarz emerged from a meeting: "Mr. Solarz said that he did not believe that changes being contemplated in apartheid 'would be seen as terribly significant by the black people of this country or by the rest of the world,' " *New York Times,* August 13, 1985.

p. 586: "I am not prepared to lead": For excerpts from P. W. Botha's speech, see *New York Times,* August 16, 1985.

p. 587: "I was less affected by the substance": Author interview with Robert McFarlane, May 23, 1990.

p. 587: McFarlane told the two men: Crocker, *High Noon,* 276.

p. 587: "The visual expression of hypocrisy": Ibid.

p. 587: draw up a list of sanctions: See author interview with Robert McFarlane, May 23, 1990.

p. 588: Governor Thomas Kean of New Jersey: See "Kean Backs Halt in Investing Tied to South Africa," *New York Times,* August 21, 1985. "Mr. Kean said that he decided to sign the bill after a speech last week by President P. W. Botha convinced him that the South African government had no intention of ending apartheid," read the account. See also "Kean Signs Curbs on Pretoria Ties," *New York Times,* August 28, 1985. Later articles speculated that Kean might have been motivated by the feeling that his opposition to divestment was seen as the only political impediment to his forthcoming reelection.

p. 588: "The recommendation comes in the wake": Press release by Columbia University Public Relations officer Fred Knubel, August 28, 1985.

p. 588: "Divestment strengthens our condemnation": "Trustees Adopt Recommendation Made in August to Divest, October 7, 1985," press release. See also the press accounts at that time, including "Columbia to Sell Stock Linked to South Africa," *New York Times,* October 8, 1985, and "Columbia to Sell Its South-Africa Related Stock," *Journal of Higher Education,* October 16, 1985.

p. 588: The State University of New York: *New York Times,* September 25, 1985.

p. 588: when Rutgers followed suit: *New York Times,* September 26, 1985.

p. 588: "a public relations disaster": "State Department Denounces Pretoria," *New York Times,* August 29, 1985.

p. 589: "a country that is making progress": *New York Times,* August 20, 1985.

p. 589: "If Bishop Tutu maintains": "Falwell Denounces Tutu As a 'Phony,' " *New York Times,* August 21, 1985.

p. 589: he had issued a public apology: *New York Times,* August 24, 1985.

p. 589: "the black majority of South Africa": "Reagan Portrays Pretoria's Rulers as Seeking Change," *New York Times,* August 27, 1985.

p. 590: apologized for being "careless": "Reagan Apologizes for Asserting That Pretoria Segregation Is Over," *New York Times,* September 7, 1985.

p. 590: The South African pro-government press: See "U.S. Says Pretoria Worsens Tensions: Calls for Talks and a Clear-Cut Policy to End Apartheid," *New York Times,* August 30, 1985.

p. 590: at a formal meeting of the National Security Council: "Reagan and Aides Review Policy on South Africa," *New York Times,* September 6, 1985. That evening Senator Robert Dole said in a speech to the Council on Foreign Relations that "we are going to pass that [sanctions] bill overwhelmingly. If there was any question on that point, it has been washed away by the events in South Africa."

p. 590: showing him the vote counts: See author interview with Robert McFarlane, May 23, 1990.

p. 590: Reagan's executive order: "Reagan in Reversal, Orders Sanctions on South Africa; Move Causes Split in Senate," *New York Times,* September 10, 1985.

p. 591: "trickery beneath the dignity of the Senate": "Dole asked me to accompany him to the parliamentarian's desk in the front of the Senate chamber," Lugar later wrote. "He asked the parliamentarian if the chairman of the committee having jurisdiction of the conference report could retain physical control of it and if there was any precedent for doing so. The parliamentarian responded that I had the right to possess the bill and that such control had occurred before. Whereupon Dole said, 'Please give me the bill,' and after laying hands on it, he gave it to me. I tucked the bill into my coat pocket and walked to the fourth floor of the Capitol for another meeting" (Lugar, *Letters to the Next President,* 222–23). Lugar's "theft" of the document, as Democrats described it, caused quite a stir. See author interview with Nancy Stetson of the Senate Foreign Relations Committee, November 1988.

p. 591: "I'm smiling ear to ear": *New York Times,* Sept 10, 1985.

p. 591: the condition of the South African economy in 1985: See SAIRR, *Survey, 1985,* 116ff.

p. 591: South Africa had accumulated thirty-four billion rand: Ibid., 117. For an analysis of South Africa's debt position in 1985, see J. H. Cooper, "The Impact of Disinvestment and the Debt Crisis on the South African Economy," author's files. See also Brian Kahn, "The Crisis and South Africa's Balance of Payments," and Vishnu Padayachee, "The Politics of South Africa's International Financial Relations, 1970–1990, both in Gelb, *South Africa's Economic Crisis.*

p. 592: Chase Manhattan . . . would not roll over: SAIRR, *Survey, 1985,* 166; Sampson, *Black and Gold,* 30ff; "Chase Ends Loans to South Africans," *New York Times,* August 1, 1985. The announcement came on the same day that the French government under President François Mitterand announced that it would bar all new investment in South Africa.

p. 592: "They got their money": Quoted in Sampson, *Black and Gold,* 31.

p. 592: South Africa was being asked to repay: "South Africa Loan Curb Tied to Increased Risks," *New York Times,* August 29, 1985.

p. 592: the rand had fallen to thirty-four cents to the dollar: SAIRR, *Survey, 1985,* 116. During the course of 1985 the rand slipped by 23.2 percent against the dollar, 38.4 percent against the British pound; 38.8 percent against the yen; and 40.1 percent against the German mark.

p. 592: police arrested Boesak: "Arrest of Cleric Protested by U.S.," *New York Times,* August 28, 1985.

p. 593: "These steps have been taken": "South Africa Bars Financial Trading As Unrest Goes On," *New York Times,* August 28, 1985.

p. 593: he could instantly have borrowed a billion dollars: du Plessis in *Wall Street Journal*, October 22, 1985; also quoted in Sampson, *Black and Gold*, 36.

p. 593: "the Achilles' heel of apartheid": "South African Economy: Achilles' Heel of Apartheid," *New York Times*, September 1, 1985.

p. 593: expressed their delight: "Our strongest leverage against the system is economic pressure, withholding what they need," said Willard Johnson at MIT. "Foreign investment has always been seen by Afrikaners as a sign of moral approval" (ibid.).

p. 593: "the spectacle of the central banker": Sampson, *Black and Gold*, 34.

p. 593: "Those whom the far left would call": Quoted in ibid.

p. 593: his government had decided to freeze the repayment: SAIRR, *Survey, 1985*, 117ff; "Pretoria Freezes Loan Repayments until End of Year," *New York Times*, September 2, 1985.

p. 594: Fritz Leutwiler: For an excellent description of Leutwiler's role in working out the debt standstill agreement, see Sampson, *Black and Gold*, chap. 2, esp. 37–45. See also SAIRR, *Survey, 1985*, 117ff; Padayachee, "Politics of South Africa's International Financial Relations," op. cit.; and Alan Hirsch, "Sanctions, Loans, and the South African Economy," in Orkin, *Sanctions*.

p. 594: "The Europeans were furious": Sampson, *Black and Gold*, 37.

p. 595: "make rescheduling of South Africa's debt": Ibid., 38.

p. 595: "Looking at this as an economist": Author interview with *Wall Street Journal* reporter Steve Mufson, October 1985; quoted in Sampson, *Black and Gold*, 39.

p. 596: "There is a perceived vacuum in our nation's policy": *New York Times*, September 6, 1985.

p. 596: "The comptroller came in the next day": Author interview with Thomas Pandick, February 1989.

p. 596: a grim study from the Senate Finance Committee: Anthony F. Chetko, "The Cost of Divestment: An Analytical Framework. A Staff Report of the New York State Senate Finance Committee, John J. Marchi, Chairman," December 1985, author's files.

p. 596: whose pessimism about divestment was well known: Wilshire Associates had published a highly critical assessment of divestment in the November–December 1985 issue of *Financial Analysts Journal*. See Wayne H. Wagner, "An Analysis of the Effect of South African Divestment on the New York State Common Retirement Fund"; for comparison, see Wayne H. Wagner, Allen Emkin, and Richard L. Dixon, "South Africa Divestiture: The Investment Issues," *Financial Analysts Journal*, November–December 1984.

p. 597: "What's the difference between boycotting": *New York Times*, October 13, 1985.

p. 597: a speech to a group of institutional investors: The following quotations are from "Remarks Prepared for Delivery by State Comptroller Edward V. Regan before the Institutional Investors Luncheon, Grand Hyatt Hotel, January 9, 1986," author's files.

p. 598: the Congress of South African Trade Unions: For the most detailed discussion of the formation and history of COSATU, see Baskin, *Striking Back*.

p. 598: "The struggle of workers on the shop floor": SAIRR, *Survey, 1985*, 577.

p. 598: "A giant has risen": Baskin, *Striking Back*, 54.

p. 598: "All forms of international pressure": SAIRR, *Survey, 1985*, 180.

p. 598: "Those who have supported sanctions": Ibid., 22.

p. 599: The End Conscription Campaign: For a discussion of its formation and activities, see ibid., 419–22.

p. 599: "its evil goals": Ibid., 421.

p. 599: "the EEC has never had, nor will have": Ibid.

p. 599: Day of Prayer for Unjust Rule: There was a controversy over what had actually been prayed for. Allan Boesak and the SACC had called for the "downfall" of the government while the Western Province Council of Churches had changed the wording to "removal" (see ibid., 574).

p. 599: "repentance, mourning, and prayer": Ibid., 576.

p. 599: a meeting for international church leaders: I am grateful to Bishop James Ault, former president of the United Methodist Board of Global Ministries, for providing me with copies of his notes and other materials from the Harare gathering.

p. 599: "prevent the extension": "Harare Declaration," author's files.

p. 599: the American church representatives disseminated the document: On January 13, 1986, less than six weeks after the Harare conference, the U.S. church representatives convened a group of 120 church leaders from across the country to seek support for the implementation of the Harare Declaration. See "Church's Emergency Committee on Southern Africa," provided by James Ault, author's files.

p. 600: More than two dozen Afrikaner faculty members: See author interview with Professor Sampie Terreblanche of the Economics Department at the University of Stellenbosch, June 12, 1993.

p. 600: proposed that the government repeal the Group Areas Act: SAIRR, *Survey, 1985,* 351.

p. 600: Treurnicht's and Terreblanche's comments about Botha: Ibid., 12, 15.

p. 600: U.S. Corporate Council on South Africa: "U.S. Companies Bid to End Apartheid," *New York Times,* September 22, 1985. The number of participants in the U.S. Corporate Council soon grew to fifty-two. On October 27, the U.S. Corporate Council added its voice to a call by South African business leaders for the abolition of statutory race discrimination.

p. 600: executives from 186 American firms signed a letter: "186 Companies Ask Botha to "Lower Tensions" in Schools," *New York Times,* November 19, 1985.

p. 600: "committee of ten": SAIRR, *Survey 1985,* 563.

p. 601: "The things that men have in common": Tony Bloom, "Notes of Meeting at Mfuwe Game Lodge: 13 September 1985," 17, author's files.

p. 602: "I do not know what the businessmen achieved": "Pretoria Assails Parley in Zambia," *New York Times,* September 15, 1985. Allan Hendrickse, the leader of the Coloured Labour Party and minister without portfolio in Botha's cabinet, echoed the state president's views. "I could not understand why people who consistently made known their belief in the capitalist system could run across the border to talk with those who aim to destroy them and South Africa" (ibid.). For Crocker's views on Botha's reaction to the Lusaka visits, see *High Noon,* 308–9.

p. 602: a delegation . . . from the Progressive Federal Party: See SAIRR, *Survey, 1985,* 34; see also *New York Times,* October 12, 1985. The delegation included party head F. van Zyl Slabbert and Colin Eglin, Alex Borraine, and Peter Gastrow.

p. 602: "I think it's the beginning of the end": "South Africa's Violence and Memories of Selma," *New York Times,* October 23, 1985.

p. 602: draconian regulations: The rule read as follows: "1. No person shall, without the permission of the South African police, or of a commissioned officer . . . in any manner make, take, record, manufacture, reproduce, publish, broadcast, or distribute, or take or send to any place within or outside the Republic any film . . . or photograph, drawing, or other representation, or any sound recording of a) any public disturbance, disorder, riot, public violence, strike, or boycott; or any damage to any property, or any assault or killing of a person; b) Any person present at or involved in any public disturbance, disorder, riot, public violence, strike, or boycott, or damaging of any property or any assault on or killing of any person; c) Any conduct of a force or any member of a force with regard to the maintenance of the safety of the public or the public order or for the termination of the state of emergency, or cause to be made, taken, recorded, manufactured, produced, published, broadcast, or distributed, or to be taken or sent to any such place or attempt to commit any such act. 2. Any persons who contravene a provision of subregulation 1 shall be guilty of an offense." Reporters found guilty of defying the rule could face jail sentences of up to ten years. See "South Africa Puts Wide Restrictions on All Reporters," *New York Times,* November 3, 1985.

p. 602: "the most stupid thing": Sampson, *Black and Gold,* 39.

p. 603: The "Trojan horse" killings: SAIRR, *Survey, 1985,* 488.

p. 603: Crocker flew to Cape Town: *New York Times,* January 14, 1986.

p. 603: Botha's reply to Reagan: Crocker, *High Noon,* 312.

p. 604: Botha's opening address to parliament: See SAIRR, *Survey, 1986,* 6. For Crocker's discussion, see *High Noon,* 312–13.

p. 604: in exchange for the freedom of Andrei Sakharov: SAIRR, *Survey, 1986,* xix.

p. 604: a turbulent meeting in the Bahamas: For the text of the agreement, see "The Commonwealth Accord on Southern Africa," released in Nassau, October 20, 1985. Reprinted in Commonwealth Committee of Foreign Ministers on Southern Africa, *South Africa: The Sanctions Report* (London: Penguin, 1989), appendix 2. For additional contemporary accounts, see *New York Times,* October 17, 18, and 22, 1985.

p. 604: quiet negotiations between the government and the ANC: This was not the only such initiative. In addition to the many meetings which were taking place between the ANC and various delegations that traveled to Lusaka, there were also clandestine meetings in third countries. The Ford Foundation, for example, arranged for J. P. de Lange, the chairman of the Broederbond, to meet with senior ANC officials at Glen Cove, Long Island, in early June 1986.

p. 604: Obasanjo was an unusual man: The material on Obasanjo and the Eminent Persons Group mission is drawn from Sparks, *Mind of South Africa,* 351–54.

p. 605: meetings of the Eminent Persons Group: See SAIRR, *Survey, 1986,* 132, 179.

p. 605: "confidence-building steps": Sparks, *Mind of South Africa,* 352.

p. 605: "For years the government had claimed": Ibid., 353.

p. 605: they would have to reach a decision: The return of the Eminent Persons Group in May had been prompted by a message from P. W. Botha through Carl von Hirschberg of the South African Foreign Ministry to the Commonwealth team that Botha was still willing to negotiate with the ANC. See "Pretoria Gives Signal on Talks on Rebels," *New York Times,* May 3, 1986.

p. 605: South African Defense Forces had once against swept into Zimbabwe: *New York Times,* May 20, 1986. The "coordinated raids are the most major military action in South Africa's 25-year campaign," said the newspaper report. The strike against the ANC office in Harare was launched by a commando team that had driven up from the southwestern city of Bulawayo in three Hertz rental cars.

p. 605–6: the Reagan administration expressed "outrage": "We vigorously condemn these attacks by South Africa," said Larry Speakes at the White House. "The United States stands with the governments and peoples of those countries in expressing our sense of outrage at these events." "Shultz felt very strongly," said a key White House official. "There's some feeling that the South Africans may have torpedoed their own peace talks. It makes us doubt their sincerity, their commitment to peace" ("U.S. Voices Outrage," *New York Times,* May 20, 1986).

p. 606: Botha had taken his cue from Reagan himself: The Afrikaner newspaper *Die Beeld* argued two days after the strike that if Reagan could order the bombing of Libya and if Western nations at the Tokyo summit could decide that "terrorism must be eradicated once and for all, then they should not threaten South Africa with sanctions when she protects her own interests." *New York Times* editor John Oakes built a critique of U.S. foreign policy along similar lines in an op-ed piece on May 29. Such strikes represent "Soviet-style problem-solving, not the American. It is a dangerously ill-suited posture for the United States, traditional upholder of the rule of law among nations. It is one that other law-breakers such as South Africa are only too happy to emulate, to our dishonor and our shame" (see "Reagan Legitimizes Botha," May 29, 1986).

p. 606: Only Margaret Thatcher remained unmoved: "Thatcher Opposes Sanctions," *New York Times,* May 21, 1986. "I totally and utterly condemn the raids on the three countries," Thatcher told Parliament, adding, "I don't believe sanctions and isolation are any more likely to succeed now than before the raids."

p. 606: 1,100 articles in 1986: Calculated from the *New York Times* index under the heading "South Africa."

p. 606: a bipartisan coalition announced: *New York Times,* May 22, 1986.

p. 606: "To those who see faint signs": "Measure Introduced to Stiffen U.S. Sanctions against Pretoria," *New York Times,* May 22, 1986.

p. 606: General Motors had announced that it would no longer sell: "G.M. Cuts Its Sales to Pretoria," *New York Times,* May 24, 1986. According to Roger Smith, the company sold about twelve hundred cars a year to the South African government, with only one hundred of those for police and military use. Smith said that the company would continue the sales to nonmilitary agencies.

p. 606: Fighting in the Crossroads township: See SAIRR, *Survey, 1986,* xxxiii, and *New York Times,* May 26, June 3, 11, and 12, 1986.

p. 606: Afrikaner extremists mobilized: See *New York Times,* May 23 and June 1, 1986. For a detailed description of the meeting on May 22, see Sparks, *Mind of South Africa,* 324–25.

p. 606: COSATU announced . . . a one-day general strike: *New York Times,* June 4, 1986.

p. 606: largest one-day strike: "1.5 Million Black Workers Stage Biggest Strike Ever in South Africa," *New York Times,* May 2, 1986.

p. 606: Tutu publicly urged the churches to defy the order: "I will instruct my clergy to organize church services on June 16th and I will certainly participate in such services," Tutu said on June 5. "I hope that other denominations throughout the country will likewise arrange services of commemoration" (see "Clerics Vow to Defy Pretoria Protest Ban," *New York Times,* June 6, 1986).

p. 606: the United Democratic Front joined Tutu: "Disobedience Urged on Soweto Anniversary," *New York Times,* June 12, 1986.

p. 607: "such force as . . . under the circumstances": "State of Emergency Imposed throughout South Africa; More Than 1,000 Rounded Up," *New York Times,* June 13, 1986.

p. 607: "well aware that stricter security action": Ibid.

p. 607: "South Africans will not allow themselves": Ibid.

p. 607: "The senator's message was stark": Crocker, *High Noon,* 304.

p. 607: "awfully hard when you are not involved": "Reagan, Citing 'Civil War,' Urges Restraint for All South Africans," *New York Times,* June 14, 1986.

p. 608: Obasanjo and Fraser were in the middle of their press conference: "Commonwealth Delegates Chart Drive for South Africa Sanctions," *New York Times,* June 13, 1986.

p. 608: the substitution was approved: For a description of the passage of the Dellums bill, see author interview with Robert Brauer, special counsel to Ronald Dellums, April 14, 1989.

p. 608: "the American answer": "House Votes Bill to Cut Off Investment in South Africa," *New York Times,* June 19, 1986.

p. 608: At Dartmouth College . . . the shantytown debate: The controversy attracted national attention. See *New York Times,* January 23 and 24; February 6, 10, 12, and 26; March 28; April 13; May 4; and June 9, 1986.

p. 609: In April police arrested sixty-one protesters: *New York Times,* April 2, 1986.

p. 609: a special investigating team, composed of Yale trustees: One of those who went on the trip was the Right Reverend Paul Moore Jr., the bishop of New York. See *New York Times,* April 27, 1986.

p. 609: the purchase of two vans: For background on Harvard's relationship with Joy Manufacturing, see the Minutes of the Meeting of the Harvard Advisory Committee on Shareholder Responsibility, April 5, 1984; and the Corporation Committee on Shareholder Responsibility Annual Report, September 1984. For the description of Calkins's encounter with the president of Joy Manufacturing and his subsequent trip to South Africa, see author interview with Hugh Calkins, September 11, 1988.

p. 609: Though he came back disturbed: "Few corporate personnel from the United States were involved in the implementation and monitoring of corporate social responsibility in South Africa. At only four of the twenty-one corporate operations I visited were the top decision makers from the United States," wrote Wilson in his report to the board of TIAA-CREF. "In some instances there was no direct reporting to U.S. headquarters, but rather the reporting was directed to other overseas offices of the corporation. . . . Few or no blacks in decison-making positions and total lack of non–South African black role models in U.S. operations." Corporate philanthropy was limited and paternalistic. One executive told Wilson that his company had built a golf course near a township. Had the firm asked any black leaders whether the community wanted or needed a golf course? Wilson asked. No, replied the executive, who appeared perplexed at the question. When Wilson returned to New York, he persuaded the TIAA-CREF trustees to use the proxy mechanism and push companies to reform their South African practices. Wilson suggested that "TIAA-CREF continue to monitor conditions in South Africa and in the voting of proxies to support the U.S. corporate presence there for corporations that: 1. are committed to change; 2. find ways to escalate quality of mass black education; 3. sign and fully implement Sullivan; 4. Actively support projects such as PACE; 5. Deny support of the homeland concept; 6. Refrain from entering into joint business ventures; 7. Remain consistent with the other aspects of TIAA-CREF's existing South African policy statement" (report by Albert Wilson on his 1982 trip, 4, author's files).

p. 609: "One man looked at me": Author interview with Albert Wilson, January 28, 1988.

p. 610: "The black servants came from the townships": Ibid.

p. 610: "believed that the National Party would hold on to power": Report by Albert Wilson on his 1986 trip, author's files.

p. 611: sanctions as a tool of influence: For a historical comparison of the use of sanctions in the twentieth century, see Hufbauer and Schott, *Economic Sanctions,* and *Economic Sanctions Reconsidered.*

p. 611: the Schlemmer studies: The first Schlemmer study was among 551 male production workers in three major industrial centers; the second among a general sample of 1,000 blacks from all major metropolian areas, covering women, young people, pensioners, and unemployed as well as workers. For a discussion, see Orkin, *Disinvestment, the Struggle,* chap. 2.

p. 611: the Markinor Polls: See *New York Times,* August 26, 1985, and August 3, 1986.

p. 612: a feverish dispute about samples, questions, and organizational bias: Mark Orkin, the director of the CASE study, explained the shift by pointing to the large number of people who had shifted over the previous year from advocating "free" investment to supporting the moderate position of conditional disinvestment. Closer examination of the data showed that while some ardently supported or opposed disinvestment under any circumstances, a growing number favored a conditional approach. Disinvestment should not be used indiscriminately but should be targeted to have the maximum effect on the South African government. Part of the disparity thus arose from the eagerness of both extremes to claim the middle group as their supporters. See Orkin, *Disinvestment, the Struggle.*

p. 612: his daughter, Naomi Tutu Seavers: For a profile of Seavers, see "Tutu's Daughter Takes an Activist's Role," *New York Times,* January 26, 1986.

p. 612: four or five speeches a day: For a description of the entire trip, see "An 'Elated' Bishop Winds Up Tour of the United States," *New York Times,* January 26, 1986.

p. 612: "When did white people suddenly become": "Tutu, in New York, Calls for Economic Sanctions," *New York Times,* January 7, 1986.

p. 612: a letter of support signed by a million Americans: The letter had been organized in response to Jerry Falwell's claim that Tutu was a "phony." See "Bishop Tutu Hails Demonstrators Near the South African Embassy," *New York Times,* January 9, 1986.

p. 612: "If those who died were white": "In Newark, Tutu Praises Jersey's Divestiture," *New York Times,* January 13, 1986.

p. 612: "Bishop Tutu's actions and statements": "Bishop Tutu Faces Taunts of Treason," *New York Times,* August 22, 1986.

p. 612: "There is no greater thorn": Ibid.

p. 613: The *Pretoria News* expressed hope . . . the *Citizen* that he would "moderate": Quoted in du Boulay, *Tutu,* 249.

p. 613: "If sanctions don't work": Desmond M. Tutu, "Sanctions vs. Apartheid," *New York Times,* June 16, 1986.

p. 613: "the protests, shareholder proposals": See Crocker, *High Noon,* 317.

p. 613: "siege mentality": See *New York Times,* June 23 and July 11, 1986.

p. 614: "The counsel of disengagement": "Shultz Rules Out Moves Damaging South African Economy," *New York Times,* July 1, 1986.

p. 614: "apartheid must end": "Bush, at NAACP, Attacks Pretoria," *New York Times,* July 4, 1986.

p. 614: Reagan might appoint . . . Robert J. Brown: For information on Robert J. Brown, see *New York Times* July 15, 16, 17, 19, and 20, 1986. Brown later forged close ties with the Mandela family. Brown helped to finance the education of Mandela's daughters, and Mandela later gave him the power of attorney to protect the Mandela name from commercial misuse in the United States.

p. 614: "Permitting Communications Director Buchanan": Crocker, *High Noon,* 321.

p. 615: "where are you going to get your chrome": "Regan Pretoria Remarks Evokes Furious Outcry," *New York Times,* July 18, 1993. For Crocker's reaction to this remark, see *High Noon,* 321.

p. 615: a new storm of protest: Four liberal groups, including the National Organization for Women, the National Women's Political Caucus, the National Political Congress of Black Women, and TransAfrica, called for Donald Regan's resignation because of the remark. See *New York Times,* July 22, 1986.

p. 615: "Alongside our vibrant language": Crocker, *High Noon,* 322.

p. 615: "clear that Africa policy issues": Lugar, *Letters to the Next President,* 227.

p. 615: "the president's own South Africa lobby": Crocker, *High Noon,* 322–23.

pp. 615–16: "The root cause of South Africa's disorder": "The United States cannot maintain cordial relations with a government whose power rests upon the denial of rights to a majority of its people based on race," said the president. "If South Africa wishes to belong to the family of Western nations, an end to apartheid is a precondition." President Ronald Reagan, "Ending Apartheid in South Africa: An Address before Members of the World Affairs Council and Foreign Policy Association in the East Room of the White House," July 22, 1986, *Department of State Bulletin,* September 1986, 1–4; see also the Weekly Compilation of Presidential Documents, July 28, 1986. For Chester Crocker's reaction, see *High Noon,* 322ff.

p. 616: the speech unleashed a gale of criticism: "Perhaps no other speech in the Reagan presidency had stirred as much international opposition and bipartisan criticism," wrote reporter Bernard Weinraub early the next week. See "The Speech that Launched a Thousand Critics," *New York Times,* July 28, 1993. For the NSC reaction to the speech, see author interview with Nancy Stetson of the Senate Foreign Relations Committee, November 2, 1988.

p. 616: "I had hoped the president would take the occasion": "Reaction in Congress to Speech Is Mostly Negative," *New York Times,* July 23, 1986.

p. 616: "I think the West, for my part, can go to hell": du Boulay, *Tutu,* 254; see "Tutu Denounces Reagan," *New York Times,* July 23, 1986.

p. 616: Shultz delivered the message he had hoped: See Crocker, *High Noon,* 324.

p. 617: "the market is speaking clearly": U.S. Secretary of State George Shultz, "The U.S. Approach to South Africa: A Statement before the Senate Foreign Relations Committee," July 23, 1986, *Department of State Bulletin,* Septmber 1986, 5ff.

p. 617: the President had met with key Republican senators: See *New York Times,* July 22, 1993. After the meeting Robert Dole told reporters that it would be difficult to prevent Senate enactment of additional sanctions without some "new credible initiative." "We need something, some positive thing to forestall action," Dole said.

p. 617: "strident pro-Pretoria tilt": Crocker, *High Noon,* 325.

p. 617: "If the Senate needed any more reason": "How America Stands on South Africa," *New York Times,* August 15, 1986.

p. 617: thirty-seven Republicans crossed the aisle: "Senate Votes Bill to Prod Pretoria," *New York Times,* August 16, 1986.

p. 618: South Africa working group: See author interview with Nancy Stetson of the Senate Foreign Relations Committee, November 2, 1988.

p. 618: Buzzing in and around all of these proceedings: Robinson had particularly strong influence in the office of William Gray, where his wife, Hazel Ross Robinson, served as a legislative assistant.

p. 618: they should accept the Lugar bill: See author interview with Robert Brauer, special counsel to Dellums, April 14, 1989.

p. 618: Lugar wrote an op-ed piece: "The President has an opportunity to take bold action, adding his enormous influence to the will of Congress," wrote Lugar. "I pray that he will do so before it is too late." Richard Lugar, "Speaking with One Voice on South Africa," *New York Times,* August 24, 1986.

p. 618: Lugar told the press that if the president chose to veto it: "Lugar Says He'd Lead Fight to Override Sanctions Veto," *New York Times,* September 17, 1986.

p. 619: the appointment of Edward Perkins: "Reagan Names a Black Diplomat U.S. Ambassador to South Africa," *New York Times,* October 1, 1986.

p. 619: "a day late and a dollar short": "House, 313 to 83, Affirms Sanctions on South Africa," *New York Times,* September 30, 1986.

p. 619: two of his farm belt colleagues: The senators were Ed Zorinsky (Democrat of Nebraska) and Charles Grassley (Republican of Iowa). For Lugar's account, see *Letters to the Next President,* 238–39.

p. 619: Leland grabbed Randall Robinson: See photograph in the *New York Times,* October 3, 1986, A8. For Lugar's more somber reaction to the vote, see *Letters to the Next President,* 239–40.

CHAPTER FIFTEEN: The Effect of Sanctions

p. 620: "Once the taps of international capital investment": de Klerk, *F. W. De Klerk,* 60.

p. 620: "become a domestic civil rights issue": Pauline Baker, "The Sanctions Vote: A G.O.P. Milestone," *New York Times,* August 26, 1986.

p. 620: met several conditions: Congressional staff used the mnemonic *PRUNE* to recall the conditions (release *P*risoners; *R*epeal laws; *U*nban parties; *N*egotiate; and *E*nd the state of emergency). Author interview with Don Steinberg, former staff assistant for Richard Gephardt and later chief economic officer in Pretoria, April 28, 1993.

p. 621: "No reason or argument": "Pretoria Says Senate Acted on 'Emotional Basis,'" *New York Times,* October 3, 1986.

p. 621: just over $400 million: Annual purchases of coal, iron, uranium, agricultural products, coal, and textiles came to $420 million in 1985 dollars.

p. 621: "There is no question": "U.S. Sanctions May Not Hurt South African Economy Much," *New York Times,* October 4, 1986.

p. 621: many feared: Ibid.

p. 621: 19 states, 68 cities, and 119 colleges: "California Senate Passes Bill to Sell Pretoria-Linked Stock," *New York Times,* August 26, 1986.

p. 621: University of California divestment: *New York Times,* July 19, 1986.

p. 621: equal to roughly two-thirds: Republican Governor George Deukmejian of California, who had opposed the measure at first, had switched sides two days before the decision by the University of California regents. Some saw the move as politically motivated. Deukmejian was locked in a reelection battle with Mayor Tom Bradley of Los Angeles, a strong proponent of divestment. Others insisted that Deukmejian, an Armenian American who was sensitive to the problems of persecuted ethnic groups, had experienced a genuine change of heart at the time of the imposition of the state of emergency *(New York Times,* July 21, 1986). Bradley, for his part, had been so inspired by a meeting with Desmond Tutu in May 1985 that he had threatened to fire his city commissioners if they refused to divest city funds *(New York Times,* May 11, 1985).

p. 621: $500 million in IBM stock: "California Senate Passes Bill to Sell Pretoria-Linked Stock," *New York Times,* August 26, 1986.

p. 622: "This was a reluctant decision": "Divestment Ends a Five Year Struggle," *New York Times,* October 21, 1986.

p. 622: "GMSA has been losing money": See "Automaker's Statement," *New York Times,* October 21, 1986.

p. 622: "a watershed for change": "Sullivan Principles' Author Hopes for Change," *New York Times,* October 22, 1993.

p. 622: "This is a tremendously significant decision": "GM Plans to Sell South Africa Unit to a Local Group," *New York Times,* October 21, 1986.

p. 622: "If we elect to leave": "South African Prospects Leave IBM Chief Glum," *New York Times,* April 23, 1986.

p. 622: economic pressure: "IBM Is Shedding South Africa Unit: Pressure Is Cited," *New York Times,* October 22, 1986.

p. 622: "This isn't a buyout": Ibid.

p. 623: "We dare not yield": "Botha Announces Early White Vote," *New York Times,* January 1, 1987.

p. 623: increased its parliamentary margin: See SAIRR, *Survey, 1987,* xxxiii, 745; Helen Suzman's Progressive Federal Party lost seven seats, reducing its total to twenty. The Conservative Party, meanwhile, increased its representation to twenty-three, thus becoming the official opposition party. Suzman blamed the loss in part on the United Democratic Front's campaign urging white voters, particularly, not to participate in an unjust election. See SAIRR, *Survey, 1987–1988,* 763.

p. 623: claim that sanctions had failed: Twelve months after the passage of the Comprehensive Anti-Apartheid Act, the Reagan White House sent a formal report to Congress which concluded that sanctions had not achieved their objectives ("Pretoria Sanctions Didn't Work, Reagan Report to Congress Says," *New York Times,* October 1, 1987). Conservative analysts in both countries churned out articles in 1987 and 1988 arguing that sanctions had backfired. For examples of the backlash thesis, see Doug Bandow, "Break Relations with South Africa," *New York Times,* February 27, 1987; Lester Venter, "Multiracialism Is the Curse of South Africa," *Sunday Times,* November 11, 1987; John Kane-Berman, "Die Trefkrag van Sanskies," and Christiaan van Wyk, "Die Uitdaging van die Negentigerjare—die saketoneel te midde van sanskies en disinvestering," *Suid Afrika-Stigting Oorsig,* vol. 14, July 1988.

The claim was echoed by those close to the Reagan administration: in 1987, for example, former U.S. ambassador to South Africa Herman Nickel said that sanctions had "substantially reduced" American leverage on Pretoria. "It is hard to think of any U.S. policy more perverse and self-defeating than the policy of trade sanctions and disinvestment against South Africa," wrote Marshall Loeb in *Fortune* magazine in July 1988. "Designed to end the abomination of apartheid, they are instead inspiring a thuggish government to roll back reforms. Worse still, they are moving the white electorate still further to the right" (Marshall Loeb, "What the U.S. Must Do in South Africa," *Fortune,* July 18, 1988). In support of his views, Loeb quoted a host of white liberals, including Helen Suzman. "Sanctions and disinvestment only make the government more recalcitrant," Suzman said, "and make its supporters tougher than ever." For additional comments by Suzman, see "Sanctions Won't End Apartheid," *New York Times,* October 4, 1987. Suzman repeated her views in speeches across the United States in late 1987; see "Suzman: Sanctions Backfired," *Business Day,* November 17, 1987.

p. 623: slowly and steadily sinking: For journalistic commentary on South Africa's slowing growth rate, see Robert S. Greenberger, "U.S. Trade Sanctions on South Africa Starting to Pay Long-Term Dividends," *Wall Street Journal,* September 21, 1987. For the most thorough examination of the imposition of sanctions by different countries in the twentieth century, see Hufbauer and Schott, *Economic Sanctions.*

p. 624: still resembled that of a Third World country: Writing in 1991, Brian Kahn, an economist at the University of Cape Town, commented that "manufacturing's contribution to exports has not increased since 1968 and in fact had fallen till 1985. . . . It is apparent that South Africa's place in the international division of labour has not changed from being a raw material supplier" (Brian Kahn, "The Crisis of South Africa's Balance of Payments," in Gelb, *South Africa's Economic Crisis,* 72).

p. 624: annual new passenger car sales: Total population: SAIRR, *Survey, 1987–1988,* 11; new car sales: the peak year was 1981.

p. 624: Whites, in general, didn't want them: "The poor purchasing power of the mass of black consumers has retarded the growth of mass demand for most manufactured consumer goods," wrote Richard Moorsom in a 1989 article, "Foreign Trade and Sanctions." "Conversely, affluent white consumers have demanded a broad range of goods in relatively small quantities, with a bias towards high quality imports" (Richard Moorsom, "Foreign Trade and Sanctions," in Orkin, *Sanctions,* 254). For white preference for foreign goods and the problem of the declining exchange rate, see "Vulnerable to the Sanctions Game," *Business Day,* November 11, 1987.

p. 624: eighty percent of its annual imports: Margaret P. Doxey, *International Sanctions,* 132.

p. 624: Paying back billions in bank loans: For a discussion of the balance of payments problems, see Brian Kahn, "The Crisis and South Africa's Balance of Payments," op. cit.

p. 625: Denmark's coal purchases: "Major Sanctions Report—Cut Exports by 7%," *Business Day,* August 3, 1988.

p. 625: 351 million rand in 1986 to zero: "SA Exports 'Have Taken Heavy Knock from US Sanctions,' " *Johannesburg Star,* October 23, 1987.

p. 625: U.S. purchases of South African goods: SAIRR, *Survey, 1987–1988,* 418.

p. 625: slipped a painful 7 percent: "Major Sanctions Report," *Business Day,* August 3, 1988.

p. 625: former director of the Rhodesian Reserve Bank: The director, Desmond Krogh, offered some provocative explanations for South Africa's economic and political crisis in an interview with the author in Pretoria on January 15, 1990. The head of the second office, designed to help South Africa circumvent the restrictions on technology, was Fred Bell, the former head of ARMSCOR. For an article on Bell, see "The Former ARMSCOR Chief Takes on Role of Mr. Sanctions Buster," *Johannesburg Star,* January 3, 1987.

p. 625: a 5 billion rand annual penalty: For a South African assessment of the effect of trade sanctions, see Carolyn Jenkins, "The Effectiveness of Trade Sanctions As a Form of Pressure for Change in South Africa," unpublished paper, Department of Economics, University of Natal. For additional estimates of the impact of trade sanctions, see various writings by American economist Stephen Lewis.

p. 626: Shipping Research Bureau: See the following, all published by the Shipping Research Bureau, Amsterdam: *Secret Oil Deliveries to South Africa, 1981–1982* (June 1984); *South Africa's Lifeline: Violations of the Oil Embargo, 1983–84* (1986); *Oil To South Africa: Apartheid's Friends and Partners, 1985–86* (1988); *Fuel for Apartheid: Oil Supplied to South Africa, 1987–88* (September 1990). See also the *Newsletter on the Oil Embargo against South Africa.*

p. 626: South Africa paid about $2 billion a year: See *Fuel for Apartheid,* op. cit., 33 (table 10).

p. 626: some of the chief executives tried to deflect attention: Many chief executives continued to be opposed to disinvestment on principle. A 1988 survey conducted by Kellogg Graduate School of Management (Northwestern University) studied the attitudes the chief executives of 120 of the biggest U.S. firms and found that thirty-one percent considered apartheid to be an "internal political issue" and that eighty-six percent opposed disinvestment. See "Divestment Is Opposed," *New York Times,* April 25, 1988.

p. 626: "You can debate the moral question": *Wall Street Journal,* October 31, 1986.

p. 627: "the potential negative impact": *Business Week,* March 17, 1986.

p. 627: The most prominent of these was Eastman Kodak: Kibbe and Hauck, *Leaving South Africa,* 9. When Eastman Kodak later purchased Sterling Drug, which had a subsidiary with 324 employees in South Africa, the new parent sold it off to the Premier Group, a South African conglomerate, for an extremely low price. See also *New York Times,* March 5 and May 12, 1987. For the sale price, see Debbie Budlender, *Assessing US Corporate Disinvestment: The CASE Report for the Equal Opportunity Foundation* (Cape Town: Community Agency for Social Enquiry, 1989), 20.

p. 627: IBM . . . sold its subsidiary: Kibbe and Hauck, 43.

p. 627: the full IBM product line: Ibid., 44. See also Duncan Innes, "Multinational Companies and Disinvestment," in Orkin, *Sanctions,* 229; "U.S. Goods in South Africa; Little Impact of Divestiture," *New York Times,* July 27, 1987.

p. 627: "We are absolutely committed": *New York Times,* October 22, 1986.

p. 627: "a very favorable contract": *Computer Mail,* February 26, 1988, quoted in Kibbe and Hauck, *Leaving South Africa,* 43. See also James M. Leas, "IBM Still Bolsters Apartheid," *New York Times,* April 4, 1988.

p. 627: "It's not doing what we want": *New York Times,* October 22, 1986.

p. 627: "IBM might have gone much farther": Ibid.

p. 627: South African auto industry: Glenn Adler, *Withdrawal Pains: General Motors and Ford Disinvest from South Africa,* (New York: Center for Labor-Management Studies, City University of New York, November 1989), 3.

p. 628: they staged a sit-in: Ibid., 6.

p. 629: Adam Opel and Isuzu: See General Motors' 1987 proxy statement, quoted by Kibbe and Hauck, *Leaving South Africa,* 42.

p. 629: "Nineteen eighty-seven was the year": Author interview with Wayne Fredericks, October 15, 1991.

p. 629: sales to the military and police: Richard Knight, "Sanctions, Disinvestment, and U.S. Corporations in South Africa," in Robert E. Edgar, ed. *Sanctioning Apartheid* (Trenton, N.J.: Africa World Press, 1990), 76. See also "South Africa Sales by Ford Will Give Blacks Big Stake," *New York Times,* June 15, 1987.

p. 629: a rival union ran to the Ford workers: The rival union was the Motor Assembly and Component Workers' Union of South Africa (MACWUSA). The two unions later combined into the National Union of Metal-workers in South Africa (NUMSA). For a discussion of the dispute, see Kibbe and Hauck, *Leaving South Africa,* 40; Adler, *Withdrawal Pains,* op. cit., 11ff.

p. 630: two smaller community trusts: See author interview with Wayne Fredericks, October 15, 1991.

p. 630: a concentrate factory in Durban: Kibbe and Hauck, *Leaving South Africa,* 35. The bottling firm was Amalgamated Beverage Industries (ABI) and the canning company was Amalgamated Beverages Canners (ABC). Coca-Cola held a majority position in ABI until 1976, when it began gradually reducing its exposure. In 1986 it held a thirty percent share. See Budlender, *Assessing US Corporate Disinvestment,* op. cit., 11.

The fruit juice company was mentioned by Donald McHenry; see author interview with Donald McHenry, September 6, 1990.

p. 630: because of the political situation: See Budlender, *Assessing US Corporate Disinvestment,* op. cit., 14; see also author interview with Donald McHenry, who made the same point.

p. 631: components of the Coca-Cola disinvestment: See Kibbe and Hauck, 35–37. With regard to the sale of the bottling plant to black investors, Donald McHenry said in his interview with the author that Coca-Cola "went out and bought a franchise and sold it to the Kilimanjaro group," whereas Kibbe and Hauck report that "Coca-Cola encouraged an independent franchiser in East London to sell a bottling plant to Kilimanjaro Investments" (37).

p. 631: Coca-Cola was not really disinvesting by moving . . . into Swaziland: Coca-Cola defended the move by insisting that its decision was designed to show support for the frontline states. See Budlender, *Assessing US Corporate Disinvestment,* op. cit., 14.

p. 631: whether it was proper for community organizations to accept: In 1988 the Equal Opportunity Foundation asked the Community Agency for Social Enquiry (CASE), an anti-apartheid research group in Johannesburg, to find out how anti-apartheid organizations both inside and outside South Africa felt about the transfer of Coca-Cola money through the foundation to community groups. The report showed widespread distrust of both the process and the motives of Coca-Cola and other American firms. See Budlender, *Assessing US Corporate Disinvestment,* op. cit.

p. 631: "We support an end": "Guidelines for Disinvestment Proposed by Five Anti-Apartheid Groups," included as appendix 2 in Kibbe and Hauck, *Leaving South Africa,* 47.

p. 632: Anglo-American had taken over: Innes, *Power and Profit,* 234.

p. 632: Ford Motor Company gave $61 million: Kibbe and Hauck, 39; Edgar, *Sanctioning Apartheid,* 27.

p. 632: "I Ain't Gonna Play Sun City": See David Marsh, *Sun City: The Making of the Record* (New York: Viking Penguin, 1985).

p. 633: *Graceland*: South African performers in exile found themselves newly in demand. When Paul Simon took the *Graceland* music on tour, for example, he performed with Miriam Makeba, who had been popular in the early 1960s and had married Stokely Carmichael. "Mapping South Africa's Pop Music from Afar," *New York Times,* February 28, 1988.

p. 633: Home Box Office aired *Mandela:* See *New York Times,* September 19 and 22, 1988.

p. 633: *South Africa Now:* See "In 'South Africa Now,' Daily Life under Apartheid," *New York Times,* June 13, 1988.

p. 633: *Cry, Freedom:* For various articles on the film, including an interview with Attenborough in which he talks about the effect he hoped the film would have on public opinion, see *New York Times,* November 1, 6, 15, and 28, 1987; December 26, 1987.

p. 633: the film arrived in South Africa: See SAIRR, *Survey, 1987–1988,* xli.

p. 634: In March 1987 the original debt standstill: For the terms of the arrangement, see "The South African Debt Accord: Second Interim Arrangements," compiled by First National Bank of South Africa and by Deloitte Haskins and Sells in 1987.

p. 634: "We thought we were on strong moral grounds": "We have done the best we could to make a careful assessment of the business loss due to opposition to our position," the spokesperson said. "We obviously could not be oblivious to them, but they did not add up to a significant factor in our decision-making process." See "Citibank Is Leaving South Africa: Foes of Apartheid See Major Gain," *New York Times,* June 17, 1987.

p. 634: "This is really bad news": Ibid.

p. 635: the withdrawal of Barclays: For a detailed case study of the Barclays case, see Smith, *Morality.*

p. 635: tremendous pressure on its balance of payments: The balance on current account actually swung negative in the second quarter of 1988. See *New York Times,* July 1, 1988.

p. 635: maximum use of foreign trade credits: SAIRR, *Survey, 1987–1988,* lvii. See also Richard Moorsom, "Foreign Trade and Sanctions," op. cit.

p. 635: foreign reserves had come under severe pressure: SAIRR, *Survey, 1987–1988,* lvii.

p. 635: "In the present international climate: Ibid., lvii.

p. 635: severely damaged the South African economy: For various South African studies on the cumulative effects of sanctions, see J. H. Cooper, "The Impact of Disinvestment and the Debt Crisis on the South African Economy," unpublished manuscript.

p. 635: ESKOM . . . mothballing thirteen power stations: SAIRR, *Survey, 1987–88,* lviii.

p. 636: eliminate 9.5 billion rand set aside for black "upliftment": Ibid., lix.

p. 636: South Africa's economic structure was grossly distorted: See David Lewis, "Unemployment and the Current Crisis," in Gelb, *South Africa's Economic Crisis.*

p. 637: governments take even more aggressive steps: In Washington in May 1988, the House Foreign Affairs Committee approved new legislation barring all trade with South Africa and forwarded the proposal to the full House, which passed the bill in August ("Panel Approves Bans on Pretoria," *New York Times,* May 4, 1988; see also June 6, August 12, and September 15, 1988).

p. 637: the Israeli cabinet, under pressure from the United States: SAIRR, *Survey, 1987–1988,* 412.

p. 637: the Japanese Ministry of International Trade and Industry: "Japan's Sales to Pretoria," *New York Times,* August 13, 1988.

p. 637: increase external pressure: For example, in August 1988 the foreign ministers of the Commonwealth countries announced that they would ask financial institutions in their countries to not increase trade financing for South Africa because of apartheid. In early September Pope John Paul II endorsed sanctions as an "acceptable" strategy for promoting change in South Africa. See *New York Times,* August 5 and September 11, 1988.

p. 637: the death of Samora Machel: Crocker, *High Noon,* 248.

p. 638: "constructive engagement has failed to achieve its objectives": "Applause for piecemeal reforms has been counterproductive," said the panel. "We recommend that the President begin urgent consultations with our allies . . . to enlist their support for a multilateral program for sanctions" (see "A U.S. Policy toward South Africa: The Report of the Secretary of State's Advisory Committee on South Africa," January 1987, Publication 9537 (Washington, D.C.: Department of State, April 1987), vi, 10, 13. The other members of the panel were Griffin Bell, Owen F. Bieber, Timothy Healy, John Dellenback, Vernon Jordan, Lawrence S. Eagleburger, and Helene Kaplan. For press reports, see "U.S. Panel Asserts the Reagan Policy on Pretoria Failed," *New York Times,* February 11, 1987, and "Epitaph for Constructive Engagement," *New York Times,* February 14, 1987.

p. 638: he now supported total U.S. corporate withdrawal: "Up until the time I made the decision, no one knew which direction I was going to go," Sullivan recalled. "I had the companies in one room, the press in another. Even that was part of the strategy" (author interview with Leon Sullivan, August 26, 1991). Sullivan began by praising American companies' "notable record" against segregation, but noted that despite their efforts "the main pillars of apartheid still remain, and blacks are still denied basic human rights in their own country" ("Sullivan Asks End of Business Links with South Africa," *New York Times,* June 4, 1987).

p. 638: "U.S. companies remaining in South Africa": Ibid.

p. 638: "The last fig leaf": Jennifer Davis, "Only Sanctions Can Dismantle Apartheid," *New York Times,* June 7, 1987. Others, such as Randall Robinson, were more generous in their assessment of Sullivan. "We have always said that Reverend Sullivan operated in good faith, but that the companies were using his principles to rationalize their desire to stay," Robinson told reporters. "The South African government would never respond to moral suasion. You have to remove the economic underpinning provided by Western oil, computers, and machinery ("Sullivan Asks End of Business Links With South Africa," *New York Times,* June 4, 1987).

p. 638: "We owe a great debt": S. G. Marzullo, "The Principles Still Offer the Best Hope," *New York Times,* June 7, 1987.

p. 638: constructive engagement had been permanently repudiated: Crocker wrote that "one of my closest colleagues urged me to resign swiftly. My resignation could be seen as an act of protest at the sheer incoherence within the Administration as well as the terminal sanctimoniousness sweeping the land" *(High Noon,* 331).

p. 639: met with George Shultz: "Shultz Meets with Leader of Rebels in South Africa," *New York Times,* January 29, 1987. The conservatives included Senator Robert Dole of Kansas. In an editorial on January 30, the *New York Times* editors attacked Dole's actions as "less concerned with terrorism . . . than with currying favor with his party's right wing" in preparation for the 1988 Republican presidential primaries.

p. 639: the whites came away moved and impressed: "I feel emotional being in Africa and accepted as an African," said Theunis Eloff, the chaplain of the University of Pretoria, at the end of the visit. "I have developed a much deeper insight and understanding into the ANC moral foundations for the armed struggle" ("Black Guerrillas and White Foes of Pretoria Find Common Ground," *New York Times,* July 13, 1987). Professor André du Toit of the University of Stellenbosch, a philosopher and longtime opponent of apartheid ideology, noted that none of the participants would ever be the same again. "This will be a very important watershed in the lives of all of us," he said. For descriptions of a similar trip in July 1989, see Chris Louw, ed. *Journey to the ANC—Op Reis Na Die ANC: Reports on a Visit to Windhoek, Harare, and Lusaka* (Kaapstad: Voorbrand Publikasies, 1989).

p. 639: **many of them received death threats:** SAIRR, *Survey, 1987–1988,* 39.

p. 639: **a succession of American visitors:** Jackson and Young visited in 1986; Wolpe went with a delegation of American members of Congress in June 1987; see "Angolan Says Cubans May Be Asked to Leave," *New York Times,* June 30, 1987.

p. 640: **the battle at Cuito Cuanavale:** For descriptions of the battle, see various articles in A. J. Venter, ed., *Challenge: Southern Africa within the African Revolutionary Context* (Gibraltar: Ashanti Publishing, 1989), particularly Willem Steenkamp, "Politics of Power: The Border War," 205; Christopher Coker, "South Africa and the Soviet Union," 314; and Douglas McClure, "Through the Looking Glass: The South African Point of View," 433.

p. 640: **"Castro's decision in late 1987":** Crocker, *High Noon,* 368. One op-ed piece even argued that Crocker had *encouraged* the Cuban escalation in order to persuade the South Africans to come to the table (see Pamela S. Falk, "A Wink and a Nod in Southern Africa," *New York Times,* August 10, 1988).

p. 640: **it metamorphosed into a standoff:** For press accounts of the military struggle, see *New York Times,* February 17, 20, 21, 23, 1988; March 23, 1988; April 20, 1988; and May 18, 1988.

p. 640: **"The risk of hairtrigger reactions":** Crocker, *High Noon,* 368. That spark nearly came in June 1988 when South African artillery batteries and armored units pounded a Cuban/Angolan/SWAPO column that was advancing south. The South Africans claimed to have killed more than two hundred of their opponents while the Cubans said they had lost only ten men. In response, Cuban MiGs killed eleven South African soldiers in a strike that destroyed a dam and pumping station in Namibia. For a short time it seemed as though full-scale war would break out. Instead of moving forward, however, South African armored artillery units pulled back across the Namibian border, creating a new buffer zone between them and their opponents.

p. 641: **a rumble of dissatisfaction:** "Afrikaner Church Questions South Africa's Angola Role," *New York Times,* July 8, 1988. Writing on August 31, John Battersby reported that "South African officials have acknowledged that the loss of about 60 young white conscripts in combat over the last year and the financial drain of the war on the ailing South African economy have played a major role in the decision to settle." In November 1988, dissident Afrikaners launched a new newspaper, *Die Vrye Weekblad,* to oppose the Nationalist government's policies.

p. 641: **even in P. W. Botha's Afrikaner base:** Crocker, *High Noon,* 380.

p. 641: **elite South African circles discussed:** For the type of arguments that were used, see Christopher Coker, "The Soviet Union," in Venter, *Challenge,* op. cit.

p. 641: **"In the wishful thinking":** Crocker, *High Noon,* 380.

p. 642: **overt advocacy:** When Savimbi visited Washington, D.C., in late June 1988, he spoke at the National Press Club, visited Ronald Reagan at the White House, and received enthusiastic support from many American conservatives (see "Angolan Rebel Chief Meets Reagan," *New York Times,* July 1, 1988).

In the literature on negotiation and mediation, the central attribute of a mediator is that of impartiality. Mediation is most commonly described as the ability to design a mutually accepted procedure that allows the participants to arrive at an acceptable agreement on substance. (See, for example, Christopher Moore, *The Mediation Process* [San Francisco: Jossey-Bass, 1986]; Laurie M. Laubich, "Neutrality vs. Fairness: Can the Mediator's Conflict Be Resolved?," Harvard Program on Negotiation, Working Papers Series; Lawrence Susskind and Jeffrey Cruikshank, *Breaking the Impasse: Consensual Approaches to Resolving Public Disputes* [New York: Basic Books, 1989].) The central dilemma for mediators is what they should do when they discover that they have a strong personal or moral preference for one outcome over others. If they disclose this preference, they undermine the impartiality for which they are valued by both of the negotiating parties. If they fail to disclose it, they are concealing relevant information and may, perhaps unconsciously, be skewing the process to achieve their preferred outcome.

p. 643: "we had broken the back of the settlement": Crocker, *High Noon,* 441.

p. 643: to sign their tripartite agreement: After an hour of speeches, in which the Cuban and South African foreign ministers exchanged bitter remarks about which country had the worst human rights violations, the men finally signed the agreement. As the American delegation left the hall, the secretary of state turned to Crocker. "That's some bunch of characters you've been working with!" he observed (Crocker, *High Noon,* 446; see also *New York Times,* December 23, 1988).

p. 644: actions inside South Africa: One was Botha's approval, in November 1987, of the formation of the Joint Executive Authority for KwaZulu-Natal, which was an outgrowth of Buthelezi's earlier initiatives. While an important precedent—that whites and blacks could work together in the implementation of government policy in a common region—Botha made it clear that the approval of a coordinated *executive* authority did not mean he was willing to accept a combined *legislature.*

p. 644: banning of organizations: The groups included AZAPO, the Soweto Civic Association, the Port Elizabeth Black Civic Association, and the National Education Crisis Committee, among others. "South Africa Bans Most Anti-Apartheid Activities," *New York Times,* February 25, 1988.

p. 644: "a major disappointment": " 'Shock and Distress' in West over Pretoria's Action," *New York Times,* February 25, 1988.

p. 644: "tribal differences": "U.S. Officials Move to Clarify Reagan Remarks," *New York Times,* February 26, 1988.

p. 644: 1,148 job actions: SAIRR, *Survey, 1987–1988,* 667.

p. 644: One strike, in August 1987: See *New York Times,* August 10, 13, 21, 23, 27, 28, 29, and 31, 1987; September 1, 6, and 7, 1987.

p. 644: In March and again in June: *New York Times,* March 22, 1988; June 7 and 9, 1988.

p. 645: residents stopped paying their rent: For discussions of the effect of the rent boycotts, see SAIRR, *Survey, 1988–1989,* 208–13; SAIRR, *Survey, 1989–1990,* 116–20. See also Mark Swilling et al., "Finance, Electricity Costs, and the Rent Boycott," in Swilling, Humphries, and Shubane, *Apartheid City.*

p. 645: authorities threatened to evict him: "Pretoria Says Tutu Faces Eviction at Soweto Home," *New York Times,* May 29, 1987.

p. 645: the government decided to reach into its own pockets: "Blacks Pressing a Rent Boycott in South Africa," *New York Times,* February 22, 1988.

p. 645: the Boksburg boycotts: See SAIRR, *Survey, 1988–1989,* xxxvii, 379, 594,

656; SAIRR, *Survey, 1989–1990,* 12, 13 230. See also " 'Whites Only' Is One Thing the Blacks Won't Buy," *New York Times,* March 17, 1989.

p. 645: "If the president of the external mission": SAIRR, *Survey, 1987–1988,* 30. In 1996, a major trial of South African military officials revealed that this attack had been carried out by Inkatha soldiers trained and led by a white government officer.

p. 646: "an eye for an eye": SAIRR, *Survey, 1987–1988,* 31.

p. 646: had claimed more than thirty-one hundred lives: SAIRR, *Survey, 1989–1990,* 235.

p. 646: "black on black" violence: The foreign press continued to use such terms for years, until the carnage in the former Yugoslavian states (which was characterized as "ethnic" rather than "tribal" conflict) demonstrated to all that white-on-white violence could be equally barbaric and loathsome.

p. 646: he intended to create an Afrikaner *volkstaat:* See SAIRR, *Survey, 1988–1989,* 645, 657. Andries Treurnicht rejected Boshoff's idea on the grounds that the proposed territory excluded too many whites. The Conservative Party viewed "the land now in white ownership as the basis on which the final borders between the white fatherland and the national states for nonwhites should be determined" (SAIRR, *Survey, 1988–1989,* 657).

p. 646: "was going to capitulate": SAIRR, *Survey, 1987–1988,* 710.

p. 646: "would be like banning Christ himself": SAIRR, *Survey, 1988–1989,* 647.

p. 646: Strydom's lunchtime attacks: "A Neo-Facist Kills 3 in Pretoria," *New York Times,* November 16, 1988.

p. 647: "to see if I was physically capable of killing people": Quoted in Rose Moss, *Shouting at the Crocodile: Popo Molefe, Patrick Lekota, and the Freeing of South Africa* (Boston: Beacon Press, 1990), 1.

p. 647: "stand back to allow a tyrant": SAIRR, *Survey, 1988–1989,* 647.

p. 647: the attack on Albie Sachs: Ibid., 607. See also *New York Times,* May 17, 1988. For Sachs's account of the incident and his poignant description of his recuperation, see Sachs, *Soft Vengeance.*

p. 647: the assassination of Dulcie September: SAIRR, *Survey, 1988–1989,* 607; *New York Times,* March 30, 1988.

p. 647: reported external assassination attempts to forty-six: SAIRR, *Survey, 1988–1989,* 606.

p. 647: unsolved murders . . . to nearly a hundred: SAIRR, *Survey, 1988–1989,* 606.

p. 647: the African National Congress would close its Angolan bases: "South African Insurgents Agree to Shut Their Bases, Angola Says" *New York Times,* January 6 and 10, 1989; see also Crocker, *High Noon,* 442. At the time that Angola made this announcement, Jesse Jackson, who was in Luanda visiting Angolan President Jose Eduardo dos Santos, urged the United States to recognize Angola. "If we can have relations with South Africa," said Jackson, "we can have diplomatic ties with Angola."

p. 648: "short-term predictions": de Klerk, *F. W. de Klerk,* 156.

p. 649: "Is a discussion between the government": "Afrikaner Paper Urges Talk with Mandela," *New York Times,* January 17, 1989. The *Beeld* had already formally called for Mandela's release the previous July.

p. 649: curt disdain or flat rage: See Ottaway, *Chained Together,* 52.

p. 649: Botha was in Cape Town to prepare: "South African Leader Has Mild Stroke," *New York Times,* January 19, 1989.

p. 650: "binding power in our country": Kamsteeg and van Dijk, *F. W. de Klerk,* 47; see also Ottaway, *Chained Together,* 53.

p. 650: De Klerk beat du Plessis: For various accounts of this historic party caucus, see Kamsteeg and Van Dijk, *F. W. de Klerk,* 46–47; "Botha Quits As Head of National Party; and to Remain President," *New York Times,* February 3, 1989. David Ottaway suggests that de Klerk won because his strong ties to the National Party made it less likely that he would turn to the security system that P. W. Botha had assembled for power (Ottaway, *Chained Together,* 54).

p. 650: hymns and other evangelical contaminants: Kamsteeg and van Dijk, *F. W. de Klerk,* 14.

p. 650: His aunt was married: Ibid., 21; Ottaway, *Chained Together,* 61.

p. 650: "Don't be afraid": Kamsteeg and van Dijk, *F. W. de Klerk,* 23.

p. 650: "We often talked politics": de Klerk, *F. W. de Klerk,* 140. For other reflections by Willem de Klerk, see Margaret A. Novicki, "Willem de Klerk: A View of the Future," *Africa Report,* July–August 1989, 36ff.

p. 651: de Klerk attended Potchefstroom: "I found law studies absorbing because of their exactness, the thorough analysis and the foundation of principles that underpins each legal subject," de Klerk recalled (de Klerk, *F. W. de Klerk,* 149).

p. 651: "People keep calling me": This quotation is from a conversation between F. W. de Klerk, Professor Ann Braude and the author which took place in April 1993 at the residence of the U.S. ambassador in Cape Town. Several South Africa scholars have pointed out that Dopper theology, which holds the Bible as the cardinal source of ethical principle, can be extremely conservative as long as the biblical basis for a position is well established. If a Dopper theologian can be persuaded that a new principle has biblical grounding, however, he or she is more likely to seize on a new course of action; this approach is unlike that of adherents to the main branch of the Dutch Reformed Church, whose loyalties are more evenly divided between scripture and culture. For Willem de Klerk's comments on his brother's piety, see *F. W. de Klerk,* 29–30.

p. 651: paid for her own wedding ring: Ottaway, *Chained Together,* 65.

p. 651: reportedly had a profound effect: The author heard several unconfirmed stories about de Klerk's amazement at the ease with which Americans of different races interacted. I wrote to F. W. de Klerk and asked if he had written a report of his trip. The state president responded that he had not. F. W.'s brother reports in his book that the visits to Germany, England, America, and Israel "greatly helped him [F. W.] to develop an overseas perspective" (de Klerk, *F. W. de Klerk,* 152).

p. 651: Vorster . . . told Willem de Klerk: Ibid., 153.

p. 651: de Klerk defended it: SAIRR, *Survey, 1983,* 12, 23, 37. "It would be political nonsense to suggest that Africans outside the homelands should be given political rights outside their own tribal groups," de Klerk announced in a rebuff to the Progressive Party (SAIRR, *Survey, 1983,* 94).

p. 652: "most hated political adversary": de Klerk, *F. W. de Klerk,* 18.

p. 652: He spent hours in intense discussion: Ibid., 29–30.

p. 652: could no longer be defended morally: The interviewer was David Frost, who spoke to de Klerk on South African television in April 1993.

p. 652: torpedoed by de Klerk: This allegation was extremely widespread; the author heard it from numerous sources during his visits to South Africa. See Ottaway, *Chained Together,* 55–56.

p. 652: "It had been leaked abroad": de Klerk, *F. W. de Klerk,* 20.

p. 652: provoked a spirited debate: See, for example, Harold Packendorf, "New Personality, Old Policies?," *Africa Today,* May–June 1989.

p. 652: "I can't see him removing the foundation stones": Quoted in Ottaway, *Chained Together,* 54.

p. 652: "Just as President Nixon": Robert Rotberg, "Has South Africa Found Its Nixon?," *New York Times,* March 14, 1989; also quoted in Ottaway, *Chained Together,* 55.

p. 653: "I am basically a team man": "A New Face for Old Policies in South Africa," *New York Times,* February 4, 1989.

p. 653: "When President Botha is rough": Quoted in de Klerk, *F. W. de Klerk,* 139.

p. 653: Botha . . . went on television to promise: " 'I am not an old man clinging to power," he told an interviewer. "I am clinging to the Constitution of the country; I am clinging to good order and I am clinging to the idea of discipline" (see "Botha Again Rejects Pressure to Give Up Pretoria Presidency," *New York Times,* March 13, 1989). See also Ottaway, *Chained Together,* 69–71, for another description of the clash between Botha and de Klerk, as well as *New York Times,* March 10 and 13, 1989.

p. 653: the parliamentary caucus unanimously voted: "Ouster of Botha Urged in South Africa," *New York Times,* March 14, 1989.

p. 653: after extended negotiations: For foreign coverage of the dispute, see *New York Times* March 19 and 24, 1989; April 7, 1989; and May 4, 1989.

p. 653: the formation of the Democratic Party: "New Party Meets in South Africa," *New York Times,* April 9, 1989; de Klerk, *F. W. de Klerk,* 23.

p. 654: the Rangel amendment: For South African commentary on the Rangel amendment, see Wally Horak, "Hoekom slaag Rangel-wysigings nie?" *Finansies & Tegniek,* June 24, 1988, 32.

p. 654: "very foolish laws": "Mobil to Sell South African Units," *New York Times,* April 29, 1989. Rangel was delighted. "I regard the Mobil withdrawal as particularly significant because of Mobil's leading role as a corporate apologist for continued U.S. investment in South Africa," said Rangel, adding that he hoped Mobil would "invest the resources they have been spending justifying their presence in South Africa on a new campaign explaining why it is no longer good business to remain under apartheid."

p. 654: "the atmosphere would change completely": *New York Times,* June 22, 1989.

p. 655: had been secretly meeting with Mandela: Ottaway, *Chained Together,* 26–28.

p. 655: had even written Botha a lengthy brief: See "Excerpts from Essay by Mandela for Botha," *New York Times,* January 26, 1990. See also Mandela's comments at his first press conference, on February 12, 1990, in which he insists that the meeting was not a "propaganda ploy" by Botha but had been at Mandela's request.

p. 655: "What really impressed me": *New York Times,* June 23, 1990. See also Ottaway, *Chained Together,* 29, and Mandela, *Long Walk,* 479.

p. 655: Botha announced publicly: "Pretoria Leader and Mandela Meet in Hint of Release," *New York Times,* July 9, 1989. See also Robert Rotberg, "South Africa's Tide Shifts," *New York Times,* August 3, 1989.

p. 655: De Klerk wanted to fly to Zambia: "Zambian Chief to Meet Head of Pretoria Party," *New York Times,* August 11, 1989.

p. 655: "We believe that the least painful solution: Ottaway, *Chained Together,* 70.

p. 655: "After all the years": "Botha, Rebuffed by His Party, Quits South Africa Presidency," *New York Times,* August 15, 1989.

p. 656: They sent more than two hundred ailing Africans: "Blacks Fight Race Laws at South Africa Hospitals," *New York Times,* August 3, 1989.

p. 656: tried to cross into the whites-only beaches: "Apartheid Protest at Two Beaches," *New York Times,* August 20, 1989.

p. 656: The police also raided the home and office of Richard Kraft: Ibid.

p. 656: a young white veteran: The young man, Philip Ivey, succeeded in eluding the police for several months, in part because Desmond Tutu persuaded the Cape Town newspapers to cover his face in the photographs they printed of the incident. Ivey was caught and put on trial, but the charges were eventually dropped by the state prosecutor.

p. 656: ninety-three seats in the white House of Assembly: SAIRR, *Survey, 1989– 1990,* 548.

p. 657: symbolic and substantive reforms: See Ottaway, *Chained Together,* 72–74.

p. 657: De Klerk's first steps: to stop using whips, *New York Times,* September 12, 1989; granted legal permission for outdoor protest, September 13, 1989.

p. 657: the possible release of Nelson Mandela: See "Mandela Expects to Be Released Soon, His Wife Says," *New York Times,* January 9, 1990.

p. 657: "faceless man with a fax": See *New York Times,* January 30, 1990.

p. 658: to display some of South Africa's military might: de Klerk, *F. W. de Klerk,* 1.

p. 658: some of them gasped: Kamsteed and van Dijk, *F. W. de Klerk,* 59.

p. 658: "I had no doubts": de Klerk, *F. W. de Klerk,* 2.

p. 658: de Klerk's speech: For the full text of F. W. de Klerk's speech, see ibid., 34–46, and Kamsteg and van Dijk, *F. W. de Klerk,* 91–108. For a discussion of the event, see SAIRR, *Survey, 1989–1990,* 215.

p. 659: "I admire the courage of F. W.": Kamsteg and van Dijk, *F. W. de Klerk,* 62.

p. 659: "It can't be true": "Hope in South Africa," *New York Times,* February 4, 1993.

p. 659: "Are you ready?": See the Associated Press photograph on the front page of the *New York Times,* February 3, 1990.

p. 659: Thabo Mbeki welcomed the development: See Thabo Mbeki, "The Rebels Answer to Pretoria," *New York Times,* February 4, 1990.

p. 660: Treurnicht promised that his Conservative Party: "South Africa's Rightists Vows to Defend Apartheid," *New York Times,* February 6, 1990.

p. 660: the Johannesburg Stock Exchange: "Hopes Run High for South Africa," *New York Times,* February 6, 1990. For a discussion of the high expectations among business leaders for the immediate elimination of sanctions, see Massie, "Great Expectations," *New Republic,* February 1990.

p. 660: Warrant Officer Gregory: At his press conference the day after his release, Mandela attributed his lack of bitterness to some of his jailers, men "who are very good in the sense that they understand your point of view and do everything to try and make you as happy as possible." Tallie Dotwana, the daughter of Mandela's adoptive parents, commented at the time that she was sure he was referring to Gregory. "He has often said that Gregory was a very nice man. Yesterday, when we left the prison, he was the last person he hugged as we said goodbye" *(New York Times,* February 13, 1990).

p. 661: Betty Shabazz . . . heard the news: See interview with Shabazz on the video *Mandela in America,* produced by Danny Schecter (A*Vision Entertainment, 1990).

p. 661: "Welcome Home, Mandela": "Has de Klerk Devised His Own Fall?," *New York Times,* February 13, 1993; see also *New York Times,* February 20, 1993.

p. 661: he had left both his reading glasses and the text of his speech: The oversight was described the next day by Tallie Dotwana to John Burns. "After Three Decades Mandela Measures Up to the Legend," *New York Times,* February 13, 1993.

p. 661: "We have waited too long": The quotations from Mandela's Cape Town city hall speech were transcribed directly by the author from a videotape of the live broadcast.

p. 661: "We sang '*Masi Wu*' ": Author interview with Desmond Tutu, March 1993.

p. 662: more than a thousand interview requests: "Mandela's Day: Exercise and Uproar," *New York Times,* February 15, 1993.

p. 663: "The most pleasant memory": For a clip of this exchange between Mandela and Sparks, see the video *Mandela in America,* op. cit.

p. 663: urged his followers to stop the factional warfare: "Mandela Urges Blacks of Natal to End Deadly Rivalry," *New York Times,* February 26, 1990.

p. 664: who had been dreaming about the moment: Crocker, *High Noon,* 485.

p. 664: "the first time in 78 years": See "Excerpts from Mandela and de Klerk Remarks as Talks Open," *New York Times,* May 5, 1990.

p. 664: De Klerk hopped around nine European countries: "De Klerk Begins Major Tour of West Europe," *New York Times,* May 9, 1990.

p. 665: began dialing their friends: See "Pretoria's Leader Puts Off U.S. Trip," *New York Times,* May 30, 1990. See also Jacob Weisberg, "Mandela's Men," *New Republic,* July 9 and 16, 1990.

p. 665: Randall Robinson: This was not Robinson's first meeting with Mandela, which had taken place several weeks earlier when Robinson had gone to South Africa to work with the ANC to plan the trip.

p. 665: "To enjoy the support of the youth": Quoted from the video *Mandela in America,* op. cit.

p. 666: importing truckloads of ticker tape: See the interview with David Dinkins on ibid.; see also the coverage of the parade in the *New York Times,* June 21, 1990.

p. 666: "feeling of joy and warmth": See the interview with Mpho Tutu on the video *Mandela in America,* op. cit.

p. 666: "on a more transcendent plane": See "A Hero's Welcome," *Time,* July 2, 1990, 14.

p. 666: "I identify myself so directly": The exchange is captured on the video *Mandela in America,* op. cit.

p. 667: "The form of economy will be decided": *New York Times,* June 22, 1990.

p. 667: "Eddie! Good God!": The sequence and exchange are recorded on the video *Mandela in America,* op. cit.

p. 667: "complete identity with the peoples of this country": Ibid.

p. 668: "Mr. Mandela is a George Washington": Ibid.

p. 668: "Never in this history of humankind": Ibid.

p. 668: "I couldn't imagine that I could attract": Ibid.

p. 669: an honor normally reserved for heads of state: Despite this honor, the White House remained far more concerned about finding ways to support F. W. de Klerk. De Klerk "is something of a visionary," one top White House official was quoted as saying. "The problem is he may be out too far in front of his people" *(New York Times,* June 24, 1990).

p. 669: Mandela's speech to Congress: The text has been transcribed from the video *Mandela in America,* op. cit.

EPILOGUE: **Legacy and Future**

p. 672: "If such things can happen": Desmond Tutu, "Hope and Despair," in *A Book of Hope* (Cape Town: David Philip, 1992), 21.

p. 672: Thousands of exiled South Africans: Estimates of the number of South African political exiles ranged from thirty thousand to forty thousand. See SAIRR, *Survey, 1990–91,* xl; *New York Times,* March 12, 1991, and March 22, 1991. In December 1993 government records showed that only 11,226 exiles had returned since February 1990. See SAIRR, *Survey, 1993–94,* 26.

p. 674: Congress for Democratic South Africa: See SAIRR, *Survey, 1990–91,* xlviii.

p. 674: only a democratically elected constituent assembly: As Joe Slovo put it in 1991, "We don't want to negotiate the constitution at CODESA. That's the task of a representative body." SAIRR, *Survey, 1990–91,* lii.

p. 674: a gaggle of international experts: For example, Harvard Law Professor Roger Fisher, the author of *Getting to Yes,* joined by his associates from the Cambridge firm of Conflict Management Inc., spent many weeks offering negotiation training to the leadership of the ANC, the National Party government, and Inkatha and in some cases brought South Africa leaders (such as UDF activist and ANC leader Popo Molefe) for training at Harvard.

p. 674: more than ten thousand people died: The numbers were as follows: 1,403 in 1989; 3,699 in 1990; 2,706 in 1991; and 2,820 through the end of November 1992. See SAIRR, *Survey, 1991–92,* lxiii; SAIRR, *Survey, 1992–93,* 27.

p. 674: murder rate grew to ten times: Ottaway, *Chained Together,* 6.

p. 674: political violence in Natal: According to a confidential police report submitted to the Transitional Executive Council in late 1993, Inkatha Freedom Party supporters were most frequently the aggressors *(Business Day,* January 10, 1994). For a statistical analysis, see Graham Howe, "The Trojan Horse: Natal's Civil War, 1987–1993," *Indicator SA* 10.2 (1993). Starting in mid-1990 the clashes between Inkatha and its opponents spread to urban townships, particularly in the Transvaal. The newspapers were full of reports of battles and massacres, as the residents of the hostels controlled by Inkatha pushed out and seized pieces of townships by force. "By the middle of 1990," writes David Ottaway, "it had become clear that the Inkatha-controlled hostels had become the centers of the perpetual explosions of violence rocking the townships" *(Chained Together,* 125). In March 1991, for example, Inkatha men took control of a chunk of the Alexandra township to the north of Johannesburg in a fierce battle that left forty-five people dead. From then on raids by Inkatha men and retaliation by ANC "civil defense units" kept blood flowing at a steady pace (see SAIRR, *Survey, 1990–91,* xxxvi).

p. 675: peace agreement between Mandela and Buthelezi: For the text of the agreement see SAIRR, *Survey, 1991–92,* app. E, 519.

p. 675: National Peace Accord: See SAIRR, *Survey, 1991–92,* xxxiv, lxviff, 467. For the text, see app. F, "The National Peace Accord," final version dated October 16, 1991.

p. 675: "third force": SAIRR, *Survey, 1990–91,* xxxvii.

p. 675: Civil Cooperation Bureau: Ottaway, *Chained Together,* 123. For detailed evidence and discussion of the CCB and other covert operations, see the comprehensive range of articles in Minnaar, *Hidden Hand.*

p. 676: receiving more than one million dollars: "Zulu Ex-Aide Tells of Arms Training," *New York Times,* March 1, 1992.

p. 676: Ramaphosa demanded: SAIRR, *Survey, 1992–93,* 462.

p. 676: "I have wondered": Quoted in "Mandela's Wife Becomes Estranged from the Cause," *Washington Times,* February 16, 1989.

p. 676: she turned to alcohol: See Ottaway, *Chained Together,* 141. This persistent rumor was reliably confirmed to the author during a visit to South Africa in 1990.

p. 677: "With our boxes of matches": Ibid., 141.

p. 677: Winnie's authority within the anti-apartheid movement: See "Winnie's Team of Trouble," *Johannesburg Star,* February 11, 1989; Ottaway, *Chained Together,* 143. For a chronology of the events, see "Mandela and Her Football Club," *Business Day,* February 24, 1989.

p. 677: sent a report to Oliver Tambo: Her attitude, they continued, was endangering the whole liberation struggle. "She seems to think she is above the community," they wrote. "She shows utter contempt for both the crisis committee and the community" (quoted in Ottaway, *Chained Together,* 146).

p. 677: "We are not prepared": Ibid., 146.

p. 678: he blamed himself: In an interview two days before the 1994 election, Mandela was asked by a political team from the *Johannesburg Star* whether, if he were to live his life over, he would make the same choices. "I hope I would do the same again," he replied, "though it has not been easy. To see your family, your children being persecuted, when you are absolutely helpless in jail, this is one of the most bitter experiences, most painful experiences I have had. Your wife being hounded from job to job, your children being taken out of coloured schools, police breaking into your house at night and even assaulting your wife. So I wondered sometimes whether I had made the correct decision. I had not anticipated the repression in relation to my family. But at the end of the agonizing I felt, no, it was correct. My commitment was proper" *(Johannesburg Star,* April 25, 1994).

p. 678: the specter of national collapse: According to local moving companies, the rate of immigration to South Africa decreased by sixty percent after the assassination of Hani, and the ratio by March 1994 was one family arriving for every ten leaving. SAIRR, *Survey, 1994–95,* 16.

p. 678: apprehension of the assassin: Ibid., 643.

p. 678: most of the American constraints: For a contemporary discussion, see Robert Kinloch Massie, "Great Expectations," *New Republic,* February 26, 1990, and "An End to Sanctions and Divestment?" *Die Suid Afrikaan,* April 1990. See also the survey of South African trade with the United States in *Financial Mail,* October 11, 1991, supplement.

p. 678: state and local divestment: This information, which comes from the Investor Responsibility Research Center, *A Guide to American State and Local Laws on South Africa, 1993,* was widely reported in the South African press. See *Weekly Mail,* September 24, 1993, and September 28, 1993. The cities that had restrictions were New York, Los Angeles, Chicago, Houston, Philadelphia, San Diego, Detroit, and Dallas. The two that did not were Phoenix and San Antonio. See "U.S. Companies Quietly Moving Back," *Johannesburg Star,* March 5, 1993.

p. 678: Harry Schwarz's report: April 8, 1993, April 12, 1993.

p. 678: international economics experts: Mandela, for example, had decided to rein in the ANC's plans for nationalization of industries after listening to international investors at a meeting in Davos, Switzerland. Trevor Manuel, Tito Mboweni, and other senior economics officials spent three days listening to stern realities at a conference on South Africa's place in the global economy organized by IDASA and the Aspen Institute in April 1993. For the published proceedings, see Baker, Borraine, and Krafchik, *South Africa and the World Economy*.

p. 679: "participate freely in politics": Established by parliament in Septmeber 1993, the Transitional Executive Council was created, according to a contemporary document, "to prepare for and help during the changeover to a new democratic order in South Africa. The TEC does not take over the powers of the existing government but functions in conjunction with all legislative and executive structures at all levels of government in South Africa" *(Transitional Executive Council,* pamphlet printed by the TEC, Private Bag 878, Pretoria, early 1994). For a discussion of its work by one of the co-chairs, see Colin Eglin, "TEC-nical Transition," *Indicator SA* 11.2 (1994).

p. 679: the Medal of Liberty: "Sanctions Row Mars Medal Day," *Argus,* July 5, 1993.

p. 679: the "lunacy" of apartheid: *Johannesburg Star,* January 26, 1993.

p. 680: "building a culture of democratic accountability": For the proceedings of the conference, see André du Toit, ed., *Toward Democracy: Building a Culture of Accountability in South Africa* (Cape Town: Institute for a Democratic Alternative for South Africa, 1991).

p. 680: The Commission of Inquiry: SAIRR, *Survey, 1993–94,* 314, 361, 663. The PAC officially suspended the activities of APLA, its armed wing, in January 1994. See reports in the *Citizen* and *Sowetan,* January 17, 1994. See Mark Shaw, "The Goldstone Commission: In the Public Eye," *Indicator SA* 11.1 (1993). For a discussion of the "Third Force" allegations, see Paulus Zulu, "Behind the Mask: South Africa's 'Third Force,' " *Indicator SA* 10.1 (1992).

p. 680: the board of the powerful South African Broadcasting Corporation: SAIRR, *Survey, 1994–95,* 651.

p. 680: IEC membership: For a discussion of the politics of choosing the members, see "Wanted: Fair People for Free Elections," *Sunday Times,* March 21, 1993.

p. 681: minuscule time span: "The IEC—and particularly its headquarters—is a cross-cultural mishmash," wrote one reporter at the time, "thrown together without warning or preparation, set a task of immense organizational difficulty and massive significance for the country's survival, with no time even to get acquainted" ("Inside the IEC—A Frantic Jumpstart to Democracy," *Weekly Mail,* April 22–28, 1994).

p. 681: international mediation: *Business Day,* March 3, 1994.

p. 681: "erratic, fickle, obstructionist": Adele Tait, ed., *Portfolio of South Africa, 1995: The Nation's Leaders, Its Challenges and Opportunities* (Gauteng: Portfolio Business Publications, 1995), 134.

p. 681: Buthelezi . . . backed down: "Why Buthelezi Backed Down," *Weekly Mail,* April 22–28, 1994. See other reports in the *Citizen,* April 20, 1994, and the *Sowetan,* April 21, 1994.

p. 681: eighteen parties: *Business Day,* February 2, 1994.

p. 681: millions of stickers: Independent Electoral Commission, *End to Waiting,* 64.

p. 681: airlifted by SADF helicopters: Ibid., 29.

p. 682: strain of fear: "It is generally accepted," wrote the editors of the *Star,* "that the election . . . will not be totally free of violence" (April 7, 1994).

p. 682: "add to the unnecessary suffering": *Citizen,* April 25, 1994.

p. 682: "last ditch attempts": *Johannesburg Star,* April 25, 1994.

p. 682: quarter of a million overseas South Africans: *Business Day,* April 25, 1994.

p. 682: "One of the most poignant": *Sowetan,* April 28, 1994.

p. 683: their faces bearing a range of emotions: The descriptions of the voting are drawn from press reports and from the author's eyewitness experiences as an international observer on behalf of the World Council of Churches at fifteen polling sites in the Western Cape, April 26–28.

p. 683: people came out of their homes: See Robert Kinloch Massie, *Boston Globe,* April 30, 1994.

p. 683: fear of intimidation: Independent Electoral Commission, *End to Waiting,* 199.

p. 684: doctored the outcome: Ibid., 33.

p. 684: Nelson Mandela promised to go to work: See the text of Mandela's address in the *Boston Globe,* May 8, 1994.

p. 684: national election results: See SAIRR, *Survey, 1994–95,* 339; also results published in the *Cape Times,* May 7, 1994.

p. 684: provincial 1994 election results: See "National Assembly Election Results by Region," *Indicator SA* 11.3 (1994).

p. 684: carnival atmosphere: See the description in the *Natal Mercury,* May 12, 1994.

p. 684: "The moment to bridge the chasms": *Boston Globe,* May 14, 1994.

p. 685: "president of the people": *Citizen,* May 11, 1994.

p. 685: "Mandela has expressed an inspired, positive, and attainable vision": *Business Day,* May 25, 1994.

p. 686: cabinet appointments: See *This Week in South Africa,* May 10–16, 1994. For a detailed profile of each cabinet minister, see Tait, *Portfolio,* op. cit.

p. 686: Dullah Omar: Tait, *Portfolio,* op. cit., 151.

p. 686: Of the nine provinces: See SAIRR, *Survey, 1994–95,* 341.

p. 686: unemployment figures: SAIRR, *Survey, 1990–91,* xliii.

p. 687: the poorest forty percent: SAIRR, *Survey, 1994–95,* 377.

p. 687: relatively high manufacturing wages: "Global Game Imposes Harsh Rules," *Financial Mail,* March 17, 1995, foreign trade special report; "Moving the Goal Posts," *Financial Mail,* August 12, 1994.

p. 688: business fraud: See Robert Kinloch Massie, "Understanding Corruption," *Die Suid-Afrikaan,* August–September 1993; see also *Financial Mail,* November 5, 1993.

p. 688: the RDP: African National Congress, *TheReconstruction and Development Programme: A Policy Framework* (Johannesburg: Umanyano Publications, 1994), 14.

p. 689: increased U.S. aid: *Business Day,* February 8, 1994, and March 2, 1994.

p. 689: U.S. embassy figures: See speech by U.S. Ambassador Princeton Lyman, March 10, 1993, author's files.

p. 689: When Chase Manhattan returned: *Johannesburg Star,* February 19, 1995.

p. 690: the emergence of codes of conduct: COSATU, May 17, 1993; SACC; Sullivan, April 28, 1994. See also material from the SACC WCC conference on the South African economy held in Utrecht, Holland, June 1993, author's files.

p. 690: continued to file shareholder resolutions: See "U.S. Business and Recent Events in South Africa," Social Issues Service Report B (Washington, D.C.: IRRC, 1995).

p. 691: Truth and Reconciliation Commission: SAIRR, *Survey, 1994–95,* 345; see André du Toit's reading list for his course "Justice in Transition" at the University of Cape Town, including citations for Chilean National Commission on Truth and Reconciliation; André du Toit, "Laying the Past to Rest," *Indicator SA* 11.4 (1994);

Truth and Reconciliation Commission, explanatory booklet, published by Justice in Transition on behalf of the Ministry of Justice; Gareth Newham, "Truth and Reconciliation: Realising the Ideals," *Indicator SA* 12.4 (1995); Richard Wilson, "Manufacturing Legitimacy: The Truth and Reconciliation Commission and the Rule of Law," *Indicator SA* 13.1 (1995); Charles Villa-Vicencio, "On Taking Responsibility," draft manuscript.

p. 692: Slovo . . . succumbed to cancer: The lifelong Communist received one of his most unexpected and heartfelt eulogies from the editors of *Business Day.* "In his few months in the cabinet, Slovo displayed an ability to tackle and solve daunting political problems in a remarkably practical and efficient way," they wrote. "Had such talent been at the disposal of the country for longer, many other pressing issues would doubtless have been dealt with. The same can be said for others whose productive years were blighted by apartheid" *(Business Day,* January 9, 1995).

p. 692: allegations against Allan Boesak: *Financial Mail,* April 7, 1995.

p. 692: "one long debate about divestment": *Harvard,* June 1992, 23.

p. 692: Jennifer Davis and her colleagues: Author interview with Jennifer Davis, October 1996.

p. 693: He spoke out against: TransAfrica news release, March 19, 1993; *New York Times,* March 17, 1995.

p. 693: TransAfrica's new headquarters: *Washington Post,* June 5, 1993.

p. 693: "as we look to pass the baton of leadership": *Washington Post,* September 15, 1993.

p. 693: 1996 shareholder resolutions: *The Proxy Resolutions Book* (New York: Interfaith Center on Corporate Responsibility, January 1996).

p. 693: two other codes of conduct: See South African Council of Churches, *Towards a Code of Investment: A Report on the Conference on Ethics for South Africa's International Economic Relations* (Johannesburg: SACC, 1992).

Selected Bibliography

The following are abbreviations used in the notes and bibliography for frequently cited archival sources:

ACOA Amistad   American Committee on Africa, Amistad Collection, Tulane University
ICCR   Interfaith Center on Corporate Responsibility
ICEOP   International Council for Equality of Opportunity Principles
JFKL   John F. Kennedy Presidential Library
NSF   National Security Files (JFKL)
OH   Oral History (JFKL)
OIC   Opportunities Industrialization Center
POF   Presidential Office Files (JFKL)
SAIRR   South African Institute of Race Relations
SASO   South African Students' Association
SPRO-CAS   Study Project on Christianity in Apartheid Society

BOOKS

ABEDIAN, IRAJ, and BARRY STANDISH, eds. *Economic Growth in South Africa: Selected Policy Issues.* Cape Town: Oxford University Press, 1992.

ACKERMAN, BRUCE. *Social Justice in the Liberal State.* New Haven: Yale University Press, 1980.

ACKERMAN, ROBERT W. *The Social Challenge to Business.* Cambridge: Harvard University Press, 1975.

———, and RAYMOND BAUER. *Corporate Social Responsiveness: The Modern Dilemma.* Reston, Va.: Reston Publishing, 1976.

ACKERMANN, DENISE, et al., eds. *Women Hold Up Half the Sky: Women in the Church in Southern Africa.* Pietermaritzburg: Cluster Publications, 1991.

ADAM, HERIBERT. *Modernizing Racial Domination: The Dynamics of South African Politics.* Berkeley: University of California Press, 1971.

———, and KOGILA MOODLEY. *South Africa without Apartheid: Dismantling Racial Domination.* Cape Town: Maskew Miller Longman, 1986.

African National Congress. *The Reconstruction and Development Programme: A Policy Framework.* Johannesburg: African National Congress, 1994.

AGUILAR, FRANCIS J. *Scanning the Business Environment.* New York: Macmillan, 1967.

ALBERTS, LOUW, and FRANK CHIKANE. *The Road to Rustenberg: The Church Looking Forward to a New South Africa.* Cape Town: Struik Christian Books, 1991.

ALLISON, GRAHAM T. *The Essence of Decision.* Boston: Little, Brown, 1971.

ANDREWS, KENNETH R. *The Concept of Corporate Strategy.* Homewood, Ill.: Richard D. Irwin, 1980.

ANSTEY, MARK. *Practical Peacemaking: A Mediator's Handbook.* Port Elizabeth, South Africa: Juta and Company, 1993.

Arthur D. Little, Inc. *Reports on the Signatory Companies to the Statement of Principles for South Africa.* Cambridge, Mass.: Arthur D. Little, Inc., annual issues.

BACKMAN, JULES, ed. *Social Responsibility and Accountability.* New York: New York University Press, 1975.

BAKER, PAULINE H. *The United States and South Africa: The Reagan Years.* South Africa Update Series. New York: Ford Foundation, Foreign Policy Association, 1989.

————, ALEX BORRAINE, and WARREN KRAFCHIK, eds. *South Africa and the World Economy in the 1990s.* Cape Town: David Philip, in conjunction with the Brookings Institution, IDASA, and the Aspen Institute, 1993.

BALDWIN, FRED D. *Conflicting Interests: Corporate Governance Controversies.* Lexington, Mass.: Lexington Books, 1984.

BALDWIN, STUART, et al. *Pension Funds and Ethical Investment: A Study of Investment Practices and Opportunities for the State of California Retirement Systems.* New York: Council on Economic Priorities, 1980.

BALIA, DARYL. *Christian Resistance to Apartheid: Ecumenism in South Africa, 1960–1987.* Braamfontein, South Africa: Skotaville Publishers, 1989.

BALL, GEORGE W. *The Discipline of Power.* Boston: Little, Brown, 1968.

BALLINGER, MARGARET. *From Union to Apartheid: A Trek to Isolation.* Cape Town: Juta and Company, 1969.

BARBER, JAMES. *South Africa's Foreign Policy, 1945–1970.* London: Oxford University Press, 1973.

BARKER, LUCIUS J. *Our Time Has Come: A Delegate's Diary of Jesse Jackson's 1984 Presidential Campaign.* Chicago: University of Illinois Press, 1988.

————, and RONALD WATERS, eds. *Jesse Jackson's 1984 Presidential Campaign: Challenge and Change in American Politics.* Chicago: University of Illinois Press, 1989.

BARNARD, CHESTER I. *The Functions of the Executive.* Introduction by Kenneth R. Andrews. 1938. Reprint, Cambridge: Harvard University Press, 1968.

BARRY, VINCENT. *Moral Issues in Business.* Belmont, Calif.: Wadsworth, 1979.

BASKIN, JEREMY. *Striking Back: A History of COSATU.* Johannesburg: Ravan Press, 1991.

BEAUCHAMP, THOMAS. *Case Studies in Business, Society, and Ethics.* Englewood Cliffs, N.J.: Prentice-Hall, 1983.

————, and NORMAN BOWIE. *Ethical Theory and Business.* 3rd ed. Englewood Cliffs, N.J.: Prentice-Hall, 1988.

BENSON, MARY. *Nelson Mandela: The Man and the Movement.* New York: Norton, 1986.

BERGER, PETER L., and BOBBY GODSELL, eds. *A Future South Africa: Visions Strategies and Realities.* Boulder, Colo.: Westview Press, 1988.

BERLE, ADOLF A., and GARDINER C. MEANS. *The Modern Corporation and Private Property.* New York: Macmillan, 1932.

BERNSTEIN, HILDA. *No. 46—Steve Biko.* London: International Defence and Aid Fund, April 1978.

————. *For Their Triumphs and for Their Tears: Women in Apartheid South Africa.* London: International Defence and Aid Fund, 1985.

————. *The World That Was Ours: The Story of the Rivonia Trial.* London: SAWriters, 1989.

BIKO, STEPHEN. *I Write What I Like.* New York: Harper and Row, 1978.

BINDMAN, GEOFFREY, ed. *South Africa: Human Rights and the Rule of Law.* London: Pinter Publishers, 1988.

BLACK, DUNCAN, and R. A. EWING. *Committee Decisions with Complementary Valuation.* London: William Hodge and Company, 1951.

————. *The Theory of Committees and Elections.* Cambridge: Cambridge University Press, 1963.

BLINDER, ALAN S. *Private Pensions and Public Pensions: Theory and Fact.* Ann Arbor: University of Michigan Institute of Public Policy Studies, 1981.

BLOOM, JACK BRIAN. *Black South Africa and the Disinvestment Dilemma.* Johannesburg: Jonathan Ball Publishers, 1986.

BOGUE, MARCUS C., and ELWOOD S. BUFFA. *Corporate Strategic Analysis.* New York: Free Press, 1986.

BOK, SISSELA. *Alva Myrdal.* Reading, Mass.: Addison-Wesley, 1991.

BOOTH, ALAN R. *The United States Experience in South Africa, 1784–1870.* Cape Town: A. A. Balkema, 1976.

————, ed. *Journal of the Rev. George Champion, American Missionary in Zululand.* Cape Town: C. Struik, 1967.

BOSHOFF, ANNATJIE. *Betsie Verwoerd: Die Vrou.* Pretoria: Afrikanervolkswag-publikasie, 1993.

BOTHA, JAN. *Verwoerd Is Dead.* Cape Town: Books of Africa, 1967.

BOWEN, HOWARD R. *Social Responsibilities of the Businessman.* New York: Harper and Bros., 1953.

BOWER, JOSEPH L. *Managing the Resource Allocation Process.* 1970. Reprint, Boston: Harvard Business School Press, 1986.

————. *The Two Faces of Management.* Boston: Houghton Mifflin, 1983.

BRADSHAW, THORNTON, and DAVID VOGEL. *Corporations and Their Critics.* New York: McGraw-Hill, 1981.

BRANCH, TAYLOR. *Parting the Waters: America in the King Years, 1954–1963.* New York: Simon and Schuster, 1988.

BRAYBOOKE, DAVID. *Ethics in the World of Business.* Totowa, N.J.: Rowman and Allanhead, 1983.

BRIDGLAND, FRED. *Jonas Savimbi: A Key to Africa.* Edinburgh: Mainstream Publishing, 1986.

BROWN, ROGER. *Social Psychology: The Second Edition.* New York: Free Press, 1986.

BROZEN, Y., E. JOHNSON, and C. POWERS. *Can the Market Sustain an Ethic?* Chicago: University of Chicago Press, 1978.

BRUYN, SEVERYN T. *The Field of Social Investment.* New York: Cambridge University Press, 1987.

BURNS, JAMES MACGREGOR. *Leadership.* New York: Harper and Row, 1978.

BUTHELEZI, MANGOSUTHU GATSHA. *Power Is Ours: The Collected Speeches of South African Statesman Gatsha Buthelezi.* New York: Books in Focus, 1979.

————. *South Africa: My Vision of the Future.* London: Weidenfeld and Nicolson, 1990.

BUTLER, JEFFREY, ROBERT I. ROTBERG, and JOHN ADAMS. *The Black Homelands of South Africa: The Political and Economic Development of Bophuthatswana and KwaZulu.* Berkeley: University of California Press, 1977.

CALLAHAN, DANIEL, and SISSELA BOK. *Ethics Teaching in Higher Education.* New York: Plenum Press, 1980.

CALVOCORESSI, PETER. *South Africa and World Opinion.* London: Oxford University Press, under the auspices of the Institute of Race Relations, 1961.

CAMPBELL, JAMES T. *Songs of Zion: The African Methodist Episcopal Church in the United States and South Africa.* New York: Oxford University Press, 1995.

CAMPSCHREUR, WILLEM, and JOOST DIVENDAL. *Culture in Another South Africa.* New York: Olive Branch Press, 1989.

CAMPTON, HARVEY. *The New Transkei.* Sandton: Valiant Publishers, 1976.

Carnegie Commission of Investigation of the Poor White Question in South Africa. *The Poor White Problem in South Africa: A Report of the Carnegie Commission.* 5 vols. Stellenbosch: Pro Ecclesia-Drukkery, 1932.

CARROLL, ARCHIE B. *Managing Corporate Social Responsibility.* Boston: Little, Brown, 1977.

CARSON, CLAYBORNE. *In Struggle: SNCC and the Black Awakening of the 1960s.* Cambridge: Harvard University Press, 1981.

CARTER, BARRY E. *International Economic Sanctions: Improving the Haphazard U.S. Legal Regime.* New York: Cambridge University Press, 1988.

CARTER, GWENDOLYN, and PATRICK O'MEARA, eds. *African Independence: The First Twenty-Five Years.* Bloomington: Indiana University Press, 1986.

CARY, W. L., and C. B. BRIGHT. *The Law and the Lore of Endowment Funds.* New York: Ford Foundation, 1969.

CAWTHRA, GAVIN. *Brutal Force: The Apartheid War Machine.* London: International Defence and Aid Fund, 1986.

CELL, JOHN. *The Highest Stage of White Supremacy: The Origins of Segregation in South Africa and the American South.* New York: Cambridge University Press, 1982.

CHANDLER, ALFRED D. *Strategy and Structure.* New York: Doubleday and Co., 1966.

CHURCH, FRANK, GALE W. MCGEE, and FRANK E. MOSS. *Study Mission to Africa.* Report to the Senate Committee on Foreign Relations, Committee on Appropriations, and Committee on the Interior and Insular Affairs. Washington, D.C.: GPO, 1961.

CLARK, DICK. *U.S. Corporate Interests in South Africa.* Washington, D.C.: GPO, 1978.

COCHRANE, JAMES. *Servants of Power: The Role of English-Speaking Churches, 1903–1930.* Johannesburg: Ravan Press, 1987.

COFFEE, JOHN C. Jr., LOUIS LOWENSTEIN, and SUSAN ROSE-ACKERMAN. *Knights, Raiders, and Targets: The Impact of the Hostile Takeover.* New York: Oxford University Press, 1988.

COHEN, BARRY, and MOHAMED A. EL-KHAWAS. *The Kissinger Study on Southern Africa.* London: Spokesman Books, 1975.

COKER, CHRISTOPHER. *The United States and South Africa, 1968–1985: Constructive Engagement and Its Critics.* Durham: Duke University Press, 1986.

COLE, JOSETTE. *Crossroads: The Politics of Repression and Reform 1976–1986.* Johannesburg: Ravan Press, 1987.

COLTON, ELIZABETH O. *The Jackson Phenomenon: The Man, the Power, the Message.* New York: Doubleday, 1989.

Commission on U.S. Policy toward Southern Africa. *South Africa: Time Running Out.* Berkeley: University of California Press, 1981.

Commonwealth Committee of Foreign Ministers on Southern Africa. *South Africa: The Sanctions Report.* London: Penguin Books, 1989.

CONE, JAMES. *Black Theology and Black Power.* New York: Seabury Press, 1969.

———. *Martin and Malcolm in America: A Dream or a Nightmare?* Maryknoll, N.Y.: Orbis Books, 1992.

CONNOLLY, WILLIAM, ed. *Legitimacy and the State.* London: Basil Blackwell, 1984.

CORDER, HUGH, ed. *Democracy and the Judiciary.* Cape Town: Institute for a Democratic Alternative for South Africa, 1989.

Corporate Data Exchange, *U.S. Bank Loans to South Africa.* New York: Corporate Data Exchange, 1978.

CRAPANZANO, VINCENT. *Waiting: The Whites of South Africa.* New York: Random House, 1985.

CULL, PATRICK, ed. *Economic Growth and Foreign Investment in South Africa.* Cape Town: Institute for a Democratic Alternative for South Africa, 1992.

CYERT, RICHARD M., and JAMES G. MARCH. *A Behavioral Theory of the Firm.* Englewood Cliffs, N.J.: Prentice-Hall, 1963.

DAVENPORT, T. R. H. *South Africa: A Modern History.* 2nd ed. Toronto: University of Toronto Press, 1977; 4th ed. Toronto: University of Toronto Press, 1991.

DAVID, KEITH, WILLIAM FREDERICK, and ROBERT BLOMSTROM. *Business and Society: Concepts and Policy Issues.* New York: McGraw-Hill, 1980.

DAVIDOW, JEFFREY. *A Peace in Southern African: The Lancaster Conference on Rhodesia.* Boulder, Colo.: Westview Press, under the auspices of the Center for International Affairs, Harvard University, 1984.

DAVIS, RICHARD HARDING. *With Both Armies in South Africa.* New York: Scribner's, 1900.

DAVIS, STEPHEN M. *Apartheid's Rebels: Inside South Africa's Hidden War.* New Haven: Yale University Press, 1987.

DE BEER, CEDRIC. *The South African Disease: Apartheid Health and Health Services.* Trenton, N.J.: Africa World Press, 1986.

DE GRUCHY, JOHN W. *The Church Struggle in South Africa.* 2nd ed. Cape Town: David Philip, 1986.

———. *Faith for a Time like This: South African Sermons.* Cape Town: Rondebosch United Church, 1992.

———. *Christianity and Democracy: A Theology for a Just World.* Cape Town: David Philip, 1995.

DE KLERK, WILLEM. *F. W. de Klerk: The Man in His Time.* Johannesburg: Jonathan Ball Publishers, 1991.

DE KOCK, WESSEL. *Usuthu! Cry Peace! Inkatha and the Fight for a Just South Africa.* Cape Town: Open Hand Press, 1986.

DE VILLIERS, DAWID. *The Case for South Africa.* London: Tom Stacey, 1970.

DE VILLIERS, LES. *In Sight of Surrender: The U.S. Sanctions Campaign against South Africa, 1946–1993.* Westport, Conn.: Greenwood, 1995.

DEGEORGE, RICHARD T., and J. A. PICHLER. *Ethics, Free Enterprise, and Public Policy.* New York: Oxford University Press, 1978.

DESJARDINS, J., and J. MCCALL. *Contemporary Issues in Business Ethics.* Belmont, Calif.: Wadsworth, 1984.

D'OLIVEIRA, JOHN. *Vorster: The Man.* Johannesburg: Ernest Stanton Publishers, 1977.

DOMHOFF, G. WILLIAM. *The Powers That Be: Processes of Ruling Class Domination in America.* New York: Vintage, 1978.

DOMINI, AMY L., with PETER D. KINDER. *Ethical Investing.* Reading, Mass.: Addison-Wesley, 1984.

DONALDSON, GORDON, and JAY LORSCH. *Decision-Making at the Top.* New York: Basic Books, 1983.

DONALDSON, THOMAS. *Case Studies in Business Ethics.* Englewood Cliffs, N.J.: Prentice-Hall, 1984.

DOXEY, MARGARET P. *International Sanctions in Contemporary Perspective.* New York: St. Martin's Press, 1987.

DU BOULAY, SHIRLEY. *Tutu: Voice of the Voiceless.* Grand Rapids: Eerdmans, 1988.

DU PLESSIS, J. *A History of Christian Missions in South Africa.* London: Longmans, Green, 1911.

DU TOIT, ANDRÉ, and HERMANN GILIOMEE. *Afrikaner Political Thought: Analysis and Documents.* Vol. 1, *1780–1850.* Cape Town: David Philip, 1983.

EDGAR, ROBERT, ed. *An African American in South Africa: The Travel Notes of Ralph Bunche.* Athens: Ohio University Press, 1992.

EELLS, RICHARD. *The Government of Corporations.* New York: Free Press of Glencoe, Illinois, 1960.

EINHORN, HERBERT. *Shareholder Meetings: Dealing with Management and Shareholder Proposals.* New York: Practicing Law Institute.

ELLIS, STEPHEN, and TSEPO SECHABA. *Comrades against Apartheid: The ANC and the South African Communist Party in Exile.* Bloomington: Indiana University Press, 1992.

EMERSON, FRANK D., and FRANKLIN C. LATCHAM. *Shareholder Democracy.* Cleveland: Press of Western Reserve University, 1954.

EPSTEIN, EDWIN M., and DON VOTAW, eds. *Rationality, Legitimacy, Responsibility: Search for New Directions in Business and Society.* Santa Monica: Goodyear Publishing Company, 1978.

ETZIONI, AMITAI. *A Comparative Analysis of Complex Organizations: On Power, Involvement, and Their Correlates.* New York: Free Press, 1961.

———. *The Moral Dimension: Toward a New Economics.* New York: Free Press, 1988.

FAIRCLOUGH, ADAM. *To Redeem the Soul of America: The Southern Christian Leadership Conference and Martin Luther King.* Athens: University of Georgia Press, 1987.

FARISANI, TSHENUWANI SIMON. *Diary from a South African Prison.* Philadelphia: Fortress Press, 1987.

FIRST, RUTH. *117 DAYS.* New York: Stein and Day, 1965; New York: Monthly Review Press, 1989.

———, JONATHAN STEELE, and CHRISTABEL GURNEY. *The South African Connection: Western Investment in Apartheid.* London: Temple Smith, 1972.

FORD, GERALD R. *A Time to Heal.* New York: Harper and Row, 1979.

FOURIE, STEPHEN. *Strategies for Change.* Cape Town: David Philip Publishers and IDASA, 1989.

FRAMEL, PHILIP. *Pretoria's Praetorians: Civil-Military Relations in South Africa.* Cambridge: Cambridge University Press, 1984.

FREDERICKSON, GEORGE M. *White Supremacy: A Comparative Study in American and South African History.* Cambridge: Oxford University Press, 1981.

FREEMAN, R. EDWARD. *Strategic Management: A Stakeholder Approach.* London: Pitman, 1984.

FREY, ALEXANDER H., JESSE H. CHOPER, NOYES E. LEECH, and C. ROBERT MORRIS Jr. *Cases and Materials on Corporate Law.* 2nd ed. Boston: Little, Brown, 1977.

GABRIELLI, GILBERTO, and DANIELE FANO, eds. *The Challenge of Private Pension Funds: Present Trends and Future Prospects in Industrialised Countries.* London: Economist Publications, 1986.

GARROW, DAVID. *Bearing the Cross: Martin Luther King Jr. and the Southern Christian Leadership Conference.* New York: Morrow, 1986.

———, ed. *Martin Luther King Jr.: Civil Rights Leader, Theologian, Orator.* Brooklyn: Carlson Publishers, 1989.

GASTROW, SHELAGH. *Who's Who in South African Politics, Number Two.* Johannesburg: Ravan Press, 1987.

GELB, STEPHEN, ed. *South Africa's Economic Crisis.* Cape Town: David Philip, 1991.

GELDENHUYS, D. *The Diplomacy of Isolation: South Africa's Foreign Policy Making.* Johannesburg: Macmillan, 1984.

GERHART, GAIL M. *Black Power in South Africa: The Evolution of an Ideology.* Berkeley: University of California Press, 1978.

GHERSI, STEFANO, and PETER MAJOR. *South Africa: The 51st State.* Randburg: Fastdraft, 1989.

GILBERT, LEWIS D. *Dividends and Democracy.* Larchmont, N.Y.: American Research Council, 1956.

GOODE, WILLIAM J. *The Celebration of Heroes: Prestige as a Social Control System.* Berkeley: University of California Press, 1978.

GREEN, NICK, and REG LASCARIS. *Third World Destiny: Recognizing and Seizing the Opportunities Offered by a Changing South Africa.* Cape Town: Human and Rousseau, 1988.

GREGORY, THEODORE. *Ernest Oppenheimer and the Economic Development of Southern Africa.* Cape Town: Oxford University Press, 1962.

GROBBELAAR, PIETER W. *This Was a Man.* Cape Town: Human and Rousseau, 1967.

———, ed. *Strategic Management.* New York: John Wiley, 1983.

HAMPTON, HENRY, and STEVE FAYER. *Voices of Freedom.* New York: Bantam Books, 1990.

HANLON, JOSEPH, and ROGER OMOND. *The Sanctions Handbook.* London: Penguin Books, 1987.

HARBER, ANTON, and BARBARA LUDMAN, eds. *A–Z of South African Politics: The Essential Handbook.* London: Penguin Books, 1995.

HARRIS, SEYMOUR E., ed. *American Economic History.* New York: McGraw-Hill, 1961.

HAUCK, DAVID, and MEG VOORHES. *Two Decades of Debate.* Washington, D.C.: Investor Responsibility Research Center, 1983.

HAYSOM, NICHOLAS. *Apartheid's Private Army: The Rise of Right-Wing Vigilantes in South Africa.* Johannesburg: Center for Applied Legal Studies, University of the Witwatersrand, distributed by the Catholic Institute for International Relations, 1986.

HEESE, J. A. *Die Herkoms van die Afrikaner, 1657–1867.* Cape Town: A. A. Balkema, 1971.

HEPPLE, ALEXANDER. *Verwoerd.* London: Penguin Books, 1967.

HERO, ALFRED O. Jr., and JOHN BARRATT, eds. *The American People and South Africa.* Lexington, Mass.: Lexington Books, 1981.

HEUNIS, JAN C. *United Nations versus South Africa: A Legal Assessment of United Nations and United Nations Related Activities in Respect of South Africa.* Johannesburg: Lex Patria, 1986.

HIRSCHMAN, ALBERT O. *Exit, Voice, and Loyalty.* Cambridge: Harvard University Press, 1970.

———. *The Rhetoric of Reaction.* Cambridge: Harvard University Press, 1991.

HOFER, CHARLES W., and DAN SCHENDEL. *Strategy Formulation: Analytical Concepts.* St. Paul: West Publishing, 1978.

HOFFMANN, W. MICHAEL, ed. *Business Values and Social Justice: Compatibility or Contradiction?* Proceedings of the First National Conference on Business Ethics, March 11–12, 1977. Waltham, Mass.: Center for Business Ethics, Bentley College, 1977.

———. *Power and Responsibility in the American Business System.* Proceedings of the Second National Conference, 1979. Waltham, Mass.: Center for Business Ethics, Bentley College, 1979. See Dharmenda T. Verma, "Polaroid in South Africa."

———. *The Work Ethics in Business.* Proceedings of the Third National Conference, 1981. Waltham, Mass.: Center for Business Ethics, Bentley College, 1981. See Charles Powers, "Individual Dignity and Institutional Identity: The Paradoxical Needs of the Corporate Employee." (1981)

———. *Corporate Governance and Institutionalizing Ethics.* Proceedings of the Fifth National Conference, 1983. Waltham, Mass.: Center for Business Ethics, Bentley College, 1983. See Ken Andrews, "Overseeing Ethical Policy"; Ralph Nader, "Reforming Corporate Governance"; David Vogel, "Shareholder Activism: An Update"; Daniel Purnell, "Sullivan Principles."

HOLLAND, HEID. *The Struggle: A History of the African National Congress.* London: Grafton Books, 1989.

HOPE, MARJORIE, and JAMES YOUNG. *The South African Churches in a Revolutionary Situation.* Maryknoll, N.Y.: Orbis Books, 1981.

HOPKINS, DWIGHT N. *Black Theology, U.S.A. and South Africa: Politics, Culture, and Liberation.* Maryknoll, N.Y.: Orbis Books, 1990.

HOUGHTON, D. HOBART. *The South African Economy.* Cape Town: Oxford University Press, 1976.

HOUSER, GEORGE M. *No One Can Stop the Rain.* New York: Pilgrim Press, 1989.

HUDDLESTON, TREVOR. *Naught for Your Comfort.* London: Collins, 1956.

HUFBAUER, GARY CLYDE, and JEFFREY J. SCHOTT. *Economic Sanctions in Support of Foreign Policy Goals.* Washington, D.C.: Institute for International Economics, 1983.

———. *Economic Sanctions Reconsidered: History and Current Policy.* Washington, D.C: Institute for International Economics, 1985.

HUIZENGA, C. J., ed. *Corporate Governance: A Definitive Exploration of the Issues.* Proceedings of UCLA conference, January 8–9, 1981. Los Angeles: UCLA Press, 1981.

HURST, JAMES WILLARD. *The Legitimacy of the Business Corporation.* Charlottesville: University Press of Virginia, 1970.

Independent Electoral Commission. *An End to Waiting: The Story of South Africa's Elections.* Johannesburg: Independent Electoral Commission, 1995.

Inkatha. *Year Book 1987.* Durban: Inkatha Institute for South Africa, 1987.

INNES, DUNCAN, et al., eds. *Power and Profit: Politics, Labour, and Business in South Africa.* Cape Town: Oxford University Press, 1992.

Institute for Policy Studies. *Black South Africa Explodes.* Washington, D.C.: Transnational Institute, Institute for Policy Studies, 1977.

Interfaith Center on Corporate Responsibility. *Church Investments, Corporations, and South Africa.* New York: Corporate Information Center, 1973.

IPPOLITO, RICHARD A. *Pensions, Economics, and Public Policy.* Homewood, Ill.: Dow Jones-Irwin for the Pension Research Council, Wharton School, 1986.

JOHNS, SHERIDAN, and R. HUNT DAVIS Jr. *Mandela, Tambo, and the African National Congress: The Struggle against Apartheid, 1948–1990: A Documentary Survey.* New York: Oxford University Press, 1991.

JOHNSON, SHAUN, ed. *South Africa: No Turning Back.* Bloomington: Indiana University Press, 1989.

KAMSTEEG, AAD, and EVERT VAN DIJK. *F. W. de Klerk: Man of the Moment.* Cape Town: Vlaeberg Publishers, 1990.

KANE-BERMAN, JOHN. *South Africa: The Method in the Madness.* Johannesburg: Ravan Press, 1979.

————, et al., eds. *Beating Apartheid and Building the Future.* Johannesburg: South African Institute of Race Relations, 1990.

KANTER, ROSABETH MOSS. *The Change Masters.* New York: Simon and Schuster, 1983.

KANTROW, ALAN M. *The Constraints of Corporate Tradition: Doing the Correct Thing, Not Just What the Past Dictates.* New York: Harper and Row, 1984.

KARIS, THOMAS A., and GWENDOLEN M. CARTER, eds. *From Protest to Challenge: A Documentary History of African Politics in South Africa, 1882–1964.* 4 vols. (Vol. 4 edited by Thomas A. Karis and Gail M. Gerhart.) Stanford, Calif.: Hoover Institution Press, 1977.

KENNEY, HENRY. *Architect of Apartheid.* Johannesburg: Jonathan Ball Publishers, 1980.

KIBBE, JENNIFER, and DAVID HAUCK. *Leaving South Africa: The Impact of U.S. Corporate Disinvestment.* Washington, D.C.: IRRC, 1988.

KING, MARTIN LUTHER Jr. *Where Do We Go from Here?: Chaos or Community.* Boston: Beacon Press, 1967.

KISSINGER, HENRY M. *White House Years.* New York: Little, Brown, 1979.

————. *Years of Upheaval.* New York: Little, Brown, 1982.

KOENDERMAN, TONY. *Sanctions: The Threat to South Africa.* Johannesburg: Jonathan Ball Publishers, 1982.

KOTTER, JOHN P. *The General Managers.* New York: Free Press, 1982.

KUPER, LEO. *Passive Resistance in South Africa.* New Haven: Yale University Press, 1957.

LAKE, ANTHONY. *Caution and Concern: The Making of American Policy toward South Africa, 1946–1971.* Unpublished doctoral dissertation, Princeton University, 1974.

————. *The Tar Baby Option.* New York: Columbia University Press, 1976.

LAURENCE, PATRICK. *The Transkei: South Africa's Politics of Partition.* Johannesburg: Ravan Press, 1976.

LAWRENCE, PAUL R., and JAY W. LORSCH. *Organization and Environment.* Cambridge: Division of Research, Harvard University, 1967.

LEAPE, JONATHAN, BO BASKIN, and STEFAN UNDERHILL, eds. *Business in the Shadow of Apartheid.* Lexington, Mass.: Lexington Books, 1985.

LEARNED, EDMUND P., C. ROLAND CHRISTENSEN, KENNETH R. ANDREWS, and WILLIAM D. GUTH. *Business Policy: Text and Cases.* Homewood, Ill.: Richard D. Irwin, 1965.

LEGUM, COLIN. *The Battlefields of Southern Africa.* New York: Africana Publishing Company, 1988.

LEGUM, COLIN, and MARGARET LEGUM. *South Africa: Crisis for the West.* London: Pall Mall Press, 1964.

LELYVELD, JOSEPH. *Move Your Shadow.* New York: New York Times Books, 1985.

LEONARD, RICHARD. *South Africa at War: White Power and the Crisis in Southern Africa.* Westport, Conn.: Lawrence Hill, 1983.

LEVIN, NOEL ARNOLD, and MARK E. BROSSMAN. *Social Investing for Pension Funds: For Love or Money.* Brookfield, Wisc.: International Foundation of Employee Benefit Plans, 1982. (18700 West Bluemond Road, P.O. Box 69, Brookfield, Wisconsin 53005.)

LEVINE, JANET. *Inside Apartheid: One Woman's Struggle in South Africa.* Chicago: Contemporary Books, 1988.

LEWIS, STEPHEN R. Jr. *The Economics of Apartheid.* New York: Council on Foreign Relations Press, 1990.

LIBBY, RONALD T. *The Politics of Economic Power in Southern Africa.* Princeton: Princeton University Press, 1987.

LINDBLOM, CHARLES E. *Politics and Markets.* New York: Basic Books, 1977.

LIPTON, MERLE. *Capitalism and Apartheid: South Africa 1910–1984.* Aldershot, Eng.: Gower House, 1985.

LITVAK, LAWRENCE. *Pension Funds and Economic Renewal.* Vol. 12, *Studies in Development Policy.* Michael Barker, general ed. Washington, D.C.: Council of State Planning Agencies, 1981.

LOCKWOOD, EDGAR. *South Africa's Moment of Truth.* New York: Friendship Press, 1988.

LODGE, TOM. *Black Politics in South Africa since 1945.* London: Longman Group, 1983.

———, BILL NASSON, et al. *All, Here, and Now: Black Politics in South Africa in the 1980s.* South Africa Update Series. New York: Ford Foundation, 1991.

LONGSTRETH, BEVIS, and H. DAVID ROSENBLOOM. *Corporate Social Responsibility and the Institutional Investor: A Report to the Ford Foundation.* New York: Praeger, 1973.

LOVE, JANICE. *The U.S. Anti-Apartheid Movement: Local Activism in Global Politics.* New York: Praeger, 1985.

LOWENSTEIN, LOUIS. *What's Wrong with Wall Street: Short-Term Gain and the Absentee Shareholder.* Reading, Mass.: Addison-Wesley, 1988.

LUGAR, RICHARD G. *Letters to the Next President.* New York: Simon and Schuster, 1988.

LULAT, Y. G-M. *U.S. Relations with South Africa: An Annotated Bibliography.* 2 vols. Boulder, Colo.: Westview Press, 1991.

LUTHULI, ALBERT. *Let My People Go.* London: Collins, 1962.

MACCOBY, MICHAEL. *The Gamesman.* New York: Simon and Schuster, 1976.

MACDONALD, DWIGHT, and FRANCIS X. SUTTON. *The Ford Foundation: The Men and the Millions.* New Brunswick, N.J.: Transaction Books, 1988.

MACE, MYLES L. *Directors: Myth and Reality.* Boston: Harvard Business School Press, 1971, 1986.

MACKLER, IAN. *Pattern for Profit in Southern Africa.* Lexington, Mass.: Lexington Books, 1972.

MACMILLAN, HAROLD. *Pointing the Way, 1959–1961.* London: Macmillan, 1972.

MACSHANE, DENNIS, et al. *Power! Black Workers, Their Unions, and the Struggle for Freedom in South Africa.* Boston: South End Press, 1984.

MAGAT, RICHARD. *The Ford Foundation at Work: Philanthropic Choices, Methods, and Styles.* New York: Plenum Press, 1979.

MAHONEY, RICHARD D. *JFK: Ordeal in Africa.* New York: Oxford University Press, 1983.

MAKGETLA, NEVA, and ANN SEIDMAN. *Outposts of Monopoly Capitalism: Southern Africa in the Changing Global Economy.* Westport, Conn.: Lawrence Hill, 1980.

MALAN, RIAN. *My Traitor Heart.* New York: Atlantic Monthly Press, 1990.

MANDELA, NELSON. *The Struggle Is My Life.* London: International Defence and Aid Fund, 1978.

———. *Long Walk to Freedom.* Boston: Little, Brown, 1994.

MANDELA, WINNIE. *Part of My Soul Went with Him.* New York: Norton, 1985.

MANDY, NIGEL. *A City Divided.* Johannesburg: Macmillan South Africa, 1984.

MANROSS, WILLIAM. *A History of the American Episcopal Church.* New York: Morehouse, 1935.

MARCH, JAMES G., and HERBERT A. SIMON. *Organizations.* New York: John Wiley and Sons, 1958.

MARCUM, JOHN. *The Angolan Revolution.* Vol. 1, *The Anatomy of an Explosion, 1950–1962.* Vol. 2, *Exile Politics and Guerrilla Warfare, 1962–1976.* Cambridge: MIT Press, 1978.

MARÉ, GERHARD, and GEORGINA HAMILTON. *An Appetite for Power: Buthelezi's Inkatha and South Africa.* Johannesburg: Ravan Press, 1987.

MARKS, SHULA. *The Ambiguities of Dependence in South Africa: Class, Nationalism, and the State in Twentieth Century Natal.* Johannesburg: Ravan Press, 1986.

MARTIN, DAVID, and PHYLLIS JOHNSON. *The Struggle for Zimbabwe: The Chimurenga War.* London: Faber and Faber, 1981.

MARX, ANTHONY W. *Lessons of Struggle: South African Internal Opposition, 1960–1990.* New York: Oxford University Press, 1992.

MASSIE, ROBERT KINLOCH (Jr.). *Moral Deliberation and Policy Formulation: Eight Institutional Investors' Approaches to South African Disinvestment.* Unpublished doctoral dissertation. Harvard Graduate School of Business Administration, 1989.

MATANZIMA, KAIZER D. *Independence My Way.* Pretoria: Foreign Affairs Association, 1976.

MATTES, ROBERT. *The Election Book: Judgement and Choice in South Africa's 1994 Election.* Cape Town: IDASA Public Information Center, 1995.

MATTHEWS, JOHN B., KENNETH E. GOODPASTER, and LAURA L. NASH. *Policies and Person: A Casebook in Business Ethics.* New York: McGraw-Hill, 1985.

MATTHEWS, Z. K. *Freedom for My People.* London: Rex Collins, 1981.

MBALI, ZOLILE. *The Churches and Racism: A Black South African Perspective.* London: SCM Press, 1987.

MCCOY, CHARLES. *The Management of Values: The Ethical Difference in Corporate Performance and Policy.* London: Pitman, 1985.

MCCRAW, THOMAS K. *Prophets of Regulation.* Cambridge: Harvard University Press, 1984.

MCGREGOR, DOUGLAS M. *The Human Side of Enterprise.* New York: McGraw-Hill, 1985.

MCHENRY, DONALD. *United States Firms in South Africa.* Study Project on External Investment in South Africa and Namibia (South-West Africa). Bloomington: African Studies Program, Indiana University, for Africa Publications Trust, 1975.

MEANS, GARDINER C. *The Corporate Revolution in America.* New York: Collier Books, 1964.

MEER, FATIMA. *Higher than Hope: The Authorized Biography of Nelson Mandela.* New York: Harper and Row, 1990.

MELI, FRANCIS. *South Africa Belongs to Us: A History of the ANC.* London: James Currey, 1988.

MEREDITH, MARTIN. *In the Name of Apartheid: South Africa in the Postwar Era.* New York: Harper and Row, 1988.

MERMELSTEIN, DAVID, ed. *The Anti-Apartheid Reader.* New York: Grove Press, 1987.

MICOU, ANNE MCKINSTRY. *The U.S. Independent Sector As It Relates to South African Initiatives: A Directory.* New York: Institute of International Education, June 1993.

MIDGLEY, KENNETH, ed. *Management Accountability and Corporate Governance.* London: Macmillan, 1982. See "The Question of Ownership and the Role of Institutional Shareholders" and "Social Responsibility and the Institutional Investor."

MILES, RAYMOND E., and CHARLES C. SNOW. *Organizational Strategy, Structure, and Process.* New York: McGraw-Hill, 1978.

MILLSTEIN, IRA M., and SALEM M. KATSH. *The Limits of Corporate Power.* New York: Macmillan, 1981.

MINNAAR, ANTHONY, et al., eds. *The Hidden Hand: Covert Operations in South Africa.* Pretoria: Human Sciences Research Council, 1994.

MINTER, WILLIAM. *King Solomon's Mines Revisited: Western Interests and the Burdened History of Southern Africa.* New York: Basic Books, 1986.

MINTZBERG, HENRY. *The Nature of Managerial Work.* New York: Harper and Row, 1973.

———. *The Structuring of Organizations.* Englewood Cliffs, N.J.: Prentice-Hall, 1979.

———. *Power in and around Organizations.* Englewood Cliffs, N.J.: Prentice-Hall, 1983.

MOODIE, T. DUNBAR. *The Rise of Afrikanerdrom: Power, Apartheid, and the Afrikaner Civil Religion.* Los Angeles: University of California Press, 1975.

MORANO, ROY W. *The Protestant Challenge to Corporate America: Issues of Social Responsibility.* Ann Arbor: UMI Research Press, 1984.

MORRIS, ALDON D. *The Origins of the Civil Rights Movement.* New York: Free Press, 1984.

MORRIS, ROGER. *Uncertain Greatness: Henry Kissinger and American Foreign Policy.* New York: Harper and Row, 1977.

MOSALA, ITUMELENG J., and BUTI TLHAGALE, eds. *The Unquestionable Right to Be Free: Black Theology from South Africa.* Maryknoll, N.Y.: Orbis Books, 1986.

MOSKOWITZ, MILTON, ed., with MICHAEL KATZ and ROBERT LEVERING. *Everybody's Business: An Almanac.* New York: Harper and Row, 1980.

MTOLO, BRUNO. *Umkhonto We Sizwe: The Road to the Left.* Durban: Drakensberg Press, 1966.

MYERS, DESAIX III. *Labor Practices of U.S. Corporations in South Africa.* New York: Praeger, 1977.

———, et al. *U.S. Business in South Africa: The Economic, Political, and Moral Issues.* Bloomington: University of Indiana Press, 1980.

MYRDAL, GUNNAR. *An American Dilemma: The Negro Problem and Modern Democracy.* New York: Harper and Row, 1944.

MZALA. *Gatsha Buthelezi: Chief with a Double Agenda.* London: Zed Books, 1988.

NADER, RALPH, MARK GREEN, and JOEL SELIGMAN. *Taming the Giant Corporation.* New York: Norton, 1976.

NATTRASS, JILL. *The South African Economy: Its Growth and Change.* 2nd ed. Cape Town: Oxford University Press, 1988.

Nedbank Limited. *South Africa, an appraisal: The Sovereign Risk Criteria.* Johannesburg: Nedbank Group Economic Unit, 1977.

NIELSEN, WALDEMAR. *Great Powers and Africa.* New York: Praeger, 1969.

———. *The Big Foundations.* New York: Columbia University Press, 1972.

———. *The Golden Donors: A New Anatomy of the Great Foundations.* New York: Dutton, 1985.

NIXON, RICHARD M. *The Memoirs of Richard Nixon.* New York: Grosset and Dunlap, 1978.

NOVAK, MICHAEL. *The Spirit of Democratic Capitalism.* New York: Simon and Schuster, 1982.

————, and JOHN W. COOPER, eds. *The Corporation: A Theological Inquiry.* Proceedings of the third annual seminar sponsored by the American Enterprise Institute and Syracuse University Department of Religion. Washington, D.C.: American Enterprise Institute, 1981.

NÜRNBERGER, KLAUS, et al., eds. *The Cost of Reconciliation in South Africa.* National Initiative for Reconciliation reader number 1. Pietermaritzburg: Encounter Publications, 1988.

————. *Conflict and the Quest for Justice.* National Initiative for Reconciliation reader number 2. Pietermaritzburg: Encounter Publications, 1989.

————. *A Democratic Vision for South South Africa: Political Realism and Christian Responsibility.* National Initiative for Reconciliation reader number 3. Pietermaritzburg: Encounter Publications, 1991.

OLIVER, ROLAND, and J. D. FAGE. *A Short History of Africa.* 6th ed. London: Penguin Books, 1988.

O'MEARA, DANIEL. *Volkskapitalisme: Class, Capital, and Ideology in the Development of Afrikaner Nationalism, 1934–1948.* New York: Cambridge University Press, 1983.

OMOND, ROGER. *The Apartheid Handbook: A Guide to South Africa's Everyday Racial Policies.* 2nd ed. London: Penguin Books, 1986.

ORKIN, MARK. *Disinvestment, the Struggle, and the Future: What Black South Africans Really Think.* Johannesburg: Ravan Press, 1986.

————, ed. *Sanctions against Apartheid.* Cape Town: David Philip, 1989.

OTTAWAY, DAVID. *Chained Together: Mandela, de Klerk, and the Struggle to Remake South Africa.* New York: Random House, Times Books, 1993.

PALLISTER, DAVID, et al. *South Africa Inc.: The Oppenheimer Empire.* Braamfontein: Lowry Publishers, 1987.

PATON, ALAN. *Cry, the Beloved Country.* New York: Scribner's, 1950.

PEART-BINNS, JOHN S. *Archbishop Joost de Blank: Scourge of Apartheid.* London: Muller, Blond, and White, 1987.

PENNINGS, JOHANNES M., ed. *Organizational Strategy and Change.* San Francisco: Jossey-Bass, 1985.

PERROW, CHARLES. *Complex Organizations: A Critical Essay.* 3rd ed. New York: Random House, 1986.

PETERSEN, JOHN E. *A Summary of State and Local Government Public Employee Retirement System Investment Practices and Policies.* Washington, D.C.: Government Finance Officers Association, December 1980.

PFEFFER, JEFFREY. *Organizations and Organization Theory.* London: Pitman, 1982.

PIENAAR, S. *Glo in U Volk: Dr. D. F. Malan as Redenaar.* Kaapstad: Tafelberg-Uitgewers, 1964.

————, and ANTHONY SAMPSON. *South Africa: Two Views of Separate Development.* London: Oxford University Press, 1960.

PITYANA, BARNEY N., and CHARLES VILLA-VICENCIO, eds. *Being the Church in South Africa Today.* Johannesburg: South African Council of Churches, 1995.

PITYANA, BARNEY N., et al., eds. *Bounds of Possibility: The Legacy of Steve Biko and Black Consciousness.* Cape Town: David Philip, 1991.

POLLEY, JAMES A., ed. *The Freedom Charter and the Future.* Proceedings of the National IDASA Conference on the Freedom Charter and the Future, Cape Town, July 1988. Cape Town: A. D. Donker Publisher, 1988.

POTTINGER, BRIAN. *The Imperial Presidency: P. W. Botha, the First Ten Years.* Johannesburg: Southern Book Publishers, 1988.

Practising Law Institute. *Stockholder Derivative Actions: The Investor and the Corporation, New Developments and Tactics.* New York: Practising Law Institute, 1983.

――――. *Competitive Advantage.* New York: Free Press, 1985.

PRATT, JOHN W., and RICHARD J. ZECKHAUSER, eds. *Principals and Agents: The Structure of Business.* Boston: Harvard Business School Press, 1985.

QUINN, JAMES B. *Strategies for Change.* Illinois: Richard D. Irwin, 1981.

RAZIS, VIC. *The American Connection: The Influence of United States Business on South Africa.* New York: St. Martin's Press, 1986.

Reader's Digest Association. *Illustrated Guide to Southern Africa.* 4th ed. Cape Town: Reader's Digest Association, 1985.

REES, MERVYN, and CHRIS DAY. *Muldergate: The Story of the Info Scandal.* Johannesburg: Macmillan South Africa, 1980.

Republic of South Africa, Consular Office. *Prospects and Progress in South Africa.* Pretoria: Government Information Office, 1976.

REYNOLDS, ANDREW, ed. *Election '94 South Africa: The Campaigns, Results, and Future Prospects.* Cape Town: David Philip, 1994.

ROETHLISBERGER, F. J. *The Elusive Phenomena.* Cambridge: Harvard University Press, 1977.

ROGERS, BARBARA. *White Wealth and Black Poverty: American Investments in Southern Africa.* Westport, Conn.: Greenwood Press, 1976.

ROSENTHAL, ERIC. *Stars and Stripes in Africa.* Cape Town: National Books Limited, 1968.

ROTBERG, ROBERT. *The Founder: Cecil Rhodes and the Pursuit of Power.* New York: Oxford University Press, 1988.

RUMELT, RICHARD P. *Strategy, Structure, and Economic Performance.* Boston: Harvard Business School Press, 1974.

RYAN, COLLEEN. *Beyers Naudé: Pilgrimage of Faith.* Cape Town: David Philip, 1990.

SACHS, ALBIE. *Justice in South Africa.* Berkeley: University of California Press, 1973.

――――. *The Soft Vengeance of a Freedom Fighter.* London: Paladin, 1991.

――――. *Advancing Human Rights in South Africa.* Cape Town: Oxford University Press, 1992.

SCHELLING, THOMAS C. *International Economics.* Boston: Allyn and Bacon, 1958.

SCHLATTER, RICHARD. *Private Property: The History of an Idea.* New Brunswick: Rutgers University Press, 1951.

SCHLESINGER, ARTHUR M. JR. *Robert Kennedy and His Times.* Boston: Houghton Mifflin, 1978.

――――. *A Thousand Days.* New York: Houghton Mifflin, 1965.

SCHMIDT, ELIZABETH. *Decoding Corporate Camouflage: U.S. Business Support for Apartheid.* Washington, D.C.: Institute for Policy Studies, 1980.

SCHNEIDMAN, WITNEY WRIGHT. *American Foreign Policy and the Fall of the Portuguese Empire, 1961–1976.* Unpublished doctoral dissertation, University of Southern California, 1987.

SCHOLTZ, J. J. J. *Fighter and Reformer: Extracts from the Speeches of P. W. Botha.* Pretoria: South African Bureau of Information, 1989.

SEIDMAN, ANN W. *South Africa and Multinational Corporations.* Westport, Conn.: Lawrence Hill, 1978.

――――. *The Roots of Crisis in Southern Africa.* Trenton, N.J.: Africa World Press, 1985.

SELZNICK, PHILIP. *Leadership in Administration.* New York: Harper and Row, 1957.

SERFONTEIN, J. H. P. *Apartheid, Change, and the NG Kerk.* Emmarentia, South Africa: Taurus Publishers, 1982.

SETHI, F. PRAKASH. *Business Corporations and the Black Man: An Analysis of Social Conflict, the Kodak-FIGHT Controversy.* Scranton: Chandler Publishing Company, 1970.

————. *Up Against the Corporate Wall.* Englewood Cliffs, N.J.: Prentice-Hall, 1971.

————. *The South African Quagmire: In Search of a Peaceful Path of Democratic Pluralism.* Cambridge, Mass.: Ballinger Publishing, 1987.

SIMON, HERBERT. *Administrative Behavior.* 3rd ed. New York: Free Press, 1976.

SIMON, JOHN, CHARLES POWERS, and JON GUNNEMANN. *The Ethical Investor.* New Haven: Yale University Press, 1972.

SITKOFF, HARVARD. *The Struggle for Black Equality, 1954–1992.* Rev. ed. New York: Hill and Wang, 1993.

SJOLLEMA, BALDWIN. *Isolating Apartheid.* Geneva: World Council of Churches, 1982.

SLOCUM, JOSHUA. *Sailing Alone around the World.* 1900. Reprint, New York: Dover Publications, 1956.

SMITH, N. CRAIG. *Morality and the Market: Consumer Pressure for Corporate Accountability.* London: Routledge, 1989.

SNUTS, DENE, et al., ed. *The Purple Shall Govern: A South African A to Z of Nonviolent Action.* Cape Town: Centre for Intergroup Studies and Oxford University Press, 1991.

South African Institute of Race Relations [SAIRR]. *Race Relations Survey.* All years from 1960 to 1994–1995. Cited as SAIRR, *Survey.*

SOUTHALL, ROGER. *South Africa's Transkei: The Political Economy of an "Independent" Bantustan.* New York: Monthly Review Press, 1983.

SPARKS, ALLISTER. *The Mind of South Africa.* New York: Knopf, 1990.

SPENCE, J. E. *The Political and Military Framework.* The Study Project on External Investment in South Africa and Namibia (South-West Africa). London: African Publications Trust, 1975.

STOCKWELL, JOHN. *In Search of Enemies: A CIA Story.* New York: Norton, 1978.

STRANGWAYES-BOOTH, JOANNA. *The Cricket in the Thorn Tree: Helen Suzman and the Progressive Party of South Africa.* London: Hutchinson and Company, 1976.

STREEK, BARRY, and RICHARD WICKSTEED. *Render under Kaiser: A Transkei Dossier.* Johannesburg: Ravan Press, 1981.

SULLIVAN, LEON H. *Build Brother Build.* Philadelphia: Macrae Smith Company, 1969.

SUZMAN, HELEN. *In No Uncertain Terms: A South African Memoir.* New York: Knopf, 1993.

SWILLING, MARK, RICHARD HUMPHRIES, and KHEHLA SHUBANE, eds. *Apartheid City in Transition.* London: Oxford University Press, 1991.

TALNER, LAUREN. *The Origins of Shareholder Activism.* Washington, D.C.: Investor Responsibility Research Center, 1983.

TAMARKIN, M. *The Making of Zimbabwe: Decolonization in Regional and International Politics.* London: Frank Cass and Company, 1990.

TEMKIN, BEN. *Gatsha Buthelezi: Zulu Statesman.* Cape Town: Purnell, 1976.

THOMPSON, LEONARD. *The Political Mythology of Apartheid.* New Haven: Yale University Press, 1985.

————. *A History of South Africa.* New Haven: Yale University Press, 1990.

TRIPLETT, THOMAS, and SUSAN JON MOSCH. *Tools for the Strategic Investing of Pension Funds.* Minneapolis: Minnesota Project, November 1982. 618 E. 22nd Street, Minneapolis, Minnesota, 55404.

TUCKER, BOB, and BRUCE R. SCOTT, eds. *South Africa: Prospects for Successful Transition.* Cape Town: Juta and Company, 1992.

TURNER, RICHARD. *The Eye of the Needle.* Johannesburg: Ravan Press, 1980.

TUTU, DESMOND MPILO. *Hope and Suffering.* Grand Rapids, Mich.: Eerdmans, 1983.

———. *The Rainbow People of God: The Making of a Peaceful Revolution.* New York: Doubleday, 1994.

TYLER, JOSIAH. *Forty Years among the Zulus.* Boston: Congregational Sunday School and Publishing Society, 1891.

United Nations, International Labour Office. *Apartheid and Labour.* Geneva: International Labour Office, 1983.

VANDENBOSCH, AMRY. *South Africa and the World: The Foreign Policy of Apartheid.* Lexington: University of Kentucky Press, 1970.

VAN RENSBURG, J. F. J. *Their Paths Crossed Mine: Memoirs of the Commandant General of the Ossewa Brandwag.* Cape Town: Central News Agency, 1956.

VILLA-VICENCIO, CHARLES. *Trapped in Apartheid: A Socio-Theological History of the English-Speaking Churches.* Cape Town: David Philip, 1988.

———. *Civil Disobedience and Beyond: Law, Resistance, and Religion in South Africa.* Cape Town: David Philip, 1990.

———. *The Spirit of Hope: Conversations on Politics, Religion, and Values.* Braamfontein: Skotaville Publishers, n.d.

———. *A Theology of Reconstruction: Nation-Building and Human Rights.* New York: Cambridge University Press, 1992.

———, and JOHN W. DE GRUCHY, eds. *Resistance and Hope: South African Essays in Honour of Beyers Naudé.* Grand Rapids, Mich.: Eerdmans, 1985.

VOGEL, DAVID. *Lobbying the Corporation: Citizen Challenges to Business Authority.* New York: Basic Books, 1979.

WALSHE, PETER. *The Church versus State in South Africa: The Case of the Christian Institute.* London: C. Hurst and Company, 1983.

WALTERS, RONALD W. *South Africa and the Bomb: Responsibility and Deterrence.* Lexington, Mass.: Lexington Books, 1987.

WARD, HARRY F. *The Social Creed of the Churches.* New York: Abingdon Press, 1914.

WASHINGTON, JAMES M., ed. *A Testament of Hope.* San Francisco: Harper and Row, 1986.

WHITE, THEODORE H. *The Making of the President, 1960.* New York: Atheneum, 1961.

———. *The Making of the President, 1964.* New York: Atheneum, 1965.

WILKSINS, IVOR, and HANS STRYDOM. *The Super-Afrikaners: Inside the Afrikaner Broederbond.* Johannesburg: Jonathan Ball, 1978.

WILLIAMS, BERNARD. *Ethics and the Limits of Philosophy.* Cambridge: Harvard University Press, 1985.

WILLIAMS, G. MENNEN. *Africa for the Africans.* Grand Rapids, Mich.: Eerdmans, 1969.

WILLIAMS, OLIVER F., and JOHN HOUCK, eds. *The Judeo-Christian Vision and the Modern Corporation.* Notre Dame: University of Notre Dame Press, 1982.

———. *The Apartheid Crisis: How Can We Do Justice in a Land of Violence?* San Francisco: Harper and Row, 1986.

WILLIAMSON, OLIVER E. *Markets and Hierarchies.* New York: Free Press, 1975.

WILMORE, GAYRAUD S., and JAMES H. CONE, eds. *Black Theology: A Documentary History, 1966–1979.* Maryknoll, N.Y.: Orbis Books, 1990.

WILSON, FRANCIS. *Labour in the South African Gold Mines, 1911–1969.* Cambridge: Cambridge University Press, 1972.

———, and MAMPHELA RAMPHELE. *Uprooting Poverty: The South African Challenge.*

Report of the Second Carnegie Inquiry into Poverty and Development in Southern Africa. New York: Norton, 1989.

WOFFORD, HARRIS. *Of Kennedys and Kings.* New York: Farrar Straus Giroux, 1980.

WOLPE, HAROLD. *Race, Class, and the Apartheid State.* Trenton, N.J.: Africa World Press, 1988.

WOODS, DONALD. *Biko.* London: Paddington Press, 1978.

————. *Asking for Trouble: The Education of a White South African.* Boston: Beacon Press, 1980.

World Council of Churches, Programme to Combat Racism. *From Cottesloe to Cape Town: Challenges for the Church in a Post-Apartheid South Africa.* Geneva: World Council of Churches, 1991.

YOST, CHARLES. *The Conduct and Misconduct of Foreign Affairs.* New York: Random House, 1972.

ARTICLES

Most article references are contained in the notes. The following is a selected list of additional articles that were consulted.

ACKERMAN, ROBERT. "Public Responsibility and the Businessman: A Review of the Literature." Harvard Business School Working Paper 4-371-520.

ANDREWS, KENNETH R. "Corporate Strategy As a Vital Function of the Board." *Harvard Business Review,* November–December 1981.

BERNSTEIN, SHELDON E., and HENRY G. FISCHER. "The Regulation of the Solicitation of Proxies: Some Reflections on Corporate Democracy." *University of Chicago Law Review* 7 (1940): 226.

BLACK, P. A., and J. H. COOPER. "Economic Sanctions and Interest Group Analysis: Some Reservations." *South African Journal of Economics* 57 (June 1989).

BLASHILL, JOHN. "The Proper Role of U.S. Corporations in South Africa." *Fortune,* July 1972.

BLUMBERG, PHILLIP I. "Introduction to the Politicalization of the Corporation." *Conference Board Record,* 1972.

BUTHELEZI, MANAS. "Six Theses: Theological Problems of Evangelism in the South African Context." *Journal of Theology of Southern Africa* 3 (June 1973).

CAMPBELL, BEVERLY ROSS, and WILLIAM JOSEPHSON. "Public Pension Fund Trustees' Pursuit of Social Goals." *Journal of Urban and Contemporary Law* 24 (1983): 43–120.

CAPLIN, MORTIMER M. "Proxies, Annual Meeting, and Corporate Democracy." *Virginia Law Review* 37 (1951): 653. (See also "Stockholder Participation in Corporate Affairs" in the same issue.)

CARSTENS, KENNETH. Testimony before the African Subcommittee of the Committee on Foreign Affairs of the United States House of Representatives. Manuscript, March 1966.

CHETTLE, JOHN. "The Evolution of U.S. Policy toward South Africa." *Modern Age,* Summer 1972.

CLARK, ROBERT C. "Agency Costs versus Fiduciary Duties." In John W. Pratt and Richard J. Zeckhauser, eds. *Principals and Agents: The Structure of Business.* Boston: Harvard Business School Press, 1985.

Congressional Black Caucus. "The African-American Manifesto on Southern Africa." *Black Scholar,* January–February 1977.

CROCKER, CHESTER A. "The Nixon-Kissinger National Security Council System,

1969–1972: A Study in Foreign Policy Management." In vol. 6, Appendices, of Commission on the Organization of the Government for the Conduct of Foreign Policy. Washington, D.C.: GPO, 1975.

———. "South Africa: Strategy for Change." *Foreign Affairs* 59 (Winter 1980–1981): 323–51.

———, and WILLIAM H. LEWIS. "Missing Opportunities in Africa." *Foreign Policy* (1979–1980): 34–37.

DODD, E. MERRICK Jr. "For Whom Are Corporate Managers Trustees?" *Harvard Law Review* 45 (1932): 1145. See also response by A. A. Berle Jr., *Harvard Law Review* 45 (1932): 1365.

DOUGLAS, WILLIAM O. "Directors Who Do Not Direct." *Harvard Law Review* 47 (1934): 1305.

DOWLING, JOHN, and JEFFERY PFEFFER. "Organizational Legitimacy: Social Values and Organizational Behavior." *Pacific Sociological Review,* January 1975.

DUBIN, ROBERT. "Theory Building in Applied Areas." In Marvin D. Dunnette, ed. *Handbook of Industrial and Organizational Psychology.* New York: John Wiley, 1983.

DUNLOP, JOHN T., ALFRED D. CHANDLER Jr., GEORGE P. SHULTZ, and IRVING S. SHAPIRO. "Business and Public Policy." *Harvard Business Review,* November–December 1979.

DU PLESSIS, LOURENS M. "Between Reform and Transformation: Shalom for South Africa?" Paper presented at the Consultation on Evangelicals and American Public Life, Philadelphia, May 4–6, 1989.

Dutch Reformed Churches of South Africa. "Statements on Race Relations." Johannesburg: Information Bureau of the Dutch Reformed Church, November 1960.

DU TOIT, ANDRÉ. "No Chosen People: The Myth of the Calvinist Origins of Afrikaner Nationalism and Racial Ideology." *American Historical Review* 88.4 (October 1983): 920–52.

EISENBERG, MELVIN. "The Legal Roles of Shareholders and Management in Modern Corporate Decision-making." *California Law Review* 57 (1969).

EMERSON, F. D. "The Roles of Management and Shareholder in Corporate Government." *Law and Contemporary Problems* 23 (1958): 231.

ETZIONI, AMITAI. "The Case for a Multiple Utility Conception." *Economics and Philosophy* 2 (1986).

FIERCE, MILFRED C. "Black and White American Opinions towards South Africa." *Journal of Modern Africa Studies* 20.4 (1982).

FRIEDMAN, MILTON. "The Social Responsibility of Business Is to Increase Its Profits." *New York Times Magazine,* September 13, 1970.

GARRETT, RAY. "Attitudes on Corporate Democracy: A Critical Analysis." *Northwestern University Law Review* 51 (1956): 310.

GILBERT, LEWIS D. "Wanted: A Program for Fair Corporate Suffrage." *Investor,* June 1953.

GOODE, WILLIAM. "Individual Choice and Social Order." In James Short, ed. *The Social Fabric.* Beverly Hills: Sage Publications, 1984. Based on papers presented at the 79th Annual Meeting of the American Sociological Association.

HOUSER, GEORGE. "Relations between the United States and South Africa." *Black Scholar,* November–December 1984.

JACKSON, JESSE. "Don't Adjust to Apartheid." *Black Scholar,* November–December 1984.

JACOBY, NEIL H. "The Myth of the Corporate Economy: A Statistical Profile of the Evolution of the American Corporate Enterprise." *Conference Board Record,* June 1971.

JENSEN, MICHAEL C., and WILLIAM H. MECKLING. "The Theory of the Firm: Managerial Behavior, Agency Costs, and Ownership Structure." *Journal of Financial Economics* 3 (1976): 305–60.

———. "The Market for Corporate Control: The Scientific Evidence." *Journal of Financial Economics* 11 (1983): 5–50.

———. "Takeovers: Folklore and Science." *Harvard Business Review,* November–December 1984.

KATZ, WILBER G. "The Philosophy of MidCentury Corporation Statutes." *Law and Contemporary Problems* 23 (1958): 177.

KAYSEN, CARL. "The Social Significance of the Modern Corporation." *American Economic Review Proceedings* 47 (May 1957): 311.

KIEWIET, CORNELIS DE. "The Revolution That Disappeared." *Virginia Quarterly Review* 46.2 (Spring 1970).

LANCASTER, PAUL. "Champion among the Heathen: An American Missionary Caught in South African Conflict 140 Years Ago." *American Heritage* 29.2 (1978).

LANDAU, PETER. "Do Institutional Investors Have a Social Responsibility?" *Institutional Investor,* July 1970.

LEVITT, THEODORE. "The Dangers of Social Responsibility." *Harvard Business Review,* 36 (1958): 41.

LINDBLOM, CHARLES E. "The Science of Muddling Through." *Public Administration Review* 19 (1959): 79–88.

LINDBLOM, CRISTI K. "The Concept of Organizational Legitimacy and Its Implications for Corporate Social Responsibility Disclosure." Working paper. Sarasota, Fla.: American Accounting Association, 1983.

MANNE, HENRY G. "The 'Higher Criticism' of the Modern Corporation." *Columbia Law Review* 62 (1962): 399.

———. "Some Theoretical Aspects of Share Voting." *Columbia Law Review* 64 (1964): 1427.

———. "Our Two Corporation Systems: Law and Economic." *Virginia Law Review* 53 (March 1967): 259.

MANNING, BAYLESS. "Corporate Power and Individual Freedom: Some General Analysis and Particular Reservations." *Northwestern Law Review* 55 (1960): 38.

MANNING, CHARLES W. "In Defense of Apartheid." *Foreign Affairs,* October 1964.

MASSIE, ROBERT K. "The Jameson Raid and the Kruger Telegram." In *Dreadnought: Britain, Germany, and the Coming of the Great War.* New York: Random House, 1991.

MASSIE, ROBERT KINLOCH. "Local Churches in the New South Africa." *Journal of Theology for Southern Africa* 85 (December 1993).

MILLER, ROBERTA BALSTAD. "Science and Society in the Early Career of H. F. Verwoerd." *Journal of Southern African Studies* 10.4 (December 1993).

"The Moral History of U.S. Business." *Fortune,* May 1949.

MUNGER, EDWIN S. "Christians and Race Relations in South Africa." Part 1, "The Anglican Church." Part 2, "The Dutch Reformed Church." New York: American Universities Field Staff Reports Service, January and March, 1961.

PAUL, KAREN. "The Inadequacy of Sullivan Reporting." *Business and Society Review* (1985).

PFEFFER, JEFFREY. "The Amibiguity of Leadership." *Academy of Management Review* (January 1977): 104–12.

PORTER, MICHAEL. "The Contributions of Industrial Organization to Strategic Management." *Academy of Management Review* (October 1981): 609–20.

RAZIS, VIC. "Early Perceptions of United States Corporations Regarding the Sullivan Principles." *IR Journal* (Third Quarter 1987).

SCHOMER, HOWARD. "South Africa: Beyond Fair Employment." *Harvard Business Review,* May–June 1983.

SCHWARTZ, DONALD E. "Towards New Corporate Goals: Co-Existence with Society." *Georgetown Law Review* 60 (1971): 57.

———, and ELLIOTT J. WEISS. "An Assessment of the SEC Shareholder Proposal Rule." *Georgetown Law Journal* 65.3 (February 1977).

SEIDMAN, ANN. "Why U.S. Corporations Should Get Out of South Africa." *Issue* 9.1–2 (1979).

SIMON, HERBERT A. "Rational Decision Making in Business Organizations." *American Economic Review* 69.4 (1979): 493–513.

TRAUB, JAMES. "Shareholder Power: A Swift Kick in the Corporate Shins." *Saturday Review,* November 11, 1978.

United Nations. "Apartheid in South Africa." Summary of the Report of the United Nations Special Committee on the Policies of Apartheid of the Government of South Africa. New York: United Nations Office of Public Information, 1963.

VAN WYK, KOOS, and M. ANTON BELOW. "The Debate on South Africa's Strategic Minerals Revisited." *Comparative Strategy* 7 (1988).

WAGNER, WAYNE H., ALLEN EMKIN, and RICHARD L. DIXON. "South Africa Divestiture: The Investment Issues." *Financial Analysts Journal,* November–December 1984.

World Student Christian Federation. "The Banks and Apartheid." An open letter from the World Student Christian Federation. New York: University Christian Movement, 1968.

WRAPP, H. EDWARD. "Good Managers Don't Make Policy Decisions." *Harvard Business Review,* September–October 1967.

WRIGHT, KENNETH M. "Social Concerns, Public Policy, and Life Insurance Investments." Presentation to the 5th Biennial Meeting of the Pacific Insurance Conference, September 1971.

CASE STUDY SOURCES

EPISCOPAL CHURCH

Church and Society: Social Policy of the Episcopal Church. Executive Council and General Convention, December 1967–April 1979. New York: The Executive Council of the Episcopal Church, 1979. Supplements, December 1979, February, June, and November 1980.

Journal of General Convention of the Protestant Episcopal Church in the United States for the years 1964, 1967, 1970, 1973, 1976, 1982, 1985, and 1988.

MARTIN, HAROLD C. *Outlasting Marble and Brass: The History of the Church Pension Fund.* (New York: Church Hymnal Corporation, 1986.

Minutes, annual reports, and reports to General Convention of the Committee on Social Responsibility in Investments, 1970–1987.

Minutes and other documents from the Committee on Fiduciary and Social Responsibility in Investments of the Church Pension Funds, 1972–1987.

UNITED CHURCH OF CHRIST

CHAVIS, BENJAMIN F., and AUDREY CHAPMAN SMOCK, eds. *Implementation of the United Church of Christ Full Divestment of All Financial Resources from All Corporations Doing Business in South Africa.* Committee Report to the Sixteenth General Synod, June 1987.

Constitution and By-Laws, 1984 edition.

Corporate Social Responsibility Actions. Reports by United Church Board for Homeland Ministries, United Church Board for World Ministries, Pensions Board—United Church of Christ, and United Church Foundation to the Twelfth (1977–1979), Thirteenth (1979–1981), Fourteenth (1981–1983), and Fifteenth (1983–1985) General Synods of the United Church of Christ.

Corporate Social Responsibility Updates, 1982–1984.

Fifteenth General Synod. *Pronouncement on Full Divestment of All Financial Resources from All Corporations Doing Business in South Africa,* 1985.

"The History and Program of the United Church of Christ." 5th ed. New York: United Church of Christ Press, 1986.

"The Role of Transnational Business in Mass Economic Development." A Working Group report prepared at the request of the United Church Board for Homeland Ministries, United Church Board for World Ministries, Pensions Board—United Church of Christ, United Church of Christ Center for Social Action, and United Church Foundation, February 1, 1975.

HARVARD UNIVERSITY

Advisory Committee on Shareholder Responsibility

ASCR annual reports, 1973–1987.

Report on South Africa Shareholder Responsibility, Spring 1978.

ACSR Report on Portfolio Companies with Operations in South Africa, March 30, 1979.

Corporation Committee on Shareholder Responsibility CCSR annual and midyear reports, 1973–1987.

CCSR Progress Report on Policy Implementation Regarding Portfolio Companies Doing Business in South Africa, February 13, 1985.

Report of the Committee on University Relations with Corporate Enterprise, January 1971.

Statements and Open Letters by President Derek Bok and/or the Fellows of Harvard College

Statement of the President and Fellows of Harvard College, April 1978.

"Reflections on the Ethical Responsibilities of the University in Society: An Open Letter to the Harvard Community," March 9, 1979.

"Reflections on the Divestment of Stock: An Open Letter to the Harvard Community," April 6, 1979.

"Reflections on Boycotts: An Open Letter to the Harvard Community," May 18, 1979.

"The Problem with Divestment," October 1984.

"The Crisis in South Africa: One University's Response," March 14, 1986.

Columbia University

The sections on Columbia University were based on a review of the key policy statements by the ad hoc investment committees, the president's office, and the board of trustees; on interviews with members of the administration and a review of proxy voting materials provided by the university; and on an examination of twenty years' worth of articles in the *Columbia Spectator*. Some of the most important documents include the following.

Ad Hoc Committee Regarding Investment in Companies with Operations in South Africa, report to the trustees, July 17, 1985.

Investment Policy Committee, Menelaos Hassialis, Chairman, 1970–1971, report (University Senate Archives).

McGill, William J. "Ethical Guidelines for Business Dealings, Investments, and Relations with Foreign Governments." Report to the Trustees Committee on Finance, March 23, 1977.

———. Letter from the president to members of the Columbia University community, May 3, 1978.

Press release by Columbia University public relations officer Fred Knubel, August 28, 1985.

Report of the Board of Trustees on Decision to Divest.

Standby Committee on University Investments in Corporate Securities, report, April 28, 1978.

University Senate Committee on Investments in Companies with Operations in South Africa, report, 1984.

TIAA-CREF

The primary materials on TIAA-CREF were the annual reports, the public statements of the proxy committee, the two reports submitted by Albert Wilson about his trips to South Africa, and copies of correspondence between William Greenough and various corporate executives included in the annual response by TIAA-CREF to the survey circulated by IRRC.

New York City

Correspondence between City Council President Carol Bellamy and various trustees of NYCERS.

New York City Employee's Retirement System, annual reports, 1984–1987.

Reports and other material received from the South African Investment Responsibility Unit.

Testimony and public statements by Comptroller Harrison Goldin, including the monthly newsletter put out by the comptroller's office.

New York State

Annual Reports (1985–1988), each of which includes several pages on the actions of the proxy committee and the Office of Investor Affairs.

Report of the New York State Senate Finance Committee, 1985.
Testimony and public statements by New York Governor Mario Cuomo.
Testimony and public statements by State Comptroller Edward V. Regan.
Testimony and public statements of Office of Investor Affairs Director Thomas Pandick.

OTHER ORGANIZATIONAL DOCUMENTS

AMERICAN COMMITTEE ON AFRICA

BOYER, SANDY. "Divesting from Apartheid: A Summary of State and Municipal Legislative Action on South Africa," March 1983.
MassDivest. "Make It in Massachusetts, Not in South Africa: How We Won Divestment Legislation," March 1983.

BUSINESS ROUNDTABLE

Statement on Corporate Responsibility, 1981.
Report on Boards of Directors.

INTERFAITH CENTER ON CORPORATE RESPONSIBILITY

BARNES, HANNAH, and FANTU CHERU. *A History of ICCR Resolutions on South Africa,* 1984.
Church Investments, Corporations, and Southern Africa. New York: Corporate Information Center, 1973.
Church Proxy Resolutions, annual editions, 1974–1995.
The Corporate Examiner (monthly newsletter), 1974–1995.

INVESTOR RESPONSIBILITY RESEARCH CENTER

Annual Reports, 1975–1990.
COOPER, ALISON. *U.S. Business in South Africa: A Directory of U.S. Corporations with Business Links to South Africa* (various years).
Divestment Action Roundup, November 1987.
"Does the Signing of the Sullivan Principles Matter? A Comparison of the Labor Practices and Public Affairs Activities of Signers and Non-Signers," June 1985.
GRAY, HILLEL. "New Directions in the Investment and Control of Pension Funds," 1983.
HAUCK, DAVID. "Can Pretoria Be Moved? The Emergence of Business Activism in South Africa," 1986.
South Africa Review Service.
"U.S. Corporate Withdrawal from South Africa: The Likely Impact on Political Change," August 1986.
VOORHES, MEG. "Black South African Views on Disinvestment," July 1986.
"What Happens When U.S. Companies Sell Their South African Operations?," May 1987.

Presbyterian Church

Boycotts: Policy Analysis and Criteria. New York: General Assembly Mission Council, United Presbyterian Church, 1979.

"Declaration of Conscience on South Africa and Namibia," 193rd General Assembly, 1981.

Investment Policy and Guidelines of the General Assembly Mission Board of the United Presbyterian Church in the U.S.A., adopted March 20, 1976.

UNITED STATES GOVERNMENT DOCUMENTS

Congress, Joint Economic Committee

U.S. Congress. Joint Economic Committee. *Abuses of Power.* Hearings before the Subcommittee on Priorities and Economy in Government. 94th Cong., 2nd sess., 1976.

House of Representatives

Committee on Banking, Finance, and Urban Affairs

U.S. Congress. House. Committee on Banking, Finance, and Urban Affairs. Subcommittee on Domestic Monetary Policy. *Impact of Withdrawal and Disinvestment from South Africa on the U.S. Economy.* Washington D.C.: GPO, 1985, 268 pp.

U.S. Congress. House. Committee on Banking, Finance, and Urban Affairs. Subcommittee on Financial Institutions, Supervision, Regulation, and Insurance. *South African Restrictions.* Washington, D.C.: GPO, 1983, 289 pp.

Committee on the District of Columbia

U.S. Congress. House. Committee on the District of Columbia. *U.S. Investments and Bank Loans in South Africa.* Staff report and supplemental material to the hearings and markups of January 31 and February 7, 1984. Serial no. 98-14. Washington, D.C.: GPO, 1985.

U.S. Congress. House. Committee on the District of Columbia. Subcommittee on Fiscal Affairs and Health. *South Africa Divestment.* Washington, D.C.: GPO, 1984.

Committee on Education and Labor

U.S. Congress. House. Committee on Education and Labor. *Pension Task Force Report on Public Employee Retirements Systems.* 95th Cong., 2nd sess., 1978.

Committee on Foreign Affairs/International Relations

U.S. Congress. House. Committee on Foreign Affairs. *Anti-Apartheid Act of 1985 together with Minority Views to Accompany H.R. 1460, Including Cost Estimate of the Congressional Budget Office.* 99th Cong., 1st sess. Report #99-76.

U.S. Congress. House. Committee on Foreign Affairs. *Enforcement of the U.S. Arms Embargo against South Africa.* 97th Cong., 2nd sess., March 1982.

U.S. Congress. House. Committee on Foreign Affairs. Subcommittee on Africa.

Developments in South Africa: United States Policy Responses. Hearing. 99th Cong., 2nd sess., March 12, 1986.

U.S. Congress. House. Committee on Foreign Affairs. Subcommittee on Africa. *Economic Sanctions and Their Potential Impact on U.S. Corporate Involvement in South Africa.* Washington, D.C.: GPO, 1985.

U.S. Congress. House. Committee on Foreign Affairs. Subcommittee on Africa. *Hearings on U.S. Business in South Africa, 1971–1973.* Washington, D.C.: GPO, 1973.

U.S. Congress. House. Committee on Foreign Affairs. Subcommittee on Africa. *Implementation of the U.S. Arms Embargo (against Portugal, South Africa, and Related Issues).* 93rd Cong., 1st sess., March 1973.

U.S. Congress. House. Committee on Foreign Affairs. Subcommittee on Africa. *United States–South African Relations.* 89th Cong., 2nd sess., 1966.

U.S. Congress. House. Committee on Foreign Affairs. Subcommittee on Human Rights and International Organizations and Subcommittee on Africa. *The Human Rights Situation in South Africa, Zaire, the Horn of Africa, and Uganda.* 98th Cong., 2nd sess., 1985.

U.S. Congress. House. Committee on Foreign Affairs. Subcommittee on International Economic Policy and Trade. *U.S. Corporate Activities in South Africa.* Washington, D.C.: GPO, 1983.

U.S. Congress. House. Committee on Foreign Affairs. Subcommittee on International Organizations and Movements. *Sanctions as an Instrumentality of the United Nations—Rhodesia As a Case Study.* Washington, D.C.: GPO, 1972.

U.S. Congress. House. Committee on International Relations. Subcommittee on Africa. *The Rhodesian Sanctions Bill.* 95th Cong., 1st sess., 1977.

U.S. Congress. House. Committee on International Relations. Subcommittees on Africa and International Economic Policy and Trade. *United States Private Investment in South Africa.* 95th Cong., 2nd sess., 1978.

U.S. Congress. House. Committee on International Relations. Subcommittee on Africa. *U.S. Policy toward South Africa.* 95th Cong., 1st sess., 1977.

SENATE

Committee on Banking, Housing, and Urban Affairs

U.S. Congress. Senate. Banking Committee. Subcommittee on Citizens and Shareholder Rights and Remedies. *The Role of the Shareholder in the Corporate World.* Hearings. 95th Cong., 1st sess., 1977.

U.S. Congress. Senate. Committee on Banking, Housing, and Urban Affairs. Subcommittee on Financial Institutions, Supervision, Regulation, and Insurance. *Anti-Apartheid Act of 1986.* Washington, D.C.: GPO, 1986.

U.S. Congress. Senate. Committee on Banking, Housing, and Urban Affairs. Subcommittee on Intergovernmental Relations. *Disclosure of Corporate Ownership.* Washington, D.C.: GPO, 1973.

U.S. Congress. Senate. Committee on Banking, Housing, and Urban Affairs. Subcommittee on International Finance and Monetary Policy. *The Anti-Apartheid Act of 1985.* Washington, D.C.: GPO, 1985.

U.S. Congress. Senate. Committee on Banking, Housing, and Urban Affairs. Subcommittee on Securities. *Institutional Investors Full Disclosure Act.* Washington, D.C.: GPO, 1973.

Committee on Foreign Relations

U.S. Congress. Senate. Committee on Foreign Relations. *Setting U.S. Policy toward Apartheid: Report together with Additional Views to Accompany S. 2701.* 99th Cong., 2nd sess., 1986, no. 99-370.

U.S. Congress. Senate. Committee on Foreign Relations. *Situation in South Africa.* Washington, D.C.: GPO, 1986.

U.S. Congress. Senate. Committee on Foreign Relations. *U.S. Policy toward South Africa.* Washington, D.C.: GPO, 1985.

U.S. Congress. Senate. Committee on Foreign Relations. Subcommittee on African Affairs. *U.S. Corporate Interests in South Africa.* 95th Cong., 2nd sess., January 1978.

U.S. Congress. Senate. Committee on Foreign Relations. Subcommittee on African Affairs. *U.S. Policy on South Africa.* 96th Cong., 2nd sess., 1980.

U.S. Congress. Senate. Committee on Foreign Relations. Subcommittee on African Affairs. *U.S. Policy toward South Africa.* 98th Cong., 2nd sess., 1982.

Committee on Finance

U.S. Congress. Senate. Committee on Finance. *The Role of Institutional Investors in the Stock Market.* Washington, D.C.: GPO, 1973.

U.S. Congress. Senate. Committee on Finance. Subcommittee on Financial Markets. *Financial Markets.* Washington, D.C.: GPO, 1973.

Committee on Governmental Affairs

U.S. Congress. Senate. Committee on Governmental Affairs. *Structure of Corporate Concentration: Institutional Shareholders and Interlocking Directorates among Major U.S. Corporations: A Staff Study.* Washington, D.C.: GPO, 1980.

U.S. Congress. Senate. Committee on Governmental Affairs. Subcommittee on Oversight of Government Management. *Department of Labor's Enforcement of the Employee Retirement Income Security Act (ERISA).* Washington, D.C.: GPO, 1985.

U.S. Congress. Senate. Committee on Governmental Affairs. Subcommittee on Reports, Accounting, and Management. *Voting Rights in Major Corporations.* Washington D.C.: GPO, 1978.

Committee on the Judiciary

U.S. Congress. Senate. Committee on the Judiciary. Subcommittee on Citizens and Shareholder Rights and Remedies. *Citizens and Shareholder Rights and Remedies.* Washington, D.C.: GPO, 1978.

Executive Branch

Department of State

Advisory Committee. Report on Policy towards Southern Africa. 1987.

Bureau of African Affairs. "Employment Practices of U.S. Firms in South Africa." February 1973.

CROCKER, CHESTER A., assistant secretary of state for African affairs. "Regional Strategy for Southern Africa." Address to the American Legion, Honolulu, August 29, 1981. Department of State Bulletin 81:2055 (October 1981).

———. "United States and Southern Africa." Address to the Council on Foreign Relations, New York, October 5, 1981. *Southern Africa Record* 27 (June 1982).

KISSINGER, HENRY M., secretary of state. "The Challenge of Africa." Address to the Convention of Opportunities Industrialization Centers, July 31, 1976. Department of State Bulletin 75:1943 (September 20, 1976).

MOOSE, RICHARD, assistant secretary of state for African affairs. "U.S. Policy Toward South Africa." Department of State Bulletin 80:2040 (July 1980).

———. "Southern Africa: Four Years Later." Department of State Bulletin 81:2046 (January 1981).

NEWSOM, DAVID, assistant secretary of state for African affairs. "U.S. Options in Southern Africa." Address at Northwestern University, December 8, 1971. Department of State Bulletin 64:1647 (January 7, 1971).

———. "Southern Africa: Constant Themes in U.S. Policy." Address to Mid-American Committee, Chicago, June 28, 1972. Department of State Bulletin 72:1726 (July 24, 1972).

President's Commission on Corporate Pension Funds and Other Private Retirement and Welfare Programs. *Public Policy and Private Pension Programs: A Report to the President on Private Employee Retirement Plans.* Washington, D.C.: GPO, 1965.

SCHAUFELE, W., assistant secretary of state for African affairs. "U.S. Relations in Southern Africa." Address to the American Academy of Political and Social Science, Philadelphia, April 16, 1977. Department of State Bulletin 76:1976 (May 7, 1977).

YOUNG, ANDREW, ambassador to the United Nations. "Developments Concerning Apartheid." Department of State Bulletin 77:1997 (October 3, 1977).

Department of Labor

Labor-Management Services Administration. Office of Employee Benefits Security. "Fiduciary Standards: Employee Retirement Income Security Act."

Securities and Exchange Commission

Securities and Exchange Commission. *Recent Trends in the Stockholdings and Market Participations of Institutional Investors.* June 26, 1975.

Securities and Exchange Commission. Division on Corporate Finance. *Staff Report on Corporate Accountability: A Re-examination of the Rules Relating to Shareholder Communications, Shareholder Participation in the Electoral Process, and Corporate Governance.* Washington, D.C.: GPO, 1983.

OTHER UNITED STATES GOVERNMENT PUBLICATIONS

United States. Bureau of Foreign Commerce (1953–1961). Near Eastern and African Division. *Conditions and Outlook for United States Investors in South Africa.* New York: Greenwood Press, 1969.

United States. Congress. Conference Committees. *Anti-Apartheid Act of 1985: Conference Report to Accompany H.R. 1460.* Washington, D.C.: GPO, 1985.

U.S. Congress. House. *Progress toward Ending the System of Apartheid: Communication from the President of the United States Transmitting the First Annual Report on the Extent to Which Significant Progress Has Been Made toward Ending Apartheid in South Africa, Pursuant to 22 U.S.C. 5091(b).* 100th Cong., 1st sess., 1987.

ARCHIVES, THINK TANKS, AND SPECIAL COLLECTIONS

American Committee on Africa, Amistad Collection, Tulane University. Cited as ACOA Amistad. The ACOA also has important historical materials in its active files in its New York City office. Cited as ACOA New York.

Andover Library, Harvard Divinity School, Howard Schomer Collection.

Center for Nonviolent Change, Martin Luther King Jr. Library and Archives, Atlanta, Georgia.

Centre for Intergroup Studies, Cape Town.

Centre for Policy Studies, Graduate School of Business Administration, University of the Witwatersrand.

Gail Gerhart Black Consciousness Movement Collection. Cited as Gerhart BCM Collection.

Institute for Democratic Alternatives in South Africa (IDASA), Cape Town.

John F. Kennedy Presidential Library, Boston, Massachusetts. Cited as JFKL.

Martin Luther King Jr. Collection, Boston University.

Moorland-Spingarn Research Center, Howard University, Charles C. Diggs Jr. Collection. Cited as Diggs Collection.

Temple University, Philadelphia, Pennsylvania, Leon Sullivan Collection; Opportunities Industrialization Center (OIC) Collection; International Council for Equality of Opportunity Principles (ICEOP) Collection. Cited as OIC and ICEOP, respectively.

University of Cape Town, Department of Economics; Graduate School of Business; South African Labor and Development Research Unit.

University of the Witwatersrand, Business School.

Historical materials provided to the author by the following:

American Committee on Africa, New York
James Ault
Charles C. Diggs Jr.
André du Toit
Ford Foundation, New York
Interfaith Center on Corporate Responsibility, New York. Cited as ICCR.
Investor Responsibility Research Center, Washington, D.C.
Robert F. Kennedy Center for Human Rights, New York
TransAfrica, Washington, D.C.
Paul Deats
Wayne Fredericks
Jon Gunnemann
Bevis Longstreth
Sal Marzullo
Robert Monks
Charles Powers
Howard Schomer

NEWSPAPERS, JOURNALS, AND OTHER REGULAR PUBLICATIONS

SOUTH AFRICAN NEWSPAPERS

The Argus
Business Day
The Cape Times
The Citizen
Drum
The East London Dispatch
The Financial Times
The Guardian
The Johannesburg Star
The Rand Daily Mail
The Sowetan
The Sunday Times (Johannesburg)
The Weekly Mail

U.S. NEWSPAPERS

The Boston Globe
The Columbia Spectator
The Daily Princetonian
The Harvard Crimson
The Los Angeles Times
The New York Times
The Wall Street Journal
The Washington Post
The Yale Daily News

JOURNALS, PERIODICALS, AND NEWSLETTERS

African Studies Review
Africa Report
AmCham News Line (American Chamber of Commerce in Southern Africa newsletter)
The Black Scholar
Business Alert (Centre for Business Studies, University of the Witwatersrand)
Clarion Call (Inkatha)
Democracy in Action (Institute for a Democratic Alternative for South Africa)
Die Suid Afrikaan
Ebony
Ecunews (South African Council of Churches)
Foreign Affairs
Foreign Policy
Financial Mail
Finance Week
Foreign Policy
Harvard Gazette
Indicator S.A.

Institute of International Education, South African Information Exchange Working
   Papers
Journal of South African Studies
Journal of Theology for Southern Africa
Leadership
Mayibuye
Paratus
Naval War College Review
The New Republic
Sechaba
Shared Interest (FREESA Development Fund for South Africa)
South African Information Exchange (Institute of International Education)
South Africa Pressclips
South African Reserve Bank Quarterly Bulletin
South African Review
Southern Africa Update
This Week in South Africa
Track Two
Weekly Mail and Guardian

Acknowledgments

TO ATTEMPT to express my gratitude to all those who have had an effect on a project that has occupied much of my adulthood is a task I approach with great humility. I must begin in 1971, when I was a young student living in Paris and I was invited by Phyllis and Henri Glaeser to meet a South African friend, Nana Mahomo, and to see the rough cut of his documentary film about apartheid *The Last Grave at Dimbaza*. The film's powerful images—and the questions they raised—launched me on a path of inquiry that has influenced my intellectual life ever since.

During my years as an undergraduate at Princeton University and later at Yale Divinity School I saw firsthand—and in some cases participated in—the debate about the degree to which these universities' ownership of stock created obligations to oversee and influence corporate behavior. To me such questions drove to the heart of the intersection of morality and markets, of politics and principle. By the time I reached the doctoral program at Harvard Business School in the early 1980s, my interest had focused on exploring how moral deliberations and policy formulation come together in large organizations, and, in choosing a topic through which to explore such interactions, I returned to my long-standing interest in South Africa.

In this pursuit I benefited beyond measure from the intellectual and material resources offered by Harvard University. I am grateful to the faculty with whom I worked—Malcolm Salter, Howard Stevenson, Thomas McCraw, and especially the late John B. Matthews—who helped to hone my thinking at vital points. I am also indebted to Associate Dean Thomas Piper, Patricia Khederian, and the HBS Division of Research for providing me with funds to visit facilities in the United States and South Africa. I thank the Albert Einstein Institute for an early grant to expand the scope of my research. While writing my dissertation I also benefited immensely from being chosen as one of the first Harvard University Fellows in Ethics and the Professions, a program that allowed me to expand my knowledge of moral philosophy and political theory. I particularly want to thank the director of this program,

Professor Dennis F. Thompson, for his guidance and support over several years.

After completing my dissertation in 1989 I was invited by Dean Ronald F. Thiemann to come to Harvard Divinity School to teach courses on the intersection of economics, ethics, and public policy. Dean Thiemann graciously provided me with the time, space, and resources to work on this book over several years; his steady friendship and encouragement were vital to its completion. While at Harvard Divinity School I was honored to have been the Henry Luce Fellow in Theology and to have served as the director of the Project on Business, Values, and the Economy of the Center for the Study of Values in Public Life. I deeply appreciate the intellectual and personal support I received from my friends on the faculty, particularly Clarissa Atkinson, Constance Buchanan, Allen Callahan, Harvey Cox, Ralph Potter, Timothy Weiskel, and Preston Williams. I value Missy Daniel's willingness to listen and respond to the torrent of ideas that sometimes overtook me. I could not have functioned without the secretarial assistance of Phyllis Stevens, Brian Murphy, and the late Sara Hazel. I also want to thank Margaret Studier, Julie Bisbee, Maria Cedargren, Cheryl Henderson, and Laura Whitney for providing important help along the way.

I benefited more than I can express from my interactions with my students, particularly those in my course on the history of U.S. relations with South Africa. I also enjoyed working with a host of talented teaching fellows and research assistants, many of whom have already gone on to leadership in their own fields, including Cathy Bowers, Pulane Evans, Pedro Gonzalez, Betsy Grossman, Caroline Moon, Joanne Park, Matthew Pinsker, Tom Riedlinger, Kathleen Skerrett, Margaret Smith, Molly Teas, Jennifer Wu, and Karen-Marie Yust.

As I tracked down the many strands of this story I was greatly assisted by those who offered their reminiscences and interpretations in more than 150 interviews. Some also helped me piece together the record by sending me documents or whole collections of material, among them James Ault, Jon Gunnemann, Paul Deats, Johan Heyns, Willard Johnson, Sal Marzullo, Charles Powers, Witney Schneidman, and Howard Schomer.

In 1993 I had the privilege of serving for six months as a senior Fulbright research scholar at the University of Cape Town's Graduate School of Business. I thank Kate Jowell, Norman Faull, and other members of the faculty and staff for their hospitality and assistance. Francis Wilson, Dudley Horner, and the other members of the Department of Economics, as well as the staff of the South Africa Labour Development Research Unit, could not have been more helpful. I am also grateful to my many friends in UCT's Department of Religion, especially Charles

Villa-Vicencio, who was unfailingly gracious and supportive, and John de Gruchy, who generously provided his home while he was on sabbatical. I also want to thank Barney and Dimza Pityana, two inspiring friends for whom I feel deep admiration and affection. Professor Nicholas Binedell of the School of Management of the University of the Witwatersrand gave me invaluable insights and encouragement along the way. Tembisa Mnqumevu not only helped in our home but offered me an important window into her life. Jacques and Carol Kriel and the members of their family offered help and hospitality on numerous occasions.

My debt to the du Toit family is immeasurable; without them this book would not exist. Professor André du Toit of the University of Cape Town first became a friend at Harvard, where I quickly came to respect his brilliance and integrity. He introduced me to many people and ideas, particularly to South African political philosophy, both historical and contemporary. His wife, Maretha, one of the most gracious human beings I have ever met, not only taught me Afrikaans but opened her home and helped me in innumerable ways during every visit. Their daughter, Marijke, was a superb research assistant who relentlessly tracked down material and was my reliable companion as we drove around the Western Cape during some of South Africa's most turbulent days. A talented historian in her own right, Marijke read the manuscript with a skillful eye, helped me understand some of the nuances of South African history, and saved me from many, but perhaps not all, the oversimplifications to which an external observer is prone. To all three of them, and to the rest of the members of their family, I offer my most profound gratitude.

To trace the story of how the anti-apartheid movement affected American institutions I needed the assistance of many librarians and archivists in both countries. I extend my appreciation to the staffs of the John F. Kennedy Presidential Library, the Amistad Research Center at Tulane University, the Moorland-Spingarn Center at Howard University, the Mayibuye Center of the University of the Western Cape, the American Committee on Africa, the Interfaith Center on Corporate Responsibility, the Investor Responsibility Research Center, the Leon Sullivan Collection at Temple University, Andover, Baker, and Widener Libraries at Harvard University, the South African Research Program at Yale University, the Columbia University library, and all of the other institutions where I examined records. Because the history of the anti-apartheid movement is so fresh, many of these institutions are still gathering and sorting their abundant materials, a development that I hope will attract new scholarship in both countries. I particularly hope that someone will write a more detailed history of the work of TransAfrica, whose historical files were unfortunately not available for examination during the writing of this book.

I owe a special debt to those who helped move my research from its more narrow academic formulation into a book for a wider audience. I want to thank Professor Rosabeth Moss Kanter of Harvard Business School, who, by telling me that in her view life was too short for small projects, emboldened me to embark on such a massive work. I am profoundly grateful to my agent, Melanie Jackson, who not only instantly understood what I was attempting to do but skillfully shepherded the work through some of its most hazardous and demoralizing moments. I thank Harriet Rubin for her early enthusiasm about the project and Nan Talese for her leadership, vitality, and wisdom in its publication. Jesse Cohen and I worked so closely together on paring and polishing the manuscript that I often felt he knew the work better than I did; I am grateful to have had the benefit of his friendship and his extraordinary editorial eye.

At a moment of personal trial that threatened to interrupt my progress, Clara Bingham and David Michaelis stepped in to help me in ways for which I will always be grateful. I similarly acknowledge Ralph Taylor's support and counsel at key moments. If one could earn a Nobel Prize in the category of friendship, Lynda Wik would win handily; her generosity to me and to legions of her other friends is legendary. I thank Dana L. Robert for the support she provided during the period our interests converged. I regret that Henri Nouwen, my close friend and mentor, did not live to see the final version of this book, since he followed its progress with such avid interest. My sister Susanna Thomas and her husband, Jim, offered their farm in Kentucky as a place of refuge and reflection, and my sister Elizabeth cheered me with her wit and spunk. My mother, Suzanne Massie, and her husband, Seymour Papert, expressed their faith in me and in this project in innumerable ways. My father, Robert K. Massie, and his wife, Deborah Karl, offered assistance and advice at important moments. I owe a debt to both of my parents for teaching me the discipline and craft of writing and for instilling in me strong convictions about the urgency, excitement, and relevance of historical research.

Finally, I am more thankful than I can say to my sons, Samuel and John, to whom this book is dedicated, for their irrepressible wonder at life and for the way they have deepened my capacity to love. And I thank my wife, Anne, whose intelligence, passion, commitment, and courage regularly stun her voluble spouse into the most profound and grateful of silences.

Index

Throughout this index ANC refers to African National Congress.

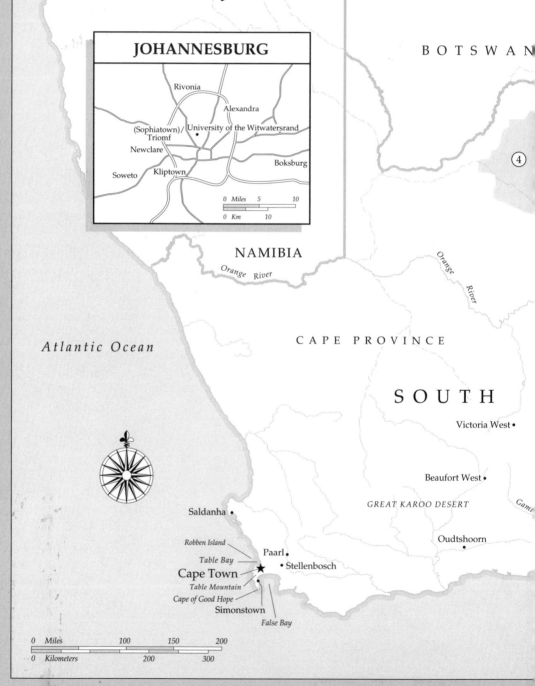

South Africa, circa 1980

★ Windhoek

Walvis
Bay

BOTSWANA

④

JOHANNESBURG

Rivonia

Alexandra

(Sophiatown)/ University of the Witwatersrand
Triomf

Newclare

Soweto   Kliptown

Boksburg

0 Miles   5   10
0 Km   10

NAMIBIA

Orange River

Orange River

Atlantic Ocean

CAPE PROVINCE

SOUTH

Victoria West •

Beaufort West •

GREAT KAROO DESERT

Gam

Saldanha •

Robben Island

Table Bay

Cape Town

Table Mountain

Cape of Good Hope

Paarl •

★

• Stellenbosch

Simonstown

False Bay

0 Miles   100   150   200
0 Kilometers   200   300